Special Edition Using

Using Java™ 2 Platform

QUE®

Joseph Weber

Special Edition Using Java 2 Platform

International Standard Book Number: 0-7897-2018-3

Library of Congress Catalog Card Number: 98-68732

Printed in the United States of America

First Printing: January 1999

00 99 4 3 2 1

Trademarks

All terms mentioned in this book that are known to be trademarks or service marks have been appropriately capitalized. *Que Publishing* cannot attest to the accuracy of this information. Use of a term in this book should not be regarded as affecting the validity of any trademark or service mark. Java is a trademark of Sun Microsystems, Inc.

Warning and Disclaimer

Every effort has been made to make this book as complete and as accurate as possible, but no warranty or fitness is implied. The information provided is on an "as is" basis. The authors and the publisher shall have neither liability or responsibility to any person or entity with respect to any loss or damages arising from the information contained in this book or from the use of the CD or programs accompanying it.

Contents at a Glance

IV IO

V Databases

VI Component-Based Development

VII Advanced Java

VIII Debugging Java

Table of Contents

V Databases

VI Component-Based Development

X Java Resources

XI Appendix

Credits

EXECUTIVE EDITOR
Tim Ryan

ACQUISITIONS EDITOR
Jeffrey W. Taylor

DEVELOPMENT EDITOR
Benjamin Milstead

MANAGING EDITOR
Patrick Kanouse

PROJECT EDITOR
Andrew Cupp

COPY EDITORS
Geniel Breeze
Kelli Brooks
Michael Brumitt
Cheri Clark
Keith Cline
Dana Lesh
Theresa Mathias
San Dee Phillips
Heather Urschel

INDEXER
Erika Millen

TECHNICAL EDITORS
Joe Carpenter
Jodi Cornelius

SOFTWARE DEVELOPMENT SPECIALIST
Dan Scherf

PRODUCTION
Carol Bowers
Mona Brown
Michael Dietsch
Ayanna Lacey
Gene Redding

Dedication

To my parents, Emmet and Ruth, who taught me faith and dedication. I love them dearly.

About the Authors

Joe Weber is a frequent contributor to a variety of Java books, magazines, and other resources. He has been working with Java full-time since its early alpha stages and has helped advise a number of Fortune 500 companies on the goals of Java. He has also helped to generate adoption in those organizations. Mr. Weber is a V.P. of MagnaStar Inc., a Java consulting firm; serves as the senior technical advisor to Soren Technologies, a medial software company whose systems are written in Java; and currently is the director of the DocuLink product division for XLink Corporation. Joe has also served on advisory committees for and taught classes at universities in the Midwest. He continues to be a strong advocate for Java in the educational environment. Mr. Weber is a cofounder of the *Java™ology Magazine* and has contributed articles to several other Java magazines. Mr. Weber loves to hear from his readers and can be reached via e-mail at `weber@inc.net`.

Mark Wutka is a senior systems architect who refuses to give up his programming hat. For the past three years he has worked as the chief architect on a large, object-oriented distributed system providing automation for the flight operations division of a major airline. Over the past nine years, he has designed and implemented numerous systems in Java, C, C++, and Smalltalk for that same airline. He is currently Vice President of Research and Development for Pioneer Technologies, a consulting firm specializing in distributed systems and legacy system migration. He can be reached via email at `wutka@netcom.com`. He also claims responsibility for the random bits of humor at `www.webcom.com/wutka`.

Acknowledgments

I would like to thank and acknowledge the huge numbers of individuals who have worked on this book. A volume like the one that you hold in your hands right now is not the work of a single individual, but is a collaboration of the efforts of the writers, editors, and the developer. So many people contribute to a work like this behind the scenes, and unfortunately I don't even know all of their names, but their efforts are greatly appreciated.

In particular I would like to thank Ben Milstead, who has developed this work and, along with Joe Carpenter and Jodi Cornelius, helped to insure that what you read is accurate. It would be impossible for this book to have the degree of accuracy that it has with out these people's efforts.

I would like to thank Jeff Taylor, who was the last in a string of acquisition editors on this book, and who has stuck through it and made life so much easier.

I would be remiss if I did not single out the efforts of Mark Wutka. Mark has helped to write portions of this book since its first edition and his skills and work have helped to add volume and understanding to this book. Mark deserves my immense gratitude and thanks for his contributions.

I would also like to acknowledge

Stephanie Gould, my first Acquistions Editor, who convinced me to work on my first book and showed me that I like writing.

Mark Arend and Gene deGroot who, when I was not so much younger, each taught me perseverance and creativity.

Shawn Gubine, my oldest and dearest friend, for reasons not even he probably knows.

Scott Morris, who taught me that the correct answer to why most software works the way it does is, "because they didn't ask me," and that confidence is 99 percent of success.

David and Dorothy, my siblings, who have added humanity.

Finally, last, but most importantly, I would like to thank my wife, Kim, whose patience, understanding, and love have allowed this book to come into existence. Kim deserves as much credit as I for making this book happen.

Tell Us What You Think!

As the reader of this book, *you* are our most important critic and commentator. We value your opinion and want to know what we're doing right, what we could do better, what areas you'd like to see us publish in, and any other words of wisdom you're willing to pass our way.

As the Executive Editor for the Java team at Macmillan Computer Publishing, I welcome your comments. You can fax, email, or write me directly to let me know what you did or didn't like about this book—as well as what we can do to make our books stronger.

Please note that I cannot help you with technical problems related to the topic of this book, and that due to the high volume of mail I receive, I might not be able to reply to every message.

When you write, please be sure to include this book's title and author as well as your name and phone or fax number. I will carefully review your comments and share them with the author and editors who worked on the book.

Fax: 317-817-7070

E-mail: `java@mcp.com`

Mail: Tim Ryan, Executive Editor
Java Team
Macmillan Computer Publishing
201 West 103rd Street
Indianapolis, IN 46290 USA

Introduction

In this chapter

Welcome to the amazing and dynamic world of Java! If you are brand new to Java, you're in for a treat. Java is an extremely rich language that is simple and easy to learn. Java gives the programmer unprecedented access to even the most complex of tasks.

What is Java? Java is a revolutionary programming language that was introduced by Sun Microsystems in June 1995. Since then, hundreds of thousands of programmers have picked up books just like the one you hold in your hands now and have realized just how powerful the language is.

Java is an object-oriented programming language, which means that people programming in Java can develop complex programs with great ease. In addition, Java has built-in support for threads, networking, and a vast variety of other tools.

A note about version numbers: The final release of Java in December 1998 was called Java 2. At that time, however, the JDK was still being called JDK 1.2. Don't be confused; JDK 1.2 is part of Java 2, and this book covers both.

This Book Is for You

If you're new to Java, this book is for you. Don't be intimidated by the size of this book. It contains a vast amount of rich information about every facet of the Java programming language, along with easy-to-follow chapters that are designed to get you started.

If you're already a Java expert, this book will become a treasured item on your shelf. Actually, it may never leave your desk. This book puts into one source the most complete reference and set of examples on every aspect of the Java programming language ever compiled. No currently available API has gone unexplored; no programming method has gone undocumented. Between the covers of this book, you find examples and explanations that will make your life as a programmer immensely easier.

How This Book Is Organized

This book is organized into 11 parts. Each part covers a large chunk of information about how the Java programming language is organized.

Part I, "Introduction to Java," introduces you to the design of the Java language and the Virtual Machine. It shows you what Java can do for you, and how it's being implemented in some programs today. Clear instructions have been included to help you get started by downloading the Java Development Kit and installing it. Finally, this part teaches you how each of the free tools included in the Java Development Kit (JDK) work.

Part II, "The Java Language," shows how Java's syntax is developed. The fundamental aspects of Java are found in its language syntax. Every program is built using the fundamentals of the language, and this part walks you through each segment. The second half of this part talks about building specific Java programs, such as applets and applications. For the beginner, each of the chapters has been structured to help you become familiar with Java programming. For the expert, the individual aspects of the language are explored in great detail, making Part II a great reference as well as a learning tool.

Part III, "User Interface," teaches you the details of building a graphical user interface in Java. It shows you how to do this using the traditional AWT interfaces, and then demonstrates the new features of Java 1.2 with the Java Foundation Classes (also know as Swing). In addition, this part explores how to build and manipulate images, and then discusses Java 1.2's 2D graphics system.

Part IV, "IO," walks you through reading and writing data into your Java application. The part begins by teaching you the fundamental components and techniques of streaming and reading files. Then you learn how to build networked applications. You'll find priceless information about the internet's TCP/IP protocol. The part finishes by teaching you about the more advanced features, such as making sure your data transfers are secure. It covers using Java's serialization for sending and retrieving whole Java objects, and using Remote Method Invocation to run entire Java programs on remote machines. Finally, the part wraps up by discussing the new management API in Java 1.2 that allows you to talk to advanced devices, such as routers.

Part V, "Databases," walks you through the details of one of the most important aspects of building modern business applications. Databases are the core to almost all business applications, and Java's JDBC (Java DataBase Connectivity) eases the burden of communicating between your Java applications and the database. In this part, you are introduced to how databases work, given a bit of history, and then you learn the terminology required to go on. Next, you explore Java's JDBC interface, which allows you to connect, send, and store data to any JDBC-compliant database. Welcome to the world of platform-independent and DBMS-independent systems!

Part VI, "Component-Based Development," will be fascinating to anyone interested in learning how to make the development cycle faster and easier. Component-based development has been around for many years now, but it has never been as easy to do as with Java. In this part, you will learn how to use three different component models: Java's own JavaBeans specification, CORBA (which is rapidly becoming an industry standard, and maps very nicely to JavaBeans), and COM (Microsoft's interface for talking to Windows).

Part VII, "Advanced Java," teaches you about some very complex technologies surrounding Java when you're ready to take the next step. Part VII shows you advanced techniques. You learn how to take advantage of the server-side capabilities of Java and how to use the Java Wallet for building commerce applications. You also learn about Java's built-in data structures and utilities, and how to build native applications. This part finishes with a comparison of Java to C++.

Part VIII, "Debugging Java," teaches you all the tricks of the trade. This part will quickly become invaluable as you learn how important good debugging technique is when developing applications. You will find great references on every aspect of the `sun.tools.debug` package, as well as on the op-codes for Java's Virtual Machine.

Part IX, "JavaScript," talks about the distant cousin to Java, JavaScript, which can help you do tasks with great ease. Because it can control the browser, it can even do some things Java can't. This part teaches you JavaScript programming, so you'll be multilingual.

Part X, "Java Resources," is a perfect source for additional material beyond this book. You'll find some terrific Web sites and other material to help you stay up to date and on top of the Java community.

Part XI, "Appendix," gives you an overview of all of the resources on the CD-ROM included with this book.

Conventions Used in This Book

This book uses various stylistic and typographic conventions to make it easier to use.

NOTE When you see a note in this book, it indicates additional information that may help you avoid problems or that should be considered in using the described features.

Tip paragraphs suggest easier or alternative methods of executing a procedure. Tips can help you see that little extra concept or idea that can make your life so much easier.

CAUTION

Cautions warn you of hazardous procedures (for example, activities that delete files).

Special Edition Using Java 2 uses cross-references to help you access related information in other parts of the book.

See "The Object Class," **p. 1081**

PART I

Introduction to Java

CHAPTER 1

What Java Can Do for You

In this chapter

The Many Types of Java Applications

By now you have probably heard enough hype about Java to go out and buy this book. The good news is that the hype is well-justified. Java is probably everything you have heard that it is and more.

In this chapter, you examine the various possibilities provided by the Java language by taking a look at the different types of applications you can develop with it. To drive the point home, you then take a look at several examples of Java applets that are currently on the Web. You also examine examples of a Java Graphical User Interface (GUI) application and a Java command line application. By the end of this chapter, you should have a fairly good idea of what you can accomplish with Java and be excited about this language, the incredible new enhancements with JDK 1.2, and how Java is changing the computing world.

Java is not used only to create applets or servlets. The amazing thing about Java is that it can be used to create a huge variety of applications. The following are a few of the types of applications you can build in Java:

- Applets (mini applications)
- GUI applications
- Command line applications
- Servlets (server side applications)
- Packages (libraries)
- Embedded applications (such as oscilloscopes and other embedded computers)
- Pen-based programs

Applets are essentially applications that run inside a Java-enabled browser, such as Netscape Navigator, Microsoft Internet Explorer, or HotJava.

GUI applications developed in Java have graphical interfaces and stand on their own. They operate like any other GUI application, for instance the Windows Notepad application, which does not require a Web browser to execute it.

Command line applications can be run from an MS-DOS command prompt or a UNIX shell prompt, just like the `xcopy` command in MS-DOS or the `ls` command in UNIX.

Packages are not applications per se. Rather, packages are more like a collection of classes (portable Java-bytecode files) that belong to one package (similar to a C++ class library). There is no custom format for packages like those used with static and dynamic libraries on the various operating systems. The implementation in Java is much simpler and more portable.

Basically, all classes belonging to a package are placed in one directory. For example, all classes belonging to Java's Abstract Window Toolkit (AWT) package, java.awt, are placed in a directory called `AWT` under the `C:\jdk1.2\src` directory. This is a directory tree of various packages provided with the Java Development Kit:

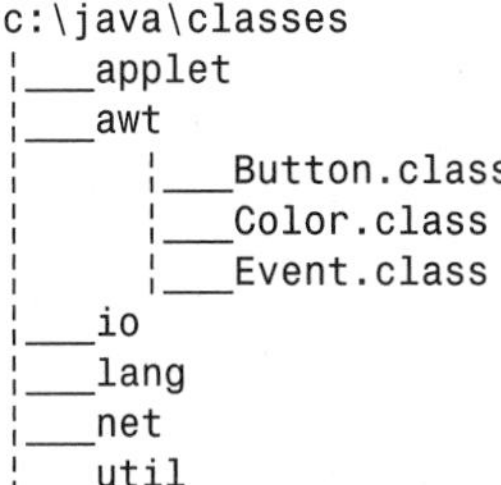

```
c:\java\classes
|___applet
|___awt
|       |___Button.class
|       |___Color.class
|       |___Event.class
|___io
|___lang
|___net
|___util
```

A few examples of class files under the AWT directory are also shown to illustrate the point here (in actuality, there are several dozen class files under the AWT directory).

Learning About the Java Language

When Java was first created, Sun Microsystems released a white paper that described Java with a series of buzzwords to make your head spin:

> Java is a simple, object-oriented, robust, secure, portable, high-performance, architecturally neutral, interpreted, multithreaded, dynamic language.

Phew! Try saying all that in one breath. Anyway, the language itself is discussed in more detail in the remainder of this book, but the one buzzword you need to learn for this chapter is *interpreted.*

Java source code compiles into portable bytecodes that require an interpreter to execute them. For applets, this task is handled by the browser. For GUI and command line applications, the Java interpreter program is required to execute the application. The examples shown in the section "Java Command Line Applications" later in this chapter illustrate both methods.

The Java Development Kit

The reason Java is so popular is not simply because of the benefits of the language itself. The rich sets of packages (or class libraries to you C++ programmers) that come bundled with the Java Development Kit (JDK) from Sun Microsystems also contribute to its popularity. These prewritten objects get you up and running with Java quickly, for two main reasons:

- You do not need to develop the functionality they provide.
- The source code is available for all.

Here is a brief description of some of the more significant packages provided with Java:

Package	Description
`java.applet`	Classes for developing applets.
`java.awt`	Abstract Window Toolkit (AWT) classes for the GUI interface, such as windows, dialog boxes, buttons, text fields, and more.

Package	Description
`java.net`	Classes for networking, URLs, client/server sockets.
`java.io`	Classes for various types of input and output.
`java.lang`	Classes for various data types, running processes, strings, threads, and much more.
`java.util`	Utility classes for dates, vectors, and more.
`java.awt.image`	Classes for managing and manipulating images.

Java Applets

As mentioned previously, Java applets run within a Java-enabled Web browser. Because Web browsers were primarily developed for displaying HTML documents, incorporating Java applets inside a Web browser requires an HTML tag to invoke an applet. This HTML tag is the `<APPLET>` tag, as shown in the following example:

```
<applet code=TextEdit.class width=575 height=350></applet>
```

You will explore all the details of Applets in Chapters 14 and 15.

Real-World Examples of Java Applets on the Web

Because pictures truly say more than a thousand words, you will enjoy taking a look at some examples of real-world Java applets on the Web today. Figures 1.2 through 1.11 are examples of these applets.

Figure 1.1 shows a Java application called NetProphet. NetProphet is a wonderful utility that allows you to chart and graph all of your stocks. It is a wonderful example of how having a Java client interacting with a server (client/server) can be used to create dynamic information. Netprofit is available from Neural Applications at `http://www.neural.com/NetProphet/NetProphet.html`.

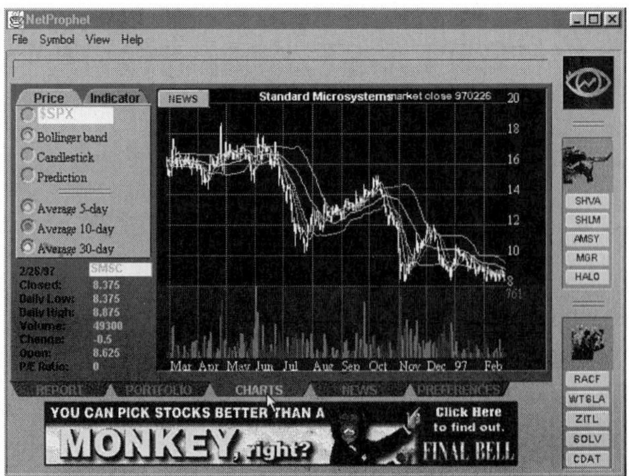

FIG. 1.1
NetProphet is a wonderful example of client/server Java.

Figure 1.2 shows how Eastland Data Systems's Internet Shopping Applet (`http://www.eastland.com/shoptech.html`) has been applied by Blossom Flowers (`http://www.blossomflowers.com/shopping_frame.html`).

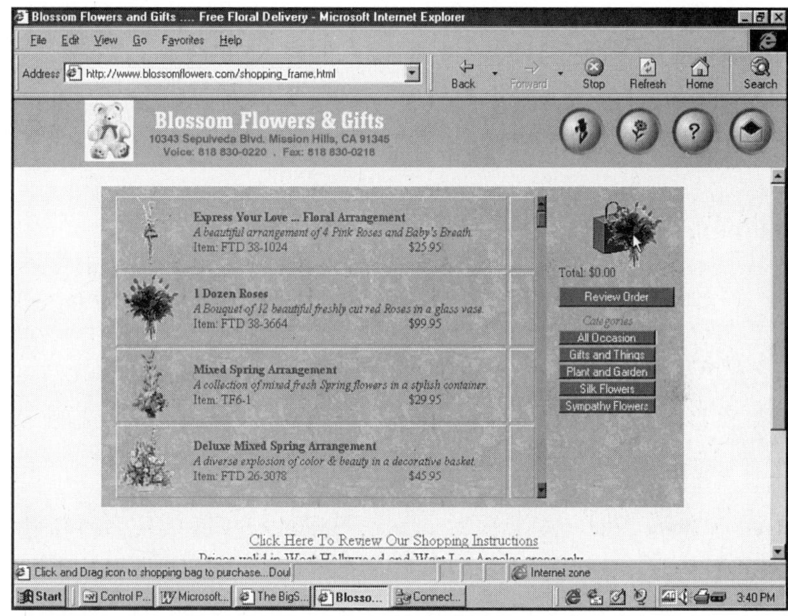

FIG. 1.2
Internet shopping by Eastland.

This applet is unique because it implements drag-and-drop features on the Internet.

Java has been shown to be a great language to write Internet games in. Figure 1.3 shows the famous Rubik's Cube that amused everyone a few years ago. This is a fully functional Rubik's cube developed in Java. You can play with it live on the Internet at `http://www.tdb.uu.se/~karl/java/rubik.html`.

Figure 1.4 below shows another game that uses 3D graphics. Palle Pedalpost (`http://www.zapper.kd/postpil/postgame.html`) performs with smooth animation, and is definitely worth a look.

Lotus has been very innovative in its use of the Java language with the eSuite program. eSuite is a collection of tools for building groupware applications, and is shown in Figure 1.5.

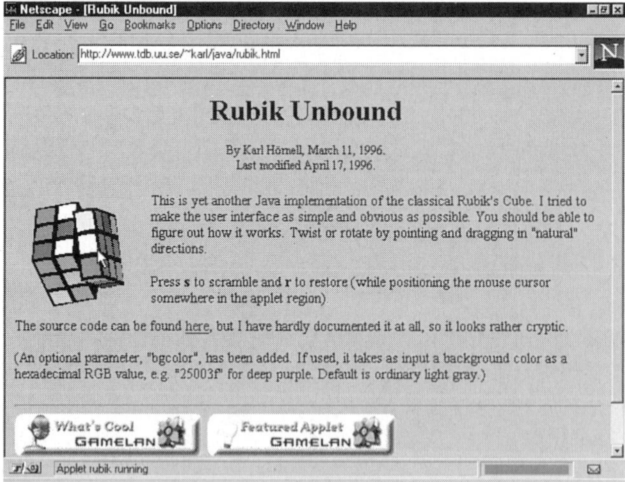

FIG. 1.3
Rubik's Cube.

FIG. 1.4
Pelle Pedalpost.

One of the wonderful enhancements with JDK 1.2 is the capability to have applications display multimedia. Figure 1.6 shows an MPG movie playing within a Java program.

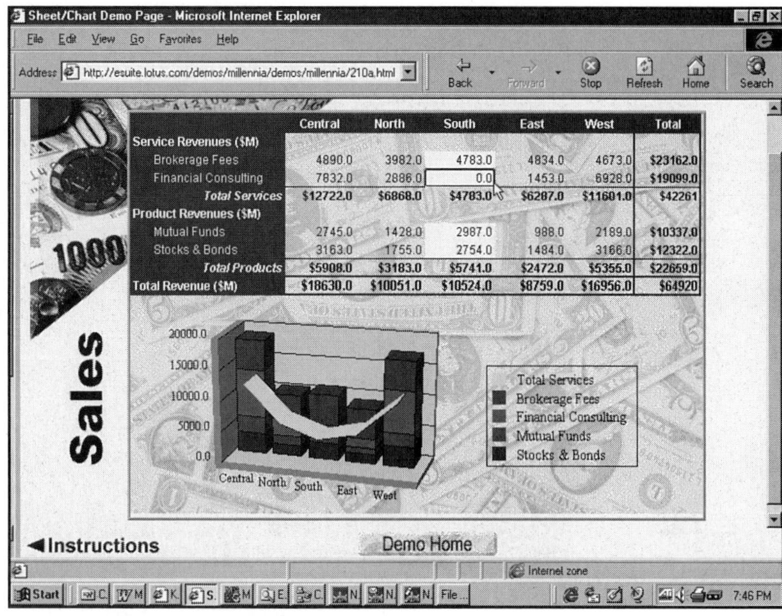

FIG. 1.5
Lotus eSuite.

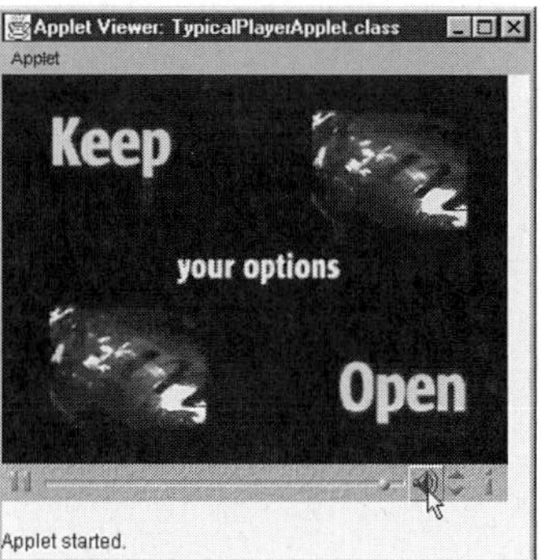

FIG. 1.6
This MPG movie is playing in a Java program.

The *Chicago Tribune* has used Java Servlets to create a wonderful site called Metromix. Metromix, shown in Figure 1.7, is a source of entertainment in the Chicago area.

A group of students from Harvard has created a truly innovative system for scheduling classes. This system, shown in Figure 1.8, can be viewed from `http://www.digitas.harvard.edu`.

FIG. 1.7
Metromix Web site.

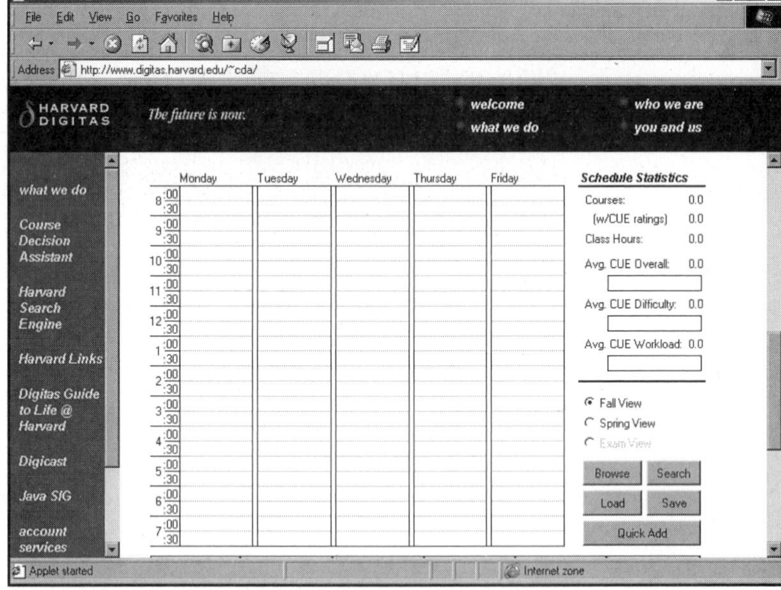

FIG. 1.8
Digitas Course Decision Assistant.

Java GUI Applications

While Java applets have stolen most of Java's thunder, Java goes a lot further than applets. Java can be used to develop portable GUI applications across all supported platforms. In fact, the same Java source code can be used for both an applet and an application.

To illustrate this, look at an application called Text Editor that was developed for demonstration purposes. As the name implies, this application is used for editing text files, similar to the Windows Notepad application. Figure 1.9 shows the applet version of the Text Editor, Figure 1.10 shows the application version on Windows 95, and Figure 1.11 shows the application version under Solaris.

All three versions of the Text Editor were generated using the same Java source files. In fact, all three versions are executed using the same bytecode files that were compiled only once under Windows 95 and copied to Solaris without requiring a recompilation.

Notice how the Java interpreter is used on the MS-DOS prompt to execute the application.

Notice the File dialog box in Figures 1.10 and 1.11. If you are a Windows 95 or Solaris user, you know they are the standard File dialog boxes used on these operating systems. As a developer, you do not need to custom code anything to get the native look and feel. All you have to do is ensure that the class (bytecode) files are available from where the applet or application needs to be invoked. The rest (the native look and feel, system-specific features, and so on) is handled by Java's dynamic link libraries.

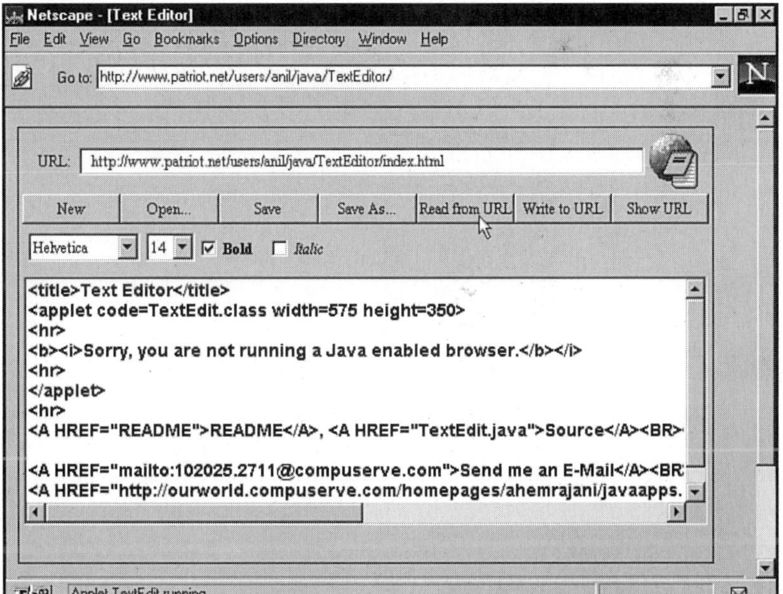

FIG. 1.9
The Text Editor application running as an applet.

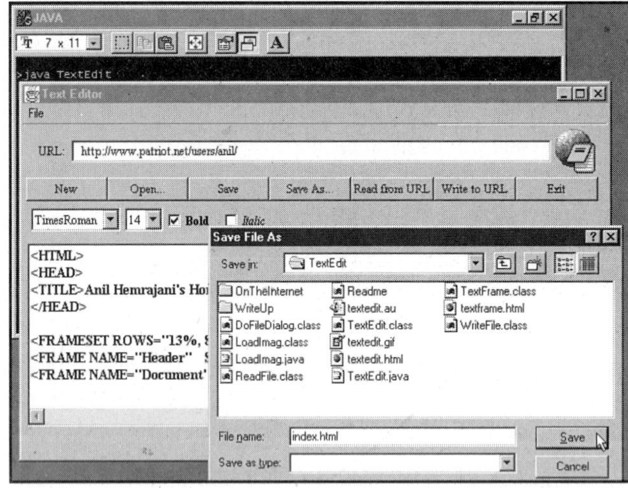

FIG. 1.10
The Text Editor application on Windows 95 runs using the Java interpreter.

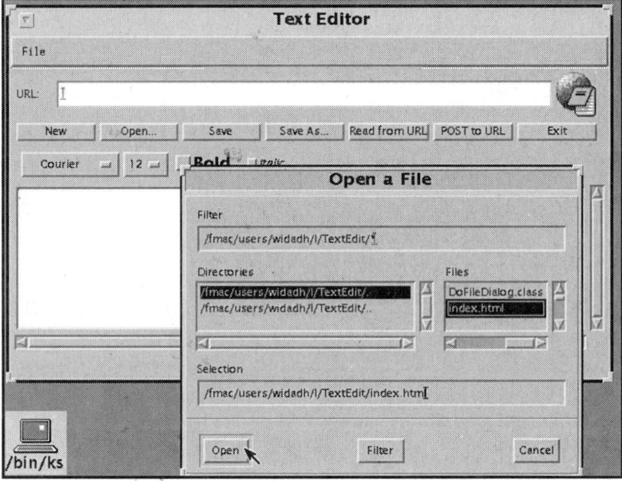

FIG. 1.11
The Text Editor application on Solaris.

Java Command Line Applications

Even in today's world, where GUI applications have become a standard on practically every type of computer, there are times when you might need to drop down to the command line to perform some tasks. For these times, Java provides the capability to develop command line applications.

The only difference between command line and GUI applications is that command line applications do not use any of the GUI features provided in Java. In other words, command line applications do not use the `java.awt` package.

Figure 1.12 shows an example of a command line application, `copyURL`, which essentially is a copy utility for copying files from the Internet to a local disk. This application uses the `java.net` package to obtain information about a resource (file) on the Internet. Then `copyURL` uses the `java.io` package to read the bytes of data from the file on the Internet and write them to a local file.

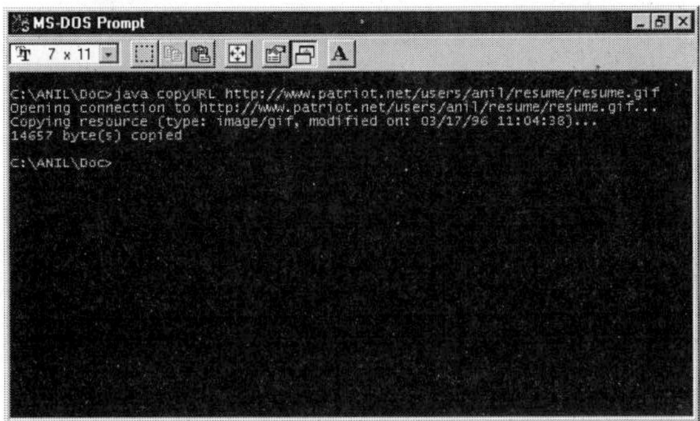

FIG. 1.12 `copyURL.class` is an Internet command line copy utility.

Java Is Client/Server

In today's computing world, client/server technology has found a place in most corporations. The biggest benefit of this technology is that the processing load is shared between the client and the server. A client can be any program (GUI application, Telnet, and so on) that requests services from a server application. Examples of server applications include database servers, application servers, communication (FTP, Telnet, Web) servers, and more.

In this chapter, you have seen several examples of Java client-side applets and applications. However, Java provides classes for server-side processing as well. Java applications can be used as clients or servers, whereas applets can only be used for client-side processing.

The `java.net` package provides classes necessary for developing client/server applications. Figure 1.13 shows a Java applet, `javaSQL`, that sends free-form SQL queries typed in by the user to a server application, `javaSQLd`. `javaSQLd` in turn queries a database and returns the query results to the `javaSQL` applet.

Figure 1.14 illustrates the relationship between `javaSQL` and `javaSQLd`. Imagine querying a database at work from home via a Java-enabled browser. With Java, the possibilities are endless!

How to Stay Current

Web-related technology is progressing so rapidly that it is difficult to stay on top of new events. The pace of innovation on the Internet is extremely rapid, and Java has been growing at a rate at least as astounding as the rest of the technology.

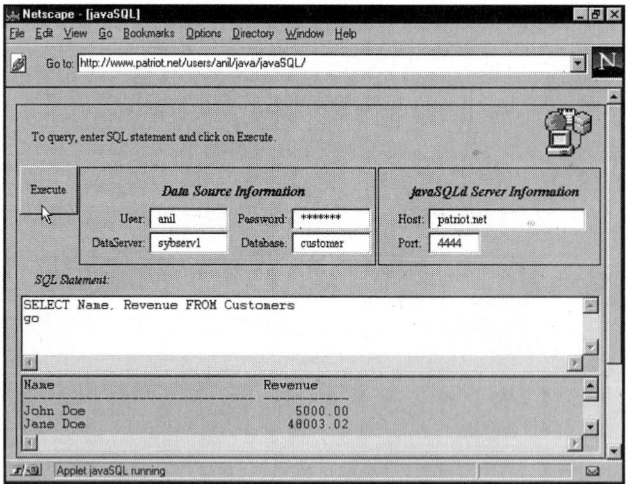

FIG. 1.13
`javaSQL` client applet.

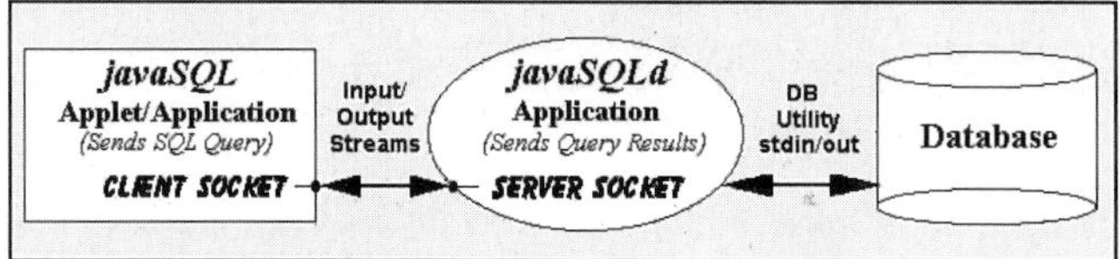

FIG. 1.14
`javaSQL` and `javaSQLd`.

About the only way to stay current is to visit certain Web sites that post the latest news and Java examples. While there are dozens of Java-related Web sites that provide timely information, you will find a list of some of those that have a history of providing great information in Chapter 56, "Java Resources." ●

CHAPTER 2

Java Design

In this chapter

Java Is Interpreted

Before you write any applets or programs with Java, it is important to understand how Java works. This chapter introduces you to the actual language, the limitations of the language (intentional and unintentional), and how code can be made reusable.

Strictly speaking, Java is interpreted, although in reality Java is both interpreted and compiled. In fact, only about 20 percent of the Java code is interpreted by the browser, but this is a crucial 20 percent. Both Java's security and its ability to run on multiple platforms stem from the fact that the final steps of compilation are handled locally.

A programmer first compiles Java source into bytecode using the Java compiler. These bytecodes are binary and architecturally neutral (or platform-independent—both work equally well). The bytecode isn't complete, however, until it's put together with a Java runtime environment, usually a browser. Because each Java runtime environment is for a specific platform, the bytecodes can be interpreted for the specific platform and the final product will work on that specific platform.

This platform-specific feature of Java is good news for developers. It means that Java code is Java code is Java code, no matter what platform you're developing for or on. You could write and compile a Java applet on your UNIX system and embed the applet into your Web page. Three different people on three different machines, each with different environments, can take a peek at your new applet. Provided that each of those people runs a Java-capable browser, it won't matter whether he or she is on an IBM, HP, or Macintosh. Using Java means that only one source of Java code needs to be maintained for the bytecode to run on a variety of platforms. One pass through a compiler for multiple platforms is good news for programmers.

The one drawback that comes with interpretation, however, is that there is a performance hit. This is caused by the fact that the browser has to do some work with the class files (interpret them) before they can be run. Under traditional programming, such as with C++, the code that is generated can be run directly by the computer. The performance hit that interpretation causes means that Java programs tend to run about 1/2 to 1/6 the speed of their native counterparts.

This deficiency is largely overcome using a tool called a just-in-time (JIT) compiler. A just-in-time compiler compiles Java methods to native code for the platform you're using. It is embedded with the Java environment for a particular platform (such as Netscape). Without the JIT compiler, methods are not translated to native code but remain in the original machine-independent bytecode. This bytecode is interpreted on any platform by the Java Virtual Machine. A Java application is portable, but the just-in-time compiler itself cannot be portable because it generates native code specific to a platform, exactly as you need a different version of the virtual machine for each new platform. Generally, you don't even need to concern yourself with JITs. Both the Netscape Navigator and Microsoft's Internet Explorer browsers have JIT compilers in them.

Why is this combination of compilation and interpretation a positive feature?

- It facilitates security and stability. The Java environment contains an element called the linker, which checks data coming into your machine to make sure it doesn't contain deliberately harmful files (security) or files that could disrupt the functioning of your computer (robustness).
- More importantly, this combination of compilation and interpretation alleviates concern about version mismatches.

The fact that the final portion of compilation is being accomplished by a platform-specific device, which is maintained by the end user, relieves you of the responsibility of maintaining multiple sources for multiple platforms. Interpretation also enables data to be incorporated at runtime, which is the foundation of Java's dynamic behavior.

Java Is Object Oriented

Java is an object-oriented language. Therefore, it's part of a family of languages that focuses on defining data as objects and the methods that may be applied to those objects. As explained, Java and C++ share many of the same underlying principles; they just differ in style and structure. Simply put, object-oriented programming languages (OOP, for short) describe interactions among data objects.

▶ **See** Chapter 50, "Java Versus C(++)," to learn more about the similarities of Java with C++, **p. 1161**

Many OOP languages support multiple inheritance, which can sometimes lead to confusion or unnecessary complications. Java doesn't. As part of its less-is-more philosophy, Java supports only single inheritance, which means each class can inherit from only one other class at any given time. This type of inheritance avoids the problem of a class inheriting classes whose behaviors are contradictory or mutually exclusive. Java enables you to create totally abstract classes, known as interfaces. Interfaces allow you to define methods you can share with several classes, without regard for how the other classes are handling the methods.

▶ **See** Chapter 5, "Object-Oriented Programming," to learn more, **p. 71**

NOTE Although Java does not support multiple inheritance, Java does allow a class to implement more than one interface.

Each class, abstract or not, defines the behavior of an object through a set of methods. All the code used for Java is divided into classes. Methods can be inherited from one class to the next, and at the head of the class hierarchy is the class called Object. The Object class belongs to the java.lang package of the Java Core API. You are introduced in the last section of this chapter to the Java Core API.

▶ **See** Chapter 11, "Classes," to learn more about classes and objects, **p. 157**

Objects can also implement any number of interfaces (or abstract classes). The Java interfaces are a lot like the Interface Definition Language (IDL) interfaces. This similarity means it's easy to build a compiler from IDL to Java.

That compiler could be used in the Common Object Request Broker Architecture (CORBA) system of objects to build distributed object systems. Is this good? Yes. Both IDL interfaces and the CORBA system are used in a wide variety of computer systems and this variety facilitates Java's platform independence.

▶ **See** Chapter 42, "JavaIDL: A Java Interface to CORBA," to learn more about CORBA, **p. 939**

As part of the effort to keep Java simple, not everything in this object-oriented language is an object. Booleans, numbers, and other simple types are not objects, but Java does have wrapper objects for all simple types. Wrapper objects enable all simple types to be implemented as though they are classes.

It is important to remember that Java is unforgivingly object oriented; it simply does not allow you to declare anything that is not encapsulated in an object. Even though C++ is considered an OOP language, it enables you to develop bad habits and not encapsulate types.

▶ **See** Chapter 7, "Data Types and Other Tokens," to learn more about types, **p. 97**

Object-oriented design is also the mechanism that allows modules to "plug and play." The object-oriented facilities of Java are essentially those of C++, with extensions from Objective C for more dynamic method resolution.

The Java Virtual Machine

The heart of Java is the Java Virtual Machine, or JVM. The JVM is a virtual computer that resides in memory only. The JVM enables Java programs to be executed on a variety of platforms as opposed to only the one platform for which the code is compiled. The fact that Java programs are compiled for the JVM is what makes the language so unique, but in order for Java programs to run on a particular platform, the JVM must be implemented for that platform.

▶ **See** Chapter 53, "Inside the Java Virtual Machine," to learn more about the JVM, **p. 1253**

The JVM is the very reason that Java is portable. It provides a layer of abstraction between the compiled Java program and the underlying hardware platform and operating system.

The JVM is actually very small when implemented in RAM. It is purposely designed to be small so that it can be used in a variety of consumer electronics. In fact, the whole Java language was originally developed with household electronics in mind. Gadgets such as phones, PCs, appliances, television sets, and so on will soon have the JVM in their firmware and allow Java programs to run. Cool, huh?

Java Source Code

Java source code is compiled to the bytecode level, as opposed to the bitcode level. The JVM executes the Java bytecode. The javac program, which is the Java compiler, reads files with the .java extension, converts the source code in the .java file into bytecodes, and saves the resulting bytecodes in a file with a .class extension.

The JVM reads the stream of bytecode from the .class file as a sequence of instructions. Each instruction consists of a one-byte opcode, which is a specific and recognizable command, and zero or more operands (the data needed to complete the opcode). The opcode tells the JVM what to do. If the JVM needs more than just the opcode to perform an action, then an operand immediately follows the opcode.

See Chapter 52, "Understanding the `.class` File," to learn about opcodes, **p. 1233**

There are four parts to the JVM:

- Stack
- Registers
- Garbage-collection heap
- Method area

The Java Stack

The size of an address in the JVM is 32 bits. Therefore, it can address up to 4G of memory, with each memory location containing one byte. Each register in the JVM stores one 32-bit address. The stack, the garbage-collection heap, and the method area reside somewhere within the 4G of addressable memory. This 4G of addressable memory limit isn't really a limitation now, because most PCs don't have more than 32M of RAM. Java methods are limited to 32K in size for each single method.

Java Registers

All processors use registers. The JVM uses the following to manage the system stack:

- *Program counter* Keeps track of where exactly the program is in execution.
- *Optop* Points to the top of the operand stack.
- *Frame* Points to the current execution environment.
- *Vars* Points to the first local variable of the current execution environment.

The Java development team decided that Java would only use four registers because if Java had more registers than the processor it was being ported to, that processor would take a serious reduction in performance.

The stack is where parameters are stored in the JVM. The JVM is passed to the bytecode from the Java program and creates a stack frame for each method. Each frame holds three kinds of information:

- *Local variables* An array of 32-bit variables that is pointed to by the vars register.
- *Execution environment* Where the method is executed and is pointed to by the frame register.
- *Operand stack* Acts on the first-in, first-out principle, or FIFO. It is 32 bits wide and holds the arguments necessary for the opcodes. The top of this stack is indexed by the optop register.

Garbage-Collection Heap

The heap is the collection of memory from which class instances are allocated. Any time you allocate memory with the new operator, that memory comes from the heap. You can call the garbage collector directly, but it is not necessary or recommended under most circumstances. The runtime environment keeps track of the references to each object on the heap and automatically frees the memory occupied by objects that are no longer referenced. Garbage collections run as a thread in the background and clean up during CPU inactivity.

The Java Method Area

The JVM has two other memory areas:

- Method
- Constant pool

There are no limitations as to where these memory areas must actually exist, making the JVM more portable and secure. The fact that memory areas can exist anywhere makes the JVM more secure in the fact that a hacker couldn't forge a memory pointer.

The JVM handles the following primitive data types:

- byte (8 bits)
- float (32 bits)
- int (32 bits)
- short (16 bits)
- double (64 bits)
- char (16 bits)
- long (64 bits)

Security and the JVM

This section is organized into six parts. You will explore the issue of security of networked computing in general and define the security problem associated with executable content. I propose a six-step approach to constructing a viable and flexible security mechanism. How the architecture of the Java language implements security mechanisms will also be covered. As with any new technology, there are several open questions related to Java security, which are still being debated on the Net and in other forums.

Executable Content and Security

In this section, you will analyze the concept of security in the general context of interactivity on the Web and security implementation via executable content.

Let's examine the duality of security versus interactivity on the Web and examine the evolution of the Web as a medium in the context of this duality. To do this, let's create a definition of the security problem in the context of executable content.

The Security Problem Defined A program arriving from outside the computer via the network has to be greeted by the user with a certain degree of trust and allowed a corresponding degree of access to the computer's resources to serve any useful purpose. The program is written by someone else, however, under no contractual or transactional obligation to the user. If this someone is a hacker, the executable content coming in could be a malicious program with the same degree of freedom as a local program.

See Chapter 34, "Java Security in Depth," to learn more about Java Security, **p. 769**

Does the user have to restrict completely the outside program from accessing any resource whatsoever on the computer? Of course not. This would cripple the ability of executable content to do anything useful at all. A more complete and viable security solution strategy would be a six-step approach:

1. Anticipate all potential malicious behavior and attack scenarios.
2. Reduce all such malicious behavior to a minimal orthogonal basis set.
3. Construct a programming environment/computer language that implicitly disallows the basis set of malicious behavior and, hence, by implication, all potential malicious behavior.
4. Logically or, if possible, axiomatically prove that the language/environment is indeed secure against the intended attack scenarios.
5. Implement and allow executable content using only this proven secure language.
6. Design the language such that any new attack scenarios arising in the future can be dealt with by a corresponding set of countermeasures that can be retrofitted into the basic security mechanism.

Working backwards from the previous solution strategy, the security problem associated with executable content can be stated as consisting of the following six subproblems:

- What are the potential target resources and corresponding attack scenarios?
- What is the basic, minimal set of behavioral components that can account for the previous scenarios?
- How should a computer language/programming environment that implicitly forbids the basis set of malicious behavior be designed?
- How can you prove that such a language/environment is, indeed, secure as claimed?
- How can you make sure that incoming executable content has, indeed, been implemented in and originated from the trusted language?
- How can you make the language future proof (extensible) to co-opt security strategies to counter new threats arising in the future?

As you will learn, Java has been designed from the ground up to address most (but probably not all) of the security problems as defined here. Before you move on to Java security architecture itself, the attack targets and scenarios are identified next.

Potential Vulnerability In this subsection, I list the various possible attack scenarios and resources on a user's computer that are likely to be targeted by a potentially malicious, external, executable content module.

Attack scenarios could belong to one of the following categories and have one of the following goals (this is not an exhaustive list):

- Damage or modify integrity of data and/or the execution state of programs.
- Collect and smuggle out confidential data.
- Lock up resources, making them unavailable for legitimate users and programs.
- Steal resources for use by an external, unauthorized party.
- Cause nonfatal but low-intensity unwelcome effects, especially on output devices.
- Usurp identity and impersonate the user or the user's computer to attack other targets on the network.

Table 2.1 lists the resources that could be potentially targeted and the type of attack they could be subject to. A good security strategy assigns security/risk weights to each resource and designs an appropriate access policy for external executable content.

Table 2.1 Potential Targets and Attack Scenarios

Targets	Damage Integrity	Smuggle Information	Lock Up/ Deny Usage	Steal Resource	Nonfatal Distraction	Impersonate
File system	X	X	X	X	X	
Confidential data	X	X	X		X	X
Network	X	X	X	X		X
CPU		X	X	X		
Memory	X	X	X	X		
Output devices		X	X	X	X	
Input devices		X	X		X	
OS, program state	X		X	X	X	

Java Approach to Security

This following discussion is in reference to the six-step approach outlined in the previous section.

Step 1: Visualize All Attack Scenarios Instead of coming up with every conceivable attack scenario, the Java security architecture posits potential targets of a basic set of attack categories very similar to the previous attack scenario matrix.

Specifically, the Java security model covers the following potential targets:

- Memory
- OS/program state
- Client file system
- Network

against the following attack types listed in Table 2.1:

- Damage integrity of software resources on the client machine. Achieved by what is usually called a virus. A virus is usually written to hide itself in memory and corrupt specific files when a particular event occurs or on a certain date.
- Lock up/deny usage of resource on the client machine. Usually achieved by a virus.
- Smuggle information out of the client machine. Can be done easily with UNIX SENDMAIL, for example.
- Impersonate the client machine. Can be done through IP spoofing. This style of attack was brought to the attention of the world by Kevin Mitnick when he hacked into one of computer security guru Tsutumo Shimura's personal machines. The whole incident is well-documented in the *New York Times* best-selling book *Takedown* by Tsutumo Shimura.

Step 2: Construct a Basic Set of Malicious Behavior Instead of arriving at a basic set of malicious behavior, Java anticipates a basic set of security hotspots and implements a mechanism to secure each of these:

- Java language mechanism and compiler.
- Java-compiled class file.
- Java bytecode verifier and interpreter.
- Java runtime system, including class loader, memory manager, and thread manager.
- Java external environment, such as Java Web browsers and their interface mechanisms.
- Java applets and the degrees of freedom allowed for applets (which constitute executable content).

Step 3: Design Security Architecture Against Previous Behavior Set Construct a programming environment/computer language that implicitly disallows the basic set of malicious behavior and hence, by implication, all potential malicious behavior. You guessed it—this language is Java!

Step 4: Prove the Security of Architecture This step involves logically or, if possible, axiomatically proving that the language/environment is indeed secure against the intended attack scenarios.

Security mechanisms built into Java have not (yet) been axiomatically or even logically proven to be secure. Instead, Java encapsulates all its security mechanism into distinct and well-defined layers. Each of these security loci can be observed to be secure by inspection in relation to the language design framework and target execution environment of Java language programs and applets.

Step 5: Restrict Executable Content to Proven Secure Architecture The Java class file checker and bytecode verifier achieve this objective.

Step 6: Make Security Architecture Extensible This step requires that the language be designed. Design the language such that any new attack scenarios arising in the future can be dealt with by a corresponding set of counter-measures, which can be retrofitted into the basic security mechanism.

The encapsulation of security mechanisms into distinct and well-defined loci, combined with the provision of a Java SecurityManager class, provides a generic mechanism for incremental enhancement of security.

Security at the Java Language Level

The first tier of security in Java is the language design itself—the syntactical and semantic constructs allowed by the language. The following is an examination of Java language design constructs with a bearing on security.

Strictly Object Oriented Java is fully object oriented, with every single primitive data structure (and, hence, derived data structure) being a first-class, full-fledged object. Having wrappers around each primitive data structure ensures that all the theoretical security advantages of OOP permeate the entire syntax and semantics of programs written in Java:

- Encapsulation and hiding of data behind private declarations.
- Controlled access to data structures via public methods only.
- Incremental and hierarchical complexity of program structure.
- No operator overloading.

Final Classes and Methods Classes and methods can be declared as final, which disallows further subclassing and method overriding. This declaration prevents malicious modification of trusted and verified code.

Strong Typing and Safe Typecasting Typecasting is security checked both statically and dynamically, which ensures that a declared compile-time type of an object is strictly compatible with eventual runtime type, even if the object transitions through typecasts and coercions. Typecasting prevents malicious type camouflaging.

No Pointers This is possibly the strongest guarantor of security that is built right into the Java language. Banishment of pointers ensures that no portion of a Java program is ever anonymous. Every single data structure and code fragment has a handle that makes it fully traceable.

Language Syntax for Thread-Safe Data Structures Java is multithreaded. Java language enforces thread-safe access to data structures and objects. Chapter 13, "Threads," examines Java threads in detail, with examples and application code.

Unique Object Handles Every single Java object has a unique hash code that is associated with it. This means that the state of a Java program can be fully inventoried at any time.

Security in Compiled Java Code

At compile time, all the security mechanisms implied by the Java language syntax and semantics are checked, including conformance to private and public declarations, typesafeness, and the initialization of all variables to a guaranteed known value.

Class Version and Class File Format Verification Each compiled class file is verified to conform to the currently published official class file format. The class file is checked for both structure and consistency of information within each component of the class file format. Cross-references between classes (via method calls or variable assignments) are verified for conformance to public and private declarations.

Each Java class is also assigned a major and minor version number. Version mismatches between classes within the same program are checked.

Bytecode Verification Java source classes are compiled into bytecodes. The bytecode verifier subjects the compiled code to a variety of consistency and security checks. The verification steps applied to bytecode include:

- Checking for stack underflows and overflows.
- Validating of register accesses.
- Checking for correctness of bytecode parameters.
- Analyzing dataflow of bytecode generated by methods to ensure integrity of a stack, objects passed into and returned by a method.

Namespace Encapsulation Java classes are defined within packages. Package names qualify Java class names. Packages ensure that code which comes from the network is distinguished from local code. An incoming class library cannot maliciously shadow and impersonate local trusted class libraries, even if both have the same name. This also ensures unverified, accidental interaction between local and incoming classes.

Very Late Linking and Binding Late linking and binding ensures that the exact layout of runtime resources, such as stack and heap, is delayed as much as possible. Late linking and binding constitutes a road block to security attacks by using specific assumptions about the allocation of these resources.

Java Runtime System Security

The default mechanism of runtime loading of Java classes is to fetch the referred class from a file on the local host machine. Any other way of loading a class—including from across the network—requires an associated ClassLoader. A ClassLoader is a subtype of the standard Java ClassLoader class, which has methods that implement all the consistency and security mechanisms and applies them to every class that is newly loaded.

For security reasons, the ClassLoader cannot make any assumptions about the bytecode, which could have been created from a Java program compiled with the Java compiler. The bytecode could also have been created by a C++ compiler modified to generate Java bytecode. This means the ClassLoader kicks in only after the incoming bytecode has been verified.

ClassLoader has the responsibility of creating a namespace for downloaded code and resolving the names of classes referenced by the downloaded code. The ClassLoader enforces package-delimited namespaces.

Automatic Garbage Collection and Implicit Memory Management In C and C++, the programmer has the explicit responsibility to allocate memory, deallocate memory, and keep track of all the pointers to allocated memory. This often is a maintenance nightmare and a major source of bugs that result from memory leaks, dangling pointers, null pointers, and mismatched allocation and deallocation operations.

Java eliminates pointers and, with it, the programmer's obligation to manage memory explicitly. Memory allocation and deallocation are automatic, strictly structured, and fully typesafe. Java uses garbage collection to free unused memory instead of explicit programmer-mediated deallocation. Garbage collection eliminates memory-related bugs as well as potential security holes. Manual allocation and deallocation allows unauthorized replication, cloning, and impersonation of trusted objects, as well as attacks on data consistency.

SecurityManager Class SecurityManager is a generic and extensible locus for implementing security policies and providing security wrappers around other parts of Java, including class libraries and external environments (such as Java-enabled browsers and native methods). The SecurityManager class itself is not intended to be used directly (each of the checks defaults to throwing a security exception). It is a shell class that is intended to be fleshed out via subclassing to implement a specific set of security policies.

Among other features, SecurityManager has methods to determine whether a security check is in progress and also checks the following:

- To prevent the installation of additional ClassLoaders.
- If dynamic libraries can be linked (used for native code).
- If a class file can be read from.
- If a file can be written to.
- If a network connection can be created.
- If a certain network port can be listened to for connections.
- If a network connection can be accepted.
- If a certain package can be accessed.
- If a new class can be added to a package.
- The security of a native OS system call.

Security of Executable Code

The major source of security threats from and to Java programs is Java code that comes in across the network and executes on the client machine. This class of transportable Java programs is called the Java applet class. A Java applet has a very distinct set of capabilities and restrictions within the language framework, especially from the security standpoint.

File System and Network Access Restrictions Applets loaded over the network have the following restrictions imposed on them:

- They cannot read or write files on the local file system.
- They cannot create, rename, or copy files and directories on the local file system.
- They cannot make arbitrary network connections, except to the host machine they originally came from. The host machine would be the host domain name specified in the URL of the HTML page that contains the `<APPLET>` tag for the applet, or the host name specified in the `CODEBASE` parameter of the `<APPLET>` tag. The numeric IP address of the host does not work.

The previous strict set of restrictions on access to a local file system applies to applets running under Netscape Navigator. The JDK AppletViewer slightly relaxes the restrictions by letting the user define a specific, explicit list of files that can be accessed by applets.

Now, as you will learn in Chapter 16, "JAR," it is possible to overcome the limitations on applets in 1.1-compliant browsers by "signing" the files. This enables applets that need to perform one of these functions this capability while maintaining a security framework.

External Code Access Restrictions Applets cannot do the following:

- Call external programs via such system calls as fork or exec.
- Manipulate any Java thread groups except their own thread group that is rooted in the main applet thread.

System Information Access Applets can read some system properties by invoking System.getProperty (String key). Applets under Netscape have unrestricted access to these properties. Sun's JDK AppletViewer enables individual control over access to each property. Table 2.2 lists the type of information returned for various values of key.

Table 2.2 System Variable Availability

Key	Information Returned
java.version	Java version number
java.vendor	Java vendor-specific string
java.vendor.url	Java vendor URL
java.class.version	Java class version number
os.name	Operating system name

continues

Table 2.2 Continued

Key	Information Returned
os.arch	Operating system architecture
file.separator	File separator (such as /)
path.separator	Path separator (such as :)
line.separator	Line separator

Inaccessible System Information The information provided in Table 2.3 is not accessible to applets under Netscape. AppletViewer and the HotJava browser enable user-controllable access to one or more of these resources.

Table 2.3 System Variables Restricted from Applets

Key	Information Returned
java.home	Java installation directory
java.class.path	Java classpath
user.name	User's account name
user.home	User's home directory
user.dir	User's current working directory

Applets Loaded from the Local Client There are two different ways that applets are loaded by a Java system (note: this applies only to AppletViewer). An applet can arrive over the network or be loaded from the local file system. The way an applet is loaded determines its degree of freedom.

If an applet arrives over the network, it is loaded by the ClassLoader and is subject to security checks imposed by the ClassLoader and SecurityManager classes. If an applet resides on the client's local file system in a directory listed in the user's `CLASSPATH` environment variable, then it is loaded by the file system loader.

From a security standpoint, locally loaded applets can:

- Read and write the local file system.
- Load libraries on the client.
- Execute external processes on the local machine.
- Exit the JVM.
- Skip being checked by the bytecode verifier.

Open Issues

Having examined the issue of security of executable content both in general and specifically in the framework of Java, you now examine some aspects of security that are not fully addressed by the current version of the Java architecture. You also learn if, for some types of threats, 100 percent security can be achieved.

The following components of the Java architecture are the loci of security mechanisms:

- Language syntax and semantics.
- Compiler and compiled class file format and version checker.
- Bytecode verifier and interpreter.
- Java runtime system, including ClassLoader, SecurityManager, memory, and thread management.
- Java external environment, such as Java Web browsers and their interface mechanisms.
- Java applets and the degrees of freedom allowed for applets (which constitute executable content).

Security provided by each of these layers, however, can be diluted or defeated in some ways with varying degrees of difficulty:

- Data layout in the source code can be haphazard and exposed despite hiding and control mechanisms provided by Java syntax. This situation can lead to security breaches if, for instance, access and assignment to objects are not thread safe or data structures that ought to be declared private are instead exposed as public resources.
- The runtime system is currently implemented in a platform-dependent, non-Java language, such as C. The only way to ensure the system is not compromised is by licensing it from Sun or comparing it with a reference implementation.

  Using runtime systems written in non-Java languages can lead to a security compromise if, instead of using Sun's own runtime system or a verified clone, someone uses a home-brew or no-name version of the runtime that has diluted versions of the class loader or bytecode verifier.
- The interface between Java and external non-Java environments, such as Web browsers, may be compromised.

Security issues that cannot easily be addressed within Java (or any other mechanism of executable content, for that matter) include:

- CPU resources on the client side can be stolen. A user can send an applet to your computer that uses your CPU to perform some computation and returns the results back to the user.
- Applets can contain nasty or annoying content (images, audio, or text). If this happens often, users have to block applets on a per-site basis. User-definable content filtering should be integrated into the standard Java class library.
- An applet can allocate an arbitrary amount of memory.

- An applet can start up an arbitrary number of threads.
- Security compromises can arise out of inherent weaknesses in Internet protocols, especially those that were implemented before Java and executable content burst on the scene.

One generic way to deal with security problems is for Java applet classes to be sent encrypted and digitally signed. The ClassLoader, SecurityManager, and even the bytecode verifier can include built-in decryption and signature verification methods.

NOTE These and other open issues related to Java security are topics of ongoing debate and exploration of specific and involved security breach scenarios, especially on online forums. The next and final section of this chapter points to references and sources of further information on this topic.

The Java API

The Java Application Programming Interface, or API, is a set of classes developed by Sun for use with the Java language. It is designed to assist you in developing your own classes, applets, and applications. With these sets of classes already written for you, you can write an application in Java that is only a few lines long, as opposed to an application that would be hundreds of lines long if it were written in C. Which would you rather debug?

The classes in the Java API are grouped into packages, each of which may have several classes and interfaces. Furthermore, each of these items may also have several properties, such as fields and/or methods.

Although it is possible to program in Java without knowing too much about the API, every class that you develop will be dependent on at least one class within the API, with the exception of java.lang.Object, which is the superclass of all other objects. Consequently, when you begin to develop more complex programs that deal with strings, sockets, and graphical interfaces, it is extremely helpful for you to know the objects provided to you by Sun, as well as the properties of these objects.

I suggest downloading the Core API in HTML format from JavaSoft and reading through it to really get a good feel of how the language works. As you go through each package, you will begin to understand how easy to use and powerful an object-oriented language like Java can be.

Java Core API

The Core API is the API that is currently shipped with Java 1.1. These packages make up the objects that are guaranteed to be available, regardless of the Java implementation, so long as the implementation supports at least version 1.1:

- java.lang
- java.lang.reflect

- java.bean
- java.rmi, java.rmi.registry, and java.rmi.server
- java.security, java.security.acl, and java.security.interfaces
- java.io
- java.util
- java.util.zip
- java.net
- java.awt
- java.awt.image
- java.awt.peer
- java.awt.datatransfer
- java.awt.event
- java.applet
- java.sql
- java.text

NOTE Those packages that were added under 1.1 are only guaranteed to be available on machines supporting the 1.1 API.

java.lang The java.lang package consists of classes that are the core of the Java language. It provides you not only with the basic data types, such as Character and Integer, but also the means of handling errors through the Throwable and Error classes. Furthermore, the SecurityManager and System classes supply you with some degree of control over the Java Runtime System.

See Chapter 47, "java.lang," to learn more about java.lang, **p. 1079**

java.io The java.io package serves as the standard input/output library for the Java language. This package provides you with the ability to create and handle streams of data in several ways. It provides you with types as simple as a String and as complex as a StreamTokenizer.

java.util The java.util package is composed essentially of a variety of useful classes that do not truly fit in any of the other packages. Among these handy classes are:

- Date class, designed to manage and handle operations with dates.
- Hashtable class.
- Classes to develop ADTs, such as Stack and Vector.

See Chapter 46, "Data Structures and Java Utilities," to learn more about the java.util package, **p. 1049**

java.net The java.net package is the package that makes Java a networked-based language. It provides you with the capability to communicate with remote sources by creating or connecting to sockets or using URLs. You can write your own Telnet, Chat, or FTP clients and/or servers, for example, by using this package.

java.awt The java.awt package is also known as the Java Abstract Window Toolkit (AWT). It consists of resources that enable you to create rich, attractive, and useful interfaces in your applets and standalone applications. The AWT not only contains managerial classes, such as GridBagLayout, but it also has several concrete interactive tools, such as Button and TextField. More importantly, however, is the Graphics class that provides you with a wealth of graphical abilities, including the ability to draw shapes and display images.

java.awt.image The java.awt.image package is closely related to the java.awt package. This package consists of tools that are designed to handle and manipulate images coming across a network.

java.awt.peer java.awt.peer is a package of interfaces that serve as intermediaries between your code and the computer on which your code is running. You probably won't need to work directly with this package.

java.applet The java.applet package is the smallest package in the API, but it is also the most notable as a result of the Applet class. This class is full of useful methods, as it lays the foundation for all applets and is also able to provide you with information regarding the applet's surroundings via the AppletContext interface.

1.1 Packages The following packages were added to Java during the 1.1 upgrade:

java.awt.datatransfer java.awt.datatransfer provides classes for dealing with the transfer of data. This includes new classes for clipboards and the capability to send Java strings.

java.awt.event Under JDK 1.0, all events used a single class called java.awt.event. This mechanism proved to be fairly clumsy and difficult to extend. To combat this, the java.awt.event package provides you the ability to use events any way you want.

JavaBean API

The JavaBean API defines a portable, platform-neutral set of APIs for software components. JavaBean components are also able to plug into existing component architectures, such as Microsoft's OLE/COM/ActiveX architecture, OpenDoc, and Netscape's LiveConnect. The advantage of JavaBean is that end users are able to join JavaBean components using application builders, such as the BeanBox. A button component could trigger a bar chart to be drawn in another component, for example, or a live data feed component could be represented as a chart in another component.

java.rmi, java.rmi.registry, and java.rmi.server The java.rmi, java.rmi.registry, and java.rmi.server packages provide all the tools you need to perform Remote Method Invocation (RMI). Using RMI you can create objects on a remote computer (server) and use them on a local computer (client) seamlessly.

▶ **See** Chapter 36, "Remote Method Invocation," to learn more about RMI, **p. 809**

java.lang.reflect The java.lang.reflect package provides the tools you need to reflect objects. Reflection enables you to inspect a runtime object to determine what its constructors, methods, and fields are.

▶ **See** Chapter 48, "Reflection," to learn more, **p. 1129**

java.security, java.security.acl, and java.security.interfaces The java.security packages provide the tools necessary for you to use encryption in your Java programs. By using the java.security packages, you can securely transfer data back and forth from a client to a server.

▶ **See** Chapter 34, "Java Security in Depth," to learn more about the java.security packages, **p. 769**

java.sql The java.sql package encompasses what is known as JDBC, or the Java DataBase Connectivity. JDBC enables you to access relation databases, such as Microsoft SQL Server or Sybase SQL Anywhere.

▶ **See** Chapters 38 to 40 to learn more about JDBC, **p. 855**

NOTE Printed documentation for all the APIs is available from the JavaSoft Web site at **http://www.javasoft.com**.

New to JDK 1.2

The following packages were added during the upgrade to 1.2:

Java Enterprise API The Java Enterprise API supports connectivity to enterprise databases and legacy applications. With these APIs, corporate developers are building distributed client/server applets and applications in Java that run on any OS or hardware platform in the enterprise.

Java Database Connectivity, or JDBC, is a standard SQL database access interface that provides uniform access to a wide range of relational databases. You have probably heard of ODBC. Sun has left no stone unturned in making Java applicable to every standard in the computing industry today.

Java IDL is developed to the OMG Interface Definition Language specification as a language-neutral way to specify an interface between an object and its client on a different platform.

Java RMI is a remote-method invocation between peers or the client and server when applications at both ends of the invocation are written in Java.

Java Commerce API The JavaCommerce API brings secure purchasing and financial management to the Web. JavaWallet is the initial component, which defines and implements a client-side framework for credit card, debit card, and electronic cash transactions. Just imagine—surfing the Internet will take up all of your spare time…and money!

Java Server API Java Server API is an extensible framework that enables and eases the development of a whole spectrum of Java-powered Internet and intranet servers. The Java Server API provides uniform and consistent access to the server and administrative system resources. This API is required for developers to quickly develop their own Java servlets—executable programs that users upload to run on networks or servers.

Java Media API The Java Media API easily and flexibly allows developers and users to take advantage of a wide range of rich, interactive media on the Web. The Media Framework has clocks for synchronizing and media players for playing audio, video, and MIDI. Two-D and 3D provide advanced imaging models. Animation provides for motion and transformations of 2D objects. Java Share provides for sharing of applications among multiple users, such as a shared white board. Finally, Telephony integrates the telephone with the computer. This API is probably the most fun of all to explore.

Java Security API The Java Security API is a framework for developers to include security functionality easily and securely in their applets and applications. This functionality includes cryptography with digital signatures, encryption, and authentication.

Java Management API Java Management API provides a rich set of extensible Java objects and methods for building applets that can manage an enterprise network over the Internet and intranets. It has been developed in collaboration with SunSoft and a broad range of industry leaders including AutoTrol, Bay Networks, BGS, BMC, Central Design Systems, Cisco Systems, Computer Associates, CompuWare, LandMark Technologies, Legato Systems, Novell, OpenVision, Platinum Technologies, Tivoli Systems, and 3Com.

Java Embedded API

The Java Embedded API specifies how the Java API may be subsetted for embedded devices that are incapable of supporting the full Java Core API. It includes a minimal embedded API based on java.lang, java.util, and parts of java.io. It then defines a series of extensions for particular areas, such as networking and GUIs. ●

CHAPTER 3

Installing The JDK and Getting Started

In this chapter

Why You Need Sun's Java Development Kit to Write Java

This chapter intends to help you install Java, give you a basic introduction to the Java Development Kit, and give you several Java-enabled browsers. By the end of the chapter, you will have installed what you need to get going and you'll have compiled and run your first Java application.

The Java Development Kit (JDK) is a software package that Sun has made available to the public for free. This package gives you all the tools you need to start writing and running Java programs. It includes all the basic components that make up the Java environment, including the Java compiler, the Java interpreter, an applet viewer that lets you see applets without opening a Java-compatible Web browser, as well as a number of other programs useful in creating Java programs. The JDK represents the bare minimum of what you need to work with Java.

If there's no such thing as a free lunch, then JDK is more of a free light snack. Although it does contain all the tools you really need to work with Java, it isn't the integrated development environment many programmers are used to working with. The tools that come with the JDK are command-line driven and they don't have a nice graphical user interface like those of Visual C++ or Borland C++. The tools are intended to be executed from the command prompt (the DOS prompt, for Windows 95 and NT systems). The files that contain your source code are plain ASCII text files you create with a text editor (which you need to supply), such as the NotePad (for Win32 systems), vi (on UNIX), or BBEdit (on the Macintosh).

NOTE A growing number of integrated development environments (IDEs) are available from various third-party companies, each with various features that make life easier on the programmer. If you decide to do your Java development with an IDE, you will probably get a code editor that can colorize Java code, a project file manager, and a faster compiler. Most of the major development companies have IDEs for Java. Microsoft (Visual J++), Borland (JBuilder), Symantec (Cafe), IBM (Visual Age for Java), Metroworks (CodeWarrior), and Aysmetrix (SuperCede) are just a few of the commercial Java development environments available. Each has strengths and weaknesses. If you plan on doing serious Java development, check them out and see which fits your programming needs the best. Even if you plan to use an integrated development environment (IDE) like Visual J++, Visual Café or Visual Age for Java, you will want to learn about the JDK because it's the reference by which all others are compared.

More on How Java Is Both Compiled and Interpreted

A C++ compiler takes high-level C++ code and compiles it into instructions a computer's microprocessor can understand (Machine Code). This means that every different type of computer platform will need a separate compiling of a given C++ program in order to be able to run it. Taking a C++ program and compiling it on different types of computers is not an easy task. Because different computers do things in different ways, the C++ program has to be able to handle those differences. This is a significant problem when dealing with the wide variety of computer platforms available today.

The Java environment overcomes this problem by putting a middleman between the compiler and the computer called the Java Virtual Machine (JVM). Instead of compiling directly for one type of computer, the Java compiler, javac, takes the high-level, human-readable Java source code in a text file and compiles it into lower-level Java bytecodes that the JVM understands. The JVM then takes that bytecode and interprets it so that the Java program runs on the computer the JVM is running on. The only platform-specific program is the JVM itself. Similarly, Web browsers that support Java applets all have JVMs built into them.

The JVM concept provides a number of advantages, the main one being cross-platform compatibility. Java programmers don't need to worry about how a computer platform handles specific tasks and they don't need to worry about how to compile different versions of their program to run on different platforms. The only platform that programmers need to worry about is the JVM. Programmers can be reasonably confident that their program will run on whatever platforms have JVMs, such as Windows 95, Solaris, and Macintosh.

CAUTION

Even with Java, there are slight differences between platforms. When working with Java, it's a good idea to test a program on as many different types of computers as possible.

On the other hand, languages like Basic are not compiled. In order to run the program, you need a basic interpreter, which reads each line of code, parses out what you've written, and figures out all the machine-code necessary to run the program. The major disadvantage of this type of interpreter is that it requires a lot of processing power, so inevitably it is very slow.

Because Java is compiled, it meets you halfway. The amount of interpretation is therefore greatly reduced. The main disadvantage of this system is that interpreting code is still slower than running a program that is native to the host computer. For each instruction in the Java bytecode, the JVM must figure out what the equivalent is for the system it is running on. This creates a slowdown in processing a Java program.

To overcome the speed limitation of Java, a number of Just-In-Time compilers (JITs) are available. JITs make the Java system even more confusing, but they make it run much faster by taking the already compiled Java bytecode and compiling it into instructions that are native to a given computer. It's all done transparently to the user from within the JVM. The JIT, because it's part of the JVM, is also platform-specific but runs any Java bytecode, regardless of what type of machine it comes from. Using a JIT, a Java program can achieve speeds close to that of a native C++ program.

Getting and Installing Sun's JDK

Now that you know a little bit more about what Java and the JDK are, you're now ready to get going on actually installing and using it.

If you haven't done so already, sit down at your computer, turn it on, and load the CD-ROM from the back of the book. On the CD-ROM is a directory called JDK. Inside the directory "JDK" are three subdirectories: `MACINTOSH`, `SOLARIS`, and `WINDOWS`. Each of these subdirectories contains the complete installation of Sun's Java Developer's Kit for each of those three platforms. Table 3.1 shows what those refer to.

Table 3.1 Contents of the JDK Folder on the CD-ROM

Directory	Contents
MACINTOSH	Contains the JDK for the Macintosh platform, both 68k and PowerPC.
SOLARIS	Contains two subdirectories, one for the SPARC Solaris JDK and one for the x86 Solaris JDK.
WINDOWS	Contains the JDK for x86 32-bit Windows systems, namely Windows 95 and Windows NT.

NOTE Alternately, you can use a Web browser and a connection to the Internet to receive the JDK. If you are going to download it, see the section "Downloading the JDK" later in this chapter.

What if you're not using one of those three platforms? You may or may not be in luck. A number of other JDKs exist for other platforms, but you may need to look around the Internet for them. The three previous ones are supported by Sun; any other platforms are not. There are ports for systems such as Linux, DEC Alpha, Amiga, OS/2 and many others. The best place to look for information on those releases is the list of third party ports on Sun's list: `http://www.javasoft.com/products/jdk/1.2/`.

Now you'll look at how to install the JDK onto 32-bit Windows systems from the CD-ROM. The setup is fairly easy, but you should be familiar with the Windows and DOS environments before attempting to install the JDK.

Installing the JDK Off the CD-ROM for Windows 95 and NT

Step 1: Remove Previous Versions of the JDK There should not be any copies of previous versions of the Java Developers Kit on your computer. If you have stored any additional Java source code files (files you have written or files you have received from someone else) in a directory under the main JDK Java directory, you should move those files to a new directory before deleting previous versions of the JDK. You can delete the entire Java directory tree using Windows Explorer or the File Manager.

Step 2: Unpacking the JDK After removing the previous version of the JDK, execute the self-extracting archive to unpack the JDK files. You should unpack the file in the root directory of the C drive to create C:\JDK1.2. If you want the JDK in some other directory, unpack the archive file in that directory. Unpacking the archive creates a Java parent directory and all the necessary subdirectories for this release.

If you look through the files that are installed with the JDK you will find a several files in the lib and jre\lib files with the extension `.jar`. The `.jar` files contain the runtime API classes necessary for the Java VM to operate successfully. Note: prior to JDK 1.2 the setup program created a file called lib/classes.zip instead of the various `.jar` files. DO NOT UNZIP THE `CLASSES.ZIP` FILE.

Step 3: Update Environment Variables After unpacking, you should add the `JAVA\BIN` directory onto the path. The easiest way to accomplish this is to edit the `AUTOEXEC.BAT` file and make the change to the path statement there.

If you have set the `CLASSPATH` environment variable, you may need to update it. For instance, you may have to make a `CLASSPATH` entry that points to the `jdk1.2\jre\lib\rt.jar` file. Again, the easiest way to accomplish this is to edit the `AUTOEXEC.BAT` file and make the change to the `CLASSPATH` environment variable there, or you can let the setup program make the changes for you.

After completing these changes to `AUTOEXEC.BAT`, save the file and reboot so the changes take effect.

The next section covers the installation of the JDK for x86 and SPARC Solaris UNIX Systems. This installation procedure is similar to some of the other UNIX operating system installations. For more information about getting ports of the JDK for other UNIX systems (such as Linux) see Chapter 49, "Java Resources."

Installing the JDK Off the CD-ROM for x86 and SPARC Solaris

The setup for installing the JDK onto a 32-bit Windows system is fairly easy, but you should be familiar with the Windows and DOS environments before attempting to install the JDK.

Step 1: Copy the Directory to Your Hard Drive Copy the appropriate directory (either the x86 or Sparc Solaris release directory) onto your hard drive. Depending on how your file system is configured and the privileges on your system, you might want to either copy the directory into a public area, such as `/usr/local/` or into your home directory. The command to copy the Sparc release from the Solaris directory on the CD-ROM to your home directory is

```
>cp -r sparc ~/
```

Step 2: Set Your Environment Variables The `CLASSPATH` variable is an environment variable that defines a path to the `rt.jar` file. Most of the tools that come with the JDK use the `CLASSPATH` variable to find that file, so having it set correctly is fairly important. You can set the `CLASSPATH` variable at the command prompt by entering the following:

```
% setenv CLASSPATH .:/usr/local/jdk1.2/jre/lib/rt.jar
```

Or you can put this line of text in your `.login` or `.profile` files, so it's called every time you log in:

```
setenv CLASSPATH .:/usr/local/jdk1.2/jre/lib/rt.jar
```

NOTE If you are using a version of Java prior to JDK 1.2, you will need to substitute `jre/lib/rt.jar` with `lib/classes.zip` in all of the examples through out this book.

Downloading the JDK

You can download the JDK off the Internet instead of getting it from the CD-ROM in the back of the book. When you download the JDK off the Internet, you can be fairly certain that you're getting the latest version of it.

What You Need to Download the JDK The first item you need to download the JDK is a computer with a connection to the Internet that can use a Web browser. The particular browser doesn't really matter all that much, but the Netscape Navigator browser is used for these examples.

The second item you need is some (well, actually, quite a bit) of free hard disk space on the machine to which you are planning to download the JDK. Table 3.3 contains the amounts of disk space you need to download and uncompress the JDK for each platform.

Table 3.3 Disk Space Requirements for the JDK 1.1

Platform	Disk Space Compressed	Disk Space Uncompressed
Solaris	13.7 MB	16.5 MB
Windows	5.77 MB	12.1 MB

Starting Your Download If you have some free disk space and a browser handy, you're ready to download. Now you can get started!

1. Launch your Net connection (if you need to do that) and your Web browser. If you are unsure of how to do this, consult your system administrator, your friends who know how to use computers, the manuals, or a book on using the Web, such as Que's *Special Edition Using the World Wide Web*.
2. Point your browser at the JavaSoft JDK download site at
   `http://www.javasoft.com/products/jdk/1.2/`
3. Scroll down to the pop-up menu that says "Download JDK Software" lists the various operating systems on which the JDK is available from Sun. Pick your operating system of choice in that pop-up menu.
4. Click the "Download Software" button just below the pop-up menu.

5. You'll hit a page that has a number of restrictions on the distribution of the JDK. Read each and, if you comply to all the restrictions, click the "Yes" button to go to the download page.
6. The page that now comes up has a list of various sites the JDK is available to download from. If there are options available, use the one closest to your location. Click the link to start the download.

The JDK is a pretty big file and downloading is going to take a while. How long it takes depends on how fast your connection is, the user load on the FTP server at that particular moment, the network load on the Internet at the time of day you are downloading the file, the beating of a butterfly's wings somewhere on the planet, sunspots, blind luck, and a large number of other factors that are even more difficult to predict. If the file transfer is going too slow for your taste, try connecting at another time. Depending on where you are on the planet, good times to connect will vary, again depending on many of the same factors that control the transfer rate.

Installing a Downloaded JDK

Now that you have the appropriate installer file for your computer somewhere handy on your hard drive, it is time to actually install the software so you can get to work programming. Each platform has its own standard installation procedures and the 1.2 release of the JDK is pretty good at following them to make installation a simple and straightforward procedure.

Solaris x86 and SPARC Platforms

For Solaris, the JDK 1.2 is normally distributed as a self-extracting shell script (a file with a .sh extension); the name of the file indicates its version.

CAUTION

Use tar or your standard system backup process to back up any previous releases of the JDK before beginning installation of a new version. You don't want to lose all that work you put into it and you'll have a copy of the previous release in the event something goes wrong with your new copy.

Installing the JDK on a Solaris machine can be done in one of two ways. It can either be installed into a user's home directory for individual use or it can be installed into a public bin directory, such as `/usr/local/bin/`, so that all users on a system can use it. The installation process is the same for both.

1. Choose a directory for the installation. These instructions assume an installation location of `/usr1/JDK1.2`. If you choose a different base directory, simply replace USR with the name of your installation directory. For example, if you choose to install under your home directory, everywhere you see `usr`, replace it with ~ or `$HOME`.

2. Verify that you have write permissions for the installation directory. Use this command to check the current permissions:

   ```
   ls -ld /usr1
   ```

   The options to the `ls` command specify a long listing, which includes information about ownership and permission, and also specifies to `ls` to not list the contents of the directory, which is the default. For more information about the `ls` command, see your system manuals.

   The output of the command should be similar to the following:

   ```
   drwxr-xr-x  root  other  512   Feb 18  21:34   /usr
   ```

   In this case, the directory is owned by root (the system administrator) and neither the group nor the general user community has permission to write to this directory. If you run into this situation and you are not root, you need the assistance of your system administrator to install in that directory.

3. Move or copy the JDK distribution file to `/USR1`.

4. Extract the JDK by typing a period, a space, and then the `jdk.sh` filename (such as `jdk1.2-solaris2-sparc.sh`).

   ```
   > . jdk1.2-solaris2-sparc.sh
   ```

   This executes the shell script, which then automatically uncompresses the file you need into the directories that you need them in.

5. Verify that the following subdirectories were created under `/USR1`:

   ```
   jdk1.2
   jdk1.2/bin
   jdk1.2/classes
   jdk1.2/demo
   jdk1.2/lib
   jdk1.2/src
   ```

6. Set your `PATH` environment variable. For the C shell and its derivatives, use:

   ```
   setenv PATH $PATH:/usr1/jdk1.2/bin
   ```

   For the Korn shell and its derivatives, use:

   ```
   PATH= $PATH;/usr1/jdk1.2/bin
   export PATH
   ```

7. Set your `CLASSPATH` environment variable. For the C shell and its derivatives, use:

   ```
   setenv CLASSPATH /usr1/jdk1.2/jre/lib/rt.jar
   ```

   For the Korn shell and its derivatives, use:

   ```
   CLASSPATH = CLASSPATH /usr1/jdk1.2/jre/lib/rt.jar
   export CLASSPATH
   ```

Rather than set these variables from the command line each time, you probably should add the commands to set the PATH and CLASSPATH variables in your shell resource file—`.shrc`, `.cshrc`, `.profile`, and so on. If you are a system administrator installing the JDK as a network development tool, you may want to add these parameters to the default configuration files.

Windows Installation

You need Windows 95 or Windows NT to run Java. For Windows 3.1, see "Installing IBM's Applet Developer's Kit for Windows 3.1" later in this chapter.

Installing the JDK is a fairly simple procedure, but you should know your way around the Windows and DOS environments. For Windows, the JDK is provided in a standard windows setup format; the name of the file indicates its version.

1. Choose a directory for the installation. These instructions assume an installation location of `C:\JDK1.2`. If you choose a different base directory, simply append the appropriate path (and change the drive letter, if appropriate). If you want to install to `E:\TOOLS\JAVA`, for example, replace `C:` with `e:\tools` whenever it shows up in the instructions.

CAUTION

Rename the JAVA directory (for example, to OLDJAVA) using the Explorer in Windows 95 or Windows NT. If the installation fails for any reason, you can restore the previous version directly from OLDJAVA. Otherwise, after the installation is complete, you can move any additional files, such as documentation, from your old installation into your new installation before removing it from your system.

2. If you plan on installing to a networked drive, make sure you have permission to write to the desired directory.
3. Extract the JDK by running the self-extracting program (double-clicking the icon in Explorer or File Manager works just fine).
4. Verify that the following subdirectories were created on drive C:\.

```
C:\JDK1.2
C:\JDK1.2\BIN
C:\JDK1.2\CLASSES
C:\JDK1.2\DEMO
C:\JDK1.2\LIB
```

For Windows NT 4.0 and later, you can skip steps 6, 7, and 8, and set the CLASSPATH from a properties sheet. You do not need to reboot, but you may have to close any DOS Prompt windows that you had open to use the new variable.

6. Add `C:\JDK1.2\BIN` to your `PATH` statement in your autoexec.bat file:

```
set PATH=c:\windows;c:\dos;...;c:\java\bin
```

7. Set your `CLASSPATH` environment variable in your autoexec.bat file:

```
set CLASSPATH=c:\java\jre\lib\rt.jar
```

8. Reboot your computer for the environment variables to take effect.

Macintosh Installation

For Macintosh, the JDK is normally distributed as a stuffed, bin-hexed archive (a file with a `HQX.SIT` extension). The file version is indicated in its name.

CAUTION

Make sure to archive your current version of the JDK before installing a newer version. You don't want to lose all that work you put into it and you'll have a copy of the previous release in the event something goes wrong with your new copy.

To install the JDK for Macintosh, follow the following steps.

1. After following the instructions earlier in this chapter for downloading the MacJDK 1.2, you should have an installer titled MacJDK.SEA. Double-click this installer so that it launches into a fairly standard Macintosh installer dialog box.

CAUTION

The Macintosh enables you to name directories and files in a manner that choke UNIX. Filenames that UNIX can't handle include the naming of directories with slashes (/). This causes problems with the JDK because it uses a mixed UNIX/Mac method of tracking paths when the JDK attempts to locate your files. Thus, a slash in the name of a directory is interpreted as a change of directory.

UNIX also has a few problems with names that include spaces. As of this release, you should follow the UNIX file and directory naming conventions used by the developers. This means you shouldn't use spaces, slashes, asterisks, and most other punctuation characters in your file and directory names. You can, however, use as many periods as you want, and the filename can be as long as you want it (as long as it's less than 32 characters).

For example, the following is a perfectly good Macintosh filename but will not work under UNIX:

```
/../..../Stuff \/\/..java
```

To work under UNIX and the Mac, the filename should look like this:

```
Stuff.java
```

2. In the lower-left corner of the installer dialog box in the Install Location area, you can specify where you want to install the JDK. After selecting the appropriate drive and directory, click the Install or hit "return" button to run the installer. It puts all the Mac JDK in a directory called `MACJDK` at whatever location you specify in the installer. The default installation location is the root level of your startup disk.

You now have a working copy of the JDK on your hard drive folder. This includes two essential programs: the Java compiler and the AppletViewer. You are now ready to move onto the next (and much more fun) parts of Java development.

Testing the Java Compiler and JVM

Now you're ready to write a small Java application to test your installation of the JDK.

Creating a New Java Project

Somewhere on your hard drive, create a new directory to store your projects. I call mine `PROJECTS` and I keep it out of the JDK directory, so that I don't need to move it around whenever I install a new version of the JDK. Inside that directory, create another directory called `HELLOWORLD`.

Now, using your favorite text editor (such as the NotePad, vi, emacs, SimpleText, or something else), create a file called `HelloWorld.java` (double-check your capitalization—Java is case-sensitive), and type into it:

```
public class HelloWorld {
    public static void main(String[] args) {
        System.out.println("Hello, World!");
    }
};
```

Don't worry about the details of syntax right now; just type that in, save it, and exit your text editor. Make sure it's saved as a standard ASCII text file.

Running a Java Application for UNIX or Windows

If you're on a UNIX or Windows machine, at the command (DOS) prompt, type the following:

```
javac HelloWorld.java
```

Your system should pause for a moment, then return you to your prompt.

Get a directory listing in a DOS window to make sure you have the following files:

```
>dir
HelloWorld.class     HelloWorld.java
```

Or, in UNIX, get a directory listing to make sure you have the following files:

```
>ls
HelloWorld.class     HelloWorld.java
```

If you get any errors, check the HelloWorld.java code to make sure it looks exactly as it does here.

If you get an error that javac was not found, you didn't set the `JAVA/BIN` directory in your `PATH` variable. Go back and check your installation.

Now you're ready to run your first Java program! At your command prompt, type the following:

```
>java HelloWorld
```

You should see the following:

```
Hello, World!
```

If you did, congratulations. You've run your first Java application, but more importantly, you've correctly and successfully installed the JDK.

If you didn't see "Hello, World!", there is something wrong with your installation. Check to make sure your `CLASSPATH` variable is set to point at both the current working directory (a period "`.`") and to the `rt.jar` file. Check to make sure you typed the name of the file correctly, keeping in mind that Java is case-sensitive. If none of that works, you may need to reinstall the JDK.

Running a Java Application for the Macintosh

The procedure for compiling and running a Java application is a bit different for a Macintosh because it doesn't have a command prompt.

1. On your Mac, open your HELLOWORLD folder so that your `HelloWorld.java` file appears.
2. Then open the MACJDK folder so that the Java compiler icon appears (it should be a little "Duke" with a "C" on his chest). Drag the `HelloWorld.java` file onto the Java compiler icon. The Java compiler then launches and begins compiling the program. When it's finished, a file called `HelloWorld.class` should appear in your HELLOWORLD folder.
3. If you received compile time errors, check the `HelloWorld.java` code to make sure it looks exactly the same as the previous code.
4. Double-click the `HelloWorld.class` file. The java runner application launches, loads the HelloWorld program, and runs the program. A window titled `stdout` should appear, with the words `Hello, World!` in them.

If it did, congrats. You've installed the JDK and run your first Java program.

If you didn't see `Hello, World!`, there is something wrong with your installation. Check to make sure you are running System 7, that the JDK installed completely, and that the filename and the name of the class generated match, keeping in mind that Java is case-sensitive. If you still can't get it to work, you may need to reinstall the JDK.

NOTE The authors of the Macintosh Java Runner application have cleverly hidden the Quit command in the Apple menu. Why they did that isn't known. If you want to free up the memory that the Java Runner is taking up after it's finished running your program, choose Apple, Java Runtime, Quit. Not very Mac-like, but at least it's not a command line.

To quit, you can just hit command-Q, like any other normal Mac program.

Installing IBM's Applet Developer's Kit for Windows 3.1

Why isn't there a Sun JDK for Windows 3.1? Well, a number of technical issues make porting the JDK tools to Windows 3.1 difficult, and with the release of Windows 95, Windows 3.1 was seen as a dying platform, so the decision was made to not directly support it. Some of these issues include the fact that Java needs long filenames such as the ".java" and ".class" filenames. The eight-character file name and three-character extension of Window's 3.1 naming system just couldn't fully support Java file names. A more difficult problem to solve, however, is the fact that Java is a multi-threaded language, meaning it can run more than one process at the same time, but Windows 3.1 doesn't support multithreading. In order to support Java in Windows 3.1, several groups undertook projects to port the JDK to 3.1, the most successful of which is IBM's ADK.

With IBM's release of their ADK, Windows 3.1 users now have a way to develop Java applets and applications without upgrading to Windows 95 or NT. It includes a number of programs that help get around the problems previously described, as well as improving upon the tools that come with the JDK.

Downloading the ADK

To get to the main ADK Web page, you first need to launch your Web browser and go to `http://www.alphaworks.ibm.com/`. This is the main Web page for a number of IBM's projects that are currently under development. To get to the ADK Web page, you'll need to pick the "ADK for Win 3.1" entry in the pop-up menu in the "Select" selection.

To completely install the ADK and use all its features, you need three components: the ADK itself, the Windows 32-bit extension Win32s, and the WinG graphics extension.

To download and install the two windows components, ftp to `ftp://ftp.microsoft.com/softlib/mslfiles/` and get the following two files:

```
pw1118.exe
wing10.exe
```

The WinG extension file name is wing10.exe and it is about 830k.

The Win32s file name is pw1118.exe and it is about 2.4 MB. You need to get and install both of these before installing the ADK.

To install these two system enhancements, make a temporary directory for each of the two and put the .exe files into them. Use either a DOS prompt or the Run command in the File menu of the program manager, to execute the .exe files. If you put the wing10.exe file in a directory called wingtemp on your C: drive, for example, the DOS prompt command would look like:

```
C:\wingtemp\>wing10.exe
```

This decompresses all the files to do the complete install. Each should decompress to a large number of files with an executable called setup.exe. After it is done decompressing, execute the setup program, again using either a DOS prompt or the File, Run menu. The setup program prompts you for some information and then installs all the needed files. After you are done installing these, you can delete the temporary directories you put the installer programs in.

When you have WinG and Win32s installed, you can proceed with the installation of the ADK itself. You will first need to read the ADK license agreement at `http://www.alphaWorks.ibm.com/ADK`.

At the bottom of the page is a button labeled "I Agree." If you read the license and agree to its terms, you can click that button, which takes you to the download page where you can download the ADK installer. The actual ADK file is rather large, about 4 MB, and will take a while to download, especially over a modem connection.

Once you've gotten the ADK installer, you can then execute it from the Windows program manager File, Run menu. It asks you for an installation directory (for example: `C:\java\`) and then it does its stuff, installing all the files you'll need to get up and running with the ADK.

When the ADK is completely installed, it creates a program group with the items in Table 3.4.

Table 3.4 Files in the ADK Program Group

Name	Description
Configure AppletViewer	This runs the AppletViewer and displays a license document.
ADK.WRI	The ADK User Guide—read this for more information on the ADK.
ADK File	A file manager type application that lets you manipulate files with long file names, rather than the Win 3.1 standard 8.3 file names.
ADK Edit	A small editor that integrates the ADK tools into one program, so you can work with Java code without having to switch between a number of other programs.
ADK Console	The guts of the ADK, this is the program that runs all the Java environment-based tools, such as AppletViewer and javac.

To set up the ADK, run the "Configure AppletViewer" program, agree to the license agreement, follow the instructions to configure the AppletViewer, and then close the applet.

To test your installation, follow these steps:

1. Launch the "ADK Console" program.
2. Select AppletViewer from the Tools menu.

3. Type **`C:\java\demo\Animator\`** into the Working Directory Field (or whatever directory you installed the ADK).
4. Type **`example1.html`** into the Command Options field.
5. Press OK.

This should launch the Animator applet and put a dancing Duke on your screen. If it did, then you're all set to develop Java programs on your Windows 3.1 machine. If it didn't, make sure that the path you put in the Working Directory field is actually the path that has the Animator applet and that there is a example1.html file in that directory. If not, you may need to go back through the installation process and try again. ●

CHAPTER 4

JDK Tools

In this chapter

JDK Tools Reference

This chapter is intended to cover all the tools that are included in the Java Developer's Kit. You'll learn about each tool, what it does, all its associated options, and the environment variables it references. If you're just beginning programming in Java, this chapter serves as an introduction to the tools of the JDK. If you're a hard-core Java hacker, this chapter is more of a reference tool, so you don't have to waste precious CPU cycles bringing the rather ugly man page reference materials. Either way, reading this chapter gives you a pretty good idea of what the JDK tools can do and how to make them do it.

AppletViewer

Applets are programs written in Java that are designed to run embedded in an HTML document, just like a Web page. Under most circumstances, they don't have the ability to run by themselves. The AppletViewer tool is a small program that lets you run applets without the overhead of launching a system that hogs the Web browser. It's a quick and easy way to test your applets as you're developing them.

You call the AppletViewer with the following command:

```
AppletViewer [ options ] URLs...
```

The URLs in the command line are the Uniform Resource Locators to HTML files that contain applet tags (such as `http://www.javasoft.com/index.html`). Alternatively, if you're in a directory that has an HTML file that references an applet, you can call AppletViewer simply by typing in the name of the HTML file that contains the applet tag. The following option is available:

Option	**Description**
-debug	Starts the AppletViewer in the Java debugger, jdb, thus allowing you to debug the applets in the HTML document.

The AppletViewer also has an Applet menu in the AppletViewer window that enables you to set a number of different functions of the AppletViewer. Those menu options are as follows:

- *Restart* Restarts the applet using the current settings.
- *Reload* Reloads the applet. Changes in the class file are applied upon reload.
- *Stop* Causes the `stop()` method of the applet to be called and halts the applet. Note the applet is not destroyed in this example as it is with *Reload.*
- *Save* Saves the serialized state of the applet.
- *Start* Starts the applet. This is useful when the *Stop* option has been utilized. If the applet has not been stopped, it has no action.
- *Clone* Clones (duplicates) the current applet, using the same settings to create another AppletViewer instance.
- *Tag* Shows the HTML applet tag that is used to run the current applet, as well as any parameters that are passed to the applet from the HTML tag (see Figure 4.1).

- *Info* Shows special information about the applet, which is set within the applet's program (see Figure 4.2).
- *Edit* This doesn't appear to do anything; it has been grayed out since the first beta.
- *Print* Causes the applet's PrintGraphics to be sent to a printer.
- *Properties* Shows the AppletViewer security properties. These settings enable you to configure AppletViewer for a network environment that includes a firewall proxy, or an HTTP proxy, using the relative proxy server and proxy port boxes. The Network Access box allows you to select the type of network access that AppletViewer is allowed. The choices are No Network Access, Applet Host (default), and Unrestricted. The Class Access box enables you to choose what kind of access—Restricted or Unrestricted—you would like AppletViewer to have on other classes (see Figure. 4.3)
- *Close* Closes the AppletViewer window and terminates the applet.
- *Quit* Closes the AppletViewer window and terminates the applet.

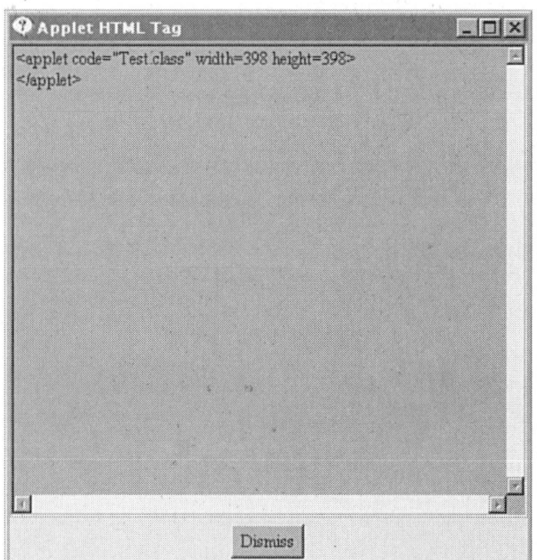

FIG. 4.1
The AppletViewer's Tag window.

java, The Java Interpreter

The Java interpreter is what you use to run your compiled Java application.

The syntax for the interpreter is:

```
java [options] classname
```

where classname only includes the name of the class and not the extension (.class). The Java interpreter options are listed in Table 4.1.

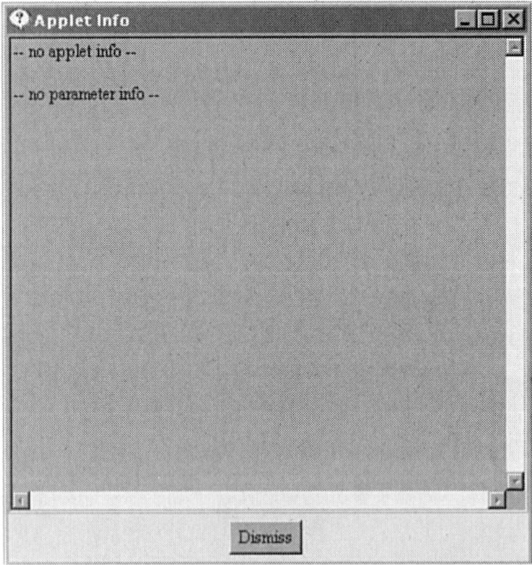

FIG. 4.2
The AppletViewer's Applet Info window.

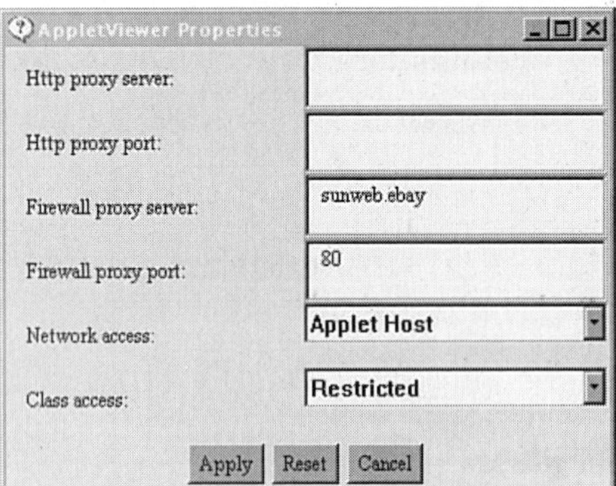

FIG. 4.3
The AppletViewer's Properties window.

Table 4.1 Java Interpreter Options

Option	Description
-help	Displays all the options.
-version	Displays the version of the JDK that is used to compile the source code.
-v (also -verbose)	Displays all the classes as they are loaded. (Performs the same functions as in the javac tool.)
-cs (also -checksource)	Checks to see if the source code is newer (not yet compiled) than its class file. If this is the case, then the new version of source is compiled.

Option	Description
-debug	Used with remote Java files that are to be debugged later with the jdb tool. The interpreter generates a password for you, which is used in the jdb's password option (see the section "jdb, The Java Debugger" later in this chapter.)
-prof	Output profiling information to file \JAVA.PROF.
-classpath dirs	java looks for class files in the specified directories, DIRS. For multiple directories, a colon (in UNIX) or semicolon (in DOS) is used to separate each directory. For example, on a DOS machine, the classpath might look like `set CLASSPATH=.;C:\users\dac\classes;C:\tools\java\classes`.
-noasyncgc	Turns off asynchronous garbage collection.
-verbosegc	Prints out a message each time a garbage collection occurs.
-noclassgc	Disables class garbage collection.
-verify	Verifies all classes that are loaded.
-verifyremote	Verifies classes that are imported or inherited. This is the default setting.
-noverify	Turns off class verification.
-mx val	Sets the maximum Java heap size to the value specified by val. The minimum heap size is 1K (-mx 1k) and the default is 16M (-mx 16m). (Use the letters m and k to specify megabytes or kilobytes for the value of val.)
-ms val	Sets the initial Java heap size to the value specified by val. The minimum heap size is 1K (-mx 1k) and the default is 1M (-mx 1m). (Use the letters m and k to specify megabytes or kilobytes for the value of val.)
-ss val	Sets the value of the stack size for a C process to the value specified in val. The stack size must be greater than 1K (-ss 1k). (Use the letters m and k to specify megabytes or kilobytes for the value of val.)
-oss val	Sets the stack size of a Java process to the specified value in val. (Use the letters m and k to specify megabytes or kilobytes for the value of val.)

javac, The Java Compiler

The javac program is the tool you use to convert .java files into class files that can be run by the interpreter. Table 4.2 lists the Java compiler options.

Table 4.2 Java Compiler Options

Option	Description
-O	Displays the current version of the JDK.
-classpath <path>	Overrides the default CLASSPATH environment variable and specifies a new path to look up classes. Make certain you always include library classes, such as `jdk1.2\jre\rt.jar`.
-d <directory>	Specifies the directory to place the resulting class files in. Note the directory specifies the root location.
-g	Using this option causes debugging tables to be generated with the class files. This information is necessary to provide complete debugging information when you use jdb.
-nowarn	Turns off warnings. When this is turned out, the Compiler does not generate any warning messages. Note: this option is available in JDK 1.1 and above, but not in JDK 1.0
-O	Turns optimization on. This causes all static, final, and prive methods to be placed inline. Although this can result in faster performance, it may also cause your class files to become larger.
-verbose	Turn verbose compilation on. This causes the compiler to print out the source files that are being compiled and loaded.
-depend	Using the depend option causes the compiler to consider recompiling class files that are referenced from other class files. Ordinarily, recompilation is only done based on file dates. Note: this is JDK 1.2 and is not available in JDK 1.0
-Jjavaoption	This option can be used to pass a single argument through to the Java interpreter that is actually running the compiler. The *javaoption* should not contain any spaces; if spaces are required, multiple –J parameters should be used. This option can be used to enable you to pass options like mx or ms to alter the amount of memory used during the compiler's execution.

javap, The Java Disassembler

The Java disassembler is used to disassemble Java bytecode that has already been compiled. After disassembling the code, information about the member variables and methods is printed. The syntax for the Java disassembler is:

```
javap [options] classnames
```

Multiple classes can be disassembled. Use a single space to separate each class. The options available for the disassembler are shown in Table 4.3.

Table 4.3 javap Options

Option	Description
-version	Displays the version of the JDK that javap is being executed from.
-c	Disassembles the source file and displays the bytecodes produced by the compiler.
-l	Prints the local variable tables.
-public	Shows only public classes and members.
-protected	Shows protected and public classes and members.
-package	Prints out private, protected, and public member variables and methods. (By default, javap uses this option.)
-private	Shows all classes and members.
-s	Print internal type signatures.
-verbose	Prints stacks, local variables, and member methods as the javap works.
-classpath dirs	Looks for class files in the specified directories, _DIRS. For multiple directories, a colon (UNIX) or semicolon (DOS) is used to separate each directory. For example, on a DOS machine the classpath might look like set `CLASSPATH=.;C:\users\dac\classes;C:\tools\java\classes`.
-verify	Runs the verifier on the source, and checks the classes being loaded.

javah C-Header and Stub File Creation

The javah tool creates C-header and stub files needed to extend your Java code with the C language.

The syntax of the javah tool is:

```
javah [options] classname
```

where classname is the name of the Java class file without the .class extension. See Table 4.4 for a list of javah options.

Table 4.4 javah Options

Option	Description
-version	Prints out the build version.
-help	Prints out the help screen. This is the same as typing javah by itself.
-jni	Creates a header file for use in JNI.

continues

Table 4.4 Continued

Option	Description
-td	Identifies the temporary directory for javah to use.
-trace	Causes trace information to be added to the stub files.
-classpath	Specifies the classpath for use with javah.
-stubs	Creates stub files instead of the default header files.
-d dir	Tells the javah tool in what directory to create the header or stub files.
-v	Prints out the status as it creates the header or stub file.
-o filename	Puts both the stub and header files into the file specified by file name. This file could be a regular text file or even a header (FILENAME.H) or stub (FILENAME.C) file.

The javadoc Tool (Documentation Generator)

The javadoc tool creates an HTML file based on the tags that are embedded in the `/** */` type of comments within a Java source file. These HTML files are used to store information about the classes and methods that you can easily view with any Web browser.

Javadoc was actually used by the creators of the JDK to create the Java API Documentation (refer to `http://www.javasoft.com/doc` for more information). You can view the API online and you can also see the source code used to generate it in your \JDK1.2\SRC\JAVA directory. See Tables 4.5 and 4.6 for information regarding options and tags.

Table 4.5 javadoc Options

Option	Description
-verbose	Displays more information about what files are being documented.
-d directory	Specifies the directory where javadoc stores the generated HTML files. For example, javadoc `-d C:\usrs\dac\public_html\doc java.lang`.
-classpath dirs	Looks for class files, included in the source file, in the specified directories, DIRS. For multiple directories, a colon (UNIX) or semicolon (DOS) is used to separate each directory. For example, on a DOS machine, the classpath might look like `set CLASSPATH=.;C:\users\dac\classes;C:\tools\java\classes`.
-sourcefile dirs	Specifies in colon-separated directories the list of files to use.
-doctype	Specifies the type of file to output the information in. The default is HTML, but it can be set to MIF.
-nodepreciated	Causes javadoc to ignore @depreciated paragraphs.

Option	Description
-author	Causes javadoc to utilize the @author paragraphs.
-noindex	Javadoc does not create an index file.
-notree	Javadoc does not create a tree file.
-J<flag>	The specified flag is passed directly to the Java runtime.

Table 4.6 javadoc Tags

Tag	Description
@see class	Puts a See Also link in the HTML file to the class specified by class.
@see class#method	Puts a See Also link in the HTML file to the method specified by method.
@param param descr	Describes method arguments.
@version ver	Specifies the version of the program.
@author name	Includes the author's name in the HTML file.
@return descr	Describes a method's return value.
@exception class	Creates a link to the exceptions thrown by the class specified by class.

jdb, The Java Debugger

The Java debugger is the debugging tool for the Java environment and is completely command-line driven. You can use the debugger to debug files located on your local system or files that are located on a remote system. For remote Java files, the jdb must be used with the -host and -password options described in the table of options. The jdb also consists of a list of commands that are not covered in this chapter. See Table 4.7 for information regarding jdb options.

Table 4.7 jdb Options

Options	Description
-host hostname	Tells the jdb where the remote Java program resides. hostname is the name of the remote computer (such as well.com or sun.com).
-password password	Passes to the jdb the password for the remote Java file, issued by the Java interpreter using the -debug option.

Now that you've covered the JDK tools, look at the one variable upon which they all depend—the `CLASSPATH` variable.

The *CLASSPATH* Environment Variable

There is really only one environment variable used by the various tools of the JDK, which is the `CLASSPATH` variable and it is essential that it is set correctly. If it is not, the compiler, interpreter, and other JDK tools will not be able to find the .class files they need to complete their tasks.

The `CLASSPATH` variable points to the directories where all the classes that are available to import from reside. `CLASSPATH` lets you put your own class files in various directories and lets the JDK tools know where they are.

On UNIX machines, the `CLASSPATH` variable is a colon-separated list of directories in the form:

```
setenv CLASSPATH .:/users/java/:/usr/local/jdk1.2/classes/
```

This command can be put in your .login file, so it's set properly every time you log in.

In DOS land, it's a semicolon-separated list of directories in the form:

```
set CLASSPATH=.;C:\users\dac\classes;C:\tools\jdk1.2\classes
```

This line can be put in your `AUTOEXEC.BAT` file so that the `CLASSPATH` is set properly every time you boot your machine.

The first period points the `CLASSPATH` at the current working directory, which is quite helpful if you don't feel like typing in full path names every time you want to do something with the Java program you're working on at a given moment.

The UNIX and Win32 versions of the JDK are quite similar and most of the commands that work for one work for the other. The Macintosh version of the JDK has some significant differences, however.

Macintosh Issues

Because the Mac doesn't have a command-line interface, the tools for the JDK are slightly different on the Mac than they are on other platforms.

NOTE The most notable difference is that fewer tools come with the Mac JDK than for other platforms. Hopefully, this will change soon, but until then, Mac users have to make due without some of the most basic tools, such as the Java debugger, javadoc, and the Java disassembler.

The Mac JDK includes four tools:

- *AppletViewer* The applet viewer program to run applets outside of a browser.
- *Java Compiler* Compiles the .java files into .class bytecodes.

- *Java Runner* The Java interpreter, basically the "java" described previously.
- *JavaH* C-header creator, with stub file creation, otherwise known as javah.

For the most part, these do the same things as their non-GUI counterparts but have some interface issues that make them different. Some tools, like the AppletViewer, are quite similar to the versions on other platforms. Other tools, like the Java Runner, are completely different. Here's the basic information on those tools and where they differ from their cross-platform counterparts.

AppletViewer for the Macintosh

When opened, the Mac AppletViewer has the standard Mac File and Edit menus. There is also a status box, which shows the current amount of memory allotted to the Applet-viewer's Java Virtual Machine, and how much of that memory is taken. That box also shows progress bars indicating the status of any information being loaded into the AppletViewer, like .class files or GIF image files.

NOTE If you are running a Mac that supports drag and drop (supported in Mac OS 7.1 and above), you can launch applets off your hard drive by simply dragging the HTML file that contains the `<applet>` tag onto the little Duke icon of the AppletViewer. You can also double-click the AppletViewer Duke icon and use one of the two Open menus to open an applet.

The AppletViewer File menu contains the following options:

- *Open URL* Opens a URL to a Web page that contains an applet.
- *Open Local* Brings up a standard Mac Open dialog box that lets you open an HTML file on your local hard drive.
- *Save* Doesn't do anything; it's there to comply with the Mac human interface guidelines.
- *Close* Closes the topmost window, if that window can be closed.
- *Properties* Shows the AppletViewer security properties. These settings enable you to configure AppletViewer for a network environment that includes a firewall proxy, or an HTTP proxy, using the relative proxy server and proxy port boxes. The Network Access box allows you to select the type of network access that AppletViewer is allowed. The choices are No Network Access, Applet Host (default), and Unrestricted. The Class Access box enables you to choose what kind of access—restricted or unrestricted you would like AppletViewer to have on other classes.
- *Quit* Closes all the open applets and exits the AppletViewer.

The AppletViewer also has an Edit menu, but this is not enabled as of this writing. Hopefully, it will be enabled soon, at the very least, so you don't have to type in long URLs in the Open URL dialog box.

When an applet is running, an Applet menu also appears. The commands available in that menu are as follows:

- *Restart* Restarts the applet using the current settings.
- *Reload* Reloads the applet. Changes in the class file are applied upon reload.
- *Clone* Clones (duplicates) the current applet, using the same settings to create another AppletViewer instance.
- *Tag* Shows the HTML applet tag that is used to run the current applet, as well as any parameters that are passed to the applet from the HTML tag (refer to Figure 4.1).
- *Info* Shows special information about the applet, which is set within the applet's program (refer to Figure 4.2).
- *Properties* Shows the AppletViewer security properties. These settings enable you to configure AppletViewer for a network environment that includes a firewall proxy, or an HTTP proxy, using the relative proxy server and proxy port boxes. The Network Access box allows you to select the type of network access that AppletViewer is allowed. The choices are No Network Access, Applet Host (default), and Unrestricted. The Class Access box enables you to choose what kind of access—Restricted or Unrestricted—you would like AppletViewer to have on other classes (refer to Figure 4.3).
- *Quit* Closes the AppletViewer window and terminates the applet.

Java Runner, The Mac Java Interpreter

The Mac Java Runner is the Mac equivalent of the java command described earlier. Because the Mac has no command line, it has a very rudimentary GUI to set the various options. To make matters slightly worse, that GUI doesn't quite follow the Apple Human Interface Guidelines, which means there's a menu where you wouldn't normally expect it.

You normally launch the Java Runner by double-clicking a `.class` file that has a `main()` method. You use the Java compiler to create that `.class` file, and so it appears on the desktop, or in the folder from which it was launched, as a document icon with Duke in the middle, and 1s and 0s in the upper-left corner of the icon.

Alternatively, you can drag the .class file onto the Java Runner icon, or double-click the Java Runner icon and select the .class file in the Open File dialog box that appears.

The Java Runner's menus are cleverly hidden as a submenu in the Apple, Java Runtime menu so that they don't interfere with any menus created by the Java application that is running:

- *Edit Mem* Lets you set the maximum and minimum heap sizes and disable asynchronous garbage collection (to speed things up).
- *Edit Classpath* This option is not currently enabled.
- *Redirect Stderr* Redirects error messages to a file that you specify in the Create File dialog box that appears after selecting this menu option.
- *Redirect Stdout* Redirects program messages to a file that you specify in the Create File dialog box that appears after selecting this menu option.
- *Save Options* Saves your other menu settings.

- *Save Text Window* Saves the frontmost text window (for example, the output window of the HelloWorld program) to a file.
- *Close Text Window* Closes the topmost text window.
- *Quit* Quits the Java Runner and kills any running Java applications.

The Java Compiler

The Java compiler has a basic GUI that lets you set the options that are available as command-line arguments to the other systems. You can compile files by either dragging the .java files onto the compiler, or by choosing File, Compile File. Other menu options are as follows:

- *Close* Seems to return an error when selected. Hopefully, this will be fixed in a future release.

CAUTION

As of version 1.02 of the MacJDK, the Close menu item appears to have a bug that causes a method not found exception when used. Until that bug is fixed, do not use the Close menu item.

- *Properties* Opens a dialog box that lets you set—using check boxes and other items—most of the options available to the other systems. It also lets you select an outside editor from a list of popular editors. The default is simple text. This dialog box also lets you set the CLASSPATH for the compiler, the target folder where .class files will be written, and disable threaded compiles to speed up the compiler in situations where multithreading is slowing things down.
- *Quit* Quits the compiler.

JavaH: C-Header File Generator

JavaH is provided so that you can link native methods into Java code. At this time, it only works for PowerPC-based Macs. It has no menus of its own outside of the standard Java Runner in the Apple menu, such as the all-important Quit command. To use JavaH, you need a third-party compiler, such as Metrowerks CodeWarrior, in order to generate the C code to actually link in with the Java. ●

PART II

The Java Language

CHAPTER 5

Obejct-Oriented Programming

In this chapter

Object-Oriented Programming: A New Way of Thinking

By now, as a programmer, you have no doubt heard of a marvelous term called OOP—object-oriented programming. OOP is truly the hottest method of software development today. It isn't a totally new concept, but it has been a long time in coming to the masses. While Java doesn't impose OOP programming like some languages (such as SmallTalk), it does embrace it and allow you to dance with the technology seamlessly.

Object-oriented programming is a completely new way of programming. At the same time, in many ways OOP is much the same as structured programming. After you learn and embrace the new terms and concepts associated with object programming, the switch can be so easy that you might not even notice you are doing it. You see, OOP's goal is to provide you, the programmer, with a few new ways to actually write code and a whole lot of new ways to think about programming.

After you have embraced the new ways OOP teaches you to think about programming, the *lexical changes*, or how you actually write code grammatically, come quite naturally. Unfortunately, truly embracing these changes can take some time. For others, the realization of how OOP works comes in flashes of inspiration. With each new realization, you open up a whole new set of programming possibilities.

A Short History of Programming

To understand why object-oriented programming is of such great benefit to you as a programmer, it's necessary to take a look at the history of programming as a technology.

In the early days of computing, programming was an extremely labored process. Each step the computer needed to take had to be meticulously (and flawlessly) programmed. The early languages were known as Machine Language, which later evolved to Assembly Language.

If you have ever tried giving another person directions for how to tie their shoes, you probably found that it was very difficult—especially if they had never seen shoelaces before. As a simple exercise, ask a coworker (one that won't think this is too weird) to take his or her shoes off. Ask that person to do exactly what you tell him or her to do, and no more. You find that it is necessary to give very precise, step-by-step directions. "Lift up the left shoelace, move it to the right side below the right shoelace. Pick up the right shoelace," and so on.

If you can grasp the number of instructions you need to teach someone how to tie a shoe, you might be able to grasp what this type of programming was like. For programmers, the instructions were a bit more cryptic (and the computer was much less forgiving about imprecise directions). It was necessary to give directions such as "Push the contents of register 1 onto the stack," "Take the contents of the accumulator and place them in register 1," and so on.

Procedural Languages

Programmers soon saw the need for more stylized procedural languages. These procedural languages placed code into blocks called procedures or functions. The goal of each of these blocks was to act like a black box that completed one task or another. For instance, you might create a procedure to write something to the screen, like `writeln` in Pascal or `printf` in C. The purists of this type of programming believed that you could always write these functions without modifying external data. In the example of `printf` or `writeln`, the string that you print to the screen is the same string before and after you print the string out. In essence, the ideal was not only to build a black box, but to weld the box shut when you were done testing it.

One of the problems with this method, though, is to write all functions in such a way that they actually do not modify data outside their boundary. This can be very difficult. For instance, what if you want to pass in a value that you want to have updated while it "lives" inside the method (but not one that is returned)? Frequently, constraining a procedure in this manner turns out to be too difficult a restriction. So, as functions began changing data outside their scope (in C this is done by passing a pointer), a problem called ***coupling*** began to surface. Because the functions were now changing data outside of their scope, testing became more and more difficult. Coupling meant that each method had to be tested—not only individually, but also to make sure that it wasn't used in such a way that a value it changed wasn't corrupted as a result. In addition, it meant that each black box had to be tested with all of its black boxes in place. If any of those boxes where changed, the parent box had to be retested because the other box may have changed a value and the parent box may not work any longer. (Starts to sound pretty complicated doesn't it?)

As large programs were developed, the problem of coupling reared its ugly head. Testing these programs begot a whole sub-industry, and software managers lost most of their hair. If they were lucky enough to keep their hair, you could spot them just as easily because they never cut it.

Structured Development

The next solution was to try structured development. Structured development didn't necessarily change the languages that were being used, but rather provided a new process. Using structured development, programmers were expected to plan 100 percent of their program before ever writing a single line of code. When a program was developed, huge schematics and flow charts were developed showing the interaction of each function with every other and how each piece of data flowed through the program. This heavy pre-code work proved to be effective in some cases, but limiting for most. This pitfall might have come in large part because the emphasis in programming became good documentation and not necessarily great design.

In addition, when programmers were pushed to predesign all of their code before actually writing any of it, a bad thing happened. Programming became institutionalized. You see, good programs tended to be as much experimentation as real development. Structured development pulled at this portion of the development cycle. Because the program needed to be completely designed before anything was implemented, programmers were no longer free to sit and experiment with individual portions of the system.

Ahh...Object-Oriented Programming

Finally, along came object-oriented programming. Object-oriented programming did require a few language changes, but also changed the way that programmers think about programming. The resulting programming technique goes back to procedural development by emphasizing black boxes, embraces structured development (and actually pushes it further), and most importantly, encourages creative programming design.

Objects under an OOP paradigm are represented in a system, not just their acquainted data structures. Objects aren't just numbers, like integers and characters; they are also the methods that relate and manipulate the numbers. In OOP programming, rather than passing data around a system openly (such as to a function), messages are passed to and from objects. Rather than taking data and pushing it through a function, a message is passed to an object telling it to perform its task.

Object-oriented programming really isn't all that new; it was developed in the 1970s by the same group of researchers at Xerox Parc that brought us GUI (graphical user interfaces), EtherNet, and a host of other products that are commonplace today. Why has OOP taken so long to enter into the masses? OOP requires a paradigm shift in development. In addition, because the computer ends up doing much more work, programs developed using OOP do tend to require a bit more computing horsepower to obtain the same performance results—but what a difference those little breaks can make.

Objects themselves are the cornerstone of object-oriented programming. The concept of objects is perhaps the first and most significant change each programmer who wants to do OOP design must understand.

Objects are robust packages that contain both data and methods. Objects can be replicated and adjusted without damaging the predefined code. Instead of being trapped under innumerable potential additional uses, a method's purpose is easily definable, as is the data upon which it will work. As the needs of new programs begin to grow, the method can be replicated or adjusted to fit the needs of the new system taking advantage of the current method, but not necessarily altering it (by overloading or overriding the method).

Objects themselves can be expanded and, by deriving new objects from existing ones, code time is greatly reduced. Equally important, if not more important, debug time is greatly reduced by localizing bugs, because coupling changes are limited, at worst, to new classes.

A Lesson in Objects

As you work, you are familiar with objects all the time: calculators, phones, computers, fax machines, and stereos are all examples of objects in the real world. When you deal with these objects, you don't separate the object from its quantities and methods. For example, when you turn on your stereo, you don't think about the quantities (such as the station number) from the methods (such as turning the dial or making sound). You simply turn it on, select a station, and sit back to listen to the music.

By using object-oriented programming, you can approach the same simplicity of use. As a structured programmer, you are used to creating data structures to hold data and to defining methods and functions to manipulate this data. Objects, however, take and combine the data with the code. The synergistic relationship that comes out is one object that knows everything necessary to exist and work.

Take a look at an example using your car. When you describe a car, there are a number of important physical factors: the number of people a car can hold, the speed the car is going, the amount of horsepower the engine has, the drag coefficient, and so on. In addition, the car has several functional definitions: It accelerates, decelerates, turns, and parks. Neither the physical nor the functional definitions alone embody the definition of your car—it is necessary to define them both.

Traditional Program Design

In a traditional program, you might define a data structure called `MyCarData` to look like this:

```
public class MyCarData {
    int weight;
    float speed;
    int hp;
    double dragCoef;
    }
}
```

Then you would create a set of methods to deal with the data:

```
public class RunCar {
    public void speedUp(MyCarData m){
    ...
    }

    public void slowDown(MyCarData m){
    ...
    }

    public void stop(MyCarData m){
    ...
    }
}
```

The OOP Way

In OOP programming, the methods for the car to run and the actual running of the car are combined into one object:

```
public class Car{
int weight;
float speed;
int hp;
double dragCoef;

public void speedUp(){
    speed += hp/weight;
}
```

```
public void slowDown(){
    speed -= speed * dragCoef;
}

public void stop(){
    speed=0;
}
}
```

Within each of the new methods, there is no need to either reference the variables using dot notation (such as `m.speed`) or pass in a reference to variables (such as `(MyCarData m)`). The methods implicitly know about the variables of their own class. (These variables are also known as *field variables.*)

Extending Objects Through Inheritance

The next step in developing objects is to create multiple objects based on one super object. Return to the car example. A Saturn SL 2 is a car, and yet certainly it has several attributes that not all cars have. When building a car, manufacturers don't typically start from scratch. They know their cars are going to need several things: tires, doors, steering wheels, and more. Frequently, the same parts can be used between cars. Wouldn't it be nice to start with a generic car, build up the specifics of a Saturn, and from there (because each Saturn has its own peculiarities) build up the SL 2?

Inheritance is a feature of OOP programming that enables you to do just this. By inheriting all the common features of a car into a Saturn, it's not necessary to reinvent the object (car) every time.

In addition, by inheriting a car's features into the Saturn—through an added benefit called *polymorphism*—the Saturn is also a car. Now that might seem obvious, but the reach and scope of that fact is enormous. Under traditional programming techniques, you would have to separately deal with each type of car—Fords here, GMCs there, and so on. Under OOP, the features all cars have are encapsulated in the car object. When you inherit car into Ford, GMC, and Saturn, you can then polymorph them back to car, and much, if not all, of this work is eliminated.

For instance, say you have a race track program. On the race track, you have a green light, yellow light, and red light. Now, each race car driver comes to the race with a different type of car. Each driver has accessible to him each of the peculiarities of his individual car (such as some fancy accelerator in your Volvo). As you put each car on the track, you give a reference of your car to the track itself. The track controller doesn't need access to any methods that access that fancy accelerator of yours or the CD player; those methods are individual to each of the cars. However, the person sitting in the control tower does want to be able to tell both drivers to slow down when the yellow light is illuminated. Because the makes are cars, the control tower program has received them as cars. Take a look at this hypothetical code.

Here are two cars:

```
class Lamborghini extends Car{
    public void superCharge(){
```

```
    for (int x=0;x<infinity;x++)
    speedUp();
   }
}

class Volvo extends Car{
CDPlayer cd;

public void goFaster(){
    while(I_Have_Gas){
         speedUp();
    }
}

public void jam(){
    cd.turnOn();
}

}
```

Here is the race track itself:

```
class RaceTrack {
    Car  theCars[] = new Car[3];
    int  numberOfCars = 0;

    public void addCar(Car newCar){
        theCars[numberOfCars]=newCar;
        numberOfCars++;
    }

    public void yellowLight(){
         for (int x=0;x<numberOfCars;x++)
            theCars[x].slowDown();
    }
}
```

Here is the program that puts it all together:

```
class RaceProgram{
Lamborghini me = new Lamborghini();
Volvo      you = new Volvo();
RaceTrack rc = new RaceTrack();

public void start(){
rc.addCar(me);
rc.addCar(you);
while(true){
if (somethingIsWrong)
rc.yellowLight();
}
}
}
```

How can this work? In the `RaceProgram` class, you created two different objects: me (of type `Lamborghini`) and you (of type `Volvo`). How can you call `rc.addCar`, which takes a `Car` as a parameter type? The answer lies in polymorphism. Because both of the cars extended `Car`, they can be used as `Cars` as well as their individual types. This means that if you create yet another type of car (`Saturn`), you could call `rc.addCar` (the `Saturn`) without having to make any changes to `RaceTrack` whatsoever. Notice that this is true, even though `Volvo` effectively is a different structure, because it now also contains a `CDPlayer` variable!

Objects as Multiple Entities

One of the pitfalls you have probably fallen into as a procedural programmer is thinking of the data in your program as a fixed quantity. A perfect example of this is the screen. Usually procedural programs tend to write something to the (one) screen. The problem with this method is that when you switch to a windowing environment and have to write to multiple screens, the whole program is in jeopardy. It takes quite a bit of work to go back and change the program so that the right data is written to the appropriate window.

In contrast, OOP programming treats the screen not as *the* screen but as *a* screen. Adding windows is as simple as telling the function it's writing to a different screen object.

This demonstrates one of the aspects of OOP that saves the most real programming time immediately. When you become an OOP programmer, you begin thinking of dealing with objects. No matter if there's 1 or 100 of them, it doesn't affect the program in any way. If you're not familiar with OOP programming, this might not make sense. After all, what you are saying to yourself is, "If I have two screens, when I go to print something to the screen, I need to be sure to position it correctly on the correct screen, and pay attention to user interaction to each different window."

Believe it or not, under OOP the need to do this is washed away. After the elements of a window or screen are abstracted sufficiently, when you write the method, it's irrelevant which screen you're writing to. The window object handles all of that for you. This is actually the flip side of polymorphism, because all you care about is that the item is a screen, and not any of the extra capabilities any one particular screen has.

Organizing Code

OOP organizes your code elegantly because of two key factors:

- When used correctly, OOP forces you to organize your code into many manageable pieces.
- By using OOP, each piece is organized naturally, without you having to actually think about the organization. Given that you are forced to organize your code and the organization is natural, this is an amazingly powerful feature.

Objects and How They Relate to Java Classes

At the heart of Java is support for these objects you have been hearing about. They come in a form called a *class*. (Actually, there is a Java class called `Object`, which all classes inherit from, so all classes literally are `Objects`.)

Objects are instances of classes. In this sense, classes can be thought of as a template for creating an object. Take a rectangle as an example. A rectangle you want to create should have an x,y location, height, width, move method, and resize method (for shrinking or enlarging the rectangle). When you write the code for the rectangle, you create it in a class. However, to take advantage of the code, you need to create an instance of that class. The instance is a single `Rectangle` object.

Building a Hierarchy: A Recipe for OOP Design

When setting out to develop an OOP program for the first time, it is often helpful to have a recipe to follow. Developing good OOP structures is a lot like baking a pie. It's first necessary to gather all the ingredients, then begin assembling each portion of the pie.

Break Down Code to Its Smallest Entities

When writing an OOP program, it's first necessary to figure out which ingredients are needed. For instance, if you were writing an arcade game, it would be necessary to figure out everything that would be in that game: creatures, power pieces, the main character, bullets, and so on.

After you have assembled these pieces, you need to break them down into all of their entities, both data and functional. For this example, if you were setting out to write the arcade game, you might create a list like this for the four items:

Piece	Entity
Creatures	Location, size, power level, attack capability to, and maneuverability
Power Pieces	Must be drawn, location, power level
Bullets	Capability to be fired, size, and quantity
Main Character	Capability to receive commands from the user, capability to move around the maze according to these commands, capability to attack, location, and size

Look for Commonality Between the Entities

The next phase of developing an OOP structure is to look for all the common relationships between each of the entities. For instance, right away you might recognize that the primary difference between the creatures and the main character (aside from how they look) is who controls each. Namely, the creatures are controlled by the computer, and the main character is controlled by the user. Wouldn't it be great if you could write most of the code for both the creatures and the main character once, and then just write separate code for moving them?

If that's how you feel, but you really don't think it could be that easy, keep reading. Treating objects this way is exactly what the OOP paradigm is all about.

Look for Differences Between Entities

The next step is to find the differences between the entities. For instance, the bullets move and the power pieces stay put. Creatures are controlled by the computer, and the main character is controlled by the user. You are looking for relationships that unite and separate all of those entities in your program.

Find the Largest Commonality Between All Entities

The third step is to find the largest common relationship between all the entities in your program. Rarely is it impossible to find any common relationships among all objects. It is possible, however, to find one entity so completely different that it doesn't share anything with any other object.

Looking at the game example, what do you see that all four objects have in common? A quick list might include size, the capability to move around (the power piece doesn't really need to move, but it wouldn't hurt if it could), and location.

Is that all they have in common? Perhaps the most obvious commonality wasn't even (intentionally) listed before—the capability to be drawn to the screen. This capability is so obvious you might just miss it. Don't forget to look at the obvious.

With these entities, you could create a class called `Draw_Object`. The class would contain all the items just listed.

Put Remaining Common Objects Together and Repeat

The next phase is to put objects that still have things in common together (after you have eliminated the aspects that were just grouped into the previous class). You use these commonalties to produce another level of classes, each of which inherits from the class that contains all the completely common information (`Draw_Object`).

Going back to the example, at this point the power pieces and the bullets probably split from the creatures and the main character. Now, take the remaining objects and repeat the recipe again.

Going through the next phase, you find that the only real difference between the power pieces and the bullets is their size and how fast they move (the power pieces at speed 0). Because these are primarily minor differences, you combine them into one class.

When you look at the creatures and the main character, you have decided that the main character contains everything that a creature does plus some, so you inherit the `Creature` class in the `Main_Character` class.

The final class hierarchy is shown in Figure 5.1. Try this on your own. There are countless variations to the chart developed here; see what you come up with.

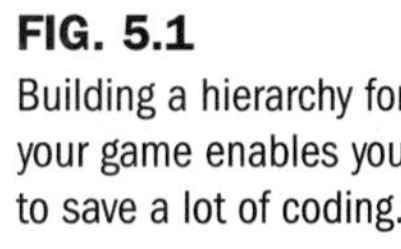

FIG. 5.1
Building a hierarchy for your game enables you to save a lot of coding.

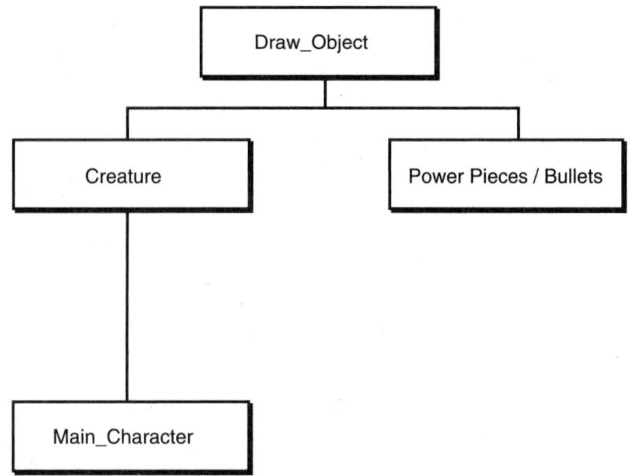

Using Objects to Add As Many As Desired

When writing a game, it is often desirable to be able to add as many attack creatures as a particular board wants. Because the `creature` class encapsulates, all that you need to create a creature and a new board with more creatures is to add those creatures to the list. Again, this might seem obvious, but it's extremely powerful; it means you don't need to create a string of variables like `creature1Speed`, `creature2Speed`, `creature1Power`, `creature2Power`, and so on.

You can think of this step as if you were creating any other variable. For instance, assuming that you're already a programmer in a different language, you're probably very used to just creating an integer variable any time you need one. Now you can create a whole new creature any time you need one.

Java Isn't a Magic OOP Bullet

The focus of this chapter has been to introduce the concepts of good OOP. The chapter has intentionally avoided complicated coding implementations; the rest of this book should help you fill in that portion.

Now that you have seen many of the fundamentals of OOP programming at a surface level, establish why you went through all of this. Java isn't a magic bullet to creating OOP programs. While Java embraces the OOP paradigm, it is still possible (and not unusual) to write structured programs using Java. It's not unusual to see Java programs written without any acknowledgment of some of the OOP tools just covered, like polymorphism and encapsulation.

By introducing OOP at this stage, hopefully you can break the bad habits of structured programming before they begin. You need to remember that OOP is as much a different way of thinking as it is a different way of programming. Throughout this book, there are applets and applications written both ways. Look for those programs that are broken into multiple pieces. Then, when you think you understand OOP, reread this chapter and see if any more insights are brought to mind. ●

CHAPTER 6

HelloWorld!: Your First Java Program

In this chapter

HelloWorld Application

When learning to program, it is often useful to jump in headfirst, learn how to write a short application, and then step back and learn the rest of the fundamentals. In this chapter you do just that, and by the end you should be able to write your own Java programs.

You have already seen the simplest Java program, HelloWorld, in Chapter 3, "Installing the JDK and Getting Started." Take a closer look at each of the components. Listing 6.1 shows the HelloWorld application.

Listing 6.1 The HelloWorld Application

```
public class HelloWorld {
  public static void main(String args[]){
    System.out.println("Hello World!!");
  }
}
```

As you can see, there really isn't a lot to this program, which may be why it's called the easiest Java application. Nevertheless, you take a close look at the program from the inside out. Before you do that, though, compile the program and run it.

Create the File

The first step to creating the HelloWorld application is to copy the text from Listing 6.1 into a file called HelloWorld.java using your favorite text editor (Windows NotePad, or SimpleText on the Macintosh will work if you don't have another). It is very important to call the file HelloWorld.java, because the compiler expects the filename to match the class identifier (see "Declaring a Class" later in this chapter).

CAUTION

If you use a program such as Microsoft Word to type the code, make sure that you save the file as text only. If you save it as a Word document, Word adds a lot of information about formatting the text that simply doesn't apply to your situation, and only causes you grief.

Compile the Code

To compile the program, you need to first install the JDK. Then, use the program javac included with the JDK to convert the text in Listing 6.1 to a form the computer can run. To run javac on a Macintosh, drag the source file over the javac icon. On any other computer, type the following at a command prompt: **`javac HelloWorld.java`**.

The javac program creates a file called HelloWorld.class from the HelloWorld.java file. Inside this file (HelloWorld.class) are what is known as bytecodes. *Bytecodes* are special instructions that can be run by the Java interpreter.

▶ **See** "Installing a Downloaded JDK," **p. 45**

Run the Program

Now that you have compiled the program, you can run it by typing the following at the command prompt: **`java HelloWorld`**.

NOTE The HelloWorld used in the command prompt java HelloWorld is not HelloWorld.class or HelloWorld.java, just the name of the class.

After you do this, the computer should print the following to the screen:

```
Hello World!!
```

That may not seem very interesting, but then it's a simple program. If you don't see that on the screen, go back and make sure you have typed in the file exactly as it is shown in Listing 6.1, and make sure that you called the file HelloWorld.java.

Understanding HelloWorld

Now that you have seen the results of the HelloWorld program, go back to the original source code and see if you can understand how it works. As you should begin to see, there are a lot of parts to the HelloWorld program. After you understand all of them, you're a long way to being able to write any program.

Declaring a Class

The first task when creating any Java program is to create a class. Take a look at the first line of the HelloWorld application:

```
public class HelloWorld {
```

This declares a class called `HelloWorld`.

See "Classes in Java," **p. 160**

To create any class, simply write a line that looks like:

```
public class ClassName
```

Here, `ClassName` is the name of the program you are writing. In addition, `ClassName` must correspond to the filename. It's a good idea to make all your class names descriptive, so that it's easier to remember for what they are used.

NOTE It is an accepted practice that class names should always begin with a capital letter. This is not required, but considered good style. There are also a number of limitations on the names you can assign to a class, but you learn more about that later in Chapter 11, "Classes."

Next, notice the brace (`{`) that is located before the class declaration. If you look at the end of the class, there is also a closing brace (`}`). The braces tell the compiler where your class will begin and end. Any code between those two braces is considered to be in the `HelloWorld` class.

Don't be confused. Braces are used for a number of things called blocks, which are covered in more detail in Chapter 8, "Methods." The braces are matched in a LIFO (Last In, First Out) format. That means that the next closing brace closes the open brace that was closest to it. In the case of the HelloWorld program, there are two open braces, so the one that closes the class is the very last one.

main Method

The next line in the HelloWorld program reads like the following:

```
public static void main(String args[]){
```

This line declares what is known as the `main` method. *Methods* are essentially mini-programs. Each method performs some of the tasks of a complete program. The `main` method is the most important one with respect to applications, because it is the place that all Java applications start. For instance, when you run `java HelloWorld`, the Java interpreter starts at the first line of the `main` method.

When creating any Java application, you need to create a `main` method as shown. In Chapter 8 you learn more about declaring and using methods.

Writing to the Screen

How does the text `Hello World!!` appear when you run the HelloWorld program? The answer (as you have probably guessed) lies in the next line of the program:

```
System.out.println("Hello World!!");
```

You can replace any of the text within the quotation marks (`""`) with any text you would like.

The `System.out` line is run because, the interpreter looks at the first line of code (namely the printout) and executes it when the application starts. If you place any other code there, it runs that code instead.

System.out and *System.in*

You have just seen how `System.out.println` was used to print text to the screen. In fact, `System.out.println` can be used at any time to print text to what is known as Standard Out. In almost all cases, *Standard Out* is the screen.

The `system.out.println` serves approximately the same purpose as the `writeln` in Pascal. In C, the function is `printf`, and in C++, `cout`.

println* Versus *print There is one minor variation on `println` that is also readily used: `print("Hello World!!")`. The difference between `println` and `print` is that `print` does not add a carriage return at the end of the line, so any subsequent printouts are on the same line. Strictly speaking, `print` is the true cousin to `printf` and `cout` for C/C++ programmers.

To demonstrate this, expand your HelloWorld example a bit by copying Listing 6.2 into a file called HelloWorld2.java and compiling it with the line `java HelloWorld2.java`.

Listing 6.2 A HelloWorld Program with Two Printouts

```
public class HelloWorld2 {
  public static void main(String args[]){
    System.out.println("Hello World!");
    System.out.println("Hello World Again!");
  }
}
```

To run the program, type **java HelloWorld2**. You should see output that looks like the following:

```
Hello World!
Hello World Again!
```

Notice that each phrase appears on its own line. Now, for comparison, try the program again using `print` instead of `println`. Copy Listing 6.3 into a file called HelloWorld3, compile, and run it.

Listing 6.3 A HelloWorld Output Using *print* Statements

```
public class HelloWorld3 {
  public static void main (String args[]){
    System.out.print ("Hello World!");
    System.out.print ("Hello World Again!");
  }
}
```

You should notice that the output looks like this:

```
Hello World!Hello World Again!
```

What caused the change? When you use `print`, the program does not add the extra carriage return.

Extending the String: Writing More Than *HelloWorld* One of the features Java has inherited from C++ is the capability to add strings together. Although this might not seem completely mathematically logical, it is awfully convenient for a programmer. Revisit your last HelloWorld program and get the same output using one `println` and the + operator (see Listing 6.4).

Listing 6.4 HelloWorld Output Adding Two Strings

```
public class HelloWorld4 {
  public static void main (String Args[]){
    System.out.print ("Hello World!" + "Hello World Again!");
  }
}
```

When you compile and run HelloWorld4, you should see the same output that was produced from HelloWorld3. This might not seem too interesting, so take a look at one more extensions of the ability to add to strings—you can also add numbers. For instance, say you want to add the number 43 to the string. Listing 6.5 shows an example of just such a situation.

Listing 6.5 HelloWorld with a Number

```
public class HelloWorld5 {
  public static void main (String args[]){
    System.out.print ("Hello World! " + 43);
  }
}
```

Listing 6.5 produces the following:

```
Hello World! 43
```

Getting Information from the User with *System.in* `System.out` has a convenient partner called `System.in`. While `System.out` is used to print information to the screen, `System.in` is used to get information into the program.

Requesting Input from the User Use `System.in.read()` to get a character from the user. This is not covered in too much depth, because `System.in` isn't used that often in Java programs; that is primarily, because (as you learn in the upcoming section "HelloWorld as an Applet") it really doesn't apply to applets. Nevertheless, Listing 6.6 shows an example of a Java application that reads a letter from the user.

Listing 6.6 ReadHello: An Application that Reads Input from the User

```
import java.io.*;

public class ReadHello {
public static void main (String args[]){
  int inChar;
  System.out.println("Enter a Character:");
  try {
     inChar = System.in.read();
     System.out.println("You entered " + inChar);
     } catch (IOException e){
       System.out.println("Error reading from user");
       }
  }
}
```

You've probably already noticed that there is a lot more to this code than there was to the last one. Before that's explained, you should compile the program and prove to yourself that it works:

```
Enter a Character:
A
You entered 65
```

First things first. The code you are most interested in is the line that reads:

```
inChar = System.in.read();
```

`System.in.read()` is a method that takes a look at the character that the user enters. It then performs what is known as a ***return*** on that value. A value that is returned by a method can then be used in an expression. In the case of `ReadHello`, a variable called `inChar` is set to the value that is returned by the `System.in.read()` method.

In the next line, the value of the `inChar` variable is added to the `System.out` string, just as you did in Listing 6.5. By adding the variable into the string, you can see the results of your work. It's not necessary to use a variable. If you prefer, you can print it out directly in the second `System.out` line, by changing it to the following:

```
System.out.println("You entered "+ System.in.read());
```

Notice that the program displays a number instead of a character for what you entered. This is because the `read()` method of `System.in` returns an integer, not an actual character. The number corresponds to what is known as the *ASCII character set.*

Converting an Integer to a Character You need to do what is known as a *cast* to convert the number that is returned from `System.in` into a character. Casting effectively converts a given datatype to another one. Change ReadHello to look like Listing 6.7.

Listing 6.7 ReadHello: An Application that Reads in a Character from the User

```
import java.io.*;
public class ReadHello {
  public static void main (String args[]){
    char inChar;
    System.out.println("Enter a Character:");
    try {
       inChar =(char) System.in.read();
       System.out.println("You entered " + inChar);
       } catch (IOException e){
         System.out.println("Error reading from user");
         }
  }
}
```


Notice the characters before `System.in.read()`.The `(char)` causes the integer to be changed into a character.

The Rest of the Extra Code—*try* and *catch* What does the rest of all that code do? There is a sequence there called a `try-catch` block in this code.

In some programming languages, when a problem occurs during execution, there is no way for you as a programmer to catch it and deal with the problem. When a problem occurs, the system halts and ends the program (usually with some nasty message like `General Protection Fault`, or `Core Dump`). In some languages, it's a bit complicated. In Java, most problems cause what are known as *exceptions*, which can be handled by you, so your program doesn't stop working.

▶ **See** "Java's Exceptions," **p. 364**

▶ **See** "Java's Events," **p. 381**

When a method states that it will throw an exception, it is your responsibility to try to perform that method, and if it throws the exception, you need to catch it. Do you see the line of code right after the `catch` phase? If there is an error while reading, an exception called an `IOException` is thrown. When that happens, the code in the `catch` block is called.

HelloWorld as an Applet—Running in Netscape

If you are reading this book, odds are you are most interested in using Java to write programs called *applets*. Applets can be run in a browser, such as Netscape Navigator.

Several differences exist between applets and applications. The most important is that Java applet classes extend an existing class. This class is called `java.applet.Applet`. For now, it's enough to say that you have to extend `Applet` for a class to be usable as such. This is covered in more detail in a later chapter.

▶ **See** "Applets Versus Applications," **p. 775**

The New Source Code—Compiling It

One of the simplest applets is the `HelloWorld` applet, the source code for which is shown in Listing 6.8. Right away you should see that the applet `HelloWorld` is quite different from the HelloWorld application in Listing 6.1. You break down the source code to understand it a little later in this chapter. For now, copy Listing 6.8 into a file called HelloApplet.java and compile it.

Listing 6.8 HelloWorld as an Applet

```
import java.applet.Applet;
import java.awt.Graphics;
public class HelloApplet extends Applet {
  public void paint (Graphics g) {
     g.drawString ("Hello World!",0,50);
  }
}
```

Creating an HTML File

When you created the HelloWorld application in Listings 6.1 through 6.5, you ran them using the Java interpreter. Applets, however, don't run from the command line; they are executed within a browser—but how do you tell the browser to open the applet?

If you have already written Web pages, you are familiar with HTML. HTML pages are what a browser such as Netscape is used to dealing with. To get the applet into the browser, you need to embed what are known as HTML *tags* into an HTML file. The HTML file can then be read into a browser.

The simplest HTML file for the `HelloApplet` class is shown in Listing 6.9. Copy this text into a file called HelloApplet.html.

▶ **See** "Including a Java Applet in an HTML Page," **p. 228**

Take a look at the third line of Listing 6.9. Notice the <APPLET> tag? The <APPLET> tag is a new HTML tag that is used to include Java applets. When creating your own HTML files, don't forget to include the closing </APPLET> tag as well, or your applets won't appear.

NOTE With Java files, it is necessary that the filename be the same as the class file. This is not necessary with the HTML file. In fact, a single HTML file can contain several <APPLET> tags.

Listing 6.9 HelloApp.html—HTML File to Use for Applet

```
<HTML>
<BODY>
<APPLET CODE="HelloApplet.class" WIDTH = 200 HEIGHT=200> </APPLET>
</BODY>
</HTML>
```

Running the Program in AppletViewer

To run the applet, the JDK includes a very simplified version of a browser called AppletViewer. AppletViewer looks for <APPLET> tags in any given HTML file and opens a new window for each of them.

When you run the HTML file in AppletViewer, you see output such as that in Figure 6.1. To run the HelloApplet program using AppletViewer, type **`appletviewer HelloApplet.html`** on the command line.

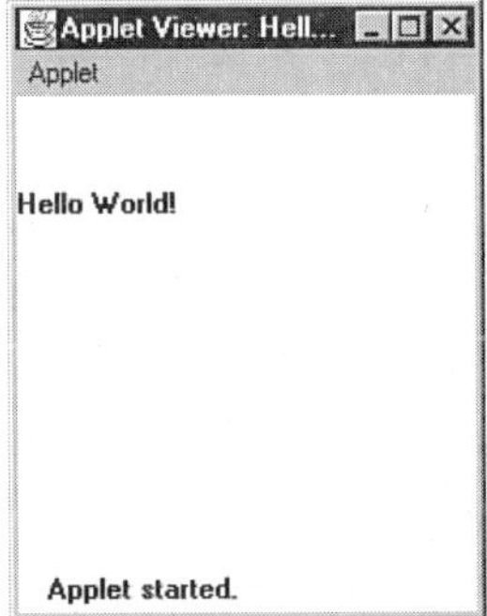

FIG. 6.1
AppletViewer opens a new window and runs HelloApplet in it.

Running HelloWorld in Netscape

Another option for running applets is with Netscape Communicator. You're probably already familiar with using the Navigator. To open the HelloApplet program in Netscape, choose File, Open File, then select the HelloApplet.html file, as shown in Figure 6.2.

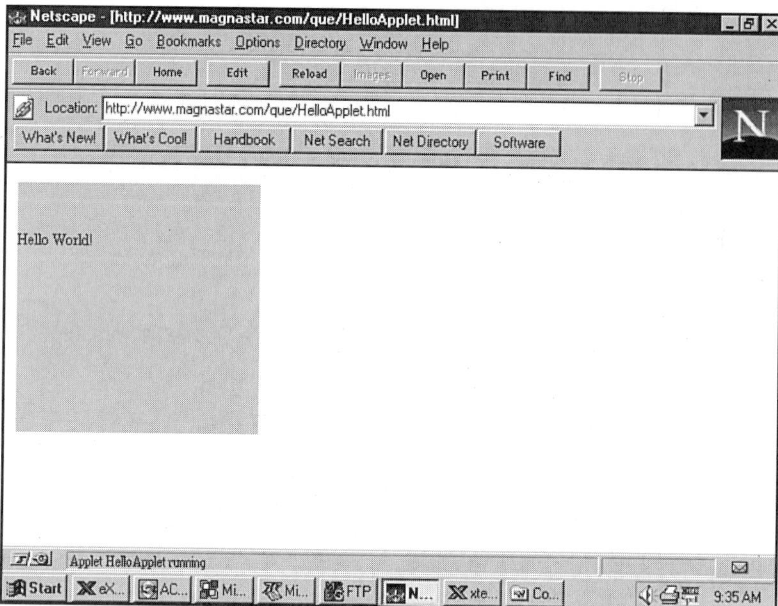

FIG. 6.2
HelloApplet can also be run by using Netscape Navigator.

Understanding the Source Code

Now that you have seen how to run the HelloApplet program, go back and see how the program works.

Importing Other Classes The first thing to notice are the top two lines of the code:

```
import java.applet.Applet;
import java.awt.Graphics;
```

The `import` statement is a new one. It is often necessary or easier to use the contents of a class file that have already been created, rather than try to reproduce that work yourself. The `import` statement enables you to use these other classes. If you are familiar with the C/C++ `#include` declaration, the `import` statement works in somewhat the same way.

In the case of the HelloApplet program, there are two classes used, other than HelloApplet. The first is the `java.applet.Applet` class. The `Applet` class contains all the information that is specific to applets. In fact, any class run in a browser as an applet must extend `java.applet.Applet`.

The second class that is imported into HelloApplet is the `java.awt.Graphics` class. `java.awt.Graphics` contains all kinds of tools for drawing things to the screen. In fact, the screen is treated as a `Graphics` object.

Declaring an *Applet* Class You might have noticed that there is a slight difference between this class declaration for the `HelloApplet` class compared with the HelloWorld application. `HelloApplet` extends `Applet`. Remember in the last chapter how you learned about building a class structure? `extends` is the keyword that indicates that a class should be entered into that class hierarchy. In fact, a class that extends another class is placed at the bottom of the existing chain:

```
public class HelloApplet extends Applet {
```

▶ **See** "Super Classes—Extending Another Class," **p.164**

You might think this harps the issue, but it's important: All applets must extend `java.applet.Applet`. However, because you imported the `Applet` class, you can simply call it `Applet`. If you had not imported `java.applet.Applet`, you could still have extended it using the full name:

```
public class HelloApplet extends java.applet.Applet {
```

Applet Methods—*paint* The next item to notice about the `HelloApplet` class versus `HelloWorld` is that `HelloApplet` doesn't have a `main` method. Instead, this applet only has a `paint` method. How is this possible?

The answer lies in the fact that the applets don't start themselves. They are being added to an already running program (the browser). The browser has a predefined means for getting each applet to do what it wants. It does this by calling methods that it knows the applet has. One of these is `paint`:

```
public void paint (Graphics g) {
```

The `paint` method is called any time the browser needs to display the applet on the screen; you can use the `paint` method to display anything. The browser helps by passing a `Graphics` object to the `paint` method. This object gives the `paint` method a way to display items directly to the screen.

The next line shows an example of using the `Graphics` object to draw text to the screen:

```
        g.drawString ("Hello World!",0,50);
    }
}
```


The Brief Life of an Applet

The `paint` method is not the only method that the browser calls of the applet. You can override any of these other methods just like you did for the `paint` method in the HelloWorld example.

When the applet is loaded, the browser calls the `init()` method. This method is only called once no matter how many times you return to the same Web page.

After the `init()` method, the browser first calls the `paint()` method. This means that if you need to initialize some data before you get into the `paint()` method, you should do so in the `init()` method.

Next, the `start()` method is called. The `start()` method is called every time an applet page is accessed. This means that if you leave a Web page and then click the Back button, the `start()` method is called again. However, the `init()` method is not.

When you leave a Web page (for example, by clicking a link), the `stop()` method is called.

Finally, the `destroy()` method is called when the browser exits all together.

NOTE Notice that unlike the `paint(Graphics g)` method, the `init()`, `start()`,`stop()`, and `destroy()` methods do not take any parameters between the parentheses.

Keywords

Before you set off on a more in-depth exploration of each of the topics discussed in this chapter, there are a few other housekeeping matters you need to learn.

The most important of these is the use of keywords in Java. There are certain sequences of characters, called ***keywords***, that have special meaning in Java. Some of them are like verbs, some like adjectives, and some like pronouns. Some of them are tokens that are saved for later versions of the language, and one (`goto`) is a vile oath from ancient procedural tongues that may never be uttered in polite Java.

The following is a list of the 56 keywords you can use in Java. When you know the meanings of all these terms, you will be well on your way to being a Java programmer.

```
abstract      boolean      break          byte
case          cast         catch          char
class         const        continue       default
do            double       else           extends
final         finally      float          for
future        generic      goto           if
implements    import       inner          instanceof
int           interface    long           native
new           null         operator       outer
package       private      protected      public
rest          return       short          static
super         switch       synchronized   this
throw         throws       transient      try
var           void         volatile       while
```

The keywords `byvalue`, `cast`, `const`, `future`, `generic`, `goto`, `inner`, `operator`, `outer`, `rest`, and `var` are the reserved words that have no meaning in Java. Programmers experienced with other languages such as C, C++, Pascal, or SQL may know for what these terms might eventually be used. For the time being, you won't use these terms, and Java is much simpler and easier to maintain without them.

The tokens `true` and `false` are not on this list; technically, they are literal values for `Boolean` variables or constants.

The reason you care about keywords is these terms have specific meaning in Java; you can't use them as identifiers for something else. This means that you can't create classes with any of these names. If `HelloApplet` had been on the list, the compiler never would have compiled that program for you. In addition, they cannot be used as variables, constants, and so on. However, they can be used as part of a longer token, for example:

```
public int abstract_int;
```

NOTE Because Java is case sensitive, you can use an initial uppercase letter if you are bent on using one of these words as an identifier of some sort. Although this is possible, it is a very bad idea in terms of human readability, and it results in wasted manhours when the code must be improved later to this:

```
public short Long;
```

It can be done, but for the sake of clarity and mankind's future condition, please don't do it.

In addition, there are numerous classes defined in the standard packages. Although their names are not keywords, the overuse of these names can make your meaning unclear to people who work on your application or applet in the future.

API

In this chapter, you learned how to use several classes other than the one you were writing. The most important of these was `java.applet.Applet`.

Why were you told what methods were in `java.applet.Applet`? The answer is that all the classes in what is known as the Java API are well documented. Although it's unlikely that you will have great success understanding the API until you have finished reading several more chapters, it's important to start looking at it now.

As you progress as a Java programmer, the API will probably become one of your best friends. In fact, it may well be that Java's rich API is one of the reasons for its success.

You can access a hyperlink version of the API documentation on Sun's site at `http://www.javasoft.com/products/JDK/CurrentRelease/`.

When exploring the API, you should notice how various classes inherit from others using the `extends` keyword. Sun has done a great deal of work to keep you from having to write nearly as much code; you simply must learn to make good use of the classes.

CHAPTER 7

Data Types and Other Tokens

In this chapter

Java Has Two Data Types

When working with computers—either for something as simple as writing a college paper or as complex as solving quantum theory equations—the single most important thing the computer does is deal with data. Data to a computer can be numbers, characters, or simply values. Java has several types of data it can work with, and this chapter covers some of the most important.

In Java, there are two categories into which data types have been divided.

- Primitive types
- Reference types

Java has eight primitive types, each with its own purpose and use.

- `Boolean`
- `char`
- `float`
- `byte`
- `int`
- `double`
- `short`
- `long`

As you proceed through this chapter, each of these types is covered in detail. For now, take a look at Table 7.1, which shows the numerical limits each type has.

Table 7.1 Primitive Data Types in the Java Language

Type	Description
`Boolean`	These have values of either `true` or `false`.
`byte`	7-bit 2s-complement integer with values between -2^7 and 2^7-1 (-128 to 127).
`short`	16-bit 2s-complement integer with values between -2^{15} and $2^{15}-1$ (-32,768 to 32,767).
`char`	16-bit Unicode characters. For alphanumerics, these are the same as ASCII with the high byte set to `0`. The numerical values are unsigned 16-bit values between `0` and `65535`.
`int`	32-bit 2s-complement integer with values between -2^{31} and $2^{31}-1$ (-2,147,483,648 to 2, 147,483,647).
`long`	64-bit 2s-complement integer with values between -2^{63} and $2^{63}-1$ (-9,223,372,036,854,775,808 to 9,223,372,036,854,775,807).

Type	Description
`float`	32-bit single precision floating-point numbers using the IEEE 754-1985 standard (+/- about 10^{39}).
`double`	64-bit double precision floating-point numbers using the IEEE 754-1985 standard (+/- about 10^{317}).

Primitive types in Java are unique because, unlike many other languages, the values listed in Table 7.1 are always as shown here, regardless of what type of computer you are working on. This gives you, as a programmer, added security and portability you might not always have in other languages.

Learning About *boolean* Variables

The simplest data type available to you in Java is that of the `boolean`. `boolean` variables have two possible values—`true` or `false`. In some other languages, `Booleans` are `0` or `1`; or, as in C(++), false is `0` and all other numbers are `true`. Java has simplified this a bit, and made actual values `true` and `false`.

`boolean` variables are used mostly when you want to keep track of the state an object is in. For instance, a piece of paper is either on or off the table. A simple piece of code might say:

```
boolean on_the_table = true;
```

Declaring a Variable

You should understand what the line of code in the last section means before you go any further. When you create a variable in Java, you must know at least a few things:

- You must know what data type you are going to use. In this case, that was `Boolean`.
- You must know what you want to call the variable (`on_the_table`).
- You might also want to know the value with which the variable should start. In this case, assume the paper is on the table initially, so you set the variable to `true`. If you do not specify a value for the variable, the Java compiler automatically makes your `Boolean` variables `false`.

You can create any variable in Java in the same way as was just shown:

1. State the data type that you will be using (`boolean`).
2. State the name the variable will be called (`on_the_table`).
3. Assign the variable a value (`= true`).
4. As with every other line of code in Java, terminate the line with a semicolon (;).

Identifiers: The Naming of a Variable

Refer to the first example:

```
boolean on_the_table = true;
```

How does the computer work with the characters that make up `on_the_table`? `on_the_table` is called an identifier in programming lexicology. Identifiers are important because they are used to represent a whole host of things. In fact, *identifiers* are any phrases chosen by the programmer to represent variables, constants, classes, objects, labels, or methods. After an identifier is created, it represents the same object in any other place it is used in the same code block.

There are several rules that must be obeyed when creating an identifier:

- The first character of an identifier must be a letter. After that, all subsequent characters can be letters or numerals.
- The characters do not need to be Latin numerals or digits; they can be from any alphabet. Because Java is based on the Unicode, standard identifiers can be in any language, such as Arabic-Indic, Devanagari, Bengali, Tamil, Thai, or many others.
- The underscore (_) and the dollar sign ($) are considered letters and can be used as any character in an identifier, including the first one.
- In Java, as in C and most other modern languages, identifiers are case sensitive and language sensitive. This means that `on_the_table` is not the same as `On_The_Table`. Changing the case changes the identifier by which the variable is known.
- Make your identifier names long enough so that they are descriptive. Most application developers are forever walking the line of compromise between choosing identifiers that are short enough to be quickly and easily typed without error and those that are long enough to be descriptive and easily read. Either way, in a large application, it is useful to choose a naming convention that reduces the likelihood of accidental reuse of a particular identifier. It is not generally a good idea to create four variables called x, x1, x2, and x4, because it would be difficult to remember the purpose of each variable. In addition, identifiers cannot be keywords.

Table 7.2 shows several legal and illegal identifiers. The first illegal identifier is forbidden because it begins with a numeral. The second has an illegal character (`&`) in it. The third also has an inappropriate character: the blank space. The fourth is a literal number (`216`) and cannot be used as an identifier. The last one contains yet another bad character: the hyphen, or minus sign. Java would try to treat this last case as an expression containing two identifiers and an operation to be performed on them.

Table 7.2 Examples of Legal and Illegal Identifiers

Legal Identifiers	Illegal Identifiers
`HelloWorld`	`9HelloWorld`
`counter`	`count&add`

Legal Identifiers	Illegal Identifiers
`HotJava$`	`Hot Java`
`ioc_Queue3`	`65536`
`ErnestLawrenceThayers`	`non-plussed` `FamousPoemOfJune1888`

Changing *Boolean* Variables

In Chapter 10, "Control Flow," you see how `Boolean` variables can be used to change the behavior of a program. For instance, if the paper is on the table, you do nothing, but if it has fallen onto the floor, you can tell the computer to pick it up.

There are two ways in which you can change a `Boolean` variable. Because `Booleans` are not represented by numbers, you must always set a `Boolean` to either `true` or `false`. The first way to do this is explicitly. For instance, if you have a variable called `My_First_Boolean`, to change this variable to false, you would type:

```
My_First_Boolean = false;
```

If you compare this line to the declaration of `on_the_table` earlier, you might notice that they are very similar.

The next way to assign a Boolean variable is based on an equation or other variable. For instance, if you want `My_First_Boolean` to have the same value as `on_the_table`, you might type a line like this:

```
My_First_Boolean= on_the_table;
```

You can also make the variable have a value based on the equality of other numbers. For instance, the following line would make `My_First_Boolean false`:

```
My_First_Boolean = 6>7;
```

Because 6 is not greater than 7, the equation on the right would evaluate `false`. You learn more about this type of equation later in Chapter 10.

NOTE Boolean types are a new feature in Java, not found in C and C++. To some, this stricter adherence to typing may seem oppressive. On the other hand, pervasive ambiguity, which has resulted in countless lost man-hours from the world's intellectual workforce in the form of chasing many hard-to-detect programming errors, may be eliminated.

The Various Flavors of Integer

The next set of primitive types in Java are all known as *integer types*:

- `byte`
- `int`

- `char`
- `short`
- `long`

As you saw in Table 7.1, each of these types has a different limit to the numbers it can carry. For instance, a `byte` cannot hold any number that is greater than 127, but a `long` can easily hold the amount of the national debt. It can actually hold one million times that number.

There are different reasons to use each type, and you should not use a `long` for every variable just because it is the biggest. It is unlikely that most of the programs you write will need to deal with numbers large enough to take advantage of that size. More importantly, large variables such as `longs` take up much more space in the computer's memory than do variables like `short`.

Limits on Integer Values

Integers can have values in the ranges shown in Table 7.3.

Table 7.3 Integer Types and Their Limits

Integer Type	Minimum Value	Default Value	Maximum Value
`byte`	-128	(byte) 0	127
`short`	-32,768	(short) 0	32,767
`int`	-2,147,483,648	0	2,147,483,647
`long`	-9,223,372,036,854,775,808	0	9,223,372,036,854,775,807
`char`	0	0	65535

NOTE The maximum number for a `long` is enough to provide a unique ID for one transaction per second for every person on the planet for the next 50 years. It is also the number of grains in about a cubic mile of sand. Yet, if a project to count the black flies in Maine is undertaken, surely the cry will arise for 128-bit integers.

NOTE If some operation creates a number exceeding the ranges shown here, no overflow or exception is created. Instead, the 2s-complement value is the result. (For a byte, it's `127+1=-128`, `127+9 =-120`, and `127+127=-2`.) However, an `ArithmeticException` is thrown if the right-hand operand in an integer divide or modulo operation is zero.

Creating Integer Variables

All of the main four integer types can be created in nearly the same way (you learn about `char` later in this chapter). The following lines show how to create a variable of each of these types:

```
byte My_First_Byte = 10;
short My_First_Short = 15;
int My_First_Int = 20;
long My_First_Long = 25;
```

Notice that the declaration of the integer types is nearly identical to that for the `Boolean` variable and that it is exactly the same for all integer types. The one main difference is that an integer variable must be assigned a number, not `true` or `false`. Also, notice that an integer must be assigned a whole number, not a fraction. In other words, if you want to have a number like 5.5 or 5 2/3, you cannot do so with an integer. You learn more about these types of numbers in the section "Floating-Point Variables" later in this chapter.

Operations on Integers

You can perform a wide variety of operations on integer variables. Table 7.4 shows a complete list.

Table 7.4 Operations on Integer Expressions

Operation	Description
=, +=, -=, *=, /=	Assignment operators
==, !=	Equality and inequality operators
<, <=, >, >=	Inequality operators
+, -	Unary sign operators
+, -, *, /, %	Addition, subtraction, multiplication, division, and modulus operators
+=, -=, *=, /=	Addition, subtraction, multiplication, division, and assign operators
++, —	Increment and decrement operators
<<, >>, >>>	Bitwise shift operators
<<=, >>=, >>>=	Bitwise shift and assign operators
~	Bitwise logical negation operator
&, ¦, ^	Bitwise AND, OR, and exclusive or (XOR) operators
&=, ¦=, ^=	Bitwise AND, OR, exclusive or (XOR), and assign operators

Later in Chapter 10 you learn about the equality and inequality operators that produce `Boolean` results. For now, concentrate on the arithmetic operators.

Operators

Operators are used to change the value of a particular object. For instance, say you want to add or subtract 5 from 10. As you soon see, you would use the addition or subtraction operator.

They are described here in several related categories. C and C++ programmers should find the operators in Table 7.4 very familiar.

Arithmetic Operators

Arithmetic operators are used to perform standard math operations on variables. These operators include:

- `+` Addition operator
- `-` Subtraction operator
- `*` Multiplication operator
- `/` Division operator
- `%` Modulus operator (gives the remainder of a division)

Probably the only operator in this list that you are not familiar with is the modulus operator. The modulus of an operation is the remainder of the operand divided by the operandi. In other words, in the equation 10 % 5, the remainder is 0 because 5 divides evenly into 5. However, the result of 11 % 5 is 1 because (if you can remember your early math classes), 11 divided by 5 is 2 R 1, or 2 remainder 1.

Listing 7.1 shows an example of these operators in use.

Listing 7.1 Examples Using Arithmetic Operators

```
int j = 60;                  // set the byte j's value to 60
int k = 24;
int l = 30;
int m = 12L;
int result = 0L;

result = j + k;              // result gets 84: (60 plus 24)
result = result / m;         // result gets 7: (84 divided by 12)
result = j - (2*k + result); // result gets 5: (60 minus (48 plus 7))
result = k % result;         // result gets 4: (remainder 24 div by 5)
```

Assignment Operators

The simplest assignment operator is the standard assignment operator. This operator is often known as the `gets` operator, because the value on the left gets the value on the right:

- `=` Assignment operator

The arithmetic assignment operators provide a shortcut for assigning a value. When the previous value of a variable is a factor in determining the value that you want to assign, the arithmetic assignment operators are often more efficient:

+= Add and assign operator

-= Subtract and assign operator

*= Multiply and assign operator

/= Divide and assign operator

%= Modulus and assign operator

Except for the assignment operator, the arithmetic assignment operators work as if the variable on the left of the operator were placed on the right. For instance, the following two lines are essentially the same:

```
x = x + 5;
x += 5;
```

Listing 7.2 shows more examples of the operators in use.

Listing 7.2 Examples Using Arithmetic Assignment Operators

```
byte j = 60;                    // set the byte j's value to 60
short k = 24;
int l = 30;
long m = 12L;
long result = 0L;

result += j;                    // result gets 60: (0 plus 60)
result += k;                    // result gets 84: (60 plus 24)
result /= m;                    // result gets 7: (84 divided by 12)
result -= l;                    // result gets -23: (7 minus 30))
result = -result;               // result gets 23: (-(-23))
result %= m;                    // result gets 11: (remainder 23 div by 12)
```

Increment/Decrement Operators

The increment and decrement operators are used with one variable (they are known as *unary operators*):

++ Increment operator

— Decrement operator

For instance, the increment operator (++) adds one to the operand, as shown in the next line of code:

```
x++;
```

This is the same as:

```
x+=1;
```

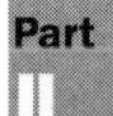

The increment and decrement operators behave slightly differently based on the side of the operand they are placed on. If the operand is placed before the operator (for example, ++x), the increment occurs before the value is taken for the expression. The result of `y` is `6` in the following code fragment:

```
int x=5;
int y=++x;        // y=6 x=6
```

If the operator appears after the operand, the addition occurs after the value is taken. `y` is `5` as shown in the next code fragment. Notice that in both examples, `x` is `6` at the end of the fragment:

```
int x=5;
int y = x++;    //y=5 x=6
```

Similarly, the decrement operator (—) subtracts one from the operand, and the timing of this is in relation to the evaluation of the expression in which it occurs.

Character Variables

Characters in Java are a special set. They can be treated as either a 16-bit unsigned integer with a value from `0` to `65535`, or as a Unicode character. The Unicode standard makes room for the use of many different languages' alphabets. The Latin alphabet, numerals, and punctuation have the same values as the ASCII character set (a set that is used on most PCs and with values between `0` and `256`). The default value for a `char` variable is `\u0000`.

The syntax to create a character variable is the same as for integers and `Booleans`:

```
char myChar = 'b';
```

In this example, the `myChar` variable has been assigned the value of the letter `'b'`. Notice the tick marks (`'`) around the letter `b`? These tell the compiler that you want the literal value of `b` rather than an identifier called `b`.

Floating-Point Variables

Floating-point numbers are the last category of native types in Java. *Floating-point numbers* are used to represent numbers that have a decimal point in them (such as 5.3 or 99.234). Whole numbers can also be represented, but as a floating point, the number 5 is actually 5.0.

In Java, floating-point numbers are represented by the types `float` and `double`. Both of these follow a standard floating-point specification: *IEEE Standard for Binary Floating-Point Arithmetic*, ANSI/IEEE Std. 754-1985 (IEEE, New York). The fact that these floating-point numbers follow this specification—no matter what machine the application or applet is running on—is one of the details that makes Java so portable. In other languages, floating-point operations are defined for the floating-point unit (FPU) of the particular machine the program is executing on. This means that the representation of 5.0 on an IBM PC is not the same as on, for example, a DEC VAX, and the limits on both machines are shown in the following table:

Floating-Point Type	Minimum Positive Value	Default Value	Maximum Value
`float`	1.40239846e–45f	0	3.40282347e+38f
`double`	4.94065645841246544e–324d	0	1.7976931348623157e+308d

In addition, there are four unique states that floating-point numbers can have:

- Negative infinity
- Positive infinity
- Zero
- Not a number

These states are required, due to how the 754-1985 standard works, to account for number rollover. For instance, adding 1 to the maximum number of a floating point results in a positive infinity result.

Many of the operations that can be done on integers have an analogous operation that can be done on floating-point numbers. The main exceptions are the bitwise operations. The operators that may be used in expressions of `type`, `float`, or `double` are given in Table 7.5.

Table 7.5 Operations on *float* and *double* Expressions

Operation	Description
`=, +=, -=, *=, /=`	Assignment operators
`==, !=`	Equality and inequality operators
`<, <=, >, >=`	Inequality operators
`+, -`	Unary sign operators
`+, -, *, /`	Addition, subtraction, multiplication, and division operators
`+=, -=, *=, /=`	Addition, subtraction, multiplication, division, and assign operators
`++, —`	Increment and decrement operators

Arrays

There are three types of reference variables:

- Classes
- Interfaces
- Arrays

Classes and interfaces are so complicated that each gets its own chapter, but arrays are comparatively simple and are covered here with the primitive types.

An *array* is simply a way to have several items in a row. If you have data that can be easily indexed, arrays are the perfect means to represent them. For instance, if you have five people in a class and you want to represent all of their IQs, an array would work perfectly. An example of such an array is:

```
int IQ[] = {123,109,156,142,131};
```

The next line shows an example of accessing the IQ of the third individual:

```
int ThirdPerson = IQ[3];
```

Arrays in Java are somewhat tricky. This is mostly because, unlike most other languages, there are really three steps to filling out an array, rather than one.

1. Declare the array. There are two ways to do this: Place a pair of brackets after the variable type or place brackets after the identifier name. The following two lines produce the same result:

   ```
   int MyIntArray[];
   int[] MyIntArray;
   ```

2. Create space for the array and define the size. To do this, you must use the keyword `new`, followed by the variable type and size:

   ```
   MyIntArray = new int[500];
   ```

3. Place data in the array. For arrays of native types (like those in this chapter), the array values are all set to `0` initially. The next line shows how to set the fifth element in the array:

   ```
   MyIntArray[4] = 467;
   ```

At this point, you may be asking yourself how you were able to create the five-element array and declare the values with the IQ example. The IQ example took advantage of a shortcut. For native types only, you can declare the initial values of the array by placing the values between braces (`{`,`}`) on the initial declaration line.

Array declarations are composed of the following parts:

Array modifiers	Optional	The keywords `public`, `protected`, `private`, or `synchronized`
Type name	Required	The name of the type or class being arrayed
Brackets	Required	`[ ]`
Initialization	Optional	See Chapter 11 for more details about initialization
Semicolon	Required	`;`

Listing 7.3 shows several more examples of using arrays.

Listing 7.3 Examples of Declaring Arrays

```
long Primes[] = new long[1000000];      // Declare an array and assign
                                        // some memory to hold it.
long[] EvenPrimes = new long[1];        // Either way, it's an array.
EvenPrimes[0] = 2;                      // Populate the array.

// Now declare an array with an implied 'new' and populate.

long Fibonacci[] = {1,1,2,3,5,8,13,21,34,55,89,144};

long Perfects[] = {6, 28};              // Creates two element array.

long BlackFlyNum[];                     // Declare an array.
                                        // Default value is null.

BlackFlyNum = new long[2147483647];     // Array indexes must be type int.

// Declare a two dimensional array and populate it.
long TowerOfHanoi[][]={{10,9,8,7,6,5,4,3,2,1},{},{}};

long[][][] ThreeDTicTacToe;             // Uninitialized 3D array.
```

There are several additional points about arrays you need to know:

- Indexing of arrays starts with `0` (as in C and C++). In other words, the first element of an array is `MyArray[0]`, not `MyArray[1]`.
- You can populate an array on initialization. This only applies to native types and allows you to define the value of the array elements.
- Array indexes must either be type `int` (32-bit integer) or be able to be cast as an `int`. As a result, the largest possible array size is 2,147,483,647. Most Java installations would fail with arrays anywhere near that size, but that is the maximum defined by the language.
- When populating an array, the rightmost index sequences within the innermost curly braces.

Whitespace

Of some importance to most languages is the use of whitespace. *Whitespace* is any character that is used just to separate letters on a line—a space, tab, line feed, or carriage return.

In Java, whitespace can be declared anywhere within the application's source code without affecting the meaning of the code to the compiler. The only place that whitespace cannot be is between a token, such as a variable or class name. This may be obvious, because the following two lines are obviously not the same:

```
int myInt;
int my   Int;
```

Whitespace is optional, but because proper use of it has a big impact on the maintainability of the source code for an application or applet, its use is highly recommended. Let's take a look at the ever popular `HelloWorld` application written with minimal use of whitespace:

```
public class HelloWorld{public static void main(String args
➥[]){System.out.println("Hello World!!");}}
```

Clearly, it is a little harder to ferret out what this application does, or even that you have started at the beginning and finished at the end. Choose a scheme for applying meaningful whitespace and follow it. You stand a better chance of knowing which close curly brace (`}`) matches which open brace (`{`).

Comments

Comments are an important part of any language. *Comments* enable you to leave a message for other programmers (or yourself) as a reminder of what is going on in that particular section of code. They are not tokens and neither are any of their contents.

Java supports three styles of comments:

- Traditional (from the C language tradition)
- C++ style
- javadoc (a minor modification on traditional comments)

Traditional Comments

A traditional comment is a C-style comment that begins with a slash-star (`/*`) and ends with a star-slash (`*/`). Take a look at Listing 7.4, which shows two traditional comments.

Listing 7.4 Example Containing Two Traditional Comments

```
/* The following is a code fragment
 * that is here only for the purpose
 * of demonstrating a style of comment.
 */

double pi = 3.141592654  /* close enough for now */ ;
```

As you can see, comments of this sort can span many lines or can be contained within a single line (outside a token). Comments cannot be nested. Thus, if you try to nest them, the opening of the inner one is not detected by the compiler, the closing of the inner one ends the comment, and subsequent text is interpreted as tokens. Listing 7.5 shows how this can become very confusing.

Listing 7.5 An Example of a Single Comment That Looks Like Two

```
/* This opens the comment
/* That looked like it opened another comment but it is the same one
* This will close the entire comment                                   */
```

C++ Style Comments

The second style of comment begins with a slash-slash (//) and ends when the current source code line ends. These comments are especially useful for describing the intended meaning of the current line of code. Listing 7.6 demonstrates the use of this style of comment.

Listing 7.6 An Example Using Traditional and C++ Style Comments

```
for (int j = 0, Boolean Bad = false; // initialize outer loop
   j < MAX_ROW;                      // repeat for all rows
   j++) {
     for (int k = 0;   // initialize inner loop
     k < MAX_COL;      // repeat for all columns
     k++) {
          if (NumeralArray[j][k] > '9') { // > highest numeric?
               Bad = true;     // mark bad
          }                            // close if > '9'
          if (NumeralArray[j][k] < '0') { // < lowest numeric?
               Bad = true;     // mark bad
          }                            // close if < '0'
     }                                 // close inner loop
}                                      // close outer loop
```

javadoc Comments

The final style of comment in Java is a special case of the first. It has the properties mentioned previously, but the contents of the comment may be used in automatically generated documentation by the javadoc tool.

CAUTION

Avoid inadvertent use of this style if you plan to use javadoc. The javadoc program will not be able to tell the difference.

javadoc comments are opened with /**, and are closed with */. By using these comments in an appropriate manner, you can use javadoc to automatically create documentation pages similar to those of the Java API. Listing 7.7 shows a javadoc comment.

Listing 7.7 An Example of a javadoc Comment

```
/** This class is for processing databases
  * Example use:
  *  xdb myDB = new xdb (myDbFile);
*  System.out.println(xdb.showAll()); */
```

Literals: Assigning Values

When you learned about assigning a `Boolean` variable, there were only two possible values: `true` and `false`. For integers, the values are nearly endless. In addition, there are many ways an integer value can be represented using literals.

The easiest way to assign a value to an integer value is with its traditional Roman numeral:

```
int j = 3;
```

However, what happens when you want to assign a number that is represented in a different form, such as hexadecimal? To tell the computer that you are giving it a hexadecimal number, you need to use the hexadecimal literal. For a number like 3, this doesn't make much difference, but consider the number 11. Represented in hexadecimal (`0x11`), it has a value of `16`! Certainly, you need a way to make sure the computer gets this right.

The following statements all contain various literals:

```
int j=0;
long GrainOfSandOnTheBeachNum=1L;
short Mask1=0x007f;
static String FirstName = "Ernest";
static Char TibetanNine = '\u1049'
Boolean UniverseWillExpandForever = true;
```

Clearly, there are several types of literals. In fact, there are five major types of literals in the Java language:

- `Boolean`
- Integer
- Character
- String
- Floating-point

Integer Literals

Integer literals are used to represent numbers of integer types. Because integers can be expressed as decimal (base 10), octal (base 8), or hexadecimal (base 16) numbers, each has its own literal. In addition, integer numbers can be represented with an optional uppercase L (`'L'`) or lowercase L (`'l'`) at the end, which tells the computer to treat that number as a long (64-bit) integer.

As with C and C++, Java identifies decimal integer literals as any number beginning with a non-zero digit (for example, any number between 1 and 9). Octal integer literal tokens are recognized by the leading zero (045 is the same as 37 decimal); they may not contain the numerals 8 or 9. Hexadecimal integer literal tokens are known by their distinctive `'zero-X'` at the beginning of the token. Hex numbers are composed of the numerals 0 through 9—plus the Latin letters A through F (case is not important).

The largest and smallest values for integer literals are shown in each of these three formats:

Largest 32-bit integer literal	2147483647 017777777777 0x7fffffff
Most negative 32-bit integer literal	-2147483648 020000000000 0x80000000
Largest 64-bit integer literal	9223372036854775807L 0777777777777777777777L 0x7fffffffffffffffL
Most negative 64-bit integer literal	-9223372036854775808L 01777777777777777777777L 0xffffffffffffffffL

CAUTION

Attempts to represent integers outside the range shown in this table result in compile-time errors.

Character Literals

Character literals are enclosed in single quotation marks. This is true whether the character value is Latin alphanumeric, an escape sequence, or any other Unicode character. Single characters are any printable character except hyphen (-) or backslash (\). Some examples of these literals are `'a'`, `'A'`, `'9'`, `'+'`, `'_'`, and `'~'`.

Some characters, such as the backspace, would be difficult to write out like this, so to solve this problem, these characters are represented by what are called escape characters. The escape sequence character literals are in the form of `'\b'`. These are found within single quotation marks—a backslash followed by one of the following:

- Another character (`b`, `t`, `n`, `f`, `r`, `"`, `'`, or `\`)
- A series of octal digits
- A `u` followed by a series of hex digits expressing a nonline-terminating Unicode character

The Escape characters are shown in Table 7.6.

Table 7.6 Escape Characters

Escape Literal	Meaning
`'\b'`	`\u0008` backspace
`'\t'`	`\u0009` horizontal tab
`'\n'`	`\u000a` linefeed

continues

Table 7.6 Continued

Escape Literal	Meaning
`'\f'`	`\u000c` form feed
`'\r'`	`\u000d` carriage return
`'\"'`	`\u0022` double quotation mark
`'\''`	`\u0027` single quotation mark
`'\\'`	`\u005c` backslash

CAUTION

Don't use the `\u` format to express an end-of-line character. Use the `\n` or `\r` characters instead.

Character literals mentioned in Table 7.6 are called *octal escape literals*. They can be used to represent any Unicode value from `'\u0000'` to `'\u00ff'` (the traditional ASCII range). In octal (base 8), these values are from `\000` to `\377`. Note that octal numerals are from 0 to 7 inclusive. Table 7.7 shows some examples of octal literals.

Table 7.7 Octal Values and Their Meaning

Octal Literal	Meaning
`'\007'`	`\u0007 bell`
`'\101'`	`\u0041 'A'`
`'\141'`	`\u0061 'a'`
`'\071'`	`\u0039 '9'`
`'\042'`	`\u0022` double quotation mark

CAUTION

Character literals of the type in the previous table are interpreted very early by javac. As a result, using the escape Unicode literals to express a line termination character—such as carriage return or line feed—results in an end-of-line appearing before the terminal single quotation mark. The result is a compile-time error. Examples of this type of character literal appear in the Meaning heading listed in the previous table.

Floating-Point Literals

Floating-point numbers can be represented in a number of ways. The following are all legitimate floating-point numbers:

1003.45 .00100345e6 100.345E+1100345e-2

1.00345e3 0.00100345e+6

Floating-point literals have several parts, which appear in the following order as shown in Table 7.8.

Table 7.8 Floating-Point Requirements

Part	Is It Required?	Examples
Whole Number	Not if fractional part is present.	0, 1, 2,..., 9, Number Part 12345
Decimal Point	Not if exponent is present; must be there if there is a fractional part.	
Fractional	Can't be present if there is no decimal point. Must be there if there is no whole number part.	0, 1, 14159, 718281828,41421, 9944
Exponent	Only if there is no decimal point.	e23, E-19, E6, e+307, e-1
Type Suffix	No. The number is assumed to be double precision in the absence of a type suffix.	f, F, d, D

The whole number part does not have to be a single numeral; case is not important for the `E` which starts the exponent, or for the `F` or `D`, which indicate the type. As a result, a given number can be represented in several different ways as a literal:

- Single precision floating-point literals produce compile-time errors if their values are non-zero and have an absolute value outside the range from 1.40239846e-45f through 3.40282347e+38f.
- The range for the non-zero absolute values of double precision literals is 4.94065645841246544e-324 through 1.79769313486231257e+308.

String Literals

Strings are not really native types. However, it is also necessary to talk about them to finish the discussion of literals. String literals have zero or more characters enclosed in double quotation marks. These characters may include the escape sequences listed in the "Character Literals" section earlier in this chapter. Both double quotation marks must appear on the same line of the source code, so strings may not directly contain a newline character. To achieve the new line effect, you must use an escape sequence such as `\n` or `\r`.

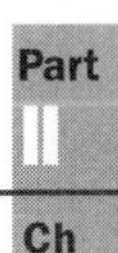

The double-quotation mark (`"`) and backslash (`\`) characters must also be represented using the escape sequences (`\"` and `\\`).

One nice feature Java inherits from C++ is that if you need to use a longer string, a string may be created from concatenating two or more smaller strings with the string concatenation operator (+).

CAUTION

Although it is often convenient to use the + operator for strings, the current implementation of the `String` class isn't very efficient. As a result, doing lots of string concatenations can waste memory resources.

Some examples of string literals include:

```
 "Java"
 "Hello World!\n"
 "The Devanagari numeral for 9 is \u096f "
 "Do you mean the European Swallow or the African Swallow?"
 "*** *ERROR 9912 Date/Time 1/1/1900 00:01"
+ " predates last backup: all files deleted!"
 "If this were an actual emergency"
```

Creating and Destroying Objects

Memory management is a topic that is very important to all computer languages. Whenever you create a new instance of a class, the Java runtime system sets aside a portion of memory in which to store the information pertaining to the class. However, when the object falls out of scope or is no longer needed by the program, this portion of memory is freed to be used again by other objects.

While Java hides most of these operations from the programmer, it does provide you some chances to optimize your code by performing certain additional tasks. While requiring you to allocate memory explicitly for each new object with the new operator, it also enables you to specialize your new object (by using its constructor methods) and ensures that it leaves no loose ends when it is destroyed.

NOTE Unlike C and C++, which provide the programmer with a great deal of control over memory management, Java performs many of these tasks for you. Most notably, in its aptly called *garbage collection*, Java automatically frees objects when there are no references to the given object, thereby making the C++ `free()` method unnecessary.

Creating Objects with the *new* Operator

When creating an instance of a class, it is necessary to set aside a piece of memory to store its data. However, when you declare the instance at the beginning of a class, you are merely telling the compiler that a variable with a certain name will be used in the class, not to actually allocate memory for it. Consequently, it is necessary to create the memory for the variable using the `new` operator. Examine the following code:

```
public class Checkers
{
    private GameBoard board;
    public Checkers() {
    board = new GameBoard("Checkers");
    board.cleanBoard();
}
...
```

You see that although the variable `board` is declared in the third line, you must also allocate memory for it using the `new` operator. The syntax of a statement involving the `new` operator is:

```
instanceofClass = new ClassName(optional_parameters);
```

Quite simply, the line tells the compiler to allocate memory for an instance of the class and points the variable to the new section of memory. In the process of doing this, the compiler also calls the class's constructor method and passes the appropriate parameters to it.

Pointers: Fact or Fiction?

Java claims not to possess pointers and, as a result, prevents the programmer from making some of the mistakes associated with pointer handling. Nevertheless, although it chooses not to adopt the pointer-based mindset, Java is forced to deal with the same issues of allocating memory and creating references to these locations in memory.

Thus, although assigned a different name, references are Java's version of pointers. Although you cannot perform some of the intrusive operations with pointers as you can with C, there are striking parallels between pointer assignment and object creation. You must first declare a variable (the reference). Then you must allocate adequate memory and assign the reference to it. Furthermore, because you may later decide to set a reference equal to another type of the same variable (or null), Java's reference system is extremely similar to C's system of pointers.

While Java's implementation effectively hides the behavior of pointers from the programmer and shields you from their pitfalls, it is nevertheless a good idea to consider what is occurring behind the scenes when you create and refer to a variable.

CHAPTER 8

Methods

In this chapter

Parts of a Method

Methods are truly the heart and soul of Java programs. Methods serve the same purpose in Java that functions do in C, C++, Pascal. All execution, which takes place in any applet or application, takes place within a method, and only by combining multiple dynamic methods are large-scale quality Java applications written.

Like C and C++ functions, Java methods are the essence of the class and are responsible for managing all tasks that will be performed. A method has two parts: a declaration and a body. While the actual implementation of the method is contained within the method's body, a great deal of important information is defined in the method declaration.

The simplest method (and least useful) would look like this:

```
void SimpleMethod(){
```

Declaration

The declaration for a method is similar to the first line in the previous section. At the very least, it specifies what the method will return, and the name the method will be known by. Ordinarily, as you will soon see, more options than these two are used. In general, method declarations have the form

```
access_specifier modifier return_value   nameofmethod   (parameters)
throws ExceptionList
```

where everything in italics is optional.

Access Specifiers The first option for a method is the access specifier. Access specifiers are used to restrict access to the method. Regardless of what the access specifier is, though, the method is accessible from any other method in the same class. However, although all methods in a class are accessible by all other methods in the same class, there are certain necessary tasks that you might not want other objects to be able to perform. You learn more about classes in Chapter 11, "Classes." For now you look at how the access modifiers can change a method.

Public The public modifier is the most relaxed modifier possible for a method. By specifying a method as `public`, it becomes accessible to all classes regardless of their lineage or their package. In other words, a `public` method is not restricted in any way. For example:

```
public void toggleStatus()
```

Protected The second possible access modifier is protected. Protected methods can be accessed by any class that extends the current class. For instance, the class `java.awt.Component` has a `protected` method `paramString()`, which is used in classes such as `java.awt.Button`, but is inaccessible to any class that you might create that does not extend `Component`. For example:

```
protected void toggleStatus()
```

▶ **See** "Using Packages to Organize Your Code," **p.189**

NOTE If you are having a compile-time error caused by an attempt to access a method not visible to the current scope, you might have trouble diagnosing the source of your problems. This is because the error message does not tell you that you are attempting to access a protected method. Instead it resembles the following:

```
No method matching paramString() found in class java.awt.Button.
```

`java.awt.Button.paramString()` is a protected method in `java.awt.Button`. This is because the restricted methods are effectively hidden from the non-privileged classes. Therefore, when compiling a class that does not meet the security restrictions, such methods are hidden from the compiler.

Also note that you encounter a similar error message when trying to access a private or protected method outside of its range of access, as well as when you attempt to access a field from an unprivileged class.

Private Private is the highest degree of protection that can be applied to a method.

A private method is only accessible by those methods in the same class. Even classes that extend from the current class do not have access to a private class. For example:

```
private void toggleStatus()
```

Default Those methods that do not declare their access level have a special accessibility in Java. These methods are accessible to any class in the rest of the current package, but not any classes outside the current package. For example:

```
package abc;
public class NetworkSender {
  void sendInfo(String mes) {
    system.out.println(mes)
  }
}

package abc;
public class NetworkSenderTest {
  String mes = "test";
  void informOthers(String mes) {
    NetworkSender messenger;
    messenger = new NetworkSender();
 messanger.sendInfo(mes); // this is legal
}
}

package xyz;
import NetworkSender;
public class NetworkSenderTest2 extends NetworkSender{
  String mes = "test";
  void informOthers(String mes) {
    NetworkSender messenger;
    messenger = new NetworkSender();
    messanger.sendInfo(mes); // this is NOT legal
  }
}
```

The first statement invokes `sendInfo()` as a method belonging to the `NetworkSender`. This is legal because `default` methods are accessible to other classes in the same package (both `NetworkSender` and `NetworkSenderTest` are in the package abc). However, in `NetworkSenderTest2` the statement is illegal because it attempts to invoke `sendInfo()` on an instance of the `NetworkSender` class, but `NetworkSenderTest2` is in a different package (xyz). Even though `NetworkSenderTest2` is a subclass of `NetworkSender`, it is referencing `sendInfo()` not as a method belonging to its superclass, but rather as a method belonging to an instance of `NetworkSender`.

Modifiers Method modifiers enable you to set properties for the method, such as where it will be visible and how subclasses of the current class will interact with it.

Static Static, or class, variables and methods are closely related. For example:

```
static void toggleStatus()
```

It is important to differentiate between the properties of a specific instance of a class and the class itself. In the following code (see Listing 8.1), you create two instances of the `Elevator` class and perform some operations with them.

Listing 8.1 Hotel.java—Hotel Example with Instance Methods

```
class Elevator {
   boolean running = true;
   void shutDown() {
      running = false;
   }
}

class FrontDesk {
   private final int EVENING = 8;
   Elevator NorthElevator, SouthElevator;

   FrontDesk() {                      // the class constructor
      NorthElevator = new Elevator();
      SouthElevator = new Elevator();
   }

   void maintenance(int time) {
      if (time == EVENING)
         NorthElevator.shutDown();
   }

   void displayStatus() {
      // code is very inefficient, but serves a purpose
      System.out.print("North Elevator is ");
      if (!(NorthElevator.running ))
         System.out.print("not ");
      System.out.println("running.");
      System.out.print("South Elevator is ");
      if (!(SouthElevator.running ))
```

```
            System.out.print(" not ");
         System.out.println("running.");
          }
   }

public class Hotel {
   public static void main(String args[]) {
      FrontDesk lobby;
      lobby = new FrontDesk();
      System.out.println("It's 7:00.  Time to check the elevators.");
      lobby.maintenance(7);
      lobby.displayStatus();

      System.out.println();
      System.out.println("It's 8:00.  Time to check the elevators.");
      lobby.maintenance(8);
      lobby.displayStatus();
   }
}
```

Both `NorthElevator` and `SouthElevator` are instances of the `Elevator` class. This means that each is created with its own `running` variable and its own copy of the `shutDown()` method. Although these are initially identical for both elevators, as you can see from the preceding example, the status of `running` in `NorthElevator` and `SouthElevator` does not remain equal once the `maintenance()` method is called.

Consequently, if compiled and run, the preceding code produces the following output:

```
C:\dev>\JDK1.2\java\bin\java Hotel
It's 7:00.  Time to check the elevators.
North Elevator is running.
South Elevator is running.
It's 8:00.  Time to check the elevators.
North Elevator is not running.
South Elevator is running.
```

NOTE In the preceding example, you might notice a rather funny looking method named `FrontDesk()`. What is it? As you learn in the "Constructors" section in Chapter 11, this is the constructor method for the `FrontDesk` class. Called whenever an instance of `FrontDesk` is created, it provides you the ability to initialize fields and perform other such preparatory operations.

Variables and methods such as `running` and `shutDown()` are called instance variables and instance methods. This is because every time the `Elevator` class is instantiated, a new copy of each is created. In the preceding example, while the value of the `running` variable certainly can change because there are two copies of it, changing one does not change the other. Therefore, you can track the status of the `NorthElevator` and `SouthElevator` separately.

However, what if you want to define and modify a property for all elevators? Examine the example in Listing 8.2 and note the additions.

Listing 8.2 Hotel2.java—Hotel Example with Static Methods

```
class Elevator {
   boolean running = true;
   static boolean powered = true;
   void shutDown() {
      running = false;
   }
   static void togglePower() {
      powered = !powered;
   }
}

class FrontDesk {
   private final int EVENING = 8;
   private final int CLOSING = 10;
   private final int OPENING = 6;
   Elevator NorthElevator, SouthElevator;
   FrontDesk() {
      NorthElevator = new Elevator();
      SouthElevator = new Elevator();
   }

   void maintenance(int time) {
      if (time == EVENING)
         NorthElevator.shutDown();
      else if ( (time == CLOSING) || (time == OPENING) )
         Elevator.togglePower();
   }

   void displayStatus() {
      // Code is very inefficient, but serves a purpose.
      System.out.print("North Elevator is ");
      if (!(NorthElevator.running ))
         System.out.print("not ");
      System.out.println("running.");
      System.out.print("South Elevator is ");
      if (!(SouthElevator.running ))
         System.out.print(" not ");
      System.out.println("running.");
      System.out.print("The elevators are ");
      if (!(Elevator.powered  ))
         System.out.print("not ");
      System.out.println("powered.");
   }

public class Hotel2 {
   public static void main(String args[]) {
      FrontDesk lobby;
      lobby = new FrontDesk();
      System.out.println("It's 7:00.  Time to check the elevators.");
      lobby.maintenance(7);
      lobby.displayStatus();

      System.out.println();
      System.out.println("It's 8:00.  Time to check the elevators.");
```

```
        lobby.maintenance(8);
        lobby.displayStatus();

        System.out.println();
        System.out.println("It's 10:00.  Time to check the elevators.");
        lobby.maintenance(10);
        lobby.displayStatus();
    }
}
```

In this case, the variable `powered` is now a static variable, and the method `togglePower()` is a static method. This means that each is now a property of all `Elevator` classes, not the specific instances. Invoking either the `NorthElevator.togglePower()`, `SouthElevator.togglePower()`, or `Elevator.togglePower()` method would change the status of the `powered` variable in both classes.

Consequently, the code would produce the following output:

```
C:\dev>\JDK1.2\java\bin\java Hotel2
It's 7:00.  Time to check the elevators.
North Elevator is running.
South Elevator is running.
The elevators are powered.
It's 8:00.  Time to check the elevators.
North Elevator is not running.
South Elevator is running.
The elevators are powered.
It's 10:00.  Time to check the elevators.
North Elevator is not running.
South Elevator is running.
The elevators are not powered.
```

Placing the `static` modifier in front of a method declaration makes the method a static method. While nonstatic methods can also operate with static variables, static methods can only deal with static variables and static methods.

Abstract Abstract methods are simply methods that are declared, but are not implemented in the current class. The responsibility of defining the body of the method is left to subclasses of the current class. For example:

```
abstract void toggleStatus();
```

CAUTION

Neither static methods nor class constructors can be declared to be `abstract`. Furthermore, you should not make abstract methods `final`, because doing so prevents you from overriding the method.

Final By placing the keyword `final` in front of the method declaration, you prevent any subclasses of the current class from overriding the given method. This ability enhances the degree of insulation of your classes, and you can ensure that the functionality defined in this method will never be altered in any way. For example:

```
final void toggleStatus()
```

Native Native methods are methods that you want to use, but do not want to write in Java. Native methods are most commonly written in C++ and can provide several benefits such as faster execution time. Like abstract methods, they are declared simply by placing the modifier `native` in front of the method declaration and by substituting a semicolon for the method body.

However, it is also important to remember that the declaration informs the compiler as to the properties of the method. Therefore, it is imperative that you specify the same return type and parameter list as can be found in the native code.

Synchronized By placing the keyword `synchronized` in front of a method declaration, you can prevent data corruption that may result when two methods attempt to access the same piece of data at the same time. Although this might not be a concern for simple programs, after you begin to use threads in your programs, this can become a serious problem. For example:

```
synchronized void toggleStatus()
```

▶ **See** "What Are Threads?" **p. 208**

Returning Information Although returning information is one of the most important things a method can do, there is little to discuss by way of details about returning information. Java methods can return any data type ranging from simple ones, such as integers and characters, to more complex objects. (This means that you can return things such as strings as well.)

Keep in mind that unless you use the keyword `void` as your return type, you must return a variable of the type specified in your declaration.

For example, the following method is declared to return a variable of type `boolean`. The return is actually accomplished by employing the `return` (either `true` or `false`) statement in the third and fourth lines:

```
public synchronized boolean isEmpty(int x, ét y) {
   if (board[x][y] == EMPTY)
      return true;
   return false;
}
```

Method Name The rules regarding method names are quite simple and are the same as any other Java identifier: Begin with a Unicode letter (or an underscore or dollar sign) and continue with only Unicode characters.

Parameter Lists Simply put, the parameter list is the list of information that will be passed to the method. It is in the following form and can consist of as many parameters as you want:

```
DataType VariableName, DataType VariableName,...
```

NOTE If you have no parameters, Java requires that you simply leave the parentheses empty. (This is unlike other languages that permit you to omit a parameter list, or C, which requires the keyword `void`.) Therefore, a method that took no parameters would have a declaration resembling the following:

```
public static final void cleanBoard()
```

Passing Parameters in Java

In C and C++, variables are always passed by value. In Pascal, they are always passed by reference. In Java, however, it depends on what data type you are using. This is probably the single most ambiguous part of the entire Java language. Here is the rule: If the type being passed is a primitive type (such as `int`, `char`, or `float`), the result is passed by value. If, however, the type being passed is an object (such as a class you created), the object is passed by reference.

What does this mean? As shown in Listing 8.2, if you pass an `int` to a method and that method changes the `int`, in the old class the `int` still has the value it did before. However, when a class is passed and a variable is changed, the variable is changed in the old method, too. Take a look at Listing 8.3.

Listing 8.3 PassingDemo.java—The Difference Between Passing an Object and a Primitive Type

```
public class passingDemo {

        public void first(){
                xObject o = new xObject ();
                o.x   = 5;
                int x = 5;

                changeThem (x, o);
                System.out.println();
                System.out.println("Back in the original method");
                System.out.println("The value of o.x is "+o.x);
                System.out.println("But, The value of x is now "+x);
        }


        public void changeThem (int x, xObject o){
                x =9;
                o.x = 9;
                System.out.println("In the changThem method");
                System.out.println("The value of o.x is "+o.x);
                System.out.println("The value of x is now "+x);
        }

        public static void main(String args[]){
                passingDemo myDemo = new passingDemo();
                myDemo.first();
        }
}


class xObject {
        public int x =5;
}
```

The resulting output from this code is

```
In the changeThem method
The value of o.x is 9
The value of x is 9
```

Back in the original method

```
The value of o.x is 9
The value of x is 5
```

Pass by Reference or Pass by Value? One important thing to understand about any programming language is whether the values are passed into a method by value or by reference. If a language uses pass by reference, when you pass a value into a method as a parameter, and then change the value it is changed back in the calling program as well. On the other hand, if a language uses pass by value, only the value is passed into the method and any changes aren't present in the calling method.

Java is actually a mixed system. Native types (byte,short,char,int,long,float,double and boolean) are passed by value. All objects however are passed by reference. This is why in the example in the previous section the value of x (a native) is not changed in the original method. On the other hand since o (an object) is passed by reference, o.x has been changed when it's printed out in the original method.

Blocks and Statements

Methods and static initializers in Java are defined by blocks of statements. A *block* of statements is a series of statements enclosed within curly-braces `{}`. When a statement's form calls for a statement or substatement as a part, a block can be inserted in the substatement's place.

The simplest block `{}` is shown in the following example:

```
public void HiThere() {
}
```

The next example is only slightly more complex:

```
public void HiThere(){
    int Test;
    Test = 5;
}
```

Code blocks are not only integral for defining the start and end of a method, but they can also be used in a variety of locations throughout your code. One very important aspect of a block is that it is treated lexically as one instruction. This means that you can put together large blocks of code that will be treated as one instruction line.

There is nothing in the definition of Java that prevents the programmer from breaking code into blocks even though they are not specifically called for, but this is seldom done. The following code fragment demonstrates this legal but seldom-performed technique:

```
String Batter;
Short Inning, Out, Strikes;
Batsman Casey;                       // Object of class Batsman.
...
if ((Inning == 9) && (Out==2) && (Batter.equals("Casey"))) {
   Casey.manner("ease");
   Casey.bearing("pride");
   {                                 // Begins new block for no reason.
      int OnlyExistsInThisBlock = 1;
      Casey.face("smile");
      Casey.hat("lightly doff");
   }                                 // Ends superfluous blocking.
}
```

Notice that this fragment contains two complete blocks. One is the substatement of the `if` statement, and the other is the unneeded block, which contains the unused integer `OnlyExistsInThisBlock`.

Labeled Statements

Any statement in Java can have a label. The actual label has the same properties as any other identifier; it cannot have the same name as a keyword or already declared local identifier. If it has the same name as a variable, method, or type name that is available to this block, then within that block, the new label takes precedence and that outside variable, method, or type is hidden. The label has the scope of the current block. The label is followed by a colon.

Labels are only used by the `break` and `continue` statements.

An example of labeled statements appears in the following code fragment:

```
writhing:
   Pitcher.GrindsBall("Hip");
   Casey.eye("Defiance Gleams");
   Casey.lip("Curling Sneer");
pitch:  while (strike++ < 2) {
      if (strike < 2) continue pitch;
         break writhing;
}
```

The `writhing` statement is simple labeling of an expression statement, in this case, a method call from a rather complicated object called `Pitcher`. The `pitch` statement is labeling an iteration statement (`while`). This label is used as a parameter for the `continue` statement.

Scope

Another use of blocks is to control what is known as the scope of an object. When you declare a variable, it is only available for your use within a given code block. For instance, say you had the following block:

```
{
   int x= 5;
}
System.out.println ("X is ="+x); // This line is not valid.
```

The last line of this code would not be valid, because the computer creates the `x` variable, but when the computer reaches the closing brace, it gets rid of `x`.

Separators

Separators are single-character tokens, which (as their name implies) are found between other tokens. There are nine separators, which are loosely described as follows:

- (Used both to open a parameter list for a method and to establish a precedence for operations in an expression
-) Used both to close a parameter list for a method and to establish a precedence for operations in an expression
- { Used both to open a parameter list or used to begin a block of statements or an initialization list
- } Used to close a block of statements or an initialization list
- [Used both to open a parameter list for a Precedes an expression used as an array index
-] Follows an expression used as an array index
- ; Used both to end an expression statement and to separate the parts of a `for` statement
- , Used as a list delimiter in many contexts
- . Used both as a decimal point and to separate such things as package name from class name from method or variable name

CHAPTER 9

Using Expressions

In this chapter

What Is an Expression?

Expressions—combinations of operators and operands—are one of the key building blocks of the Java language, as they are of many programming languages. Expressions allow you to perform arithmetic calculations, concatenate strings, compare values, perform logical operations, and manipulate objects. Without expressions, a programming language is dead—useless and lifeless.

You've already seen some expressions, mostly fairly simple ones, in other chapters in this book. Chapter 7, "Data Types and Other Tokens," in particular showed you that operators—one of the two key elements in an expression—form one of the main classifications of Java tokens, along with such things as keywords, comments, and so on. In this chapter, you take a closer look at how you can use operators to build expressions—in other words, how to put operators to work for you.

There are all kinds of technical definitions of what an expression is, but at its simplest, an expression is what results when operands and operators are joined together. Expressions are usually used to perform operations—manipulations—on variables or values. In Table 9.1, you see several legal Java expressions.

Table 9.1 Legal Java Expressions

Name of Expression	Example
Additive expression	`x+5`
Assignment expression	`x=5`
Array indexing	`sizes[11]`
Method invocation	`Triangle.RotateLeft(50)`

How Expressions Are Evaluated

When an expression is simple, like those shown in Table 9.1, figuring out the result of the expression is easy. When the expression becomes more detailed and more than one operator is used, things get more complicated.

In Chapter 7, you learned that expressions are just combinations of operators and operands. And while that definition may be true, it's not always very helpful. Sometimes you need to create and use pretty complex expressions—maybe to perform some kind of complicated calculation or other involved manipulation. To do this, you need a deeper understanding of how Java expressions are created and evaluated. In this section, you look at three major tools that will help you in your work with Java expressions: operator associativity, operator precedence, and order of evaluation.

Operator Associativity

The easiest of the expression rules is associativity. All the arithmetic operators are said to associate left-to-right. This means that if the same operator appears more than once in an expression—as the plus in a+b+c does—then the leftmost occurrence is evaluated first, followed by the one to its right, and so on. Consider the following assignment statement:

```
x = a+b+c;
```


In this example, the value of the expression on the right of the = is calculated and assigned to the variable x on the left. In calculating the value on the right, the fact that the + operator associates left-to-right means that the value of a+b is calculated first, and the result is then added to c. The result of that second calculation is what is assigned to x. So if you were to write it using explicit parentheses, the line would read:

```
x=((a+b)+c);
```

NOTE Notice that in the previous example, a+b+c, the same operator appears twice. It's when the same operator appears more than once–as it does in this case–that you apply the associativity rule.

You would use the associativity rule in evaluating the right sides of each of the following assignment statements:

```
volume = length * width * height ;

OrderTotal = SubTotal + Freight + Taxes ;

PerOrderPerUnit = Purchase / Orders / Units ;
```

Of these expressions, only the last one would result in a different way if you associated the expression incorrectly. The correct answer for this expression is

```
(Purchase / Orders)/ Units
```

However, evaluated incorrectly the result would be

```
Purchase / (Orders/Units)
```

which can also be written as

```
(Purchase * Units)/ Orders
```

which is obviously not the same as the correct expression.

Precedence of Java Operators

When you have an expression that involves different operators, the associativity rule doesn't apply, because the associativity rule only helps figure out how combinations of the same operator would be evaluated. Now you need to know how expressions using combinations of different operators are evaluated.

Precedence helps to determine which operator to act on first. If you write A+B*C, by standard mathematics you would first multiply B and C and then add the result to A. Precedence helps the computer to do the same thing. The multiplicative operators (`*`, `/`, and `%`) have higher precedence than the additive operators (+ and -). So, in a compound expression that incorporates both multiplicative and additive operators, the multiplicative operators are evaluated first.

Consider the following assignment statement, which is intended to convert a Fahrenheit temperature to Celsius:

```
Celsius = Fahrenheit - 32 * 5 / 9;
```

The correct conversion between Celsius and Fahrenheit is that the degrees Celsius are equal degrees Fahrenheit minus 32 times 5 divided by 9. However, in the equation, because the * and / operators have higher precedence, the sub-expression 32*5/9 is evaluated first (yielding the result 17) and that value is subtracted from the Fahrenheit variable.

To correctly write this equation, and whenever you need to change the order of evaluation of operators in an expression, you can use parentheses. Any expression within parentheses is evaluated first. To perform the correct conversion for the preceding example, you would write:

```
Celsius = ( Fahrenheit - 32 ) * 5 / 9;
```

NOTE Interestingly, there are some computer languages that do not use rules of precedence. Some languages, like APL for example, use a straight left-to-right or right-to-left order of evaluation, regardless of the operators involved.

Use of parentheses would also help with the following examples:

```
NewAmount = (Savings + Cash) * ExchangeRate ;

TotalConsumption = (Distance2 - Distance1) * ConsumptionRate ;
```

The precedence of the unary arithmetic operators—in fact all unary operators—is very high; it's above all the other arithmetic operators. In the following example, you multiply the value –5 times the value of Xantham, and not Xantham times five negated (although the results are the same):

```
Ryman = -5 * Xantham;
```

Summary—The Operator Table

Table 9.2 is what is known as the precedence table. The operators with the highest precedence are at the top. Operators on the same line are of equal precedence.

All these operators associate left-to-right, except the unary operators, assignments, and the conditional. For any single operator, operand evaluation is strictly left-to-right, and all operands are evaluated before operations are performed.

Table 9.2 The Complete Java Operator Precedence Table

<table>
<tr><th>Description</th><th>Operators</th></tr>
<tr><td>High Precedence</td><td><code>. [] ()</code></td></tr>
<tr><td>Instance Of Unary</td><td><code>+ - ~ ! ++ - -</code></td></tr>
<tr><td>Multiplicative</td><td><code>* / %</code></td></tr>
<tr><td>Additive</td><td><code>+ -</code></td></tr>
<tr><td>Shift</td><td><code><< >> >>></code></td></tr>
<tr><td>Relational</td><td><code>< <= >= > ></code></td></tr>
<tr><td>Equality</td><td><code>== !=</code></td></tr>
<tr><td>Bitwise AND</td><td><code>&</code></td></tr>
<tr><td>Bitwise XOR</td><td><code>^</code></td></tr>
<tr><td>Bitwise OR</td><td><code>|</code></td></tr>
<tr><td>Conditional-AND</td><td><code>&&</code></td></tr>
<tr><td>Conditional-OR</td><td><code>||</code></td></tr>
<tr><td>Conditional</td><td><code>?:</code></td></tr>
<tr><td>Assignment</td><td><code>= op=</code></td></tr>
</table>

Order of Evaluation

Many people, when they first learn a language, confuse the issue of operator precedence with order of evaluation. The two are actually quite different. The precedence rules help you determine which operators come first in an expression and what the operands are for an operator. For example, in the following line of code, the operands of the `*` operator are `a` and `(b+c)`:

```
d = a * (b+c) ;
```

The order of evaluation rules, on the other hand, help you to determine not when operators are evaluated, but when operands are evaluated.

Here are three rules that should help you remember how an expression is evaluated:

- For any binary operator, the left operand is evaluated before the right operand.
- Operands are always evaluated fully before the operator is evaluated; for example, before the operation is actually performed.
- If a number of arguments are supplied in a method call, separated by commas, the arguments are evaluated strictly left-to-right.

Of Special Interest to C Programmers

Because Java is an evolutionary outgrowth of C and C++, it's understandable that the expression syntax for the three languages is so similar. If you already know C, it's important that you keep in mind that the three languages are only similar—not identical.

One very important difference is that order of evaluation is guaranteed in Java, and is generally undefined or implementation-specific in C. In Java, the remainder (`%`), increment (++), and decrement (- -) operators are defined for all primitive data types (except Boolean); in C, they are defined only for integers.

Relational and equality operators in Java produce a Boolean result; in C, they produce results of type `int`. Furthermore, the logical operators in Java are restricted to Boolean operands.

Java supports native operations on strings—including string concatenation and string assignment. C does not have this support for strings.

In C, using the right-shift operator (>>) on a signed quantity results in implementation-specific behavior. Java avoids this confusion by using two different right-shift operators—one that pads with zeroes and the other that does sign-extension.

Bitwise Operators

If you have a number, such as 0x0F2 (which is a hexadecimal number equal to 242), do you know how to get rid of just the 2? Do you know how to find out which of the bits of 0x0F2 are set the same as they are for the number 0x0A1? Bitwise operators allow you to solve these problems easily. (To answer the question: 0x0F2&0x0F0 and 0x0F2&0x0A1.)

The bitwise operators are a set of operators that are either very important or completely unimportant to you depending on what you are doing. When you need a bitwise operator, it is rarely the case that you can substitute any other operation to easily reproduce the same results. But, at the same time, it's highly likely that most of the work you do will not require you to perform such esoteric calculations.

So what are bitwise operators? Bitwise operators work on the fundamental level of how values are stored in a computer. Numbers are stored in sequences of on and off, known as bits, which are most often translated to the binary numbers 1 and 0. A typical variable such as an `int` has 32 of these 1s and 0s in order to make up a complete number. It is often helpful to be able to manipulate these values directly, and bitwise operators are the means to do that.

Consider a simple example using bytes. A byte comprises eight bits of memory. Each of the eight bits can have the value of 0 or 1, and the value of the whole quantity is determined by using base 2 arithmetic, meaning that the rightmost bit represents a value of 0 or 1; the next bit represents the value of 0 or 2; the next represents the value 0 or 4, and so on, where each bit has a value of 0 and 2^n and n is the bit number. Table 9.3 shows the binary representation of several numbers.

Table 9.3 Some Base 10 Values and Their Base 2 Equivalents

Base 10	Value	128	64	32	16	8	4	2	1
17	0	0	0	0	1	0	0	0	1
63	0	0	0	1	1	1	1	1	1
75	0	0	1	0	0	1	0	1	1
131	0	1	0	0	0	0	0	1	1

To find the Base 10 value of the numbers in Table 9.3, you need to add together the number at the top of the column for each of the columns containing a 1. For instance, the first row would be

```
16+1 = 17
```

The numeric quantities in Table 9.3 are all positive integers, and that is on purpose. Negative numbers are a little more difficult to represent. For any integer quantity in Java, except `char`, the leftmost bit is reserved for the sign-bit. If the sign-bit is 1, then the value is negative. The rest of the bits in a negative number are also determined a little differently, in what is known as two's-complement, but don't worry about that now. Floating-point numbers also have their own special binary representation, but that's beyond the scope of this book.

The three binary bitwise operators perform the logical operations of AND, OR, and Exclusive OR (sometimes called XOR) on each bit in turn. The three operators are:

- Bitwise `AND: &`
- Bitwise `OR: |`
- Bitwise Exclusive `OR: ^`

Each of the operators produces a result based on what is known as a truth table. Each of the operators has a different truth table, and the next three tables show them.

To determine the results of a bitwise operator, it is necessary to take a look at each of the operands as a set of bits and compare the bits to the appropriate truth table.

First Value (A) (A&B)	Second Value (B)	Resulting Value
0	0	0
0	1	0
1	0	0
1	1	1

First Value (a)	Second Value (b)	Resulting Value (AIB)
0	0	0
0	1	1
1	0	1
1	1	1

First Value (a)	Second Value (b)	Resulting Value (A ^ B)
0	0	0
0	1	1
1	0	1
1	1	0

The operands of the bitwise operators can also be Boolean, in addition to being any other integer type.

Table 9.4 shows the results of each of these operations performed on two sample values. First, you see the Boolean values of the two numbers 11309 and 798, and then the resulting bit sequences after the various bit operators are applied.

Table 9.4 Bitwise Operation Examples

Expression	Binary Representation
`11309`	0010 1100 0010 1101
`798`	0000 0011 0001 1110
`11309 & 798`	0000 0000 0000 1100
`11309 ¦ 798`	0010 1111 0011 1111
`11309 ^ 798`	0010 1111 0011 0011

The Shift Operators

There are three shift operators in Java, as follows:

- Left shift: <<
- Signed right shift: >>
- Unsigned right shift: >>>

The shift operators move (shift) all of the bits in a number to the left or the right. The left operand is the value to be shifted, while the right operand is the number of bits to shift by, so in the equation

```
17<<2
```

the number 17 will be shifted two bits to the left. The left shift and the unsigned right shift populate the vacated spaces with zeroes. The signed right shift populates the vacated spaces with the sign bit. The following table shows two 8-bit quantities, 31 and -17, and what happens when they are shifted:

Quantity	x	x<<2	x>>2	x>>>2
31	00011111	01111100	00000111	00000111
–17	11101111	10111100	11111011	00111011

The precedence of the shift operators is above that of the relational operators, but below the additive arithmetic operators.

Type Conversions

One very critical aspect of types in general in any language is how they interrelate. In other words, if you have a `float` such as 1.2, how does that relate to, say, an integer? How does the language handle a situation where a byte (8 bits) is added to an `int` (32 bits)? To deal with these problems, Java performs type conversions. Java is called a strongly typed language, because at compile time the type of every variable is known. Java performs extensive type-checking (to help detect programmer errors) and imposes strict restrictions on when values can be converted from one type to another.

There are really two different kinds of conversions:

- Explicit conversions occur when you deliberately change the data type of a value.
- Implicit conversions occur any time two unequal types are represented in an equation, and they can be adjusted to be the same time. This can happen without your intervention, even without your knowledge.

Briefly then, casting and converting are the way Java allows the use of a variable of one type to be used in an expression of another type.

NOTE In C, almost any data type can be converted to almost any other across an assignment statement. This is not the case in Java, and implicit conversions between numeric data types are only performed if they do not result in loss of precision or magnitude. Any attempted conversion that would result in such a loss produces a compiler error, unless there is an explicit cast.

Implicit Type Conversions

Java performs a number of implicit type conversions when evaluating expressions, but the rules are simpler and more controlled than in the case of C or even C++.

For unary operators (such as ++ or - -), the situation is very simple: Operands of type `byte` or `short` are converted to `int`, and all other types are left as is.

For binary operators, the situation is only slightly more complex. For operations involving only integer operands, if either of the operands is `long`, then the other is also converted to `long`; otherwise, both operands are converted to `int`. The result of the expression is an `int`, unless the value produced is so large that a `long` is required. For operations involving at least one floating-point operand, if either of the operands is `double`, then the other is also converted to `double` and the result of the expression is also a `double`; otherwise, both operands are converted to `float`, and the result of the expression is also a `float`. Consider the expressions in Listing 9.1.

Fortunately, implicit conversions take place almost always without your wanting or needing to know. The compiler handles all the details of adding bytes and `ints` together so you don't have to.

Listing 9.1 Some Mixed Expressions Showing Type Conversions

```
short Width;
long Length, Area;
double TotalCost, CostPerFoot;

// In the multiplication below, Width will be converted to a
// long, and the result of the calculation will be a long.
Area = Length * Width;

// In the division below, Area will be converted to a double,
// and the result of the calculation will be a double.
CostPerFoot = TotalCost / Area ;
```

Cast Operator

Normally with implicit conversion, the conversion is so natural that you don't even notice. Sometimes, though, it is important to make sure a conversion occurs between two types. Doing this type of conversion requires an explicit cast, by using the cast operator.

The cast operator consists of a type name within round brackets. It is a unary operator with high precedence and comes before its operand, the result of which is a variable of the type specified by the cast, but which has the value of the original object. The following example shows an example of an explicit cast:

```
float x = 2.0;
float y = 1.7;
x = ( (int)(x/y) * y)
```

When `x` is divided by `y` in this example, the type of the result is a floating-point number. However, the value of `x/y` is explicitly converted to type `int` by the cast operator, resulting in a 1, not 1.2. So the end result of this equation is that `x` equals 1.7.

Not all conversions are legal. For instance, Boolean values cannot be cast to any other type, and objects can only be converted to a parent class.

See "Declaring a Class," **p. 85**

NOTE Because casting involves an unconditional type conversion (if the conversion is legal), it is also sometimes known as type coercion.

Casting and Converting Integers

The four integer types can be cast to any other type except Boolean. However, casting into a smaller type can result in a loss of data, and a cast to a floating-point number (`float` or `double`) will probably result in the loss of some precision, unless the integer is a whole power of two (for example, 1, 2, 4, 8,...).

Casting and Converting Characters

Characters can be cast in the same way 16-bit (`short`) integers are cast; that is, you can cast them to be anything. But, if you cast into a smaller type (byte), you lose some data. In fact, even if you convert between a character and a short, you can lose some data.

NOTE If you are using the Han character set (Chinese, Japanese, or Korean), you can lose data by casting a `char` into a `short` (16-bit integer), because the top bit will be lost.

Casting and Converting Booleans

There are not any direct ways to cast or convert a Boolean to any other type. However, if you are intent on getting an integer to have a 0 or 1 value based on the current value of a Boolean, use an `if-else` statement, or imitate the following code.

```
int j;
boolean tf;
...
j = tf?1:0;          // Integer j gets 1 if tf is true, and 0 otherwise.
```

Conversion the other way can be done with zero to be equal to false, and anything else equal to true as follows:

```
int j;
boolean tf;
...
tf = (j!=0);     // Boolean tf is true if j is not 0, false otherwise.
```

Addition of Strings

Before you can finally leave the subject of operators, it is important to also cover a special use of the addition operator as it relates to strings.

In general, Java does not support operator overloading; however, in Java, the concatenation of strings is supported by using the + operator. The behavior of the + operator with strings is just what you'd expect if you're familiar with C++. The first and second string are concatenated to produce a string that contains the values of both. In the following expression, the resulting string would be "Hello World":

```
"Hello" + " World"
```

If a non-string value is added to a string, it is first converted to a string using implicit typecasting before the concatenation takes place. This means, for example, that a numeric value can be added to a string. The numeric value is converted to an appropriate sequence of digit characters, which are concatenated to the original string. All the following are legal string concatenations:

```
"George " + "Burns"

"Burns" + " and " + "Allen"

"Fahrenheit" + 451

"Answer is: " + true
```

CHAPTER 10

Control Flow

In this chapter

Controlling the Execution

Controlling the flow of execution is perhaps the most important aspect of any programming language. Control flow allows you to direct the computer in different directions depending on conditions. So, if you're lost, you might turn in a random direction. Otherwise, you would follow the map.

You can also think about control flow like a stoplight. If the light is red, you want to stop your car, but if the light is green, you want all cars to go through the intersection. Without this type of decision making, programs would be flat and lifeless. This chapter teaches you how to make the computer follow the map and traffic laws.

true and *false* Operators on Booleans

Almost all control flow expressions in Java control the flow based on a `true` or `false` value. For instance, as you learn later in this chapter, an `if (value)` statement causes the next statement to be executed only if the value is `true`. You can actually write something like `if (true)`, but there is little value in it. Instead, usually the value is a Boolean expression.

Operators in Java have particular meanings for use with Boolean expressions. Many of the same operator symbols are used with other types of expressions. In most cases, the meanings are a natural extension from the operations performed on integer types. The operations shown in Table 10.1 can be performed on Booleans.

Table 10.1 Operations on Boolean Expressions

Operation	Name	Description
=	Assignment	As in `tf = true;`.
==	Equality	This produces a `true` if the two Boolean operands have the same value (`true` or `false`). It produces `false` otherwise. This is equivalent to *NOT EXCLUSIVE OR* (NXOR).
!=	Inequality	This produces a `true` if the two Boolean operands have different values (one `true`, the other `false`). It produces `false` otherwise. This is equivalent to *EXCLUSIVE OR* (XOR).
!	Logical NOT	If the operand is `false`, the output is `true`, and vice versa.
&	AND	Produces a `true` if and only if both operands are `true`. Note: This is only valid for Boolean operands. For other values, it's a bitwise operator.
|	OR	Produces a `false` if and only if both operands are `false`. Note: This is only valid for Boolean operands. For other values, it's a bitwise operator.

Operation	Name	Description
^	XOR	Produces `true` only if exactly one (exclusive OR) operand is `true`. Note: This is only valid for Boolean operands. For other values, it's a bitwise operator.
&&	Logical AND	Same result for Booleans as described for &.
¦¦	Logical OR	Same result for Booleans as described for ¦.
?:	if-then-else	Requires a Boolean expression before the question mark.

The Relational Operators

The most intuitive comparative operators are those that fall into a category known as *relational operators*. Relational operators include those standard greater-than and less-than symbols you learned about back in third grade. Conveniently enough, they work the same as they did back in third grade, too. For instance, you know that if you write (3>4), you wrote something wrong (`false`). On the other hand, (3<4) is correct (`true`). In Java and most other languages, you are not limited to evaluating constants; you are free to use variables, so the statement (Democrats>Republicans) is also valid. The complete list of relational operators is shown here:

Operator	Boolean Result
<	Less than
<=	Less than or equal to
>	Greater than
>=	Greater than or equal to

The precedence of the relational operators is below that of the arithmetic operators, but above that of the assignment operator. Thus, the following two assignment statements produce identical results:

```
result1 = a+b < c*d ;
result2 = (a+b) < (c*d) ;
```

The associativity is left-to-right, but this feature isn't really very useful. It may not be immediately obvious why, but consider the following expression:

```
a < b < c
```

The first expression, `a<b`, is evaluated first, and produces a value of `true` or `false`. This value then would have to be compared to `c`. Because a Boolean cannot be used in a relational expression, the compiler generates a syntax error.

NOTE In C and C++, the relational operators produce an integer value of `0` or `1`, which can be used in any expression expecting an integer. Expressions like the following are legal in C or C++, but generate compiler errors in Java:

```
RateArray [ day1 < day2 ]
NewValue = OldValue + ( NewRate > OldRate ) * Interest;
```

Try a very basic program to test some of what you have just learned. Listing 10.1 shows a list of printouts that tell if the things you learned in grade school were true. Here, we're using another convenient fact of Java—you can add Boolean values to a string and the answer `true` or `false` will be displayed for you.

Listing 10.1 QuickTest.java—A Simple Lesson from the Third Grade

```
public class QuickTest
{
     public static void main(String args[]){
          System.out.println("5 is greater than 6:"+(5>6));
          System.out.println("6 is greater than or equal to 3:"+(6>=3));
          System.out.println("8 is less than 10:"+(8<10));
     }
}
```

To run this program, first copy Listing 10.1 to a file called `QuickTest.java`. As discussed in previous chapters, it's important the file be called `QuickTest.java` with all capitalization the same. Next, compile the program using `javac`:

```
javac QuickTest.java
```

After the file is compiled, you're ready to run it:

```
java QuickTest
```

As you may have already guessed, the output you get should look like this:

```
5 is greater than 6:false
6 is greater than or equal to 3:true
8 is less than 10:true
```

The Equality Operators

The equality operators are the next set of evaluation operators in Java. Equality operators enable you to compare one value to another and find out if they are equal. In third grade, you might have written this as (3=3). Unfortunately, in Java, this statement would cause the compiler to use the assignment operator (also known as `gets`) rather than evaluate the equation. `gets` is used in traditional computing as a substitute for the = operator when reading text, as shown here. So, if you were to read out loud the line 3=3, you would say "three gets three."

The problem is that this is not the result you are looking for. To solve this problem, a separate two-character operator (==) is used. In Java then, you would write the equation as (3==3). This would be read out loud as "three equals three."

On the other hand, obviously the equation (3==4) would result in an incorrect equation (`false`).

The following equality operators are very similar to the relational operators, with slightly lower precedence:

Operator	Boolean Result
`==`	Is equal to
`!=`	Is not equal to

The equality operators can take operands of virtually any type. In the case of the primitive data types, the values of the operands are compared. However, if the operands are some other type of object (such as a class you created), the evaluation determines if both operands refer to exactly the same object. Consider the following example:

```
String1 == String2
```

In this example, `String1` and `String2` must refer to the same string—not to two different strings that happen to contain the same sequence of characters. Consider the lines shown in Listing 10.2.

Listing 10.2 ObjectEquals.java—Comparing Objects in Java

```
public class ObjectEquals
{
     public static void main(String args[]){
          String String1 = new String("Hi Mom");
          String String2 = new String("Hi Mom");
          //At this point String1 is not equal to String2
          System.out.println("String1 == String2 :"+(String1==String2));

          String String3=String1;
          //Now String1 is equal to String2
          System.out.println("String1 == String3 :"+(String1==String3));
     }
}
```

Given this sequence, `String1==String2` would return `false` after the first two lines because despite the fact that they contain the same letters, they are not the same object. On the other hand, `String1=String3` would return `true` because they refer to exactly the same object. So as you may have already guessed, the output of this program is as follows:

```
String1 == String2 :false
String1 == String3 :true
```

NOTE If you want to compare `String1` to `String2` in the first two lines of this example, you can use the `equals` method of `String`. This would be written `String1.equals(String2)`. The `equals()` method compares the strings character by character.

The associativity of these operators is again left-to-right. You've seen that the associativity of the relational operators is really not useful to you as a programmer. The associativity of the equality operators is only slightly more useful. Take a look at the following example:

```
StartTemp == EndTemp == LastRace
```

Here, the variables `StartTemp` and `EndTemp` are compared first, and the Boolean result of that comparison is compared to `LastRace`, which must be Boolean. If `LastRace` is of some non-Boolean type, the compiler generates an error.

CAUTION

Writing code that depends on this kind of subtlety is considered extremely poor form. Even if you understand it completely when you write it, chances are you'll be as mystified as everyone else when you try to read it a few weeks or months later. Try to use constructs in your code that are easily read. If there is some reason that you must use an expression like the one just given, be sure to use comments to explain how the expression operates and, if possible, why you've chosen to implement your algorithm that way.

Logical Expressions

The third set of evaluation operators falls into a category known as *logical expressions*. Logical expressions work a bit differently than the previous operators and are probably not something you covered in your third-grade math class.

Logical expressions operate either on a pair of Booleans or on the individual bits of an object. There are two types of logical operators which are divided roughly along these lines:

- Boolean operators Only operate on Boolean values
- Bitwise operators Operate on each bit in a pair of integral operands

You have already seen in Chapter 9, "Using Expressions," how bitwise operators work. This chapter covers only the conditional half of the logical expression operators. However, it is interesting to note that, with some minor exceptions, bitwise operators and conditional operators will produce the same result if the operands are Boolean.

Conditional-AND and *Conditional-OR* Operators

There are two primary Boolean operators:

- `Conditional-AND: &&`
- `Conditional-OR: ||`

Oddly, in most computer languages (including Java) there is no `conditional-XOR` operator.

These operators obey the same truth table that was constructed in Chapter 9 for the bitwise operators. They also tend to be fairly easy to read. For instance, `true && true` when read "both true and true" is obviously `true`. For your convenience, the truth tables for `AND` and `OR` are reproduced:

When A is	And when B is	(A && B)	(A II B)
false	false	false	false
false	true	false	true
true	false	false	true
true	true	true	true

The operands of a conditional-OR or a conditional-AND expression are evaluated left-to-right; if the value of the expression is determined after evaluating the left operand, the right operand will not be evaluated. So, in the following example, if x is indeed less than y, then m and n are not compared:

```
(x<y) || (m>n)
```

If the left side of this expression produces the Boolean value true, then the result of the whole expression is true, regardless of the result of the comparison m>n. Note that in the following expression, if you instead used a bitwise operator, m and n are compared regardless of the values of x and y:

```
(x<y) | (m>n)
```

The precedence of the two conditional operators is below that of the bitwise operators.

The Unary Logical Operators

There are two unary logical operators:

- Logical negation of Boolean operand: !
- Bitwise negation of integral or Boolean operand: ~

NOTE For integer operands, this operator is the *bit flipper*—each bit in its operand is toggled. (What was 0 becomes 1; what was 1 becomes 0.)

By placing a negation operator in front of any value, the expression continues with the opposite value of that which the value had originally. For instance, !true would be false.

Both these operators have high precedence, equivalent to that of the other unary operators. Take a look at the following example, which shows a combination of the logical negation and the conditional-AND:

```
if (!dbase.EOF && dbase.RecordIsValid() )
```

Because the logical negation has high precedence, it is evaluated first. If EOF refers to End of File, you first check to see if you have reached the end of the file on this database. If you haven't, the second operand is evaluated, which in this case is a method invocation that might determine the validity of the record. The key to understanding this is to realize that if the first operand is false—in other words, you have reached the end of the file—then you won't check to see if the record is valid.

The Conditional Operator

The conditional operator is unique because it is the one ternary or triadic operator meaning that there are three operands to the expression (instead of the typical two). It operates in Java, as it does in C and C++, and takes the following form:

```
expression1 ? expression2 : expression3
```

In this syntax, `expression1` must produce a Boolean value. If this value is `true`, then `expression2` is evaluated, and its result is the value of the conditional. If `expression1` is `false`, then `expression3` is evaluated, and its result is the value of the conditional. You can look at the ternary operator just as if it was a typical `if` statement:

```
If (expression1)
     expression2;
else
     expression3;
```

Consider the following examples. The first is using the conditional operator to determine the maximum of two values; the second is determining the minimum of two values; the third is determining the absolute value of a quantity.

```
BestReturn = Stocks > Bonds ? Stocks : Bonds ;
LowSales = JuneSales < JulySales ? JuneSales : JulySales ;
Distance = Site1-Site2 > 0 ? Site1-Site2 : Site2 - Site1 ;
```

In reviewing these examples, think about the precedence rules and convince yourself that none of the three examples requires any brackets to be evaluated correctly.

Booleans in Control Flow Statements

Booleans (and Boolean expressions) are the only type that may be used in the `true` clause of the control flow statements as seen in the following code fragment:

```
Boolean TestVal = false;
int IntVal = 1;
...
if (TestVal) {} else {}
if (IntVal != 1) {} else {}
...
while (TestVal) {}
while (IntVal == 0) {}
...
do {} while (TestVal)
do {} while (IntVal == 0)
for (int j=0; TestVal; j++) {}
for (int j=0; IntVal < 5; j++) {}
```

In this code fragment, the comparisons of the integer `IntVal` to an integer constant value are very simple Boolean expressions. Naturally, much more complicated expressions could be used in the same place.

Control Flow Functions

Control flow is the heart of any program. *Control flow* is the ability to adjust (control) the way that a program progresses (flows). By adjusting the direction that a computer takes, the programs that you build become dynamic. Without control flow, programs would not be able to do anything more than several sequential operations.

if Statements

The simplest form of control flow is the `if` statement. An `if` takes a look at a conditional expression (probably derived through any of the means described the first half of this chapter) and if the value is `true`, the next block of code is executed. The general syntax for the `if` is as follows:

```
if (expression)
statement;
```


If the value is `false`, the computer skips the statement and continues on. An example of an `if` statement is shown in the following code fragment:

```
if (myNameIsFred)
System.out.println("Hi Fred");
System.out.println("Welcome to the system");
```

If the value of `myNameIsFred` is `true`, when this fragment runs the computer prints out the following:

```
Hi Fred
Welcome to the system
```

However, if the value is `false`, the program skips over the line after the `if` and the result is as follows:

```
Welcome to the system
```

In most situations, you will want to execute more than one line of code based on an evaluation. To do this, you can place a code block after the `if`, which begins and ends with a pair of curly braces. The following code fragment shows just such an example:

```
if (umpire.says.equals("Strike two")){      //equals method returns Boolean
Crowd.cry("Fraud");                         // method call
Strike++;                                   // last statement in if block.
}
Casey.face("Christian charity");                  // 1st statement after if block.
```

if-else Statements

Only slightly more advanced than a simple `if`, the `if-else` expression passes execution to the `else` statement if the `if` evaluates to `false`. The code in the `else` block is not run if the `if` is `true`. Only one or the other set of code is run. The general syntax for an `if-else` is as follows:

```
if (expression)
if_statement;
else
else_statement;
```

An example of an `if-else` statement is as follows:

```
if (strike != 2)
Casey.lip("Curling Sneer");          // single substatement (could have// been a
block)
else {
Casey.teeth("Clenched in hate");          // block of substatements// (could have
been single)
Casey.bat.pound("Plate");
}
```

One important aspect of `if-else` blocks is how `else` blocks are evaluated when there are nested `ifs`. In other words, consider the following code:

```
if (firstVal==0)
if (secondVal==1)
firstVal++;
else
firstVal—;
```

When is the `else` executed? In this example, the tabbing shows you that the `else` is associated with the inner (second) `if`. An `if-else` expression counts as one statement, so the `else` belongs to the most recent `if` and is part of the `if` statement for the first `if`. Another way to put this is that `ifs` are evaluated to `elses` in a First In First Out (FIFO) fashion. You can change this by placing the second `if` in a block:

```
if (firstVal==0){
if (secondVal==1)
firstVal++;
}
else
firstVal—;
```

Because a block counts as a single statement, the `else` is associated with the first `if`.

Another equally valid `if-else` statement is known as the compound `if`:

```
if (firstVal==0)
  if (secondVal==1)
    firstVal++;
  else  if (thirdVal==2)
    firstVal-—;
```

In this example, the `firstVal` statement is only executed when `firstVal` is `0`, `secondVal` is not `1`, and the `thirdVal` is `2`. Follow this last example through to verify to yourself that this is the case.

Iteration Statements

Programmers use iteration statements to control sequences of statements that are repeated according to runtime conditions.

Java supports five types of iteration statements:

- while
- for
- break
- do
- continue

These are very similar to the statements of the same type found in C and C++, with the exception that continue and break statements in Java have optional parameters that can change their behavior (compared with C and C++, where these statements have no parameters) within the substatement blocks.

while Statements

The while statement tests an expression and, if it is true, executes the next statement or block repeatedly until the expression becomes false. When the variable or expression is false, control is passed to the next statement after the while statement. The syntax for a while loop looks very similar to that of an if statement:

```
while (expression)
statement;
```

while loops can become endless, either intentionally or by accident, if the expression is made so that it will never become false. The following example shows a while loop in action:

```
while (Casey.RoundingTheBasepads==true) {
Crowd.cry("Hooray for Casey");
}
```

In this example, it is clear that the expression might not be true initially, and if not, the block in the substatement will never be executed. If it is true, this block of code is executed repeatedly until it is not true.

do Statements

The do statement is similar to the while statement. In fact, it has a while clause at the end. Like the while expression in the previous section, the expression in the while statement must be a Boolean. The execution of a do loop processes the statement and then evaluates the while. If the while is true, execution returns to the do statement until the expression becomes false. The complete syntax for a do-while loop is as follows:

```
do
statement;
while  (expression)
```

The primary reason a programmer chooses to use a `do` statement instead of a `while` statement is that the statement will always be executed at least once, regardless of the value of the expression. This is also known as *post-evaluation*. For example:

```
do {
Crowd.cry("Kill the Umpire!");
} while (umpire.says.equals("Strike two"));
```

In this example, the method `Crowd.cry` is invoked at least once no matter what. As long as the `umpire.says` method returns the string `"Strike two"`, the `Crowd.cry` method is called over and over again.

for Statements

The most complicated of the four iteration statements is the `for` loop. The `for` statement gives the programmer the capability of all three of the other iteration statements. The complete syntax of a `for` loop is as follows:

```
for (initialization, expression , step )
statement;
```

The `for` loop first runs the initialization code (like a `do`) and then evaluates the expression (like an `if` or `while`). If the expression is `true`, the statement is executed and then the step is performed. A `for` loop can also be written with a `while` loop as follows:

```
initialization;
while (expression){
statement;
step;
}
```

An example of a `for` loop appears in the following code fragment:

```
for (int ball=0, int strike=0; (ball<4) && (strike<3);Ump.EvaluateSwing()) {
Pitcher.pitch();
Player.swing();
}
```

This example demonstrates the fact that the initialization clause can have more than one statement, and that the statements are separated by commas. Both the initialization and step clauses can have multiple statements this way. On the flip side, the statements can also be empty, with no statements.

switch Statements

The next type of control flow is the `switch` statement. The `switch` statement is the first control flow statement that does not require a Boolean evaluation. A `switch` passes control to one of many statements within its block of substatements, depending on the value of the expression in the statement. Control is passed to the first statement following a case label with the same value as the expression. If there are none, control passes to the default label. If there is no default label, control passes to the first statement after the `switch` block.

The syntax for a switch is as follows:

```
switch (expression){
case V1:       statement1;
break;
case V2:       statement2;
break;
default:       statementD;
}
```

Unique to switches, the expression must be of an integer type. You may use bytes, shorts, chars, or ints, but not floats or Booleans.

The break statements are not really required. However, because of the way a switch works, breaks frequently end up being used. As soon as a value matches the expression, execution continues from that point. The execution falls through all the other statements. Take a look at the following example:


```
switch (1){
case 1: System.out.println ("one");
case 2: System.out.println ("two");
case default: System.out.println("Default");
}
```

In this example, the resulting output would be as follows:

```
one
two
Default
```

This happens because as soon as a case match is made, the execution falls through, or continues through, to the end of the switch. It is likely, however, that you don't want to print all three results. The break can be used to only produce the one printout. To do this, the code should be changed to the following:

```
switch (1){
case 1: System.out.println ("one");
break;
case 2: System.out.println ("two");
break;
case default: System.out.println("Default");
break;
}
```

NOTE Notice that unlike if, while, do, and for statements, the case statement is not limited to a single statement, and no blocks are required. Execution simply begins after the case and continues until a break.

The switch expression and case label constants must all evaluate to either byte, short, char, or int. In addition, no two case labels in the same switch block can have the same value.

Another example of the switch statement is included in the following code fragment:

```
switch (strike) {
case 0:
case 1:
```

```
Casey.lip("Curling Sneer");
break;
case 2:
Casey.teeth("Clenched in hate");
Casey.bat.pound("Plate");
break;
default:
System.out.println("Strike out of range");
}
```

In this example, assume that `strike` is a compatible integer type (for example, `int`). Control passes to the correct line, depending on the value of `strike`. If `strike` doesn't have one of the values it should have, a programmer-defined error message is printed.

Jump Statements

In addition to the more common control flow functions, Java also has three kinds of jump statements: `break`, `continue`, and `return`.

break Statements

The substatement blocks of loops and `switch` statements can be broken out of by using the `break` statement. An unlabeled `break` statement passes control to the next line after the current (innermost) iteration (`while`, `do`, `for`, or `switch` statement).

With a label, control may be passed to a statement with that label within the current method. If there is a `finally` clause to a currently open `try` statement, that clause is executed before control is passed on.

continue Statements

A `continue` statement may only appear within the substatement block of an iteration statement (`while`, `do`, or `for`). The effect of the unlabeled `continue` statement is to skip the remainder of the statements in the innermost iteration statement's block and go on to the next pass through the loop. The label parameter permits the programmer to choose which level of nested iteration statements to continue with.

If there is a `finally` clause for a currently open `try` statement within the indicated level of nesting, that clause is executed before control is passed on.

return Statements

A `return` statement passes control to the caller of the method, constructor, or static initializer containing the `return` statement. If the `return` statement is in a method that is not declared void, it may have a parameter of the same type as the method.

If there is a `finally` clause for a currently open `try` statement, that clause is executed before control is passed.

▶ **See** "Returning Information," **p. 126**

CHAPTER 11

Classes

In this chapter

What Are Classes?

Classes are the major building block of an object-oriented structure. In fact, classes are what make objects possible, and without objects, object-oriented programming would just be oriented programming which, well, would not make sense. There are several major advantages to using objects. They enable you to encapsulate data, keeping all information and actions about a particular item separate from the rest of your code. They allow you to build class hierarchies, which enables you to build up more and more complex structures from simpler ones. Lastly, through a technique called polymorphism, dissimilar objects that share a common attribute can be utilized by their similarities.

From a common-sense view, classes are a way to assemble a set of data and then determine all of the methods needed to access, use, and change that data.

Fundamentally, every class has two major portions. The first portion is that of state. The state of an object is nothing more than the values of each of its variables. If, for instance, you had a class `StopLight` with one variable, `RedGreenYellow`, the state of the `StopLight` would be determined by the value of `RedGreenYellow`. For example:

```
public class StopLight{
      int RedGreenBlue;
}
```

The second portion of a class is its tools, or methods. The methods of a class determine the utility the class has. In the case of the `StopLight`, it is likely that you would have a method called `changeLight()`, which would cause the light to change from red to green (probably by changing the `RedGreenYellow` variable).

```
public class StopLight{
      int RedGreenBlue;
      changeLight(){
            RedGreenBlue = ++RedGreenBlue%3;
      }
}
```

NOTE To distinguish class variables with variables that are parts of methods, class variables are often referred to as fields, or class scope variables. In the previous example, the `RedGreenYellow` variable would be a field of the `StopLight` class.

Why Use Classes?

When dealing with classes, it is important to remember that classes do not enable programmers to do anything more than what they would be able to do without them. While it might be significantly more work, you could write all OOP programs structurally.

So why use classes? The answer to this question is similar to the reason why large companies are divided into departments and sub-departments. By organizing hundreds of people with thousands of tasks, the department architecture provides for a simple distribution of tasks and responsibilities. Furthermore, because the billing department knows how to bill customers, the sales department does not need to worry about those details. By doing this work, the billing department has effectively encapsulated the work of billing within itself.

However, the power of object-oriented programming extends beyond the simple capability to encapsulate functionality in objects. A great deal of the appeal of OOP is its capability to provide inheritance—the capability to create new classes based on old classes. As an example of inheritance, consider a game board. Assume that you wrote a Checkers game a couple of months ago, and would now like to write a chess game. By using traditional programming techniques, you would start from scratch, or maybe cut and paste some of your old code. Using inheritance can eliminate most of this work. Instead, you build upon the code you wrote for your Checkers game. Override only those methods that behave differently in Checkers instead of Chess, and add only those methods that Checkers simply doesn't need.

NOTE When new classes inherit the properties of another class, they are referred to as child classes or subclasses. The class from which they are derived is then called a parent or superclass.

Another benefit of enclosing data and methods in classes is the OOP characteristic of encapsulation—the capability to isolate and insulate information effectively from the rest of your program. By creating isolated modules, after you have developed a complete class that performs a certain task, you may effectively forget the intricacies of that task and simply use the methods provided by the class. Because the class mechanisms are isolated, even if you have to significantly change the inner workings of a given class later, you do not need to modify the rest of your program as long the methods used to gain access to the class do not change. A side benefit of this is that by placing the data within the class and creating the appropriate methods to manipulate it, you may seal off the data from the rest of the program, thereby preventing accidental corruption of the data.

Finally, the allure of the OOP approach to creating self-sustaining modules is further enhanced by the fact that children of a given class are still considered to be of the same "type" as the parent. This feature, called polymorphism, enables you to perform the same operation on different types of classes as long as they share a common trait. Although the behavior of each class might be different, you know that the class will be able to perform the same operation as its parent because it is of the same family tree. For example, if you were to create a `Vehicle` class, you may later choose to create `Truck` and `Bike` classes, each extending the `Vehicle` class. Although bikes and trucks are very different, they are both still vehicles! Therefore, everything that you are permitted to do with an instance of the `Vehicle` class you may also do with an instance of the `Truck` or `Bike` classes. A car dealership, then, need not worry if it is selling a Volvo or Saturn. The lot is simply full of vehicles.

What's So New About Object-Oriented Programming?

OOP emphasizes a modular view of programming by forcing you to break down your task into manageable components, each with a specific function. However, unlike procedural functions, which are simply pieced together to form a program, objects are living "creatures" that have the capability to manage themselves, running concurrently with other operations and even existing after the rest of the program has terminated. It is this capability to exist and work with objects as a separate entity that makes OOP a nice match for Java, a network-based language.

CAUTION

In the previous example, while every bike and truck is also a vehicle, a vehicle is not necessarily a bike or a truck. Thus, while the `Bike` and `Truck` classes can be treated just like the `Vehicle` class in Java, you may not perform an operation reserved for the `Bike` class on an instance of the `Vehicle` class.

Classes in Java

As stated at the beginning of this chapter, classes are the essential building block in any Java applet or application. Classes are used to create objects. When you create an instance of a class, you create an object. You can include all the code for that object within the class. In accordance with the object-oriented paradigm, you can later choose to build upon that class to build new programs or enhance your current program.

Bigger and Better Java

Java itself is built from classes that are made available to the general public in the JDK. While there are some limitations, a large number of the classes that make up the Java architecture may themselves be extended. By doing this, you may tailor the classes in the Java API library—especially those in the AWT—to meet your particular needs.

Before you start creating large programs, you must first learn how to create simple classes. In terms of syntax, there are two parts to a class in Java: the declaration and the body. Listing 11.1 is a simple class that fulfills some of the requirements of the simple game board discussed earlier. Examine this listing to get an idea of what constitutes a class. You can refer to this listing again later as your understanding of classes grows.

Listing 11.1 GameBoard.java—A General Class for Creating a 10×10 Board Game

```
public class GameBoard
{
/* This is the beginning of a simple game board class that provides the basic */
/* structures necessary for a game board.  It may easily be */
/* extended to create a richer game board. */
```

```
    private static final int WIDTH =      10;  /* These are constants */
    private static final int HEIGHT = 10;  /* that you want to */
    private static final int EMPTY = 0;   /* keep as standards */

    private int board[][];
       // This array will keep track of the board

    public String myname;                  // what game is being played

    public GameBoard (String gamename) {
         board = new int[WIDTH][HEIGHT];
         myname = new String(gamename);
    }

    public final void cleanBoard() {
         for (int i = 0; i < WIDTH; i++)
              for (int j = 0; j < HEIGHT; j++)
                   board[i][j] = EMPTY;
    }

    public synchronized void setSquare(int x, int y, int value) {
         board[x][y] = value;
    }

    public synchronized boolean isEmpty(int x, int y) {
         if (board[x][y] == EMPTY)
              return(true);
         return(false);
    }
}
```


Take a quick look through this class. The first part of any class is the class declaration. Most classes you write will look very similar to `GameBoard`:

```
public class GameBoard
```

Declaring a class states several things, but probably the most important one is the name of the class (`GameBoard`). In the case of any public class, the name of the class must also match up with the name of the file it is in. In other words, this class must appear in the file GameBoard.java.

The next part of the class is the opening brace. You should notice that there is a brace ({) at the beginning of the class, and if you look all the way down at the bottom there is also a closing brace (}). The braces define the area in the file where the class definitions will exist.

A bit farther down you will see several comments. As you learned in "Comments" (Chapter 7), comments can exist anywhere in the file and are ignored by the compiler, but they help you leave messages for yourself or other programmers. Next, you will see several fields declared. Each of these variables is accessible from any of the methods in the class. When you change them in one method, all the other methods will see the new value.

```
private static final int WIDTH =     10;  /* These are constants */
private static final int HEIGHT = 10;  /* that you want to */
private static final int EMPTY = 0;  /* keep as standards */
private int board[][];
// This array will keep track of the board

public String myname;                // what game is being played
```

Finally, you should see four methods:

```
        public GameBoard (String gamename) {
             board = new int[WIDTH][HEIGHT];
             myname = new String(gamename);
        }

        public final void cleanBoard() {
             for (int i = 0; i < WIDTH; i++)
                  for (int j = 0; j < HEIGHT; j++)
                       board[i][j] = EMPTY;
        }

        public synchronized void setSquare(int x, int y, int value) {
             board[x][y] = value;
        }

        public synchronized boolean isEmpty(int x, int y) {
             if (board[x][y] == EMPTY)
                  return(true);
             return(false);
        }
}
```

Declaring a Class

In general, Java class declarations have the form

AccessSpecifier class NewClass *extends NameofSuperClass implements NameofInterface*

where everything in italics is optional. As you can see, there are four properties of the class that may be defined in the declaration:

- Modifiers
- Class name
- SuperClasses
- Interfaces

Access Specifiers

The access specifiers in a class declaration determine how the class can be handled in later development and are very similar to those four access specifiers discussed in Chapter 8, "Methods." Although they are usually not extremely important in developing the class itself, they become very important when you decide to create other classes, interfaces, and exceptions that involve that class.

When creating a class, you may choose to accept the default status or you may employ one of the three specifiers: `public`, `final`, or `abstract`.

Public Classes By placing the modifier `public` in front of the class declaration, the class is defined to be public. Public classes are, as their name implies, accessible by all objects. This means that they can be used or extended by any object, regardless of its package. Here's an example:

```
public class PictureFrame
```

Also note that public classes must be defined in a file called ClassName.java (for example, PictureFrame.java).

Protected Classes If you choose not to place a modifier in front of the class declaration, the class is created with the default properties. Therefore, you should be aware of what these properties are.

By default, all classes are assigned the protected level of access. This means that while the class may be extended and employed by other classes, only those objects within the same package may make use of this class. Here's an example of a friendly class:

```
class PictureFrame
```


Final Classes Final classes may not have any subclasses and are created by placing the modifier `final` in front of the class declaration.

The reason for creating final classes may not be not be evident at first. Why would you want to prevent other classes from extending your class? Isn't that one of the appeals of the object-oriented approach?

It is important to remember that the object-oriented approach effectively enables you to create many versions of a class (by creating children that inherit its properties but nevertheless change it somewhat). Consequently, if you are creating a class to serve as a standard (for example, a class that will handle network communications), you would not want to allow other classes to handle this function in a different manner. Thus, by making the class `final`, you eliminate this possibility and ensure consistency.

In addition, telling the compiler that this is the final version of a class allows the compiler to perform a number of performance optimizations that otherwise would not be possible. Here's an example:

```
final class PictureFrame
```

Abstract Classes An abstract class, denoted by the modifier abstract, is a class in which at least one method is not complete. This state of not being finished is referred to as abstract. For example:

```
abstract class PictureFrame
```

How can a finished class not be complete? In the case of a grammar-checking class that is to be implemented in many languages, there are several methods that would have to be changed for each language-dependent version class. To create a cleaner program, instead of creating an `EnglishChecker`, a `FrenchChecker`, and a `SpanishChecker` class from scratch, you could simply create a `GrammarChecker` class in which the language-specific methods are declared as `abstract` and left empty. When ready, you could then create the language-specific classes that would extend the abstract `GrammarChecker` class and fill in the blanks by redefining these methods with actual code. Although you would still end up with separate classes for each language, the heart of your code would be in the `GrammarChecker` class, leaving only the language-dependent portions for the specific classes.

NOTE Because they are not complete, you may not create instances of abstract classes.

The class declaration need not be very complex and most often is very simple. In this example, only one modifier, `public`, was used; no other classes or interfaces were required.

Class Name

Like all other Java identifiers, the only requirements on a class name are that it:

- Begin with a letter or the characters - or $
- Contain only Unicode characters above hex 00C0 (basic letters and digits, as well as some other special characters)
- Not be the same as any Java keyword (such as `void` or `int`)

Also, it is general practice to capitalize the first letter in the name of any class.

Although only required for public classes, it is generally a good practice to name the file in which class `NewClass` is defined NewClass.java. Doing so helps the compiler find `NewClass`, even if `NewClass` has not been compiled yet.

Super Classes—Extending Another Class

One of the most important aspects of OOP is the ability to use the methods and fields of a class you have already built. By building upon these simpler classes to build bigger ones, you can save yourself a lot of coding. Possibly even more important, you can greatly reduce the work of finding and fixing bugs in your code. To build upon a previous class, you must extend the class in the class `declaration`.

By extending a super class, you are making your class a new copy of that class but are allowing for growth. If you were simply to leave the rest of the class blank (and not do anything different with the modifiers), the new class would behave identically to the original class. Your new class will have all of the fields and methods declared or inherited in the original class.

NOTE Does this example look familiar?

```
public class MyClass extends Applet {
```

If you look at the source of any applet, you see that its declaration resembles the example. In fact, you probably have been extending the `java.applet.Applet` class without even knowing what you were doing.

Remember the methods you have been able to use in your applets, such as `showStatus()`, `init()`, and `keyDown()`? Did they appear out of thin air? No, they are drawn from the `java.applet.Applet` class or one of the classes that it extends, such as `java.awt.Component`.

By extending the `java.applet.Applet` class, your applet class is able to access and implement these methods, thereby providing your applet with a great deal of power.

Every class in Java is considered to be an object. By default, every class is derived from the `java.lang.Object` class. So if your class does not extend any other class, it still extends `java.lang.Object`.

NOTE Multiple-inheritance does not exist in Java. Thus, unlike C++, Java classes may only extend one class.

Constructors

Constructors are very special methods with unique properties and a unique purpose. Constructors are used to set certain properties and perform certain tasks when instances of the class are created. For instance, the constructor for the `GameBoard` class is:

```
public GameBoard (String gamename) {
     board = new int[WIDTH][HEIGHT];
     myname = new String(gamename);
}
```

Constructors are identified by having the same name as the class itself. Thus, in the `GameBoard` class, the name of the constructor is `GameBoard()`. Secondly, constructors do not specify a return argument because they are not actually called as a method. For instance, if you wanted to create an instance of the `GameClass`, you would have a line that looked like this:

```
GameClass myGame = new GameClass();
```

When the `new GameClass()` is actually instantiated, the constructor method is called.

In general, constructors are used to initialize the class's fields and perform various tasks related to creation, such as connecting to a server or performing some initial calculations.

Also note that overloading the constructor enables you to create an object in several different ways. For example, by creating several constructors, each with a different set of parameters, you enable yourself to create an instance of the `GameBoard` class by specifying the name of the game, the values of the board, both, or neither. This practice is prevalent in the Java libraries themselves. As a result, you can create most data types (such as `java.lang.String` and `java.net.Socket`) while specifying varying degrees and types of information.

Most programmers choose to make their constructors public. This is because if the level of access for the constructor is less than the level of access for the class itself, another class may be able to declare an instance of your class but will not actually be able to create an instance of that class.

However, this loophole may actually be used to your advantage. By making your constructor private, you may enable other classes to use static methods of your class without enabling them to create an instance of it.

Finally, constructors cannot be declared to be `native`, `abstract`, `static`, `synchronized`, or `final`.

Overriding Methods

It is not legal to create two methods within the same class that have both the same name and the same parameter list. After all, doing so would just confuse the whole system (which method would you really want to be calling?). However, one of the purposes of extending a class is to create a new class with added functionality. To allow you to do this, when you inherit another class, you can override any of its methods by defining a method with the same name and parameter list as a method in the superclass. For instance, consider an `Elevator` class, shown in Listing 11.2.

Listing 11.2 Elevator.java—A Simple *Elevator* Class

```
        class Elevator {
              ...
              private boolean running = true;
              ...
             public void shutDown() {
                  running = false;
              }
}
```

At some point you realize that this elevator just isn't very safe, so you decide to create a safer one. You want to extend the old `Elevator` class and maintain most of its properties, but change some as well. Specifically, you want to check to make sure the elevator car is empty before stopping, so you override the `shutDown()` method as shown in Listing 11.3.

Listing 11.3 SaferElevator.java—A Safer Elevator That Extends *Elevator*

```
class SaferElevator extends Elevator {
    ...
    public void shutDown() {
         if ( isEmpty() )
              running = false;
```

```
            else
                 printErrorMessage();
            }
}
```

Note that overriding is accomplished only if the new method has the same name and parameter signature as the method in the parent class. If the parameter signature is not the same, the new method will overload the parent method, not override it. For example, look at Listing 11.4.

Listing 11.4 SaferElevator.java—Safer Elevator with an Overloaded *shutDown()* Not an Overridden One

```
class SaferElevator extends Elevator {
      ...
          public void shutDown(int delay) {
               if ( isEmpty() )
                    running = false;
               else
                    printErrorMessage();
               }
      }
```

The `shutDown` method from the `Elevator` class would not have changed. Adding the parameter `(int delay)` to the method changes what is known as the method signature. The new `shutDown` method is still valid, though, and can be called because it has overloaded the original `shutDown`, as you learned in Chapter 8, "Methods."

NOTE When you override a method, you may not make it more protected than the original method. Because the `shutDown` method is public in `Elevator`, you cannot make it private in `SaferElevator`.

Creating an Instance of a Class

To actually use a class you have created, you need to be able to create an instance of that class. An instance is an object of the type of the class. Any class you create can be instantiated, just like any other data type in Java. For example, to create an instance of the `GameBoard`, you would generally declare a variable of that type. Listing 11.5 shows a class called `Checkers` creating an instance of the `GameBoard` class.

Listing 11.5 Checkers.java—Creates an Instance of *GameBoard*

```
public class Checkers{
  GameBoard myBoard = new GameBoard();
     ....
}
```

NOTE Technically, it's not necessary to create an instance of a class in order to use it. If the method or variable you are calling is static, no instance is necessary. However, remember that a static method can only refer to static class variables.

This exception is what allows you to access the `out` variable of `System` without actually instantiating a `System` variable. In other words, you can type:

```
System.out.println("Note, System was not instantiated!!");
```

As you may have noticed, the one primary difference between declaring an Object type, like `GameBoard`, and a primitive type, like `int`, is the use of the `new` keyword. In Listing 11.5, we used the phrase `new GameBoard()` to create a new instance of `GameBoard`. `new` performs several key tasks:

- Tells the computer to allocate the space necessary to store a `GameBoard`
- Causes the constructor method of `GameBoard` to be called
- Returns a reference to the object (which is then assigned to `myBoard`)

You may be wondering in all of this, how does the very first instance of my class get created? After all, when you create an applet or an application, you don't have any way to actually instantiate that class, so how does it come to be? The answer lies with the virtual machine.

When a browser encounters an `<APPLET>` tag (see Chapter 14, "Writing an Applet," to learn more about applets) or the Java program is run on an application (see Chapter 17, "Applets Versus Applications"), the virtual machine does a few things. In the case of an application, when you type `java MyClass`, the virtual machine calls the static method `main()` in `MyClass`. That doesn't actually create an instance of `MyClass`, but, because it's static (see the preceding note), an instance isn't necessary. That's why you typically need to create an instance of your class in the `main()` method. In the case of an applet, the browser does create an instance of `MyClass` when it encounters `<APPLET CODE="MyClass">` and automatically calls the `init()` method.

NOTE One additional difference in Java between objects and primitive types is how they are referenced. Primitive types are always referred to by their value. Object types are always referred to by their reference. This means that in the following code, `x` and `y` are not equal at the end, but in `w` and `z`, `myName` is the same:

```
int x = 5;
int y = x;
y++;  // x = 5, y =6;
GameBoard w = new GameBoard();
GameBoard z =  w;
w.myName = "newString"; //Since z and w point to the same object, they now
both have the same myName
```

Referring to Parts of Classes

Now that you have begun to develop classes, examine how they can be used in other classes. As discussed earlier in the section "Why Use Classes?", Java classes may contain instances of other classes that are treated as variables. However, you may also deal with the fields and methods of these class type reference variables. To do so, Java uses the standard dot notation used in most OOP languages. Listing 11.6 is an example.

Listing 11.6 Checkers.java—The *GameBoard* is Accessed by its Instance *Board*

```
import java.awt.*;
     public class Checkers
     {
          private GameBoard board;

          public Checkers() {
               board = new GameBoard("Checkers");
               board.cleanBoard();
          }
          ...

          public void movePiece(int player, int direction) {
               java.awt.Point    destination;
               ...
               if (board.isEmpty(destination.x, destination.y) )
                   // code to move piece
          }

          private void showBoard(Graphics g) {
               g.drawString(board.myname,100,100);
               drawBoard(g);
          }

          private void drawBoard(Graphics g){
          ....
          }
}
```

Notice that `board` is an instance in the `GameBoard` class, and the variable `myname` in the `GameBoard` class is referenced by `board.myname`. The general notation for this type of access is `instanceName.methodOrVariableName`.

CAUTION

Notice that the variable `myname` is referred to as `board.myname`, not as `GameBoard.myname`. If you try to do so, you get an error resembling:

```
Checkers.java:5: Can't make a static reference to non-static variable
myname in class GameBoard.
```

This is because `GameBoard` is a type of class, while `board` is an instance of the class. As discussed in the previous section, when you deal with `board`, you deal with a specific copy of the `GameBoard` class. Because `myname` is not a static variable, it is not a property of the `GameBoard` class, but rather a property of the instances of that class. Therefore, it cannot be changed or referenced by using `GameBoard` as the variable name.

This Special Variable You have seen how to refer to other classes. However, what if you want the class to refer to itself? Although the reasons to do so may not seem so obvious at first, being able to refer to itself is a capability that is very important for a class. To solve this problem, a unique variable called `this` is used whenever it is necessary to explicitly refer to the class itself.

In general, there are two situations that warrant use of the `this` variable:

- When there are two variables in your class with the same name—one belonging to the class and one belonging to a specific method.
- When a class needs to pass itself as an argument to a method. Often when you create applets that employ other classes, it is desirable to provide those classes with access to such methods as `showStatus()`. For example, if you are creating a `Presentation` applet class and want to use a simple `TextScroll` class to display some text across the status bar at the bottom of the screen, you need to provide the `TextScroll` class with some means of using the `showStatus()` method belonging to the applet. The best way to enable the `TextScroll` to do this is to create the `TextScroll` class with a constructor method that accepts an instance of the `Presentation` applet class as one of its arguments.

As seen in Listing 11.7, the `TextScroll` class would then be able to display the information across the bottom of the `Presentation` class's screen.

Listing 11.7 Presentation.java—An Instance of the Presentation Is Passed to a *TextScroll* Constructor

```
public class Presentation extends Applet {
        TextScroll scroller;

        public void init() {
             ...
             scroller = new TextScroll(this, length_of_text);
             scroller.start();
        }
             ...
    }

    class TextScroll extends Thread {
         Presentation screen;
         String newMessage;
         boolean running;
         int size;
```

```
        TextScroll(Presentation appl, int size) {
            screen = appl;
        }

        public void run() {
              while (running) {
              displayText();
             }
        }

        void displayText() {
             // perform some operations to update what should
             // be displayed (newMessage)

             screen.showStatus(newMessage);
        }
    }
```

▶ **See** "What Are Threads?" **p. 208**

Note the use of the special `this` variable in the `init()` method of the `Presentation` class as well as the result. This technique is extremely useful and powerful.

***super* Special Variable** Along the same lines as `this`, the special variable `super` provides access to a class's super class. This is useful when overriding a method, because when doing so you may want to use code from the old method as well. For example, if you were creating a new class `NewGameBoard` that extended the `GameBoard` class and were overriding the `setSquare()` method, you might employ the `super` variable to use the former code without recopying all of it (see Listing 11.8).

Part II Ch 11

Listing 11.8 NewGameBoard.java—Extending the *setSquare* Method, but Still Using the Results of the Existing Method

```
class NewGameBoard extends game board {

          private static int FIXEDWALL  = 99;
          // permanent wall, cannot be moved

public static synchronized void setSquare(int x, int y, int value){
    if (board[x][y] != FIXEDWALL) {
         super.setSquare(x,y,val);
    }
}
```

In the preceding example, you use the `super` variable to refer to the original version of the `setSquare()` method, found in the `GameBoard` class. By doing so, you save yourself the headache of recopying the entire method, while at the same time adding to the functionality of the `setSquare` method. This allows you to keep the functionality of `setSquare` encapsulated in the original `GameBoard` class. If, down the road you discover an error in some of the logic, you won't be forced to change it in both the `GameBoard` and the `NewGameBoard` classes.

You should also examine how to call the super method if the method you are dealing with is a constructor. It is necessary to call the constructor for a parent class, just as you need to call the constructor for any class. Although calling a super constructor is not much different from any other super method, its syntax may seem confusing at first:

```
public NewGameBoard(String gamename) {
     // new code would go here
     super(gamename);
}
```

Note that on a simplistic level, super can be considered equivalent to GameBoard. Consequently, because GameBoard() is the name of the original constructor method, it may be referred to as super().

Variables

Obviously, variables are an integral part of programs and, thus, classes as well. In Chapter 7, "Data Types and Other Tokens," you examined the various types of variables, but now you must also consider how they are employed in your programs and the different roles they may assume.

When creating variables, whether they are as simple as integers or as complex as derived classes, you must consider how they will be used, what processes will require access to the variables, and what degree of protection you want to provide to these variables.

The ability to access a given variable is dependent on two things: the access modifiers used when creating the variable and the location of the variable declaration within the class.

▶ **See** "Literals—Assigning Values," p. **1307**

Class Fields Versus Method Variables

In a class, there are two types of variables: those belonging to the class itself and those belonging to specific methods.

Those variables declared outside of any methods, but within a given class (usually immediately after the class declaration and before any methods), are referred to as fields of the class and are accessible to all methods of it.

In addition, one may declare variables within a method. These variables are local to the method and may only be accessed within that method.

Because method variables exist only for the lifetime of the method, they cannot be accessed by other classes. Consequently, you cannot apply any access modifiers to method variables.

Although it is possible to make every field accessible to every class, this is not a prudent practice. First of all, you would be defeating a great deal of the purpose of creating your program from classes. Why do you choose appropriate class names instead of class1, class2, class3, and so on? You do so simply to create a clean program that is easy to code, follow, and debug. For the same reason, by creating various levels of protection, you encapsulate your code into self-sufficient and more logical chunks.

Furthermore, inasmuch as OOP is heavily dependent on the modification of code that you have written beforehand, access restrictions prevent you from later doing something that you shouldn't. (Keep in mind that preventing access to a field does not prevent the use of it.) For example, if you were creating a `Circle` class, there would most likely be several fields that would keep track of the properties of the class, such as `radius`, `area`, `border_color`, and so on—many of which may be dependent on each other. Although it may seem logical to make the `radius` field public (accessible by all other classes), consider what would happen if a few weeks later you decided to write the code shown in Listing 11.9.

Listing 11.9 Circle.java—Code Fragment Showing What Direct Access to a Class Field Looks Like

```
import java.awt.*;
class Circle {
  public int radius, area;
  public Color border_color;
...
}

class GraphicalInterface {
Circle ball;
...
void animateBall() {
    for (int update_radius = 0; update_radius <= 10; update_radius++){
        ball.radius = update_radius;
        paintBall(ball.area, ball.border_color);
        ...
    }
}
void paintBall(int area,Color color){
    ...
}
}
```

This code would not produce the desired result. Although the

```
ball.radius = update_radius;
```

statement would change the radius, it would not affect the `area` field. As a result, you would be supplying the `paintBall()` method with incorrect information. Now, instead, if the radius and area variables are protected, and any update to the radius forced the area to be recomputed, the problem would disappear as shown in Listing 11.10.

Listing 11.10 Circle.java—Providing Access to the Circle Fields Through Methods

```
class Circle {
      protected int radius, area;

      public void newRadius (int rad){
```

continues

Listing 11.10 Continued

```
            radius = rad;
            area = rad *2 * Math.PI;
      }

       public int radius(){
            return radius;
       }

       public int area (){
            return area;
       }
}

      class GraphicalInterface {
      Circle ball;
      ...
      void animateBall() {
        for (int update_radius = 0; update_radius <= 10; update_radius++){
           ball.newRadius (update_radius);
             paintBall(ball.area(), ball.border_color);
                  ...
                  }
             }
        }
```

In the next few sections, you examine the various ways of regulating access and solving this problem.

Although it is important to consider the level of access that other objects will have to your fields, it is also important to consider how visible the fields and method variables will be within your class. Where the variable is accessible, a property called scope is very important. In general, every variable is accessible only within the block (delimited by the curly braces { and }) in which it is declared. However, there are some slight exceptions to this rule. Examine Listing 11.11.

Listing 11.11 CashRegister.java—Variables Have Scope Based on Where They Are Declared

```
class  CashRegister {
     public int total;
     int sales_value[];
     Outputlog log;

     void printReceipt(int total_sale) {
          Tape.println("Total Sale = $"+ total_sale);
           Tape.println("Thank you for shopping with us.");
     }
```

```
    void sellItem(int value) {
         log.sale(value);
         total += value;
    }

    int totalSales() {
         int num_of_sales, total = 0;
         num_of_sales = log.countSales();

        for (int i = 1; i <= num_of_sales; i++)
             total += sales_value[i];
         re
turn(total);
    }
}
```

Now examine some of the variables and their scope:

Variable Name	Declared As	Scope
`total`	Field global to `CashRegister` class	Entire class
`total`	Local to `totalSales()` method	Within `totalSales()`
`log`	Field global to `CashRegister` class	Entire class
`value`	Parameter to `sellItem()`	Within `sellItem()`
`i`	Local to `totalSales()` within `for` loop	Within the `for` loop

There are several things to note from the table. Start with the simplest variable, `log`. `log` is a field of the `CashRegister` class and is, therefore, visible throughout the entire class. Every method in the class (as well as other classes in the same package) may access `log`. Similarly, `value`, although declared as a parameter, is nevertheless local to the method `sellItem()` in which it was declared. Although all statements in `sellItem()` may access `value`, it may not be accessed by any other methods. Slightly more confusing is the variable `i`, which is declared not at the beginning of a method but within a `for` statement. Like `log` and `value` that exist only within the block in which they were defined, `i` exists only within the `for` statement in which it was defined. In fact, if you consider a complex `for` loop like that shown in the following example, `i` is recreated (in this case, 10 times).

```
for (int x = 0; x<10 ;x++){
      for (int i =0;i < num_of_sales; i++ )
            ...
}
```

To understand why this is the case, it may be helpful to look at how this code might look if you "unwound it" into a `while` loop.

```
{
        int x = 0; //declare x and set it's initial value
        while (x <10) {
                { //start the next for loop
                        int i = 0; //declare i and set it's initial value
                        while (i < num_of_sales) {
                                … //do whatever is in the inner for loop
                                i++; //perform the increment of i
                        }
                }
                x++; //increment x
        }
}
```

As you can see, even though the `for` loop looks fairly simple, the scope of the variables is actually quite complicated if you add all the implied braces.

Finally, you arrive at the problem of having two `total` variables with overlapping scope. While the `total` field is accessible to all methods, a problem seems to arise in the `totalSales()` method. In such cases, using the multiply-defined identifier refers to the most local definition of the variable. Therefore, although having no impact on the rest of the class, within the `totalSales()` the identifier `total` actually refers to the local variable `total`, not the global one. This means that after exiting the `totalSales()` method, the `total` class variable is unchanged. In such a situation, you can access the class by using the `this` keyword. So, to set the class variable `total` to the value of the local variable `total`, you would type:

```
this.total = total;
```

Although using the same identifier as a field and method variable name does not cause many problems and is considered an acceptable practice, it is preferable to choose a different (and more descriptive) identifier, such as `total_sales`. Another equally valid way to make your code easier to read is to come up with a unique naming scheme for all your class variables. The following are two common ways to do this:

- Add the letter `m` (for my) as the first letter to all class field variables
- Add an underscore (_) to the beginning of the all field variables

Personally, I prefer the second option because it doesn't cause the confusion that can come from the former solution. If we were to have used this naming scheme in the previous example, it would have looked like this:

```
class  CashRegister {
     public int _total;
     int _sales__value[];
     Outputlog _log;
```

NOTE Although you can use the same identifier as a class field and as a local variable within a method, this does not apply to all code blocks within your code. For example, declaring `num_of_sales` as your counter within the `for` block would produce an error.

Modifiers

Like the modifiers for classes and methods, access modifiers determine how accessible certain variables are to other classes. However, it is important to realize that access modifiers apply only to the global fields of the class. It makes little sense to speak of access modifiers for variables within methods because they exist only while the method is executing. Afterwards, they are collected to free up memory for other variables.

Why Not Make All Variables Fields?

Because all class variables (fields) are accessible to all methods in a given class, why not make all variables fields global to all methods in the class?

The first reason is that you would be wasting a great deal of memory. Although local variables (those variables declared within the methods themselves) exist only while the method is executing, fields must exist for the lifetime of the Object. Consequently, instead of allocating memory for dozens of fields by making many of your variables local, you are able to use the same piece of memory over and over again.

The second reason is that making all your variables global would create sloppy programs that would be hard to follow. If you are going to be using a counter only in one method, why not declare it in that method? Furthermore, if all of your variables are global, someone reviewing your code (or you, a few weeks later) would have no idea from where the variables were obtaining their values, because there would be no logical path of values being passed from method to method.

Default By default, fields are assigned a level of access that, although accessible to other classes within the same package, are not accessible to subclasses of the current class or classes outside of the current package. For example:

```
int size;
```

public Identical to the `public access` modifier for methods, the `public` modifier makes fields visible to all classes, regardless of their package, as well as all subclasses. Again, you should make an effort to limit `public` fields. For example:

```
public int size;
```

protected `protected` fields may be accessed by all subclasses of the current class, but are not visible to classes outside of the current package. For example:

```
protected int size;
```

private The highest degree of protection, `private` fields are accessible to all methods within the current class. They are, however, not accessible to any other classes, nor are they accessible to the subclasses of the current class. For example:

```
private int size;
```

static As with methods, placing the modifier `static` in front of the field declaration makes the field static. `static` fields are fields of the class whose values are the same in all instances of the class. Consequently, changing a `static` field in one class will affect that field in all instances of the given class. `static` fields may be modified in both `static` and non-`static` methods. For example:

```
static int size;
```

▶ **See** Chapter 8, "Methods," **p. 119**

final Although Java does not have preprocess, `#define`-type statements, or constants, there is a very simple way of creating constants—fields whose values cannot change while the program is running. By placing the modifier `final` in front of a field declaration, you tell the compiler that the value of the field cannot change during execution. Furthermore, because it cannot change elsewhere, you must set the actual value of all final fields as soon as they are declared, as seen in the next example:

```
final int SIZE = 5;
```

If the value cannot change, why not use the value itself within the program? The answer to this question is twofold:

- While you cannot change the value of constants within your code, as a programmer, you may later change the value of a constant without having to change the value of each use of the constant. For instance, if `SIZE` is used in 10 locations, you only need to change the number 5 in one location, not in 10.
- By using constants, your code becomes a lot cleaner and easier to follow. For example, in the `GameBoard` class, using 0 as a check for an empty space would not always make sense to a reader of your code. However, using the final field `EMPTY` and assigning it the value 0 makes the code a lot easier to follow.

NOTE By convention, all letters of constants are capitalized. Furthermore, to save memory, constants are usually made static as well.

NOTE There are two additional modifiers for fields.

When dealing with many threads, there are several problems that can result when multiple threads attempt to access the same data at the same time. Although a majority of these problems can be solved by making certain methods synchronized, in future releases of Java, you will be able to declare certain fields as `threadsafe`. Such fields will be handled extra carefully by the Java runtime environment. In particular, the validity of each volatile field will be checked before and after each use.

The other heralded keyword, `transient`, is related closely to the capability to enable the creation of persistent Java applets and Beans. In such an environment, transient fields would not be part of the persistent object.

Using Methods to Provide Guarded Access

Although it may be advantageous to restrict access to certain fields in your class, it is nevertheless often necessary to provide some form of access to those fields. A very intelligent and useful way of doing this is to allow access to restricted fields through less restricted methods (often referred to as `set` and `get` methods), such as in Listing 11.12.

Listing 11.12 Circle.java—A Circle with Protected Fields

```
class Circle {
     private int radius, area;
     private Color border_color;

     public void setRadius(int update_radius) {
          radius = update_radius;
          area = Math.PI * radius * 2;
     }

     public Color getColor() {
          return(border_color);
     }
     public int getRadius() {
          return(radius);
     }
     public int getArea() {
          return(area);
     }
}
class GraphicalInterface {
     Circle ball;
     ...
     void animateBall() {
     for (int update_radius = 0; update_radius <= 10;
                              update_radius++){
               ball.setRadius(update_radius);
               paintBall(ball.getArea(), ball.getColor() );
          }
          ...
     }
}
```

By limiting access to the `radius` field to the `setRadius()` method, you ensure that any change of the radius will be followed by an appropriate change of the `area` variable. Because you have made the two fields private, you must also provide yourself with the means of accessing them through the various `get`-type methods. These methods are commonly referred to as accessor methods because they provide access to otherwise inaccessible fields. Although at first this may seem a bit cumbersome, its benefits by far outweigh its disadvantages. As a result, it is a very widely used approach that is extremely prevalent in the Java API libraries on which Java is heavily dependent.

Using the *finalize()* Method

Belonging to the `java.lang.Object` class, and thus present in all classes, is the `finalize()` method. Empty by default, this method is called by the Java runtime system during the process of garbage collection and, may be used to clean up any ongoing processes before the object is destroyed. For example, in a class that deals with sockets, it is good practice to close all sockets before destroying the object defined by the class. Therefore, you could place the code to close the sockets in the `finalize()` method. After the instance of the class is no longer being used in the program and is destroyed, this method would be invoked to close the sockets as required.

NOTE The `finalize()` method is very similar to the `~classname()` method in C++.

For example, take a look at the `finalize()` method in Listing 11.13.

Listing 11.13 NetworkSender.java—Using *finalize()*

```
import java.io.*;
Import java.net.*;
public class NetworkSender
{
    private Socket me;
    private OutputStream out;

    public NetworkSender(String host, int port) {
       try {
          me = new Socket(host,port);
          out = me.getOutputStream();
       }
       catch (Exception e) {
          System.out.println(e.getMessage();
       }
    }

      public void sendInfo(char signal) {
         try {
               out.write(signal);
               out.flush();
          }
          catch (Exception e) {
                System.out.println(e.getMessage());
          }
        }

        public void disconnect() {
           System.out.println("Disconnecting...");
           try {
               me.close();
           }

           catch (Exception e)
           System.out.println("Error on Disconnect" + e.getMessage());

      System.out.println("done.");
   }

/* In this case finalize() is the identical to disconnect() /*
/* and only attempts to ensure closure of the socket in the /*
/* case that disconnect() is not called. */
```

```
   protected void finalize() {
      System.out.println("Disconnecting...");
      try {
           me.close();
       }
       catch (Exception e)
          System.out.println("Error on Disconnect" + e.getMessage());

       System.out.println("done.");
    }

}
```

NOTE `finalize()` is declared to be protected in `java.lang.Object` and must remain protected or become less restricted.

CAUTION

While the `finalize()` method is a legitimate tool, it should not be relied upon too heavily because garbage collection is not a completely predictable process. This is because garbage collection runs in the background as a low-priority thread and is generally performed when you have no memory left.

Consequently, it is a good practice to attempt to perform such clean-up tasks elsewhere in your code, resorting to `finalize()` only as a last resort and when failure to execute such statements will not cause significant problems.

Inner Classes

With the Java 1.1 compiler, Sun added several new features to the language. One of these was nested classes. Nested classes can only be compiled using a Java 1.1 or 1.2 compiler.

What Are Inner Classes?

Inner classes are classes that are actually included within the body of another class. In fact, you can even include a class within the body of a method. Nested classes are primarily useful to programmers because they can help you structure your code in a more organized fashion. In addition, in some cases they can add to the readability of the code.

You may wonder why you would ever want to do this. The reality is that you are never required to develop anything using inner classes. However, inner classes provide you with the ability to organize your code in a more understandable fashion, and occasionally provide the compiler with a means to further optimize the final code. It is also true that you can produce identical results by placing the inner classes in their own scope.

At this point, if you're one of those programmers who rode out the evolution of C++, you might be wondering whether or not inner classes are just one of those concepts that seemed like a good idea to the designers at the time, but that ends up only causing confusion. Wasn't Java supposed to avoid these pitfalls? Wasn't that the rationalization for avoiding operator overloading, multiple inheritance and other useful but confusing aspects of languages such as C++? Well, the unfortunate answer is maybe. Time will tell how well inner classes are accepted by the developer community as a whole. Regardless of what your own view is, it's very important to understand how to utilize inner classes in case you find yourself editing code from individuals who do utilize the power of inner classes. With that spirit, forge ahead and look at how inner classes work.

Creating a Program with Inner Classes

The major advantage of inner classes is the ability to create what are known as adapter classes. Adapter classes are classes that implement an interface. By isolating individual adapters into nested classes, you can, in essence, build a package-like structure right within a single top-level class.

Take a look at an example that uses an adapter class. Listing 11.14 demonstrates how two individual and separate `Runnable` interfaces can be created in the same class. Both of these interfaces need access to the variable `currentCount` of the top-level class.

Listing 11.14 BigBlue—An Application that Utilizes an Inner Class (*Apple*)

```
/*
 *
 * BigBlue
 *
 */
public class BigBlue implements Runnable{
     int currentCount;

     class Apple implements Runnable {
          public void run(){
               while(true){
                    System.out.println("count="+currentCount);
                    try{
                         Thread.sleep(100);
                    }catch (Exception e){}
               }
          }
     }

     public Runnable getApple(){
          return new Apple();
     }

     public void run(){
          while(true){
               currentCount+=5;
               try{
                    Thread.sleep(75);
               }catch (Exception e){}
          }
     }

     public static void main(String argv[]){
          BigBlue b = new BigBlue();
```

```
            Thread appleThread = new Thread (b.get Apple());

            appleThread.start();
            Thread thisThread = new Thread (b);
            thisThread.start();
        }
})
```

As you look at the preceding example, notice that the `run()` method of `BigBlue` has access directly to the `currentCount` variable, because `currentCount` is a field of the `BigBlue` class. This works just like any other method. Now take a look at the `Apple` class. This class also has access to the `currentCount` variable, and it accesses it just like it was its own, only it's not; it's received from the top-level class `BigBlue`.

To compile this program, it's not necessary to compile both `Apple` and `BigBlue`, just the `BigBlue` class:

```
javac BigBlue.java
```

To run the program, type:

```
java BigBlue
```

What you end up seeing are a sequence of numbers. Notice that because the sleep time in the `BigBlue` thread is a bit shorter than the `Apple` one, every once in a while the numbers increment faster. This was done to demonstrate that they were in fact two different threads, running in two completely different loops.

CAUTION

If, when you compile a class containing an inner class, you get an error similar to:

```
bigBlue.java:30 :
no enclosing instance of class bigBlue is in scope; an explicit one must be
provided when creating class bigBlue. apple, as in outer. new inner() or
outer.super().
Thread appleThread = new Thread (new apple());
```

You may be very confused. To explain this error, look at what a `main` method would look like that might generate this error:

```
public static void main(String argv[]){
      bigBlue b = new bigBlue();

      Thread appleThread = new Thread (new apple());
      appleThread.start();
      Thread thisThread = new Thread (b);
      thisThread.start();
}
```

What causes this error is an attempt to create a new `apple()` inside of the static `main` method. To be able to access the `apple` class, you must do so in a non-static instance of `BigBlue`.

Synchronization with Inner Classes

From time to time, it is necessary to be able to synchronize a method on the parent class of an inner class. Ordinarily, you might just declare a method to be synchronized or create a block that is synchronized (`this`). However, because `this` is a new class, how are you to specify a synchronization on the parent class? Consider the situation where we create an enumeration, as in Listing 11.15.

Listing 11.15 Enumeration of Elements

```
public class FixedStack {
int array[] = new int[10];
int top=0;

synchronized public void push(int item) {
      array[top++] = item;
}

class Enumerator implements java.util.Enumeration {
public int nextElement() {
         synchronized (FixedStack.this) {
               if (count > top)
                    count = top;
               if (count == 0)
                    throw new NoSuchElementException("FixedStack");
               return array[--count];
         }
}
}
}
```

NOTE In Listing 11.15, make sure you don't try to access an element in the array with the `nextElement()` method of the Enumeration at the same time an element is added with the `push()` method. To do this, the example uses the qualified `FixedStack.this` variable. The qualified name refers to the super class of `this`. The inner class implicitly knows that the qualified `this` refers to the instance that instantiated the inner class. ■

So How Do Inner Classes Work?

At this point, you're probably wondering how inner classes work. Under Java 1.0, inner classes were not available. So, how did Java designers make the programs that you write using inner classes work with virtual machines that were designed from the 1.0 specification? The answer is that inner classes aren't really new. The solution lies in the fact that when you write a class with an inner class in it, the compiler takes the inner class outside of the main class and just adjusts the compiled result.

Again, if you're one of those programmers who rode the change in the early days of C++, inner classes will spark a note. The reason is that in the beginning of C++, C++ was really C wrapped in an object-oriented shroud. When you wrote a C++ program, the C++ compiler actually just converted your C++ code into C code, and then a C compiler did the real compilation. Well, with Java, you don't actually need two compilers, but the end result is very similar.

Why Use Inner Classes?

You might be saying to yourself, "Why should I ever use an inner class?" The answer, as indicated at the beginning of this section, is to organize your code in a more suitable fashion. Sun's documentation refers to these inner classes as Adapter classes. To understand why, look at what inner classes are usually used for.

An inner class can extend or implement any interface you would like—so can an ordinary class. The only problem is that when a standard class implements an interface, it's often difficult to locate where the methods associated with the interface are located within the code. However, because the declaration and the code are together with an inner class, this is generally much clearer.

Packages

When you start creating a large number of classes for a program, it is helpful to keep them together. A clutter of class files is not unlike how your hard drive would look without subdirectories or folders. Imagine if all the files on your hard drive were placed in a single folder. You would have thousands of files, and you would have to make sure that none of them had the same name.

Class files by themselves must comply with this same arrangement. That's a fairly rigid requirement. To overcome this, Java has a system called packages. You can think of each package as a subdirectory. You have already seen how a number of packages are used in the Java API. For example, java.awt is a package, java.lang is another package, and so on.

Packages in Java are groups of classes. These are similar to libraries in many computer languages. A package of Java classes typically contains related classes. You can imagine a package called `Transportation`, which would have numerous classes defined in it such as `Car`, `Boat`, `Airplane`, `Train`, `Rocket`, `AmphibiousCar`, `SeaPlane`, and so on. Applications that deal with items of this sort might benefit from importing the imaginary `Transportation` package.

To make a class a member of a package, you must declare it using the `package` statement:

```
package Transportation;
```

Some unique requirements go along with the `package` statement, however:

- For a class to be included in a package, its source code must be in the same directory as the rest of the package files. You can get around this requirement, but it's not really a good idea.

- The `package` statement itself must be the very first statement in the file. In other words, you can have comments and whitespace before the package line, but nothing else. The following table shows an example of a valid and an invalid `package` statement:

Legal	**Illegal**
`package Transportation`	`import java.applet.Applet;`
`import java.applet.Applet;`	`package Transportation;`

Importing Classes in Packages

After a file has been declared to be part of a package, the actual name for the class is the package name dot (.) and the name of the class. In other words, in our `Transportation` example, the `Car` class would be `Transportation.Car`, where before it would have been simply `Car`.

This leads to a small problem with an easy solution. If you write a program and then later decide to make all of the classes a member of a package, how does the compiler find the other files? Before, they were called `Car` and `Van`. Now, you must import them as `Transportation.Car` in order to use them. In other words, as shown here, where before you imported `Car`, you must now import `Transportation.Car`:

Old	**New**
import `Car;`	import `Transportation.Car`

Importing Entire Packages

It is also possible to import the entire contents of a package or all of the classes in that package. You have probably already seen this done with some of the JDK classes such as `java.awt`. To import all the classes, replace the individual class name with the wild card (*):

```
import java.awt.*;
```

By importing entire packages, you give yourself access to every class in the package. This can be very convenient, because you don't need to make up a big list like:

```
import java.awt.Graphics;
import java.awt.Image;
import java.awt.Button;
import java.awt.Canvas;
...
```

Now, if you're thinking, "That seems simple; why don't I just import the entire package all the time?" The answer lies in the fact that there are a couple of drawbacks to importing the entire package:

- When you import an entire package, the virtual machine has to keep track of the names of all of the elements in the package. Using extra RAM to store class and method names is not terribly important right now because your computer probably has 16M or more of RAM. However, as more and more small, Java-based computers come into play, this could become an issue. In addition, this slows the system down slightly.

- If you import several packages and they happen to share a class file name, things start to fall apart. Which class do you really want? For instance, if you import `YourCorp.*`, which has a `Button` class, and import `java.awt.*`, which also contains a `Button` class, the two `Button` classes will collide.
- The most important drawback deals with the bandwidth over the Internet. When you import an entire package that is not on the computer already (this excludes the `java.*` packages) the Appletviewer or other browser has to drag all of the class files for the entire package across the Net before it can continue. If you have 30 classes in a package and are only using two, your applets aren't going to load nearly as fast, and you would be wasting a lot of resources.

Using a Class Without Importing It

You may have not realized this before, but it is not necessary to actually import a class before you use it. Ordinarily, classes in the `null` package (default) and that reside in the same physical directory can be used without doing anything. For instance, if there are two classes `Car` and `Van` in the same directory, you can create an instance of `Car` in the `Van` class without actually importing the `Car` class. Listings 11.16 and 11.17 show two such classes.

Listing 11.16 A Simple Class File for the *Car* Class

```
//Car is just a generic class with a few variables
public class Car {
 int wheels;
 int tires;
 int speed;
 //simple constructor
 public Car (int inWheels, int inTires, int inSpeed){
  wheels=inWheels;
  tires = inTires;
  speed = inSpeed;
 }
}
```

Listing 11.17 A Simple Class File for *Van* that Uses the *Car* Class

```
//The Van class is another simple class, but uses the Car class
public class Van {
  //The Car class is used here without being imported
  Car theCar;
  int doors;
  //simple constructor
  public Van (Car inCar, int inDoor){
    theCar= inCar;
    doors= inDoor;
  }
}
```

When you place a class in a package, you can still use the class without importing it. The only difference is that you must use the full class name when declaring the instance. Listings 11.18 and 11.19 are identical to 11.15 and 11.16 except that `Car` is a member of the `Transportation` package.

Listing 11.18 A Simple Class File for the *Car* Class in a Package

```
package Transportation;
//Car is just a generic class with a few variables
public class Car {
 int wheels;
 int tires;
 int speed;
 //simple constructor
 public Car (int inWheels, int inTires, int inSpeed){
  wheels=inWheels;
  tires = inTires;
  speed = inSpeed;
 }
}
```

Listing 11.19 A Simple Class File for *Van* that Uses the *Car* Class in a Package

```
//The Van class is another simple class, but uses the Car class
public class Van {
  //The Car class is used here without being imported
  Transportation.Car theCar;
  int doors;
  //simple constructor
  public Van (Car inCar, int inDoor){
    theCar= inCar;
    doors= inDoor;
  }
}
```

NOTE Although you do not need to import a package to use the classes, doing so affords a shorthand way to refer to classes defined in the package. Specifically, in the previous example, if the package was imported:

```
import Transportation.Car;
```

to create an object of Class `Car`, you would not need `Transportation` in front of every `Car` reference, and the code would look otherwise identical to Listing 11.18.

Using Packages to Organize Your Code

Packages are more than just a shortcut. They are a way of keeping things organized.

Java itself comes with a built-in set of packages, as shown in Table 11.1.

Table 11.1 Standard Java Packages

Package	Description
`java.applet`	Contains classes needed to create Java applets that run under Netscape 2.0 (or greater), HotJava, or other Java-compatible browsers.
`java.awt`	Contains classes helpful in writing platform-independent graphic user interface (GUI) applications. This comes with several subpackages including `java.awt.peer` and `java.awt.image`.
`java.io`	Contains classes for doing I/O (input and output). This is where the data stream classes are kept.
`java.lang`	Contains the essential Java classes. `java.lang` is implicitly imported, so you don't need to import its classes.
`java.net`	Contains the classes used for making network connections. These are used in tandem with `java.io` for reading and writing data from the network.
`java.util`	Contains other tools and data structures, such as encoding, decoding, vectors, stacks, and more.

Additional packages are also available commercially.

The one feature to notice about these classes is how Sun Microsystems has used the packages to group similar classes together. When you set out to construct a program, you might be tempted to place the entire program in a package. For instance, say you were writing a Pac Man game. You might be tempted to place all of the classes in a package called `Pac`. Would this be a good idea? Probably not, but it all depends on your implementation.

The odds are that your Pac Man game will include a lot of code that is likely to be used by other arcade-style games you have written. For instance, you might create what is known as a game sprite engine. It's probably a more far-sighted approach to place all of the elements for the game-sprite in their own package and then place only those classes that are specific to the Pac Man game in the `Pac` package. Later you can go back and add to the game-sprite package without disrupting the readability of your Pac Man game.

Implicit Import of All *java.lang* Classes

You might have noticed from reading the code throughout this book that there is another set of classes that you don't need to import to use. The classes in the `java.lang` package are always imported for you. This means that you can use the `java.lang.System` class as if it was part of the system—without importing it in statements like this:

```
System.out.println("Hi there, System hasn't been imported");
```

This can be a very convenient thing as in the case of `System`, but it can also be a source of confusion. For instance, look back at Listing 11.10; the `Math` class is also used without instantiating it to access the value of PI. However, if you're not familiar with how `Math` got imported (automatically), this may have caused you some confusion. The only way to overcome this is to become familiar with the `java.lang` package and learn what classes are available to you. ●

CHAPTER 12

Interfaces

In this chapter

What Are Interfaces?

Interfaces are Java's substitute for C++'s feature of multiple inheritance, the practice of allowing a class to have several superclasses. Although it is often desirable to have a class inherit several sets of properties, for several reasons the creators of Java decided not to allow multiple inheritance. Java classes, however, can implement several interfaces, thereby enabling you to create classes that build upon other objects without the problems created by multiple inheritance.

Somewhat resembling classes in syntax, interfaces are used when you want to define a certain functionality to be used in several classes, but are not sure exactly how this functionality will be defined by each of these classes. By placing such methods in an interface, you are able to outline common behavior and leave the specific implementation to the classes themselves. This makes using interfaces instead of classes a better choice when dealing with advanced data handling.

Interfaces are the underprivileged first cousins of classes. In fact, they are extremely similar to pure abstract classes. Although classes have the capability to define an object, interfaces define a set of methods and constants to be implemented by another object. From a practical viewpoint, interfaces help to define the behavior of an object by declaring a set of characteristics for the object. For example, knowing that a person is an athlete does not define her entire personality, but does ensure that she has certain traits and capabilities.

As an example, say an athlete will always have a 100-meter time, be able to perform the task of running a mile, and be able to lift weights. By later implementing the athlete interface, you ensure that a person will possess these abilities.

Thinking of interfaces in another way, consider your radio, TV, and computer speakers. Each of them has one common control: volume. For this reason, you might want all these devices to implement an interface called `VolumeControl`.

Interfaces have one major limitation: They can define abstract methods and final fields, but cannot specify any implementation for these methods. For methods, this means that the body is empty. The classes that implement the interface are responsible for specifying the implementation of these methods. This means that, unlike extending a class, when you implement an interface, you must override every method in the interface.

In general, interfaces enable you as a programmer to define a certain set of functionality without having any idea as to how this functionality will be later defined. For example, if a class implemented the `java.lang.Runnable` interface (an interface with one method—`run()`), the class is known to have a `run()` method. Because the VM can be assured that any `Runnable` class has a `run()` method, the VM can blindly call the `run()` method. At the same time, when the designers were writing the VM, they did not have to know anything about what would happen in the `run()` method. So, you could be doing an animation, or calculating the first 1,000 prime numbers. It doesn't matter; all that does matter is that you will be running, and you have established that by implementing the `Runnable` interface.

Another excellent example is the `java.applet.AppletContext` interface. This interface defines a set of methods that returns information regarding the environment in which an applet is running. For instance, the `AppletContext` defines a method called `getImage`. Any viewer capable of running an applet has a means to load an image through the implementation of this method.

The problem is that different viewers such as the Appletviewer or Netscape Navigator get images differently. Worse yet, even the same browser varies based on the platform it is running on. Fortunately, every Java-enabled browser implements the `AppletContext` interface, so although the `java.applet.Applet` class depends on the methods declared in the `AppletContext` interface, it does not need to worry about how these methods work. That means, you can use the same applet class and the same methods (such as `java.applet.Applet.getImage()`) in a variety of environments and browsers without worrying about whether the `getImage()` method will be there.

Creating an Interface

The syntax for creating an interface is extremely similar to that for creating a class. However, there are a few exceptions. The most significant difference is that none of the methods in your interface may have a body, nor can you declare any variables that will not serve as constants.

An example interface is shown in Listing 12.1. It shows three items: an interface, a class that implements the interface, and a class that uses the derived class. Look it over to get an idea as to how interfaces are used and where we are going in this chapter.

Listing 12.1 Product.java: Product Interface

```
public interface Product {
   static final String MAKER = "My Corp";
   static final String PHONE = "555-123-4567";

   public int getPrice(int id);

}

***begin Listing 12.1a: Shoe.java: Class Shoe which implements the Product
Interface
public class Shoe implements Product {
   public int getPrice(int id) {
   if (id == 1)
      return(5);
   else
      return(10);
   }
   public String getMaker() {
      return(MAKER);
   }
}
```

continues

Listing 12.1 Continued

```
***Begin Listing 12.1b: Store.java: Class Store extends Shoe(which implements
Product)
public class Store {
   static Shoe hightop;

   public static void init() {
      hightop = new Shoe();
   }

   public static void main(String argv[]) {
      init();
      getInfo(hightop);
      orderInfo(hightop);
   }

   public static void getInfo(Shoe item) {
      System.out.println("This Product is made by "+ item.MAKER);
      System.out.println("It costs $" + item.getPrice(1) + '\n');
   }

   public static void orderInfo(Product item) {
      System.out.println("To order from " + item.MAKER + " call " +
                 ➥item.PHONE + ".");
System.out.println("Each item costs $" + item.getPrice(1));
   }
}
```

The Declaration

Interface declarations have the syntax

`public` interface NameofInterface `extends InterfaceList` (where *public*, *extends* and *InterfaceList* are in italics)

where everything in italics is optional.

Public Interfaces By default, interfaces may be implemented by all classes in the same package. But if you make your interface public, you allow classes and objects outside of the given package to implement it as well.

Just like public classes, public interfaces must be defined in a file named NameOf Interface.java.

Interface Name The rules for an interface name are identical to those for classes. The only requirements on the name are that it begin with a letter, an underscore character, or a dollar sign; contain only Unicode characters (basic letters and digits, as well as some other special characters); and not be the same as any Java keyword (such as `extends` or `int`). Again, like classes, it is common practice to capitalize the first letter of any interface name.

▶ **See** "Keywords," **p. 94**

TIP Although only required for public interfaces, it is a good practice to place all interfaces in a file named NameOf Interface.java. This enables both you and the Java compiler to find the source code for your class.

Thus, while the `Product` interface is not public, you should still declare it in a file named Product.java.

Extending Other Interfaces In keeping with the OOP practice of inheritance, Java interfaces may also extend other interfaces as a means of building larger interfaces upon previously developed code. The new sub-interface inherits all the methods and static constants of the super-interfaces just as subclasses inherit the properties of superclasses.

▶ **See** "Object-Oriented Programming: A New Way of Thinking," **p. 72**

The one major rule that interfaces must obey when extending other interfaces is that they may not define the body of the parent methods, any more than they can define the body of their own methods. Any class that implements the new interface must define the body of all of the methods for both the parent and child interface.

As an example, the following lines show a new interface that extends a previously defined interface (`Runnable`):

```
interface MonitoredRunnable extends java.lang.Runnable {
   boolean isRunning() {
   }
}
```

The declaration shows a more detailed `Runnable` interface, including some of the features that can be found in `java.lang.Thread`.

NOTE Interfaces cannot extend classes. There are a number of reasons for this, but probably the easiest to understand is that any class that the interface would be extending would have its method bodies defined. This violates the "prime directive" of interfaces. ■

Remember that if you implement an extended interface, you must override both the methods in the new interface and the methods in the old interface, as seen in Listing 12.2.

Listing 12.2 ***Fireworks*** **Class Implementing the** ***MonitoredRunnable*** **Derived Interface**

```
class Fireworks implements MonitoredRunnable {
   private boolean running;        // Keeps track of state.

   void run() {
      shootFireWorks();
   }
```

continues

Listing 12.2 Continued

```
   boolean isRunning() {          // Provides access to other objects without
      return(running);      //allowing them to change the value of running.
   }

}
```

Because `Fireworks` implements `MonitoredRunnable`, it must override `isRunning()`, declared in `MonitoredRunnable`. Because `MonitoredRunnable` extends `Runnable`, it must also override `run()`, declared in `Runnable`.

NOTE Although classes implement interfaces to inherit their properties, interfaces extend other interfaces. When extending more than one interface, separate each by a comma. This means that although classes cannot extend multiple classes, interfaces are allowed to extend multiple interfaces:

```
interface MonitoredRunnable extends java.lang.Runnable,java.lang.Cloneable {
    boolean isRunning() {
    }
}
```

The Interface Body

The body of an interface cannot specify the specific implementation of any methods, but it does specify their properties. In addition, interfaces may also contain final variables.

For example, declaring the `MAKER` variable in the `Product` interface allows you to declare a constant that will be employed by all classes implementing the `Product` interface.

Another good example of final fields in interfaces can be found in the `java.awt.image.ImageConsumer` interface. The interface defines a set of final integers that serve as standards for interpreting information. Because the `RANDOMPIXELORDER` variable equals 1, classes that implement the `ImageConsumer` interface can make reference to the variable and know that the value of 1 means that the pixels will be sent in a random order. This is shown in the `setHints` method of Listing 12.3.

Listing 12.3 Pseudocode for a Class Implementing *ImageConsumer*

```
public class MagnaImage implements ImageConsumer{
   imageComplete(int status) {
      ...
   }

   setColorModel(ColorModel cm) {
      ...
   }

   setDimensions(int x, int y) {
      ...
   }
   setHints(int hints) {
```

```
        if ((hints & RANDOMPIXELORDER)!=0){
            ...
        }
    }

setPixels(int x, int y, int w , int h, ColorModel cm , byte pixels[],
➥int off, int scansize) {
        ...
    }

setPixels(int x, int y, int w, int h, ColorModel cm, int pixels[], int off,
➥int scansize) {      ...
    }

    setProperties(Hashtable props) {
        ...
    }
}
```

Methods The main purpose of interfaces is to declare abstract methods that will be defined in other classes. As a result, if you are dealing with a class that implements an interface, you can be assured that these methods will be defined in the class. Although this process is not overly complicated, there is one important difference that should be noticed.

The syntax for declaring a method in an interface is extremely similar to declaring a method in a class, but in contrast to methods declared in classes, methods declared in interfaces cannot possess bodies. An interface method consists of only a declaration. For example, the following two methods are complete if they are defined in an interface:

```
public int getPrice(int id);

public void showState();
```

However, in a class, they would require method bodies:

```
public int getPrice(int id) {
  if (id == 1)
    return(5);
  else
    return(10);
}

public void showState() {
  System.out.println("Massachusetts");
}
```

The method declaration does not determine how a method will behave; it does define how it will be used by defining what information it needs and what (if any) information will be returned. The method that is actually defined later in a class must have the same properties as you define in the interface. To make the best use of this fact, it is important to carefully consider factors like return type and parameter lists when defining the method in the interface.

Method declarations in interfaces have the following syntax:

```
public  return_value   nameofmethod   (parameters)   throws ExceptionList;
```

where everything in italics is optional. Also note that unlike normal method declarations in classes, declarations in interfaces are immediately followed by a semicolon.

NOTE All methods in interfaces are public by default, regardless of the presence or absence of the public modifier. This is in contrast to class methods which default to friendly.

It's actually illegal to use any of the other standard method modifiers (including native, static, synchronized, final, private, protected, or private protected) when declaring a method in an interface.

Variables in Interfaces Although interfaces are generally employed to provide abstract implementation of methods, you may also define variables within them. Because you cannot place any code within the bodies of the methods, all variables declared in an interface must be global to the class. Furthermore, regardless of the modifiers used when declaring the field, all fields declared in an interface are always public, final, and static.

Although all fields will be created as public, final, and static, you do not need to explicitly state this in the field declaration. All fields default to public, static, and final regardless of the presence of these modifiers. It is, however, a good practice to explicitly define all fields in interfaces as public, final, and static to remind yourself (and other programmers) of this fact.

As seen in the `Product` interface, interface fields—like final static fields in classes—are used to define constants that can be accessed by all classes that implement the interface:

```
public interface Product {
//This variable is static and final.
static final String MAKER = "My Corp";

//This variable is also static and final by default, even though not
//stated explicitly.
String PHONE = "555-123-4567";

public int getPrice(int id);
}
```

Implementing Interfaces

Now that you know how to create interfaces, let's examine how they are used in developing classes. Listing 12.4 shows an example of a class that implements our `Product` interface.

Listing 12.4 *Shoe* Class Implementing the *Product* Interface

```
class Shoe implements Product {
     public int getPrice(int id) {
          if (id == 1)
               return(5);
          else
               return(10);
     }
```

```
        public String getMaker() {
            return(MAKER);
        }
}
```

Of course, the code in the class can deal with functions other than those relating to the interface (such as the `getMaker()` method). But, to fulfill the requirements of implementing the `Product` interface, the class must override the `getPrice(int)` method.

Overriding Methods

Declaring a method in an interface is a good practice. However, the method cannot be used until a class implements the interface and overrides the given method.

Remember that if you implement an interface, you are required to override all methods declared in the interface. Failure to do so will make your class abstract.

Modifiers

As discussed earlier, methods declared in interfaces are by default assigned the public level of access. Consequently, because you cannot override a method to be more private than it already is, all methods declared in interfaces and overridden in classes must be assigned the public access modifier, unless they are explicitly made less public in the interface.

Of the remaining modifiers that may be applied to methods, only `native` and `abstract` may be applied to methods originally declared in interfaces.

Parameter List

Interface methods define a set of parameters that must be passed to the method. Consequently, declaring a new method with the same name but a different set of parameters than the method declared in your interface overloads the method, not overrides it.

Although there is nothing wrong with overloading methods declared in interfaces, it is also important to implement the method declared in the interface. Therefore, unless you declare your class to be abstract, you must override each method, employing the same parameter signature as in your interface (see Listing 12.5). By the way, only one method satisfies the `run()` method required for `Runnable`.

Listing 12.5 Runner.java—A Class (Runner) that Implements *Runnable* and Has Two *run* Methods

```
public void Runner implements Runnable {

//This method overloads the run() method; it does not
//fulfill the requirements for Runnable.
```

continues

Listing 12.5 Continued

```
public void run(int max){
   int count =0;
   while (count++<max){
      try{
         Thread.sleep(500);
      } catch (Exception e){}
   }
}

//This method fulfills the requirement for Runnable.
//You must have this method.
public void run(){
   while (true){
      try{
         Thread.sleep(500);
      } catch (Exception e){}
   }
}

}
```

If the method `String createName(int length, boolean capitalized)` is declared in an interface, here are some valid and invalid examples of how to override it. The invalid methods can exist (as overloaded versions of the method) in addition to the valid ones, but will not be related to the interface:

Valid

`String createName(int a, boolean b)`

`String createName(int width, boolean formatted)`

Invalid

`String createName (boolean capitalized, int length)`

`String createName(int length)`

Body

When creating a class that implements an interface, one of your chief concerns will be creating bodies for the methods originally declared in the interface. Unless you decide to make the method native, it is necessary to create the body for every method originally declared in your interface if you do not want to make your new class abstract.

The actual implementation and code of the body of your new method is entirely up to you. This is one of the good things about using interfaces. Although the interface ensures that, in a non-abstract class, its methods will be defined and will return an appropriate data type, the interface places no further restrictions or limitations on the method bodies.

Using Interfaces from Other Classes

You've learned how to create interfaces and build classes based on interfaces. However, interfaces are not useful unless you can develop classes that will either employ the derived classes or the interface itself.

Using an Interface's Fields

Although the fields of an interface must be both static and final, they can be extremely useful in your code.

The following example demonstrates that any variable from an interface can be referenced by using the same dot notation you use with classes. That means you can use `java.awt.image.ImageConsumer.COMPLETESCANLINES` just as with the class `java.awt.Event` you use with `java.awt.Event.MOUSE_DOWN`. This provides you with access to constants. Listing 12.6 shows an example of another `ImageConsumer` variable being used.

Listing 12.6 Using the Constant Fields of an Interface

```
import java.awt.image.*;
class MyImageHandler {
/* The java.awt.image.ImageConsumer interface defines certain constants to serve
as indicators. STATICIMAGEDONE, which  is set to equal 3, informs the consumer
that the image is complete.*/
     ImageConsumer picture;

     void checkStatus(boolean done) {
          if (done)
               picture.imageComplete(ImageConsumer.STATICIMAGEDONE);
          }
}
```


Using Interfaces as Types

One of the most important features of an interface is that it can be used as a data type. An interface variable can be used just as you would any class.

As a Parameter Type In Listing 12.7, you create a simple application that employs the `Shoe` class developed earlier. Because the `Shoe` class implements the `Product` interface, you may deal with the instances of the `Shoe` class either as standard `Shoe` objects or as objects based on the `Product` interface. Although both approaches produce the same results, treating the instance as an object based on the `Product` interface provides you with a more flexible and useful way of using the resources provided by the `Product` interface.

Listing 12.7 Using the Product Interface as a Parameter Type

```
class Store {
     static Shoe hightop;
```

continues

Listing 12.7 Continued

```
        public static void init() {
                hightop = new Shoe();
        }

        public static void main(String argv[]) {
                init();
                getInfo(hightop);
                orderInfo(hightop);
               }

        public static void getInfo(Shoe item) {
System.out.println("This Product is made by "+ item.MAKER);
              System.out.println("It costs $" + item.getPrice(1) + '\n');
        }

        public static void orderInfo(Product item) {
              System.out.println("To order from " +item.MAKER + " call " +
              ➥item.PHONE + ".");
              System.out.println("Each item costs $" + item.getPrice(1));
        }
}
```

Output In the following example, the `getInfo()` method treats `hightop` as a simple class with certain methods and fields. However, the interesting example is `orderInfo()`, which extracts almost the same information without knowing anything about a `Shoe`. Because a `Shoe` meets the requirements of a `Product`, you are able to implicitly cast a `Shoe` to become a `Product`. As a result, because you know that the `Product` interface declares certain features, you can be sure that these features, such as the `getPrice()` method, are present in the parameter `item`:

```
C:\dev>\jdk\java\bin\java Store
This Product is made by My Corp
It costs $5

To order from My Corp call 555-123-4567.
Each item costs $5
```

NOTE Notice that in treating `hightop` as a `Product`, you are implicitly casting it as a new data type without specifically stating so in your code. Although the compiler has no trouble doing this, you could substitute that line of code in the `Store` class for the following:

```
orderInfo( (Product)hightop);
```

This statement would accomplish the same goal and is often easier for other programmers to read, because it shows that `orderInfo()` accepts a `Product`, not a `Shoe` as its argument.

Although it is not necessary to use the `Product` type as your argument in this simplistic example, its use becomes apparent when you have multiple classes, each of which implements the same interface. For example, consider a more elaborate `Store` class with several items, all of which implemented the `Product` interface, such as in Listing 12.8.

Listing 12.8 Using an Interface as a Type to Deal with Several Classes

```
interface Product {
     static final String MAKER = "My Corp";
     static final String PHONE = "555-123-4567";
     public int getPrice(int id);
     public void showName();
}
class Book implements Product {
     public int getPrice(int id) {
          if (id == 1)
               return(20);
          else
               return(30);
     }
     public void showName() {
           System.out.println("I'm a book!");
     }
}
class Shoe implements Product {
     public int getPrice(int id) {
          if (id == 1)
               return(5);
          else
               return(10);
     }
     public void showName() {
           System.out.println("I'm a shoe!");
     }
}
class store {
     static Shoe hightop;
     static Book using_java;

     public static void init() {
          hightop = new Shoe();
          using_java = new Book();
     }

     public static void main(String argv[]) {
          init();
          orderInfo(hightop);
          orderInfo(using_java);
     }

     public static void orderInfo(Product item) {
          item.showName();
          System.out.println("To order from " + item.MAKER + " call " +
          ➥item.PHONE + ".");
          System.out.println("Each item costs $" + item.getPrice(1));
     }
}
```

Part II
Ch 12

continues

Listing 12.8 Continued

```
Output:
C:\dev>\JDK1.2\java\bin\java Store
I'm a shoe!
To order from My Corp call 555-123-4567.
Each item costs $5
I'm a book!
To order from My Corp call 555-123-4567.
Each item costs $20
```

Exceptions

For an interface method to throw an exception, the exception type (or one of its superclasses) must be listed in the exception list for the method as defined in the interface. Here are the rules for overriding methods that throw exceptions:

- The new exception list may only contain exceptions listed in the original exception list, or subclasses of the originally listed exceptions.
- The new exception list does not need to contain any exceptions, regardless of the number listed in the original exception list. (This is because the original list is inherently assigned to the new method.)
- The new method may throw any exception listed in the original exception list or derived from an exception in the original list, regardless of its own exception list.

In general, the exception list of the method—which is declared in the interface, not the redeclared method—determines which expectations can and cannot be thrown. In other words, when a redeclared method changes the exception list, it cannot add any exceptions that are not included in the original interface declaration.

As an example, examine the interface and method declarations in Listing 12.9.

Listing 12.9 Alternate Exception Lists

```
interface Example {
     public int getPrice(int id) throws java.lang.RuntimeException;
}

class User implements Example {
     public int getPrice(int id) throws java.awt.AWTException {
     // Illegal - Reason 1
     // java.awt.AWTException is not a subclass of java.lang.RuntimeException
     /// method body
     }
     public int getPrice(int id) {
          if (id == 6)
               throw new java.lang.IndexOutOfBoundsException();
                         // Legal - Reason 2
                         // IndexOutOfBoundsException is derived from
```

```
                    // RuntimeException
        else
            ...
    }
    public int getPrice(int id) throws java.lang.IndexOutOfBoundsException {
        // Legal - Reason 1
        // IndexOutOfBoundsException is derived from
        //RuntimeException
        if (id == 6)
            throw new java.lang.ArrayIndexOutOfBoundsException();
                // Legal - Reason 3
                //      ArrayIndexOutOfBoundsException is derived from
                //IndexOutOfBoundsException
        ...
    }
}
```

CHAPTER 13

Threads

In this chapter

What Are Threads?

A unique property of Java is its built-in support for *threads*. Threads allow you to do many things at the same time. If you could only move one arm or leg at a time, you would probably feel fairly limited. Threads are the computer's answer to this problem. This chapter covers how threads can be used in Java programs.

Think about a typical corporation. In almost every company there are at least three interdependent departments: management, accounting, and manufacturing/sales. For an efficient company to run, all three of these operations need to work at the same time. If accounting fails to do its job, the company will go bankrupt. If management fails, the company will simply fall apart, and if manufacturing doesn't do its job, the company will have nothing with which to make money.

Many software programs operate under the same conditions as your company. In a company, you complete all the tasks at the same time by assigning them to different people. Each person goes off and does his or her appointed task. With software, you (usually) only have a single processor, and that single processor has to take on the tasks of all these groups. To manage this, a concept called *multitasking* was invented. In reality, the processor is still only doing one thing at any one time, but it switches between them so fast that it seems like it is doing them all simultaneously. Fortunately, modern computers work much faster than human beings, so you hardly even notice that this is happening.

Now, let's go one step further. Have you ever noticed that the accounting person is really doing more than one thing? For instance, that person spends time photocopying spreadsheets, calculating how many widgets the company needs to sell to corner the widget market, adding up all the books, and making sure the bills get paid.

In operating system terms, this is known as *multithreading*. Think about it in this way: Each program is assigned a particular person to carry out a group of tasks, called a *process*. That person then breaks up his or her time even further into threads.

Why Use Threads?

So, you're saying to yourself, "Why should I care how the computer works, so long as it runs my programs?" Multithreading is important to understand because one of the great advances Java makes over other programming languages is its built-in, native support for threading. By using threading, you can avoid long pauses between what your users do and when they see things happen. Better yet, you can send tasks such as printing off into the background where users don't have to worry about them—they can continue typing their dissertation or perform some other task.

In Java, currently the most common use of a thread is to allow your applet to go off and do something while the browser continues to do its job. Any application you're working on that requires two things to be done at the same time is probably a great candidate for threading.

How to Make Your Classes Threadable

You can make your applications and classes run in separate threads in two ways:

- Extending the `Thread` class
- Implementing the `Runnable` interface

It should be noted that making your class able to run as a thread does not automatically make it run as such. A section later in this chapter explains this.

Extend Thread

You can make your class runnable as a thread by extending the class `java.lang.Thread`. This gives you direct access to all the thread methods directly:

```
public class GreatRace extends Thread
```

Implement *Runnable*

Usually, when you want to make a class able to run in its own thread, you also want to extend the features of some other class. Because Java doesn't support multiple inheritance, the solution to this is to implement the `Runnable` interface. In fact, `Thread` actually implements `Runnable` itself. The `Runnable` interface has only one method: `run()`. Any time you make a class implement `Runnable`, you need to have a `run()` method in your class. In the `run()` method you actually do all the work you want to have done by that particular thread:

```
public class GreatRace extends java.applet.Applet implements Runnable
```

The Great Thread Race

Now that you have seen how to make your class runnable, let's take a look at a thread example. The source code for two classes follows (see Listings 13.1 and 13.2):

- *`GreatRace`*. A class that adds several items of the class `Threader`.
- *`Threader`*. Operates in its own thread and races along a track to the finish line.

Listing 13.1 *GreatRace.java*

```
import java.awt.Graphics;
import java.awt.GridLayout;
import java.awt.Frame;
import Threader;

public class GreatRace extends java.applet.Applet implements Runnable{
  Threader theRacers[];
  static int racerCount = 3;
  Thread    theThreads[];
  Thread    thisThread;
  static boolean inApplet=true;
```

continues

Listing 13.1 Continued

```
int    numberofThreadsAtStart;

public void init(){
  //we will use this later to see if all our Threads have died.
  numberofThreadsAtStart = Thread.activeCount();

  //Specify the layout. We will be adding all of the racers one on top
  //of the other.

  setLayout(new GridLayout(racerCount,1));

  //Specify the number of racers in this race, and make the arrays for the
  //Threaders and the actual threads the proper size.
  theRacers = new Threader [racerCount];
  theThreads = new Thread[racerCount];

  //Create a new Thread for each racer, and add it to the panel.
  for (int x=0;x<racerCount;x++){
    theRacers[x]=new Threader ("Racer #"+x);
    theRacers[x].setSize(getSize().width,getSize().height/racerCount);
    add (theRacers[x]);
    theThreads[x]=new Thread(theRacers[x]);

  }
}

public void start(){
  //Start all of the racing threads
  for (int x=0;x<racerCount;x++)
    theThreads[x].start();

  //Create a thread of our own. We will use this to monitor the state of
  //the racers and determine when we should quit altogether.
  thisThread= new Thread (this);
  thisThread.start();
}


public void stop(){
  for (int x= 0;x<theRacers.length;x++){
    theRacers[x].stop();
  }
}

public void run(){
  //Loop around until all of the racers have finished the race.
  while(Thread.activeCount()>numberofThreadsAtStart+2){
    try{
      thisThread.sleep(100);
    }  catch (InterruptedException e){
      System.out.println("thisThread was interrupted");
    }
  }
```

```
    //Once the race is done, end the program.
    if (inApplet){
      stop();
      destroy();
    }
    else
      System.exit(0);
  }


  public static void main (String argv[]){
    inApplet=false;

    //Check to see if the number of racers has been specified on the command
    //line.
    if (argv.length>0)
      racerCount = Integer.parseInt(argv[0]);

    //Create a new frame and place the race in it.
    Frame theFrame = new Frame("The Great Thread Race");
    GreatRace theRace = new GreatRace();
    theFrame.setSize(400,200);
    theFrame.add ("Center",theRace);
    theFrame.show();
    theRace.init();
    theFrame.pack();
    theRace.start();
  }

}//end class GreatRace.
```

Listing 13.2 ***Threader.java***

```
import java.awt.Graphics;
import java.awt.Color;

public class Threader extends java.awt.Canvas implements Runnable {
  int myPosition =0;
  String myName;
  int numberofSteps=600;
  boolean keepRunning = true;

  //Constructor for a Threader. We need to know our name when we
  //create the Threader.
  public Threader (String inName){
    myName=new String (inName);
  }

  public synchronized void paint(Graphics g){
    //Draw a line for the 'racing line'.
    g.setColor (Color.black);
    g.drawLine (0,getSize().height/2,getSize().width,getSize().height/2);
```

continues

Listing 13.2 Continued

```
    //Draw the round racer.
    g.setColor (Color.yellow);
    g.fillOval((myPosition*getSize().width/
   ➥numberofSteps),0,15,getSize().height);
  }

  public void stop(){
    keepRunning = false;
  }

  public void run(){
    //Loop until we have finished the race.
    while ((myPosition <numberofSteps)&& keepRunning){
      //Move ahead one position.
      myPosition++;
      repaint();

      //Put ourselves to sleep so the paint thread can get around to painting.
      try{
        Thread.currentThread().sleep(10);
      }catch (Exception e){System.out.println("Exception on sleep");}
    }
    System.out.println("Threader:"+myName+" has finished the race");
  }


}//end class Threader.
```

Understanding the *GreatRace*

Most of the code in `Threader.java` and `GreatRace.java` should be fairly easy for you to understand by now. Let's take a look at the key sections of the code that deal with the actual threads. The first one to look at is the `for` loop in the `init()` method of `GreatRace` (see Listing 13.3).

Listing 13.3 *for* Loop from *init()* in *GreatRace*

```
for (int x=0;x<racerCount;x++){
    theRacers[x]=new Threader ("Racer #"+x);
    theRacers[x].resize(size().width,size().height/racerCount);
    add (theRacers[x]);
    theThreads[x]=new Thread(theRacers[x]);
}
```

In the `for` loop, the first thing to do is create an instance of the class `Threader`. As you can see from Listing 13.2, `Threader` is an ordinary class that happens to also implement the `Runnable` interface. After an instance of `Threader` is created, it is added to the panel, and the new thread is created with your `Threader` argument. Don't confuse the `Threader` class with the `Thread` class.

CAUTION

The new `Thread` can only be called using an object extending `Thread` or one that implements `Runnable`. In either case, the object must have a `run()` method. However, when you first create the thread, the `run()` method is not called. That only happens when the thread is `started`.

The next important set of code is in the `start()` method, again of `GreatRace.java` (see Listing 13.4).

Listing 13.4 *start()* Method of *GreatRace*

```
public void start(){
  //Start all of the racing threads.
  for (int x=0;x<racerCount;x++)
   // start() will call the run() method.
   theThreads[x].start();

//Create a thread of our own. We will use this to monitor the state of
//the racers and determine when we should quit altogether.
  thisThread= new Thread (this);
  thisThread.start();
}
```

The first task is to start up all the threads created in the `init()` method. When the thread is started, it calls the `run()` method on its `Runnable` right away. In this case, that's the `run()` method of the `Threader` object that was passed to the constructor back in the `init()` method.

Notice that after the racers have started, a thread is created for the actual applet. This thread will be used to monitor what is going on with all the threads. If the race finishes (that is, all the other threads have died and are no longer active), you might as well end the program.

Finally, take a look at the last set of important code—the `run()` method of `Threader` (see Listing 13.5).

Listing 13.5 *run()* Method of *Threader* (racer)

```
public void run(){
  //Loop until we have finished the race.
  while ((myPosition <numberofSteps)&& keepRunning){
    //Move ahead one position.
    myPosition++;
    repaint();

    //Put ourselves to sleep so the paint thread can get around to painting.
    try{
      Thread.currentThread().sleep(10);
      }catch (Exception e){System.out.println("Exception on sleep");}
    }
  System.out.println("Threader:"+myName+" has finished the race");
}
```

Notice that the `while` loop is fairly long. `run()` is only called once when the thread is started. If you plan to do a lot of repetitive work—which is usually the case in a thread—you need to stay within the confines of `run()`. In fact, it isn't a bad idea to think of the `run()` method as being a lot like typical `main()` methods in other structured languages.

Look down a few lines and notice that you put the thread to sleep a bit, in the middle of each loop (`Thread.currentThread().sleep(10)`). This is an important task. You should almost always put your threads to sleep once in a while to prevent other threads from going into starvation.

It is true that under Windows you can get away without doing this in some cases. This works because Windows doesn't really behave like it should with respect to the priority of a thread, as discussed later in the section "A Word About Thread Priority, Netscape, and Windows." However, this is a bad idea, and it probably will not be portable. UNIX machines in particular will look like the applet has hung, and the Macintosh will do the same thing. This has to do with the priority assigned to the paint thread, but there are many other reasons to give the system a breather from your thread.

Thread Processing

To better understand the importance of putting a thread to sleep, it is important to first understand how it is that a computer actually performs threading. How does a computer handle threads so that it seems to us that it is doing more than one thing at a time? The answer lies at the heart of what is known as *task swapping*.

Inside a computer is a periodic clock. For this example, say that the clock ticks every millisecond (in reality, the period is probably much shorter). Now, every millisecond the computer looks at its process table. In the table are pointers to each of the processes (and threads) currently running. It then checks to see whether there are any threads that want to run, and if not goes back to the one it was previously running. This is shown in the timeline of Figure 13.1.

If the Task Manager looks at the process table and there are more threads that are not sleeping, it then goes round-robin between them if they are the same priority. This activity is shown in Figure 13.2.

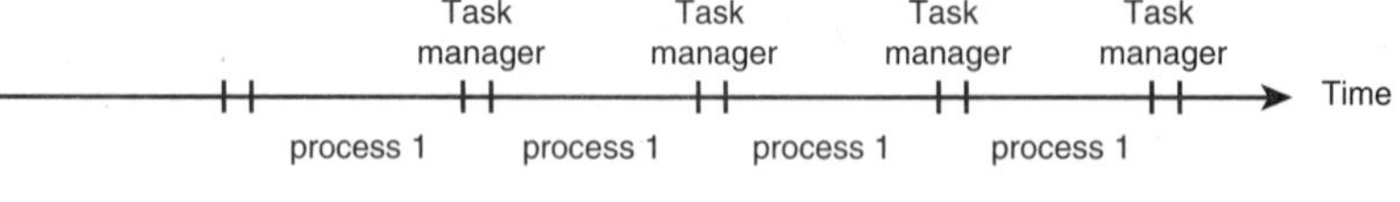

FIG. 13.1 With only one process running, the Task Manager always goes back to that process.

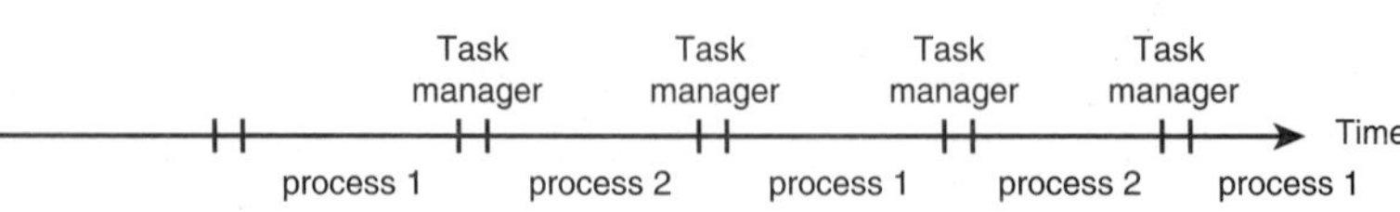

FIG. 13.2 With two processes of the same priority running, the Task Manager swaps between them.

The third option that the Task Manager might find is that there are two threads running, but process 2 is of a lower priority than process 1. In this case, the Task Manager runs only the thread that is the higher priority. The timeline for this session is shown in Figure 13.3.

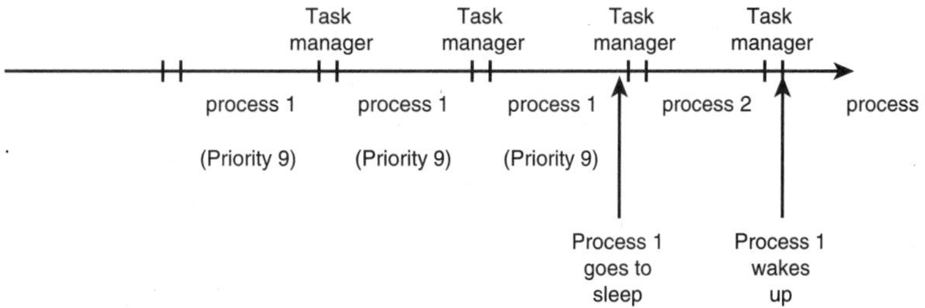

FIG. 13.3
The Task Manager always returns to the higher priority thread (1) until it decides to go to sleep.

Try Out the Great Thread Race

Go ahead and compile the `GreatRace` and run it as shown in Figure 13.4 by typing

```
java GreatRace
```

You can also access it using your browser, by opening the `index.html` file.

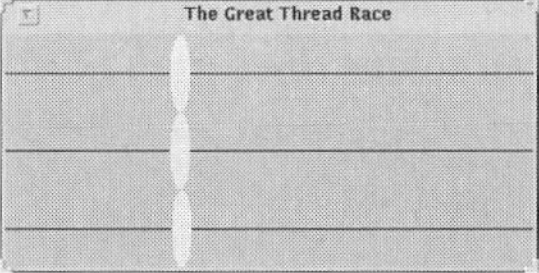

FIG. 13.4
`GreatRace` runs as an application.

You just saw three rather boring ovals run across the screen. Did you notice that they all ran at almost the same speed, yet they were really all processing separately? You can run the `GreatRace` with as many racers as you want by typing

```
java GreatRace 5
```

The racers should all make it across the screen in about the same time (see Figure 13.5).

If you run the race a number of times, you see that the race is actually quite fair, and each of the racers wins just about an equal number of times. If you show the Java Console under Netscape or look at the window you ran `Java GreatRace` from, you can actually see the order in which the racers finish, as shown in Figure 13.6.

Changing the Priority

There are two methods in `java.lang.Thread` that deal with the priority of a thread:

- `setPriority(int)`—used to set a new priority for a thread.
- `getPriority()`—used to obtain the current priority of a thread.

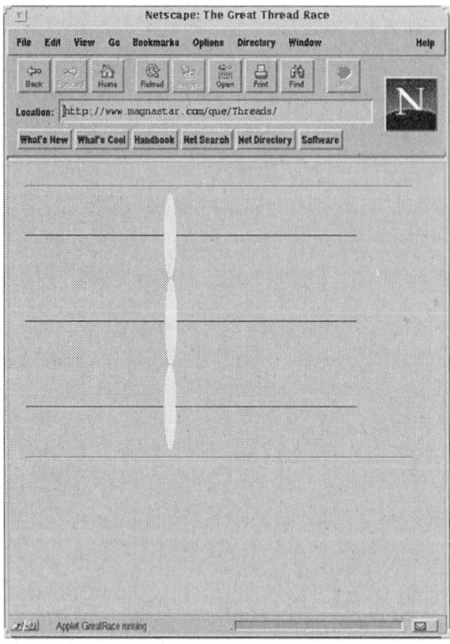

FIG. 13.5
`GreatRace` as an applet.

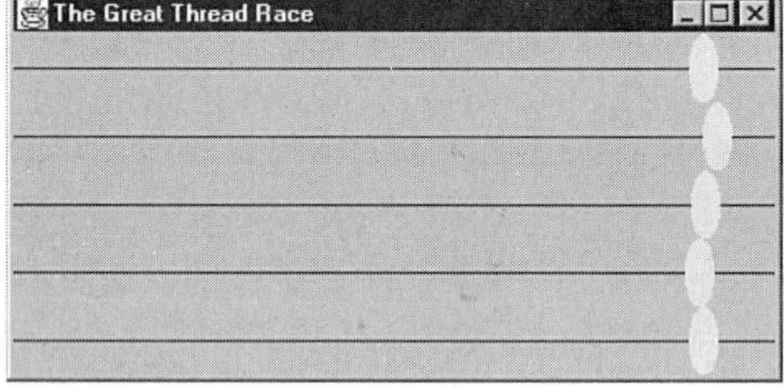

FIG. 13.6
A window shows `GreatRace` and the DOS window it was run from.

Let's see what happens when you tell the computer you want it to treat each of the racers a bit differently by changing the priority.

Change the `init()` method in `GreatRace.java` by adding the following line into the `for` loop:

```
theThreads[x].setPriority(Thread.MIN_PRIORITY+x);
```

The `for` loop now looks like Listing 13.6.

Listing 13.6 New *for* Loop for *init()* Method

```
//Create a new Thread for each racer, and add it to the panel.
for (int x=0;x<racerCount;x++){
    theRacers[x]=new Threader ("Racer #"+x);
    theRacers[x].setSize(getSize().width,getSize().height/racerCount);
    add (theRacers[x]);
    theThreads[x]=new Thread(theRacers[x]);
    theThreads[x].setPriority(Thread.MIN_PRIORITY+x);
}
```

Recompile GreatRace now, and run it again, as shown in Figure 13.7.

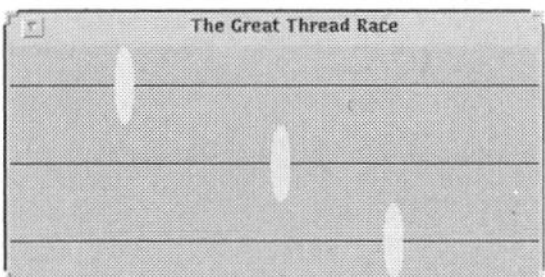

FIG. 13.7 The New GreatRace shown as it is run—mid-race.

By changing the priority of the racers, all of a sudden the bottom racer always wins. Why? The highest priority thread always gets to use the processor when it is not sleeping. This means that every 10ms, the bottom racer gets to advance towards the finish line, stopping the work of the other racers. The other racers get a chance to try to catch up only when that racer decides to go to sleep. Unlike the hare in the fable about the tortoise and the hare, though, the highest priority thread always wakes up in 10ms, and rather quickly outpaces the other racers all the way to the finish line. As soon as that racer finishes, the next racer becomes the highest priority and gets to move every 10ms, leaving the next racer farther behind.

NOTE The priority of the thread was changed with the method `setPriority(int)` from `Thread`. Note that you did not just give it a number. The priority was set relative to the `MIN_PRIORITY` variable in `Thread`. This is an important step. The `MIN_PRIORITY` and `MAX_PRIORITY` are variables that could be set differently for a particular machine. Currently, the `MIN_PRIORITY` on all machines is 1, and the `MAX_PRIORITY` is 10. It is important not to exceed these values. Doing so will cause an `IllegalArgumentException` to be thrown.

A Word About Thread Priority, Netscape, and Windows

If you ran the updated version of GreatRace under Windows, you saw something like Figure 13.8. No doubt you're wondering why your race did not turn out the same as was shown in Figure 13.7. The trailing two racers stayed very close together until the first one won.

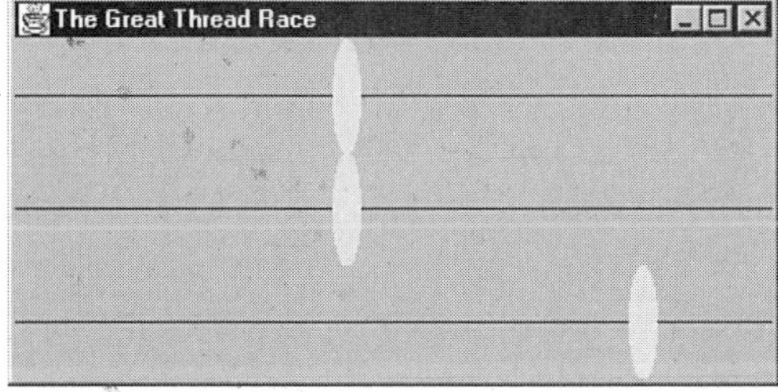

FIG. 13.8 The New GreatRace as it appears running under Windows 95.

With Netscape under Windows, as shown in Figure 13.9, you may be wondering why your last racer didn't even win!

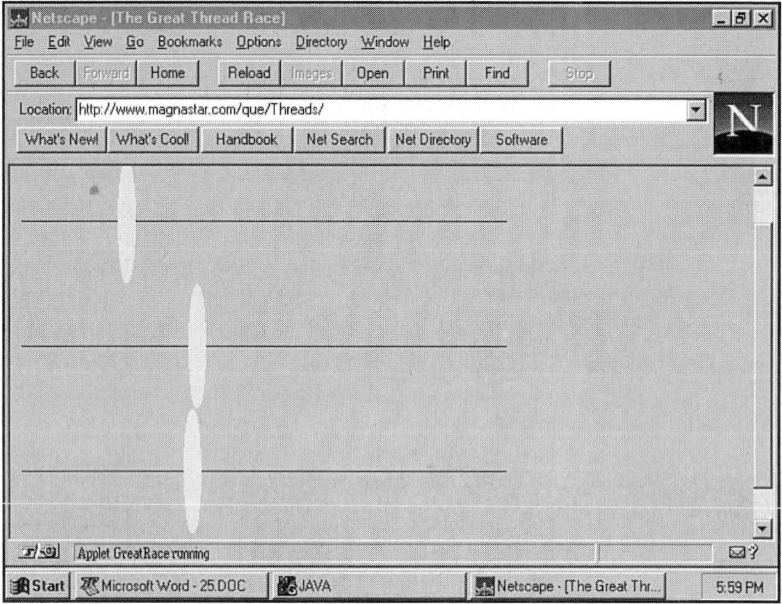

FIG. 13.9
New `GreatRace` run as an applet running under Windows 95.

The reason for this discrepancy is that threads under Windows don't have nearly the amount of control in terms of priority as do threads under UNIX or Macintosh machines. In fact, threads that have nearly the same priority are treated almost as if they had the same priority with the Windows version of Netscape. That is the reason why under Netscape the last two racers seem to have a nearly equal chance at winning the race. To make the last racer always win, you must increase the priority difference. Try changing the line in the `GreatRace` `init()` method to read like this:

```
theThreads[x].setPriority(Thread.MIN_PRIORITY+x*2);
```

Now if you try the race under Windows 95, the last racer should always win by a good margin, as seen in Figure 13.10.

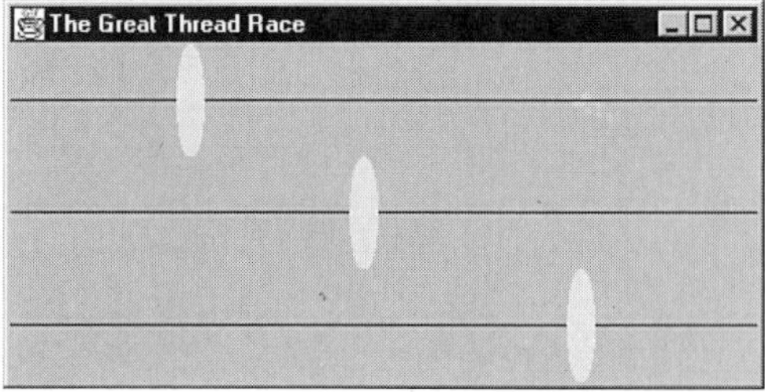

FIG. 13.10
`GreatRace` with increased priorities under Windows 95.

If you run it again under Netscape, the last racer also wins, but just barely (see Figure 13.11).

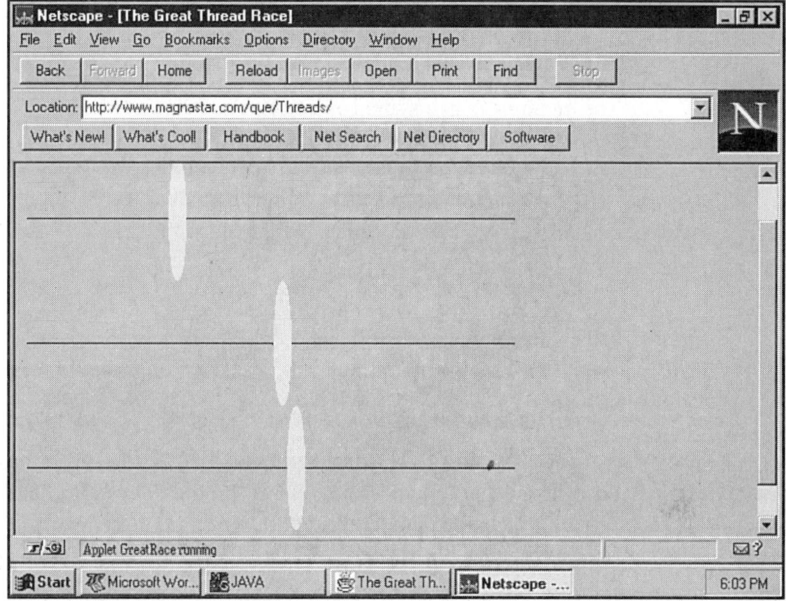

FIG. 13.11
`GreatRace` with increased priorities as an applet under Windows 95.

This difference is important to realize. If you're going to depend on the priority of your threads, make sure that you test the application on both a Windows and Macintosh or UNIX machine. If you don't have the luxury of a UNIX machine or Macintosh, it seems that running the program as a Java application rather than a Java applet is a closer approximation to how the thread priorities should be handled, as you saw in the last two figures.

CAUTION

These thread priority differences make it dangerous to not put your threads to sleep occasionally if you're only using a Windows 95 machine. The paint thread, which is a low-priority thread, will get a chance at the processor under Windows, but only because it will be able to keep up just as the racers did. However, this does not work under a Macintosh or UNIX machine.

Synchronization

When dealing with multiple threads, consider this: What happens when two or more threads want to access the same variable at the same time, and at least one of the threads wants to change the variable? If they were allowed to do this at will, chaos would reign. For example, while one thread reads Joe Smith's record, another thread tries to change his salary (Joe has earned a 50-cent raise). The problem is that this little change causes the thread reading the file in the middle of the other update to see something somewhat random, and it thinks Joe has gotten a $500 raise. That's a great thing for Joe, but not such a great thing for the company, and probably a worse thing for the programmer who will lose his job because of it. How do you resolve this?

The first thing to do is declare the method that will change the data and the method that will read to be synchronized. Java's keyword, `synchronized`, tells the system to put a lock around a particular method. At most, one thread may be in any `synchronized` method at a time. Listing 13.7 shows an example of two synchronized methods.

Listing 13.7 Two *synchronized* Methods

```
public synchronized void setVar(int){
  myVar=x;
}

public synchronized int getVar (){
  return myVar;
}
```

Now, while in `setVar()`, the JVM sets a condition lock, and no other thread will be allowed to enter a `synchronized` method, including `getVar()`, until `setVar()` has finished. Because the other threads are prevented from entering `getVar()`, no thread will obtain incorrect information because `setVar()` is in mid-write.

Don't make all your methods synchronized or you won't be able to do any multithreading at all because the other threads will wait for the lock to be released and only one thread will be active at a time. But even with only a couple of methods declared as `synchronized`, what happens when one thread starts a `synchronized` method, stops execution until some condition happens that needs to be set by another thread, and that other thread would itself have to go into a (blocked) `synchronized` method? The solution lies in the dining philosopher's problem.

Speaking with a Forked Tongue

What is the dining philosopher's problem? Well, I won't go into all the details, but let me lay out the scenario for you.

Five philosophers are sitting around a table with a plate of food in front of them. One chopstick lies on the table between each philosopher, for a total of five chopsticks. What happens when they all want to eat? They need two chopsticks to eat the food, but there are not enough chopsticks to go around. At most, two of them can eat at any one time—the other three will have to wait. How do you make sure that each philosopher doesn't pick up one chopstick, and none of them can get two? This will lead to starvation because no one will be able to eat. (The philosophers are too busy thinking to realize that one of them can go into the kitchen for more chopsticks; that isn't the solution.)

There are a number of ways to solve this ancient problem (at least in terms of the life of a computer). I won't even try to solve this problem for you. But it's important to realize the consequences. If you make a method `synchronized`, and it is going to stop because of some condition that can only be set by another thread, make sure that you exit the method and return the chopstick to the table. If you don't, it is famine waiting to happen. The philosopher won't return his chopstick(s) to the table, and he will be waiting for something to happen that can't happen because his fellow thinkers don't have utensils to be able to start eating.

Changing the Running State of the Threads

Threads have a number of possible states. Let's take a look at how to change the state and what the effects are. The methods covered here are:

- `start()`
- `yield()`
- `destroy()`
- `sleep(long)`, `sleep(long,int)`
- `*stop()`
- `*resume()`
- `*suspend()`

*These methods have been deprecated, so generally speaking don't use them.

`start()` and `stop()` are relatively simple operations for a thread. `start()` tells a thread to start the `run()` method of its associated `Runnable` object.

`stop()` tells the thread to stop. There is more that goes into `stop()`—it actually throws a `ThreadDeath` object at the thread. In almost every situation, you should not try to catch this object. The only time you need to consider doing so is if you have a number of extraordinary things you need to clean up before you can stop.

CAUTION

`stop()`,`suspend()`, and `resume()` have all been deprecated in JDK 1.2. This is because they can inherently lead to thread deadlocks, like we talked about with the philosophers. Instead of using these methods, you should use conditions in the `run()` method to produce the same result.

CAUTION

If you catch the `ThreadDeath` object, be sure to throw it again. If you don't do this, the thread will not actually stop, and, because the error handler won't notice this, nothing will ever complain.

You have already briefly looked at the `sleep()` method, when putting the `Threadable` to sleep in the `GreatRace`. Putting a thread to sleep essentially tells the VM, "I'm done with what I am doing right now; wake me up in a little while." By putting a thread to sleep, you are allowing lower-priority threads a chance to get a shot at the processor. This is especially important when very low-priority threads are doing tasks that, although not as important, still need to be done periodically. Without stepping out of the way occasionally, your thread can put these threads into starvation.

The `sleep()` method comes in two varieties. The first is `sleep(long)`, which tells the interpreter that you want to go to sleep for a certain number of milliseconds:

```
thisThread.sleep(100);
```

The only problem with this version is that a millisecond, although only an instant for humans, is an awfully long time for a computer. Even on a 486/33 computer, this is enough time for the processor to do 25,000 instructions. On high-end workstations, hundreds of thousands of instructions can be done in one millisecond.

As a result, there is a second incantation: `sleep(long,int)`. With this version of the `sleep` command, you can put a thread to sleep for a number of milliseconds, plus a few nanoseconds:

```
thisThread.sleep(99,250);
```

`suspend()` and `resume()` are two methods that you can use to put threads to sleep until some other event has occurred. One such example is if you were about to start a huge mathematical computation, such as finding the millionth prime number, and you don't want the other threads to be taking up any of the processor until the answer had been computed. (Incidentally, if you're really trying to find the millionth prime number, I would suggest you write the program in a language other than Java. Fortran still is king for this type of calculation—and get yourself a very large computer.)

Again, as of JDK 1.2, `suspend()` and `resume()` have been deprecated. You should have your thread monitor its status and use a `wait()`, `notify()` scheme.

`yield()` works a bit differently from `suspend()`. `yield()` is much closer to `sleep()`. With `yield()` you're telling the interpreter that you want to get out of the way of the other threads, but when they are done, you want to pick back up. `yield()` does not require a `resume()` to start back up when the other threads have stopped, gone to sleep, or died.

The last method to change a thread's running state is `destroy()`. In general, don't use `destroy()`. `destroy()` does not do any cleanup on the thread; it just destroys it. Because it is essentially the same as shutting down a program in progress, you should use `destroy()` only as a last resort.

Obtaining the Number of Threads That Are Running

`Java.lang.Thread` has one method that deals with determining the number of threads that are running: `activeCount()`.

`Thread.activeCount()` returns the integer number of the number of threads that are running in the current `ThreadGroup`. This is used in the `GreatRace` to find out when all the threads have finished executing. Notice that in the `init()` method, you check the number of threads that are running when you start your program. In the `run()` method, you then compare this number plus two to the number of threads currently running to see whether your racers have finished the race:

```
while(Thread.activeCount()>numberofThreadsAtStart+2){
```

NOTE Why add +2? You need to account for two additional threads that do not exist before the race starts. The first one is made out of `GreatRace(thisThread)`, which actually runs through the main loop of `GreatRace`. The other thread that has not started up at the point the `init()` method is hit is the `Screen_Updater` thread. This thread does not start until it is required to do something.

As with most programming solutions, you have many ways to determine whether all the racers have finished. You can use thread messaging with `PipedInputStream` and `PipedOutputStream`, or check to see whether the threads are alive.

Finding All the Threads That Are Running

Sometimes it's necessary to be able to see all the threads that are running. For instance, what if you did not know that there were two threads you needed to account for in the `main()` loop of the `GreatRace`? There are three methods in `java.lang.Thread` that help you show just this information:

- `enumerate(Thread[])`
- `getName()`
- `setName(String)`

`enumerate(Thread[])` is used to get a list of all the threads that are running in the current `ThreadGroup`. `getName()` is used to get the name assigned to the thread, whereas its counterpart `setName(String)` is used to actually set this name. By default, if you do not pass in a name for the thread to the constructor of a thread, it is assigned the default name `Thread-`*x* where *x* is a unique number for that thread.

Let's modify the `GreatRace` a bit to show all the threads that are running. Change the `run()` method to look like what's shown in Listing 13.8.

Part II
Ch 13

Listing 13.8 New *run()* Method for *GreatRace*

```
public void run(){
  Thread allThreads[];
  //Loop around until all of the racers have finished the race.
  while(Thread.activeCount()>1){
    try{
      //Create a Thread array for allThreads.
      allThreads = new Thread[Thread.activeCount()];
      //Obtain a link to all of the current Threads.
      Thread.enumerate (allThreads);
      //Display the name of all the Threads.
      System.out.println("****** New List ***** ");
      for (int x=0;x<allThreads.length;x++)
        System.out.println("Thread:"+allThreads[x].getName()
➥+":"+allThreads[x].getPriority()+":"+allThreads[x].isDaemon());
```

continues

Listing 13.8 Continued

```
          thisThread.sleep(1000);
        }  catch (InterruptedException e){
           System.out.println("thisThread was interrupted");         }
      }

    //Once the race is done, end the program.
    if (inApplet){

      destroy();
      }
    else
      System.exit(0);
  }
```

The new set of lines is at the beginning of the `while()` loop. These lines create an array of threads, use the `enumerate` method, which was just talked about, and write out the name of each of the threads to `System.out`.

Now recompile the program and run it. Under Netscape, make sure that you show the Java Console by choosing Options, Show Java Console (see Figure 13.12).

As the race progresses and each of the racers completes the race, you can see that the number of active threads really does decrease. In fact, run the application and give it a number higher than three (see Figure 13.13). In other words, try:

```
java GreatRace 5
```

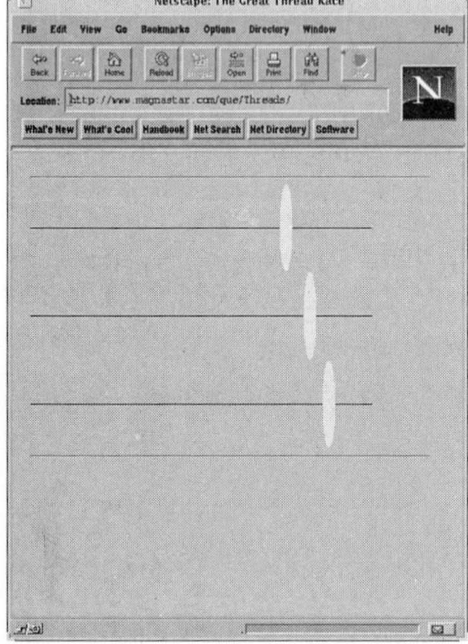

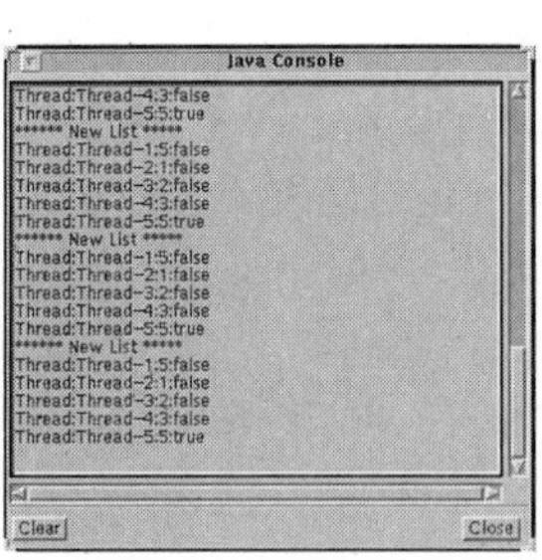

FIG. 13.12 The `GreatRace` running under Netscape with the Java Console showing.

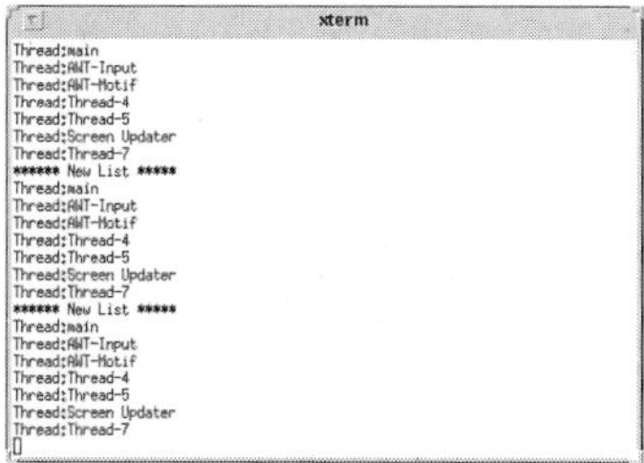

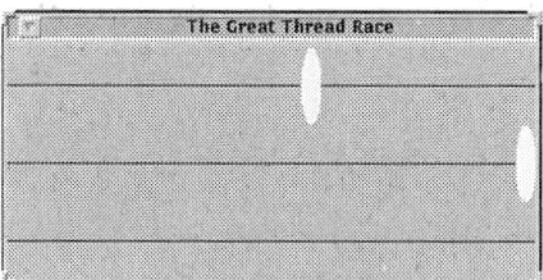

FIG. 13.13
GreatRace can be run with five racers.

The Daemon Property

Threads can be one of two types: either a user thread or a daemon thread.

So what is a daemon? Well, *Webster's Dictionary* says it is "a supernatural being or force, not specifically evil."

In a sense, *Webster's* is right, even with respect to daemon threads. Although the thread is not actually supernatural and it is definitely not evil, a daemon thread is not a natural thread, either. You can set off daemon threads on a path without ever worrying whether they come back. After you start a daemon thread, you don't need to worry about stopping it. When the thread reaches the end of the tasks it was assigned, it stops and changes its state to inactive, much like user threads.

An important difference between daemon threads and user threads is that daemon threads can run all the time. If the Java interpreter determines that only daemon threads are running, it will exit, without worrying whether the daemon threads have finished. This is useful because it enables you to start threads that do things such as monitoring; they die on their own when there is nothing else running.

The usefulness of this technique is limited for graphical Java applications because, by default, several base threads are not set to be daemon. These include:

- `AWT-Input`
- `Main`
- `AWT-Motif`
- `Screen_Updater`

Unfortunately, this means that any application using the `AWT` class will have non-daemon threads that prevent the application from exiting.

Two methods in `java.lang.Thread` deal with the daemonic state assigned to a thread:

- `isDaemon()`
- `setDaemon(boolean)`

The first method, `isDaemon()`, is used to test the state of a particular thread. Occasionally, this is useful to an object running as a thread so that it can determine whether it is running as a daemon or a regular thread. `isDaemon()` returns `true` if the thread is a daemon, and `false` otherwise.

The second method, `setDaemon(boolean)`, is used to change the daemonic state of the thread. To make a thread a daemon, you indicate this by setting the input value to `true`. To change it back to a user thread, you set the `Boolean` value to `false`.

If you had wanted to make each of the racers in the `GreatRace` daemon threads, you could have done so. In the `init() for` loop, this would have looked like Listing 13.9.

Listing 13.9 New *for* Loop for *init()* Method in *GreatRace.java*

```
for (int x=0;x<racerCount;x++){
    theRacers[x]=new Threader ("Racer #"+x);
    theRacers[x].resize(size().width,size().height/racerCount);
    add (theRacers[x]);
    theThreads[x]=new Thread(theRacers[x]);
    theThreads[x].setDaemon(true);
}
```

CHAPTER 14

Writing an Applet

In this chapter

Java's Children

In the beginning there was FTP, and then came Telnet; years later Telnet begot the Web. The Web was static and without life until there came CGI, but CGI required a submit button and whole new pages to be downloaded, and the world saw that this was not good. Then a few visionaries saw a product called Oak lying in the ashes, and like a phoenix, they resurrected it to make the Web dynamic and client/server. They renamed this product Java, with children they called applets. The world paused and saw that it was good.

If you're new to Java, one thing you're probably dying to learn how to do is write applets. Applets are those Java programs you have seen running all over the World Wide Web. They provide a fascinating layer on top of the already dynamic Java language, which extends far beyond traditional programming architecture and methodology. When you write an applet, you create a program that can not only be run on just about any computer but also can be included in a standard HTML page. Now that you've learned the Java language, you are no doubt excited to start creating applets, those dynamic creatures you see all over the Internet. In this chapter, you will learn to apply your new knowledge toward writing Java applets.

Applets and HTML

Because you're interested in writing Java applets, you're probably already familiar with using HTML (Hypertext Markup Language) to create Web pages. If not, it's probably not a bad idea to pick up a book on HTML such as Que's *Special Edition Using HTML 4*, Fourth Edition, to get some idea of how that markup language actually works.

As you now know, Java can be used to create two types of programs: applets and standalone applications. An applet must be included as part of a Web page, such as an image or a line of text. When your Java-capable Web browser loads an HTML document containing a reference to an applet, the applet is also loaded and executed. (See Chapter 1, "What Java Can Do for You," for more information.)

Let's quickly review how an applet's code comes to run on your computer. When the browser detects an `<APPLET>` tag in an HTML file, it will retrieve the class files for the applet from the server. The bytecode verifier then determines whether the class is a legitimate one. Assuming that the class is legit, the verifier will start to process the class file. As the VM detects import statements, it will continue to go back to the server for more class files until it has downloaded all the code for the applet. For a visual depiction of this cycle see Figure 14.1.

Including a Java Applet in an HTML Page

If your primary goal with this chapter is to be able to display the "Java Compliant" logo on your pages, this section is for you. The simplest means to obtain a Java applet is to get one that has already been built, or that you contract to have built for you. If you have not had time to read the rest of this book and learn to program in Java yourself, this is probably the direction you will take. Look at how to include in a Web page a simple applet from MagnaStar, Inc., called Muncher.

FIG. 14.1
The bytecode verifier will continue to return to the server until all the applet code has been downloaded.

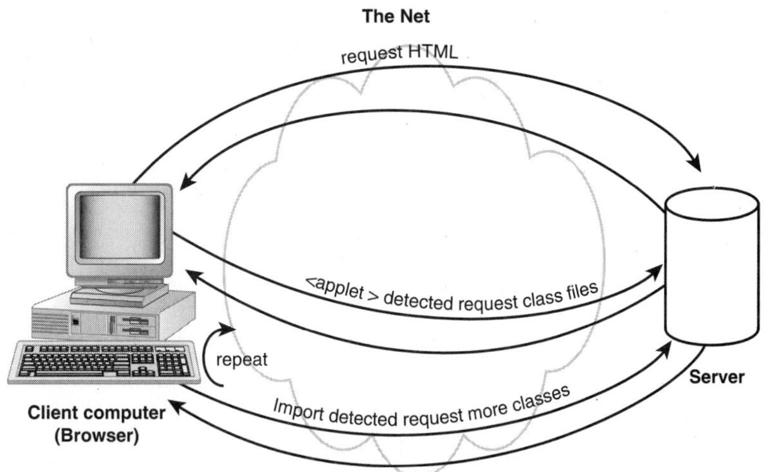

Listing 14.1 shows the simplest version of an HTML file that could be used to display `Muncher`.

Listing 14.1 An HTML File that Includes the *Muncher* Applet

```
<HTML>
<BODY>
<APPLET  CODE="GobLoader.class" HEIGHT=0 WIDTH=0></APPLET>
</BODY>
</HTML>
```

Notice the `<APPLET>` tag on the third line. The `<APPLET>` tag is used to indicate to the browser that you want it to include an applet on your page. In many ways the `<APPLET>` tag is similar to the `<IMG>` tag. There are three key attributes to notice about the `<APPLET>` tag: `CODE`, `HEIGHT`, and `WIDTH`.

NOTE Like most HTML tags, the `<APPLET>` tag is mostly case-insensitive. In other words, all three of the following tags perform the same thing:

```
<APPLET  CODE="GobLoader.class" height=0 width=0></APPLET>
<Applet  code="GobLoader.class" HEIGHT=0 WIDTH=0></Applet>
<apPlEt  cOdE="GobLoader.class" height=0 width=0></ApPlET>
```

However, an important distinction needs to be made. Although the `<APPLET>` tag itself is case-insensitive, its attribute values are not. This means that you cannot enter `GobLoader` as `gobloader` or `GOBLOADER`.

The first attribute of the `<APPLET>` tag is the `CODE` statement. The `CODE` value of `<APPLET>` is similar to the `SRC` value of `<IMG>`. In the case of `<APPLET>`, the `CODE` value must be set to the name of the main class file of the applet. In the case of `Muncher`, there are a number of classes, but the only one you should include in the HTML file is `GobLoader.class` (`Muncher` used to be called `Gobbler`, so the name is a hold over). This is important to realize; including the wrong class name can cause some strange and disastrous problems. It's also important to remember that having a `CODE` value is a required portion of an `<APPLET>` tag, unless an alternative `OBJECT` attribute is not present.

NOTE Most applets come with either a description of which class file to include, or a sample HTML file you can look at to find this answer. Alternatively, the class name is the one thing you can see when viewing the HTML document source on another site.

The second and third attributes to notice are the `HEIGHT` and `WIDTH` attributes. These are identical to those in the `<IMG>` tag. There is one unique thing about an applet, though, that is not exactly the same as an image. Some applets, such as `Muncher`, don't actually take up any space on the Web page. Instead they create their own windows. This means that the size should be set to `0`. In addition, unlike images, for almost all applets, the `HEIGHT` and `WIDTH` attributes should be set. With images, if you do not specify the height and width, the browser can figure them out on its own eventually. With applets, this is usually not the case.

The final thing to notice about the `<APPLET>` tag is the closing `</APPLET>` tag. The ending tag is required for an applet. In addition, as you will see in Listing 14.2, because the `<APPLET>` tag does not have an `ALT` attribute like `<IMG>`, the space before the `</APPLET>` tag can be used to include alternative information.

Including Alternative Information

Listing 14.2 shows a more complete version of the HTML for `Muncher` (see Figure 14.2).

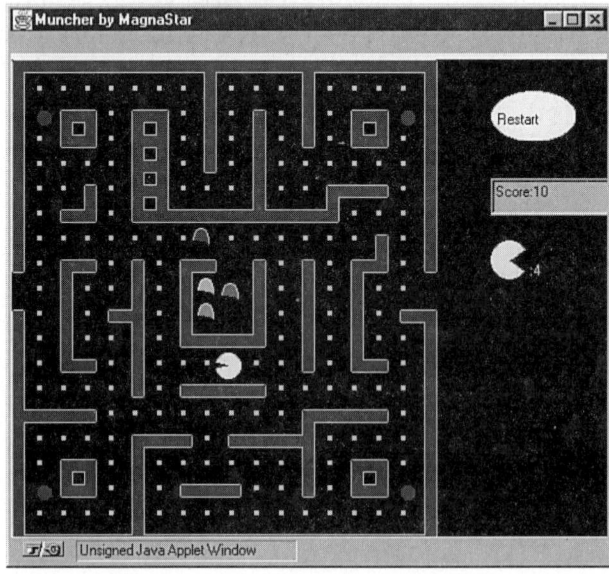

FIG. 14.2
`Muncher` is a shareware applet available on the Internet.

Listing 14.2 An HTML File That Includes an Applet Plus Alternative Information for Non-Java Browsers

```
<HTML>
<BODY>
<APPLET CODE="GobLoader.class" HEIGHT=0 WIDTH=0>
Warning: You are not using a Java browser. There is an applet on this
page you cannot see.
If you had a Java-enabled browser you would see something similar to the picture
➥below<BR>
<IMG SRC="gobbler.gif" ALT="Game Picture">
</APPLET>
</BODY>
</HTML>
```

As you can see, you can include any standard HTML between the `<APPLET>` and `</APPLET>` tag. A non-Java browser will ignore the `<APPLET>` tag and only read this information.

The <*PARAM*> Tag Java applets have a tag in addition to `<APPLET>`. This HTML tag is `<PARAM>`. Many applets use the parameter tag to specify additional information about the applet's behavior. Take a look at another applet that does this. `GrayButton`, also from MagnaStar, Inc., provides a simple means of adding some interaction to your Web pages (see Figure 14.3).

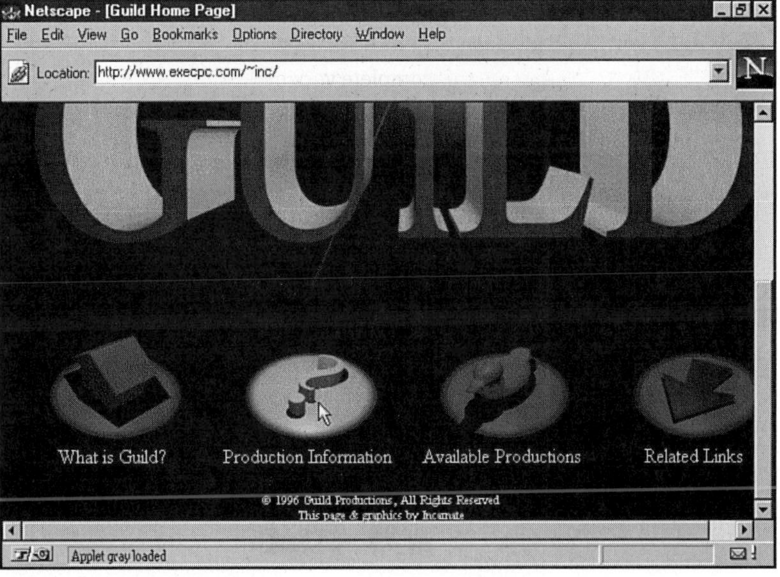

FIG. 14.3
The `GrayButton` applet is used on this page to provide some limited interaction.

The complete listing for including `GrayButton` on your Web page is shown in Listing 14.3.

Listing 14.3 An HTML File for an Applet That Uses *<PARAM>* Tags

```
<HTML>
<BODY>
<APPLET CODE="gray.class"  WIDTH=300 HEIGHT=300>
<PARAM NAME="graphic" VALUE ="http://www.magnastar.com/NOW.GIF">
<PARAM NAME ="link" VALUE="http://www.magnastar.com/GrayButton/license.html">
<A HREF="license.html"><IMG SRC="NOW.GIF"></a>
</APPLET>
</BODY>
</HTML>
```

This example demonstrates two important things. First note the `<PARAM>` tags on lines 4 and 5. To get this applet to run, you must specify a graphic for it to load and a place for it to link to if the user clicks that button. Take a look at the syntax for the `<PARAM>` tag.

The `<PARAM>` tag must be included between the `<APPLET>` and the `</APPLET>` tags. A `<PARAM>` tag anywhere else has no point of reference, so the browser ignores it.

In general, the `<PARAM>` tag has two attributes of its own: `NAME` and `VALUE`. The `NAME` attribute is used to specify which parameter you are setting. In the case of the `GrayButton`, there are two `NAME`s that must be set, `"graphic"` and `"link"`.

The second attribute of the `<PARAM>` tag is `VALUE`. The `VALUE` attribute is used to dictate the `VALUE` that should be associated with the `NAME`. The `VALUE` does not have to be a string, although both of them with `GrayButton` are. The `VALUE` could easily be a number if the applet called for that type of data.

NOTE In addition to the `<PARAM>` tags, the example in Listing 14.3 also shows the use of an image link before the `</APPLET>`. This is another example of an alternative display. If the viewer does not have a Java-enabled browser, the graphic will be displayed instead. In the case of `GrayButton`, this works out especially nice, because the only thing that is lost without a Java browser is the level of interaction.

Additional *<APPLET>* Attributes

In addition to the attributes already mentioned, you can use several attribute values to further customize how an applet will behave, as shown in Table 14.1.

Table 14.1 Attributes for the *<APPLET>* Tag

Attribute	Value	Description
`CODE*`	Class name	Defines the name of the class file that extends `java.applet.Applet`.
`HEIGHT^`	Number	Height in pixels that the applet occupies vertically on the Web page.

Attribute	Value	Description
WIDTH^	Number	Width in pixels that the applet occupies horizontally on the Web page.
VSPACE	Number	Vertical space in pixels between the applet and the rest of the HTML. Behaves identically to the Vspace value of an <IMG> tag.
HSPACE	Number	Horizontal space in pixels between the applet and the rest of the HTML. Behaves identically to the HSpace value of an <IMG> tag.
ALIGN	Any of: LEFT, RIGHT, TOP, TEXTTOP, MIDDLE, ABSMIDDLE, BASELINE, BOTTOM, ABSBOTTOM	Indicates the alignment of the applet in relationship to the rest of the page. These values work the same as their <IMG> counterparts.
ALT	String	Specifies alternate text to be displayed by the browser if it is unable to display the actual applet. This attribute is only utilized if the browser understands the <APPLET> tag but is unable to display the applet. Otherwise, the open HTML between the <APPLET> and </APPLET> tags is displayed.
ARCHIVE	Archive list	Contains a list of archives and other resources that should be "preloaded" by the browser before it begins execution.
OBJECT	Serialized applet	Contains the name of the file that has a serialized representation of the applet. The init() method of the applet is not called because it is presumed to have been called on the serialized applet; however, the start() method is. Note: If an OBJECT attribute is present, a CODE attribute need not be; however, one or the other is required.
CODEBASE	URL	URL of base directory where the class files for the applet are located (under the security manager). This host, and the host where the HTML with the <APPLET> tag is located, are the only hosts that can be accessed by the applet.

** Required*
^ Highly Recommended

To sum up, look at Listing 14.4. The text in normal characters is typed literally; the text shown in italics is replaced by whatever is appropriate for the applet you're including in the document. The first and last lines are required. Other lines in the tag are optional. Figure 14.4 shows how attributes can affect an applet's placement.

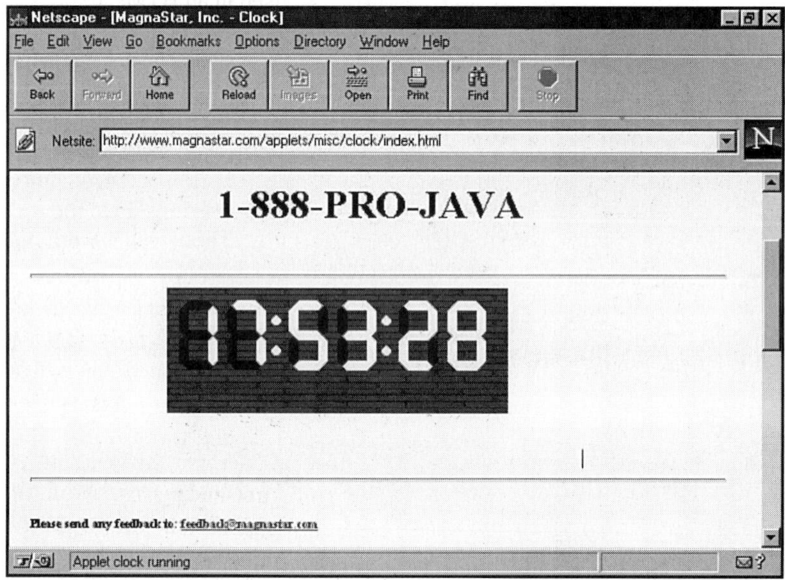

FIG. 14.4 As you look at this figure, you can see how the various attributes affect the applet's placement.

Listing 14.4 ***LST14_04.TXT*—The <*APPLET*> Tag**

```
<APPLET attributes>
parameters
alternate-content
</APPLET>
```

Using Java Plug-in

One of the best innovations that Sun Microsystems, Inc. has added in a while is known as the Java Plug-in. Java Plug-in was designed to directly address the fragmentation of the Java Virtual Machine in the variety of browsers. Over time, each browser started to include its own version of the VM. This led to minor differences between each of the browsers. In addition, Microsoft chose not to implement some of the key features of the JDK.

To use the Java Plug-in, users must download the Java Plug-in first and plug it into their browsers. Adding the Java Plug-in gives the browser full support for the latest JDK. As an added benefit, the way the Java Plug-in is used it will actually upgrade itself. The great thing about this is it means in the future you will no longer have to concern yourself with using JDK 1.2 and future JDKs because browsers will already be upgraded.

Using Java Plug-in in Internet Explorer

Using Java Plug-in in Internet Explorer requires that you use a different pattern other than the one that you just learned with the <APPLET> tag. Java Plug-in is actually a different program for Internet Explorer altogether, so you need to include it just like any other ActiveX component. Listing 14.5 shows how Java Plug-in can be used in an HTML page designed for Internet Explorer, with the same applet used previously in Listing 14.3.

Listing 14.5 Using Java Plug-in in Internet Explorer

```
<OBJECT CLASSID="clsid:8AD9C840-044E-11D1-B3E9-00805F499D93"
WIDTH="300" HEIGHT="300" ALIGN="baseline"
codebase="http://java.sun.com/products/plugin/1.1/jinstall-11-
win32.cab#Version=1,1,0,0">
<PARAM NAME="code" VALUE="gray.class">
<PARAM NAME="codebase" VALUE="html/">
<PARAM NAME="graphic" VALUE ="http://www.magnastar.com/NOW.GIF">
<PARAM NAME ="link" VALUE="http://www.magnastar.com/GrayButton/license.html">
No JDK 1.2 support for APPLET!!
</OBJECT>
```

The <OBJECT> tag in Listing 14.5 has many of the same attributes as the <APPLET> tag in Listing 14.3. There are some differences, however. First, and perhaps most obvious, is the CLASSID parameter. This ID identifies not the Java class, but rather the Java Plug-in. It should always be this number, so you don't have to worry about where this came from. The number will actually be different for each different version of the Java Plug-in, so you may need to find out what the latest version is and get its CLASSID.

Now, the CODEBASE in the <OBJECT> tag that you see is not the CODEBASE for the java class, but it's the CODEBASE for the Java Plug-in. Because both the code and CODEBASE parameters can't be specified in the <OBJECT> tag itself, they end up in the <PARAM> tags between <OBJECT> and </OBJECT>.

Using Java Plug-in in Netscape

Netscape. does not use ActiveX components like Internet Explorer. Instead, you need to use a Netscape plug-in. Listing 14.6 shows how to use Java Plug-in in Netscape.

Listing 14.6 Using Java Plug-in in Netscape.

```
<EMBED TYPE="application/x-java-applet;version=1.2" WIDTH="300" HEIGHT="300"
ALIGN="baseline" CODE="gray.class" CODEBASE="html/"
GRAPHIC="http://www.magnastar.com/NOW.GIF"
LINK="http://www.magnastar.com/GrayButton/license.html"
pluginspage="http://java.sun.com/products/plugin/1.1/plugin-install.html">
<NOEMBED>
No JDK 1.2 support for APPLET!!
</NOEMBED>
</EMBED>
```

With the <EMBED> tag, the new parameter isn't CLASSID; instead it's the TYPE value. You might notice that there is a VERSION value in the type. The VERSION allows you to specify the Java version you wish to use. Note the PLUGINSPAGE parameter, which specifies where Netscape can find the plug-in if it hasn't already downloaded it.

One of the interesting things about using an <EMBED> tag is that there are no equivalents to the <PARAM> tag. Instead, you see all of the values listed inside of the <EMBED> tag itself. Look at the LINK parameter for an example of how this is used.

Setting Up the HTML for All Browsers

You can combine the <EMBED> and <OBJECT> tags as shown in Listing 14.7 so that both Netscape and Internet Explorer will use Java Plug-in.

Listing 14.7 Using Java Plug-in in Both Internet Explorer and Netscape

```
<OBJECT CLASSID="clsid:8AD9C840-044E-11D1-B3E9-00805F499D93"
WIDTH="300" HEIGHT="300" ALIGN="baseline"
codebase="http://java.sun.com/products/plugin/1.1/jinstall-11-win32.cab
➥#Version=1,1,0,0"><PARAM NAME="code" VALUE="gray.class">
<PARAM NAME="codebase" VALUE="html/">
<PARAM NAME="graphic" VALUE ="http://www.magnastar.com/NOW.GIF">
<PARAM NAME ="link" VALUE="http://www.magnastar.com/GrayButton/license.html">
<PARAM NAME="type" VALUE="application/x-java-applet;version=1.1">
<COMMENT>
<EMBED TYPE="application/x-java-applet;version=1.1" WIDTH="300" HEIGHT="300"
ALIGN="baseline" CODE="gray.class" CODEBASE="html/"
GRAPHIC=http://www.magnastar.com/NOW.GIF
LINK="http://www.magnastar.com/GrayButton/license.html"
pluginspage="http://java.sun.com/products/plugin/1.1/plugin-install.html">
<NOEMBED>
</COMMENT>
No JDK 1.2 support for APPLET!!
</NOEMBED></EMBED>
</OBJECT>
```

But Listing 14.7 tries to use Java Plug-in, even if it's on a browser that doesn't support the ActiveX or plug-in. So to be truly accurate, the best thing to do is use Listing 14.8. This listing includes the necessary JavaScript code to have the browser properly look for the right system. Under Internet Explorer and Netscape on a Windows machine the browser will use the Java Plug-in, and on all other platforms it will use the built-in VM. Normally you can just copy Listing 14.8 into your HTML and replace all of the correct parameters, so even though this looks complicated, you really just need to copy and paste.

Listing 14.8 Using the Best Java VM Regardless of Platform

```
<SCRIPT LANGUAGE="JavaScript"><!--
if (_ie == true) document.writeln('<OBJECT
CLASSID="clsid:8AD9C840-044E-11D1-B3E9-00805F499D93"
```

```
WIDTH="300" HEIGHT="300" ALIGN="baseline"
codebase="http://java.sun.com/products/plugin/1.1/jinstall-11-
➥win32.cab#Version=1,1,0,0">
<NOEMBED><XMP>');
else if (_ns == true) document.writeln('<EMBED
TYPE="application/x-java-applet;version=1.1" WIDTH="200" HEIGHT="200"
ALIGN="baseline" CODE="gray.class" CODEBASE="html/"
GRAPHIC=http://www.magnastar.com/NOW.GIF
LINK ="http://www.magnastar.com/GrayButton/license.html"
pluginspage="http://java.sun.com/products/plugin/1.1/plugin-install.html">
<NOEMBED><XMP>');
//--></SCRIPT>
<APPLET CODE="gray.class" CODEBASE="html/" ALIGN="baseline"
WIDTH="300" HEIGHT="300"></XMP>
<PARAM NAME="code" VALUE="gray.class">
<PARAM NAME="codebase" VALUE="html/">
<PARAM NAME="graphic" VALUE ="http://www.magnastar.com/NOW.GIF">
<PARAM NAME ="link" VALUE="http://www.magnastar.com/GrayButton/license.html">
No JDK 1.2 support for APPLET!!
</APPLET></NOEMBED></EMBED></OBJECT>
```

Begin Developing Java Applets

Now that you have explored how to include an applet in an HTML page, take a look at how to write some of your own.

Many years ago, two programming visionaries named Kernie and Richie invented a language called C. The first program they wrote was called Hello World. Since that time, the first program that any programmer writes in any language simply displays "Hello World" to the screen. So, take a look at how to write the `HelloWorld` applet in Java.

In the preceding several chapters, you have learned about each of the parts of the Hello World application, but let's review it one more time, as shown in Listing 14.9.

Listing 14.9 Hello World as an Applet

```
import java.applet.Applet;
import java.awt.Graphics;
/*
 *
 * HelloWorld
 *
 */
public class HelloWorld extends Applet {
     public void paint (Graphics g){
          g.drawString ("HelloWorld",5,20);
     }
}
```

To create the `HelloWorld` applet, copy the contents of Listing 14.9 into a file called `HelloWorld.java`. It is important that you call the file `HelloWorld.java`, or you will be unable to compile the program. Now, assuming that you have installed the JDK from Sun in your path, compile the program by typing the following at a command prompt:

```
javac HelloWorld.java
```

NOTE Windows users, for this to work, you will need to open a DOS prompt window.

If everything has worked correctly, you should now have an additional file in your directory called `HelloWorld.class`. This file is the Java equivalent of an `.exe` file. Before you can run the applet, though, you will need to create an HTML file as discussed in the previous section. In the case of the `HelloWorld` applet, the HTML file should look like Listing 14.10.

NOTE Technically, the class file is not an executable file by itself. However, several products such as Asymetric's SuperCede and Microsoft's Visual J++ now include native compilers for Java that actually produce `.exe` files. These compilers are also known as *static compilers* and will generate `.exe` files, but are no longer platform independent.

Listing 14.10 An HTML File for the *HelloWorld* Applet

```
<HTML>
<BODY>
<APPLET CODE="HelloWorld.class" HEIGHT=100 WIDTH=100></APPLET>
</BODY>
</HTML>
```

After you have created the HTML file, you can open it in a browser like Netscape Navigator, or use one of the tools that come with the JDK called `appletviewer`. Figure 14.5 shows what happens when you load this file in Netscape.

Notice that when a Java applet is loaded, the Navigator has to go back to the server (or in this case, your hard drive) to download the `HelloWorld.class` file before it can be run. This is done exactly the same way that a GIF file is grabbed for an image, but it does take an extra second or two.

Understanding Hello World—Building Applets

Now, go back and break down the code in the `HelloWorld` applet, so you can understand it.

The first thing that you should have noticed is that `HelloWorld` extends `java.applet.Applet`. Every applet in the world must extend `Applet`. As you can see, you take advantage of object-oriented programming (OOP) inheritance to declare your applet class by subclassing Java's `Applet` class. For more information on inheritance, check out Chapter 11, "Classes."

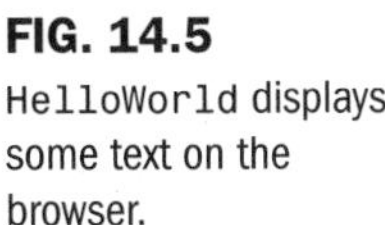

FIG. 14.5
`HelloWorld` displays some text on the browser.

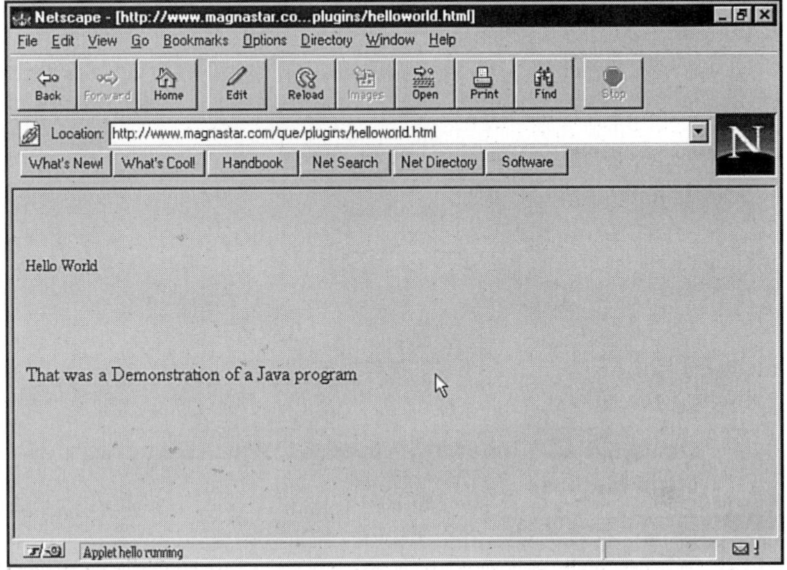

NOTE The reason it is necessary to extend `Applet` is because every browser expects to receive an `Applet` class from the `CODE` attribute. By using the polymorphic characteristics of inheritance, your custom applet, such as `HelloWorld`, is both a `HelloWorld` class and an `Applet` class.

Exploring the Life Cycle of an Applet

It might surprise you to learn that an applet actually has a life cycle. This means that throughout the time that an applet exists, certain methods will be called on that applet. To be precise, four methods are called on an applet:

`init()`—Called the first time that an applet is loaded

`start()`—Called after the `init()` method, and thereafter each time a browser returns to a page on which the applet is contained

`stop()`—Called any time a browser leaves a Web page containing the applet

`destroy()`—Called before a browser completely shuts down

Figure 14.6 shows the life cycle of an applet. To better understand how the life cycle of an applet works, take a look at a program designed to show when these methods are called. Listing 14.11 contains a program that prints out a message each time one of the methods is called and puts up a graph of this activity.

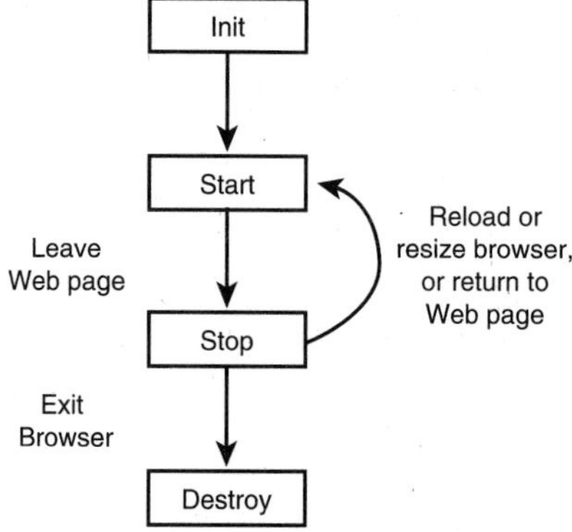

FIG. 14.6
A visual representation of the life cycle of an applet.

Listing 14.11 *InitStartStop* Applet, Which Demonstrates the Use of the Life Cycle Methods

```
import java.applet.Applet;
import java.awt.*;

/*
 *
 * InitStartStop
 *
 */
public class InitStartStop extends Applet{
     int initCount = 0;
     int startCount = 0;
     int stopCount = 0;
     int destroyCount = 0;

     public void paint (Graphics g){
          //clear the area
          g.setColor(Color.white);
          g.fillRect(0,0,size().width,size().height);
          //paint all the standard parts of the graph
          g.setColor (Color.red);
          g.drawLine (120,20,120,220);
          g.drawLine (120,220,300,220);
          //draw the labels
          g.setColor (Color.gray);
          g.drawString ( "Init Count", 5,50);
          g.drawString ( "Start Count", 5,100);
          g.drawString ( "Stop Count", 5,150);
          g.drawString ( "Destroy Count", 5,200);
          //paint the grid lines
          g.setColor(Color.lightGray);
          for (int x=(120+25);x<300;x+=25){
               g.drawLine(x,20,x,199);
          }
```

```
        //draw the bars for each of the stats
        g.setColor (Color.black);
        g.fillRect (120,30,initCount * 25,40);
        g.fillRect (120,80,startCount * 25,40);
        g.fillRect (120,130,stopCount * 25, 40);
        g.fillRect (120,180,destroyCount * 25, 40);
    }

    public void update(Graphics g){
        paint(g);
    }


    public void init(){
        initCount++;
        System.out.println("init");
        repaint();
    }

    public void start(){
        startCount++;
        System.out.println("start");
        repaint();
    }

    public void stop(){
        stopCount++;
        System.out.println("stop");
        repaint();
    }

    public void destroy(){
        destroyCount++;
        System.out.println("destroy");
        repaint();
    }

}
```

Compiling the *InitStartStop* Applet

To be able to run the `InitStartStop` applet, just like the `HelloWorld` applet, you must compile it and generate an HTML file that references the applet. To do this, first copy the contents of Listing 14.11 to a file called `InitStartStop.java`. Then compile this file using `javac`:

```
javac InitStartStop.java
```

Now, before you can actually use the `InitStartStop` applet, you must first create the HTML for it. The `InitStartStop.html` file is as follows:

```
<HTML>
<BODY>
<APPLET code="InitStartStop.class" HEIGHT=300 WIDTH=400></APPLET>
</BODY>
</HTML>
```

Finally, you're set to run the `InitStartStop` applet. To do this, load the `InitStartStop.html` file into a browser such as Netscape Navigator. The first time you load the program you will see something that looks like Figure 14.7. The `init()` method has been called once, as has the `start()` method. This should be exactly what you expected to see.

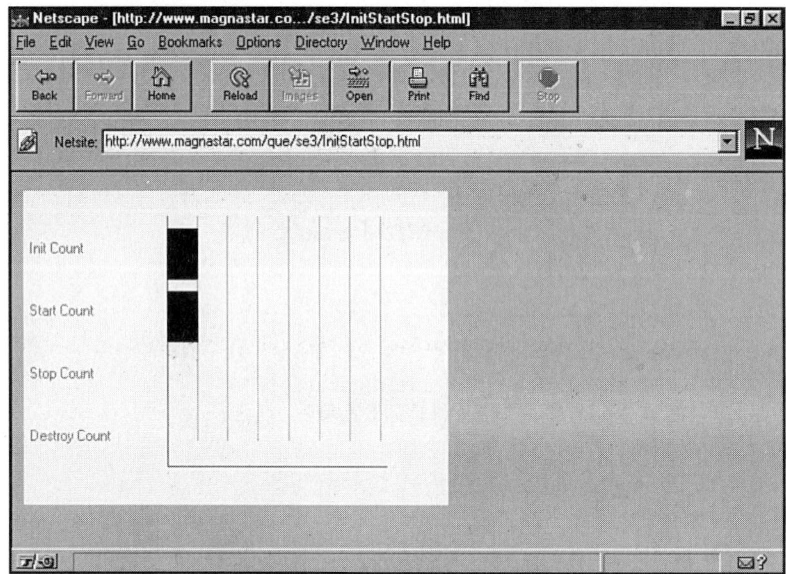

FIG. 14.7 When `InitStartStop` first starts, it has run the `init()` method and the `start()` method once.

Now click the reload button a couple of times. Each time you do, the number of times that `stop()` is called and the number of times that `start()` is called will both increment once, as demonstrated in Figure 14.8. However, the `init()` count will stay the same because the `init()` method is only called the first time the browser loads the applet.

As you run the applet, you can also look at those printout statements you were generating. To do this in Netscape 3.1 and earlier, select Options, Show Java Console. Users of Netscape 4.0 can get to the Java Console by accessing Communicator, Java Console. This should produce yet another window, as shown in Figure 14.9. Inside this window, you can see all the `System.out` messages as they appear. Try clicking reload a few more times. Now, try going to a different Web page. What happened? Well of course, `stop()` was called, and `start()` wasn't. Now click the back button. `start()` is called.

Understanding the *InitStartStop* Applet

To understand the `InitStartStop` applet, take it step by step.

```
import java.applet.Applet;
import java.awt.*;
```

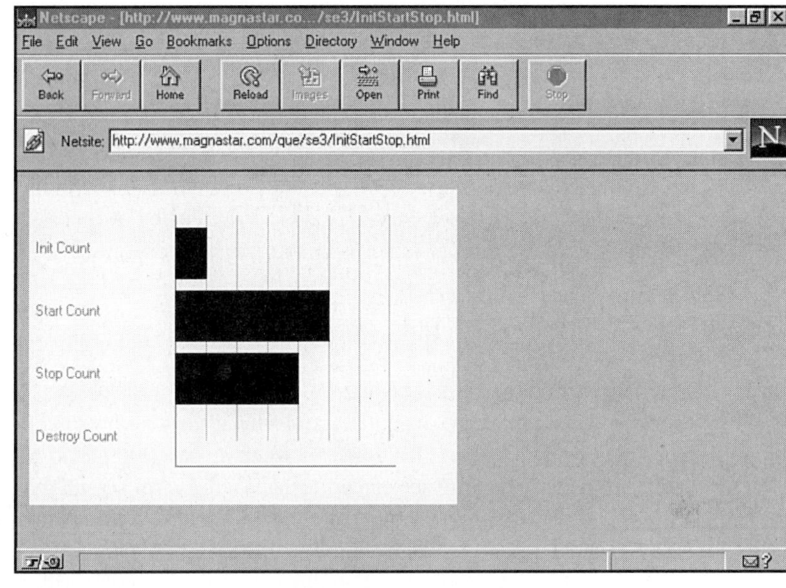

FIG. 14.8 After leaving the page and coming back several times, `start()` and `stop()` will have incremented. Notice that the applet has always started one more time than it has stopped.

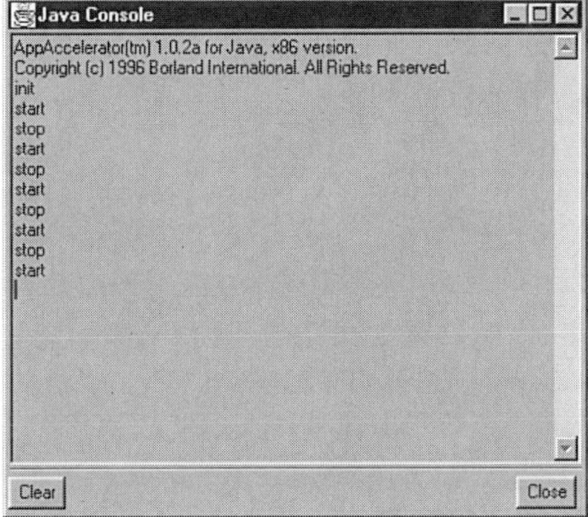

FIG. 14.9 The Java Console in Netscape shows you the `System.out` messages as they appear.

The first thing in the file are several import statements. As you learned in Chapter 11, for a class to be used (without fully qualifying its name each time), the class must first be imported. Just like the `HelloWorld` applet, `InitStartStop` needs access to the `java.awt.Graphics` class. In addition, `InitStartStop` will need access to a couple of other `java.awt` classes. So rather than import each individual class separately, the entire package of `java.awt` is imported here.

The first method in `InitStartStop` is the `paint` method. This method paints a number of things to the screen using methods available in the `java.Graphics` class. You will learn more about the `Graphics` class in Chapter 27, "Files, Streams, and Java," so for now, just concentrate on the last part of the `paint()` method.

```
//draw the bars for each of the stats
g.setColor (Color.black);
g.fillRect (120,30,initCount * 25,40);
g.fillRect (120,80,startCount * 25,40);
g.fillRect (120,130,stopCount * 25, 40);
g.fillRect (120,180,destroyCount * 25, 40);
```

The purpose of this section is to draw the actual bars that you saw indicating how many times each of the methods had been called. This is accomplished by increasing the width of the bar by 25 times the count number (such as `initCount*25`).

```
public void update(Graphics g){
     paint(g);
}
```

The next method in the class is `update()`. `update()` just calls `paint()`, so you might be wondering what it is doing there. To understand why, it's necessary to understand the relationship between `update()` and `paint()`. Ordinarily when an applet needs to be painted, either because it's just been displayed to the screen, or perhaps a different screen that had been covering the applet was just removed, the `paint()` method is called. However, when an applet only needs to be partially painted, such as when another window has only partially obscured the applet or when the `repaint()` method was called, the `update()` method is called. By default, `update()` clears the panel and then calls `paint()`. However, this can cause an annoying flicker (try running `InitStartStop` with this method removed). To get around this, it's become routine for programmers to insert an `update()` method, which does not clear the screen but calls `paint()` right away.

The next several methods are really the ones you want to see something from. Each method increments a counter, does a printout, and calls `repaint()` (which causes the `update/paint()` method to be called).

```
     public void init(){
          initCount++;
          System.out.println("init");
          repaint();
     }

     public void start(){
          startCount++;
          System.out.println("start");
          repaint();
     }

     public void stop(){
          stopCount++;
          System.out.println("stop");
          repaint();
     }
```

```
    public void destroy(){
        destroyCount++;
        System.out.println("destroy");
        repaint();
    }

}
```

Java *Animator* Applet

One of the fun things to do with Java is create simple animations. It should be pointed out that Java is not the best medium to do this. If all you want to do is create an animation, there are much better ways to do so, such as GIF89a Cel Frame animations. Or you can use the Java Media Framework discussed in Chapter 44, "Java Media Framework." However, because derivations of animations are so frequently done in Java, an animator is shown here. Listing 14.12 shows a complete version of an animator written in Java.

Listing 14.12 *Animator* Class Cycles Through Images

```
import java.awt.*;
import java.util.Vector;

public class Animator extends java.applet.Applet implements Runnable {
Vector images;
int imgNumber;
int currentImage=1;
Thread thisThread;

  public void init(){
    //Read in the number of images in the animation
    imgNumber = new Integer(getParameter("imgNumber")).intValue();

    //Load the images
    for (int x=0;x<imgNumber;x++){
      Image img = getImage(getDocumentBase(),"images/img"+(x+1));
      images.addElement(img);
      }
  }

  public void paint(Graphics g){
    g.drawImage((Image)images.elementAt(currentImage++),0,0,null);
    currentImage%=imgNumber;
    }

  public void update(Graphics g){
    paint(g);
  }

  public void start(){
    thisThread = new Thread(this);
    thisThread.start();
    }
```


continues

Listing 14.12 Continued

```
  public void stop(){
    thisThread.stop();
  }

  public void run(){
    while(true){
      try{
        thisThread.sleep(100);
        }
        catch (Exception e){}
    }
   }
}
```

You can probably tell that there is much more to this applet than to the `HelloWorld` one. To compile this program, first copy all of Listing 14.12 into a file called `Animator.java`. To run it, you will need to create an HTML file that should look something like Listing 14.13.

Listing 14.13 HTML File for Including *Animator*

```
<HTML>
<BODY>
<APPLET code="Animator.class" HEIGHT=200 WIDTH=200>
<PARAM NAME="imgNumber" VALUE="5">
</APPLET>
</BODY>
</HTML>
```

In addition to these files, you will also need to have several images that you want to animate, and you will need to place them in a subdirectory called `images`. The images must be called `img1.gif`, `img2.gif`, and so on, where `img1.gif` is the first image of the animation. You will also want to change the `imgNumber` parameter to have the correct number of images. With all that done, you should see something similar to Figure 14.10.

Now, to understand how `Animator` works, break Listing 14.12 into some more manageable chunks. First, take the first three lines of the code:

```
import java.awt.*;
import java.util.Vector;

public class Animator extends java.applet.Applet implements Runnable {
```

The first two lines serve to import other Java classes. Java is an extensible language, and the object-oriented nature of the language allows you to take advantage of prebuilt classes. The first two lines of the `Animator` code import such classes.

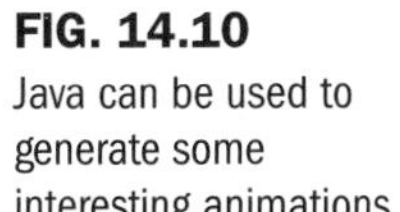

FIG. 14.10
Java can be used to generate some interesting animations.

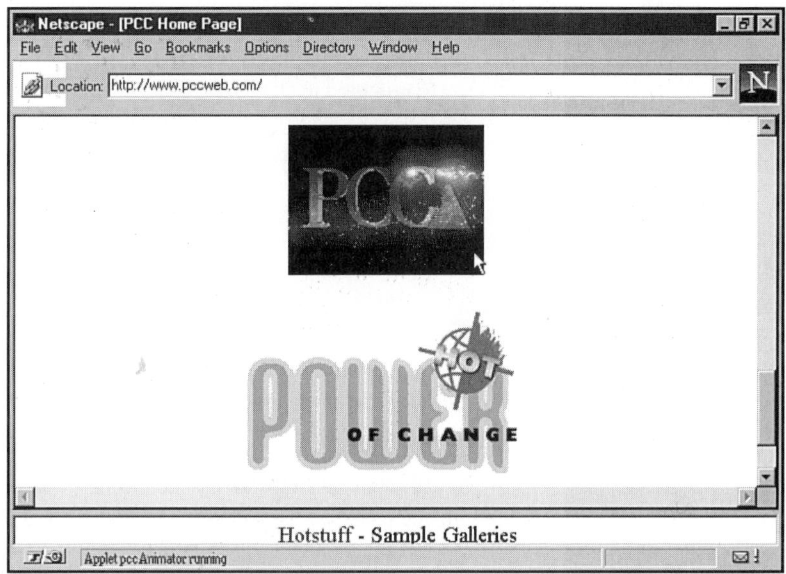

The third line of code is the class declaration. At the end of the line you will notice that the `Animator`, like `HelloWorld`, `extends java.applet.Applet`. `java.applet.Applet` is the name of the class from which all applets extend. Immediately after the class declaration is the statement `implements Runnable`, which indicates that the application can be run as a thread. It is important that `Animator` be able to run as a thread because it will continue to process even after the rest of the page is finished loading.

Immediately after these lines of code, `Animator` declares several variables of its own.

```
Vector images;
int imgNumber;
int currentImage=1;
Thread thisThread;
```

Remember from Chapter 10, "Control Flow," that Java is a strongly typed language. This means that each variable must be declared to be a specific type. In some other languages, such as JavaScript, you would have created the variables with only the `var` keyword.

```
var images;
var imgNumber;
var currentImage=1;
var thisThread;
```

For a variety of reasons, this is not really the best way to work, and Java requires that you declare the type that each variable will be. As you can see, you are creating four variables. The `Vector` is a class type that is convenient to contain a number of elements, especially if you do not know ahead of time how many you will be adding. The `thread` variable will be used to control the activity of the applet later on.

The `Animator` applet has several methods. The first of these is the `init()` method.

```
public void init(){
  //Read in the number of images in the animation
  imgNumber = new Integer(getParameter("imgNumber")).intValue();

  //Load the images
  for (int x=0;x<imgNumber;x++){
    Image img = getImage(getDocumentBase(),"images/img"+(x+1));
    images.addElement(img);
    }
}
```

The `init()` method is called when the page is initially loaded into the browser. It is convenient to use the `init()` method to set up variables that only have to be initialized once. In the case of the `Animator` class, all the images only need to be loaded once. Notice that after the `getImage` method is called, the image is added to the `Vector of images`.

The next method is the `paint()` method. The `paint()` method is called each time the applet needs to be displayed on the Web page. This can happen if the user scrolls the applet off the screen and then scrolls back, or if you specifically cause the applet to be repainted,

```
public void paint(Graphics g){
  g.drawImage((Image)images.elementAt(currentImage++),0,0,null);
  currentImage%=imgNumber;
  }
```

Without breaking the `paint()` method apart completely, break the `drawImage` line apart a bit. `drawImage()`is a method that obviously draws an image to the graphics screen. Four parameters must be given the `drawImage()` method. First, the name of the image, next the `x` and `y` locations, and finally the `imageObserver`, which should pay attention to the image.

So why is the image name `((Image)images.elementAt(currentImage++)` so complicated? Well, take it from the right side back. First, you want to display the current image (`currentImage`). It is convenient to increment the `currentImage` number so that the next time through you will display the next image and you automatically increment the `currentImage` variable (`currentImage++`). Now you have stored the images in a vector, and the way to get the current image from the vector is to use the method `elementAt` on the image object (`elementAt(CurrentImage++)`). The only problem at this point is that the vector does not really know it is holding an image. The vector only knows that it has something, and so it returns the image to you in a way that isn't quite right, so you need to perform what is known as a cast. The `(Image)` in front of the `images.elementAt` performs the cast for you, and now you have retrieved an image.

The next method is `start()`. `start()` is called each time the user goes to a specific page. But wait, isn't that when the `init()` method is called? No, not exactly. You see, the `init()` method is only called the first time the page is loaded. From that point on, each time the page is loaded, the only method called is `start()`. `start()` is called the first time too, after the `init()` method, but on successive loads only `start()` is called.

```
public void start(){
  thisThread = new Thread(this);
  thisThread.start();
  }
```

The `start()` method is a great place to put the applet into a known state. In the case of `Animator`, a thread is created. Without a complete explanation of threads, this means that the applet will continue to run as the rest of the browser does other things.

```
public void stop(){
  thisThread.stop();
}
```

See Chapter 13, "Threads." **p. 207**

A close cousin to the `start()` method is the `stop()` method, which is called each time the user leaves the page. It is important to clean up what you have started when the page is exited. The `stop()` method of `Animator` takes the thread it was running and stops it.

The last method for `Animator` is `run()`. `run()` is the method that actually runs in the thread.

```
public void run(){
  while(true){
    repaint();
    try{
      thisThread.sleep(100);
      }
      catch (Exception e){}
  }
}
```

Essentially what occurs in `Animator`'s `run` method is a constant loop that consists of first telling the `Animator` to repaint and then to place the `Animator` thread in a state known as sleep for 100ms. The result of this is that 10 times a second (1/100ms) the next frame of the animation is displayed.

An Applet That Uses Controls

As you saw in the previous applet example, applets are interactive applications that can handle messages generated by both the system and the user. Another way, besides the mouse, that you can enable user interaction is by including controls—such as buttons, menus, list boxes, and text boxes—in your applet's display. Although controls are covered thoroughly in Chapter 19, "`java.awt`: Components," you'll get an introduction to them now, as you create an applet that can connect you to various Web sites on the Internet.

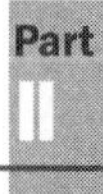

Listing 14.14 is the Java source code for the applet in question, and Listing 14.15 is the applet's HTML document. Before running this applet (by loading its HTML document into a Java-compatible browser), make your Internet connection. Then, when you run the applet, you see a window something like Figure 14.16, which shows `InternetApplet` running in Netscape Navigator 3.1. Just click one of the connection buttons, and you automatically log on to the Web site associated with the button. Figure 14.12 shows where you end up when you click the CNet button.

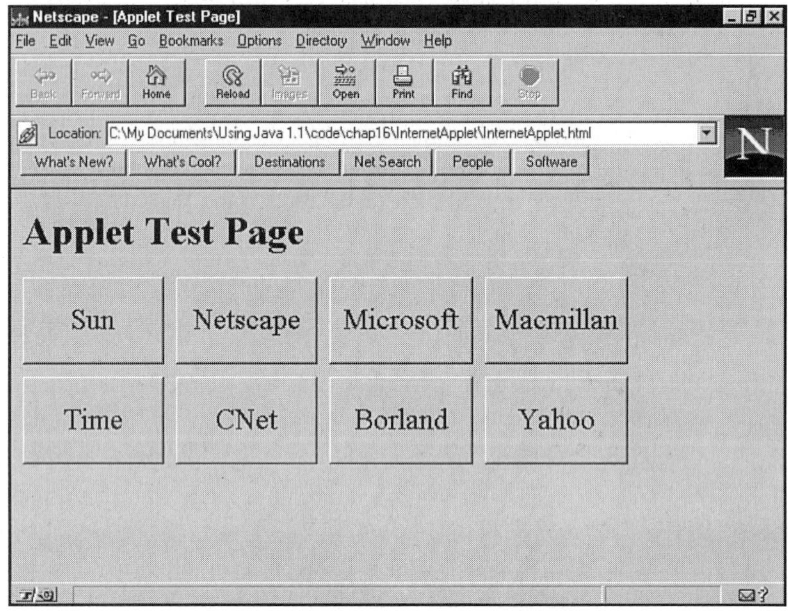

FIG. 14.11 The `InternetApplet` applet uses buttons to provide an instant connection to eight different Web sites.

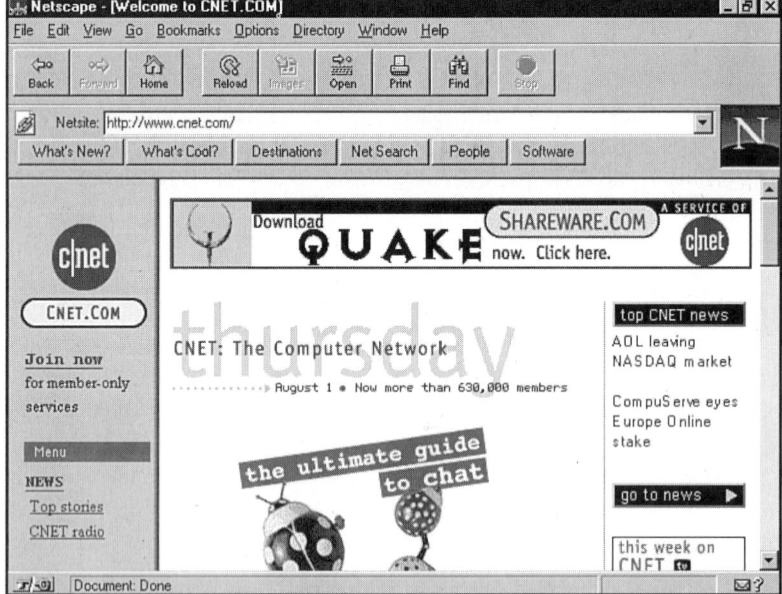

FIG. 14.12 The CNet button, for example, connects to CNet's terrific site.

Listing 14.14 ***InternetApplet.java*—The *InternetApplet* Applet**

```
import java.awt.*;
import java.awt.event.*;
import java.applet.*;
import java.net.*;
public class InternetApplet extends Applet implements ActionListener {
  boolean badURL;
  public void init() {
    GridLayout layout = new GridLayout(2, 4, 10, 10);
    setLayout(layout);
    Font font = new Font("TimesRoman", Font.PLAIN, 24);
    setFont(font);
    Button button = new Button("Sun");
    button.setActionCommand("http://www.sun.com");
    button.addActionListener(this);
    add(button);
    button = new Button("Netscape");
    button.setActionCommand("http://www.netscape.com");
    button.addActionListener(this);
    add(button);
    button = new Button("Javasoft");
    button.setActionCommand("http://www.javasoft.com");
    button.addActionListener(this);
    add(button);
    button = new Button("Macmillan");
    button.setActionCommand("http://www.mcp.com");
    button.addActionListener(this);
    add(button);
    button = new Button("Time");
    button.setActionCommand("http://www.pathfinder.com");
    button.addActionListener(this);
    add(button);
    button = new Button("CNet");
    button.setActionCommand("http://www.cnet.com");
    button.addActionListener(this);
    add(button);
    button = new Button("Borland");
    button.setActionCommand("http://www.borland.com");
    button.addActionListener(this);
    add(button);
    button = new Button("Yahoo");
    button.setActionCommand("http://www.yahoo.com");
    button.addActionListener(this);
    add(button);
    badURL = false;
  }

  public void paint(Graphics g) {
    if (badURL)
      g.drawString("Bad URL!", 60, 130);
  }
  public void actionPerformed(ActionEvent event) {
    String pageName = event.getActionCommand();
```

continues

Listing 14.14 Continued

```
    try {
      URL url = new URL(pageName);
      AppletContext context = getAppletContext();
      context.showDocument(url);
    }
    catch (MalformedURLException e) {
      badURL = true;
      repaint();
    }
  }
}
```

NOTE The preceding applet works only in browsers that support Java 1.1 or better. So, if you need to use an older browser that has not been upgraded, you will want to look through the following code in Listing 14.15, which supports the 1.0 model.

Listing 14.15 *InternetApplet.java*—The *InternetApplet* Applet

```
import java.awt.*;
import java.applet.*;
import java.net.*;
public class InternetApplet extends Applet
{
    boolean badURL;
    public void init()
    {
        GridLayout layout = new GridLayout(2, 4, 10, 10);
        setLayout(layout);
        Font font = new Font("TimesRoman", Font.PLAIN, 24);
        setFont(font);
        Button button = new Button("Sun");
        add(button);
        button = new Button("Netscape");
        add(button);
        button = new Button("Microsoft");
        add(button);
        button = new Button("Macmillan");
        add(button);
        button = new Button("Time");
        add(button);
        button = new Button("CNet");
        add(button);
        button = new Button("Borland");
        add(button);
        button = new Button("Yahoo");
        add(button);
        badURL = false;
```

```
    }
    public void paint(Graphics g)
    {
        if (badURL)
            g.drawString("Bad URL!", 60, 130);
    }
    public boolean action(Event evt, Object arg)
    {
        String str;
        if (arg == "Sun")
            str = "http://www.sun.com";
        else if (arg == "Netscape")
            str = "http://www.netscape.com";
        else if (arg == "Microsoft")
            str = "http://www.microsoft.com";
        else if (arg == "Macmillan")
            str = "http://www.mcp.com";
        else if (arg == "Time")
            str = "http://www.pathfinder.com";
        else if (arg == "CNet")
            str = "http://www.cnet.com";
        else if (arg == "Borland")
            str = "http://www.borland.com";
        else
            str = "http://www.yahoo.com";
        try
        {
            URL url = new URL(str);
            AppletContext context = getAppletContext();
            context.showDocument(url);
        }
        catch (MalformedURLException e)
        {
            badURL = true;
            repaint();
        }

        return true;
    }
}
```

Listing 14.16 ***InternetApplet.html—InternetApplet*'s HTML Document**

```
<TITLE>Applet Test Page</TITLE>
<H1>Applet Test Page</H1>
<APPLET
    CODE="InternetApplet.class"
    WIDTH=500
    HEIGHT=150
    NAME="InternetApplet">
</APPLET>
```

Understanding the *InternetApplet* Applet

Now take a look at the applet's source code. The first three lines enable the program to access the classes stored in Java's `awt`, `applet`, and `net` packages:

```
import java.awt.*;
import java.awt.event.*;
import java.applet.*;
import java.net.*;
```

You're already familiar with the `awt` and `applet` packages. The `net` package contains the classes needed to log on to the Internet.

The applet's main class, which is derived from `Applet`, begins in the next line:

```
public class InternetApplet extends Applet
```

`InternetApplet` then declares its single data member:

```
boolean badURL;
```

The `badURL` data member is used in the program to notify the applet that the currently selected URL is no good.

Exploring the *init()* Method

Next comes the familiar `init()` method, where the applet can perform whatever initialization it requires. In this case, the applet first declares and sets a layout manager:

```
GridLayout layout = new GridLayout(2, 4, 10, 10);
setLayout(layout);
```

Java programs use layout managers to control where components in the program will appear on the screen. Java offers many types of layout managers, each represented by its own class in the `awt` package. (See Chapter 21, "Containers and Layout Managers," for more information on layout managers.) If you don't create and set your own layout manager, Java uses the `FlowLayout` manager—which places components horizontally one after the other—by default. In `InternetApplet`, you're using a `GridLayout` manager, which organizes components into a grid. `GridLayout`'s constructor takes four arguments:

- Number of rows in the grid
- Number of columns in the grid
- Horizontal space between cells in the grid
- Vertical space between the cells

These latter two arguments have default values of 0 if you want to leave them off.

The `setLayout()`function is a member of the `Container` class, which is a superclass (a parent class in the class hierarchy) of the `Applet` class. Its single argument is a reference to a layout-manager object. After calling `setLayout()`, Java knows to use the new layout manager rather than the default one.

After setting the applet's layout manager, the program creates and sets the font that'll be used for all text in the applet:

```
Font font = new Font("TimesRoman", Font.PLAIN, 24);
setFont(font);
```

The constructor for the `Font` class takes three arguments—the font's name, attribute, and size. The font's name can be `Dialog`, `Helvetica`, `TimesRoman`, `Courier`, or `Symbol`, whereas the attribute can be `Font.PLAIN`, `Font.ITALIC`, or `Font.BOLD`. The `setFont()`method sets the new font for the applet.

The next task is to create and add to the applet the button controls used to select Web sites. Listing 14.17 shows a sample of the code that accomplishes this task.

Listing 14.17 *LST14_17.TXT*—Creating Button Controls

```
Button button = new Button("Sun");
button.setActionCommand("http://www.sun.com");
button.addActionListener(this);
add(button);
```

The `Button` class's constructor takes a single argument, which is the text label that appears in the button when it's displayed. If you want your buttons to be more interesting with graphics as well as text, you will probably want to read about JFC in Chapters 34, "Java Security in Depth," and 35, "Object Serialization." JFC includes more advanced buttons, but because there is more involved, we haven't used them in this chapter.

ActionCommand and *ActionListeners*

When you create a button, you have the option of specifying the command that will be issued when the button is clicked. By default, this command is the same as the label you put on the button. However, in this case, when the button is clicked you want it to specify an URL. So, the next line after each button is created specifies the action command for that button.

For the command to be useful, though, you must establish a listener for the button. After a listener is registered with the applet, it will receive a notification any time the indicated event occurs. In this case, we want to listen to the `Action` event.

The `add()` method adds the button to the next available cell in the `GridLayout` manager.

Finally, `init()`sets the `badURL` flag to `false`. In the event that one of the URLs you've entered doesn't work out, the `badURL` flag will help you notify the user.

```
badURL = false;
```


The *actionPeformed()* Method

Before you can add `this` as an action listener, you must first implement the `ActionListener` interface. The `ActionListener` requires you to create an `actionPeformed()` method.

When the user clicks one of the applet's buttons, the `actionPeformed()` method is called. Because you've specified the URL as the command for the button, you can use the `action` command to obtain the selected URL as shown below.

```
String pageName = event.getActionCommand();
```

After obtaining the selected URL, the applet can connect to the Web site. Before doing this, though, the program must set up a `try` and `catch` program block because the `URL` class's constructor throws a `MalformedURLException`, which must be caught by your program. (You learn more about exceptions in Chapter 20, "Exceptions and Events in Depth.") The `try` program blocks attempts to create the `URL` object and connects to the Web site, as shown in Listing 14.18.

Listing 14.18 ***LST14_18.TXT*****—Connecting to a Web Site**

```
try
{
    URL url = new URL(pageName);
    AppletContext context = getAppletContext();
    context.showDocument(url);
}
```

In the `try` block, the program first tries to create an `URL` object from the `URL` text string. If the construction fails, the `URL` class throws a `MalformedURLException`, and program execution continues at the `catch` program block, which you look at soon. If the `URL` object gets constructed successfully, the program calls the `getAppletContext()` method to get a reference to the applet's `AppletContext` object. This object's `showDocument()` method connects the applet to the chosen URL.

If the `URL` class's constructor throws an exception, program execution jumps to the `catch` program block, which is shown in Listing 14.19.

Listing 14.19 ***LST14_19.TXT*****—The Catch Program Block**

```
catch (MalformedURLException e)
{
    badURL = true;
    repaint();
}
```

In the `catch` program block, the program simply sets the `badURL` flag to `true` and calls `repaint()` to display an error message to the user.

Exploring the *paint()* Method

Listing 14.20 shows the applet's `paint()` method, which does nothing more than display an error message if the `badURL` flag is set to `true`.

NOTE Because the URLs are hard-coded into the program, it's not likely that the URL will construct improperly. If you were to change a button's URL, though, the error message lets you know whether you typed the URL incorrectly.

Listing 14.20 *LST14_20.TXT*—The *paint()* Method

```
public void paint(Graphics g)
{
    if (badURL)
        g.drawString("Bad URL!", 60, 130);
}
```

The `drawString()` function, which is a method of the `Graphics` class, displays a text string on the screen. Its three arguments are the string to display, and the X,Y coordinates at which to display the string.

CHAPTER 15

Advanced Applet Code

In this chapter

Using the <*PARAM*> Tag

The most utilized `java.applet.Applet` feature is the capability to get information from the HTML file. This information can be useful because it enables you to use the HTML file almost as a batch file, containing the runtime parameters for a particular applet. This also enables you to write an applet once, which can be customized by people unfamiliar with Java coding. This information is placed in what are known as <PARAM> tags.

In Chapter 14, "Writing an Applet," you learned that <PARAM> tags are part of the <APPLET> tag included in HTML files. In addition, you learned that the syntax for a <PARAM> tag is

```
<PARAM NAME="parameter_name" VALUE=value_of_parameter>
```

where the items in italics are replaced by specific information for your case. In this chapter, you learn how to use this information within an applet.

▶ **See** "Writing an Applet," **p. 227**

To access the parameter data, `java.applet.Applet` has a method called `getParameter()`. The method prototype for this method looks like this:

```
public String getParameter(String name)
```

As you can see from the prototype, `getParameter()` requires a parameter—a name. That name corresponds directly to the NAME value in the <PARAM> tag, so if you had a tag that looked like

```
<PARAM NAME="Stars" VALUE=50>
```

you could retrieve the result with a line of code similar to this:

```
String starCount = getParameter("Stars");
```

NOTE Normally, you will actually develop the program and then the HTML file, so this example will probably be backward for most of your development.

If what you had wanted to get from the parameter was a string value, the previous code might be enough to satisfy your needs. However, odds are that what you really wanted was an integer with a value of 50. Because `getParameter()` returns a string, how can you obtain the `int` value 50? The answer lies in the `Wrapper` class for `int` called `java.lang.Integer`. `Integer` can take a string that represents a number and "parse" through it to get the number value. Using `Integer`, you can retrieve the value into an `int` by using `Integer`'s `parseInt()` method, as shown here:

```
int starCountInt = Integer.parseInt(starCount);
```

How to put this whole thing together in a complete applet that paints the stars in random places on the screen is shown in Listing 15.1.

Listing 15.1 *StarPainter* Reads in a Value for the Number of Stars and Paints Them to the Screen

```
import java.applet.Applet;
import java.awt.*;

/*
 *
 * StarPainter
 *
 */
public class StarPainter extends Applet{
     int starCount;
     public void init(){
          starCount = Integer.parseInt(getParameter("Stars"));
     }

     public void paint(Graphics g){
          g.setColor(Color.black);
          for (int count=0;count<starCount;count++){
               int xValue = (int)(getSize().width*Math.random());
                int yValue = (int)(getSize().height*Math.random());
               g.drawLine(xValue,yValue,xValue,yValue);
          }
     }
}
```

When you compile `StarPainter`, you also need to create an HTML file for it. In Listing 15.2, you see one possible version of this HTML file. Figure 15.1 shows what `StarPainter` looks like with those parameter values. Try changing the number of stars to see what happens (you might want to increase it by a large number because it's difficult to see small changes in this applet).

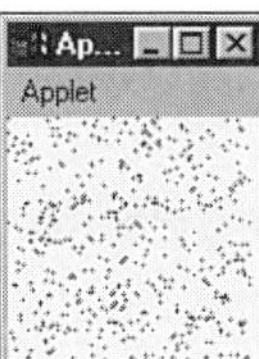

FIG. 15.1
`StarPainter` paints stars at random places on the screen.

Listing 15.2 An HTML File for the *StarPainter* Applet

```
<HR>
<APPLET CODE="StarPainter.class" WIDTH=100 HEIGHT=100>
<PARAM NAME=Stars VALUE=500>
</APPLET>
<HR>
```

Understanding the *StarPainter* Source Code

Because you're still fairly new to applet programming, take a look at Listing 15.1 and walk through how the `StarPainter` applet works.

```
import java.applet.Applet;
import java.awt.*;
```

The first thing to notice is, like all Java classes, the `StarPainter` program needs to import several classes. This is really an important step. When you're just starting to program in Java, you may get frustrated by an error that looks like the following:

```
StarPainter.java:14 Class Graphics not found in type declaration.
     public void paint(Graphics g){
                 ^
```

This error occurs because you failed to import the `Graphics` class.

```
public void init(){
     starCount = Integer.parseInt(getParameter("Stars"));
}
```

The `init()` method of `StarPainter` should look just like you thought it would, except for one minor change. You have combined the two lines of code you saw earlier into one. Notice that this demonstrates the fact that it is perfectly legitimate to use a method (`getParameter()`) as a parameter to a second method (`parseInt()`) when the proper value is being returned.

```
     public void paint(Graphics g){
          g.setColor(Color.black);
          for (int count=0;count<starCount;count++){
               int xValue = (int)(getSize().width*Math.random());
                int yValue = (int)(getSize().height*Math.random());
               g.drawLine(xValue,yValue,xValue,yValue);
          }
     }
}
```

The `paint()` method of `StarPainter` is not too involved but does contain some methods you haven't seen until now. The first thing that the `paint()` method does is set the paint color to black.

▶ **See** "Graphics," **p. 431**

Using the *getSize()* Method

Now concentrate on the `xValue=` and the `yValue=` lines.

```
int xValue = (int)(getSize().width*Math.random());
```

To help you understand this line, break it up into several lines of equivalent code:

```
int width = getSize().width;
double randomLoc = Math.random();
double location = width * randomLoc;
int xValue = (int) location;
```

Go through the code on your own and verify that it does get you the same result as the `xValue=` line in `StarPainter`.

The first line of code uses a method you haven't seen before—`getSize()`. `getSize()` is a method that an applet inherits from the `java.awt.Component` class. `getSize()` can be a useful method for applets because it allows you to find out how much room you have to work with. To understand how the applet obtained the `getSize()` method, take a look at the API for the applet at `http://www.javasoft.com/products/jdk/1.2/docs/api/packages.html`.

When you visit the Web site, you see a structure at the top of the applet, called an inheritance tree, which looks like the following:

```
Class java.applet.Applet

java.lang.Object
   |
   +----java.awt.Component
           |
           +----java.awt.Container
                   |
                   +----java.awt.Panel
                           |
                           +----java.applet.Applet
```

An inheritance tree helps you to see all the classes `Applet` inherits from. You see that, just like when you create your applets by extending the `java.applet.Applet` class (and in so doing you obtain all the methods of `Applet`), when `Applet` extends `Panel`, it obtains all of `Panel`'s methods. So even though you aren't extending `Component`, because `Container` does and because `Panel` extends `Container`, and `Applet` extends `Panel`, and `PaintStars` extends `Applet`, you have effectively inherited all those classes and can use the methods present in all of them.

At the top of the tree, you will see `Component`, which is a rich class with a lot of methods. You will want to get to know `Component` very well. `Component` has a method called `getSize()`, which is the method you were looking for.

Going back to your equivalent code, the next line after the `width = getSize().width;` is a line that says:

```
double randomLoc = Math.random();
```

`Math` is a class in the `java.lang` package (that is, `java.lang.Math`). `Math` has a number of valuable methods, one of which is `random()`. `random()` returns a random number from 0.0–1.0. This can be useful because, as you used it here, you can use that number to generate any random number you need. The rest of the code should be easy to follow after you understand `random()` and `getSize()`.

NOTE Notice that when you call `random()`, you are doing this on the class `Math` and not on an actual instance of `Math`. In other words, what you are NOT doing is

```
Math myMathVar = new Math();
double randomLoc = myMathVar.random();
```

How can you do this? Ordinarily you cannot call methods just using their class names. However, if a method is defined as static, the method can be invoked without having to create an instance object of the class `first`. It just so happens that all of `Math`'s methods are static, so you can use them without having to actually invoke `Math`. If you're following along using Sun Microsystems's API, you may have noticed that `random()` is preceded by a green dot rather than a red one. This is to indicate that `random()` is a static method.

See "Methods," **p. 119**

Adding Images to an Applet

Another common task when building an applet is displaying an image. As you saw in the `StarPainter` applet, you can create images on your own using the `Graphics` class, but you can also load images stored in `.gif` or `.jpg` formats. `getImage()` is the method that has been added to `java.applet.Applet` for the purpose of loading such images.

```
public Image getImage(URL url)
```

`getImage()` is an easy method to use. All you need to know is the URL where the image can be found. So to get the image called `banner.gif` from the Web site `www.magnastar.com`, all you would need to do is use a line similar to this:

```
Image testImage = getImage (new URL("http://www.magnastar.com/banner.gif");
```

To put this in an applet, see Listing 15.3.

Listing 15.3 ***PaintBanner*** **Loads an Image and Displays It**

```
import java.applet.Applet;
import java.awt.*;
import java.net.URL;

/*
 *
 * PaintBanner
 *
 */
public class PaintBanner extends Applet{
     Image testImage;
     public void init(){
          testImage = getImage("http://www.magnastar.com/banner.gif");
     }

     public void paint(Graphics g){
          g.drawImage(testImage,0,0,this);
     }
}
```

PaintBanner is an effective applet if what you want to do is paint one image: banner.gif. However, it's unlikely that you will have too many requirements for banner.gif. Because of the URL restrictions imposed on applets, you would not even be able to load the banner.gif image from www.magnastar.com unless the applet actually resides on the www.magnastar.com computer.

You can get away from this requirement by using the getParameter() method you learned about in the preceding section, embedding a parameter that would be used for the URL. For limited cases, this might actually work. However, what if you want to load the banner.gif graphic, and you want to always load it off the current computer? In other words, what if you create an applet that relies on a number of graphics, but when somebody from www.jars.com loads the applet, they need to get the image from www.jars.com, not from www.magnastar.com.

java.applet.Applet has two methods that can help you in this pursuit. It has the capability to tell you the relative URL of either the location where the class files for the applet were retrieved, or where the HTML file the applet was contained in are from. These two methods are getDocumentBase() and getCodeBase().

```
public URL getDocumentBase()
public URL getCodeBase()
```

The getDocumentBase() method will return the relative URL where the applet is contained. getCodeBase() returns the relative URL where the applet's class files are located.The key here is the term *relative*. The two methods return only the relative location for the file. For instance, the relative URL for the banner.gif file talked about before would be http://www.magnastar.com/. Had it been located in a subdirectory called Images, the URL would be http://www.magnastar.com/Images/. To get to the whole URL, you need to create an URL from both this URL and the name of the actual file you're looking for. How do you do this? The answer is twofold; first you could use the two-parameter constructor for an URL, which would look like new URL(getDocumentBase(),"banner.gif"). It just so happens that getImage() itself has been overloaded to provide this same functionality as well. Listing 15.4 shows Listing 15.3 again using the getDocumentBase() method.

Listing 15.4 Loading an Image from the Current Directory

```
import java.applet.Applet;
import java.awt.*;
import java.net.URL;

/*
 *
 * PaintBanner
 *
 */
public class PaintBanner extends Applet{
     Image testImage;
     public void init(){
          testImage = getImage(getDocumentBase(),"banner.gif");
     }
```

continues

Listing 15.4 Continued

```
    public void paint(Graphics g){
        g.drawImage(testImage,0,0,this);
    }
}
```

Figure 15.2 shows the result of adding the `getDocumentBase()` method.

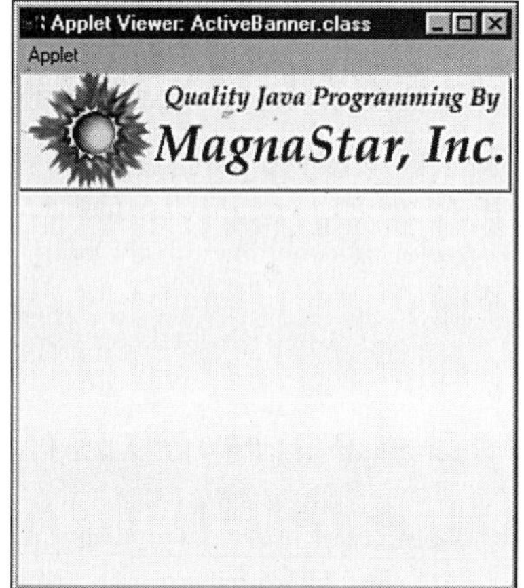

FIG. 15.2
The `getDocumentBase()` method will return the relative URL where the applet is contained.

Now when you run `PaintBanner`, the browser will look for the graphic `banner.gif` in the same directory where it found the HTML file. When you move `PaintBanner` to another system or directory, there is no need to change either the HTML or the source code.

NOTE One interesting characteristic of `getImage()` is that it returns immediately. In other words, your program starts to process the next file right away. `getImage()` does not wait until after the image has been dragged across the Net; in fact, the image isn't actually even retrieved until it is first used. Be aware of this fact because you'll likely see images paint slowly at times. You learn more about this in Chapter 22, "Graphics."

Adding Sound to an Applet

Another useful feature of applets is their capability to load and use sounds. One new feature of Java 1.2 is the capability to load many sound files. In the past, Java only had support for one format—the AU format. Now you can use many file formats, including WAVE, AU, AIFF, MIDI, and a great format—RMF.

Audio is abstracted in Java in a class called `java.applet.AudioClip`. `Applet` provides several methods to load the audio files, the `getAudioClip()` method is available in a variety of formats, and a new method—`newAudioClip()`—allows you to load an audio file without needing to have the browser's support.

```
public AudioClip getAudioClip(URL url)
public AudioClip getAudioClip(URL url, String name)

public static final AudioClip newAudioClip(URL r)
```

`newAudioClip()` and `getAudioClip()` work similarly to `getImage()`. In fact, just as with `getImage()`, `getAudioClip()` has two possibilities, one with just the URL, and one with a relative URL and a name. To actually use the `AudioClip`, you will need to use one of `AudioClip`'s methods: `play()`, `loop()`, or `stop()`. Each of these methods works exactly as you would think it would. `play()` plays the clip once, whereas `loop()` plays it over and over. Please use courtesy when using `loop()`. There is nothing worse than hearing the same clip over and over, so don't arbitrarily loop an `AudioClip` endlessly. Put these together in a small applet, as shown in Listing 15.5.

Listing 15.5 Play *AudioClip*—When You Click This Applet It Plays a Sound

```
import java.applet.Applet;
import java.applet.AudioClip;
import java.awt.Event;

/*
 *
 * PlayAudio
 *
 */
public class PlayAudio extends java.applet.Applet{
     AudioClip audio;

     public void init(){
          audio = getAudioClip(getDocumentBase(),"welcome.au");
     }

     public booleanmouseDown(Event evt, int x, int y){
          audio.play();
          returns true;
     }
}
```

One major difference between `getAudioClip()` and `getImage()` is that `getAudioClip()` will go out to the Net and return the actual audio clip. `getImage()` does not do this, instead `getImage()` returns immediately and only loads the image when you need it. However, when you get an audio clip, the rest of your program will have to wait until that audio file has been downloaded.

One more audio-related method in `Applet` is called `play()`. `play()` is overloaded the same way that `getAudioClip()` and `getImage()` are. The difference between `play()` and `getAudioClip()` is that `play()` grabs the audio clip and plays it right away. However, it doesn't save the audio clip so, if you need it again, it will have to be re-downloaded from the Net.

Using the Applet to Control the Browser

Another thing you can use an applet to do is provide control over the browser. This is important because it allows the applets that you write to extend the capabilities of a standard browser, actually changing the experience of a user to fit your new needs.

One difference between the methods used to control the browser, as opposed to the rest of the methods discussed in this chapter, is that `java.applet.Applet` doesn't have the capability to change the Web page itself. Instead, a class called `AppletContext`, which is basically a link to the browser itself, actually controls the browser environment in which the applet lives.

To retrieve the `AppletContext` for the browser, you need to use the following method:

```
public AppletContext getAppletContext()
```

After you have the `AppletContext` for the applet, you can begin to manipulate the browser.

Changing the Status Message

An applet can cause the browser to change Web pages or display a different message. The first method for doing this is `showStatus()`. `showStatus()` causes the message to be displayed in the status window, normally at the bottom of the page, as seen in Figure 15.3.

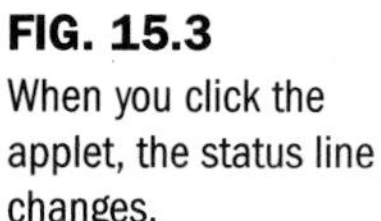

FIG. 15.3
When you click the applet, the status line changes.

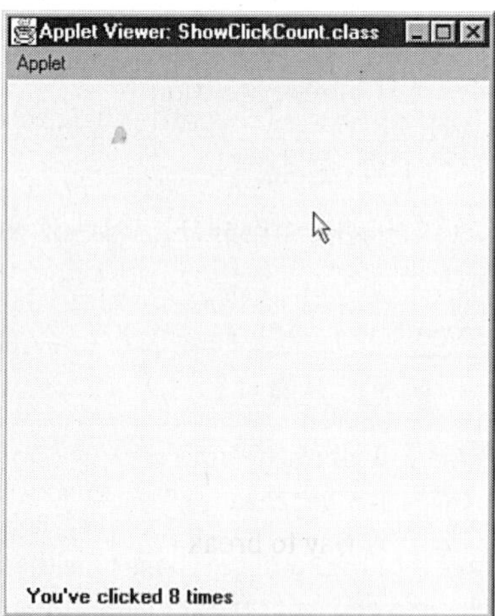


```
public void showStatus(String msg)
```

Using `showStatus()`, you can change the value of this output to be any string you want. Listing 15.6 shows a sample program that changes the status to indicate the number of times you've clicked the applet.

Listing 15.6 The Status Window of This Browser Is Changed by the Applet

```
import java.applet.Applet;
import java.awt.Event;

/*
 *
 * ShowClickCount
 *
 */
public class ShowClickCount extends Applet
{

     int count=0;

     public boolean mouseDown(Event evt, int x, int y){
          getAppletContext().showStatus("You've clicked "+(count++)+" times");
          return true;
     }

}
```

When you run the `ShowClickCount` applet, you will notice the status message changes each time you click the applet. Changing the status message at the bottom of the page can be a useful way to give feedback to your users. Notice how the browser uses the status area to tell you about where a link goes, or the status of a download.

Changing the Page the Browser Displays

Another thing you can do with the browser is change the Web page it is displaying. This can be useful because it means you can now add navigation capabilities to your applet. `AppletContext`'s method for doing this comes in two varieties:

```
showDocument(URL)
showDocument(URL, String)
```

If you're jumping ahead, you're thinking to yourself, "Ahh huh, `showDocument()` has the same relative URL and final document options that `getImage()` and `getAudioClip()` did." If that's what you're thinking—well, there's no easy way to break this to you—you're wrong. The two versions of `showDocument()` do not work the same way as `getImage()` and `getAudioClip()`, so read on.

First, `showDocument(URL)` does change the browser window to the URL you've pointed it to, just as you might have guessed. So, if you want to create a simple applet that just changes to the Web page, you could put something together like Listing 15.7.

Listing 15.7 Show Document Displaying a Different Web Page in the Browser

```
import java.applet.Applet;
import java.awt.Event;
import java.net.*;

/*
 *
 * ShowDocument
 *
 */
public class ShowDocument extends Applet {
     public boolean mouseDown(Event evt, int x, int y){
          try{
          getAppletContext().showDocument(new URL("http://www.magnastar.com"));
          } catch (MalformedURLException urlException){
               System.out.println("Sorry but there was an error creating the
➥URL:"+urlException);
          }
          return true;
     }

}
```

When you run the `ShowDocument` applet and then click it, your browser changes to the `www.magnastar.com` Web page. Notice the `try-catch` sequence in the preceding example. Do you realize why you need it? It's required because the constructor for URL throws an exception if the URL isn't valid. For instance, if you point to `http://www.magnastar.com`, this would not be a valid URL because URL doesn't know what to do with http.

So what, then, is the difference between the two `showDocument()` methods? Well, the first method takes the URL you want to show, as just covered. The second takes the URL you want to point to and the name of the target frame to display the document in. You can use the actual name of the frame you want to display in (if you are using frames on the Web page) or the values `"_self"`, `"_parent"`, and `"_blank"` to refer to either the current frame (default), the parent frame, or a new window, respectively.

Putting It All Together

Now, try to construct a more complete example using each of the methods you learned about in this chapter. For this complete example, first display a graphic. Then, each time the mouse enters the applet, play a sound. When the mouse button is pressed, display a message, and when the button is released, change pages. Listing 15.8 shows you how to create this application; see if you can work through the source code on your own.

Listing 15.8 *ActiveBanner* Displays an Image and Plays a Sound When the Mouse Enters the Area and Switches Web Pages When It's Clicked

```
import java.applet.*;
import java.awt.*;
import java.net.*;

/*
 *
 * ActiveBanner
 *
 */
public class ActiveBanner extends Applet{
     Image banner;
     AudioClip welcome;

     public void init(){
          banner = getImage(getDocumentBase(),"banner.gif");
          welcome = getAudioClip(getDocumentBase(),"welcome.au");
     }

     public void paint(Graphics g){
          g.drawImage(banner,0,0,this);
     }

     public void update (Graphics g){
          paint(g);
     }

     public boolean mouseEnter(Event e, int x, int y){
          welcome.play();
          return true;
     }

     public boolean mouseDown(Event e, int x, int y){
          getAppletContext().showStatus("Release the mouse button to go to
ÂMagnaStar");
          return true;
     }

     public boolean mouseUp(Event e, int x, int y){
          try{
               getAppletContext().showDocument(new URL("http://
Âwww.magnastar.com"));
          } catch (MalformedURLException urlException){
               System.out.println("Sorry but there was an error creating the
ÂURL:"+urlException);
          }
          return true;
     }

}
```

CHAPTER 16

JAR Archive Files

In this chapter

Why JAR?

The JAR file format brings several important advantages to applets. These include performance improvements and enhanced portability. JAR files also implement the Security Model that was introduced with JDK 1.1, described in detail in Chapter 34, "Java Security in Depth."

JAR archives are not the first Java archive format to be supported. Since version 1.0, the JDK has used the uncompressed ZIP file `classes.zip` to store the JDK system class files as a single disk file. Netscape Navigator 3.0, following this procedure, allowed the `<APPLET>` tag to load an applet from a similar ZIP file. Starting with version 3.0, Microsoft Internet Explorer started allowing you to load Java applets from Microsoft's CAB files, like ActiveX controls.

JAR files have been replacing these other mechanisms over time. They offer the following benefits which make them the preferred choice.

Bundling

A complex applet may consist of dozens or hundreds of Java classes, each stored in a separate class file (recall that each public class must be stored in a separate file). To run the applet, the Web browser makes an HTTP connection to load each file, as needed, from the server. Establishing an HTTP connection entails overhead, and if the class files are small, as they typically are, much of the time spent loading an applet can be spent establishing the multiple HTTP connections required to load all the class files.

The first and most obvious benefit of a JAR file is that it combines several class files into one archive file, which can then be transmitted from the server to the Web browser over a single HTTP connection. Furthermore, JAR files can contain not only class files but also audio and image files, allowing an entire applet to be downloaded in one transaction. This is useful not only for improved performance, but also because it simplifies applet distribution.

Compression

JAR files, like CAB files (but unlike `classes.zip`), are compressed using a variant of the standard Lempel-Ziv algorithm. For example, the JDK `TicTacToe` demo is 20 percent smaller when archived as a JAR file; the ImageMap demo is 5 percent smaller (it contains more image files, which are already compressed). By not only aggregating multiple files but also compressing them, JAR files can greatly reduce the time needed to download an applet.

Backward Compatibility

Because JAR archives preserve the directory hierarchy of their files, and because they can be loaded through a simple change to the `<APPLET>` tag, JAR archives can be used transparently with existing Java applets, with no change to the applet code.

Portability

Portability, in this case, refers to two things: portability between browsers, and portability between Web servers.

Browser incompatibility between Netscape Navigator, Microsoft Internet Explorer, and other browsers is a familiar bugaboo to anyone who has developed Web pages or Java applets. Prior to Java 1.1, a Web developer had no portable archiving mechanism.

JAR files solve this problem by providing a single, browser-independent archive file format. Because JAR support and tools are implemented entirely in Java, any browser supporting the standard Java 1.1+ library will be able to support JAR files.

The other side of the portability question becomes clear when you try to move an applet from one Web server to another. For example, imagine that you have developed an applet running on a Windows 95–based Web server. Your files have descriptive names such as `NavigationBarAnimationPanel.class`—a legal filename under Windows 95. Now you need to move your Web site to a Macintosh-based Web server. Unfortunately, you discover that Macintosh filenames are limited to 31 characters, and you are forced to rename not only your Java source files, but also your classes within them (because filenames must match the names of classes they contain).

(To see this firsthand, try downloading and installing the JDK 1.1 beta 2 documentation files on a Macintosh. Many of the filenames will be truncated, and your browser won't be able to navigate links to those files.)

By storing an applet's various class files and other resource files in a single JAR file, you make the applet immune to any idiosyncrasies of the Web server's underlying file system.

Security

As of JDK 1.1, the Java Security Model has been extended. It is now possible, by using authenticated JAR archives, for the user to verify the origin of an applet, mark it as trusted, and give it additional privileges. This makes it possible for new types of applets to be written, such as word processors that store files on the local user's hard disk.

When to Use JAR Archives

You should consider using a JAR archive for your applet if any of the following apply:

- You wish to decrease your applet's loading time, especially if your applet consists of many files.
- You wish to simplify the distribution of your applet or make it portable to more Web servers.
- Your applet needs to be authenticated as trusted code.

JAR files are useful chiefly for applets. If you are developing a Java application, JAR files won't be as useful to you, although you may still use them as a general-purpose archiving format.

The *jar* Tool

The jar tool allows you to create, list, and extract files from JAR archives. It deliberately resembles the UNIX tar tool, both in function and in usage. Like other tools in the JDK, the jar tool is implemented as a Java application, making it portable to any platform supporting Java.

Creating a New Archive To create a new archive, use the options cvf. The c option tells jar to create a new archive. The v option tells jar to output verbose diagnostic messages to the console while it is working so you can see what is being added. The f option tells jar to create an archive file of the given name. For example, the following

```
jar cvf Foo.jar *.class images
```

will create a new JAR archive named Foo.jar in the current directory. The archive will contain all the class files in the current directory, as well as the complete images directory and all its contents.

As an example, connect to the directory containing the JDK demo TicTacToe.

A listing of the directory contents reveals a class file and two subdirectories containing audio and image files:

```
D:\java\demo\TicTacToe>dir
 Volume in drive D is NTFS20
 Volume Serial Number is 6C98-56B4

 Directory of D:\JDK1.2\demo\TicTacToe

01/13/97  10:04a        <DIR>          .
01/13/97  10:04a        <DIR>          ..
12/16/96  11:29a        <DIR>          audio
11/19/96  12:34p                   139 example1.html
12/16/96  11:29a        <DIR>          images
11/19/96  12:34p                 3,454 TicTacToe.class
12/06/96  10:27a                 7,593 TicTacToe.java
               7 File(s)        11,186 bytes
                         1,575,772,160 bytes free
```

Create a new subdirectory that will contain the JAR file version of this applet:

```
D:\JDK1.2\demo\TicTacToe>mkdir jar
```

Now create the JAR archive:

```
D:\JDK1.2\demo\TicTacToe>jar cvf jar\TicTacToe.jar *.class audio images
adding: TicTacToe.class
adding: audio/beep.au
adding: audio/ding.au
adding: audio/return.au
adding: audio/yahoo1.au
adding: audio/yahoo2.au
adding: images/cross.gif
adding: images/not.gif
```

Notice that when directories are listed as input files to the jar tool, their contents are added to the archive and the directory names are preserved.

When the `jar` tool creates a new archive, it automatically adds a manifest file to the archive. In most cases, this will suffice. However, should you wish to create your own manifest file, and have the `jar` tool use that, you can do so by specifying the `m` option.

Listing Archive Contents The `jar` tool can also list the contents of a JAR archive. For example

```
jar tvf Foo.jar
```

will list the contents of `Foo.jar`.

To continue with the `TicTacToe` demo applet, connect to the `jar` subdirectory you created previously. Use the `t` option to obtain a listing.

```
D:\JDK1.2\demo\TicTacToe\jar>jar tf TicTacToe.jar
META-INF/MANIFEST.MF
TicTacToe.class
audio/beep.au
audio/ding.au
audio/return.au
audio/yahoo1.au
audio/yahoo2.au
images/cross.gif
images/not.gif
```

Notice that a manifest file has been added to the archive automatically. See the section "Manifest File," later in this chapter, for more information about manifest files. You can obtain more information by using the `v` option.

```
D:\JDK1.2\demo\TicTacToe\jar>jar tvf TicTacToe.jar
  1045 Mon Jan 13 11:52:18 PST 1997 META-INF/MANIFEST.MF
  3454 Tue Nov 19 12:34:26 PST 1996 TicTacToe.class
  4032 Tue Nov 19 12:34:26 PST 1996 audio/beep.au
  2566 Tue Nov 19 12:34:26 PST 1996 audio/ding.au
  6558 Tue Nov 19 12:34:26 PST 1996 audio/return.au
  7834 Tue Nov 19 12:34:26 PST 1996 audio/yahoo1.au
  7463 Tue Nov 19 12:34:26 PST 1996 audio/yahoo2.au
   157 Tue Nov 19 12:34:24 PST 1996 images/cross.gif
   158 Tue Nov 19 12:34:24 PST 1996 images/not.gif
```

Extracting Files from an Archive Finally, the `jar` tool can extract files from an archive file. For example, to extract the `TicTacToe.class` file, type the following:

```
D:\JDK1.2\demo\TicTacToe\jar>jar xvf TicTacToe.jar TicTacToe.class
extracted: TicTacToe.class, 3454 bytes
```

If you are following along on your computer, remove the file you just extracted so that upcoming examples will work:

```
D:\JDK1.2\demo\TicTacToe\jar>del TicTacToe.class
```

You cannot use the `x` option to extract a single file within a subdirectory of the JAR archive. Instead, specify the entire subdirectory and, after it has been extracted, discard those files that you do not need.

The *APPLET* Tag

The APPLET tag embeds a Java applet into an HTML file. It has a number of attributes that specify the name of the applet to be loaded, the URL to use to locate the applet, and the size of the applet on the page. In addition to these attributes, any number of parameters can be specified. For example, in the following

```
<APPLET CODE="FooMain.class" WIDTH=100 HEIGHT=120>
<PARAM NAME="color" VALUE="red">
<PARAM NAME="background" VALUE="blue">
</APPLET>
```

the CODEBASE attribute indicates the URL base from which to load the class file. If no CODEBASE is specified, the URL of the referring page is used. For example, the browser will try to load the following applet from `http://www.foo.com/applets/FooMain.class`:

```
<APPLET CODE="FooMain.class" CODEBASE="http://www.foo.com/applets/" WIDTH=100
➥HEIGHT=120>
...
</APPLET>
```

Beginning with JDK 1.1, Sun specified changes to the <APPLET> tag which enable the class to be loaded from a JAR archive that is downloaded before the Java applet class is located.

Loading from a JAR archive can be specified in two ways: using an attribute or using a parameter. First, an attribute named ARCHIVES can be used, as follows:

```
<APPLET ARCHIVES="Foo.jar" CODE="FooMain.class">
...
</APPLET>
```

When the browser reads this tag, it first downloads the `Foo.jar` file from the server, then tries to find the `FooMain.class` in `Foo.jar`. If the browser cannot find the class in the archive, it looks at the location specified by the CODEBASE, as usual.

Alternatively, the JAR archive can be specified as a parameter. This parameter should have the name ARCHIVES. The parameter's value is the name of the JAR file, as follows:

```
<APPLET CODE="FooMain.class">
<PARAM NAME=ARCHIVES VALUE="Foo.jar">
...
</APPLET>
```

It's possible to specify more than one JAR archive to be loaded. To do so, insert the string ` + ` (a plus sign surrounded by spaces) between the archive filenames, as follows:

```
<APPLET ARCHIVES="foo.jar + foo_images.jar + foo_sounds.jar"
CODE="FooMain.class">
...
</APPLET>
```

Specifying a JAR archive in an APPLET tag is a performance optimization, instructing the browser to preload a specified archive and use that archive, if possible, when locating classes. If the JAR file is not found, or if a required class file is not found in the archive, the usual search procedure, as defined by JDK 1.0, will be followed. Specifying a JAR file to preload does not prevent the usual search paths from being tried and used if necessary.

As a final example, look at the <APPLET> tag used by the TicTacToe demo in JDK 1.1. The file example1.html, in Listing 16.1, contains this <APPLET> tag.

LISTING 16.1 ***example1.html*—Without JAR Archive Loading**

```
<title>TicTacToe</title>
<hr>
<applet code=TicTacToe.class width=120 height=120>
</applet>
<hr>
<a href="TicTacToe.java">The source.</a>
```

Copy this to the subdirectory jar that you created previously.

```
D:\JDK1.2\demo\TicTacToe>copy example1.html jar
        1 file(s) copied.
```

Now edit it to add the APPLETS attribute. It should look like Listing 16.2 when you're done.

LISTING 16.2 ***example1.html*—With JAR Archive Loading**

```
<title>TicTacToe</title>
<hr>
<applet code=TicTacToe.class archives=TicTacToe.jar width=120 height=120>
</applet>
<hr>
<a href="TicTacToe.java">The source.</a>
```

Now you should be able to run the TicTacToe applet from the JAR archive created earlier:

```
D:\java\demo\TicTacToe\jar>appletviewer example1.html
loading d:\jdk11b2\java\bin\..\lib\awt.properties
```

Compatible Browsers

To use a JAR file, you must be using a JDK 1.1 browser, which means you can use Navigator 3.0 or Internet Explorer 3.0 if you've added the Java Activator. If you're using a 4.0+ browser though, worry not—you're already set.

JAR Archives and Security

The Web allows content to be downloaded, and the Java architecture extends the Web to allow executable content to be downloaded. Although this opens up tremendous new possibilities, it also opens up new risks. A static text or image file can do little to harm its receiver (Snow Crash notwithstanding), but a piece of code can, potentially, do a lot of damage—witness computer viruses.

In order to protect recipients of downloaded code, Java implements a security model known as the *sandbox*. This is a domain within which an untrusted piece of Java code may do whatever it wishes. By restricting the applet's activities to a well-defined area, a browser can run an untrusted applet while still protecting everything outside the sandbox—typically, the local machine's memory, files, and disks, and the network.

Running within the sandbox is not a hindrance to an applet that displays a clock, a stock ticker, or an animated navigation bar. But what about an applet that implements a word processor or a spreadsheet? For such an applet to be useful, it needs to interact with the user's local machine in order to read and write files (unless the applet wants to tackle the formidable task of maintaining user data files on a remote server). To do this, it needs to leave the sandbox. Under JDK 1.0, it was difficult for applets to do this. However, using authenticated JAR archives, applets have a standard way to easily gain trusted status.

The Manifest File

The first entry in any JAR file is a collection of meta-information about the archive. The `jar` tool generates this meta-information automatically and stores it in a top-level directory named `META-INF`. This directory always contains what is known as the manifest file, `META-INF/MANIFEST.INF` (see Listing 16.3).

Normally, if no authentication is applied, the manifest file contains checksums for the other files in the archive. For example, you can extract the manifest file for the `TicTacToe.jar` archive, created previously, as follows:

```
D:\JDK1.2\demo\TicTacToe\jar>jar xvf TicTacToe.jar META-INF
extracted: META-INF/MANIFEST.MF, 1045 bytes
```

LISTING 16.3 Manifest File *MANIFEST.MF* of *TicTacToe.jar*

```
Manifest-Version: 1.0

Name: TicTacToe.class
Hash-Algorithms: MD5 SHA
MD5-Hash: TsjcL1vWU7k4/HDkwOnvHg==
SHA-Hash: IGRKfYKD8Cpef7+or5ZKqYp3bh0=

Name: audio\beep.au
Hash-Algorithms: MD5 SHA
MD5-Hash: kZv279ZIA/H6mOw4t8W8XA==
SHA-Hash: JgfdUl4/uzNq5yUy3e07ZXwvNOc=

Name: audio\ding.au
Hash-Algorithms: MD5 SHA
MD5-Hash: 23oJDEp/LqCZC70AEIOsVQ==
SHA-Hash: dpRUB8DKzEP0Grc7DIrXclPMjJ8=

Name: audio\return.au
Hash-Algorithms: MD5 SHA
MD5-Hash: tBUwkF2qeyor/nmPeF81hg==
SHA-Hash: ABV7Ar1gRYQmpp7kSbkH3GN+YOA=
```

```
Name: audio\yahoo1.au
Hash-Algorithms: MD5 SHA
MD5-Hash: Bq9PhKz6zAWrgQvtGWS8zQ==
SHA-Hash: qUO3jWxRvJWIp25S9XRQk5lbLaY=

Name: audio\yahoo2.au
Hash-Algorithms: MD5 SHA
MD5-Hash: 6lhsclKkFy5iBu+km+DAVQ==
SHA-Hash: Gfc7hOmtTmM31JJlHJZgkMm2elo=

Name: images\cross.gif
Hash-Algorithms: MD5 SHA
MD5-Hash: gTJaDGQtdz1Y4W+hHWxjgA==
SHA-Hash: plA3I8zoS3u8XXj9+vutZupQo0U=

Name: images\not.gif
Hash-Algorithms: MD5 SHA
MD5-Hash: SJsp04DooHqq9ndFnn6S6w==
SHA-Hash: MmqEk9R8pMigNK3xDi2yK1cyyZ8=
```


The manifest file lists all the files in the archive, together with values labeled `MD5-Hash` and `SHA-Hash`. Listing 16.3 shows a typical manifest file. `MD5` and `SHA` are *message digests,* also known as *one-way hash functions*. A hash function takes an arbitrary piece of input data and produces a piece of output data of a fixed size. `MD5` hashes are 128 bits; `SHA` hashes are 160 bits. The term *one-way* refers to the fact that it is difficult to produce the same hash from two different inputs.

The message digests in this manifest can be used to confirm that the archive has not undergone accidental corruption: As a browser reads each file from the archive, it can compute its `MD5` and `SHA` hash values and check them against those in the file. Deliberate corruption, on the other hand, cannot be ruled out, because anyone who intentionally corrupts an archive file can also modify the manifest file's corresponding hash.

It is possible, however, to detect deliberate corruption of the files in a JAR archive. To do so, the JAR archive must be "signed." This is analogous to signing a paper document with a pen. It indicates, with certainty, that the given JAR archive came from the indicated source. In fact, a digital signature is stronger than a physical one; it is harder to forge, it cannot be repudiated by the signer, and the signed document cannot be modified.

Private Keys, Public Keys, and Certificates

In order to sign a JAR archive, you must first create a private key, a public key, and a certificate. The *public* and *private keys* are paired pieces of data used to create digital signatures and to encrypt data. A *certificate* is a guarantee by one entity, usually a trusted public organization, that another entity's public key is valid. (In this case, more specifically, a certificate conforms to the X.509 standard published by CCITT.) The combination of a public key and a certificate can be used to confidently verify a digital signature.

keytool

The keytool tool handles the creation and management of identities, public and private keys, and certificates. The details of key and certificate creation and management are beyond the scope of this chapter, but they are covered in Chapter 34.

Very quickly, the keytool program can create files called *keystore databases*. These databases are actually files that reside generally in the root of your JDK installation and contain the certificates that you have created or used.

keytool itself has a variety of parameters, used to specify the manipulation of a key. However, for now look at just one scenario, generating a key. To do this, you need to know several things. First, you need an alias by which this key will be known. For now, let's use javajoe. Next, you need a distinguishing name by which you will be known. This name is part of the X.509 standard for specifying your name and follows this format:

```
CN=commonName OU=organizationUnit O=organizationName L=locality
➥Name S=stateName C=country
```

Each of these fields helps spell out who you are; for example, my -dname might be

```
"CN=Joe Weber, OU=QUE, O=Macmillan Publishing, L=Milwaukee, S=Wisconsin, C=US"
```

Now you can use both of these values to generate a new key:

```
keytool -genkey -dname "CN=Joe Weber, OU=QUE, O=Macmillan Publishing,
➥L=Milwaukee, S=Wisconsin, C=US" -alias javajoe
```

As you probably already guessed, the -genkey command tells keytool that you are generating a new key, -dname specifies distinguishing name, and -alias specifies the alias you will be using. Note that the alias is case-sensitive, so javajoe is not the same alias as JavaJoe.

When you run keytool like this, you are prompted to enter a password for the keystore and a password for your new key. These passwords will be required each time you use the key later down the road. You could also have specified the key password on the command line using the -storepass -keypass parameter. If you want to, you can set the -storepass to mystorepassword and the -keypass to privatekeypassword using the following command:

```
keytool -genkey -dname "CN=Joe Weber, OU=QUE, O=Macmillan Publishing,
➥ L=Milwaukee, S=Wisconsin, C=US" -alias javajoe -storepass
➥ mystorepassword -keypass privatekeypassword
```

In general, the parameters for use when generating a key are

```
keytool -genkey {-alias alias} {-keyalg keyalg} {-keysize keysize}
➥ {-sigalg sigalg} [-dname dname] [-keypass keypass] {-validity valDays}
➥ {-keystore keystore} [-storepass storepass] {-v}
```

jarsigner

Now that you have generated a key, you can digitally sign your JAR file. Signing a file is useful so that you and users of the file can be sure that you are the person who sent the file and that it hasn't been tampered with.

Before you can sign the JAR file, you need to know a couple of details. First, you need to know the alias for the key you wish to use. Next, you need to know the `-keystore` password and the private key password for the key you will be using. Finally, you optionally need to know the location of the `keystore` file. If you've left it in the default location, you don't need this, but if you've moved it elsewhere, you need to specify that information.

Using the key that you created under the `keytool` section, you can now sign the `TicTacToe.jar` file using the following command line:

```
jarsigner -storepass mystorepassword -keypass privatekeypassword
➥ TicTacToe.jar javajoe
```

When you sign the JAR file, it adds two files to the manifest for the file. The first file is an `.SF` file. The `.SF` file contains information very similar to the manifest file that is always included with a JAR file. However, the `.SF` file's digest includes not the hash of the binary data in the file (as the manifest's does) but rather a hash of the data in the manifest. This locks in the manifest information.

The second file is a `.DSA` file. The `.DSA` file contains a signature of the `.SF` file and also contains, encoded inside it, a copy of the `.SF` file and a certificate authenticating the public key corresponding to the private key used for signing.

Wow, that's a mouthful. Fortunately, you should never have to know any of those details. However, you should know that both files by default are named via the first eight characters in the alias (converted to uppercase); so in this case, you would have `JAVAJOE.DSA` and `JAVAJOE.SF`. As this implies, you can sign a JAR file more than once and chain these signatures together, resulting in an `.SF` and `.DSA` file for each person who signed the file.

`jarsigner` has a number of additional options that you can use, depending on your particular situation, as outlined in Table 16.1.

TABLE 16.1 ***jarsigner*** **Options**

Option	Description
`-keystore` *`file`*	Specify the `keystore` (database file) location. By default, this file refers to *`.keystore`* in the user's home directory. This directory is specified by the `user.home` system property. For Windows systems, `user.home` is the path specified by concatenating the `HOMEDRIVE` and `HOMEPATH` environment variables, if they produce a valid path; otherwise, it is the root of the JDK installation directory.
`-storepass` *`password`*	Specify the `keystore` password. You need this password only when signing a JAR file, not when verifying it. If you fail to specify this command option, you are prompted to enter it. Normally, you should not specify this password on the command line for security reasons.

continues

TABLE 16.1 Continued

Option	Description
`-keypass` *password*	Specify the password for the individual key entry. You need this password only when signing a JAR file, not when verifying it. If you fail to specify this command option you will be prompted to enter it. Normally, you should not specify this password on the command line for security reasons. Note: The `keypass` password can be the same as the `keystore` password. If it is, the `keypass` is not required.
`-sigfile` *file*	Specifies the base filename for the `.SF` and `.DSA` files. If none is specified, the first eight characters of the alias (converted to uppercase) are used.
`-signedjar` *file*	Specifies the name to be used for the signed JAR file (output). If this is not specified, the new JAR file contains the same name as its source (and overwrites it).
`-verify`	Specifies that you want to verify the signatures in the file. This is basically the opposite of signing the file. Assuming the verification was successful, `jar verified` will be displayed. If an unsigned JAR file is verified, or one is signed with an unsupported algorithm (for example, RSA when you don't have an RSA provider installed), the following is displayed: `jar is unsigned. (signatures missing or not parsable).`
`-ids`	This option can be used only if the `-verify` and `-verbose` options are also used. If it is, the distinguished names of the JAR file signer(s) and the alias name for the `keystore` entry are also displayed.
`-verbose` *idOrSigner*	Puts `jarsigner` into verbose mode. In this mode, the signer outputs additional information as the signing or verification progresses.

NOTE Under JDK 1.1, the functionality of `keytool` and `jarsigner` was embedded in a tool called `javakey`. If you haven't upgraded to 1.2, you use `javakey` instead. However, note that there is no backward compatibility to `javakey` with `keytool`, so you can't interchange them.

With `javakey`, when you have a public key, a private key, and a certificate, you need one more thing to sign an archive. This is the directive file, which specifies the signer, certificate, and the name to be used for the signature file. The directive file consists of fields of name-value pairs. The required fields are given in Table 16.2. For a sample directive file, see Listing 16.4.

TABLE 16.2 Required JAR Directive File Fields

Field Name	Field Value
`signer`	Name of the signer. This name must already be registered in the persistent database maintained by `javakey`.
`cert`	Certificate number to use for the given signer. The first certificate is number `1`.
`chain`	Chain depth for a chain of certificates. This is currently not supported; use `0`.
`signature.file`	A name, 8 characters or shorter, to assign the signature and certificate files that will be created in the `META-INF` directory of the signed JAR archive.

LISTING 16.4 Example JAR Directive File *LiuJDF.txt*

```
signer=liu
cert=1
chain=0
signature.file=LIUSIGN
```

To sign a JAR file, use the `javakey` tool with option `-gs` and two arguments: the name of the directive file and the name of the JAR archive file. For example, the following command signs the archive `Foo.jar` using the directive file `LiuJDF.txt`:

```
javakey -gs LiuJDF.txt Foo.jar
```

In response to this command, `javakey` creates two entries in the `META-INF` directory of the archive: the signature file `LIUSIGN.SF` and the certificate file `LIUSIGN.DSA`.

NOTE Although a purported feature of JAR archives is the capability of signing individual files, the current release of the `jarsigner` tool does not seem to support this.

The *java.util.zip* Package

The `java.util.zip` package contains a number of classes that manipulate JAR archive files. Although you will typically not need to use these classes, it is helpful to understand them at a general level. You do not need to use these classes to create or load JAR files; you can use the `jar` tool and the `APPLET` tag for that.

The `java.util.zip` package defines the `Checksum` interface. The `Checksum` interface defines a protocol for a class that computes the checksum of a stream. `java.util.zip` provides two classes that implement the Checksum interface: `Adler32` and `CRC32`.

Classes

The package `java.util.zip` defines the following 14 classes.

ZipFile The `ZipFile` class represents a ZIP archive file. It provides methods that read the file's entries. This class does not allow you to create a new archive file or to edit an existing file's contents. You must use the `jar` tool for that.

ZipEntry `ZipEntry` represents an entry in an archive file and has methods that get and set various attributes of the entry, such as its name, modification time, and CRC checksum. In addition, by calling the method `ZipFile.getInputStream()` with a `ZipEntry` object, you can obtain an `InputStream` object that you can use to read the entry's contents.

Adler32* and *CRC32 The `Adler32` and `CRC32` classes implement the `Checksum` interface. They compute two different checksums of a data stream. `CRC-32` is a standard industry algorithm; `Adler-32` is a checksum developed by one of the ZLIB authors, Mark Adler, with similar characteristics but lower computational costs. To use these classes, you instantiate them and pass them to the constructor of `CheckedInputStream` or `CheckedOutputStream`. In fact, this is just what `DeflaterOutputStream` and `InflaterInputStream` do, using the `Adler32` class.

CheckedInputStream* and *CheckedOutputStream `CheckedInputStream` and `CheckedOutputStream` extend `java.io. FilterInputStream` and `java.io. FilterOutputStream`. They maintain a checksum of the data being read or written. The constructor for each of these classes takes a stream object, and an object implementing the `Checksum` interface, which allows the caller to specify different checksum algorithms for different streams.

Deflater* and *Inflater `Deflater` and `Inflater` implement general-purpose compression and decompression using the standard `deflate` compression algorithm. For more information, see RFC 1951, available at `http://www.internic.net/rfc/rfc1951.txt`.

DeflaterOutputStream* and *InflaterInputStream `DeflaterOutputStream` and `InflaterInputStream` extend `java.io. FilterInputStream` and `java.io. FilterOutputStream`. `DeflaterOutputStream` compresses its output stream; `InflaterInputStream` decompresses its input stream. These classes form the basis for other compression and decompression streams that use other protocols, including `GZIP` (`GZIPOutputStream` and `GZIPInputStream`) and `ZIP` (`ZipOutputStream` and `ZipInputStream`).

GZIPOutputStream* and *GZIPInputStream `GZIPOutputStream` and `GZIPInputStream` extend `DeflaterOuputStream` and `InflaterInputStream`. They use the standard `GZIP` compression algorithm to compress the output stream and decompress the input stream. For more information, see RFC 1952, available at `http://www.internic.net/rfc/rfc1951.txt`.

ZipOutputStream* and *ZipInputStream `ZipOutputStream` and `ZipInputStream` extend `DeflaterOuputStream` and `InflaterInputStream`. They use the ZIP compression algorithm to compress the output stream and decompress the input stream.

Reading a JAR File Programmatically

Typically, you will not use the classes in `java.util.zip` to read a JAR file; you will specify the archive to be read in your `APPLET` tag, and the browser will do the rest. However, should you need to read a JAR file yourself, this section will get you started.

First, enter Listing 16.5, named `DumpJAR.java`.

LISTING 16.5 Source Code for *DumpJAR.java*

```
import java.util.zip.ZipFile;
import java.util.zip.ZipEntry;
import java.util.Enumeration;

class DumpJAR
{
     public static void main(String[] args)
     {
          String file_name = args[0];
          try
          {
               ZipFile zip = new ZipFile(file_name);
               PrintEntryNames(zip);
          }
          catch (java.io.IOException e)
          {
               System.out.println("Exception " + e);
          }
     }

     public static void PrintEntryNames(ZipFile zip)
     {
          for (Enumeration e = zip.entries(); e.hasMoreElements(); )
          {
               ZipEntry entry = (ZipEntry)e.nextElement();
               System.out.println(entry.getName());
          }
     }
}
```

Now compile it:

```
D:\JDK1.2\demo\TicTacToe\jar>javac DumpJAR.java
```

If you run this application on the `TicTacToe.jar` file created earlier, you will see a listing of its contents. Notice that the entries are not shown in the same order that the `jar` tool produces. You should not depend on the order of entries returned by the `ZipFile.entries()` method:

```
D:\JDK1.2\demo\TicTacToe\jar>java DumpJAR TicTacToe.jar
audio/return.au
audio/ding.au
TicTacToe.class
audio/yahoo1.au
```

```
audio/yahoo2.au
images/not.gif
audio/beep.au
images/cross.gif
META-INF/MANIFEST.MF
```

JAR File Format

The JAR file format is based on the general-purpose, freely usable ZLIB file format, which is based on the ZIP file format. This is a portable file format designed to store multiple files in a directory hierarchy. The ZLIB format is not specific to any single compression method; however, the `deflate` compression scheme is commonly used. This is the compression method used in JAR files. The `deflate` protocol is based on a variant of the Lempel-Ziv algorithm, LZ77, and features low compression overhead and well-defined runtime memory requirements. This makes it a good general-purpose compression protocol. For more information about ZLIB, refer to RFC 1950 and RFC 1951, available at `ftp://ds.internic.net/rfc/`.

In general, you won't need to concern yourself with the details of the JAR file format, because you interact with JAR files through the `jar` and `javakey` tools and possibly the `java.util.zip` package.

CHAPTER 17

Applets Versus Applications

In this chapter

Applications Explored

Although Java became famous for its capability to create applets, it is also an equally powerful language to develop full-fledged applications. In fact, the ability to use Java to create applications may be the more powerful attribute. Applications written in Java do not suffer from the numerous pitfalls that traditional programming paradigms present.

It's almost ironic that the most overlooked portion of Java is the capability to create applications. When programming in other languages, such as C, C++, or any other traditional language, what you always create are standard programs. Oddly enough, the hype surrounding applets has created an environment where most people interested in Java completely overlook the possibility of using Java to create applications in addition to applets.

The difference between applications and applets is at once very subtle and at the same time very profound. In fact, as you will learn later in the chapter, applications can at the same time be applets and vice versa. The most fundamental difference between applets and applications is their operating environment. Applets must "live" within a browser such as Netscape Navigator, Microsoft Internet Explorer, or AppletViewer. Applications can be run directly from the command prompt with the use of the Java interpreter. (If you're using the JDK, that would be java.exe.)

NOTE In the future, you will be able to run Java applications directly from your operating system without having to invoke the Java interpreter. Microsoft, IBM, and Apple have all signed a letter of intent to embed the Java Virtual Machine into upcoming versions of their operating systems. In addition, Sun has a project currently code-named Kona, which will be an entirely Java-based OS. When the JVM becomes part of the OS, Java applications will become even more crucial.

Advantages of Applications

The application model offers a number of advantages over the applet. For one thing, applications can be faster. This is caused by a couple of things. First, an application does not have the overhead of the browser to deal with. In addition, when run as an applet, the browser generally has control of the amount of memory an applet may utilize. As an application, you have complete control over the entire environment the program is running in. These items combine to result in slightly faster execution of Java applications, which are free of some of the burdens of their applet counterparts.

The Sandbox

The more substantial difference between applications and applets is the lack of what is known as a *sandbox*. The sandbox restricts the operation of an applet. Under ordinary circumstances, an applet is forbidden from trying to write or read from your local file system, for instance, and the applet cannot open an URL to any host on the Internet that it pleases, only to the host from which the HTML and class files came. In contrast, an application is under no such restrictions. When a Java program is run as an application, it has all the rights and capabilities that any program written in, say C++, would have.

NOTE If you read chapters 16 and 34, you will learn how to create signed applets. These applets can open the security box and allow the applet to perform additional operations.

In addition, the new JDK 1.2 security features allow you to do just the opposite. You can restrict an application or a part of the application so that it has no more rights than an applet.

This means that applications can run what are known as trusted methods. You can find a number of these methods in the `java.lang.RunTime` class. However, they also include all native methods, and a host of others.

So, assuming that you don't care about the minor performance boost, and you don't need access to elements outside the sandbox, why not just bundle AppletViewer with your applet? Applications have four additional advantages:

- Windows generated from an application do not display the `Warning applet window`, which can be a source of confusion to inexperienced users.
- Applications do not require an HTML file to tell them what to load.
- Applications are much cleaner because they are executed just like normal executable programs.
- Your clients undoubtedly will consider applications to be full-fledged programs, and based on the name alone, they will consider applets to be miniature programs. Generally, this means that they will be willing to pay more for something that they perceive to be a complete program as compared to a partial one.

Developing Java Applications

When you learned about writing Java applets in Chapter 14, "Writing an Applet," one of the first things you learned is that any applet must extend the `java.applet.Applet` class. Unlike applets, applications do not need to extend any other class in order to be usable. In fact, the reason that applets need to extend the `java.applet.Applet` class is so that an application (known as a browser) can use the class through polymorphism.

▶ **See** "Extending Objects Through Inheritance." **p. 76**

Any Java class can be run as an application. There is really only one restriction to this: To run a class as an application, it must have a `main` method with the following prototype:

```
public static void main (String args[])
```

So an application can be thought of as just a normal class that has one unique feature: a `static public main` method. In Java the `main()` method has the same purpose as the `main()` function in C and C++—it's where the application starts.

HelloWorld—The Application

As you have done in previous chapters and will continue to do throughout this book, take a look at the infamous "Hello World" program as it would be written as a Java application, as shown in Listing 17.1.

Listing 17.1 The Simplest Application Is *HelloWorld*

```
public class Hello{
    public static void main(String args[]){
         System.out.println("Hello World!");
    }
}
```

You can compile the `Hello` class just as you have the others in this book. From a command prompt type:

```
javac Hello.java
```

Alternatively, on a Macintosh drag the `Hello.java` file over the `javac` icon.

NOTE As with any standard public class, `Hello` must be defined within a file that carries its name followed by the extension `.java`. Therefore, in this case `Hello` must be in a file called `Hello.java`.

To invoke a Java application, you will use the syntax `[java ClassName]`. Note that you use the `ClassName` only, not the `ClassName.class` or the `ClassName.java`. `java` will search the existing classpath (which includes your current directory [.]) to try to locate the class that you have indicated. Therefore, to run your `Hello` application from the command prompt, type the following:

```
java Hello
```

What you should see is the message `Hello World` appear onscreen. Note that you did not type `Hello.class`, only `Hello`. The Java Virtual Machine implicitly knows that the `Hello` class is located within the file `Hello.class`, and that it should start off right away with the `main()` method.

NOTE On the Macintosh, things work a bit differently, as you have already learned when you learned to compile Java programs. In the case of running a Java application, double-click the Java icon and enter the class name you wish to run. Alternatively, you can drag the class file for the application over the Java icon.

Also, for users of Windows, to get a command prompt you need to start the program MS-DOS Prompt.

Passing Parameters to an Application

As you saw with the "HelloWorld" application, applications, unlike applets, do not rely on an HTML file to be loaded. This can be a benefit because it decreases the complexity of the system, but how then do you pass parameters into the application?

In C/C++ you will typically utilize the values in the arrays of `argv` and `argc`. The `argv/argc` system tends to be one that is a bit obtuse, and many programmers look up how to utilize the variables each time they need them. In Java, the parameter set is much simpler.

You will recall from laying out the prototype for the `main()` method that main has a parameter—an *array of strings*. This array of strings contains the values of the additional parameters left on the command line. If you are a DOS user, for example, you're probably familiar with the `/?` option. For instance:

```
dir /?
```

The `/?` is an additional parameter to the `dir` program. Now, take a look at how to do this with the Hello World program. Instead of having the program say hello to the whole world, change it so that it only says hello to you. Listing 17.2 shows just how to do this.

Listing 17.2 *HelloWorld* Using a Command-Line Parameter

```
public class Hello{
    public static void main(String args[]){
         System.out.println("Hello "+args[0]+"!");
    }
}
```

To compile the program, type:

```
javac Hello.java
```

But to run this version of `Hello` is slightly different because you need to use the additional parameter:

```
java Hello Weber
```

Now, what you should see is:

```
     Hello Weber!
```

Preventing Null Pointer Exceptions

If you accidentally did not type the additional parameter at the end of the command line, what you saw was:

```
java.lang.ArrayIndexOutOfBoundsException:
    at Hello.main(Hello.java):3
```

To prevent this message, if a user happens to forget to add his or her name at the end of the line, you need to put in some error checking. Probably the best way to do this is to add an `if` statement. Make one more change to the Hello World program, as shown in Listing 17.3.

Listing 17.3 *HelloWorld* with a Parameter and Some Error Checking

```
public class Hello{
    public static void main(String args[]){
         if (args.length <1){
              System.out.println("Syntax for running Hello is:");
              System.out.println("        java  Hello  <Name>");
              System.out.println("\n\nWhere <Name> is the person to greet");
         } else
              System.out.println("Hello "+args[0]+"!");
    }
}
```

Now, if you happen to run the Hello World program without any parameters, what you will see should look like this:

```
Syntax for running Hello is:
       java  Hello  <Name>
```

Where `<Name>` is the person to greet

Limitations Imposed Due to the Static Nature of *main()*

The `main` method of a class has characteristics very similar to the `main()` function in C or C++. Unlike C and C++, however, because the `main` method must be static, it cannot utilize nonstatic methods or variables of its class directly. The following code, for instance, would not compile:

```
public class fooBar {
    int foo;
    public static void main(String args[]){
         foo = 50;
    }
}
```

The problem, of course, is that the `foo` variable is not static, and the compiler will refuse to allow the static method `main()` to modify it. To understand why this occurs, review what it means for any method or variable to be static. When a static method is loaded into memory, the virtual machine looks at it and essentially says: "Okay, well there is only going to be one of these, regardless of how many instances of the class the user creates, so I'm going to assign it to a special place in memory. I might as well do that now." This happens not when the class is first instantiated, but as soon as the class is loaded. Later, when the `fooBar` class is actually instantiated, what would happen if the `main` method were allowed to access the `foo` variable?

When the `fooBar` class is instantiated, the machine allocates space for the `foo` variable, and then calls the `main` method. But wait, the `main` method was already placed into memory with a reference to the foo variable...but which `foo` variable? Of course this is assuming that you had actually been able to compile this class. So there is no real answer, but you can see why the compiler won't let you perform this type of activity.

You can solve this problem in one of two ways. First, you can declare the `foo` variable to be static, as shown in Listing 17.4.

Listing 17.4 *fooBar* Written so that *foo* Is Static

```
public class fooBar {
    static int foo;

    public init(){
         System.out.println("Init method");
    }

    public static void main(String args[]){
         foo = 50;
    }
}
```


The `fooBar` class will now compile, but what about calling methods, such as the `init` method in the preceding example? Because the `init()` method is not itself static, the compiler would again refuse to compile the `fooBar` class. Of course, you could declare the `init` method to be static as well, but this can quickly become quite cumbersome, and it would be difficult, if not impossible, to actually perform many of the useful tasks you want to do as a programmer. Instead, it is probably a good idea to have the `fooBar`'s `main` method instantiate another copy of `fooBar`, as shown in Listing 17.5.

Listing 17.5 *fooBar* Creates an Instance of Itself in the *main* Method

```
public class fooBar {
    int foo;

    public init(){
         System.out.println("Init method");
    }

    public static void main(String args[]){
         fooBar f = new fooBar();
         f.foo = 50;
         f.init();
    }
}
```

Now, because the `f` variable is actually created within the `main` method, you can perform operations on the `f` instance. The major difference here is that you are performing operations not on the `this` variables, but on the `f.this` variables, and this distinction helps the compiler understand how to deal with such methods. In other words, `f` is actually an *instance* of `fooBar`.

Converting an Applet to an Application

Now that you have briefly looked at how to create an application, consider another very important aspect of application programming—converting an applet to an application. You see, there is really no reason why a program you have already written as an applet can't also be run as an application. This section provides a step-by-step walkthrough that shows you how to convert the clock applet (shown in Figure 17.1) into an application.

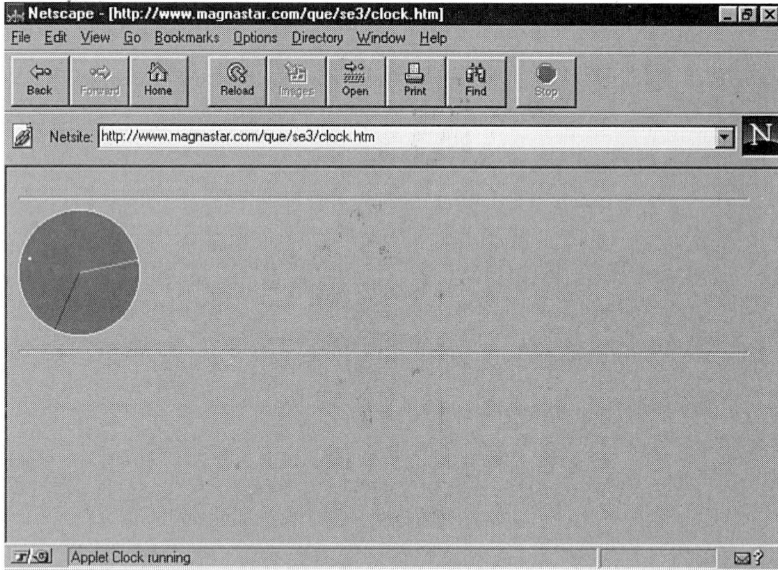

FIG. 17.1
The clock applet running in Navigator.

Why Convert an Applet to an Application?

An applet cannot be run from the command prompt without a browser.

So why convert an applet to an application? Well for one thing, believe it or not, not everyone in the world has realized that the Internet exists. Some people and companies do, but do not yet have access to the Internet, and many companies have access to the Internet but do not allow their users to surf the World Wide Web. More important, though, many people do not have access to the World Wide Web all of the time. For those people who don't have access to the World Wide Web all the time, applications on the Web aren't as useful.

As a result, before long you probably will want to present your applets to people and companies that are not yet familiar with the Internet, or you may want to present your applets to people without forcing them to be connected to the Internet. One perfect example of this is when you want to deliver your applets on a CD-ROM. With Java, there is no reason why the application you deliver on the CD should be any different from what you display on the Internet. Imagine being able to develop a single application that will run on every platform and that can work over the World Wide Web, Enterprise Network, and CD-ROM, all without changing a single line of code or performing a single recompilation.

Changing the Applet Code to an Application

For this chapter, you will change the simple clock applet into an application. Listing 17.6 shows the source code for the applet.

Listing 17.6 A Simple Application That Displays a Clock

```
/*
*
* Clock
*
*/
import java.applet.Applet;
import java.awt.*;
import java.util.*;

public class Clock extends Applet implements Runnable{
    Thread thisThread;

    Color faceColor,borderColor,minuteColor,hourColor,secondColor;

    public void init(){
         //read in the colors for each of the hands and for the face/border
         faceColor = readColor (getParameter("faceCol"));
         borderColor = readColor (getParameter("borderCol"));
         minuteColor = readColor (getParameter("minuteCol"));
         hourColor = readColor(getParameter("hourCol"));
         secondColor = readColor(getParameter("secondCol"));
    }

    // This method creates a color based on a  string.
    // The string is assumed to be "red,green,blue"  where each
    // of the colors is represented by its integer equivalent.
    public Color readColor(String aColor) {
     if (aColor == null) {
           return Color.black;
      }

     int r;
     int g;
     int b;

      //break the string apart into each number
      StringTokenizer st = new StringTokenizer(aColor, ",");

     try {
         r = Integer.valueOf(st.nextToken()).intValue();
         g = Integer.valueOf(st.nextToken()).intValue();
         b = Integer.valueOf(st.nextToken()).intValue();
         return new Color(r,g,b);
```

continues

Listing 17.6 Continued

```
        }
        catch (Exception e) {
            System.out.println("An exception occurred trying
➥ to convert a parameter to a color:"+e);
            return Color.black;
        }
    }


    public void start(){
        thisThread = new Thread(this);
        thisThread.start();
    }

    public void run(){
        while(true){
            repaint();
            try{
                thisThread.sleep(1000);
            }catch (Exception e){}
        }
    }

    public void update(Graphics g){
        paint(g);
    }

    public void paint(Graphics g){
        //fill clock face
        g.setColor(faceColor);
        g.fillOval(0,0,100,100);
        g.setColor(borderColor);
        g.drawOval(0,0,100,100);

        //get the current time
        Calendar d = Calendar.getInstance();
        //draw the minute hand
        g.setColor(minuteColor);
        double angle = (((double)(90 - d.get
➥(Calendar.MINUTE)))/60)*2 * Math.PI;
        g.drawLine(50,50,50+(int)(Math.sin(angle)*50),50 +
➥(int)(Math.cos(angle)*50));
        //draw the hour hand
        g.setColor(hourColor);
        angle = ((((double)18 - d.get(Calendar.HOUR_OF_DAY)
➥+(double)d.get(Calendar.MINUTE)/60))/12)*2 * Math.PI;
       g.drawLine(50,50,50+(int)(Math.sin(angle)*40),50 +
➥(int)(Math.cos(angle)*40));
       //draw the second hand
       g.setColor(secondColor);
       angle = (((double)(90 - d.get(Calendar.SECOND)))/60)*2 * Math.PI;
       g.drawLine(50,50,50+(int)(Math.sin(angle)*50),50 +
➥(int)(Math.cos(angle)*50));
```

```
    }
}
```

The first task is to add a `main()` method to the `Clock` class to make it into an application. To do so, open `Clock.java` in your favorite text editor. Page all the way down until you reach the closing brace (}). Directly before that brace, add the code shown in Listing 17.7.

Listing 17.7 New *main* Method for *Clock.java*

```
static boolean inApplet =true;
public static void main(String args[]){
        /*set a boolean flag to show if you are in an applet or not */
        inApplet=false;

        /*Create a Frame to place our application in. */
        /*You can change the string value to show your desired label*/
        /*for the frame */
        Frame myFrame = new Frame ("Clock as an Application");

        /*Create a clock instance. */
        Clock myApp = new Clock();


        /*Add the current application to the Frame */
        myFrame.add ("Center",myApp);

        /*Resize the Frame to the desired size, and make it visible */
        myFrame.setSize(100,130);
        myFrame.show();

        /*Run the methods the browser normally would */
        myApp.init();
        myApp.start();
}
```


Here is a line-by-line breakdown of this code fragment:

```
inApplet=false;
```

The first statement in this code creates a status variable, so you can tell if the program is being run as an applet or as an application. As you will learn later, you often must do a few things differently when you have an applet that is not actually running in a browser such as AppletViewer or Netscape. As a result, a Boolean variable (`inApplet`) has been added to the class. Technically, for good programming structure, the declaration for this variable should be placed at the top with the rest of your variables, but it's easier to see it here. Notice that the variable is declared to be `static`. If you miss this keyword, the compiler growls at you about referencing a nonstatic variable in a static method. `main()` must be static and public for you to run the method as an application.

```
Frame myFrame = new Frame ("Clock as an Application");
```

Next, you create a frame in which to put your new clock. The parameter `"Clock as an Application"` is placed in the title bar of `Frame`. Indicating that the program is being run as an application is good practice; this indication helps eliminate confusion on the part of the user. If you don't want to set the title in the `Constructor` for some reason, you can create an untitled `Frame` and change the title later, using `setTitle(String)`, if you prefer.

```
Clock myApp = new Clock();
```

The next line indicates that you want to create a new instance of the class `Clock`. A perfectly legitimate question at this point is, why not use `this`? After all, `this` is an instantiation of the class `Clock` already, right? The primary reason to create a new instance of `Clock` is to avoid rewriting any of the applet methods to make them static. Just as it is not legitimate to change the variable `inApplet` if it is nonstatic, it is not legitimate to try to access a nonstatic method. It is, however, legitimate to access the nonstatic methods of a variable. Bearing that in mind, create a new instance variable of the class `Clock` called `myApp` and add it to the frame.

```
myFrame.add ("Center",myApp);
```

The next line adds the new `Clock` variable to the frame. This is important because before you attach the `Clock` to something, it can't be displayed.

▶ **See** "Layout Managers," **p. 406**

Next, you add the lines `myFrame.resetSize(100,130) and myFrame.show()` to the `Clock.java` file. `myFrame.setSize(100,130)` tells the application to make the frame's size 100×100, but you also need to account for a 30-pixel title bar that the frame has vertically. Normally, when you convert an applet to an application, you know the ideal size for your applet. When in doubt, go ahead and copy the `WIDTH` and `HEIGHT` values from your most commonly used HTML file. On those rare occasions when you want the size to be adjustable, use the techniques covered later in this chapter when you learn how to account for parameter data, to read in the size from the command line.

```
myFrame.resize(100,100);
myFrame.show();
```

CAUTION

Technically, when the applet has been added to the frame, you could go through the normal applet methods `init()` and `start()` right there. Contrary to popular belief, however, this procedure is not a good idea. If your applet uses double buffering or requires any other image that is built with the `createImage(x,y)` method, the procedure will not work until the frame has been shown. The drawback is that you will see a flicker as the frame comes up with nothing in it. Keep this fact in the back of your mind, even if you're not using `createImage(x,y)` now because this minor fact is not documented anywhere and has caused this author hours of headaches because it's easy to forget.

Finally, you add the lines myApp.init() and myApp.start() to your function. Because your application is not running in the browser, the init() and start() methods are not called automatically, as they would be if the program were running as an applet. As a result, you must simulate the effect by calling the methods explicitly. It should be pointed out that if your application does not appear, you may want to add the line myApp.repaint() to the end of the main() method.

```
myApp.init();
myApp.start();
```

Before you save your new copy of Clock.java, you need to make one more change. Go to the top of the file in which you are performing your imports and make sure that you are importing java.awt.Frame. Then go ahead and save the file.

```
import java.awt.Frame
```


Accounting for Other Applet Peculiarities

The most difficult problem to deal with when you convert applets to applications has to do with duplicating the effect of a parameter tag and other applet-specific tasks. You can handle this situation in many ways; the following sections discuss two of the most common solutions.

Defaulting The first solution is defaulting. In defaulting, the idea is to provide the application with all the information that it would be getting anyway from the HTML file. In a sense, this solution is exactly what you did when you told the Frame what size you wanted to use with resize(x,y). To do this for the <param> items requires rewriting the getParameter method.

Clock has several parameters it receives in <param> tags. Take a look at the number of <param> tags from the Clock's HTML file in Listing 17.8.

Listing 17.8 *Clock.html*

```
<TITLE>Clock</TITLE>
<H1>Clock </H1>
<hr>
<applet code="Clock.class" width=100 height=100>
<param name=hourCol value=255,00,00 >
<param name=minuteCol value=00,255,00>
<param name=secondCol value=00,00,255>
<param name=borderCol value=255,255,255>
<param name=faceCol value=125,125,125>
</applet>
<hr>
```

To mimic these effects in your new application, add the method shown in Listing 17.9 to your current Clock.java file.

Listing 17.9 *getParameter()* Method for *Clock.java*

```
public String getParameter (String name){
    String ST;
    if (inApplet)
         return super.getParameter(name);
    //If you are not in an applet you default all of the values.
    if (name == "hourCol")
         return "255,00,00" ;
    if (name == "minuteCol")
         return "00,255,00";
    if (name == "secondCol")
         return "00,00,255";
    if (name == "borderCol")
         return "255,255,255";
    if (name == "faceCol")
         return "125,125,125";
    return null;
}
```

CAUTION

If you are going to have several parameters, you should use a `switch` statement. A `switch` requires an integer, however, which you can get by using the `hashCode()` of the string. Unfortunately, because multiple strings can have the same `hashCode()`, you must then make sure you really have the correct string. This makes the solution much more involved. Still, if you are working with several `<param>` tags, consider using this alternative method.

This method replaces the duties normally performed by the `java.applet.Applet` class with your own default values.

Notice that the first thing you do is check to see whether you are in an applet (`if (inApplet)`). If so, you use the `getParameter(String)` method from your super class (`java.applet.Applet`). Doing this maintains your normal pattern of operation when you go back and use `Clock` as an applet again. The idea is to have one program that can run as both an application and an applet.

NOTE A better way to handle the `getParameter()` is to implement `appletStub`. However, without a complete explanation of interfaces, explaining how to do this would be purely academic. If you plan to implement several aspects of `java.applet.Applet`, refer to Chapter 12, "Interfaces," for more information.

Recompiling the Application

The next step is recompiling the application. Recompiling an application is no different from compiling an applet. In this case, type the following:

```
javac Clock.java
```

Testing the Application

Now you can test your application (see Figure 17.2). To do so, you need to invoke the Java Virtual Machine, followed by the class name, as follows:

```
java Clock
```

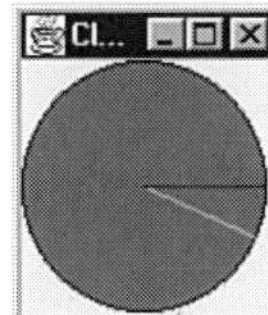

FIG. 17.2
The `Clock` running as an application

TIP Be sure to maintain proper capitalization at all times.

Second Way to Add *<param>* Information Defaulting is a quick and easy way to get the extraneous information into an application that you normally leave in an HTML file. Odds are, however, that if you took the time to include a parameter tag in the first place, you don't want the values to be fixed. After all, you could have hard-coded the values to start with, and then you never would have had this problem in the first place. How do you get information into your application from the outside world? The easiest answer is to get it from the command line.

As you recall, the `main()` method takes an array of strings as an argument. You can use this array to deliver information to an application at runtime. This section addresses one of the simplest cases: sending the `WIDTH` and `HEIGHT` information to the application from the command line. Although this section doesn't also explain how to insert the information for a `<param>`, hopefully you can deduce from this example how to do it for `<param>` tags on your own.

To use the information from the command line, you need to make a few modifications in the `main()` method. Listing 17.10 shows the new version.

Listing 17.10 New *main()* Method

```
public static void main(String args[]){
    /*set a boolean flag to show if you are in an applet or not */
    inApplet=false;

    /*Create a Frame to place your application in. */
    /*You can change the string value to show your desired label*/
    /*for the frame */
    Frame myFrame = new Frame ("Clock as an Application");

    /*Create a clock instance. */
    Clock myApp = new Clock();
```

continues

Listing 17.10 Continued

```
    /*Add the current application to the Frame */
    myFrame.add ("Center",myApp);

    /*Resize the Frame to the desired size, and make it visible */
    /*Resize the Frame to the desired size, and make it visible */
    if (args.length>=2)
      /*resize the Frame based on command line inputs */
      myFrame.setSize(Integer.parseInt(args[0]),Integer.parseInt(args[1]));
    else
      myFrame.setSize(100,130);
    myFrame.show();

    /*Run the methods the browser normally would */
    myApp.init();
    myApp.start();
  }
```

Make the necessary changes and recompile the program. Now you can run the `Clock` at any size you want. Try the following:

```
java Clock 100 100
```

At first glance, your new `main()` method is almost identical to the one in Listing 17.3. The main difference is a group of six lines:

```
/*Resize the Frame to the desired size, and make it visible */
if (argv.length>=2)
     /*resize the Frame based on command line inputs */
     myFrame.setSize(Integer.parseInt(args[0]),Integer.parseInt(args[1]));
else
     myFrame.setSize(100,130);
```

The first line of actual code checks to see whether the user put enough information in the command line. This check prevents null pointer exceptions caused by accessing information that isn't really there. Besides, you probably want the user to be able to run `Clock` at its normal size without specifying the actual size.

The next line is the one that does most of the work. It should be fairly obvious to you what is happening in this code, but you should know why you need to use `Integer.parseInt` on the array values. At runtime, the Java machine isn't aware of what is coming in from the command line; it just sees a string. To convert a string to an `int`, you need to use the class `Integer's` `parseInt(String)` method. (Note, use the `Integer` class, not `int`. If you're confused, refer to Chapter 7, "Data Types and Other Tokens.")

CAUTION

To be complete, the `parseInt` method should be surrounded by a `try{} catch{}` block, in case something other than an integer is typed in the command line.

Making the Window Close Work

By now, you probably have noticed that to close your new `Clock` application you have to press Ctrl+C or in some other way cause the operating system to close your application. To allow the user to close the window the normal way, you need to catch the `windowClosing()` event that is generated. You can do this by creating a window listener and performing an exit in the `windowClosing()` method.

The `WindowListener` interface requires you to implement several methods, so it's not always the most convenient thing to do. Fortunately, the `java.awt.event` package includes several convenience adapters that take care of some of the work for you. In the case of `WindowListener`, the class `WindowAdapter` implements the interface and provides default behavior for each of the methods. So, now you can extend the WindowAdapter class and just override whatever method you are interested in.

In the case of the Clock program, now you can create an anonymous class and add a `WindowAdapter` to the `myFrame` variable:

```
myFrame.addWindowListener(new WindowAdapter(){
  public void windowClosing(WindowEvent event){
    System.exit(0);
  }
});
```

Finally, the complete `Clock` applet should look like Listing 17.11.

Listing 17.11 The Final *Clock* Application with Everything in Place

```
/*
*
* Clock
*
*/
import java.applet.Applet;
import java.awt.*;
import java.awt.event.*;
import java.util.*;

public class Clock extends Applet implements Runnable{
  Thread thisThread;

  Color faceColor ,borderColor,minuteColor,hourColor,secondColor;

  public void init(){
    //read in the colors for each of the hands and for the face/border
    faceColor = readColor (getParameter("faceCol"));
    borderColor = readColor (getParameter("borderCol"));
    minuteColor = readColor (getParameter("minuteCol"));
    hourColor = readColor(getParameter("hourCol"));
    secondColor = readColor(getParameter("secondCol"));
  }
```

continues

Listing 17.11 Continued

```
// This method creates a color based on a  string.
// The string is assumed to be "red,green,blue"  where each
// of the colors is represented by it's integer equivalent.
public Color readColor(String aColor) {
  if (aColor == null) {
    return Color.black;
  }

  int r;
  int g;
  int b;

  //break the string apart into each number
  StringTokenizer st = new StringTokenizer(aColor, ",");

  try {
    r = Integer.valueOf(st.nextToken()).intValue();
    g = Integer.valueOf(st.nextToken()).intValue();
    b = Integer.valueOf(st.nextToken()).intValue();
    return new Color(r,g,b);
  }
  catch (Exception e) {
    System.out.println("An exception occurred trying to
➥ convert a parameter to a color:"+e);
    return Color.black;
  }
}


public void start(){
  thisThread = new Thread(this);
  thisThread.start();
}

public void run(){
  while(true){
    repaint();
    try{
      thisThread.sleep(1000);
    }catch (Exception e){}
  }
}

public void update(Graphics g){
  paint(g);
}

public void paint(Graphics g){
  //fill clock face
  g.setColor(faceColor);
  g.fillOval(0,0,100,100);
  g.setColor(borderColor);
  g.drawOval(0,0,100,100);
```

```
    //get the current time
    Calendar d = Calendar.getInstance();
    //draw the minute hand
    g.setColor(minuteColor);
    double angle = (((double)(90 - d.get(Calendar.MINUTE)))/60)*2 * Math.PI;
    g.drawLine(50,50,50+(int)(Math.sin(angle)*50),50 +
➥(int)(Math.cos(angle)*50));
    //draw the hour hand
    g.setColor(hourColor);
    angle = ((((double)18 - d.get(Calendar.HOUR_OF_DAY)+
➥(double)d.get(Calendar.MINUTE)/60))/12)*2 * Math.PI;
    g.drawLine(50,50,50+(int)(Math.sin(angle)*40),50 +
➥(int)(Math.cos(angle)*40));
    //draw the second hand
    g.setColor(secondColor);
    angle = (((double)(90 - d.get(Calendar.SECOND)))/60)*2 * Math.PI;
    g.drawLine(50,50,50+(int)(Math.sin(angle)*50),50 +
➥(int)(Math.cos(angle)*50));
  }


  static boolean inApplet =true;
  public static void main(String args[]){
    /*set a boolean flag to show if you are in an applet or not */
    inApplet=false;

    /*Create a Frame to place your application in. */
    /*You can change the string value to show your desired label*/
    /*for the frame */
    Frame myFrame = new Frame ("Clock as an Application");
    myFrame.addWindowListener(new WindowAdapter(){
      public void windowClosing(WindowEvent event){
      System.exit(0);
      }
      });


    /*Create a clock instance. */
    Clock myApp = new Clock();


    /*Add the current application to the Frame */
    myFrame.add ("Center",myApp);

    /*Resize the Frame to the desired size, and make it visible */
    /*Resize the Frame to the desired size, and make it visible */
    if (args.length>=2)
      /*resize the Frame based on command line inputs */
      myFrame.setSize(Integer.parseInt(args[0]),Integer.parseInt(args[1]));
    else
      myFrame.setSize(100,130);
    myFrame.show();
```

continues

Listing 17.11 Continued

```
    /*Run the methods the browser normally would */
    myApp.init();
    myApp.start();
  }

  public String getParameter (String name){
    String ST;
    if (inApplet)
      return super.getParameter(name);
    //If you are not in an applet you default all of the values.
    if (name == "hourCol")
      return "255,00,00" ;
    if (name == "minuteCol")
      return "00,255,00";
    if (name == "secondCol")
      return "00,00,255";
    if (name == "borderCol")
      return "0,0,0";
    if (name == "faceCol")
      return "125,125,125";
    return null;
  }


}
```

Now, recompile and run `Clock` one last time. If you click the Window Close icon, `Clock` exits like a normal program.

Checking All the Applet Methods

When you convert your own applets to applications, you need to perform one final step. You need to search for all methods in `java.applet.Applet` that are valid only with respect to a browser. Most commonly, you need to search for the methods described in the following sections.

getAppletContext() Fortunately, most of the things you will do with `getAppletContext()` you can ignore with applications. `showDocument()`, for example, has no meaning without a browser. Attempting to execute `getAppletContext().showDocument()` produces an error on `System.out`, but the application shouldn't crash because of it.

Similarly, `showStatus()` usually is not relevant with applications. In applets that use the applet context to display information, the easiest thing to do usually is to surround the specific code with an `if (inApplet){}` block and ignore it if you're not in an applet.

What do you do if you really have to see that information? You can select the top and bottom 17 lines of the `Frame` and write into the `paint` method a section that displays the applet-context information there. Why do you select the top and the bottom? Due to a strange quirk between the UNIX version of `Frame` peer and the Windows 95 version of `Frame` peer, each system chops out a 17-line area in which it can display its `Warning applet` message. On Windows machines, this area is the top 17 lines; on UNIX machines, it is the bottom 17 lines.

If you're not convinced, go to the following URL:

```
http://www.magnastar.com/ultra_nav
```

UltraNav is a program by MagnaStar Inc. which aids in the navigation of Web pages. Notice the yellow "information" line. Its location moves based on your platform.

If you are on a Windows machine, you should see an information bar at the top of the `Frame`. If you're on a UNIX machine, that bar is at the bottom. The bar is being drawn at both the top and the bottom; you are just seeing only one.

getCodeBase() and getDocumentBase() `getCodeBase()`and `getDocumentBase()` are a bit trickier to deal with. Both of these methods return an URL, and you don't want to limit yourself to having the user connected to the Internet. After all, if the user can access your Web site, you probably have him or her downloading the applet directly from you, so you would have no need to turn the applet into an application.

You will usually deal with `getCodeBase()` and `getDocumentBase()` on a case-by-case basis. If you can get away without the information, ignore it. If you really need the information from `getCodeBase()` or `getDocumentBase()`, you may have to give it a hard-coded URL or one that you read from the command line.

Paying Attention to Your *Constructor* Frequently, when converting applets, you will find yourself creating a `Constructor` for your class other than the null `Constructor`. Creating a custom `Constructor` is a perfectly desirable thing to do to pass information from the command line or other information. If you do this, however, make sure you add the null `Constructor` back in manually (the null `Constructor` is the `Constructor` that does not take any parameters on input). If you create another `Constructor`, Java doesn't automatically generate a null one for you. You won't even notice that you need one until you are working on a project and another class needs to create an instance of your applet, for a thread or something. When this situation occurs, the class attempts to access the null `Constructor`. Now, even though you didn't actually delete the null `Constructor` from the class, it is no longer there. The error message that you get will look something like this:

```
java.lang.NoSuchMethodError
      at sun.applet.AppletPanel.run(AppletPanel.java:170)
      at java.lang.Thread(Thread.java)
```

Notice that nothing in the error message tells you anything about your classes. The error doesn't even look like one that involves your class; it looks like a bug in `AppletPanel`. If you encounter this situation, the first thing to do is delete `*.class` and recompile the whole program. Then the compiler will be able to catch the missing `Constructor` call.

createImage If you are using `createImage`, and the `Image` variable is being returned as null when you convert your applet to an application, make sure you have made the `Frame` visible first. See the caution under "Changing the Applet Code to an Application," earlier in this chapter.

Packaging Your Applications in Zip Format

Now that you have converted your applets to applications, you can send them to your clients. The best way to deliver the applications is in a single JAR file. To package the file as a JAR, just follow the directions in Chapter 16, "JAR Archive Files." Once you have the JAR file, you just need to add it to the classpath. Then you will be able to run the program just as if all the classes had been spread about the directory.

Converting an Application to an Applet

Converting an application to an applet is on one side much less complicated than converting an applet and on another almost impossible. The easy part of converting an application to an applet is getting the basic functionality of the application running. To do this, you really only have one design decision. The question at hand is this: Do you want to start and stop your application when the person leaves your Web page, or do you want to start it once and leave it at that?

The Simplest Conversion

Assuming that you want to start the application once, all you need to do is extend `java.applet.Applet` and call the `static main` method in the `init()` method:

```
public void init(){
    main(null);
}
```

NOTE What do you do if you are already extending another class? Well, unfortunately there's no good answer to this question unless you are extending `Panel`, `Container`, or `Component`. In the case of those three classes, just extend `Applet` instead (that is, change extends xxxx to extends `Applet`). Polymorphism will leave your application virtually unchanged. If you're not so lucky, however, you will need to find another way to be able to extend `Applet`. The two more common classes which are extended may have fairly easy solutions depending on your situation.

`Thread`—Change your applet to implement `Runnable`. If you need access to `Thread` methods, you will need to keep an instance variable for your running `Thread`.

`Frame`—Depending on what you are doing with the `Frame`, you may just be able to extend `Applet`, but odds are you will need to create an instance `Frame` and add the `Applet` to it:

```
Frame fr = new Frame();
fr.add(this);
```

All `Frame` calls will then need to be directed at the `fr` variable.

Handling Command-Line Parameters

Now, of course, if you accept command-line parameters, you can set up `<PARAM>` tags to account for this and pass them into an array which you would then deliver to the application as follows:

```
public void init(){
    String args[] = new String[2];
    args[1] = getParameter("param1");
    args[2]= getParameter("param2");
    main(args);
}
```

Maintaining a Single Instance of the Application

If, instead of starting the application once and letting it go on infinitely, you want to start and stop your application as the user enters and exits the Web site, you have got some things to think about. The easy solution is to create a new instance of the application each time in the `start()` method by changing the method to `start()` rather than `init()`. In the `stop()` method, you would perform the exiting procedures you normally have in place for your application.

On the other hand, if you want to leave the instance of the application up, but you just want to put it to sleep, you will have to do some extra work. How you do this depends entirely on your program. If your application is in a `Frame()`, however, you may just be able to hide and show the `Frame` as in the next instance:

```
public void init(){
    String args[] = new String[2];
    args[1] = getParameter("param1");
    args[2]= getParameter("param2");
    main(args);
}

public void start(){
    myApp.show();
}

public void stop(){
    myApp.hide();
}
```

Note that for this to work, you will need to keep an instance method of `myApp` which you generate in the `main()` method.

The More Difficult Problems for Application-to-Applet Conversion

There is, however, a very sticky problem when converting applications to applets that is not so easily dealt with: replacing security-protected methods in applets. Unfortunately, for some problems there is just no solution. `System.exec()`, for example, cannot be called from an applet.

The most common problem, however, is accessing files. Unfortunately, there is no real way to completely replace access to files—especially if you need to write to the file as well as read from it. A possible replacement does exist for you, however, if all you need to do is read from the file: the `URL` class. You see the following two code fragments produce `InputStreams` (the `is` variable) which can both read from a file.

```
try{
    FileInputStream fs = new FileInputStream("myFile.txt");
    InputStream is = new InputStream (fs);
}catch (

try{
    URL us = new URL("http:"//www.magnastar.com/myFile.txt");
    InputStream is = us.openStream();
} catch {
```

One difference here is that the `myFile.txt` file is located in a different location. In the first case, it is on the local file system; in the latter, it is on a Web server. For configuration files, however, this may be okay.

If you need to write to a file too, you're stuck. Either you can sign the applet and restrict yourself to 1.1 browsers with support for local files (at the time of this writing only HotJava does), or you can write a client/server application, with the server side storing the information to a file. ●

CHAPTER 18

Managing Applications

In this chapter

Installing Applications

Java applications are a very powerful way to deliver your Java programs. Before you can use Java applications, however, you have to know how to install them. This chapter discusses how to install and maintain applications. The chapter also provides directions for turning your applets into applications.

Java applications come in many forms, but this chapter discusses the two most common: applications that come packaged as a series of .class files and applications that come as a single .zip file.

CAUTION

When you install someone else's Java applications, you are giving up the security protection that you are guaranteed with an applet. Giving up this security is not necessarily a bad thing; in fact, you may need to violate it. Just be aware that installing random Java applications can expose you to all the problems you encounter with traditional software schemes, such as viruses and other malicious software.

Installing Applications from *.class* Files

Installing applications that come as a set of .class files is a bit less entangling than installing applications for .zip files. In time, most applications will come with their own installation programs, but for now you must perform the installation manually. The following sections explain how to install the Clock application, which is on the CD-ROM that comes with this book, that you worked with in the previous chapter.

Create a Directory for the Application First, you need to designate a directory in which to place your Clock. This directory need not be associated with the directory where you put your Java JDK; however, having a deployment plan for your applications is important. This plan can be the same one you use for installing more traditional programs, such as Netscape, or something unique to your Java applications.

CAUTION

Keeping backup copies of applications you value is important, just like with any other program or data that you value. Don't expect applications to become corrupted, but don't ignore that possibility either.

Copy the Files After you create the directory in which you want to place the application, copy all the *.class* files to it. You should make sure you maintain any directory structure that has already been set up for the application. If you have subdirectories for packages, make sure you keep the classes in them.

NOTE To copy an entire subdirectory on a Windows machine from a DOS prompt, use the following command:

```
xcopy c:\original\directory\*.class c:\destination\directory /s
```

You can also drag-and-drop the whole directory structure within the Windows Explorer system.

On UNIX machines, the command is

```
cp -r /original/directory /destination/directory
```

CAUTION

If you are deploying an application you have written and you are still updating the program, don't make your working copy the same one that you have users accessing. If you happen to be compiling your application at the same time that a user tries to start it, unexpected and undesirable effects may occur.

Make Sure That Everything Works Now make sure that everything is running the way it should. Go to the directory in which you placed the Clock application and type **java Clock**. If everything is going as planned, a clock window should appear onscreen, as shown in Figure 18.1. If not, something has gone wrong. Make sure that you followed all the procedures correctly. You should also make sure that you have the java executable in your path. If you have been following through the rest of the book and you have installed the Java Development Kit, the java executable should already be in your classpath; if not, refer to Chapter 3, "Installing the JDK and Getting Started," for information on installing the JDK.

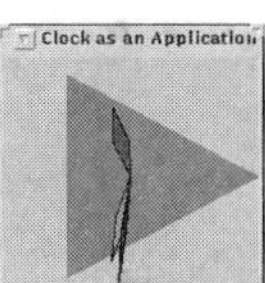

FIG. 18.1 The Clock application as it appears under Solaris.

Finishing the Installation

After you copy all the .class files to the correct directory, the next task is to create a script or batch file that you will use to run the application.

You can automate this process so your users don't always have to type **java Clock**. Your users will be much happier if they can just type **Clock** to invoke the Clock program, without having to also type **java**. Making this possible, however, takes you in a different direction, depending on your platform. Ideally, you will be able to follow the same path you would use for UNIX and Windows 95/NT.

Finishing Installing Applications for UNIX

In explaining how to install an application under UNIX, this section covers specifically how to do this under Solaris 2.4 using Korn shell. Your implementation may differ slightly, based on your particular operating system and shell.

Create a Wrapper Script Automating the usage of a Java application under UNIX is done by creating a wrapper script. The wrapper script is essentially a standard script file that "wraps" all the commands for a Java application together. The first task is creating the script. You can create it with vi, nedit, or your favorite text editor. Listing 18.1 shows an example script for Clock. Note that there are several variables you may need to change for your particular installation.

Listing 18.1 Clock

```
#Add the applications directory to the CLASSPATH
#set to the directory you have placed the application
#Note, I insert the application directory first to avoid
#having classes from other applications getting called first

CLASSPATH=/ns-home/docs/que/Clock/:$CLASSPATH

#Set the location in which you hold java.
#This directory is probably the same as below
#If you have java in your global path, this line is
#not really necessary

Java_Home=/optl/java/bin/java

#Specify the name of the application.
#Important: Remember this is the name of the class, not the
#file

App=Clock

#Now run the actual program.
#If you have any additional parameters which you need to
#pass to the application, you can add them here.

$Java_Home $App
```

Test the Script Copy the text from Listing 18.1 to a file called Clock and make sure that the script is functioning correctly. To test it, simply type the name of the wrapper script, as follows:

```
Clock &
```

Your application should start and look something like Figure 18.2; if it doesn't, make sure that you made the script executable. You can make the script executable by typing the following:

chmod a+x Clock

Don't do this if you don't want everyone to execute your script. If that is the case, type **chmod u+x Clock**, or check with your system administrator to determine the proper parameters to use with `chmod`.

Copy the Script to a Common Location It is probably a good idea to place your new wrapper script in the /usr/bin directory so that anyone who has access to the system can run the new script.

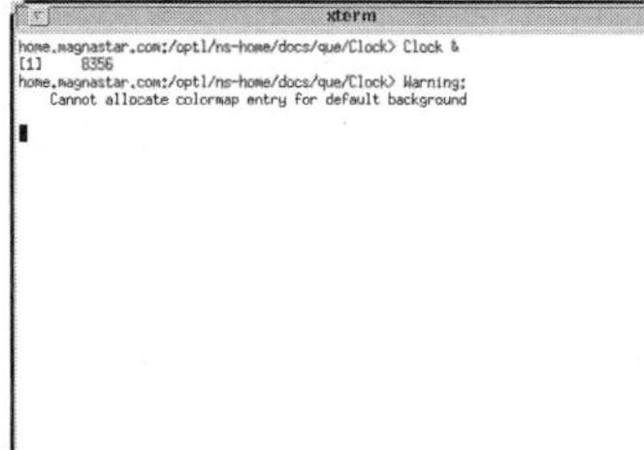

FIG. 18.2 Testing the Clock application.

Finishing Installing an Application for Windows

This section discusses how to install applications under Windows 95. Aside from a few particulars, the procedures are the same under Windows NT.

You can install an application under Windows in two ways: by creating a batch file or by using the .pif file.

Creating a Wrapper Batch File To install the application with a batch file, use your favorite editor. You can use the Edit command supplied with DOS, Notepad under Windows, or any other text editor. Create a batch file called Clock.bat that contains the lines shown in Listing 18.2.

TIP If your application does not use the Windows environment, or if you need to be able to see the output on `System.out`, use `java` instead of `javaw`.

Listing 18.2 Clock.bat

```
rem add the location where java.exe is located. If it
rem is already in your path don't add this line.
rem change c:\java\bin to the directory you have
rem installed for the JDK - see chapter 3

set PATH=%PATH%;c:\java\bin

rem Set this line to be the directory where your new
rem application is located.

set CLASSPATH = c:\appdir\;%CLASSPATH%

rem Run the actual application, change the applClass to be
rem the correct class for the application you are installing

javaw applClass
```

NOTE If your application does not run and you see an error message similar to `Can't find class classname`, first make sure that the .zip file is included in your `CLASSPATH` variable. Next, make sure that the length of the `CLASSPATH` variable does not exceed the maximum limit, which on Windows machines is 128 characters.

CAUTION

Unlike Solaris and Macintosh machines, the CLASSPATH on Windows machines is not separated by a colon (:). The separation between the elements in the CLASSPATH is accomplished with a semicolon (;). In short, the syntax of CLASSPATH is the same syntax that you use to set your PATH variable.

Incorrect syntax:

```
set CLASSPATH=c:\java\jre\lib\rt.jar:c:\application\
```

Correct syntax:

```
CLASSPATH=c:\java\jre\lib\rt.jar;c:\application\
```

Under JDK 1.2, either option will technically work; however, do not expect this to be backward-compatible for users still using JDK 1.0.

NOTE If you are using a previous version of the JDK, you must substitute `lib\classes.zip` for all instances of `jre\lib\rt.jar` throughout this chapter.

Test the Batch File To run the application, type **Clock** at a DOS prompt. The application should start, as shown in Figure 18.3. Pay special attention to any extra parameters you have to send to the application. Note that because Clock is a DOS batch file, it is actually case insensitive, so you can run the file as Clock, clock, or cLOCK if you would like.

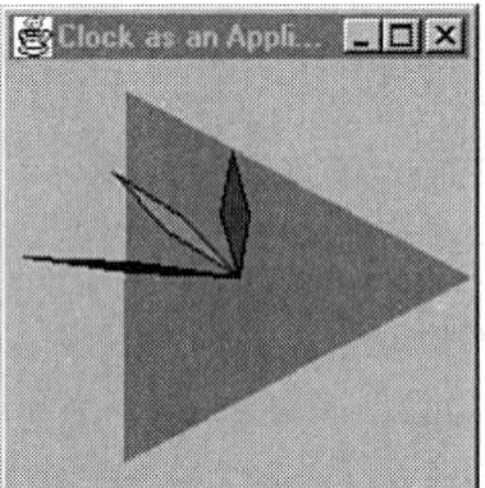

FIG. 18.3
The Clock application running under Windows.

Add the Application to Windows To add this batch file to your Windows environment, switch back to the Windows environment, if necessary, and select the folder in which you want to place the application. Make sure you can actually see the folder's contents, and not just the folder icon.

Now create a new shortcut (File, New, Shortcut). Fill in the information for your new batch file (in this case c:\que\Clock.bat) as shown in Figure 18.4 and specify the name under which you want the application to appear on your desktop.

When you finish creating the shortcut, double-click it. An MS-DOS window appears and your Clock should start. Now, if you're like most people, having a DOS window pop up to start an application is downright annoying. Normally, you don't care what is going to System.out and having a big black obstruction on the screen causes most people just to close it. Here are a few pointers to make this a bit less obtrusive for you and your users.

FIG. 18.4
The Shortcut window.

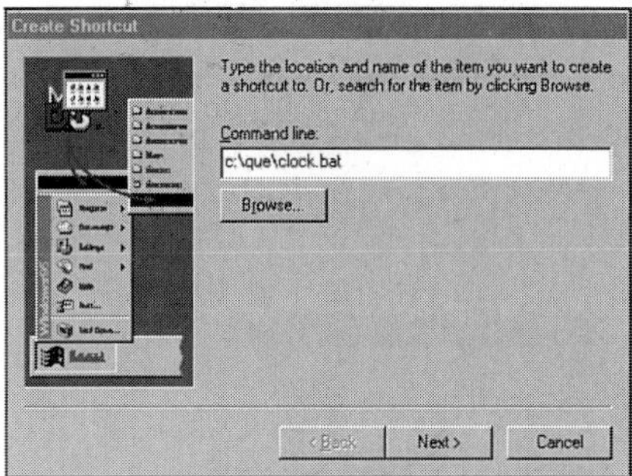

To make the MS-DOS window less obtrusive, first stop the DOS window from appearing on the screen, and second, have the DOS window exit on its own as soon as the Java application has started. To make these changes, open the properties for your new application. Move your mouse over to the Clock icon and use your right mouse button to click the Clock icon. A pop-up menu should appear; choose Properties. The properties window shown in Figure 18.5 should appear. Now switch to the Program tab. Change the Run option to Minimized; this makes it so that the DOS Window does not appear. Next, select Close on Exit, which forces the DOS session to exit automatically after the Java application has started. Finally, click OK.

FIG. 18.5
In the Properties Window, change the Run option and select Close on Exit.

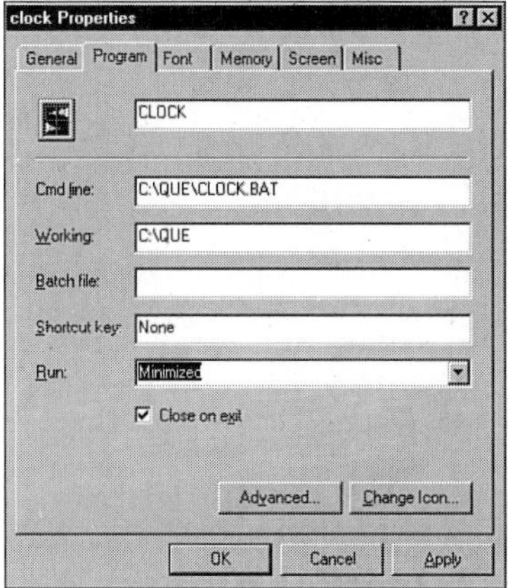

Now, if you double-click the Clock icon, the application starts without the obtrusive DOS window.

The other method of adding an application to Windows requires that you know the following:

- Where java.exe is located. Alternatively, java.exe must be in the path.
- Where the rt.jar file is located.
- Where your new application is located.

First, select the folder in which you want your new application to appear. Then create a new shortcut, as described in the preceding section. When you are prompted to enter the command line option, however, enter the following line as seen in Figure 18.6:

```
c:\java\bin\javaw.exe -classpath c:\java\jre\lib\rt.jar;c:\appDir\
applicationClass
```

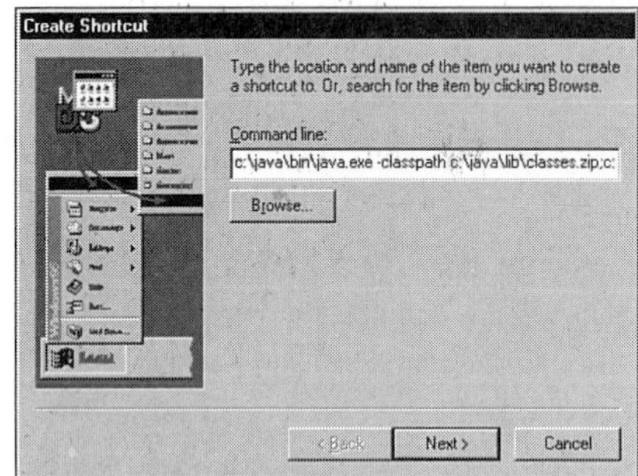

FIG. 18.6
In the Shortcut window, enter the complete command line.

You want to replace all the directories and the class name with ones that apply to your application. If your application does not seem to load, try using `java.exe` instead of `javaw.exe`. `javaw.exe` is an alternative version of java that returns right away and ignores all the error messages that ordinarily are generated when an application starts. `javaw.exe` is great for distracting your users from what is going on, but it makes it difficult to see what is really happening when things don't work correctly.

Installing Applications from a .jar File

With the advent of JDK 1.1, support was added to deliver Java applications with a single .jar file. This addition makes it easier to deliver an application because only the .jar file and the wrapper are required.

When you install an application from a .jar file, be aware of the following things:

- When you run an application from a .jar file, you must include the file in the `CLASSPATH` environment variable. You must actually specify the .jar file, not just the path in which the file is located.
- When you include multiple applets in your `CLASSPATH` variable, make sure that the applications you are installing do not use classes that have the same name but refer to different classes.

The second point here is important. Suppose that you have the applet SkyTune installed in `CLASSPATH`. SkyToon, which calculates the likelihood that the sky will fall today, has a class called `Tune`, which deals with the color of the sky. You also have an applet called CDTunes installed; you use this applet to play music CDs in your CD-ROM drive. CDTunes has a class called `Tune` that handles all the audio input and output from the CD. What happens in this situation where two applications have a class called `Tune`? When you run CDTunes, the Java interpreter looks down your classpath, finds the first instance of the class `Tune`, finds the class in SkyToons—and chokes.

You can prevent this problem by carefully naming all your classes or putting them in packages. The best solution, of course, is to use well-named packages. If you are running someone else's program, however, there is no guarantee that this problem won't occur. You need to be aware of the possibility in case your applications stop working one day. (You may have this problem when you run applications that come in .class form, too, but the problem is a bit more obvious when it occurs.)

Now you are ready to install an application sent in .jar format. Although .jar-distributed classes are somewhat trickier to deal with in a management sense than .class distributions, you have to make only one change in your wrapper script or batch file.

If you are using UNIX, refer to the script in Listing 18.1, and change

```
CLASSPATH="/ns-home/docs/appDir/:$CLASSPATH"
```

to

```
CLASSPATH="/ns-home/docs/appDir/application.zip:$CLASSPATH"
```

If you are using Windows, refer to the batch file in Listing 18.2 and change

```
set CLASSPATH = c:\appdir\;%CLASSPATH%
```

to

```
set CLASSPATH = c:\appdir\application.jar;%CLASSPATH%
```

These examples assume that the .jar file you received with the application is called application.jar. In reality, the file probably is called classes.jar. The examples simply demonstrate the fact that the file may have any name.

Maintaining Multiple Applications on the Same System

Maintaining multiple Java applications on a single system is not as simple as maintaining several normal programs compiled in binary code, for the following reasons:

- Java bytecode depends on the Virtual Machine (see Chapter 1, "What Java Can Do for You"). As a result, changes in the VM can cause bugs to appear and disappear in all your Java programs.
- Java programs are not compiled to a single file. Each class for the program is contained in its own file. Code is installed based on its class name.
- Java applications that reuse parts of other programs are affected if those other programs are changed.

You can solve the last two problems yourself. The first problem, however, will have to be resolved by the Virtual Machine vendors.

Consider an example situation. You have been using a Java-based word processor for months. One night, you or your system administrator installs a new version of Java (.exe). This new version of Java is 300 times faster (which is the minimum that you can expect from the next generation of VMs), but it has an interesting side effect: It switches the characters a and z. This switch probably is the result of a bug, but what happens to your word processor? Worse, what happens if you don't notice the change for a few days, and you have saved several old documents in the new format? Only one thing can completely prevent such an event: Don't upgrade without making absolutely certain that your new Java machine is 100 percent compatible with previous versions. Developers, working before the final Java release, went through some growing pains with each new release of the JDK (from JDK pre-beta to JDK beta 1, and so on; never mind what happened from alpha to beta, 1.02 to 1.1, or now from 1.1 to 1.2). Lest you be scared off from upgrading your VM, most of the problems were very minor, but they almost always required a small code change and, if you don't have the source code, you may not have this luxury.

The second problem deals with the fact that Java is compiled to files that bear the name Something.class. Each class for an applet is contained in its own .class file, and each application can contain dozens of class files.

With each of your Java applications having dozens of classes, it's often difficult to avoid the situation where applications don't just happen to have classes that bear the same name as a class from another application, and thus the wrong class gets loaded. One solution is to place the classes in packages and give each of the packages a unique name. What happens, however, when package names overlap? This situation should not occur if you follow good programming practice, but the world isn't perfect.

To prevent this problem from crashing your applications, you should always place the current application directory or .jar file at the beginning of the classpath list. In situations where there is code sharing, make sure that the items you include in the `CLASSPATH` are correct for the application you are actually running. If you ever think you are pulling the wrong class, strip your `CLASSPATH` down to nothing and rebuild it with only the required directories. Ultimately, though, you have to put your faith in the programmers. As with upgrading your Virtual Machine, time will tell if good methods are developed to prevent these situations.

Finally, what do you do about applications that share code with other applications or that load part of their code from the Internet? When you make changes in one application, you must ensure that the changes are backward-compatible. Normally, code that is being deployed is not subject to frequent change. But, when you are installing a new version of an application, you need to make sure that no other programs depend on the code in the old version.

If some programs do depend on code from the old version, maintain the legacy code, just in case you need to reinstall the code for other applications.

In all, the procedure is not quite as simple as installing a new version of Microsoft Word, but it isn't like reinstalling your operating system, either. The key when installing applications is being aware of the downwind effects that every change will cause. ●

PART III

User Interface

CHAPTER 19

java.awt: Components

In this chapter

Building GUI with *java.awt*

Components are the building blocks of the AWT. The end-user interacts directly with these components. The components provided by the AWT are

- Buttons
- Text fields
- Labels
- Text areas
- Check boxes
- Menus
- Radio buttons
- Canvases
- Lists
- Scrollbars
- Choices

Figure 19.1 shows a Java applet with a sample of some of the components of the AWT.

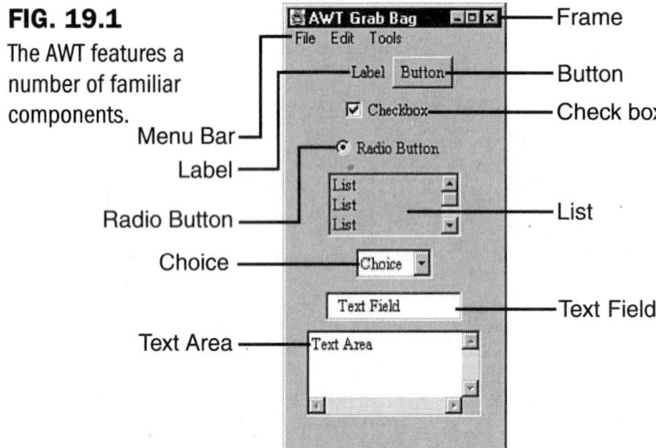

FIG. 19.1
The AWT features a number of familiar components.

Figure 19.2 shows you a portion of the AWT's inheritance hierarchy.

Buttons

Although buttons are simple mechanisms, they are some of the workhorses of any graphical interface. You find buttons on toolbars, dialog boxes, windows, and even in other components, such as scrollbars.

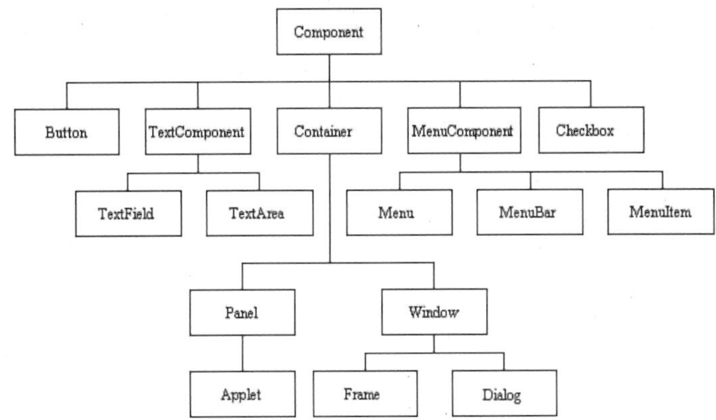

FIG. 19.2
The AWT inherits all its user interface components from `Component`.

Creating Buttons

The only decision you must make when creating a button is whether you want the button to be labeled. There are no other options for buttons.

To create an unlabeled button, use the empty constructor:

```
public Button()
```

Creating a labeled button is an equally simple task:

```
public Button(String label)
```

After you have created a button, you need to add it to a container. Because an applet is already a container, you can add a button directly to an applet:

```
Button myButton = new Button("Press Me");

add(myButton);
```

To change the label of a button, use `setLabel`:

```
public void setLabel(String newLabel)
```

To get the label for a button, use `getLabel`:

```
public String getLabel()
```

NOTE You might notice the lack of image buttons—that is, buttons that contain an image instead of text. These types of buttons are almost a necessity for creating toolbars. Unfortunately, they are not supported in the AWT. If you want an image button, you have to implement it yourself or search one of the Java archives on the Internet for someone else's implementation of an image button. Alternatively, if you choose to use the Java Foundation Classes (covered in Chapters 23 and 24) the JButton does have image support.

Using Buttons

Now that you can create a button and add it to your applet, it's time to learn how to make the button do something. There are two ways to handle events in Java. Under the Java 1.0 event model, all the components within the AWT have an `action` method that is called when an action is taken on the component. In the case of the button, `action` is called when the button is pressed. The `action` method is similar to some of the event-handling methods you might have come across already, such as `keyDown` or `mouseDown`.

NOTE The AWT does not call the `action` method directly. Instead, it calls the `handleEvent` method, which is responsible for handling all the events for a component. The `handleEvent` method acts as an event dispatcher. When it receives an `Event.ACTION_EVENT` event, it calls the `action` method. When it receives a `KEY_PRESS` event, it calls the `keyDown` method. If a method called by `handleEvent` returns a value of `false`, the `handleEvent` method will pass the event up to the `handleEvent` method in the parent container, which again performs the same dispatching duties. This process continues until `handleEvent` calls a method that returns `true`, or until the event reaches the topmost container. ■

The format of the `action` method in all components is

```
public boolean action(Event event, Object whatAction)
```

where `event` is the event that has occurred in the component, and `whatAction` indicates what has occurred.

For buttons, `whatAction` is the label of the button that has been pressed. The `event` parameter contains other information specific to the action, such as the component where (`event.target`) and when (`event.when`) the action occurred.

CAUTION

You should always check the `event.target` variable using the `instanceof` operator to make sure that the action is for the object you expect. For instance, if you expect that the action is for a `Button`, then you need to make sure that (`event.target instanceof Button`) is `true`.

Now that you know how to create a button and check for an action, you can create a button applet. A very simple example is an applet with buttons that change its background color. One way to do this is to put the name of the color in the button label. Then, in the `action` method, you look at the label of the button that was pressed and set the applet's background color based on the label. For example, the button to turn the background blue could be labeled `Blue`. The `action` method would set the background to blue if the button's label was Blue. The applet in Listing 19.1 demonstrates how to do this.

Listing 19.1 Source Code for *Button1Applet.java*

```
import java.applet.*;
import java.awt.*;
```

```
// Example 19.1 - Button1Applet
//
// This applet creates two buttons named "Red" and "Blue". When a
// button is pressed, the background color of the applet is set to
// the color named by that button's label.
//

public class Button1Applet extends Applet
{
     public void init()
     {
          add(new Button("Red"));

          add(new Button("Blue"));

     }

     public boolean action(Event evt, Object whatAction)
     {
// Check to make sure this is a button action. If not,
// return false to indicate that the event has not been handled.
          if (!(evt.target instanceof Button))
          {
               return false;
          }
          String buttonLabel = (String) whatAction;

          if (buttonLabel == "Red")
          {
               setBackground(Color.red);
          }
          else if (buttonLabel == "Blue")
          {
               setBackground(Color.blue);
          }
          repaint();     // Make the change visible immediately
          return true;
     }
}
```

Figure 19.3 shows you the `Button1Applet` in operation.

NOTE When you compile this application with JDK 1.2 (or JDK 1.1, for that matter), you get a warning that reads

```
Note: Button1Applet.java uses or overrides a deprecated API.
Recompile with "-d " for details.
1 warning
```

This error is caused because JavaSoft has marked the `action` method to be removed from the API at some point in the future. For now, `action` will continue to work, but there is no guarantee that it will work in future additions of Java.

Using Buttons with the 1.1 Event Model

The Java 1.0 event model does not promote good object-oriented design. In the case of the `Button1Applet`, all the application logic is in the applet itself. There really isn't any part of this example that you can reuse as a compiled unit. You would have to cut and paste pieces out of the example to reuse any part of it.

FIG. 19.3 The buttons in `Button1Applet` change the applet's background color.

Although there is a slightly better way to approach the application under Java 1.0, the Java 1.1 event model (which carries through in Java 1.2) makes it much easier to make a reusable piece of the application. The 1.1 model relies on a model of Listeners and Adaptors. This allows you to decentralize your program control. Ideally, your applet should just create some objects and set them in motion, occasionally handling things that come up.

In `Button1Applet`, the main action is the setting of the applet's background color. Under the 1.1 event model, you can create an object that listens for actions, such as the button being pressed, and responds to those actions by setting the background color of the applet. Because any component can have its background color changed, it seems silly to restrict the object to only changing applets. Listing 19.2 shows the `BGSetter` object that reacts to an action event by changing the background color on a specific component.

Listing 19.2 Source Code for *BGSetter.java*

```
import java.applet.*;
import java.awt.*;
import java.awt.event.*;

// This class listens for an action event and then changes the
// background color of a specified component.

public class BGSetter extends Object implements ActionListener
{
```

```
        Component component;
        Color color;

        public BGSetter(Component component, Color color)
        {
             this.component = component;
             this.color = color;
        }


        public void actionPerformed(ActionEvent evt)
        {
             component.setBackground(color);
             component.repaint();
        }
   }
```

Now all the applet needs to do is create some buttons and some `BGSetters`. Listing 19.3 shows the new version of the applet. Notice that an instance of `BGSetter` is set as an `ActionListener` for `red`.

Listing 19.3 Source Code for *Button2Applet.java*

```
import java.applet.*;
import java.awt.*;

public class Button2Applet extends Applet
{
     public void init()
     {
          Button red = new Button("Red");
          add(red);
          red.addActionListener(new BGSetter(this, Color.red));

          Button blue = new Button("Blue");
          add(blue);
          blue.addActionListener(new BGSetter(this, Color.blue));
     }
}
```

Labels

Labels are the simplest of the AWT components. They are text strings that are used only for decoration. Because they are components, labels have an `action` method, but because they are display only, they do not generate an action event.

There are three different ways to create a label. The simplest is to create an empty label:

```
public Label()
```

Of course, an empty label isn't going to do you much good because there is nothing to see. You can create a label with some text by passing the text to the constructor:

```
public Label(String labelText)
```

Labels can be left-justified, right-justified, or centered. The variables `Label.LEFT`, `Label.RIGHT`, and `Label.CENTER` can be used to set the alignment of a label when you create it:

```
public Label(String labelText, int alignment)
```

Here is an example of how to create a right-justified label:

```
Label myLabel = new Label("This is a right-justified label", Label.RIGHT);
```

You can change the text of a label with `setText`:

```
public void setText(newLabelText)
```

You can also get the text of a label with `getText`:

```
public String getText()
```

You can change the alignment of a label with `setAlignment`:

```
public void setAlignment(int alignment)
throws IllegalArgumentException
```

You can also get the alignment of a label with `getAlignment`:

```
public int getAlignment()
```

Figure 19.4 shows you a sample label.

FIG. 19.4
Labels are simply text strings.

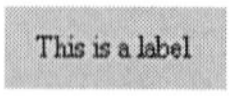

This is a label

Check Boxes and Radio Buttons

Check boxes are similar to buttons except that they are used as yes/no or on/off switches. Every time you click a check box, it changes from off to on or from on to off. A close cousin to the check box is the radio button. Radio buttons are also on/off switches, but they are arranged in special, mutually exclusive groups where only one button in a group can be on at a time. Imagine what a radio would sound like if more than one station could be on at a time!

Creating Check Boxes

A check box contains two parts: a label and a state. The label is the text that is displayed next to the check box itself, while the state is a Boolean variable that indicates whether the box is checked. By default, the state of a check box is `false`, or off.

The `Checkbox` class has five constructors:

```
public Checkbox()
```

creates a check box with no label.

```
public Checkbox(String label)
```

creates a labeled check box.

```
public Checkbox(String label, boolean state)
```

creates a check box with the specified label and initial state (if the state is `true`, the check box is checked initially).

```
public Checkbox(String label, boolean initialState, CheckboxGroup group)
```

and

```
public Checkbox(String label, CheckboxGroup group, boolean initialState)
```

create a labeled check box that is checked if `initialState` is `true`. The `group` parameter indicates what check box group this check box belongs to. The `CheckboxGroup` class allows you to group check boxes into mutually exclusive radio buttons. If you are creating a check box and not a radio button, pass `null` as the `group`.

Checking and Setting the State of a Check Box

You can check whether a check box has been checked by using `getState`:

```
public boolean getState()
```

For example:

```
if (myCheckbox.getState()) {
// The box has been checked
} else {
// The box has not been checked
}
```

On the other hand, you can also set the state of the check box using the `setState(boolean)` method. To cause the check box to be checked, you can use the following:

```
MyCheckBox(true);
```

Listening to Changes in the Check Box

Like `Button`, you can monitor changes in `Checkbox` using the 1.0 event model action methods. However, the preferred method is to use the `ItemListener`. `Checkbox` has two related methods to add and remove listeners:

```
addItemListener((ItemListener)
```

```
removeItemListner(ItemListener)
```

The java.awt.Event.ItemListener interface has a single method (`itemStateChanged(ItemEvent)`). Listing 19.4 shows a simple example of using check boxes. Note the user of the inner adapter class that implements `ItemListener`.

Listing 19.4 Source Code for *CheckBoxExample.java*

```
/*
 *
 * CheckBoxExample
 *
 */

import java.applet.*;
import java.awt.*;
import java.awt.event.*;


public class CheckboxExample extends Applet
{
     public void init()
     {

               Checkbox redBlue = new Checkbox("Red/Blue");
               add(redBlue);
               //Add an ItemListener to the red checkbox.
               //Note, the ItemListener that is added here is
               //actually an inner class.
               redBlue.addItemListener(  new ItemListener(){
                       public void itemStateChanged(ItemEvent evt){
                               if (evt.getStateChange()==ItemEvent.SELECTED)
                                       setColor(Color.red);
                               else
                                       setColor(Color.blue);
                       }
               });

     }

          public void setColor(Color color){
               setBackground(color);
               repaint();
          }
}
```

In Listing 19.4, the listener that is added is an inner class. Unlike the `Button2Applet` example in Listings 19.3 and 19.4, this does not require two separate .java files. Although this limits the reuse of the event handling mechanisms, it is often useful to define the event routines with the components declaration.

▶ **See** Chapter 11, "Classes," for more information on inner classes, **p. 157**.

Creating Radio Buttons

A radio button is just a special case of a check box. No `RadioButton` class exists. Instead, you create a set of radio buttons by creating check boxes and putting them in the same check box group. The constructor for `CheckboxGroup` takes no arguments:

```
public CheckboxGroup()
```

After you have created a check box group, you add check boxes to the group by passing the group to the check box constructor. In other words, instead of adding existing check boxes to a group explicitly, you create new check boxes that belong to the group.

Listing 19.5 creates a check box group, creates some check boxes that belong to the group, and then adds them to the applet.

Listing 19.5 ***RadioExample.java*** **Creates a Group of Check Boxes**

```
import java.awt.*;
import java.applet.*;

public class RadioExample extends Applet{
    public void init(){
        //create the CheckboxGroup, all the checkboxes
        //will be a member of this group
        CheckboxGroup myCheckBoxGroup = new CheckboxGroup();

        //create the checkboxes, making them members of the group
        Checkbox cb1 = new Checkbox("Favorite language is Java",
 myCheckboxGroup, true)
        Checkbox cb2 = new Checkbox("Favorite language is Visual Cobol",
 myCheckboxGroup, false);
        Checkbox cb3 = new Checkbox("Favorite language is Backtalk",
myCheckboxGroup, false);

        //add the checkboxes to the applet
        add(cb1);
        add(cb2);
        add(cb3);
    }
}
```

NOTE When you add check boxes to a `checkbox` group, the last check box added as `true` is the box that is checked when the group is displayed.

You can find out which radio button is selected by either calling `getState` on each check box or calling `getSelectedCheckbox` on the `CheckboxGroup`. The `getSelectedCheckbox` method returns the check box that is currently selected:

```
public Checkbox getSelectedCheckbox()
```

NOTE For users of Java 1.0, you need to use the `getCurrent()` and `setCurrent()` methods instead of `getSelectedCheckbox()` and `setSelectedCheckbox()`, respectively.

Using Radio Buttons

An item event for a check box or radio button is called whenever it is clicked. As with check boxes, you must create an object that implements the `ItemListener` interface to find out when a radio button has been selected.

The `itemStateChanged` method, which is called when a check box or radio button is selected or deselected, is passed an `ItemEvent` object.

The `ItemEvent` object can tell you the object where the event occurred, the item selected, and the kind of selection. The `getItemSelectable` returns the object where the event occurred:

```
public ItemSelectable getItemSelectable()
```

The `getItem` method in `ItemEvent` tells you the value of the selected item. In this case, it returns the label of the check box or radio button:

```
public Object getItem()
```

As you saw in Listing 19.4, the `getStateChange` method returns either `ItemEvent.SELECTED` or `ItemEvent.DESELECTED`, depending on whether the object has been selected or deselected:

```
public int getStateChange()
```

Listing 19.6 shows how you can receive notification of a change in a radio button and determine which item was selected. Notice the use of the event variable in the `myItemListener.itemStateChanged` method.

Listing 19.6 Source code for *RadioExample.java*

```
import java.awt.*;
import java.awt.event.*;
import java.applet.*;

public class RadioExample extends Applet{
    public void init(){
        //create the CheckboxGroup, all the checkboxes
        //will be a member of this group
        CheckboxGroup myCheckboxGroup = new CheckboxGroup();

        //create the checkboxes, making them members of
        //the group
        Checkbox cb1 = new Checkbox("Favorite language is
➥Java", myCheckboxGroup, true);
        Checkbox cb2 = new Checkbox("Favorite language is
➥Visual Cobol", myCheckboxGroup, false);
        Checkbox cb3 = new Checkbox("Favorite language is
➥Backtalk", myCheckboxGroup, false);

        //add the checkboxes to the applet
```

```
        add(cb1);
        add(cb2);
        add(cb3);

        //create an ItemListner, NOTE: myItemListener is defined
        //in listing 19.6
        ItemListener listener = new myItemListener();

        //add listener to the checkboxes item list
        cb1.addItemListener(listener);
        cb2.addItemListener(listener);
        cb3.addItemListener(listener);
    }
}


class myItemListener implements ItemListener{
    public void itemStateChanged(ItemEvent event)
    {
        if (event.getStateChange() == ItemEvent.SELECTED) {
            System.out.println(event.getItem() + " has been selected.");
        } else {
          System.out.println(event.getItem() + " has been deselected.");
        }
    }
}
```

TROUBLE SHOOTING

Remember that the 1.1 events are contained in the java.awt.event package. This means that you must import both the java.awt and java.awt.event packages when creating a class that implements one of the listeners. If you fail to do this, you receive an error:

```
RadioExample.java:31: Interface ItemListener of class myItemListener not found.
class myItemListener implements ItemListener{
                                ^
RadioExample.java:21: Class ItemListener not found in type declaration.
        ItemListener listener = new myItemListener();
        ^
2 errors
```


NOTE Under the Java 1.0 event model, the `whichAction` parameter of the `action` method is an instance of a `Boolean` class that is `true` if the check box was clicked on or `false` if the check box was clicked off.

If you create an `action` method for a radio button, you should not rely on the `whichAction` parameter to contain the correct value. If a radio button is clicked when it is already on, the `whichAction` contains a `false` value, even though the button is still on. You are safer using the `getState` method to check the state of the radio button or the check box.

continues

continued

You can also use the `getLabel` method to determine which check box has been checked. The following code fragment shows an `action` method that responds to a box being checked and retrieves the current state of the box:

```
public boolean action(Event evt, Object whichAction)
{
    if (evt.target instanceof Checkbox)  // make sure this is a check box
    {
        Checkbox currentCheckbox = (Checkbox)evt.target;
        boolean checkboxState = currentCheckbox.getState();

        if (currentCheckbox.getLabel() == "Check me if you like Java")
        {
            if (checkboxState)
        {
            // Code to handle "Check me if you like Java" being set to on
        } else {
            // Code to handle "Check me if you like Java" being set to off
        }
        return true;  // the event has been handled
        }
    }
    return false;  // the event has not been handled
}
```

Figure 19.5 shows you some check boxes and a group of three radio buttons.

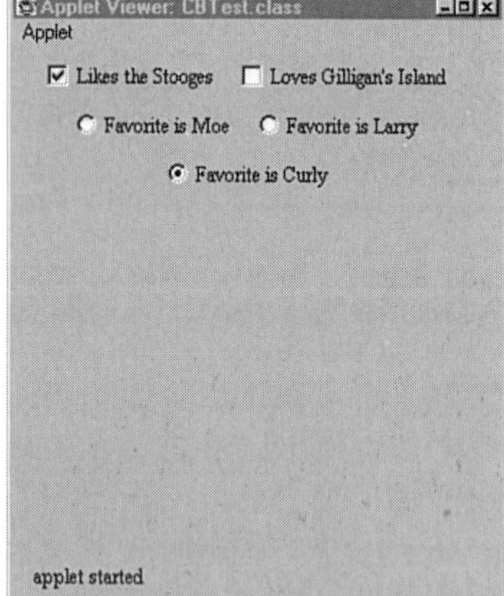

FIG. 19.5 Check boxes are square boxes with checks in them. Radio buttons are round and checked with dots.

Choices

The `Choice` class provides a pop-up menu of text string choices. The current choice is displayed as the menu title.

Creating Choices

To create a choice pop-up menu, you must first create an instance of the `Choice` class. Because there are no options for the choice constructor, the creation of a choice should always look something like this:

```
Choice myChoice = new Choice();
```

After you have created the choice, you can add string items using the `addItem` method:

```
public synchronized void addItem(String item)
throws NullPointerException
```

For example:

```
myChoice.addItem("Moe");
myChoice.addItem("Larry");
myChoice.addItem("Curly");
```

You can also remove items from the choice list by using either of the following methods:

```
public synchronized void remove(int position)
public synchronized void removeAll()
```

To change the item that is currently selected programmatically, you can use

```
public synchronized void select(int pos)
throws IllegalArgumentException

public void select(String str)
```

If you want `Curly` to be selected, for instance, you could select him by name:

```
myChoice.select("Curly");      // Make "Curly" become selected item
```

You could also select `Curly` by his position in the list. Because he was added third and the choices are numbered starting at 0, `Moe` would be 0, `Larry` would be 1, and `Curly` would be 2:

```
myChoice.select(2);      // Make the third list entry become selected
```

The `getSelectedIndex` method returns the position of the selected item:

```
public int getSelectedIndex()
```

Again, if `Curly` was selected, `getSelectedIndex` would return 2. Similarly, the `getSelectedItem` method returns the string name of the selected item:

```
public String getSelectedItem()
```

If `Curly` was selected, `getSelectedItem` would return `Curly`.

If you have an index value for an item and you want to find out the name of the item at that index, you can use `getItem`:

```
public String getItem(int index)
```

Figure 19.6 shows a choice in its usual form, while Figure 19.7 shows a choice with its menu of choices pulled down.

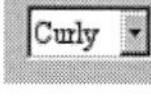

FIG. 19.6
The choice box displays its current selection.

FIG. 19.7
The button on the right of a choice pops up a menu of the possible choices.

Using Choices

Like radio buttons, check boxes, and other components that generate item events, you need to set up an `ItemListener` object to handle action events from a `Choice` object. An item event is generated whenever a choice is selected, even if it is the same choice.

NOTE Under the 1.0 event model, the `action` method for a choice is called whenever a choice is made, even if it is the same choice. The `whatAction` parameter contains the name of the selected item. The following code fragment gives an example `action` method for a choice where the selection is stored in a `String` variable within the applet:

```
String currentStooge;

public boolean action(Event event, Object whatAction)
{
        // Check to make sure this is a choice object, if not
        // indicate that the event has not been handled.
        if (!(event.target instanceof Choice))
        {
                return false;
        }
        Choice whichChoice = (Choice) event.target;
        // See if this is an action for myChoice
        if (whichChoice == myChoice)
        {
                currentStooge = (String) whatAction;
                return true; // the event has been handled
        }
        return false;  // it must have been a different Choice
}
```

Lists

The `List` class allows you to create a scrolling list of values that can be selected either individually or many at a time. You can add and delete items from the list at any time, and even change which items are selected. The AWT handles all the scrolling for you.

Creating Lists

You have three options when creating a list. The default constructor for the `List` class allows you to create a list that does not allow multiple selections:

```
public List()
```

You can also set the number of list entries that are visible in the list window at any one time:

```
public List(int rows)
```

Finally, you can set the number of rows as well as determine whether to allow multiple selections:

```
public List(int rows, boolean multipleMode)
```

The following code fragment creates a list with 10 visible entries and multiple selections turned on:

```
List myList = new List(10, true);    // True means allow multiple selections
```

After you have created the list, you can add new entries with the `add` method:

```
public synchronized void add (String item)
```

For example:

```
myList.add ("Moe");
myList.add ("Larry");
myList.add ("Curly");
```

You can also add an item at a specific position in the list:

```
public synchronized void add (String item, int index)
```

The list positions are numbered from 0, so if you add an item at position 0, it goes to the front of the list. If you try to add an item at position –1 or at a position higher than the number of positions, the item will be added to the end of the list. The following code adds `Shemp` to the beginning of the list and `Curly Joe` to the end:

```
myList.add ("Shemp", 0);        // Add Shemp at position
myList.add ("Curly Joe", -1);   // Add Curly Joe to the end of the list
```

NOTE If you are using Java 1.0, you need to use the `addItem()` method instead of `add()`.

List Features

The `List` class provides a number of different methods for changing the contents of the list. The `replaceItem` method replaces an item at a given position with a new item:

```
public synchronized void replaceItem(String newValue, int position)
```

```
myList.replaceItem("Dr. Howard", 0);
// Replace the first item in the list with "Dr. Howard"
```

You can delete an item in the list with `remove`:

```
public synchronized void remove(int position)
```

You can delete all of the items in the list with the `removeAll` method:

```
public synchronized void removeAll()
```

NOTE Java 1.0 users, use `delItem()` instead of `remove()` and use `clear()` instead of `removeAll()`.

The `getSelectedIndex` method returns the index number of the currently selected item or –1 if no item is selected:

```
public synchronized int getSelectedIndex()
```

You can also get the selected item directly with `getSelectedItem`:

```
public synchronized String getSelectedItem()
```

For lists with multiple selections turned on, you can get all the selections with `getSelectedIndexes`:

```
public synchronized int[] getSelectedIndexes()
```

The `getSelectedItems` returns all the selected items:

```
public synchronized String[] getSelectedItems()
```

CAUTION

You should only use `getSelectedIndex` and `getSelectedItem` on lists without multiple selections. If you allow multiple selections, you should always use `getSelectedIndexes` and `getSelectedItems`.

You select any item by calling the `select` method with the index of the item you want selected:

```
public synchronized void select(int index)
```

If the list does not allow multiple selections, the previously selected item is deselected.

You can deselect any item by calling the `deselect` method with the index of the item you want deselected:

```
public synchronized void deselect(int index)
```

The `isSelected` method tells you whether the item at a particular index is selected:

```
public synchronized boolean isSelected(int index)
```

For example:

```
if (myList.isSelected(0)){
    // the first item in the list is selected
}
```

You can turn multiple selections on and off with the `setMultipleSelections` method:

```
public void setMultipleSelections(boolean allowMultiples)
```

The `isMultipleMode` method returns `true` if multiple selections are allowed:

```
public boolean isMultipleMode()
```

For example:

```
if (myList.isMultipleMode()){
   // multiple selections are allowed
}
```

NOTE Java 1.0 users, use `allowsMultipleSelections` instead of `isMultipleMode()`.

Sometimes, you might want to make sure a particular item is visible in the list window. You can do that by passing the index of the item you want to make visible to `makeVisible`:

```
public void makeVisible(int index)
```

For example, suppose the list was positioned on item 0, but you want to make sure item 15 is showing in the window instead. You would call

```
myList.makeVisible(15);          // Make item 15 in the list visible
```

Using Lists

The `List` object generates an `ItemEvent` whenever an item is selected or deselected. The `getItem` method in the `ItemEvent` returns the index of the selected item and not the item itself. The `List` object generates an action event when you double-click an item. The `getActionCommand` method in the `ActionEvent` returns the string label of the item selected.

Listing 19.7 shows a complete example. Notice the `ItemListener` inner class, which handles the events.

Listing 19.7 Using Lists

```
// This applet creates a scrolling list with several choices and
// informs you of selections and deselections using a label.
//

import java.applet.*;
import java.awt.*;
import java.awt.event.*;

public class ListExample extends Applet {
       Label   listStatus;
       List scrollingList;

       public void     init() {
```

continues

Listing 19.7 Continued

```
            // First, create the List

            scrollingList = new List(3, true);
            // Now add a few items to the list
            scrollingList.add("Moe");
            scrollingList.add("Larry");
            scrollingList.add("Curly");
            scrollingList.add("Shemp");
            scrollingList.add("Curly Joe");

            // Set Shemp to be selected
            scrollingList.select(3);

            // Finally, add the list to the applet
            add(scrollingList);

            // Now create a label to show the last event that occurred
            listStatus = new Label("You selected entry Shemp");
            add(listStatus);

            scrollingList.addItemListener( new ItemListener(){
                    public void itemStateChanged (ItemEvent evt){
                            String selectionString;
                            String selection;
                            int selectionNum;

        if (evt.getStateChange() == ItemEvent.SELECTED){
                // selection is the index of the selected item
                selectionNum = ((Integer)evt.getItem()).intValue();
                selection = scrollingList.getItem(selectionNum);
                // use getItem to get the actual item.
                SelectionString = You selected entry " + selection;
                // Update the label
                listStatus.setText(selectionString);
        } else {
                // If this is a deselection, get the deselected item
                // selection is the index of the selected item
                selectionNum = ((Integer)evt.getItem()).intValue();
                selection = scrollingList.getItem(selectionNum);
                // use getItem to get the actual item.
                SelectionString = "You deselected entry " + selection;
                // Update the label
                listStatus.setText(selectionString);
        }
                    }
            });
        }
}
```

NOTE If you are using the 1.0 event model, unlike the previous user interface components you have encountered in the Java 1.0 event model, the `List` class does not make use of the `action` method. Instead, you must use the `handleEvent` method to catch list selection and deselection events. The `handleEvent` method is called whenever you select or deselect an item in a list. The format of `handleEvent` is

```
public boolean handleEvent(Event event)
```

When an item on a list is selected, `event.id` will be equal to `Event.LIST_SELECT`, and `event.arg` will be an instance of an integer whose value is the index of the selected item. The deselect event is identical to the select event except that `event.id` is `Event.LIST_DESELECT`. `LIST_SELECT` and `LIST_DESELECT` are declared in the `Event` class as static variables, as are all other event types.

The applet in Listing 19.8 sets up a list containing several values and uses a label to inform you whenever an item is selected or deselected.

Listing 19.8 Source Code for *ListApplet.java*

```
// Example 19.8 - ListApplet
//
// This applet creates a scrolling list with several choices and
// informs you of selections and deselections using a label.
//

import java.applet.*;
import java.awt.*;

public class ListApplet extends Applet
{
     Label listStatus;
     List scrollingList;

     public void init()
     {

// First, create the List

          scrollingList = new List(3, true);

// Now add a few items to the list

          scrollingList.addItem("Moe");

          scrollingList.addItem("Larry");

          scrollingList.addItem("Curly");

          scrollingList.addItem("Shemp");

          scrollingList.addItem("Curly Joe");
```

Part III Ch 19

continues

Listing 19.8 Continued

```
// Set Shemp to be selected

          scrollingList.select(3);

// Finally, add the list to the applet

          add(scrollingList);
// Now create a label to show the last event that occurred

          listStatus = new Label("You selected entry Shemp");
          add(listStatus);

     }

     public boolean handleEvent(Event evt)
     {
          String selectionString;
          Integer selection;

// Since you are handling events in the applet itself,
// you need to check to make sure the event is for the scrollingList.

          if (evt.target == scrollingList)
          {

// Check to see if this is a selection event

               if (evt.id == Event.LIST_SELECT)
               {
// selection is the index of the selected item
                    selection = (Integer) evt.arg;
// use getItem to get the actual item.
                    selectionString = "You selected entry "+
                         scrollingList.getItem(
                              selection.intValue());
// Update the label
                    listStatus.setText(selectionString);
               }
               else if (evt.id == Event.LIST_DESELECT)
               {
// If this is a deselection, get the deselected item
// selection is the index of the selected item
                    selection = (Integer) evt.arg;
// use getItem to get the actual item.
                    selectionString = "You deselected entry "+
                         scrollingList.getItem(
                              selection.intValue());
// Update the label
                    listStatus.setText(selectionString);
               }
          }
          return true;
     }
}
```

Figure 19.8 shows the output from `ListApplet`.

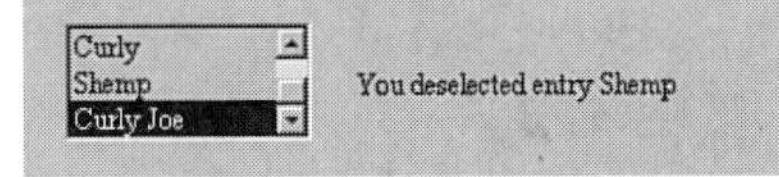

FIG. 19.8
The `ListApplet` program lets you select and deselect list items.

Text Fields and Text Areas

The AWT provides two different classes for entering text data—`TextField` and `TextArea`. The `TextField` class handles only a single line of text, while the `TextArea` handles multiple lines. Both of these classes share many similar methods because both are derived from a common class called `TextComponent`.

Creating Text Fields

The easiest way to create a text field is with the empty constructor:

```
public TextField()
```

The empty constructor creates an empty text field with an unspecified number of columns. If you want to control how many columns are in the text field, you can do so with

```
public TextField(int numColumns)
```

Sometimes you might want to initialize the text field with some text when you create it:

```
public TextField(String initialText)
```

Rounding out these combinations is a method for creating a text field that is initialized with text and has a fixed number of columns:

```
public TextField(String initialText, int numColumns)
```


Creating Text Areas

It should come as no surprise that the methods for creating text areas are similar to those for text fields. In fact, they are identical, except that when giving a fixed size for a text area, you must give both columns and rows. You can create an empty text area with an unspecified number of rows and columns by using the empty constructor:

```
public TextArea()
```

You can initialize an area that contains some text with

```
public TextArea(String initialText)
```

You can give a text area a fixed number of rows and columns with

```
public TextArea(int numRows, int numColumns)
```

Finally, you can create a text area that has some initial text and a fixed size with

```
public TextArea(String initialText, int numRows, int numColumns)
```

Common Text Component Features

`TextArea` actually extends a class called `TextComponent` (along with `TextField`). The `TextComponent` abstract class implements a number of useful methods that can be used on either `TextArea` or `TextField` classes.

You will probably want to put text into the component at some point. You can do that with `setText`:

```
public void setText(String newText)
```

You will certainly want to find out what text is in the component. You can use `getText` to do that:

```
public String getText()
```

You can find out what text has been selected (highlighted with the mouse) by using `getSelectedText`:

```
public String getSelectedText()
```

You can also find out where the selection starts and ends. The `getSelectionStart` and `getSelectionEnd` methods return integers that indicate the position within the entire text where the selection starts and ends:

```
public int getSelectionStart()
```

```
public int getSelectionEnd()
```

For instance, if the selection started at the very beginning of the text, `getSelectionStart` would return 0:

```
int selectionStart, selectionEnd;
selectionStart = myTextField.getSelectionStart();
selectionEnd = myTextField.getSelectionEnd();
```

You can also cause text to be selected with the `select` method:

```
public void select(int selectionStart, int selectionEnd)
```

If you want to select the entire text, you can use `selectAll` as a shortcut:

```
public void selectAll()
```

You can also use `setEditable` to control whether the text in the component can be edited (if not, it is read only):

```
public void setEditable(boolean canBeEdited)
```

The `isEditable` method returns `true` if the component is editable or `false` if it is not:

```
public boolean isEditable()
```

Text Field Features

Text fields have some features that text areas do not. The `TextField` class allows you to set an echo character that is printed instead of the character that was typed. Echo characters are useful when making fields for entering passwords where you might make * the echo character. That way, you don't see the password on the screen—only a line of asterisks. Setting up an echo character is as easy as calling `setEchoCharacter`:

```
public void setEchoChar(char ch)
```

One of the most common uses of `setEchoChar` is printing asterisks for a password. The following code fragment sets the echo character to an asterisk:

```
myTextField.setEchoCharacter('*'); // Print *s in place of what was typed
```

You can find out the echo character for a field with `getEchoChar`:

```
public char getEchoChar()
```

The `echoCharIsSet` method returns `true` if an echo character is set for the field or `false` if not:

```
public boolean echoCharIsSet()
```

Finally, you can find out how many columns are in the text field (how many visible columns, not how much text is there) by using the `getColumns` method:

```
public int getColumns()
```

Text Area Features

Text areas also have their own special features. Text areas are usually used for editing text, so they contain some methods for inserting, appending, and replacing text. You can add text to the end of the text area with `appendText`:

```
public void appendText(String textToAdd)
```

You can also insert text at any point in the current text with `insertText`. For instance, if you add text at position 0, you add it to the front of the area:


```
public void insertText(String newText, int position)
```

You can also use `replaceText` to replace portions of the text:

```
public void replaceText(String str, int start, int end)
```

Here is an example that uses the `getSelectionStart` and `getSelectionEnd` functions from `TextComponent` to replace selected text in a `TextArea` with `"[CENSORED]"`:

```
myTextArea.replaceText("[CENSORED]", myTextArea.getSelectionStart(),
myTextArea.getSelectionEnd());
```

Finally, you can find out the number of columns and the number of rows in a text area with `getColumns` and `getRows`:

```
public int getColumns()
public int getRows()
```

Using Text Fields and Text Areas

Like the `List` class, the `TextArea` class does not use the `action` method. However, in this case, you probably do not need to use the `handleEvent` method, either. The events you would get for the TextArea would be keyboard and mouse events, and you want the TextArea class to handle those itself. What you should do instead is create a button for users to press when they have finished editing the text. Then you can use getText to retrieve the edited text.

The TextField class either generates an ActionEvent or uses the action method (depending on whether you're using the Java 1.1 or Java 1.0 event model) only when the user presses Return. You may find this useful, but again, you could create a button for the user to signal that he or she finished entering the text (especially if a number of text fields must be filled out).

Listing 19.9 creates two text fields—a text area with an echo character defined, and a text area that displays the value of the text entered in one of the text fields.

Listing 19.9 Two Text Fields

```
import java.awt.*;
import java.awt.event.*;
import java.applet.*;

// TextFieldExample
// This applet creates some text fields and a text area
// to demonstrate the features of each.
//

public class TextFieldExample extends Applet
{
     protected TextField passwordField;

     protected TextArea textArea;

     public void init()
     {
          passwordField = new TextField(10); // 10 columns
          passwordField.setEchoChar('*'); // print '*' for input
          add(passwordField);

          textArea = new TextArea(5, 40); // 5 rows, 40 cols
          textArea.append("This is some initial text for the text area.");
          textArea.select(5, 12); // select "is some"

          add(textArea);

              passwordField.addActionListener(new ActionListener(){
                      public void actionPerformed(ActionEvent event){
                                // Now, change the text in the textArea to "Your
                              ➥password is: "
                                // followed by the password entered in the
                              ➥passwordField
                               textArea.setText("Your password is: "+
                              ➥event.getActionCommand());
                              }
                 });
     }
}
```

NOTE Listing 19.10 shows how to create Listing 19.9 with the 1.0 event model.

Listing 19.10 Source Code for *TextApplet.java*

```
import java.awt.*;
import java.applet.*;

// TextApplet
// This applet creates some text fields and a text area
// to demonstrate the features of each.
//

public class TextApplet extends Applet
{
     protected TextField inputField;
     protected TextField passwordField;

     protected TextArea textArea;

     public void init()
     {
          inputField = new TextField();     // unspecified size
          add(inputField);

          passwordField = new TextField(10); // 10 columns
          passwordField.setEchoCharacter('*'); // print '*' for input
          add(passwordField);

          textArea = new TextArea(5, 40); // 5 rows, 40 cols
          textArea.appendText(
               "This is some initial text for the text area.");
          textArea.select(5, 12); // select "is some"

          add(textArea);
     }

// The action method looks specifically for something entered in the
// password field and displays it in the textArea

     public boolean action(Event evt, Object whichAction)
     {
// Check to make sure this is an event for the passwordField
// if not, signal that the event hasn't been handled
          if (evt.target != passwordField)
          {
               return false;  // Event not handled
          }

// Now, change the text in the textArea to "Your password is: "
// followed by the password entered in the passwordField

          textArea.setText("Your password is: "+
               event.getText());
          return true;     // Event has been handled
     }
}
```

If, at some point, you want to receive notification of all keyboard activity, you can use another type of event listener: the `TextListener`. `TextListener`'s method is `textValueChanged(TextEvent)`, and because `addTextListener()` is a `TextComponent` method, you can add `TextListeners` to either `TextFields` or `TextAreas`.

Scrollbars

The `Scrollbar` class provides a basic interface for scrolling that can be used in a variety of situations. The controls of the scrollbar manipulate a position value that indicates the scrollbar's current position. You can set the minimum and maximum values for the scrollbar's position as well as its current value. The scrollbar's controls update the position in three ways:

- `line`
- `page`
- `absolute`

The arrow buttons at either end of the scrollbar update the scrollbar position with a `line` update. You can tell the scrollbar how much to add to the position (or subtract from it). For a `line` update, the default is 1.

A `page` update is performed whenever the mouse is clicked on the gap between the slider button and the scrolling arrows. You may also tell the scrollbar how much to add to the position for a page update.

The `absolute` update is performed whenever the slider button is dragged in one direction or another. You have no control over how the position value changes for an absolute update, except that you can control the minimum and maximum values.

An important aspect of the `Scrollbar` class is that it is only responsible for updating its own position. It is unable to cause any other component to scroll. If you want the scrollbar to scroll a canvas up and down, you must add code to detect when the scrollbar changes and update the canvas as needed.

Creating Scrollbars

You can create a simple vertical scrollbar with the empty constructor:

```
public Scrollbar()
```

You can also specify the orientation of the scrollbar as either `Scrollbar.HORIZONTAL` or `Scrollbar.VERTICAL`:

```
public Scrollbar(int orientation)
```

You can create a scrollbar with a predefined orientation, position, page increment, minimum value, and maximum value:

```
public Scrollbar(int orientation, int position, int pageIncrement,
int minimum, int maximum)
```

The following code creates a vertical scrollbar with a minimum value of 0, a maximum value of 100, a page size of 10, and a starting position of 50:

```
Scrollbar myScrollbar = new Scrollbar(Scrollbar.VERTICAL, 50, 10, 0, 100);
```

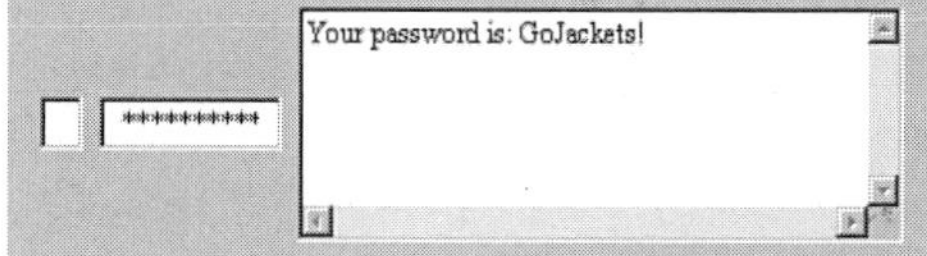

FIG. 19.9
Text fields and text areas allow the entry of text.

Scrollbar Features

You can set the scrollbar's line increment with `setUnitIncrement`:

```
public void setUnitIncrement(int increment)
```

You can query the current line increment with `getUnitIncrement`:

```
public int getUnitIncrement()
```

You can set the page increment with `setBlockIncrement`:

```
public void setBlockIncrement()
```

You can also query the page increment with `getBlockIncrement`.

```
public int getBlockIncrement()
```

You can find out the scrollbar's minimum and maximum position values with `getMinimum` and `getMaximum`:

```
public int getMinimum()

public int getMaximum()
```

The `setValue` method sets the scrollbar's current position:

```
public void setValue()
```

You can query the current position with `getValue`:

```
public int getValue()
```

The `getOrientation` method returns `Scrollbar.VERTICAL` if the scrollbar is vertical or `Scrollbar.HORIZONTAL` if it is horizontal:

```
public int getOrientation()
```

You can also set the position, page increment, minimum value, and maximum value with `setValues`:

```
public void setValue(int position, int pageIncrement,
int minimum, int maximum)
```

The following code sets the position to 75, the page increment to 25, the minimum value to 0, and the maximum value to 500:

```
myScrollbar.setValues(75, 25, 0, 500);
```

Using Scrollbars

The `Scrollbar` class generates `AdjustmentEvents` and sends them to an `AdjustmentListener` object. The lone method defined by the `AdjustmentListener` interface is `adjustmentValueChanged`:

```
public void adjustmentValueChanged(AdjustmentEvent event)
```

A scrollbar can change three ways—in single units, in block units, or by absolute positioning (tracking). A single unit adjustment occurs when you click the arrows at either end of the scrollbar. A block adjustment occurs when you click the area between an arrow and the slider. An absolute adjustment occurs when you drag the slider around.

The `getAdjustmentType` in the `AdjustmentEvent` object returns either `AdjustmentEvent.UNIT_INCREMENT`, `AdjustmentEvent.UNIT_DECREMENT`, `AdjustmentEvent.BLOCK_INCREMENT`, `AdjustmentEvent.BLOCK_DECREMENT`, or `AdjustmentEvent.Track`:

```
public int getAdjustmentType()
```

Like the `List` class, the `Scrollbar` class does not make use of the `action` method under the Java 1.0 event model. You must use the `handleEvent` method to determine when a scrollbar has moved. The possible values of `evt.id` for events generated by the `Scrollbar` class are

- `Event.SCROLL_ABSOLUTE` when the slider button is dragged
- `Event.SCROLL_LINE_DOWN` when the up arrow or left arrow button (depending on the scrollbar's orientation) is pressed
- `Event.SCROLL_LINE_UP` when the down arrow or right arrow button (depending on the scrollbar's orientation) is pressed
- `Event.SCROLL_PAGE_DOWN` when the user clicks in the area between the slider and the bottom or left arrow
- `Event.SCROLL_PAGE_UP` when the user clicks in the area between the slider and the top or right arrow

You may not care which of these events is received. In many cases, you may only need to know that the scrollbar position is changed. You would call the `getValue` method to find out the new position.

Canvases

The `Canvas` class is a component with no special functionality. It is mainly used for creating custom graphic components. You create an instance of a `Canvas` with

```
Canvas myCanvas = new Canvas();
```

However, you will almost always want to create your own special subclass of `Canvas` that does whatever special function you need. You should override the `Canvas` paint method to make your `Canvas` do something interesting.

NOTE By default, a `Canvas` has no size. This is very inconvenient when you are using a layout manager that needs to have some idea of a component's required size. At the minimum, you should implement your own size method in a canvas. It is even nicer to implement `minimumSize` and `preferredSize`.

Listing 19.11 creates a `CircleCanvas` class that draws a filled circle in a specific color.

Listing 19.11 Source Code for *CircleCanvas.java*

```
import java.awt.*;

// Example 29.6 CircleCanvas class
//
// This class creates a canvas that draws a circle on itself.
// The circle color is given at creation time, and the size of
// the circle is determined by the size of the canvas.
//

public class CircleCanvas extends Canvas
{
     Color circleColor;

// When you create a CircleCanvas, you tell it what color to use.

     public CircleCanvas(Color drawColor)
     {
          circleColor = drawColor;
     }

     public void paint(Graphics g)
     {
          int circleDiameter, circleX, circleY;
          Dimension currentSize = getSize();

// Use the smaller of the height and width of the canvas.
// This guarantees that the circle will be drawn completely.


          if (currentSize.width < currentSize.height)
          {
               circleDiameter = currentSize.width;
          }
          else
          {
               circleDiameter = currentSize.height;
          }
```


continues

Listing 19.11 Continued

```
            g.setColor(circleColor);

// The math here on the circleX and circleY may seem strange. The x and y
// coordinates for fillOval are the upper-left coordinates of the rectangle
// that surrounds the circle. If the canvas is wider than the circle, for
// instance, we want to find out how much wider (i.e. width - diameter)
// and then, since we want equal amounts of blank area on both sides,
// we divide the amount of blank area by 2. In the case where the diameter
// equals the width, the amount of blank area is 0.

            circleX = (currentSize.width - circleDiameter) / 2;
            circleY = (currentSize.height - circleDiameter) / 2;

            g.fillOval(circleX, circleY, circleDiameter, circleDiameter);
        }
}
```

The `CircleCanvas` is only a component, not a runnable applet. In the next chapter, in the section "Grid Bag Layouts," you use this new class in an example of using the `GridBagLayout` layout manager.

Common Component Methods

The `Component` class defines a large number of methods that are common to all AWT components and containers. Almost all of the methods deal with either displaying the component or receiving input events.

Component Display Methods

You can control many simple things in a component, such as the foreground and background colors, the font, and whether the component is even shown. The `setForeground` and `setBackground` methods change the foreground and background colors of the component:

```
public void setForeground(Color c)
```

```
public void setBackground(Color c)
```

Although `setForeground` and `setBackground` are defined for all components, they may not always work at the moment as advertised under some Java implementations. Many Java implementations actually rely on the underlying windowing system to draw the components, and they may not be able to change the foreground and background colors for components easily.

You can query the foreground and background colors of any component with `getForeground` and `getBackground`:

```
public Color getForeground()
```

```
public Color getBackground()
```

The `hide` and `show` methods control whether or not a component is visible on the screen.

```
public void hide()
```

keeps a component from being displayed. The component still exists, however.

```
public void show()
```

makes a component display itself. This method is important for frames because they are hidden by default:

```
public void setVisable(boolean showComponent)
```

NOTE For Java 1.0, the `setVisable()` method should be replaced with `show()`.

If `showComponent` is `true`, the component is displayed. If `showComponent` is `false`, the component is hidden.

The `setFont` method changes a component's font. This method is only useful for components that display text:

```
public void setFont(Font f)
```

You can query a component's current font with `getFont`:

```
public Font getFont()
```

The `Component` class also gives you access to the font metrics for a font:

```
public FontMetrics getFontMetrics(Font font)
```


Component Positioning and Sizing

The size and position are usually dictated to a component by the layout manager. The component can return its preferred and minimum size, but the layout manager still makes the decision on the actual size. The layout manager also decides a component's position (its x and y coordinates). After the layout manager decides the position and size of a component, it invokes methods in the component to resize and position it.

The `getMinimumSize` method returns the minimum width and height a component must be given, while `preferredSize` returns the preferred width and height:

```
public Dimension getMinimumSize()


public Dimension preferredSize()
```

The `getSize` method returns a component's actual width and height:

```
public Dimension getSize()
```

The `setLocation` method sets the x and y coordinates for the upper-left corner of the component's display area:

```
public void setLocation(int x, int y)
```

These coordinates are relative to the parent component's space. For example, if a component was moved to 0,0 and its parent was located on the screen at 100,150, the component would really be drawn at 100,150. Figure 19.10 illustrates the relationship between a component's coordinates, the parent's coordinates, and the real screen coordinates.

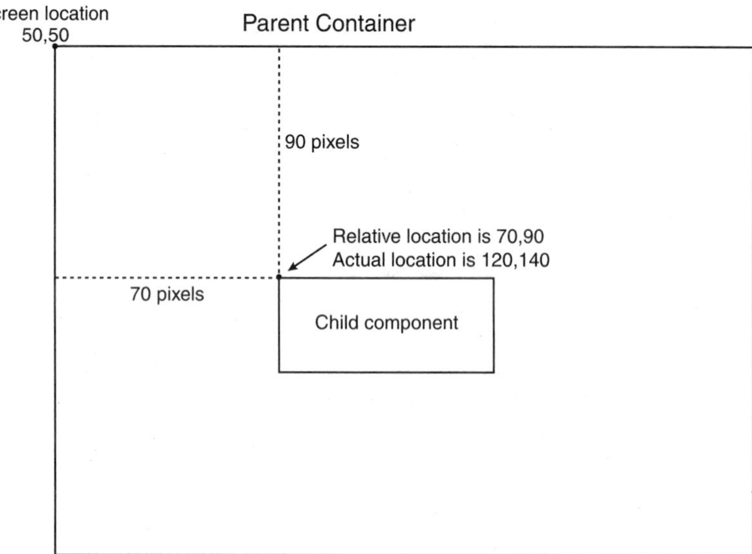

FIG. 19.10
A component's coordinates are relative to its parent container.

If you want to query a component's position relative to its parent's display area, use the `location` method:

```
public Point location()
```

The `getComponentAt` method finds the component that contains a particular x,y point:

```
public Component getComponentAt(int x, int y)
```

If the point is not within this component, the `locate` method returns `null`. If the point is within this component and the component contains subcomponents, it looks for a child component that contains the point. If one is found, `locate` returns that component. If not, it returns the current component. Note that `locate` only searches one level deep into the children. After you get a child component, you can repeat the search.

The following method finds the component on the screen that occupies a particular x,y coordinate. If `locate` returns a container, it searches through that container's components until it finds the correct component.

```
public Component findComponent(int x, int y)
{

        // Find out which component this x,y is inside
         Component whichComp = getComponentAt(x, y);
```

```
        // If the component is a container, descend into the container and
        // find out which of its components contains this x,y

         while (whichComp instanceof Container) {
               // If you have to search within a container, adjust
➥ the x,y to be relative
               // to the container.
                x -= whichComp.getLocation().x;
                y -= whichComp.getLocation().y;
                Component nextComp = whichComp.getComponentAt(x, y);

               // if locate returns the component itself, we're done
                if (nextComp == whichComp) break;
                whichComp = nextComp;
        }
        return whichComp;
}
```

NOTE If you are using Java 1.0, the methods listed above need to be replaced according to the following table:

Java 1.1 & 1.2	Java 1.0
`getSize`	`size`
`getMinimumSize`	`minimumSize`
`getComponentAt`	`locate`
`setLocation`	`move`

This substitution should result in the following method:

```
public Component findComponent(int x, int y)
{

// Find out which component this x,y is inside
Component whichComp = locate(x, y);

// If the component is a container, descend into the container and
// find out which of its components contains this x,y

while (whichComp instanceof Container) {

      // If you have to search within a container, adjust the x,y to be relative
      // to the container.
      x -= whichComp.location().x;
      y -= whichComp.location().y;
      Component nextComp = whichComp.locate(x, y);

      // if locate returns the component itself, we're done
      if (nextComp == whichComp) break;
          whichComp = nextComp;
      }
      return whichComp;
}
```

Component Layout and Rendering Methods

You may already be familiar with the key methods for component rendering (drawing on the screen). They are `repaint`, `update`, and `paint`.

```
public void repaint()
```

requests that this image be repainted as soon as possible. This results in an eventual call to update, but maybe not immediately.

```
public void repaint(int x, int y, int width, int height)
```

repaints only the portion of the component within the rectangle specified by the parameters.

```
public void repaint(long tm)
```

requests that the component be repainted within `tm` milliseconds.

```
public void repaint(long tm, int x, int y, int width, int height)
```

requests that a specific portion of the component be repainted within `tm` milliseconds.

```
public void update(Graphics g)
```

initiates a repaint of the component onto graphics context `g`. The `default update` method erases the graphics context and calls the `paint` method.

```
public void paint(Graphics g)
```

redraws the component onto graphics context `g`.

When components are laid out by a layout manager, they are marked as being valid. That is, they have been examined and laid out. If a component changes size or some other aspect that requires the current layout to be altered, the component can be marked invalid by the `invalidate` method:

```
public void invalidate()
```

Invalidating a component marks it as changed. The next time the `validate` method in the component or its parent is called, the component layout is performed again. The format of the `validate` method is

```
public void validate()
```

The `validate` method also makes use of the `doLayout` method in each child component of this component:

```
public void doLayout()
```

The default `layout` method for a component does nothing. In a container, however, the `layout` method causes the layout manager to recompute the position of each contained component.

You can get a reference to the parent container of your component by using the `getParent` method:

```
public Container getParent()
```

You can get a reference to the parent frame of an applet by tracing back through the applet's parent containers until you find a frame. You can get unpredictable results this way, but sometimes you can have fun with it. The following loop tries to find an applet's parent frame:

```
Container parent = getParent();

// Trace back up getting parents until there
// are no more parents or we hit a Frame
//
while ((parent != null) && !(parent instanceof Frame))
{
        parent = parent.getParent();
}

// At this point, parent will either be null or it will
// be the parent frame for the applet
```

Component Input Events

Components can receive a large number of actions, so component has a number of methods to add event listeners. These include each of the following:

```
public void addComponentListener(ComponentListener)
public void addFocusListener(FocusListener)
public void addKeyListener(KeyListener)
public void addMouseListener(MouseListener)
public void addMouseMotionListener(MouseMotionListener)
```

As you may have already guessed, `FocusListeners` listen for focus changes (either gained or lost), `KeyListeners` listen for keyboard input, `MouseListeners` listen for the mouse to enter, exit, or click on an area, and `MouseMotionListeners` listen for the mouse to move. But what does the `ComponentListener` do?

`ComponentListeners` listen for changes to the component's position, size, or for the component to be shown or hidden. With all these different listeners, you can monitor just about any activity with any component.

Part III Ch 19

NOTE Under the 1.0 event model, the `handleEvent` method notifies a component of incoming input. The `handleEvent` method is actually part of a longer chain of event-handling methods.

```
public void deliverEvent(Event evt)
```

sends an event to this component. This is the initial entry point for an event in the event-handling chain. This method passes the event on to the `postEvent` method.

```
public boolean postEvent(Event evt)
```

passes the event on to the `handleEvent` method. If the `handleEvent` method returns `false`, this method passes the event on to the parent component using the parent's `postEvent` method. If `postEvent` returns `true`, the event has been handled successfully.

```
public boolean handleEvent(Event evt)
```

examines the event and calls one of the following methods based on the event type: `mouseEnter`,

continues

continued

`mouseExit`, `mouseMove`, `mouseDrag`, `mouseDown`, `mouseUp`, `keyDown`, `keyUp`, `action`, `gotFocus`, or `lostFocus`.

You can keep a component from receiving input events by disabling it with the `disable` method:

```
public void disable()
```

To enable it again, call the `enable` method:

```
public void enable()
```

The `isEnabled` method returns `true` if a component is enabled:

```
public boolean isEnabled()
```

CHAPTER 20

Exceptions and Events in Depth

In this chapter

Java's Exceptions

When you write applets or applications using Java, sooner or later (and probably much sooner) you're going to run into exceptions. An *exception* is a special type of object that is created when something goes wrong in a program. After Java creates the `exception` object, it sends it to your program, an action called *throwing* an exception, and it's up to your program to catch the exception. Catching the exception is done in what is known as exception-handling code. In this chapter, you get the inside information on these important error-handling objects.

Another important type of activity in Java is an *event*. Events represent actions that the user performs while running your program, such as clicking a button or moving the mouse. As you will soon see, there are several ways your programs can handle events. This chapter gives you an in-depth look at the `Event` class and how it's used in your Java projects.

In some of the previous chapters, you've gotten a quick look at exceptions and how they are handled in a program. Exceptions are thrown because the method call may not be able to complete successfully (such as when trying to put a thread to sleep). In this case, Java throws an exception object called `InterruptedException` (see Listing 20.1).

Listing 20.1 Handling an Exception

```
try
{
    Thread.sleep(500);
}
catch (InterruptedException e)
{
    String err = e.toString();
    System.out.println(err);
}
```

As you can see in Listing 20.1, you place the code that may cause the exception in a `try` block, and the exception-handling code goes into a `catch` program block. In this case, the first line of the `try` block attempts to put the current thread to sleep for 500 milliseconds. If the `Thread` `sleep` is unsuccessful, the `sleep()` method throws an `InterruptedException`. When this happens, Java ignores the rest of the code in the `try` block and jumps to the `catch` block, where the program handles the exception. On the other hand, if the sleep goes okay, Java executes all the code in the `try` block and skips the `catch` block.

NOTE The `catch` block does more than direct program execution. It actually catches the `exception` object thrown by Java. In Listing 20.1, you can see the `exception` object being caught inside the parentheses following the `catch` keyword. This is very similar to a parameter being passed to a method. In this case, the type of the "parameter" is `InterruptedException`, and the name of the parameter is `e`. If you need to, you can access the `exception` object's methods through the `e` object. In this example, the program calls `e`'s `toString()` method in order to get a string representing the `exception` object.

Java defines many `exception` objects that may be thrown by the methods in Java's classes. How do you know which exceptions you have to handle? If you try to call a method that explicitly states that it may throw an exception, Java insists that you handle the exception in one way or another. If you fail to do so, your class does not compile. Instead, you receive an error message indicating where your program may generate the exception (see Figure 20.1).

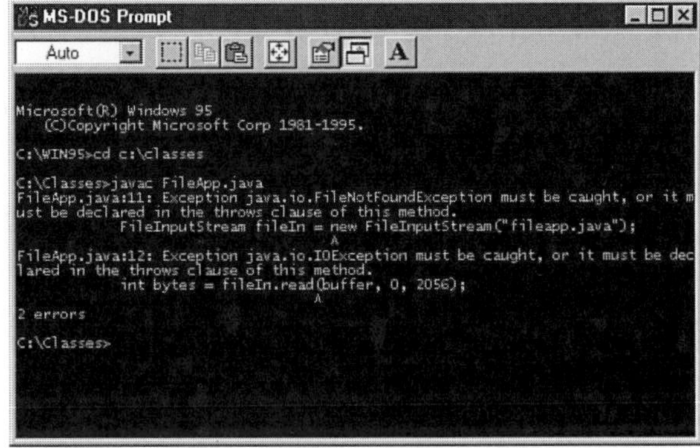

FIG. 20.1 Java's compiler gives you an error message if you fail to handle an exception in your applet.

Although the compiler's error messages are a clue that something is amiss, the clever programmer will look up a method in Java's documentation before using the method. Then the programmer will know in advance whether that method requires exception-handling code. If you're interested in seeing the exceptions that are defined by a package, find the package's section in Java's online documentation where the classes and exceptions are listed (see Figure 20.2).

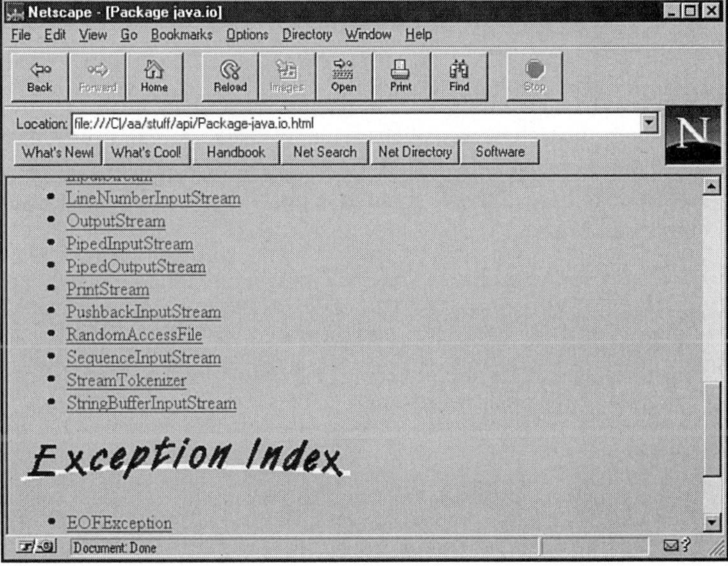

FIG. 20.2 Java's online documentation lists the exception objects that may be thrown by methods in a class.

The online documentation on Sun's Web site is constantly being updated. To stay up to date, set a bookmark in your browser for `http://www.javasoft.com/products/JDK/` and visit the site often.

The online documentation also lists all the methods that comprise a particular package. By looking up the method in the documentation (see Figure 20.3), you can see what types of arguments the method expects, the type of value the method returns, and whether the method may throw an exception. If the method shows that it can throw an exception, your code must handle the right type of exception or the program will not compile.

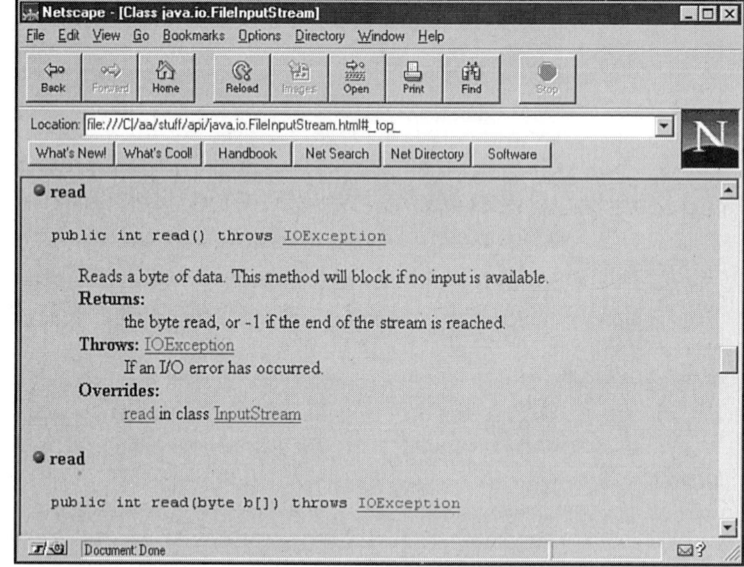

FIG. 20.3 The online documentation for a method shows the exception the method may throw.

Throwing an Exception

One handy thing about exceptions is that you don't have to handle them in the same method in which the exception is generated. For example, when the program in Listing 20.1 tries to put the thread to sleep, if the sleep fails, the method throws an exception that the program handles in its `catch` block.

But what if, for some reason, you don't want to catch the exception the same way you did with the `read()` method? If you don't know what to do with the exception, you may not want to catch it. In that case, Java enables you to simply pass the buck, so to speak, by throwing the exception up the method hierarchy. Listing 20.2 shows one way you might do this with the `IOException` exception.

Listing 20.2 *LST20-02.TXT*—Throwing an Exception

```
protected void MyMethod(){
    try
    {
        DoRead();
    }
    catch (IOException e)
    {
        String err = e.toString();
        System.out.println(err);
    }
}

protected void DoRead() throws IOException
{
    System.in.read(buffer, 0, 255);
}
```

The `read()` method throws an `IOException`, so you could have called it within a `try/catch` block. However, in Listing 20.2, the call to the `read()` method has been moved to a method called `DoRead()` that doesn't directly handle the `IOException` exception. Instead, `DoRead()` states that it can throw an `IOException` and passes the exception back to the calling method. Java knows that `DoRead()` wants to pass the exception, because `DoRead()` adds the phrase `throws IOException` to its signature. Throwing the exception, however, doesn't relieve you from handling it eventually. Notice that in Listing 20.2, the exception still gets handled in the `myMethod()` calling method.

In short, you can handle an exception in two ways:

- Write `try` and `catch` program blocks exactly where you call the function that may generate the exception.
- Declare the method as throwing the exception, in which case you must write the `try` and `catch` program blocks in the method that calls the "throwing" method, as shown in Listing 20.2.

A Combined Approach

There may be times in your programs when you want to both handle an exception in your code and pass it on to the calling function. Java enables you to construct your code this way so that different parts of a program can handle an exception as is appropriate for that part of the program. To use this combined approach to exception handling, include both `try/catch` program blocks and a `throws` clause in the method. Listing 20.3 shows an example of this handy technique.

Listing 20.3 *LST20-03.TXT*—Code That Both Handles and Passes on an Exception

```
protected void MyMethod() throws IOException{
    try
    {
        DoRead();
    }
    catch (IOException e)
    {
        String err = e.toString();
        System.out.println(err);
          throw e;
    }
}
```

As you've seen in the last few examples, `exception` objects can do a lot of traveling. They jump from method to method, up the hierarchy of method calls until someone finally deals with them. If the exception makes its way up to the Java system, the system handles it in some default manner, usually by generating an error message. However, when running applets in a browser, the user may not get a chance to see the error messages. Worse, some Java-compatible browsers handle exceptions differently from others. One browser may just ignore the exception and keep on chugging, whereas another may be driven to its digital knees. The best approach is to handle any exceptions that may occur in your program. That way, you can be pretty sure that the browser will remain unaffected by the error.

Types of Exceptions

Java defines many different exception objects. Some of them you must always handle in your code if you call a function that may throw the exception. Others are generated by the system when something like memory allocation fails, an expression tries to divide by zero, a null value is used inappropriately, and so on. You can choose to watch for this second kind of exception or let the VM deal with them. All of these types of exceptions are derived from the `RuntimeException` class.

Just as with programming before exceptions existed, you should always be on the lookout for places in your program where an exception could be generated. These places are usually as sociated with user input, which is infamously unpredictable. However, programmers also have been known to make mistakes in their programs that lead to exception throwing. Some common exceptions you may want to watch out for at appropriate places in your applet are listed in Table 20.1.

Table 20.1 Common Java Exceptions

Exception	Caused By
`ArithmeticException`	Math errors, such as division by zero
`ArrayIndexOutOfBoundsException`	Bad array indexes
`ArrayStoreException`	A program trying to store the wrong type of data in an array
`FileNotFoundException`	An attempt to access a nonexistent file
`IOException`	General I/O failures, such as inability to read from a file
`NullPointerException`	Referencing a null object
`NumberFormatException`	A failed conversion between strings and numbers
`OutOfMemoryException`	Too little memory to allocate a new object
`SecurityException`	An applet trying to perform an action not allowed by the browser's security setting
`StackOverflowException`	The system running out of stack space
`StringIndexOutOfBoundsException`	A program attempting to access a nonexistent character position in a string

You can catch all exceptions by setting up your `catch` block for exceptions of type `Exception`, like this:

```
catch (Exception e)
```

Call the exception's `getMessage()` method (inherited from the `Throwable` superclass) to get information about the specific exception that you've intercepted.

All Java's exceptions are really just classes that are extended from the `Throwable` class, to which all exception and error objects can trace their ancestry. (You learn about `error` objects later in this chapter in the section "Java's Error Classes.") The `Throwable` class defines three useful methods that you can call to get information about an exception:

- `getMessage()` Gets a string that details information about the exception
- `toString()` Converts the object to a string that you can display onscreen
- `printStackTrace()` Displays the hierarchy of method calls that leads to the exception

Listing 20.4 shows a `catch` clause that calls these various methods, whereas Figure 20.4 shows the output from the `catch` clause. (Notice that in the case of `NumberFormatException`, the `getMessage()` method returns an empty string.)

Listing 20.4 *LST20-04.TXT*—Calling a *throwable* Object's Methods

```
catch (NumberFormatException e)
{
    System.out.println();
    System.out.println("Here's getMessage()'s string:");
    System.out.println("---------------------------");
    String str = e.getMessage();
    System.out.println(str);
    System.out.println();
    System.out.println("Here's toString()'s string:");
    System.out.println("-------------------------");
    str = e.toString();
    System.out.println(str);
    System.out.println();
    System.out.println("Here's the stack trace:");
    System.out.println("---------------------");
    e.printStackTrace();
}
```

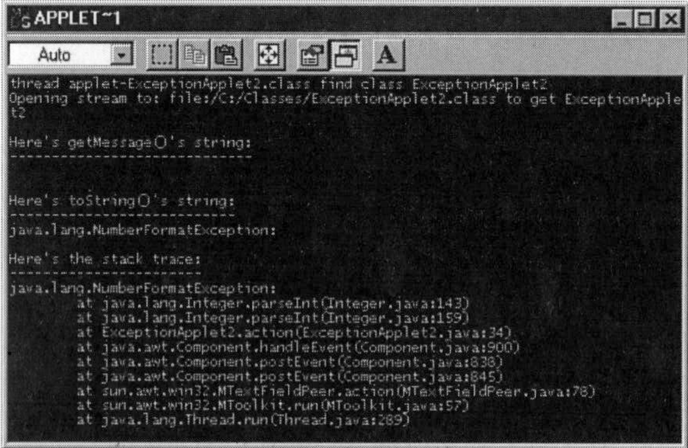

FIG. 20.4 Here's the output generated by the `catch` block in Listing 20.4.

Exceptions are divided into three main categories:

- Exception classes that are directly derived from `Exception`
- Runtime exception classes
- I/O exception classes

Java's many exception classes are listed as they appear in the class hierarchy. The package in which a class is defined is shown in parentheses after the class name.

```
Throwable (java.lang)
Exception (java.lang)
AWTException (java.awt)
NoSuchMethodException (java.lang)
InterruptedException (java.lang)
InstantiationException (java.lang)
ClassNotFoundException (java.lang)
CloneNotSupportedException (java.lang)
```

```
IllegalAccessException (java.lang)
IOException (java.io)
EOFException (java.io)
FileNotFoundException (java.io)
InterruptedIOException (java.io)
UTFDataFormatException (java.io)
MalformedURLException (java.net)
ProtocolException (java.net)
SocketException (java.net)
UnknownHostException (java.net)
UnknownServiceException (java.net)
RuntimeException (java.lang)
ArithmeticException (java.lang)
ArrayStoreException (java.lang)
ClassCastException (java.lang)
IllegalArgumentException (java.lang)
IllegalThreadStateException (java.lang)
NumberFormatException (java.lang)
IllegalMonitorStateException (java.lang)
IndexOutOfBoundsException (java.lang)
ArrayIndexOutOfBoundsException (java.lang)
StringIndexOutOfBoundsException (java.lang)
NegativeArraySizeException (java.lang)
NullPointerException (java.lang)
SecurityException (java.lang)
EmptyStackException (java.util)
NoSuchElementException(java.util)
```

NOTE The list of exceptions shown here was created from the original Java classes. The latest version of Java adds many new classes and therefore adds many new exceptions as well.

Determining the Exceptions to Handle

Experienced programmers usually know when their code may generate an exception of some sort. However, when you first start writing applets with exception-handling code, you may not be sure what type of exceptions to watch out for. One way to discover this information is to see what exceptions are generated as you test your applet.

Listing 20.5, for example, is an applet called `ExceptionApplet` that divides two integer numbers obtained from the user and displays the integer result (dropping any remainder). Because the applet must deal with user input, the probability of disaster is high. `ExceptionApplet`, however, contains no exception-handling code.

Listing 20.5 *ExceptionApplet.java*—An Applet with No Exception Handling

```
import java.awt.*;
import java.awt.event.*;
import java.applet.*;

public class ExceptionApplet extends Applet
{
```

continues

Listing 20.5 Continued

```
    TextField textField1, textField2;
    String answerStr;
    public void init()
    {
        textField1 = new TextField(15);
        add(textField1);
        textField2 = new TextField(15);
        add(textField2);
        answerStr = "Undefined";

               //create an inner ActionListener class
               ActionListener listener = new ActionListener(){
                      public void actionPerformed(ActionEvent evt){
                             performAction();
                      }
               };

               textField1.addActionListener(listener);
               textField2.addActionListener(listener);
    }

    public void paint(Graphics g)
    {
        Font font = new Font("TimesRoman", Font.PLAIN, 24);
        g.setFont(font);
        g.drawString("The answer is:", 50, 100);
        g.drawString(answerStr, 70, 130);
    }

    public void performAction()
    {
        String str1 = textField1.getText();
        String str2 = textField2.getText();
        int int1 = Integer.parseInt(str1);
        int int2 = Integer.parseInt(str2);
        int answer = int1 / int2;
        answerStr = String.valueOf(answer);
        repaint();
    }
}
```

NOTE Users of the 1.0 event model need to eliminate the inner class and replace the performAction method with the following:

```
public boolean action(Event evt, Object arg)
    {
        String str1 = textField1.getText();
        String str2 = textField2.getText();
        int int1 = Integer.parseInt(str1);
        int int2 = Integer.parseInt(str2);
```

```
        int answer = int1 / int2;
        answerStr = String.valueOf(answer);
        repaint();
        return true;
    }
```

You'll use this applet as the starting point for a more robust applet. When you run the applet using AppletViewer, you see the window shown in Figure 20.5. Enter a number into each of the two text boxes and then press Enter. The program then divides the first number by the second number and displays the result (see Figure 20.6).

As long as the user enters valid numbers into the text boxes, the program runs perfectly.

What happens, though, if the user presses Enter when either or both of the text boxes are empty? Java immediately throws a `NumberFormatException` when the `action()` method attempts to convert the contents of the text boxes to integer values. You can see this happening by watching the command-line window from which you ran AppletViewer, as shown in Figure 20.7. As you can see in the figure, Java has displayed quite a few lines that trace the exception. The first line (the one that starts with the word `Exception`) tells you the type of exception you've encountered.

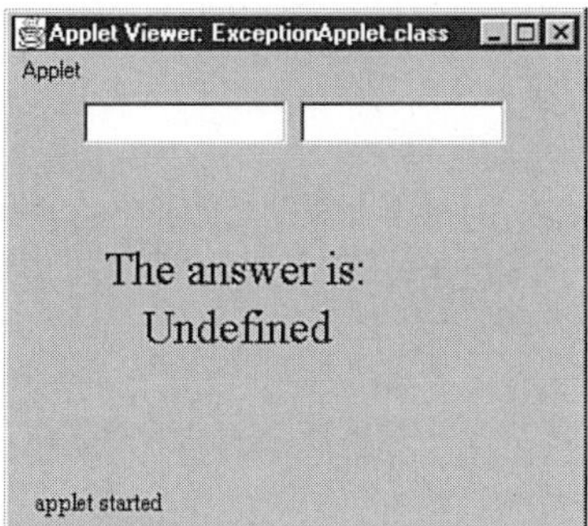

FIG. 20.5 `ExceptionApplet` is running under AppletViewer.

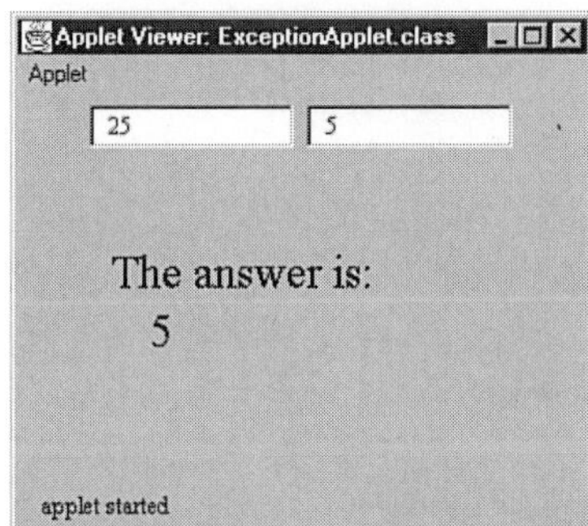

FIG. 20.6 `ExceptionApplet` divides the first number by the second.

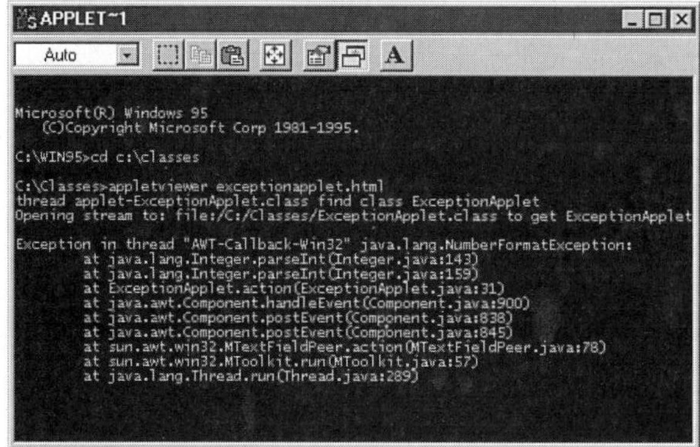

FIG. 20.7
Here, Java reports a `NumberFormatException`.

NOTE As you now know, you don't have to catch every exception that Java can produce. When you fail to provide code for an exception that doesn't require catching, Java catches the exception internally. When this happens to an applet running under AppletViewer, you see an exception error appear in the command-line window. However, if an applet generates an exception while running in a Web browser, the user is probably never aware of it because the applet doesn't usually crash or display errors; it just fails to perform the command that generated the exception.

Catching a Runtime Exception

You now know that users can cause a `NumberFormatException` if they leave one or more text boxes blank or enter an invalid numerical value, such as the string one. In order to ensure that your applet is not caught by surprise, you now need to write the code that will handle this exception. Follow these steps to add this new code:

1. Load `ExceptionApplet` into your text editor.
2. Replace the `action()` method with the new version shown in Listing 20.6.

Listing 20.6 *LST20-06.TXT*—Handling the *NumberFormatException* Exception

```
public boolean action(Event evt, Object arg)
{
    String str1 = textField1.getText();
    String str2 = textField2.getText();
    try
    {
        int int1 = Integer.parseInt(str1);
        int int2 = Integer.parseInt(str2);
        int answer = int1 / int2;
        answerStr = String.valueOf(answer);
    }
    catch (NumberFormatException e)
    {
        answerStr = "Bad number!";
```

```
        }
        repaint();
        return true;
    }
```

3. In the class declaration line, change the name of the class to `ExceptionApplet2`.
4. Save the new applet under the name `ExceptionApplet2.java`.
5. Load the `EXCEPTIONAPPLET.HTML` file.
6. Change all occurrences of `ExceptionApplet` to `ExceptionApplet2`.
7. Save the file as `EXCEPTIONAPPLET2.HTML`.

In Listing 20.6, the `action()` method now uses `try` and `catch` program blocks to handle the `NumberFormatException` gracefully. Figure 20.8 shows what happens now when the user leaves the text boxes blank. When the program gets to the first call to `String.valueOf()`, Java generates the `NumberFormatException` exception, which causes program execution to jump to the `catch` block. In the `catch` block, the program sets the display string to `Bad number!`. The call to `repaint()` ensures that this message to the user is displayed onscreen.

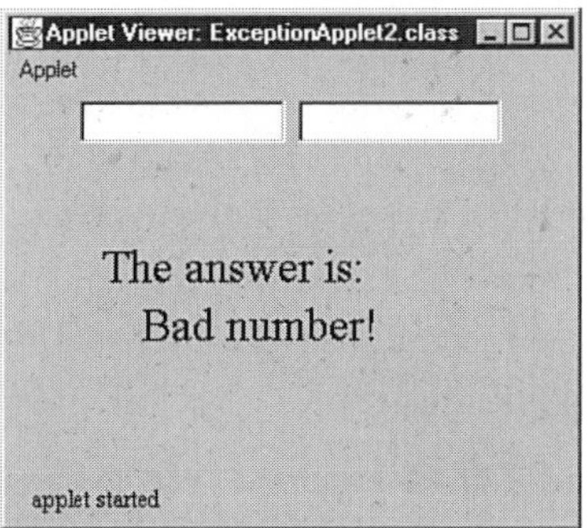

FIG. 20.8 `ExceptionApplet2` handles the `NumberFormatException` gracefully.

Handling Multiple Exceptions

So, here you are, having a good time entering numbers into `ExceptionApplet2`'s text boxes and getting the results. Without thinking, you enter a zero into the second box, Java tries to divide the first number by the zero, and pow!—you've got yourself an `ArithmeticException` exception. What to do? You're already using your `catch` block to grab `NumberFormatException`; now, you've got yet another exception to deal with.

The good news is that you're not limited to only a single `catch` block. You can, in fact, create `catch` blocks for any exceptions you think the program may generate. To see how this works with your new applet, follow these steps:

1. Load `ExceptionApplet2` into your text editor.
2. Replace the `action()` method with the new version shown in Listing 20.7.

Listing 20.7 *LST20-07.TXT*—Handling Multiple Exceptions

```
public boolean action(Event evt, Object arg)
{
    String str1 = textField1.getText();
    String str2 = textField2.getText();
    try
    {
        int int1 = Integer.parseInt(str1);
        int int2 = Integer.parseInt(str2);
        int answer = int1 / int2;
        answerStr = String.valueOf(answer);
    }
    catch (NumberFormatException e)
    {
        answerStr = "Bad number!";
    }
    catch (ArithmeticException e)
    {
        answerStr = "Division by 0!";
    }
    repaint();
    return true;
}
```

3. In the class declaration line, change the name of the class to `ExceptionApplet3`.
4. Save the new applet under the name `ExceptionApplet3.java`.
5. Load the `EXCEPTIONAPPLET.HTML` file.
6. Change all occurrences of `ExceptionApplet` to `ExceptionApplet3`.
7. Save the file as `EXCEPTIONAPPLET3.HTML`.

If you examine Listing 20.7, you can see that the `action()` method now defines two `catch` program blocks, one each for the `NumberFormatException` and `ArithmeticException` exceptions. In this way, the program can watch for both potential problems from within a single `try` block. Figure 20.9 shows what `ExceptionApplet3` looks like when the user attempts a division by zero. If you discover another exception that your program may cause, you can add yet another `catch` block.

It's important to make sure that you catch the most specific exception first. For instance, if you want to catch the exception `FileNotFoundException`, you should do so before catching the more generic `IOException`.

NOTE Although handling exceptions is a powerful tool for creating crash-proof programs, you should use them only in situations in which you have little control over the cause of the exception, such as when dealing with user input. If your applet causes an exception because of a program bug, you should track down and fix the problem rather than try to catch the exception.

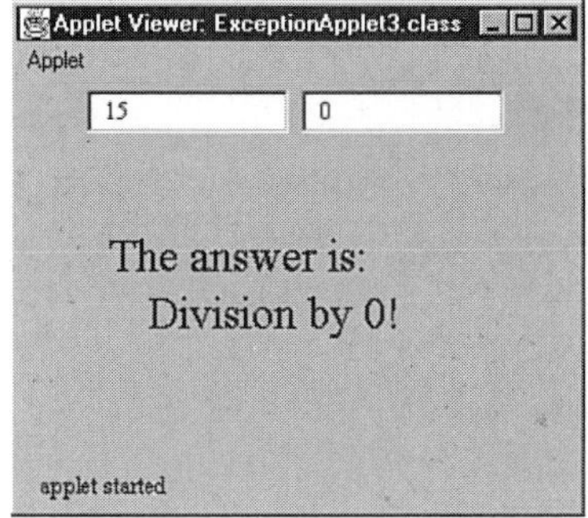

FIG. 20.9
`ExceptionApplet3` catches division-by-zero errors.

There may be times when you want to be sure that a specific block of code gets executed whether or not an exception is generated. You can do this by adding a `finally` program block after the last `catch`. The code in the `finally` block gets executed after the `try` block or `catch` block finishes its thing. Listing 20.8 shows an example.

Listing 20.8 *LST20-08.TXT*—Using the *finally* Program Block

```
try
{
    // The code that may generate an exception goes here.
}
catch (Exception e)
{
    // The code that handles the exception goes here.
}
finally
{
    // The code here is executed after the try or
    // catch blocks finish executing.
}
```


Creating Your Own Exception Classes

Although Java provides exception classes for just about every general error you can imagine, the designers of the language couldn't possibly know what type of code you're going to write and what kinds of errors that code may experience. For example, you may write a method that sums two numbers within a specific range. If the user enters a value outside the selected range, your program could throw a custom exception called something like `NumberRangeException`.

To create and throw your own custom exceptions, you must first define a class for the exception. Usually, you derive this class from Java's `Exception` class. Listing 20.9 shows how you might define the aforementioned `NumberRangeException` class.

Listing 20.9 NumberRangeException.java—The *NumberRangeException* Class

```
public class NumberRangeException extends Exception
{
    public NumberRangeException(String msg)
    {
     super(msg);
    }
}
```

As you can see, defining a new exception requires little work. In fact, you can get by with just creating a constructor for the class. Notice that the `NumberRangeException` class's constructor receives a `String` parameter. This string is the detail message that the class returns if you call its `getMessage()` method (which the class inherits from `Throwable` through `Exception`). Inside the constructor, this string is passed on up to `NumberRangeException`'s superclass (`Exception`), which itself passes the string on up to the `Throwable` class, where it is stored as a data member of the class. Now, inside your program, wherever you determine that your custom-exception condition has occurred, you can create and throw an object of your exception class.

Listing 20.10 is an applet that puts the new `NumberRangeException` to the test. When you run the applet, type a number into each text box. If you follow the directions, typing two numbers within the range 10–20, the applet sums the numbers and displays the results. Otherwise, the applet generates a `NumberRangeException` exception and displays an error message, as shown in Figure 20.10.

When you compile the `ExceptionApplet4` applet, make sure the `NumberRangeException.java` file is in the same directory as the applet's source code. Otherwise, the Java compiler may not be able to find it. You may also need to add the applet's path to the `CLASSPATH` environment variable.

Listing 20.10 *ExceptionApplet4.java*—An Applet That Incorporates a Custom Exception Class

```
import java.awt.*;
import java.awt.event.*;
import java.applet.*;

public class ExceptionApplet4 extends Applet
{
    TextField textField1, textField2;
    String answerStr;
    public void init()
    {
        textField1 = new TextField(15);
        add(textField1);
        textField2 = new TextField(15);
        add(textField2);

        //create an ActionListener.  This will be registered with
        //the TextFields and when 'enter' is pressed the actionPerformed()
```

```
    //method will be called.
    ActionListener listener = new ActionListener(){
           public void actionPerformed(ActionEvent evt)
           {
                    try
                    {
                           int answer = CalcAnswer();
                           answerStr = String.valueOf(answer);
                    }
                    catch (NumberRangeException e)
                    {
                           answerStr = e.getMessage();
                    }
                    repaint();
                    return true;
           }
    };

    //register the listener with the TextFields
    textField1.addActionListener(listener);
    textField2.addActionListener(listener);


    answerStr = "Undefined";
    resize(500, 200);
}

public void paint(Graphics g)
{
    Font font = new Font("TimesRoman", Font.PLAIN, 24);
    g.setFont(font);
    g.drawString("Enter numbers between", 40, 70);
    g.drawString("10 and 20.", 70, 90);
    g.drawString("The answer is:", 40, 130);
    g.drawString(answerStr, 70, 150);
}


public int CalcAnswer() throws NumberRangeException
{
    int int1, int2;
    int answer = -1;
    String str1 = textField1.getText();
    String str2 = textField2.getText();
    try
    {
        int1 = Integer.parseInt(str1);
        int2 = Integer.parseInt(str2);

                  //check to make sure both integers are within the range
        if ((int1 < 10) || (int1 > 20) ||
            (int2 < 10) || (int2 > 20))
        {
            //since they are not, throw our custom exception
```

continues

Listing 20.10 Continued

```
                NumberRangeException e = new NumberRangeException
                   ("Numbers not within the specified range.");
                throw e;
            }
            answer = int1 + int2;
        }
        catch (NumberFormatException e)
        {
           answerStr = e.toString();
        }
        return answer;
    }
}
```

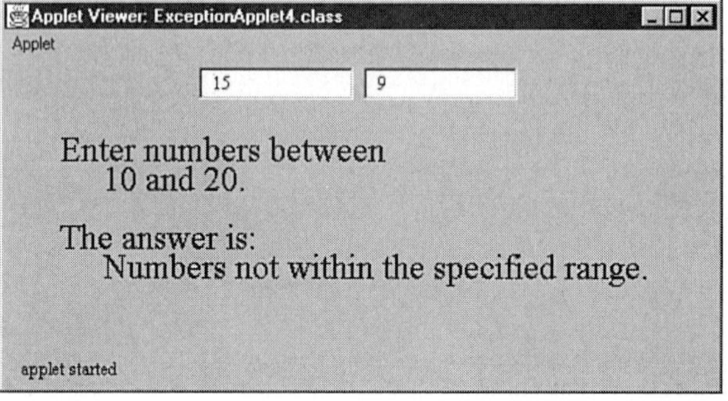

FIG. 20.10
The applet catches NumberRangeException.

In the ExceptionApplet4 applet's action() method, the program calls the local CalcAnswer() method. The action() method must enclose this method call in try and catch program blocks because CalcAnswer() throws a NumberRangeException exception (the exception class you just created). In CalcAnswer(), the program extracts the strings the user typed into the text boxes and converts the returned strings to integers. Because the parseInt() method calls can throw NumberFormatException exceptions, CalcAnswer() encloses the calls to parseInt() within a try program block. In the try block, the program not only converts the strings to integers, but also checks whether the integers fall within the proper range of values. If they don't, the program creates and throws an object of the NumberRangeException class.

Java's Error Classes

So far, you've had a look at the exception classes you can handle in your own programs. Java also defines a set of Error classes that are really little more than special types of exceptions. Like the class Exception, the class Error is derived from Throwable. However, the more specific error classes that are derived from Error represent serious errors, such as internal errors or problems with a class, that your program shouldn't fool with. The Java system handles these errors for you.

The following is a list of the error classes organized into their inheritance hierarchy. The package in which a class is defined is shown in parentheses after the class's name (all but one are defined in `java.lang`).

```
Throwable (java.lang)
Error (java.lang)
AWTError (java.awt)
ThreadDeath (java.lang)
LinkageError (java.lang)
ClassCircularityError (java.lang)
ClassFormatError (java.lang)
NoClassDefFoundError (java.lang)
UnsatisfiedLinkError (java.lang)
VerifyError (java.lang)
IncompatibleClassChangeError (java.lang)
AbstractMethodError (java.lang)
IllegalAccessError (java.lang)
InstantiationError (java.lang)
NoSuchFieldError (java.lang)
NoSuchMethodError (java.lang)
VirtualMachineError (java.lang)
InternalError (java.lang)
OutOfMemoryError (java.lang)
StackOverflowError (java.lang)
UnknownError (java.lang)
```

Java's Events

As you've already learned, events represent all the activity that goes on between a program, the system, and the program's user. When the user does something with the program, such as click the mouse in the program's window, the system creates an event representing the action and ships it off to your program's event-handling code. This code determines how to handle the event so that the user gets the appropriate response.

For example, when the user clicks a button, he expects the command associated with that button to be executed. In Chapter 15, "Advanced Applet Code," you got a quick look at how you can use events in your applets. Now, it's time to examine Java's events in depth by exploring the classes that deal with events and how to create and handle events.

Event-Handling Techniques

Java has two different event-handling systems. Java 1.1 introduced a Listener-Adapter system, which is included in Java 1.2. Later in this chapter, you will learn about the Java 1.0 event model, under which the `Component` class is where most event-handling occurs. This means that any Java 1.0 class that needs to handle events has to be able to trace its ancestry back to the `Component` class. Version 1.1 revised the event model so that any class can receive and manage events, regardless of whether that class has `Component` as a superclass.

The 1.1 event model makes the important observation that an event is often handled by another object. For instance, when you press a button, you want to perform the processing for the action event in some object other than the button. In order to support this, the event model supports the notion of event listeners as defined in `java.util.EventListener`.

An *event listener* is any object that implements one or more listener interfaces. There are different listeners for each category of `AWT` event. For instance, the `MouseListener` interface defines methods such as `mouseClicked`, `mousePressed`, and `MouseReleased`. In order to receive events from a component, an object adds itself as a listener for that component's events. If an object implements the `MouseListener` interface, it listens for a component's mouse events by calling `addMouseListener` on that component. This enables you to handle a component's events without having to create a subclass of the component, and without handling the events in the parent container.

The `MusicalButton` object, for instance, would implement the `ActionListener` interface, which would receive `ActionEvent` objects through the `actionPerformed` method. Because `MusicalButton` is no longer a subclass of button, you can hook it up to any type of button without adding additional code. All buttons support the `addActionListener` method to add listeners.

For each type of listener in the Java 1.1 event model, there is also an adapter object. The adapters are very simple objects that implement a specific interface, containing empty methods for each method defined in the interface. If you are creating an object specifically to implement the `KeyListener` interface, you can just create an object that is a subclass of `KeyAdapter` and then override whichever methods you are interested in. The same is true for all listener interfaces.

One of the other complaints against the Java 1.0 event model was that there was one big `Event` object that contained attributes for all possible events. Under Java 1.2, there are different event objects for different events. Keyboard events are delivered in a `KeyEvent` object, while actions are delivered in an `ActionEvent` object. This enables the events to stay relatively small, because they don't have to contain all possible variations of events.

CAUTION

Although the Java 1.0 event model is supported in the current Java release, you should not intermix the 1.0 event model with the 1.1 event model in the same program. They are not guaranteed to work at the same time.

Event Listeners

In Java 1.2, events are managed by event listeners. *Event listeners* are classes that have been registered with the Java system to receive specific events. Only the types of events that are registered with an event listener will be received by that listener.

In this section, you modify the `EventApplet` applet so that it uses the Java 1.1 event model. The original version of the program, developed in the previous section, used the more familiar Java 1.0 event model.

The first step in changing `EventApplet` into `EventApplet2` is to add the following line to the top of the source-code file:

```
import java.awt.event.*;
```

This line gives the program access to the new classes defined in the event package. If you fail to include this package, a program using the Java 1.1 event model will not compile.

Next, you must determine which events your program handles and which components generate those events. To keep things simple, write `EventApplet2` so that it responds only to `action` events, which are the most common events handled in an applet. Table 20.2 provides the information you need to convert any applet to the Java 1.1 event model. The table lists all the events, showing which components generate those events and which interface to use for the Java 1.1 event model.

Table 20.2 Summary of the Java 1.1 Event Model

Event	Components	Interface
ACTION_EVENT	Button, List, MenuItem	ActionListener
ACTION_EVENT	CheckBox, Choice	ItemListener
ACTION_EVENT	TextField	ActionListener
GOT_FOCUS	Component	FocusListener
KEY_ACTION	Component	KeyListener
KEY_ACTION_RELEASE	Component	KeyListener
KEY_PRESS	Component	KeyListener
KEY_RELEASE	Component	KeyListener
LIST_DESELECT	Checkbox, CheckboxMenuItem	ItemListener
LIST_DESELECT	Choice, List	ItemListener
LIST_SELECT	Checkbox, CheckboxMenuItem	ItemListener
LIST_SELECT	Choice, List	ItemListener
LOST_FOCUS	Component	FocusListener
MOUSE_DOWN	Canvas, Dialog, Frame	MouseListener
MOUSE_DOWN	Panel, Window	MouseListener
MOUSE_DRAG	Canvas, Dialog, Frame	MouseMotionListener
MOUSE_DRAG	Panel, Window	MouseMotionListener
MOUSE_ENTER	Canvas, Dialog, Frame	MouseListener

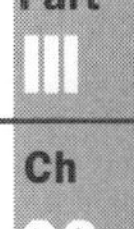

continues

Table 20.2 Continued

Event	Components	Interface
MOUSE_ENTER	Panel, Window	MouseListener
MOUSE_EXIT	Canvas, Dialog, Frame	MouseListener
MOUSE_EXIT	Panel, Window	MouseListener
MOUSE_MOVE	Canvas, Dialog, Frame	MouseMotionListener
MOUSE_MOVE	Panel, Window	MouseMotionListener
MOUSE_UP	Canvas, Dialog, Frame	MouseListener
MOUSE_UP	Panel, Window	MouseListener
SCROLL_ABSOLUTE	Scrollbar	AdjustmentListener
SCROLL_BEGIN	Scrollbar	AdjustmentListener
SCROLL_END	Scrollbar	AdjustmentListener
SCROLL_LINE_DOWN	Scrollbar	AdjustmentListener
SCROLL_LINE_UP	Scrollbar	AdjustmentListener
SCROLL_PAGE_DOWN	Scrollbar	AdjustmentListener
SCROLL_PAGE_UP	Scrollbar	AdjustmentListener
WINDOW_DEICONIFY	Dialog, Frame	WindowListener
WINDOW_DESTROY	Dialog, Frame	WindowListener
WINDOW_EXPOSE	Dialog, Frame	WindowListener
WINDOW_ICONIFY	Dialog, Frame	WindowListener
WINDOW_MOVED	Dialog, Frame	ComponentListener

So you can see that the `ACTION_EVENT` produced by the `Button` component should be handled by the `ActionListener` interface. This means that you must declare `EventApplet2` as implementing the `ActionListener` interface, like this:

```
public class EventApplet2 extends Applet
implements ActionListener
```

Now, in order to receive events from the `Button` component, the program must create the button, register the button as an `ActionListener`, and add the button to the applet. All this is done in the `init()` method, like this:

```
button1 = new Button("Test Button");
button1.addActionListener(this);
add(button1);
```

As you can see, the Button class now has a method called addActionListener() that registers the button as an ActionListener. Other components have similar new methods. For example, the Scrollbar class now has a method called addAdjustmentListener() that registers the scrollbar as an AdjustmentListener.

Because the applet implements the ActionListener interface, it must also implement every method declared in the interface. Luckily, ActionListener declares only a single method: actionPerformed(). This method replaces the old action() method as the place where the program handles the action events. Listing 20.11 shows the old action() method, whereas Listing 20.12 shows the new actionPerformed() method.

Listing 20.11 ***lst20-16.txt*—The Old *action()* Method**

```
public boolean action(Event evt, Object arg)
{
    if (arg == "Test Button")
    {
        if (color == Color.black)
            color = Color.red;
        else
            color = Color.black;
        repaint();
        return true;
    }
    return false;
}
```

Listing 20.12 ***lst20-17.txt*—The New *actionPerformed()* Method**

```
public void actionPerformed(ActionEvent event)
{
    String arg = event.getActionCommand();
    if (arg == "Test Button")
    {
        if (color == Color.black)
            color = Color.red;
        else
            color = Color.black;
        repaint();
    }
}
```

If you examine the two listings closely, you discover that there are really only two main differences. First, action() returns a Boolean value, whereas actionPerformed() returns no value. Second, the arg variable that holds the button's text label is passed to action() as a parameter, whereas in actionPerformed(), you get the text label by calling the ActionEvent object's getActionCommand() method. Listing 20.13 shows the complete EventApplet2, which handles its button component using the Java 1.1 event model.

Listing 20.13 ***EventApplet2.java*****—An Applet That Incorporates the Java 1.1 Event Model**

```
import java.awt.event.*;
import java.awt.*;
import java.applet.*;

public class EventApplet2 extends Applet
    implements ActionListener
{
    Button button1;
    Color color;

    public void init()
    {
        button1 = new Button("Test Button");
        button1.addActionListener(this);
        add(button1);
        color = Color.black;
        resize(400, 200);
    }

    public void paint(Graphics g)
    {
        Font font = new Font("TimesRoman", Font.PLAIN, 48);
        g.setFont(font);
        g.setColor(color);
        g.drawString("TEST COLOR", 55, 120);
    }

    //*************************************************
    // Here is the method implementation for the
    // ActionListener interface.
    //*************************************************

    public void actionPerformed(ActionEvent event)
    {
        String arg = event.getActionCommand();
        if (arg == "Test Button")
        {
            if (color == Color.black)
                color = Color.red;
            else
                color = Color.black;
            repaint();
        }
    }
}
```

NOTE To determine what methods your Java program must implement for a listener interface, load the interface's source code and copy the method declarations into your own program. Then, finish implementing the methods by writing code for the methods you need and changing the remaining declarations into empty methods.

Keyboard and Mouse Events

Let's continue looking at the 1.1 event model. As you know, you can be notified when a key is pressed and when it is released; when the mouse enters the applet window and when it leaves the applet window; when the mouse button is pressed and when it is released; and when the mouse moves and when it is dragged (moved with the button held down).

Keyboard Events

To listen for keyboard events from an object under Java 1.2, you need to implement the `KeyListener` interface. The `KeyListener` interface contains three methods: `keyPressed`, `keyReleased`, and `keyTyped`. The `keyPressed` method is called whenever a key is pressed, and the `keyReleased` method is called whenever a key is released. The `keyTyped` method is a combination of `keyPressed` and `keyReleased`. When a key is pressed and then released (as in normal typing), the `keyTyped` method is called. Here are the method declarations for the `KeyListener` interface:

```
public abstract void keyTyped(KeyEvent event)
public abstract void keyPressed(KeyEvent event)
public abstract void keyReleased(KeyEvent event)
```

Every keyboard event has an associated key code, which is returned by the `getKeyCode` method in `KeyEvent`:

```
public int getKeyCode()
```

A keycode can be the character typed, in the case of a normal letter, or it can be a special key (function keys, cursor movement keys, keyboard control keys, and so on). Certain keys are also considered action keys. The *action keys* are the cursor movement keys (arrows, Home, End), the function keys F1–F12, the Print Screen key, and the Lock keys (Caps Lock, Num Lock, and Scroll Lock). The `isActionKey` method in `KeyEvent` returns `true` if the key involved is an action key:

```
public boolean isActionKey()
```

Because keycodes vary from system to system, the AWT defines its own codes for common keys. The keycodes defined in the `KeyEvent` class are shown in the following table. Note that the values in the table can be single keys or combination of keys.

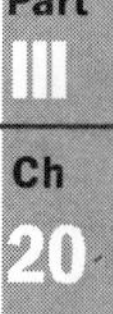

Key Codes	Key
`KeyEvent.F1–KeyEvent.F12`	Function keys F1–F12
`KeyEvent.VK_LEFT`	Left-arrow key
`KeyEvent.VK_RIGHT`	Right-arrow key
`KeyEvent.VK_LEFT`	Up-arrow key
`KeyEvent.VK_DOWN`	Down-arrow key
`VK_KP_UP`	Up key on the keypad
`VK_KP_DOWN`	Down key on the keypad

continues

continued

Key Codes	Key
VK_KP_LEFT	Left key on the keypad
VK_KP_RIGHT	Right key on the keypad
VK_END	End key
VK_HOME	Home key
VK_PAGE_DOWN	Page Down key
VK_PAGE_UP	Page Up key
VK_PRINTSCREEN	Print Screen key
VK_SCROLL_LOCK	Scroll Lock key
VK_CAPS_LOCK	Caps Lock key
VK_NUM_LOCK	Num Lock key
PAUSE	Pause key
VK_INSERT	Insert key
VK_DELETE	Delete key
VK_ENTER	Enter key
VK_TAB	Tab key
VK_BACK_SPACE	Backspace key
VK_ESCAPE	Escape key
VK_CANCEL	Cancel key
VK_CLEAR	Clear key
VK_SHIFT	Shift key
VK_CONTROL	Control key
VK_ALT	Alt key
VK_PAUSE	Pause key
VK_SPACE	Space key
VK_COMMA	Comma key
VK_SEMICOLON	Semicolon key
VK_COLON	: key
VK_AMPERSAND	& key
VK_EXCLAMATION_MARK	! key
VK_INVERTED_EXCLAMATION_MARK	The inverted exclamation key

Key Codes	Key
VK_AT	@ key
VK_CIRCUMFLEX	^ key
VK_NUMBER_SIGN	# key
VK_DOLLAR	$ key
VK_UNDERSCORE	_ key
VK_PLUS	+ key
VK_EURO_SIGN	Constant for Euro currency
VK_EQUALS	= key
VK_LESS	< key
VK_GREATER	> key
VK_PERIOD	. key
VK_SLASH	/ key
VK_BACK_SLASH	\ key
VK_0-VK_9	0 through 9 keys
VK_A–VK_Z	A–Z keys (equivalent to ASCII values)
VK_OPEN_BRACKET	[key
VK_CLOSE_BRACKET	] key
VK_BRACELEFT	{ key
VK_BRACERIGHT	} key
VK_LEFT_PARENTHESIS	(key
VK_RIGHT_PARENTHESIS	) key
VK_NUMPAD0-VK_NUMPAD9	0 through 9 keys on keypad
VK_MULTIPLY	Multiply key
VK_ADD	Add key
VK_SUBTRACT	Subtraction key
VK_DIVIDE	Divide key
VK_DECIMAL	. key
VK_SEPARATER	Separator key
VK_HELP	Help key
VK_META	Meta key

continues

continued

Key Codes	Key
VK_QUOTE	' key
VK_BACK_QUOTE	Back quote key
VK_QUOTEDBL	" key
VK_CUT	Cut key
VK_COPY	Copy key
VK_PASTE	Paste key
VK_UNDO	Undo key
VK_AGAIN	Again key
VK_FIND	Find key
VK_PROPS	Props key
VK_STOP	Stop key
VK_COMPOSE	Compose key
VK_ALT_GRAPH	AltGraph key
VK_UNDEFINED	Key typed did not have keycode value

NOTE Many of the constants in `KeyEvent` changed their name in JDK 1.2, so if you're using a previous JDK you will need to refer to the API to get the correct values.

Because many keycodes are really just normal characters, you can retrieve the character code for a keystroke with `getKeyChar()`:

```
public char getKeyChar()
```

Modifier Keys in Java 1.2

You might think that the modifier keys (Control, Alt, Shift, Meta) are keyboard events, but they aren't. Under most windowing systems, you can use these keys in conjunction with the mouse as well. The Java 1.2 event hierarchy contains an `InputEvent` class, which is the superclass of both `KeyEvent` and `MouseEvent`. The `getModifiers()` method in `InputEvent` returns a bitmap indicating which modifier keys were active when the event occurred:

```
public int getModifiers()
```

You can use the `SHIFT_MASK`, `CTRL_MASK`, `META_MASK`, and `ALT_MASK` attributes of `InputEvent` to examine the modifier bits returned by `getModifiers()`. For example, the following code snippet checks an event to see if the Alt key was pressed when the event occurred:

```
InputEvent evt;
if ((evt.getModifiers() & InputEvent.ALT_MASK) != 0) {
```

```
// the alt key was down
}
```

Because this can be a cumbersome way to check for modifiers, the `InputEvent` class also defines the following shortcuts:

```
public boolean isShiftDown()
public boolean isControlDown()
public boolean isMetaDown()
```

The mouse buttons are also considered modifier keys. The `BUTTON1_MASK`, `BUTTON2_MASK`, and `BUTTON3_MASK` attributes of `InputEvent` enable you to check whether any buttons were pressed when the event occurred. There are no shortcuts for these methods, however.

In addition to the modifier information, you can also find out when an input event occurred by calling `getWhen()`, which returns a timestamp similar to the one returned by `System.currentTimeMillis`:

```
public long getWhen()
```

Mouse Events in Java 1.2

There are two different listener interfaces in Java 1.2 that listen to mouse events. Most of the time, you only need the `MouseListener` interface, which defines methods that are not related to the motion of the mouse.

The `mousePressed` and `mouseReleased` methods indicate that a mouse button has been pressed or released:

```
public abstract void mousePressed(MouseEvent event)
public abstract void mouseReleased(MouseEvent event)
```

If you don't want to keep track of when a button is pressed and then released, you can use the `mouseClicked()` method, which is called when a button is pressed and then released:

```
public abstract void mouseClicked(MouseEvent event)
```

The `getClickCount()` method in the `MouseEvent` object tells you how many times the button was clicked, so you can detect double-clicks:

```
public int getClickCount()
```

The `mouseEntered()` and `mouseExited()` methods are called whenever the mouse enters a component and when it leaves the component:

```
public abstract void mouseEntered(MouseEvent event)
public abstract void mouseExited(MouseEvent event)
```

At any time, you can get the x,y coordinate where the event occurred (relative to the component's x,y) by calling the `getPoint()` method in the `MouseEvent` object, or by calling `getX()` and `getY()`:

```
public synchronized Point getPoint()
public int getX()
public int getY()
```

Because most applications do not need to track mouse motion, the mouse motion methods have been placed in a separate listener interface. This enables you to listen for simple button presses without getting an event every time someone sneezes near the mouse. The `MouseListenerInterface` implements two methods for tracking mouse movement. The `mouseMoved()` method is called whenever the mouse is moved but no buttons have been pressed, while `mouseDragged()` is called when the mouse is moved while a button is pressed:

```
public abstract void mouseMoved(MouseEvent event)
public abstract void mouseDragged(MouseEvent event)
```

The 1.0 Event Model

Prior to JDK 1.1, the event model was quite different from what you've seen so far in this chapter. This model is maintained in JDK 1.1 and 1.2, but it is deprecated (meaning it may be removed in the future). Unfortunately, older browsers (Netscape 2.0–4.0 and Internet Explorer 2.0–3.0) do not support the 1.1 event model. For this reason it's often necessary to code to the 1.0 event model, so I will cover it here.

The *Event* Class

Under Java 1.0, events are actually objects of a class. This class—called, appropriately enough, `Event`—defines all the events to which a program can respond, as well as defining default methods for extracting information about the event. When all is said and done, `Event` is a fairly complex class, as you will soon see.

The first thing the `Event` class does is define constants for the many keys that can either constitute an event (such as a key-down event) or be used to modify an event (such as holding down Shift when mouse-clicking). Table 20.3 lists these constants and their descriptions.

Table 20.3 Keyboard Constants of the *Event* Class in 1.0

Constant	Key
ALT_MASK	Alt (Alternate) key
CTRL_MASK	Ctrl
DOWN	Down arrow
END	End
F1	F1
F10	F10
F11	F11
F12	F12
F2	F2

Constant	Key
F3	F3
F4	F4
F5	F5
F6	F6
F7	F7
F8	F8
F9	F9
HOME	Home
LEFT	Left arrow
META_MASK	Meta
PGDN	Page Down
PGUP	Page Up
RIGHT	Right arrow
SHIFT_MASK	Shift
UP	Up arrow

Next, the `Event` class defines constants for all the events that can be handled in a Java program. These events include everything from basic mouse and keyboard events to the events generated by moving, minimizing, or closing windows. Table 20.4 lists these event constants, which are used as IDs for `Event` objects.

Table 20.4 *Event* Constants of the *Event* Class in 1.0

Constant	Description
ACTION_EVENT	Used in support of the `action()` method
GOT_FOCUS	Generated when a window (or component) gets the input focus
KEY_ACTION	Similar to `KEY_PRESS`
KEY_ACTION_RELEASE	Similar to `KEY_RELEASE`
KEY_EVENT	A general keyboard event
KEY_PRESS	Generated when a key is pressed
KEY_RELEASE	Generated when a key is released

continues

Table 20.4 Continued

Constant	Description
LIST_DESELECT	Generated by deselecting an item in a list
LIST_EVENT	A general list box event
LIST_SELECT	Generated by selecting an item in a list
LOAD_FILE	Generated when a file is loaded
LOST_FOCUS	Generated when a window (or component) loses focus
MISC_EVENT	A miscellaneous event
MOUSE_DOWN	Generated when the mouse button is pressed
MOUSE_DRAG	Generated when the mouse pointer is dragged
MOUSE_ENTER	Generated when the mouse pointer enters a window
MOUSE_EVENT	A general mouse event
MOUSE_EXIT	Generated when the mouse pointer exits a window
MOUSE_MOVE	Generated when the mouse pointer is moved
MOUSE_UP	Generated when the mouse button is released
SAVE_FILE	Generated when a file is saved
SCROLL_ABSOLUTE	Generated by moving the scroll box
SCROLL_EVENT	A general scrolling event
SCROLL_LINE_DOWN	Generated by clicking the scrollbar's down arrow
SCROLL_LINE_UP	Generated by clicking the scrollbar's up arrow
SCROLL_PAGE_DOWN	Generated by clicking below the scroll box
SCROLL_PAGE_UP	Generated by clicking above the scroll box
WINDOW_DEICONIFY	Generated when a window is restored
WINDOW_DESTROY	Generated when a window is destroyed
WINDOW_EVENT	A general window event
WINDOW_EXPOSE	Generated when a window is exposed
WINDOW_ICONIFY	Generated when a window is minimized
WINDOW_MOVED	Generated when a window is moved

Like most classes, the `Event` class declares a number of data members that it uses to store information about an event object. You might examine one or more of these data members when responding to an event. For example, when responding to most mouse events, you usually want to know the x and y coordinates of the mouse when the event occurred. Table 20.5 lists the data members and their descriptions.

Table 20.5 Data Members of the *Event* Class

Data Member	Description
`arg`	Additional information about the event
`clickCount`	Number of mouse clicks associated with the event
`evt`	Next event in the list
`id`	Event's ID (refer to Table 20.4)
`key`	Keyboard event's key
`keyChar`	Character key that was pressed
`modifiers`	Event's modifier keys (refer to Table 20.3)
`target`	Component that generated the event
`when`	Event's timestamp
`x`	Event's x coordinate
`y`	Event's y coordinate

Last, but surely not least, the `Event` class defines a number of methods that you can use to retrieve information about the event. Table 20.6 lists these methods and their descriptions.

Table 20.6 Methods of the *Event* Class

Method	Description
`controlDown()`	Gets the status of the Ctrl key
`metaDown()`	Gets the status of a Meta key
`paramString()`	Gets the event's parameter string
`shiftDown()`	Gets the status of the Shift key
`toString()`	Gets a string representing the object's status
`translate()`	Translates the event so that its x and y positions are increased or decreased

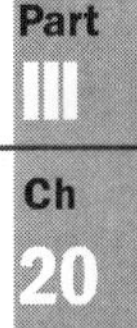

An Event's Genesis

You may wonder exactly where the events that arrive at your program come from. An operating system such as Microsoft Windows or Macintosh's System 7 tracks all the events occurring in the system. The system routes these events to the appropriate target objects. For example, if the user clicks your applet's window, the system constructs a mouse-down event and sends it off to the window for processing. The window can then choose to do something with the event or just pass it back to the system for default processing.

In the case of Java, the Java 1.0 event model intercepts events that are meant for Java components, translating and routing them as appropriate. Because all of this event-handling stuff is dependent on the current windowing system being used, Java deals with events in the classes defined in the `java.awt` package. Specifically, the `Component` class receives and processes events for any class derived from `Component`. Because virtually every visible object (buttons, panels, text boxes, canvases, and more) in a Java 1.0 application or applet can trace its ancestry back to `Component`, `Component` is the event-handling granddaddy of them all. As such, the `Component` class defines many event-related methods. Table 20.7 lists these methods and their descriptions.

Table 20.7 Event-Handling Methods of the *Component* Class

Method	Description
`action()`	Responds to components that have action events
`deliverEvent()`	Sends an event to the component
`handleEvent()`	Routes events to the appropriate handler
`keyDown()`	Responds to key-down events
`keyUp()`	Responds to key-up events
`mouseDown()`	Responds to mouse-down events
`mouseDrag()`	Responds to mouse-drag events
`mouseEnter()`	Responds to mouse-enter events
`mouseExit()`	Responds to mouse-exit events
`mouseMove()`	Responds to mouse-move events
`mouseUp()`	Responds to mouse-up events
`postEvent()`	Similar to `deliverEvent()`

NOTE If you use the 1.0 event model under JDK 1.1 or JDK 1.2, the compiler will issue warnings that these methods are deprecated. These warnings are not actually problems but let you know these methods may not be supported in the future.

In the `Component` class, event-handling methods such as `action()`, `mouseDown()`, and `keyDown()` don't actually do anything except return `false`, which indicates to Java that the event hasn't yet been handled. These methods are meant to be overridden in your programs so that the program can respond to the event as is appropriate. For example, if you haven't overridden `mouseDown()` in an applet, the default version of `mouseDown()` returns `false`, which tells Java that the message needs to be handled further on down the line. In the case of a mouse-down event, Java probably returns the unhandled event to the system for default handling (meaning that the event is effectively ignored).

The applet in Listing 20.11 responds to mouse clicks by printing the word `Click!` wherever the user clicks in the applet. It does this by overriding the `mouseDown()` method and storing the coordinates of the mouse click in the applet's `coordX` and `coordY` data fields. The `paint()` method then uses these coordinates to display the word. Listing 20.14 shows `MouseApplet` running under AppletViewer.

Listing 20.14 *MouseApplet.java*—Using Mouse Clicks in an Applet

```
import java.awt.*;
import java.applet.*;
public class MouseApplet extends Applet
{
    int coordX, coordY;
    public void init()
    {
        coordX = -1;
        coordY = -1;
        Font font =
        ➥   new Font("TimesRoman", Font.BOLD, 24);
        setFont(font);
        resize(400, 300);
    }
    public void paint(Graphics g)
    {
        if (coordX != -1)
            g.drawString("Click!", coordX, coordY);
    }
    public boolean mouseDown(Event evt, int x, int y)
    {
        coordX = x;
        coordY = y;
        repaint();
        return true;
    }
}
```

NOTE When you run `MouseApplet`, you discover that the applet window gets erased each time the `paint()` method is called. That's why only one `Click!` ever appears in the window.

The Keyboard

The keyboard has been around even longer than the mouse, and has been the primary interface between humans and their computers for decades. Given the keyboard's importance, obviously there may be times when you want to handle the keyboard events at a lower level than you can with something like a `TextField` component. Java responds to two basic key events, which are represented by the `KEY_PRESS` and `KEY_RELEASE` constants. As you will soon see, Java defines methods that make it just as easy to respond to the keyboard as it is to respond to the mouse. You received an introduction to keyboard events in Chapter 15. In this section, you learn even more about how to deal with the keyboard in your Java programs.

Whenever the user presses a key while an applet is active, Java sends the applet a `KEY_PRESS` event. In your Java program, you can respond to this event by overriding the `keyDown()` method, whose signature looks like this:

```
public boolean keyDown(Event evt, int key)
```

As you can see, this method receives two arguments, which are an `Event` object and an integer representing the key that was pressed. This integer is actually the ASCII representation of the character represented by the key. In order to use this value in your programs, however, you must first cast it to a `char` value, like this:

```
char c = (char)key;
```

Some of the keys on your keyboard issue commands rather than generate characters. These keys include all the F keys, as well as keys like Shift, Ctrl, Page Up, Page Down, and so on. In order to make these types of keys easier to handle in your applets, Java's `Event` class defines a set of constants that represent these keys' values (refer to Table 20.3).

The `Event` class also defines a number of constants for modifier keys that the user might press along with the basic key. These constants, which are also listed in Table 20.3, include `ALT_MASK`, `SHIFT_MASK`, and `CTRL_MASK`, which represent the Alt (or Alternate), Shift, and Ctrl (or Control) keys on your keyboard. The `SHIFT_MASK` and `CTRL_MASK` constants are used in the `Event` class's methods `shiftDown()` and `controlDown()`, each of which returns a Boolean value indicating whether the modifier key is pressed. (There currently is no `altDown()` method.) You can also examine the `Event` object's `modifiers` field to determine whether a particular modifier key was pressed. For example, if you want to check for the Alt key, you might use a line of Java code like this:

```
boolean altPressed = (evt.modifiers & Event.ALT_MASK) != 0;
```

By using `AND` on the mask with the value in the `modifiers` field, you end up with a non-zero value if the Alt key was pressed and a `0` if it wasn't. You convert this result to a Boolean value by comparing the result with 0.

Handling Events Directly

All of the events received by your applet using the Java 1.0 event model are processed by the `handleEvent()` method, which is inherited from the `Component` class. When this method is not overridden in your program, the default implementation is responsible for calling the many methods that respond to events. Listing 20.15 shows how the `handleEvent()` method is implemented in the `Component` class. By examining this listing, you can easily see why you only have to override methods like `mouseDown()` to respond to events. In the next section, you see how to customize `handleEvent()` in your own programs.

Listing 20.15 ***LST20-12.TXT*—The Default Implementation of *handleEvent()***

```
public boolean handleEvent(Event evt) {
switch (evt.id) {
  case Event.MOUSE_ENTER:
    return mouseEnter(evt, evt.x, evt.y);
  case Event.MOUSE_EXIT:
    return mouseExit(evt, evt.x, evt.y);
  case Event.MOUSE_MOVE:
    return mouseMove(evt, evt.x, evt.y);
  case Event.MOUSE_DOWN:
    return mouseDown(evt, evt.x, evt.y);
  case Event.MOUSE_DRAG:
    return mouseDrag(evt, evt.x, evt.y);
  case Event.MOUSE_UP:
    return mouseUp(evt, evt.x, evt.y);
  case Event.KEY_PRESS:
  case Event.KEY_ACTION:
    return keyDown(evt, evt.key);
  case Event.KEY_RELEASE:
  case Event.KEY_ACTION_RELEASE:
    return keyUp(evt, evt.key);

  case Event.ACTION_EVENT:
    return action(evt, evt.arg);
  case Event.GOT_FOCUS:
    return gotFocus(evt, evt.arg);
  case Event.LOST_FOCUS:
    return lostFocus(evt, evt.arg);
}
return false;
}()
```


Overriding the *handleEvent()* Method

Although the default implementation of `handleEvent()` calls special methods that you can override in your program for each event, you might want to group all your event handling into one method to conserve on overhead, change the way an applet responds to a particular event, or even create your own events. To accomplish any of these tasks (or any others you might come up with), you can forget the individual event-handling methods and override `handleEvent()` instead.

In your version of `handleEvent()`, you must examine the `Event` object's `id` field in order to determine which event is being processed. You can just ignore events in which you're not interested. However, be sure to return `false` whenever you ignore a message so that Java knows that it should pass the event on up the object hierarchy. Listing 20.16 is an applet that overrides the `handleEvent()` method in order to respond to events.

Listing 20.16 ***DrawApplet2.java*—Using the *handleEvent()* Method**

```
import java.awt.*;
import java.applet.*;
public class DrawApplet2 extends Applet
{
    Point startPoint;
    Point points[];
    int numPoints;
    boolean drawing;
    public void init()
    {
        startPoint = new Point(0, 0);
        points = new Point[1000];
        numPoints = 0;
        drawing = false;
        resize(400, 300);
    }
    public void paint(Graphics g)
    {
        int oldX = startPoint.x;
        int oldY = startPoint.y;
        for (int x=0; x<numPoints; ++x)
        {
            g.drawLine(oldX, oldY, points[x].x, points[x].y);
            oldX = points[x].x;
            oldY = points[x].y;
        }
    }
    public boolean handleEvent(Event evt)
    {
        switch(evt.id)
        {
            case Event.MOUSE_DOWN:
                drawing = true;
                startPoint.x = evt.x;
                startPoint.y = evt.y;
                return true;
            case Event.MOUSE_MOVE:
                if ((drawing) && (numPoints < 1000))
                {
                    points[numPoints] = new Point(evt.x, evt.y);
                    ++numPoints;
                    repaint();
                }
                return true;
```

```
default:
                    return false;
            }
        }
}
```

NOTE In Listing 20.13, the program overloads `handleEvent()` in order to be able to handle events at a lower level. However, one side effect of this technique is that events other than those explicitly handled in the new version of `handleEvent()` are ignored. If you still want to respond normally to all other events, you have to be sure to include them in your version of `handleEvent()`, or, even easier, just call the original version of `handleEvent()` from your new version, using the line `super.handleEvent(evt)` in place of the return `false`.

Sending Your Own Events

There may be times when the events created and routed by Java don't completely fit your program's needs. In those cases, you can create and send your own events. For example, you may want the user to be able to select a command both by clicking a button or pressing a key. One way you could handle this need is to have almost exactly the same event-handling code in your `action()` and `keyDown()` methods. The code in `action()` would handle the button click, and the code in `keyDown()` would handle the key press, as shown in Listing 20.17.

Listing 20.17 *LST20-14.TXT*—Handling Events with Duplicate Code

```
public boolean action(Event evt, Object arg)
{
    if (arg == "Test Button")
    {
        if (color == Color.black)
            color = Color.red;
        else
            color = Color.black;
        repaint();
        return true;
    }
    return false;
}
public boolean keyDown(Event evt, int key)
{
    if ((key == LOWERCASE_T) || (key == UPPERCASE_T))
    {
        if (color == Color.black)
            color = Color.red;
        else
            color = Color.black;
        repaint();
        return true;
    }
    return false;
}
```

A more elegant solution to the problem presented in Listing 20.14 is to create your own event in response to a key press and then deliver that event to the button component. You can create your own event by calling the `Event` class's constructor, like this:

```
Event event = new Event(button1, Event.ACTION_EVENT, "Test Button");
```

The three required arguments are the event's target component, the event ID, and the additional information that's appropriate for the type of event. For a button action event, the third argument should be the button's label.

After you have the event constructed, sending it is as easy as calling the `deliverEvent()` method, like this:

```
deliverEvent(event);
```

This method's single argument is the `event` object you want to deliver.

Listing 20.18 is an applet that creates and sends its own events in order to link key presses to button clicks. In the applet, when you click the button, the text color changes. The color also changes when you press the keyboard's T key. This is because the `keyDown()` method watches for T key presses (both upper- and lowercase). When `keyDown()` gets a T key press, it creates an `ACTION_EVENT` event and delivers it. This causes Java to call the `action()` method with the event, same as if the user had clicked the button. Figure 20.11 shows `EventApplet` running under AppletViewer.

Listing 20.18 ***EventApplet.java*****—Creating and Delivering Events**

```
import java.awt.*;
import java.applet.*;
public class EventApplet extends Applet
{
    Button button1;
    String str;
    Color color;
    final int LOWERCASE_T = 116;
    final int UPPERCASE_T = 84;
    public void init()
    {
        button1 = new Button("Test Button");
        add(button1);
        str = "TEST COLOR";
        color = Color.black;
        resize(400, 200);
    }
    public void paint(Graphics g)
    {
        Font font = new Font("TimesRoman", Font.PLAIN, 48);
        g.setFont(font);
        g.setColor(color);
        g.drawString(str, 55, 120);
    }
    public boolean action(Event evt, Object arg)
```

```
        {
            if (arg == "Test Button")
            {
                if (color == Color.black)
                    color = Color.red;
                else
                    color = Color.black;
                repaint();
                return true;
            }
            return false;
        }
        public boolean keyDown(Event evt, int key)
        {
            if ((key == LOWERCASE_T) || (key == UPPERCASE_T))
            {
                Event event = new Event(button1,
                    Event.ACTION_EVENT, "Test Button");
                deliverEvent(event);
                return true;
            }
            return false;
        }
    }
```

FIG. 20.11
`EventApplet` creates and delivers its own events.

CHAPTER 21

Containers and Layout Managers

In this chapter

Organizing Components

AWT components implement the basic interface widgets you expect to find in a windowing system. Containers and layout managers handle the difficult task of organizing the components into a reasonable structure. In order to display a component, you must place it in a container. An applet, for instance, is a container because it is a subclass of the `Panel` container.

A layout manager is like a set of instructions for placing a component within a container. Whenever you add a component to a container, the container consults its layout manager to find out where it should put the new component. While it may be difficult to abandon the old techniques of placing components by absolute coordinates, you need to adapt to this new model, because your applets may be running on screens with unusual layouts in the future. It is better to leave the placement to the container and layout manager.

Containers

You need more than just components to create a good user interface; the components need to be organized into manageable groups. That's where containers come in. *Containers* contain components. You cannot use a component in the AWT unless it is contained within a container. A component without a container is like a refrigerator magnet without a refrigerator. The containers defined in the AWT are:

- Windows
- Panels
- Frames
- Dialogs

Even if you don't create a container in your applet, you are still using one. The `Applet` class is a subclass of the `Panel` class.

Containers not only contain components; they are components themselves. This means that a container can contain other containers.

Layout Managers

Even though a container is a place where your user interface (UI) components can be stored neatly, you still need a way to organize the components within a container. That's where the layout managers come in. Each container is given a layout manager that decides where each component should be displayed. The layout managers in the AWT are:

- Flow layout
- Border layout
- Grid layout

- Card layout
- Grid bag layout

Containers

In addition to all of these wonderful components, the AWT provides several useful containers:

- `Panel` A pure container. It is not a window in itself. Its sole purpose is to help you organize your components in a window.
- `Frame` A fully functioning window with its own title and icon. Frames may have pull-down menus and may use a number of different cursor shapes.
- `Dialog` A pop-up window that is not quite as fully functioning as the frame. Dialogs are used for things such as "Are you sure you want to quit?" pop-ups.
- `ScrollPane` A window with optional scrollbars to enable you to display areas too large to fit on the screen.

Container Basics

All containers perform the same basic function, which is that they contain other components. You place a component in a container by calling one of the `add` methods in the container. For example, the statement

```
public synchronized Component add(Component newComponent)
```

adds `newComponent` to the end of the container. A container is like an array or a vector in that each component contained in it has a specific position or index value. On the other hand,

```
public synchronized Component add(Component newComponent, int pos)
```

adds `newComponent` at position `pos` in the container. The components from position `pos` to the end are all shifted up in position. In other words, this method does not replace the component at `pos`; it inserts the new component right before it.

```
public synchronized Component add(String name, Component newComponent)
```

adds `newComponent` to the end of the container. The component is also added to the container's layout manager as a component named `name`. Some layout managers, such as the `BorderLayout`, require each component to have a specific name in order to be visible. Other layout managers ignore the name if they do not require it.

The `remove` method removes a component from a container, as shown in the following snippet:

```
public synchronized void remove(Component comp)
```

The `removeAll` method removes all of the components from a container:

```
public synchronized void removeAll()
```

You can get the `n`th component in the container using the `getComponent` method:

```
public synchronized Component getComponent(int n)
throws ArrayIndexOutOfBoundsException
```

Or, you can get all of the components with `getComponents`:

```
public synchronized Component[] getComponents()
```

The `countComponents` method returns the total number of components stored in this container:

```
public int countComponents()
```

Panels

Because panels are only used for organizing components, there are very few things you can actually do to a panel. You create a new panel with the following:

```
Panel myPanel = new Panel();
```

You can then add the panel to another container. For instance, you might want to add it to your applet:

```
add(myPanel);
```

You can also nest panels—one panel containing one or more other panels:

```
Panel mainPanel, subPanel1, subPanel2;
subPanel1 = new Panel();   // create the first sub-panel
subPanel2 = new Panel();   // create the second sub-panel
mainPanel = new Panel();   // create the main panel

mainPanel.add(subPanel1);  // Make subPanel1 a child (sub-panel) of mainPanel
mainPanel.add(subPanel2);  // Make subPanel2 a child of mainPanel
```

You can nest panels as many levels deep as you like. For instance, in the previous example, you could have made `subPanel2` a child of `subPanel1` (obviously with different results).

Listing 21.1 shows how to create panels and nest sub-panels within them.

Listing 21.1 Source code for *PanelApplet.java*

```
import java.awt.*;
import java.applet.*;


// PanelApplet
//
// The PanelApplet applet creates a number of panels and
// adds buttons to them to demonstrate the use of panels
// for grouping components.

public class PanelApplet extends Applet
{
     public void init()
     {
// Create the main panels
```

```
        Panel mainPanel1 = new Panel();
        Panel mainPanel2 = new Panel();

// Create the sub-panels
        Panel subPanel1 = new Panel();
        Panel subPanel2 = new Panel();

// Add a button directly to the applet
        add(new Button("Applet Button"));

// Add the main panels to the applet
        add(mainPanel1);
        add(mainPanel2);

// Give mainPanel1 a button and a sub-panel
        mainPanel1.add(new Button("Main Panel 1 Button"));
        mainPanel1.add(subPanel1);

// Give mainPanel2 a button and a sub-panel
        mainPanel2.add(new Button("Main Panel 2 Button"));
        mainPanel2.add(subPanel2);

// Give each sub-panel a button
        subPanel1.add(new Button("Sub-panel 1 Button"));

        subPanel2.add(new Button("Sub-panel 2 Button"));
    }
}
```

Figure 21.1 shows the output from `PanelApplet`.

FIG. 21.1
Panels, like other containers, help group components together.

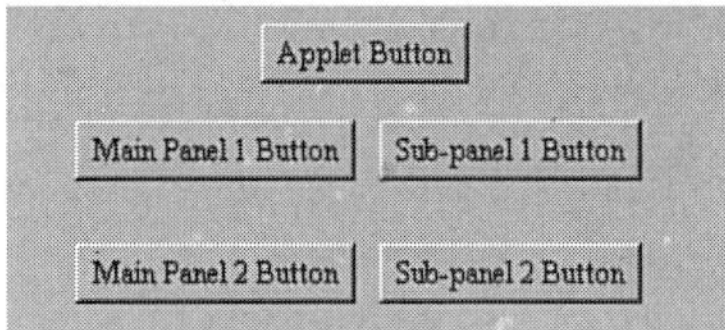

Frames

Frames are powerful features of the AWT. They enable you to create separate windows for your application. For instance, you might want your application to run outside the main window of a Web browser. You can also use frames to build stand-alone graphical applications.

Creating Frames

You can create a frame that is initially invisible and has no title with the empty constructor:

```
public Frame()
```

You can give the frame a title when you create it, but it will still be invisible:

```
public Frame(String frameTitle)
```

Frame Features

After you create a frame, you will probably want to see it. Before you can see the frame, you must give it a size. Use the `resize` method to set the size:

```
myFrame.resize(300, 100);  // Make the frame 300 pixels wide, 100 high
```

Then you can use the `show` method to make it visible:

```
myFrame.show();      // Show yourself, Frame!
```

You can send a frame back into hiding with the `hide` method. Even though the frame is invisible, it still exists:

```
myFrame.hide();
```

As long as a frame exists, invisible or not, it is consuming some of the resources in the windowing system it is running on. If you are finished with a frame, you should get rid of it with the `dispose` method:

```
public synchronized void dispose()
```

You can change the title displayed at the top of the frame with `setTitle`:

```
public void setTitle(String newTitle)
```

For example:

```
myFrame.setTitle("With Frames like this, who needs enemies?");
```

The `getTitle` method will return the frame's title:

```
public String getTitle()
```

The `Frame` class has a number of different cursors. You can change the frame's cursor with `setCursor`:

```
public void setCursor(int cursorType)
```

The available cursors are:

```
Frame.DEFAULT_CURSOR
Frame.CROSSHAIR_CURSOR
Frame.TEXT_CURSOR
Frame.WAIT_CURSOR
Frame.HAND_CURSOR
Frame.MOVE_CURSOR
Frame.N_RESIZE_CURSOR
Frame.NE_RESIZE_CURSOR
Frame.E_RESIZE_CURSOR
```

```
Frame.SE_RESIZE_CURSOR
Frame.S_RESIZE_CURSOR
Frame.SW_RESIZE_CURSOR
Frame.W_RESIZE_CURSOR
Frame.NW_RESIZE_CURSOR
```

The `getCursorType` method will return one of these values indicating the current cursor type:

```
public int getCursorType()
```

If you do not want to allow your frame to be resized, you can call `setResizable` to turn resizing on or off:

```
public void setResizable(boolean allowResizing)
```

The `isResizable` method will return `true` if a frame can be resized:

```
public boolean isResizable()
```

You can change a frame's icon with `setIconImage`:

```
public setIconImage(Image image)
```

Using Frames to Make Your Applet Run Standalone

You can create applets that can run either as an applet or as a standalone application. All you need to do is write a `main` method in the applet that creates a frame and then an instance of the applet that belongs to the frame. Listing 21.2 shows an applet that can run either as an applet or as a standalone application.

Listing 21.2 Source code for *StandaloneApplet.java*

```
import java.awt.*;
import java.applet.*;

// StandaloneApplet is an applet that runs either as
// an applet or a standalone application.  To run
// standalone, it provides a main method that creates
// a frame, then creates an instance of the applet and
// adds it to the frame.

public class StandaloneApplet extends Applet
{
     public void init()
     {
          add(new Button("Standalone Applet Button"));
     }

     public static void main(String args[])
     {
// Create the frame this applet will run in
          Frame appletFrame = new Frame("Some applet");
```

continues

Listing 21.2 Continued

```
// Create an instance of the applet
          Applet myApplet = new StandaloneApplet();

// Initialize and start the applet
          myApplet.init();
          myApplet.start();

// The frame needs a layout manager
          appletFrame.setLayout(new FlowLayout());

// Add the applet to the frame
          appletFrame.add(myApplet);

// Have to give the frame a size before it is visible
          appletFrame.resize(300, 100);

// Make the frame appear on the screen
          appletFrame.show();
     }
}
```

Adding Menus to Frames

You can attach a `MenuBar` class to a frame to provide drop-down menu capabilities. You can create a menu bar with:

```
MenuBar myMenuBar = new MenuBar();
```

After you create a menu bar, you can add it to a frame by using the `setMenuBar` method:

```
myFrame.setMenuBar(myMenuBar);
```

Once you have a menu bar, you can add menus to it by using the `add` method:

```
public synchronized Menu add(Menu newMenu)
```

The following code fragment creates a menu called `"File"` and adds it to the menu bar:

```
Menu fileMenu = new Menu("File");
myMenuBar.add(fileMenu);
```

Some windowing systems enable you to create menus that stay up after you release the mouse button. These are referred to as *tear-off menus*. You can specify that a menu is a tear-off menu when you create it by using the following syntax:

```
public Menu(String menuLabel, boolean allowTearoff)
```

In addition to adding submenus, you will want to add menu items to your menus. *Menu items* are the parts of a menu that the user actually selects. Menus, on the other hand, are used to contain menu items as well as submenus. For instance, the File menu on many systems contains menu items such as New, Open, Save, and Save As. If you created a menu structure with no menu items, the menu structure would be useless. There would be nothing to select. You may add menu items to a menu in two ways. You can simply add an item name:

```
fileMenu.add("Open");      // Add an "Open" option to the file menu
```

You can also add an instance of a `MenuItem` class to a menu:

```
MenuItem saveMenuItem = new MenuItem("Save");
         // Create a "Save" menu item
fileMenu.add(saveMenuItem);        // Add the "Save" option to the file menu
```

You can enable and disable menu items by using `enable` and `disable`. When you disable a menu item, it still appears on the menu, but it usually appears in gray (depending on the windowing system). You cannot select menu items that are disabled. The format for `enable` and `disable` is:

```
saveMenuItem.disable();      // Disables the save option from the file menu
saveMenuItem.enable();       // Enables the save option again
```

In addition to menu items, you can add submenus and menu separators to a menu. A separator is a line that appears on the menu to separate sections of the menu. To add a separator, just call the `addSeparator` method:

```
public void addSeparator()
```

To create a submenu, just create a new instance of a menu and add it to the current menu:

```
Menu printSubmenu = new Menu("Print");
fileMenu.add(printSubmenu);
printSubmenu.add("Print Preview");
         // Add print preview as option on Print menu
printSubmenu.add("Print Document");
         // Add print document as option on Print menu
```

You can also create special check box menu items. These items function like the check box buttons. The first time you select one, it becomes checked, or on. The next time you select it, it becomes unchecked, or off. To create a check box menu item:

```
public CheckboxMenuItem(String itemLabel)
```

The `getState` method returns `true` if a check box menu item is checked:

```
public boolean getState()
```

You can set the current state of a check box menu item with `setState`:

```
public void setState(boolean newState)
```

Normally, menus are added to a menu bar in a left-to-right fashion. Many windowing systems, however, create a special Help menu that is on the far right of a menu bar. You can add such a menu to your menu bar with the `setHelpMenu` method:

```
public synchronized void setHelpMenu(Menu helpMenu)
```


Using Menus

Whenever a menu item is selected, it either generates an action event or it calls its action method, depending on the event model you are using (Java 1.1 versus Java 1.0). Under Java 1.0, the `whichAction` parameter to the `action` method will be the name of the item selected:

```
public boolean action(Event evt, Object whichAction)
{

// First, make sure this event is a menu selection

     if (evt.target instanceof MenuItem)
     {
          if ((String)whichAction == "Save")
          {
               // Handle save option
          }
     }
     return true;
}
```

Under Java 1.1, the event model was changed (and it stays this way in 1.2); under the 1.1 event model, you must create an `ActionListener` for the menu. An object that implements `ActionListener` must support the `actionPerformed()` method to receive notification that an action has occurred:

```
public void actionPerformed(ActionEvent event)
{
    if (event.getSource() instanceOf MenuComponent)
    {
        if (event.getSource() == saveMenuComponent)
        {
            // Handle save option
        }
    }
}
```

Listing 21.3 shows the code for an application that sets up a simple File menu with New, Open, and Save menu items; a check box called Auto-Save; and a Print submenu with two menu items.

Listing 21.3 Source code for *MenuApplication.java*

```
import java.awt.*;
import java.applet.*;

public class MenuApplication extends Object
{
     public static void main(String[] args)
     {
// Create the frame and the menubar
          Frame myFrame = new Frame("Menu Example");
          MenuBar myMenuBar = new MenuBar();

// Add the menubar to the frame
          myFrame.setMenuBar(myMenuBar);

// Create the File menu and add it to the menubar
          Menu fileMenu = new Menu("File");
          myMenuBar.add(fileMenu);
```

```
// Add the New and Open menuitems
        fileMenu.add(new MenuItem("New"));
        fileMenu.add(new MenuItem("Open"));

// Create a disabled Save menuitem
        MenuItem saveMenuItem = new MenuItem("Save");
        fileMenu.add(saveMenuItem);
        saveMenuItem.disable();

// Add an Auto-Save checkbox, followed by a separator
        fileMenu.add(new CheckboxMenuItem("Auto-Save"));
        fileMenu.addSeparator();

// Create the Print submenu
        Menu printSubmenu = new Menu("Print");
        fileMenu.add(printSubmenu);
        printSubmenu.add("Print Preview");
        printSubmenu.add("Print Document");

// Must resize the frame before it can be shown
        myFrame.resize(300, 200);

// Make the frame appear on the screen
        myFrame.show();
    }
}
```

Figure 21.2 shows the output from the `MenuApplication` program with the Print Document option in the process of being selected.

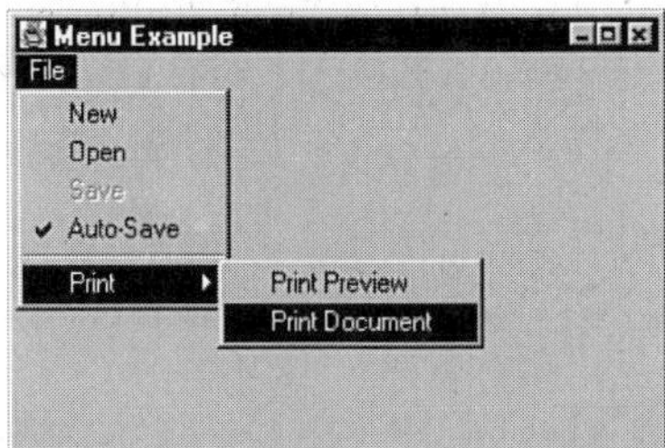

FIG. 21.2
The AWT provides a number of popular menu features including checked menu items, disabled menu items, and separators.

Pop-Up Menus

It is frequently desirable to create a pop-up menu for a component that enables you to click the component with the right or middle mouse button and bring up a menu specific to that component. Under Java 1.1, you can create such a menu.

You create a pop-up menu the same way you create a regular menu. You first instantiate a pop-up menu using either of the following constructors:

```
public PopupMenu()

public PopupMenu(String title)
```

Next, you add `MenuItem` objects to the pop-up menu, just like a regular menu. After you add all the items you want, add the pop-up menu to a component using the component's `add` method, as shown in the following snippet:

```
PopupMenu popup = new PopupMenu("Button Stuff");
popup.add("Winken");
popup.add("Blinken");
popup.add("Nodd");
Button myButton = new Button("Push Me");
myButton.add(popup);
```

Dialogs

Dialogs are pop-up windows that are not quite as flexible as frames. You can create a dialog as either modal or non-modal. The term ***modal*** means that the dialog box blocks input to other windows while it is being shown. This is useful for dialogs where you want to stop everything and get a crucial question answered, such as, "Are you sure you want to quit?" An example of a ***non-modal*** dialog box might be a control panel that changes settings in an application while the application continues to run.

Creating Dialogs

You must first have a frame in order to create a dialog. A dialog cannot belong to an applet. However, an applet may create a frame to which the dialog can then belong. You must specify whether a dialog is modal or non-modal at creation time, and you cannot change its "modality" once it has been created.

```
public Dialog(Frame parentFrame, boolean isModal)
```

The following example creates a modal dialog whose parent is `myFrame`:

```
Dialog myDialog = new Dialog(myFrame, true);      // true means modal dialog
```

You can also create a dialog with a title:

```
public Dialog(Frame parentFrame, String title, boolean isModal)
```

NOTE Because dialogs cannot belong to applets, your use of dialogs can be somewhat limited. One solution is to create a dummy frame as the dialog's parent. Unfortunately, you cannot create modal dialogs this way, because only the frame and its children would have their input blocked—the applet would continue on its merry way. A better solution is to use the technique discussed in the "Frames" section earlier in this chapter. In this case, you create a stand-alone application using frames, have a small startup applet create a frame, and then run the real applet in that frame. ■

Once you have created a dialog, you can make it visible using the `show` method:

```
myDialog.show();
```

Dialog Features

The `Dialog` class has several methods in common with the `Frame` class:

```
void setResizable(boolean);
boolean isResizable();
void setTitle(String);
String getTitle();
```

In addition, the `isModal` method will return `true` if the dialog is modal:

```
public boolean isModal()
```

A Reusable OK Dialog Box

Listing 21.4 shows the `OKDialog` class, which provides an OK dialog box that displays a message and waits for you to click OK. You normally must supply a frame for the dialog box, but you don't create a frame when running an applet. To enable applets to use the dialog box, this class provides a static `createOKDialog` method that first creates a frame for the dialog box. The frame is then saved as a static variable, so other dialog boxes can use the same frame.

Listing 21.4 Source code for *OKDialog.java*

```
import java.awt.*;

//
// OKDialog - Custom dialog that presents a message and waits for
// you to click on the OK button.
//
// Example use:
//     Dialog ok = new OKDialog(parentFrame, "Click OK to continue");
//     ok.show();     // Other input will be blocked until OK is pressed
// As a shortcut, you can use the static createOKDialog that will
// create its own frame and activate itself:
//     OKDialog.createOKDialog("Click OK to continue");
//

public class OKDialog extends Dialog
{
     protected Button okButton;
     protected static Frame createdFrame;

     public OKDialog(Frame parent, String message)
     {
          super(parent, true);     // Must call the parent's constructor

// This Dialog box uses the GridBagLayout to provide a pretty good layout.

          GridBagLayout gridbag = new GridBagLayout();
          GridBagConstraints constraints = new GridBagConstraints();

// Create the OK button and the message to display
          okButton = new Button("OK");
```


continues

Listing 21.4 Continued

```
          Label messageLabel = new Label(message);

          setLayout(gridbag);

// The message should not fill, it should be centered within this area, with
// some extra padding.  The gridwidth of REMAINDER means this is the only
// thing on its row, and the gridheight of RELATIVE means there should only
// be one thing below it.
          constraints.fill = GridBagConstraints.NONE;
          constraints.anchor = GridBagConstraints.CENTER;
          constraints.ipadx = 20;
          constraints.ipady = 20;
          constraints.weightx = 1.0;
          constraints.weighty = 1.0;
          constraints.gridwidth = GridBagConstraints.REMAINDER;
          constraints.gridheight = GridBagConstraints.RELATIVE;

          gridbag.setConstraints(messageLabel, constraints);
          add(messageLabel);

// The button has no padding, no weight, takes up minimal width, and
// Is the last thing in its column.

          constraints.ipadx = 0;
          constraints.ipady = 0;
          constraints.weightx = 0.0;
          constraints.weighty = 0.0;
          constraints.gridwidth = 1;
          constraints.gridheight = GridBagConstraints.REMAINDER;

          gridbag.setConstraints(okButton, constraints);
          add(okButton);

// Pack is a special window method that makes the window take up the minimum
// space necessary to contain its components.

          pack();

     }

// The action method just waits for the OK button to be clicked and
// when it is it hides the dialog, causing the show() method to return
// back to whoever activated this dialog.

     public boolean action(Event evt, Object whichAction)
     {
          if (evt.target == okButton)
          {
               hide();
               if (createdFrame != null)
               {
                    createdFrame.hide();
               }
          }
```

```
        return true;
    }

// Shortcut to create a frame automatically, the frame is a static variable
// so all dialogs in an applet or application can use the same frame.

    public static void createOKDialog(String dialogString)
    {
// If the frame hasn't been created yet, create it
        if (createdFrame == null)
        {
            createdFrame = new Frame("Dialog");
        }
// Create the dialog now
        OKDialog okDialog = new OKDialog(createdFrame, dialogString);

// Shrink the frame to just fit the dialog
        createdFrame.resize(okDialog.size().width,
            okDialog.size().height);

// Show the dialog
        okDialog.show();

    }
}
```

The `DialogApplet` in Listing 21.5 pops up an OK dialog whenever a button is pressed.

Listing 21.5 Source code for *DialogApplet.java*

```
import java.awt.*;
import java.applet.*;

// DialogApplet
//
// Dialog applet creates a button, and when you press
// the button it brings up an OK dialog.  The input
// to the original button should be blocked until
// the OK button in the dialog is pressed.

public class DialogApplet extends Applet
{
    protected Button launchButton;

    public void init()
    {
        launchButton = new Button("Give me an OK");
        add(launchButton);
    }

    public boolean action(Event event, Object whichAction)
    {
```


continues

Listing 21.5 Continued

```
// Make sure this action is for the launchButton
          if (event.target != launchButton)
          {
               return false;
          }

// Create and display the OK dialog
          OKDialog.createOKDialog(
               "Press OK when you are ready");

// Signal that you've handled the event
return true;
     }
}
```

Figure 21.3 shows the `DialogApplet` with the OK dialog popped up.

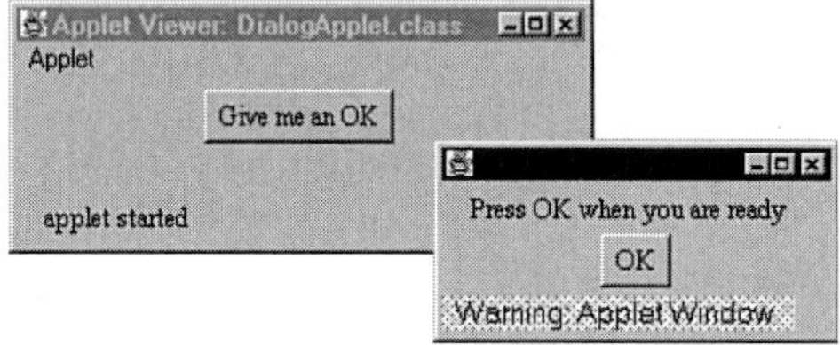

FIG. 21.3
The `OKDialog` class creates a pop-up dialog box with an OK button.

ScrollPanes

A `ScrollPane` is a special container that contains scrollbars to enable you to scroll the contents of the container. This allows you to create very large containers that don't have to be displayed all at once. A common use for a `ScrollPane` is to display a large image. You can create a canvas that displays the image and then place it in a `ScrollPane` container to provide automatic scrolling of the image.

You can control the scroll pane's use of scrollbars. By default, a scroll pane uses scrollbars only if necessary. You can specify that it should always use scrollbars, or never use scrollbars (in which case it is no different from a `Panel` object). If you use the default constructor, the scroll pane uses scrollbars if needed, otherwise you can pass either `ScrollPane.SCROLLBARS_ALWAYS`, `ScrollPane.SCROLLBARS_NEVER`, or `ScrollPane.SCROLLBARS_AS_NEEDED` to the constructor:

```
public ScrollPane()
```

```
public ScrollPane(int scrollbarOption)
```

You add components to a scroll pane the same way you do with any other container. You can set the position of the viewing area by calling `setScrollPosition` with either a `Point` object or x and y coordinates:

```
public void setScrollPosition(Point point)
```

```
public void setScrollPosition(int x, int y)
```

The `setScrollPosition` method only controls the upper-left corner of the viewing area. The rest is determined by the size of the scroll pane.

If you want to listen for events from the scroll pane's scrollbars, you can call `getHAdjustable` and `getVAdjustable` to get `Adjustable` interfaces for the horizontal and vertical scrollbars:

```
public Adjustable getHAdjustable()

public Adjustable getVAdjustable()
```

The `Adjustable` interface, in turn, enables you to listen for events with `setAdjustableListener`.

You can also determine the width and height of the viewing area with `getViewport`:

```
public Dimension getViewport()
```

Layout Managers

If you haven't noticed already, when you add components to a container you don't have to tell the container where to put a component. By using layout managers, you tell the AWT where you want your components to go relative to the other components. The layout manager figures out exactly where to put them. This helps you make platform-independent software. When you position components by absolute coordinates, it can cause a mess when someone running Windows 95 in 640×480 resolution tries to run an applet that is designed to fit on a 1280×1024 X-terminal.

The AWT provides five different types of layout managers:

- `FlowLayout` Arranges components from left to right until no more components will fit on a row. It then moves to the next row and continues going left to right.
- `GridLayout` Treats a container as a grid of identically sized spaces. It places components in the spaces in the grid, starting from the top left and continuing in left to right fashion, just like the `FlowLayout`. The difference between `GridLayout` and `FlowLayout` is that `GridLayout` gives each component an equal-sized area to work in.
- `BorderLayout` Treats the container like a compass. When you add a component to the container, you ask the `BorderLayout` to place it in one of five areas: "North," "South," "East," "West," or "Center." It figures out the exact positioning based on the relative sizes of the components.
- `CardLayout` Treats the components added to the container as a stack of cards. It places each component on a separate card, and only one card is visible at a time.
- `GridBagLayout` The most flexible of the layout managers. It is also the most confusing. `GridBagLayout` treats a container as a grid of cells, but unlike `GridLayout`, a component may occupy more than one cell. When you add a component to a container managed by `GridBagLayout`, you give it a `GridBagConstraint`, which has placement and sizing instructions for that component.

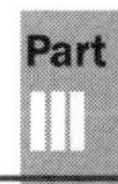

Flow Layouts

A `FlowLayout` class treats a container as a set of rows. The heights of the rows are determined by the height of the items placed in the rows. The `FlowLayout` starts adding new components from left to right. If it cannot fit the next component onto the current row, it drops down to the next row and starts again from the left. It also tries to align the rows using either left justification, right justification, or centering. The default alignment for a `FlowLayout` is centered, which means that when it creates a row of components, it will try to keep it centered with respect to the left and right edges.

The `FlowLayout` layout manager is the default layout manager for all applets.

The empty constructor for the `FlowLayout` class creates a flow layout with a centered alignment:

```
public FlowLayout()
```

You may also specify the alignment when you create the flow layout:

```
public FlowLayout(int alignment)
```

The different types of `FlowLayout` alignment are `FlowLayout.LEFT`, `FlowLayout.RIGHT`, and `FlowLayout.CENTER`.

You may also give the `FlowLayout` horizontal and vertical gap values. These values specify the minimum amount of horizontal and vertical space to leave between components. These gaps are given in units of screen pixels:

```
public FlowLayout(int alignment, int hgap, int vgap)
```

The following snippet creates a right-justified `FlowLayout` with a horizontal gap of 10 pixels and a vertical gap of five pixels:

```
myFlowLayout = new FlowLayout(FlowLayout.RIGHT, 10, 5);
```

Figure 21.4 shows five buttons arranged in a flow layout.

FIG. 21.4
The flow layout places components from left to right.

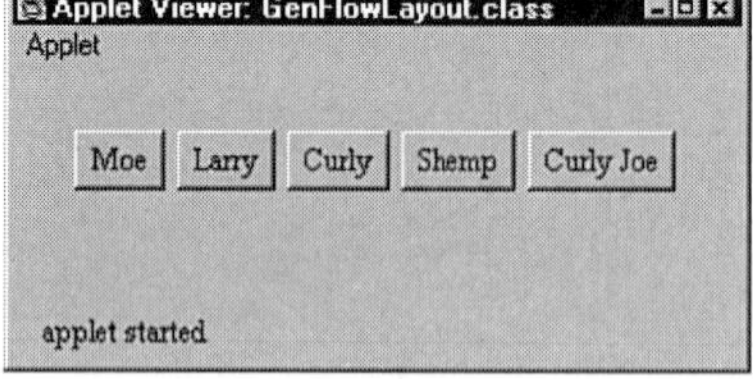

Grid Layouts

The `GridLayout` class divides a container into a grid of equally sized cells. When you add components to the container, the `GridLayout` places them from left to right starting in the top left cells. When you create a `GridLayout` class, you must tell it how many rows or columns you want. If you give it a number of rows, it will compute the number of columns needed.

If, instead, you give it a number of columns, it will compute the number of rows needed. If you add six components to a `GridLayout` with two rows, it will create three columns. The format of the `GridLayout` constructor is

```
public GridLayout(int numberOfRows, int numberOfColumns)
```

If you create a `GridLayout` with a fixed number of rows, you should use 0 for the number of columns. If you have a fixed number of columns, use 0 for the number of rows.

NOTE If you pass non-zero values to `GridLayout` for both the number of rows and the number of columns, it will only use the number of rows. The number of columns will be computed based on the number of components and the number of rows. `GridLayout(3, 4)` is exactly the same as `GridLayout(3, 0)`.

You may also specify a horizontal and vertical gap:

```
public GridLayout(int rows, int cols, int hgap, int vgap)
```

The following code creates a `GridLayout` with four columns, a horizontal gap of eight, and a vertical gap of 10:

```
GridLayout myGridLayout = new GridLayout(0, 4, 8, 10);
```

Figure 21.5 shows five buttons arranged in a grid layout.

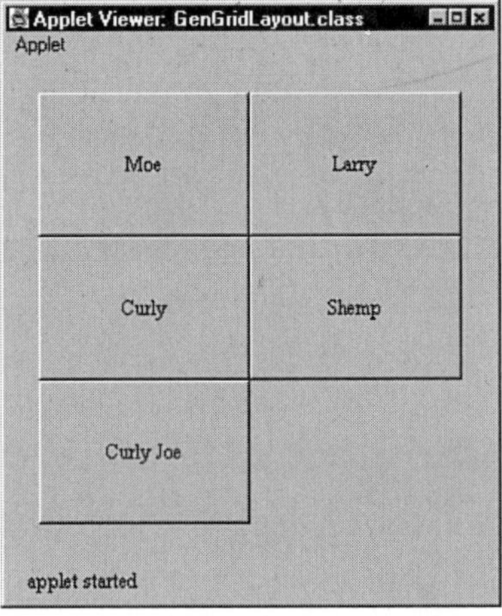

FIG. 21.5
The grid layout allocates equally sized areas for each component.

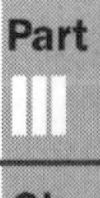

Border Layouts

The `BorderLayout` class divides a container into five areas named “North,” “South,” “East,” “West,” and “Center.” When you add components to the container, you must use a special form of the `add` method that includes one of these five area names. These five areas are arranged like the points on a compass. A component added to the “North” area is placed at the top of the container, while a component added to the “West” area is placed on the left side of the container.

The `BorderLayout` class does not allow more than one component in an area. You may optionally specify a horizontal and vertical gap. To create a `BorderLayout` without specifying a gap, use the empty constructor:

```
public BorderLayout()
```

You can also specify the horizontal and vertical gap:

```
public BorderLayout(int hgap, int vgap)
```

The following line adds `myButton` to the `"West"` area of the `BorderLayout`:

```
myBorderLayout.add("West", myButton);
```

CAUTION

The `BorderLayout` class is very picky about how and where you add components. It requires you to use the `add` method that takes a string name along with the component. If you try to add a component using the regular `add` method (without the area name), you will not see your component. If you try to add two components to the same area, you will only see the last component added.

Listing 21.6 shows a `BorderLayoutApplet` that creates a `BorderLayout`, attaches it to the current applet, and adds some buttons to the applet.

Listing 21.6 Source code for *BorderLayoutApplet.java*

```
import java.applet.*;
import java.awt.*;

//
// This applet creates a BorderLayout and attaches it
// to the applet.  Then it creates buttons and places
// in all possible areas of the layout.

public class BorderLayoutApplet extends Applet
{
     public void init()
     {

// First create the layout and attach it to the applet

          setLayout(new BorderLayout());

// Now create some buttons and lay them out

          add("North", new Button("Larry"));
          add("South", new Button("Curly Joe"));
          add("East", new Button("Curly"));
          add("West", new Button("Shemp"));
          add("Center", new Button("Moe"));
     }
}
```

Figure 21.6 shows five buttons arranged in a border layout.

FIG. 21.6
The border layout places components at the "North," "South," "East," and "West" compass points, as well as in the "Center."

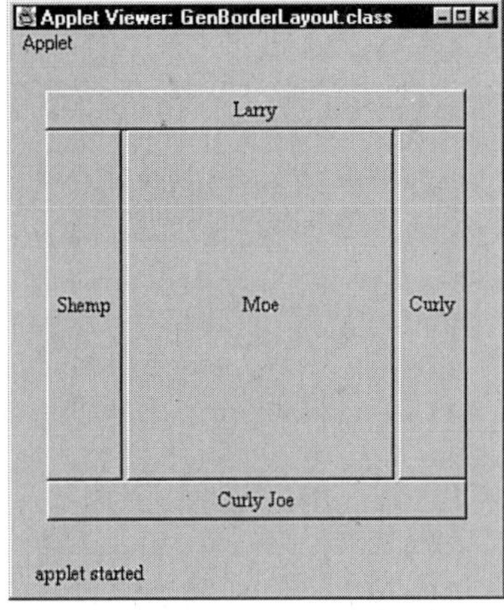

Grid Bag Layouts

The `GridBagLayout` class, like the `GridLayout`, divides a container into a grid of equally sized cells. Unlike the `GridLayout`, however, the `GridBagLayout` class decides how many rows and columns it will have and allows a component to occupy more than one cell, if necessary. The total area that a component occupies is called its *display area*. Before you add a component to a container, you must give the `GridBagLayout` a set of "suggestions" on where to put the component. These suggestions are in the form of a `GridBagConstraints` class. The `GridBagConstraints` class has a number of variables to control the placement of a component:

- `gridx` and `gridy` The coordinates of the cell where the next component should be placed (if the component occupies more than one cell, these coordinates are for the upper-left cell of the component). The upper-left corner of the `GridBagLayout` is at 0, 0. The default value for both `gridx` and `gridy` is `GridBagConstraints.RELATIVE`, which for `gridx` means the cell just to the right of the last component that was added. For `gridy`, it means the cell just below the last component added.
- `gridwidth` and `gridheight` Tell how many cells wide and tall a component should be. The default for both `gridwidth` and `gridheight` is `1`. If you want this component to be the last one on a row, use `GridBagConstraint.REMAINDER` for the `gridwidth` (use this same value for `gridheight` if this component should be the last one in a column). Use `GridBagConstraint.RELATIVE` if the component should be the next-to-last component in a row or column.
- `fill` Tells the `GridBagLayout` what to do when a component is smaller than its display area. The default value, `GridBagConstraint.NONE`, causes the component size to remain unchanged. `GridBagConstraint.HORIZONTAL` causes the component to be stretched horizontally to take up its whole display area horizontally while leaving its height unchanged. `GridBagConstraint.VERTICAL` causes the component to be stretched vertically while leaving the width unchanged. `GridBagConstraint.BOTH` causes the component to be stretched in both directions to fill its display area completely.

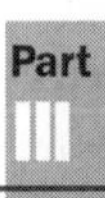

- `ipadx` and `ipady` Tell the `GridBagLayout` how many pixels to add to the size of the component in the x and y direction. The pixels will be added on either side of the component, so an `ipadx` of `4` would cause the size of a component to be increased by four on the left and also four on the right. Remember that the component size will grow by two times the amount of padding because the padding is added to both sides. The default for both `ipadx` and `ipady` is `0`.
- `insets` An instance of an `Insets` class. It indicates how much space to leave between the borders of a component and the edges of its display area. In other words, `insets` creates a "no-man's land" of blank space surrounding a component. The `Insets` class (discussed later in this chapter in the section "Insets") has separate values for the top, bottom, left, and right insets.
- `anchor` Used when a component is smaller than its display area. It indicates where the component should be placed within the display area. The default value is `GridBagConstraint.CENTER`, which indicates that the component should be in the center of the display area. The other values are all compass points:

  `GridbagConstraints.NORTH`

  `GridBagConstraints.NORTHEAST`

  `GridBagConstraints.EAST`

  `GridBagConstraints.SOUTHEAST`

  `GridBagConstraints.SOUTH`

  `GridBagConstraints.SOUTHWEST`

  `GridBagConstraints.WEST`

  `GridBagConstraints.NORTHWEST`

  As with the `BorderLayout` class, `NORTH` indicates the top of the screen, while `EAST` is to the right.
- `weightx` and `weighty` Used to set relative sizes of components. For instance, a component with a `weightx` of `2.0` takes up twice the horizontal space of a component with a `weightx` of `1.0`. Because these values are relative, there is no difference between all components in a row having a weight of `1.0` or `3.0`. You should assign a weight to at least one component in each direction, otherwise the `GridBagLayout` will squeeze your components toward the center of the container.

When you want to add a component to a container using a `GridBagLayout`, you create the component, then create an instance of `GridBagConstraints`, and set the constraints for the component. For example:

```
GridBagLayout myGridBagLayout = new GridBagLayout();
setLayout(myGridBagLayout);
        // Set the applet's Layout Manager to myGridBagLayout

Button myButton = new Button("My Button");
GridBagConstraints constraints = new GridBagConstraints();
constraints.weightx = 1.0;
constraints.gridwidth = GridBagConstraints.RELATIVE;
constraints.fill = GridBagConstraints.BOTH;
```

Next, you set the component's constraints in the `GridBagLayout`:

```
myGridLayout.setConstraints(myButton, constraints);
```

Now you may add the component to the container:

```
add(myButton);
```

The applet in Listing 21.7 uses the `GridBagLayout` class to arrange a few instances of `CircleCanvas` (created in the section "Canvases" earlier in this chapter).

Listing 21.7 Source code for *CircleApplet.java*

```
import java.applet.*;
import java.awt.*;

//
// This circle demonstrates the CircleCanvas class we
// created.  It also shows you how to use the GridBagLayout
// to arrange the circles.

public class CircleApplet extends Applet
{
     public void init()
     {
          GridBagLayout gridbag = new GridBagLayout();
          GridBagConstraints constraints = new GridBagConstraints();
          CircleCanvas newCircle;

          setLayout(gridbag);

// You'll use the weighting to determine relative circle sizes. Make the
// first one just have a weight of 1. Also, set fill for both directions
// so it will make the circles as big as possible.

          constraints.weightx = 1.0;
          constraints.weighty = 1.0;
          constraints.fill = GridBagConstraints.BOTH;

// Create a red circle and add it

          newCircle = new CircleCanvas(Color.red);
          gridbag.setConstraints(newCircle, constraints);
          add(newCircle);

// Now, you want to make the next circle twice as big as the previous
// one, so give it twice the weight.

          constraints.weightx = 2.0;
          constraints.weighty = 2.0;

// Create a blue circle and add it

          newCircle = new CircleCanvas(Color.blue);
```


continues

Listing 21.7 Continued

```
            gridbag.setConstraints(newCircle, constraints);
            add(newCircle);

// You'll make the third circle the same size as the first one, so set the
// weight back down to 1.

            constraints.weightx = 1.0;
            constraints.weighty = 1.0;

// Create a green circle and add it.

            newCircle = new CircleCanvas(Color.green);
            gridbag.setConstraints(newCircle, constraints);
            add(newCircle);

      }
}
```

Figure 21.7 shows the three circle canvases from the `GridBagApplet`.

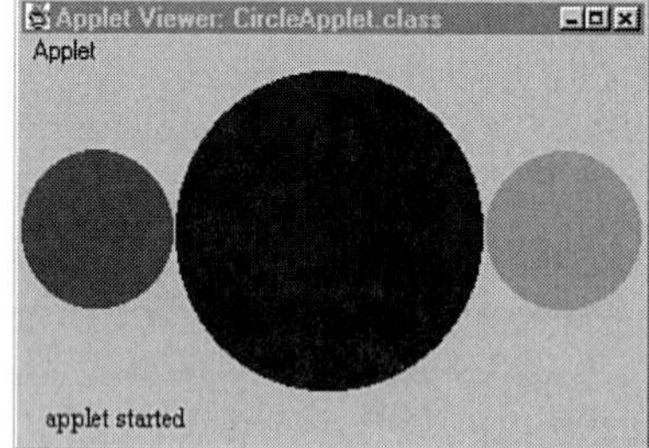

FIG. 21.7
The `GridBagApplet` creates three circle canvases.

Insets

Insets are not layout managers. They are instructions to the layout manager about how much space to leave around the edges of the container. In other words, *insets* define an empty area between the edge of a container and the components it contains. If you have an inset of 20 pixels on the left side of a container, no component will be placed closer than 20 pixels to the left edge of the container.

Insets are described by an instance of the `Insets` class. This class has instance variables for the left, top, right, and bottom inset values. The layout manager determines the inset values for a container by calling the container's `insets` method, which returns an instance of an `Insets` class. For example, if you want to leave a 20-pixel gap between the components in your applet and the applet border, you should create an `insets` method in your applet:

```
public Insets insets()
{
     return new Insets(20, 20, 20, 20);
```

```
        // Inset by 20 pixels all around
}
```

The constructor for the `Insets` class takes four inset values in the order top, left, bottom, and right.

Figure 21.8 shows what the `GridBagApplet` would look like if it used the above `insets` method. The gap between the circles is not from the `Insets` class but from the fact that the circles are smaller. The gaps on the top, bottom, left, and right are created by the `Insets` class.

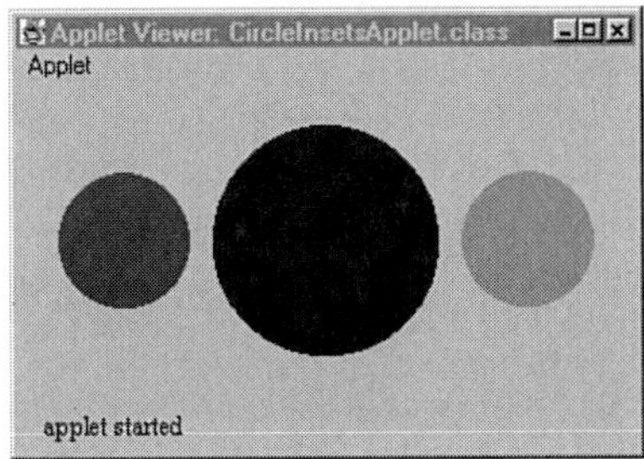

FIG. 21.8 Insets create a gap between components and the edges of their containers.

The Null Layout Manager

You aren't required to use a layout manager at all, although it is recommended. There are cases where you need to place components explicitly at certain coordinates. If you set the layout manager in a container to `null`, you can explicitly set the sizes and positions of the components using the `move` and `resize` methods in each component.

Future Extensions from Sun

Sun is developing a complete development environment for Java applications called *Solstice Workshop*, which includes a robust set of class libraries. These libraries will include a set of classes called the *Admin View Module* (*AVM*), which will address some of the shortcomings of the AWT. It does not replace the AWT; it complements the AWT. The AVM will include such useful features as:

- Image buttons
- Multicolumn lists
- Scrolling windows
- Toolbars
- Image canvases
- Many common dialogs

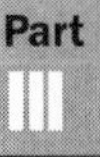

These features will be fully integrated with the rest of Solstice Workshop to enable you to develop robust applications very quickly without writing too much code. For more information on the AVM, consult the Java Management API (JMAPI) Web site at `http://www.javasoft.com/products/JavaManagement/index.html`. ●

CHAPTER 22

Graphics

In this chapter

Java Graphics

The Abstract Windowing Toolkit (AWT) provides an Application Programming Interface (API) for common User Interface components, such as buttons and menus.

One of the main goals of Java is to provide a platform-independent development environment. The area of Graphical User Interfaces has always been one of the stickiest parts of creating highly portable code. The Windows API is different from the OS/2 Presentation Manager API, which is different from the X-Windows API, which is different from the Mac API. The most common solution to this problem is to look at all the platforms you want to use, identify the components that are common to all of them (or would be easy to implement on all of them), and create a single API you can use for all of them. On each different platform, the common API would interface with the platform's native API. Applications using the common API would then have the same look and feel as applications using the native API.

The opposite of this approach is to create a single look and feel, and then implement that look and feel on each different platform. For Java, Sun chose the common API approach, which allows Java applications to blend in smoothly with their surroundings. Sun called this common API the Abstract Windowing Toolkit, or AWT for short.

The AWT addresses graphics from two different levels. At the lower level, it handles the raw graphics functions and the different input devices such as the mouse and keyboard. At the higher level, it provides a number of components like pushbuttons and scroll bars you would otherwise have to write yourself.

This chapter discusses the low-level graphics and printing features of the AWT. Chapter 28 discusses the low-level input handling, while Chapters 29 and 30 discuss the higher-level portions of the AWT.

paint, *Update*, and *repaint*

As you saw in the simple HelloWorld applet, Java applets can redraw themselves by overriding the `paint` method. Because your applet never explicitly calls the `paint` method, you may have wondered how it is called. Your applet actually has three different methods that are used in redrawing the applet, as follows:

- `repaint` can be called any time the applet needs to be repainted (redrawn).
- `Update` is called by `repaint` to signal that it is time to update the applet. The default `update` method clears the applet's drawing area and calls the `paint` method.
- `paint` actually draws the applet's graphics in the drawing area. The `paint` method is passed an instance of a `Graphics` class that it can use for drawing various shapes and images.

The *Graphics* Class

The `Graphics` class provides methods for drawing a number of graphical figures, including the following:

- Lines
- Circles and Ellipses
- Rectangles and Polygons
- Images
- Text in a variety of fonts

In addition, Graphics is extended by the Graphics2D and Graphics3D classes. To learn more about the new 2D features refer to Chapter 26, "Java 2D Graphics."

The Coordinate System

The coordinate system used in Java is a simple Cartesian (x, y) system where x is the number of screen pixels from the left-hand side, and y is the number of pixels from the top of the screen. The upper-left corner of the screen is represented by (0, 0). This is the coordinate system used in almost all graphics systems. Figure 22.1 gives you an example of some coordinates.

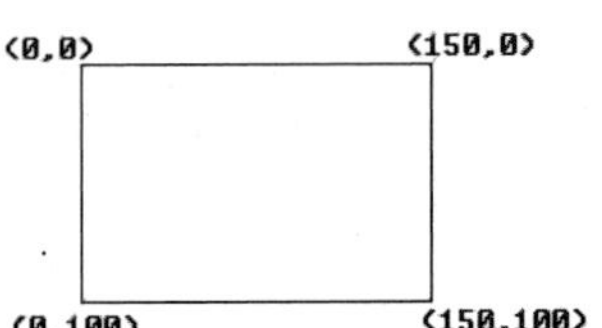

FIG. 22.1 Unlike math coordinates, where y increases from bottom to top, the y coordinates in Java increase from the top down.

Drawing Lines

The simplest Figure you can draw with the `Graphics` class is a line. The `drawLine` method takes two pairs of coordinates—x1,y1 and x2,y2—and draws a line between them:

```
public abstract void drawLine(int x1, int y1, int x2, int y2)
```

The applet in Listing 22.1 uses the `drawLine` method to draw some lines. The output from this applet is shown in Figure 22.2.

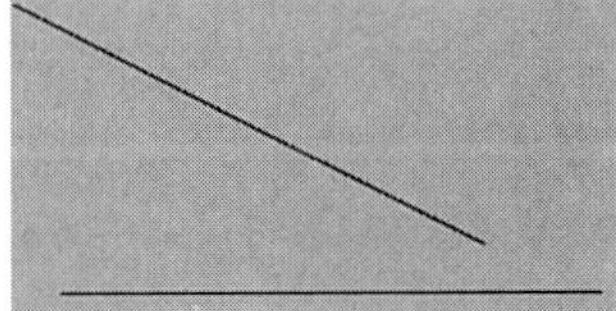

FIG. 22.2 Line drawing is one of the most basic graphics operations.

Listing 22.1 Source Code for *DrawLines.java*

```
import java.awt.*;
import java.applet.*;

//
// This applet draws a pair of lines using the Graphics class
//

public class DrawLines extends Applet
{
   public void paint(Graphics g)
   {
// Draw a line from the upper-left corner to the point at (200, 100)
     g.drawLine(0, 0, 200, 100);

// Draw a horizontal line from (20, 120) to (250, 120)
     g.drawLine(20, 120, 250, 120);
   }
}
```

Drawing Rectangles

Now that you know how to draw a line, you can progress to rectangles and filled rectangles. To draw a rectangle, you use the `drawRect` method and pass it the x and y coordinates of the upper-left corner of the rectangle, the width of the rectangle, and its height:

```
public abstract void drawRect(int x, int y, int width, int height)
```

To draw a rectangle at (150, 100) that is 200 pixels wide and 120 pixels high, your call would be:

```
g.drawRect(150, 100, 200, 120);
```

The `drawRect` method draws only the outline of a box. If you want to draw a solid box, you can use the `fillRect` method, which takes the same parameters as `drawRect`:

```
public abstract void fillRect(int x, int y, int width, int height)
```

You may also clear out an area with the `clearRect` method, which also takes the same parameters as `drawRect`:

```
public abstract void clearRect(int x, int y, int width, int height)
```

Figure 22.3 shows you the difference between `drawRect`, `fillRect`, and `clearRect`. The rectangle on the left is drawn with `drawRect`, and the center one is drawn with `fillRect`. The rectangle on the right is drawn with `fillRect`, but the `clearRect` is used to make the empty area in the middle.

FIG. 22.3
Java provides several flexible ways of drawing rectangles.

Drawing 3D Rectangles

The `Graphics` class also provides a way to draw "3D" rectangles similar to buttons that you might find on a toolbar. Unfortunately, the `Graphics` class draws these buttons with very little height or depth, making the 3D effect difficult to see. The syntax for the `draw3DRect` and `fill3DRect` is similar to `drawRect` and `fillRect`, except they have an extra parameter at the end—a Boolean indicator as to whether the rectangle is raised or not:

```
public void draw3dRect(int x, int y, int width, int height, boolean raised)
public void fill3dRect(int x, int y, int width, int height, boolean raised)
```

The raising/lowering effect is produced by drawing light and dark lines around the borders of the rectangle.

Imagine a light coming from the upper-left corner of the screen. A raised 3D rectangle would catch light on its top and left sides, while the bottom and right sides would have a shadow. A lowered 3D rectangle would have a shadow on the top and left sides, while the bottom and right sides would catch light. Both the `draw3DRect` and `fill3DRect` methods draw the top and left sides in a lighter color for raised rectangles while drawing the bottom and right sides in a darker color. They draw the top and left darker and the bottom and right lighter for lowered rectangles. In addition, the `fill3DRect` method will draw the entire button in a darker shade when it is lowered. The applet in Listing 22.2 draws some raised and lowered rectangles, both filled and unfilled.

Listing 22.2 Source Code for *Rect3d.java*

```
import java.awt.*;'
import java.applet.*;

//
// This applet draws four varieties of 3-D rectangles.
// It sets the drawing color to the same color as the
// background because this shows up well in HotJava and
// Netscape.

public class Rect3d extends Applet
{
   public void paint(Graphics g)
   {
// Make the drawing color the same as the background
      g.setColor(getBackground());

// Draw a raised 3-D rectangle in the upper-left
      g.draw3dRect(10, 10, 60, 40, true);
// Draw a lowered 3-D rectangle in the upper-right
      g.draw3dRect(100, 10, 60, 40, false);

// Fill a raised 3-D rectangle in the lower-left
      g.fill3dRect(10, 80, 60, 40, true);
// Fill a lowered 3-D rectangle in the lower-right
      g.fill3dRect(100, 80, 60, 40, false);
   }
}
```

Figure 22.4 shows the output from the Rect3d applet. Notice that the raised rectangles appear the same for the filled and unfilled. This is only because the drawing color is the same color as the background. If the drawing color were different, the filled button would be filled with the drawing color, while the unfilled button would still show the background color.

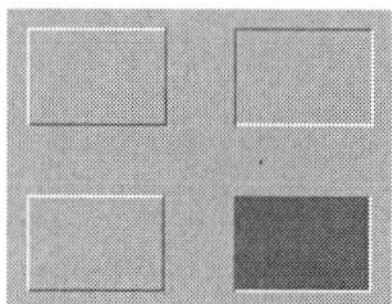

FIG. 22.4
The `draw3DRect` and `fill3DRect` methods use shading to produce a 3D effect.

Drawing Rounded Rectangles

In addition to the regular and 3D rectangles, you can also draw rectangles with rounded corners. The `drawRoundRect` and `fillRoundRect` methods are similar to `drawRect` and `fillRect` except that they take two extra parameters:

```
public abstract void drawRoundRect(int x, int y, int width, int height,
int arcWidth, int arcHeight)
public abstract void fillRoundRect(int x, int y, int width, int height,
int arcWidth, int arcHeight)
```

The `arcWidth` and `arcHeight` parameters indicate how much of the corners will be rounded. For instance, an `arcWidth` of 10 tells the `Graphics` class to round off the left-most five pixels and the right-most five pixels of the corners of the rectangle. An `arcHeight` of 8 tells the class to round off the top-most and bottom-most four pixels of the rectangle's corners.

Figure 22.5 shows the corner of a rounded rectangle. The `arcWidth` for the Figure is 30, while the `arcHeight` is 10. The Figure shows an imaginary ellipse with a width of 30 and a height of 29 to help illustrate how the rounding is done.

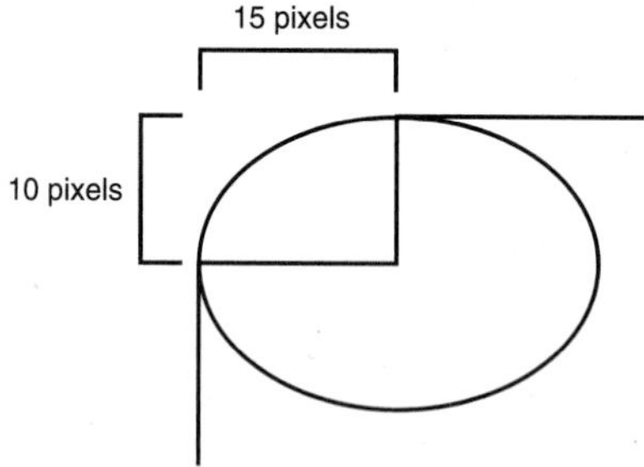

FIG. 22.5
Java uses an ellipse to determine the amount of rounding.

The applet in Listing 22.3 draws a rounded rectangle and a filled, rounded rectangle. Figure 22.6 shows the output from this applet.

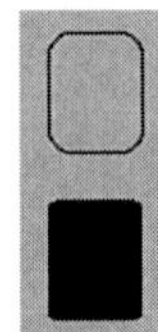

FIG. 22.6
Java's rounded rectangles are a pleasant alternative to sharp-cornered rectangles.

Listing 22.3 Source Code for *RoundRect.java*

```
import java.awt.*;
import java.applet.*;

// Example 22.3-RoundRect Applet
//
// This applet draws a rounded rectangle and then a
// filled, rounded rectangle.

public class RoundRect extends Applet
{
   public void paint(Graphics g)
   {
// Draw a rounded rectangle with an arcWidth of 20, and an arcHeight of 20
      g.drawRoundRect(10, 10, 40, 50, 20, 20);

// Fill a rounded rectangle with an arcWidth of 10, and an arcHeight of 8
      g.fillRoundRect(10, 80, 40, 50, 10, 6);
   }
}
```

Drawing Circles and Ellipses

If you are bored with square shapes, you can try your hand at circles. The `Graphics` class does not distinguish between a circle and an ellipse, so there is no `drawCircle` method. Instead, you use the `drawOval` and `fillOval` methods:

```
public abstract void drawOval(int x, int y, int width, int height)
public abstract void fillOval(int x, int y, int width, int height)
```

To draw a circle or an ellipse, first imagine that the Figure is surrounded by a rectangle that just barely touches the edges. You pass `drawOval` the coordinates of the upper-left corner of this rectangle. You also pass the width and height of the oval. If the width and height are the same, you are drawing a circle. Figure 22.7 illustrates the concept of the enclosing rectangle.

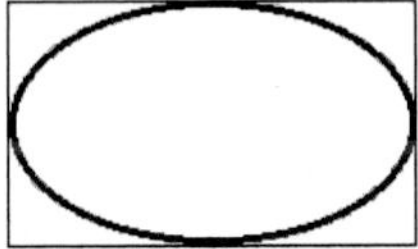

FIG. 22.7
Circles and ellipses are drawn within the bounds of an imaginary enclosing rectangle.

The applet in Listing 22.4 draws a circle and a filled ellipse. Figure 22.8 shows the output from this applet.

FIG. 22.8 Java doesn't know the difference between ellipses and circles; they're all just ovals.

Listing 22.4 Source Code for *Ovals.java*

```
import java.awt.*;
import java.applet.*;

//
// This applet draws an unfilled circle and a filled ellipse

public class Ovals extends Applet
{
   public void paint(Graphics g)
   {

// Draw a circle with a diameter of 30 (width=30, height=30)
// With the enclosing rectangle's upper-left corner at (0, 0)
      g.drawOval(0, 0, 30, 30);

// Fill an ellipse with a width of 40 and a height of 20
// The upper-left corner of the enclosing rectangle is at (0, 60)
      g.fillOval(0, 60, 40, 20);
   }
}
```

Drawing Polygons

You can also draw polygons and filled polygons by using the `Graphics` class. You have two options when drawing polygons. You can either pass two arrays containing the x and y coordinates of the points in the polygon, or you can pass an instance of a `Polygon` class:

```
public abstract void drawPolygon(int[] xPoints, int[] yPoints, int numPoints)
```

```
public void drawPolygon(Polygon p)
```

The applet in Listing 22.5 draws a polygon using an array of points. Figure 22.9 shows the output from this applet.

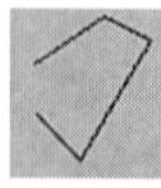

FIG. 22.9 Java allows you to draw polygons of almost any shape you can imagine.

Listing 22.5 Source Code for *DrawPoly.java*

```
import java.applet.*;
import java.awt.*;

//
// This applet draws a polygon using an array of points

public class DrawPoly extends Applet
{
// Define an array of X coordinates for the polygon
   int xCoords[] = { 10, 40, 60, 30, 10 };

// Define an array of Y coordinates for the polygon
   int yCoords[] = { 20, 0, 10, 60, 40 };

   public void paint(Graphics g)
   {
     g.drawPolygon(xCoords, yCoords, 5);   // 5 points in polygon
   }
}
```

CAUTION

Notice that in this example, the polygon is not "closed off." In other words, there is no line between the last point in the polygon and the first one. If you want the polygon to be closed, you must repeat the first point at the end of the array.

The *Polygon* Class

The `Polygon` class provides a more flexible way to define polygons. You can create a Polygon by passing it an array of x points and an array of y points:

```
public Polygon(int[] xPoints, int[] yPoints, int numPoints)
```

You can also create an empty polygon and add points to it one-at- a-time:

```
public Polygon()
public void addPoint(int x, int y)
```

Once you have created an instance of a `Polygon` class, you can use the `getBounds` method to determine the area taken up by this polygon (the minimum and maximum x and y coordinates):

```
public Rectangle getBounds()
```

The `Rectangle` class returned by `getBounds()` contains variables indicating the x and y coordinates of the rectangle and its width and height. You can also determine whether a point is contained within the polygon or outside it by calling inside with the x and y coordinates of the point:

```
public boolean contains(int x, int y)
```

For example, you can check to see if the point (5,10) is contained within `myPolygon` by using the following code fragment:

```
if (myPolygon.contains(5, 10))
{
   // the point (5, 10) is inside this polygon
}
```

You can use this `Polygon` class in place of the array of points for either the `drawPolygon` or `fillPolygon` methods. The applet in Listing 22.6 creates an instance of a polygon and draws a filled polygon. Figure 22.10 shows the output from this applet.

FIG. 22.10
Polygons created with the `Polygon` class look just like those created from an array of points.

Listing 22.6 Source Code for *Polygons.java*

```
import java.applet.*;
import java.awt.*;

//
// This applet creates an instance of a Polygon class and then
// uses fillPoly to draw the Polygon as a filled polygon.

public class Polygons extends Applet
{
// Define an array of X coordinates for the polygon
    int xCoords[] = { 10, 40, 60, 30, 10 };

// Define an array of Y coordinates for the polygon
    int yCoords[] = { 20, 0, 10, 60, 40 };

    public void paint(Graphics g)
    {
// Create a new instance of a polygon with 5 points
        Polygon drawingPoly = new Polygon(xCoords, yCoords, 5);

// Draw a filled polygon
        g.fillPolygon(drawingPoly);
    }
}
```

Drawing Text

The `Graphics` class also contains methods to draw text characters and strings. As you have seen in the "Hello World" applet, you can use the `drawString` method to draw a text string on the screen. Before plunging into the various aspects of drawing text, you should be familiar with some common terms for fonts and text, as follows:

- Baseline. Imaginary line the text is resting on.
- Descent. How far below the baseline a particular character extends. Some characters, such as g and j, extend below the baseline.
- Ascent. How far above the baseline a particular character extends. The letter d would have a higher ascent than the letter x.
- Leading. Amount of space between the descent of one line and the ascent of the next line. If there was no leading, such letters as g and j would almost touch such letters as M and H on the next line.

CAUTION

The term *ascent* in Java is slightly different from the same term in the publishing world. The publishing term *ascent* refers to the distance from the top of the letter x to the top of a character, where the Java term *ascent* refers to the distance from the baseline to the top of a character.

Figure 22.11 illustrates the relationship between the descent, ascent, baseline, and leading.

FIG. 22.11 Java's font terminology originated in the publishing field, but some of the meanings have been changed.

NOTE You may also hear the terms *proportional* and *fixed* associated with fonts. In a fixed font, every character takes up the same amount of space. Typewriters (if you actually remember those) wrote in a fixed font. Characters in a proportional font only take up as much space as they need. You can use this book as an example.

The text of the book is in a proportional font, which is much easier on the eyes. Look at some of the words and notice how the letters only take up as much space as necessary. (Compare the letters i and m, for example.) The code examples in this book, however, are written in a fixed font (this preserves the original spacing). Notice how each letter takes up exactly the same amount of space.

To draw a string using the `Graphics` class, you call `drawString`, give it the string you want to draw, and give it the x and y coordinates for the beginning of the baseline (that's why you needed the terminology briefing):

```
public abstract void drawString(String str, int x, int y)
```

You may recall the "Hello World" applet used this same method to draw its famous message:

```
public void paint(Graphics g)
{
```

```
    g.drawString("Hello World", 10, 30);
}
```

You can also draw characters from an array of characters or an array of bytes. The format for `drawChars` and `drawBytes` is:

```
void drawChars(char charArray[], int offset, int numChars, int x, int y)
void drawBytes(byte byteArray[], int offset, int numChars, int x, int y)
```

The `offset` parameter refers to the position of the first character or byte in the array to draw. This will most often be zero because you will usually want to draw from the beginning of the array. The applet in Listing 22.7 draws some characters from a character array and from a byte array.

Listing 22.7 Source Code for *DrawChars.java*

```
import java.awt.*;
import java.applet.*;

//
// This applet draws a character array and a byte array

public class DrawChars extends Applet
{
   char[] charsToDraw = { 'H', 'i', ' ', 'T', 'h', 'e', 'r', 'e', '!' };

   byte[] bytesToDraw = { 65, 66, 67, 68, 69, 70, 71 }; // "ABCDEFG"

   public void paint(Graphics g)
   {
     g.drawChars(charsToDraw, 0, charsToDraw.length, 10, 20);

     g.drawBytes(bytesToDraw, 0, bytesToDraw.length, 10, 50);
   }
}
```

The *Font* Class

You may find that the default font for your applet is not very interesting. Fortunately, you can select from a number of different fonts. These fonts have the potential to vary from system to system, which may lead to portability issues in the future; but for the moment, HotJava and Netscape support the same set of fonts.

In addition to selecting between multiple fonts, you may also select a number of font styles: `Font.PLAIN`, `Font.BOLD`, and `Font.ITALIC`. These styles can be added together, so you can use a bold italic font with `Font.BOLD + Font.ITALIC`.

When choosing a font, you must also give the point size of the font. Point size is a printing term that relates to the size of the font. There are 100 points to an inch when printing on a printer, but this does not necessarily apply to screen fonts. Microsoft Windows defines the point size as being about the same height in all different screen resolutions. In other words, a letter in a

14-point font in the 640×480 screen resolution should be about the same height on your monitor as a 14-point font in 1,024×768 resolution on the same monitor. Java does not conform to this notion, however. In Java, a font's height varies directly with the number of pixels. A 14-point font in 1,280×960 resolution would be twice as tall as a 14-point font in 640×480 mode. The point sizing is done this way in Java because many applets use absolute screen coordinates, especially when drawing raw graphics. Lines and squares have a fixed pixel height. If you draw text with these figures, make the text have a fixed height as well.

You create an instance of a font by using the font name, the font style, and the point size:

```
public Font(String fontName, int style, int size)
```

The following declaration creates the Times Roman font that is both bold and italic and has a point size of 12:

```
Font myFont = new Font("TimesRoman", Font.BOLD + Font.ITALIC, 12);
```

You can also retrieve fonts that are described in the system properties using the `getFont` methods:

```
public static Font getFont(String propertyName)
```

Returns an instance of `Font` described by the system property named `propertyName`. If the property name is not set, it will return null.

```
public static Font getFont(String propertyName, Font defaultValue)
```

Returns an instance of `Font` described by the system property named `propertyName`. If the property name is not set, it will return `defaultValue`.

The `getFont` method allows the fonts described in the system properties to have a style and a point size associated with them in addition to the font name. The format for describing a font in the system properties is

```
font-style-pointsize
```

The `style` parameter can be `bold`, `italic`, `bolditalic`, or not present. If the `style` parameter is not present, the format of the string is

```
font-pointsize
```

You might describe a bold 16-point `TimesRoman` font in the system properties as

```
TimesRoman-bold-16
```

This mechanism is used for setting specific kinds of fonts. For instance, you might write a Java VT-100 terminal emulator that used the system property `defaultVT100Font` to find out what font to use for displaying text. You could set such a property on the command line:

```
java -DdefaultVT100Font=courier-14 emulators.vt100
```

You can get information about a font using the following methods:

```
public String getFamily()
```

The family of a font is a platform-specific name for the font. It will often be the same as the font's name.

```
public String getName()
public int getSize()
public int getStyle()
```

You can also examine the font's style by checking for bold, italic, and plain individually:

```
public boolean isBold()
public boolean isItalic()
public boolean isPlain()
```

The `getFontList` method in the `Toolkit` class returns an array containing the names of the available fonts:

```
public abstract String[] getFontList()
```

You can use the `getDefaultToolkit` method in the `Toolkit` class to get a reference to the current toolkit:

```
public static synchronized ToolKit getDefaultToolkit()
```

The applet in Listing 22.8 uses `getFontList` to display the available fonts in a variety of styles. Figure 22.12 shows the results of Listing 22.8.

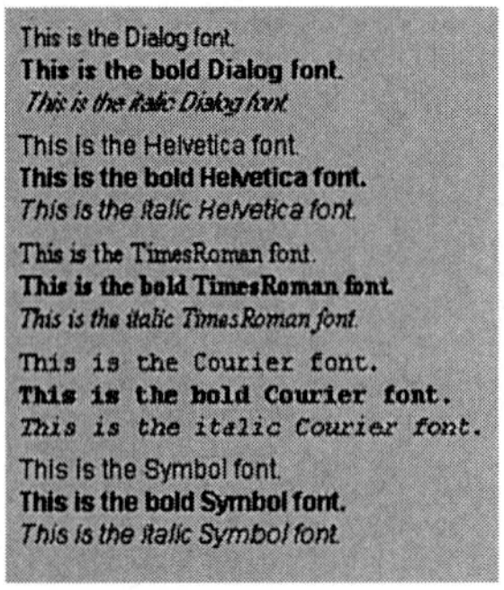

This is the Dialog font.
This is the bold Dialog font.
This is the italic Dialog font.
This is the Helvetica font.
This is the bold Helvetica font.
This is the italic Helvetica font.
This is the TimesRoman font.
This is the bold TimesRoman font.
This is the italic TimesRoman font.
This is the Courier font.
This is the bold Courier font.
This is the italic Courier font.
This is the Symbol font.
This is the bold Symbol font.
This is the italic Symbol font.

FIG. 22.12
Java provides a number of different fonts and font styles.

Listing 22.8 Source Code for *ShowFonts.java*

```
import java.awt.*;
import java.applet.*;

//
// This applet uses the Toolkit class to get a list
// of available fonts, then displays each font in
// PLAIN, BOLD, and ITALIC style.

public class ShowFonts extends Applet
{
   public void paint(Graphics g)
   {
     String fontList[];
```

```
        int i;
        int startY;

    // Get a list of all available fonts
        fontList = getToolkit().getFontList();

        startY = 15;

        for (i=0; i < fontList.length; i++)
        {
    // Set the font to the PLAIN version
           g.setFont(new Font(fontList[i], Font.PLAIN, 12));
    // Draw an example
           g.drawString("This is the "+
             fontList[i]+" font.", 5, startY);
    // Move down a little on the screen
           startY += 15;

    // Set the font to the BOLD version
           g.setFont(new Font(fontList[i], Font.BOLD, 12));
    // Draw an example
           g.drawString("This is the bold "+
             fontList[i]+" font.", 5, startY);
    // Move down a little on the screen
           startY += 15;

    // Set the font to the ITALIC version
           g.setFont(new Font(fontList[i], Font.ITALIC, 12));
    // Draw an example
           g.drawString("This is the italic "+
             fontList[i]+" font.", 5, startY);

    // Move down a little on the screen with some extra spacing
           startY += 20;
        }
      }
    }
```

The *FontMetrics* Class

The `FontMetrics` class lets you examine the various character measurements for a particular font. The `getFontMetrics` method in the `Graphics` class returns an instance of `FontMetrics` for a particular font:

```
public abstract FontMetrics getFontMetrics(Font f)
```

You can also get the font metrics for the current font:

```
public FontMetrics getFontMetrics()
```

An instance of `FontMetrics` is always associated with a particular font. To find out what font an instance of `FontMetrics` refers to, use the `getFont` method:

```
public Font getFont()
```

The `getAscent`, `getDescent`, `getLeading`, and `getHeight` methods return the various height aspects of a font.

```
public int getAscent()
```

returns the typical ascent for characters in the font. It is possible for certain characters in this font to extend beyond this ascent.

```
public int getDescent()
```

returns the typical descent for characters in the font. It is possible for certain characters in this font to extend below this descent.

```
public int getLeading()
```

returns the leading value for this font.

```
public int getHeight()
```

returns the total font height, calculated as ascent + descent + leading.

Because some characters may extend past the normal ascent and descent, you can get the absolute limits with `getMaxAscent` and `getMaxDescent`:

```
public int getMaxAscent()
public int getMaxDescent()
```

The width of a character is usually given in terms of its "advance." The advance is the amount of space the character itself takes up plus the amount of white space that comes after the character. The width of a string as printed on the screen is the sum of the advances of all its characters. The `charWidth` method returns the advance for a particular character:

```
public int charWidth(char ch)
public int charWidth(int ch)
```

You can also get the maximum advance for any character in the font with the `getMaxAdvance` method:

```
public int getMaxAdvance()
```

One of the most common uses of the `FontMetrics` class is to get the width, or advance, of a string of characters. The `stringWidth` method returns the advance of a string:

```
public int stringWidth(String str)
```

You can also get the width for an array of characters or an array of bytes.

```
public int charsWidth(char[] data, int offset, int len)
```

returns the width for `len` characters stored in data starting at position offset.

```
public int bytesWidth(char[] data, int offset, int len)
```

returns the width for `len` bytes stored in data starting at position offset.

The `getWidths` method returns an array of widths for the first 256 characters in a font:

```
public int[] getWidths()
```

Drawing Modes

The `Graphics` class has two different modes for drawing figures: paint and XOR. Paint mode means that when a Figure is drawn, all the points in that Figure overwrite the points that were underneath it. In other words, if you draw a straight line in blue, every point along that line will be blue. You probably just assumed that would happen anyway, but it doesn't have to. There is another drawing mode called XOR, short for exclusive-OR.

The XOR drawing mode dates back several decades. You can visualize how the XOR mode works by forgetting for a moment that you are dealing with colors and imagining that you are drawing in white on a black background. Drawing in XOR involves the combination of the pixel you are trying to draw and the pixel that is on the screen where you want to draw. If you try to draw a white pixel where there is currently a black pixel, you will draw a white pixel. If you try to draw a white pixel where there is already a white pixel, you will instead draw a black pixel.

This may sound strange, but it was once very common to do animation using XOR. To understand why, you should first realize that if you draw a shape in XOR mode and then draw the shape again in XOR mode, you erase whatever you did in the first draw. If you were moving a Figure in XOR mode, you would draw it once; then to move it, you'd draw it again in its old position (thus erasing it); then XOR draws it in its new position. Whenever two objects overlapped, the overlapping areas looked like a negative: black was white and white was black. You probably won't have to use this technique for animation, but at least you have some idea where it came from.

NOTE When using XOR on a color system, think of the current drawing color as the white from the above example and identify another color as the XOR color—or the black. Because there are more than two colors, the XOR mode makes interesting combinations with other colors, but you can still erase any shape by drawing it again.

To change the drawing mode to XOR, just call the `setXORMode` and pass it the color you want to use as the XOR color. The applet in Listing 22.9 shows a simple animation that uses XOR mode to move a ball past a square.

Listing 22.9 Source Code for *BallAnim.java*

```
import java.awt.*;
import java.applet.*;
import java.lang.*;

//
// The BallAnim applet uses XOR mode to draw a rectangle
// and a moving ball. It implements the Runnable interface
// because it is performing animation.

public class BallAnim extends Applet implements Runnable
{
   Thread animThread;
```

continues

Listing 22.9 Continued

```
   int ballX = 0;      // X coordinate of ball
   int ballDirection = 0;   // 0 if going left-to-right, 1 otherwise

// Start is called when the applet first cranks up. It creates a thread for
// doing animation and starts up the thread.

   public void start()
   {
     if (animThread == null)
     {
        animThread = new Thread(this);
        animThread.start();
     }
   }

// Stop is called when the applet is terminated. It halts the animation
// thread and gets rid of it.

   public void stop()
   {
     animThread.stop();
     animThread = null;
   }

// The run method is the main loop of the applet. It moves the ball, then
// sleeps for 1/10th of a second and then moves the ball again.

   public void run()
   {
     Thread.currentThread().setPriority(Thread.NORM_PRIORITY);

     while (true)
     {
        moveBall();
        try {
          Thread.sleep(100);   // sleep 0.1 seconds
        } catch (Exception sleepProblem) {
// This applet ignores any exceptions if it has a problem sleeping.
// Maybe it should take Sominex
        }
     }
   }

   private void moveBall()
   {
// If moving the ball left-to-right, add 1 to the x coord
     if (ballDirection == 0)
     {
        ballX++;

// Make the ball head back the other way once the x coord hits 100

        if (ballX > 100)
        {
```

```
          ballDirection = 1;
          ballX = 100;
        }
      }
      else
      {
// If moving the ball right-to-left, subtract 1 from the x coord
        ballX—;

// Make the ball head back the other way once the x coord hits 0
        if (ballX <= 0)
        {
          ballDirection = 0;
          ballX = 0;
        }
      }

      repaint();
    }

    public void paint(Graphics g)
    {
      g.setXORMode(getBackground());
      g.fillRect(40, 10, 40, 40);
      g.fillOval(ballX, 0, 30, 30);
    }
}
```

Figure 22.13 is a snapshot of the `BallAnim` applet in action. Notice that the ball changes color as it passes over the square. This is due to the way the XOR mode works.

FIG. 22.13
XOR drawing produces an inverse effect when objects collide.

Drawing Images

The `Graphics` class provides a way to draw images with the `drawImage` method:

```
public abstract boolean drawImage(Image img, int x,
➥ int y, ImageObserver observer)

public abstract boolean drawImage(Image img, int x,
➥ int y, int width, int height,
    ImageObserver observer)
public abstract boolean drawImage(Image img, int x,
➥ int y, Color bg, ImageObserver ob)
public abstract boolean drawImage(Image img, int x,
➥ int y, int width, int height, Color
                                bg, ImageObserver ob)
```

```
public abstract boolean drawImage(Image img, int dx1,
➥ int dy1, int dx2, int dy2, int
                                  sx1, int sy1, int sx2, int sy2, Color bg,
                                  ImageObserver ob)
public abstract boolean drawImage(Image img, int dx1, int dy1, int dx2,
➥ int dy2, int
                                  sx1, int sy1, int sx2, int sy2,
➥ ImageObserver ob)
```

The `observer` parameter in the `drawImage` method is an object that is in charge of watching to see when the image is actually ready to draw. If you are calling `drawImage` from within your applet, you can pass this as the observer because the `Applet` class implements the `ImageObserver` interface. The `bg` parameter, if present, indicates the color of the background area of the rectangle into which the image is drawn. This is often used if the image has transparent pixels where the `bg` color indicates the color used for the transparent pixels.

The `drawImage` method can draw a portion of an image and scale it as it draws. The `sx,sy` parameters indicate the top-left and bottom-right corners of the region of the original image that is to be drawn. The `dx,dy` parameters indicate the top-left and bottom-right corners of the region where the image is to be drawn. If the size of the `sx` and `'` rectangles is different, the image is scaled appropriately.

To draw an image, however, you need to get the image first. That is not provided by the `Graphics` class. Fortunately, the `Applet` class provides a `getImage` method that you can use to retrieve images. The applet in Listing 22.10 retrieves an image and draws it. Figure 22.14 shows the output from this applet.

FIG. 22.14
You can draw any GIF or JPEG in a Java applet with the `drawImage` method.

Listing 22.10 Source Code for *DrawImage.java*

```
import java.awt.*;
import java.applet.*;

//
// This applet uses getImage to retrieve an image
// and then draws it using drawImage

public class DrawImage extends Applet
{
   private Image samImage;

   public void init()
```

```
    {
      samImage = getImage(getDocumentBase(), "samantha.gif");
    }

    public void paint(Graphics g)
    {
      g.drawImage(samImage, 0, 0, this);
    }
}
```

The *MediaTracker* Class

One problem you may face when trying to display images is that the images may be coming over a slow network link (for instance, a 14.4Kbps modem). When you begin to draw the image, it may not have arrived completely. You can use a helper class called the `MediaTracker` to determine whether an image is ready for display.

To use the `MediaTracker`, you must first create one for your applet.

```
public MediaTracker(Component comp)
```

creates a new media tracker for a specific AWT component. The `comp` parameter is typically the applet using the media tracker.

For example, to create a media tracker within an applet:

```
MediaTracker myTracker = new MediaTracker(this);    // "this" refers to the applet
```

Next, try to retrieve the image you want to display:

```
Image myImage = getImage("samantha.gif");
```

Now you tell the `MediaTracker` to keep an eye on the image. When you add an image to the `MediaTracker`, you also give it a numeric `id`:

```
public void addImage(Image image, int id)
```

The `id` value can be used for multiple images so when you want to see if an entire group of images is ready for display, you can check it with a single ID. If you intend to scale an image before displaying it, you should specify the intended width and height in the `addImage` call:

```
public synchronized void addImage(Image image, int id, int width, int height)
```

As a simple case, you can just give an image an ID of zero:

```
myTracker.addImage(myImage, 0);    // Track the image, give an id of 0
```

Once you have started tracking an image, you can load it and wait for it to be ready by using the `waitForID` method.

```
public void waitForID(int id)
```

waits for all images with an ID number of `id`.

```
public void waitForID(int id, long ms)
```

waits up to a maximum of ms milliseconds for all images with an ID number of id.

You can also wait for all images using the waitForAll method:

```
public void waitForAll()
```

As with the waitForID method, you can give a maximum number of milliseconds to wait:

```
public void waitForAll(long ms)
```

You may not want to take the time to load an image before starting your applet. You can use the statusID method to initiate a load, but not to wait for it. When you call statusID, you pass the ID you want to status and a Boolean flag to indicate whether it should start loading the image. If you pass it true, it will start loading the image:

```
public int statusID(int id, boolean startLoading)
```

A companion to statusID is statusAll, which checks the status of all images in the MediaTracker:

```
public int statusAll(boolean startLoading)
```

The statusID and statusAll methods return an integer that is made up of the following flags:

- MediaTracker.ABORTED if any of the images have aborted loading
- MediaTracker.COMPLETE if any of the images have finished loading
- MediaTracker.LOADING if any images are still in the process of loading
- MediaTracker.ERRORED if any images encountered an error during loading

You can also use checkID and checkAll to see if an image has been successfully loaded. All the variations of checkAll and checkID return a Boolean value that is true if all the images checked have been loaded.

```
public boolean checkID(int id)
```

returns true if all images with a specific ID have been loaded. It does not start loading the images if they are not loading already.

```
public synchronized boolean checkID(int id, boolean startLoading)
```

returns true if all images with a specific ID have been loaded. If startLoading is true, it will initiate the loading of any images that are not already being loaded.

```
public boolean checkAll()
```

returns true if all images being tracked by this MediaTracker have been loaded, but does not initiate loading if an image is not being loaded.

```
public synchronized boolean checkAll(boolean startLoading)
```

returns true if all images being tracked by this MediaTracker have been loaded. If startLoading is true, it will initiate the loading of any images that have not started loading yet.

The applet in Listing 22.11 uses the `MediaTracker` to watch for an image to complete loading. It will draw text in place of the image until the image is complete; then it will draw the image.

Listing 22.11 Source Code for *ImageTracker.java*

```
import java.awt.*;
import java.applet.*;
import java.lang.*;
//
// The ImageTracker applet uses the media tracker to see if an
// image is ready to be displayed. In order to simulate a
// situation where the image takes a long time to display, this
// applet waits 10 seconds before starting to load the image.
// While the image is not ready, it displays the message:
// "Image goes here" where the image will be displayed.

public class ImageTracker extends Applet implements Runnable
{
   Thread animThread;   // Thread for doing animation
   int waitCount;      // Count number of seconds you have waited
MediaTracker myTracker;   // Tracks the loading of an image
   Image myImage;      // The image you are loading

   public void init()
   {
// Get the image you want to show
     myImage = getImage(getDocumentBase(), "samantha.gif");

// Create a media tracker to track the image
     myTracker = new MediaTracker(this);

// Tell the media tracker to track this image
     myTracker.addImage(myImage, 0);
   }

   public void run()
   {
     Thread.currentThread().setPriority(Thread.NORM_PRIORITY);

     while (true)
     {
// Count how many times you've been through this loop
        waitCount++;

// If you've been through 10 times, call checkID and tell it to start
// loading the image
        if (waitCount == 10)
        {
          myTracker.checkID(0, true);
        }

        repaint();
        try {
```

continues

Listing 22.11 Continued

```
// Sleep 1 second (1000 milliseconds)
            Thread.sleep(1000);   // sleep 1 second
          } catch (Exception sleepProblem) {
          }
      }
   }

   public void paint(Graphics g)
   {
     if (myTracker.checkID(0))
     {
// If the image is ready to display, display it
          g.drawImage(myImage, 0, 0, this);
     }
     else
     {
// Otherwise, draw a message where you will put the image
          g.drawString("Image goes here", 0, 30);
     }
   }

   public void start()
   {
     animThread = new Thread(this);
     animThread.start();
   }

   public void stop()
   {
     animThread.stop();
     animThread = null;
   }

}
```

Graphics Utility Classes

The AWT contains several utility classes that do not perform any drawing, but represent various aspects of geometric figures. The `Polygon` class introduced earlier is one of these. The others are `Point`, `Dimension`, and `Rectangle`.

The *Point* Class

A `Point` represents an x-y point in the Java coordinate space. Several AWT methods return instances of `Point`. You can also create your own instance of point by passing the x and y coordinates to the constructor:

```
public Point(int x, int y)
```

You can also create an uninitialized point, or initialize a point using another `Point` object:

```
public Point()
public Point(Point p)
```

The x and y coordinates of a `Point` object are public instance variables:

```
public int x
public int y
```

This means you may manipulate the x and y values of a `Point` object directly. You can also change the x and y values using either the move or translate methods:

```
public void move(int newX, int newY)
```

sets the point's x and y coordinates to `newX` and `newY`.

```
public void translate(int xChange, yChange)
```

adds `xChange` to the current x coordinate, and `yChange` to the current y.

The *Dimension* Class

A dimension represents a width and height, but not at a fixed point. In other words, two rectangles can have identical dimensions without being located at the same coordinates. The empty constructor creates a dimension with a width and height of 0:

```
public Dimension()
```

You can also specify the width and height in the constructor:

```
public Dimension(int width, int height)
```

If you want to make a copy of an existing `Dimension` object, you can pass that object to the `Dimension` constructor:

```
public Dimension(Dimension oldDimension)
```

The width and height of a dimension are public instance variables, so you can manipulate them directly:

```
public int width
public int height
```

The *Rectangle* Class

A rectangle represents the combination of a `Point` and a `Dimension`. The `Point` represents the upper-left corner of the rectangle, while the `Dimension` represents the rectangle's width and height. You can create an instance of a `Rectangle` by passing a `Point` and a `Dimension` to the constructor:

```
public Rectangle(Point p, Dimension d)
```

Rather than creating a `Point` and a `Dimension`, you can pass the x and y coordinates of the point and the width and height of the dimension:

```
public Rectangle(int x, int y, int width, int height)
```

If you want x and y to be 0, you can create the rectangle using only the width and height:

```
public Rectangle(int width, int height)
```

If you pass only a `Point` to the constructor, the width and height are set to 0:

```
public Rectangle(Point p)
```

Similarly, if you pass only a `Dimension`, the x and y are set to 0:

```
public Rectangle(Dimension d)
```

You can use another Rectangle object as the source for the new rectangle's coordinates and size:

```
public Rectangle(Rectangle r)
```

If you use the empty constructor, the x, y, width, and height are all set to 0:

```
public Rectangle()
```

The x, y, width, and height variables are all public instance variables, so you can manipulate them directly:

```
public int x
public int y
public int width
public int height
```

Like the `Point` class, the `Rectangle` class contains move and translate methods which modify the upper-left corner of the rectangle:

```
public void move(int newX, int newY)
public void translate(int xChange, yChange)
```

The `setSize` and `grow` methods change the rectangle's dimensions in much the same way that `move` and `translate` change the upper-left corner point:

```
public void setSize(int newWidth, int newHeight)
public void grow(int widthChange, int heightChange)
```

The `setBounds` method changes the x, y, width, and height all in one method call:

```
public void setBounds(int newX, int newY, int newWidth, int newHeight)
```

The `contains` method returns `true` if a rectangle contains a specific x, y point:

```
public boolean contains(int x, int y)
```

The `intersection` method returns a rectangle representing the area contained by both the current rectangle and another rectangle:

```
public Rectangle intersection(Rectangle anotherRect)
```

You can determine if two rectangles intersect at all using the `intersects` method:

```
public boolean intersects(Rectangle anotherRect)
```

The union method is similar to the intersection, except that instead of returning the area in common to the two rectangles, it returns the smallest rectangle that is contained by the rectangles:

```
public Rectangle union(Rectangle anotherRect)
```

The add method returns the smallest rectangle containing both the current rectangle and another point:

```
public void add(Point p)
public void add(int x, int y)
```

If the point is contained in the current rectangle, the add method will return the current rectangle. The add method will also take a rectangle as a parameter, in which case it is identical to the union method:

```
public void add(Rectangle anotherRect)
```

The *Color* Class

You may recall learning about the primary colors when you were younger. There are actually two kinds of primary colors. When you are drawing with a crayon, you are actually dealing with pigments. The primary pigments are red, yellow, and blue. You probably know some of the typical mixtures, such as red + yellow = orange, yellow + blue = green, and blue + red = purple. Black is formed by mixing all the pigments together; while white is the absence of pigment.

Dealing with the primary colors of light is slightly different. The primary colors of light are red, green, and blue. Some common combinations are red + green = brown (or yellow, depending on how bright it is), green + blue = cyan (light blue), and red + blue = magenta (purple). For colors of light, the concept of black and white are the reverse of the pigments. Black is formed by the absence of all light, while white is formed by the combination of all the primary colors. In other words, red + blue + green (in equal amounts) = white. Java uses a color model called the RGB color model.

You define a color in the RGB color model by indicating how much red light, green light, and blue light is in the color. You can do this either by using numbers between zero and 255 or by using floating point numbers between 0.0 and 1.0. Table 22.1 indicates the red, green, and blue amounts for some common colors.

Table 22.1 Common Colors and Their RGB Values

Color Name	Red Value	Green Value	Blue Value
White	255	255	255
Light Gray	192	192	192
Gray	128	128	128
Dark Gray	64	64	64

continues

Table 22.1 Continued

Color Name	Red Value	Green Value	Blue Value
Black	0	0	0
Red	255	0	0
Pink	255	175	175
Orange	255	200	0
Yellow	255	255	0
Green	0	255	0
Magenta	255	0	255
Cyan	0	255	255
Blue	0	0	255

You can create a custom color three ways:

```
Color(int red, int green, int blue)
```

creates a color using red, green, and blue values between zero and 255.

```
Color(int rgb)
```

creates a color using red, green, and blue values between 0 and 255, but all combined into a single integer. Bits 16–23 hold the red value, 8–15 hold the green value, and 0–7 hold the blue value. These values are usually written in hexadecimal notation, so you can easily see the color values. For instance, 0x123456 would give a red value of 0x12 (18 decimal), a green value of 34 (52 decimal), and a blue value of 56 (96 decimal). Notice how each color takes exactly 2 digits in hexadecimal.

```
Color(float red, float green, float blue)
```

creates a color using red, green, and blue values between 0.0 and 1.0.

Once you have created a color, you can change the drawing color using the `setColor` method in the `Graphics` class:

```
public abstract void setColor(Color c)
```

For instance, suppose you wanted to draw in pink. A nice value for pink is 255 red, 192 green, and 192 blue. The following paint method sets the color to pink and draws a circle:

```
public void paint(Graphics g)
{
   Color pinkColor = new Color(255, 192, 192);
   g.setColor(pinkColor);
   g.drawOval(5, 5, 50, 50);
}
```

You don't always have to create colors manually. The `Color` class provides a number of predefined colors:

- `Color.white`
- `Color.lightGray`
- `Color.gray`
- `Color.darkGray`
- `Color.black`
- `Color.red`
- `Color.pink`
- `Color.orange`
- `Color.yellow`
- `Color.green`
- `Color.magenta`
- `Color.cyan`
- `Color.blue`

Given a color, you can find out its red, green, and blue values by using the `getRed`, `getGreen`, and `getBlue` methods:

```
public int getRed()

public int getGreen()

public int getBlue()
```

The following code fragment creates a color and then extracts the red, green, and blue values from it:

```
int redAmount, greenAmount, blueAmount;
Color someColor = new Color(0x345678);    // red=0x34, green = 0x56, blue = 0x78

redAmount = someColor.getRed();    // redAmount now equals 0x34
greenAmount = someColor.getGreen();    // greenAmount now equals 0x56
blueAmount = someColor.getBlue();    // blueAmount now equals 0x78
```

You can darken or lighten a color using the `darker` and `brighter` methods:

```
public Color darker()
public Color brighter()
```

These methods return a new `Color` instance that contains the darker or lighter version of the original color. The original color is left untouched.

Clipping

Clipping is a technique in graphics systems that prevents one area from drawing over another. Basically, you draw in a rectangular area, and everything you try to draw outside the area gets "clipped off." Normally, your applet is clipped at the edges. In other words, you cannot draw beyond the bounds of the applet window. You cannot increase the clipping area; that is, you cannot draw outside the applet window, but you can further limit where you can draw inside the applet window. To set the boundaries of your clipping area, use the `clipRect` method in the `Graphics` class:

```
public abstract void clipRect(int x, int y, int width, int height)
```

You can query the current clipping area of a Graphics object with the `getClipBounds` method:

```
public abstract Rectangle getClipBounds()
```

The applet in Listing 22.12 reduces its drawing area to a rectangle whose upper-left corner is at (10, 10) and is 60 pixels wide and 40 pixels high, and then tries to draw a circle. Figure 22.15 shows the output from this applet.

FIG. 22.15 The `clipRect` method reduces the drawing area and cuts off anything that extends outside it.

Listing 22.12 Source Code for *Clipper.java*

```
import java.applet.*;
import java.awt.*;

//
// This applet demonstrates the clipRect method by setting
// up a clipping area and trying to draw a circle that partially
// extends outside the clipping area.
// I want you to go out there and win just one for the Clipper...

public class Clipper extends Applet
{
   public void paint(Graphics g)
   {
// Set up a clipping region
      g.clipRect(10, 10, 60, 40);

// Draw a circle
      g.fillOval(5, 5, 50, 50);
   }
}
```

The `clipRect` method will only reduce the current clipping region. Prior to Java 1.1, there was no way to expand the clipping region once you reduced it. Java 1.1 adds the `setClip` method that can either expand or reduce the clipping area:

```
public abstract void setClip(int x, int y, int width, int height)
```

In preparation for the possibility of non-rectangular clipping areas, Sun has added a `Shape` interface and a method to use a `Shape` object as a clipping region. The `Shape` interface currently has only one method:

```
public abstract Rectangle getBounds()
```

You can set the clipping region with any object that implements the `Shape` interface using this variation of `setClip`:

```
public abstract void setClip(Shape region)
```

Since the clipping region may one day be non-rectangular, the `getClipBounds` method will not be sufficient for retrieving the clipping region. The `getClip` method returns the current clipping region as a `Shape` object:

```
public abstract Shape getClip()
```

Although the `Shape` interface might allow you to create non-rectangular clipping regions, you cannot do it yet. The only method defined in the `Shape` interface returns a rectangular area. The `Shape` interface will need to be expanded to support non-rectangular regions.

Animation Techniques

You may have noticed a lot of screen flicker when you ran the `ShapeManipulator` applet. It was intentionally written to not eliminate any flicker so you could see just how bad flicker can be. What causes this flicker? One major cause is that the shape is redrawn on the screen right in front of you. The constant redrawing catches your eye and makes things appear to flicker. A common solution to this problem is a technique called double-buffering.

The idea behind double-buffering is that you create an offscreen image, and do all your drawing to that offscreen image. Once you are finished drawing, you copy the offscreen image to your drawing area in one quick call so the drawing area updates immediately.

The other major cause of flicker is the `update` method. The `default update` method for an applet clears the drawing area, then calls your `paint` method. You can eliminate the flicker caused by the screen clearing by overriding `update` to simply call the `paint` method:

```
public void update(Graphics g)
{
   paint(g);
}
```

CAUTION

There is a danger with changing update this way. Your applet must be aware that the screen has not been cleared. If you are using the double-buffering technique, this should not be a problem because you are replacing the entire drawing area with your offscreen image anyway.

The `ShapeManipulator` applet can be modified easily to support double-buffering and eliminate the screen-clear. In the declarations at the top of the class, you add an Image that will be the offscreen drawing area:

```
private Image offScreenImage;
```

Next, you add a line to the `init` method to initialize the offscreen image:

```
offScreenImage = createImage(size().width, size().height);
```

Finally, you create an `update` method that does not clear the real drawing area, but makes your `paint` method draw to the offscreen area and then copies the offscreen area to the screen (see Listing 22.13).

Listing 22.13 An Update Method to Support Double-Buffering

```
public void update(Graphics g)
{
// This update method helps reduce flicker by supporting off-screen drawing
// and by not clearing the drawing area first. It enables you to leave
// the original paint method alone.

// Get the graphics context for the off-screen image
    Graphics offScreenGraphics = offScreenImage.getGraphics();

// Now, go ahead and clear the off-screen image. It is O.K. to clear the
// off-screen image, because it is not being displayed on the screen.
// This way, your paint method can still expect a clear area, but the
// screen won't flicker because of it.

    offScreenGraphics.setColor(getBackground());

// You've set the drawing color to the applet's background color, now
// fill the entire area with that color (i.e. clear it)
    offScreenGraphics.fillRect(0, 0, size().width,
        size().height);

// Now, because the paint method probably doesn't set its drawing color,
// set the drawing color back to what was in the original graphics context.
    offScreenGraphics.setColor(g.getColor());

// Call the original paint method
    paint(offScreenGraphics);

// Now, copy the off-screen image to the screen
    g.drawImage(offScreenImage, 0, 0, this);
}
```

Printing

The ability to send information to a printer was one of the most glaring omissions in the 1.0 release of Java. Fortunately, Java 1.1 addresses that problem with the `PrintJob` class.

The first thing you need to do in order to print something is to create an instance of a `PrintJob` object. You can do this with the `getPrintJob` method in `java.awt.Toolkit`:

```
public abstract PrintJob getPrintJob(Frame parent, String jobname,
     Properties props)
```

As you can see, a print job must be associated with a `Frame` object. If you are printing from an applet, you must first create a `Frame` object before calling `getPrintJob`. Once you have a `PrintJob` object, you print individual pages by calling `getGraphics` in the `PrintJob` object, which creates a `Graphics` object that you can then draw on:

```
public abstract Graphics getGraphics()
```

Every new instance of `Graphics` represents a separate print page. Once you have printed all the pages you want, you call the end method in `PrintJob` to complete the job:

```
public abstract void end()
```

The `Graphics` object returned by `getGraphics` is identical to the `Graphics` object passed to your `paint` method. You can use all the drawing methods normally available to your `paint` method. In fact, you can print an image of your current screen by manually calling your `paint` method with the `Graphics` object returned by `getGraphics`. Once you finish drawing on a `Graphics` object, you invoke its `dispose` method to complete the page.

When printing, you often want to know the resolution of the page, or how many pixels per inch are on the page. The `getResolution` method in a `PrintJob` object returns this information:

```
public abstract int getPageResolution()
```

The `getPageDimension` method returns the page width and height in pixels:

```
public abstract Dimension getPageDimension()
```

Some systems and some printers print the last page first. You can find out if you will be printing in last-page-first order by calling `lastPageFirst`:

```
public abstract boolean lastPageFirst()
```

Listing 22.14 shows the printing equivalent of the famous "Hello World" program.

Listing 22.14 Source Code for *PrintHelloWorld.java*

```
import java.awt.*;
import java.applet.*;

public class PrintHelloWorld extends Applet
{
     public void init()
     {

// First create a frame to be associated with the print job
          Frame myFrame = new Frame();
```

continues

Listing 22.14 Continued

```
// Start a new print job
        PrintJob job = Toolkit.getPrintJob(myFrame, "Hello", NULL);

// Get a graphics object for drawing
        Graphics g = job.getGraphics();

// Print the famous message to the graphics object
        g.drawString("Hello World!", 50, 100);

// Complete the printing of this page by disposing of the graphics object
        g.dispose();

// Complete the print job
        job.end();
    }
}
```

The drawing functions provided by the Graphics object are fairly primitive by modern standards. These functions will eventually be superseded by the Java 2D API, which will provide a much more robust drawing model. ●

CHAPTER 23

JFC—Java Foundation Classes

In this chapter

Java Foundation Classes

The first questions you're probably asking are "Why do I even need a foundation class? What good is it going to do me?"

To understand this, you need to take a brief look at the history of Java. When Java was first created, user interfaces were developed using the AWT classes you learned about in Chapter 19, "`java.awt`: Components," and Chapter 20, "Exceptions and Events in Depth." However, the AWT design has many limitations.

To understand why, let's go back a bit and look at the decisions the original developers of Java faced. They needed a way to create screen components such as buttons on many different kinds of computers. It's reasonably easy to make two computers add one and one and get both of them to come up with two, but to get two computers to place two buttons on the screen in the same place with the same size and shape requires a fair amount of work.

Why is this the case? Well, graphics are a funny thing. If you're a Windows user, you're familiar with screen configurations such as 640×480 and 800×600. But if you're on a Macintosh, you're just as likely to be familiar with 1180×900, or on a Solaris machine 1600×1280. Now, this is just scratching the surface, but consider how you would create a button on a Macintosh and have it look the same on a Windows machine? Add to that the difference in how buttons look on various platforms. Look at Netscape 4.0 for Macintosh in Figure 23.1 and Netscape 4.0 for PC in Figure 23.2.

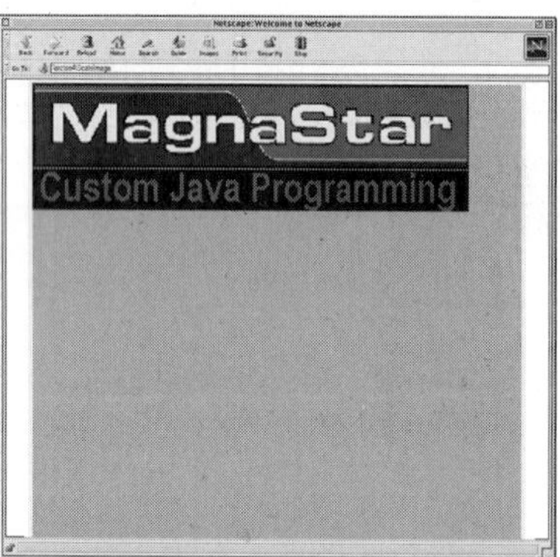

FIG. 23.1
Netscape 4.0 on a Macintosh.

If you look at the buttons on the various machines, they actually appear different. Why is this? Well, it's a concept called *look and feel*. The people who write software for the Macintosh are used to buttons looking a certain way, and Windows users are used to buttons looking a different way.

To reconcile this confusion, the designers of Java decided to use a design pattern that would give Java programmers access to the button but would use the system's own buttons for the look and feel. That means that when you put a java.awt.Button component on your screen, you're actually using a native button for the look and feel. So, on a Windows machine, a Windows button is created and on a Macintosh, a Macintosh button is created. Seems to make sense, right?

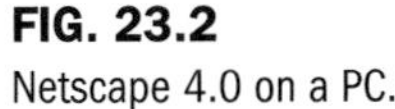

FIG. 23.2
Netscape 4.0 on a PC.

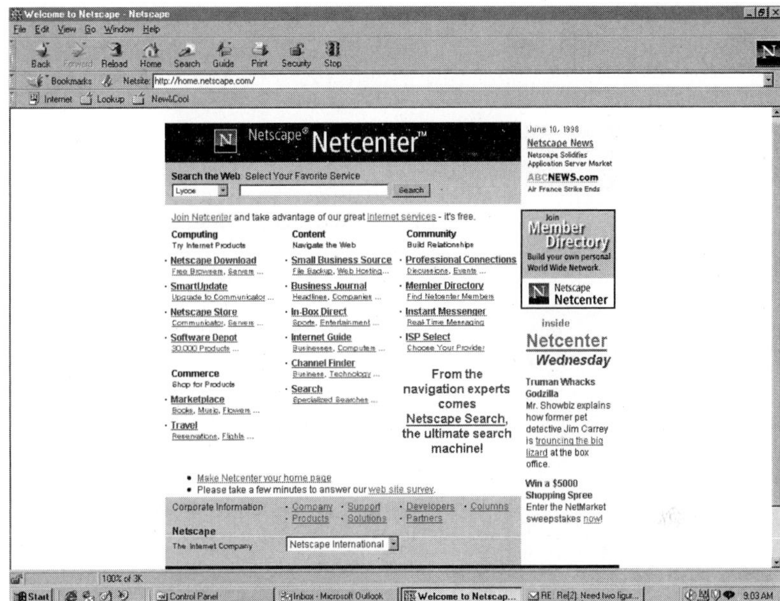

Well, unfortunately it's not quite that easy, and before long Java's implementation began to differ greatly from one computer system to another.

You see, it's also very difficult to create a truly abstract system and expect it to work the same on all systems. For instance, not all systems report mouse movements the same, or at the same time. Not all systems display characters the same, and from platform to platform individual characteristics of things such as TextAreas change. Because of all these variations, it's very difficult to actually write an AWT system for one platform that will look and behave the same as an AWT system on another.

Because not all AWT systems are alike, people like you and me who are creating applications are forced to run a lot of tests on a lot of different types of computers in order to truly achieve Sun's promise of Write Once Run Anywhere.

Unfortunately, all that testing can completely eat away all the shorter development time benefits of Java. So, several developers decided to build a different kind of system. The new systems relied on only one fairly common component—a Container (a parent of Panel). Because a Container is fairly uniform for all systems, you can paint (or draw) on one without encountering platform dependencies. Microsoft's solution of this form was AFC (Application Foundation Classes), Netscape's was IFC (Internet Foundation Classes), and there were a half dozen independent solutions. Each of these solutions had one very large limiting factor however: size. To create an entirely new windowing system takes up just too much size. 600k might not be too bad if it were on your hard drive, but it's a nasty bump if you have to download it over the Internet. In addition, without a standards body supporting one foundation class or another, many developers were left wondering which solution to adapt. So, in the spring of 1997, Sun teamed up with Netscape to offer JFC. Unfortunately, as of right now, Microsoft has decided not to adopt JFC in favor of its own WFC solution, but hopefully, in time, they too will adopt JFC.

JFC: A First Look

The JFC system is based on two primary things: first, the Container and Frame components from AWT and second, the JDK 1.1 event model. Unfortunately, because of the latter, IFC users will find the switch to JFC much more difficult than users of AWT.

Setting Up for JFC

JFC is part of the core of JDK 1.2, but it can be added to JDK 1.1 implementations by downloading the JFC package from Sun at this address:

```
http://www.javasoft.com/products/jfc/
```

After you download the JFC API, you need to unzip the file. Inside you will find several .jar files. In addition to the swing.jar file that contains the core swing classes, you will also find several look and feel–specific .jar files such as windows.jar and jlf.jar.

To make it easier to use all these .jar files, Sun has added another environment variable. The swing_home variable needs to be set to point to the directory where you have installed the swing package. For instance, on a Windows machine, you might type the following:

```
set swing_home=c:\swing
```

HelloWorld

As we have done throughout this book, we will start our look at JFC by creating the simplest application possible. In Listing 23.1, you will find the source for HelloWorldJFC.java. After you compile and run HelloWorldJFC, you should see the results in Figure 23.3.

Listing 23.1 ***HelloWorldJFC.java*—Hello World Written Using JFC**

```
import java.awt.*;
import java.awt.event.*;
import javax.swing.*;

public class HelloWorldJFC extends JComponent {
     static JFrame myFrame;


     public void paint(Graphics g){
           g.setColor(Color.black);
           g.drawString ("HelloWorld",20,15);
     }
```

```
        public static void main(String args[]){
            myFrame = new JFrame("Hello World!");
            HelloWorldJFC jt = new HelloWorldJFC();
            myFrame.getContentPane().add("Center",jt);
            myFrame.setSize(100,50);
            myFrame.setVisible(true);
        }
}
```

FIG. 23.3 The HelloWorldJFC application.

Compiling HelloWorldJFC

You can compile HelloWorldJFC just like you compile any other Java program, so long as swing.jar is included in your classpath. If you use an IDE and not the JDK, you need to add swing.jar to the systems list of classes. For some IDEs, you might have to unjar the file in order to compile with it.

Running HelloWorldJFC

At first guess, you might think that running HelloWorldJFC is identical to running any other Java program, so long as swing.jar was in your class path. Simply type the following:

```
java HelloWorldJFC
```

However, in order for this to work, you must perform one additional step: Include the look and feel .jar file for your platform. Later, in Chapter 24, "Advanced JFC," we talk more about JFC's pluggable look and feel, but for now you need to know that you must include an additional .jar file in your classpath. Under Windows, this means that windows.jar must be included because on most UNIX machines, motif.jar will do the trick—and on Macintosh, include mac.jar. Alternatively, you can use the SwingAll.jar file. This file contains all the standard look-and-feels. If you fail to include the look-and-feel .jar file, you will get an error like the following:

```
java.lang.Error: can't load javax.swing.windows.WindowsLookAndFeel
        at javax.swing.UIManager.
        ➥initializeDefaultLookAndFeel(UIManager.java:318)
        at javax.swing.UIManager.initialize(UIManager.java:386)
        at javax.swing.UIManager.maybeInitialize(UIManager.java:395)
        at javax.swing.UIManager.getDefaults(UIManager.java:146)
        at javax.swing.UIManager.getColor(UIManager.java:155)
        at javax.swing.JPanel.<init>(JPanel.java:50)
        at javax.swing.JPanel.<init>(JPanel.java:83)
        at javax.swing.JRootPane.createGlassPane(JRootPane.java:145)
        at javax.swing.JRootPane.<init>(JRootPane.java:112)
        at javax.swing.JFrame.createRootPane(JFrame.java:105)
        at javax.swing.JFrame.frameInit(JFrame.java:99)
        at javax.swing.JFrame.<init>(JFrame.java:93)
        at HelloWorldJFC.main(HelloWorldJFC.java:41)
```

If you do see this, you have failed to add the Windows look and feel (or whichever one you're having problems with) to the classpath. Because the individual look-and-feels are packaged in separate JAR files, all you need to do is add the required JAR file to your classpath.

Understanding HelloWorldJFC

As you can see, HelloWorldJFC contains really only two methods: `paint()` and `main()`. If you look at the `paint()` method, it looks nearly identical to the one in Chapter 15, "Advanced Applet Code."

The `main()` method, however, contains a few different functions.

The frame created is not a java.awt.Frame as it would be in an AWT application, but instead is a JFrame. JFrame differs from Frame in one major way: It provides several layered panes instead of one flat panel.

Pane Layering

JFC uses multiple layers upon which it can layer components. This layering enables you to overlap components and paint on top of components. Because the layering model is built into the JFC system, unlike AWT, you can do this without getting inconsistent results. For instance, if you want to put a pop-up ToolTip on a button, and you want that ToolTip to appear directly below that button, even if something else is there, you can simply paint on the glass pane. Under AWT, this is not possible because when a button (or any component) occupies a place on the screen, it generally does not allow you to paint over it.

JFC includes a number of view layers; Figure 23.4 shows the panel views and their order.

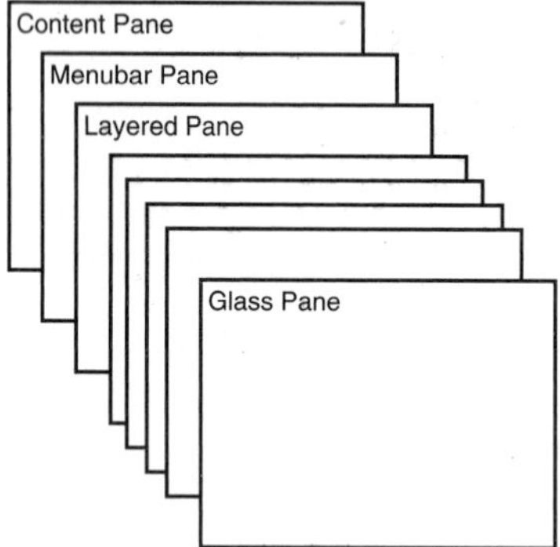

FIG. 23.4
JFC layers several panes on top of one another.

All this means is that in our HelloWorld example's `main` method, instead of simply adding the panel, we add the panel to the content pane:

```
myFrame.getContentPane().add("Center",jt);
```

Generally speaking, most of the time when you add a component to any JFC Container, you will add it to the content pane. However, if the component has a specific need to overlay other components, you need to add it to either the layered pane or the glass pane.

Improving HelloWorld

There are two things that you might have noticed about our original version of HelloWorld that need to be improved. First, if you actually ran the program, you have noticed that the program does not actually exit when you press the Close Window button (under Windows this is the X button in the upper-right corner). Just like with standard AWT, you need to create a WindowAdapter that listens for the `windowClosing` event and exits the program.

The second thing for you to be concerned with is that instead of using a component (Label) to display the "Hello World" text, the program currently draws the string directly to the screen in the `paint()` method. Although this is useful from the standpoint of an analogy with the applet's HelloWorld, it's not the best practice. In Listing 23.2, you find the code for an improved HelloWorldJFC application. HelloWorldJFC2 displays like Figure 23.5 when you run it.

Listing 23.2 *HelloWorldJFC2.java*—Hello World Improved

```
import java.awt.*;
import java.awt.event.*;
import javax.swing.*;

public class HelloWorldJFC2 extends JPanel {
  static JFrame myFrame;
  public HelloWorldJFC2(){
    JLabel label = new JLabel ("Hello World!");
    add(label);
  }

  public static void main(String args[]){
    myFrame = new JFrame("Hello World!");
    HelloWorldJFC2 hello = new HelloWorldJFC2();
    myFrame.getContentPane().add("Center",hello);
    myFrame.setSize(200,100);
    myFrame.addWindowListener(new WindowAdapter() {
      public void windowClosing(WindowEvent e) {System.exit(0);}
      });
    myFrame.setVisible(true);
  }
}
```

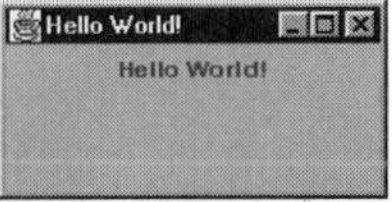

FIG. 23.5
The HelloWorldJFC2 application.

Like AWT Container classes, the HelloWorldJFC2 adds components using the `add()` method. In this case, the component being added in the constructor is a JLabel.

JLabel

The JLabel in HelloWorldJFC2's constructor is used to display the "Hello World!" text. As it is used in Listing 23.2, JLabel does not provide any additional functionality over its AWT counterpart. However, JLabel does have a couple of differences between it and Label.

First, JLabel, like most JFC components, can support not only text but also images (or both). So, although we did not use it in the HelloWorld example, we could have also added an icon that would have been displayed along with the text. There are two ways to do this:

- Use one of the constructors that accommodates the icon.
- Add the icon using the `setIcon()` method.

Adding Icons

An icon is a graphical representation in JFC. The icon can be an image but might also be a drawing created programmatically. To add an icon to almost any component in the JFC set, you can use one of the following two techniques:

▶ **See** Chapter 24: "Advanced JFC," to learn more about creating an icon programatically. **p. 499**

- Specify the icon in the constructor.
- Set the icon later using the `setIcon()` method.

In the case of our HelloWorldJFC2 example, if we had an image called feet.gif and wanted to use it alongside the "Hello World!" text, we could have added it using the ImageIcon class. To do so, modify the constructor in Listing 23.2 like this:

```
public HelloWorldJFC2(){
    Icon icon = new ImageIcon ("feet.gif");
    JLabel label = new JLabel ("Hello World!", icon, SwingConstants.RIGHT);
    add(label);
}
```

Figure 23.6 shows the results of this change.

FIG. 23.6
Labels can have both icons and text.

NOTE Note that in addition to specifying the label text and the icon, JLabel also needs to know how to align the two items. Later in Listing 23.7, we will go into more depth on how to use this alignment.

Alternatively, if you decide to specify the icon after creating the icon, you can set the icon using the `setIcon` method, in which case you can modify the constructor call to look like this:

```
public HelloWorldJFC2(){
    Icon icon = new ImageIcon ("feet.gif");
    JLabel label = new JLabel ("Hello);
    label.setIcon(icon);
    add(label);
}
```


Closing the Window

HelloWorldJFC2 includes the additional code necessary to have the window close. Like AWT's Frame class, the JFrame class can generate events when things happen to the window, such as the window being closed, activated, iconified, or opened. These events can be sent to a WindowListener if one is registered with the frame.

In HelloWorldJFC2's `main()` method, you can see the following code, which adds a nested class, which is created on the spot. In this case, when the window Close button is pressed, we simply exit the application.

```
myFrame.addWindowListener(new WindowAdapter() {
    public void windowClosing(WindowEvent e) {
        System.exit(0);
    }
});
```

Adding Buttons with JFC

Like JLabel, buttons are among the components that JFC has improved. JFC's buttons (JButton) have the added capability to know their accelerator key, programmatically simulate clicking, use both strings and icons, and have many more states than their AWT counterparts.

Listing 23.3 shows an example with two JButtons (see Figure 23.7).

Listing 23.3 *ButtonExample.java*—Two Buttons in JFC

```
import java.awt.*;
import java.awt.event.*;
import javax.swing.*;

public class ButtonExample extends JPanel {
  static JFrame myFrame;
  JLabel label;

  public ButtonExample(){
    label = new JLabel ("Hello World!");
    JButton hello = new JButton("Hello");
    hello.setMnemonic('h');
    hello.addActionListener(new ActionListener(){
      public void actionPerformed(ActionEvent ae){
```

continues

Listing 23.3 Continued

```
        System.out.println("Hello World!");
        label.setText("Hello World!");
        }
        });
      JButton bye = new JButton("Bye");
      bye.setMnemonic('b');
      bye.addActionListener(new ActionListener(){
        public void actionPerformed(ActionEvent ae){
        System.out.println("Bye World!");
        label.setText("Good Bye World!");
        }
        });
      add(bye);
      add(hello);
      add(label);
    }

    public static void main(String args[]){
      myFrame = new JFrame("Button Example");
      ButtonExample jt = new ButtonExample();
      myFrame.getContentPane().add("Center",jt);
      myFrame.setSize(300,70);
      myFrame.addWindowListener(new WindowAdapter() {
        public void windowClosing(WindowEvent e) {System.exit(0);}
        });
      myFrame.setVisible(true);
    }
  }
```

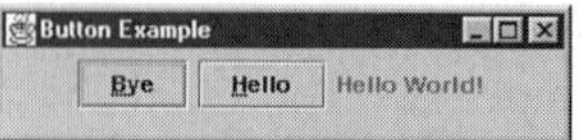

FIG. 23.7
ButtonExample, running with the Java L&F.

Understanding ButtonExample

ButtonExample's `main` method is nearly identical to the ones in Listings 23.1 and 23.2. There should not be any surprises there.

The interesting code in this example is in the constructor for ButtonExample. In this case, we have added two buttons and a label that is changed based on which button is pressed.

With the HelloWorldJFC2 example in Listing 23.2, you already saw how the JLabel works, so for this example, we will look just at one of the two buttons: the Hello button. The code to creating the JButton looks very similar to the code creating a java.awt.Button.

```
JButton hello = new JButton("Hello");
```

Setting a Shortcut Key or Mnemonic

The next line of code in HelloWorldJFC 2 establishes the mnemonic for the button. The mnemonic is the equivalent of the shortcut key. This means that the user of this application can use his mouse to press the Hello button, or he can press a combination of keys to press the button. In this case, that combination is Alt-H. All buttons can set their mnemonic using the `setMnemonic()` method:

```
hello.setMnemonic('h');
```


Listening for Actions from the Button

When a button is pressed, or its mnemonic is keyed, the button can produce an ActionEvent. To "hear" the action, add an ActionListener to the button and create an inner class that performs the actions you want to occur when the button is pressed.

```
hello.addActionListener(new ActionListener(){
    public void actionPerformed(ActionEvent ae){
        System.out.println("Hello World!");
        label.setText("Hello World!");
    }
});
```

Adding ToolTips and Icons

One of the advantages of having a layered view is that it affords JFC enhancements such as ToolTips. ToolTips can be added to any JComponent, JButtons included.

The label of a button is usually an abbreviation for what the button will actually do. This is the case with the ButtonExample in Listing 23.3.

Also, like JLabel, JButtons can use icons as part of its label, so in Listing 23.4, you see the ButtonExample modified to add the ToolTip to the buttons, and the feet.gif has been added to the Hello button (see Figure 23.8).

Listing 23.4 ***TipButtons.java*—Adding ToolTips to JFC Buttons**

```
import java.awt.*;
import java.awt.event.*;
import javax.swing.*;

public class TipButtons extends JPanel {
  static JFrame myFrame;
  protected JLabel label;

  public TipButtons(){
    label = new JLabel ("Hello World!");
    label.setOpaque(true);
```

continues

Listing 23.4 Continued

```
    JButton hello = new JButton("Hello");
    hello.setMnemonic('h');
    hello.addActionListener(new ActionListener(){
      public void actionPerformed(ActionEvent ae){
      label.setText("Hello World!");
      }
      });
    //Set the ToolTip for the hello button
    hello.setToolTipText("Select to change label to Hello World");

    JButton bye = new JButton("Bye");
    bye.setMnemonic('b');
    bye.addActionListener(new ActionListener(){
      public void actionPerformed(ActionEvent ae){
      label.setText("Good Bye World!");
      }
      });
    //Set the ToolTip for the bye button
    bye.setToolTipText("Select to change label to Good Bye World");

    add(bye);
    add(hello);
    add(label);
  }

  public static void main(String args[]){
    myFrame = new JFrame("Tooltiped Buttons");
    TipButtons tb = new TipButtons();
    myFrame.getContentPane().add("Center",tb);
    myFrame.setSize(300,75);
    myFrame.addWindowListener(new WindowAdapter() {
      public void windowClosing(WindowEvent e) {System.exit(0);}
      });
    myFrame.setVisible(true);
  }
}
```

FIG. 23.8
When you mouse over a button that has a ToolTip set, the text for the tip shows up to help the user.

Using Pop-Up Menus

Like ToolTips, another one of the advantages of JFC's design is an advanced pop-up menu capability. Often it's useful to enable the user to click with the mouse and pop up an extra menu, as shown in Figure 23.9. Listing 23.5 shows just such an example.

Listing 23.5 *PopupExample.java*—Adding Pop-Up Menus to a JFC Panel

```
import java.awt.*;
import java.awt.event.*;
import javax.swing.*;

public class PopupExample extends JPanel {
  static JFrame myFrame;
  protected JLabel label;
  JPopupMenu popup;

  public PopupExample(){
    label = new JLabel ("Hello World!");
    label.setOpaque(true);
    add(label);

    popup = new JPopupMenu();

    //create the first menu item
    JMenuItem menuItem1 = new JMenuItem("Hello World!");
    menuItem1.addActionListener(new ActionListener(){
      public void actionPerformed(ActionEvent ae){
      label.setText("Hello World!");
      }
      });

    //create the second menu item
    JMenuItem menuItem2 = new JMenuItem("Good Bye World!");
    menuItem2.addActionListener(new ActionListener(){
      public void actionPerformed(ActionEvent ae){
      label.setText("Good Bye World!");
      }
      });
    //add the menu items to the popup menu
    popup.add(menuItem1);
    popup.add(menuItem2);

    addMouseListener(new MouseAdapter(){
      public void mouseReleased(MouseEvent evt){
                //Pop up the menu at the location where the mouse was pressed
                if (evt.isPopupTrigger()){
                  popup.show(evt.getComponent(),evt.getX(),evt.getY());
        }
      }
    });
  }


  public static void main(String args[]){
    myFrame = new JFrame("Popup Example");
    PopupExample example = new PopupExample();
    myFrame.getContentPane().add("Center",example);
    myFrame.setSize(300,75);
    myFrame.addWindowListener(new WindowAdapter() {
```

continues

Listing 23.5 Continued

```
        public void windowClosing(WindowEvent e) {System.exit(0);}
        });
      myFrame.setVisible(true);
    }
  }
```

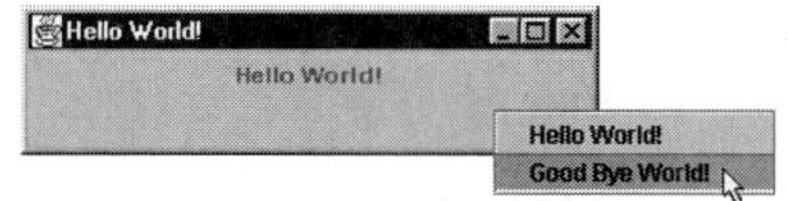

FIG. 23.9 PopupMenu—If you press the right mouse button, the pop-up appears.

Understanding PopupExample

There are three primary steps to creating and showing a pop-up menu under JFC. The first step is to create the pop-up menu itself.

```
popup = new JPopupMenu();
```

The next step is creating the menu items that will be on the pop-up. These menu items are the same items that you add to a menu on a menu bar. In the case of PopupExample, you add two menu items. Each of these menu items has an ActionListener added and created for it.

```
JMenuItem menuItem1 = new JMenuItem("Hello World!");
menuItem1.addActionListener(new ActionListener(){
    public void actionPerformed(ActionEvent ae){
        label.setText("Hello World!");
    }
});
```

NOTE JMenuItem is a JComponent (by virtue of the fact that it extends from JComponent), so like all other JComponents, JMenuItem can have ToolTips added. So, if you want, you can add a ToolTip to each of the items as well.

The final step is to actually pop up the menu. In this case, we want to pop up the menu whenever the pop-up trigger button is pressed (the right mouse button on most platforms). The `processMouseEvent()` method handles the work of popping up the menu.

```
addMouseListener(new MouseAdapter(){
    public void mouseReleased(MouseEvent evt){
    //Popup the menu at the location where the mouse was pressed
        if (evt.isPopupTrigger()){
            popup.show(evt.getComponent(),evt.getX(),evt.getY());
        }
    }
});
```

Borders

One of the unique characteristics that JFC has added to all components is the capability to have an adjustable border. What's unique about this is that any object can have an arbitrary border placed on it. So if you want a button to have a flower border or a label to have an etched border, you can do so.

Included with the JFC set, you will find a package called com.java.swing.border (java.swing.border in the 1.2 core). This package contains a number of different borders, each of which can be applied to a wide variety of swing components.

Listing 23.6 shows the two buttons from Listing 23.3 with different borders (see Figure 23.10).

Listing 23.6 ***BorderedButtons.java*—Example with Bordered Components**

```
import java.awt.*;
import java.awt.event.*;
import javax.swing.*;
import javax.swing.border.*;

public class BorderedButtons extends JPanel {
  static JFrame myFrame;
  protected JLabel label;
  JPopupMenu pm;

  public BorderedButtons(){
    label = new JLabel ("Hello World!");
    label.setBorder(new EtchedBorder());

    JButton hello = new JButton("Hello");
    hello.addActionListener(new ActionListener(){
      public void actionPerformed(ActionEvent ae){
      label.setText("Hello World!");
      }
    });

    //set the border to an image.  Note: the image will be tiled.
    Icon icon = new ImageIcon ("feet.gif");
    hello.setBorder(new MatteBorder(10, 10, 10, 10, icon));

    JButton bye = new JButton("Bye");
    bye.addActionListener(new ActionListener(){
      public void actionPerformed(ActionEvent ae){
      label.setText("Good Bye World!");
      }
    });
    bye.setBackground (SystemColor.control);
    bye.setBorder(new LineBorder(Color.green));

    add(bye);
    add(hello);
    add(label);
```

continues

Listing 23.6 Continued

```
    }

    public static void main(String args[]){
      myFrame = new JFrame("Border Example");
      BorderedButtons jt = new BorderedButtons();
      myFrame.getContentPane().add("Center",jt);
      myFrame.setSize(300,75);
      myFrame.addWindowListener(new WindowAdapter() {
        public void windowClosing(WindowEvent e) {System.exit(0);}
        });
      myFrame.setVisible(true);
    }
  }
```

FIG. 23.10 Buttons and labels with borders.

Understanding BorderedButtons

As you can see, Listing 23.6 is very similar to the other examples in this chapter. The key detail is that the label and each of the buttons have their own border. Each of them has a different kind of border attached to it. In the case of the label, the etched border was used.

```
label.setBorder(new EtchedBorder());
```

Because JComponent sports the `setBorder()` method, any JComponent can have its border set using the `setBorder()` method.

More Borders

Beyond being able to set specific borders, some borders can even be cascaded. As you saw in the BorderedButton example in Figure 23.6, the `hello` button uses the MatteBorder.

```
hello.setBorder(new MatteBorder(10, 10, 10, 10, icon));
```

The MatteBorder takes the icon image and tiles it for the border. The problem, however, is that the MatteBorder runs a bit too close to the text for most people.

You can fix this problem by using the CompoundBorder. The CompoundBorder can cascade two borders together, like this:

```
hello.setBorder(new CompoundBorder(new MatteBorder
➥(10, 10, 10, 10, icon),new EmptyBorder(10,10,10,10)));
```

In this case, the border set on the button is a CompoundBorder. The CompoundBorder is composed of two separate borders, one inside the other. The EmptyBorder is basically just a blank space. Applying this new type of border to the buttons in Listing 23.6 gives more room, as shown in Figure 23.11.

FIG. 23.11 The BorderButtons with more room around the border.

Some of the other borders also enable you to cascade them. In other words, you can combine the capabilities of certain borders. Another good example of this is the TitledBorder. The TitledBorder displays text within the border itself. So for instance, if you want to add the title "hi" to the border for the Hello button, you can change the set border lines:

```
LineBorder lb = new LineBorder(Color.green);
hello.setBorder(new TitledBorder(lb,"hi"));
```

There are quite a few borders in the borders package. Each of the borders has a slightly different look to it. Figure 23.12 shows several of the borders in the package.

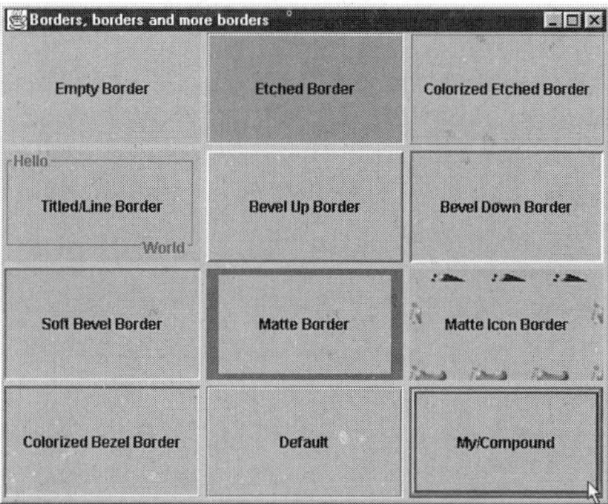

FIG. 23.12 JFC comes standard with many borders you can choose from.

Check Boxes and Radio Buttons

Under JFC, check boxes and radio buttons are very similar. The only real difference between the two is how they look. As with AWT, JFC check boxes and radio buttons come in two different forms. A single check box by itself is effectively a toggle button. However, used with a check box group, the check boxes become a selection "pool," as shown in Figure 23.13. The group class under JFC is called ButtonGroup (as opposed to AWT's CheckBoxGroup). This more generic group actually works with AbstractButton, which means it can be used with just about any button in the JFC API. Listing 23.7 shows the use of five check boxes in a group.

Listing 23.7 *CheckBoxPanel.java*—Using JFC Check Boxes

```
public class CheckBoxPanel extends JPanel implements SwingConstants{
  public CheckBoxPanel(ActionListener al){

    Box vertBox = Box.createVerticalBox();

    Box topBox = Box.createHorizontalBox();
    Box middleBox = Box.createHorizontalBox();
    Box bottomBox = Box.createHorizontalBox();

    ButtonGroup group = new ButtonGroup();

    //Create the checkboxes
    JCheckBox north = new JCheckBox("North");
    north.addActionListener(al);
    north.setActionCommand("north");
    group.add(north);
    topBox.add(north);

    JCheckBox west = new JCheckBox("West");
    west.addActionListener(al);
    west.setActionCommand("west");
    group.add(west);
    middleBox.add(west);

    JCheckBox center = new JCheckBox("Center");
    center.addActionListener(al);
    center.setActionCommand("center");
    group.add(center);
    middleBox.add(center);

    JCheckBox east = new JCheckBox("East");
    east.addActionListener(al);
    east.setActionCommand("east");
    group.add(east);
    middleBox.add(east);

    JCheckBox south = new JCheckBox("South");
    south.addActionListener(al);
    south.setActionCommand("south");
    group.add(south);
    bottomBox.add(south);

    vertBox.add (topBox);
    vertBox.add (middleBox);
    vertBox.add (bottomBox);

    add(vertBox);
  }
}
```

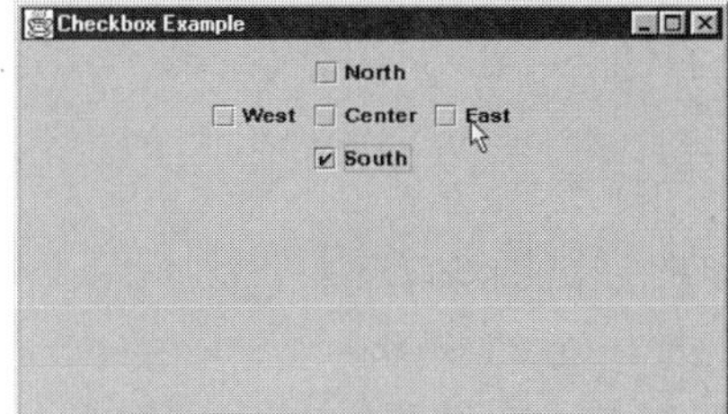

FIG. 23.13
Five check boxes in a group.

Understanding CheckBoxPanel

Listing 23.7, CheckBoxPanel.java, shows how to build a group of check boxes. Notice that each of the check boxes is added to `group` the GroupBox variable.

Using ActionListeners and Setting Action Events

The constructor for CheckBoxPanel takes as a parameter an ActionListener. Note that this action listener has been registered for each of the `CheckBoxes` in Listing 23.7 using the `addActionListener()` method. This registration is identical to how you registered the ActionListener with the JButton in Listing 23.3, only in this case, you use an ActionListener object that has been passed into the method.

In addition, note that in this example, we have explicitly specified what the ActionCommand will be, using the `setActionCommand()` method, rather than relying on the default action.

Using the BoxLayout and Boxes

You might have noticed that in this example we used a new class: Box. With JFC, you get a new LayoutManager called the BoxLayout. BoxLayout is somewhat similar to the GridLayout class, but unlike GridLayout, the BoxLayout aligns things either horizontally or vertically but does not have support for multiple columns and rows. However, BoxLayout also does not assume that all components will be the same size in the major axis.

The Box class that we use in this example is a panel that uses the BoxLayout. It's a convenient way to create a vertical or horizontal "strip" upon which we can place components.

In this example, three horizontal strips have been created, one for each "row," and these strips have then been added to one vertical strip (see Figure 23.14).

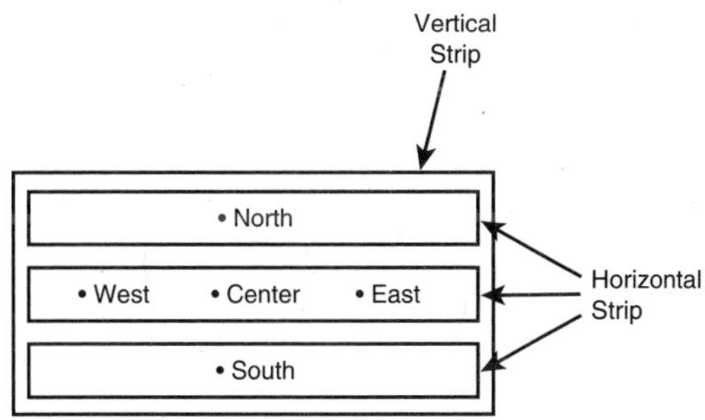

FIG. 23.14
An illustration of how each of the boxes is used.

You will notice that each of the check boxes is added to one of these boxes—for example,

```
topBox.add(north);
```

Applying CheckBoxPanel to Change Text Alignment

When you read about the JLabel earlier in this chapter, you learned that when you use both an icon and a text label, you can specify the alignment of the icon to the text. Now, let's look at how you can change that alignment.

JLabel and JButton both include two methods for specifying the position of the text, as it relates to the icon:

```
setVerticalTextPosition()

setHorizontalTextPosition()
```

Both of these methods take a parameter from the SwingConstants interface. SwingConstants contains a number of constant values such as: `TOP`, `BOTTOM`, `LEFT`, `RIGHT`, and `CENTER`. As you might already have guessed, setting the vertical text position to say `TOP` causes the text to appear above the icon.

In Listing 23.7, you saw how a group of check boxes could be placed on a panel in a group. When each button is pressed, it creates an ActionEvent that gives a direction. Now use the CheckBoxPanel to change the alignment of the text and icon on a button, as shown in Listing 23.8 and Figure 23.15.

Listing 23.8 CheckBoxPanel—Altering Alignment

```
import java.awt.*;
import java.awt.event.*;
import javax.swing.*;
import javax.swing.border.*;

public class CheckBoxExample extends JPanel implements
➥ActionListener,SwingConstants{
  static JFrame myFrame;
  protected JLabel label;
  JButton theButton;

  public CheckBoxExample(){
    Icon icon = new ImageIcon ("feet.gif");
    theButton = new JButton("My Feet",icon);
    add (theButton);
    add (new CheckBoxPanel(this));
  }

  public void actionPerformed(ActionEvent ae){
    String action = ae.getActionCommand();
```

```
        if (action.equals("north")){
          theButton.setVerticalTextPosition(TOP);
          theButton.setHorizontalTextPosition(CENTER);
        }
        else if (action.equals("south")){
          theButton.setVerticalTextPosition(BOTTOM);
          theButton.setHorizontalTextPosition(CENTER);
        }
        else if (action.equals("east")){
          theButton.setHorizontalTextPosition(RIGHT);
          theButton.setVerticalTextPosition(CENTER);
        }
        else if (action.equals("west")){
          theButton.setHorizontalTextPosition(LEFT);
          theButton.setVerticalTextPosition(CENTER);
        }
        else if (action.equals("center")){
          theButton.setHorizontalTextPosition(CENTER);
          theButton.setVerticalTextPosition(CENTER);
        }
      }

      public static void main(String args[]){
        myFrame = new JFrame("Checkbox Example");
        CheckBoxExample jt = new CheckBoxExample();
        myFrame.getContentPane().add("Center",jt);
        myFrame.setSize(400,250);
        myFrame.addWindowListener(new WindowAdapter() {
          public void windowClosing(WindowEvent e) {System.exit(0);}
          });
        myFrame.setVisible(true);
      }
    }
```


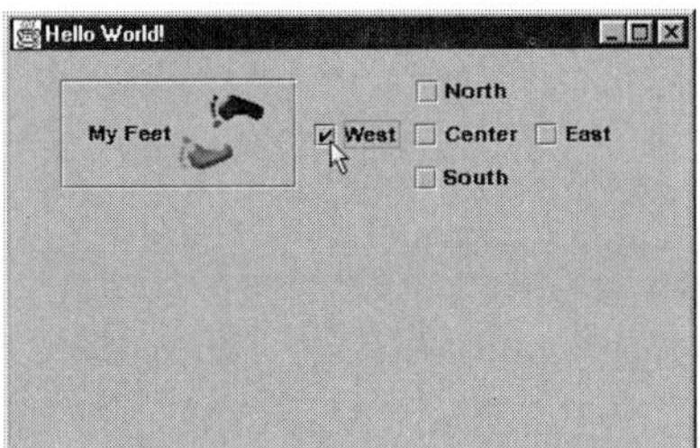

FIG. 23.15 Each time you select a different setting, the alignment of the label changes.

Understanding CheckBoxPanel

The constructor for CheckBoxPanel should look very similar to some of the earlier examples in this book. The only real difference is that here you see that you can also add classes that extend from JPanel (CheckBoxPanel) like you would expect.

Changing the Alignment

As you will recall from Listing 23.7, CheckBoxPanel.java, the constructor required you to pass in an ActionListener. You will also note that CheckBoxExample implements ActionListener. So, when the CheckBoxPanel is created, you effectively automatically register your class to receive the ActionEvents from the check boxes.

That being said, what you are really interested in here is how you go about changing the text alignment of the button. The `actionPerformed()` method first gets the actions command, proceeds to compare it to each of the known results, and then proceeds to change the alignment. So, if the command was `"north"`, you would be concerned only with the following snippet:

```
if (action.equals("north")){
      theButton.setVerticalTextPosition(TOP);
      theButton.setHorizontalTextPosition(CENTER);
}
```

Notice that both the horizontal and vertical position are set because you don't know whether either was set before. You might have already figured out that if we had wanted to allow configurations such as North-West and South-East, we could have done that as well.

At this point, you might be wondering where the `TOP` and `CENTER` variables came from. After all, earlier we mentioned that they were in the SwingConstants interface. The answer to this is quite simple: To use SwingConstants, you can either implement the interface, or as you saw earlier in the section, "Adding Icons," you can call out the qualified names such as `SwingConstants.TOP`. In this case, CheckBoxExample implements the SwingConstants interface, so the variables are directly available to us.

Tabbed Panes

Tabbed views have been a staple of GUI designs almost since the inception of the concept of GUI. AWT includes a layout manager called CardLayout, which many people have used to create their own equivalent of a tabbed layout. However, AWT is not equipped with any complete solution for tabs. JFC has added a class called JTabbedPane for just this purpose.

The JTabbedPane automatically handles the graphical side of creating the tabs. Like CardLayout, it also enables you to hide and show various pages each time you click on a tab. One of the great features of the graphic tabs themselves is that they can be placed at any of the four standard sizes (top, bottom, left, or right). Listing 23.9 shows how to create two tabs at the top.

Listing 23.9 JTabbedPane Provides a Facility to Handle Tabs in Your Interfaces

```
import java.awt.*;
import java.awt.event.*;
import javax.swing.*;
```

```
public class TabExample extends JPanel {
  static JFrame myFrame;
  public TabExample(){
    JTabbedPane tabs = new JTabbedPane(SwingConstants.BOTTOM);
    Icon icon = new ImageIcon ("feet.gif");
    JButton button = new JButton(icon);
    JLabel label = new JLabel ("Hello World!");
    tabs.addTab("Hello World",label);
    tabs.addTab("Feet",icon,button);
    setLayout(new BorderLayout());
    add(tabs,"Center");
  }

  public static void main(String args[]){
    myFrame = new JFrame("Tab Example");
    TabExample tabExample = new TabExample();
    myFrame.getContentPane().add("Center",tabExample);
    myFrame.setSize(400,200);
    myFrame.addWindowListener(new WindowAdapter() {
      public void windowClosing(WindowEvent e) {System.exit(0);}
      });
    myFrame.setVisible(true);
  }
}
```


Understanding JTabbedPane

Fig 23.16 shows the results of running JTabbedPane. As with our other examples, the `main()` method should be easy for you to figure out on your own.

In this example, two tabs have been added to the `tabs` object, using an `addTab()` method. There are three variations on the `addTab()` allowing you to label the tab with a string, an icon, or both. Here are the three methods:

```
addTab(String title, Component component);
addTab(String title, Icon icon, Component component);
addTab(String title, Icon icon, Component component, String toolTip);
```

Listing 23.9 shows the use of two of these options:

```
tabs.addTab("Hello World",label);
tabs.addTab("Feet",icon,button);
```

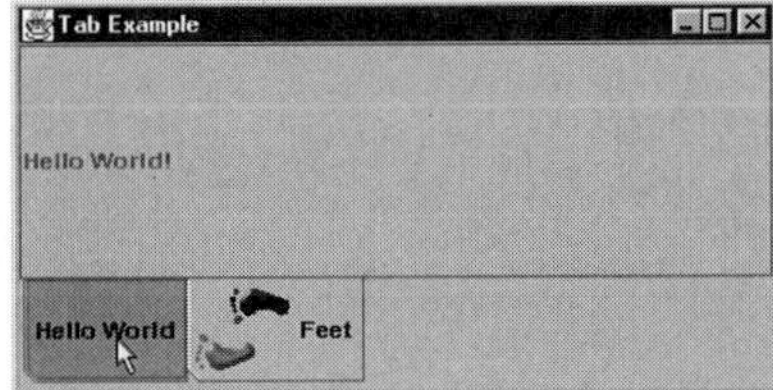

FIG. 23.16
Change the tabs to get to the various components.

The `component` object is the item to be used as the body of the tab area. In the case of this example, we used a button on one tab and a label on the other. However, you can just as easily add a JPanel or other compound object.

Other JTabbedPane Abilities

Under CardLayout, you're stuck with the insert order for the order of the cards. Unlike CardLayout, using JTabbedPane you can also specify the order of the cards. What this means is that with JTabbedPane, if you choose to put an extra tab into the system at any time, it doesn't necessarily have to be the last tab. To do so, you can use the `insertTab()` method:

```
public void insertTab(String title, Icon icon, Component
➥ component, String tip, int index)
```

Sliders

Sliders are similar to scrollbars in that they enable a user to drag a marker across the screen. However, sliders are typically used to help specify a quantity, as opposed to moving a screen view. Unfortunately, sliders were missing among the components included with AWT. JFC, however, has remedied this gap, with the JSlider class.

JSlider can display major ticks, minor ticks, both, or neither as guides for the user. In addition, the slider can be displayed either vertically or horizontally. Listing 23.10 shows several different variations on the vertical variation of the slider (see Figure 23.17).

Listing 23.10 SliderExample.java—Five Different Sliders

```
import javax.swing.*;
import javax.swing.border.*;
import javax.swing.event.*;
import java.awt.BorderLayout;
import java.awt.event.WindowAdapter;
import java.awt.event.WindowEvent;

public class SliderExample extends JPanel{
  JLabel slider5Value;
  static JFrame myFrame;
  public SliderExample() {
    Box horizBox = Box.createHorizontalBox();
    JSlider slider1 = new JSlider (JSlider.VERTICAL, 0, 50, 25);
    slider1.setPaintTicks(true);
    slider1.setMajorTickSpacing(10);
    slider1.setMinorTickSpacing(2);
    slider1.setSnapToTicks(true);
    horizBox.add(slider1);
    horizBox.add(horizBox.createHorizontalStrut(15));

    JSlider slider2 = new JSlider (JSlider.VERTICAL, 0, 50,25);
    slider2.setPaintTicks(true);
    slider2.setMinorTickSpacing(5);
```

```
    horizBox.add(slider2);
    horizBox.add(horizBox.createHorizontalStrut(15));

    JSlider slider3 = new JSlider (JSlider.VERTICAL, 0, 50,25);
    slider3.setPaintTicks(true);
    slider3.setMajorTickSpacing(10);
    horizBox.add(slider3);
    horizBox.add(horizBox.createHorizontalStrut(15));

    JSlider slider4 =  new JSlider (JSlider.VERTICAL, 0, 50,25);
    slider4.setBorder(LineBorder.createBlackLineBorder());
    horizBox.add(slider4);
    horizBox.add(horizBox.createHorizontalStrut(15));

    JSlider slider5 =  new JSlider (JSlider.VERTICAL, 0, 50,25);
    slider5.setBorder(LineBorder.createBlackLineBorder());
    slider5.setMajorTickSpacing(10);
    slider5.setPaintLabels(true);
    horizBox.add(slider5);
    horizBox.add(horizBox.createHorizontalStrut(15));

    slider5Value = new JLabel("Slider5 value = 25");
    horizBox.add(slider5Value);

    slider5.addChangeListener(new ChangeListener(){
      public void stateChanged(ChangeEvent event){
        slider5Value.setText("Slider5 value = "
        ➥+((JSlider)event.getSource()).getValue());
      }
    });


    setLayout(new BorderLayout());
    add(horizBox,"Center");
  }

  public static void main(String args[]){
    myFrame = new JFrame("Slider Example");
    SliderExample sliderExample = new SliderExample();
    myFrame.getContentPane().add("Center",sliderExample);
    myFrame.setSize(300,300);
    myFrame.addWindowListener(new WindowAdapter() {
      public void windowClosing(WindowEvent e) {System.exit(0);}
    });
    myFrame.setVisible(true);
  }
}
```

Understanding SliderExample

SliderExample uses the same box panel you saw in CheckBoxPanel. Each of the different sliders is added to this horizontal panel. Now, to create the various sliders, we used a constructor that takes four different values, like this:

```
JSlider slider1 = new JSlider (JSlider.VERTICAL, 0, 50, 25);
```

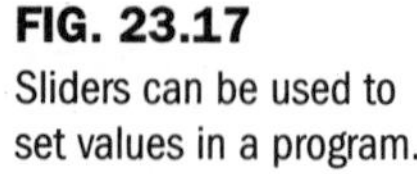

FIG. 23.17
Sliders can be used to set values in a program.

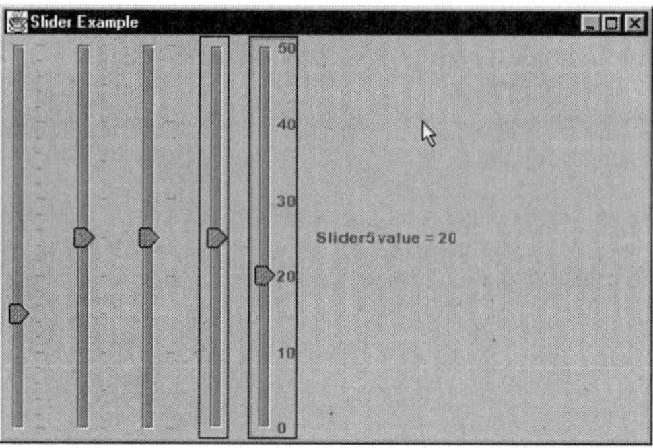

The first parameter for the constructor is obviously the direction, which can be either `SwingConstants.VERTICAL` or `SwingConstants.HORIZONTAL`. Note, that because JSlider implements the SwingConstants interface, we can also use the value like `JSlider.VERTICAL`.

The next two parameters for the constructor are the minimum and maximum values for the slider. So, can you guess what the last parameter is? It's the initial value of the slider.

Configuring the Tick Marks

By default, a slider doesn't display its tick marks (like `slider5`). However, you can turn on either the major or minor tick marks independently, using either `setMajorTickSpacing()` or `setMinorTickSpacing()` respectively. Both of these methods take an `int` parameter. This parameter specifies the number of elements between each tick.

Capturing Changes in the Slider

To capture the changes in a slider, you can use a new event in the JFC set: xxx.swing.event.ChangeEvent. The ChangeEvent occurs any time the slider is moved, so in Listing 23.10, when `slider5` is moved, the label at the far right is changed to include the value from the slider.

Progress Bars

When an activity is going to take a long time to complete, many applications use progress bars to show the current status, and to help the user know that the process is continuing. AWT does not include progress bars, but like sliders, JFC has filled this gap. The JProgressBar component is JFC's solution for the gap.

ProgressBarExample in Listing 23.11 demonstrates how a JProgressBar can be used. It creates a thread that progresses along and updates the bar, as shown in Figure 23.18.

Listing 23.11 ProgressBarExample with a Thread-Controlled ProgressBar

```
import javax.swing.*;
import javax.swing.event.*;
import java.awt.*;
import java.awt.event.*;

public class ProgressExample extends JPanel {
  ProgressThread progressThread;
  JProgressBar progressBar;
  static JFrame myFrame;

  public ProgressExample() {
    setLayout(new BorderLayout());
    progressBar = new JProgressBar();
    add(progressBar,"Center");

    JPanel buttonPanel = new JPanel();
    JButton startButton = new JButton("Start");
    buttonPanel.add(startButton);
    startButton.addActionListener(new ActionListener() {
      public void actionPerformed(ActionEvent e) {
      startRunning();
      }
      });

    JButton stopButton = new JButton("Stop");
    buttonPanel.add(stopButton);
    stopButton.addActionListener(new ActionListener() {
      public void actionPerformed(ActionEvent e) {
      stopRunning();
      }
      });
    add(buttonPanel, BorderLayout.SOUTH);
  }

  public void startRunning() {
    if(progressThread == null|| !progressThread.isAlive()) {
      progressThread = new ProgressThread(progressBar);
      progressThread.start();
    }
  }

  public void stopRunning() {
    progressThread.setStop(true);
  }

  public static void main(String args[]){
    myFrame = new JFrame("Hello World!");
    ProgressExample progressExample = new ProgressExample();
    myFrame.getContentPane().add("Center",progressExample);
    myFrame.setSize(200,100);
    myFrame.addWindowListener(new WindowAdapter() {
      public void windowClosing(WindowEvent e) {
      System.exit(0);
```

continues

Listing 23.11 Continued

```
      }
      });
    myFrame.setVisible(true);
  }
}


class ProgressThread extends Thread {
  JProgressBar progressBar;
  boolean stopStatus = false;
  boolean aliveStatus = false;

  public ProgressThread(JProgressBar progressBar){
    this.progressBar = progressBar;
  }

  public void setStop(boolean value){
    stopStatus = value;
  }

  public void run () {
    int min = 0;
    int max = 50;
    progressBar.setMinimum(min);
    progressBar.setMaximum(max);
    progressBar.setValue(min);
    for (int x=min;x<=max;x++) {
      if(stopStatus){
        break;
      }else{
        progressBar.setValue(x);
        try {
          Thread.sleep(100);
        } catch (InterruptedException e) {
          // Ignore Exceptions
        }
      }
    }
    aliveStatus = false;
  }
}
```

FIG. 23.18 Once the ProgressThread is started, the progress bar will begin to travel across the screen.

Understanding ProgressBarExample

In order to demonstrate a progress bar with any real meaning, it's necessary to have something that is actually progressing. As a result, ProgressBarExample in Listing 23.11 might seem unnecessarily complicated. However, after you take the time to digest the example, it won't seem so difficult after all.

Creating and Controlling the Progress Bar

To see all the work done with the progress bar in this example, you need to look in a couple of places. First, to see how the progress bar is created, you can look in the same place that you've seen many of the other components throughout this chapter—the constructor. You'll seen two lines that look like the following:

```
progressBar = new JProgressBar();
add(progressBar,"Center");
```

Not surprisingly, this looks very similar to the rest of the examples in this chapter. The second place to look is inside the ProgressThread's `run()` method, which is where you will find all the calls for configuring and updating the progress bar. The first set of method calls simply configures the initial state of the progress bar.

```
progressBar.setMinimum(min);
progressBar.setMaximum(max);
progressBar.setValue(min);
```

If you recall the discussion of scrollbars from Chapter 19, these methods should look very similar. Effectively what this does is set the smallest and largest value the progress bar will know about, and then it sets the initial value. The usefulness of setting min/max values might not be immediately obvious, but the implication is that you can configure your bar for whatever scale you need. For instance, if instead of counting from 0 to 50, you wanted to show the status as you read from a file, and you were going to start at the 10k mark and read 5Mb, you could set the min to 10240 and the max to 5242880. Then as you read from the file, you can just update the progress bar with your current location; the progress bar handles figuring out all the percentages and so on.

ProgressThread

The majority of the extra code in this example is dedicated to the thread that actually updates the progress bar. Obviously, the thread's sole purpose is to call `setValue()` on the progress bar every so often.

A warning is necessary at this point though. ProgressThread calls a thread safe method—`setValue`. However, most of the methods in the JFC API are not thread safe. This means that, in general, you should not call directly to one of these methods from an independent thread. To do so can result in some unexpected, and generally undesirable, results. Instead you should make most of your calls in the Swing thread.

If for some reason you need to call a nonthread safe method, you can have Swing process that thread for you using one of two techniques. In the SwingUtilities class are two methods: `invokeAndWait()` and `invokeLater()`. Both of these methods require a Runnable object to be passed into them (just like a Thread), but they will process the `run()` method within Swing's event thread. The difference between the two methods, by the way, is that `invokeAndWait()` forces the Runnable to be processed immediately, and your code will block at the `invokeAndWait()` method until it finishes. `invokeLater()` will queue the Runnable, and process it at the next opportunity, but independent of your current code process. Normally you will use `invokeLater()`.

ProgressMonitor

Because it's so common to display a progress bar in a window all its own while a particular process is running, and display the status of that process, JFC also has a convenience class that combines everything you need to do this. This class is called the ProgressMonitor.

ProgressMonitors are actually self-intelligent in that they can figure out if they will ever be needed. If within two seconds of their creation, the status of the task has already completed, the ProgressMonitor won't even bother to pop up. You can configure the time it waits before popping up if you need to, but generally speaking, two seconds is a good time.

Listing 23.12 shows how our ProgressBarExample from Listing 23.11 would be modified to use the monitor. Notice how Listing 23.12 differs from Listing 23.11. You can see the results in Figure 23.19.

Listing 23.12 ProgressMonitor Shows the Status in a Subwindow

```
import javax.swing.*;
import javax.swing.event.*;
import java.awt.*;
import java.awt.event.*;

public class ProgressMonitorExample extends JPanel {
  ProgressThread progressThread;
  static JFrame myFrame;

  public ProgressMonitorExample() {
    setLayout(new BorderLayout());
    JPanel buttonPanel = new JPanel();
    JButton startButton = new JButton("Start");
    buttonPanel.add(startButton);
    startButton.addActionListener(new ActionListener() {
      public void actionPerformed(ActionEvent e) {
           startRunning();
      }
  });

    JButton stopButton = new JButton("Stop");
    buttonPanel.add(stopButton);
    stopButton.addActionListener(new ActionListener() {
      public void actionPerformed(ActionEvent e) {
      stopRunning();
```

```
      }
      });
    add(buttonPanel, BorderLayout.SOUTH);
  }

  public void startRunning() {
    if(progressThread == null¦¦ !progressThread.isAlive()) {
      progressThread = new ProgressThread(this);
      progressThread.start();
    }
  }

  public void stopRunning() {
    progressThread.setStop(true);
  }

  public static void main(String args[]){
    myFrame = new JFrame("Hello World!");
    ProgressMonitorExample progressMonitorExample = new
    ➥ProgressMonitorExample();
    myFrame.getContentPane().add("Center",progressMonitorExample);
    myFrame.setSize(200,100);
    myFrame.addWindowListener(new WindowAdapter() {
      public void windowClosing(WindowEvent e) {
      System.exit(0);
      }
      });
    myFrame.setVisible(true);
  }
}


class ProgressThread extends Thread {
  ProgressMonitor monitor;
  boolean stopStatus = false;
  int min = 0;
  int max = 50;

  public ProgressThread(Component parent){
    monitor = new ProgressMonitor(parent,"Progress of Thread","Not Started",
    ➥min,max);
  }

  public void setStop(boolean value){
    stopStatus = value;
  }

  public void run () {
    monitor.setNote("Started");
    for (int x=min;x<=max;x++) {
      if(stopStatus){
        monitor.close();
        break;
      }else{
        monitor.setProgress(x);
```

continues

Listing 23.12 Continued

```
            monitor.setNote(""+(x*2)+"%");
            try {
              sleep(100);
            } catch (InterruptedException e) {
              // Ignore Exceptions
            }
          }
        }
      }
    }
```

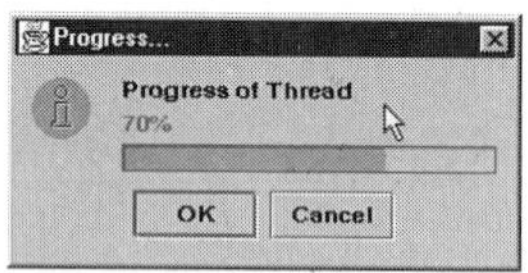

FIG. 23.19 ProgressMonitor produces a child window and shows the status in that window.

Understanding ProgressMonitorBar Unlike our ProgressBarExample program, Listing 23.12 doesn't split the work with ProgressMonitor into two classes. The 'Start' and 'Stop' buttons are used simply to trigger the creation of the ProgressMonitor in the ProgressThread object.

The ProgressThread Class The ProgressThread class is the one that is really interesting in this example. Let's start by looking at the constructor and how the `monitor` object is created.

```
public ProgressThread(Component parent){
  monitor = new ProgressMonitor(parent,"Progress of Thread",
  ➥"Not Started",min,max);
}
```

ProgressMonitor has one constructor, and it requires some items from you:

- A parent window, just like a Dialog or modal JDialog
- A label for the window
- An initial status note
- A minimum and a maximum value for the scrollbar

As you would guess, you can change any of these values after you construct the ProgressMonitor, except one: the parent. This value is used to construct the dialog and really wouldn't make sense to change later.

The *run()* Method The `run()` method in this example is where the bulk of the work is done.

As you look through the `run()` method, you will notice that you actually use more methods with the ProgressMonitor than we did with our ProgressExample.

First, in ProgressExample when the stopStatus was set, you simply ended the `run()` method. However, with this example, you tell the monitor to close. Ordinarily the ProgressMonitor will automatically close as soon as you reach or go past the maximum value. But if you want to close it before that happens, you must call the `close()` method. Of course, you can also set the progress to `max` and accomplish basically the same task.

```
if(stopStatus){
  monitor.close();
  break;
}
```

Next, notice that each time the thread updates, you update not one but two values for the monitor. The first just updates the progress status, like you did in Listing 23.11, except that ProgressMonitor's method is `setProgress()`, whereas JProgressBar's was `setValue()`.

The next method is a bit more interesting; it sets the ProgressMonitor's note. You can use the note to display updated information beyond what the progress bar shows. In this case, you'll see the completion percentage, but you can show anything you like. So if you were reading a bunch of files, you might want to show the current file you're working with.

ProgressMonitorInputStream

Another very common use of the progress bar is to show your status as you read from a stream, such as a FileInputStream. Like ProgressMonitor, as a convenience to you, JFC also adds a monitor for reading from a stream. The new class is called ProgressMonitorInputStream, and it works similarly to the ProgressMonitor in that it creates its own dialog window.

Because ProgressMonitorInputStream is so similar to ProgressMonitor, you can use the same base class you did in Listing 23.12 and substitute just the ProgressThread class shown in Listing 23.13 to see how ProgressMonitorInputStream works.

Listing 23.13 Changing the ProgressThread to Use a ProgressMonitorInputStream Instead of a ProgressMonitor

```
class ProgressThread extends Thread {
  boolean stopStatus = false;
  BufferedInputStream in;

  public ProgressThread(Component parent,String fileName){
    try{
      in = new BufferedInputStream(
          new ProgressMonitorInputStream(
              parent,
              "Reading "+fileName,
              new FileInputStream(fileName)
              )
          );
    }catch (FileNotFoundException exception){
      System.out.println("File not found:"+fileName);
    }
  }

  public void setStop(boolean value){
```

continues

Listing 23.13 Continued

```
        stopStatus = value;
    }

    public void run () {
        int readVal;
        try{
            while (!stopStatus &&((readVal = in.read())!=-1)){
                //if this was for real, you'd do something here
            }
        }catch (IOException ioe){
            System.out.println("Exception while reading");
        }
        System.out.println("done");
    }

}
```

Understanding ProgressMonitorInputStream The real work of Listing 23.13 comes in the constructor of the class. Before we dig into that, however, it's important to note that ProgressMonitorInputStream extends from InputStream, and because it does, ProgressMonitorInputStream can generally be used just like most of the custom input streams such as BufferedInputStream or ObjectInputStream.

The constructor for ProgressThread creates the ProgressMonitorInputStream based on a FileInputStream. In effect, it *wraps* the FileInputStream. Then, just to show that ProgressMonitorInputStream is no different, it is wrapped in a BufferedInputStream.

```
in = new BufferedInputStream(
          new ProgressMonitorInputStream(
              parent,
              "Reading "+fileName,
              new FileInputStream(fileName)
              )
          );
```

The constructor for the ProgressMonitorInputStream, which is contained in the middle lines, requires three components:

- The parent Container, just like the ProgressMonitor
- The message for the monitor
- The InputStream to wrap, which will provide the source of the data

Unlike ProgressMonitor, ProgressMonitorInputStream does not enable you to directly change the message it displays. However, if you need to do this, you can request the ProgressMonitor using the `getProgressMonitor()` method.

The *run()* Method The `run()` method for the ProgressThread then simply reads from the stream until it reaches the end. To make this example interesting, you need to provide the body for the `while()` loop. ●

CHAPTER 24

Advanced JFC

In this chapter

Model-View-Control—JFC's Design

JFC's entire system is based on a design concept called Model View Control, or MVC. The MVC system separates the various portions of each interface component into three separate segments, as shown in Figure 24.1.

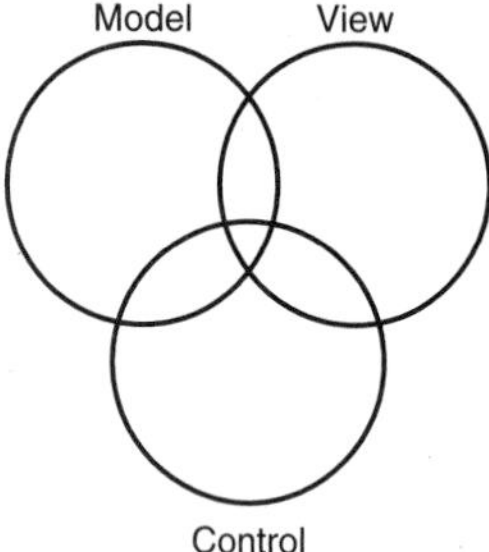

FIG. 24.1 Model View Control designs split the interface into three sections.

This design has been used very successfully in the past by other systems, but it first makes its debut in Java in JFC. Each of these components has its own set of requirements and responsibilities. Following are the three segments of MVC:

Model: The model is responsible for knowing and maintaining the state of the component. For instance, a button's model must know whether the button has been pressed, or whether the button has been armed. On the flip side, when the button is pressed, the model is responsible for notifying all the event listeners of the change.

View: The view is responsible for all display aspects of the component. This primarily involves the `paint()` method, but it also means that the view must know exactly what should be painted. So if a component has a different look when the mouse is over the component, the view must be able to display both the normal view and the view when the mouse is over the component.

Control: The control manages the actual events that are received by the component. These events can be either from the user (such as a mouse click) or from the system (such as a timer event). The control must figure out what to do with this event and inform the model, the view, and any other appropriate listeners.

Because the communication between the view and the control is very complicated, for the most part JFC has combined them into a single component called a delegate, resulting in a diagram more like Figure 24.2 than Figure 24.1.

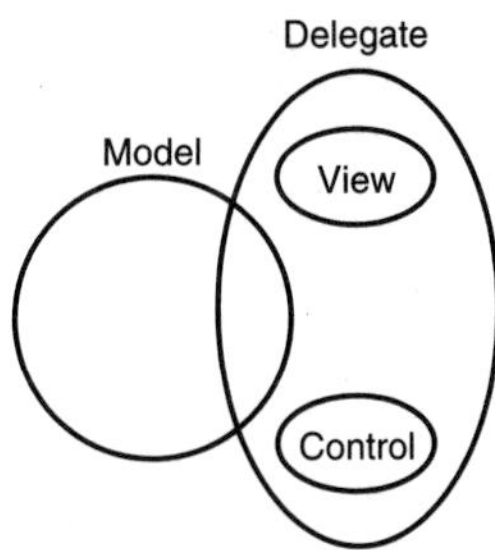

FIG. 24.2
By combining the view and the control, JFC simplifies the design.

Comparing MVC to AWT's Design

At first glance, you might think that MVC is a radical departure for Java, but in reality, AWT's design had many of the same aspects. Under AWT, components have objects called peers. The peer is actually a native component, so for example, if you run a Java app under Windows and you create a `java.awt.Button`, the button gets a button peer from Windows, which is a native Windows API button. The peer effectively has all the same features that JFC's delegate has. The primary difference between how the AWT model works and how the MVC system works is that the design of the peer makes it very difficult to change the way the button works, or how it looks. You are, after all, dependent on the button that the (Windows) system gives you.

The other major difference is that under the AWT design, the model portions of the MVC were embedded within the component itself. So if, for whatever reason, you wanted to change the way the model worked, you had to go through a fairly involved process, and your new model was generally tightly coupled to the original.

So Where Is the Component in This Model?

Perhaps the most confusing thing to try to understand about JFC's MVC design is figuring out exactly where the component fits. For instance, if you look at `JButton`, which part does `JButton` itself play? It is not the model, the view, or the controller; `JButton` is the component. Take a look at the two views shown in Figure 24.3. On the left you see a model similar to 24.2, except that the MVC is shown living inside of the component. On the right of Figure 24.3, you see an object diagram that shows that the model, the view, and the control all exist in a "has a" relationship to the component.

Digging a Bit Deeper, How Does an MVC Component Actually Work?

To understand better how the three pieces (component, model, and delegate) work together, it helps to see examples. You are probably wondering how all of these items fit together in practice, so take a look at a couple of examples and how they work in practice.

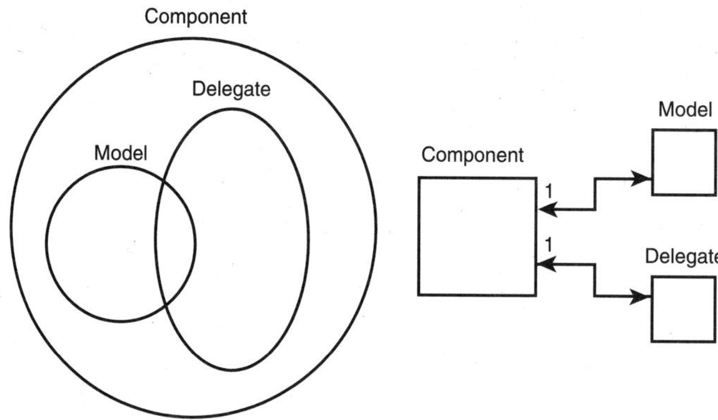

FIG. 24.3
The component "has a" model and a delegate (view and controller).

Painting to the Screen If you are an experienced Java developer and have been creating interesting applets, or if you read the earlier chapters that dealt with AWT, you will remember that `java.awt.Component` has a method called `paint()`. This method is called each time the component needs to be displayed onscreen. In fact, if you look back to the first example on how to use JFC in Chapter 23, "JFC—Java Foundation Classes" (Listing 23.1), you will see that the `paint()` method is used to display `hello world`. The same is true for the applet's "Hello World" (see Listing 14.5).

How does the `paint()` method work for a JFC component like `JButton`? You learned just moments ago that the view is responsible for painting the button. However, you also learned that the view is a "part" of the button, but it isn't actually *the* button. So you're probably wondering how all this works. After all, you are calling `add()` with the `JButton`, not the `JButton`'s view. The paint thread will want to paint the added component—it doesn't know anything about the delegate object.

Whenever any component in the Java system needs to be displayed onscreen, or it is instructed to `update()`, the screen-repainter thread proceeds to call the `paint()` method on the object. This is true for all AWT components, not just JFC ones (note: JFC `JComponent` does extend from AWT's `Component` class). Under JFC, the `JComponent` handles making sure that all the painting for the component is done correctly, including any children of the component. When it comes time for it to paint itself, the `paint()` method passes the `Graphics` object off to the view and instructs the view to paint. Effectively, you can think of `JComponent`'s `paint()` method as if its code looked like this:

```
public void paint(Graphics g){
    ui.paint(g);
}
```

Now, in reality, `JComponent`'s `paint()` method is much more complicated due to the requirements to paint all the child objects and accommodate the layered views in JFC, but for the purposes of understanding how the view fits in, it works perfectly.

Changing Values So now you understand how the `paint()` method makes its way out to the view, but you're still wondering how values are changed. For instance, if a button is pressed, how does that information get relayed?

The first part of the task is for the Controller to receive the events in the first place. This is done through the standard `java.awt.events`, such as `MouseListener` and `MouseMotionListener`. As you saw earlier, the controller is typically bundled with the view. So what happens is that the view (or more probably, an inner class of the view) receives the `mousePressed()` event.

Inside of the `mousePressed()` method, the Controller informs the model of the change in state, which performs the necessary changes, and then it might also tell the component to do something.

Take a look at how the `JButton` handles this sequence. When the `mousePressed()` event occurs, it is handled in the button's Controller. For the Basic UI, this class is called `BasicButtonListener`. Inside of the `mousePressed()` method, the controller performs two tasks. First, it tells the model to set its "pressed" state to `true`. Then it tells the component (`JButton`) to request focus. Notice that the model does not actually directly handle the event, but rather is informed of the appropriate change from the Controller.

When the model receives the change command from the Controller, it sets the flag for the pressed state, then tells the view that it needs to repaint (to reflect the new change). By having the model be responsible for calling the `repaint()` method, you have multiple sources changing the state of the button, and in all cases the view will get appropriately updated. So, for instance, you could change the button state by pressing the button (as you just saw), or you could call `JButton`'s `setSelected()` or `doClick()` methods. In either case, because the model updates the view, the change is apparent onscreen.

Obtaining Value Information Finally, you should examine what happens when you decide that you want to request some information from the component. As you've seen, the model is responsible for coming up with this information. So when you interrogate the component for its information, it will actually ask the model.

Once again, take a look at `JButton`. If you have followed the scenario set up in the preceding section, you will recall that you have pressed the mouse button on the button. Now you want to know the state of the `JButton`.

Normally, you would obtain the state of the button by querying `JButton`'s `isSelected()` method. Now, as you have probably already guessed, if you look at the internals of the `JButton` class's `isSelected()` method, it actually requests the state from the model and returns that value.

Why Understand MVC?

In many applications, you might not need to ever know how the Model-View-Controller model works. In fact, in Chapter 23 you learned about JFC without ever having to do anything with either the model or the delegate. This is not uncommon. However, for complex components such as Trees and Tables, which are discussed later in this chapter, understanding MVC is critical.

Using JFC's Pluggable Look-and-Feel

Beyond being able to tweak the system's individual pieces, one other truly fascinating side effect of JFC's Model-View-Control design comes out. The effect is that it allows JFC designs to mutate their look, and seamlessly change how they feel (react) to something completely different. This means that the entire look of the application can change without a single changed line of code, even at runtime. This whole concept is called a "pluggable look-and-feel." Figures 24.4 through 24.6 show a single application in three completely different views: the Java view, the Macintosh view, the Windows view, and the Motif view.

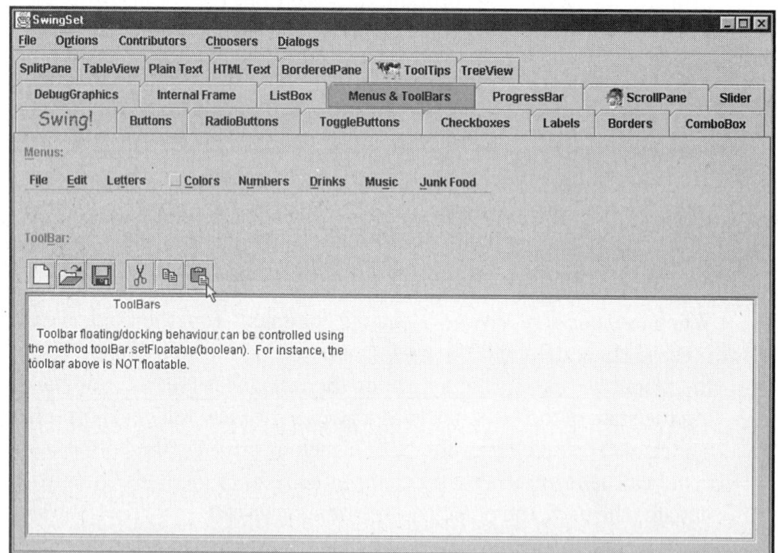

FIG. 24.4
An application rendered using the Java look-and-feel.

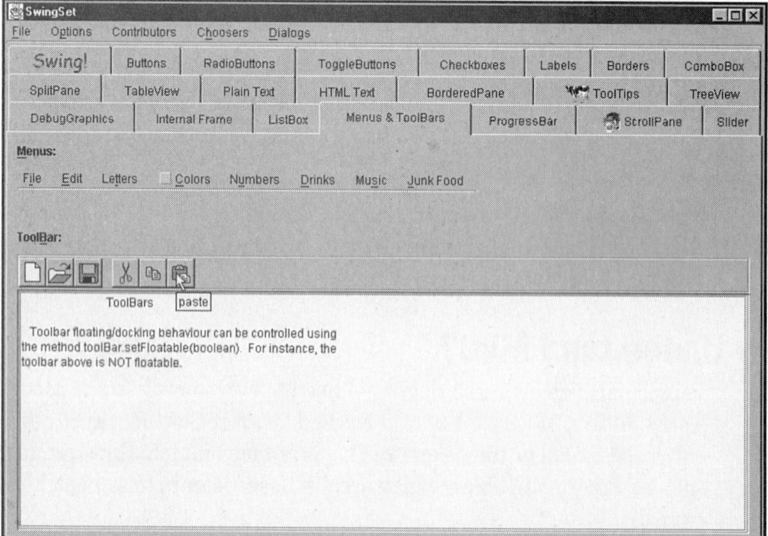

FIG. 24.5
An application rendered using the Windows look-and-feel.

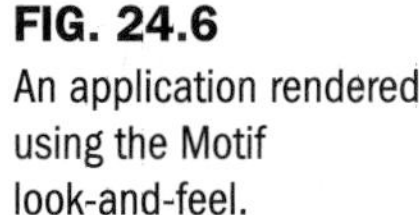

FIG. 24.6
An application rendered using the Motif look-and-feel.

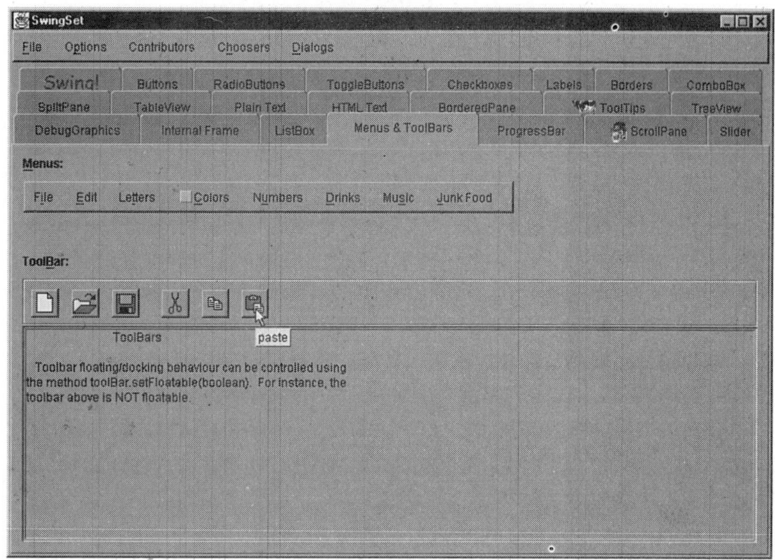

Changing the Look-and-Feel

Changing the look-and-feel of an application can be very painless. To change it, you really need to know just one thing: what is the name of the look-and-feel class responsible for providing each of the various UI components for that look-and-feel. You can think of the look-and-feel class as the driver for the look-and-feel. Various look-and-feels are bundled with JFC, and their look-and-feel classes are listed in Table 24.1.

Table 24.1 Various Look-and-Feel Drivers Shipped with JFC

Look-and-Feel Name	Class
Basic—The core to most look-and-feels.	`javax.swing.plaf.basic.BasicLookAndFeel`

continues

Table 24.1 Continued

Look-and-Feel Name	Class
Java look-and-feel—A cool new age look-and-feel. Most of the figures in this chapter and Chapter 23 have been shot using the Java look-and-feel.	`javax.swing.plaf.metal.MetalLookAndFeel`
Macintosh—A look-and-feel that resembles the way a Macintosh works. Note: By default, this look and feel is not available on any platform other than a Macintosh, for trademark reasons.	`com.sun.java.swing.plaf.mac.MacLookAndFeel`
Motif—A look-and-feel that resembles the view from many graphical UNIX machines.	`com.sun.java.swing.plaf.motif.MotifLookAndFeel`
Multiplexing look-and-feel—A look-and-feel designed to allow more than one UI to be associated with a component at a time.	`javax.swing.plaf.multi.MultiLookAndFeel`
Windows—A look-and-feel designed to simulate the look and feel of Windows 95/NT. Note: By default, this look and feel is not available on any platform other than a Windows machine, for trademark reasons.	`com.sun.java.swing.plaf.windows.Windows`

After you have found the look-and-feel you are looking for in Table 24.1, you can now proceed to change your application. Listing 24.1 shows just how to do this using the Window's look-and-feel.

Listing 24.1 JFC Allows You to Change the Look-and-Feel

```
try{
  UIManager.setLookAndFeel("com.sun.java.swing.plaf.windows.
WindowsLookAndFeel");
} catch (java.lang.ClassNotFoundException e){
  System.out.pritln("Look and feel not found");
}
```

Now, obviously you would substitute the string `"com.sun.java.swing.plaf.windows.WindowsLookAndFeel"` with the class from Table 24.1 that matches your desired look-and-feel. And, technically speaking, that's all you need to do. However, if you want to change the look-and-feel on the fly (that is, at runtime you want to support more than one L&F), you also need to notify the components that are already visible to update. You can do this in two ways. First, you can manually call the `updateUI()` method on each component in your program. `updateUI()` forces the component to reobtain its delegate and repaint itself. Obviously, going through every component could be a fairly big task if you had a lot of components in your system, and it would create a fair amount of coupling. So the `SwingUtilities` class has a way to make the task much easier. However, before you can use the swing utilities, you must know the component that is at the root of all your other views. Typically, this is either the `JFrame` or a `JApplet` your program started with. When you know this, you can call

```
SwingUtilities.updateComponentTreeUI(rootComponent);
```

In the next section, Listing 24.2 will put this all together in a complete example.

Menus and Toolbars

Menus and toolbars are common UI components in many systems. AWT provides menus, but left out toolbars. JFC has provided both. The classes in question are `JMenuBar` and `JToolBar`. Both of them are standard `JComponents`. The interesting thing about this is that it means you can put them into your UI in any location you would like. You are not bound to putting them in the standard locations. So if you want a menu bar to be located below a text field, you can do just that.

You'll create a toolbar that will allow you to change the look-and-feel of the `JTabbed` pane in Listing 24.2, and Figure 24.7. The example adds a menu bar that has a File menu and an L&F menu. The File menu won't actually do anything at this point, but it does make it look nice.

Listing 24.2 Tab Example Can Be Expanded to Support Multiple Views

```
import java.awt.*;
import java.awt.event.*;
import javax.swing.*;

public class MenuBarExample extends JPanel implements ItemListener{
  static JFrame myFrame;
```

continues

Listing 24.2 Continued

```
  Font myFont = new Font("Dialog", Font.PLAIN, 12);

  public MenuBarExample(){
//    setFont(myFont);
    JTabbedPane tabs = new JTabbedPane(SwingConstants.BOTTOM);
    Icon icon = new ImageIcon ("feet.gif");
    JButton button = new JButton(icon);
    JLabel label = new JLabel ("Hello World!");
    tabs.addTab("Hello World",label);
    tabs.addTab("Feet",icon,button);
    setLayout(new BorderLayout());
    add(tabs,"Center");
    add(createMenu(),"North");
  }

  public JMenuBar createMenu(){
    JMenuBar menuBar = new JMenuBar();
    // File Menu - create this so we have at least two menu options
    JMenu file = (JMenu) menuBar.add(new JMenu("File"));
    file.setMnemonic('F');
    JMenuItem mi; //Temporary place holder
    //Add several items under 'File' these won't do anything.
    mi = (JMenuItem) file.add(new JMenuItem("Open"));
    mi.setMnemonic('O');
    mi = (JMenuItem) file.add(new JMenuItem("Save"));
    mi.setMnemonic('S');
    mi = (JMenuItem) file.add(new JMenuItem("Save As..."));
    mi.setMnemonic('A');
    file.add(new JSeparator());
    mi = (JMenuItem) file.add(new JMenuItem("Exit"));

    // Look and Feel Menu
    JMenu options = (JMenu) menuBar.add(new JMenu("L&F"));
    options.setMnemonic('L');

    // Look and Feel Radio control
    ButtonGroup group = new ButtonGroup();
    mi = options.add(new JRadioButtonMenuItem("Windows Style Look and
➥Feel"));
    mi.setActionCommand("java.swing.plaf.windows.WindowsLookAndFeel");
    //If the current look and feel is windows, select this item.
    mi.setSelected(UIManager.getLookAndFeel().getName().equals
➥("Windows"));
    group.add(mi);
    mi.addItemListener(this);
    //  mi.setAccelerator(KeyStroke.getKeyStroke
➥(KeyEvent.VK_1, ActionEvent.ALT_MASK));

    mi = options.add(new JRadioButtonMenuItem("Motif Look and Feel"));
    mi.setActionCommand("java.swing.plaf.motif.
➥MotifLookAndFeel");
    mi.setSelected(UIManager.getLookAndFeel().getName().equals
➥("CDE/Motif"));
    group.add(mi);
```

```
    mi.addItemListener(this);
    //  mi.setAccelerator(
➥KeyStroke.getKeyStroke(KeyEvent.VK_2, ActionEvent.ALT_MASK));

    mi = options.add(new JRadioButtonMenuItem("Metal Look and Feel"));
    mi.setActionCommand(
➥"java.swing.plaf.metal.MetalLookAndFeel");
    mi.setSelected(UIManager.getLookAndFeel().getName().equals
➥("Metal"));
    //  metalMenuItem.setSelected(true);
    group.add(mi);
    mi.addItemListener(this);
    //  metalMenuItem.setAccelerator(
➥KeyStroke.getKeyStroke(KeyEvent.VK_3, ActionEvent.ALT_MASK));
    return menuBar;
  }

  public void itemStateChanged(ItemEvent e) {
    Component root = myFrame;
    //Bump the cursor into a wait mode while we make this change
    root.setCursor(Cursor.getPredefinedCursor(Cursor.WAIT_CURSOR));
    //Get the source of the event.
    JRadioButtonMenuItem button = (JRadioButtonMenuItem) e.getSource();
    try {
      if(button.isSelected()) {
        UIManager.setLookAndFeel(button.getActionCommand());
        button.setEnabled(true);
        SwingUtilities.updateComponentTreeUI(myFrame);
      }
    } catch (UnsupportedLookAndFeelException exc) {
      // Error - unsupported L&F
      button.setEnabled(false);
      System.err.println("Unsupported LookAndFeel: " +
➥button.getText());
    }catch (Exception exc2){
         System.err.println("Couldn't load Look and feel" +
➥button.getText());
    }

    root.setCursor(Cursor.getPredefinedCursor(Cursor.DEFAULT_CURSOR));
  }


  public static void main(String args[]){
    myFrame = new JFrame("MenuBar Example");
    MenuBarExample menuExample = new MenuBarExample();
    myFrame.getContentPane().add("Center",menuExample);
    myFrame.setSize(400,200);
    myFrame.addWindowListener(new WindowAdapter() {
      public void windowClosing(WindowEvent e) {System.exit(0);}
      });
    myFrame.setVisible(true);
  }
}
```

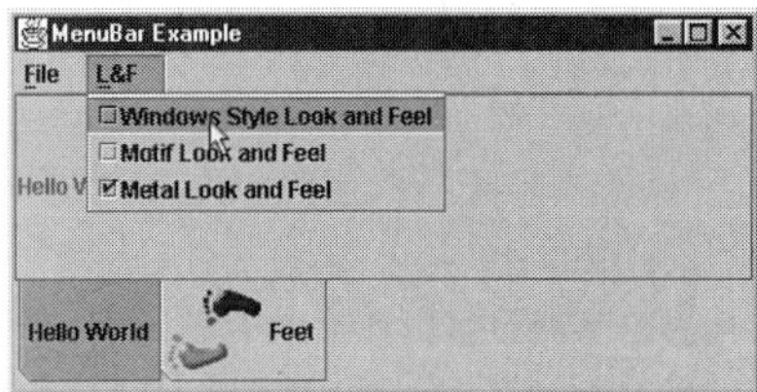

FIG. 24.7 Using the menu options, you can change the look-and-feel.

Understanding the MenuBar Example

The two primary methods you'll want to look at in this example are `createMenu()` and the `itemStateChanged()` event method. The `createMenu()` method produces the `JMenuBar`, which is then added to the "North" portion of the `JPanel`.

createMenu() To understand the `createMenu()` method, it's first important to understand the basics of `JMenuBar`. A `JMenuBar` is really just a container that runs horizontally. It contains menus that are the typical items you see on a menu bar, such as File and Edit. The menus themselves are also containers that contain `MenuItems`. `MenuItems` are the actual items that appear when you select a menu like Open or Save. Of course, if you've been building menu bars with AWT, all of this should come as old hand.

Creating Menus The first task is for you to create the MenuBar. The menu bar will hold two menus, File and L&F. To the menu bar you will add each of the `JMenus`. Now, the interesting part comes when you start adding `MenuItems`. The `JMenuItem` works very similar to a `JButton`. It can have `Mnemonics`, `ActionEvents` and `ItemEvents`. Take a look at the first couple of lines of `createMenu()`, in which the first menu (File) is created and its first item (Open) is added.

```
JMenu file = (JMenu) menuBar.add(new JMenu("File"));
file.setMnemonic('F');
JMenuItem mi; //Temporary place holder
mi = (JMenuItem) file.add(new JMenuItem("Open"));
```

In addition to menu items, you might want to add a separation between items, as is the case between the Save As and the Exit.

```
file.add(new JSeparator());
```

Adding Check Box Menu Items Later in the method, you start adding the L&F menu. In this case, you don't use the regular `MenuItem` class. Since you only want a single item to be selected at a time, and also because it would be nice to have a visual cue to show which of the options has been selected, you use the `JCheckBoxMenuItem`. This class extends the normal `JMenuItem` class and adds the capability to display both a check box and the label. This is the code for the first item:

```
ButtonGroup group = new ButtonGroup();
mi = lnf.add(new JCheckBoxMenuItem("Windows Style Look and Feel"));
mi.setActionCommand("java.swing.plaf.windows.
WindowsLookAndFeel");
//If the current look and feel is windows, select this item.
mi.setSelected(UIManager.getLookAndFeel().getName().equals("Windows"));
group.add(mi);
```

Notice that the `ButtonGroup` class has been applied to make sure that only one of each of the options is selected at any time, by adding all the check box menu items to the group.

KeyAccelerators with *KeyStroke*

You have already seen how the `Mnemonic` works with many JFC components. The menu items in Listing 24.2 each have a `Mnemonic` of their own. However, `Mnemonics` are triggered only when the components are visible. In the case of the `MenuItem`, it's convenient to use the `Mnemonic` so that as soon as the pop-up menu is shown, the user can hot-key to that selection. But what if you want to be able to press a key combination at any time?

Because the pop-up is not visible all the time, the `Mnemonic` will not work. However, you can use another trick to allow the user to press the key combination regardless of the menu's visibility. The trick is using a `KeyAccelerator`. The `KeyAccelerator` captures any keys that are pressed but that are not used by some other device. (This means that if you have an active `Mnemonic` that clashes with the accelerator, the `Mnemonic` will win.)

The `setAccelerator()` method is used for setting such a capture. `setAccelerator()` requires a `KeyStroke` object as its parameter. `KeyStroke` is yet another new class in JFC, which is used to represent a key combination, including a character and any key mask, such as Shift or Alt. So you can support a combination like Ctrl+b. The masks come from the `awt.event.ActionEvent` class. As you will recall, they are bit masks, and they include the following:

- `java.awt.ActionEvent.SHIFT_MASK`
- `java.awt.ActionEvent.CTRL_MASK`
- `java.awt.ActionEvent.META_MASK`
- `java.awt.ActionEvent.ALT_MASK`

So if you want to capture Alt+1, you can set the menu item with this:

```
mi.setAccelerator(KeyStroke.getKeyStroke(KeyEvent.VK_1, ActionEvent.
ALT_MASK));
```

Because the masks are bit flags, you can combine them using bitwise ANDs (`&`). As an example, if you want to have a combination like Shift+Ctrl+B, you can do so by combining the masks like this:

```
mi.setAccelerator(KeyStroke.getKeyStroke(KeyEvent.VK_1,
        ActionEvent.CTRL_MASK&ActionEvent.SHIFT_MASK));
```

Lists and Combo Boxes

Lists are probably one of the single-most-used UI components for displaying several items. Combo boxes are another variation on a list. AWT includes a list and a combo box (which is represented by the `Choice` class), but both are limited to displaying only strings. JFC adds `JList`, which is a completely different type of list box. `JComboBox` is different from AWT's `Choice` in several ways, and it actually uses the `JList` class for its pop-up display. Instead of displaying just strings, `JList` can display any kind of object and can include not only a string but also an associated icon. Further, the view for the list can change based on a large number of conditions. So if you want to have a different view when the item is selected, it's easy to do. First, you'll create a simple list and combo box. Often you want to just have a list from a fixed list. Listing 24.3 shows a list and a `JComboBox`, each with a fixed set of items (see Figure 24.8).

Listing 24.3 ***ListComboExample.java*** **Shows a List of People**

```
import java.awt.*;
import java.awt.event.*;
import javax.swing.*;
import javax.swing.border.*;

public class ListComboExample extends JPanel{
  static JFrame myFrame;

  String values[] = {"Joe","Shawn","Gabe","Jim","Bill","Jeremy"};
  public ListComboExample(){
    setLayout(new GridBagLayout());
    JList list = new JList(values);
    list.setVisibleRowCount(4);
    JScrollPane pane = new JScrollPane();
    pane.setViewportView(list);
    add(pane);

    JComboBox combobox = new JComboBox(values);
    add(combobox);
  }

  public static void main(String args[]){
    myFrame = new JFrame("List and ComboBox Example");
    ListComboExample jt = new ListComboExample();
    myFrame.getContentPane().add("Center",jt);
    myFrame.setSize(400,250);
    myFrame.addWindowListener(new WindowAdapter() {
      public void windowClosing(WindowEvent e) {System.exit(0);}
      });
    myFrame.setVisible(true);
  }
}
```

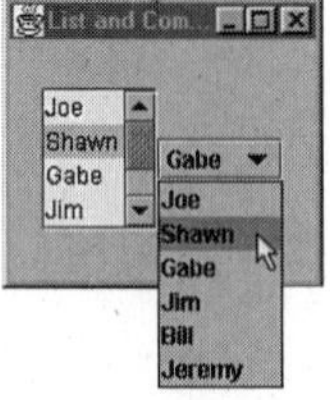

FIG. 24.8
A `JList` and `JComboBox` side by side.

Understanding *ListComboExample*

By now, most of Listing 24.3 should be intuitive to you. The most interesting part of the list is the use of the `JScrollPane`. `JList` doesn't implement scrolling on its own. It's an interesting design that allows you to do many interesting things with the `JList` without being bound to standard scrolling. However, for most uses you will simply create the `JScrollPane` and set its viewport view to the list. Notice that it's the pane, not the list, that is actually added to the panel.

List View Models

Although creating a list from a default list is useful, dynamic lists are far more interesting. As you will recall from the discussion of the Model-View-Controller earlier in this chapter, the model provides the data for a component. So to use dynamic data with a list, it makes sense that you will want to change the model. Lists use a basic list called a `ListModel`. `ListModel` is an interface that contains four methods, but it is often easier to simply extend the `AbstractListModel` class and define just two methods: `getElementAt()` and `getSize()`.

The combo box's model is slightly more complicated, however. First, it extends from `ListModel`, which means that you can base a `ComboBoxModel` on an existing `ListModel`, but after that you must define two additional methods: `setSelectedItem()` and `getSelectedItem()`. Listing 24.4 demonstrates how to modify Listing 24.3 to use models instead of a fixed list of data.

Listing 24.4 Add *ListModels* and *ComboBoxModels* to Support Dynamic Data

```
import java.awt.*;
import java.awt.event.*;
import javax.swing.*;
import javax.swing.border.*;

public class ListComboExample2 extends JPanel{
  static JFrame myFrame;

  public ListComboExample2(){
    setLayout(new GridLayout(2,2));
    JList list = new JList(new ListModelExample());
    list.setVisibleRowCount(4);
    JScrollPane pane = new JScrollPane();
    pane.setViewportView(list);
    add(pane);

    JComboBox combobox = new JComboBox(new ComboModelExample());
    add(combobox);


  public static void main(String args[]){
    myFrame = new JFrame("List and ComboBox Example");
    ListComboExample2 jt = new ListComboExample2();
    myFrame.getContentPane().add("Center",jt);
```

continues

Listing 24.4 Continued

```
    myFrame.setSize(400,250);
    myFrame.addWindowListener(new WindowAdapter() {
      public void windowClosing(WindowEvent e) {System.exit(0);}
      });
    myFrame.setVisible(true);
  }

  class ListModelExample extends AbstractListModel{
    String values[] = {"Joe","Shawn","Gabe","Jim","Bill","Jeremy"};
    public Object getElementAt(int index){
      return values[index];
    }

    public int getSize(){
      return values.length;
    }
  }

  class ComboModelExample extends ListModelExample
➥ implements ComboBoxModel{
    Object item;
    public void setSelectedItem(Object anItem){
      item = anItem;
    }
    public Object getSelectedItem(){
      return item;
    }

  }
}
```

Using Tables

It has been argued that the invention of the spreadsheet was the single innovation that caused computers to come into the mainstream. One of the key features of a spreadsheet is the capability to display two-dimensional data in a table. Although not as functional as a full-fledged spreadsheet, JFC has an extremely extensible table component called `JTable`.

You'll start by looking at the simplest version of a `JTable`, one in which you define a static set of data (Figure 24.9). Listing 24.5 shows just such an example, with a table that lists the first several chapters in this book.

Listing 24.5 *TableExample.java—JTable* Allows You to Display Two-Dimensional Data

```
import java.awt.*;
import java.awt.event.*;
import javax.swing.*;
import javax.swing.border.*;
```

```
public class TableExample extends JPanel{
  static JFrame myFrame;
  String data[][] ={{"1","Introduction"},
    {"2","What Java can Do for You"},{"3","JAVA Design"}
➥,{"4","Installing  JAVA"},
    {"5","JDK tools"},{"6","Object-Oriented Programming"}
➥,{"7","Hello world"},
    {"8","Data Types"},{"9","Methods"},{"10","Using Expressions"}};
  String columnNames[] ={"Chapter Number","Chapter Title"};

  public TableExample(){
    setLayout(new BorderLayout());
    JTable table = new JTable(data,columnNames);
    JScrollPane pane = JTable.createScrollPaneForTable(table);
    add(pane);
  }
  public static void main(String args[]){
    myFrame = new JFrame("Table Example");
    TableExample tableExample = new TableExample();
    myFrame.getContentPane().add("Center",tableExample);
    myFrame.setSize(400,250);
    myFrame.addWindowListener(new WindowAdapter() {
      public void windowClosing(WindowEvent e) {System.exit(0);}
      });
    myFrame.setVisible(true);
  }
}
```


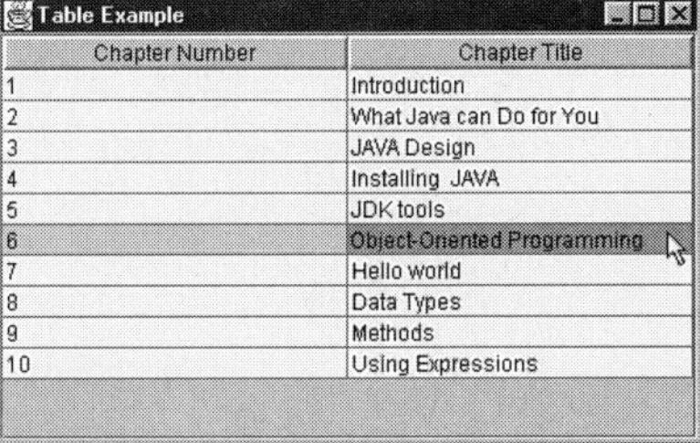

FIG. 24.9
The `JTable` displays two-dimensional data elegantly.

Understanding *TableExample*

`TableExample` takes advantage of one of `JTable`'s simplest constructors. The constructor takes a set of two-dimensional data, and a set of labels for the column heads. In `TableExample`, you see the data and column heads represented as arrays of strings. The data is by no means limited to strings, but for this example, that technique just was simplest. You can also use various components.

Also, note that like `JList`, `JTable` does not implement its own scrolling. However, unlike `JList`, `JTable` has a convenience method for creating the scroll pane and placing the table and the table header in the proper locations. Like `JList`, it's the pane, not the table itself, that gets added to the panel.

Table Models

Although a complete coverage of all the `JTable` options is unfortunately beyond the scope of this book, this text would fall short if it did not talk about using the models for tables. You see, it's often not convenient to create the data for the table at the time you create it. Beyond that, it might well be a problematic programming process to create the data as a two-dimensional array. However, the MVC model for the `JTable` is perfect for this situation. By defining the model separately, the model can take on a life of its own without affecting the table code.

Normally, you will create a table model by extending the `AbstractTableModel` class. The `AbstractTableModel` has a few methods that need to be implemented:

- `public int getRowCount();`
- `public int getColumnCount();`
- `public Object getValueAt(int row, int column);`

You should be able to guess exactly how to implement these methods. Another table model, `DefaultTableModel`, extends `AbstractTableModel` but adds the capability to edit the table. Listing 24.6 modifies the earlier example with a class that extends the `DefaultTableModel`. Notice that the `JTable` uses the new class (`TableModel`) instead of the fixed strings.

Listing 24.6 *TableExample2.java—JTable* Using a *TableModel* Instead of Fixed Arrays

```
import java.awt.*;
import java.awt.event.*;
import javax.swing.*;
import javax.swing.table.*;
import javax.swing.event.*;

public class TableExample2 extends JPanel{
  static JFrame myFrame;


  public TableExample2(){
    setLayout(new BorderLayout());
    JTable table = new JTable(new TableModel());
    JScrollPane pane = JTable.createScrollPaneForTable(table);
    add(pane);
  }
  public static void main(String args[]){
    myFrame = new JFrame("Table Example #2");
    TableExample2 tableExample = new TableExample2();
    myFrame.getContentPane().add("Center",tableExample);
    myFrame.setSize(400,250);
    myFrame.addWindowListener(new WindowAdapter() {
      public void windowClosing(WindowEvent e) {System.exit(0);}
      });
    myFrame.setVisible(true);
  }
}
```

```
class TableModel extends DefaultTableModel{
  String data[][] ={{"1","Introduction"},
            {"2","What Java can Do for You"},{"3","JAVA Design"},
            {"4","Installing  JAVA"},{"5","JDK tools"},
            {"6","Object-Oriented Programming"},{"7","Hello world"},
            {"8","Data Types"},{"9","Methods"},{"10","Using Expressions"}};
  String columnNames[] ={"Chapter Number","Chapter Title"};

  public int getRowCount(){
    return data.length;
  }

  public int getColumnCount(){
    return data[0].length;
  }

  public Object getValueAt(int row,int column){
    return data[row][column];
  }

  public String getColumnName(int column){
    return columnNames[column];
  }

  public void setValueAt(Object value, int row, int column){
    if (value instanceof String){
      data[row][column] = (String)value;
    }
    //Make sure you fire the table changed data so the view etc.
➥ will get notified of the change
    fireTableChanged(new TableModelEvent(this,row,row,column));
  }
}
```


Cell Editors

When you run `TableExample2`, you will notice that if you try to type in one of the fields, it changes to a text field and you are able to change the value. This can be very useful, but what if you want to offer the users a couple of options, like with a combo box? Well, tables support the concept of a cell editor just for this purpose. The cell editor provides you incredibly finite control over all aspects of the editing of a cell. For the scope of this chapter, though, the text will just cover how to add two columns. One will use a combo box; the other, a check box.

Listing 24.7 shows how to set one new column to be editable as a combo box. In addition, it demonstrates the fact that a Boolean can be represented as a check box.

Listing 24.7 Adding a Separate Cell Editor to the *TableExample*

```
import java.awt.*;
import java.awt.event.*;
import javax.swing.*;
import javax.swing.table.*;
import javax.swing.event.*;

public class TableExample3 extends JPanel{
  static JFrame myFrame;


  public TableExample3(){
    setLayout(new BorderLayout());
    JTable table = new JTable(new TableModel());
    JScrollPane pane = JTable.createScrollPaneForTable(table);
    add(pane);

    JComboBox comboBox = new JComboBox(new String[]{"Low","Medium","High"});
    TableColumn priorityColumn = table.getColumn("Priority");
    priorityColumn.setCellEditor(new DefaultCellEditor(comboBox));

  }
  public static void main(String args[]){
    myFrame = new JFrame("Table Example #3");
    TableExample3 tableExample = new TableExample3();
    myFrame.getContentPane().add("Center",tableExample);
    myFrame.setSize(400,250);
    myFrame.addWindowListener(new WindowAdapter() {
      public void windowClosing(WindowEvent e) {System.exit(0);}
      });
    myFrame.setVisible(true);
  }
}

class TableModel extends AbstractTableModel{
  String data[][] ={{"1","Introduction","High"},
          {"2","What Java can Do for You","Low"},
          {"3","JAVA Design","Low"},{"4","Installing  JAVA","Low"},
          {"5","JDK tools","Low"},
          {"6","Object-Oriented Programming","Low"},
          {"7","Hello world","Low"},{"8","Data Types","Low"},
          {"9","Methods","Low"},{"10","Using Expressions","Low"}};
  Boolean doneFlags[] = {new Boolean(false),new Boolean(false),
              new Boolean(false),new Boolean(false),new Boolean(false),
                          new Boolean(false),new Boolean(false),
              new Boolean(false),new Boolean(false),new Boolean(false)};
  String columnNames[] ={"Chapter Number","Chapter Title",
              "Priority","Done?"};

  public int getRowCount(){
    return data.length;
  }

  public int getColumnCount(){
```

```
      return columnNames.length;
    }

    public Object getValueAt(int row,int column){
      if (column<3)
        return data[row][column];
      else
        return doneFlags[row];
    }

    public String getColumnName(int column){
      return columnNames[column];
    }

    public void setValueAt(Object value, int row, int column){
      if (value instanceof String){
        data[row][column] = (String)value;
      }else if (value instanceof Boolean){
        doneFlags[row] =(Boolean) value;
      }
      fireTableChanged(new TableModelEvent(this,row,row,column));
    }
    public boolean isCellEditable(int row, int col) {return true;}
    public Class getColumnClass(int c)
  ➥{return getValueAt(0, c).getClass();}
  }
```


Trees

Tree displays have been a huge hit with GUI designs for years. Trees allow you to display n-dimensional data with relative ease. They are extremely popular for file listings, but they are useful in various situations. JFC's new tree class, called `JTree`, has many of the same facilities that `JTable` and `JList` have for controlling data.

Unlike with tables, it's not usual to create a tree from something as simple as an array of strings. If you want to do so, the facility is there, but what you will end up with is nothing more than a glorified list. If you want to predefine the root headers, this method might be perfect for you, but because it's not usual, we won't cover it here.

Tree Nodes

Trees are made up of nodes. Each node represents either a leaf or a branch. A leaf is a distinct element that has no sub elements or children. In other words, a leaf would not have the capability to "open" and "close" or, as it's put in tree terms, the capability to "expand" and "collapse." A branch, on the other hand, does have children and can expand or collapse to show the children. The children can be either branches or leafs. In reality, both branches and leafs are standard nodes, and there is not much difference between the two, except that a leaf has no children.

Generally speaking, you will probably find that the `DefaultMutableTreeNode` class will provide all the facilities you need for creating your tree nodes. Listing 24.8 shows how you could build a tree using just `DefaultMutableTreeNodes`. Figure 24.10 shows the results of this code.

Listing 24.8 *TreeExample.java*—You Can Build a Tree from a Set of Tree Nodes

```
import java.awt.*;
import java.awt.event.*;
import javax.swing.*;
import javax.swing.tree.DefaultMutableTreeNode;

public class TreeExample extends JPanel{
  static JFrame myFrame;

  public TreeExample(){
    setLayout(new BorderLayout());
    DefaultMutableTreeNode rootNode = createNodes();
    JTree tree = new JTree(rootNode);
    tree.setRootVisible(true);
    JScrollPane pane = new JScrollPane();
    pane.setViewportView(tree);
    add(pane);
  }

  public DefaultMutableTreeNode createNodes(){
    DefaultMutableTreeNode rootNode =
➥new DefaultMutableTreeNode ("Java Stuff");
    DefaultMutableTreeNode resources =
➥new DefaultMutableTreeNode ("Resources");
    DefaultMutableTreeNode tools =
➥new DefaultMutableTreeNode ("Tools");
    rootNode.add(resources);
    rootNode.add(tools);
    DefaultMutableTreeNode webSites =
➥new DefaultMutableTreeNode ("Web Sites");
    DefaultMutableTreeNode books =
➥new DefaultMutableTreeNode ("Books");
    resources.add(webSites);
    resources.add(books);

    DefaultMutableTreeNode magazines =
➥new DefaultMutableTreeNode ("Magazines");
    webSites.add(new DefaultMutableTreeNode ("JavaSoft"));
    webSites.add(new DefaultMutableTreeNode ("Gamelan"));
    webSites.add(magazines);
    magazines.add(new DefaultMutableTreeNode ("Javology"));
    magazines.add(new DefaultMutableTreeNode ("JavaWorld"));

    books.add(
➥new DefaultMutableTreeNode ("Special Edition Using Java 1.2"));

    tools.add(new DefaultMutableTreeNode ("JBuilder"));
    tools.add(new DefaultMutableTreeNode ("Visual J++"));
    tools.add(new DefaultMutableTreeNode ("Visual Age for Java"));
    tools.add(new DefaultMutableTreeNode ("Apptivity"));

    return rootNode;
  }

  public static void main(String args[]){
    myFrame = new JFrame("Tree Example");
```

```
        TreeExample treeExample = new TreeExample();
        myFrame.getContentPane().add("Center",treeExample);
        myFrame.setSize(400,250);
        myFrame.addWindowListener(new WindowAdapter() {
          public void windowClosing(WindowEvent e) {System.exit(0);}
          });
        myFrame.setVisible(true);
      }
    }
```

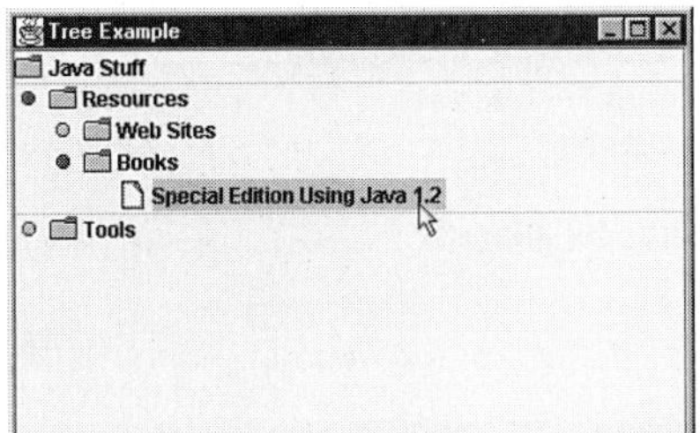

FIG. 24.10 You can expand and close the tree at will.

Understanding *TreeExample* First, take a look at the constructor. The tree is created using the `rootNode` object. You'll take a look at how the `rootNode` is created later, but the important thing to realize is that you are passing in just the root node of the tree.

The next line of code that you'll see sets the root node to be visible. This is actually the default value, but it's shown here to make the point. You see, the root node cannot have any siblings, and often this means that you will create a root node that doesn't really offer any additional information. So you can set the root to be nonvisible by using `tree.setRootVisible (false)`.

The last interesting portion of the constructor is the fact that like `JList` and `JTable`, `JTree` does not handle the scrolling on its own. Instead, like `JList` and `JTable`, it implements the `Scrollable` interface. So you create a scroll pane and add the tree to it.

Creating the Nodes The `createNodes()` method is where the nodes for the tree are actually created. Effectively, what you are doing is layering out each branch. You first create the `rootNode`, and then its children. Then the nodes for each of the children are created, and added to the parent node, and so on.

Tree Models

Building a tree out of a set of nodes as in Listing 24.8 works great when you know the data at the time you create the tree. However, it's not enough when you will be inserting or removing nodes after you first create the tree. The reason is that although you can still call the `add()` method on a visible node, the tree doesn't know about this information, and the visual portion of the tree is not updated.

Like the models for tables, the tree models can be manipulated at any time and can store various values. All the details of handling `TreeModels` is unfortunately beyond the scope of this book, so we will cover only how to add and remove nodes.

Listing 24.9 demonstrates the use of the model. It has a `TextField` at the top of the window, which allows you to add a new node with the `TextField`'s value to the item selected in the tree. On the bottom of the window is a button that removes the selected node from the tree (Figure 24.11).

Listing 24.9 Trees Can Be Manipulated Through Their Models

```
import java.awt.*;
import java.awt.event.*;
import javax.swing.*;
import javax.swing.tree.DefaultMutableTreeNode;
import javax.swing.tree.DefaultTreeModel;
import javax.swing.tree.TreePath;

public class TreeExample extends JPanel{
  static JFrame myFrame;
  JTextField tf;
  JTree tree;

  public TreeExample(){
    setLayout(new BorderLayout());
    tf= new JTextField();
    tf.addActionListener(new ActionListener(){
      public void actionPerformed(ActionEvent ae){
      addTextFieldValue();
      }
      });
    add(tf,"North");

    DefaultMutableTreeNode rootNode = createNodes();
    tree = new JTree(rootNode);
    tree.setRootVisible(true);
    JScrollPane pane = new JScrollPane();
    pane.setViewportView(tree);
    add(pane,"Center");

    JButton remove = new JButton("Remove");
    remove.addActionListener(new ActionListener(){
      public void actionPerformed(ActionEvent ae2){
      removeSelectedNode();
      }
      });
    add(remove,"South");
  }

  public void removeSelectedNode(){
    TreePath selectionPath = tree.getSelectionPath();
    DefaultMutableTreeNode selectedNode = (DefaultMutableTreeNode)
➥selectionPath.getLastPathComponent();
    ((DefaultTreeModel)tree.getModel()).removeNodeFromParent
➥(selectedNode);
  }

  public void addTextFieldValue(){
```

```
    DefaultMutableTreeNode newNode = new DefaultMutableTreeNode
➥ (tf.getText());
    TreePath selectionPath = tree.getSelectionPath();
    DefaultMutableTreeNode selectedNode = (DefaultMutableTreeNode)
➥selectionPath.getLastPathComponent();
    ((DefaultTreeModel)tree.getModel()).insertNodeInto(newNode,
➥ selectedNode, selectedNode.getChildCount());
  }

  public DefaultMutableTreeNode createNodes(){
    DefaultMutableTreeNode rootNode = new DefaultMutableTreeNode
➥ ("Java Stuff");
    DefaultMutableTreeNode resources = new DefaultMutableTreeNode
➥ ("Resources");
    DefaultMutableTreeNode tools = new DefaultMutableTreeNode
➥ ("Tools");
    rootNode.add(resources);
    rootNode.add(tools);
    DefaultMutableTreeNode webSites =new DefaultMutableTreeNode
➥ ("Web Sites");
    DefaultMutableTreeNode books = new DefaultMutableTreeNode
➥ ("Books");
    resources.add(webSites);
    resources.add(books);

    DefaultMutableTreeNode magazines = new DefaultMutableTreeNode
➥ ("Magazines");
    webSites.add(new DefaultMutableTreeNode ("JavaSoft"));
    webSites.add(new DefaultMutableTreeNode ("Gamelan"));
    webSites.add(magazines);
    magazines.add(new DefaultMutableTreeNode ("Javology"));
    magazines.add(new DefaultMutableTreeNode ("JavaWorld"));

    books.add(new DefaultMutableTreeNode
➥ ("Special Edition Using Java 1.2"));

    tools.add(new DefaultMutableTreeNode ("JBuilder"));
    tools.add(new DefaultMutableTreeNode ("Visual J++"));
    tools.add(new DefaultMutableTreeNode ("Visual Age for Java"));
    tools.add(new DefaultMutableTreeNode ("Apptivity"));

    return rootNode;
  }

  public static void main(String args[]){
    myFrame = new JFrame("Tree Example");
    TreeExample treeExample = new TreeExample();
    myFrame.getContentPane().add("Center",treeExample);
    myFrame.setSize(400,250);
    myFrame.addWindowListener(new WindowAdapter() {
      public void windowClosing(WindowEvent e) {System.exit(0);}
      });
    myFrame.setVisible(true);
  }
}
```

FIG. 24.11
Using the `TextField`, you can add values to the tree; using the remove button, you can delete from it.

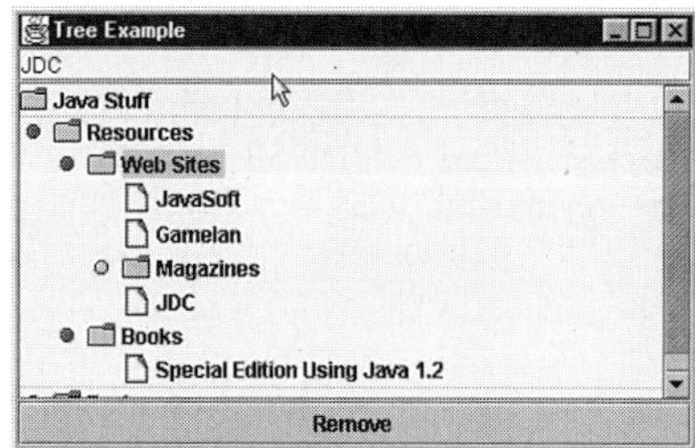

Understanding new *TreeExample*

Most of this example is left for you to look through and figure out on your own. The two key methods we need to explore, however, are `removeSelectedNode()` and `addTextFieldValue()`.

removeSelectedNode()

The `removeSelectedNode()` method is designed to delete the node that has been selected in the tree. To do this, it must first obtain the node that's been selected. The tree can provide you with the path to this node via the `getSelectionPath()` method. This method does not return the node itself, but instead returns a new class called a `TreePath`. The `TreePath` includes all the nodes from the root down to the node that has been selected. This is convenient because you can store the path and later make sure that all the folders have been opened to expose the node using tree's `expandPath()` method, or it can be used in various other ways.

In this case, the tree path is used to obtain the node that has been selected, but requesting the path's last component. `GetLastPathComponent()` actually returns an `Object`, so you will notice that the result has been casted to a `DefaultMutableTreeNode`.

Now that you know the node, you can delete it. As was mentioned earlier, the part of the tree that you want to have delete the node is the tree's model. The model will then inform all the other necessary component pieces. Fortunately, `DefaultTreeModel` has a method just for the purpose of removing the node called `removeNodeFromParent` that does the trick.

NOTE In this case, because you haven't used a special model and are using just the default, you can safely cast the `getModel()` to a `DefaultTreeModel`. If you had changed it to a custom model, though, you'd need to adjust this code.

You might also want to know that when you remove the node from the tree, the node itself is not actually deleted. If you wanted to put it somewhere else, or on another tree, you could safely do just that.

addTextFieldValue()

The other method you're interested in with this class is the `addTextFieldValue()` method. This method creates a new node with the text in the text field and adds it as a child of the selected node.

The first task in adding the node is to obtain its parent node. In the preceding section, you already saw how most of the code for this task works. What's different is the last line of the method. `DefaultTreeModel`'s `insertNodeInto()` method takes three parameters. The first one is the new node. The second is the new parent of the node, and the last is the location in the list to add the node. In this case, you will add it as the last child to the node, but you can also add it as the first element or in any other order you like. Play with this on your own to see the effect.

Displaying HTML with *JEditor*

Another one of the great innovations added to JFC was what is known as an editor. `JEditor` allows you to display formatted text, with tags that make parts of the text have special attributes, such as centering and italics. Standard with JFC are editor kits for HTML and RTF. Even better, you can define your own implementation of a class known as `EditorKit` and specify your own file format.

In Listing 24.10, you see `JEditor` being used to create what you might call a basic Web browser.Figure 24.12 shows the result of this code.

Listing 24.10 *HTMLView.java*—Using *JEditor* to Create a Browser

```
import javax.swing.*;
import javax.swing.event.*;
import java.awt.BorderLayout;
import java.awt.event.*;
import java.io.IOException;
import java.util.Date;
import java.net.URL;
import java.net.MalformedURLException;


public class HTMLView extends JPanel{
  // The initial width and height of the frame
  public static int WIDTH = 600;
  public static int HEIGHT = 400;

  protected JEditorPane _view;
  protected JTextField _commandLine;

  public HTMLView(){
    _view = new JEditorPane();
    _view.setEditable(false);
    _view.addHyperlinkListener(new HyperlinkListener(){
      //This is called if a hyperlink is clicked on
      public void hyperlinkUpdate(HyperlinkEvent event){
      setURL(event.getURL());
      }
      });

    setLayout(new BorderLayout());
    add(_view,"Center");
```

continues

Listing 24.10 Continued

```
    //Add the location line
    _commandLine = new JTextField();
    add(_commandLine,"North");
    _commandLine.addActionListener(new ActionListener(){
      public void actionPerformed(ActionEvent ae){
        try{
          URL newURL = new URL(ae.getActionCommand());
          setURL(newURL);
        }catch (MalformedURLException mue){
          System.out.println
➥("The URL you clicked on appears incorrect:"+mue);
        }
      }
    });
  }

  public void setURL(URL newURL){
    try{
      _view.setPage(newURL);
      _commandLine.setText(newURL.toExternalForm());
    }catch (IOException ioe){
      System.out.println("Error :"+ioe);
    }
  }

  public static void main(String s[]) {
    HTMLView panel = new HTMLView();

    JFrame frame = new JFrame("HTML Example");
    frame.addWindowListener(new WindowAdapter() {
      public void windowClosing(WindowEvent e) {System.exit(0);}
      });
    frame.getContentPane().add("Center", panel);
    frame.pack();
    frame.setVisible(true);
    frame.setSize(WIDTH,HEIGHT);
  }
}
```

Understanding *HTMLView*

`HTMLView` has two different components, the `JEditor` and a `JTextField`. The editor displays the current Web site and allows you to click on any standard hypertext link. The text field is used to let the user specify a Web page, just like the location field is used in Netscape Navigator or Internet Explorer.

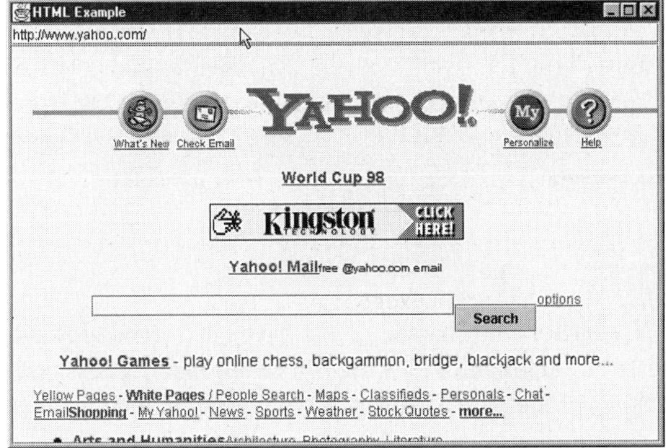

FIG. 24.12
The `HTMLView` can show Web pages such as Yahoo.com.

Listening for Hyperlink Events

When the user clicks on a hypertext link on the `JEditor`, the `JEditor` will produce an event called a `HyperlinkEvent`. Generally speaking, when this happens in a browser, you want to change the editor page to the URL pointed to by the hyperlink. Before you can achieve this effect with your little browser, you first need to capture the event. As with all events, you can capture the event with a listener, and the listener you need to implement is the `HyperlinkListener`. As you can see from the following snippet from Listing 24.10, `HyperlinkListener` has one method: `hyperlinkUpdate()`.

```
_view.addHyperlinkListener(new HyperlinkListener(){
      //This is called if a hyperlink is clicked on
      public void hyperlinkUpdate(HyperlinkEvent event){
          setURL(event.getURL());
      }
});
```

Setting a New Page

To set the new page for the `JEditor`, you need to use the `setPage()` method. The trick in doing this, however, is that the `setPage()` method can throw an `IOException`, so you need to catch the `IOException` as shown in the next code snippet from Listing 24.10:

```
public void setURL(URL newURL){
    try{
      _view.setPage(newURL);
      _commandLine.setText(newURL.toExternalForm());
    }catch (IOException ioe){
      System.out.println("Error :"+ioe);
    }
  }
```

JTextField

JFC's TextFields – JTextFields work extremely similar to their AWT counterparts. As shown in Listing 24.10, `ActionListeners` can receive notification when the user presses the Enter key, and you can use this to change the Web page by calling the same `setURL` method we used for the `HyperlinkListener`.

Creating Icons

Throughout this chapter and Chapter 23 you have used icons. However, so far you have used only icons created from graphics files. As you can probably guess, graphics icons are not always as efficient as image files. This is true from the standpoints of both size and performance. In addition, it is difficult to adjust to changing needs such as size and color. Though both changes can be accommodated using images, the results are nearly impossible to generate without losing quality, and these methods are never fast.

The preferred machanism for creating simple icons is to implement the Icon interface. Icon has three methods:

```
public abstract void paintIcon(Component c, Graphics g, int x, int y)
```

Which must draw the icon onto the Graphics object at the x,y coordiante.

```
public abstract int getIconWidth()
```

Which needs to return the width of the icon. Note: this value is fixed and cannot change later.

```
public abstract int getIconHeight()
```

Which needs to return the height of the icon. Note: this value is fixed and cannot change later.

The ImageIcon that you have become familiar with over the last two chapters simply paints the image when the paintIcon method is called. However, it is frequently the case that it will take less time, and file space to manually draw the icon. Listing 24.11 below shows an example of drawing a bulls eye icon. Figure 24.13 shows the results of this code.

Listing 24.11 Drawing Your Own Icon on the Button

```
import java.awt.*;
import java.awt.event.*;
import javax.swing.*;
import javax.swing.border.*;

public class IconButton extends JPanel {
  static JFrame myFrame;
  protected JLabel label;
  JPopupMenu pm;

  public IconButton(){
    JButton hello = new JButton("Hello");
    hello.setMnemonic('h');
```

```
    hello.addActionListener(new ActionListener(){
      public void actionPerformed(ActionEvent ae){
      label.setText("Hello World!");
      }
      });

    //set the background of the button
    hello.setBackground (SystemColor.control);

    //Set the icon for the button
    Icon icon = new MyFirstIcon ();
    hello.setIcon(icon);

    add(hello);

  }

  public static void main(String args[]){
    myFrame = new JFrame("Hello World!");
    IconButton ib = new IconButton();
    myFrame.getContentPane().add("Center",ib);
    myFrame.setSize(300,75);
    myFrame.addWindowListener(new WindowAdapter() {
      public void windowClosing(WindowEvent e) {System.exit(0);}
      });
    myFrame.setVisible(true);
  }
}

class MyFirstIcon implements Icon{

  static private final Dimension size = new Dimension( 20, 20 );


  public void paintIcon(Component c, Graphics g, int x, int y) {
    //translate g to the x,y coordiantes so you don't have to deal
    //with it through out the rest of the method
    g.translate( x, y );

    int right = size.width;
    int bottom = size.height;

    int ringWidth= right/10;
    int ringHeight = bottom/10;


    // Draw white fill
    g.setColor( Color.red );
    g.fillOval(0,0,right,bottom  );

    // Draw outer ring
    g.setColor( Color.white );
    g.fillOval(ringWidth,ringHeight,right-ringWidth*2,
➥bottom-ringHeight*2);
```

continues

Listing 24.11 Continued

```
    // Draw middle white ring
    g.setColor( Color.red);
    g.fillOval(ringWidth*2,ringHeight*2,right-ringWidth*4,
➥bottom-ringHeight*4);

    //draw middle ring
    g.setColor( Color.white );
    g.fillOval(ringWidth*3,ringWidth*3,right-ringWidth*6,
➥bottom-ringHeight*6);

    // Draw middle white ring
    g.setColor( Color.red);
    g.fillOval(ringWidth*4,ringHeight*4,right-ringWidth*8,
➥bottom-ringHeight*8);

    //draw inner ring
    g.setColor( Color.white );
    g.fillOval(ringWidth*5,ringWidth*5,right-ringWidth*10,
➥bottom-ringHeight*10);


    //Translate g back to where it was when we started the
    //method
    g.translate( -x, -y );
  }


  public int getIconWidth() { return size.width; }
  public int getIconHeight() { return size.height; }

}
```

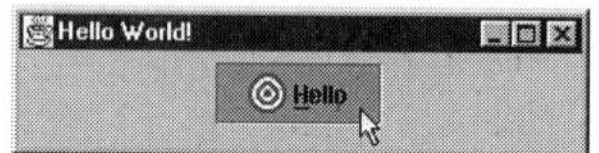

FIG. 24.13
The button has a unique icon on it.

JFC Applets

So you've gotten intrigued by all this JFC - Swing stuff, and now you want to write some applets that use JFC. Well, before you do, you need to consider one important technical issue: JFC is a fairly large package; can you afford to use it? If you're writing an intranet applet, odds are this isn't an issue, but if you're writing an Internet app, you'll want to be sure to tell your users how to put the JFC packages into their browser. If you don't do this, your users will get stuck downloading that huge file every time they run your application.

Now, to change your applet, you need to do only two things. First, you need to extend `JApplet` instead of `Applet`, and second, you need to add your components to the content pane instead of directly to the applet.

Listing 24.12 below shows how to build the HelloWorld applet with a button. Notice that the `feet.gif` icon can be used here too.

Listing 24.12 You Must Add All Components to the Content Pane of a Swing Applet

```
import java.awt.*;
import java.awt.event.*;
//import javax.swing.*;
import javax.swing.*;

public class HelloWorldJFCApplet extends JApplet {
  static JFrame myFrame;

  public void init(){

    Icon icon = new ImageIcon ("feet.gif");
    JLabel label = new JLabel ("Hello World!",icon,SwingConstants.RIGHT);

    //For an Applet you must add everything to the content pane.
    Container panel = getContentPane();
    panel.setLayout(new FlowLayout());
    panel.add(label);
  }

}
```


Configuring Netscape and Internet Explorer for JFC The best way to use JFC with either Navigator or Internet Explorer is to use the Java Plug-in. The Plug-in includes the Swing API, and insures that you are using a true Java Virtual Machine. ●

CHAPTER 25

Images

In this chapter

Drawing Images to the Screen

Java's methods for manipulating images are different from some of the more conventional graphics systems. To support network-based operations, Java has to support an imaging paradigm that supports the gradual loading of images. You don't want your applet to sit and wait for all the images to download. Java's producer-consumer model takes the gradual loading of images into account. Java also uses the concept of filters to enable you to change the image as it passes from producer to consumer. This might seem like a strange way to deal with images at first, but it is very powerful.

Just drawing basic images to the screen is easy to do in Java. The Graphics class provides a convenient method called `drawImage()` for this very purpose. The `drawImage` method was used in several programs before. In Chapter 15, "Advanced Applet Code," "Adding Images to Applets," you learned to load images from URLs and draw them in the `paint()` method. The `paint()` method enables you to do much more than this, allowing you to scale the image dynamically. And starting with Java 1.1, you can also crop and rotate the image just using the `drawImage` method.

Listing 25.1 shows how to use the `drawImage` method to double the size of the image when it appears on the screen (see Figure 25.1).

Listing 25.1 *ScaleImage.java*—Draw the Image at Twice Its Normal Size

```
import java.applet.Applet;
import java.awt.Graphics;
import java.awt.Image;
import java.net.URL;
import java.net.MalformedURLException;


public class ScaleImage extends Applet{
  Image img;

  public void init(){
    try{
      img = getImage (new URL(getDocumentBase(),"MagnaHeader.gif"));
    }catch (MalformedURLException e){
      System.out.println("URL not valid:"+e);
    }
  }

  public void paint (Graphics g){
    g.drawImage (img,0,0,img.getWidth(null)*2,img.getHeight(null)*2,this);
  }


}
```

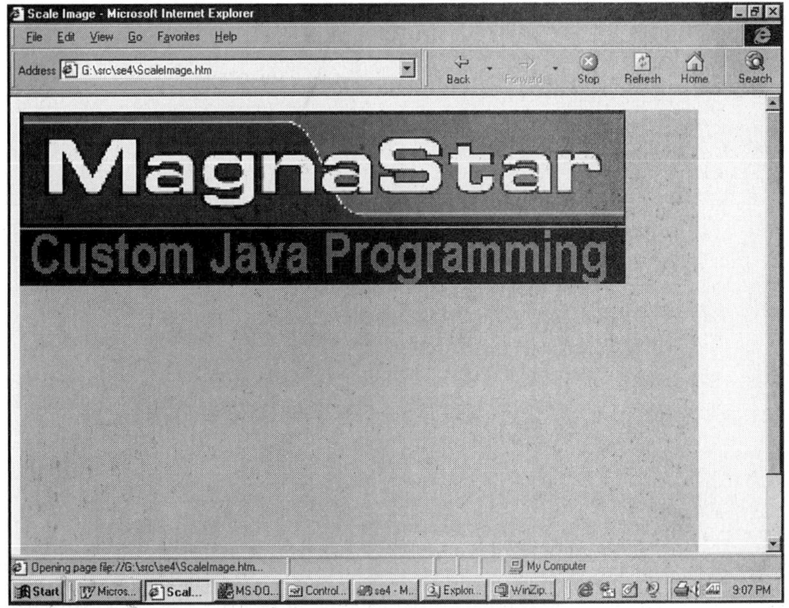

FIG. 25.1
You can draw a simple image to the screen and scale it to twice its size.

Starting with Java 1.1, an additional `drawImage` method was added that provided you even more functionality. This `drawImage` method has the following signature:

```
public abstract boolean drawImage(Image img,
int dx1,  int dy1,  int dx2,   int dy2,
int sx1, int sy1,   int sx2,   int sy2,
ImageObserver observer)
```

This `drawImage` method works quite a bit differently from its brothers. First the initial set of parameters (the `dx` variables) specify not just the x and y coordinate to start from and the height and width, but the x,y coordinate of the upper-left corner of the image and the x,y coordinate of the lower-right portion of the image. This means you can actually perform axle conversions directly. The second set of parameters (the `sx` variables) indicate the x,y coordinates of the source to start from and end at—enabling you to crop the image at will.

Look at how you can use the `drawImage` method in practice. Listing 25.2 shows how to use this `drawImage` method to flip an image upside down (see Figure 25.2).

Listing 25.2 ***FlipImage.java***

```
import java.applet.Applet;
import java.awt.Graphics;
import java.awt.Image;
import java.net.URL;
import java.net.MalformedURLException;
```

continues

Listing 25.2 Continued

```
public class FlipImage extends Applet{
  Image img;

  public void init(){
    try{
       img = getImage (new URL(getDocumentBase(),"MagnaHeader.gif"));
    }catch (MalformedURLException e){
      System.out.println("URL not valid:"+e);
    }
  }

  public void paint (Graphics g){
    g.drawImage (img,0,
                 img.getHeight(null), img.getWidth(null), 0,0,0,
                 img.getWidth(null),img.getHeight(null),this);
  }
}
```

FIG. 25.2
`drawImage` enables you to flip an image upside-down.

Next, look at how to use the `sx` variables to crop out just the center of the image. In Listing 25.3 below the center of the image is drawn upside down (see Figure 25.3).

Listing 25.3 ***FlipCropImage.java***

```
import java.applet.Applet;
import java.awt.Graphics;
import java.awt.Image;
```

```
import java.net.URL;
import java.net.MalformedURLException;


public class FlipCropImage extends Applet{
  Image    img;

  public void    init(){
    try{
      img    =    getImage (new    URL(getDocumentBase(),"MagnaHeader.gif"));
    }catch (MalformedURLException    e){
      System.out.println("URL    not    valid:"+e);
    }
  }

  public void    paint    (Graphics    g){
    g.drawImage    (img,0, img.getHeight(null)/2,img.getWidth(null)/2,
                  0,img.getWidth(null)/4, img.getHeight(null)/4,
                  img.getWidth(null)*3/4 ,img.getHeight(null)*3/4, this);
  }
}
}
```

FIG. 25.3 `drawImage` enables you to crop out a section of the image.

Producers, Consumers, and Observers

Java's model for manipulating images is more complex than other models. Java uses the concept of image producers and image consumers. An example of an image producer might be an object responsible for fetching an image over the network, or it might be a simple array of bytes that represent an image. The image producer can be thought of as the source of the image data. Image consumers are objects that make use of the image data.

Image consumers are, typically, low-level drawing routines that display the image onscreen. The interesting thing about the producer-consumer model is that the producer is "in control." The ImageProducer uses the `setPixels` method in the `ImageConsumer` to describe the image to the consumer.

The best way to illustrate this mechanism is to trace the process of loading an image over the network. First, the `ImageProducer` starts reading the image. The first thing it reads from the image is the width and height of the image. It notifies its consumers (notice that a producer can serve multiple consumers) of the dimension of the image using the `setDimensions` method. Figure 25.4 illustrates the relationship between an `ImageProducer` and an `ImageConsumer`.

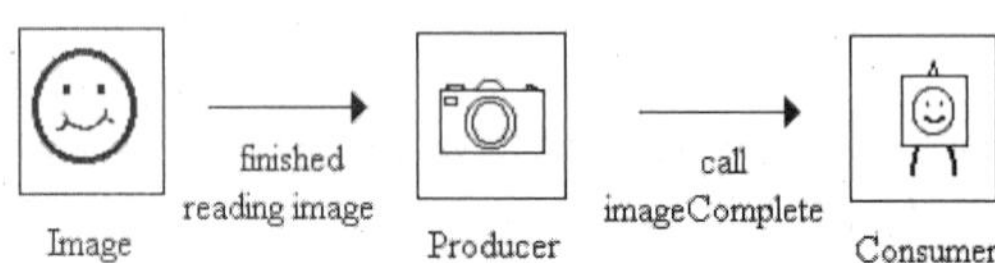

FIG. 25.4 The `ImageProducer` reads the image dimensions from the image file and passes the information to the `ImageConsumer`.

Next, the producer reads the color map for the image. From this color map, the producer determines what kind of color model the image uses, and calls the `setColorModel` method in each consumer. Figure 25.5 illustrates how the producer passes color information to the consumer.

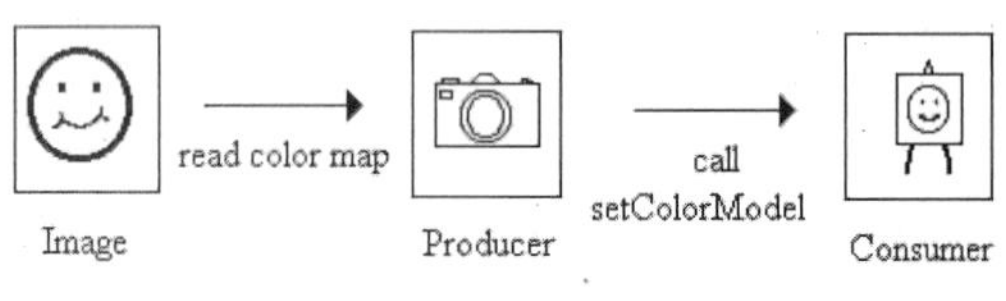

FIG. 25.5 The producer uses the `setColorModel` method to relay color information to the consumer.

The producer calls the `setHints` method in each consumer to tell the consumers how it intends to deliver the image pixels. This enables the consumers to optimize their pixel handling, if possible. Some of the values for the hints are: `ImageConsumer.RANDOMPIXELORDER`, `ImageConsumer.TOPDOWNLEFTRIGHT`, `ImageConsumer.COMPLETESCANLINES`, `ImageConsumer.SINGLEPASS`, and `ImageConsumer.SINGLEFRAME`. Figure 25.6 illustrates how the producer passes hints to the consumer.

Now the producer finally starts to "produce" pixels, calling the `setPixels` method in the consumers to deliver the image. This might be done in many calls, especially if the consumers are delivering one scan line at a time for a large image. Or it might be one single call if the consumers are delivering the image as a single pass (`ImageConsumer.SINGLEPASS`). Figure 25.7 shows the producer passing pixel information to the consumer.

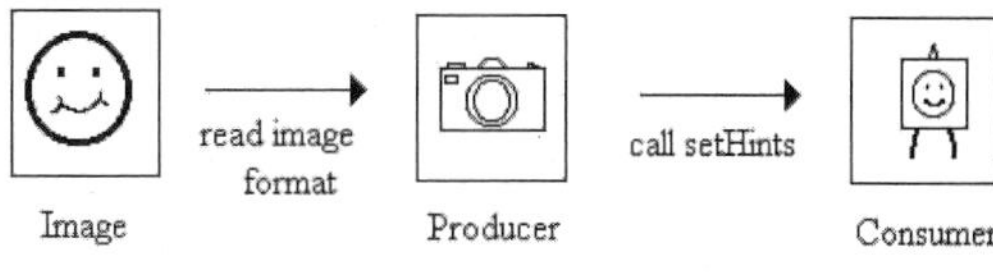

FIG. 25.6
The producer passes hints to the consumer to indicate how it will send pixels.

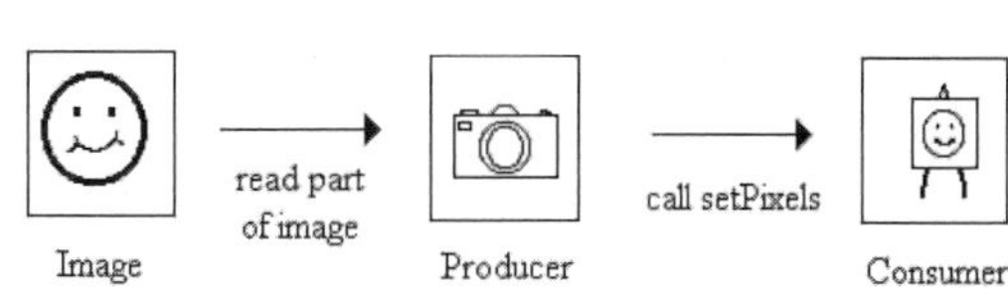

FIG. 25.7
The producer uses the `setPixels` method to pass pixel information to the consumer.

Finally, the producer calls the `imageComplete` method in the consumer to indicate that the image has been delivered. If a failure occurs in delivery—for instance, the network went down as it was being transmitted—then the `imageComplete` method will be called with a parameter of `ImageConsumer.IMAGEERROR` or `ImageConsumer.IMAGEABORT`. Another possible status is that this image is part of a multiframe image (a form of animation) and there are more frames to come. This would be signaled by the `ImageConsumer.SINGLEFRAMEDONE` parameter. When everything is truly complete, `imageComplete` is called with the `ImageConsumer.STATICIMAGEDONE` parameter. Figure 25.8 shows the producer wrapping up the image transfer to the consumer.

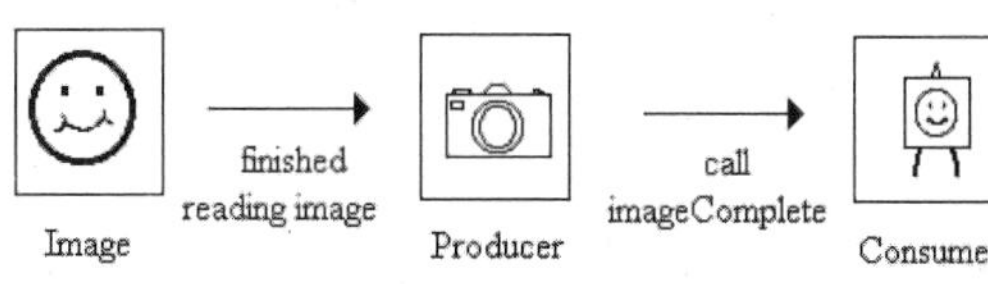

FIG. 25.8
The producer uses the `imageComplete` method to tell the consumer it is through transferring the image.

This method enables Java to load images efficiently; it does not have to stop and wait for them all to load before it begins. The `ImageObserver` interface is related to the producer-consumer interface as a sort of "interested third party." It enables an object to receive updates whenever the producer has released some new information about the image.

You might recall that when you used the `drawImage` method, you passed `this` as the last parameter. You were actually giving the `drawImage` method a reference to an `ImageObserver`. The `Applet` class implements the `ImageObserver` interface. The `ImageObserver` interface contains a single method called `imageUpdate`:

```
boolean imageUpdate(Image img, int flags, int x, int y,
   int width, int height)
```

Not all the information passed to the `imageUpdate` method is valid all the time. The `flags` parameter is a summary of flags that tell what information is now available about the image. Here are the possible flags:

`ImageObserver.WIDTH`	Width value is now valid.
`ImageObserver.HEIGHT`	Height value is now valid.
`ImageObserver.PROPERTIES`	Image properties are now available.
`ImageObserver.SOMEBITS`	More pixels are available (x, y, width, and height indicate the bounding box of the pixels now available).
`ImageObserver.FRAMEBITS`	Another complete frame is now available.
`ImageObserver.ALLBITS`	The image has loaded completely.
`ImageObserver.ERROR`	There was an error loading the image.
`ImageObserver.ABORT`	The loading of the image was aborted.

These flags are usually added together, so an `imageUpdate` method might test for the `WIDTH` flag with the following code:

```
if ((flags & ImageObserver.WIDTH) != 0) {
        // width is now available
     }
```

Image Filters

The Java image model also enables you to filter images easily. The concept of a filter is similar to the idea of a filter in photography. It is something that sits between the image consumer (the film) and the image producer (the outside world). The filter changes the image before it is delivered to the consumer. The `CropImageFilter` is a predefined filter that crops an image to a certain dimension. (It only shows a portion of the whole image.) You create a `CropImageFilter` by passing the `x`, `y`, `width`, and `height` of the cropping rectangle to the constructor:

```
public CropImageFilter(int x, int y, int width, int height)
```

After you create an image filter, you can lay it on top of an existing image source by creating a `FilteredImageSource`:

```
public FilteredImageSource(ImageProducer imageSource, ImageFilter filter)
```

The applet in Listing 25.4 takes an image and applies a `CropImageFilter` to it to display only a part of the image. Figure 25.9 contains the output from this applet, showing a full image and a cropped version of that image.

Listing 25.4 Source Code for *CropImage.java*

```
import java.awt.*;
import java.awt.image.*;
import java.applet.*;

// Example 25.4 - CropImage Applet
//
// This applet creates a CropImageFilter to create a
// cropped version of an image.  It displays both the original
// and the cropped images.
```

```
public class CropImage extends Applet
{
   private Image originalImage;
   private Image croppedImage;
   private ImageFilter cropFilter;

   public void init()
   {
// Get the original image
      originalImage = getImage(getDocumentBase(), "samantha.gif");

// Create a filter to crop the image in a box starting at (25, 30)
// that is 75 pixels wide and 75 pixels high.

      cropFilter = new CropImageFilter(25, 30, 75, 75);

// Create a new image that is a cropped version of the original

      croppedImage = createImage(new FilteredImageSource(
         originalImage.getSource(), cropFilter));
   }

   public void paint(Graphics g)
   {
// Display both images
      g.drawImage(originalImage, 0, 0, this);
      g.drawImage(croppedImage, 0, 200, this);
   }
}
```

FIG. 25.9 The `CropImageFilter` enables you to display only a portion of an image.

Copying Memory to an Image

One possible type of image producer is an array of integers representing the color values of each pixel. The `MemoryImageSource` class is just that. You create the memory image and then create a `MemoryImageSource` to act as an image producer for that memory image. Next, you create an image from the `MemoryImageSource`. `MemoryImageSource` has a number of constructors. In all of them, you must supply the width and height of the image, the array of pixel values, the starting offset of the first pixel in the array, and the number of positions that make up a scan line in the image. The pixel values are normally the RGB values for each pixel; however, if you supply your own color model, the meaning of the pixel values is determined by the color model. The scanline length is usually the same as the image width.

Sometimes, however, your pixel array might have extra padding at the end of the scanline, so you might have a scanline length larger than the image width. You cannot have a scanline length shorter than the image width. You can also pass a table of properties for the image that will be passed to the image consumer. You need the properties only if you have an image consumer that requires them. The consumers that ship with the JDK do not require any properties. Here are the constructors for the `MemoryImageSource`:

```
public MemoryImageSource(int width, int height, ColorModel model,
byte[] pixels, int startingOffset, int scanlineLength)

public MemoryImageSource(int width, int height, ColorModel model,
byte[] pixels, int startingOffset, int scanlineLength, Hashtable properties)

public MemoryImageSource(int width, int height, ColorModel model,
int[] pixels, int startingOffset, int scanlineLength)

public MemoryImageSource(int width, int height, ColorModel model,
int[] pixels, int startingOffset, int scanlineLength, Hashtable properties)

public MemoryImageSource(int width, int height, int[] pixels,
int startingOffset, int scanlineLength)

public MemoryImageSource(int width, int height, int[] pixels,
int startingOffset, int scanlineLength, Hashtable properties)
```

The applet in Listing 25.5 creates a memory image, a `MemoryImageSource`, and finally draws the image in the drawing area. Figure 25.10 shows the output from this applet.

FIG. 25.10
`MemoryImageSource` class enables you to create your own images from pixel values.

Listing 25.5 Source Code for *MemoryImage.java*

```
import java.applet.*;
import java.awt.*;
import java.awt.image.*;

// Example 25.5 - MemoryImage Applet
//
// This applet creates an image using an array of
// pixel values.

public class MemoryImage extends Applet
{
```

```
    private final static int b = Color.blue.getRGB();
    private final static int r = Color.red.getRGB();
    private final static int g = Color.green.getRGB();

// Create the array of pixel values.  The image will be 10x10
// And resembles a square bullseye with blue around the outside,
// green inside the blue, and red in the center.

    int pixels[] = {
        b, b, b, b, b, b, b, b, b, b,
        b, b, b, b, b, b, b, b, b, b,
        b, b, g, g, g, g, g, g, b, b,
        b, b, g, g, g, g, g, g, b, b,
        b, b, g, g, r, r, g, g, b, b,
        b, b, g, g, r, r, g, g, b, b,
        b, b, g, g, g, g, g, g, b, b,
        b, b, g, g, g, g, g, g, b, b,
        b, b, b, b, b, b, b, b, b, b,
        b, b, b, b, b, b, b, b, b, b};

    Image myImage;

    public void init()
    {
// Create the new image from the pixels array.  The 0, 10 means start
// reading pixels from array location 0, and there is a new row of
// pixels every 10 locations.
        myImage = createImage(new MemoryImageSource(10, 10,
            pixels, 0, 10));
    }

    public void paint(Graphics g)
    {
// Draw the image.  Notice that the width and height we give for the
// image is 10 times its original size.  The drawImage method will
// scale the image automatically.
        g.drawImage(myImage, 0, 0, 100, 100, this);
    }
}
```

Part III
Ch 25

Copying Images to Memory

The `PixelGrabber` class is sort of an inverse of the `MemoryImageSource`. Rather than taking an array of integers and turning it into an image, it takes an image and turns it into an array of integers. The `PixelGrabber` acts as an `ImageConsumer`. You create a `PixelGrabber`, give it the dimensions of the image you want and an array in which to store the image pixels, and it gets the pixels from the `ImageProducer`.

To grab pixels, you must first create a `PixelGrabber` by passing the image you want to grab, the x, y, width, and height of the area you are grabbing, an array to contain the pixel values, and the offset and scanline length for the array of pixel values:

```
public PixelGrabber(Image image, int x, int y, int width, int height,
int[] pixels, int startingOffset, int scanlineLength)
```

You can also supply an image producer instead of an image:

```
public PixelGrabber(ImageProducer producer, int x, int y, int width, int height,
int[] pixels, int startingOffset, int scanlineLength)
```

To initiate the pixel grabbing, call the `grabPixels` method.

```
public boolean grabPixels() throws InterruptedException
```

starts grabbing pixels and waits until it gets all the pixels. If the pixels are grabbed successfully, it returns `true`. If there is an error or an abort, it returns `false`.

```
public boolean grabPixels(long ms) throws InterruptedException
```

starts grabbing pixels and waits a maximum of `ms` milliseconds for all the pixels. If the pixels are grabbed successfully, it returns `true`. If there is a timeout, an error, or an abort, it returns `false`.

You can check on the status of a pixel grab with the `status` method:

```
public synchronized int status()
```

The value returned by `status` contains the same information as the `flags` parameter in the `imageUpdate` method in `ImageObserver`. Basically, if the `ImageObserver.ABORT` bit is set in the value, the pixel grab is aborted; otherwise, it should be okay.

The `PixelGrabber` is useful if you want to take an existing image and modify it. Listing 25.6 is an applet that uses the `PixelGrabber` to get the pixels of an image into an array. It then enables you to color sections of the image by picking a crayon and touching the area you want to color. To redisplay the image, it uses the `MemoryImageSource` to turn the array of pixels back into an image. The applet runs pretty slowly on a 486/100, so you need a lot of patience. It requires the `Shape` class.

Listing 25.6 Source Code for *Crayon.java*

```
import java.applet.*;
import java.awt.*;
import java.awt.image.*;

// Example 25.6 - Crayon Applet
//
// The Crayon applet uses the PixelGrabber to create an array of pixel
// values from an image.  It then allows you to paint the image using
// a set of crayons, and then redisplays the image using the
// MemoryImageSource.
// If you want to use other images with this applet, make sure that
// the lines are done in black, since it specifically looks for black
// as the boundary for an area.
// Also, beware, this applet runs very slowly on a 486/100

public class Crayon extends Applet
{
```

```
   private Image coloringBook;    // the original image
   private Image displayImage;    // the image to be displayed

   private int imageWidth, imageHeight;    // the dimensions of the image

// the following two arrays set up the shape of the crayons

   int crayonShapeX[] = { 0, 2, 10, 15, 23, 25, 25, 0 };
   int crayonShapeY[] = { 15, 15, 0, 0, 15, 15, 45, 45 };

// We use the ShapeObject class defined earlier so we can move the crayons
// to a new location easily.
   private ShapeObject crayons[];

// The color class doesn't provide a default value for brown, so we add one.
   private Color brown = new Color(130, 100, 0);

// crayonColors is an array of all the colors the crayons can be.  You can
// add new crayons just by adding to this array.

   private Color crayonColors[] = {
      Color.blue, Color.cyan, Color.darkGray,
      Color.gray, Color.green, Color.magenta,
      Color.orange, Color.pink, Color.red,
      Color.white, Color.yellow, brown };

   private Color currentDrawingColor;    // the color we are coloring with

   private int imagePixels[];    // the memory image of the picture

   boolean imageValid = false;    // did we read the image in o.k.?

// blackRGB is just used as a shortcut to get to the black pixel value
       private int blackRGB = Color.black.getRGB();

   public void init()
   {
      int i;
      MediaTracker tracker = new MediaTracker(this);

// Get the image we will color
      coloringBook = getImage(getDocumentBase(), "smileman.gif");

// tell the media tracker about the image
      tracker.addImage(coloringBook, 0);

// Wait for the image, if we get an error, flag the image as invalid
      try {
         tracker.waitForID(0);
         imageValid = true;
      } catch (Exception oops) {
         imageValid = false;
      }

// Get the image dimensions
```

continues

Listing 25.6 Continued

```
      imageWidth = coloringBook.getWidth(this);
      imageHeight = coloringBook.getHeight(this);

// Copy the image to the array of pixels
      resetMemoryImage();

// Create a new display image from the array of pixels
      remakeDisplayImage();

// Create a set of crayons.  We determine how many crayons to create
// based on the size of the crayonColors array
          crayons = new ShapeObject[crayonColors.length];

          for (i=0; i < crayons.length; i++)
          {
// Create a new crayon shape for each color
                 crayons[i] = new ShapeObject(crayonShapeX,
                        crayonShapeY, crayonShapeX.length);

// The crayons are lined up in a row below the image
             crayons[i].moveShape(i  * 30,
                    imageHeight + 10);
      }
// Start coloring with the first crayon
      currentDrawingColor = crayonColors[0];
   }

// resetMemoryImage copies the coloringBook image into the
// imagePixels array.

       private void resetMemoryImage()
       {
          imagePixels = new int[imageWidth * imageHeight];

// Set up a pixel grabber to get the pixels
          PixelGrabber grabber = new PixelGrabber(
       coloringBook.getSource(),
       0, 0, imageWidth, imageHeight, imagePixels,
       0, imageWidth);

// Ask the image grabber to go get the pixels
          try {
       grabber.grabPixels();
          } catch (Exception e) {
       // Ignore for now
       return;
          }

// Make sure that the image copied correctly, although we don't
// do anything if it doesn't.

          if ((grabber.status() & ImageObserver.ABORT) != 0)
          {
       // uh oh, it aborted
```

```
        return;
           }

        }

// getPixel returns the pixel value for a particular x and y
   private int getPixel(int x, int y)
        {
           return imagePixels[y * imageWidth + x];
        }

// setPixel sets the pixel value for a particular x and y
   private void setPixel(int x, int y, int color)
        {
           imagePixels[y*imageWidth + x] = color;
        }

// floodFill starts at a particular x and y coordinate and fills it, and all
// the surrounding pixels with a color.  It doesn't paint over black pixels,
// so they represent the borders of the fill.
// The easiest way to code a flood fill is by doing it recursively - you
// call flood fill on a pixel, color that pixel, then it calls flood fill
// on each surrounding pixel and so on.  Unfortunately, that usually causes
// stack overflows since recursion is pretty expensive.
// This routine uses an alternate method.  It makes a queue of pixels that
// it still has to fill.  It takes a pixel off the head of the queue and
// colors the pixels around it, then adds those pixels to the queue.  In other
// words, a pixel is really added to the queue after it has been colored.
// If a pixel has already been colored, it is not added, so eventually, it
// works the queue down until it is empty.

        private void floodFill(int x, int y, int color)
        {
// If the pixel we are starting with is already black, we won't paint
           if (getPixel(x, y) == blackRGB)
           {
              return;
           }

// Create the pixel queue.  Assume the worst case where every pixel in the
// image may be in the queue.
           int pixelQueue[] = new int[imageWidth * imageHeight];
           int pixelQueueSize = 0;

// Add the start pixel to the queue (we created a single array of ints,
// even though we are enqueuing two numbers.  We put the y value in the
// upper 16 bits of the integer, and the x in the lower 16.  This gives
// a limit of 65536x65536 pixels, that should be enough.)

           pixelQueue[0] = (y << 16) + x;
           pixelQueueSize = 1;

// Color the start pixel.
           setPixel(x, y, color);
```

continues

Part III Ch 25

Listing 25.6 Continued

```
// Keep going while there are pixels in the queue.
          while (pixelQueueSize > 0)
          {

// Get the x and y values of the next pixel in the queue
             x = pixelQueue[0] & 0xffff;
             y = (pixelQueue[0] >> 16) & 0xffff;

// Remove the first pixel from the queue.  Rather than move all the
// pixels in the queue, which would take forever, just take the one
// off the end and move it to the beginning (order doesn't matter here).

             pixelQueueSize--;
             pixelQueue[0] = pixelQueue[pixelQueueSize];

// If we aren't on the left side of the image, see if the pixel to the
// left has been painted.  If not, paint it and add it to the queue.
             if (x > 0) {
                    if ((getPixel(x-1, y) != blackRGB) &&
                           (getPixel(x-1, y) != color))
                    {
                           setPixel(x-1, y, color);
                           pixelQueue[pixelQueueSize] =
                                  (y << 16) + x-1;
                           pixelQueueSize++;
                    }
             }

// If we aren't on the top of the image, see if the pixel above
// this one has been painted.  If not, paint it and add it to the queue.
             if (y > 0) {
                    if ((getPixel(x, y-1) != blackRGB) &&
                           (getPixel(x, y-1) != color))
                    {
                           setPixel(x, y-1, color);
                           pixelQueue[pixelQueueSize] =
                                  ((y-1) << 16) + x;
                           pixelQueueSize++;
                    }
             }

// If we aren't on the right side of the image, see if the pixel to the
// right has been painted.  If not, paint it and add it to the queue.
             if (x < imageWidth-1) {
                    if ((getPixel(x+1, y) != blackRGB) &&
                           (getPixel(x+1, y) != color))
                    {
                           setPixel(x+1, y, color);
                           pixelQueue[pixelQueueSize] =
                                  (y << 16) + x+1;
                           pixelQueueSize++;
                    }
             }
```

```
// If we aren't on the bottom of the image, see if the pixel below
// this one has been painted.  If not, paint it and add it to the queue.
            if (y < imageHeight-1) {
                   if ((getPixel(x, y+1) != blackRGB) &&
                          (getPixel(x, y+1) != color))
                   {
                          setPixel(x, y+1, color);
                          pixelQueue[pixelQueueSize] =
                                 ((y+1) << 16) + x;
                          pixelQueueSize++;
                   }
            }
        }
    }

// remakeDisplayImage takes the array of pixels and turns it into an
// image for us to display.
    private void remakeDisplayImage()
    {
           displayImage = createImage(new MemoryImageSource(
                  imageWidth, imageHeight, imagePixels, 0, imageWidth));
  }

// The paint method is written with the assumption that the screen has
// not been cleared ahead of time, that way we can create an update
// method that doesn't clear the screen, but doesn't need an off-screen
// image.

    public void paint(Graphics g)
    {
           int i;

// If we got the image successfully, draw it, otherwise, print a message
// saying we couldn't get it.

           if (imageValid)
           {
                  g.drawImage(displayImage, 0, 0, this);
           }
           else
           {
                  g.drawString("Unable to load coloring image.", 0, 50);
           }

// Draw the crayons
               for (i=0; i < crayons.length; i++)
               {
// Draw each crayon in the color it represents
                  g.setColor(crayonColors[i]);
                  g.fillPolygon(crayons[i]);

// Get the box that would enclose the crayon
                  Rectangle box = crayons[i].getBoundingBox();
```

continues

Listing 25.6 Continued

```
// If the crayon is the current one, draw a black box around it, if not,
// draw a box the color of the background around it (in case the current
// crayon has changed, we want to make sure the old box is erased).

                    if (crayonColors[i] == currentDrawingColor)
                    {
                           g.setColor(Color.black);
                    }
                    else
                    {
                           g.setColor(getBackground());
                    }

// Draw the box around the crayon.
                        g.drawRect(box.x, box.y, box.width, box.height);
                 }
       }

// Override the update method to call paint without clearing the screen.

       public void update(Graphics g)
       {
              paint(g);
   }

   public boolean mouseDown(Event event, int x, int y)
   {
      int i;

// Check each crayon to see whether the mouse was clicked inside of it.  If so,
// change the current color to that crayon's color.  We use the "inside"
// method to see whether the mouse x,y is within the crayon shape.  Pretty
handy!

      for (i=0; i < crayons.length; i++)
      {
         if (crayons[i].inside(x, y))
         {
            currentDrawingColor = crayonColors[i];
            repaint();
            return true;
         }
      }

// If the mouse wasn't clicked on a crayon, see whether it was clicked within
// the image.  This assumes that the image starts at 0, 0.
      if ((x < imageWidth) && (y < imageHeight))
      {
// If the image was clicked, fill that section of the image with the
// current crayon color
         floodFill(x, y, currentDrawingColor.getRGB());

// Now re-create the display image because we just changed the pixels
         remakeDisplayImage();
```

```
            repaint();
            return true;
        }

        return true;
    }
}
```

Color Models

The image producer-consumer model also makes use of a `ColorModel` class. As you have seen, the images passed between producers and consumers are made up of arrays of integers. Each integer represents the color of a single pixel. The `ColorModel` class contains methods to extract the red, green, blue, and alpha components from a pixel value. You are probably already familiar with the red, green, and blue color components, but the alpha component might be something new to you.

▶ **See** "The Color Class," **p. 457**

The alpha component represents the transparency of a color. An alpha value of 255 means that the color is completely opaque, whereas an alpha of zero indicates that the color is completely transparent. The default color model is the `RGBdefault` model, which encodes the four-color components in the form 0xaarrggbb. The left-most eight bits are the alpha value; the next eight bits are the red component followed by eight bits for green and, finally, eight bits for blue. For example, a color of 0×12345678 has an alpha component of 0×12 (fairly transparent), a red component of 0×34, a green component of ×56, and a blue component of 0×78.

NOTE The alpha component is used only for images. You cannot use it in conjunction with the `Color` class. In other words, you can't use it in any of the drawing functions in the `Graphics` class.

Any time you need a color model and you are satisfied with using the `RGBdefault` model, you can use `getRGBdefault`:

```
public static ColorModel getRGBdefault()
```

You can extract the red, green, blue, and alpha components of a pixel using these methods:

```
public abstract int getRed(int pixel)
public abstract int getGreen(int pixel)
public abstract int getBlue(int pixel)
public abstract int getAlpha(int pixel)
```

You can find out the number of bits per pixel in a color model using `getPixelSize`:

```
public int getPixelSize()
```

Because many other AWT components prefer colors in RGB format, you can ask the color model to convert a pixel value to RGB format with `getRGB`:

```
public int getRGB(int pixel)
```

The *DirectColorModel* Class

The `DirectColorModel` class stores the red, green, blue, and alpha components of a pixel directly in the pixel value. The standard RGB format is an example of a direct color model. The format of the pixel is determined by a set of bitmasks that tell the color model how each color is mapped into the pixel. The constructor for the `DirectColorModel` takes the number of bits per pixel, the red, green, and blue bit masks, and an optional alpha mask as parameters:

```
public DirectColorModel(int bits, int redMask, int greenMask,
int blueMask)
```

```
public DirectColorModel(int bits, int redMask, int greenMask,
int blueMask, int alphaMask)
```

You can query the mask values using the following methods:

```
public final int getRedMask()
public final int getGreenMask()
public final int getBlueMask()
public final int getAlphaMask()
```

The bits in each mask must be contiguous, that is, they must all be adjacent. You can't have a blue bit sitting between two red bits. The standard RGB format is 0xaarrggbb where aa is the hex value of the alpha component, and rr, gg, and bb represent the hex values for the red, green, and blue components, respectively. This is represented in a direct color model as:

```
DirectColorModel rgbModel = new DirectColorModel(32,
     0xff0000, 0x00ff00, 0x0000ff, 0xff000000)
```

The *IndexColorModel* Class

Unlike the `DirectColorModel`, the `IndexColorModel` class stores the actual red, green, blue, and alpha components of a pixel in a separate place from the pixel. A pixel value is an index into a table of colors. You can create an `IndexColorModel` by passing the number of bits per pixel, the number of entries in the table, and the red, green, and blue color components to the constructor. You can optionally pass either the alpha components or the index value for the transparent pixel:

```
public IndexColorModel(int bitsPerPixel, int tableSize,
byte[] red, byte[] green, byte[] blue)
```

```
public IndexColorModel(int bitsPerPixel, int tableSize,
byte[] red, byte[] green, byte[] blue, int transparentPixel)
```

```
public IndexColorModel(int bitsPerPixel, int tableSize,
byte[] red, byte[] green, byte[] blue, byte[] alpha)
```

Instead of passing the red, green, and blue components in separate arrays, you can pass them as one big array of bytes. The `IndexColorModel` class assumes that every three bytes represents a color (every four if you tell it you are sending it alpha components). The color components should be stored in the order red, green, blue. If you specify an alpha component, it should come after the blue component. That might be counter-intuitive because the standard RGB format has the alpha component first. Here are the constructors for the packed format of colors:

```
public IndexColorModel(int bitsPerPixel, int tableSize,
byte[] packedTable, boolean includesAlpha)
```

```
public IndexColorModel(int bitsPerPixel, int tableSize,
byte[] packedTable, boolean includesAlpha, int transparentPixel)
```

Notice that you can actually have both a transparent pixel and alpha components using this last format!

You can retrieve a copy of the red, green, blue, and alpha tables with the following methods:

```
public final void getReds(byte[] redArray)
public final void getGreens(byte[] greenArray)
public final void getBlues(byte[] blueArray)
public final void getAlphas(byte[] alphaArray)
```

Each method copies the component values from the table into the array you pass it. Make sure that the array is at least as large as the table size. The `getMapSize` method returns the size of the table:

```
public final int getMapSize()
```

The `getTransparentPixel` method returns the index value of the transparent pixel, or it returns `-1` if there is no transparent pixel:

```
public final int getTransparentPixel()
```


RGBImageFilter Class

The java.awt.image package comes with two standard image filters: the `CropImageFilter` and the `RGBImageFilter`. The `RGBImageFilter` enables you to manipulate the colors of an image without changing the image itself. When you create your own custom `RGBImageFilter`, you need to create only a `filterRGB` method:

```
public abstract int filterRGB(int x, int y, int rgb)
```

For each pixel in an image, the `filterRGB` method is passed the pixel's `x` and `y` coordinates and its current RGB value. It returns the new RGB value for the pixel.

Because some images are defined with an index color model, you can set your filter to filter only the index color model. This is handy if the color adjustment has nothing to do with the x,y position of the pixel. If you filter only rgb values from the index, the `x` and `y` coordinates passed to `filterRGB` will be `-1,-1`. To indicate that you are willing to filter the index instead of the whole image, set the `canFilterIndexColorModel` variable to `true`:

```
protected boolean canFilterIndexColorModel
```

You can override the `filterIndexColorModel` method if you want to change the behavior of the index color model filtering:

```
public IndexColorModel filterIndexColorModel(IndexColorModel oldCM)
```

The `IndexColorModel` returned by this method is the new index color model that will be used by the image.

If you want to change only the color model for an image, you can use the `RGBImageFilter` to substitute one color model for another:

```
public void substituteColorModel(ColorModel oldCM, ColorModel newCM)
```

This method is used by the `RGBImageFilter` when filtering an index color model. It creates a new color model by filtering the colors of the old model through your `filterRGB` method and then sets up a substitution from the old color model to the new color model. When a substitution is set up, the `filterRGB` method is not called for individual pixels. This enables you to change the colors quickly.

Listing 25.7 shows a simple gray color model class that takes the red, green, and blue values from another color model and converts them all to gray. It takes the maximum value of the red, green, and blue components and uses it for all three components. The gray color model leaves the alpha value untouched.

Listing 25.7 Source Code for *GrayModel.java*

```
import java.awt.image.*;

// This class implements a gray color model
// scheme based on another color model. It acts
// like a gray filter. To compute the amount of
// gray for a pixel, it takes the max of the red,
// green, and blue components and uses that value
// for all three color components.

public class GrayModel extends ColorModel
{
   ColorModel originalModel;

   public GrayModel(ColorModel originalModel)
   {
      super(originalModel.getPixelSize());
      this.originalModel = originalModel;
   }

// The amount of gray is the max of the red, green, and blue
   protected int getGrayLevel(int pixel)
   {
      return Math.max(originalModel.getRed(pixel),
         Math.max(originalModel.getGreen(pixel),
            originalModel.getBlue(pixel)));
   }

// Leave the alpha values untouched
   public int getAlpha(int pixel)
   {
      return originalModel.getAlpha(pixel);
   }

// Since gray requires red, green and blue to be the same,
// use the same gray level value for red, green, and blue
```

```
   public int getRed(int pixel)
   {
      return getGrayLevel(pixel);
   }

   public int getGreen(int pixel)
   {
      return getGrayLevel(pixel);
   }

   public int getBlue(int pixel)
   {
      return getGrayLevel(pixel);
   }

// Normally, this method queries the red, green, blue and
// alpha values and returns them in the form 0xaarrggbb. To
// keep from computing the gray level 3 times, we just override
// this method, get the gray level once, and return it as the
// red, green, and blue, and add in the original alpha value.

   public int getRGB(int pixel)
   {
      int gray = getGrayLevel(pixel);
      return (getAlpha(pixel) << 24) + (gray << 16) +
         (gray << 8) + gray;
   }
}
```


Listing 25.8 shows an RGB image filter that sets up a simple substitution of the gray model for the original color model.

Listing 25.8 Source Code for *GrayFilter.java*

```
import java.awt.image.*;

// This class sets up a very simple image graying
// filter. It takes the original color model and
// sets up a substitition to a GrayModel.
public class GrayFilter extends RGBImageFilter
{
   public GrayFilter()
   {
      canFilterIndexColorModel = true;
   }

// When the color model is first set, create a gray
// model based on the original model and set it up as
// the substitute color model.

   public void setColorModel(ColorModel cm)
   {
```

continues

Listing 25.8 Continued

```
      substituteColorModel(cm, new GrayModel(cm));
   }

// This method has to be present, but it will never be called
// because we are doing a color model substitution.

   public int filterRGB(int x, int y, int pixel)
   {
      return pixel;
   }
}
```

Listing 25.9 shows a simple applet that displays an image using the gray filter.

Listing 25.9 Source Code for *Grayer.java*

```
import java.awt.*;
import java.awt.image.*;
import java.applet.*;

// This applet displays a grayed-out image by using
// a GrayFilter rgb image filter.

public class Grayer extends Applet
{
   private Image origImage;
   private Image grayImage;
   private GrayFilter colorFilter;

   public synchronized void init()
   {
// Get the name of the image to use
      String gifName = getParameter("image");

// Fetch the image
      origImage = getImage(getDocumentBase(), gifName);
      System.out.println(origImage);

// Create the gray filter
      colorFilter = new GrayFilter();

// Create a grayed-out version of the original image
      grayImage = createImage(new FilteredImageSource(
         origImage.getSource(),
         colorFilter));

      MediaTracker mt = new MediaTracker(this);
      mt.addImage(grayImage, 0);
      try {
         mt.waitForAll();
      } catch (Exception ignore) {
      }
```

```
    }

    public synchronized void paint(Graphics g)
    {
        g.drawImage(grayImage, 0, 0, this);
    }

    public void update(Graphics g)
    {
        paint(g);
    }
}
```

Animation by Color Cycling

The technique of color cycling is a little-known animation technique where an image is animated by changing its color palette without changing the actual image. This can take a number of forms—from simulating flowing water to changing text. You can use this technique on images created with an index color model. The idea is that you change the values in a color table and redraw the image with the new color table. If you continually loop through a set of colors, the image appears animated even though the image data itself hasn't changed.

Any time you perform image animation by creating new images on-the-fly, don't use `createImage` to create the new images. Instead, reuse the existing image by calling the `flush` method in the current image. This cleans out the memory used by the old image and causes it to be filtered again. Otherwise, on some systems you might use up more memory than you need to.

Listing 25.10 shows an RGB image filter that cycles the colors in an index color model.

Listing 25.10 Source Code for *CycleFilter.java*

```
import java.awt.*;
import java.awt.image.*;

//
// This class cycles the colors in an index color model.
// When you create a CycleFilter, you give the offset in
// the index color model and also the number of positions
// you want to cycle. Then every time you call cycleColors,
// it increments the cycle position. You then need to re-create
// your image and its colors will be cycled.
//
// This filter will work only on images that have an indexed
// color model.
public class CycleFilter extends RGBImageFilter {

    // The offset in the index to begin cycling
    protected int cycleStart;
```

continues

Listing 25.10 Continued

```
// How many colors to cycle
protected int cycleLen;

// The current position in the cycle
protected int cyclePos;

// A temporary copy of the color components being cycled
protected byte[] tempComp;

public CycleFilter(int cycleStart, int cycleLen) {
  this.cycleStart = cycleStart;
  this.cycleLen = cycleLen;
  tempComp = new byte[cycleLen];

  cyclePos = 0;

  // Must set this to true to allow the shortcut of filtering
  // only the index and not each individual pixel

  canFilterIndexColorModel = true;
}

// cycleColorComponent takes an array of bytes that represent
// either the red, green, blue, or alpha components from the
// index color model, and cycles them based on the cyclePos.
// It leaves the components that aren't part of the cycle intact.

public void cycleColorComponent(byte component[]) {

  // If there aren't enough components to cycle, leave this alone
  if (component.length < cycleStart + cycleLen) return;

  // Make a temporary copy of the section to be cycled
  System.arraycopy(component, cycleStart, tempComp,
                   0, cycleLen);

  // Now for each position being cycled, shift the component over
  // by cyclePos positions.
  for (int i=0; i < cycleLen; i++) {
    component[cycleStart+i] = tempComp[(cyclePos+i) %
                                      cycleLen];
  }
}

// cycleColors moves the cyclePos up by 1.

public void cycleColors() {
  cyclePos = (cyclePos + 1) % cycleLen;
}

// Can't really filter direct color model RGB this way, since we have
// no idea what rgb values get cycled, so just return the original
// rgb values.
```

```
  public int filterRGB(int x, int y, int rgb) {
    return rgb;
  }

  // filterIndexColorModel is called by the image filtering mechanism
  // whenever the image uses an indexed color model and the
  // canFilterIndexColorModel flag is set to true. This allows you
  // to filter colors without filtering each and every pixel
  // in the image.

  public IndexColorModel filterIndexColorModel(IndexColorModel icm) {

    // Get the size of the index color model
    int mapSize = icm.getMapSize();

    // Create space for the red, green, and blue components
    byte reds[] = new byte[mapSize];
    byte greens[] = new byte[mapSize];
    byte blues[] = new byte[mapSize];

    // Copy in the red components and cycle them
    icm.getReds(reds);
    cycleColorComponent(reds);

    // Copy in the green components and cycle them
    icm.getGreens(greens);
    cycleColorComponent(greens);

    // Copy in the blue components and cycle them
    icm.getBlues(blues);
    cycleColorComponent(blues);

    // See if there is a transparent pixel. If not, copy in the alpha
    // values, just in case the image should be partially transparent.

    if (icm.getTransparentPixel() == -1) {

      // Copy in the alpha components and cycle them
      byte alphas[] = new byte[mapSize];
      icm.getAlphas(alphas);
      cycleColorComponent(alphas);

      return new IndexColorModel(icm.getPixelSize(),
                                 mapSize, reds, greens, blues, alphas);
    } else {

      // If there was a transparent pixel, ignore the alpha values and
      // set the transparent pixel in the new filter
      return new IndexColorModel(icm.getPixelSize(),
                                 mapSize, reds, greens, blues,
                                 icm.getTransparentPixel());

    }
  }
}
```

To use the `CycleFilter`, set up an applet that continually calls `cycleColors` in the `CycleFilter` and then redraws an image. Listing 25.11 shows an example applet that creates a simple memory image with an index color model and uses the `CycleFilter` to cycle the colors. Figure 25.11 shows the output image generated by the `Cycler` applet.

FIG. 25.11
The `Cycler` applet performs animation by cycling the color palette.

Listing 25.11 Source Code for *Cycler.java*

```
import java.awt.*;
import java.awt.image.*;
import java.applet.*;

// This applet creates a series of moving
// lines by creating a memory image and cycling
// its color palette.

public class Cycler extends Applet implements Runnable {
  protected Image origImage; // the image before color cycling
  protected Image cycledImage;   // image after cycling
  protected CycleFilter colorFilter;    // performs the cycling

  protected Thread cycleThread;
  protected int delay = 50;    // milliseconds between cycles

  protected int imageWidth = 200;
  protected int imageHeight = 200;

  protected boolean stopStatus = false; //thread should not stop, until true

  public void init() {

    // Create space for the memory image
    byte pixels[] = new byte[imageWidth * imageHeight];

    // We're going to cycle through 16 colors, but leave position 0 alone in
    // the index color model we create, so allow room for 17 slots
    byte red[] = new byte[17];
    byte green[] = new byte[17];
    byte blue[] = new byte[17];

    // Fill slots 1-16 with varying shades of gray (when the red, green,
    // blue values are all equal you get shades of gray ranging from
    // black when all values are 0, to white when all values are 255).
```

```
    for (int i=0; i < 16; i++) {
      red[i+1] = (byte) (i * 16);
      green[i+1] = (byte) (i * 16);
      blue[i+1] = (byte) (i * 16);
    }

    // Create an index color model that supports 8 bit indices, only 17
    // colors, and uses the red, green, and blue arrays for the color values

    IndexColorModel colorModel = new IndexColorModel(8, 17,
                                                     red, green, blue);

    // Now create the image, just go from top to bottom, left to right
    // filling in the colors from 1-16 and repeating.

    for (int i=0; i < imageHeight; i++) {
      for (int j=0; j < imageWidth; j++) {
        pixels[i*imageWidth + j] =
                                (byte) ((j % 16)+1);
      }
    }

    // Create the uncycled image
    origImage = createImage(new MemoryImageSource(imageWidth,
                                              imageHeight,
                                              colorModel, pixels, 0,
imageWidth));

    // Create the filter for cycling the colors
    colorFilter = new CycleFilter(1, 16);

    // Create the first cycled image
    cycledImage = createImage(new FilteredImageSource(
                                                 origImage.getSource(),
                                                 colorFilter));
  }

  // Paint simply draws the cycled image
  public synchronized void paint(Graphics g) {
    g.drawImage(cycledImage, 0, 0, this);
  }

  // Flicker-free update
  public void update(Graphics g) {
    paint(g);
  }

  // Cycles the colors and creates a new cycled image. Uses media
  // tracker to ensure that the new image has been created before
  // trying to display. Otherwise, we can get bad flicker.

  public synchronized void doCycle() {
    // Cycle the colors
    colorFilter.cycleColors();
```

continues

Listing 25.11 Continued

```
      // Flush clears out a loaded image without having to create a
      // whole new one. When we use waitForID on this image now, it
      // will be regenerated.

      cycledImage.flush();

      MediaTracker myTracker = new MediaTracker(this);
      myTracker.addImage(cycledImage, 0);
      try {

        // Cause the cycledImage to be regenerated
        if (!myTracker.waitForID(0, 1000)) {
          return;
        }
      } catch (Exception ignore) {
      }
      // Now that we have reloaded the cycled image, ask that it
      // be redrawn.
      repaint();
    }

    // Typical threaded applet start and stop
    public void start() {
      stopStatus = false; //don't stop yet
      cycleThread = new Thread(this);
      cycleThread.start();
    }

    public void stop() {
      stopStatus = true;
    }

    public void run() {
      // Continually cycle colors and wait.
      while (!stopStatus) {
        doCycle();
        try {
          Thread.sleep(delay);
        } catch (Exception hell) {
        }
      }
    }
  }
```

When you are comfortable with Java's imaging model, you can create many wonderful images. You can write image filters to perform a wide variety of effects. You can use the `MemoryImageSource` and `PixelGrabber` to make an image editor, or a paint program. You can even use image transparency to make interesting image combinations. Whatever image manipulation you need to do, Java should be able to handle it. ●

CHAPTER 26

Java 2D Graphics

In this chapter

The *Graphics2D* Object

One of the major complaints about the early versions of Java was that the graphics API was not very robust. The functions provided by the AWT were roughly the same as those found on 8-bit microcomputers in the early 1980s. Java 1.2 introduces a powerful new 2D graphics API that provides the kinds of features one would expect from a modern graphics API. The Java 2D API provides better support for drawing shapes, filling and rotating shapes, drawing text, rendering images, and defining colors.

If you are familiar with the `Graphics` object from the Java AWT, you already have some idea of how the 2D graphics API works. All the new 2D features are provided by the `Graphics2D` class, which is a subclass of the `Graphics` object. One of the challenges faced by the Java designers when creating a new 2D API was that because so many developers were familiar with the existing graphics API, they needed to extend the old API without breaking it. Because the new `Graphics2D` object is a subclass of the `Graphics` class, you can use a `Graphics2D` object anywhere you have been using a `Graphics` object. In other words, your existing graphics code doesn't break when you use the new `Graphics2D` object.

Under the old AWT API, you didn't actually create your own `Graphics` object (at least, not usually). Instead, you relied on the `paint` method, which received a `Graphics` object as a parameter. Under the 2D API, you still use the `paint` method to get your `Graphics` object. Under Java 1.2, the `Graphics` object passed to your `paint` method is really a `Graphics2D` object! You only need to cast the `Graphics` object to a `Graphics2D` object:

```
public void paint(Graphics oldGraphics)
{
        Graphics2D newGraphics = (Graphics2D) oldGraphics;

        // now you can use the new 2-D methods
}
```

Coordinates in Java 2D

The original AWT API treated the drawing area as a simple field of pixels. Coordinate 1,1 represented a pixel location, and coordinate 2,1 was the pixel directly adjacent to 1,1. This drawing coordinate system worked for simple screen drawing, but really didn't work well if you tried to draw on a printer. The problem is that printers have much greater resolutions than screens. If you use the same number of pixels to draw an image on a printer as you do for the screen, the printer image will be tiny (or very blocky). As a developer, you don't want to keep track of how much you have to resize drawings for various devices, so the 2D API takes care of that for you.

Java 2D has the notion of a "coordinate space." A *coordinate space* is just a way of specifying coordinates. Your program normally operates in "user coordinate space," which is a virtual drawing area where coordinate 0,0 is in the upper-left corner, and the area is a certain number of pixels wide and a certain number high. Because most drawing work is done on a screen, the user coordinate space is given the same dimensions as the screen area. While your program operates in the user coordinate space, the device that displays the output uses a "device coordinate space."

To translate between user coordinates and device coordinates, the 2D system uses a "default transform" that defines how a coordinate in user space is converted to a coordinate in device space. Because the dimensions of the user space are the same as the screen dimensions, the default transform for the screen device doesn't change the coordinates at all. In other words, coordinate 100,50 in user coordinate space is also coordinate 100,50 onscreen. The default transform for a printer puts 72 user space pixels per inch. The coordinate 144,72 in user space would be to 2 inches from the left, and 1 inch down on a printer page.

Although it is sometimes okay to think of the coordinates in user space as representing pixels, it is not always correct. Coordinates in the `Graphics2D` object are specified with floating point numbers, not whole numbers. Thus you could draw a line from 50.1,100.1 to 50.4, 100.4. On the screen, this may only draw the pixel at 50,100; on a printer, however, you would get a very small line.

The fact that coordinates do not necessarily represent whole pixels is really what enables you to make very smooth printer pictures and perform complex transformations on screen images. You can now draw an image with much greater precision, and let the screen device draw it as best it can. If you have a better display device, your drawing will look better. In the past, because you were working with whole pixels, a printer device couldn't give you any better detail because there was no way to be more specific. If you wanted to draw a circle on the screen that had a 3-pixel diameter, for example, you would either draw a plus sign (+), or a 3×3 square. Using the Java 2D API, you can draw a circle with a diameter of 3 that will still look like either a square or a plus sign on the screen, but when drawn on a printer it will look like a real circle.

You shouldn't have to deal directly with coordinate spaces when writing Java programs, but it is important to remember that you can be much more specific with coordinates than you could using the old `Graphics` object.

Drawing Figures

In the original AWT `Graphics` object, there were specific methods for drawing and filling various kinds of shapes. There were very few options for specifying the kind of pen to use for drawing and how to fill the shape. In fact, the only thing you could really change was the color used to draw and fill.

The `Graphics2D` object treats all drawn figures as shapes (it treats images and text separately). There is only one `draw` method in `Graphics2D`, and it takes a shape as a parameter:

```
public void draw(Shape s)
```

Likewise, there is only one `fill` method:

```
public void fill(Shape s)
```

The trick to drawing figures in the 2D API is creating shapes. Fortunately, the `java.awt.geom` package supplies a wide variety of shape creation classes, including some common shapes.

Don't forget to import `java.awt.geom.*` when using the shape objects. Just importing `java.awt.*` won't get the subpackages.

Drawing a Line

The `java.awt.geom.Line2D` class is a *shape* that represents a simple line between two points. When you create the line, you must use either the `Float` or `Double` version of the `line` class to define the points. The `Double` version is there in case you need a lot of precision. The following code snippet creates a `Line2D` object from 50,60 to 300,320 and then draws it:

```
Line2D line = new Line2D.Float(50, 60, 300, 320);

newGraphics.draw(line);
```

NOTE In the `java.awt.geom` package, you will find that the Java designers made heavy use of Java's inner class feature. All the `shape` objects have at least one inner class that is used to specify coordinates using a particular data type. All the `shapes` have a `Float` inner class, and many have a `Double` class. `Line2D` is a `shape` class, but to specify coordinates, you use the inner class `Line2D.Float`.

You can also use the `Point2D` class to define the end points of a line:

```
Line2D line = new Line2D.Float(
    new Point2D.Float(50, 60), new Point2D.Float(300, 320));
```

Drawing a Rectangle

The `Rectangle2D` class defines a rectangle shape using an `x,y` coordinate, a width, and a height. The following code snippet creates a rectangle at 10,15 with a width of 100 and a height of 50 and draws it:

```
Rectangle2D rect = new Rectangle2D.Float( 10, 15, 100, 50);

newGraphics.draw(rect);
```

Drawing a Rounded Rectangle

The `RoundRectangle2D` draws a rectangle whose corners are rounded. In addition to the rectangle position and size, you specify the width and height of the rounding arc. If you specify a width and height of 5 for the rounding arc, for example, the rounded portion of each corner would be 5 units in width and height. The following code fragment defines a rounded rectangle at 10, 15 with a width of 100, a height of 50, and a rounding of 5 units in the x direction, and 3 in the y direction:

```
RoundRectangle2D roundRect =
        New RoundRectangle2D.Float(10, 15, 100, 50, 5, 3);
```

Drawing Ellipses and Circles

The `Ellipse2D` represents an ellipse shape, which is a circle when the width and height are the same. As with the `ellipse` methods in the `Graphics` object, the ellipse is defined using a bounding box. You specify a rectangle whose width and height represent the width and height of the ellipse (for a circle, use the circle's diameter for both width and height). You also give the `x,y` coordinate of the upper-left corner of the rectangle. The following code fragment creates an ellipse at coordinates 50, 80 with a width of 30 and a height of 10:

```
Ellipse2D ellipse =
        New Ellipse2D.Float(50, 80, 30, 10);
```

You may often need to specify the coordinates of a circle or an ellipse by using the center of the shape and not the upper-left corner of the bounding rectangle. You can compute the upper-left coordinates by `leftX = centerX - (width / 2)` and `upperY = centerY - (height / 2)`.

Drawing Arcs

In addition to drawing ellipses, you can draw partial ellipses using the `Arc2D` class. You specify the position and size of the arc the same way you specify an ellipse, using the upper-left corner, width, and height of the bounding box. In addition, you specify the starting angle and ending angle in degrees. For half an ellipse, you could use a starting angle of 0 and an ending angle of 180, or a starting angle of 90 and an ending angle of 270. Remember that unlike a compass, 0 degrees points to the right, with 90 pointing down, 180 pointing left, and 270 pointing up.

CAUTION

Angles for the `ARC2D` class go in a clockwise direction (90 degrees being at the bottom). This is the opposite of the old arc routines in the `Graphics` class, where 90 degrees was at the top and angles increased in a counter-clockwise direction.

Also, the angle positions used for specifying the start and end of the arc may not look like the angles you expect. The angles are measured from the center of the ellipse, but they are measured as if they were on a circle. If the ellipse is twice as wide as it is tall, the angle as measured on the screen will not be the same angle you specified. Figure 26.1 shows a pie wedge drawn from 0 to 45 degrees on a circle, and the same wedge drawn on an ellipse. In the second case, notice that the angle is less than 45 degrees onscreen.

Drawing Curves

In addition to arcs, the Java 2D API provides shapes that define quadratic and cubic curves. A quadratic curve is defined by two end points and a single control point that controls the shape of the curve. A cubic curve is similar to a quadratic curve except that it has two control points rather than one.

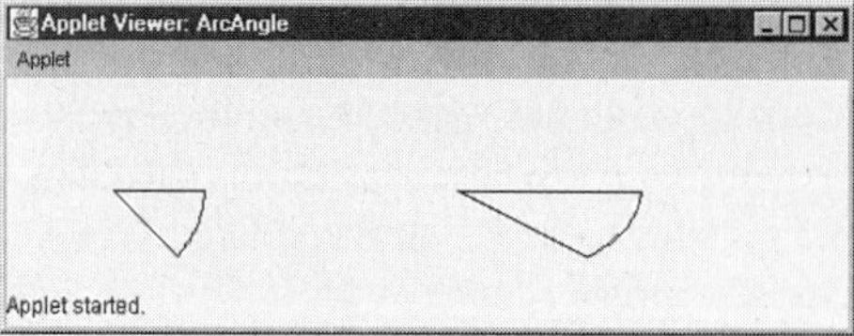

FIG. 26.1
As a circle stretches into an ellipse, the arc angles do not match the angles displayed onscreen.

The following code fragment defines a quadratic curve with end points at 50, 50 and 50, 200 with a control point at 10, 10:

```
QuadCurve2D curve = new QuadCurve2D.Float(50, 50, 10, 10, 50, 100);
```

Figure 26.2 shows the curve with a circle drawn at the control point.

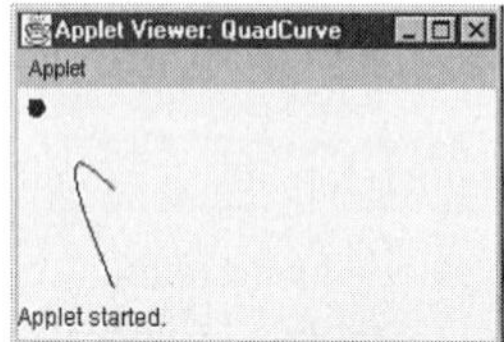

FIG. 26.2
A quadratic curve bends toward the control point.

The following code fragment defines a cubic curve with end points at 50, 50 and 50, 200, with control points at 10, 10 and 100, 100:

```
CubicCurve2D curve = new CubicCurve2D.Float(50, 50, 10, 10, 100, 100, 50, 200);
```

Figure 26.3 shows the cubic curve with circles drawn at the control points.

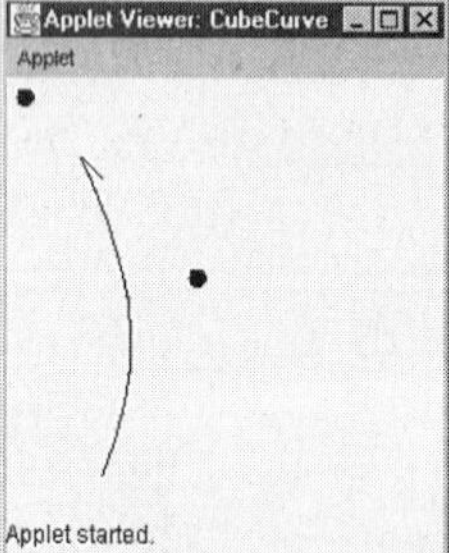

FIG. 26.3
A cubic curve bends toward both control points.

On all the curve definition functions, the control points parameters appear in between the start and end points. In other words, the first two parameters define the start point (if one is needed) and the next few pairs of parameters define the control points, and then the last two parameters are the endpoint.

Drawing Arbitrary Shapes

In addition to predefined shapes, you can also create your own shapes using the `GeneralPath` class. All you need to do to create you own shape is call the `moveTo` and `lineTo` methods in `GeneralPath` for each point in the shape, just as if you were drawing it with the `Graphics` class.

The following code fragment creates a `GeneralPath` object and defines a triangle using `moveTo` and `lineTo`:

```
GeneralPath path = new GeneralPath();
path.moveTo(0, 50);
path.lineTo(25, 0);
path.lineTo(50, 50);
```

In addition to the `lineTo` method, you can also create a curve between two points using `quadTo` and `curveTo`. The `quadTo` method starts at the current point and draws a quadratic curve to another point using a single control point. The following code defines a quadratic line to 50,50 using 100,0 as a control point:

```
path.quadTo(100, 0, 50, 50);
```

The `curveTo` method uses two control points, as shown in this statement, which is the same as the preceding `quadTo` call but with an additional control point of 40,30:

```
path.curveTo(40, 30, 100, 0, 50, 50);
```

Different Strokes

Until now, drawing different shapes hasn't been much different from the old way of doing things. The real excitement comes when you start changing the drawing stroke and the fill pattern for the shapes you are drawing. The drawing stroke defines how the border of the shape is drawn. In the old AWT `Graphics` object, the stroke was always a 1-pixel wide solid line. Now, you can change the width of the stroke and also create a wide variety of dotted lines.

The `BasicStroke` class can be created several different ways:

```
public BasicStroke()
public BasicStroke(float width, int cap, int join)
public BasicStroke(float width, int cap, int join,
float miterlimit)
public BasicStroke(float width, int cap,
int join, float miterlimit, float[] dash,
float dash_phase)
```

The `width` parameter defines the width of the stroke. The default width is 1. The `cap` parameter determines the shape of the ends of the stroke. It is important for line segments and curves that are not connected all the way around. There are three possible values for the `cap` parameter: `CAP_BUTT`, `CAP_ROUND`, and `CAP_SQUARE`.

The `CAP_BUTT` value indicates that there should be nothing extra drawn on the end of the stroke. `CAP_ROUND` indicates that the ends of the line should be rounded, and `CAP_SQUARE` indicates that the ends should be square. Figure 26.4 shows the various ends of a stroke.

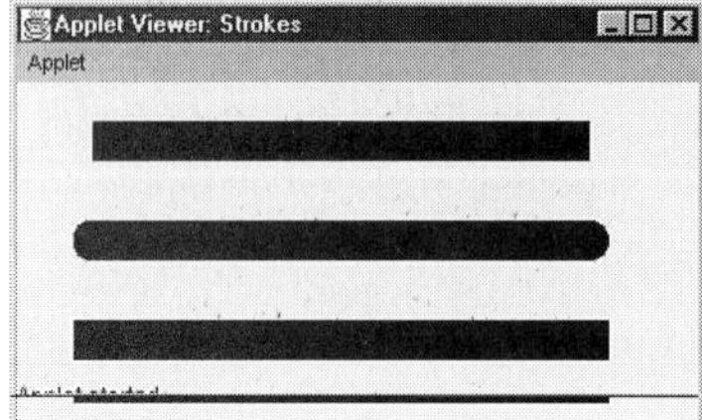

FIG. 26.4
A stroke can either be left alone, rounded-off, or squared off.

The `join` parameter determines how corners in the stroke should be handled. There are three possible values for the join parameter: `JOIN_BEVEL`, `JOIN_MITER`, and `JOIN_ROUND`.

The `JOIN_BEVEL` option draws a straight line between the outer ends of the stroke and fills in the area. This gives the corners a flattened appearance. The `JOIN_MITER` option extends the strokes until they meet at a point, making the corners sharp. The `JOIN_ROUND` option makes an arc connection between the ends of the stroke, giving the corner a rounded appearance. The `miterlimit` parameter defines how far out the miter can go. It is not used for `JOIN_ROUND` or `JOIN_BEVEL`. Figure 26.5 shows the various types of corner joins.

FIG. 26.5
Corners can be beveled, mitered, or rounded.

The `dash` array contains alternating lengths for blank space and dashes for a line. The first element of the array indicates the length of the first dash. The next element indicates the length of the first gap. The array values continue to alternate between dash length and gap length. The following array definition, for example, creates a dash-dot pattern by specifying a long dash, a small gap, an even smaller second dash, and another gap the same size as the first:

```
float[] dashValues = new float[4];
dashValues[0] = 20;
dashValues[1] = 10;
dashValues[2] = 5;
dashValues[3] = 10;
```

Figure 26.6 shows this dashed line pattern.

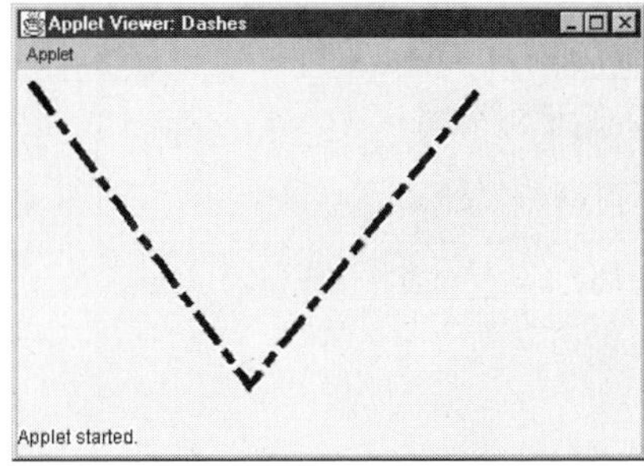

FIG. 26.6
You can define interesting dash patterns in a `stroke` object.

The `dashphase` parameter tells how far into the dash sequence to start. If you used a value of 10 for the first dash length, and you set the dash phase to 11, for example, the line would start with the first blank area.

After you have created a `BasicStroke` object, you tell the `Graphics2D` class to use it by calling `setStroke`:

```
newGraphics.setStroke(myStroke);
```

Custom Fills

The original AWT `Graphics` class only allowed solid color fills. The `Graphics2D` class adds the capability to create gradient color fills and textured patterns. The `GradientPaint` object enables you to define a gradual color change between two points. The two points you define don't need to be contained within the figure you are drawing, however. These points are only used to define the length of the gradient area in user space. If you define start and endpoints that are 100 units apart, for example, the fill starts with the color assigned to the start point, and over the course of 100 units, transforms the fill color to the color associated with the endpoint. Normally, the gradient is acyclic, so that after the color reaches the end point color, it stays at that color. You can optionally make the fill cyclic, which causes the fill color to change back to the start color after it reaches the endpoint color. The gradient pattern follows the direction of the line between the points you define. In other words, if the points you define are on a horizontal line the gradient will change color horizontally. If the points are on a vertical line, the color changes vertically. Likewise, if the points are on a diagonal, the gradient changes diagonally.

Figure 26.7 shows three gradient patterns and lines indicating the endpoints of the gradient.

The gradient sounds pretty complex, but it is very easy to set one up. The `GradientPaint` object has the following Constructors:

```
public GradientPaint(float x1, float y1, Color color1,
float x2, float y2, Color color2)
public GradientPaint(float x1, float y1, Color color1,
float x2, float y2, Color color2, boolean cyclic)
public GradientPaint(Point2D pt1, Color color1,
Point2D pt2, Color color2)
public GradientPaint(Point2D pt1, Color color1,
Point2D pt2, Color color2, boolean cyclic)
```

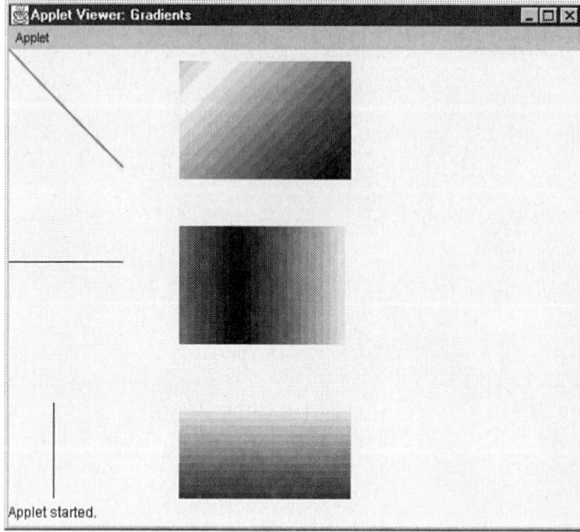

FIG. 26.7 The gradient changes colors in the direction of the line connecting the endpoints.

As you can see by the various Constructors, you can specify the endpoints of the gradient using either floating point `x,y` values, or a `Point2D` structure (which contains a floating point `x,y` pair anyway). The `cyclic` parameter should be set to `true` if you want the gradient to cycle back to the start point when it reaches the endpoint.

After you create the `GradientPaint` object, call the `setPaint` method in `Graphics2D` to use it:

```
GradientPaint gradient = new GradientPaint(0, 0, Color.red,
    50, 50, Color.blue, true);
newGraphics.setPaint(gradient);

Rectangle2D rect = new Rectangle2D.float(0, 0, 200, 200);
NewGraphics.fill(rect);
```

The `TexturePaint` object enables you to use an image for filling figures. You just provide a `BufferedImage` object containing the pattern you want to use for the fill. As you will see later in this chapter, the `BufferedImage` class is a special version of the `Image` class that is tuned for manipulating the individual pixels of the image using an array. Along with the image, you need to provide a rectangle that describes the size of the fill pattern, and a flag to indicate how `TexturePaint` should generate colors.

The `TexturePaint` object has only one Constructor:

```
public TexturePaint(BufferedImage pattern,
Rectangle2D rect2d, int interpolation)
```

The `pattern` parameter specifies the image used for the fill pattern. The `rect2d` parameter describes the size of the pattern. In other words, the pattern is replicated in blocks the size of `rect2d`. The `interpolation` parameter is used to determine how to display colors when the fill can't represent all the colors in the image. The two possible values for `interpolation` are `TexturePaint.BILINEAR` and `TexturePaint.NEAREST_NEIGHBOR`. Listing 26.1 shows an applet that draws a simple path by using a very wide stroke and a texture fill. It is a little unusual, but the texture fill in this example is an actual picture. Fills using simple bit patterns are a little more common. The program uses an image file named `katyface.gif`. Make sure you have an image with that name in the same directory as the applet before running the program.

Listing 26.1 Source Code for *TextureDemo.java*

```
import java.awt.*;
import java.applet.*;
import java.awt.geom.*;
import java.awt.image.BufferedImage;
import java.net.URL;

public class TextureDemo extends Applet
{

    public void paint(Graphics g)
    {

// Get the Graphics2D object

        Graphics2D newG = (Graphics2D) g;

// Create a path to draw

        GeneralPath path = new GeneralPath();

        path.moveTo(60, 0);
        path.lineTo(50, 300);
        path.curveTo(160, 230, 270, 140, 400, 100);

// Load an image to use as the texture

        URL imgURL = null;
        try {
            imgURL = new URL(getDocumentBase(), "katyface.gif");
        } catch (Exception ignore) {
        }

        Image img = getImage(imgURL);

        MediaTracker tracker = new MediaTracker(this);
        try {
            tracker.addImage(img, 0);
            tracker.waitForAll();
        } catch (Exception e) {
            e.printStackTrace();
        }

// Normally you would create a buffered image and set the individual
// pixels yourself, but you can also use an existing image. Rather than
// trying to convert the loaded image into a BufferedImage, it is easier
// (from a programming standpoint) to just get a Graphics2D object for
// the BufferedImage and draw the texture image into it
```

Part III Ch 26

continues

Listing 26.1 Continued

```
        BufferedImage buff = new BufferedImage(img.getWidth(this),
            img.getHeight(this), BufferedImage.TYPE_INT_RGB);

        Graphics tempGr = buff.createGraphics();

        tempGr.drawImage(img, 0, 0, this);

// The TexturePaint requires a rectangle defining the area to be filled
// In this case, just use the image size.

        Rectangle2D rect = new Rectangle2D.Float(
            0, 0, img.getHeight(this),
            img.getWidth(this));

// Create the textured paint

        TexturePaint painter = new TexturePaint(buff, rect,
            TexturePaint.NEAREST_NEIGHBOR);

        newG.setPaint(painter);

// Create a VERY wide stroke (100 pixels) round off the corners and
// make the ends square
        BasicStroke stroke = new BasicStroke(100,
            BasicStroke.CAP_SQUARE, BasicStroke.JOIN_ROUND);
        newG.setStroke(stroke);

// Draw the original path
        newG.draw(path);
    }
}
```

Figure 26.8 shows the output of the `TextureDemo` applet.

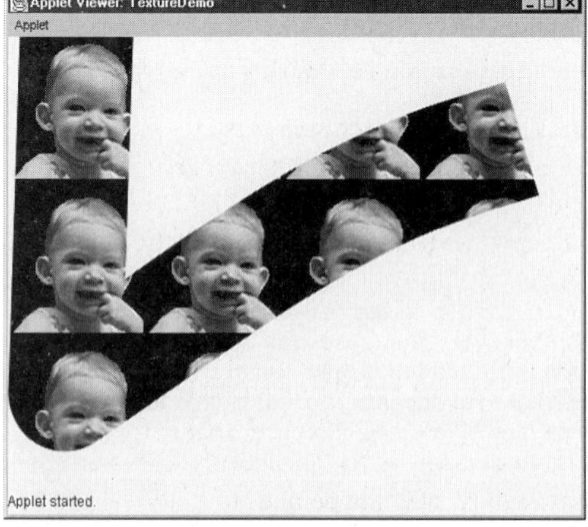

FIG. 26.8
You can use an image as a fill pattern.

Transformations

In addition to drawing shapes, you frequently need to move, rotate, and resize shapes. These operations are performed using an object called `AffineTransform`. The `AffineTransform` class contains a matrix that is used to change one `x,y` point into another. If you really like doing your own matrix operations, you can create an `AffineTransform` by supplying the six matrix entries used in the transform. The transform matrix has 3 columns and 2 rows. If you number the elements on row 0 as `m00`, `m01`, and `m02` and the elements on row 1 as `m10`, `m11`, and `m12`, the formula for translating point `xorig,yorig` to `xnew,ynew` is as follows:

```
xnew = xorig * m00 + yorig * m01 + m02

ynew = xorig * m10 + yorig * m11 + m12
```

Fortunately, for those who don't like matrix operations, the `AffineTransform` class has methods for building the transform one operation at a time. You start by creating an empty `AffineTransform` by calling the default Constructor:

```
AffineTransform myTransform = new AffineTransform();
```

You can add a translation (that is, a move) by calling the `translate` method. The following example moves the transform 5 units to the left and 10 units down:

```
myTransform.translate(-5.0, 10.0);
```

When you perform `translate`, `rotate`, and `scaling` operations on a transform, you aren't really moving the transform. Instead, you are changing what the transform does to points. It is helpful, however, to think of these operations as actually moving the transform, because whatever you think you are doing to the transform is what it does to shapes.

The `rotate` method rotates the transform in a clockwise direction (or counter-clockwise for negative angle values). The angle of rotation is specified in radians. You can specify an optional `x,y` point, which rotates the transform around a specific point rather than around the origin. The two forms of the `rotate` method are as follows:

```
public void rotate(double numRadians)

public void rotate(double numRadians, double x, double y)
```

The `scale` method multiplies the `x` and `y` coordinates by particular values. When you call the `scale` method, you always pass scale values for both `x` and `y`. If you only want to scale in one direction, use a scale value of 1.0 for the value you don't want to change. To double the size of the transform in the `x` direction and leave the `y` values alone, for example, use `2.0` for the `x` scale and `1.0` for the `y` scale:

```
myTransform.scale(2.0, 1.0);
```

The `shear` method is similar to the `scale` method, except that it changes the `x` value based on the `y` value, and the `y` value based on the `x` value. If you shear the `x` values by a factor of 2, the `x` value for each point will be increased by the shear factor times that point's `y` value. Suppose, for example, that you have an `x` shear of 2, the point `5,10` would be sheared to (5 + 2*10), 10 or in simpler terms, 25, 10. The higher the y value, the more the x points get moved. The same relationship holds true for shears in the y direction. The shear method is defined as follows:

```
public void shear(double xshear, double yshear)
```

Just manipulating an AffineTransform object doesn't change anything onscreen. You need to apply the transform to either a shape that you want to draw, or to the entire Graphics2D object. To manipulate a shape, call the createTransformedShape method, which returns a new shape with the current transform applied. The following code fragment rotates a rectangle 45 degrees, for example:

```
Rectangle2D rect = new Rectangle2D.Float(0, 0, 50, 20);
AffineTransform transform = new AffineTransform();
Transform.rotate(45.0 * 3.1415927 / 180.0);
Shape rotatedRect = transform.createTransformedShape(rect);
```

Remember that you can multiply a degree value by 3.1415927 / 180.0 or just 0.0174532928 to convert it to radians.

You can also apply a transform to the entire Graphics2D object by calling the setTransform method in Graphics2D. Transforming the Graphics object itself causes everything drawn with that Graphics object to be transformed before being displayed. The setTransform method is defined as follows:

```
public void setTransform(AffineTransform transform)
```

Drawing Text

Drawing text is one of the big three in graphics operations (drawing shapes and images being the other two). The 2D API adds some handy extensions to the original text drawing routines. One of the most notable is the ability to rotate text. The Graphics2D class implements several different versions of the drawString method. The simplest version takes a string and an x,y coordinate pair:

```
public void drawString(String textString, float x, float y)
```

This simple version of the drawString method is analogous to the drawString method in the Graphics class, except that the coordinates are specified with floating point values rather than integers. The other big difference, of course, is that all the graphics transforms in the current transform matrix are applied to the string before drawing it. This enables you to rotate text strings, and even paint them with interesting fill patterns.

Styled Strings

You can also draw a StyledString object, which is a string and an associated set of attributes (often just a font). You can even concatenate styled strings together to make a single styles string containing text of different fonts. You might want to print the ubiquitous "Hello World!" message, for example, using different fonts for each word. The following code fragment does just that:

```
Font fntCourier = new Font("courier", Font.PLAIN, 48);
StyledString ssHello = new StyledString("Hello ", fntCourier);

Font fntHelvetica = new Font("helvetica", Font.BOLD, 48);
StyledString ssWorld = new StyledString("World!", fntHelvetica);

StyledString helloWorld = ssHello.concat(ssWorld);

newGraphics.drawString(helloWorld, 100, 100);
```

Like the normal Java `String` class, the `StyledString` is immutable—you can't change its contents. Instead, you create new versions of the string by calling `concat` (to put two strings together) or `substring` (to get a portion of the string). The `substring` method is identical to the `String` `substring` method:

```
public StyledString substring(int startIndex, int endIndex)
```

Text Layouts

Although the `StyledString` class is useful, the most useful new text feature is the `TextLayout` object. One of the biggest drawbacks of the original `drawString` method in the `Graphics` class is that it only draws a single line. You often need to draw entire paragraphs of text. Until now, developers have had to create their own formatting routines to break up a paragraph into multiple lines, resulting in multiple calls to `drawString`. The `TextLayout` class can format text to fit on multiple lines, and can even handle right-to-left and top-to-bottom paragraph styles that sometimes occur when drawing non-English text. You can even use `TextLayout` to format a `StyledString`, allowing multiple fonts within the paragraph.

The `TextLayout` class has several Constructors:

```
public TextLayout(String string, Font font)
public TextLayout(String string, AttributeSet attributes)
public TextLayout(StyledString text)
public TextLayout(AttributedCharacterIterator text)
```


The two most common `TextLayout` constructors are the `String/Font` combination and the `StyledString`. If you want more complex characters, you can use a set of character attributes, or define the attributes of each character though an iterator. The program in Listing 26.2 displays a simple paragraph onscreen:

Listing 26.2 Source Code for *Paragraph.java*

```
import java.awt.*;
import java.applet.*;
import java.awt.geom.*;
import java.awt.font.*;

public class Paragraph extends Applet
{
```

continues

Listing 26.2 Continued

```
    public void paint(Graphics g)
    {

// Get the Graphics2D object

        Graphics2D newG = (Graphics2D) g;

        String message = "Harold, on the other hand, refused "+
            " to eat the chalk. He reached into his lunchbox "+
            " and removed a small block of balsa wood, which "+
            " he proceeded to chew on gleefully. Harold always "+
            " referred to balsa wood as a \"light snack\"";


        Font fntRoman = new Font("timesroman", Font.PLAIN, 24);

        TextLayout layout = new TextLayout(message, fntRoman);

        newG.drawString(layout, (float) 100, (float) 100);
    }
}
```

Character Attributes

Although you may be happy with changing just the font on a character, the need often arises to change more than that. The `StyledString` and the `TextLayout` classes enable you to specify a set of character attributes that define much more than just a different font. You specify character attributes through the `AttributeSet` object, which, like the `StyledString` object, is immutable. If you can't change it, how can you set it? That's where the `MutableAttributeSet` object comes in. You typically create a `MutableAttributeSet`, add new attributes to it, and then pass it to a method that takes an `AttributeSet` as a parameter. You can think of the relationship between `AttributeSet` and `MutableAttributeSet` like the relationship between `String` and `StringBuffer`. The `MutableAttributeSet` is used for building `AttributeSets` that cannot be changed.

A `MutableAttributeSet` is itself subclass of `AttributeSet`, and you normally pass it to methods that expect an `AttributeSet`. If any method needs to keep a reference to the `AttributeSet`, it will make a copy of it. Otherwise, because the set is really a mutable set, you could make changes later on in your program that affect existing attributes. What this boils down to is that an `AttributeSet` is immutable only in that the class has no methods to change it. An `AttributeSet` can change if it is actually a `MutableAttributeSet`.

To set character attributes, you should use the `TextAttributeSet` object. The `TextAttributeSet` object is a mutable object set that also defines a number of constants. Some of the constants represent the names of various text attributes, and other constants represent default or common values for those attributes.

The names of the valid text attributes are as follows:

Attribute Name	Meaning
LANGUAGE	The language used for the text (usually a locale)
READING	The pronunciation information for the word (used for some languages that require a pronunciation annotation)
INPUT_METHOD_SEGMENT	Used for breaking up lines into segments (usually words)
SWAP_COLORS	Whether the foreground and background colors of the text should be swapped
FAMILY	The family for the font
WEIGHT	The weight of the characters (bold text means a heavier weight)
POSTURE	The slant of the text
SIZE	The size of the font in points
TRANSFORM	The graphics transform applied to the font
FONT	An instance of `Font` to use for the characters
BIDI_EMBEDDING	Controls bi-directional text
BACKGROUND	An instance of `Color` specifying the background color of the text
FOREGROUND	An instance of `Color` specifying the foreground color of the text
UNDERLINE	Indicates whether text should be underlined
STRIKETHROUGH	Indicates whether the text should have a strikethrough
SUPERSUBSCRIPT	Makes the text either a superscript or a subscript
JUSTIFICATION	Adjusts the amount of space used in justification
RUN_DIRECTION	Controls whether text runs left-to-right, right-to-left, or top-to-bottom
BIDI_NUMERIC	Controls bi-directional layout of roman numerals
BASELINE	Adjusts the baseline for all characters

To set various attributes, you just call the `add` method with the name of the attribute and its value. Many attribute values have preset constants; others take string or numeric arguments. The following code fragment creates a text attribute set with a Times-Roman font and strikethrough:

```
Font fntRoman = new Font("timesroman", Font.PLAIN, 24);

TextAttributeSet textAttr = new TextAttributeSet();
textAttr.add(TextAttributeSet.FONT, fntRoman);
```

```
textAttr.add(TextAttributeSet.STRIKETHROUGH,
TextAttributeSet.STRIKETHROUGH_ON);
```

Drawing Images

The Java 2D API recognizes the frequent need to manipulate images by performing various mathematical operations on them. It also strengthens the ability to manipulate image data on a pixel-by-pixel basis. Although the earlier versions of the AWT did not prevent these types of operations, they were not as efficient, and many operations needed to be performed manually.

Buffered Images

In previous versions of Java, it was very difficult to manipulate images on a pixel-by-pixel basis. You had to either create an image filter and modify the pixels as they came through the filter, or you had to make a pixel grabber to grab an image and then create a `MemoryImageSource` to turn the array of pixels into an image. The `BufferedImage` class provides a quick, convenient shortcut by providing an image whose pixels can be manipulated directly.

The easiest way to create a buffered image is to specify a width, height, and a pixel type:

```
public BufferedImage(int width, int height, int pixelType)
```

The pixel type has many different options, but you usually just need `TYPE_INT_ARGB` or `TYPE_INT_RGB`. The `TYPE_INT_ARGB` pixel type is the same pixel type used in earlier versions of Java. Each pixel is represented by a 32-bit integer with 8 bits for transparency, and 8-bit red, green, and blue values, arranged as `aarrggbb`. The `TYPE_INT_RGB` format is almost identical except that it assumes that there is no transparency. The `aa` portion is assumed to be 255 at all times. If you have worked with systems that encode colors in `bbggrr` form in an integer, you can use the `TYPE_INT_BGR` format for your pixels. Given three integer `red`, `green`, and `blue` values, you can encode them in `RGB` format like this:

```
int rgb = (red << 16) + (green << 8) + blue;
```

To use this technique, you must ensure that the `red`, `green`, and `blue` values are between 0 and 255. To add an `alpha` (transparency) to the pixel, you can use the following line:

```
int argb = (alpha << 24) + (red << 16) + (green << 8) + blue;
```

To store a pixel in `bgr` format, just reverse the order of the variables like this:

```
int bgr = (blue << 16) + (green << 8) + red;
```

To extract the `alpha`, `red`, `green`, and `blue` components from an `ARGB` pixel, you can use the following statements:

```
int alpha = (argb >> 24) & 255;

int red = (argb >> 16) & 255;

int green = (argb >> 8) & 255;

int blue = argb & 255;
```

The getRGB method in BufferedImage returns a pixel in ARGB format, regardless of how the pixel is stored within the image:

```
public int getRGB(int x, int y)
```

To set a pixel in a buffered image, call setRGB (don't forget to use ARGB format for the pixel):

```
public int setRGB(int x, int y, int rgb)
```

Copying an Image into a *BufferedImage*

When you use the getImage method in java.applet.Applet or java.awt.Toolkit, the image you get back is just an Image object. There are probably a number of complicated ways to turn an image into a BufferedImage. One quick and dirty way is to create a Graphics object from a BufferedImage and draw an image onto it. Although this method is not very efficient, it is pretty easy to do and if you only need to do it once, efficiency isn't that big a deal.

The following code fragment creates a BufferedImage object, and then gets a Graphics object to draw to the buffered image, and then draws an existing image into the buffered image:

```
// Create a buffered image using the existing image's
// width and height

BufferedImage buff = new BufferedImage(img.getWidth(this),
img.getHeight(this), BufferedImage.TYPE_INT_RGB);

// Get a graphics object for drawing into the buffered image
Graphics tempGr = buff.createGraphics();

// Draw the existing image into the buffered image
tempGr.drawImage(img, 0, 0, this);
```


Filtering Buffered Images

Image filters were introduced in Java 1.0 and they have always been a useful way to manipulate images. The Java 2D API expands the existing image filtering with several pre-made filters, and special filtering for buffered images. The old AWT image filtering mechanism used the producer-consumer model where the filter was a consumer of the source image and a producer of the filtered image. Although the BufferedImage class contains a getSource method, which is required for creating a FilteredImageSource, the method returns null. Consequently, you can't really use the existing producer-consumer interface for filtering buffered images. Instead, the BufferedImageOp interface defines a way to filter a single buffered image source into a single buffered image destination by directly manipulating the buffered pixels.

The BufferedImageFilter class exists as a way to hook the image ops into the existing producer-consumer paradigm, but it is currently broken.

BufferedImageOp is only an interface, so you can't instantiate it directly. Instead, you must either create a class that implements the interface, or use one of the existing image op classes: AffineTransformOp, BandCombineOp, ColorConvertOp, ConvolveOp, LookupOp, RescaleOp, and ThresholdOp. Some of the built-in operations allow the source and destination to be the same.

Others require separate images. The rule of thumb is, if the operation uses more than one pixel in a conversion, or if it moves a pixel from one place to another, you need a separate source and destination. Color conversions, for instance, almost never need separate source and destination images.

To filter an image using any of the `BufferedImageOp` classes, just create the op and call the `filter` method with a source and destination image (which for some ops can be the same image). Here is an example call to the `filter` method:

```
op.filter(srcBuff, destBuff);
```

If you just need to draw a filtered image, the `drawImage` method in `Graphics2D` enables you to draw an image filtered by a `BufferedImageOp`:

```
public void drawImage(BufferedImage image,
    BufferedImageOp op, ImageObserver obs)
```

AffineTransformOp An `AffineTransformOp` performs an affine transform on an image. The transform can contain any combination of scaling, rotation, and translation. The following code fragment creates an `AffineTransformOp` that rotates an image 45 degrees, for example:

```
AffineTransform transform = new AffineTransform();

transform.rotate(45.0 * 3.1415927 / 180.0,
buff.getWidth() / 2, buff.getHeight() / 2);

AffineTransformOp op = new BilinearAffineTransformOp(
transform);
```

NOTE `AffineTransformOp` is an abstract class. You must choose either `BilinearAffineTransformOp` or `NearestNeighborAffineTransformOp`. These two versions differ only in how they choose colors when performing a transform.

The `AffineTransformOp` requires separate source and destination images.

BandCombineOp At first glance, the `BandCombineOp` filter seems strange and not very useful. Buffered images are stored in raster objects, which are really just arrays of pixels. Within these rasters are "bands" of colors. For a typical RGB image, there are three bands: red, green, and blue. The `BandCombineOp` filter enables you to change the color of an image by a combination of the various color bands. For a 3-band image, you specify a matrix with 4 columns and 3 rows, like this:

```
B11    B12    B13    B1OFFSET
B21    B22    B23    B2OFFSET
B31    B32    B33    B3OFFSET
```

The formula for the color of band 1 is as follows:

```
B1COLOR = B1COLOR * B11 + B2COLOR * B12 +
B3COLOR * B13 + B1OFFSET
```

The following filter would do nothing to an image (that is, it is the identity matrix for a band combine) because it just multiplies each color in the band by 1:

```
1.0     0.0     0.0     0.0
0.0     1.0     0.0     0.0
0.0     0.0     1.0     0.0
```

In a typical RGB raster, band 1 is red, band 2 is green, and band 3 is blue. The following matrix removes all the green color from a picture while leaving red and blue alone:

```
1.0     0.0     0.0     0.0
0.0     0.0     0.0     0.0
0.0     0.0     1.0     0.0
```

You can invert colors, too. To invert the red, for instance, the red row in the matrix would be this:

```
-1.0     0.0     0.0     255.0
```

This would multiply the red color by –1 and add 255, making the formula 255 – red.

The really interesting combinations come when you allow one color to contribute to another color. You could filter the red so that it is a combination of the amount of red, green, and blue in the image, for example. The following matrix leaves red and blue alone, but for green it uses half the old amount of green and one fourth the amount of red and one fourth the amount of blue. In other words, the brighter the green and blue are, the brighter the red is. Here is the matrix:

```
1.0     0.0     0.0     0.0
0.25    0.5     0.25    0.0
0.0     0.0     1.0     0.0
```

The following code fragment creates a `BandCombineOp` object:

```
float filt[][] = {
{ 1.0f, 0.0f, 0.0f, 0.0f },
{ 0.25f, 0.5f, 0.25f, 0.0f },
{ 0.0f, 0.0f, 1.0f, 0.0f }};

BandCombineOp op = new BandCombineOp(filt);
```

`BandCombineOp` can use the same image for the source and destination.

ColorConvertOp The `ColorConvertOp` class converts from one color space to another. A color space defines how a color is represented. You are probably familiar with the RGB color space, for example, where you specify colors by using the amount of red, green, and blue in the color. Publishers often use a color space called CMYK, which specifies colors by the amount of cyan, magenta, yellow, and black. The following code fragment creates a `ColorConvertOp` that converts an image into a grayscale image:

```
ColorSpace graySpace = ColorSpace.getInstance(
ColorSpace.CS_GRAY);

ColorConvertOp op = new ColorConvertOp(
graySpace);
```

ConvolveOp The `ConvolveOp` class implements a common image operation where each pixel is modified based on the pixels around it, according to a simple matrix operation. When you create a `ConvolveOp` object, you supply a `Kernel` object, which contains the matrix to be applied to the image. The `Kernel` object even has several predefined sharpening matrices that use edge-detection to enhance an image.

If you have ever used a paint program that has different image algorithms, you may have seen one called "edge detect." When you run edge detect on an image, you get a mostly black image with lines showing some of the edges in the image. You can create an edge detect using a `Kernel` and a `ConvoleOp`.

When you create a `Kernel` for image processing, you really just specify a matrix that is used to calculate the color of each pixel in the image. The matrix determines how the surrounding pixels affect the current pixel. In the case of an edge detect, you completely ignore the color of the current pixel. Instead, you look at the upper-left and lower-right pixels (you can really look at any pair of opposing pixels). Multiply the upper-left pixel by some factor and multiply the lower-right pixel by the negative of that factor. The higher the factors, the more pronounced the edges.

The matrix for the `Kernel` object should have odd-numbered dimensions, and is usually 3×3. The center value in the matrix is the multiplication factor for the current pixel. The surrounding values are the factors for the surrounding pixels. To perform an edge detect, you want the current pixel to be ignored, so the center value would be 0. The upper-left and lower-right corners of the matrix would contain the edge-detect factors. Figure 26.9 shows an image next to the result of an edge detect on the image.

FIG. 26.9
An edge detect shows sharp transitions between colors.

The following code fragment creates a fairly strong edge detector using a factor of 5:

```
float matrix[] = {
-5, 0, 0,
0, 0, 0,
0, 0, 5 };

Kernel kernel = new Kernel(3, 3, matrix);

ConvolveOp op = new ConvolveOp(kernel,
ConvolveOp.EDGE_ZERO_FILL);
```

The Kernel class has some predefined matrices for image sharpening. These matrices are SHARPEN3x3_1, SHARPEN3x3_2, SHARPEN3x3_3. These matrices are defined as follows:

SHARPEN3x3_1:

```
-1   -1   -1
-1    9   -1
-1   -1   -1
```

SHARPEN3x3_2:

```
 1   -2    1
-2    5   -2
 1   -2    1
```

SHARPEN3x3_3:

```
 0   -1    0
-1    5   -1
 0   -1    0
```

You can create a Kernel with one of these predefined matrices like this:

```
Kernel sharpen = new Kernel(Kernel.SHARPEN3x3_1);
```

After you create a Kernel, you use it to create a ConvolveOp:

```
ConvolveOp op = new ConvolveOp(sharpen);
```

Because it relies on surrounding pixels, ConvolveOp must have different source and destination images.

LookupOp The LookupOp class provides a simple table lookup to map one pixel value to another. To create a LookupOp, you need to create a LookupTable, which takes an array or byte or short values. LookupTable itself is an abstract class. You must create either a ByteLookupTable or a ShortLookupTable. The following code fragment creates a LookupOp that reverses colors (0 becomes 255, 1 becomes 254, and so on):

```
short lookupValues[] = new short[256];

for (int i=0; i < lookupValues.length; i++) {
lookupValues[i] =(short) (255 - i);
}

LookupTable table = new ShortLookupTable(0, lookupValues);

LookupOp op = new LookupOp(table);
```

Figure 26.10 shows an image before and after this reverse-color lookup.

LookupOp can have the same source and destination images.

RescaleOp The RescaleOp class enables you to change colors in an image based on a coefficient and an offset. The name might lead you to believe that it changes the size of an image, but it does not (use the AffineTransformOp for that). You create a RescaleOp by supplying a scaling factor and an offset. Each color in the image is multiplied by the scaling factor and then added to the offset. The Constructors for RescaleOp are declared as follows:

FIG. 26.10
A lookup table can be a quick way to reverse colors.

```
public RescaleOp(float factor, float offset)
```

```
public RescaleOp(float[] factors, float[] offsets)
```

When you pass an array of values to the Constructor, the values apply to each raster channel. (For an RGB image, that's the red, green, and blue channels.) If you pass singular values, they apply to all channels. You can perform a "wash" effect by halving the color values and adding 128. The following code fragment creates a wash `RescaleOp`:

```
RescaleOp op = new RescaleOp(0.5f, 128);
```

Figure 26.11 shows an image before and after the wash effect.

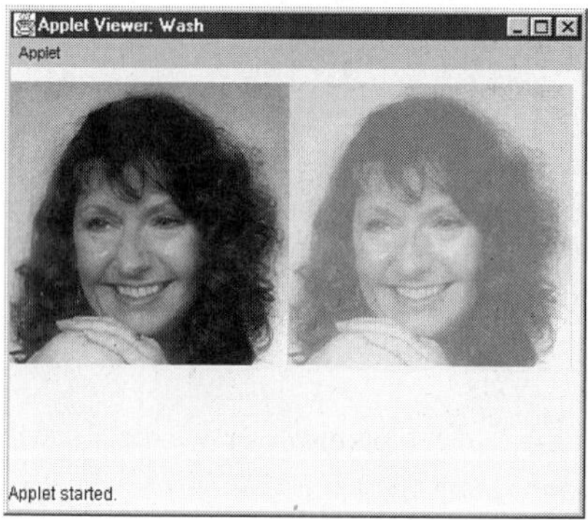

FIG. 26.11
A `RescaleOp` can make washout effects, among other things.

Because it operates only on single pixels, `RescaleOp` can use the same image for the source and destination.

CAUTION

`RescaleOp` does not adjust color values that are above 255 or below 0. Instead, it adds them into the final RGB color value as they are, causing very strange distortion effects. If you keep the coefficient of `RescaleOp` at 1 or less, you shouldn't run into any problems. Try to avoid situations where a color value might be less than 0 or greater than 255.

ThresholdOp Rounding out the list of predefined operations, `ThresholdOp` provides an on-off type filter for colors. You specify a threshold value, a low value, and a high value. Any color less than the threshold value is assigned the low value, and any color higher than the threshold is assigned the high value. The assignments are done on a per-channel basis. (That is, it works on the red, and then the green, and then the blue channels in an RGB image.) You can specify different values for each color channel by providing arrays of threshold, low, and high values. As you might guess, `ThresholdOp` really reduces the number of colors in an image. The Constructors for `ThresholdOp` are as follows:

```
public ThresholdOp(float threshold, float low, float high)
```

```
public ThresholdOp(float[] thresholds, float[] lows, float[] highs)
```

Figure 26.12 shows an image with a threshold of 128, a low value of 0, and a high value of 255. You might think that it would produce a completely black and white picture, but there are a few patches of color. These occur when some channels go to 0 and others go to 255.

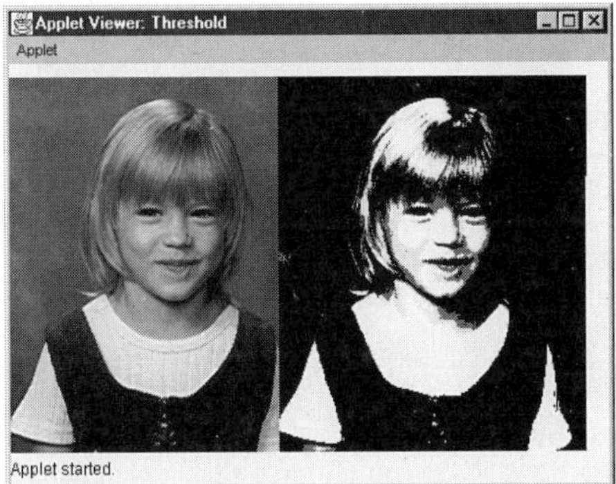

FIG. 26.12
A `ThresholdOp` reduces colors significantly in most images.

Manipulating Buffered Images

Sometimes you may want to manipulate the pixels in a buffered image without using a filter. You can use `getRGB` and `setRGB` to manipulate pixels directly. Listing 26.3 shows an applet that performs an emboss effect on an image. The operation is similar to an edge detect, but cannot be implemented using `ConvolveOp` because it needs to set the current pixel to 128 before factoring in the upper-left and lower-right pixels. Make sure the `katyface.gif` file is in the same directory as the applet.

Listing 26.3 Source Code for *Emboss.java*

```
import java.awt.*;
import java.applet.*;
import java.awt.geom.*;
import java.awt.font.*;
import java.awt.image.*;
import java.net.URL;
```

continues

Listing 26.3 Continued

```
public class Emboss extends Applet
{

    public void paint(Graphics g)
    {

// Get the Graphics2D object

        Graphics2D newG = (Graphics2D) g;

// Load an image to display

        URL imgURL = null;
        try {
            imgURL = new URL(getDocumentBase(), "katyface.gif");
        } catch (Exception ignore) {
        }

        Image img = getImage(imgURL);

        MediaTracker tracker = new MediaTracker(this);
        try {
            tracker.addImage(img, 0);
            tracker.waitForAll();
        } catch (Exception e) {
            e.printStackTrace();
        }

// Normally you would create a buffered image and set the individual
// pixels yourself, but you can also use an existing image. Rather than
// trying to convert the loaded image into a BufferedImage, it is easier
// (from a programming standpoint) to just get a Graphics2D object for
// the BufferedImage and draw the image into it

        int width = img.getWidth(this);
        int height = img.getHeight(this);

// Create a buffered version of the image by creating a graphics
// context and drawing into it.

        BufferedImage buff = new BufferedImage(width,
            height, BufferedImage.TYPE_INT_ARGB);

        Graphics tempGr = buff.createGraphics();

        tempGr.drawImage(img, 0, 0, this);

// Create a buffered image to hold the resulting embossed image

        BufferedImage outBuff = new BufferedImage(width,
            height, BufferedImage.TYPE_INT_ARGB);


        embossImage(buff, outBuff);
```

```
        newG.drawImage(outBuff, 100, 100, this);
    }

// To emboss an image, you start with a completely gray destination image.
// For each pixel in the source image, look at pixels to the upper-left and
// lower-right. Figure out the change in red, green, and blue between the
// upper-left and lower-right and look at the maximum change (either maximum
// positive or maximum negative) for any color component. For example,
// if the green changed by -5, blue changed by 10 and red changed by
// -100, the maximum change would be -100 (the red, which changed the most).
//
// Now, add the amount of change to 128 (the gray level) and create a
// pixel in the destination image with red, green, and blue values equal
// to the new gray level. Make sure you adjust the gray level so it can't
// be less than 0 or more than 255.
//
//
    public void embossImage(BufferedImage srcImage, BufferedImage destImage)
    {

        int width = srcImage.getWidth();
        int height = srcImage.getHeight();

// Loop through every pixel

        for (int i=0; i < height; i++) {
            for (int j=0; j < width; j++) {

// Assume that the upper-left and lower-right are 0
                int upperLeft = 0;
                int lowerRight = 0;

// If the pixel isn't on the upper or left edge, get the upper-left
// pixel (otherwise, the upper-left for edge pixels is the default of 0)

                if ((i > 0) && (j > 0)) {

// The & 0xffffff strips off the upper 8 bits, which is the transparency

                    upperLeft = srcImage.getRGB(j-1, i-1)
                        & 0xffffff;
                }

// If the pixel isn't on the bottom or right edge, get the lower-right
// pixel (otherwise, the lower-right for egde pixels is the default of 0)

                if ((i < height-1) && (j < width-1)) {

// The & 0xffffff strips off the upper 8 bits, which is the transparency
                    lowerRight = srcImage.getRGB(j+1, i+1)
                        & 0xffffff;
                }

// Get the differences between the red, green and blue pixels
```

continues

Listing 26.3 Continued

```
                int redDiff = ((lowerRight >> 16) & 255) -
                    ((upperLeft >> 16) & 255);
                int greenDiff = ((lowerRight >> 8) & 255) -
                    ((upperLeft >> 8) & 255);
                int blueDiff = (lowerRight & 255) -
                    (upperLeft & 255);

// Figure out which color had the greatest change

                int diff = redDiff;
                if (Math.abs(greenDiff) > Math.abs(diff))
                    diff=greenDiff;
                if (Math.abs(blueDiff) > Math.abs(diff))
                    diff=blueDiff;


// Add the greatest change to a medium gray
                int greyColor = 128 + diff;

// If the gray is too high or too low, make it fit in the 0-255 range
                if (greyColor > 255) greyColor = 255;
                if (greyColor < 0) greyColor = 0;

// Create the new color, and don't forget to add in a transparency
// of 0xff000000 making the image completely opaque

                int newColor = 0xff000000 + (greyColor << 16) +
                    (greyColor << 8) + greyColor;

                destImage.setRGB(j, i, newColor);
            }
        }
    }
}
```

Figure 26.13 shows an embossed image.

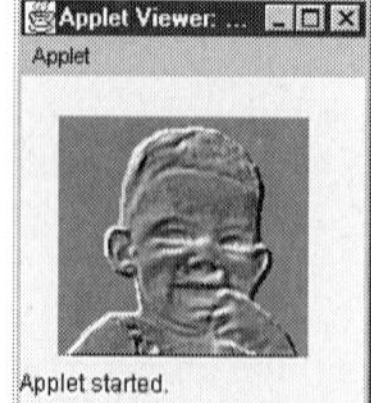

FIG. 26.13 You can use a `BufferedImage` to create an embossing effect.

Transparency

In the early versions of Java, the AWT image API allowed the use of transparent or semi-transparent pixels. In addition to the regular red-green-blue values in a color, there was a fourth value—the alpha component. An alpha component of 0 meant that the color was completely transparent (thus, the RGB values were actually unused). An alpha component of 255 meant that the color was completely opaque. When it was drawn over an existing pixel, the existing pixel was completely hidden. Alpha values between 0 and 255 gave interesting results. You could have two images overlay each other and blend together.

The Java 2D graphics API extends the transparency model to all drawing, enabling you to specify an alpha component for any color.

One term you will encounter frequently in the Java documentation is "premultiplied alpha." When Java draws pixels containing an alpha component, it really adds the various red, green, and blue values for each different figure it is drawing at a particular place. When adding these values, it multiplies them by their respective alpha values first. If an image is completely transparent, for example, it has an alpha value of 0. There is no magical check in the code to say that when alpha is 0, don't draw the pixel. Instead, it multiplies the red, green, and blue components by the alpha value of 0 and adds them to the current pixel values. Because they all multiply out to 0, they have no effect on the current color.

Sometimes, a color has a "premultipled alpha," meaning the red, green, and blue values have already been multiplied by the alpha. They are ready to be added to the current pixel color. You probably won't have to deal with premultiplied alpha values very often, however, unless you specifically want to. The default handling of colors leaves the red, green, and blue components alone.

You can create a color with a transparent component with one of the following Constructors for `Color`:

```
public Color(int red, int green, int blue, int alpha)

public Color(int rgba, boolean hasAlpha)

public Color(float red, float green, float blue, float alpha)
```


The program in Listing 26.4 draws two figures, one with a partially transparent red, the other with a partially transparent blue. The area where they overlap is magenta. If not for the alpha component, there would be no overlap and the first triangle would be hidden wherever the second triangle is drawn.

Listing 26.4 Source Code for *AlphaDraw.java*

```
import java.awt.*;
import java.applet.*;
import java.awt.geom.*;
import java.awt.image.BufferedImage;
import java.net.URL;

public class AlphaDraw extends Applet
{

    public void paint(Graphics g)
```

continues

Listing 26.4 Continued

```
    {
        Graphics2D newG = (Graphics2D) g;

// Create a partially transparent blue

        Color transBlue = new Color(0, 0, 255, 128);
        newG.setColor(transBlue);

        GeneralPath path = new GeneralPath();

        path.moveTo(60, 0);
        path.lineTo(50, 300);
        path.curveTo(160, 230, 270, 140, 400, 100);


        newG.fill(path);

        Color transRed = new Color(255, 0, 0, 128);
        newG.setColor(transRed);

        path = new GeneralPath();
        path.moveTo(200, 300);
        path.lineTo(10, 100);
        path.lineTo(300, 40);
        path.lineTo(200, 300);

        newG.fill(path);

    }
}
```

Clipping

Under the Java 2D API, you can now set up clipping regions using any `Shape` object, including text. Earlier in this chapter, you saw how to set up an image `paint` object so that when you drew text, it filled in the text with an image. You can do something similar by creating what is essentially a stencil, made of text or any shape you like. All you do is create a shape and call the `clip` method in `Graphics2D`:

```
public clip(Shape shape)
```

Listing 26.5 shows how to use a text string as a clipping area. Note that you need to translate the string before clipping with it. Make sure the `johnpat2.gif` file is in the same directory as your applet.

Listing 26.5 Source Code for *TextClip.java*

```
import java.awt.*;
import java.applet.*;
import java.awt.geom.*;
```

```
import java.awt.font.*;
import java.awt.image.BufferedImage;
import java.net.URL;

public class TextClip extends Applet
{

    public void paint(Graphics g)
    {

// Get the Graphics2D object

        Graphics2D newG = (Graphics2D) g;

// Load an image to use as the texture

        URL imgURL = null;
        try {
            imgURL = new URL(getDocumentBase(), "johnpat2.gif");
        } catch (Exception ignore) {
        }

        Image img = getImage(imgURL);

        MediaTracker tracker = new MediaTracker(this);
        try {
            tracker.addImage(img, 0);
            tracker.waitForAll();
        } catch (Exception e) {
            e.printStackTrace();
        }

        int width = img.getWidth(this);
        int height = img.getHeight(this);

        Font bigfont = new Font("Serif", Font.BOLD, 60);

        StyledString ssGrahams = new StyledString("The Grahams",
            bigfont);

// Set the clipping area to be the text string
        AffineTransform transform = new AffineTransform();
        transform.translate(0, 100);

        Shape clipShape = transform.createTransformedShape(
            ssGrahams.getStringOutline());

        newG.clip(clipShape);

// Draw the image over the clipped area
        newG.drawImage(img, 0, 0, width*2, height*2, this);

    }
}
```

The Java 2D API provides a much richer set of graphics functions, taking much of the burden off the programmer. Using this new 2D API, you can create visually stunning displays, and display information better and more efficiently.

PART IV

IO

CHAPTER 27

Files, Streams, and Java

In this chapter

Streams: What Are They?

All computer programs must accept input and generate output. That is, after all, basically what a computer is useful for. Obviously, every computer language must have a way of dealing with input and output. Otherwise it would be impossible to write a useful program. Java features a rich set of classes that represent everything from a general input or output stream to a sophisticated random-access file. You now get a chance to experiment with these important classes.

The `java.io` package provides different input and output streams for reading and writing data. There are streams for a variety of sources including access to common file system functions (such as file and directory creation, removal and renaming, as well as directory listing). The input and output streams can be connected to files, network sockets, or internal memory buffers.

The `java.io` package also contains a number of stream filters that enable you to access stream data in a variety of different formats. You can also create your own filters to add additional functionality.

All information used with a computer system flows from the input through the computer to the output. It is this idea of data flow that leads to the term *streams*. That is, a stream is really nothing more than a flow of data. There are input streams that direct data from the outside world from the keyboard, or a file for instance, into the computer, and output streams that direct data toward output devices such as the computer screen or a file. Because streams are general in nature, a basic stream does not specifically define which devices the data flows from or to. Just like a wire carrying electricity that is being routed to a light bulb, TV, or dishwasher, a basic input or output stream can be directed to or from many different devices.

In Java, streams are represented by classes. The simplest of these classes represents basic input and output streams (`InputStream` and `OutputStream`) that provide general streaming capabilities. Java derives from the basic classes other classes that are more specifically oriented toward a certain type of input or output. You can find all these classes in the `java.io` package:

- `InputStream` The basic input stream.
- `BufferedInputStream` A basic buffered input stream.
- `DataInputStream` An input stream for reading primitive data types.
- `FileInputStream` An input stream used for basic file input.
- `ByteArrayInputStream` An input stream whose source is a byte array.
- `StringBufferInputStream` An input stream whose source is a string.
- `LineNumberInputStream` An input stream that supports line numbers.
- `PushbackInputStream` An input stream that allows a byte to be pushed back onto the stream after the byte is read.

- `PipedInputStream` An input stream used for inter-thread communication.
- `SequenceInputStream` An input stream that combines two other input streams.
- `OutputStream` The basic output stream.
- `PrintStream` An output stream for displaying text.
- `BufferedOutputStream` A basic buffered output stream.
- `DataOutputStream` An output stream for writing primitive data types.
- `FileOutputStream` An output stream used for basic file output.
- `FilterInputStream` An abstract input stream used to add new behaviors to existing input stream classes.
- `FilterOutputStream` An abstract output stream used to add new behaviors to existing output stream classes.
- `ByteArrayOutputStream` An output stream whose destination is a byte array.
- `PipedOutputStream` An output stream used for inter-thread communication.
- `File` A class that encapsulates disk files.
- `FileDescriptor` A class that holds information about a file.
- `RandomAccessFile` A class that encapsulates a random-access disk file.
- `StreamTokenizer` A class that enables a stream to be input as a series of tokens.

Obviously, there are too many stream classes to be covered thoroughly in a single chapter. An entire book could be written on Java I/O alone. For that reason, this chapter covers the most useful of the stream classes, concentrating on basic input and output, as well as file handling and inter-thread communications. You begin with a brief introduction to the classes, after which sample programs demonstrate how the classes work.

The Basic Input and Output Classes

The more specific Java stream classes such as `FileInputStream` and `ByteArrayOutputStream` rely on the general base classes `InputStream` and `OutputStream` for their basic functionality, but extend them to create more specific classes. Because `InputStream` and `OutputStream` are abstract classes, you cannot use them directly. However, because all of Java's stream classes have `InputStream` or `OutputStream` in their family tree, you should know what these classes have to offer.

The *InputStream* Class

The `InputStream` class represents the basic input stream. As such, it defines a set of methods that all input streams need. Table 27.1 lists these methods, without their parameters.

Table 27.1 Methods of the *InputStream* Class

Method	Description
`read()`	Reads data into the stream.
`skip()`	Skips over bytes in the stream.
`available()`	Returns the number of bytes immediately available in the stream.
`mark()`	Marks a position in the stream.
`reset()`	Returns to the marked position in the stream.
`markSupported()`	Returns a `boolean` value indicating whether the stream supports marking and resetting.
`close()`	Closes the stream.

The `read()` method is overloaded in the class, providing three methods for reading data from the stream. The methods' signatures look like this:

```
int read()
int read(byte b[])
int read(byte b[], int off, int len)
```

The most basic method for getting data from any `InputStream` object is the `read` method.

```
public abstract int read() throws IOException
```

reads a single byte from the input stream and returns it. This method performs what is known as a *blocking read*, which means that it waits for data if there is none available. So, when a datasource doesn't have any data to be read yet the method will wait until a byte becomes available before returning. One example of this situation is when the stream is on a network and the next byte of data may not have arrived yet. You want to be careful with this situation, however, because it can cause similar problems to the synchronization problems discussed in Chapter 13, "Threads," if you are not careful.

When the stream reaches the end of a file, this method returns –1. Note that to be able to return a full 8 bits of data (a byte) and still have –1 only occur when the stream is at an end, the values are actually returned as if they were generated from an unsigned byte—that is, if you write a –1 into a stream it will actually get read back in as an integer with a value of 255. Fortunately casting that `int` back to a byte will return the value to –1.

NOTE This `read` method is the most important because it is the method that actually grabs data from the native source. All the other methods use this one to perform their work.

```
public int read(byte[] bytes) throws IOException
```

fills an array with bytes read from the stream and returns the number of bytes read. It is possible for this method to read fewer bytes than the array can hold, because there may not be enough bytes in the stream to fill it. When the stream reaches end of file this method returns –1. You will always receive all the bytes in the stream before you hit end of file. In other words, if there are 50 bytes left in the stream and you ask to read 100 bytes, this method returns the 50 bytes, and then the next time it is called it returns –1, if the stream is at an end.

```
public int read(byte[] bytes, int offset, int length)
     throws IOException
```

fills an array starting at position `offset` with up to `length` bytes from the stream. It returns either the number of bytes read or –1 for end of file.

The `read` method always blocks (it sits and waits without returning) when there is no data available. To avoid blocking, you might need to ask ahead of time exactly how many bytes you can safely read without blocking. The `available` method returns this number:

```
public int available() throws IOException
```

You can skip over data in a stream by passing the `skip` method the number of bytes you want to skip over:

```
public long skip(long n)
```

The `skip` method actually uses the `read` method to skip over bytes, so it will block under the same circumstances as `read`. It returns the number of bytes it skipped or –1 if it hits the end of file.

Some input streams enable you to place a bookmark of sorts at a point so that you can return to that location later. The `markSupported` method returns `true` if the stream supports marking:

```
public boolean markSupported()
```

The `mark` method marks the current position in the stream, so you can back up to it later:

```
public synchronized void mark(int readLimit)
```

The `readLimit` parameter sets the maximum number of bytes that can be read from the stream before the mark is no longer set. In other words, you must tell the stream how many bytes it should let you read before it forgets about the mark. Some streams may need to allocate memory to support marking, and this parameter tells them how big to make their array.

If you have set a mark, you can reposition the stream back to the mark by calling the `reset` method:

```
public synchronized void reset() throws IOException
```

After you are done with a stream, you should close it down using the `close` method:

```
public void close() throws IOException
```

Most streams get closed automatically at garbage collection time. On the majority of operating systems, however, the number of files you can have open at one time is limited. Therefore, you should close your streams when you are finished with them to free up system resources immediately without waiting for garbage collection.

The *OutputStream* Class

The counterpart to `InputStream` is the `OutputStream` class, which provides the basic functionality for all output streams. Table 27.2 lists the methods defined in the `OutputStream` class, along with their descriptions.

Table 27.2 Methods of the *OutputStream* Class

Method	Description
`write()`	Writes data to the stream.
`flush()`	Forces any buffered output to be written.
`close()`	Closes the stream.

Rather than being a source of data like the input stream, an output stream is a recipient of data. The most basic method of an `OutputStream` object is the `write` method.

```
public abstract void write(int b) throws IOException
```

writes a single byte of data to an output stream.

```
public void write(byte[] bytes) throws IOException
```

writes the entire contents of the `bytes` array to the output stream.

```
public void write(byte[] bytes, int offset, int length)
     throws IOException
```

writes `length` bytes from the `bytes` array, starting at position `offset`.

Depending on the type of stream, you may need to occasionally flush the stream if you need to be sure that the data written on the stream has been delivered. Flushing a stream does not destroy any information in the stream, it just makes sure that any data stored in internal buffers is written out onto whatever device the stream may be connected to. To flush an output stream, call the `flush` method:

```
public void flush() throws IOException
```

As with the input streams, you should close output streams when you are done with them by calling the `close` method:

```
public void close() throws IOException
```

System.in and *System.out* Objects

To support the standard input and output devices (usually the keyboard and screen, respectively), Java defines two stream objects that you can use in your programs without having to create stream objects of your own. The `System.in` object (instantiated from the `InputStream` class) enables your programs to read data from the keyboard, whereas the `System.out` object (instantiated from the `PrintStream` class) routes output to the computer's screen. You can use these stream objects directly to handle standard input and output in your Java programs, or you can use them as the basis for other stream objects you may want to create.

Listing 27.1, for example, is a Java application that accepts a line of input from the user and then displays the line onscreen. Figure 27.1 shows the application running in a DOS window.

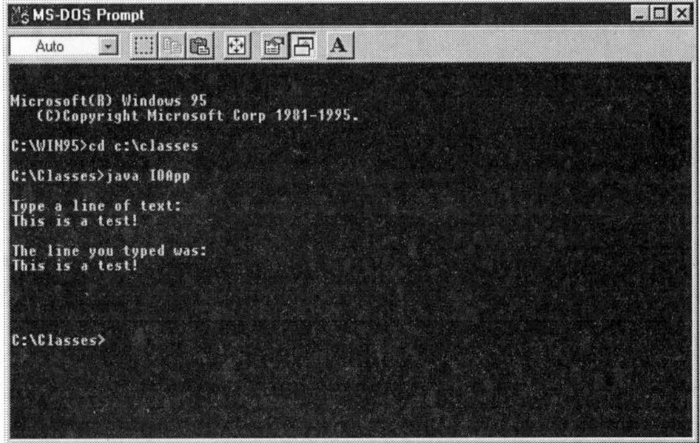

FIG. 27.1 Java's `System` class provides for standard I/O.

Listing 27.1 *IOApp.java*—**Performing Basic User Input and Output**

```
import java.io.*;
class IOApp {
  public static void main(String args[]) {
    byte buffer[] = new byte[255];
    System.out.println("\nType a line of text: ");
    try {
      System.in.read(buffer, 0, 255);
    }
    catch (Exception e) {
      String err = e.toString();
      System.out.println(err);
    }
    System.out.println("\nThe line you typed was: ");
    try{
      String inputStr = new String(buffer, "Default");
      System.out.println(inputStr);
    }catch (UnsupportedEncodingException e){
      System.out.println("e:"+e);
    }
  }
}
```

PrintWriter Class

You probably noticed in Listing 27.1 a method called `println()`, which is not a part of the `OutputStream` class. To provide for more flexible output on the standard output stream, the `System` class derives its `out` output-stream object from the `PrintWriter` class, which provides for printing values as text output. Table 27.3 lists the methods of the `PrintWriter` class, along with their descriptions.

Table 27.3 Basic Methods of the *PrintWriter* Class

Method	Description
`write()`	Writes data to the stream.
`flush()`	Flushes data from the stream.
`checkError()`	Flushes the stream, returning errors that occurred.
`print()`	Prints data in text form.
`println()`	Prints a line of data (followed by a newline character) in text form.
`close()`	Closes the stream.

As with many of the methods included in the stream classes, the `write()`, `print()`, and `println()` methods are overloaded many times and come in several versions. The `write()` method can write Strings, partial Strings, single chars or whole char arrays, whereas the `print()` and `println()` methods can display almost any type of data onscreen. The various method signatures look like this:

```
void write(int c)
void write(char c[], int off, int len)
void write(String s)
void write(String s,int off,int len)
void print(Object obj)
void print(String s)
void print(char s[])
void print(char c)
void print(int i)
void print(long l)
void print(float f)
void print(double d)
void print(boolean b)
void println()
void println(Object obj)
void println(String s)
void println(char s[])
void println(char c)
void println(int i)
void println(long l)
void println(float f)
void println(double d)
void println(boolean b)
```

Handling Files

Now that you've had an introduction to the stream classes, you can put your knowledge to work. Perhaps the most common use of I/O—outside of retrieving data from the keyboard and displaying data onscreen—is file I/O. Any program that wants to retain its status (including the status of any edited files) must be capable of loading and saving files. Java provides several classes—including `File`, `FileDescriptor`, `RandomAccessFile`, `FileInputStream`, `FileOutputStream`, `FilePermission`, `FileReader`, and `FileWriter`—for dealing with files. In this section, you examine these classes and get a chance to see how they work.

File Security

When you start reading and writing to a disk from a networked application, you have to consider security issues. Because the Java language is used especially for creating Internet-based applications, security is even more important. No user wants to worry that the Web pages he's currently viewing are capable of reading from and writing to his hard disk. For this reason, the Java system was designed to allow the user to set system security from within his Java-compatible browser and determine which files and directories are to remain accessible to the browser and which are to be locked up tight.

In most cases, the user disallows all file access on his local system, thus completely protecting his system from unwarranted intrusion. In fact the default setting on all current browsers disallows access to the local system, and until recently even volunteering access to the file system was not possible. This tight security is vital to the existence of applets because of the way they are automatically downloaded onto a user's system behind the user's back, as it were. No one would use Java-compatible browsers if he feared that such use would open his system to the tampering of nosy corporations and sociopathic programmers.

Java standalone applications, however, are a whole different story. Java applications are no different than any other application on your system. They cannot be automatically downloaded and run the way applets are. For this reason, standalone applications can have full access to the file system on which they are run. The file-handling examples in this chapter, then, are incorporated into Java standalone applications.

FileInputStream Class

If your file-reading needs are relatively simple, you can use the `FileInputStream` class, which is a simple input-stream class derived from `InputStream`. This class features all the methods inherited from the `InputStream` class. To create an object of the `FileInputStream` class, you call one of its `Constructors`, of which there are three, as shown:

```
FileInputStream(String name)
FileInputStream(File file)
FileInputStream(FileDescriptor fdObj)
```

The first `Constructor` creates a `FileInputStream` object from the given filename `name`. The second `Constructor` creates the object from a `File` object, and the third creates the object from a `FileDescriptor` object.

Listing 27.2 is a Java application that reads its own source code from disk and displays the code onscreen. Figure 27.2 shows the application's output in a DOS window.

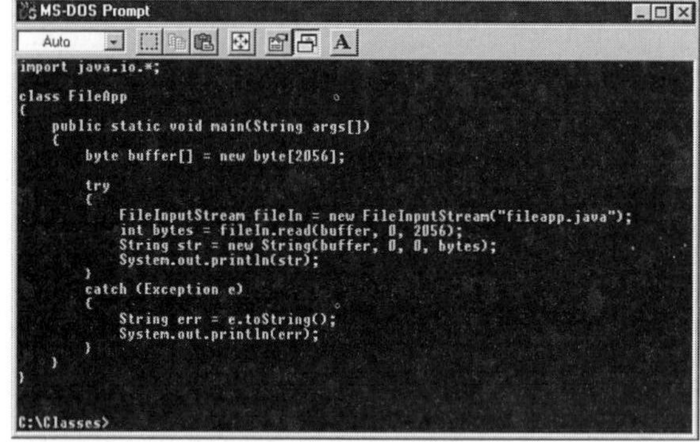

FIG. 27.2
The `FileApp` application reads and displays its own source code.

Listing 27.2 ***FileApp.java*—An Application That Reads Its Own Source Code**

```
import java.io.*;
class FileApp {
  public static void main(String args[]) {
    byte buffer[] = new byte[2056];
    try {
      FileInputStream fileIn =
                              new FileInputStream("fileapp.java");
      int bytes = fileIn.read(buffer, 0, 2056);
      try{
        String str = new String(buffer, 0, bytes, "Default");
        System.out.println(str);
      }catch (UnsupportedEncodingException e){
        System.out.println("The encoding \"Default\" was not found :"+e);
      }
    }
    catch (Exception e) {
      String err = e.toString();
      System.out.println(err);
    }
  }
}
```

Using the *FileOutputStream* Class

As you may have guessed, the counterpart to the `FileInputStream` class is `FileOutputStream`, which provides basic file-writing capabilities. Besides `FileOutputStream`'s methods, which are inherited from `OutputStream`, the class features three `Constructors`, whose signatures look like this:

```
FileOutputStream(String name)
FileOutputStream(File file)
FileOutputStream(FileDescriptor fdObj)
```

The first `Constructor` creates a `FileOutputStream` object from the given filename, `name`, whereas the second `Constructor` creates the object from a `File` object. The third `Constructor` creates the object from a `FileDescriptor` object.

Listing 27.3 is a Java application that reads a line of text from the keyboard and saves it to a file. When you run the application, type a line and press Enter. Then at the system prompt (for DOS), type **`TYPE LINE.TXT`** to display the text in the file, just to prove it's really there. Figure 27.3 shows a typical program run.

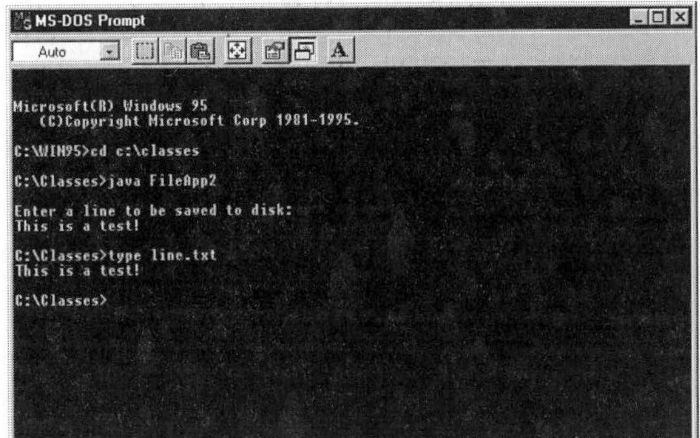

FIG. 27.3
The `FileApp2` application saves user input to a file.

Listing 27.3 ***FileApp2.java*—An Application that Saves Text to a File**

```
import java.io.*;
class FileApp2
{
    public static void main(String args[])
    {
        byte buffer[] = new byte[80];
        try
        {
            System.out.println
               ("\nEnter a line to be saved to disk:");
            int bytes = System.in.read(buffer);
            FileOutputStream fileOut =
                new FileOutputStream("line.txt");
            fileOut.write(buffer, 0, bytes);
        }
        catch (Exception e)
        {
            String err = e.toString();
            System.out.println(err);
        }
    }
}
```

Using the *File* Class

If you need to obtain information about a file, you should create an object of Java's `File` class. This class enables you to query the system about everything from the file's name to the time it was last modified. You can also use the `File` class to make new directories, as well as to delete and rename files. Create a `File` object by calling one of the class's three `Constructors`, whose signatures are as follows:

```
File(String path)
File(String path, String name)
File(File dir, String name)
```

The first `Constructor` creates a `File` object from the given full pathname (for example, `C:\CLASSES\MYAPP.JAVA`). The second `Constructor` creates the object from a separate path and a file, and the third creates the object from a separate path and filename, with the path being associated with another `File` object.

The `File` class features a full set of methods that give your program a lot of file-handling options. Table 27.4 lists these methods along with their descriptions.

Table 27.4 Methods of the File Class

Method	Description
`getName()`	Gets the file's name (as a String).
`getPath()`	Gets the file's path (as a String).
`getAbsolutePath()`	Gets the file's absolute path (as a String).
`getAbsoluteFile()`	Gets the file's absolute path (as a File).
`getCanonicalPath()`	Gets the file's canonical path. (as a String).
`getCanonicalFile()`	Gets the file's canonical path (as a File).
`getParent()`	Gets the file's parent directory (as a String).
`getParentFile()`	Gets the file's parent directory (as a File).
`exists()`	Returns `true` if the file exists, `false` otherwise.
`createNewFile()`	Creates a new file, but only if the file does not already exist (returns `true` if the file was created).
`createTempFile (String pattern, File directory)`	Creates a temporary file. The file's name is created first, by the directory, and then by using the pattern to create a unique name (returns a File).
`createTempFile (String prefix)`	Creates a temporary file. The file's name is created first, by the default system temp directory, and then by using the pattern to create a unique name (returns a File).
`deleteOnExit()`	Request that this file be deleted when the VM exits. Note: only successful by normal VM exits not by abnormal exits.

Method	Description
`canWrite()`	Returns `true` if the file can be written to.
`canRead()`	Returns `true` if the file can be read.
`setReadOnly()`	Sets the file so that it is read only.
`isFile()`	Returns `true` if the file is valid.
`isDirectory()`	Returns `true` if the directory is valid.
`isAbsolute()`	Returns `true` if the filename is absolute.
`isHidden()`	Tests to see if the file is hidden. (Returns `true` if it is.)
`lastModified()`	Returns the time the file was last changed, represented as the number of milliseconds since 00:00:00 GMT, January 1, 1970.
`setLastModified (long time)`	Sets the time when the file was last modified. The time should be represented as the number of milliseconds since 00:00:00 GMT, January 1, 1970.
`length()`	Returns the number of bytes in the file.
`mkdir()`	Makes a directory represented by this file. (Returns `true` if successful.)
`mkdirs()`	Makes a directory represented by this file, and any required but non-existent parent directories.(Returns `true` if successful.)
`renameTo(File dest)`	Renames the file to the indicated file.
`list()`	Gets a list of files in the directory. (Returns an array of strings.)
`list (FilenameFilter filter)`	Gets a list of files in the directory that match the given file filter. (Returns an array of strings.)
`listFiles()`	Gets a list of files in the directory. (Returns an array of files.)
`listFiles (FilenameFilter filter)`	Gets a list of files in the directory that match the given file filter. (Returns an array of files.)
`listRoots()`	Gets a list of the root directories for the current system. A Windows or Macintosh computer would have one root for each drive, a UNIX machine has one root (`/`). (Returned as an array of files.)
`delete()`	Deletes the file. (Returns `true` if successful.)
`hashCode()`	Gets a hash code for the file.
`equals()`	Compares the `file` object with another object. (Returns `true` if they are equal.)
`toString()`	Gets a string containing the file's path.
`toURL()`	Returns an URL object equivalent to the file.

Directory Operations Although most of the methods in the `File` class can be used on both files and directories, the `list` method is only for use in a directory:

```
public String[] list()
```

The `list` method returns an array of the names of all the files contained within the directory. You can also set up a filename filter for the `list` method, which enables you to select only certain filenames:

```
public String[] list(FilenameFilter filter)
```

The `FilenameFilter` interface defines a single method, `accept`, that returns `true` if a filename should be included in the list:

```
public abstract boolean accept(File dir, String name)
```

Listing 27.4 shows an object that implements a filename filter that allows only files ending with `.java`.

Listing 27.4 Source Code for *JavaFilter.java*

```
import java.io.*;

// This class implements a filename filter that only allows
// files that end with .java

public class JavaFilter extends Object implements FilenameFilter
{
     public JavaFilter()
     {
     }

     public boolean accept(File dir, String name)
     {

// Only return true for accept if the file ends with .java
          return name.endsWith(".java");

     }
}
```

Listing 27.5 shows a program that uses the `JavaFilter` to list out all the `.java` files in the current directory.

Listing 27.5 Source code for *ListJava.java*

```
import java.io.*;

public class ListJava extends Object
{
     public static void main(String[] args)
     {
```

```
// Create a File instance for the current directory
          File currDir = new File(".");

// Get a filtered list of the .java files in the current directory
          String[] javaFiles = currDir.list(new JavaFilter());

// Print out the contents of the javaFiles array
          for (int i=0; i < javaFiles.length; i++) {
               System.out.println(javaFiles[i]);
          }
     }
}
```

Creating Temporary Files A new JDK 1.2 feature is the ability to create temporary files. Temporary files are useful for a variety of purposes in many programs. To create a temporary file, you can use the static `createTemporaryFile` method in `File`. As shown in Listing 27.6, the temporary file is created by passing in a string that represents the naming pattern that you want to apply to the file. The string should contain the first several letters of the file name (minimum three characters) and then a pound sign (#), followed by an extension. The pound sign is replaced with a four-digit number that is guaranteed to be unique within this instance of the VM. If you do not provide the pound sign, it is automatically appended to the string; if you do not provide an extension, it is automatically assumed to be `.tmp`.

Listing 27.6 Source Code for *TestFile.java*

```
import java.io.*;
public class TestFile{
    public static void main(String args[]){
        try{
            File tempFile = File.createTempFile("test#que");
            FileOutputStream fout = new FileOutputStream(tempFile);
            PrintStream out = new PrintStream(fout);
            out.println("Place this test string in the temp file");
        }catch (IOException ioe){
             System.out.println("There was a problem creating/writing to the
➥temp file");
             ioe.printStackTrace(System.err);
        }
    }
}
```

Part IV Ch 27

After you run the `TestFile` program in Listing 27.6 you should see a file called `test????.que` in your systems temp directory (where the `????`s are actually numbers).

Deleting Files on Exit There is one additional feature commonly used with temporary files, but which can be applied to any file. The `deleteOnExit()` method was added to JDK 1.2 which allows you to schedule a file to be deleted when the VM exits. This is very useful if, for instance, you are creating a file within your program, but don't want to leave it on the system after the program quits. There are two cautions you need to be aware of with this method. First, once a file is scheduled to be deleted on exit, you cannot unschedule it. The second is that the `deleteOnExit()` method is only effective if the VM exits normally, such as by `System.exit(0)`. If the system crashes, or there is some other form of abnormal crash, the VM will not be able to delete the file.

Listing 27.7 shows how `TestFile` in Listing 27.6 would be modified to delete the file when the system exits. Notice that when you run `TestFile2` you see a file in the temp directory before the system exits, but afterwards the file is gone.

Listing 27.7 Source Code for *TestFile.java*

```
import java.io.*;
public class TestFile2{
    public static void main(String args[]){
        try{
            File tempFile = File.createTempFile("test#que");
            FileOutputStream fout = new FileOutputStream(tempFile);
            PrintStream out = new PrintStream(fout);
            out.println("Place this test string in the temp file");
            tempFile.deleteOnExit();
        }catch (IOException ioe){
             System.out.println("There was a problem creating/writing to the
➥temp file_
             ioe.printStackTrace(System.err);
        }

        System.out.println("Until you hit 'Enter' there is a temp file on the
➥system");_
        try{
            System.in.read();
        }catch (IOException ioe){
        }
        System.exit(0);
    }
}
```

RandomAccessFile Class

At this point, you may think that Java's file-handling capabilities are scattered through a lot of different classes, making it difficult to obtain the basic functionality you need to read, write, and otherwise manage a file. But Java's creators are way ahead of you. They created the `RandomAccessFile` class for those times when you really need to get serious about your file handling. By using this class, you can do just about everything you need to do with a file.

You create a `RandomAccessFile` object by calling one of the class's two `Constructors`, whose signatures are as follows:

```
RandomAccessFile(String name, String mode)
RandomAccessFile(File file, String mode)
```

The first `Constructor` creates a `RandomAccessFile` object from a string containing the filename and another string containing the `access` mode (`"` for read and `rw` for read and write). The second `Constructor` creates the object from a `File` object and the mode string.

After you have the `RandomAccessFile` object created, you can call on the object's methods to manipulate the file. Table 27.5 lists those methods.

Table 27.5 Methods of the *RandomAccessFile* Class

Method	Description
`close()`	Closes the file.
`getFD()`	Gets a `FileDescriptor` object for the file.
`getFilePointer()`	Gets the location of the file pointer.
`length()`	Gets the length of the file.
`read()`	Reads data from the file.
`readBoolean()`	Reads a `boolean` value from the file.
`readByte()`	Reads a byte from the file.
`readChar()`	Reads a `char` from the file.
`readDouble()`	Reads a `double` floating-point value from the file.
`readFloat()`	Reads a `float` from the file.
`readFully()`	Reads data into an array, completely filling the array.
`readInt()`	Reads an `int` from the file.
`readLine()`	Reads a text line from the file.
`readLong()`	Reads a long `int` from the file.
`readShort()`	Reads a short `int` from the file.
`readUnsignedByte()`	Reads an unsigned byte from the file.
`readUnsignedShort()`	Reads an unsigned short `int` from the file.
`readUTF()`	Reads a UTF string from the file.
`seek()`	Positions the file pointer in the file.
`skipBytes()`	Skips over a given number of bytes in the file.
`write()`	Writes data to the file.
`writeBoolean()`	Writes a `boolean` to the file.
`writeByte()`	Writes a byte to the file.
`writeBytes()`	Writes a string as bytes.

continues

Table 27.5 Continued

Method	Description
`writeChar()`	Writes a `char` to the file.
`writeChars()`	Writes a string as `char` data.
`writeDouble()`	Writes a `double` floating-point value to the file.
`writeFloat()`	Writes a `float` to the file.
`writeInt()`	Writes an `int` to the file.
`writeLong()`	Writes a long `int` to the file.
`writeShort()`	Writes a short `int` to the file.
`writeUTF()`	Writes a UTF string.

Listing 27.8 is a Java application that reads and displays its own source code using a `RandomAccessFile` object. Figure 27.4 shows a typical program run.

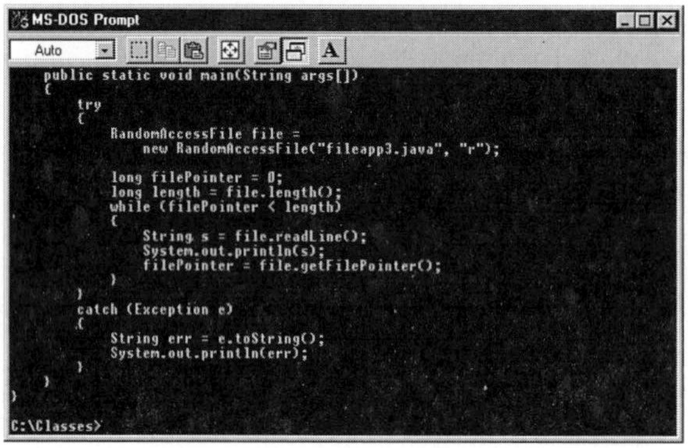

FIG. 27.4
The `FileApp3` application can read and display its own source code.

Listing 27.8 ***FileApp3.java*—Using a *RandomAccessFile* Object**

```
import java.io.*;
class FileApp3
{
    public static void main(String args[])
    {
        try
        {
            RandomAccessFile file =
                new RandomAccessFile("fileapp3.java", "r");
            long filePointer = 0;
            long length = file.length();
            while (filePointer < length)
            {
```

```
                String s = file.readLine();
                System.out.println(s);
                filePointer = file.getFilePointer();
            }
        }
        catch (Exception e)
        {
            String err = e.toString();
            System.out.println(err);
        }
    }
}
```

Using Pipes

Normal stream and file handling under Java isn't all that different than under any other computer language. The Java stream classes provide all the functions you are used to using to handle streams. However, Java also supports pipes, a form of data stream with which you may have little experience. Basically, pipes are a way to transfer data directly between different threads. One thread sends data through its output pipe, and another thread reads the data from its input pipe. By using pipes, you can share data between different threads without having to resort to things like temporary files.

Introducing the *PipedInputStream* and *PipedOutputStream* Classes

As you may have guessed, Java provides two special classes for dealing with pipes.

The first class, `PipedInputStream`, represents the input side of a pipe; the second, `PipedOutputStream`, represents the output side of the pipe. These classes work together to provide a piped stream of data in much the same way a conventional pipe provides a stream of water. If you were to cap off one end of a conventional pipe, the flow of water would stop. The same is also true of piped streams. If you don't have both an input and output stream, you've effectively sealed off one or both ends of the data pipe.

To create a piped stream, you first create an object of the `PipedOutputStream` class. Then, you create an object of the `PipedInputStream` class, handing it a reference to the piped output stream, like this:

```
pipeOut = new PipedOutputStream();
pipeIn = new PipedInputStream(pipeOut);
```

By giving the `PipedInputStream` object a reference to the output pipe, you have effectively connected the input and output into a stream through which data can flow in a single direction. Data that's pumped into the output side of the pipe can be received by another thread that has access to the input side of the pipe, as shown in Figure 27.5.

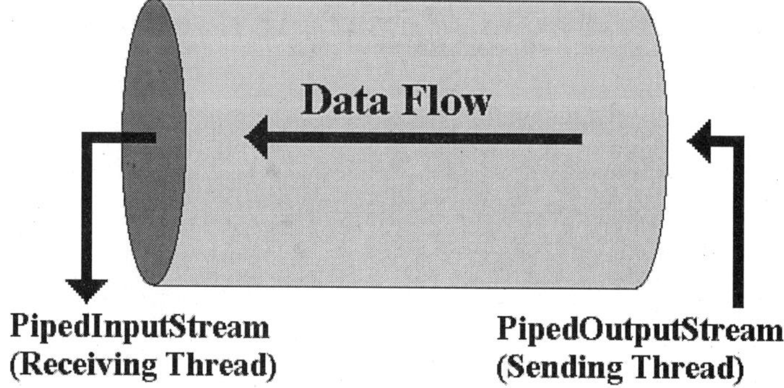

FIG. 27.5
The output stream and input stream act as two ends on a one-way pipe.

NOTE It may seem a little weird that the output side of the pipe is the side into which data is pumped, and the input side is the side from which the data flows. You have to think in terms of the threads that are using the pipe, rather than of the pipe itself. That is, the thread supplying data sends its output into the piped output stream, and the thread inputting the data takes it from the piped input stream.

After you have created the pipe, you can read and write data just as you would with a conventional file. In the following section, you get a chance to see pipes in action.

The *PipeApp* Application

Listings 27.9 and 27.10 are the source code for an application called `PipeApp` that uses pipes to process data. The application has three threads: the main thread and two secondary threads that are started by the main thread. The program takes a file that contains all Xs, and, using pipes to transfer data, first changes the data to all Ys and finally changes the data to all Zs, after which the program displays the modified data onscreen. Note that no additional files, beyond the input file, are created. All data is manipulated using pipes. Figure 27.6 shows a program run.

FIG. 27.6
The `PipeApp` application uses pipes to share data with three threads.

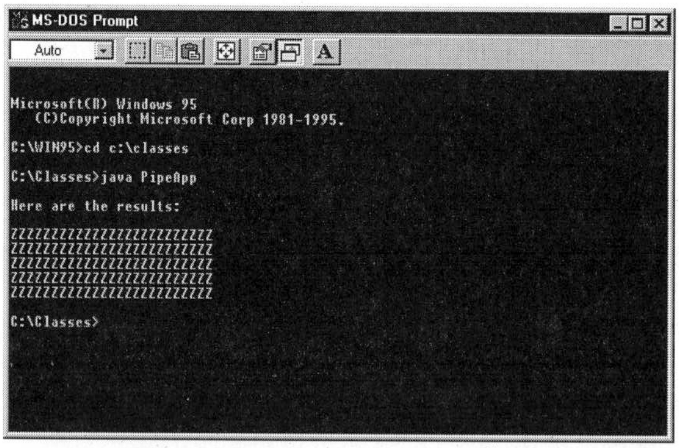

```
MS-DOS Prompt

Microsoft(R) Windows 95
   (C)Copyright Microsoft Corp 1981-1995.

C:\WIN95>cd c:\classes

C:\Classes>java PipeApp

Here are the results:

ZZZZZZZZZZZZZZZZZZZZZZZZZ
ZZZZZZZZZZZZZZZZZZZZZZZZZ
ZZZZZZZZZZZZZZZZZZZZZZZZZ
ZZZZZZZZZZZZZZZZZZZZZZZZZ
ZZZZZZZZZZZZZZZZZZZZZZZZZ

C:\Classes>
```

Listing 27.9 *PipeApp.java*—The Main *PipeApp* Application

```
import java.io.*;
public class PipeApp {
  public static void main(String[] args) {
    PipeApp pipeApp = new PipeApp();
    try {
      FileInputStream XFileIn = new FileInputStream("input.txt");
      InputStream YInPipe = pipeApp.changeToY(XFileIn);
      InputStream ZInPipe = pipeApp.changeToZ(YInPipe);
      System.out.println();
      System.out.println("Here are the results:");
      System.out.println();
      BufferedReader reader = new BufferedReader(new
➥InputStreamReader(ZInPipe));
      String str = reader.readLine();
      while (str != null) {
        System.out.println(str);
        str = reader.readLine();
      }
      reader.close();
    }
    catch (Exception e) {
      System.out.println(e.toString());
    }
  }
  public InputStream changeToY(InputStream inputStream) {
    try {
      BufferedReader XFileIn = new BufferedReader(new
➥InputStreamReader(inputStream));
      PipedOutputStream pipeOut = new PipedOutputStream();
      PipedInputStream pipeIn = new PipedInputStream(pipeOut);
      PrintWriter printWriter = new PrintWriter(pipeOut);
      YThread yThread = new YThread(XFileIn, printWriter);
      yThread.start();
      return pipeIn;
    }
    catch (Exception e) {
      System.out.println(e.toString());
    }
    return null;
  }
  public InputStream changeToZ(InputStream inputStream) {
    try {
      BufferedReader YFileIn = new BufferedReader
➥(new InputStreamReader(inputStream));
      PipedOutputStream pipeOut2 = new PipedOutputStream();
      PipedInputStream pipeIn2 = new PipedInputStream(pipeOut2);
      PrintWriter printWriter2 = new PrintWriter(pipeOut2);
      ZThread zThread = new ZThread(YFileIn, printWriter2);
      zThread.start();
      return pipeIn2;
    }
    catch (Exception e) {
      System.out.println(e.toString());
```

continues

Listing 27.9 Continued

```
    }
    return null;
  }
}
```

Listing 27.10 ***YThread.java*****—The Thread That Changes the Data to Ys**

```
import java.io.*;
class YThread extends Thread {
  BufferedReader  XFileIn;
  PrintWriter printWriter;
  YThread(BufferedReader XFileIn, PrintWriter printWriter) {
    this.XFileIn = XFileIn;
    this.printWriter = printWriter;
  }
  public void run() {
    try {
      String XString = XFileIn.readLine();
      while (XString != null) {
        String YString = XString.replace('X', 'Y');
        printWriter.println(YString);
        printWriter.flush();
        XString = XFileIn.readLine();
      }
      printWriter.close();
    }
    catch (IOException e) {
      System.out.println(e.toString());
    }
  }
}
```

Listing 27.11 ***ZThread.java*****—The Thread That Changes the Data to All Zs**

```
import java.io.*;
class ZThread extends Thread {
  BufferedReader YFileIn;
  PrintWriter printWriter;
  ZThread(BufferedReader YFileIn, PrintWriter printWriter) {
    this.YFileIn = YFileIn;
    this.printWriter = printWriter;
  }
  public void run() {
    try {
      String YString = YFileIn.readLine();
      while (YString != null) {
        String ZString = YString.replace('Y', 'Z');
        printWriter.println(ZString);
        printWriter.flush();
        YString = YFileIn.readLine();
      }
```

```
      printWriter.close();
    }
    catch (IOException e) {
      System.out.println(e.toString());
    }
  }
}
```

Exploring the *main()* Method

Seeing the `PipeApp` application work and understanding why it works are two very different things. In this section, you examine the program line by line to see what's going on. The `PipeApp.java` file is the main program thread, so you start your exploration there. This application contains three methods: the `main()` method, which all applications must have; and the `changeToY()` and `changeToZ()` methods, which start two additional threads.

Inside `main()`, the program first creates an application object for the program:

```
PipeApp pipeApp = new PipeApp();
```

This is necessary to be able to call the `ChangeToY()` and `ChangeToZ()` methods, which don't exist until the application object has been created. One way around this would be to make all the class's methods `static`, rather than just `main()`. Then, you could call the methods without creating an object of the class.

After creating the application object, the program sets up a `try` program block because streams require that `IOException` exceptions be caught in your code. Inside the `try` block, the program creates an input stream for the source text file:

```
FileInputStream XFileIn = new FileInputStream("input.txt");
```

This new input stream is passed to the `changeToY()` method so that the next thread can read the file:

```
InputStream YInPipe = pipeApp.changeToY(XFileIn);
```

The `changeToY()` method creates the thread that changes the input data to all Ys (you will see how this method works in the following section, "Exploring the `changeToY()` Method") and returns the input pipe from the thread. The next thread can use this input pipe to access the data created by the first thread. Therefore the input pipe is passed as an argument to the `changeToZ()` method:


```
InputStream ZInPipe = pipeApp.changeToZ(YInPipe);
```

The `changeToZ()` method starts the thread that changes the data from all Ys to all Zs. The main program uses the input pipe returned from `changeToZ()`to access the modified data and print it onscreen.

After the program gets the `ZInPipe` piped input stream, it prints a message onscreen:

```
System.out.println();
System.out.println("Here are the results:");
System.out.println();
```

Then, the program maps the piped input stream to a `BufferedReader` object, which enables the program to read the data using the `readLine()` method:

```
BufferedReader reader = new BufferedReader(new InputStreamReader(ZInPipe));
```

After the input stream is created, the program can read the data in, line by line, and display it onscreen (see Listing 27.12).

Listing 27.12 ***LST19_08.TXT*—Reading and Displaying the Data Line by Line**

```
String str = reader.readLine();
while (str != null)
{
    System.out.println(str);
    str = inputStream.readLine();
}
```

Finally, after displaying the data, the program closes the input stream:

```
reader.close();
```

Exploring the *changeToY()* Method

Inside the `changeToY()` method is the first place in the program you really get to see pipes in action. Like `main()`, the `changeToY()` method does most of its processing inside a `try` program block to catch `IOException` exceptions. The method first maps the source input stream, which was passed as the method's single parameter, to a `DataInputStream` object. This enables the program to read data from the stream using the `readLine()` method:

```
BufferedReader XFileIn = new BufferedReader
(new InputStreamReader(inputStream));
Next, changeToY() creates the output pipe and input pipe:
PipedOutputStream pipeOut = new PipedOutputStream();
PipedInputStream pipeIn = new PipedInputStream(pipeOut);
```

Then, to be able to use the `println()` method to output text lines to the pipe, the program maps the output pipe to a `PrintStream` object:

```
PrintWriter printWriter = new PrintWriter(pipeOut);
```

At this point, the method has four streams created:

- The first (`XFileIn`) represents the data that will be read from the file.
- The second and third (`pipeOut` and `printWriter`, which you can think of as the same stream, if you like) are the output end of the pipe into which the new thread will output its data.
- The fourth (`pipeIn`) is the input side of the pipe from which the next thread will input its data.

Figure 27.7 illustrates this situation.

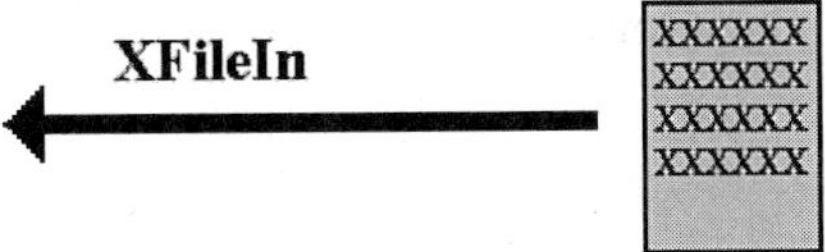

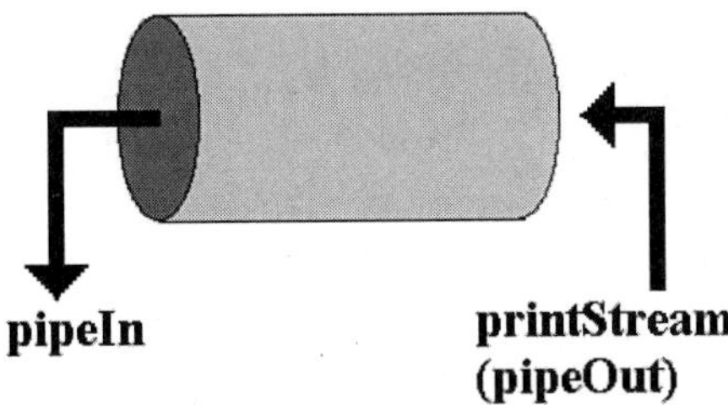

FIG. 27.7 These are the streams created in the `changeToY()` method.

Now the program can create the thread that changes the data from Xs to Ys. That thread is an object of the `YThread` class, whose `Constructor` is passed the input file (`XFileIn`) and the output pipe (now called `printWriter`) as arguments:

```
YThread yThread = new YThread(XFileIn, printWriter);
```

After creating the thread, the program starts the thread:

```
yThread.start();
```

As you soon see, the `YThread` thread reads data in from `XFileIn`, changes the data from Xs to Ys, and outputs the result into `printWriter`, which is the output end of the pipe. Because the output end of the pipe is connected to the input end (`pipeIn`), the input end contains the data that the `YThread` thread changed to Ys. The program returns that end of the pipe from the `changeToY()` method so that it can be used as the input for the `changeToZ()` method. Figure 27.8 shows the `changeToY()` portion of the chain.

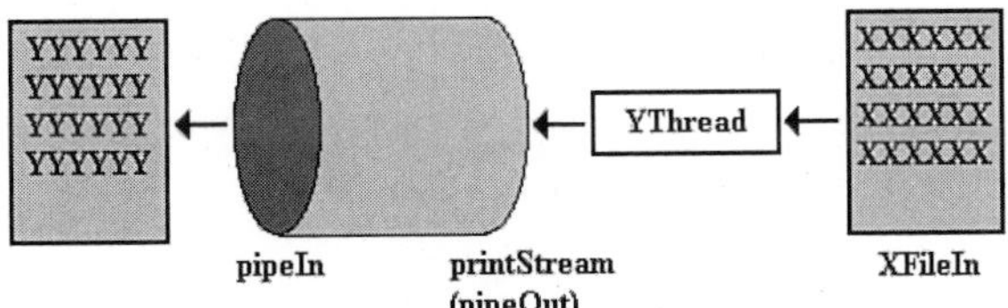

FIG. 27.8 The `changeToY()` method reads in Xs and send Ys into the pipe.

Exploring the *changeToZ()* Method

The `changeToZ()`method works similarly to the `changeToY()` method. However, because the way each method accesses its streams is important to understanding the `PipeApp` application, you examine `changeToZ()` line by line, too. The `changeToZ()` method starts by mapping its input stream, which is the input end of the pipe returned from `changeToY()`, to a

BufferedReader object so that the program can read from the stream using the readLine() method:

```
BufferedReader YFileIn = new BufferedReader(new InputStreamReader
➥(inputStream));
```

The program then creates a new pipe:

```
PipedOutputStream pipeOut2 = new PipedOutputStream();
PipedInputStream pipeIn2 = new PipedInputStream(pipeOut2);
```

This new pipe routes data from the third thread (counting the main thread) back to the main program.

After creating the pipe, the program maps the output end to a PrintStream object so that data can be sent into the pipe using the println() method:

```
PrintWriter printWriter2 = new PrintWriter(pipeOut2);
```

Next, the program creates a thread from the ZThread class, providing the input pipe created by changeToY() and the new output pipe (mapped to printWriter2) as arguments to the class's Constructor:

```
ZThread zThread = new ZThread(YFileIn, printStream2);
```

The next line starts the thread:

```
zThread.start();
```

The ZThread thread reads data from the input pipe created by changeToY() that was stuffed with data by the YThread thread, and then changes the data to Zs, and finally outputs the data to the output pipe called printWriter2. The changeToZ() method returns the input half of this pipe (pipeIn2) from the method, where the main program prints the stream's contents onscreen. You now have a stream scenario like that illustrated in Figure 27.9.

FIG. 27.9
The data travels a long path as it's changed from all Ys to all Zs.

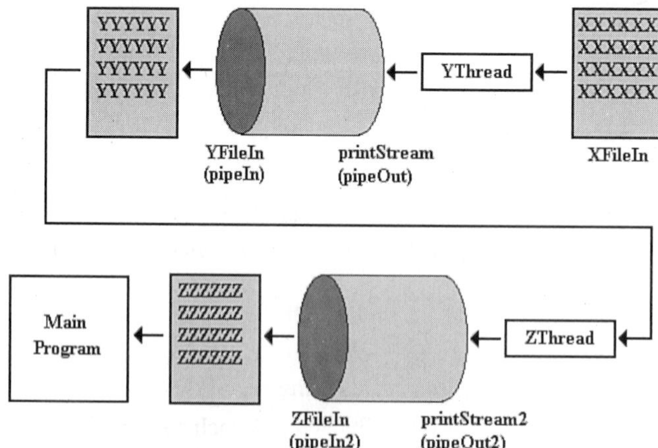

Exploring the *YThread* Class

You now should have a basic understanding of how the pipes work. The last part of the puzzle is the way that the secondary threads, `YThread` and `ZThread`, service the pipes. Because the two threads work almost identically, you examine only `YThread`.

`YThread`'s `Constructor` receives two parameters: the input file and the output end of the first pipe. The `Constructor` saves these parameters as data members of the class:

```
this.XFileIn = XFileIn;
this.printWriter = printWriter;
```

With its streams in hand, the thread can start processing the data, which it does in its `run()` method. First, the thread reads a line from the input file; then it starts a `while` loop that processes all the data in the file. The first line read from the file before the loop begins ensures that `XString` is not `null`, which would prevent the loop from executing:

```
String XString = XFileIn.readLine();
while (XString != null)
```

Inside the loop, the thread first changes the newly read data to all Ys:

```
String YString = XString.replace('X', 'Y');
```

It then outputs the modified data to the output end of the pipe:

```
printWriter.println(YString);
printWriter.flush();
```

It's important to flush the stream to ensure that all buffered data has been output into the pipe.

Next, the thread reads another line of data for the next iteration of the loop:

```
XString = XFileIn.readLine();
```

Finally, when the loop completes, the thread closes the piped output stream:

```
printWriter.close();
```

And that's all there is to it. To put it simply, the thread does nothing more than read lines from the input file, change the characters in the lines to Ys, and ship the changed data into the pipe, from which it is retrieved from the next thread.

The `ZThread` thread works almost the same way, except its input stream is the input end of the pipe into which `YThread` output its data. Finally, the input end of `ZThread`'s pipe feeds the main program as the program reads the text lines and displays them onscreen.

Filtered Streams

One of the most powerful aspects of streams is that you can chain one stream to the end of another. The basic input stream, for example, only provides a `read` method for reading bytes. If you want to read strings and integers, you can attach a special data input stream to an input stream and suddenly have methods for reading strings, integers, and even floats. The `FilterInputStream` and `FilterOutputStream` classes provide the capability to chain streams together. They don't add any new methods, however. Their big contribution is that they are "connected" to another stream. The Constructors for the FilterInputStream and FilterOutputStream classes take InputStream and OutputStream objects as parameters:

```
public FilterInputStream(InputStream in)
public FilterOutputStream(OutputStream out)
```

Because these classes are themselves instances of InputStream and OutputStream, they can be used as parameters to Constructors to other filters, enabling you to create long chains of input and output filters.

The DataInputStream class, discussed later in this chapter, is a very useful filter that enables you to read strings, integers, and other simple types from an input stream. In addition, the LineNumberInputStream filter automatically counts lines as you read input. You can chain these filters together to read data while counting the lines:

```
LineNumberInputStream lineCount = new LineNumberInputStream(
    System.in);
DataInputStream dataIn = new DataInputStream(lineCount);
```

Buffered Streams

Buffered streams help speed up your programs by reducing the number of reads and writes on system resources. Suppose you have a program that is writing one byte at a time. You may not want each write call to go out to the operating system, especially if it is writing to a disk. Instead, you would like the bytes to be accumulated into big blocks and written out in bulk. The BufferedInputStream and BufferedOutputStream classes provide this functionality. When you create them, you can provide a buffer size:

```
public BufferedInputStream(InputStream in)
public BufferedInputStream(InputStream in, int bufferSize)
public BufferedOutputStream(OutputStream out)
public BufferedOutputStream(OutputStream out, int bufferSize)
```

The BufferedInputStream class tries to read as much data into its buffer as possible in a single read call; the BufferedOutputStream class only calls the write method when its buffer fills up, or when flush is called.

Data Streams

The DataInputStream and DataOutputStream filters are two of the most useful filters in the java.io package. They enable you to read and write Java primitive types in a machine-independent fashion. This is important if you want to write data to a file on one machine and read it in on another machine with a different CPU architecture. One of the most common difficulties in transferring binary data between an Intel-based PC and a Sparc-based workstation, for example, is the different way the CPUs store integers. A number stored on a Sun as 0′12345678 would be interpreted by a PC as 0′78563412. Fortunately, the DataInputStream and DataOutputStream classes take care of any necessary conversions automatically.

The *DataInput* Interface

The `DataInputStream` implements a `DataInput` interface. This interface defines methods for reading Java primitive data types, as well as a few other methods.

The `DataInput` methods for reading primitive data types are as follows:

```
public boolean readBoolean() throws IOException, EOFException
public byte readByte() throws IOException EOFException
public char readChar() throws IOException, EOFException
public short readShort() throws IOException, EOFException
public int readInt() throws IOException, EOFException
public long readLong() throws IOException, EOFException
public float readFloat() throws IOException, EOFException
public double readDouble() throws IOException, EOFException
```

Sometimes you may need to read an unsigned byte or short (16-bit integer). You can use the `readUnsignedByte` and `readUnsignedShort` to do that:

```
public int readUnsignedByte() throws IOException, EOFException
public int readUnsignedShort() throws IOException, EOFException
```

You might expect the `DataInput` interface to include a `readString` method. It does, but it isn't called `readString`. Instead, the method to read a string is called `readUTF`. UTF stands for Unicode Transmission Format and is a special format for encoding 16-bit Unicode values. UTF assumes that most of the time the upper 8 bits of a Unicode value will be 0 and optimizes with that in mind. The definition of `readUTF` is as follows:

```
public String readUTF() throws IOException
```

Many times you want to read data from a text file, often one line at a time. The `readLine` method reads in a line from a text file terminated by `\r`, `\n`, or end of file, stripping off the `\r` or `\n` before returning the line as a string:

```
public String readLine() throws IOException, EOFException
```

When you are trying to read a fixed number of bytes into an array using the standard `read` method in the `InputStream` class, you may have to call `read` several times because it may return before reading the full numbers of bytes you wanted. This is especially true when you are transferring data over the network. The `readFully` methods explicitly wait for the full number of bytes you have requested:

```
public void readFully(byte[] bytes)
     throws IOException, EOFException
public void readFully(byte[] bytes, int offset, int length)
     throws IOException, EOFException
```

Notice that the `readFully` methods do not return a number of bytes as the standard `read` methods do. This is because you should already know how many bytes will be read, either by the size of the array in the first version of the method or the `length` parameter in the second. The `skipBytes` method performs a function similar to the `readFully` method; that is, it waits until the desired number of bytes have been skipped before returning. In fact, it is better to think of the method as being called `"skipBytesFully"`.

```
public int skipBytes(int numBytes)
```

The *DataOutput* Interface

The DataOutput interface defines the output methods that correspond to the input methods defined in the DataInput interface. The methods defined by this interface are as follows:

```
public void writeBoolean(boolean b) throws IOException
public void writeByte(int b) throws IOException
public void writeChar(int c) throws IOException
public void writeShort(int c) throws IOException
public void writeInt(int i) throws IOException
public void writeLong(long l) throws IOException
public void writeFloat(float f) throws IOException
public void writeDouble(double d) throws IOException
public void writeUTF(String s) throws IOException
```

You can also write a string as a series of bytes or chars using the writeBytes and writeChars methods:

```
public void writeBytes(String s) throws IOException
public void writeChars(String s) throws IOException
```

The *DataInputStream* and *DataOutputStream* Classes

The DataInputStream and DataOutputStream classes are just stream filters that implement the DataInput and DataOutput interfaces. Their Constructors are typical stream filter Constructors in that they just take the stream to filter as an argument:

```
public DataInputStream(InputStream in)
public DataOutputStream(OutputStream out)
```

Byte Array Streams

You don't always have to write to a file or the network to use streams. You can write to and read from arrays of bytes using the ByteArrayInputStream and ByteArrayOutputStream classes. These streams are not filter streams like some of the others; they are input and output streams.

When you create a ByteArrayInputStream, you must supply an array of bytes that will serve as the source of the bytes to be read from the stream.

```
public ByteArrayInputStream(byte[] bytes)
```

creates a byte input stream using the entire contents of bytes as the data in the stream.

```
public ByteArrayInputStream(byte[] bytes, int offset, int length)
```

creates a byte input stream that reads up to length bytes starting at position offset.

A ByteArrayOutputStream is an array of bytes that continually grows to fit the data stored in it. The Constructor for the ByteArrayOutputStream class takes an optional initial size parameter that determines the initial size of the array that stores the bytes written to the stream:

```
public ByteArrayOutputStream()
public ByteArrayOutputStream(int initialSize)
```

After you have written data to a `ByteArrayOutputStream`, you can convert the contents of the stream to an array of bytes by calling `toByteArray`:

```
public synchronized byte[] toByteArray()
```

The `size` method returns the total number of bytes written to the stream so far:

```
public int size()
```

Char Array Streams

One of the differences between Java and languages such as C is that Java treats characters as 16-bit values rather than 8-bit values. Unfortunately, under Java 1.0, there was no 16-bit version of the byte array streams. This encouraged programmers to treat characters as 8-bit values if they wanted to use the byte array streams. Fortunately, with Java 1.1 changes were made to include character array streams, but they are not called streams. Java 1.1 introduced a new type of stream called a "Reader" or a "Writer," depending on whether it is an input stream or an output stream. The character version of the `ByteArrayInputStream` is called a `CharArrayReader`, while the `CharArrayWriter` performs functions similar to the `ByteArrayOutputStream`.

The `CharArrayReader` and `CharArrayWriter` classes function almost identically to their byte array counterparts. They contain the same methods, only the char array streams use char values everywhere the byte array streams use byte values. The constructors for `CharArrayReader` and `CharArrayWriter` look like this, for example:

```
public CharArrayReader(char[] buf)
public CharArrayReader(char[] buf, int offset, int length)

public CharArrayWriter()
public CharArrayWriter(int size)
```

Conversion Between Bytes and Characters

Because many systems have previously treated characters as 8-bit values, you often encounter situations where you need to convert an 8-bit value into a 16-bit Java character. Java characters are 16 bits in order to support the Unicode standard, which supports a wide variety of international character sets. Currently, many programmers just take the 8-bit value and assume the upper 8 bits are 0. Unfortunately, that won't work in all situations. Java 1.1 added a standard mechanism for converting bytes into characters and characters into bytes. That doesn't mean there is a standard conversion, however. You still have to figure out what kind of conversion you should perform. After you figure that out, there is a standard way for you to tell an I/O stream how to convert characters.

The `Reader` and `Writer` classes represent a special category of input and output streams geared toward character operations. These classes perform an automatic conversion between bytes and characters. For each of the core input and output streams, there are `Reader` and

`Writer` versions for doing character operations. The following `Reader` and `Writer` classes function identically to their stream counterparts, except that they take a `Reader` rather than an `InputStream`, or a `Writer` rather than an `OutputStream`: `BufferedReader`, `BufferedWriter`, `FileReader`, `FileWriter`, `FilterReader`, `FilterWriter`, `PipedReader`, `PipedWriter`, `PrinterWriter`, and `PushbackReader`.

The `InputStreamReader` and `OutputStreamWriter` classes provide a bridge between streams and the `Reader/Writer` classes. `InputStreamReader` takes an `InputStream` and provides a `Reader` interface for it. The `Constructor` takes an optional encoding name, which is the name of the character encoding used to translate bytes into characters:

```
public InputStreamReader(InputStream in)
public InputStreamReader(InputStream in, String encoding)
```

Likewise, the `OutputStreamWriter` class provides a `Writer` interface for an `OutputStream`, and also can take an optional encoding parameter:

```
public OutputStreamWriter(OutputStream out)
public OutputStreamWriter(OutputStream out, String encoding)
```

The `Reader` and `Writer` classes enable you to support international character sets in your programs in a seamless manner. If your programs are reading and writing data that could potentially be in another language, you should use the `Reader/Writer` objects rather than streams.

The *StringBufferInputStream*

The `StringBufferInputStream` is a close cousin to the `ByteArrayInputStream`. The only difference between the two is that the `StringBufferInputStream Constructor` takes a string as the source of the stream's characters rather than a byte array:

```
public StringBufferInputStream(String str)
```

Object Streams

When Sun added Remote Method Invocation (RMI) to Java, it also added the capability to stream arbitrary objects. The `ObjectInput` and `ObjectOutput` interfaces define methods for reading and writing any object, in the same way that `DataInput` and `DataOutput` define methods for reading and writing primitive types. In fact, the `ObjectInput` and `ObjectOutput` interfaces extend the `DataInput` and `DataOutput` interfaces. The `ObjectInput` interface adds a single input method:

```
public abstract Object readObject()
throws ClassNotFoundException, IOException
```

Similarly, the `ObjectOutput` interface adds a single output method:

```
public abstract void writeObject(Object obj)
throws IOException
```

The `ObjectOutputStream` implements a stream filter that enables you to write any object to a stream, as well as any primitive type. Like most stream filters, you create an `ObjectOutputStream` by passing it an `OutputStream`:

```
public OutputStream(OutputStream outStream)
```

You can use the `writeObject` method to write any object to the stream:

```
public final void writeObject(Object ob)
throws ClassMismatchException, MethodMissingException, IOException
```

Because the `ObjectOutputStream` is a subclass of `DataOutputStream`, you can also use any of the methods from the `DataOutput` interface, such as `writeInt` or `writeUTF`.

Listing 27.13 shows a program that uses `writeObject` to stream a date and hash table to a file.

Listing 27.13 Source Code for *WriteObject.java*

```
import java.io.*;
import java.util.*;

// This class writes out a date object and a hash table object
// to a file called "writeme" using an ObjectOutputStream.

public class WriteObject extends Object
{
     public static void main(String[] args)
     {

// Create a hash table with a few entries

          Hashtable writeHash = new Hashtable();
          writeHash.put("Leader", "Moe");
          writeHash.put("Lieutenant", "Larry");
          writeHash.put("Stooge", "Curly");

          try {

// Create an output stream to a file called "writeme"
               FileOutputStream fileOut =
                    new FileOutputStream("writeme");

// Open an output stream filter on the file stream
               ObjectOutputStream objOut =
                         new ObjectOutputStream(fileOut);

// Write out the current date and the hash table
               objOut.writeObject(new Date());
               objOut.writeObject(writeHash);

// Close the stream
               objOut.close();

          } catch (Exception writeErr) {
```

continues

Listing 27.13 Continued

```
// Dump out any error information
               writeErr.printStackTrace();
          }
     }
}
```

The ObjectInputStream, as you might have guessed, implements a stream filter for the ObjectInput interface. You create an ObjectInputStream by passing it the input stream you want it to filter:

```
public ObjectInputStream(InputStream inStream)
```

The readObject method reads an object from the input stream:

```
public final Object readObject()
throws MethodMissingException, ClassMismatchException
     ClassNotFoundException, StreamCorruptedException, IOException
```

You can also use any of the methods from the DataInput interface on an ObjectInputStream.

Listing 27.14 shows a program that uses readObject to read the objects written to the "writeme" file by the example in Listing 27.13.

Listing 27.14 Source Code for *ReadObject.java*

```
import java.io.*;
import java.util.*;

// This class opens up the file "writeme" and reads two
// objects from it. It makes no assumptions about the
// types of the objects, it just prints them out.

public class ReadObject extends Object
{
     public static void main(String[] args)
     {
          try {

// Open an input stream to the file "writeme"
               FileInputStream fileIn =
                    new FileInputStream("writeme");

// Create an ObjectInput filter on the stream
               ObjectInputStream objIn =
                         new ObjectInputStream(fileIn);

// Read in the first object and print it
               Object ob1 = objIn.readObject();
               System.out.println(ob1);

// Read in the second object and print it
               Object ob2 = objIn.readObject();
               System.out.println(ob2);
```

```
// Close the stream
                objIn.close();

            } catch (Exception writeErr) {
// Dump any errors
                writeErr.printStackTrace();
            }
        }
}
```

If you do not have the latest version of Java, you can download the object serialization extensions from **www.javasoft.com**.

Other Streams

Java also provides a number of utility filters. These filters are special in that they do not exist in pairs—that is, they work exclusively for either input or output.

The *LineNumberReader* Class

The `LineNumberReader` enables you to track the current line number of an input stream. As usual, you create a `LineNumberReader` by passing it the input stream you want it to filter:

```
public LineNumberReader(new InputStreamReader(InputStream inStream))
```

The `getLineNumber` method returns the current line number in the input stream:

```
public int getLineNumber()
```

By default, the lines are numbered starting at 0. The line number is incremented every time an entire line has been read. You can set the current line number with the `setLineNumber` method:

```
public void setLineNumber(int newLineNumber)
```

Listing 27.15 shows a program that prints the contents of standard input along with the current line number.

Listing 27.15 Source Code for *PrintLines.java*

```
import java.io.*;

// This class reads lines from standard input (System.in) and
// prints each line along with its line number.

public class PrintLines extends Object {
  public static void main(String[] args) {

    // Set up a line number input filter to count the line numbers
    LineNumberReader lineCounter = new LineNumberReader
➥(new InputStreamReader(System.in));
```

continues

Listing 27.15 Continued

```
        try {
          while (true) {

            // Read in the next line
            String nextLine = lineCounter.readLine();

            // If readLine returns null, we've hit the end of the file
            if (nextLine == null) break;

            // Print out the current line number followed by the line
            System.out.print(lineCounter.getLineNumber());
            System.out.print(": ");
            System.out.println(nextLine);
          }
        } catch (Exception done) {
          done.printStackTrace();
        }
      }
    }
```

The *SequenceInputStream* Class

The `SequenceInputStream` filter enables you to treat a number of input streams as one big input stream. This is useful if you want to read from a number of data files but you don't really care where one file stops and another starts. If you have a situation where you can just as easily combine all your input files into one big file, this stream will probably be of some use. You can create a `SequenceInputStream` that combines two streams by passing both streams to the `Constructor`:

```
public SequenceInputStream(InputStream stream1, InputStream stream2)
```

If you want more than two streams, you can pass an enumeration to the `Constructor`:

```
public SequenceInputStream(Enumeration e)
```

The enumeration should return the input stream objects you want to combine. A simple way to implement this is to stick all your input streams in a vector and use the vector's `elements` method:

```
Vector v = new Vector();
v.addElement(stream1);
v.addElement(stream2);
v.addElement(stream3);
v.addElement(stream4); // and so on_
InputStream seq = new SequenceInputStream(v.elements());
```

If you want to combine three streams, you can also create a chain of `SequenceInputStreams` this way:

```
InputStream seq = new SequenceInputStream(stream1,
new SequenceInputStream(stream2, stream3));
```

The *PushbackInputStream* Class

The `PushbackInputStream` is a special stream that enables you to peek at a single character in an input stream and push it back onto the stream. This technique is often used in creating lexical scanners that peek at a character, put it back on the stream, and then read the character again as part of a larger input. You might see that the next character is a digit, for example, so you put it back and call your routine that reads in a number. At this point, you might be thinking that to create a `PushbackInputStream` filter you only need to pass the input stream you want it to filter. You are correct:

```
public PushbackInputStream(InputStream inStream)
```

The `unread` method pushes a character back into the input stream:

```
public void unread(int ch) throws IOException
```

This character is the first one read the next time the stream is read. The character that gets pushed back does not have to be the most recent character read. In other words, you can read a character off a stream, then unread a completely different character. You can only unread one character at a time, however.

The *StreamTokenizer* Class

The `StreamTokenizer` class implements a simple lexical scanner that breaks up a stream of characters into a stream of tokens. If you think of a stream of characters as being a sentence, the tokens represent the words and punctuation marks that make up the sentence. You create a `StreamTokenizer` filter by passing it the input stream you want it to filter:

```
public StringTokenizer(InputStream inStream)
```

After you have created the filter, you can use the `nextToken` method to retrieve that token from the stream:

```
public int nextToken() throws IOException
```

The `nextToken` method returns either a single character or one of the following constants:

- `StreamTokenizer.TT_WORD`
- `StreamTokenizer.TT_NUMBER`
- `StreamTokenizer.TT_EOL`
- `StreamTokenizer.TT_EOF`

If the token value returned is `TT_WORD`, the `sval` instance variable contains the actual value of the word:

```
public String sval
```

If the token value is `TT_NUMBER`, the `nval` instance variable contains the numeric value of the token:

```
public double nval
```

The `TT_EOL` and `TT_EOF` tokens represent the end of a line and the end of a file respectively.

You can specify which characters make up a word by calling the `wordChars` method with the starting and ending characters for a range of characters:

```
public void wordChars(int lowChar, int highChar)
```

The `wordChars` calls are additive, so subsequent calls to `wordChars` add to the possible word characters instead of replacing them. The default set of word characters is defined by the following calls:

```
tokenizer.wordChars('A', 'Z');      // All upper-case letters
tokenizer.wordChars('a', 'z');      // All lower-case letters
tokenizer.wordChars(150, 255);      // Other special characters
                                    // outside 7-bit ascii range
```

If you were writing a program to parse Java programs, you might also want to add `'$'` and `'_'` to the valid word `chars`, because these may appear in Java identifiers. You would do this with the following pair of calls:

```
tokenizer.wordChars('$', '$');
tokenizer.wordChars('_', '_');
```

One of the things that delimits a token is whitespace. Whitespace is not a token itself, but it can define where one token starts and another stops. The phrase "Nyuk nyuk nyuk," for example, contains three `TT_WORD` tokens, separated by whitespace. The phrase "Nyuk, nyuk, nyuk" actually contains five tokens—three nyuks and two `','` tokens. In each case, the whitespace is ignored. The typical whitespace characters are as follows:

- `' '`
- `'\t'` (tab)
- `'\n'` (newline)
- `'\r'` (carriage return)
- `'\f'` (form feed)
- The end of the file

You can define the whitespace characters with the `whitespaceChars` method, which is also additive like the `wordChars` method:

```
public void whitespaceChars(int lowChar, int highChar)
```

You can define the default set of whitespace characters with:

```
tokenizer.whitespaceChars(' ', ' ');
tokenizer.whitespaceChars('\t', '\t');
tokenizer.whitespaceChars('\n', '\n');
tokenizer.whitespaceChars('\r', '\r');
tokenizer.whitespaceChars('\f', '\f');
```

Sun took a shortcut, however, and defined all control characters as whitespace, along with the space character. In other words, characters such as escape and backspace are considered to be whitespace by the `StreamTokenizer`. Doing this allows the tokenizer to set its whitespace characters with a single call:

```
tokenizer.whitespaceChars(0, ' ');
```

The `StreamTokenizer` can also handle comments. It does not deal very well with multicharacter comment characters, or with quote-like comments other than those that Java uses. It can handle `//`-style comments, and also the `/*-*/` comments found in Java and C++, but it cannot handle the `(*-*)` comments found in Pascal. To allow the `//`-style comments to be parsed, pass `true` to the `slashSlashComments` method:

```
public void slashSlashComments(boolean allowSlashSlash)
```

To activate the `/*-*/` comments, pass `true` to `slashStarComments`:

```
public void slashStarComments(boolean allowSlashStar)
```

In addition to these two methods, you can also flag an individual character as a comment character with the `commentChar` method:

```
public void commentChar(int commentChar)
```

The comment characters are considered to be single-line comments, which means that when one is encountered, the rest of the line is ignored and parsing begins again on the next line. The `commentChar` method is additive, so you can set multiple comment characters by calling this method multiple times.

CAUTION

The `StreamTokenizer` sets `/` as a comment character by default. You may want to set it to be an ordinary character with the `ordinaryChar` method. Otherwise, any time the tokenizer encounters a single `/`, it will skip it and everything else up to the end of line.

You can undo any special settings for a character or a range of characters by calling the `ordinaryChar` or `ordinaryChars` methods:

```
public void ordinaryChar(int ch)
public void ordinaryChars(int loadChar, int highChar)
```

These methods undo any special significance to a character. If you set the `'$'` and `'_'` characters to be word characters and then decide that they shouldn't be, you can make them ordinary characters again by using the following:

```
tokenizer.ordinaryChar('$');
tokenizer.ordinaryChar('_');
```


The `StreamTokenizer` also recognizes characters as quote characters. When the tokenizer encounters a quote character, it takes all the other characters up to the next quote character and puts them in the string value stored in `sval`, and then it returns the quote character as the token value. You can flag a character as being a quote character by calling `quoteChar`:

```
public void quoteChar(int ch)
```

The default quote characters are `'` and `"`.

Normally the words returned for a `TT_WORD` token are stored exactly as they appear in the input stream. However, if you want tokens to be non–case-sensitive—in other words, if you want FOO, Foo, and foo to be the same—you can ask the tokenizer to automatically convert words to all lowercase by passing `true` to the `lowerCaseMode` method:

```
public void lowerCaseMode(boolean shiftToLower)
```

The `parseNumbers` method tells the tokenizer to accept floating-point numbers:

```
public void parseNumbers()
```

If this method is not called, the tokenizer treats the number 3.14159 as three separate tokens—3, ., and 14159. This method is called automatically by the `StreamTokenizer Constructor`. The only time you need to call it is if you call `resetSyntax`.

The `resetSyntax` method completely clears out the tokenizer's tables:

```
public void resetSyntax()
```

CAUTION

Because of the way `StreamTokenizer` is designed, it requires the space character (`' '`) to be something other than an ordinary character. If you call `resetSyntax`, you must then set space to be either whitespace, a word character, a comment character, or a quote character. Otherwise, the tokenizer cannot read characters from the stream.

CHAPTER 28

Using Strings and Text

In this chapter

Introducing Strings

String handling in C or C++ (the languages that inspired Java) is infamously clunky. Java solves that problem the same way many C++ programmers do: by creating a `String` class. Java's `String` class enables your programs to manage text strings effortlessly, using statements similar to those used in simpler languages such as BASIC or Pascal. Java also makes it easy to handle fonts, which determine the way that your text strings appear onscreen.

So, what exactly is a *string*, anyway? In its simplest form, a string is nothing more than one or more text characters arranged consecutively in memory. You can think of a string as an array of characters, with this array having an index that starts at zero. (That is, the first character in the string is at array index 0.) Unfortunately, few computer languages deal with strings in such a simple form. This is because a program needs to know where a string ends, and there are several different solutions to the length problem. Pascal, for example, tacks the length of the string onto the front of the characters, whereas C++ expects to find a null character (a zero) at the end of the string.

In Java, strings are represented by one of two classes:

- `String` Best used for string constants—that is, for strings that are not going to change after they're created.
- `StringBuffer` Used for strings that require a lot of manipulation.

NOTE With the `String` class, although you can do operations such as find, compare, and concatenate characters, you cannot insert new characters into the string or change the length of the string (except through concatenation–which actually creates a new string anyway).

Within an object of the `String` or `StringBuffer` class, Java creates an array of characters much like that used for strings in C++ programs. Because this character array is hidden within the class, however, it cannot be accessed except through the class's methods. This data encapsulation (a key feature of object-oriented programming, by the way) ensures that the string will be maintained properly and will be manipulated in accordance with the rules of the class (represented by the methods).

Figures 28.1 and 28.2 illustrate this concept. In Figure 28.1, a conventional C++ string is left hanging in memory where the program can manipulate it at will, regardless of whether said manipulation makes sense or results in a fatal error. In Figure 28.2, the string is protected by the methods of the class—the only way through which the program can access the string.

Using the *String* Class

In Java, you create strings by creating an object of the `String` or `StringBuffer` class. This `String` object can be created implicitly or explicitly depending on how the string is being used in the program. To create a string implicitly, you just place a string literal in your program, and

Java goes ahead and creates a `String` object for the string automatically. This is because, even internally, Java uses `String` objects to represent string literals. Look at this line, for example:

```
g.drawString("This is a string", 50, 50);
```

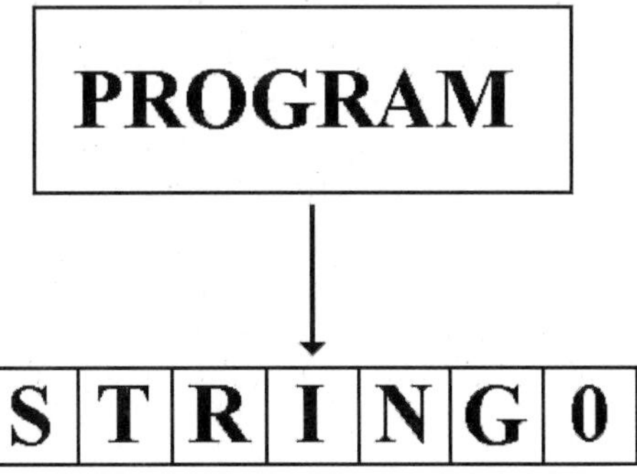

FIG. 28.1 In conventional programs, strings can be accessed directly by the program, leading to complications and errors.

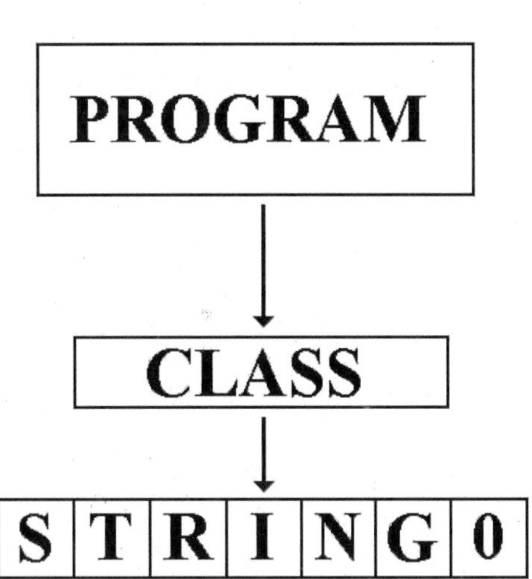

FIG. 28.2 By using a `String` class, the string can be accessed only through the class's methods, which eliminates many potential errors.

You are (or rather Java is) implicitly creating a `String` object for the string literal `"This is a string"`. Every time you refer to a string this way in a Java program, you're creating a `String` object.

The other way to create a `String` object is to explicitly instantiate an object of the `String` class. The `String` class has seven `Constructors`, so there are plenty of ways to explicitly create a `String` object, the most obvious way being this:

```
String str = new String("This is a string");
```

You can also declare a `String` object and then set its value later in the program, like this:

```
String str;
str = "This is a string";
```

Or, you can combine both of the approaches and end up with this:

```
String str = "This is a string";
```

Finally, any of the following lines create a null string:

```
String str = new String();
String str = "";
String str = "";
```

Although the preceding examples are the most common ways of explicitly creating `String` objects, the `String` class offers several alternatives. The seven `String` class's constructors look like this:

```
public String()
public String(String value)
public String(char value[])
public String(char value[], int offset, int count)
public String(byte ascii[], int hibyte, int offset, int count)
public String(byte ascii[], int hibyte)
public String (StringBuffer buffer)
```

These constructors create, respectively, the following:

- Null string
- `String` object from another `String` object (including from a string literal)
- `String` from an array of characters
- `String` from a subarray of characters
- Unicode `String` from a subarray of bytes using `hibyte` as the high byte for each Unicode character
- Unicode `String` from an array of bytes using `hibyte` as the high byte for each Unicode character
- `String` from a `StringBuffer` object

CAUTION

There's a big difference between a null `String` object and a null string. When you declare a `String` object with a line such as `String str;`, you are declaring an object of the `String` class that has not yet been instantiated. That is, there is not yet a `String` object associated with `str`, meaning that the `String` object is null. When you create a `String` object with a line such as `String str = "";`, you are creating a fully instantiated `String` object whose string contains no characters (has a string length of zero). This is called a null string.

Getting Information About a String Object

After you have your `String` object constructed, you can call upon the `String` class's methods to obtain information about the string. To get the length of the string, for example, you can call the `length()` method, like this:

```
String str = "This is a string";
int len = str.length();
```

These lines set `len` to 16, which is the length of the string (including spaces, of course).

If you want to know whether a string starts with a certain prefix, you can call the `startsWith()` method, like this:

```
String str = "This is a string";
boolean result = str.startsWith("This");
```

Here, the `boolean` variable `result` is equal to `true`, because `str` does indeed start with `"This"`. In the following example, `result` is `false`:

```
String str = "This is a string";
boolean result = str.startsWith("is");
```

A similar method is `endsWith()`, which determines whether the `String` object ends with a given set of characters. You use that method as follows:

```
String str = "This is a string";
boolean result = str.endsWith("string");
```

In this example, `result` ends up equal to `true`, whereas the following code segment sets `result` equal to `false`:

```
String str = "This is a string";
boolean result = str.endsWith("This");
```

If you're setting up a table for strings that you want to be able to locate quickly, you can use a hash table. To get a hash code for a string, you can call the `hashCode()` method:

```
String str = "This is a string";
int hashcode = str.hashCode();
```

▶ **See** "The Hashtable Class," **p. 1059**

If you want to find the location of the first occurrence of a character within a string, use the `indexOf()` method:

```
String str = "This is a string";
int index = str.indexOf('a');
```

In this example, `index` is equal to 8, which is the index of the first `a` in the string.

To find the location of subsequent characters, you can use two versions of the `indexOf()` method. To find the first occurrence of 'i', for example, you might use these lines:

```
String str = "This is a string";
int index = str.indexOf('i');
```

This gives `index` a value of 2. To find the next occurrence of "i," you can use a line similar to this:

```
index = str.indexOf('i', index+1);
```

By including the `index+1` as the method's second argument, you're telling Java to start searching at `index 3` in the string (the old value of `index`, plus 1). This results in `index` being equal to 5, which is the location of the second occurrence of "i" in the string. If you called the previous line again, `index` would be equal to 13, which is the location of the third "i" in the string.

You can also search for characters backward through a string, using the `lastIndexOf()` method:

```
String str = "This is a string";
int index = str.lastIndexOf("i");
```

Here, `index` is equal to 13. To search backward for the next "i," you might use a line like this:

```
index = str.lastIndexOf('i', index-1);
```

Now, `index` is equal to 5, because the `index-1` as the second argument tells Java where to begin the backward search. The variable `index` was equal to 13 after the first call to `lastIndexOf()`, so in the second call, `index-1` equals 12.

There are also versions of `indexOf()` and `lastIndexOf()` that search for substrings within a string. The following example sets `index` to 10, for instance:

```
String str = "This is a string";
int index = str.indexOf("string");
```

Listing 28.1 is an applet that gives you a chance to experiment with the `indexOf()` method. Listing 28.2 is the HTML document that loads the applet. When you run the applet, enter a string into the first text box and a substring for which to search in the second box. When you click the Search button, the applet displays the index at which the substring is located (see Figure 28.3).

FIG. 28.3
The `StringApplet` applet searches for substrings.

Listing 28.1 *StringApplet.java*—An Applet That Searches for Substrings

```
import java.awt.*;
import java.applet.*;
public class StringApplet extends Applet
{
```

```
    TextField textField1;
    TextField textField2;
    Button button1;
    String displayStr;
    public void init()
    {
        Label label = new Label("String:");
        add(label);
        textField1 = new TextField(20);
        add(textField1);
        label = new Label("substr:");
        add(label);
        textField2 = new TextField(20);
        add(textField2);
        button1 = new Button("Search");
        add(button1);
        displayStr = "";
        resize(230, 200);
    }
    public void paint(Graphics g)
    {
        g.drawString(displayStr, 80, 150);
    }
    public boolean action(Event evt, Object arg)
    {
        if (arg == "Search")
        {
            String str = textField1.getText();
            String substr = textField2.getText();
            int index = str.indexOf(substr);
            displayStr = "Located at " + str.valueOf(index);
            repaint();
            return true;
        }
        else
            return false;
    }
}
```

Listing 28.2 *STRINGAPPLET.HTML*—StringApplet's HTML Document

```
<title>Applet Test Page</title>
<h1>Applet Test Page</h1>
<applet
    code="StringApplet.class"
    width=200
    height=200
    name="StringApplet">
</applet>
```

Comparing Strings

Often, you need to know when two strings are equal. You might want to compare a string entered by the user to another string hard-coded in your program, for example. There are two basic ways you can compare strings:

- Calling the `equals()` method
- Using the normal comparison operator

The `equals()` method returns `true` when the two strings are equal and `false` otherwise. Here's an example:

```
String str = "This is a string";
boolean result = str.equals("This is a string");
```

Here, the `boolean` variable `result` is equal to `true`. You could also do something similar using the comparison operator:

```
String str = "This is a string";
if (str == "This is a string")
    result = true;
```

This also results in `result` being `true`.

Although these two methods are the easiest way to compare strings, the `String` class gives you many other options. The `equalsIgnoreCase()` method compares two strings without regard for upper- or lowercase letters. That is, the following code sets `result` to `false` because `equals()` considers the case of the characters in the string:

```
String str = "THIS IS A STRING";
boolean result = str.equals("this is a string");
```

This code fragment, however, sets `result` to `true`:

```
String str = "THIS IS A STRING";
boolean result = str.equalsIgnoreCase("this is a string");
```

If you want to know more than just whether the strings are equal, you can call on the `compareTo()` method, which returns a value less than zero when the `String` object is less than the given string, zero when the strings are equal, and greater than zero if the `String` object is greater than the given string. The comparison is done according to alphabetic order (or, if you want to be technical about it, according to the ASCII values of the characters). So, this code segment sets `result` to a value greater than zero because `"THIS IS A STRING"` is greater than `"ANOTHER STRING"`:

```
String str = "THIS IS A STRING";
int result = str.compareTo("ANOTHER STRING");
```

The following comparison, however, results in a `result` being set to a value less than zero, because `"THIS IS A STRING"` is less than `"ZZZ ANOTHER STRING"`:

```
String str = "THIS IS A STRING";
int result = str.compareTo("ZZZ ANOTHER STRING");
```

Finally, the following comparison results in zero because the strings are equal:

```
String str = "THIS IS A STRING";
int result = str.compareTo("THIS IS A STRING");
```

C and C++ programmers will be very familiar with this form of string comparison.

If you really want to get fancy with your string comparisons, you can dazzle your Java programming buddies by using the `regionMatches()` method, which enables you to compare part of one string with part of another. Here's an example:

```
String str = "THIS IS A STRING";
boolean result = str.regionMatches(10, "A STRING", 2, 6);
```

The `regionMatches()` method's four arguments are as follows:

- Where to start looking in the source string
- The string to compare to
- The location in the comparison string at which to start looking
- The number of characters to compare

The preceding example sets `result` to `true`. In this case, Java starts looking in `"THIS IS A STRING"` at the tenth character (starting from 0), which is the *S* in *STRING*. Java also starts its comparison at the second character of the given string "A STRING," which is also the *S* in *STRING*. Java compares six characters starting at the given offsets, which means it is comparing *STRING* with *STRING*, a perfect match.

There's also a version of `regionMatches()` that is non–case-sensitive. The following example sets `result` to `true`:

```
String str = "THIS IS A STRING";
boolean result = str.regionMatches(true, 10, "A string", 2, 6);
```

The new first argument in this version of `regionMatches()` is a `boolean` value indicating whether the comparison should be non–case-sensitive. A value of `true` tells Java to ignore the case of the characters. A value of `false` for this argument results in exactly the same sort of case-sensitive comparison you get with the four-argument version of `regionMatches()`.

Listing 28.3 is an applet that gives you a chance to experiment with the `compareTo()` method. Listing 28.4 is the HTML document that runs the applet. When you run the applet, enter a string into each text box. When you click the Compare button, the applet determines how the strings compare and displays the results (see Figure 28.4).

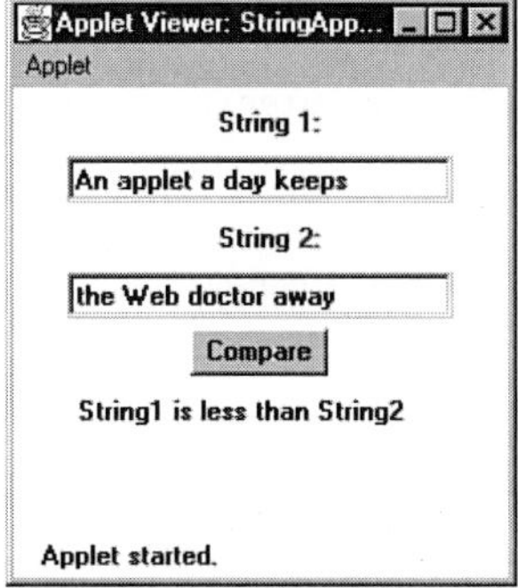

FIG. 28.4
Here's `StringApplet2` comparing two strings.

Listing 28.3 *StringApplet2.java*—An Applet That Compares Strings

```
import java.awt.*;
import java.applet.*;
public class StringApplet2 extends Applet
{
    TextField textField1;
    TextField textField2;
    Button button1;
    String displayStr;
    public void init()
    {
        Label label = new Label("String 1:");
        add(label);
        textField1 = new TextField(20);
        add(textField1);
        label = new Label("String 2:");
        add(label);
        textField2 = new TextField(20);
        add(textField2);
        button1 = new Button("Compare");
        add(button1);
        displayStr = "";
        resize(230, 200);
    }
    public void paint(Graphics g)
    {
        g.drawString(displayStr, 30, 150);
    }
    public boolean action(Event evt, Object arg)
    {
        if (arg == "Compare")
        {
            String str1 = textField1.getText();
            String str2 = textField2.getText();
            int result = str1.compareTo(str2);
            if (result < 0)
                displayStr = "String1 is less than String2";
            else if (result == 0)
```

```
                displayStr = "String1 is equal to String2";
            else
                displayStr = "String1 is greater than String2";
            repaint();
            return true;
        }
        else
            return false;
    }
}
```

Listing 28.4 *STRINGAPPLET2.HTML*—StringApplet2's HTML Document

```
<title>Applet Test Page</title>
<h1>Applet Test Page</h1>
<applet
    code="StringApplet2.class"
    width=200
    height=200
    name="StringApplet2">
</applet>
```

String Extraction

There may be many times in your programming career when you want to extract portions of a string. The `String` class provides for these needs with a set of methods for just this purpose. You can determine the character at a given position in the string, for example, by calling the `charAt()` method, like this:

```
String str = "This is a string";
Char chr = str.charAt(6);
```

In these lines, the character variable `chr` ends up with a value of "s", which is the fifth character in the string. Why didn't `chr` become equal to "i"? Because, as in C and C++, you start counting array elements at zero rather than one.

A similar method, `getChars()`, enables you to copy a portion of a `String` object to a character array:

```
String str = "This is a string";
char chr[] = new char[20];
str.getChars(5, 12, chr, 0);
```

In this code sample, the character array `chr` ends up containing the characters "is a st." The `getChars()` method's arguments are the index of the first character in the string to copy, the index of the last character in the string, the destination array, and where in the destination array to start copying characters.

The method `getBytes()` does the same thing as `getChars()`, but uses a byte array as the destination array:

```
String str = "This is a string";
byte byt[] = new byte[20];
str.getBytes(5, 12, byt, 0);
```

Another way to extract part of a string is to use the `substring()` method:

```
String str1 = "THIS IS A STRING";
String str2 = str1.substring(5);
```

In this case, the `String` object `str2` ends up equal to the substring `"IS A STRING"`. This is because `substring()`'s single argument is the index of the character at which the substring starts. Every character from the index to the end of the string gets extracted.

If you don't want to extract all the way to the end of the string, you can use the second version of the `substring()` method, whose arguments specify the beginning and ending indexes:

```
String str1 = "THIS IS A STRING";
String str2 = str1.substring(5, 9);
```

These lines set `str2` to the substring `IS A`.

Listing 28.5 is an applet that gives you a chance to experiment with the `indexOf()` method. Listing 28.6 is the HTML document that runs the applet. When you run the applet, enter a string into the first text box. Then, enter the starting and ending indexes for a substring in the second and third boxes. When you click the Extract button, the applet finds and displays the selected substring (see Figure 28.5).

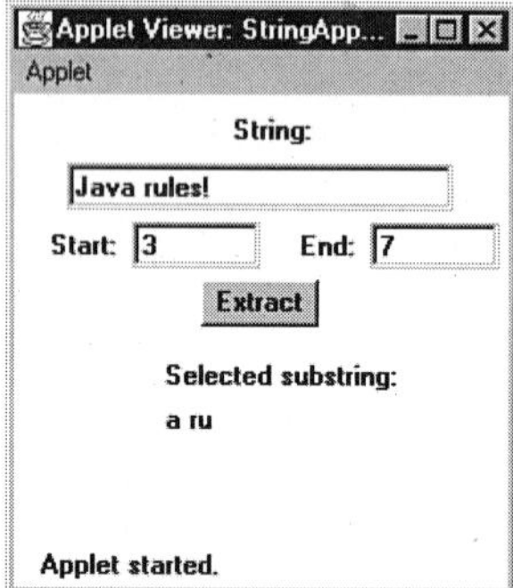

FIG. 28.5 `StringApplet3` is running under AppletViewer.

> **CAUTION**
>
> There's no error checking in Listing 28.5, so make sure your indexes are correct. Otherwise, Java generates an exception.

Listing 28.5 *StringApplet3.java*—An Applet That Extracts Substrings

```
import java.awt.*;
import java.applet.*;
public class StringApplet3 extends Applet
{
    TextField textField1;
    TextField textField2;
    TextField textField3;
    Button button1;
    String displayStr;
    public void init()
    {
        Label label = new Label("String:");
        add(label);
        textField1 = new TextField(20);
        add(textField1);
        label = new Label("Start:");
        add(label);
        textField2 = new TextField(5);
        add(textField2);
        label = new Label("End:");
        add(label);
        textField3 = new TextField(5);
        add(textField3);
        button1 = new Button("Extract");
        add(button1);
        displayStr = "";
        resize(230, 200);
    }
    public void paint(Graphics g)
    {
        g.drawString("Selected substring:", 70, 130);
        g.drawString(displayStr, 70, 150);
    }
    public boolean action(Event evt, Object arg)
    {
        if (arg == "Extract")
        {
            String str1 = textField1.getText();
            String str2 = textField2.getText();
            String str3 = textField3.getText();
            int start = Integer.parseInt(str2);
            int end = Integer.parseInt(str3);
            displayStr = str1.substring(start, end);
            repaint();
            return true;
        }
        else
            return false;
    }
}
```

Listing 28.6 *STRINGAPPLET3.HTML*—StringApplet3's HTML Document

```
<title>Applet Test Page</title>
<h1>Applet Test Page</h1>
<applet
    code="StringApplet3.class"
    width=200
    height=200
    name="StringApplet3">
</applet>
```

String Manipulation

Although the `String` class is intended to be used for string constants, the class does provide some string-manipulation methods that "modify" the `String` object. The word *modify* is in quotation marks here because these string-manipulation methods don't actually change the `String` object, but rather create an additional `String` object that incorporates the requested changes. A good example is the `replace()` method, which enables you to replace any character in a string with another character:

```
String str1 = "THIS IS A STRING";
String str2 = str1.replace('T', 'X');
```

In this example, `str2` contains `"XHIS IS A SXRING"` because the call to `replace()` requests that every occurrence of a *T* be replaced with an *X*. Note that `str1` remains unchanged and that `str2` is a brand new `String` object.

Another way you can manipulate strings is to concatenate them. *Concatenate* is just a fancy term for "join together." So, when you concatenate two strings, you get a new string that contains both of the original strings. Look at these lines of Java source code, for example:

```
String str1 = "THIS IS A STRING";
String str2 = str1.concat("XXXXXX");
```

Here, `str2` contains `"THIS IS A STRINGXXXXXX"`, whereas `str1` remains unchanged. As you can see, the `concat()` method's single argument is the string to concatenate with the original string.

To make things simpler, the `String` class defines an operator, the plus sign (+), for concatenating strings. By using this operator, you can join strings in a more intuitive way. Here's an example:

```
String str1 = "THIS IS A STRING";
String str2 = str1 + "XXXXXX";
```

This code segment results in exactly the same strings as the preceding `concat()` example. Note that you can use the concatenation operator many times in a single line, like this:

```
String str = "This " + "is " + "a test";
```

If you want to be certain of the case of characters in a string, you can rely on the `toUpperCase()` and `toLowerCase()` methods, each of which returns a string whose characters have been converted to the appropriate case. Look at these lines, for example:

```
String str1 = "THIS IS A STRING";
String str2 = str1.toLowerCase();
```

Here, `str2` is `"this is a string"` because the `toLowerCase()` method converts all characters in the string to lowercase. The `toUpperCase()` method, of course, does just the opposite—converting all characters to uppercase.

Sometimes you have strings that contain leading or trailing spaces. The `String` class features a method called `trim()` that removes both leading and trailing whitespace characters. You use it like this:

```
String str1 = "    THIS IS A STRING    ";
String str2 = str1.trim();
```

In this example, `str2` contains the string `"THIS IS A STRING"`, missing all the spaces before the first *T* and after the *G*.

Finally, you can use the `String` class's `valueOf()` method to convert just about any type of data object to a string, thus enabling you to display the object's value onscreen. The following lines convert an integer to a string, for example:

```
int value = 10;
String str = String.valueOf(value);
```

Notice that `valueOf()` is a static method, meaning that it can be called by referencing the `String` class directly, without having to instantiate a `String` object. Of course, you can also call `valueOf()` through any object of the `String` class, like this:

```
int value = 10;
String str1 = "";
String str2 = str1.valueOf(value);
```

Using the *StringBuffer* Class

The `StringBuffer` class enables you to create `String` objects that can be changed in various ways, unlike the `String` class, which represents string constants. When you modify a string of the `StringBuffer` class, you're not creating a new `String` object, but rather operating directly on the original string itself. For this reason, the `StringBuffer` class offers a different set of methods than the `String` class, all of which operate directly on the buffer that contains the string.

Creating a *StringBuffer* Object

The `StringBuffer` class offers several `Constructors` that enable you to construct a `StringBuffer` object in various ways. Those `Constructors` look like this:

```
StringBuffer()
StringBuffer(int length)
StringBuffer(String str)
```

These Constructors create an empty StringBuffer, an empty StringBuffer of the given length, and a StringBuffer from a String object (or string literal), respectively.

Getting Information About a *StringBuffer* Object

Just as with regular strings, you might need to know the length of a string stored in a StringBuffer object. The class provides the length() method for this purpose. StringBuffer objects, however, also have a capacity() method that returns the capacity of the buffer. Simply put, a StringBuffer's length is the number of characters stored in the string, whereas capacity is the maximum number of characters that fits in the buffer. In the following code example, length is 2 and capacity is 28:

```
StringBuffer str = new StringBuffer("XX");
int length= str.length();
int capacity = str.capacity();
```

StringBuffer Object

You've already had some experience with string extraction when you learned about the String class. The StringBuffer class has two of the same methods for accomplishing this task. Those methods are charAt() and getChars(), both of which work similarly to the String versions. Here's an example of using charAt():

```
StringBuffer str = new StringBuffer("String buffer");
char ch = str.charAt(5);
```

And here's an example of using getChars():

```
StringBuffer str = new StringBuffer("String buffer");
char ch[] = new char[20];
str.getChars(7, 10, ch, 0);
```

In addition, with JDK 1.2 you can also obtain a subString() from a StringBuffer, just like with the String class as shown in the next example:

```
StringBuffer str = new StringBuffer("String buffer");
String buffer = str.subString(8);
String rin = str.subString(3,6);
```

Manipulating a *StringBuffer* Object

There are several ways you can modify the string that's stored in a StringBuffer object. Unlike with the string-modification methods in the String class, which create a new string, the methods in the StringBuffer class work directly on the buffer in which the original string is stored. The first thing you can do with a string buffer is set its length. You do this by calling the setLength() method:

```
StringBuffer str = new StringBuffer("String buffer");
str.setLength(40);
```

This method's single argument is the new length. If the new length is greater than the old length, both the string and buffer length are increased, with the additional characters being filled with zeroes. If the new length is smaller than the old length, characters are chopped off the end of the string, but the buffer size remains the same.

If you want to be guaranteed a specific buffer size, you can call the `ensureCapacity()` method, like this:

```
StringBuffer str = new StringBuffer("String buffer");
str.ensureCapacity(512);
```

The `ensureCapacity()` method's argument is the new capacity for the buffer.

You can change a character in the string buffer by calling the `setCharAt()` method:

```
StringBuffer str = new StringBuffer("String buffer");
str.setCharAt(3, 'X');
```

The `setCharAt()` method's arguments are the index of the character to change and the new character. In the preceding example, the string buffer becomes "`StrXng buffer"`. As of JDK 1.2 you can also replace sections of the `String` with `Strings` or other native types using the `replace()` methods. `replace()` works similar to `setCharAt()`, only instead of requiring a character, you can replace sections of the other string types as well; this is shown in the next example. Notice that with `insert()` you must provide the begin (inclusive) and end (exclusive) index of the characters to replace, instead of just the single character index you need with `setCharAt()`.

```
StringBuffer str = new StringBuffer("String buffer"); str.replace(3,6, 'XYZ');
```

You can add characters to the end of the string with the `append()` method and insert characters anywhere in the string with the `insert()` method. Both of these methods come in several versions that enable you to handle many different types of data. To add a character version of an integer to the end of the string, for example, do something like this:

```
StringBuffer str = new StringBuffer("String buffer");
int value = 15;
str.append(value);
```

After this code executes, `str` contains `"String buffer15"`. Similarly, you insert characters like this:

```
StringBuffer str = new StringBuffer("String buffer");
int value = 15;
str.insert(6, value);
```

This code results in a string of `"String15 buffer"`. The two arguments in the previous version of `insert()` are the index at which to insert the characters and the data object to insert.

As of JDK 1.2 you can also delete characters from the `StringBuffer` using `deleteCharAt()` and `delete()`. `deletCharAt()` requires the index of the character you want to delete, while `delete()` requires the start (inclusive) index and the end (exclusive) index, as shown in the next example:

```
StringBuffer str = new StringBuffer("String buffer");
str.deleteCharAt(6);
str.delete(3,6);
```

Using the *StringTokenizer* Class

If you've been using your computer for a while, you may remember the old-fashioned text adventure games where you would enter a command from the keyboard such as `GET KEY AND OPEN DOOR`, and the computer would follow your instructions. Programs like these had to parse a text string and separate the string into separate words. These words are called tokens, and you may run into times when you would like to extract tokens from a text string. Java provides the `StringTokenizer` class for just this purpose.

Because `StringTokenizer` is not part of the `java.lang` package as `String` and `StringBuffer` are, you must include the correct package in your applet. That package is `java.util`, and you import it like this:

```
import java.util.StringTokenizer;
```

Or, if you want to import the entire `util` package, you could write this:

```
import java.util.*;
```

You can construct a `StringTokenizer` object in several ways, but the easiest is to supply the string you want to tokenize as the `Constructor's` single argument, like this:

```
StringTokenizer tokenizer =
    new StringTokenizer("One Two Three Four Five");
```

This type of string tokenizer uses space characters as the separators (called delimiters) between the tokens. To get a token, you call the `nextToken()` method:

```
String token = tokenizer.nextToken();
```

Each time you call `nextToken()`, you get the next token in the string. Usually, you extract tokens using a `while` loop. To control the `while` loop, you call the `hasMoreTokens()` method, which returns `true` as long as there are more tokens in the string. A typical tokenizer loop might look like this:

```
while (tokenizer.hasMoreTokens())
    String token = tokenizer.nextToken();
```

You can also determine how may tokens are in the string by calling the `countTokens()` method:

```
StringTokenizer tokenizer =
    new StringTokenizer("One Two Three Four Five");
int count = tokenizer.countTokens();
```

In this example, `count` equals 5.

Listing 28.7 is an applet that tokenizes any string you enter. When you run the applet, enter a string into the first text box. Then, click the Tokenize button to get a list of tokens in the string (see Figure 28.6).

Listing 28.7 *TokenApplet.java*—An Applet That Tokenizes Strings

```
import java.awt.*;
import java.applet.*;
import java.util.StringTokenizer;
public class TokenApplet extends Applet
{
    TextField textField1;
    Button button1;
    public void init()
    {
        textField1 = new TextField(30);
        add(textField1);
        button1 = new Button("Tokenize");
        add(button1);
        resize(300, 300);
}
    public void paint(Graphics g)
    {
        String str = textField1.getText();
        StringTokenizer tokenizer =
            new StringTokenizer(str);
        int row = 110;
        while (tokenizer.hasMoreTokens())
        {
            String token = tokenizer.nextToken();
            g.drawString(token, 80, row);
            row += 20;
        }
    }
    public boolean action(Event evt, Object arg)
    {
        if (arg == "Tokenize")
        {
            repaint();
            return true;
        }
        else
            return false;
    }
}
```

FIG. 28.6
The `TokenApplet` can extract individual words from a string.

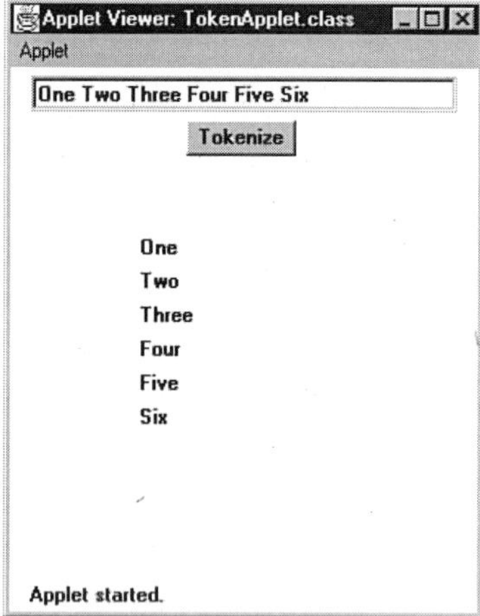

Dealing with Fonts

Because every system handles fonts in a different way, you have to be careful with how you use fonts in your applets. Although Java does its best to match fonts, you have to handle fonts carefully to be sure that your displays look right. To help in this task, Java has a `Font` class that enables you to not only create and display fonts, but also to retrieve information about fonts. Because all text displayed in a Java program uses the current font (including the text used in components such as buttons), no chapter on strings would be complete without a discussion of fonts.

Getting Font Attributes

Every font that you can use with your Java applets is associated with a group of attributes that determines the size and appearance of the font. The most important of these attributes is the font's name, which determines the font's basic style. You can easily get information about the currently active font. Start by calling the `Graphics` object's `getFont()` method, like this:

```
Font font = g.getFont();
```

The `getFont()` method returns a `Font` object for the current font. After you have the `Font` object, you can use the `Font` class's various methods to obtain information about the font. Table 28.1 shows the most commonly used public methods of the `Font` class and what they do.

Table 28.1 Most Commonly Used Public Methods for the Font Class

Method	Description
`getFamily()`	Returns the family name of the font.
`getName()`	Returns the name of the font.
`getSize()`	Returns the size of the font.

Method	Description
`getStyle()`	Returns the style of the font, where 0 is plain, 1 is bold, 2 is italic, and 3 is bold italic.
`isBold()`	Returns a Boolean value indicating whether the font is bold.
`isItalic()`	Returns a Boolean value indicating whether the font is italic.
`isPlain()`	Returns a Boolean value indicating whether the font is plain.
`toString()`	Returns a string of information about the font.

NOTE Most of the general font handling methods are also available inside your applet class. For example, you can call `getFont()` from within your applet's `init()` method, without having to worry about `Graphics` objects. The same is true for `getFontMetrics()` and `setFont()`, which you learn about in the sections "Getting Font Metrics" and "Using the Font."

As always, the best way to see how something works is to try it out yourself. With that end in mind, Listing 28.8 is an applet that displays information about the currently active font using many of the methods described in Table 28.1. Figure 28.7 shows the applet running under AppletViewer.

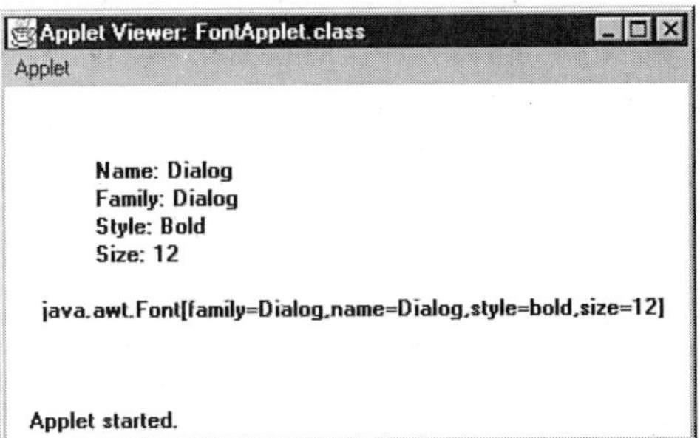

FIG. 28.7 This is `FontApplet` running under AppletViewer.

Listing 28.8 ***FontApplet.java*—Getting Information About a Font**

```
import java.awt.*;
import java.applet.*;
public class FontApplet extends Applet
{
    public void paint(Graphics g)
    {
        Font font = getFont();
        String name = font.getName();
        String family = font.getFamily();
        int n = font.getStyle();
        String style;
```

Part IV Ch 28

continues

Listing 28.8 Continued

```
        if (n == 0)
            style = "Plain";
        else if (n == 1)
            style = "Bold";
        else if (n == 2)
            style = "Italic";
        else
            style = "Bold Italic";
        n = font.getSize();
        String size = String.valueOf(n);
        String info = font.toString();
        String s = "Name: " + name;
        g.drawString(s, 50, 50);
        s = "Family: " + family;
        g.drawString(s, 50, 65);
        s = "Style: " + style;
        g.drawString(s, 50, 80);
        s = "Size: " + size;
        g.drawString(s, 50, 95);
        g.drawString(info, 20, 125);
    }
}
```

As you can see from Listing 28.8, using the `Font` class's methods is fairly straightforward. Just call the method, which returns a value that describes some aspect of the font represented by the `Font` object.

Getting Font Metrics

In many cases, the information you can retrieve from a `Font` object is enough to keep you out of trouble. By using the size returned by the `getSize()` method, for example, you can properly space the lines of text. Sometimes, however, you want to know more about the font you are using. You might want to know the width of a particular character, for example, or even the width in pixels of an entire text string. In these cases, you need to work with text metrics, which are more detailed font attributes.

True to form, the Java Developer's Kit includes the `FontMetrics` class, which makes it easy to obtain information about fonts. You create a `FontMetrics` object like this:

```
FontMetrics fontMetrics = getFontMetrics(font);
```

The `getFontMetrics()` method returns a reference to a `FontMetrics` object for the active font. Its single argument is the `Font` object for which you want the font metrics.

After you have the `FontMetrics` object, you can call its methods to obtain detailed information about the associated font. Table 28.2 lists the most commonly used methods.

Table 28.2 Commonly Used *FontMetrics* Methods

Method	Description
`charWidth()`	Returns the width of a character.
`getAscent()`	Returns the font's ascent.
`getDescent()`	Returns the font's descent.
`getFont()`	Returns the associated `Font` object.
`getHeight()`	Returns the font's height.
`getLeading()`	Returns the font's leading (line spacing).
`stringWidth()`	Returns the width of a string.
`toString()`	Returns a string of information about the font.

If you haven't used fonts before, some of the terms—leading, ascent, and descent—used in Table 28.2 may be unfamiliar to you. *Leading* (pronounced "ledding") is the amount of whitespace between lines of text. *Ascent* is the height of a character, from the baseline to the top of the character. *Descent* is the size of the area that accommodates the descending portions of letters, such as the tail on a lowercase g. Height is the sum of ascent, descent, and leading. Refer to Figure 28.8 for examples of each.

FIG. 28.8
Ascent, descent, and leading determine the overall height of a font.

Creating Fonts

You may think an applet that always uses the default font is boring to look at. In many cases, you would be right. An easy way to spruce up an applet is to use different fonts. Luckily, Java enables you to create and set fonts for your applet. You do this by creating your own `Font` object, like this:

```
Font font = new Font("TimesRoman", Font.PLAIN, 20);
```

The `Constructor` for the `Font` class takes three arguments: the font name, style, and size. The style can be any combination of the font attributes defined in the `Font` class. Those attributes are `Font.PLAIN`, `Font.BOLD`, and `Font.ITALIC`.

Although you can create fonts with the plain, bold, or italic styles, you may at times need to combine font styles. Suppose, for example, that you wanted to use both bold and italic styles. The line

```
Font font = new Font("Courier", Font.BOLD + Font.ITALIC, 18);
```

gives you an 18-point, bold, italic, Courier font.

NOTE A point is a measurement of a font's height and is equal to 1/72 of an inch.

Using the Font

After you've created the font, you have to tell Java to use the font. You do this by calling the `setFont()` method, like this:

```
setFont(font);
```

The next text displayed in your applet uses the new font. Although you request a certain type and size of font, however, you can't be sure of what you will get. The system tries its best to match the requested font, but you still need to know at least the size of the font you end up with. You can get all the information you need by creating a `FontMetrics` object, like this:

```
FontMetrics fontMetrics = getFontMetrics(font);
```

To get the height of a line of text, call the `FontMetrics` object's `getHeight()` method, like this:

```
int height = fontMetrics.getHeight();
```

CAUTION

When creating a font, be aware that the user's system may not have a particular font loaded. In that case, Java chooses a default font as a replacement. This possible font substitution is a good reason to use methods such as `Font.getName()` to see whether you got the font you wanted. You especially need to know the size of the font, so you can be sure to position your text lines properly.

You would not create a font unless you had some text to display. The problem is that before you can display your text, you need to know at least the height of the font. Failure to consider the font's height may give you text lines that overlap or that are spaced too far apart. You can use the height returned from the `FontMetrics` class's `getHeight()` method as a row increment value for each line of text you need to print. Listing 28.9, which is the source code for the `FontApplet2` applet, shows how this is done. Figure 28.9 shows what the applet looks like.

Listing 28.9 ***FontApplet2.java*—Displaying Different-Sized Fonts**

```
import java.awt.*;
import java.applet.*;
public class FontApplet2 extends Applet
{
```

```
    TextField textField;
    public void init()
    {
        textField = new TextField(10);
        add(textField);
        textField.setText("32");
    }
    public void paint(Graphics g)
    {
        String s = textField.getText();
        int height = Integer.parseInt(s);
        Font font = new Font("TimesRoman", Font.PLAIN, height);
        g.setFont(font);
        FontMetrics fontMetrics = g.getFontMetrics(font);
        height = fontMetrics.getHeight();
        int row = 80;
        g.drawString("This is the first line.", 70, row);
        row += height;
        g.drawString("This is the second line.", 70, row);
        row += height;
        g.drawString("This is the third line.", 70, row);
        row += height;
        g.drawString("This is the fourth line.", 70, row);
    }
    public boolean action(Event event, Object arg)
    {
        repaint();
        return true;
    }
}
```

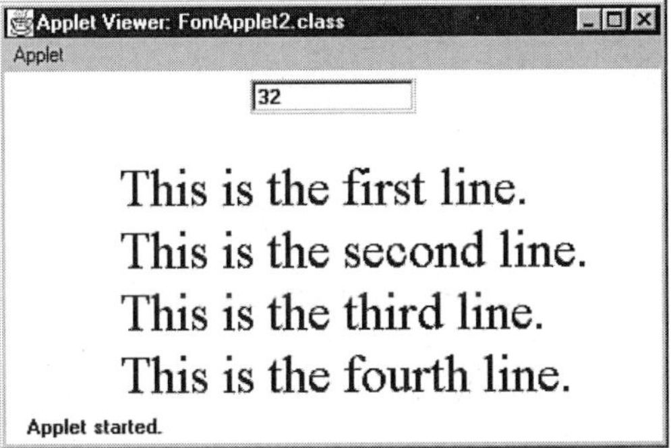

FIG. 28.9
This is AppletViewer running `FontApplet2`.

When you run `FontApplet2`, you see the window shown in Figure 28.9. The size of the active font is shown in the text box at the top of the applet, and a sample of the font appears below the text box. To change the size of the font, type a new value into the text box and press Enter.

The spacing of the lines is accomplished by first creating a variable to hold the vertical position for the next line of text:

```
int row = 80;
```

Here, the program not only declares the row variable, but also initializes it with the vertical position of the first row of text.

The applet then prints the first text line, using row for drawString()'s third argument:

```
g.drawString("This is the first line.", 70, row);
```

In preparation for printing the next line of text, the program adds the font's height to the row variable:

```
row += height;
```

Each line of text is printed, with row being incremented by the font's height in between, like this:

```
g.drawString("This is the second line.", 70, row);
row += height;
g.drawString("This is the third line.", 70, row);
```

CHAPTER 29

Using Internationalization

In this chapter

Internationalization Scenario

Joe Programmer is a Java developer for Company X. His distributed sales application is a huge success in California, where his company is based, mainly because he follows good object-oriented design and implementation: keeping his objects portable, reusable, and independent. One day, Company X decides to start selling its product in Japan. Joe Programmer, who does not know Japanese, gets a Java-literate translator to go through his code and make all the necessary changes using some custom Japanese language character set that Joe doesn't really understand. But he happily compiles this Japanese-language version of his code and sends it off to Japan, where it is a big success. Encouraged by this result, Company X starts moving into other markets; France and Canada are next. To Joe's dismay, he finds that he has to maintain several completely different versions of his code because France and Canada, although they share a common language, have a completely different culture! Poor Joe now has five compiled versions of his code: an American English, Japanese, French, Canadian French, and Canadian English. Now, when he makes even the slightest change to his code, he has to make the same change five times, and then hire several translators to make language changes directly in the source code. Clearly, Joe is in an unacceptable situation.

What Is Internationalization?

In the previous scenario, Joe Programmer is said to have written a *myopic* program, one that is only suited to one locale. A locale is a region (usually geographic, but not necessarily so) that shares customs, culture, and language. Each of the five versions of Joe's program was localized for one specific locale and was unusable outside that locale without major alteration. This violates the fundamental principle of OOP design, because Joe's program is no longer portable or reusable. The process of isolating the culture-dependent code (text, pictures, and so on) from the language-independent code (the actual functionality of the program) is called internationalization. After a program has been through this process, it can easily be adapted to any locale with a minimum amount of effort. Version 1.1 of the Java language added built-in support for internationalization, which makes writing truly portable code easy.

Java Support for Internationalization

Internationalization required several changes to the Java language. In the past, writing internationalized code required extra effort and was substantially more difficult than writing myopic code. One of the design goals was to reverse this paradigm. Java seeks to make writing internationalized code easier than its locale-specific counterpart. Internationalization mainly affects three packages:

- `java.util` Includes the `Locale` class. A `Locale` encapsulates certain information about a locale, but does not provide the actual locale-specific operations. Rather, affected methods can now be passed a `Locale` object as a parameter that will alter their behavior.

If no `Locale` is specified, a default `Locale` is taken from the environment. This package also provides support for `ResourceBundles`, objects that encapsulate locale-sensitive data in a portable, independent way.

- `java.io` All of the classes in java.io that worked with `InputStreams` and `OutputStreams` have corresponding classes that work with class `Reader` and `Writer`. `Readers` and `Writers` work like `Streams`, except they are designed to handle 16-bit Unicode characters instead of 8-bit bytes.
- `java.text` An entirely new package that provides support for manipulating various kinds of text. This includes collating (sorting) text, formatting dates and numbers, and parsing language-sensitive data.

The *Locale* class

A `Locale` object encapsulates information about a specific locale. This consists of just enough information to uniquely identify the locale's region. When a locale-sensitive method is passed a `Locale` object as a parameter, it attempts to modify its behavior for that particular locale. A `Locale` is initialized with a language code, a country code, and an optional variant code. These three things define a region, although you need not specify all three. For example, you could have a `Locale` object for American English, California variant. If you ask the `Calendar` class what the first month of the year is, the `Calendar` tries to find a name suitable for Californian American English. Because month names are not affected by what state you are in, the `Calendar` class has no built-in support for Californian English, and it tries to find a best fit. It next tries American English, but because month names are constant in all English-speaking countries, this fails as well. Finally, the `Calendar` class returns the month name that corresponds to the English `Locale`. This best-fit lookup procedure allows the programmer complete control over the granularity of internationalized code.

You create a `Locale` object using the following syntax:

```
Locale theLocale = new Locale("en", "US");
```

where `"en"` specifies English, and `"US"` specifies United States. These two-letter codes are used internally by Java programs to identify languages and countries. They are defined by the ISO-639 and ISO-3166 standards documents respectively. More information on these two documents can be found at:

```
http://www.ics.uci.edu/pub/ietf/http/related/iso639.txt
http://www.chemie.fu-berlin.de/diverse/doc/ISO_3166.html
```

Currently, the JDK supports the following language and country combinations in all of its locale-sensitive classes, such as `Calendar`, `NumberFormat`, and so on. This list may change in the future, so be sure to check the latest documentation (see Table 29.1).

Table 29.1 Locales Supported by the JDK

Locale	Country	Language
da_DK	Denmark	Danish
DE_AT	Austria	German
de_CH	Switzerland	German
de_DE	Germany	German
el_GR	Greece	Greek
en_CA	Canada	English
en_GB	United Kingdom	English
en_IE	Ireland	English
en_US	United States	English
es_ES	Spain	Spanish
fi_FI	Finland	Finnish
fr_BE	Belgium	French
fr_CA	Canada	French
fr_CH	Switzerland	French
fr_FR	France	French
it_CH	Switzerland	Italian
it_IT	Italy	Italian
ja_JP	Japan	Japanese
ko_KR	Korea	Korean
nl_BE	Belgium	Dutch
nl_NL	Netherlands	Dutch
no_NO	Norway	Norwegian (Nynorsk)
no_NO_B	Norway	Norwegian (Bokmål)
pt_PT	Portugal	Portuguese
sv_SE	Sweden	Swedish
tr_TR	Turkey	Turkish
zh_CN	China	Chinese(Simplified)
zh_TW	Taiwan	Chinese (Traditional)

Programmers can also create their own custom Locales, simply by specifying a unique sequence of country, language, variant. Multiple variants can be separated by an underscore character. To create a variant of Californian American English running on a Windows machine, use the following code:

```
Locale theLocale = new Locale("en", "US", "CA_WIN");
```

Remember that methods that do not understand this particular variant will try to find a best fit match, in this case probably "en_US".

The two-letter abbreviations listed here are not meant to be displayed to the user; they are meant only for internal representation. For display, use one of the Locale methods listed in Table 29.2. You will notice that these methods are generally overloaded so that you can get the parameter either for the current locale or the one specified.

Table 29.2 Locale Display Methods

Method Name	Description
getDisplayCountry()	
getDisplayCountry(Locale)	Country name, localized for default Locale, or specified Locale.
getDisplayLanguage()	
getDisplayLanguage(Locale)	Language name, localized for default Locale, or specified Locale.
getDisplayName()	
getDisplayName(Locale)	Name of the entire locale, localized for default Locale, or specified Locale.
getDisplayVariant()	
getDisplayVariant(Locale)	Name of the Locale's variant. If the localized name is not found, this returns the variant code.

These methods are very useful when you want to have a user interact with a Locale object. Here's an example of using the getDisplayLanguage() method:

```
Locale.setDefault( new Locale("en", "US") ); //Set default Locale to American
                                             //English
Locale japanLocale = new Locale("ja:, "JP"); //Create locale for Japan
System.out.println( japanLocale.getDisplayLanguage() );
System.out.println( japanLocale.getDisplayLanguage( Locale.FRENCH ) );
```

This code fragment prints out the name of the language used by japanLocale. In the first case, it is localized for the default Locale, which has been conveniently set to American English. The output would therefore be Japanese. The second print statement localizes the language name for display in French, which yields the output Japonais. All of the Locale "display" methods use this same pattern. Almost all Internationalization API methods allow you to explicitly control the `Locale` used for localization, but in most cases, you'll just want to use the default `Locale`.

Another thing to note in the preceding example is the use of the static constant `Locale.FRENCH`. The `Locale` class provides a number of these useful constants, each of which is a shortcut for the corresponding `Locale` object. A list of these objects is shown in Table 29.3.

Table 29.3 Locale Static Objects

Constant Name	Locale	Shortcut for
`CANADA`	English Canada	`new Locale("en", "CA", "")`
`CANADA_FRENCH`	French Canada	`new Locale("fr", "CA", "")`
`CHINA SCHINESE PRC`	Chinese (Simplified)	`new Locale("zh", "CN", "")`
`CHINESE`	Chinese Language	`new Locale("zh", "", "")`
`ENGLISH`	English Language	`new Locale("en", "", "")`
`FRANCE`	France	`new Locale("fr", "FR", "")`
`FRENCH`	French Language	`new Locale("fr", "", "")`
`GERMAN`	German Language	`new Locale("de", "", "")`
`GERMANY`	Germany	`new Locale("de", "DE", "")`
`ITALIAN`	Italian Language	`new Locale("it", "", "")`
`ITALY`	Italy	`new Locale("it", "IT", "")`
`JAPAN`	Japan	`new Locale("jp", "JP", "")`
`JAPANESE`	Japanese Language	`new Locale("jp", "", "")`
`KOREA`	Korea	`new Locale("ko", "KR", "")`
`KOREAN`	Korean Language	`new Locale("ko", "", "")`
`TAIWAN TCHINESE`	Taiwan (Traditional Chinese)	`new Locale("zh", "TW", "")`
`UK`	Great Britain	`new Locale("en", "GB", "")`
`US`	United States	`new Locale("en", "US", "")`

Packaging *Locale*-Sensitive Data

The `Locale` class allows you to easily handle `Locale`-sensitive methods. However, most programs (especially applets and GUI-based applications) require the use of Strings, data, and other resources that also need to be localized. For instance, most GUI programs have OK and Cancel buttons. This is fine for the United States, but other locales require different labels for these buttons. In Germany, for instance, you might use Gut and Vernichten instead. Traditionally, information such as this was included in the source code of an application, which, as Programmer Joe found out earlier, can lead to many problems when trying to simultaneously support many localized versions of one program. To solve this problem, Java provides a way to encapsulate this data into objects that are loaded by the VM upon demand. These objects are called `ResourceBundles`.

***ResourceBundles*—Naming Conventions** `ResourceBundle` is an abstract class that must be extended to provide any functionality. `ResourceBundles` are loaded by a class loader by name, and must follow a very strict naming convention to be loaded properly. This is best illustrated by example. Let's say you have a class called `LabelBundle` that extends `ResourceBundle` and contains the names of all GUI labels you use in an application. The class called `LabelBundle` provides default information; `LabelBundle_fr` provides French labels; `LabelBundle_ge_GE` provides German labels; and `LabelBundle_en_US_MAC` provides Macintosh-specific American English labels. You request a `ResourceBundle` using the following static method:

```
ResourceBundle getResourceBundle(String baseName, Locale locale, ClassLoader
loader)
```

This method uses the specified `ClassLoader` to search for a class that matches `baseName`, plus certain attributes of the specified `Locale`. There is a very specific search pattern that is used to find the closest match to the `Bundle` you request:

```
bundleName + "_" + localeLanguage + "_" + localeCountry + "_" + localeVariant
bundleName + "_" + localeLanguage + "_" + localeCountry
bundleName + "_" + localeLanguage
bundleName + "_" + defaultLanguage + "_" + defaultCountry + "_" + defaultVariant
bundleName + "_" + defaultLanguage + "_" + defaultCountry
bundleName + "_" + defaultLanguage
bundleName
```

In our example, if you request the `baseName` `LabelBundle` with a `fr_FR_WIN` (French language, France, Windows platform) `Locale`, the `getResourceBundle()` method performs the following steps:

1. Searches for the class `LabelBundle_fr_FR_WIN`, which fails because you have defined no such class.
2. Searches for the class `LabelBundle_fr_FR`, which also fails because you did not define a France-only `Bundle`.
3. Searches for class `LabelBundle_fr`. This succeeds and returns the class with this name. However, if this search had failed (if you had not supplied a French-language Bundle), the search would have continued, using the language, country, and variant codes supplied in the default `Locale`.

Creating *ResourceBundles* Now that you understand the naming convention used with `ResourceBundles`, take a look at how they are created. The simplest form of `ResourceBundles` extends the `ResourceBundle` class directly, and then overrides one method:

```
Object handleGetObject(String key)
```

This method returns an object that corresponds to the specified key. These keys are internal representations of the content stored in the `ResourceBundle` and should be the same for all localized versions of the same data. An extremely simple version of your `LabelBundle` might be defined as follows:

```
class LabelBundle extends ResourceBundle {
public Object handleGetObject(String key) {
if( key.equals("OK") )
return "OK";
else if( key.equals("Cancel") )
return "Cancel";

// Other labels could be handled here

return null; // If the key has no matches, always return null
}
}
```

Other versions of the same bundle might return values translated into different languages. You can see, however, that this method of handling key-value pairs is very inefficient if you have more than a few keys. Luckily, Java provides two subclasses of `ResourceBundle` that can make life easier: `ListResourceBundle` and `PropertyResourceBundle`.

`ListResourceBundles` use an array of two-element arrays to store the key-value pairs used earlier. All you have to do is override the default `getContents()` method, like this:

```
class LabelBundle extends ListResourceBundle {
static final Object[][] labels = {
{"OK", "OK"},
{"Cancel", "Cancel"},
("AnotherKey", "Another Value"}
//More key-value pairs can go here
};

public Object[][] getContents() {
return labels;
}
}
```

You could also provide your own similar functionality using a hashtable, but that's only worthwhile if you want the contents to change dynamically over time.

`PropertyResourceBundles` are created as needed from predefined "property" files stored on disk. These are usually used for systemwide settings, or when large amounts of data need to be stored in a key-value pair. `PropertyResourceBundles` are built from files with the same name as the corresponding class file, but with the `.properties` extension instead. To implement the `LabelBundle_de_DE` class, you might provide a file called `LabelBundle_de_DE.properties` with the following content:

```
OK=Gut
Cancel=Vernichten
AnotherKey=This value has a lot of text stored within it. Of course, it really
ought to be translated into German first...
```

Contents are always specified in the form "key=value" and are assumed to be Strings (although they can be cast into other appropriate objects). This functionality is based on the `java.util.Properties` class. See Chapter 47, "`java.lang`," for more information on the `java.util` package.

NOTE Although the examples given here all deal with String objects, `ResourceBundles` can store objects of any type, including `Dates`, `Applets`, GUI elements, or even other `ResourceBundles`!

Accessing *ResourceBundles* As previously mentioned, you load `ResourceBundles` by name using the static method `getResourceBundle()`. Assuming this succeeds (it throws an exception otherwise), you can then query individual values within the bundle using the `getObject()` method. Of course, this also usually requires an explicit cast to the kind of object you want, so you need to know this information ahead of time. As a matter of convenience, `ResourceBundle` also provides the following methods that return already-cast objects:

- `getMenu(String)`
- `getMenuBar(String)`
- `getObject(String)`
- `getString(String)`
- `getStringArray(String)`

Other Internationalization Pieces in *java.util*

Internationalization required a couple of other changes to be made to `java.util` classes. For instance, under Java 1.0, the `Date` class was used for time manipulation. However, since then, it is simply a wrapper for one particular instant in time. For creating `Date` objects, you should now use the `Calendar` class. `Calendar` is an abstract class that provides culture-independent methods for manipulating the epoch, century, year, month, week, day, and time in various ways. To instantiate the `Calendar` class, you have to extend it and provide methods based on a particular `Calendar` standard. The only one that (so far) comes with the JDK is the `GregorianCalendar` class, which provides very sophisticated functionality for the world's most popular calendar system. Future releases may include support for various lunar, seasonal, or other calendar systems. An adjunct to the `Calendar` class, which is not usually used directly by the programmer, is the `TimeZone` (and `SimpleTimeZone`) class, which allows dates and times to be properly adjusted for other time zones.

The `Date`, `Calendar`, and `TimeZone` classes provide a huge amount of functionality that most programmers will never need to know about. You don't need to understand the intricacies of temporal arithmetic to make use of these classes; they all contain default methods that allow you to get the current time and date, and display it in a `Locale`-sensitive way. By merely using the provided methods, your programs will become localized by default, requiring no added effort on your part.

NOTE There are many more methods in these few classes than are worth discussing here. If you are interested, a simple example of the `Calendar` and `Date` classes interacting is provided in the example at the end of the chapter. For a more complete discussion, you should consult the Java API documentation directly.

Input-Output (I/O) for Internationalization

Originally, the `java.io` package operated exclusively on byte streams, a continuous series of 8-bit quantities. However, Java's Unicode characters are 16 bits, which makes using them with byte streams difficult. Therefore, if you look at the `java.io` package, there is also a whole series of 16-bit character stream `Readers` and `Writers`, which correspond to the old `InputStream` and `OutputStream`. The two sets of classes can work together or separately, depending on whether your program needs to input or output text of any kind.

Character Set Converters

The way in which characters are represented as binary numbers is called an encoding scheme. The most common scheme used for English text is called the ISO Latin-1 encoding. The set of characters supported by any one encoding is said to be its character set, which includes all possible characters that can be represented by the encoding. Usually, the first 127 codes of an encoding correspond to the almost universally accepted ASCII character set, which includes all of the standard characters and punctuation marks. Nevertheless, most encodings can vary radically, especially because some, like Chinese and Japanese encodings, have character sets that bear little resemblance to English!

Luckily, Java 1.1 provides classes for dealing with all of the most common encodings around. The `ByteToCharConverter` and `CharToByteConverter` classes are responsible for performing very complex conversions to and from the standard Unicode characters supported by Java. Each encoding scheme is given its own label by which it can be identified. A complete list of supported encodings and their labels is shown in Table 29.4.

Table 29.4 JDK 1.1–Supported Character Encodings

Label	Encoding Scheme Description
8859_1	ISO Latin-1
8859_2	ISO Latin-2
8859_3	ISO Latin-3
8859_4	ISO Latin-4
8859_5	ISO Latin/Cyrillic
8859_6	ISO Latin/Arabic
8859_7	ISO Latin/Greek

Label	Encoding Scheme Description
8859_8	ISO Latin/Hebrew
8859_9	ISO Latin-5
Big5	Big 5 Traditional Chinese
CNS11643	CNS 11643 Traditional Chinese
Cp1250	Windows Eastern Europe/Latin-2
Cp1251	Windows Cyrillic
Cp1252	Windows Western Europe/Latin-1
Cp1253	Windows Greek
Cp1254	Windows Turkish
Cp1255	Windows Hebrew
Cp1256	Windows Arabic
Cp1257	Windows Baltic
Cp1258	Windows Vietnamese
Cp437	PC Original
Cp737	PC Greek
Cp775	PC Baltic
Cp850	PC Latin-1
Cp852	PC Latin-2
Cp855	PC Cyrillic
Cp857	PC Turkish
Cp860	PC Portuguese
Cp861	PC Icelandic
Cp862	PC Hebrew
Cp863	PC Canadian French
Cp864	PC Arabic
Cp865	PC Nordic
Cp866	PC Russian
Cp869	PC Modern Greek
Cp874	Windows Thai
EUCJIS	Japanese EUC

continues

Table 29.4 Continued

Label	Encoding Scheme Description
GB2312	GB2312-80 Simplified Chinese
JIS	JIS
KSC5601	KSC5601 Korean
MacArabic	Macintosh Arabic
MacCentralEurope	Macintosh Latin-2
MacCroatian	Macintosh Croatian
MacCyrillic	Macintosh Cyrillic
MacDingbat	Macintosh Dingbat
MacGreek	Macintosh Greek
MacHebrew	Macintosh Hebrew
MacIceland	Macintosh Iceland
MacRoman	Macintosh Roman
MacRomania	Macintosh Romania
MacSymbol	Macintosh Symbol
MacThai	Macintosh Thai
MacTurkish	Macintosh Turkish
MacUkraine	Macintosh Ukraine
SJIS	PC and Windows Japanese
UTF8	Standard UTF-8

Java also provides ways for developers to create their own encodings and to create converters for already-existing but unsupported encodings. The details of how character conversion is done are actually quite complex, and those who are interested are referred to Java's Web pages.

Readers and Writers

Character streams make heavy use of character set converters. Fortunately, they also hide the underlying complexity of the conversion process, making it easy for Java programs to be written without knowledge of the internationalizing process. Again, you see that programs are internationalized by default.

The advantages of using character streams over byte streams are many. Although they have the added overhead of doing character conversion on top of byte reading, they also allow for more efficient buffering. Byte streams are designed to read information one byte at a time, while character streams read one buffer at a time. According to Sun, this, combined with a new efficient locking scheme, more than compensates for the speed loss caused by the conversion process. Every input or output stream in the old class hierarchy now has a corresponding `Reader` or `Writer` class that performs similar functions using character streams (see Table 29.5).

Table 29.5 Input/Output Streams and Corresponding *Reader* and *Writer* Classes (from Sun Microsystems, Inc.)

Byte Stream Class (*InputStream/ OutputStream*)	Corresponding Character Stream Class (*Reader/ Writer*)	Function
`InputStream`	`Reader`	Abstract class from which all other classes inherit methods, and so on
`BufferedInputStream`	`BufferedReader`	Provides a buffer for input operations
`LineNumberInputStream`	`LineNumberReader`	Keeps track of line numbers
`ByteArrayInputStream`	`CharArrayReader`	Reads from an array
N/A	`InputStreamReader`	Translates a byte stream into a character stream
`FileInputStream`	`FileReader`	Allows input from a file on disk
`FilterInputStream`	`FilterReader`	Abstract class for filtered input
`PushbackInputStream`	`PushbackReader`	Allows characters to be pushed back into the stream
`PipedInputStream`	`PipedReader`	Reads from a process pipe
`StringBufferInputStream`	`StringReader`	Reads from a String
`OutputStream`	`Writer`	Abstract class for character-output streams
`BufferedOutputStream`	`BufferedWriter`	Buffers output, uses platform's line separator
`ByteArrayOutputStream`	`CharArrayWriter`	Writes to a character array
`FilterOutputStream`	`FilterWriter`	Abstract class for filtered character output
N/A	`OutputStreamWriter`	Translates a character stream into a byte stream

continues

Table 29.5 Continued

Byte Stream Class (*InputStream/ OutputStream*)	Corresponding Character Stream Class (*Reader/ Writer*)	Function
`FileOutputStream`	`FileWriter`	Translates a character stream into a byte file
`PrintStream`	`PrintWriter`	Prints values and objects to a `Writer`
`PipedOutputStream`	`PipedWriter`	Writes to a `PipedReader`
N/A	`StringWriter`	Writes to a `String`

The impact of these changes is actually quite minor if you're developing new programs. All you have to do is remember to use `Reader` and `Writer` classes where before you used `InputStream` and `OutputStream`. The biggest change you'll have to worry about relates to the `DataInputStream` and `PrintStream`, which used to be the classes of choice for sending text input and output. The `DataInputStream.readLine()` method has been deprecated—you should use `BufferedReader.readLine()` instead. Furthermore, you can no longer instantiate a new `PrintStream` object, although you can still use pre-existing `PrintStreams` (such as `System.out`) for debugging purposes. To output line-terminated strings, you should use the `PrintWriter` class instead. The main offshoot of this is that all code that is used to communicate with the `DataInputStream` and `PrintStream` classes (which includes much `Socket`, `File`, and `Piped` code) will have to be updated to use the proper `Reader` and `Writer` classes. To make this easier, Java provides classes called `InputStreamReader` and `OutputStreamWriter`, which are used to create a new Writer or Reader based on a byte stream. This makes the Reader/ Writer system compatible with all of the other classes that currently use byte streams (like `URL`, `Socket`, `File`, and so on).

The New Package *java.text*

The most advanced and complex Internationalization API features are found in the `java.text` package. They include many classes for formatting and organizing text in a language-independent way. For instance, date formatting can be quite problematic for programmers. In America, dates are written in month-day-year order, but in Europe, dates are written in day-month-year order. This makes interpreting a date like 10/2/97 difficult: Does this represent October 2, 1997 or February 10, 1997? This is the purpose of properly formatted text. Most of these classes are not intended to be instantiated directly and can be accessed through static `getDefault()` methods.

Text collating, on the other hand, is the process of sorting text according to particular rules. In English, sorting in alphabetical order is relatively easy because English lacks many special characters (such as accents) that could complicate things. In French, however, things are not so simple. Two words that look very similar (like péché and pêche) have entirely different meanings. Which should come first alphabetically? And what about characters like hyphenation or punctuation? The Java `Collation` class provides a way of defining language-specific sort criteria in a robust, consistent manner.

Text boundaries can also be ambiguous across languages. Where do words, sentences, and paragraphs begin and end? In English, a period generally marks the end of a sentence, but is this always the case? Certainly not. The `TextBoundary` and `CharacterIterator` classes can intelligently break up text into various sub-units based on language-specific criteria. Java comes with built-in support for some languages, but you can always define your own set of rules, as well. `TextBoundary` works by returning the integer index of boundaries that occur within a String, as demonstrated by the following example, which breaks up a String by words:

```
String str = "This is a line of text. It contains many words, sentences, and
➥formatting.";
TextBoundary byWord = TextBoundary.getWordBreak();
int from, to;
from = byWord.first();
while( (to = byWord.next()) != DONE ) {
System.out.println( byWord.getText().substring(from, to) );
        from = to;
}
```

This snippet of code prints out each word on its own line. Although this example is trivial, text boundaries can be extremely important, especially in GUI applications that require text selection, intelligent word-wrapping, and so on.

An Example: *InternationalTest*

To better understand how all of this fits together, take a look at this very simple Java application that makes use of several of the features discussed in this chapter. It is included on the CD-ROM accompanying this book, if you'd like to play with it yourself.

The application is a very simple one. It takes up to three command-line parameters that specify a locale. It uses this information to

1. Display some information about the default locale and the one entered
2. Try to load a `ResourceBundle` corresponding to the specified locale and print out what the Bundle contains
3. Display the date, localized to the specified locale

Besides the main application class (`InternationalTest`), the program requires several other classes. Most are `ResourceBundles` that correspond to different locales (currently, `ResourceBundles` must be created as public classes, but this may change in a future release of the JDK). Another thing to note is that this application passes "null" as the `ClassLoader` parameter to the `getResourceBundle()` method. This is because applications are loaded from the `CLASSPATH` environment variable, and do not have an explicit `ClassLoader`. As long as the `ResourceBundles` are also available via `CLASSPATH`, you don't need a separate `ClassLoader` to load them. If you were making an applet, on the other hand, you would need a `ClassLoader` to load the classes across the Internet. You can use the same `ClassLoader` instance that loaded the applet like this:

```
ClassLoader loader = this.getClass().getClassLoader();
```

The complete listing of `InternationalTest` follows in Listing 29.1.

Listing 29.1 *InternationalTest.java*

```
import java.util.*;
import java.lang.*;
import java.text.DateFormat;

class InternationalTest extends Object {

public static void main(String args[]) {


String lang = "", country = "", var = "";

   try {
      lang = args[0];
      country = args[1];
      var = args[2];
   } catch(ArrayIndexOutOfBoundsException e) {
      if( lang.equals("") ) {
         System.out.println("You must specify at least one parameter");
         System.exit(1);
         }
   }

   Locale locale = new Locale(lang, country, var);
   Locale def = Locale.getDefault();

   System.out.println( "Default Locale is: "+ def.getDisplayName() );
   System.out.println("You have selected Locale: "+locale.getDisplayName() );
   System.out.println("Default language, localized for your locale is: " +
           def.getDisplayLanguage( locale ) );
   System.out.println("Default country name, localized: " +
                      locale ) );

   ClassLoader loader = null;

   ResourceBundle bundle = null;
   try {
      bundle = ResourceBundle.getResourceBundle( "TestBundle", locale, loader );
   } catch( MissingResourceException e) {
      System.out.println( "No resources available for that locale." );
   } finally {
         System.out.println( "Resources available are: ");
         System.out.println(" r1: " + bundle.getString("r1") );
         System.out.println(" r2:" + bundle.getString("r2") );
   }
```

```
   DateFormat myFormat = DateFormat.getDateTimeFormat(DateFormat.FULL,
DateFormat.FULL, locale);
   Calendar myCalendar = Calendar.getDefault( locale );
   System.out.println("The localized date and time is: " +
         myFormat.format( myCalendar.getTime() ) );

   }
}
```

Figures 29.1, 29.2, and 29.3 show output from the `InternationalTest` program.

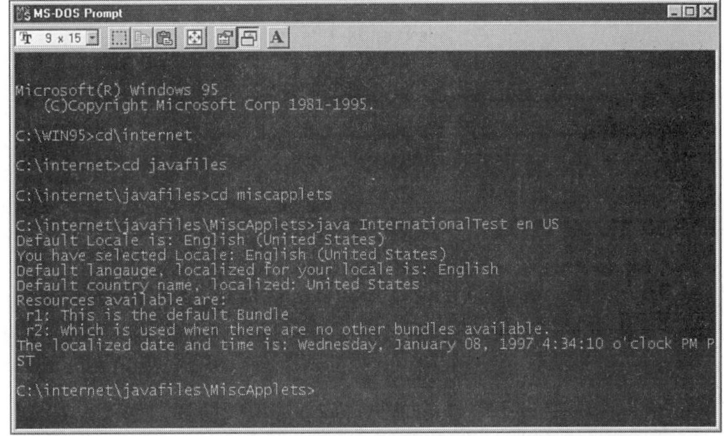

FIG. 29.1
American English locale.

FIG. 29.2
Canadian French and Canadian French Macintosh locales.

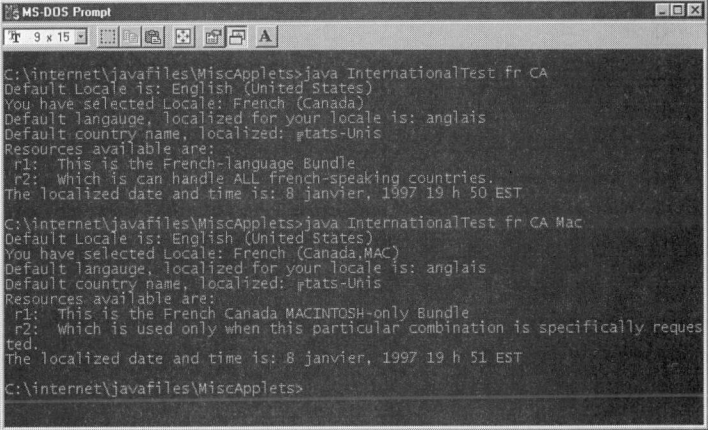

```
C:\internet\javafiles\MiscApplets>java InternationalTest fr CA
Default Locale is: English (United States)
You have selected Locale: French (Canada)
Default langauge, localized for your locale is: anglais
Default country name, localized: ╒tats-Unis
Resources available are:
 r1:  This is the French-language Bundle
 r2:  Which is can handle ALL french-speaking countries.
The localized date and time is: 8 janvier, 1997 19 h 50 EST

C:\internet\javafiles\MiscApplets>java InternationalTest fr CA Mac
Default Locale is: English (United States)
You have selected Locale: French (Canada,MAC)
Default langauge, localized for your locale is: anglais
Default country name, localized: ╒tats-Unis
Resources available are:
 r1:  This is the French Canada MACINTOSH-only Bundle
 r2:  Which is used only when this particular combination is specifically reques
ted.
The localized date and time is: 8 janvier, 1997 19 h 51 EST

C:\internet\javafiles\MiscApplets>
```

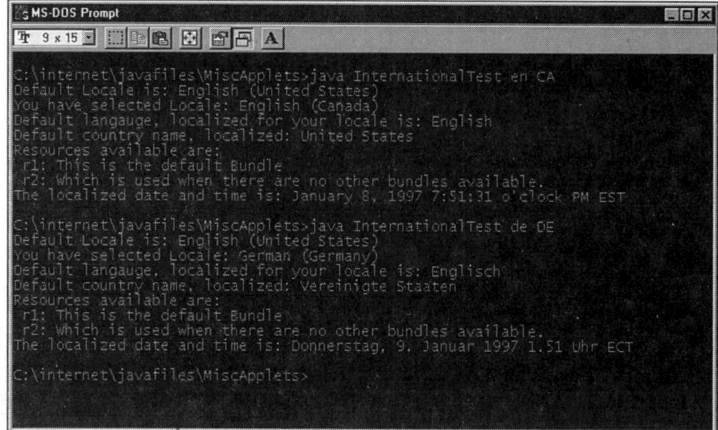

FIG. 29.3
Canadian English and Germany locales.

So where does this leave Joe Programmer? Well, he's got some work to do to convert his application to the Internationalization API. His labels, text, and localized resources need to be encapsulated into `ResourceBundles` for each locale he supports. He also needs to adjust a few methods and objects to use localized date, time, and message formats. When this process is complete, he'll find that not only will his program be localized for many locales, but he also does not need to support multiple versions of the same program. Even better, when a new locale needs to be supported, he doesn't need to modify his source code at all—he just needs to get his locale-specific resources translated to this new language/customs. His program is now, once again, portable, reusable, and independent. ●

CHAPTER 30

Communications and Networking

In this chapter

Overview of TCP/IP

Despite all its other merits, the rapid embrace of Java by the computing community is primarily due to its powerful integration with Internet networking. The Internet revolution has forever changed the way the personal computer is used, empowering individuals to gather, publish, and share information in a vast resource with millions of participants. Building on top of this foundation, Java could be the next major revolution in computing.

The Java execution environment is designed so that applications can be easily written to efficiently communicate and share processing with remote systems. Much of this functionality is provided with the standard Java API within the `java.net` package.

This is the first of four chapters that will demonstrate clear and practical uses of the classes within `java.net`, explaining the programming concepts on which they are based. As a foundation of these discussions, the design of the Internet network protocol suite—TCP/IP—is illustrated within this chapter.

TCP/IP is a suite of protocols that interconnects the various systems on the Internet. TCP/IP provides a common programming interface for diverse and foreign hardware. The suite supports the joining of separate physical networks implementing different network media. TCP/IP makes a diverse, chaotic, global network like the Internet possible.

Models provide useful abstractions of working systems, ignoring fine detail while enabling a clear perspective on global interactions. Models also facilitate a greater understanding of functioning systems and also provide a foundation for extending that system. Understanding the models of network communications is an essential guide to learning TCP/IP fundamentals.

OSI Reference Model

The network protocol architecture known as the *Open Systems Interconnect (OSI) Reference Model* is often used to describe network systems. The OSI scheme was one part of a larger project by the International Organization for Standardization (ISO). The OSI protocols never proved as successful as TCP/IP, making the Reference Model perhaps the most enduring aspect of this ISO endeavor.

The model consists of seven layers providing specific functionality. Each layer has defined characteristics, and together the whole enables network communication. The software implementation of such a layered model is appropriately termed a *protocol stack.*

The OSI model is illustrated in Figure 30.1. User applications insert information into one layer and each encapsulates the data until the last is reached. The information is then transmitted to the destination, sometimes having the layers translated from the bottom up as the data is transported.

The following layers have specific roles, each refraining from intruding into the domain of the other, all depending upon the others:

- Application Layer Contains network applications within which people interact, such as mail, file transfer, and remote login.

FIG. 30.1
The OSI Reference Model consists of seven layers.

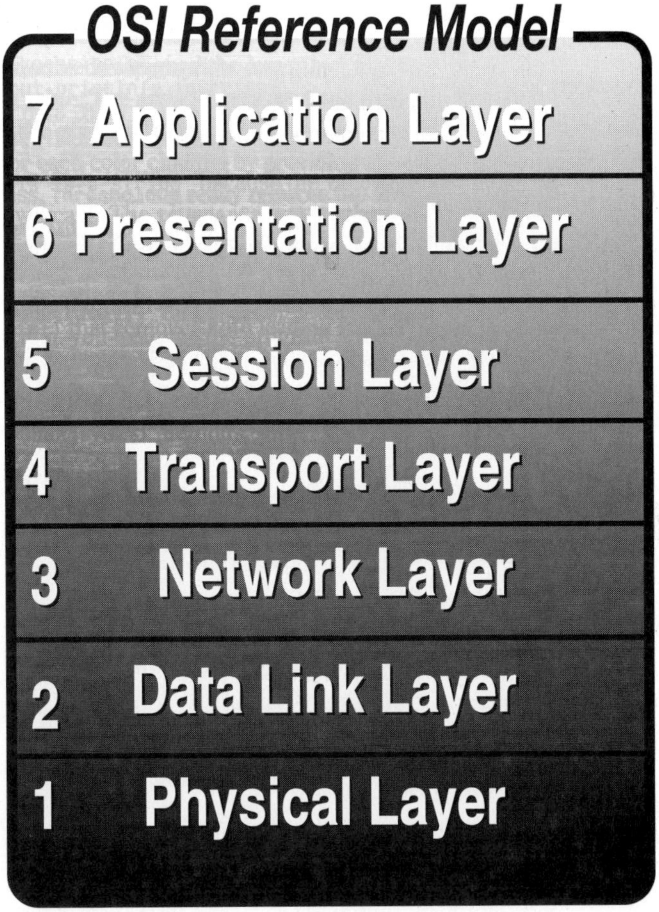

OSI Reference Model
7 Application Layer
6 Presentation Layer
5 Session Layer
4 Transport Layer
3 Network Layer
2 Data Link Layer
1 Physical Layer

- Presentation Layer   Creates common data structures.
- Session Layer   Manages connections between network applications.
- Transport Layer   Ensures that data is received exactly as it is sent.
- Network Layer   Routes data through various physical networks while traveling to a known host.
- Data Link Layer   Transmits and receives packets of information reliably across a uniform physical network.
- Physical Layer   Defines the physical properties of the network, such as voltage levels, cable types, and interface pins.

TCP/IP Network Model

The OSI model helps when trying to understand the TCP/IP communication architecture. When viewed as a layered model, TCP/IP is usually seen as being composed of four layers:

- Application
- Network
- Transport
- Link

These layers are illustrated in Figure 30.2. Attempts to map these layers to the OSI model are inexact and confuse matters, so this chapter refrains from such an endeavor.

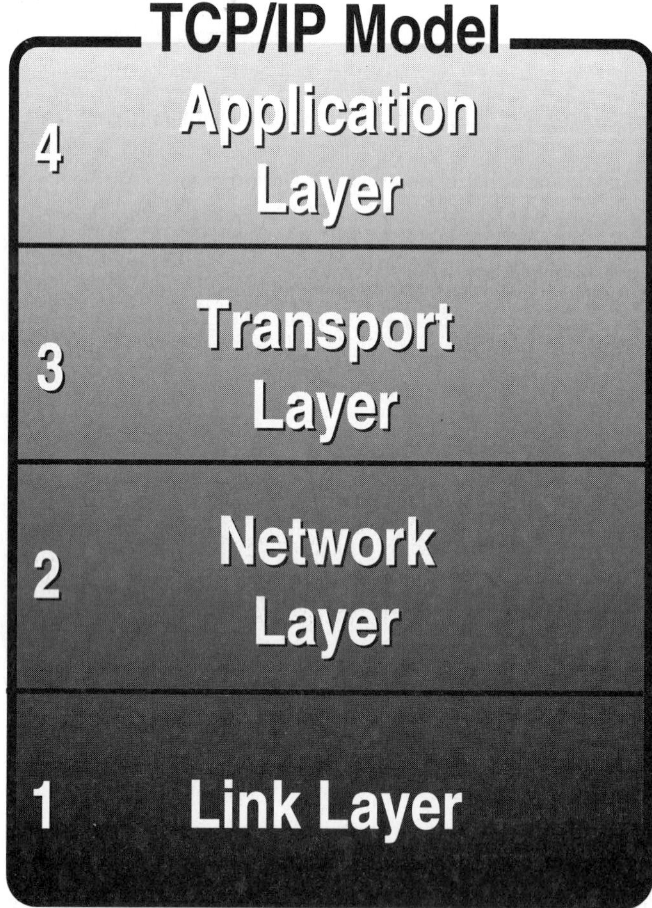

FIG. 30.2 The TCP/IP network model can be broken down into four layers.

As in the OSI model, each TCP/IP layer plays a specific role, each of which is described in the following four sections.

Application Layer Network applications depend on the definition of a clear dialog. In a client-server system, the client application knows how to request services, and the server knows how to appropriately respond. Protocols that implement this layer include HTTP, FTP, and Telnet.

Transport Layer The Transport Layer enables network applications to obtain messages over clearly defined channels and with specific characteristics. The two protocols within the TCP/IP suite that generally implement this layer are Transmission Control Protocol (TCP) and User Datagram Protocol (UDP).

Network Layer The Network Layer enables information to be transmitted to any machine on the contiguous TCP/IP network, regardless of the different physical networks that intervene. Internet Protocol (IP) is the mechanism for transmitting data within this layer.

Link Layer The Link Layer consists of the low-level protocols used to transmit data to machines on the same physical network. Protocols that aren't part of the TCP/IP suite, such as Ethernet, Token Ring, FDDI, and ATM, implement this layer.

Data within these layers is usually encapsulated with a common mechanism: protocols have a header that identifies meta information such as the source, destination, and other attributes, and a data portion that contains the actual information. The protocols from the upper layers are encapsulated within the data portion of the lower ones. When traveling back up the protocol stack, the information is reconstructed as it is delivered to each layer. Figure 30.3 shows this concept of encapsulation.

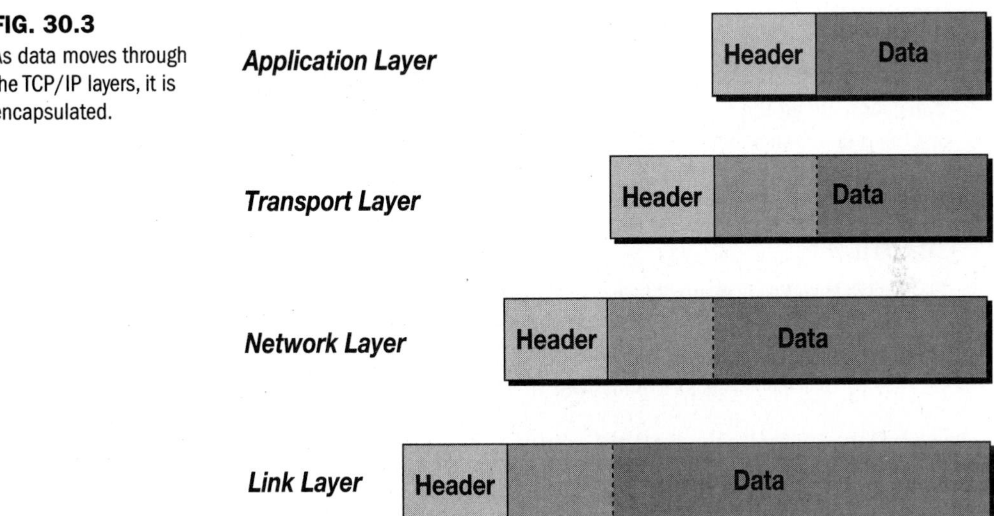

FIG. 30.3
As data moves through the TCP/IP layers, it is encapsulated.

TCP/IP Protocols

Three protocols are most commonly used within the TCP/IP scheme, and a closer investigation of their properties is warranted. Understanding how these three protocols (IP, TCP, and UDP) interact is critical to developing network applications.

Internet Protocol (IP)

IP is the keystone of the TCP/IP suite. All data on the Internet flows through IP packets, the basic unit of IP transmissions. IP is termed a connectionless, unreliable protocol. As a connectionless protocol, IP does not exchange control information before transmitting data to a remote system—packets are merely sent to the destination with the expectation that they will be treated properly. IP is unreliable because it does not retransmit lost packets or detect corrupted data. These tasks must be implemented by higher level protocols, such as TCP.

IP defines a universal addressing scheme called IP addresses. An IP address is a 32-bit number, and each standard address is unique on the Internet. Given an IP packet, the information can be routed to the destination based upon the IP address defined in the packet header. IP addresses are generally written as four numbers, between 0 and 255, separated by a period (for example, `124.148.157.6`).

While a 32-bit number is an appropriate way to address systems for computers, humans understandably have difficulty remembering them. Thus, a system called the Domain Name System (DNS) was developed to map IP addresses to more intuitive identifiers and vice versa. You can use `www.netspace.org` instead of `128.148.157.6`.

It is important to realize that these domain names are not used or understood by IP. When an application wants to transmit data to another machine on the Internet, it must first translate the domain name to an IP address using the DNS. A receiving application can perform a reverse translation, using the DNS to return a domain name given an IP address. There is not a one-to-one correspondence between IP addresses and domain names: a domain name can map to multiple IP addresses, and multiple IP addresses can map to the same domain name.

CAUTION

Even more important to note is that the entire body of DNS data cannot be trusted. Varied systems through the world are responsible for maintaining DNS records. DNS servers can be tricked, and servers can be set up that are populated with false information. In fact, a security hole in early Java implementations was created by an inappropriate trust of the DNS.

Transmission Control Protocol (TCP)

Most Internet applications use TCP to implement the transport layer. TCP provides a reliable, connection-oriented, continuous-stream protocol. The implications of these characteristics are:

- Reliable When TCP segments, the smallest unit of TCP transmissions, are lost or corrupted, the TCP implementation will detect this and retransmit necessary segments.
- Connection-oriented TCP sets up a connection with a remote system by transmitting control information, often known as a handshake, before beginning a communication. At the end of the connect, a similar closing handshake ends the transmission.
- Continuous-stream TCP provides a communications medium that allows for an arbitrary number of bytes to be sent and received smoothly; once a connection has been

established, TCP segments provide the application layer the appearance of a continuous flow of data.

Because of these characteristics, it is easy to see why TCP would be used by most Internet applications. TCP makes it very easy to create a network application, freeing you from worrying how the data is broken up or about coding error correction routines. However, TCP requires a significant amount of overhead and perhaps you might want to code routines that more efficiently provide reliable transmissions, given the parameters of your application. Furthermore, retransmission of lost data may be inappropriate for your application, because such information's usefulness may have expired. In these instances, UDP serves as an alternative, described in the following section, "User Datagram Protocol (UDP)."

An important addressing scheme that TCP defines is the port. Ports separate various TCP communications streams that are running concurrently on the same system. For server applications, which wait for TCP clients to initiate contact, a specific port can be established from where communications will originate. These concepts come together in a programming abstraction known as sockets.

▶ **See** "TCP Socket Basics," **p. 700**

User Datagram Protocol (UDP)

UDP is a low-overhead alternative to TCP for host-to-host communications. In contrast to TCP, UDP has the following features:

- Unreliable UDP has no mechanism for detecting errors, nor retransmitting lost or corrupted information.
- Connectionless UDP does not negotiate a connection before transmitting data. Information is sent with the assumption that the recipient will be listening.
- Message-oriented UDP enables applications to send self-contained messages within UDP datagrams, the unit of UDP transmission. The application must package all information within individual datagrams.

For some applications, UDP is more appropriate than TCP. For instance, with the Network Time Protocol (NTP), lost data indicating the current time would be invalid by the time it was retransmitted. In a LAN environment, Network File System (NFS) can more efficiently provide reliability at the application layer and thus uses UDP.

As with TCP, UDP provides the addressing scheme of ports, allowing for many applications to simultaneously send and receive datagrams. UDP ports are distinct from TCP ports. For example, one application can respond to UDP port 512 while another unrelated service handles TCP port 512.

Uniform Resource Locator (URL)

While IP addresses uniquely identify systems on the Internet, and ports identify TCP or UDP services on a system, URLs provide a universal identification scheme at the application level. Anyone who has used a Web browser is familiar with URLs, though their complete syntax may not be self-evident. URLs were developed to create a common format of identifying resources on the Web, but they were designed to be general enough so as to encompass applications that predated the Web by decades. Similarly, the URL syntax is flexible enough to accommodate future protocols.

URL Syntax

The primary classification of URLs is the scheme, which usually corresponds to an application protocol. Schemes include HTTP, FTP, Telnet, and Gopher. The rest of the URL syntax is in a format that depends on the scheme. These two portions of information are separated by a colon:

```
scheme-name:scheme-info
```

Thus, while **mailto:dwb@netspace.org** indicates "send mail to user 'dwb' at the machine netspace.org," **ftp://dwb@netspace.org/** means "open an FTP connection to netspace.org and log in as user dwb."

General URL Format

Most URLs conform to a general format that follows this pattern:

```
scheme-name://host:port/file-info#internal-reference
```

`Scheme-name` is an URL scheme such as HTTP, FTP, or Gopher. `Host` is the domain name or IP address of the remote system. `Port` is the port number on which the service is listening; because most application protocols define a standard port, unless a non-standard port is being used, the port and the colon that delimits it from the host are omitted. `File-info` is the resource requested on the remote system, which often is a file. However, the file portion may actually execute a server program and it usually includes a path to a specific file on the system. The `internal-reference` is usually the identifier of a named anchor within an HTML page. A named anchor enables a link to target a particular location within an HTML page. Usually this is not used, and this token with the `#` character that delimits it is omitted.

Realize that this general format is very much an over-simplification that only agrees with common use. For more complete information on URLs, read the following resource:

http://www.netspace.org/users/dwb/url-guide.html

Java and URLs

Java provides a very powerful and elegant mechanism for creating network client applications, allowing you to use relatively few statements to obtain resources from the Internet. The `java.net` package contains the sources of this power, the `URL` and `URLConnection` classes.

NOTE The Security Manager of Java browsers generally prohibits applets from opening a network connection to a machine other than the one from which the applet was downloaded. This security feature significantly limits what applets can accomplish. This holds true for all Java networking described in this and subsequent chapters. Java applications, however, are under no such restrictions.

The *URL* Class

This class enables you to easily create a data structure containing all the necessary information to obtain the remote resource. After an `URL` object has been created, you can obtain the various portions of the URL according to the general format. The `URL` object also enables you to obtain the remote data.

The `URL` class has four constructors:

```
public URL(String spec) throws MalformedURLException;
public URL(String protocol, String host, String file)
throws MalformedURLException;
public URL(String protocol, String host, int port, String file)
throws MalformedURLException;
public URL(URL context, String spec)
throws MalformedURLException;
```

The first constructor is the most commonly used and enables you to create an `URL` object with a simple declaration like:

```
URL myURL = new URL("http://www.yahoo.com/");
```

The second and third constructors enable you to specify explicitly the various portions of the URL. The last constructor enables you to use relative URLs. A relative URL only contains part of the URL syntax; the rest of the data is completed from the URL to which the resource is relative. This will often be seen in HTML pages, where a reference to merely `more.html` means "`get more.html` from the same machine and directory where the current document resides."

Here are examples of these constructors:

```
URL firstURLObject - new URL("http://www.yahoo.com/");
URL secondURLObject = new URL("http","www.yahoo.com","/");
URL thirdURLObject =
   new URL("http","www.yahoo.com",80,"/");
URL fourthURLObject = new URL(firstURLObject,"text/suggest.html");
```

The first three statements create URL objects that all refer to the Yahoo! home page, while the fourth creates a reference to `"text/suggest.html"` relative to Yahoo's home page (such as `http://www.yahoo.com/text/suggest.html`). All of these constructors throw a `MalformedURLException`, which you will generally want to catch. The example shown later in Listing 30.1 illustrates this. Note that once you create an `URL` object, you can change to which resource it points. To accomplish this, you must create a new `URL` object.

Connecting to an URL

Now that you've created an `URL` object, you will want to actually obtain some useful data. There are two main avenues of so doing: reading directly from the `URL` object or obtaining an `URLConnection` instance from it.

Reading directly from the URL object requires less code, but is much less flexible, and it only allows a read-only connection. This is limiting, as many Web services enable you to write information that will be handled by a server application. The URL class has an openStream() method that returns an InputStream object through which the remote resource can be read byte-by-byte.

Handling data as individual bytes is cumbersome, so you will often want to embed the returned InputStream within a DataInputStream object, allowing you to read the input line-by-line. This coding strategy is often referred to as using a decorator, as the DataInputStream decorates the InputStream by providing a more specialized interface. The fo=towing code fragment obtains an InputStream directly from the URL object and then decorates that stream:

```
URL whiteHouse = new URL("http://www.whitehouse.gov/");
InputStream undecoratedInput = whiteHouse.openStream();
DataInputStream decoratedInput =
   new DataInputStream(undecoratedInput);
```

Another more flexible way of connecting to the remote resource is by using the openConnection() method of the URL class. This method returns an URLConnection object that provides a number of very powerful methods that you can use to customize your connection to the remote resource.

For example, unlike the URL class, an URLConnection enables you to obtain both an InputStream and an OutputStream. This has a significant impact upon the HTTP protocol, whose access methods include both GET and POST. With the GET method, an application merely requests a resource and then reads the response. The POST method is often used to provide input to server applications by requesting a resource, writing data to the server with the HTTP request body, and then reading the response. In order to use the POST method, you can write to an OutputStream obtained from the URLConnection prior to reading from the InputStream. If you read first, the GET method will be used and a subsequent write attempt will be invalid.

The following code fragment demonstrates using an URLConnection object to contact a remote server application using the HTTP POST method by writing to an OutputStream decorated by a PrintStream instance. www.javasoft.com makes a CGI server application available to test out these methods. The code connects to a CGI application which reverses the POST data and then reads the reversed data from a decorated InputStream.

```
URL reverseURL =
new URL("http://www.javasoft.com/cgi-bin/backwards");
URLConnection reverseConn = reverseURL.openConnection();
PrintStream output =
new PrintStream(reverseConn.getOutputStream());
DataInputStream input =
new DataInputStream(reverseConn.getInputStream());
output.println("string=TexttoReverse");
String reversedText = input.readLine();
```

HTTP-Centric Classes

After reading this overview of the URL and URLConnection classes, you may begin to suspect that the methods of these classes are designed with HTTP (Hypertext Transport Protocol) in mind. If you look at the complete class specifications, this notion is confirmed. Though the `http` scheme is only one of many classifications of URLs, these classes are very HTTP-centric.

HTTP is likely to be the most used standard protocol for your communications on the Web and Internet, so this is not a significant concern. You should be aware, however, that many of these methods are useful only when working with HTTP URLs.

An Example: Customized AltaVista Searching

Now that you've learned the basics of Java networking, it would be nice to do something actually useful. The AltaVista search engine provides a very powerful way of searching for documents on the Web; however, it is designed to only return a few hits at a time to optimize performance. As other astute and sagacious programmers have pointed out, developing a small client to automatically request all of the search results and then present them at once is very useful. The `AltaVistaList` Java application does just that.

AltaVista is a powerful search engine that allows you to find documents on the Web. The AltaVista home page is available at `http://www.altavista.digital.com/`.

When designing this application, first consider what public methods this class should have. It needs:

- A method to start the application.
- A method to initialize the object.
- A method to print out all of the results.
- A number of protected methods to be used by the object itself: a method to create a query to send to AltaVista, a method to get a single HTML page from AltaVista, and a method to parse out the hit results from the rest of the returned HTML page.

Listing 30.1 shows the entire code of the `AltaVistaList` application. When executed with a series of keywords, it returns an HTML page that contains all of the hits returned by AltaVista.

B„ETION

Note that this application is limited by the specific mechanisms AltaVista uses to receive and present information. These mechanisms are not guaranteed to remain static—thus, if AltaVista changes, this program fails.

Listing 30.1 ***AltaVistaList.java***

```
import java.net.*;    // Import the names of the classes
import java.io.*;     // to be used.

/**
 * This application creates a single, concise HTML page
```

continues

Listing 30.1 Continued

```
 * of hits from the AltaVista search engine given a
 * search string.
 * @author David W. Baker
 * @version 1.1
 */
public class AltaVistaList {
   private static final String AGENT_NAME =
      "java-alta-search";
   private static final String AGENT_VERSION = "1.0";
   private static final String SEARCH_URL =
       "http://www.altavista.digital.com/cgi-bin/query";
   private int totalHits = 0;
   private StringBuffer outputList = new StringBuffer();

   /**
    * This starts the application.
    * @param args Program arguments - the search string.
    */
   public static void main(String[] args) {
      if (args.length == 0) {
         System.out.println(
            "Usage: AltaVistaList search string");
         System.exit(1);
      }
      AltaVistaList runApp = new AltaVistaList(args);
      runApp.printOutput(System.out);
      System.exit(0);
   }

   /**
    * This constructor connects to AltaVista and obtains
    * all of the relevant hits.
    * @param args The search tokens.
    */
   public AltaVistaList(String[] args) {
      String hitData;      // Store incoming data.
      int startHits = 0;   // Get the next 10 hits from here.
      String searchSyntax = createQuery(args);

      URLConnection.setDefaultRequestProperty("User-Agent",
         AGENT_NAME + "/" + AGENT_VERSION);
      while (true) {
         hitData = getPage(SEARCH_URL + "?" + searchSyntax +
            startHits); // Go get a page of hits.
         hitData = getHits(hitData);  // Extract the hits.
         // If there were no hits in the page, hitData will
         // be null. If there were hits, append them to
         // the outputList, increment to the next 10 hits,
         // and go through the loop again.
         if (hitData != null) {
            outputList.append(hitData + "\n");
            startHits += 10;
         // Otherwise, break from the loop.
         } else {
```

```
            break;
         }
      }
   }

   /**
    * This method builds an AltaVista search query
    * string.
    * @param searchTokens An array of search tokens.
    * @return The search query string built.
    */
   protected String createQuery(String[] searchTokens) {
      StringBuffer searchString = new StringBuffer();

      // Append the tokens to a single string.
      for(int index = 0; index < searchTokens.length;
            index++) {
         searchString.append(searchTokens[index]);
         // Add a space if there's another token coming up.
         if (index < searchTokens.length-1) {
            searchString.append(" ");
         }
      }
      // URL encode the string.
      String encodedSearchString =
         URLEncoder.encode(searchString.toString());
      // Return the proper query string.
      return "what=web&fmt=c&pg=q&q=" + encodedSearchString
         + "&stq=";
   }

   /**
    * This method obtains a page from the Web.
    * @param url The URL of the page to obtain.
    * @return The page obtained.
    */
   protected String getPage(String url) {
      // A buffer for the incoming page.
      StringBuffer page = new StringBuffer();
      String nextLine;  // The next line in the input stream.

      try {
         URL urlObject = new URL(url);
         URLConnection agent = urlObject.openConnection();
         DataInputStream input =
            new DataInputStream(agent.getInputStream());
         // While readLine() doesn't return null, append
         // then next line to the buffer.
         while((nextLine = input.readLine()) != null) {
            page.append(nextLine+"\n");
         }
         input.close();
      } catch(MalformedURLException excpt) {
         System.out.println("Badly formed URL: " + excpt);
      } catch(IOException excpt) {
```


continues

Listing 30.1 Continued

```
            System.out.println("Failed I/O: " + excpt);
        }
        // Convert the buffer to a string and return.
        return page.toString();
    }

    /**
     * This method extracts the list of hits from a returned
     * AltaVista results page.
     * @param hitPage The page returned from AltaVista.
     * @return The list of hits.
     */
    protected String getHits(String hitPage) {
        int first,last;     // Begin/end of a substring.
        int notFound = -1;  // Not found return for indexOf().
        String hitSection = null;  // The hits part of page.

        // Go to the first "<a href=" after "<pre>".
        first = hitPage.indexOf("<pre>") + "<pre>".length();
        first = hitPage.indexOf("<a href=",first);
        // End pointer at "</pre>".
        last = hitPage.indexOf("</pre>");

        // If our beginning is after our end, return.
        if (last < first) {
            return hitSection;
        }
        // If neither substring is found, return.
        if (first == notFound || last == notFound) {
            System.err.println("Bad search page format");
            return hitSection;
        }

        // Cut out the substring.
        hitSection = hitPage.substring(first,last);
        first = last = 0;
        totalHits += 1;    // Found one hit.
        // Go through the page line by line.
        while((last = hitSection.indexOf("\n",first))
                  != notFound) {
            // Find the next "<a href=" which should be
            // immediately after the \n.
            first = hitSection.indexOf("<a href=",last);
            // If it's not, return the current substring.
            if (first != (last+1)) {
                return hitSection.substring(0,last);
            // Otherwise, another hit has been found.
            } else {
                totalHits += 1;
            }
        }
        return hitSection; // Return the substring.
    }
```

```
    /**
     * This method prints the list of hits obtained from
     * AltaVista.
     * @param sendOutput Where to print the output.
     */
    public void printOutput(PrintStream sendOutput) {
       sendOutput.print("<!DOCTYPE HTML PUBLIC \"-//IETF//" +
          "DTD HTML//EN\">\n<HTML>\n<HEAD>\n<TITLE>" +
          AGENT_NAME + "</TITLE>\n</HEAD>\n<BODY>\n<H1>" +
          "Search Results</H1>\n<P><STRONG>Total number of " +
          "hits: " + totalHits + "</STRONG></P>\n<PRE>\n" +
          outputList + "</PRE>\n</BODY>\n</HTML>\n");
    }
}
```


The *main()* Method: Starting the Application First, the application imports the two packages it will be using, allowing its method invocations of the Java API to be more brief. Then the class is declared and a number of private instance variables are initialized: `search_URL` is the URL to the AltaVista search engine, `totalHits` maintains a count of the hits returned, and `outputList` is a buffer for the HTML of the returned hits.

The `main()` method enables this code to be executed as an application. This method checks for an appropriate set of arguments and creates an instance of the `AltaVistList` class. It then tells that instance to print its output, passing the `printOutput()` method `System.out`. `System.out` is a static reference to a `PrintStream` object within the `java.lang.System` class. By passing this `PrintStream` to `printOutput()`, it indicates that the `AltaVistaList` instance should send its data to standard output. Finally, `main()` exits the application with a return value of `0`, indicating that the execution completed normally.

The *AltaVistaList* Constructor The class' only constructor takes an argument of a reference to an array of `String` objects. It passes this array reference to the `createQuery()` method, described below, which builds a query for the AltaVista search engine. The constructor then invokes a static method of the `URLConnection` class, `setDefaultRequestProperty()`:

```
URLConnection.setDefaultRequestProperty("User-Agent",
AGENT_NAME + "/" + AGENT_VERSION);
```

Note that because this is a static method, it is not invoked through an instance of `URLConnection`. Instead, the method is invoked through the class itself. This method indicates that all HTTP requests should specify the `"User-Agent"` field as being equal to a string that identifies this application. The HTTP `User-Agent` is a field that Web clients use to tell servers their program name, allowing servers to keep track of what clients are visiting the site. For instance, Netscape browsers send a `User-Agent` field that includes "Mozilla," while the Internet Explorer sends "Explorer." Unfortunately, as of the writing of this chapter, the JDK has yet to implement this method, and the `User-Agent` remains the default `Java<version>`. This code has been left in with the assumption that the JDK will soon complete its implementation of the Java API.

The constructor then enters an infinite loop. In this loop, it calls the `getPage()` method with an URL of a page to receive. This URL is the URL of the AltaVista search engine appended by a question mark, the query returned by `createQuery()`, and a number from where the hit list should start. AltaVista lists hits 10 at a time, and the `startHits` counter enables the `AltaVistaList` application to increment throughout the entire list of hits. The returned page is passed to `getHits()`, which strips out the hits from the rest of the HTML page. If what remains is a null `String` reference, the application breaks from the loop. Otherwise, it appends the data to a `StringBuffer` and then increments the `startHits` counter to set up for retrieving the next ten hits.

The *createQuery()* Method: Building the Query String This protected method is used internally by an instance of the `AltaVistaList` class, building the query syntax for the AltaVista search engine. This query string follows this format:

```
what=web&fmt=c&pg=q&q=<search string>&stq=<n>
```

While this appears confusing, this is merely a set of five parameters separated by ampersands. `what=web` tells AltaVista to search its index of Web pages. `fmt=c` asks for output to be returned in a compact format, facilitating parsing and efficient presentation. `pq=q` indicates that you are doing a simple query using the basic syntax language. `q=` identifies your search string, which must be encoded in the URL format, encoding spaces, and other special characters. Finally, `stq=` tells AltaVista which query result item to start from when returning its data. AltaVista returns results 10 at a time, and `stq=` enables you to obtain the results after the first 10n.

`createQuery()` takes an array of `String` objects and appends the entire array to a `StringBuffer` object. The contents of each `String` are separated by a space. Another static method is used, this time `encode()` from the `URLEncoder` class. This is a very useful method:

```
String encodedSearchString =
URLEncoder.encode(searchString.toString());
```

The `URLEncoder.encode()` static method takes a `String` as an argument and returns a corresponding `String` that is in URL encoded format. This format allows spaces and other special characters to be encapsulated within an URL.

`createQuery()` then returns the appropriate query with this encoded `String` embedded. Note that `createQuery()` omits the number for the `stq=` parameter, as that information is appended within the `main()` method.

The *getPage()* Method: Retrieving a Web Page `getPage()` is a method that demonstrates the concepts learned to this point regarding Java and networking. Passed a `String` that contains an URL, the method creates an `URL` instance and then obtains an `URLConnection` from that instance. It sets up a `DataInputStream` to read data from that connection line-by-line, and then enters a loop. This `while` loop reads the next line of data, exiting the loop if the next line is null. The method appends each line to a `StringBuffer` object, and once completed, uses that class' `toString()` method to return a `String`.

The *getHits()* Method: Parsing Out the Hits The logic of this method is a little hard to follow, but its goal is to take a `String` containing an HTML page from the AltaVista search engine and strip out the returned hits. It accomplishes this by using two pointers, `first` and `last`, to indicate the beginning and end of appropriate substrings within the page.

`getHits()` looks for the first instance of `<a href=` after the first occurrence of `<pre>`, which is where the hit list should begin. The end of the hit list should be at the first `</pre>` tag. If no such string is found, the method returns with a null `String` reference, indicating that the page was devoid of hits.

Otherwise, the method pares down the HTML page to a substring and iterates through that data. Each hit should be a new line starting with `<a href=`. While this is the case, the method keeps looping until it comes to the end of the data. Each line that it encounters indicates a new hit has been found, and the method increments an instance variable used to keep track of the total number of hits. Once completed, the method returns the `String` containing the hits.

The *printOutput* Method: Displaying the Results The `printOutput()` method is very simple. It takes a `PrintStream` as an argument and then prints an HTML page to that stream. Instead of hard-coding `System.out`, this method is flexible and enables output to be easily directed to some other stream. The HTML page printed includes the total number of hits and then a preformatted section containing each hit on a separate line.

Running *AltaVistaList* To run the `AltaVistaList` application, first compile it with javac. Then, execute it with the Java interpreter, passing it an appropriate set of arguments. For instance, to see what additional information is available on the Web with both `Java` and `URL` on the same page, use the following command:

```
java AltaVistaList Java URL
```

CHAPTER 31

TCP Sockets

In this chapter

TCP Socket Basics

Sockets are a programming abstraction that isolates your code from the low-level implementations of the TCP/IP protocol stack. TCP sockets enable you to quickly develop your own custom client/server applications. Although the `URL` class described in Chapter 30, "Communications and Networking," is very useful with well-established protocols, sockets allow you to develop your own modes of communication.

Sockets, as a programming interface, were originally developed at the University of California at Berkeley as a tool to easily accomplish network programming. Originally part of UNIX operating systems, the concept of sockets has been incorporated into a wide variety of operating environments, including Java.

What Is a Socket?

A socket is a handle to a communications link over the network with another application. A TCP socket uses the TCP protocol, inheriting the behavior of that transport protocol. Four pieces of information are needed to create a TCP socket:

- The local system's IP address
- The TCP port number the local application is using
- The remote system's IP address
- The TCP port number to which the remote application is responding

The original TCP specification, RFC 793, used the term socket to mean the combination of a system's IP address and port number. A pair of sockets identified a unique end-to-end TCP connection. In this discussion, the term socket is used at a higher level, and a socket is your interface to a single network connection. RFC 793 is available at:

```
ftp://ftp.internic.net/rfc/rfc793.txt
```

Sockets are often used in client/server applications. A centralized service waits for various remote machines to request specific resources, handling each request as it arrives. For clients to know how to communicate with the server, standard application protocols are assigned well-known ports. On UNIX operating systems, ports below 1024 can only be bound by applications with super-user (for example, `root`) privileges; thus, for control, these well-known ports lie within this range, by convention. Some well-known ports are shown in Table 31.1.

The Internet Assigned Numbers Authority (IANA) assigns well-known ports to application protocols. At the time of this writing, the current listing of the well-known ports is within RFC 1700, available from:

```
ftp://ftp.internic.net/rfc/rfc1700.txt
```

Table 31.1 Well-Known TCP Ports and Services

Port	Service
21	FTP
23	Telnet
25	SMTP (Standard Mail Transfer Protocol)
79	Finger
80	HTTP

For many application protocols, you can merely use the Telnet application to connect to the service port and then manually emulate a client. This may help you understand how client/server communications work.

Client applications must also obtain, or bind, a port to establish a socket connection. Because the client initiates the communication with the server, such a port number could conveniently be assigned at runtime. Client applications are usually run by normal, unprivileged users on UNIX systems, and thus these ports are allocated from the range above 1024. This convention has held when migrated to other operating systems, and client applications are generally given a dynamically allocated or ephemeral port above 1024.

Because no two applications can bind the same port on the same machine simultaneously, a socket uniquely identifies a communications link. Realize that a server may respond to two clients on the same port, because the clients will be on different systems and/or different ports; the uniqueness of the link's characteristics are preserved. Figure 31.1 illustrates this concept.

Figure 31.1 shows a server application responding to three sockets through port 80, the well-known port for HTTP. Two sockets are communicating with the same remote machine, while the third is to a separate system. Note the unique combination of the four TCP socket characteristics.

Figure 31.1 also shows a simplified view of a client-server connection. Many machines are configured with multiple IP interfaces—they have more than one IP address. These distinct IP addresses allow for separate connections to be maintained. Thus, a server may have an application accept connections on port 80 for one IP address while a different application handles connections to port 80 for another IP address. These connections are distinct. The Java socket classes, described within the next section, "Java TCP Socket Classes," allow you to select a specific local interface for the connection.

Java TCP Socket Classes

Java has a number of classes that allow you to create socket-based network applications. The two classes you use include `java.net.Socket` and `java.net.ServerSocket`.

The `Socket` class is used for normal two-way socket communications and has four commonly used constructors:

```
public Socket(String host, int port)
➥throws UnknownHostException, IOException;
public Socket(InetAddress address, int port)
➥throws IOException;
public Socket(String host, int port, InetAddress localAddr,
➥int localPort) throws UnknownHostException, IOException;
public Socket(InetAddress address, int port,
➥InetAddress localAddr, int localPort)
➥throws UnknownHostException, IOException
```

The first constructor allows you to create a socket by just specifying the domain name of the remote machine within a `String` instance and the remote port. The second enables you to create a socket with an `InetAddress` object. The third and fourth are similar to the first two, except they allow you to choose the local interface and port number for the connection. If your machine has multiple IP addresses, you can use these constructors to choose a specific interface to use.

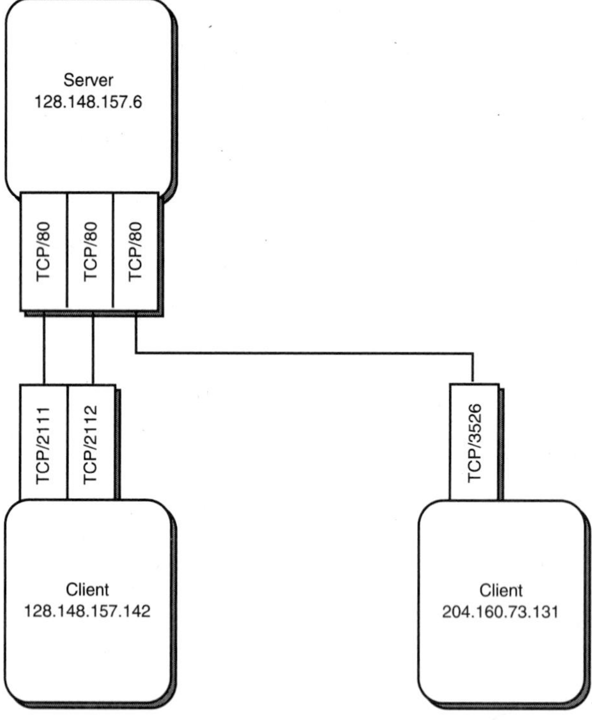

FIG. 31.1
Many clients can connect to a single server through separate sockets.

An `InetAddress` is an object that stores an IP address of a remote system. It has no public constructor methods, but does have a number of static methods that return instances of `InetAddress`. Thus, `InetAddress` objects can be created through static method invocations:

```
try {
InetAddress remoteOP =
InetAddress.getByName("www.microsoft.com");
InetAddress[] allRemoteIPs =
InetAddress.getAllByName("www.microsoft.com");
InetAddress myIP = InetAddress.getLocalHost();
} catch(UnknownHostException excpt) {
System.err.println("Unknown host: " + excpt);
}
```

The first method returns an `InetAddress` object with an IP address for `www.microsoft.com`. The second obtains an array of `InetAddress` objects, one for each IP address mapped to `www.microsoft.com`. (Recall from Chapter 30 that the same domain name can correspond to several IP addresses.) The last `InetAddress` method creates an instance with the IP address of the local machine. All of these methods throw an `UnknownHostException`, which is caught in the previous example.

TIP The DNS, described in Chapter 30, is a distributed database whose information changes over time. The `InetAddress` class, however, is written so that it only performs DNS resolution once for each hostname over the life of the Java runtime. All subsequent `InetAddress` objects created for a particular hostname will be returned from a persistent cache.

Thus, if you have a long-running Java application, the IP address contained within an InetAddress object may become inappropriate. The comments within the JDK code indicate that this was done for security reasons. In your programming, this may become an important fact to be aware of.

▶ **See** "Internet Protocol (IP)," **p. 686**

The `Socket` class has methods that allow you to read and write through the socket—the `getInputStream()` and `getOutputStream()` methods. To make applications simpler to design, the streams these methods return are usually decorated by another `java.io` object, such as `BufferedReaderandPrintWriter`, respectively. Both `getInputStream()` and `getOutputStream()` throw an `IOException`, which should be caught. Note the following:

```
try {
Socket netspace = new Socket("www.netspace.org",7);
BufferedReader input = new BufferedReader(
new InputStreamReader(netspace.getInputStream()));
PrintWriter output = new PrintWriter(
netspace.getOutputStream(), true);
} catch(UnknownHostException expt) {
System.err.println("Unknown host: " + excpt);
System.exit(1);
} catch(IOException excpt) {
System.err.println("Failed I/O: " + excpt);
System.exit(1);
}
```

To write a one-line message and then read a one-line response, you need only use the decorated stream:

```
output.println("test");
String testResponse = input.readLine();
```

After you have completed communicating through the socket, you must first close the `InputStream` and `OutputStream` instances, and then close the socket.

```
output.close();
input.close();
netspace.close();
```

To create a TCP server, it is necessary to understand a new class, `ServerSocket`. `ServerSocket` allows you to bind a port and wait for clients to connect, setting up a complete `Socket` object at that time. `ServerSocket` has three constructors:

```
public ServerSocket(int port) throws IOException;
public ServerSocket(int port, int count)
➥throws IOException;
public ServerSocket(int port, int count,
➥InetAddress localAddr) throws IOException;
```

The first constructor creates a listening socket at the port specified, allowing for the default number of 50 clients waiting in the connection queue. The second constructor enables you to change the length of the connection queue, allowing greater or fewer clients to wait to be processed by the server. The final constructor allows you to specify a local interface to listen for connections. If your machine has multiple IP addresses, this constructor allows you to provide services to specific IP addresses. Should you use the first two constructors on such a machine, the `ServerSocket` will accept connections to any of the machine's IP addresses.

After creating a `ServerSocket`, the `accept()` method can be used to wait for a client to connect. The `accept()` method blocks until a client connects, and then returns a `Socket` instance for communicating to the client. Blocking is a programming term that means a routine enters an internal loop indefinitely, returning only when a specific condition occurs. The program's thread of execution does not proceed past the blocking routine until it returns—that is, when the specific condition happens.

The following code creates a `ServerSocket` at port 2222, accepts a connection, and then opens streams through which communication can take place once a client connects:

```
try {
    ServerSocket server = new ServerSocket(2222);
    Socket clientConn = server.accept();

    BufferedReader input = new BufferedReader(
    new InputStreamReader(clientConn.getInputStream()));
    PrintWriter output = new PrintWriter(
    clientConn.getInputStream(), true);
} catch(IOException excpt) {
    System.err.println("Failed I/O: " + excpt);
    System.exit(1);
}
```

After communications are complete with the client, the server must close the streams and then close the `Socket` instance, as previously described.

NOTE The socket classes in the Java API provide a convenient stream interface by using your host's TCP implementation. Within the JDK, a subclass of the abstract class `SocketImpl` performs the interaction with your machine's TCP. It is possible to define a new `SocketImpl` that could use a different transport layer than plain TCP. You can change this transport layer implementation by creating your own subclass of `SocketImpl` and defining your own `SocketImplFactory`. However, in this chapter, it is assumed that you are using the JDK's socket implementation, which uses TCP.

Customizing Socket Behavior

The JDK allows you to specify certain parameters that affect how your TCP sockets behave. These parameters mimic the behavior of some of the options available within the Berkeley sockets API and are often referred to by the names within that API: `SO_SNDBUF`, `SO_RCVBUF`, `SO_TIMEOUT`, `SO_LINGER`, and `TCP_NODELAY`.

The `Socket` class has a method `setSoTimeout(int timeout)` that allows you to specify a timeout in milliseconds. Any subsequent attempts to read from the `InputStream` of this socket waits for data only until this timeout expires. If the timeout expires, an `InterruptedIOException` is thrown. By default, the timeout is 0, indicating that a `read()` call should block forever or until an `IOException` is thrown.

The `ServerSocket` class also has a `setSoTimeout(int timeout)` method, but the timeout applies to the `accept()` method. If you set a timeout, a subsequent call to `accept()`waits only the specified number of milliseconds for a client to connect. When the timeout expires, an `InterruptedIOException` is thrown. For most applications, it is appropriate for a server to wait indefinitely for clients to connect, but in certain instances, the ability to timeout is valuable. When the exception is thrown, the `ServerSocket` instance is still valid, and, if you want, you can call `accept()` again.

The `setSoLinger(boolean on, int linger)` method of the `Socket` class allows you to modify how the `close()` method behaves. Normally, when you `close()` the socket, any data that is queued by your machine's TCP or has yet to be acknowledged by the recipient is dealt with in the background; the `close()` function does not block until TCP has completed the transmission. If you enable the `setSoLinger()` option, this changes. When the option is enabled with a timeout of 0, a `close()` causes any data queued for transmission to be discarded, and the recipient is sent a reset segment. To wit, the connection abruptly aborts. When the option is enabled with a positive timeout, `close()`blocks until all of the data has been sent and acknowledged by the recipient, or the timeout expires, in which case an `IOException` is thrown. This option allows your
application to become more aware of how successful TCP is at sending all of the data to the recipient.

The Socket class was improved in JDK 1.2 to allow you to get and manipulate the size of the send and receive buffers (`SO_SNDBUF` and `SO_RCVBUF`, respectively). `Socket's` `getSendBufferSize()` and `getReceiveBufferSize()` obtain the size of the send or receive buffers. The `setSendBufferSize(int size)` and `setReceiveBufferSize(int size)`, on the other hand, are used to specify hints to the socket factory as to what size these buffers should be.

For high-volume sockets, setting the size higher tends to increase performance, while on lower-volume sockets, or those with known block sizes, setting the number lower tends to decrease the backlog of data. All four methods can throw a `SocketException` if something goes wrong.

The last socket option that Java TCP sockets support is set within the `setTcpNoDelay(boolean on)` option of the `Socket` class. This allows you to disable the use of the Nagle algorithm in your machine's TCP implementation. The Nagle algorithm instructs a TCP implementation to limit the number of unacknowledged small segments to one. When sending data a small piece at a time, TCP using the Nagle algorithm waits until each piece is acknowledged before sending another. This greatly reduces congestion on networks, and in most instances, it is to your advantage to leave the Nagle algorithm enabled. However, there are times when an application must have small messages transmitted without delay, and the `setTcpNoDelay()` method allows you to disable the standard behaviors.

NOTE The Nagle algorithm was originally proposed within RFC 896, available from:

`ftp://ftp.internic.net/rfc/rfc896.txt`

Creating a TCP Client/Server Application

Having understood the building blocks of TCP socket programming, the next challenge is to develop a practical application. To demonstrate this process, you will create a stock quote server and client. The client will contact the server and request stock information for a set of stock identifiers. The server will read data from a file, periodically checking to see if the file has been updated, and send the requested data to the client.

Designing an Application Protocol

Given the needs of our system, our protocol has six basic steps:

1. Client connects to server.
2. Server responds to client with a message indicating the currentness of the data.
3. The client requests data for a stock identifier.
4. The server responds.
5. Repeat steps 3 and 4 until the client ends the dialog.
6. Terminate the connection.

Implementing this design, you come up with a more detailed protocol. The server waits for the client on port 1701. When the client first connects, the server responds with:

```
+HELLO time-string
```

`time-string` indicates when the stock data to be returned was last updated. Next, the client sends a request for information. The server follows this by a response providing the data, as follows:

```
STOCK: stock-id
+stock-id stock-data
```

`stock-id` is a stock identifier consisting of a series of capital letters. `stock-data` is a string of characters detailing the performance of the particular stock. The client can request information on other stocks by repeating this request sequence.

Should the client send a request for information regarding a stock of which the server is unaware, the server responds with:

```
-ERR UNKNOWN STOCK ID
```

If the client sends a command requesting information about a stock, but omits the stock ID, the server sends:

```
-ERR MALFORMED COMMAND
```

Should the client send an invalid command, the server responds with:

```
-ERR UNKNOWN COMMAND
```

When the client is done requesting information, it ends the communication and the server confirms the end of the session:

```
QUIT
+BYE
```

The next example demonstrates a conversation using the following protocol. All server responses should be preceded by a + or - character, while the client requests should not. In this example, the client is requesting information on three stocks: ABC, XYZ, and AAM. The server has information only regarding the last two:

```
+HELLO Tue, Jul 16, 1996 09:15:13 PDT
STOCK: ABC
-ERR UNKNOWN STOCK ID
STOCK: XYZ
+XYZ Last: 20 7/8; Change -0 1/4; Volume 60,400
STOCK: AAM
+AAM Last 35; Change 0; Volume 2,500
QUIT
+BYE
```

Developing the Stock Client

The client application to implement the preceding protocol should be fairly simple. The code is shown in Listing 31.1.

Listing 31.1 *StockQuoteClient.java*

```
import java.io.*;     // Import the names of the packages
import java.net.*;    // to be used.

/**
 * This is an application which obtains stock information
 * using our new application protocol.
 * @author David W. Baker
 * @version 1.2
 */
public class StockQuoteClient {
   // The Stock Quote server listens at this port.
   private static final int SERVER_PORT = 1701;
   // Should your quoteSend PrintWriter autoflush?
   private static final boolean AUTOFLUSH = true;
   private String serverName;
   private Socket quoteSocket = null;
   private BufferedReader quoteReceive = null;
   private PrintWriter quoteSend = null;
   private String[] stockIDs;    // Array of requested IDs.
   private String[] stockInfo;   // Array of returned data.
   private String currentAsOf = null;  // Timestamp of data.

   /**
    * Start the application running, first checking the
    * arguments, then instantiating a StockQuoteClient, and
    * finally telling the instance to print out its data.
    * @param args Arguments which should be <server> <stock ids>
    */
   public static void main(String[] args) {
      if (args.length < 2) {
         System.out.println(
            "Usage: StockQuoteClient <server> <stock ids>");
         System.exit(1);
      }
      StockQuoteClient client = new StockQuoteClient(args);
      client.printQuotes(System.out);
      System.exit(0);
   }

   /**
    * This constructor manages the retrieval of the
    * stock information.
    * @param args The server followed by the stock IDs.
    */
   public StockQuoteClient(String[] args) {
      String serverInfo;

      // Server name is the first argument.
      serverName = args[0];
      // Create arrays as long as arguments - 1.
      stockIDs = new String[args.length-1];
      stockInfo = new String[args.length-1];
      // Copy the rest of the elements of the args array
      // into the stockIDs array.
```

```
   for (int index = 1; index < args.length; index++) {
      stockIDs[index-1] = args[index];
   }
   // Contact the server and return the HELLO message.
   serverInfo = contactServer();
   // Parse out the timestamp, which is everything after
   // the first space.
   if (serverInfo != null) {
      currentAsOf = serverInfo.substring(
                      serverInfo.indexOf(" ")+1);
   }
   getQuotes();   // Go get the quotes.
   quitServer();  // Close the communication.
}

/**
 * Open the initial connection to the server.
 * @return The initial connection response.
 */
protected String contactServer() {
   String serverWelcome = null;

   try {
      // Open a socket to the server.
      quoteSocket = new Socket(serverName,SERVER_PORT);
      // Obtain decorated I/O streams.
      quoteReceive = new BufferedReader(
                       new InputStreamReader(
                          quoteSocket.getInputStream()));
      quoteSend = new PrintWriter(
                        quoteSocket.getOutputStream(),
                        AUTOFLUSH);
      // Read the HELLO message.
      serverWelcome = quoteReceive.readLine();
   } catch (UnknownHostException excpt) {
      System.err.println("Unknown host " + serverName +
                            ": " + excpt);
   } catch (IOException excpt) {
      System.err.println("Failed I/O to " + serverName +
                            ": " + excpt);
   }
   return serverWelcome;   // Return the HELLO message.
}

/**
 * This method asks for all of the stock info.
 */
protected void getQuotes() {
   String response;  // Hold the response to stock query.

   // If the connection is still up.
   if (connectOK()) {
      try {
         // Iterate through all of the stocks.
         for (int index = 0; index < stockIDs.length;
```

continues

Listing 31.1 Continued

```
                 index++) {
               // Send query.
               quoteSend.println("STOCK: "+stockIDs[index]);
               // Read response.
               response = quoteReceive.readLine();
               // Parse out data.
               stockInfo[index] = response.substring(
                                   response.indexOf(" ")+1);
            }
         } catch (IOException excpt) {
            System.err.println("Failed I/O to " + serverName
                                 + ": " + excpt);
         }
      }
   }

   /**
    * This method disconnects from the server.
    * @return The final message from the server.
    */
   protected String quitServer() {
      String serverBye = null;   // BYE message.

      try {
         // If the connection is up, send a QUIT message
         // and receive the BYE response.
         if (connectOK()) {
            quoteSend.println("QUIT");
            serverBye = quoteReceive.readLine();
         }
         // Close the streams and the socket if the
         // references are not null.
         if (quoteSend != null) quoteSend.close();
         if (quoteReceive != null) quoteReceive.close();
         if (quoteSocket != null) quoteSocket.close();
      } catch (IOException excpt) {
         System.err.println("Failed I/O to server " +
                              serverName + ": " + excpt);
      }
      return serverBye; // The BYE message.
   }

   /**
    * This method prints out a report on the various
    * requested stocks.
    * @param sendOutput Where to send output.
    */
   public void printQuotes(PrintStream sendOutput) {
      // Provided that you actually received a HELLO message:
      if (currentAsOf != null) {
         sendOutput.print("INFORMATION ON REQUESTED QUOTES"
            + "\n\tCurrent As Of: " + currentAsOf + "\n\n");
         // Iterate through the array of stocks.
         for (int index = 0; index < stockIDs.length;
               index++) {
```

```
                sendOutput.print(stockIDs[index] + ":");
                if (stockInfo[index] != null)
                   sendOutput.println(" " + stockInfo[index]);
                else sendOutput.println();
             }
          }
       }

       /**
        * Conveniently determine if the socket and streams are
        * not null.
        * @return If the connection is OK.
        */
       protected boolean connectOK() {
          return (quoteSend != null && quoteReceive != null &&
                   quoteSocket != null);
       }
    }
```


The *main()* Method: Starting the Client The `main()` method first checks to see that the application has been invoked with appropriate command-line arguments, quitting if this is not the case. It then instantiates a `StockQuoteClient` with the `args` array reference and runs the `printQuotes()` method, telling the client to send its data to standard output.

The *StockQuoteClient* Constructor The goal of the constructor is to initialize the data structures, connect to the server, load the stock data from the server, and terminate the connection. The constructor creates two arrays, one into which it copies the stock IDs and the other which remains uninitialized to hold the data for each stock.

It uses the `contactServer()` method to open communications with the server, returning the opening string. Provided the connection opened properly, this string contains a timestamp indicating the currentness of the stock data. The constructor parses this string to isolate that timestamp, gets the stock data with the `getQuotes()` method, and then closes the connection with `quitServer()`.

The *contactServer()* Method: Starting the Communication Like the examples seen previously in this chapter, this method opens a socket to the server. It then creates two streams to communicate with the server. Finally, it receives the opening line from the server (for example, `+HELLO time-string`) and returns that as a String.

The *getQuotes()* Method: Obtaining the Stock Data This method performs the queries on each stock ID with which the application is invoked, now stored within the `stockIDs` array. First it calls a short method, `connectOK()`, which merely ensures that the `Socket` and streams are not null. It iterates through the `stockIDs` array, sending each in a request to the server. It reads each response, parsing out the stock data from the line returned. It stores the stock data as a separate element in the `stockInfo` array. After it has requested information on each stock, the `getQuotes()` method returns.

The *quitServer()* Method: Ending the Connection This method ends the communication with the server, first sending a `QUIT` message if the connection is still valid. Then it performs the essential steps when terminating a socket communication: it closes the streams and then the `Socket`.

The *printQuotes()* Method: Displaying the Stock Quotes Given a `PrintStream` object, such as `System.out`, this method prints the stock data. It iterates through the array of stock identifiers, `stockIDs`, and then prints the value in the corresponding `stockInfo` array.

Developing the Stock Quote Server

The server application is a bit more complex than the client that requests its services. It actually consists of two classes. The first loads the stock data and waits for incoming client connections. When a client does connect, it creates an instance of another class that implements the `Runnable` interface, passing the newly created `Socket` to the client.

This secondary object, a handler, is run in its own thread of execution. This allows the server to loop back and accept more clients, rather than perform the communications with clients one at a time. When a server handles requests one after the other, it is said to be iterative; one that deals with multiple requests at the same time is concurrent. For TCP client/server interactions, which can often last a long time, concurrent operation is often essential. The handler is the object that performs the actual communication with the client, and multiple instances of the handler allow the server to process multiple requests simultaneously.

This is a common network server design—using a multi-threaded server to allow many client connects to be handled simultaneously. The code for this application is shown in Listing 31.2.

Listing 31.2 *StockQuoteServer.java*

```
import java.io.*;     // Import the package names to be
import java.net.*;    // used by this application.
import java.util.*;

/**
 * This is an application that implements our stock
 * quote application protocol to provide stock quotes.
 * @author David W. Baker
 * @version 1.2
 */
public class StockQuoteServer {
   // The port on which the server should listen.
   private static final int SERVER_PORT = 1701;
   // Queue length of incoming connections.
   private static final int MAX_CLIENTS = 50;
   // File that contains the stock data of format:
   // <stock-id> <stock information>
   private static final File STOCK_QUOTES_FILE =
      new File("stockquotes.txt");
   private ServerSocket listenSocket = null;
   private Hashtable stockInfo;
   private Date stockInfoTime;
   private long stockFileMod;
   // A boolean used to keep the server looping until
```

```
// interrupted.
private boolean keepRunning = true;

/**
 * Starts up the application.
 * @param args Ignored command line arguments.
 */
public static void main(String[] args) {
   StockQuoteServer server = new StockQuoteServer();
   server.serveQuotes();
}

/**
 * The constructor creates an instance of this class,
 * loads the stock data, and then our server listens
 * for incoming clients.
 */
public StockQuoteServer() {
   // Load the quotes and exit if it is unable to do so.
   if (!loadQuotes()) System.exit(1);
   try {
      // Create a listening socket.
      listenSocket =
         new ServerSocket(SERVER_PORT,MAX_CLIENTS);
   } catch(IOException excpt) {
      System.err.println("Unable to listen on port " +
                         SERVER_PORT + ": " + excpt);
      System.exit(1);
   }
}

/**
 * This method loads in the stock data from a file.
 */
protected boolean loadQuotes() {
   String fileLine;
   StringTokenizer tokenize;
   String id;
   StringBuffer value;

   try {
      // Create a decorated stream to the data file.
      BufferedReader stockInput = new BufferedReader(
         new FileReader(STOCK_QUOTES_FILE));
      // Create the Hashtable in which to place the data.
      stockInfo = new Hashtable();
      // Read in each line.
      while ((fileLine = stockInput.readLine()) != null) {
        // Break up the line into tokens.
        tokenize = new StringTokenizer(fileLine);
        try {
          id = tokenize.nextToken();
          // Ensure the stock ID is stored in upper case.
          id = id.toUpperCase();
          // Now create a buffer to place the stock value in.
```

continues

Listing 31.2 Continued

```
          value = new StringBuffer();
          // Loop through all remaining tokens, placing them
          // into the buffer.
          while(tokenize.hasMoreTokens()) {
            value.append(tokenize.nextToken());
            // If there are more tokens to come, then append
            // a space.
            if (tokenize.hasMoreTokens()) {
              value.append(" ");
            }
          }
          // Create an entry in our Hashtable.
          stockInfo.put(id,value.toString());
        } catch(NullPointerException excpt) {
          System.err.println("Error creating stock data " +
                             "entry: " + excpt);
        } catch(NoSuchElementException excpt) {
          System.err.println("Invalid stock data record " +
                             "in file: " + excpt);
        }
      }
      stockInput.close();
      // Store the last modified timestamp.
      stockFileMod = STOCK_QUOTES_FILE.lastModified();
   } catch(FileNotFoundException excpt) {
      System.err.println("Unable to find file: " + excpt);
      return false;
   } catch(IOException excpt) {
      System.err.println("Failed I/O: " + excpt);
      return false;
   }
   stockInfoTime = new Date();   // Store the time loaded.
   return true;
}

/**
 * This method waits to accept incoming client
 * connections.
 */
public void serveQuotes() {
   Socket clientSocket = null;

   try {
     while(keepRunning) {
         // Accept a new client.
         clientSocket = listenSocket.accept();
         // Ensure that the data file hasn't changed; if
         // so, reload it.
         if (stockFileMod !=
            STOCK_QUOTES_FILE.lastModified()) {
            loadQuotes();
         }
         // Create a new handler.
         StockQuoteHandler newHandler = new
            StockQuoteHandler(clientSocket,stockInfo,
```

```
                                  stockInfoTime);
            Thread newHandlerThread = new Thread(newHandler);
            newHandlerThread.start();
         }
         listenSocket.close();
      } catch(IOException excpt) {
         System.err.println("Failed I/O: "+ excpt);
      }
   }

   /**
    * This method allows the server to be stopped.
    */
   protected void stop() {
      if (keepRunning) {
         keepRunning = false;
      }
   }
}

/**
 * This class is used to manage a connection to
 * a specific client.
 */
class StockQuoteHandler implements Runnable {
   private static final boolean AUTOFLUSH = true;
   private Socket mySocket = null;
   private PrintWriter clientSend = null;
   private BufferedReader clientReceive = null;
   private Hashtable stockInfo;
   private Date stockInfoTime;

   /**
    * The constructor sets up the necessary instance
    * variables.
    * @param newSocket Socket to the incoming client.
    * @param info The stock data.
    * @param time The time when the data was loaded.
    */
   public StockQuoteHandler(Socket newSocket,
                            Hashtable info, Date time) {
      mySocket = newSocket;
      stockInfo = info;
      stockInfoTime = time;
   }

   /**
    * This is the thread of execution that implements
    * the communication.
    */
   public void run() {
      String nextLine;
      StringTokenizer tokens;
      String command;
      String quoteID;
```

continues

Listing 31.2 Continued

```
      String quoteResponse;

      try {
         clientSend =
            new PrintWriter(mySocket.getOutputStream(),
                            AUTOFLUSH);
         clientReceive =
            new BufferedReader(new InputStreamReader(
                                 mySocket.getInputStream()));
         clientSend.println("+HELLO "+ stockInfoTime);
         // Read in a line from the client and respond.
         while((nextLine = clientReceive.readLine())
               != null) {
            // Break the line into tokens.
            tokens = new StringTokenizer(nextLine);
            try {
              command = tokens.nextToken();
              // QUIT command.
              if (command.equalsIgnoreCase("QUIT")) break;
              // STOCK command.
              else if (command.equalsIgnoreCase("STOCK:")) {
                 quoteID = tokens.nextToken();
                 quoteResponse = getQuote(quoteID);
                 clientSend.println(quoteResponse);
              }
              // Unknown command.
              else {
                 clientSend.println("-ERR UNKNOWN COMMAND");
              }
           } catch(NoSuchElementException excpt) {
             clientSend.println("-ERR MALFORMED COMMAND");
           }
         }
         clientSend.println("+BYE");
      } catch(IOException excpt) {
         System.err.println("Failed I/O: " + excpt);
      // Finally close the streams and socket.
      } finally {
         try {
            if (clientSend != null) clientSend.close();
            if (clientReceive != null) clientReceive.close();
            if (mySocket != null) mySocket.close();
         } catch(IOException excpt) {
            System.err.println("Failed I/O: " + excpt);
         }
      }
   }

   /**
    * This method matches a stock ID to relevant information.
    * @param quoteID The stock ID to look up.
    * @return The releveant data.
    */
   protected String getQuote(String quoteID) {
      String info;
```

```
        // Make sure the quote ID is in upper case.
        quoteID = quoteID.toUpperCase();
        // Try to retrieve from out Hashtable.
        info = (String)stockInfo.get(quoteID);
        // If there was such a key in the Hashtable, info will
        // not be null.
        if (info != null) {
          return "+" + quoteID + " " + info;
        }
        else {
          // Otherwise, this is an unknown ID.
          return "-ERR UNKNOWN STOCK ID";
        }
    }
}
```


Starting the Server The `main()` method allows the server to be started as an application and instantiates a new `StockQuoteServer` object. It then uses the `serveQuotes()` method to begin accepting client connections.

The constructor first calls the `loadQuotes()` method to load in the stock data. The constructor ensures that this process succeeds, and if not, quits the application. Otherwise, it creates a `ServerSocket` at port 1701. Now the server is waiting for incoming clients.

The *loadQuotes()* Method: Read in the Stock Data This method uses a `java.io.File` object to obtain a `DataInputStream`, reading in from the data file called `"stockquotes.txt"`. `loadQuotes()` goes through each line of the file, expecting that each line corresponds to a new stock with a format of:

```
stock-ID stock-data
```

The method parses the line and places the data into a `Hashtable` instance; the uppercase value of the stock ID is the key while the stock data is the value. It stores the file's modification time with the `lastModified()` method of the `File` class, so the server can detect when the data has been updated. It stores the current date using the `java.util.Date` class, so it can tell connecting clients when the stock information was loaded.

In a more ideal design, this method would read data from the actual source of the stock information. Because you probably haven't set up such a service within another company yet, a static file will do for now.

The *serveQuotes()* Method: Respond to Incoming Clients This method runs in an infinite loop, setting up connections to clients as they come in. It blocks at the `accept()` method of the `ServerSocket`, waiting for a client to connect. When this occurs, it checks to see if the file in which the stock data resides has a different modification time since it was last loaded. If this is the case, it calls the `loadQuotes()` method to reload the data.

The `serveQuotes()` method then creates a `StockQuoteHandler` instance, passing it the `Socket` created when the client connected and the `Hashtable` of stock data. It places this handler within a `Thread` object and starts that thread's execution. After this has been performed, the `serveQuotes()` method loops back again to wait for a new client to connect.

Creating the *StockQuotesHandler* This class implements the `Runnable` interface so it can run within its own thread of execution. The constructor merely sets some instance variables to refer to the `Socket` and stock data passed to it.

The *run()* Method: Implementing the Communication This method opens two streams to read from and write to the client. It sends the opening message to the client and then reads each request from the client. The method uses a `StringTokenizer` to parse the request and tries to match it with one of the two supported commands, `STOCK:` and `QUIT`.

If the request is a `STOCK:` command, it assumes the token after `STOCK:` is the stock identifier and passes the identifier to the `getQuote()` method to obtain the appropriate data. `getQuote()` is a simple method that tries to find a match within the `stockInfo Hashtable`. If one is found, it returns the line. Otherwise, it returns an error message. The `run()` method sends this information to the client.

If the request is a `QUIT` command, the server sends the `+BYE` response and breaks from the loop. It then terminates the communication by closing the streams and the `Socket`. The `run()` method ends, allowing the thread in which this object executes to terminate.

Should the request be neither of these two commands, the server sends back an error message, waiting for the client to respond with a valid command.

Running the Client and Server

Compile the two applications with `javac`. Then make sure you've created the stock quote data file `stockquotes.txt`, as specified within the server code, in the proper format. Run the server with the Java interpreter, and it will run until interrupted by the system.

Finally, run the client to see how your server responds. Try running the client with one or more of the stock identifiers you placed into the data file. Then, update the data file and try your queries again; the client should show that the data has changed. ●

CHAPTER 32

UDP Sockets

In this chapter

Overview of UDP Messaging

For many Internet developers, UDP (User Datagram Protocol) is used much less often than TCP. UDP does not isolate you as neatly from the details of implementing a continuous network communication. For many Java applications, however, choosing UDP as the tool to create a network linkage may be the most prudent option.

Programming with UDP has significant ramifications. Understanding these factors will guide and educate your network programming efforts.

UDP is a good choice for applications in which communications can be separated into discrete messages, where a single query from a client invokes a single response from a server. Time-dependent data is particularly suited to UDP. UDP requires much less overhead, but the burden of engineering any necessary reliability into the system is your responsibility. For instance, if clients never receive responses to their queries—perfectly possible and legitimate with UDP—you might want to program the clients to retransmit the request or perhaps display an informative message indicating communication difficulties.

UDP Socket Characteristics

As discussed in Chapter 30, "Communications and Networking," UDP behaves very differently than TCP. UDP is described as unreliable, connectionless, and message-oriented. A common analogy that explains UDP is that of communicating with postcards.

A dialog with UDP must be quanticized into small messages that fit within a small packet of a specific size, although some packets can hold more data than others. When you send out a message, you can never be certain that you will receive a return message. Unless you do receive a return message, you have no idea if your message was received—your message could have been lost en route, the recipient's confirmation could have been lost, or the recipient might be ignoring your message.

The postcards you will be exchanging between network programs are referred to as *datagrams*. Within a datagram, you can store an array of bytes. A receiving application can extract this array and decode your message, possibly sending a return datagram response.

As with TCP, you program in UDP using the socket programming abstraction. However, UDP sockets are very different from TCP sockets. Extending the postcard analogy, UDP sockets are much like creating a mailbox.

A mailbox is identified by your address, but you don't construct a new one for each person to whom you will be sending a message. (However, you might create a new mailbox to receive newspapers, which shouldn't go into your normal mailbox.) Instead, you place an address on the postcard that indicates to whom the message is being sent. You place the postcard in the mailbox, and it is (eventually) sent on its way.

When receiving a message, you could potentially wait forever until one arrives in your mailbox. After one arrives, you can read the postcard. Meta information appears on the postcard that identifies the sender through the return address.

As the previous analogies suggest, UDP programming involves the following general tasks:

- Creating an appropriately addressed datagram to send
- Setting up a socket to send and receive datagrams for a particular application
- Inserting datagrams into a socket for transmission
- Waiting to receive datagrams from a socket
- Decoding a datagram to extract the message, its recipient, and other meta information

Java UDP Classes

The `java.net` package has the tools that are necessary to perform UDP communications. For creating datagrams, Java provides the `DatagramPacket` class. When receiving a UDP datagram, you also use the `DatagramPacket` class to read the data, sender, and meta information.

To create a datagram to send to a remote system, the following constructor is provided:

```
public DatagramPacket(byte[] ibuf, int length,
InetAddress iaddr, int iport);
```

`ibuf` is the array of bytes that encodes the data of the message, while `length` is the length of the byte array to place into the datagram. This factor determines the size of the datagram. `iaddr` is an `InetAddress` object, which stores the IP address of the intended recipient. `port` identifies which port the datagram should be sent to on the receiving host.

▶ **See** "Java TCP Socket Classes," **p. 701**

To receive a datagram, you must use another `DatagramPacket` constructor in which the incoming data will be stored. This constructor has the prototype of

```
public DatagramPacket(byte[] ibuff, int ilength);
```

`ibuf` is the byte array into which the data portion of the datagram will be copied. `ilength` is the number of bytes to copy from the datagram into the array corresponding to the size of the datagram. If `ilength` is less than the size of the UDP datagram received by the machine, the extra bytes will be silently ignored by Java.

NOTE Programming with TCP sockets relieves you from breaking your data down into discrete chunks for transmission over a network. When creating a UDP-based client/server protocol, you must specify some expected length of the datagrams or create a means for determining this at runtime.

According to the TCP/IP specification, the largest datagram possible is one that contains 65,507 bytes of data. However, a host is only required to receive datagrams with up to 548 bytes of data. Most platforms support larger datagrams of at least 8,192 bytes in length.

Large datagrams are likely to be fragmented at the IP layer. If, during transmission, any one of the IP packets that contains a fragment of the datagram is lost, the entire UDP datagram will be silently lost.

The point is you must design your application with the datagram size in mind. It is prudent to limit this size to a reasonable length.

After a datagram has been received, as illustrated later in this section, you can read that data. Other methods allow you to obtain meta information regarding the message:

```
public int getLength();
public byte[] getData();
public InetAddress getAddress();
public int getPort();
```

The `getLength()` method is used to obtain the number of bytes contained within the data portion of the datagram. The `getData()` method is used to obtain a byte array containing the data received. `getAddress()` provides an `InetAddress` object identifying the sender, while `getPort()` indicates the UDP port used.

Performing the sending and receiving of these datagrams is accomplished with the `DatagramSocket` class, which creates a UDP socket. Three constructors are available:

```
public DatagramSocket() throws IOException;
public DatagramSocket(int port) throws IOException;
public DatagramSocket(int port, InetAddress localAddr)
➥throws IOException;
```

The first constructor allows you to create a socket at an unused ephemeral port, generally used for client applications. The second constructor allows you to specify a particular port, which is useful for server applications. As with TCP, most systems require super-user privileges to bind UDP ports below 1024. The final constructor is useful for machines with multiple IP interfaces. You can use this constructor to send and listen for datagrams from one of the IP addresses assigned to the machine. On such a host, datagrams sent to any of the machine's IP addresses are received by a `DatagramSocket` created with the first two constructors, while the last constructor obtains only datagrams sent to the specific IP address.

You can use this socket to send properly addressed `DatagramPacket` instances created with the first constructor described by using this `DatagramSocket` method:

```
public void send(DatagramPacket p) throws IOException;
```

After a `DatagramPacket` has been created with the second constructor described, a datagram can be received:

```
public synchronized void receive(DatagramPacket p)
➥throws IOException;
```

Note that the `receive()` method blocks until a datagram is received. Because UDP is unreliable, your application cannot expect `receive()` ever to return unless a timeout is enabled. Such a timeout, named the `SO_TIMEOUT` option from the name of the Berkeley sockets API option, can be set with this method from the `DatagramSocket` class:

```
public synchronized void setSoTimeout(int timeout)
➥throws SocketException;
```

`timeout` is a value in milliseconds. If set to 0, the `receive()` method exhibits an infinite timeout—the default behavior. When greater than zero, a subsequent `receive()` method invocation waits only the specified timeout before an `InterruptedIOException` is thrown.

NOTE Your host's UDP implementation has a limited queue for incoming datagrams. If your application cannot process these datagrams rapidly enough, they will be silently discarded. Neither the sender nor the receiver is notified when datagrams are dropped from a queue overflow. Such is the unreliable nature of UDP.

After communications through the UDP socket are completed, that socket should be closed:

```
public synchronized void close();
```

Creating a UDP Server

In this section, you learn how to create a basic UDP server that responds to simple client requests. The practical example used here is to create a daytime server.

Daytime is a simple service that runs on many systems. For example, most UNIX systems run daytime out of `inetd`, as listed in `/etc/inetd.conf`. On Windows NT, the daytime server is available through the Simple TCP/IP Services within the Services Control Panel. Daytime is generally run on UDP port 13. When sent a datagram, it responds with a datagram containing the date in a format such as

```
Friday, July 30, 1993 19:25:00
```

Listing 32.1 shows the Java code used to implement this service.

Listing 32.1 *DaytimeServer.java*

```
import java.net.*;   // Import the package names used
import java.util.*;
import java.io.*;
import java.text.*;

/**
 * This is an application that runs the
 * daytime service.
*/
public class DaytimeServer {
   // The daytime service runs on this well known port.
   private static final int TIME_PORT = 13;
   private DatagramSocket timeSocket = null;
   private static final int SMALL_ARRAY = 1;
   private static final int TIME_ARRAY = 100;
   // A boolean to keep the server looping until stopped.
   private boolean keepRunning = true;

   /**
 * This method starts the application, creating an
    * instance and telling it to start accepting
    * requests.
    * @param args Command line arguments - ignored.
    */
   public static void main(String[] args) {
```

continues

Listing 32.1 Continued

```
      DaytimeServer server = new DaytimeServer();
      server.startServing();
   }

   /**
    * This constructor creates a datagram socket to
    * listen on.
    */
   public DaytimeServer() {
      try {
         timeSocket = new DatagramSocket(TIME_PORT);
      } catch(SocketException excpt) {
         System.err.println("Unable to open socket: " +
                            excpt);
      }
   }

   /**
    * This method does all of the work of listening for
    * and responding to clients.
    */
   public void startServing() {
      DatagramPacket datagram;    // For a UDP datagram.
      InetAddress clientAddr;     // Address of the client.
      int clientPort;             // Port of the client.
      byte[] dataBuffer;          // To construct a datagram.
      String timeString;          // The time as a string.

      // Keep looping while you have a socket.
      while(keepRunning) {
         try {
            // Create a DatagramPacket to receive query.
            dataBuffer = new byte[SMALL_ARRAY];
            datagram = new DatagramPacket(dataBuffer,
                                          dataBuffer.length);
            timeSocket.receive(datagram);
            // Get the meta-info on the client.
            clientAddr = datagram.getAddress();
            clientPort = datagram.getPort();
            // Place the time into byte array.
            dataBuffer = getTimeBuffer();
            // Create and send the datagram.
            datagram = new DatagramPacket(dataBuffer,
               dataBuffer.length,clientAddr,clientPort);
            timeSocket.send(datagram);
         } catch(IOException excpt) {
            System.err.println("Failed I/O: " + excpt);
         }
      }
      timeSocket.close();
   }

   /**
```

```
     * This method is used to create a byte array
     * containing the current time in the special daytime
     * server format.
     * @return The byte array with the time.
     */
    protected byte[] getTimeBuffer() {
       String timeString;
       SimpleDateFormat daytimeFormat;
       Date currentTime;

       // Get the current time.
       currentTime = new Date();
       // Create a SimpleDateFormat object with the time
       // pattern specified.
       //   EEEE - print out complete text for day
       //   MMMM - print out complete text of month
       //   dd   - print out the day in month in two digits
       //   yyyy - print out the year in four digits
       //   HH   - print out the hour in the day, from 0-23
       //            in two digits
       //   mm   - print out the minutes in the hour in two
       //             digits
       //   ss   - print out the seconds in the minute in
       //             two digits
       daytimeFormat =
         new SimpleDateFormat("EEEE, MMMM dd, yyyy HH:mm:ss");

       // Create the special time format.
       timeString = daytimeFormat.format(currentTime);
       // Convert the String to an array of bytes using the
       // platform's default character encoding.
       return timeString.getBytes();
    }

    /**
     * This method provides an interface to stopping
     * the server.
     */
    protected void stop() {
       if (keepRunning) {
          keepRunning = false;
       }
    }

   /**
    * Just in case, do some cleanup.
    */
   public void finalize() {
     if (timeSocket != null) {
       timeSocket.close();
     }
   }
}
```

Part IV

Ch 32

Starting the Server

The `DaytimeServer` class uses a number of static final variables as constants, many of which are used to create the date string in the proper format. The `main()` method creates a `DaytimeServer` object and then invokes its `startServing()` method so that it accepts incoming requests.

The `DaytimeServer` constructor merely creates a UDP socket at the specified port. Note that as written, the server may require super-user privileges to run because it binds port 13. If you don't have permission to bind this port, the attempt to create a `DatagramSocket` throws an exception. The constructor catches this and fails gracefully, informing you of the problem.

The `DaytimeServer` is an iterative server, whereas the server created in Chapter 31, "TCP Sockets," is a concurrent server. `DaytimeServer` processes each request in serial as they come in. Given the nature of the protocol—a single datagram comes in and the server immediately sends back a datagram with the time—an iterative server is most appropriate and is simpler to program.

The *startServing()* Method Handling Requests

The `startServing()` method is where the serving logic is implemented. Although the application is intended to be running, it loops through a number of steps: It creates a small byte array and uses this array to create a `DatagramPacket`. The application then receives a datagram from the `DatagramSocket`. From the datagram, it obtains the IP address and port of the requesting application. The `startServing()` method need not read any information from the incoming datagram, as the datagram's arrival plus the meta-information it contains is sufficient for the server to understand the request.

The `getTimeBuffer()` method is called to obtain a byte array that contains the time in an appropriate format. By using this information, this method creates a new `DatagramPacket`. Finally, it sends this information through the `DatagramSocket`. The server loops through this process until interrupted externally.

The *getTimeBuffer()* Method Creating the Byte Array

This protected method creates an instance of `Date` class containing the current time and then instantiates a `SimpleDateFormat` with a specific time pattern. It uses the `SimpleDateFormat` object to create a `String` with the data in the proper format. Finally, it returns the byte array corresponding to that `String`.

Running the Daytime Server

To run the server, first compile it with `javac`. Then, if necessary, log in as the super user (for example, "root") and use `java` to run the server. If this is not possible, modify the `TIME_PORT` variable so that it binds to a port over 1024.

In the next example, you create a client to connect to this server.

Creating a UDP Client

The example used to create a UDP client makes use of the daytime server demonstrated previously but also illustrates communications with multiple servers through a single UDP socket. TimeCompare is a Java program that requests the time from a series of servers, receives their responses, and displays the difference between the remote system's times and the time of the local machine.

One of the most important aspects of this client is designing it so that an unanswered query does not hang the program. You cannot expect that every query will be answered. Thus, you need to use the `setSoTimeout()` method of the `DatagramSocket` instance before you call `receive()`.

Listing 32.2 shows this application.

Listing 32.2 *TimeCompare.java*

```
import java.io.*;     // Import the package names used.
import java.net.*;
import java.util.*;
import java.text.*;

/**
 * This is an application to obtain the times from
 * various remote systems via UDP and then report
 * a comparison.
*/
public class TimeCompare {
   private static final int TIME_PORT = 13;  // Daytime port.
   private static final int TIMEOUT = 10000; // UDP timeout.
   // This is the size of the datagram data to send
   // for the query - intentially small.
   private static final int SMALL_ARRAY = 1;
   // This is the size of the datagram you expect to receive.
   private static final int TIME_ARRAY = 100;
   // A socket to send and receive datagrams.
   DatagramSocket timeSocket = null;
   // An array of addresses to the machines to query.
   private InetAddress[] remoteMachines;
  // The time on this machine.
   private Date localTime;
  // An array of datagram responses from remote machines.
   private DatagramPacket[] timeResponses;

   /**
    * This method starts the application.
    * @param args Command line arguments - remote hosts.
    */
   public static void main(String[] args) {
      if (args.length < 1) {
         System.out.println(
            "Usage: TimeCompare host1 (host2 ... hostn)");
```

continues

Listing 32.2 Continued

```
         System.exit(1);
      }
      // Create an instance.
      TimeCompare runCompare = new TimeCompare(args);
      // Tell it to print out its data.
      runCompare.printTimes();
      System.exit(0);            // Exit.
   }

   /**
    * The constructor looks up the remote hosts and
    * creates a UDP socket.
    * @param hosts The hosts to contact.
    */
   public TimeCompare(String[] hosts) {
      remoteMachines = new InetAddress[hosts.length];
      // Look up all hosts and place in InetAddress[] array.
      for(int hostsFound = 0; hostsFound < hosts.length;
            hostsFound++) {
         try {
            remoteMachines[hostsFound] =
               InetAddress.getByName(hosts[hostsFound]);
         } catch(UnknownHostException excpt) {
            remoteMachines[hostsFound] = null;
            System.err.println("Unknown host " +
               hosts[hostsFound] + ": " + excpt);
         }
      }
      try {
         timeSocket = new DatagramSocket();
      } catch(SocketException excpt) {
         System.err.println("Unable to bind UDP socket: " +
                            excpt);
         System.exit(1);
      }
      // Perform the UDP communications.
      getTimes();
   }

   /**
    * This method is the thread of execution where you
    * send out requests for times and then receive the
    * responses.
    */
   public void getTimes() {
      DatagramPacket timeQuery; // A datagram to send as a query.
      DatagramPacket response;  // A datagram response.
      byte[] emptyBuffer;       // A byte array to build datagrams.
      int datagramsSent = 0;    // # of queries successfully sent.

      // Send out a small UDP datagram to each machine,
      // asking it to respond with its time.
      for(int ips = 0;ips < remoteMachines.length; ips++) {
        if (remoteMachines[ips] != null) {
```

```
        try {
          emptyBuffer = new byte[SMALL_ARRAY];
          timeQuery = new DatagramPacket(emptyBuffer,
             emptyBuffer.length, remoteMachines[ips],
             TIME_PORT);
          timeSocket.send(timeQuery);
          datagramsSent++;
        } catch(IOException excpt) {
          System.err.println("Unable to send to " +
                     remoteMachines[ips] + ": " + excpt);
        }
      }
    }
    // Get current time to base the comparisons.
    localTime = new Date();
    // Create an array in which to place responses.
    timeResponses = new DatagramPacket[datagramsSent];
    // Set the socket timeout value.
    try {
      timeSocket.setSoTimeout(TIMEOUT);
    } catch(SocketException e) {}
    // Loop through and receive the number of responses
    // you are expecting. You break from this loop prematurely
    // if an InterruptedIOException occurs - that is, if
    // you wait more than TIMEOUT to receive another datagram.
    try {
      for(int got = 0; got < timeResponses.length; got++) {
        // Create a new buffer and datagram.
        emptyBuffer = new byte[TIME_ARRAY];
        response = new DatagramPacket(emptyBuffer,
                                      emptyBuffer.length);
        // Receive a datagram, timing out if necessary.
        timeSocket.receive(response);
        // Now that you've received a response, add it
        // to the array of received datagrams.
        timeResponses[got] = response;
      }
    } catch(InterruptedIOException excpt) {
      System.err.println("Timeout on receive: " + excpt);
    } catch(IOException excpt) {
      System.err.println("Failed I/O: " + excpt);
    }
    // Close the socket.
    timeSocket.close();
    timeSocket = null;
 }

 /**
  * This prints out a report comparing the times
  * sent from the remote hosts with the local
  * time.
  */
 protected void printTimes() {
    Date remoteTime;
    String timeString;
```

Part IV
Ch 32

continues

Listing 32.2 Continued

```
        long secondsOff;
        InetAddress dgAddr;
        SimpleDateFormat daytimeFormat;

        System.out.print("TIME COMPARISON\n\tCurrent time " +
                         "is: " + localTime + "\n\n");
        // Iterate through each host.
        for(int hosts = 0;
            hosts < remoteMachines.length; hosts++) {
           if (remoteMachines[hosts] != null) {
              boolean found = false;
              int dataIndex;
              // Iterate through each datagram received.
              for(dataIndex = 0; dataIndex < timeResponses.length;
                  dataIndex++) {
                 // If the datagram element isn't null:
                 if (timeResponses[dataIndex] != null) {
                    dgAddr = timeResponses[dataIndex].getAddress();
                    // See if there's a match.
                    if(dgAddr.equals(remoteMachines[hosts])) {
                       found = true;
                       break;
                    }
                 }
              }
              System.out.println('Host: ' +
                                     remoteMachines[hosts]);
              // If there was a match, print comparison.
              if (found) {
                 timeString =
                    new String(timeResponses[dataIndex].getData());
                 int endOfLine = timeString.indexOf("\n");
                 if (endOfLine != -1) {
                    timeString =
                       timeString.substring(0,endOfLine);
                 }
                 // Create a SimpleDateFormat object with the time
                 // pattern specified.
                 //   EEEE - print out complete text for day
                 //   MMMM - print out complete text of month
                 //   dd   - print out the day in month in two digits
                 //   yyyy - print out the year in four digits
                 //   HH   - print out the hour in the day, from 0-23
                 //            in two digits
                 //   mm   - print out the minutes in the hour in two
                 //             digits
                 //   ss   - print out the seconds in the minute in
                 //             two digits
                 daytimeFormat =
                   new SimpleDateFormat("EEEE, MMMM dd, yyyy HH:mm:ss");
                 // Parse the string based on the pattern into a
                 // Date object.
                 remoteTime = daytimeFormat.parse(timeString,
                                                  new ParseStatus());
```

```
                // Find the difference.
                secondsOff = (localTime.getTime() -
                              remoteTime.getTime()) / 1000;
                secondsOff = Math.abs(secondsOff);
                System.out.println("Time: " + timeString);
                System.out.println("Difference: " +
                   secondsOff + " seconds\n");
             } else {
                System.out.println("Time: NO RESPONSE FROM "
                                   + "HOST\n");
             }
          }
       }
    }

    /**
     * This method performs any necessary cleanup.
     */
    protected void finalize() {
       // If the socket is still open, close it.
       if (timeSocket != null) {
          timeSocket.close();
       }
    }
}
```


Starting *TimeCompare*

The `main()` method instantiates a `TimeCompare` object, passing it the command-line arguments that correspond to the hosts to query. `main()` instructs the instance to print out its data and then exits.

The `TimeCompare` constructor uses the `InetAddress.getByName()` `static` method to look up the set of remote hosts, placing the returned `InetAddress` instances into an array of these objects. If it is unable to look up one of the hosts, this constructor ensures that the element is set to null and loops through the other hosts. The constructor creates a `DatagramSocket` at a dynamically allocated port and finally calls the `getTimes()` method to perform the queries.

The *getTimes()* Method *TimeCompare*'s Execution Path

The first thing this method does is iterate through the `remoteMachines` array. For each element that is not null, the `getTimes()` method creates a small byte array, uses it to construct an appropriately addressed `DatagramPacket`, and then sends the datagram using the UDP socket. After it's sent, the method uses `datagramsSent` to keep track of how many queries were successfully sent.

Now that a datagram has been sent to each remote host, `TimeCompare` prepares to receive the responses. At this point, `getTimes()` collects the current time, used as a basis for comparison against the remote systems' times. It creates an array of type `DatagramPacket`. The length of this array is equal to the number of successful queries sent, which is the number of expected responses. `getTimes()` then invokes the `setSoTimeout()` method of the `DatagramSocket` instance so that `accept()` will not block forever if a server fails to respond.

`getTimes()` next enters a loop, attempting to receive a `DatagramPacket` for each query successfully sent. When a response is obtained, it places it into the `timeResponses` array. If the timeout on the `receive()` method expires, it breaks out of the loop.

After `getTimes()` has completed the loop to receive responses, it closes the `DatagramSocket`.

The *printTimes()* Method Showing the Comparison

This method takes an array of UDP packets and prints out a comparison of the times contained therein. The outer `for` loop iterates through the machines contacted, while the inner `for` loop matches the host to a received datagram. If a match is found, `printTimes()` calculates the difference in times and prints the data. If no match is found, `printTimes()` indicates that a response from that host was not received.

Running the Application

Compile `TimeCompare.java` with the Java compiler and then execute it with the Java interpreter. Each argument to `TimeCompare` should be a host name of a remote machine to include in the comparison. For instance, to check your machine's time against `www.sgi.com` and `www.paramount.com`, you would type

```
java TimeCompare www.sgi.com www.paramount.com
```

and you would see a report that appeared as

```
TIME COMPARISON
Current time is: Mon Aug 19 08:03:09 PDT 1996

Host: www.sgi.com/204.94.214.4
Time: Mon Aug 19 08:02:55 1996
Difference: 14 seconds

Host: www.paramount.com/192.216.189.10
Time: Mon Aug 19 08:07:58 1996
Difference: 288 seconds
```

Using IP Multicasting

Internet Protocol (IP) is the means by which all information on the Internet is transmitted. UDP datagrams are encapsulated within IP packets to send them to the appropriate machines on the network.

▶ **See** "Internet Protocol (IP)," **p. 686**

Most uses of IP involve unicasting—sending a packet from one host to another. However, IP is not limited to this mode and includes the capability to multicast. With multicasting, a message is addressed to a targeted set of hosts. One message is sent, and the entire group can receive it.

Multicasting is particularly suited to high-bandwidth applications, such as sending video and audio over the network, because a separate transmission need not be established (which could saturate the network). Other possible applications include chat sessions, distributed data storage, and online, interactive games. Also, multicasting can be used by a client searching for an appropriate server on the network; it can send a multicast solicitation, and any listening servers could contact the client to begin a transaction.

To support IP multicasting, a certain range of IP addresses is set aside solely for this purpose. These IP addresses are class D addresses, those within the range of 224.0.0.0 and 239.255.255.255. Each of these addresses is referred to as a *multicast group*. Any IP packet addressed to that group is received by any machine that has joined that group. Group membership is dynamic and changes over time. To send a message to a group, a host need not be a member of that group.

When a machine joins a multicast group, it begins accepting messages sent to that IP multicast address. Extending the previous analogy from the section "UDP Socket Characteristics," joining a group is similar to constructing a new mailbox that accepts messages intended for the group. Each machine that wants to join the group constructs its own mailbox to receive the same message. If a multicast packet is distributed to a network, any machine that is listening for the message has an opportunity to receive it. That is, with IP multicasting, there is no mechanism for restricting which machines on the same network may join the group.

Multicast groups are mapped to hardware addresses on interface cards. Thus, IP multicast datagrams that reach an uninterested host can usually be rapidly discarded by the interface card. However, more than one multicast group maps to a single hardware address, making for imperfect hardware-level filtering. Some filtering must still be performed at the device driver or IP level.

Multicasting has its limitations, however—particularly the task of routing multicast packets throughout the Internet. A special TCP/IP protocol, Internet Group Management Protocol (IGMP), is used to manage memberships in a multicast group. A router that supports multicasting can use IGMP to determine if local machines are subscribed to a particular group; such hosts respond with a report about groups they have joined using IGMP. Based on these communications, a multicast router can determine if it is appropriate to forward on a multicast packet.

CAUTION

Realize that there is no formal way of reserving a multicast group for your own use. Certain groups are reserved for particular uses, assigned by the Internet Assigned Numbers Authority (IANA). These reserved groups are listed in RFC 1700, which can be obtained from

`ftp://ftp.internic.net/rfc/rfc1700.txt`

Other than avoiding a reserved group, there are few rules to choosing a group. The groups from 224.0.0.0 through 224.0.0.225 should never be passed on by a multicast router, restricting communications using them to the local subnet. Try picking an arbitrary address between 224.0.1.27 and 224.0.1.225.

If you happen to choose a group already being used, your communications will be disrupted by those other machines. Should this occur, quit your application and try another address.

Besides the multicast group, another important facet of a multicast packet is the time-to-live (TTL) parameter. The TTL is used to indicate how many separate networks the sender intends the message to be transmitted over. When a packet is forwarded on by a router, the TTL within the packet is decremented by one. When a TTL reaches zero, the packet is not forwarded on further.

Choose a TTL parameter as small as possible. A large TTL value can cause unnecessary bandwidth use throughout the Internet. Furthermore, you are more likely to disrupt other multicast communications in diverse areas that happen to be using the same group.

If your communications should be isolated to machines on the local network, choose a TTL of 1. When communicating with machines that are not on the local network, try to determine how many multicast routers exist along the way and set your TTL to one more than that value.

The Multicast Backbone, or MBONE, is an attempt to create a network of Internet routers that are capable of providing multicast services. However, multicasting today is by no means ubiquitous. If all participants reside on the same physical network, routers need not be involved, and multicasting is likely to prove successful. For more distributed communications, you may need to contact your network administrator.

Java Multicasting

The Java `MulticastSocket` class is the key to utilizing this powerful Internet networking feature. `MulticastSocket` allows you to send or receive UDP datagrams that use multicast IP. To send a datagram, you use the default constructor:

```
public MulticastSocket() throws IOException;
```

Then you must create an appropriately formed `DatagramPacket` addressed to a multicast group between 224.0.0.0 and 239.255.255.255. After it is created, the datagram can be sent with the `send()` method, which requires a TTL value. The TTL indicates how many routers the packets should be allowed to go through. Avoid setting the TLL to a high value, which could cause the data to propagate through a large portion of the Internet. Here is an example:

```
int multiPort = 2222;
int ttl = 1;
InetAddress multiAddr =
➥InetAddress.getByName("239.10.10.10");
byte[] multiBytes = new byte[256];
DatagramPacket multiDatagram =
➥new DatagramPacket(multiBytes, multiBytes.length,
multiAddr,multiPort);
MulticastSocket multiSocket = new MulticastSocket();
➥multiSocket.send(multiDatagram, ttl);
```

To receive datagrams, an application must create a socket at a specific UDP port. Then, it must join the group of recipients. Through the socket, the application can then receive UDP datagrams:

```
MulticastSocket receiveSocket =
➥new MulticastSocket(multiPort);
receiveSocket.joinGroup(multiAddr);
receiveSocket.receive(multiDatagram);
```

When the `joinGroup()` method is invoked, the machine now pays attention to any IP packets transmitted along the network for that particular multicast group. The host should also use IGMP to appropriately report the usage of the group. For machines with multiple IP addresses, the interface through which datagrams should be sent can be configured:

```
receiveSocket.setInterface(oneOfMyLocalAddrs);
```

To leave a multicast group, the `leaveGroup()` method is available. A `MulticastSocket` should be closed when communications are done:

```
receiveSocket.leaveGroup(multiAddr);
receiveSocket.close();
```

As is apparent, using the `MulticastSocket` is very similar to using the normal UDP socket class `DatagramSocket`. The essential differences are

- The `DatagramPacket` must be addressed to a multicast group.
- The `send()` method of the `MulticastSocket` class takes two arguments: a `DatagramPacket` and a TTL value.
- To begin listening for multicast messages, after creating the `MulticastSocket` instance, you must use the `joinGroup()` method.
- The `receive()` method is used just as with the `DatagramSocket` to obtain incoming messages, though there is no method to set a timeout, like `setSoTimeout()` in `DatagramSocket`.

Multicast Applications

The following two examples show a very simple use of multicasting. Listing 32.3 is a program that sends datagrams to a specific multicast IP address. The program is run with two arguments: the first specifying the multicast IP address to send the datagrams, the other specifying the UDP port of the listening applications. The `main()` method ensures that these arguments have been received and then instantiates a `MultiCastSender` object.

The constructor creates an `InetAddress` instance with the `String` representation of the multicast IP address. It then creates a `MulticastSocket` at a dynamically allocated port for sending datagrams. The constructor enters a `while` loop, reading in from standard input line by line. The program packages the first 256 bytes of each line into an appropriately addressed `DatagramPacket`, sending that datagram through the `MulticastSocket`.

Listing 32.3 *MultCastSender.java*

```
import java.net.*;    // Import package names used.
import java.io.*;

/**
 * This is a program that sends data from the command
 * line to a particular multicast group.
 */
class MultiCastSender {
   // The number of Internet routers through which this
   // message should be passed. Keep this low. 1 is good
   // for local LAN communications.
   private static final byte TTL = 1;
   // The size of the data sent - basically the maximum
   // length of each line typed in at a time.
   private static final int DATAGRAM_BYTES = 512;
   private int mcastPort;
   private InetAddress mcastIP;
   private BufferedReader input;
   private MulticastSocket mcastSocket;

   /**
    * This starts up the application.
    * @param args Program arguments - <ip> <port>
    */
   public static void main(String[] args) {
      // This must be the same port and IP address used
      // by the receivers.
      if (args.length != 2) {
         System.out.print("Usage: MultiCastSender <IP addr>"
            + " <port>\n\t<IP addr> can be one of 224.x.x.x "
            + "- 239.x.x.x\n");
         System.exit(1);
      }
      MultiCastSender send = new MultiCastSender(args);
      System.exit(0);
   }

   /**
    * The constructor does all of the work of opening
    * the socket and sending datagrams through it.
    * @param args Program arguments - <ip> <port>
    */
   public MultiCastSender(String[] args) {
      DatagramPacket mcastPacket;     // UDP datagram.
      String nextLine;                // Line from STDIN.
      byte[] mcastBuffer;             // Buffer for datagram.
      byte[] lineData;                // The data typed in.
      int sendLength;                 // Length of line.

      input =
        new BufferedReader(new InputStreamReader(System.in));
      try {
         // Create a multicasting socket.
```

```
            mcastIP = InetAddress.getByName(args[0]);
            mcastPort = Integer.parseInt(args[1]);
            mcastSocket = new MulticastSocket();
         } catch(UnknownHostException excpt) {
            System.err.println("Unknown address: " + excpt);
            System.exit(1);
         } catch(IOException excpt) {
            System.err.println("Unable to obtain socket: "
                                    + excpt);
            System.exit(1);
         }
         try {
            // Loop and read lines from standard input.
            while ((nextLine = input.readLine()) != null) {
               mcastBuffer = new byte[DATAGRAM_BYTES];
               // If line is longer than your buffer, use the
               // length of the buffer available.
               if (nextLine.length() > mcastBuffer.length) {
                  sendLength = mcastBuffer.length;
               // Otherwise, use the line's length.
               } else {
                  sendLength = nextLine.length();
               }
               // Convert the line of input to bytes.
               lineData = nextLine.getBytes();
               // Copy the data into the blank byte array
               // which you will use to create the DatagramPacket.
               for (int i = 0; i < sendLength; i++) {
                 mcastBuffer[i] = lineData[i];
               }
               mcastPacket = new DatagramPacket(mcastBuffer,
                   mcastBuffer.length,mcastIP,mcastPort);
               // Send the datagram.
               try {
                  System.out.println("Sending:\t" + nextLine);
                  mcastSocket.send(mcastPacket,TTL);
               } catch(IOException excpt) {
                  System.err.println("Unable to send packet: "
                                          + excpt);
               }
            }
         } catch(IOException excpt) {
            System.err.println("Failed I/O: " + excpt);
         }
         mcastSocket.close(); // Close the socket.
      }
   }
```

Listing 32.4 complements the sender by receiving multicasted datagrams. The application takes two arguments that must correspond to the IP address and port with which the `MultiCastSender` was invoked. The `main()` method checks the command-line arguments and then creates a `MultiCastReceiver` object.

Part IV Ch 32

The object's constructor creates an `InetAddress` and then a `MulticastSocket` at the port used to invoke the application. It joins the multicast group at the address contained within the `InetAddress` instance and then enters a loop. The object's constructor receives a datagram from the socket and prints the data contained within the datagram, indicating the machine and port from where the packet was sent.

Listing 32.4 ***MultiCastReceiver.java***

```
import java.net.*;    // Import package names used.
import java.io.*;

/**
 * This is a program that allows you to listen
 * at a particular multicast IP address/port and
 * print out incoming UDP datagrams.
*/
class MultiCastReceiver {
   // The length of the data portion of incoming
   // datagrams.
   private static final int DATAGRAM_BYTES = 512;
   private int mcastPort;
   private InetAddress mcastIP;
   private MulticastSocket mcastSocket;
   // Boolean to tell the client to keep looping for
   // new datagrams.
   private boolean keepReceiving = true;

   /**
    * This starts up the application
    * @param args Program arguments - <ip> <port>
    */
   public static void main(String[] args) {
      // This must be the same port and IP address
      // used by the sender.
      if (args.length != 2) {
         System.out.print("Usage: MultiCastReceiver <IP "
            + "addr> <port>\n\t<IP addr> can be one of "
            + "224.x.x.x - 239.x.x.x\n");
         System.exit(1);
      }
      MultiCastReceiver send = new MultiCastReceiver(args);
      System.exit(0);
   }

   /**
    * The constructor does the work of opening a socket,
    * joining the multicast group, and printing out
    * incoming data.
    * @param args Program arguments - <ip> <port>
    */
   public MultiCastReceiver(String[] args) {
      DatagramPacket mcastPacket;    // Packet to receive.
      byte[] mcastBuffer;            // byte[] array buffer
```

```
        InetAddress fromIP;             // Sender address.
        int fromPort;                   // Sender port.
        String mcastMsg;                // String of message.

        try {
           // First, set up your receiving socket.
           mcastIP = InetAddress.getByName(args[0]);
           mcastPort = Integer.parseInt(args[1]);
           mcastSocket = new MulticastSocket(mcastPort);
           // Join the multicast group.
           mcastSocket.joinGroup(mcastIP);
        } catch(UnknownHostException excpt) {
           System.err.println("Unknown address: " + excpt);
           System.exit(1);
        } catch(IOException excpt) {
           System.err.println("Unable to obtain socket: "
                              + excpt);
           System.exit(1);
        }
        while (keepReceiving) {
           try {
              // Create a new datagram.
              mcastBuffer = new byte[DATAGRAM_BYTES];
              mcastPacket = new DatagramPacket(mcastBuffer,
                               mcastBuffer.length);
              // Receive the datagram.
              mcastSocket.receive(mcastPacket);
              fromIP = mcastPacket.getAddress();
              fromPort = mcastPacket.getPort();
              mcastMsg = new String(mcastPacket.getData());
              // Print out the data.
              System.out.println("Received from " + fromIP +
                 " on port " + fromPort + ": " + mcastMsg);
           } catch(IOException excpt) {
              System.err.println("Failed I/O: " + excpt);
           }
        }
        try {
           mcastSocket.leaveGroup(mcastIP); // Leave the group.
        } catch(IOException excpt) {
           System.err.println("Socket problem leaving group: "
                              + excpt);
        }
        mcastSocket.close(); // Close the socket.
     }

     /**
      * This method provides a way to stop the program.
      */
     public void stop() {
        if (keepReceiving) {
           keepReceiving = false;
        }
     }
  }
```

To run the applications, first compile `MultiCastSender` and `MultiCastReceiver`. Then, transfer the `MultCastReceiver` to other machines, so you can demonstrate more than one participant receiving messages. Finally, run the applications with the Java interpreter.

For instance, to send multicast messages to the group 224.0.1.30 on port 1111, you could do the following:

```
~/classes -> java MultiCastSender 224.0.1.30 1111
This is a test multicast message.
Sending:        This is a test multicast message.
Have you received it?
Sending:        Have you received it?
```

To receive these messages, you would run the `MultiCastReceiver` application on one or more systems. You join the same multicast group, 224.0.1.30, and listen to the same port number, 1111:

```
~/classes -> java MultiCastReceiver 224.0.1.30 1111
Received from 204.160.73.131 on port 32911: This is a test multicast message.
Received from 204.160.73.131 on port 32911: Have you received it?
```

CHAPTER 33

java.net

In this chapter

The *URL* Class

The `java.net` package provides low-level and high-level network functionality. The high-level networking classes enable you to access information by specifying the type and location of the information. You can access information from a Web server, for instance. The high-level classes take care of the drudgery of networking protocols and enable you to concentrate on the actual information. If you need finer control than this, you can use the low-level classes. These classes let you send raw data over the network. You can use them to implement your own networking protocols.

The `URL` class represents a Uniform Resource Locator, which is the standard address format for resources on the World Wide Web as defined in the Internet standard RFC 1630. A URL is similar to a filename in that it tells where to go to get some information, but you still have to open and read it to get the information. After you create a URL, you can retrieve the information stored at that URL in one of three ways:

- Use the `getContent` method in the `URL` class to fetch the URL's content directly.
- Use the `openConnection` method to get a `URLConnection` to the URL.
- Use the `openStream` method to get an `InputStream` to the URL.

You have a number of options when it comes to creating a `URL` object. You can call the `Constructor` with a string representing the full URL:

```
public URL(String fullURL) throws MalformedURLException
```

The full URL string is the form you are probably most familiar with. Here is an example:

```
URL queHomePage = new URL("http://www.quecorp.com");
```

You can also create a URL by giving the protocol, host name, filename, and an optional port number:

```
public URL(String protocol, String hostName, String fileName)
     throws MalformedURLException
public URL(String protocol, String hostName, int portNumber, String fileName)
     throws MalformedURLException
```

The equivalent of the Que home page URL using this notation would be as follows:

```
URL queHomePage = new URL("http", "www.quecorp.com", "que");
```

or

```
URL queHomePage = new URL("http", "www.quecorp.com", 80,
     "que"); // 80 is default http port
```

If you have already created a URL and would like to open a new URL based on some information from the old one, you can pass the old URL and a string to the URL `Constructor`:

```
public URL(URL contextURL, String spec)
```

This is most often used in applets because the `Applet` class returns a URL for the directory where the applet's `.class` file resides. You can also get a URL for the directory where the applet's document is stored. Suppose, for example, that you stored a file called `myfile.txt` in the same directory as your applet's `.html` file. Your applet could create the URL for `myfile.txt` with this:

```
URL myfileURL = new URL(getDocumentBase(), "myfile.txt");
```

If you had stored `myfile.txt` in the same directory as the applet's `.class` file (it may or may not be the same directory as the `.html` file), the applet could create a URL for `myfile.txt` with this:

```
URL myfileURL = new URL(getCodeBase(), "myfile.txt");
```

Getting URL Contents

After you create a URL, you will probably want to fetch the contents. The easiest way to do this is by calling the `getContent` method:

```
public final Object getContent()
```

This first method requires that you define a content handler for the content returned by the URL. The HotJava browser comes with some built-in content handlers, but Netscape does not use this method for interpreting content. You will likely get an `UnknownServiceException` if you use this method from Netscape.

If you would rather interpret the data yourself, you can get a `URLConnection` for a URL with the `openConnection` method:

```
public URLConnection openConnection() throws IOException
```

Your third option for getting the contents of a URL should work almost everywhere. You can get an input stream to the URL and read it in yourself by using the `openStream` method:

```
public final InputStream openStream() throws IOException
```

The following code fragment dumps the contents of a URL to the `System.out` stream by opening an input stream to the URL and reading one byte at a time:

```
try {
    URL myURL = new URL(getDocumentBase(), "foo.html");
      InputStream in = myURL.openStream(); // get input stream for URL
     int b;
     while ((b = in.read()) != -1) {     // read the next byte
          System.out.print((char)b);     // print it
     }
 } catch (Exception e) {
     e.printStackTrace();  // something went wrong
}
```

Getting URL Information

You can retrieve the specific pieces of a URL using the following methods:

```
public String getProtocol()
```

returns the name of the URL's protocol.

```
public String getHost()
```

returns the name of the URL's host.

```
public int getPort()
```

returns the URL's port number.

```
public String getFile()
```

returns the URL's filename.

```
public String getRef()
```

returns the URL's reference tag. This is an optional index into an HTML page that follows the filename and begins with a `#`.

The *URLConnection* Class

The `URLConnection` class provides a more granular interface to a URL than the `getContent` method in the `URL` class. This class provides methods for examining HTTP headers, getting information about the URL's content, and getting input and output streams to the URL. There will be a different `URLConnection` class for each type of protocol that you can use. There will be a `URLConnection` that handles the HTTP protocol, for example, as well as another that handles the FTP protocol. Your browser may not support any of them. You can feel fairly certain that they are implemented in HotJava. HotJava is written totally in Java, which uses these classes to do all of its browsing. Netscape, on the other hand, has its own native code for handling these protocols and does not use Sun's `URLConnection` classes.

This class is geared toward interpreting text that will be displayed in a browser. Consequently, it has many methods for dealing with header fields and content types.

You do not create a `URLConnection` object yourself; it is created and returned by a URL object. After you have an instance of a `URLConnection`, you can examine the various header fields with the `getHeaderField` methods:

```
public String getHeaderField(String fieldName)
```

returns the value of the header field named by `fieldName`. If this field is not present in the resource, this method returns `null`.

```
public String getHeaderField(int n)
```

returns the value of the `n`th field in the resource. If there are not that many header fields, this method returns `null`. You can get the corresponding field name with the `getHeaderFieldKey` method.

```
public int getHeaderFieldKey(int n)
```

returns the field name of the `n`th field in the resource. If there are not that many header fields, this method returns `null`.

You can also get a header field value as an integer or a date using the following methods:

```
public int getHeaderFieldInt(String fieldName, int defaultValue)
```

converts the header field named by `fieldName` to an integer. If the field does not exist or is not a valid integer, it returns `defaultValue`.

```
public int getHeaderFieldDate(String fieldName, long defaultValue)
```

interprets the header field value as a date and returns the number of milliseconds since the epoch for that date. If the field does not exist or is not a valid date, it returns `defaultValue`.

In addition to interpreting the header fields, the `URLConnection` class also returns information about the content:

```
public String getContentEncoding()

public int getContentLength()

public String getContentType()
```

As with the `URL` class, you can get the entire content of the URL as an object using the `getContent` method:

```
public Object getContent()
throws IOException, UnknownServiceException
```

This method probably won't work under Netscape, but should work under HotJava.

Sometimes a program tries to access a URL that requires user authentication in the form of a dialog box, which automatically pops up when you open the URL. Because you do not always want your Java program to require that a user be present, you can tell the `URLConnection` class whether it should allow user interaction. If a situation occurs that requires user interaction and you have turned it off, the `URLConnection` class will throw an exception.

The `setAllowUserInteraction` method, when passed a value of `true`, will permit interaction with a user when needed:

```
public void setAllowUserInteraction(boolean allowInteraction)

public boolean getAllowUserInteraction()
```

returns `true` if this class will interact with a user when needed.

```
public static void setDefaultAllowUserInteraction(boolean default)
```

changes the default setting for allowing user interaction on all new instances of `URLConnection`. Changing the default setting does not affect instances that have already been created.

```
public static boolean getDefaultAllowUserInteraction()
```

returns the default setting for allowing user interaction.

Some URLs allow two-way communication. You can tell a `URLConnection` whether it should allow input or output by using the `doInput` and `doOutput` methods:

```
public void setDoInput(boolean doInput)

public void setDoOutput(boolean doOutput)
```

You can set either or both of these values to `true`. The `doInput` flag is `true` by default, and the `doOutput` flag is `false` by default.

You can query the `doInput` and `doOutput` flags with `getDoInput` and `getDoOutput`:

```
public boolean getDoInput()

public boolean getDoOutput()
```

The `getInputStream` and `getOutputStream` methods return input and output streams for the resource:

```
public InputStream getInputStream()
    throws IOException, UnknownServiceException

public OutputStream getOutputStream()
    throws IOException, UnknownServiceException
```

The *HTTPURLConnection* Class

The HTTP protocol has some extra features that the `URLConnection` class does not address. When you send an HTTP request, for instance, you can make several different requests (`GET`, `POST`, `PUT`, and so on). The `HTTPURLConnection` class provides better access to HTTP-specific options.

One of the most important fields in the `HTTPURLConnection` is the `request` method. You can set the `request` method by calling `setRequestMethod` with the name of the method you want:

```
public void setRequestMethod(String method) throws ProtocolException
```

The valid methods are: `GET`, `POST`, `HEAD`, `PUT`, `DELETE`, `OPTIONS`, and `TRACE`. If you don't set a request method, the default method is `GET`. Calling `getRequestMethod` will return the current method:

```
public String getRequestMethod()
```

When you send an HTTP request, the HTTP server responds with a response code and message. If you try to access a Web page that no longer exists, for example, you get a `"404 Not Found"` message. The `getResponseMessage` method returns the message part of a response while the `getResponseCode` returns the numeric portion:

```
public String getResponseMessage() throws IOException

public int getResponseCode() throws IOException
```

In the case of `"404 Not Found"`, `getResponseCode` would return `404`, and `getResponseMessage` would return `"Not Found"`.

Because Web sites move around frequently, Web servers support the notion of redirection, where you are automatically sent to a page's new location. The `HTTPURLConnection` class enables you to choose whether it should automatically follow a redirection. Passing a `flag` value of `true` to `setFollowRedirects` method instructs the `HTTPURLConnection` class to follow a redirection:

```
public static void setFollowRedirects(boolean flag)
```

The `getFollowRedirects` method returns `true` if redirection is turned on:

```
public static boolean getFollowRedirects()
```

The `getProxy` method returns `true` if all HTTP requests are going through a proxy:

```
public abstract boolean usingProxy()
```

New with JDK 1.2 you can also obtain the message stream that results after an HTTP error. The `getErrorStream()` method returns an `InputStream` that will contain the data sent after an error. For instance, if the server responded with a 404, the `HTTPURLConnection` would throw a `FileNotFoundException`. However, the Web server might have sent a help page along with the 404. The `getErrorStream()` method would provide you with a handle to that help page.

```
public InputStream getErrorStream()
```

The *URLEncoder* Class

This class contains only one static method that converts a string into URL-encoded form. The URL encoding reduces a string to a limited set of characters. Only letters, digits, and the underscore character are left untouched. Spaces are converted to a `+`, and all other characters are converted to hexadecimal and written as `%xx`, where `xx` is the hex representation of the character. The format for the `encode` method is as follows:

```
public static String encode(String s)
```

The *URLDecoder* Class

JDK 1.2 has added a class to allow you to decode strings that are in MIME format (the strings that `URLEncoder` produces, for instance). When the decode process completes, all ASCII characters a through z, A through Z, and 0 through 9 remain the same, but plus signs (+) are converted into spaces. The rest of the characters in the string are changed to three-character strings. These three-character strings begin with a percent sign (%) and are followed by the two-digit hexadecimal representation of the lower 8 bits of the character. For instance, the string `"Hello+%56"` is converted to `"Hello V"`.

```
public static String decode(String s)
```

The *URLStreamHandler* Class

The `URLStreamHandler` class is responsible for parsing a URL and creating a `URLConnection` object to access that URL. When you open a connection for a URL, it scans a set of packages for a handler for that URL's protocol. The handler should be named `<protocol>.Handler`. If you open an HTTP URL, for instance, the `URL` class searches for a class named `<some package name>.http.Handler`. By default, the class only searches the package `sun.net.www.protocol`, but you may specify an alternate search path by setting the system property to `java.protocol.handler.pkgs`. This property should contain a list of alternate packages to search that are separated by vertical bars. For example:

```
mypackages.urls¦thirdparty.lib¦funstuff"
```

At the minimum, any subclass of the `URLStreamHandler` must implement an `openConnection` method:

```
protected abstract URLConnection openConnection(URL u)
     throws IOException
```

This method returns an instance of `URLConnection` that knows how to speak the correct protocol. If you create your own `URLStreamHandler` for the FTP protocol, for example, this method should return a `URLConnection` that speaks the FTP protocol.

You can also change the way a URL string is parsed by creating your own `parseURL` and `setURL` methods:

```
protected void parseURL(URL u, String spec, int start, int limit)
```

This method parses a URL string, starting at position `start` in the string and going up to position `limit`. It modifies the URL directly, after it has parsed the string, using the protected `set` method in the URL.

You can set the different parts of a URL's information using the `setURL` method:

```
protected void setURL(URL u, String protocol, String host, int port,
    String file, String ref)
```

The call to `set` looks like the following:

```
u.set(protocol, host, port, file, ref);
```

NOTE Most of the popular network protocols are already implemented in the HotJava browser. If you want to use the `URLStreamHandler` facility in Netscape and other browsers, you need to write many of these yourself.

The *ContentHandler* Class

When you fetch a document using the HTTP protocol, the Web server sends you a series of headers before sending the actual data. One of the items in this header indicates what kind of data is being sent. This data is referred to as content, and the type of the data (referred to as the MIME content-type) is specified by the `Content-type` header. Web browsers use the content type to determine what to do with the incoming data.

If you want to provide your own handler for a particular MIME content-type, you can create a `ContentHandler` class to parse it and return an object representing the contents. The mechanism for setting up your own content handler is almost identical to that of setting up your own `URLStreamHandler`. You must give it a name of the form `<some package name>.major.minor`. The `major` and `minor` names come from the MIME `Content-type` header, which is in the following form:

```
Content-type: major/minor
```

One of the most common `major/minor` combinations is `text/plain`. If you define your own `text/plain` handler, it can be named `MyPackage.text.plain`. By default, the `URLConnection` class searches for content handlers only in a package named `sun.net.www.content`. You can give additional package names by specifying a list of packages separated by vertical bars in the `java.content.handler.pkgs` system property.

The only method you must implement in your `ContentHandler` is the `getContent` method:

```
public abstract Object getContent(URLConnection urlConn)
     throws IOException
```

It is completely up to you how you actually parse the content and select the kind of object you return.

The *Socket* Class

The `Socket` class is one of the fundamental building blocks for network-based Java applications. It implements a two-way connection-oriented communications channel between programs. After a socket connection is established, you can get input and output streams from the `Socket` object. To establish a socket connection, a program must be listening for connections on a specific port number. Although socket communications are peer-to-peer—that is, neither end of the socket connection is considered the master, and data can be sent either way at any time—the connection establishment phase has a notion of a server and a client.

Think of a socket connection as a phone call. After the call is made, either party can talk at any time, but when the call is first made, someone must make the call and someone else must listen for the phone to ring. The person making the call is the client, and the person listening for the call is the server.

The `ServerSocket` class, discussed later in this chapter, listens for incoming calls. The `Socket` class initiates a call. The network equivalent of a telephone number is a host address and port. The host address can either be a host name such as netcom.com, or a numeric address such as 192.100.81.100. The port number is a 16-bit number that is usually determined by the server. When you create a `Socket` object, you pass the constructor the destination host name and port number for the server you are connecting to. For example,

```
public Socket(String host, int port)
     throws UnknownHostException, IOException
```

creates a socket connection to port number `port` at the host named by host. If the `Socket` class cannot determine the numeric address for the host name, it throws an `UnknownHostException`. If there is a problem creating the connection—for instance, if there is no server listening at that port number—you get an `IOException`.

NOTE If you want to create a connection using a numeric host address, you can pass the numeric address as a host name string. The host address 192.100.81.100, for instance, can be passed as the `host name "192.100.81.100"`.

```
public Socket(String host, int port, boolean stream)
     throws UnknownHostException, IOException
```

creates a socket connection to port number `port` at the host named by `host`. You can optionally request this connection be made by using datagram-based communication rather than stream-based. With a stream, you are assured that all the data sent over the connection will arrive correctly. Datagrams are not guaranteed, however, so it is possible that messages can be lost. The tradeoff here is that the datagrams are much faster than the streams. Therefore, if you have a reliable network, you may be better off with a datagram connection. The default mode for `Socket` objects is Stream mode. If you pass `false` for the `stream` parameter, the connection will be made in Datagram mode. You cannot change modes after the `Socket` object has been created.

```
public Socket(InetAddress address, int port)
     throws IOException
```

creates a socket connection to port number `port` at the host whose address is stored in `address`.

```
public Socket(InetAddress address, int port, boolean stream)
     throws IOException
```

creates a socket connection to port number `port` at the host whose address is stored in `address`. If the `stream` parameter is `false`, the connection is made in Datagram mode.

NOTE Because of security restrictions in Netscape and other browsers, you may be restricted to making socket connections back to the host address from where the applet was loaded.

Sending and Receiving Socket Data

The `Socket` class does not contain explicit methods for sending and receiving data. Instead, it provides methods that return input and output streams, enabling you to take full advantage of the existing classes in `java.io`.

The `getInputStream` method returns an `InputStream` for the socket; the `getOutputStream` method returns an `OutputStream`:

```
public InputStream getInputStream() throws IOException
```

```
public OutputStream getOutputStream() throws IOException
```

Getting Socket Information

You can get information about the socket connection such as the address, the port it is connected to, and its local port number.

NOTE Just as each telephone in a telephone connection has its own phone number, each end of a socket connection has a host address and port number. The port number on the client side, however, does not enter into the connection establishment. One difference between socket communications and the telephone is that a client usually has a different port number every time it creates a new connection, but you always have the same phone number when you pick up the phone to make a call.

The `getInetAddress` and `getPort` methods return the host address and port number for the other end of the connection:

```
public InetAddress getInetAddress()
```

```
public int getPort()
```

You can get the local port number of your socket connection from the `getLocalPort` method:

```
public int getLocalPort()
```

Setting Socket Options

Certain socket options modify the behavior of sockets. They are not often used, but it is nice to have them available. The `setSoLinger` method sets the amount of time that a socket will spend trying to send data after it has been closed:

```
public void setSoLinger(boolean on, int maxTime)
     throws SocketException
```

Normally, when you are sending data over a socket and you close the socket, any untransmitted data is flushed. By turning on the Linger option, you can make sure that all data has been sent before the socket connection is taken down. You can query the linger time with `getSoLinger`:

```
public int getSoLinger() throws SocketException
```

If the Linger option is off, `getSoLinger` returns `-1`.

If you try to read data from a socket and there is no data available, the `read` method normally blocks (it waits until there is data). You can use the `setSoTimeout` method to set the maximum amount of time that the `read` method will wait before giving up:

```
public synchronized void setSoTimeout(int timeout)
     throws SocketException
```

A `timeout` of `0` indicated that the `read` method should wait forever (the default behavior). If the `read` times out, rather than just returning, it will throw `java.io.InterruptedIOException`, but the socket will remain open. You can query the current timeout with `getSoTimeout`:

```
public synchronized int getSoTimeout()
     throws SocketException
```

The TCP protocol used by socket connections is reasonably efficient in network utilization. If it is sending large amounts of data, it usually packages the data into larger packets. The reason this is more efficient is that there is a certain fixed amount of overhead per network packet. If the packets are larger, the percentage of network bandwidth consumed by the overhead is much smaller. Unfortunately, TCP can also cause delays when you are sending many small packets in a short amount of time. If you are sending mouse coordinates over the network, for instance, the TCP driver will frequently group the coordinates into larger packets while it is waiting for acknowledgment that the previous packets were received. This makes the mouse movement look pretty choppy. You can ask the socket to send information as soon as possible by passing `true` to `setTcpNoDelay`:

```
public void setTcpNoDelay(boolean on)
```

The `getTcpNoDelay` method returns `true` if the socket is operating under the No Delay option (if the socket sends things immediately):

```
public boolean getTcpNoDelay()
```

CAUTION

You should be very careful when using the No Delay option. If you send a flurry of small packets, you can waste large amounts of network bandwidth. If you send a 1-byte message, given about 64 bytes of fixed overhead, 98% of the bandwidth you use is for overhead. Even for a 64-byte message, 50% of the bandwidth is overhead.

Closing the Socket Connection

The socket equivalent of "hanging up the phone" is closing down the connection, which is performed by the `close` method:

```
public synchronized void close() throws IOException
```

Waiting for Incoming Data

Reading data from a socket is not quite like reading data from a file, even though both are input streams. When you read a file, all the data is already in the file. But with a socket connection, you may try to read before the program on the other end of the connection has sent something. Because the `read` methods in the different input streams all block—that is, they wait for data if none is present—you must be careful that your program does not completely halt while waiting. The typical solution for this situation is to spawn a thread to read data from the socket. Listing 33.1 shows a thread that is dedicated to reading data from an input stream. It notifies your program of new data by calling a `dataReady` method with the incoming data.

Listing 33.1 Source Code for *ReadThread.java*

```
import java.net.*;
import java.lang.*;
import java.io.*;

/**
 * A thread dedicated to reading data from a socket connection.
 */

public class ReadThread extends Thread
{
     protected Socket connectionSocket;  // the socket you are reading from
     protected DataInputStream inStream; // the input stream from the socket
     protected ReadCallback readCallback;

/**
 * Creates an instance of a ReadThread on a Socket and identifies the callback
 * that will receive all data from the socket.
 *
```

```
 * @param callback the object to be notified when data is ready
 * @param connSock the socket this ReadThread will read data from
 * @exception IOException if there is an error getting an input stream
 *            for the socket
 */
    public ReadThread(ReadCallback callback, Socket connSock)
    throws IOException
    {
        connectionSocket = connSock;
        readCallback = callback;
        inStream = new DataInputStream(connSock.getInputStream());
    }

/**
 * Closes down the socket connection using the socket's close method
 */
    protected void closeConnection()
    {
        try {
            connectionSocket.close();
        } catch (Exception oops) {
        }
        stop();
    }

/**
 * Continuously reads a string from the socket and then calls dataReady in the
 * read callback. If you want to read something other than a string, change
 * this method and the dataReady callback to handle the appropriate data.
 */

    public void run()
    {
        while (true)
        {
            try {
// readUTF reads in a string
                String str = inStream.readUTF();
// Notify the callback that you have a string
                readCallback.dataReady(str);
            }
            catch (Exception oops)
            {
// Tell the callback there was an error
                readCallback.dataReady(null);
            }
        }
    }
}
```

Listing 33.2 shows the `ReadCallback` interface, which must be implemented by a class to receive data from a `ReadThread` object.

Listing 33.2 Source Code for *ReadCallback.java*

```
/**
 * Implements a callback interface for the ReadConn class
 */
public interface ReadCallback
{
/**
 * Called when there is data ready on a ReadConn connection.
 * @param str the string read by the read thread, If null, the
 *      connection closed or there was an error reading data
 */
     public void dataReady(String str);
}
```

A Simple Socket Client

Using these two classes, you can implement a simple client that connects to a server and uses a `read` thread to read the data returned by the server. The corresponding server for this client is presented in the following section, "The `ServerSocket` Class." Listing 33.3 shows the `SimpleClient` class.

Listing 33.3 Source Code for *SimpleClient.java*

```
import java.io.*;
import java.net.*;

/**
 * This class sets up a Socket connection to a server, spawns
 * a ReadThread object to read data coming back from the server,
 * and starts a thread that sends a string to the server every
 * 2 seconds.
 */

public class SimpleClient extends Object implements Runnable, ReadCallback
{
     protected Socket serverSock;
     protected DataOutputStream outStream;
     protected Thread clientThread;
     protected ReadThread reader;

     public SimpleClient(String hostName, int portNumber)
     throws IOException
     {
          Socket serverSock = new Socket(hostName, portNumber);

// The DataOutputStream has methods for sending different data types
// in a machine-independent format. It is very useful for sending data
// over a socket connection.
          outStream = new DataOutputStream(serverSock.getOutputStream());

// Create a reader thread
          reader = new ReadThread(this, serverSock);
```

```
// Start the reader thread
          reader.start();
     }

// These are generic start and stop methods for a Runnable

     public void start()
     {
          clientThread = new Thread(this);
          clientThread.start();
     }

     public void stop()
     {
          clientThread.stop();
          clientThread = null;
     }

// sendString sends a string to the server using writeUTF

     public synchronized void sendString(String str)
     throws IOException
     {
          System.out.println("Sending string: "+str);
          outStream.writeUTF(str);
     }

// The run method for this object just sends a string to the server
// and sleeps for 2 seconds before sending another string

     public void run()
     {
          while (true)
          {
               try {
                    sendString("Hello There!");
                    Thread.sleep(2000);
               } catch (Exception oops) {
// If there was an error, print info and disconnect
                    oops.printStackTrace();
                    disconnect();
                    stop();
               }
          }
     }

// The disconnect method closes down the connection to the server

     public void disconnect()
     {
          try {
               reader.closeConnection();
          } catch (Exception badClose) {
               // should be able to ignore
          }
```


continues

Listing 33.3 Continued

```
     }

// dataReady is the callback from the read thread. It is called
// whenever a string is received from the server.

     public synchronized void dataReady(String str)
     {
          System.out.println("Got incoming string: "+str);
     }

     public static void main(String[] args)
     {
          try {
/* Change localhost to the host you are running the server on. If it
   is on the same machine, you can leave it as localhost. */

               SimpleClient client = new SimpleClient("localhost",
                    4331);
               client.start();
          } catch (Exception cantStart) {
               System.out.println("Got error");
               cantStart.printStackTrace();
          }
     }
}
```

The *ServerSocket* Class

The `ServerSocket` class listens for incoming connections and creates a `Socket` object for each new connection. You create a server socket by giving it a port number to listen on:

```
public ServerSocket(int portNumber) throws IOException
```

If you do not care what port number you are using, you can have the system assign the port number for you by passing in a port number of `0`.

Many socket implementations have a notion of connection backlog. That is, if many clients connect to a server at once, the number of connections that have yet to be accepted are the backlog. After a server hits the limit of backlogged connections, the server refuses any new clients. To create a `ServerSocket` with a specific limit of backlogged connections, pass the port number and backlog limit to the `Constructor`:

```
public ServerSocket(int portNumber, int backlogLimit)
throws IOException
```

NOTE Because of current security restrictions in Netscape and other browsers, you may not be able to accept socket connections with an applet.

Accepting Incoming Socket Connections

After the server socket is created, the `accept` method will return a `Socket` object for each new connection:

```
public Socket accept() throws IOException
```

If no connections are pending, the `accept` method will block until there is a connection. If you do not want your program to block completely while you are waiting for connections, you should perform the `accept` in a separate thread.

When you no longer want to accept connections, close down the `ServerSocket` object with the `close` method:

```
public void close() throws IOException
```

The `close` method does not affect the existing socket connections that were made through this `ServerSocket`. If you want the existing connections to close, you must close each one explicitly.

Getting the Server Socket Address

If you need to find the address and port number for your server socket, you can use the `getInetAddress` and `getLocalPort` methods:

```
public InetAddress getInetAddress()

public int getLocalPort()
```

The `getLocalPort` method is especially useful if you had the system assign the port number. You may wonder what use it is for the system to assign the port number because you somehow must tell the clients what port number to use. There are some practical uses for this method, however. One use is implementing the FTP protocol. If you have ever watched an FTP session in action, you will notice that when you `get` or `put` a file, a message such as `PORT command accepted` appears. What has happened is that your local FTP program created the equivalent of a server socket and sent the port number to the FTP server. The FTP server then creates a connection back to your FTP program using this port number.

Writing a Server Program

You can use many models when writing a server program. You can make one big server object that accepts new clients and contains all the necessary methods for communicating with them, for example. You can make your server more modular by creating special objects that communicate with clients but invoke methods on the main server object. Using this model, you can have clients who all share the server's information but can communicate using different protocols.

Listing 33.4 shows an example client handler object that talks to an individual client and passes the client's request up to the main server.

Listing 33.4 Source Code for *ServerConn.java*

```
import java.io.*;
import java.net.*;

/**
 * This class represents a server's client. It handles all the
 * communications with the client. When the server gets a new
 * connection, it creates one of these objects, passing it the
 * Socket object of the new client. When the client's connection
 * closes, this object goes away quietly. The server doesn't actually
 * have a reference to this object.
 *
 * Just for example's sake, when you write a server using a setup
 * like this, you will probably have methods in the server that
 * this object will call. This object keeps a reference to the server
 * and calls a method in the server to process the strings read from
 * the client and returns a string to send back.
 */

public class ServerConn extends Object implements ReadCallback
{
     protected SimpleServer server;
     protected Socket clientSock;
     protected ReadThread reader;
     protected DataOutputStream outStream;

     public ServerConn(SimpleServer server, Socket clientSock)
     throws IOException
     {
          this.server = server;
          this.clientSock = clientSock;
          outStream = new DataOutputStream(clientSock.getOutputStream());
          reader = new ReadThread(this, clientSock);
          reader.start();
     }

/**
 * This method received the string read from the client, calls
 * a method in the server to process the string, and sends back
 * the string returned by the server.
 */
     public synchronized void dataReady(String str)
     {
          if (str == null)
          {
               disconnect();
               return;
          }

          try {
               outStream.writeUTF(server.processString(str));
          } catch (Exception writeError) {
               writeError.printStackTrace();
               disconnect();
               return;
          }
```

```
    }

/**
 * This method closes the connection to the client. If there is an error
 * closing the socket, it stops the read thread, which should eventually
 * cause the socket to get cleaned up.
 **/
    public synchronized void disconnect()
    {
         try {
              reader.closeConnection();
         } catch (Exception cantclose) {
              reader.stop();
         }
    }
}
```

With the `ServerConn` object handling the burden of communicating with the clients, your server object can concentrate on implementing whatever services it should provide. Listing 33.5 shows a simple server that takes a string and sends back the reverse of the string.

Listing 33.5 Source Code for *SimpleServer.java*

```
import java.io.*;
import java.net.*;

/**
 * This class implements a simple server that accepts incoming
 * socket connections and creates a ServerConn instance to handle
 * each connection. It also provides a processString method that
 * takes a string and returns the reverse of it. This method is
 * invoked by the ServerConn instances when they receive a string
 * from a client.
 */

public class SimpleServer extends Object
{
     protected ServerSocket listenSock;

     public SimpleServer(int listenPort)
     throws IOException
     {
// Listen for connections on port listenPort
          listenSock = new ServerSocket(listenPort);
     }

     public void waitForClients()
     {
          while (true)
          {
               try {
// Wait for the next incoming socket connection
                    Socket newClient = listenSock.accept();
```

continues

Listing 33.5 Continued

```
// Create a ServerConn to handle this new connection
                    ServerConn newConn = new ServerConn(
                        this, newClient);
                } catch (Exception badAccept) {
                    badAccept.printStackTrace();
                    // print an error, but keep going
                }
            }
        }

// This method takes a string and returns the reverse of it

        public synchronized String processString(String inStr)
        {
            StringBuffer newBuffer = new StringBuffer();
            int len = inStr.length();

// Start at the end of the string and move down towards the beginning
            for (int i=len-1; i >= 0; i--) {

// Add the next character to the end of the string buffer
// Since you started at the end of the string, the first character
// in the buffer will be the last character in the string

                newBuffer.append(inStr.charAt(i));
            }
            return newBuffer.toString();
        }

        public static void main(String[] args)
        {
            try {
// Crank up the server and wait for connection
                SimpleServer server = new SimpleServer(4321);
                server.waitForClients();
            } catch (Exception oops) {

// If there was an error starting the server, say so!
                System.out.println("Got error:");
                oops.printStackTrace();
            }
        }
}
```

The *InetAddress* Class

The `InetAddress` class contains an Internet host address. Internet hosts are identified one of two ways:

- Name
- Address

The address is a 4-byte number usually written in the form a.b.c.d, like 192.100.81.100. When data is sent between computers, the network protocols use this numeric address for determining where to send the data. Host names are created for convenience. They keep you from having to memorize a lot of 12-digit network addresses. It is far easier to remember netcom.com, for example, than it is to remember 192.100.81.100.

As it turns out, relating a name to an address is a science in itself. When you make a connection to netcom.com, your system needs to find out the numeric address for netcom. It will usually use a service called Domain Name Service, or DNS. DNS is the telephone book service for Internet addresses. Host names and addresses on the Internet are grouped into domains and subdomains, and each subdomain may have its own DNS—that is, its own local phone book.

You may have noticed that Internet host names are usually a number of names that are separated by periods. These separate names represent the domain a host belongs to. netcom5.netcom.com, for example, is the host name for a machine named netcom5 in the netcom.com domain. The netcom.com domain is a subdomain of the .com domain. A netcom.edu domain could be completely separate from the netcom.com domain, and netcom5.netcom.edu would be a totally different host. Again, this is not too different from phone numbers. The phone number 404-555-1017 has an area code of 404, for example, which could be considered the Atlanta domain. The exchange 555 is a subdomain of the Atlanta domain, and 1017 is a specific number in the 555 domain, which is part of the Atlanta domain. Just as you can have a netcom5.netcom.edu that is different from netcom5.netcom.com, you can have an identical phone number in a different area code, such as 212-555-1017.

The important point to remember here is that host names are only unique within a particular domain. Don't think that your organization is the only one in the world to have named its machines after The Three Stooges, Star Trek characters, or characters from various comic strips.

Converting a Name to an Address

The `InetAddress` class handles all the intricacies of name lookup for you. The `getByName` method takes a host name and returns an instance of `InetAddress` that contains the network address of the host:

```
public static synchronized InetAddress getByName(String host)
     throws UnknownHostException
```

A host can have multiple network addresses. Suppose, for example, that you have your own LAN at home as well as a Point-to-Point Protocol connection to the Internet. The machine with the PPP connection has two network addresses: the PPP address and the local LAN address. You can find out all the available network addresses for a particular host by calling `getAllByName`:

```
public static synchronized InetAddress[] getAllByName(String host)
     throws UnknownHostException
```

The `getLocalHost` method returns the address of the local host:

```
public static InetAddress getLocalHost()
     throws UnknownHostException
```

Examining the *InetAddress*

The `InetAddress` class has two methods for retrieving the address that it stores. The `getHostName` method returns the name of the host, and `getAddress` returns the numeric address of the host:

```
public String getHostName()

public byte[] getAddress()
```

The `getAddress` method returns the address as an array of bytes. Under the current Internet addressing scheme, an array of four bytes would be returned. If and when the Internet goes to a larger address size, however, this method just returns a larger array. The following code fragment prints out a numeric address using the dot notation:

```
byte[] addr = someInetAddress.getAddress();
System.out.println((addr[0]&0xff)+"."+(addr[1]&0xff)+"."+
     (addr[2]&0xff)+"."+(addr[3]&0xff));
```

You may be wondering why the address values are ANDed with the hex value `ff` (255 in decimal). The reason is that byte values in Java are signed 8-bit numbers. That means when the leftmost bit is 1, the number is negative. Internet addresses are not usually written with negative numbers. By ANDing the values with 255, you do not change the value, but you suddenly treat the value as a 32-bit integer value whose leftmost bit is 0, and whose rightmost 8 bits represent the address.

Getting an Applet's Originating Address

Under many Java-aware browsers, socket connections are restricted to the server where the applet originated. In other words, the only host your applet can connect to is the one it was loaded from. You can create an instance of an `InetAddress` corresponding to the applet's originating host by getting the applet's document base or code base URL and then getting the URL's host name. The following code fragment illustrates this method:

```
URL appletSource = getDocumentBase(); // must be called from applet
InetAddress appletAddress = InetAddress.getByName(
     appletSource.getHost());
```

The *DatagramSocket* Class

The `DatagramSocket` class implements a special kind of socket that is made specifically for sending datagrams. A datagram is somewhat like a letter in that it is sent from one point to another and can occasionally get lost. Of course, Internet datagrams are several orders of magnitude faster than the postal system. A datagram socket is like a mailbox. You receive all your datagrams from your datagram socket. Unlike the stream-based sockets you read about earlier, you do not need a new datagram socket for every program you must communicate with.

If the datagram socket is the network equivalent of a mailbox, the datagram packet is the equivalent of a letter. When you want to send a datagram to another program, you create a

`DatagramPacket` object that contains the host address and port number of the receiving `DatagramSocket`, just like you must put an address on a letter when you mail it. You then call the `send` method in your `DatagramSocket`, and it sends your datagram packet off through the ethernet network to the recipient.

Not surprisingly, working with datagrams involves some of the same problems as mailing letters. Datagrams can get lost and delivered out of sequence. If you write two letters to someone, you have no guarantee which letter the person will receive first. If one letter refers to the other, it could cause confusion. There is no easy solution for this situation, except to plan for the possibility.

Another situation occurs when a datagram gets lost. Imagine that you have mailed off your house payment, and a week later the bank tells you it hasn't received it. You don't know what happened to the payment—maybe the mail is very slow, or maybe the payment was lost. If you mail off another payment, maybe the bank will end up with two checks from you. If you don't mail it off and the payment really is lost, the bank will be very angry. This, too, can happen with datagrams. You may send a datagram, not hear any reply, and assume it was lost. If you send another one, the server on the other end may get two requests and become confused. A good way to minimize the impact of this kind of situation is to design your applications so that multiple datagrams of the same information do not cause confusion. The specifics of this design are beyond the scope of this book. You should consult a good book on network programming.

You can create a datagram socket with or without a specific port number:

```
public DatagramSocket() throws SocketException

public DatagramSocket(int portNumber) throws SocketException
```


As with the `Socket` class, if you do not give a port number, one will be assigned automatically. You only need to use a specific port number when other programs need to send unsolicited datagrams to you. Whenever you send a datagram, it has a return address on it, just like a letter. If you send a datagram to another program, it can always generate a reply to you without you explicitly telling it what port you are on. In general, only your server program needs to have a specific port number. The clients who send datagrams to the server and receive replies from it can have system-assigned port numbers because the server can see the return address on their datagrams.

The mechanism for sending and receiving datagrams is about as easy as mailing a letter and checking your mailbox—most of the work is in writing and reading the letter. The `send` method sends a datagram to its destination (the destination is stored in the `DatagramPacket` object):

```
public void send(DatagramPacket packet) throws IOException
```

The `receive` method reads in a datagram and stores it in a `DatagramPacket` object:

```
public synchronized void receive(DatagramPacket packet)
     throws IOException
```

When you no longer need the datagram socket, you can close it down with the `close` method:

```
public synchronized void close()
```

Finally, if you need to know the port number of your datagram socket, the `getLocalPort` method gives it to you:

```
public int getLocalPort()
```

The *DatagramPacket* Class

The `DatagramPacket` class is the network equivalent of a letter. It contains an address and other information. When you create a datagram, you must give it an array to contain the data as well as the length of the data. The `DatagramPacket` class is used in two ways:

- *As a piece of data to be sent out over a datagram socket.* In this case, the array used to create the packet should contain the data you want to send, and the length should be the exact number of bytes you want to send.
- *As a holding place for incoming datagrams.* In this case, the array should be large enough to hold whatever data you are expecting, and the length should be the maximum number of bytes you want to receive.

To create a datagram packet that is to be sent, you must give not only the array of data and the length, but you must also supply the destination host and port number for the packet:

```
public DatagramPacket(byte[] buffer, int length, InetAddress destAddress,
     int destPortNumber)
```

When you create a datagram packet for receiving data, you only need to supply an array large enough to hold the incoming data, as well as the maximum number of bytes you wish to receive:

```
public DatagramPacket(byte[] buffer, int length)
```

The `DatagramPacket` class also provides methods to query the four components of the packet:

```
public InetAddress getAddress()
```

For an incoming datagram packet, `getAddress` returns the address that the datagram was sent from. For an outgoing packet, `getAddress` returns the address where the datagram will be sent.

```
public int getPort()
```

For an incoming datagram packet, this is the port number that the datagram was sent from. For an outgoing packet, this is the port number where the datagram will be sent.

```
public byte[] getData()
```

```
public int getLength()
```

Broadcasting Datagrams

A datagram broadcast is the datagram equivalent of junk mail. It causes a packet to be sent to a number of hosts at the same time. When you broadcast, you always broadcast to a specific port number, but the network address you broadcast to is a special address.

Recall that Internet addresses are in the form a.b.c.d. Portions of this address are considered your host address, and other portions are considered your network address. The network address is the left portion of the address; the host address is the right portion. The dividing line between them varies based on the first byte of the address (the a portion). If a is less than 128, the network address is just the a portion, and the b.c.d is your host address. This address is referred to as a Class A address. If a is greater than or equal to 128 and less than 192, the network address is a.b, and the host address is c.d. This address is referred to as a Class B address. If a is greater than or equal to 192, the network address is a.b.c, and the host address is d. This address is referred to as a Class C address.

Why is the network address important? If you want to be polite, you should only broadcast to your local network. Broadcasting to the entire world is rather rude and probably won't work anyway because many routers block broadcasts past the local network. To send a broadcast to your local network, use the numeric address of the network and put in 255 for the portions that represent the host address. If you are connected to Netcom, for example, which has a network address that starts with 192, you should only broadcast Netcom's network of 192.100.81, which means the destination address for your datagrams should be 192.100.81.255. On the other hand, you might be on a network such as 159.165, which is a Class B address. On that network, you would broadcast to 159.165.255.255. You should consult your local system administrator about this, however, because many Class A and Class B networks are locally subdivided. You are safest just broadcasting to a.b.c.255 if you must broadcast at all.

A Simple Datagram Server

Listing 33.6 shows a simple datagram server program that just echoes back any datagrams it receives.

Listing 33.6 Source Code for *DatagramServer.java*

```
import java.net.*;

/**
 * This is a simple datagram echo server that receives datagrams
 * and echoes them back untouched.
 */

public class DatagramServer extends Object
{
     public static void main(String[] args)
     {
          try {
// Create the datagram socket with a specific port number
               DatagramSocket mysock = new DatagramSocket(5432);

// Allow packets up to 1024 bytes long
               byte[] buf = new byte[1024];
```

continues

Listing 33.6 Continued

```
// Create the packet for receiving datagrams
               DatagramPacket p = new DatagramPacket(buf,
                    buf.length);
               while (true) {
// Read in the datagram
                    mysock.receive(p);

                    System.out.println("Received datagram!");

// A nice feature of datagram packets is that there is only one
// address field. The incoming address and outgoing address are
// really the same address.  This means that when you receive
// a datagram, if you want to send it back to the originating
// address, you can just invoke send again.

                    mysock.send(p);
               }
          } catch (Exception e) {
               e.printStackTrace();
          }
     }
}
```

Listing 33.7 shows a simple client that sends datagrams to the server and waits for a reply. If the datagrams get lost, however, this program will hang because it does not resend datagrams.

Listing 33.7 Source Code for *DatagramClient.java*

```
import java.net.*;

/**
 * This program sends a datagram to the server every 2 seconds and waits
 * for a reply. If the datagram gets lost, this program will hang since it
 * has no retry logic.
 */

public class DatagramClient extends Object
{
     public static void main(String[] args)
     {
          try {
// Create the socket for sending
               DatagramSocket mysock = new DatagramSocket();


// Create the send buffer
               byte[] buf = new byte[1024];

// Create a packet to send. Currently just tries to send to the local host.
// Change the inet address to make it send somewhere else.
```

```
                DatagramPacket p = new DatagramPacket(buf,
                     buf.length, InetAddress.getLocalHost(), 5432);
                while (true) {
// Send the datagram
                     mysock.send(p);
                     System.out.println("Client sent datagram!");
// Wait for a reply
                     mysock.receive(p);
                     System.out.println("Client received datagram!");
                     Thread.sleep(2000);
                }
           } catch (Exception e) {
                e.printStackTrace();
           }
     }
}
```

Multicast Sockets

IP multicasting is a fairly new technology that represents an improvement over simple broadcasting. A multicast functions like a broadcast in that a single message gets sent to multiple recipients, but it is only sent to recipients that are looking for it.

The idea behind multicasting is that a certain set of network addresses are set aside as being multicast addresses. These addresses are in the range 225.0.0.0 to 239.255.255.255.

NOTE Actually, network addresses between 224.0.0.0 and 224.255.255.255 are also IP multicast addresses, but they are reserved for non-application uses.

Each multicast address is considered a group. When you want to receive messages from a certain address, you join the group. You may have set up the address 225.11.22.33 as the multicast address for your stock quote system, for example. A program that wanted to receive stock quotes would have to join the 225.11.22.33 multicast group.

To send or receive multicast data, you must first create a multicast socket. A multicast socket is similar to a datagram socket (in fact, `MulticastSocket` is a subclass of `DatagramSocket`). You can create the multicast socket with a default port number or you can specify the port number in the `Constructor`:

```
public MulticastSocket() throws IOException

public MulticastSocket(int portNumber) throws IOException
```

To join a multicast address, use the `joinGroup` method; to leave a group, use the `leaveGroup` method:

```
public void joinGroup(InetAddress multicastAddr) throws IOException

public void leaveGroup(InetAddress multicastAddr) throws IOException
```

On certain systems, you may have multiple network interfaces. This can cause a problem for multicasting because you need to listen on a specific interface. You can choose which interface your multicast socket uses by calling `setInterface`:

```
public void setInterface(InetAddress interface) throws SocketException
```

If your machine had IP addresses of 192.0.0.1 and 193.0.1.15, and you wanted to listen for multicast messages on the 193 network, for example, you would set your interface to the 193.0.1.15 address. Of course, you need to know the host name for that interface. You might have host names of `myhost_neta` for the 192 network and `myhost_netb` for the 193 network. In this case, you would set your interface this way:

```
mysocket.setInterface(InetAddress.getByName("myhost_netb"));
```

You can query the interface for a multicast socket by calling `getInterface`:

```
public InetAddress getInterface() throws SocketException
```

The key to multicast broadcasting is that you must send your packets out with a "time to live" value (also called TTL). This value indicates how far the packet should go (how many networks it should jump to). A TTL value of 0 indicates that the packet should stay on the local host. A TTL value of 1 indicates that the packet should only be sent on the local network. After that, the TTL values have more nebulous meanings. A TTL value of 32 means that the packet should only be sent to networks at this site. A TTL value of 64 means the packet should remain within this region, and a value of 128 means it should remain within this continent. A value of 255 means that the packet should go everywhere. Like broadcast datagrams, it is considered rude to send your packets to everyone. Try to limit the scope of your packets to the local network or, at least, the local site.

When you send a multicast datagram, you use a special version of the `send` method that takes a TTL value (if you use the default `send` method, the TTL is always 1):

```
public synchronized void send(DatagramPacket packet,
     byte timeToLive) throws IOException
```

You should also bear in mind that untrusted applets are not allowed to create `MulticastSocket` objects. ●

CHAPTER 34

Java Security in Depth

In this chapter

What Necessitates Java Security?

In any description of the features of the Java environment, a phrase such as "Java is secure" will be found. Security can mean a lot of different things, and when you're developing Java applets, it is critical to understand the implications of Java security. Your applets are restricted to functioning within the Java security framework, which affects your design while enabling the safe execution of network-loaded code.

To ensure an uncompromised environment, the Java security model errs on the side of caution. All applets loaded over the network are assumed to be potentially hostile and are treated with appropriate caution. This fact will greatly restrict your design. To enable Java applets to expand beyond these limitations, the Java Security API has been developed.

To appreciate the intent and rationale behind the framework on which Java is based, you must investigate what makes security an issue at all. Java provides many solutions to matters of security, many of which will have ramifications on how you approach the installation and authoring of Java applications in your Internet network solutions.

The Internet forms a vast shared medium, allowing machines throughout the world to communicate freely. Trusted and untrusted computers, allowing access to millions of individuals with unknown intentions, are linked together. One computer can send information to almost any other on the Internet. Furthermore, Internet applications and protocols are not foolproof; at various levels, the identities can be concealed through various techniques.

Adding Java to this scene opens tremendous potential for abuse. Java's strengths present the most problematic issues, specifically these:

- Java is a full-fledged programming language that allows applications to use many resources on the target machine, such as manipulating files, opening network sockets to remote systems, and spawning external processes.
- Java code is downloaded from the network, often from machines over which you have no control. Such code could contain fatal flaws or could have been altered by a malicious intruder. The original author could even have questionable motives that would have an impact on your system.
- Java code is smoothly, seamlessly downloaded by Java-enabled browsers such as HotJava, Netscape, or Internet Explorer. These special programs, known as applets, can be transferred to your machine and executed without your knowledge or permission.

  This "executable content" can have capabilities that extend far beyond the original limitations of your Web browser's design, precisely because Java is intended to allow your browser's capabilities to be extended dynamically.

Given these characteristics, it is easy to see why Java code should be treated with great care. Without a tightly controlled environment, one could envision a number of problematic scenarios:

- A malicious piece of code damages files and other resources on your computer.
- While perhaps presenting a useful application, code silently retrieves sensitive data from your system and transmits it to an attacker's machine.
- When you merely visit a Web page, a virus or worm is loaded that proceeds to spread from your machine to others.
- A program uses your system as a launching pad for an attack on another system, thus obscuring the identity of the real villain while perhaps misidentifying you as the true source of the attack.
- Code created by a programmer whose abilities are not equal to yours creates a buggy program that unintentionally damages your system.

With these problems in mind, the overall problem can be seen. To be practical, Java must provide a controlled environment in which applications are executed. Avenues for abuse or unintended damage must be anticipated and blocked. System resources must be protected. To be safe, Java must assume code that is loaded over the network comes from an untrusted source; only those capabilities known to be secure should be permitted. However, Java should not be so restricted that its value goes unrealized.

For those who are familiar with Internet security systems, the issues Java faces are not new. This situation presents the old paradox in which computers must have access to capabilities and resources to be useful. However, in an inverse relationship, the more power you provide to such systems, the greater the potential for abuse. In such a situation, a paranoid stance will render the system useless. A permissive stance will eventually spell doom. A prudent stance strives to find an intelligent middle ground.

The Java Security Framework

The security framework provides Java with a clear API to create secure execution environments. As you know, Java consists of many different layers that create the complete Java execution environment:

- Java language
- Feature-rich, standard API
- Java compiler
- Bytecode
- Dynamic loading and checking libraries at runtime
- Garbage collector
- Bytecode interpreter

At critical points throughout this structure, specific features help ensure a safe execution environment. In isolation, each portion might provide little or no benefit to the system. In concert, these features work to create the solid and secure framework that makes Java a practical solution to executable content.

Part One: The Safety Provided by the Language

The Java language itself provides the first layer of network security. This security provides the features that are necessary to protect data structures and limit the likelihood of unintentionally flawed programs.

Java-Enforced Adherence to the Object-Oriented Paradigm Private data structures and methods are encapsulated within Java classes. Access to these resources is provided only through a public interface that is furnished by the class. Object-oriented code often proves to be more maintainable and follows a clear design. This helps ensure that your program does not accidentally corrupt itself, or clobber other Java elements running in the same VM.

No Pointer Arithmetic Java references cannot be incremented or reset to point to specific portions of the JVM's memory. This means that you cannot unintentionally (or maliciously) overwrite the contents of an arbitrary object. Nor can you write data into sensitive portions of the system's memory. Furthermore, every object that isn't waiting for garbage collection must have a reference defined to it, so objects can't be accidentally lost.

Array-Bounds Checking Arrays in Java are bound to their known size. So in Java, if you have an array `int[5]` and you attempt to reference `[8]`, your program will throw an exception (`ArrayIndexOutOfBoundsException`). Historically, because other languages did not pay attention to array bounds, many security problems were created. For instance, a flawed application could be induced to iterate beyond the end of an array, and when beyond the end of the array, the program would be referring to data that did not belong to the array. Java prevents this problem by ensuring that any attempt to index an element before the beginning or after the end of an array will throw an exception.

Java's Typecasting System Java ensures that any cast of one object to another is actually a legal operation. An object cannot be arbitrarily cast to another type. So, assuming that you have an object such as a `Thread`, if you try to cast it to an incompatible class such as a `System` (that is, `System s = (System) new Thread()`), the runtime will throw an exception (`ClassCastException`). In languages that do not check for cast compatibility, it is possible to cast two objects, and incorrectly manipulate objects, or thwart inheritance restrictions.

Language Support for Thread-Safe Programming Multithreaded programming is an intrinsic part of the Java language, and special semantics ensure that different threads of execution modify critical data structures in a sequential, controlled fashion.

Final Classes and Methods Many classes and methods within the Java API are declared `final`, preventing programs from further subclassing or overriding specific code.

Part Two: The Java Compiler

The Java compiler converts Java code to bytecode for the JVM. The compiler ensures that all the security features of the language are imposed. A trustworthy compiler establishes that the code is safe and establishes that a programmer has used many of the security features. The compiler makes sure that any information that is known at compile time is legitimate—for instance, by checking for typecasting errors.

Part Three: The Verifier

Java bytecode is the essence of what is transmitted over the network. It is machine code for the JVM. Java's security would be easy to subvert if only the policies defined previously were assumed to have been enforced. A hostile compiler could be easily written to create bytecode that would perform dangerous acts that the well-behaved Java compiler would prevent.

Thus, security checks on the browser side are critical to maintaining a safe execution environment. Bytecode cannot be assumed to be created from a benevolent compiler, such as javac, within the JDK. Instead, a fail-safe stance assumes that class files are hostile unless clearly proven otherwise.

To prove such an assertion, when Java bytecode is loaded, it first enters into a system known as the verifier. The verifier performs several checks on all class files loaded into the Java execution environment. The verifier goes through these steps before approving any loaded code:

1. The first pass-over ensures that the class file is of the proper general format.
2. The second check ensures that various Java conventions are upheld, such as checking that every class has a superclass (except the `Object` class) and that final classes and methods have not been overridden.
3. The third step is the most detailed inspection of the class file. Within this step, the bytecodes themselves are examined to ensure their validity. This mechanism within the verifier is generally referred to as the bytecode verifier.
4. The last step performs some additional checks, such as ensuring the existence of class fields and the signature of methods.

NOTE For more detailed information on the verifier, read the paper by Frank Yellin titled "Low Level Security," available at `http://java.sun.com/sfaq/verifier.html`.

Part Four: The *ClassLoader*

Bytecode that has reached this stage has been determined to be valid; it then enters the `ClassLoader`, an object that subclasses the abstract class `java.lang.ClassLoader`. The `ClassLoader` loads applets incoming from the net and subjects them to the restrictions of the Applet Security Manager, described in the section titled "Part Five: Establishing a Security Policy," later in this chapter. It strictly allocates namespaces for classes that are loaded into the runtime system. A namespace is conceptual real estate in which an object's data structures can reside.

The `ClassLoader` ensures that objects don't intrude into each other's namespaces in unauthorized fashions. Public fields and methods can be accessed, but unless such an interface is defined, another object has no visibility to the variables. This point is important because system resources are accessed through specific classes—ones that are trusted to behave well and are installed within the JDK. If untrusted code was able to manipulate the data of the core Java API, disastrous results would ensue.

The ClassLoader also provides a strategic gateway for controlling which class code can be accessed. For example, applets are prevented from overriding any of the built-in Java classes, such as those that are provided within the Java API. Imported classes are prevented from impersonating built-in classes that are allowed to perform important system-related tasks. When a reference to an object is accessed, the namespace of built-in classes is checked first, thwarting any spoofing by network-loaded classes.

Part Five: Establishing a Security Policy

The previous pieces of the Java security framework ensure that the Java system is not subverted by invalid code or a hostile compiler. Basically, they ensure that Java code plays by the rules. Given such an assurance, you are now able to establish a higher-level security policy. This security policy exists at the application level, allowing you to dictate what resources a Java program can access and manipulate.

The Java API provides the `java.lang.SecurityManager` class as a means of creating a clearly defined set of tasks an application can and cannot perform, such as access files or network resources. Java applications don't start out with a `SecurityManager`, meaning that all resources it could restrict are freely available. However, by implementing a `SecurityManager`, you can add a significant measure of protection.

Java-enabled browsers use the `SecurityManager` to establish a security policy that greatly distinguishes what Java applets and Java applications can do. Later in this chapter, in the section "The `SecurityManager` Class," such special restrictions are described in detail.

Putting It All Together

Figure 34.1 illustrates how these separate pieces of the framework interlock to provide a safe, secure environment. This careful structure establishes an intelligent, fail-safe stance for the execution of Java programs:

- The Java language provides features that make a safe system possible.
- Such code is compiled into bytecode, where certain compile-type checks are enforced.
- Code is loaded into the Java execution environment and checked for validity by the verifier, which performs a multistep checking process.
- The `ClassLoader` ensures separate namespaces for loaded class files, allowing the Java interpreter to actually execute the program.
- The `SecurityManager` maintains an application-level policy, selectively permitting or denying certain actions.

Applet Restrictions

Java applets are programs that extend the `java.applet.Applet` class. They can be seamlessly downloaded and executed by a Java-enabled browser, such as HotJava or Netscape. Prior to the JDK 1.1, there was no mechanism for establishing proof of ownership and trust of authorship. Thus, all applets were assumed to be from an untrustworthy source.

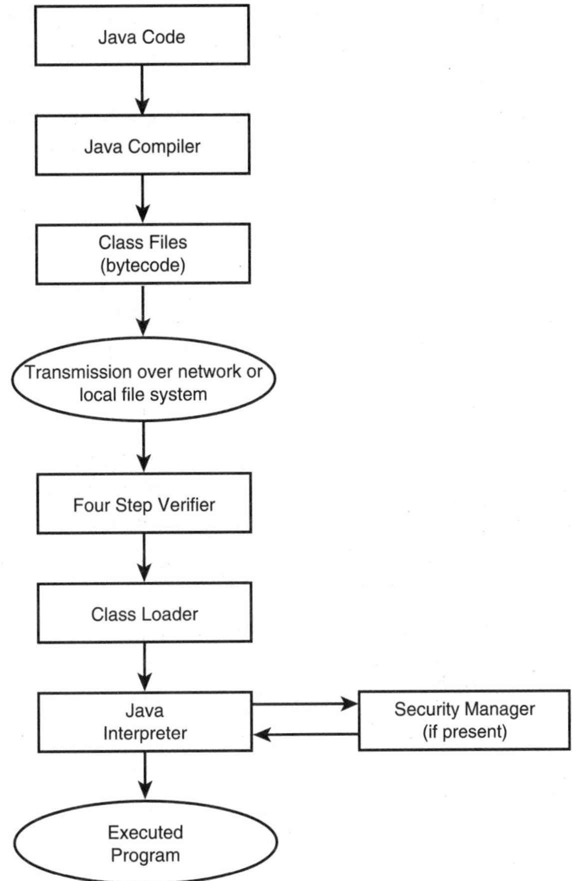

FIG. 34.1
A safe environment is created by different pieces working in a smooth fashion.

Then in JDK 1.1, Sun added the concept of a trusted applet. However, you could establish an applet source as only completely trusted or completely untrusted. JDK 1.2 has added fine-grained control to allow a particular applet source to be either partially trusted (so that it can read a particular file, for instance, but not others), completely trusted, or untrusted.

Applets Versus Applications

An important point to realize when investigating Java security is the distinction between Java applets and Java applications. Applets are special programs that extend the `Applet` class. They can be dynamically executed within a browser merely by loading an HTML page that contains an APPLET element.

Applications, on the other hand, are executed directly by the Java interpreter. They must be manually installed on the local system and consciously executed by the user on that system. A Java browser does not execute these programs.

▶ **See** "Developing Java Applications," **p. 291**

Before JDK 1.2, because of the differences between applets and applications, the two were allowed to execute under different security policies. It was assumed that during the manual installation process, the user had approved of the application's potential access to system resources. The application was trusted to the degree that it could open and write files, connect to various network resources, and execute various programs on the local system. Such a policy was consistent with just about any other application that you would install on your personal computer, and if you wanted, you could establish policies to mimic this. However, the fact was that all applications were considered trusted, and there was no way to establish a limited security policy for applications. The new security API for JDK allows you to establish a security policy for an application, just as you do for applets.

The *SecurityManager* Class

Most of the security features that are added to Java applets are imposed by the class `java.lang.SecurityManager`, although (as previously mentioned) the use of a `ClassLoader` instance plays a significant role as well. The `SecurityManager` class allows you to establish a specific security policy that is appropriate to the level of trust given to a particular program. This abstract class provides the capability to create an object that determines whether an operation that a program intends to perform is permitted.

The `SecurityManager` has methods for performing the following acts to enforce a security policy:

- Determine whether an incoming network connection from a specific host on a specific port can be accepted.
- Check whether one thread can manipulate another thread of `ThreadGroup`.
- Check whether a socket connection can be established with a remote system on a specific port.
- Prevent a new `ClassLoader` from being created.
- Prevent a new `SecurityManager` from being created, which could override the existing policy.
- Check whether a file can be deleted.
- Check whether a program can execute a program on the local system.
- Prevent a program from exiting the Java Virtual Machine.
- Check whether a dynamic library can be linked.
- Check whether a certain network port can be listened to for an incoming connection.
- Determine whether a program can load in specific Java packages.
- Determine whether a program can create new classes within a specific Java package.
- Identify which system properties can be accessed through the `System.getProperty()` method.
- Check whether a file can be read.

- Check whether data can be written to a file.
- Check whether a program can create its own implementation of network sockets.
- Establish whether a program can create a top-level window. If prevented from doing so, any windows that are allowed to be created should include some sort of visual warning.

The Security Policy of Java Browsers

Within Web browsers, a specific policy has been identified for the loading of untrusted applets. The `SecurityManager` performs various checks on a program's allowed actions; the `ClassLoader`, which loads Java classes over the network, ensures that classes loaded from external systems do not subvert this security stance. By default, the following restrictions apply:

- Applets are not allowed to read files on the local system. For example, this fails in an applet:

```
File readFile = new File("/etc/passwd");
FileInputStream readIn = new FileInputStream(readFile);
```

- Applets are not allowed to create, modify, or delete files on the local system. For example, this fails in an applet:

```
File writeData = new File("write.txt");        // Can't create files.
FileOutputStream out = new FileOutputStream(writeData);
out.write(1);
File oldName = new File("one.txt");            // Can't modify files,such as
File newName = new File("two.txt");            // by changing their names
oldName.renameTo(newName);                     // within directories.
File removeFile = new File("import.dat");      // Can't delete files.
removeFile.delete();
```

- Applets cannot check for the existence of a file on the local system. For example, this fails in an applet:

```
File isHere = new File("grades.dbm");
isHere.exists();
```

- Applets cannot create a directory on the local system. For example, this fails in an applet:

```
File createDir = new File("mydir");
createDir.mkdir();
```

- Applets cannot inspect the contents of a directory. For example, this fails in an applet:

```
String[] fileNames;
File lookAtDir = new File("/users/hisdir");
fileNames = lookAtDir.list();
```

- Applets cannot check various file attributes, such as a file's size, its type, or the time of the last modification. For example, this fails in an applet:

```
File checkFile = new File("this.dat");
long checkSize;
boolean checkType;
long checkModTime;
```

```
checkSize = checkFile.length();
checkType = checkFile.isFile();
checkModTime = checkFile.lastModified();
```

- Applets cannot create a network connection to a machine other than the one from which the applet was loaded. This rule holds true for connections that are created through any of the various Java network classes, including `java.net.Socket`, `java.net.URL`, and `java.net.DatagramSocket`.

  For example, assuming that the applet was downloaded from `www.untrusted.org`, the following code will fail in an applet:

  ```
  // Can't open TCP socket.
  Socket mailSocket = new Socket("mail.untrusted.org",25);
  // The URL objects are similarly restricted.
  URL untrustedWeb = new URL("http://www.untrusted.org/");
  URLConnection agent = untrustedWeb.openConnection();
  agent.connect();
  // As are UDP datagrams.
  InetAddress thatSite = new InetAddress("www.untrusted.org");
  int thatPort = 7;
  byte[] data = new byte[100];
  DatagramPacket sendPacket =
  new DatagramPacket(data,data.length,thatSite,thatPort);
  DatagramSocket sendSocket = new DatagramSocket();
  sendSocket.send(sendPacket);
  ```

- Applets cannot act as network servers, listening for or accepting socket connections from remote systems. For example, this fails in an applet:

  ```
  ServerSocket listener = new ServerSocket(8000);
  listener.accept();
  ```

- Applets are prevented from executing any programs that reside on the local computer. For example, this fails in an applet:

  ```
  String command = "DEL \AUTOEXEC.BAT";
  Runtime systemCommands = Runtime.getRuntime();
  systemCommands.exec(command);
  ```

- Applets are not allowed to load dynamic libraries or define native method calls. For example, this fails in an applet:

  ```
  Runtime systemCommands = Runtime.getRuntime();
  systemCommands.loadLibrary("local.dll");
  ```

- Within the Java environment, various standard system properties are set. These properties can be accessed with the `java.lang.System.getProperty(String key)` method. Applets are allowed to read only certain system properties and are prevented from accessing others. Table 34.1 shows these system properties.
- Applets cannot manipulate any Java threads other than those within their own thread group.
- Applets cannot shut down the JVM. For example, this fails in an applet:

  ```
  // This mechanism fails.
  Runtime systemCommands = Runtime.getRuntime();
  ```

```
systemCommands.exit(0);
// As does this mechanism.
System.exit(0);
```

- Applets cannot create a `SecurityManager` or `ClassLoader` instance. The Java browser creates such an object and uses it to impose the security policy on all applets.
- The `java.net` package uses factories to establish particular implementations of specific concepts: protocol handlers, content handlers, and sockets. Applets cannot override the specification of these classes: `java.net.URLStreamHandlerFactory`, `java.net.ContentHandlerFactory`, and `java.net.SocketImplFactory`.

Table 34.1 System Properties and Java Applets

Key	Purpose	Normally Accessible to Applets?
`file.separator`	The token used to separate files and directories on the filesystem (for example, / on UNIX and \ on Windows NT/95)	yes
`java.class.path`	The `CLASSPATH` value used to search for classes to load	no
`java.class.version`	The version of the Java API used	yes
`java.home`	The directory in which the Java environment is installed	no
`java.vendor`	A vendor-specific string used for identification purposes	yes
`java.vendor.url`	The URL of a resource identifying the vendor	yes
`java.version`	The version number of the Java interpreter	yes
`line.separator`	The character(s) that separate lines on the system (for example, the line-feed character on UNIX, or a line-feed, carriage-return pair on Windows NT/95)	yes
`os.arch`	The operating system's hardware architecture	yes
`os.name`	The name of the operating system	yes
`os.version`	Operating system version	yes

continues

Table 34.1 Continued

Key	Purpose	Normally Accessible to Applets?
`path.separator`	The token used to separate directories in a search-path specification (for example, : on UNIX and ; on Windows NT/95)	yes
`user.dir`	The current working directory	no
`user.home`	The user's home directory	no
`user.name`	The account name of the user	no

As you might imagine, this policy presents some severe limitations that affect what your applets can and cannot do. One particular problem is that the Internet, by its very nature, is a distributed system. However, Java applets are prevented from accessing this web of computers—they can connect only to the machine from which they were downloaded.

Furthermore, because data cannot be written to the local system, applets cannot maintain a persistent state across executions on the client. As a workaround, applets must connect to a server to store state information, reloading that information from the original server when executed later.

The current Java API provides the framework for creating specialized security policies for trusted applets loaded from known sources. This latter solution is described later in this chapter.

Java Security Problems

Despite its success and significant attention, Java is still not a completely mature system. Since the release of the first version of Java, various practical flaws have been identified, and subsequently fixed. Understanding these flaws will provide you with a feel for the medium into which you are immersing yourself.

An important point to note in this regard is the degree of openness that has been encouraged within the Java development arena. Obviously, companies such as Sun and others that have a significant stake in promoting Java suffer when a bug or flaw is revealed. Nevertheless, public scrutiny and critiques have been encouraged and generally well received.

Based on the experience of most security professionals, such public review is an essential component of the development of a secure system. In most cases, it is impossible to prove that a system is secure. A safe stance is to assume that a system with no known flaws is merely one with flaws that are waiting to be exposed and exploited. Peer review allows for various experts to search for these hidden flaws—a process that is very familiar within the Internet community.

Java's evolution has followed this philosophy, and from most practical observations, it appears that everyone has benefited.

The opposing argument is that exposing the implementation of the system to the public allows untrusted and malicious individuals to identify and act on flaws before others can rectify the situation; by keeping a system secret, it is less likely that abusive hackers will discover these problems. Many people experienced with Internet security disagree, believing that obscuring the implementation is unwise: secrecy in design creates a system that is ultimately poorer, while providing more opportunity for malevolence.

CAUTION

A word to the wise: Always treat with caution any supposedly secure system whose designer claims that the system's security would be subverted by revealing the details of its implementation.

Known Flaws

During the first few months after the release of the Java Development Kit, a number of problematic issues were revealed. The following list is an overview of some of the flaws discovered in Java since its release:

- In February 1996, Drew Dean, Edward W. Felton, and Dan S. Wallach discovered a flaw in the Java Applet Security Manager. This flaw inappropriately trusted data from the Domain Name System—the Internet mechanism for associating IP addresses with human-understandable host names. As an example, this flaw is further examined later in this section.

  This problem was fixed by a patch within the Netscape Navigator 2.01 and the JDK 1.0.1.
- In March 1996, Dean, Felton, and Wallach discovered a flaw that allowed arbitrary machine code to be executed by an applet loaded over the network. This exploitation resided on the capability to load a new `ClassLoader` from within an applet. Although the Java compiler within the JDK would not permit this operation, the Java verifier did not prevent this problem. Thus, a hostile compiler was able to subvert the Java security framework. After the new `ClassLoader` was created by the applet, arbitrary machine code could be executed.

  This issue was addressed within a patch in the Netscape Navigator 2.02 and the JDK 1.0.2.
- In June 1996, David Hopwood of Oxford University identified a flaw in the way object typecasting was implemented. The problem allows casting between arbitrary data types. With this flaw, local files can be read from and written to. In addition, arbitrary native code can be executed.

  This problem was fixed in Java 1.1.

Of the three mentioned flaws, the DNS attack identified first received perhaps the most public attention. The basic problem lies within the enforcement of the security policy by the `SecurityManager`.

The applet policy enforced by Web browsers dictates that a network connection can be opened only by the applet to the machine from which it was downloaded. As indicated in Chapter 30, "Communications and Networking," network computers identify each other on the Internet with IP addresses. The Domain Name System allows IP addresses to be associated in various ways, primarily enabling the use of human-understandable host names.

▶ **See** "Internet Protocol (IP)," p. **686**

In the flawed `SecurityManager`, the IP address of the incoming applet would be used to look up the host name of the remote machine. Then this host name would be used to look up the set of IP addresses to which it is mapped. Such a lookup should return at least the original IP address, but it might contain other IP addresses; such IP addresses can correspond to the same physical machine or completely separate machines.

Such a system might allow some flexibility in designing applets, allowing machines that share the same host name to spread out the responsibility for handling connections initiated from downloaded applets. However, such a system subtly violates the original security policy in a very significant way.

The DNS is a distributed resource. Various systems throughout the Internet are responsible for maintaining the integrity of specific parts. You have no ability to guarantee that a specific DNS server will not be broken into by hackers, and malicious individuals could easily set up their own DNS servers, providing information that could exploit this leniency in the `SecurityManager`.

By design, the DNS is insecure. One could claim that Java should not be to blame for the limitations of such a commonly used system. This nature of the DNS is well-known to Internet security specialists, however, and this problem should have been anticipated.

One final point should be made about the problems found with the Java security system. The design of the system appeared inherently sound. It was the implementation of that design that was not completely flawless.

Denial-of-Service Attacks

The term denial-of-service is a standard way of describing a particular type of security attack. Such attacks are aimed at preventing you or anyone else from using your own computer, rather than attempting to obtain sensitive data from your systems. These attacks often utilize "brute force" to overload a system.

Denial-of-service attacks in areas other than Java include such factors as these:

- A mail-bomb attack in which an individual is repeatedly mailed large documents to fill up his or her mail system.
- Use of an application such as `ping` to flood a particular system.
- Use of an automated browser to repeatedly request resources from a Web server.

Most of these attacks exploit a resource's own usefulness to make the system effectively useless. Because of this, it's not completely practical or possible to completely prevent such attacks. Only by removing the features that make the system useful can it be protected.

Denial-of-service attacks are quite possible with Java applets. These attacks don't require much imagination:

- An applet can attempt to use your CPU so much that other applications slow to a crawl.
- An applet can continually create objects, allocating more and more memory.
- An applet can create a number of windows, exhausting the GUI system on your machine.

Currently, these types of attacks are identified as out of the scope of the Java security model. Java must continue to be useful. If applets have interesting and powerful capabilities, they could potentially exhaust the practical limitations of your computer. However, Sun continues to investigate the feasibility of controlling more closely the amount of system resources an applet can use.

The Java Security API: Expanding the Boundaries for Applets

By now, you have come to realize the significant, though prudent, default limitations to which Java applets are held. These policies create a safe but restricted environment. When you're designing an applet to accomplish certain tasks, you must create cumbersome workarounds, and other goals just can't be accomplished through applets.

This situation is necessary because all applets are treated as hostile—a fail-safe stance. In many situations, however, you are able to assert that certain programs are not hostile. For instance, applets distributed by a faithful vendor or provided from within your firewall can be reasonably expected to have greater access to system resources than a random applet loaded from someone's Web page.

One of the key capabilities missing from the initial Java implementations was the capability to establish trust relationships. Java 1.1 added the foundation of the Java Security API. Using the Security API, you have the ability to create trusted relationships with program developers and verify that code from these sources is not altered by an outside party. However, the 1.1 solution simply said that a program was either trusted or untrusted; there was no incremental control over how trusted an applet could be. With 1.2, the security model has been extended to enable finite trusted control.

The features of the Java Security API are based on computer cryptography designs and algorithms. A quick investigation of these concepts can help you understand how the Security API works.

Symmetric Cryptography

The cryptographic scheme that is most familiar to many is symmetric cryptography, or private-key encryption. The concept is that a special formula or process takes a piece of data and uses a special key, such as a password, to produce an encrypted block of data.

Given only the encrypted data, or ciphertext, it is difficult or impossible to reproduce the original copy. With the key, however, you can decrypt the ciphertext into the original message.

Thus, anyone with access to the key can easily decrypt the data. Because the security of this system depends on the secrecy of this key, this scheme is referred to as private key encryption. It is symmetrical in nature because the same key that is used to encrypt the data is required to decrypt the message. Figure 34.2 illustrates the private key encryption scheme.

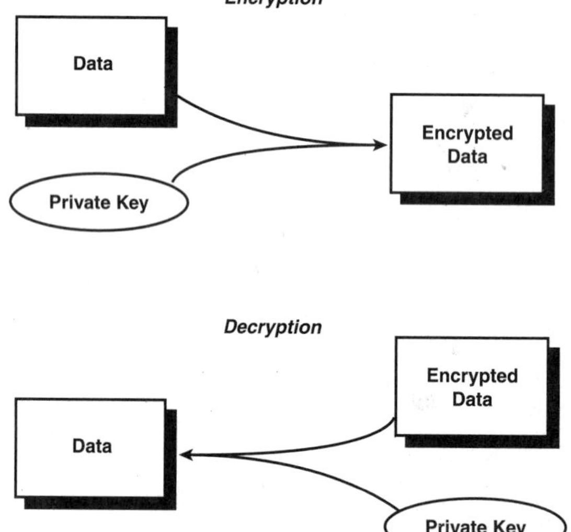

FIG. 34.2
Private key cryptography uses the same key for encryption and decryption. To be secure, the key must be kept secret.

A number of cryptographic systems use private key cryptography. Data Encryption Standard (DES) is a widely used system; however, cracking it is practical with today's technology. IDEA is a much newer algorithm and is believed to be much more secure than DES, although it has not been as thoroughly tested as DES. RC2 and RC4 are propriety algorithms distributed by RSA Data Security.

One of the problems with using private key encryption to protect communications is that both parties must have the same key. However, this exchange of private keys must be protected. Thus, to securely transmit documents, a secure mechanism of exchanging information must already exist.

Public Key Cryptography

Public key cryptography is a phenomenal idea. It is a radical system that is based on breakthroughs made during the 1970s. The concept is based on special mathematical algorithms.

A special formula is used to create two keys that are mathematically related, but neither can be induced from the other. One key is used to encrypt a particular message to produce a ciphertext. The other key is used to decrypt the message; however, the original key cannot be used to decrypt the ciphertext. Thus, this type of cryptography is referred to as asymmetric.

This system solves the problem of key distribution that limits private key cryptography. An individual who expects to receive protected documents can advertise one of the keys, generally referred to as the public key. Anyone who wants to send an encrypted message to this person merely picks up the public key and creates the ciphertext. This encrypted message can be safely transmitted because only the other key can decrypt it. The recipient keeps the corresponding, or secret, key hidden from others because it is the only key that can be used to read messages encrypted by the public key. Figure 34.3 shows this mechanism.

FIG. 34.3
Public key cryptography provides a solution to key distribution.

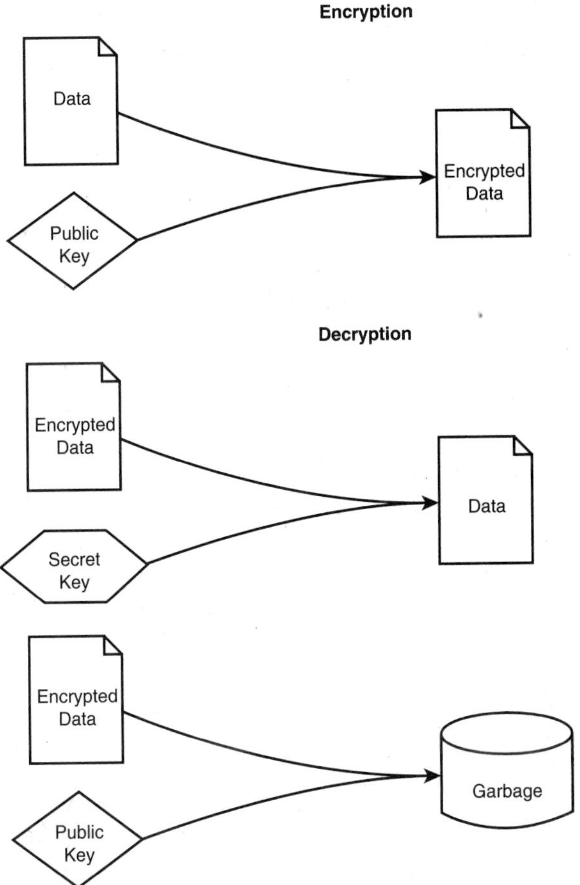

Part IV Ch 34

Perhaps of more usefulness to Java applets, however, is the converse operation that is known as signing. Given a message, the secret key is used to create an encrypted signature. The unencoded message is transmitted along with the signature, and if the message is altered, the signature cannot be decrypted. Anyone who receives the message can obtain the freely available public key to ensure two things:

- The message truly was from the supposed author.
- The message was not altered in any way after being signed.

The process of signing messages through public key cryptography is shown in Figure 34.4.

FIG. 34.4
Digital signatures can establish identity and data integrity.

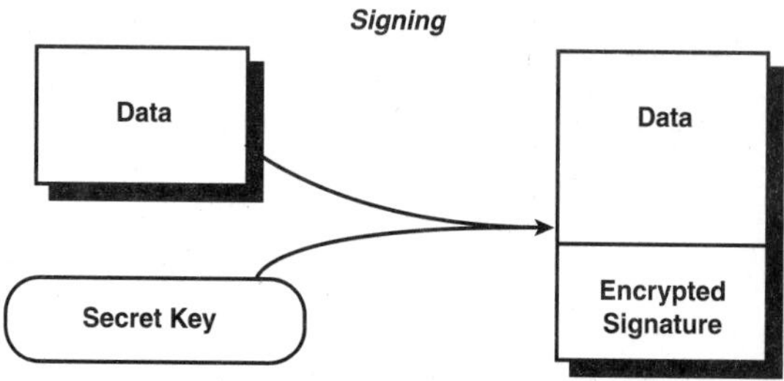

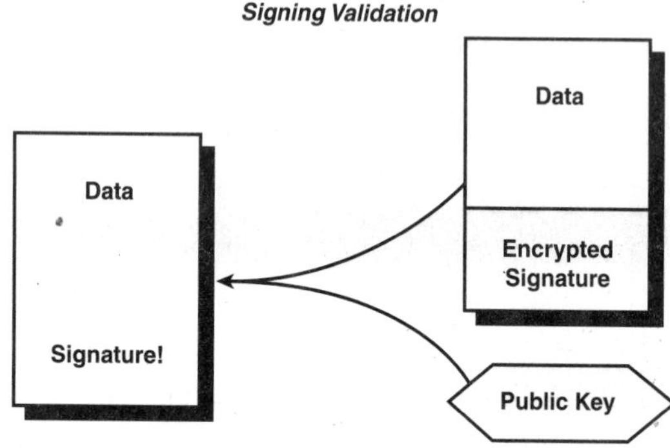

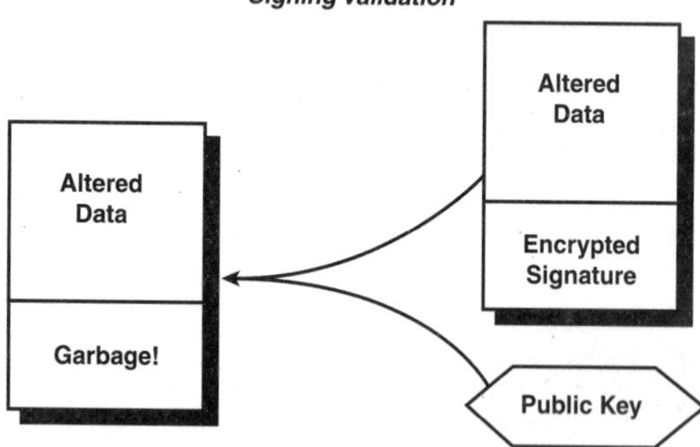

Certification Authorities

One of the limitations in the public key system is verifying that a public key truly belongs to the individual you believe it belongs to. It is conceivable that a hostile individual could send you a message signed with a secret key, claiming to be from another party. This attacker then advertises a public key as belonging to the impersonated person. You retrieve this key and decrypt the signature. Believing that you have verified the author, you now trust information that, unbeknownst to you, is written by a hostile source.

Secure transmission systems on the Web have turned to a system known as Certification Authorities (CA) to overcome this limitation. Basically, a CA is an organization or company that is very well known and goes to great lengths to ensure that its public key is properly advertised. The CA then signs the key of other agencies that conclusively prove their identity. When you receive the public key of this agency, you can use the CA's public key to verify it. If successful, you know that the CA believes that this agency is what it claims to be. Thus, the CA certifies the agency.

If your Web browser implements a mechanism of secure communications, such as SSL, you can see a list of some certificate authorities. Navigator is SSL enabled—if you choose Options, Security Preferences, Site Certificates, you can see the certificates of the CAs distributed with the browser.

What Is Accomplished

After this lengthy discussion, you might be wondering why encryption can expand the capabilities of applets. As mentioned before, applets are assumed to be untrusted and potentially hostile. However, if an applet was digitally signed with public key cryptography, you could identify the company that created the applet and ensure that a hacker has not somehow altered what the company claims to have written.

Now you can establish trust relationships. You can assign specific roles to applets from known agents. For instance, you might purchase a stock quote service from a company. To use that service, you download an applet. Because you already have a relationship with that company and you want to trust the information it provides, you can feel comfortable in allowing the applet greater access to your local system:

- You can allow the applet to save its configuration on your local disk.
- You can allow the applet to connect to various stock servers located throughout the Internet.
- You can allow the applet to write stock information into a spreadsheet residing on your computer.

It is important to note that other parts of the Java security framework are still in place. The bytecode is still verified to ensure validity. Furthermore, this isn't an all-or-nothing proposition. Applets from trusted sources can be given incrementally greater access to your computer. (Review the various checks the `SecurityManager` class has available to get a feel for the gradations of increased access that could be allowed.) Finally, unsigned applets are still untrusted; they will still be subject to the same limitations that were in place before the release of the Java Security API.

Key Management

Key management is an extremely important aspect of security. You must keep your database of certificates up to date and keep your private keys secret. If you keep keys and certificates in separate files scattered around your system, you might accidentally place a private key in a public directory where someone could steal it. To help you with key management, Java 1.1 included a key database and a key management tool called javakey. Now, with JDK 1.2, the database and the capability to sign code have been split into two separate tools: keytool and jarsigner.

NOTE Unfortunately, the keytool and jarsigner tools are not compatible with the javakey tool from JDK 1.1. So if you are using 1.1 for any reason, you need to look into how the javakey works, and not use keytool and jarsigner.

The keytool program included with JDK 1.2 is designed to allow you to create, modify, and remove keys and certificates. It stores these records in a new type of database called a keystore.

A certificate is a digitally signed object that is issued by a known entity, which identifies the public key of another entity. For instance, you could have a certificate from RSA that tells you what someone's public key is. Then, when data is digitally signed, you can verify that the signature was really generated by that person by checking the certificate.

You can do two things when verifying a signature. First, using the certificate, you can check the data's integrity. The integrity of the data means that the data has not been modified or tampered with since the time it was signed. Second, you can verify the authenticity of the data. Authenticity verifies that the person who signed the document is really who he claims to be.

A certificate is generally held by an entity. An entity is a person or an organization that is able to digitally sign information. Because signing requires a key set, a signer has both a public key and a private key, as well as a certificate authenticating the public key.

A key is a number that is associated with the entity. The public key is designed so that everyone who needs to interact with the entity can have access to the number. A private key, on the other hand, is designed so that only the entity will know it. The two keys are mathematically matched so that when a value is encrypted by the public key, it can be unencrypted only by the private key. In addition, they are designed so that the private key cannot be derived just by knowing the public key.

To store keys for an entity, you must first create an entry in the keystore database. When you create the entry, you must give the entity a name, and a password to access the entity. The following command creates an entry for a signer named `mark`:

```
keytool -genkey -alias usingjava -keypass goodbooks
➥ -dname "cn=QUE" -storepass zippydoda
```

The `-genkey` option indicates that you are creating an entry for a signer. The `-aliase` option indicates that you are creating an entry for an alias that is identified directly after the option. The `-keypass` is used to identify the password that will be required any time you want to access or modify the key.

After you have created an entry for an entity, you can add keys and certificates for that entity. For example, suppose you received Verisign's public key in a file called `vskey.key` and the certificate for that key in a file called `vskey.cer`. Use the `-import` flag on the `keytool` command to import the public key into the key database:

```
keytool -import -alias verisign -file vskey.cer -keypass verisignpas
```

You can list the entities in the database with the `-list` option:

```
keytool -list -storepass zippydoda
-keytool -list
```

To remove an entity, use the `-delete` option:

```
keytool -delete -alias usingjava -storepass abcdefgh
```

Digitally Signing a JAR File

When you store your applet or application in a JAR file, you can digitally sign the JAR file. If an applet is loaded from a JAR file signed by a trusted entity, the applet is not subject to the usual security restrictions. In future releases of Java, you will be able to configure what a signed applet can do, even assigning permissions based on who signed the applet.

To sign a JAR file, you first need to add an entry in the keystore database for an alias. After you have defined the signer, you can use the jarsigner tool to sign the JAR file. To sign the `test.jar` file with the alias `usingjava` that was created in the preceding "Key Management" section, type this:

```
jarsigner -storepass abcdefgh test1.jar usingjava
```

Defining a Policy

The last piece of the puzzle for signing a JAR file is creating a policy file to define the permissions to assign to a file. There are two ways to create a permissions file. The first method is to create it manually. Listing 34.1 shows how to create a policy file that allows a JAR file signed by `"usingjava"` to write to a file called `newfile`.

Listing 34.1 *write.jp*—Allow *usingjava* to Write to the New File

```
grant SignedBy "usingjava" {
  permission java.util.PropertyPermission "user.home", "read";
  permission java.io.FilePermission "${user.home}/newfile","write";
};
```

The second way to write a policy is by using the policytool utility bundled with JDK 1.2. Policytool is designed to ease the efforts of defining the policy file.

Running the Applet

Now that you have signed a JAR file and defined a policy file, you can run the program with the new capabilities. To run the Test program with `appletviewer`, you can type this:

```
appletviewer -J-Djava.policy=Write.jp file:///test.html
```

The Security API

The Security API is focused on providing support for digitally signed applets. There is some level of support for generating and checking digital signatures from a program, and future versions will provide classes for encrypting and decrypting information.

The Security API exists for two reasons: to allow your programs to perform security functions and to allow manufacturers of security software to create their own security provider services. Java 1.1 ships with a single security provider, which is simply called "Sun." Other vendors might provide their own security services. These providers might provide additional services beyond those defined in the Java 1.2 Security API.

Public and Private Key Classes

The Security API revolves around the manipulation of keys. As you might guess, interfaces are defined for both public and private keys. Because these keys share many common features, they both derive from a common super interface called `Key`. The three important features of a key are its algorithm, its format, and the encoded key value. You can retrieve these values from any key by using the following methods:

```
public String getAlgorithm()
public  String getFormat()
public byte[] getEncoded()
```

The *Signature* Class

The `Signature` class performs two different roles—it can digitally sign a sequence of bytes, or it can verify the signature of a sequence of bytes. Before you can perform either of these functions, you must create an instance of a `Signature` class. The constructor for the `Signature` class is protected. The public method for creating signatures is called `getInstance`, and it takes the name of the security algorithm and the name of the provider as arguments:

```
public static Signature getInstance(String algorithm,
String provider)
```

For the default package provided with Java 1.2, the most common call to `getInstance` is this:

```
Signature sig = Signature.getInstance("DSA", "SUN")
```

If you are creating a digital signature, call the `initSign` method in `Signature` with the private key you are using to create the signature:

```
public final void initSign(PrivateKey key)
```

If you are verifying a signature, call `initVerify` with the public key you are verifying against:

```
public final void initVerify(PublicKey key)
```

Whether you are creating a signature or verifying one, you must give the `Signature` class the sequence of bytes you are concerned with. For instance, if you are digitally signing a file, you must read all the bytes from the file and pass them to the `Signature` class. The `update` method allows you to pass data bytes to the `Signature` class:

```
public final void update(byte b)
public final void update(byte[] b)
```

The `update` methods are additive; that is, each call to `update` adds to the existing array of bytes that will be signed or verified. The following code fragment reads bytes from a file and stores them in a `Signature` object:

```
Signature sig = new Signature("DSA");
sig.initSign(somePrivateKey);
FileInputStream infile = new FileInputStream("SignMe");
int i;
while ((i = infile.read()) >= 0) {
sig.update(i);
}
byte signature[] = sig.sign();      // Do the signing
```

After you have stored the bytes in the `Signature`, use the `sign` method to digitally sign them, or use `verify` to verify them:

```
public final byte[] sign()

public final boolean verify(byte[] otherSignature)
```

Identities and Signers

As you already know, two types of entities are stored in the key database: identities (public keys only) and signers (public/private key pairs). The `Identity` class represents an identity, whereas the `Signer` class represents a signer. These two classes are abstract classes; you cannot create your own instances. Instead, you must go through your security provider to create and locate these classes.

When you have an instance of an `Identity`, you can retrieve its public key with `getPublicKey` or set its public key with `setPublicKey`:

```
public PublicKey getPublicKey()

public void setPublicKey(PublicKey newKey)
```

In addition, you can retrieve all the identity's certificates using the `certificates` method:

```
public Certificate[] certificates()
```

You can add and remove certificates with `addCertificate` and `removeCertificate`:

```
public void addCertificate(Certificate cert)
```

```
public void removeCertificate(Certificate cert)
```

The `Signer` class is a subclass of `Identity`, and it adds methods for retrieving the private key and setting the key pair:

```
protected PrivateKey getPrivateKey()
```

```
protected final void setKeyPair(KeyPair pair)
```

Certificates

A certificate is little more than a digitally signed public key. It also contains the owner of the key, and the signer. The owner and the signer are called principals, and they are generally entities that are stored in the key database. You can retrieve the public key from a certificate with `getPublicKey`:

```
public abstract PublicKey getPublicKey()
```

You can also retrieve the principals from a certificate. The `Guarantor` is the entity who is signing the public key (guaranteeing its authenticity), and the `Principal` is the owner of the key that is being guaranteed:

```
public abstract Principal getPrincipal()
public abstract Principal getGuarantor()
```

The only interesting method in the `Principal` interface is `getName`, which returns the name of the principal:

```
public abstract String getName()
```

The *IdentityScope* Class

The `IdentityScope` class represents a set of identities. Generally, this class represents the identities in the key database. When you have an instance of an `IdentityScope`, you can add entities, remove entities, and find entities. The `getSystemScope` method returns the default identity scope for the security system:

```
public static IdentityScope getSystemScope()
```

You can locate identities by name, by public key, or using a `Principal` reference:

```
public Identity getIdentity(String name)
public Identity getIdentity(PublicKey key)
public Identity getIdentity(Principal principal)
```

The `identities` method returns an enumeration that allows you to enumerate through all the identities in the scope:

```
public abstract Enumeration identities()
```

The `addIdentity` and `removeIdentity` methods allow you to add new identities to the scope, or to remove old ones:

```
public abstract void addIdentity(Identity id)
public abstract void removeIdentity(Identity id)
```

Listing 34.2 shows a sample program that creates a digital signature for a file and writes the signature to a separate file.

Listing 34.2 Source Code for *SignFile.java*

```
import java.security.*;
import java.io.*;
import java.util.*;

public class SignFile {
  public static void main(String[] args) {
    try {

      // Get the default identity scope
      IdentityScope scope = IdentityScope.getSystemScope();

      // Locate the entity named trustme
      Identity identity = scope.getIdentity("usingjava");

      // Create a signature and initialize it for creating a signature
      Signature sig = Signature.getInstance("DSA", "SUN");
      Signer signer = (Signer) identity;
      sig.initSign(signer.getPrivateKey());

      // Open the file that will be signed
      FileInputStream infile = new FileInputStream("SignFile.java");

      // Read the bytes from the file and add them to the signature
      int i;
      while ((i = infile.read()) >= 0) {
        sig.update((byte)i);
      }

      infile.close();

      // Open the file that will receive the digital signature of the
      // input file
      FileOutputStream outfile = new FileOutputStream(
                                                      "SignFile.sig");

      // Generate and write the signature
      outfile.write(sig.sign());
      outfile.close();

    } catch (Exception e) {
      e.printStackTrace();
    }
  }
}
```

The capability to generate digital signatures and verify them from a program allows you to provide new levels of security in your programs. This is especially useful in the area of electronic commerce because you can now digitally sign orders and receipts. ●

CHAPTER 35

Object Serialization

In this chapter

What Is Object Serialization?

Up to this point you have been working with objects, and you have learned to create classes so you can manipulate the objects using their methods. However, when you have had to write an object to a different source, say out to a network via a socket or to a file, you have only written out native types like `int` or `char`. Object serialization is the tool that was added to Java to allow you to fully utilize the OOP nature of Java and write those objects you've labored to produce to a file or other stream.

To understand object serialization, first look at an example of how you would go about reading in a simple object, such as a string, from another source. Normally when you open a stream to and from a client program, the odds are fairly good that you are sending/receiving a byte. You're probably then adding that byte to a string. To do this you might have some code similar to that in Listing 35.1.

Listing 35.1 Notice How Much Work the Computer Has to Do to Generate a String This Way

```
/*
 *
 * GetString
 *
 */

import java.net.*;
import java.io.*;

public class GetString
{

     //Read in a String from an URL
     public String getStringFromUrl (URL inURL){
          InputStream in;
          try{
               in = inURL.openStream();
          } catch (IOException ioe){
               System.out.println("Unable to open stream to URL:"+ioe);
               return null;
          }
          return getString(in);
     }

     public String getStringFromSocket (Socket inSocket){
          InputStream in;
          try{
               in = inSocket.getInputStream();
          } catch (IOException ioe){
               System.out.println("Unable to open stream to Socket:"+ioe);
               return null;
          }
```

```
            return getString(in);
        }

        public String getString (InputStream inStream){
            String readString = new String();
            DataInputStream in = new DataInputStream (inStream);
            char inChar;
            try{
                while (true){
                    inChar = (char)in.readByte();
                    readString = readString + inChar;
                }
            } catch (EOFException eof){
                System.out.println("The String read was:"+readString);
            } catch (IOException ioe) {
                System.out.println("Error reading from stream:"+ioe);
            }
            return readString;
        }
}
```

Most important in Listing 35.1, take a look at the `getString()` method. Inside of this method you will see an indefinitely long `while` loop (which breaks once an exception is thrown). If you look closely at what is happening here, you will realize you are reading character-by-character each letter in the string and appending it until you reach the end of the file (EOF). Java has no way without object serialization to actually read in a string as an object.

NOTE `DataInputStream` does have a `readLine()` which returns a String, but this is not really the same for two reasons. First, `readLine` does not read in an entire file; second, the `readLine()` method itself is actually very similar to `readString()` in Listing 35.1.

An even more dire situation arises when you want to read a heterogeneous object such as that shown in Listing 35.2.

Listing 35.2 A Heterogeneous Object

```
class testObject {
     int x;
     int y;
     float angle;
     String name;
     public testObject (int x, int y, float angle, String name){
     this.x = x ;
     this.y = y;
     this.angle= angle;
          this.name = name;
}
```

To read and write `testObject` without object serialization, you would open a stream, read in a bunch of data, and then use it to fill out the contents of a new object (by passing the read-in elements to the constructor). You might even be able to deduce directly how to read in the first three elements of `testObject`. But how would you read in the name? Well, because you just wrote a `readString` class in Listing 35.1 you could use that, but how would you know when the string ends and the next object starts? Even more importantly, what if `testObject` had even more complicated references? For instance, if `testObject` looked like Listing 35.3, how would you handle the constant recursion from `nextObject`?

Listing 35.3 *testObject* Becomes Even More Complicated

```
class testObject {
     int x;
     int y;
     float angle;
     String name;
     testObject nextNode;
     public testObject (int x, int y, float angle, String name, testObject
nextNode){
     this.x = x ;
             this.y = y;
             this.angle= angle;
          this.name = name;
                          this.nextNode = nextNode;
        }
}
```

If you really wanted to, you could write a method (or methods) to read and write Listing 35.3, but wouldn't it be great if, instead, you could grab an object a whole class at a time?

That's exactly what object serialization is all about. Do you have a class structure that holds all of the information about a house for a real estate program? No problem—simply open the stream and send or receive the whole house. Do you want to save the state of a game applet? Again, no problem. Just send the applet object down the stream.

The ability to store and retrieve whole objects is essential to the construction of all but the most ephemeral of programs. While a full-blown database might be what you need if you're storing large amounts of data, frequently that's overkill. Even if you want to implement a database, it would be easier to store objects as BLOB types (byte streams of data) than to break out an `int` here, a `char` there, and a `byte` there.

How Object Serialization Works

The key to object serialization is to store enough data about the object to be able to reconstruct it fully. Furthermore, to protect the user (and programmer), the object must have a "fingerprint" that correctly associates it with the legitimate object from which it was made. This is an aspect not even discussed when looking at writing our own objects. But it is critical for a complete system so that when an object is read in from a stream, each of its fields will be placed back into the correct class in the correct location.

NOTE If you are a C or C++ programmer, you're probably used to accomplishing much of object serialization by taking the pointer to a class or struct, doing a `sizeOf()`, and writing out the entire class. Unfortunately, Java does not support pointers or direct-memory access, so this technique will not work in Java, and object serialization is required.

It's not necessary, however, for a serialization system to store the methods or the transient fields of a class. The class code is assumed to be available any time these elements are required. In other words, when you restore the class `Date`, you are not also restoring the method `getHours()`. It's assumed that you have restored the values of the `Date` into a `Date` object and that object has the code required for the `getHours()` method.

Dealing with Objects with Object References

Objects frequently refer to other objects by using them as class variables (fields). In other words, in the more complicated `testObject` class (refer to Listing 35.3), a nextNode field was added. This field is an object referenced within the object. In order to save a class, it is also necessary to save the contents of these reference objects. Of course, the reference objects may also refer to yet even more objects (such as with `testObject` if the `nextNode` also had a valid `nextNode` value). So, as a rule, to serialize an object completely, you must store all of the information for that object, as well as every object that is reachable by the object, including all of the recursive objects.

CAUTION

Object serialization and Remote Method Invocation are not available under Netscape Navigator 3.0, Microsoft Internet Explorer 3.0, or the Java Develpment Kit 1.0. The first version of the JDK that supports object serialization and RMI is JDK 1.02, and that only with a patch. It is recommended that you use the JDK 1.1 when trying any of these features.

If you are using the JDK 1.02, you must obtain the object serialization and RMI classes separately, and these must be added to your existing class library. These classes can be downloaded from the following URL:

`http://chatsubo.javasoft.com/current/download.html`

Object Serialization Example

As a simple example, store and retrieve a `Date` class to and from a file. To do this without object serialization, you would probably do something on the order of `getTime()` and write the resulting long integer to the file. However, with object serialization the process is much, much easier.

An Application to Write a Date Class

Listing 35.4 shows an example program called DateWrite. DateWrite creates a Date Object and writes the entire object to a file.

Listing 35.4 *DateWrite.java*—An Application that Writes a Date Object to a File

```
import java.io.FileOutputStream;
import java.io.ObjectOutputStream;
import java.util.Date;
public class DateWrite {
        public static void main (String args[]){
               try{
                  // Serialize today's date to a file.
                  FileOutputStream outputFile = new
                  FileOutputStream("dateFile");
                  ObjectOutputStream  serializeStream  =  new
                 ➥ObjectOutputStream(outputFile);
                  serializeStream.writeObject("Hi!");
                  serializeStream.writeObject(new Date());
                  serializeStream.flush();
              } catch (Exception e) {
                  System.out.println("Error during serialization");
              }
      }
}//end class DateWrite
```

Take a look at the code in Listing 35.4. First, notice that the program creates a `FileOutputStream`. In order to do any serialization it is first necessary to declare an `outputStream` of some sort to which you will attach the `ObjectOutputStream`. (As you see in Listing 35.5, you can also use the `OutputStream` generated from any other object, including a URL.)

Once you have established a stream, it is necessary to create an `ObjectOutputStream` with it. The `ObjectOutputStream` contains all of the necessary information to serialize any object and to write it to the stream.

In the example of the previous short code fragment, you see two objects being written to the stream. The first object that is written is a `String` object; the second is the `Date` object.

NOTE To compile Listing 35.4 using the JDK 1.02, you need to add some extra commands that you're probably not used to. Before you do this, though, first verify that you have downloaded the RMI/object serialization classes and unzipped the file into your Java directory. Now, type the following command:

```
javac -classpathc:\java\lib\classes.zip;c:\java\lib\
➥objio.zip;. DateWrite.java
```

The previous compiler command assumes you are using a Windows machine and that the directory in which your Java files exist is C:\JAVA. If you have placed it in a different location or are using a system other than Windows, you need to substitute C:\JAVA\LIB with the path that is appropriate for your Java installation. As always, it's a good idea to take a look at the README file included with your installation, and to read the release notes to learn about any known bugs or problems.

This should compile `DateWrite` cleanly. If you receive an error, though, make sure that you have a `OBJIO.ZIP` file in your `JAVA\LIB` directory. Also, make sure that you have included both the `CLASSES.ZIP` and the `OBJIO.ZIP` files in your class path. ■

Running *DateWrite* Under JDK 1.02

Once you have compiled the `DateWrite` program you can run it. However, just as you had to include the `OBJIO.ZIP` file in the classpath when you compiled the `DateWrite` class, you must also include it in order to run the class.

```
java -classpath c:\java\lib\classes.zip;c:\java\lib\objio.zip;. DateWrite
```

NOTE If you fail to include the `OBJIO.ZIP` file in your class path, you will likely get an error such as:

```
java.lang.NoClassDefFoundError: java/io/ObjectOutputStream
          at DateWrite.main (DateWrite.java: 9)
```

This is the result of the virtual machine being unable to locate the class files that are required for object serialization.

Compiling and Running *DateWrite*

To compile and run `DateWrite` using the JDK 1.1, simply copy the contents of Listing 35.4 to a file called `DateWrite` and compile it with `javac` as you would any other file:

```
javac DateWrite.java
```

You can run it just as you would any other Java application as well:

```
java DateWrite
```

No real output is generated by the `DateWrite` class, so when you run this program you should be returned to the command prompt fairly quickly. However, if you now look in your directory structure, you should see a file called `dateFile`. This is the file you just created. If you attempt to type out the file, you will see something that looks mostly like gobbledygook.

However, a closer inspection reveals that this file contains several things. The stuff that looks like gobbledygook is actually what the serialization uses to store information about the class, such as the value of the fields and the class signature that was discussed earlier.

A Simple Application to Read in the Date

The next step, of course, is to read the `Date` and `String` back in from the file. See how complicated this could be. Listing 35.5 shows an example program that reads in the `String` and `Date`.

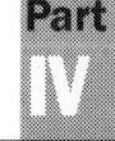

Listing 35.5 ***DateRead.java*—An Application that Reads the *String* and *Date* Back In**

```
import java.io.FileInputStream;
import java.io.ObjectInputStream;
import java.util.Date;
public class DateRead {
      public static void main (String args[]){
            Date wasThen;
            String theString;
```

continues

Listing 35.5 Continued

```
            try{
                  // Serialize date from a file.
                  FileInputStream inputFile = new FileInputStream("dateFile");
                  ObjectInputStream  serializeStream  =  new
            ObjectInputStream(inputFile);
                  theString  = (String) serializeStream.readObject();
            } catch (Exception e) {
                  System.out.println("Error during serialization");
                  return;
            }
            System.out.println("The string is:"+theString);
            System.out.println("The old date was:"+wasThen);
        }
}
```

Listings 35.4 and 35.5 differ primarily in the ways that you would expect. Listing 35.4 is writing, and Listing 35.5 is reading. In `DateRead`, you first declare two variables to store the objects in. You need to remember to do this because if you were to create the variables inside the `try-catch` block, they would go out of scope before reaching the `System.out` line. Next, a `FileInputStream` and `ObjectInputStream` are created, just as the `FileOutputStream` and `ObjectOutputStreams` were created for `DateWrite`.

The next two lines of the code are also probably fairly obvious, but pay special attention to the casting operator. `readObject()` returns an `Object` class. By default, Java does not polymorph-cast any object, so you must implicitly direct it to do so. The rest of the code should be fairly obvious to you by now.

You can compile and run `DateRead`, so simply follow the same directions for `DateWrite`.

NOTE To compile the code using JDK 1.02, this time set a `classpath` variable so that you don't always have to use the `-classpath` option with `javac`. You can use the `-classpath` option as done in the previous example, but this solution is a bit more efficient. In either case these solutions are interchangeable. To set the classpath this way do the following:

On a Windows machine, type:

```
set classpath=c:\java\lib\classes.zip;c:\java\lib\objio.zip;.
```

On other platforms, the syntax is slightly different. For instance, under UNIX you might type:

```
classpath=/usr/java/lib/classes.zip:/usr/java/lib/objio.zip:.
export classpath
```

In either case, don't forget to add the current directory (.) to the end of the classpath statement. `javac` will run without the current directory being listed, but the `java` command won't work.

Compiling and Running *DateRead*

You can compile and run `DateRead`, simply by following the same directions for `DateWrite`.

```
javac DateRead.java
```

You can also run it by using the familiar `java` command:

```
java DateRead
```

Here's an example of the resulting output from this code:

```
The String is:Hi!
The old date was:Wed Dec 1 23:36:26 edt 1996
```

Notice that the `String` and `Date` are read in just as they were when you wrote them out. Now you can write out and read entire objects from the stream without needing to push each element into the stream.

CAUTION

As you may have already guessed, it is imperative that you read in objects in exactly the same order as you wrote them out. If you fail to do this, a runtime error will occur that says something such as the following:

```
Error during serialization
```

Reading In the Date with an Applet

Object serialization is not limited to applications. Listing 35.6 shows `DateRead` changed so that it can also be run as an applet.

Listing 35.6 *DataReadApp.java*—An Applet That Reads a *Date* Object to a File

```
import java.io.FileInputStream;
import java.io.ObjectInputStream;
import java.util.Date;
import java.awt.Graphics;
public class DateReadApp extends java.applet.Applet {
      public void paint (Graphics g){
            Date wasThen;
            String theString;
            try{
                  // Serialize date from a file.
                  FileInputStream inputFile = new FileInputStream("dateFile");
                  ObjectInputStream  serializeStream  =  new
            ObjectInputStream(inputFile);
                  theString  = (String) serializeStream.readObject();
                  wasThen = (Date)serializeStream.readObject();
            } catch (Exception e) {
                  System.out.println("Error during serialization");
                  return;
            }
            g.drawString(("The string is:"+theString),5,100);
            g.drawString(("The old date was:"+wasThen),5,150);
      }
}
```

After you have compiled Listing 35.6, the resulting output should look like Figure 35.1. Remember that you will have to use Applet Viewer to run this applet, because other browsers don't yet support object serialization.

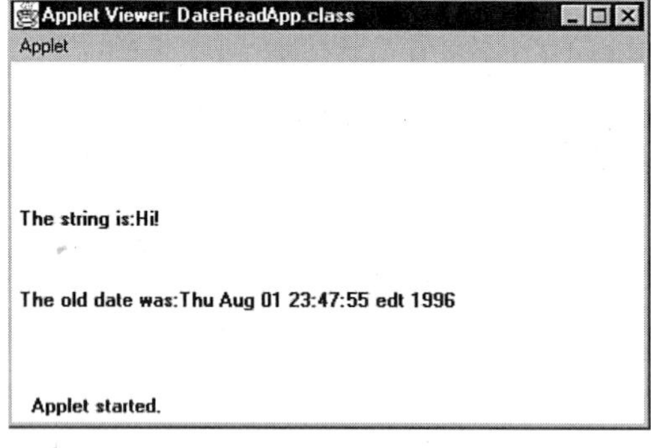

FIG. 35.1 The `Date` and `String` have been read in using serialization.

NOTE While you can run `DateReadApp` with Applet Viewer, you cannot run it using Netscape because some changes need to be made to the virtual machine in order to make object serialization possible. These changes have not yet been adopted by Netscape.

Writing and Reading Your Own Objects

By default, you have the ability to write and read most of your own objects, just as you did with the `Date` class. There are certain restrictions right now (such as if the object refers to a native peer), but for the most part, any class that you create can be serialized.

Listings 35.7 through 35.9 show the source code for serializing an example class called `SerializeObject`.

Listing 35.7 *SerializeObject*—A Simple Class with a Couple of Fields

```
public class SerializeObject implements java.io.Serializable{
      public int first;
      public char second;
      public String third;
      public SerializeObject (int first, char second, String third){
            this.first= first;
            this.second = second;
            this.third = third;
      }
}
```

Listing 35.8 *ObjWrite*—Write Out a Sample *SerializeObject* to a File

```
import java.io.FileOutputStream;
import java.io.ObjectOutputStream;
import SerializeObject;
public class ObjWrite {
      public static void main (String args[]){
            try{
                  FileOutputStream outputFile = new FileOutputStream("objFile");
                  ObjectOutputStream  serializeStream  =  new
ObjectOutputStream(outputFile);
                  SerializeObject obj = new SerializeObject (1,'c',new String
("Hi!"));
                  serializeStream.writeObject(obj);
                  serializeStream.flush();
            } catch (Exception e) {
                  System.out.println("Error during serialization");
            }
      }
}
```

Listing 35.9 *ObjRead*—Read in the Same Object from the File

```
import java.io.FileInputStream;
import java.io.ObjectInputStream;
import SerializeObject;
public class ObjRead extends java.applet.Applet {
      public void init(){
            main(null);
      }

      public static void main (String args[]){
            SerializeObject obj;
            try{
                  FileInputStream inputFile = new FileInputStream("objFile");
                  ObjectInputStream  serializeStream  =  new
ObjectInputStream(inputFile);
                  obj = (SerializeObject)serializeStream.readObject();
            } catch (Exception e) {
                  System.out.println("Error during serialization");
                  return;
            }
            System.out.println("first is:"+obj.first);
            System.out.println("second is:"+obj.second);
            System.out.println("third is:"+obj.third);
      }
}
```

In the previous example classes, notice that the `SerializeObject` class refers to a number of things, including another class—`String`. As you might already suspect, once you have compiled and run each of these classes, the resulting output is

```
First is:1
Second is:c
Third is:Hi!
```

What's most amazing about all this code is how easy it is to transfer the object.

Customizing Object Serialization

Sometimes it is useful, or even necessary, to control how an individual object is serialized. If for instance you want to encrypt the data held by this object in a proprietary form to control access to the objects data, you would not want to use the default serialization mechanisms.

NOTE Special Serialization changed in JDK 1.2. If you are using a previous version of the JDK, the methods shown here will not work for you. Instead, you should refer to the API to learn how to change the serialization for your objects. Look for the interfaces `java.io.Replaceable` and `java.io.Resolvable`.

To override how an object is serialized, you must define two methods in your class with the signatures:

```
private void writeObject(java.io.ObjectOutputStream out)
     throws IOException
 private void readObject(java.io.ObjectInputStream in)
     throws IOException, ClassNotFoundException;
```

The first question you're probably asking yourself at this point is, if `writeObject()` and `readObject()` are not in the `Serializable` interface, how does the serialization system manage to call these methods? The answer is that it uses what is know as Reflection. Reflection is covered in Chapter 48, "Reflection," but essentially it allows programs to access methods and constructors of components based on knowing their signature. Reflection is generally a complicated API, and for most of your programs you will not need to be concerned with actually getting Reflection to work. However, you do need to know that Reflection requires the signatures of the methods to be exact. Therefore, it is critical that you use exactly these signatures. Failure to make the methods private will cause the serialization mechanism to use it's default algorithms.

Your classes do not need to be concerned with calling `super.writeObject()` or `super.readObject()`, nor do you need to be concerned about how subclasses will serialize the class as each portion of the object will be handled separately by the serialization mechanism.

On the other hand, if you want to use the default mechanism within the `writeObject()` method, you can do so by calling `out.defaultWriteObject()`. Or from the `readObject()` method you can call `in.defaultReadObject()`.

Listing 35.10 contains a class called `DateTest` that writes out the value of a date as three separate integers—the year, the month, and the day of the month—instead of using the default serialization. Listings 35.11 and 35.12 contain sample classes for testing the `DateTest` class.

Listing 35.10 *DateTest*—A Class with Special Serialization

```
import java.io.*;
import java.util.*;
import java.text.*;

public class DateTest implements Serializable{
  transient GregorianCalendar myDate;

  public void newDate(){
        myDate = new GregorianCalendar();
  }

  private void writeObject(ObjectOutputStream out) throws IOException{
        int year = myDate.get(Calendar.YEAR);
        int month = myDate.get(Calendar.MONTH);
        int day = myDate.get(Calendar.DAY_OF_MONTH);
        out.writeInt(year);
        out.writeInt(month);
        out.writeInt(day);
  }

  private void readObject(ObjectInputStream in) throws IOException,
➥ClassNotFoundException{
        int year = in.readInt();
        int month = in.readInt();
        int day = in.readInt();
        myDate = new GregorianCalendar(year,month,day);
}

  public String toString(){
        DateFormat df = DateFormat.getDateInstance();
        return "DateTest:"+df.format(myDate.getTime());
  }

}
```

Listing 35.11 *DateWriter*—A Class That Writes Out a *DateTest*

```
import java.io.*;

public class DateWriter{
  public static void main(String args[]){
        try{
        DateTest test = new DateTest();
        test.newDate();
        System.out.println("Writting test:"+test);
```

continued

Listing 35.11 Continued

```
        FileOutputStream fout = new FileOutputStream("test.out");
        ObjectOutputStream oout = new ObjectOutputStream (fout);
        oout.writeObject(test);
        }catch (Exception ioe){
            ioe.printStackTrace(System.err);
        }
  }
}
```

Listing 35.12 ***DateReader*—A Class That Reads in a *Datetest***

```
import java.io.*;
public class DateReader{
  public static void main(String args[]){
        try{
        FileInputStream fin = new FileInputStream("test.out");
        ObjectInputStream oin = new ObjectInputStream (fin);
        DateTest test = (DateTest)oin.readObject();
        System.out.println("Read dateTest as "+test);
        }catch (Exception e){
                e.printStackTrace(System.err);
        }
  }
}
```

CHAPTER 36

Remote Method Invocation

In this chapter

What Is Remote Method Invocation?

One of the features that really helps push forward the client/server model in many systems is known as Remote Procedure Calls (RPC). Since JDK 1.1, Java has a similar feature called Remote Method Invocation, which allows you to create objects that actually exist and process on machines other than the client computer. This chapter covers this exciting and extremely powerful feature.

First, it's necessary to define Remote Method Invocation (RMI). With object serialization, you learned that you could take an entire object and pass it along a stream. RMI is a sister to object serialization that allows you to pass an object along a stream, and to allow that object to exist on a separate computer and invoke methods on those other systems as well.

In other words, RMI allows you to create Java objects whose methods can be invoked by the Virtual Machine on a different computer. Although these objects live and process on a different computer, they are used on the remote machine just like any local object.

Creating a Remote Object

Any object that can be called remotely must implement the Remote interface. However, the Remote interface itself does not have any methods, so obviously just implementing Remote isn't going to buy you a whole lot.

In order to have a useful interface you must create a new interface for your object, that interface must extend Remote. The new interface will contain all of the methods that can be called remotely. As you have probably already guessed, the remote object must then implement your new interface. Since the new interface extends the Remote interface, implementing the new interface fulfills the requirement for the remote object to implement Remote. Each of these implementing objects is then referred to as a remote object. So, to create and implement Remote Object there are five simple steps:

1. Define an interface that extends the Remote interface. Each method of this new interface must declare that it will throw a `RemoteExecption`.

▶ **See** "Extending Other Interfaces," **p. 195**

2. Define a class that implements the interface. Because the new interface extends Remote, this fulfills the requirements for making the new class a remote object. The class must provide a means to marshal references to the instances of the class.
3. Generate the stubs and skeletons that are needed for the remote implementations by using the `rmic` program.
4. Create a client program that will make RMI calls to the server.
5. Start the Registry and run your remote server and client.

NOTE When parameters are required by an RMI method, the objects are passed using object serialization, as discussed in Chapter 35, "Object Serialization."

A Sample RMI Application

To understand RMI, take a look at a complete example. As is so frequently the case, the example used is a fairly simple one, which simply creates a string and returns it.

Creating a Remote Interface

The first step to creating an RMI application is to create an interface, which extends the Remote interface. Each of the methods in this interface will be able to be called remotely. If you're already thinking ahead, you may have realized that the use of an interface in this system is an amazingly elegant use of object-oriented programming. With an interface, the system that calls the Remote object works with the interface just like any other class, but the compiler doesn't need to know anything about the code within the body of the methods. Just as when you create any interface, you want to make sure that the prototype for each of the methods matches exactly with the method headers you will use in the final class. Listing 36.1 shows a simple remote interface for this example.

Listing 36.1 *RemoteInterface*—A Sample Interface that Extends Remote

```
public interface RemoteInterface extends java.rmi.Remote {
    String message (String message) throws java.rmi.RemoteException;
}
```

Here, you have defined an interface with a single method. Remember that the Remote interface does not actually have any methods of its own, so message is the only method that needs to be defined by any class that implements the `RemoteInterface`.

NOTE An interface that will be utilized remotely can use any class as a parameter or a return type, so long as that type implements the Serializable.

Creating an Implementing Class

The second step is to define a class that implements your new `RemoteInterface`. This class is defined in Listing 36.2. In this example you will have `message` simply return a string, which will contain information from both the passed in string and one that is local to the object (name). Doing this should help to prove that you are, in fact, doing the processing on the remote computer. To further emphasize the point, you will do a `println`, which you will see later is displayed on the remote computer, not the client one.

Listing 36.2 *RemoteObject*—A Sample Remote Object that Receives and Sends a String

```
import java.rmi.Naming;
import java.rmi.server.UnicastRemoteObject;
```

continues

Listing 36.2 Continued

```
import java.rmi.RemoteException;
import java.rmi.RMISecurityManager;

public class RemoteObject extends UnicastRemoteObject implements
RemoteInterface{
  String name;
  public RemoteObject(String name) throws RemoteException{
    super();
    this.name = name;
  }

  public String message(String message) throws RemoteException{
    String returnString = "My Name is:"+name+",thanks for your
message:"+message;
    System.out.println("Returning:"+returnString);
    return "My Name is:"+name+",thanks for your message:"+message;
  }

  public static void main (String args[]){
    System.setSecurityManager (new RMISecurityManager());
    try{
      String myName = "ServerTest";
      RemoteObject theServer = new RemoteObject (myName);
      Naming.rebind(myName,theServer);
      System.out.println("Ready to continue");
    } catch (Exception e){
      System.out.println("An Exception occured while creating server");
    }
  }
}
```

Several key things need to be noticed about the `RemoteObject` class. First, the `RemoteObject` extends the `UnicastRemoteObject`. For the scope of this chapter, you can think of the `UnicastRemoteObject` as the `java.applet.Applet` for RMI servers. You can create your own `RemoteObject` classes, but that's beyond the scope of this chapter. Next, the server implements the `RemoteInterface` that you defined in Listing 36.1.

CAUTION

Under JDK 1.02, you will need to import and extend `java.rmi.UnicastRemoteObject`, not `java.rmi.server.UnicastRemoteObject`. So the header for the class under JDK 1.02 is

```
public class RemoteObject extends UnicastRemoteObject implements
RemoteInterface{
```

Unfortunately, this change can cause a number of incompatibilities if, for some reason, you must use a JDK 1.02 VM.

Each method in the `RemoteObject` that can be called via RMI must declare that it will throw a `RemoteException`. Notice that even the constructor method must be defined to throw a `RemoteException`. The reason for this isn't immediately obvious. After all, which of the commands in the constructor method could possibly throw an exception? It's certainly not the assignment of name, so that leaves: the `super()` constructor call, of course. Sure enough, what `UnicastRemoteObject`'s constructor does is export the remote object (the one just created) by listening for incoming requests for the object on the anonymous port (1099). Unfortunately, this export may fail if the resources to do communication are unavailable, causing an `Exception`, which your class must throw.

NOTE As with all classes which extend other classes, the `super()` call occurs implicitly by default (assuming one is available) but, to help you see where the exception is called from, it's included here explicitly.

Of course the `RemoteObject` must define the `message` method of `RemoteInterface` because it implemented `RemoteInterface`. You are most concerned with this method because this is the method you try to call using RMI. To make things simple, the `message` method simply returns a String, which includes the message that is received. If our client program receives the String back, you can be sure that the server received your original String.

The first thing the `main` method does is establish a new `SecurityManager`. This security manager does not necessarily have to be `RMISecurityManager`, but the new security manager does have to allow RMI objects to be loaded. This is important to make sure that RMI objects do not perform operations that might be considered sensitive. The default security manager does not allow any RMI objects to be exported.

The next thing the `main` method does is create an instance of `RemoteObject`, which will actually be the instance that is "attached" to by the client program. This object must then be bound into the Registry. Now, there are some important things to notice about how this is done. The `rebind()` method has two parameters. The first is the name by which the object will be known, the second is the object itself. In this case you are binding the object to the local machine and it's not really necessary to fully qualify the name. To use a fully qualified URL, the syntax would be

```
//host.name.com/bindname
```

However, as in the previous example, only the bind name is really required.

NOTE Using 1.02, you could have a space in the name of the object; however, this is no longer supported.

CAUTION

If you happen to still be using JDK 1.02, you will need to set the security manager to `java.rmi.server.StubSecurityManager`, not `java.rmi.RMISecurityManager`. So you will need to change the first line of the `main()` method to read:

```
System.setSecurityManager (new StubSecurityManager());
```

Also note that you must import this class, and not the `RMISecurityManager` one, as well.

Compiling the RemoteSever

As with Object Serialization, it is once again necessary to include additional classes when compiling `RemoteObject`.

NOTE For users of JDK 1.02, before compiling `RemoteObject`, you will need to download the `Remote Method` patch as detailed in the previous chapter with Object Serialization, and add the `rmi.zip` file to your classpath as indicated here:

```
set classpath=c:\java\lib\classes.zip;c:\java\lib\rmi.zip;c:\objio.zip;.
```

It's not technically necessary to include the `OBJIO.ZIP` file at this point, but it's not a bad idea to keep it there for good measure.

You can now compile the `RemoteObject` by typing the following:

```
javac RemoteObject.java
```

Creating the Stubs

The next step to creating an RMI server is to create the stubs and skeletons for the `RemoteObject`. You can do this using the `rmic` compiler by typing the following:

```
rmic RemoteObject
```

As you can see, the syntax for the `rmic` compiler is nearly identical to that for the `java` command. In fact, many of the same command-line options that you have available to you when running the `java` command are available to you when running `rmic`.

NOTE Unfortunately, under JDK 1.1 a small quirk in the Windows version of the JDK did not automatically include the current directory (.) in the classpath as it does in `java` or `javac`. If you are running JDK 1.1, you will need to use the classpath option as shown below (which assumes you have the JDK1.1 installed in the c:\java directory).

```
rmic -classpath c:\java\lib\classes.zip;. RemoteObject
```

Fortunately, JDK 1.2 does not have this same problem.

The `rmic` compiler produces two files for you:

```
RemoteObject_Skel.class
RemoteObject_Stub.class
```

Creating a Client

The next step to creating an RMI program is to create the client that will actually invoke the remote methods. Listing 36.3 shows an example class.

Listing 36.3 *RemoteClient.java*—An Example Client that Interfaces to the *RemoteObject* Class

```
import java.rmi.RMISecurityManager;
import java.rmi.Naming;
public class RemoteClient {
  public static void main(String args[]){
    System.setSecurityManager(new RMISecurityManager());
    try{
      RemoteInterface server = (RemoteInterface)
                             ➥Naming.lookup("ServerTest");
      String serverString = server.message("Hello There");
      System.out.println("The server says :\n"+serverString);
    } catch (Exception e){
      System.out.println("Error while performing RMI");
    }
  }
}
```

The most important portions of the `RemoteClient` class are the two lines in the middle of the `try-catch` block:

```
RemoteInterface server = (RemoteInterface) Naming.lookup("Server Test");
String serverString = server.message("Hello There");
```

The first line of code looks to the Registry to locate the stub called "Server Test" (if you look back to the `RemoteObject` program in Listing 36.2, line 21, you will see that you bound it using this name). Once the program has created an instance of the `RemoteInterface`, it then calls the message method with the string `"Hello There"`. Notice that this is actually a method call. You are invoking a method on a completely different system. The method then returns a string that is stored in `serverString` and later printed out.

You can now compile the client program just as you did for `RemoteObject`:

```
javac RemoteClient.java
```

This, of course, assumes that you have already set your classpath for the `RemoteObject` class.

Starting the Registry and Running the Code

Before you can actually run the `RemoteObject` and `RemoteClient` classes, you must first start the RMI Registry program on the computer that will be hosting the `RemoteObject`. This step is required even if the computer that you will be running the `RemoteObject` on is the same as the `RemoteClient` (as you will do in this case for demonstration purposes). In order for the Registry to work, the directory with the stub and skeleton files must be in the classpath for the `rmiregistry` program.

To start the Registry under Windows type:

```
start rmiregistry
```

TROUBLESHOOTING

If after typing `start rmiregistry` you get a `"Bad command or file name"` error, it's not because of the Registry, but rather because you don't have Windows' start program in your path. Since start is generally located in your `windows\command` directory, try adding that to your path or typing:

```
C:\windows\command\start rmiregistry
```

NOTE Unfortunately, for JDK 1.1 users under Windows, just as with `rmic`, the Registry program does not even include the current directory in the path, so if you haven't upgraded to 1.2, to start the Registry program, type:

```
set classpath=c:\java\lib\classes.zip;.
start rmiregistry
```

On most UNIX machines, you can start the Registry and push it into the background by typing:

```
set classpath=/usr/java/lib/classes.zip;.
rmiregistry &
```

If you want to start the Registry out of a different directory than the `skeleton/stub` directory, you should substitute the period (.) with the directory containing these files. Also, you should make sure that the location of `classes.zip` matches your installation.

NOTE If you are still using JDK 1.02, you need to start the Registry in a slightly different fashion. Under 1.02, the following command will start the Registry up.

```
java java.rmi.registry.RegistryImpl
```

Binding *RemoteObject* into the Registry

Once the Registry has been started, you need to start the `RemoteObject` program.

In this case start the `RemoteObject` like you would any other Java program:

```
java RemoteObject
```

In the future, you will probably want to push the object into the background. Under Windows you can start the `RemoteObject` program in the background by typing:

```
javaw RemoteObject
```

You can start it in the background on a UNIX machine by running instead as:

```
java RemoteObject &
```

Running the Client Program

The last task is to start the `RemoteClient`. However, before you do, make sure that the `RemoteObject` program has printed:

```
Ready to continue
```

This is your clue that the `RemoteObject` has been exported and bound into the Registry. Be patient, especially if you don't have an active Internet connection, because this can take a while. Also, if you started the object in the background obviously you will never see the output.

Once the `RemoteObject` has let you know it's okay to continue, you want to start the `RemoteClient`. To do this, if you're running under Windows you will need to open another DOS prompt window. If you're using a UNIX machine, even if you have put the `RemoteObject` in the background, you will probably want another session (or x-terminal) so that you can tell the difference between the outputs from the server and the client.

Finally, to run the `RemoteClient` type:

```
java RemoteClient
```

The following output should appear on the screen.

```
The Server Says:
My Name is:ServerTest, thanks for your message:Hello There
```

Notice that the string was produced on the server and returned to you. If you look at the RemoteObject window, what you will see is output that says:

```
Ready to continue

Returning: My Name is:ServerTest, thanks for your message:Hello There
```

Creating an Applet Client

Now that you have created an application that utilizes the `RemoteObject`, try doing this with an Applet as shown in Listing 36.4. As you will soon see, there really isn't much difference.

NOTE Due to the changes in the Virtual Machine that are required for RMI and Object Serialization, at the time of this writing you can only run these applets using `Appletviewer`. Neither Netscape Navigator nor Microsoft Internet Explorer have support for RMI or Object Serialization.

Listing 36.4 *RemoteAppletClient.java*—An Applet that Uses a Remote Object

```
/*
 *
 * RemoteAppletClient
 *
 */
import java.applet.Applet;
import java.rmi.RMISecurityManager;
import java.rmi.Naming;

public class RemoteAppletClient extends Applet {
  public void init(){
    System.setSecurityManager(new RMISecurityManager());
    try{
      RemoteInterface server = (RemoteInterface) Naming.lookup("ServerTest");
      String serverString = server.message("Hello There");
      System.out.println("The server says :\n"+serverString);
      } catch (Exception e){
        System.out.println("Error while performing RMI:"+e);
        }
   }
}
```

Creating a Custom Socket

Occasionally, you may want to change the way that RMI communicates from one machine to the other. In Chapters 30 through 34, you explored the use of sockets and learned about Java's built-in networking capabilities. Some of these capabilities are exploited by default with RMI. However, the default implementation may not provide some features you would like such as compression or security.

You can now create a custom socket implementation for your RMI connections. To do this you need to follow three steps:

1. Create a custom socket, or choose one to use.
2. Create a custom `RMISocketFactory` with the new socket.
3. Set the socket factory in both your client and server.

Creating a Custom Socket

To create a custom socket, generally, you need to go through two steps. First, create a custom stream and second, create a socket which uses that stream. You can skip this step if you are actually using a socket from a third party, such as Sun's `SSLSocket` class.

Creating a Custom Stream The real goal of using a custom socket with RMI is to provide some additional functionality such as compression or security. Since the socket itself doesn't do much good without a stream that provides the additional functionality, you must first define a `Stream` for your purposes. Actually you must define two streams: an `InputStream` and an `OutputStream`.

For this example, you will create a set of sockets that perform perhaps the simplest set of security, you will perform a Boolean `NOT` on each byte as it goes in and out. It's a convenient little algorithm, because it's so simple. However, since Java doesn't have a bytewise `NOT` operator instead you will `XOR` the byte with `0xFF` which has the same net result.

In this case, since you want to see the simplest example, you'll extend `java.io.InputStream`; however, if you were doing this for real you'd likely extend a more appropriate stream such as `BufferedInputStream`, `FilteredInputStream`, or `ObjectInputStream`, depending on what would make the most sense for your particular implementation.

Listing 36.6 shows the new `CustomOutputStream`. For more information about `Stream` classes please refer back to Chapter 27.

Listing 36.5 ***CustomInputStream.java*****—Creates a Stream that Reads a *NOT*ed Stream**

```
import java.io.*;
public class CustomInputStream extends FilterInputStream{

  public CustomInputStream(InputStream in) {
    super(in);
  }

  public int read() throws IOException {
    int code;
    try{
      code = in.read();
    } catch (EOFException e) {
      System.out.println("EOF");
      return -1;
    }
    //Don't invert a negative one, leave it as is.
    if (code != -1){
      //NOT the result
      code = (0xff^code);
      //mask off the top bits
      code = (0xff)& code;
    }
    return code;
  }


  public int read(byte b[], int off, int len)   throws IOException {
    int num = in.read(b,off,len);
    if (len <= 0) {
      return 0;
    }

    int i = 0;
    //convert the bytes
    for (;i<num;i++){
      b[off+i]= (byte)(b[off+i]^0xff);
```

continues

Listing 36.5 Continued

```
    }
    return num;

  }

}
```

Listing 36.6 *CustomOutputStream.java*—Creates a Stream that Writes a *NOT*ed Stream

```
import java.io.*;
public class CustomOutputStream extends FilterOutputStream {
  public CustomOutputStream (OutputStream out){
    super(out);
  }

  public void write(int b) throws IOException{
    out.write(b ^ 0xff);
    out.flush();
  }

  public void write (byte b[],int off, int len) throws IOException{
    for (int i = 0; i < len; i++) {
      byte b2 = b[off + i];
      write(b2);//[off + i]);
    }
  }
}
```

Creating a Custom Socket Now that you have a new type of stream, you can create the new `Socket` classes. Your new `Socket` class will use the new streams, but otherwise isn't much different from a standard `Socket` class. Listing 36.7 shows just such an implementation. Notice in the `getInputStream()` and `getOutputStream()` methods that your new custom streaming classes are returned instead of the original (`super.getInputStream()` or `super.getOutputStream()`).

Listing 36.7 *CustomSocket.java*—Extends Socket and Uses the New Streams

```
import java.io.*;
import java.net.*;
public class CustomSocket extends Socket {
  //The InputStream of the socket
  private InputStream in;
  //The output stream for the socket.
  private OutputStream out;
```

```
  //null constructor, since you want to support both types of
➥socket constructors
  //you need to prototype both of them.
  public CustomSocket() {
    super();
  }

  public CustomSocket(String host, int port) throws IOException {
    super(host, port);
  }


  public InputStream getInputStream()   throws IOException     {
    if (in == null) {
      //create a new stream from the normal socket stream
      in = new CustomInputStream(super.getInputStream());
    }
    return in;
  }

  public OutputStream getOutputStream() throws IOException{
    if (out == null) {
      //create a new stream from the normal socket stream
      out = new CustomOutputStream(super.getOutputStream());        }
    return out;
  }

}
```

Creating a Custom ServerSocket The RMI System must be able to listen for new connections (`ServerSockets`). Clearly, you want these connections to be of the same `Socket` class that you just created. Therefore, you must also create a custom `ServerSocket` which will utilize the `CustomSocket` class. To do this the new class really only needs to override the `accept()` method and force it to use the `CustomSocket` in Listing 36.7. Listing 36.8 shows how the new `ServerSocket` should look for our `CustomSocket` implementation.

Listing 36.8 *CustomServerSocket.java*—Extends *ServerSocket* and Uses the *CustomSocket* Class

```
import java.io.*;
import java.net.*;
public class CustomServerSocket extends ServerSocket {
    public CustomServerSocket(int port) throws IOException     {
        super(port);
  }

  public Socket accept() throws IOException {
        Socket s = new CustomSocket();
        implAccept(s);
        return s;
  }
}
```

Creating a Custom *RMISocketFactory*

Now that you have created your own `Socket` class, you can use it to create the `RMISocketFactory`. The `RMISocketFactory` actually provides the sockets that will be used in the RMI application. `RMISocketFactory` has two abstract methods that your new socket factory must provide implementations for: `createSocket()` and `createServerSocket()`. Obviously the goal here is to have the methods return either `CustomSockets` or `CustomServerSockets`. So, in Listing 36.9 you will see that `CustomRMISocketFactory` does just that.

NOTE When you read Listing 36.9 you will notice that there are actually four methods. The last two should make sense to you (they create sockets of a particular type), and in Listing 36.9 they are overridden to provide `CustomSockets` and `CustomServerSockets`. What may throw you for a loop though are the first two methods. These methods must return the default sockets. Why is this? Well, the answer is that the RMI system still needs to be able to get "clean" sockets when it performs its initial "look up" with the Registry. You see, the Registry doesn't care how the remote object and the client talk, but it expects you to talk to it on a standard socket.

The Registry is really only responsible for letting each of the objects know where the other one is. After that the objects talk directly to each other without having the Registry in the middle. To make this work though, you must still provide a default socket implementation if the specific socket type is not known.

Listing 36.9 *CustomRMISocketFactory*—Extends the *RMISocketFactory* Class and Uses the Custom Sockets

```
import java.io.*;
import java.net.*;
import java.rmi.server.*;
public class CustomRMISocketFactory extends RMISocketFactory {


    private RMISocketFactory defaultFactory  =
➥ RMISocketFactory.getDefaultSocketFactory();

    public Socket createSocket(String host, int port) throws IOException {
      return  defaultFactory.createSocket(host, port);
    }

    public ServerSocket createServerSocket(int port) throws IOException {
          return defaultFactory.createServerSocket(port);
    }

  public Socket createSocket(String host, int port,
➥SocketType type)     throws IOException    {
    String protocol = type.getProtocol();
    if(protocol.equals("custom"))
        // Use default bit pattern for the XorSocket.
        return new CustomSocket(host, port);
    return createSocket(host,port);
  }
```

```
  public ServerSocket createServerSocket(int port,SocketType type)
➥    throws IOException    {
    String protocol = type.getProtocol();
    if(protocol.equals("custom"))
      return new CustomServerSocket(port);
    return createServerSocket(port);
  }
}
```

Specifying the Socket Factory in Your Applications

The last step in the process is to actually tell your applications to use the new socket factory. The only real trick to this is that you need to be sure to modify both the client and server components. If you fail to do this, obviously you'll end up with corrupted data on one end or the other.

To change the socket factory all you need to do is call the `setSocketFactory()` method. `setSocketFactory()` is a static method of `RMISocketFactory`. So the line of code your going to add will look like:

```
RMISocketFactory.setSocketFactory(new CustomRMISocketFactory());
```

The `setSocketFactory()` method will generally be the first line in the main methods for both your new client and server pieces. Listings 36.10 and 36.11 below show our HelloWorld application from Listings 36.2 and 36.3. Notice the only change is the insertion of the one line (that and `RMISocketFactory` now needs to be imported).

The second change that you must make is in calling the constructor for `UnicastRemoteObject`. This constructor can either be called without any parameters (like you will do normally if you aren't using a custom socket), or you can specify the port and socket type.

In this case you can specify the port to be `0` (which will refer to the default port), and then you must provide a `SocketType` object. The `SocketType` will tell the `RMISocketFactory` what type of socket you want to use for this transaction. The `SocketType` constructor looks like this:

```
public SocketType(String protocol, byte[] refData, Object serverData)
```

The `refData` can provide some additional protocol data, and the `serverData` can provide additional server protocol information. But in this case, you don't need to worry about either. The only thing you need to be concerned with is the protocol name, which I've chosen to call "custom" through out this chapter. Now, to actually be able to call the `UnicastRemoteObject`'s constructor you need to modify the `RemoteObject`'s constructor as follows.

```
public RemoteObject(String name) throws RemoteException{
    super(0, new SocketType("custom", null, null));
    this.name = name;
  }
```

You'll find a complete listing of all these changes in Listings 36.10 and 36.11. Once you have compiled Listings 36.10 and 36.11, you can run the application just as you did earlier in this chapter with the normal socket implementation. Don't forget to compile the stub before you start it up, though.

Listing 36.10 ***RemoteObject.java*****—Uses the New *CustomSocket***

```
import java.rmi.server.SocketType;

public class RemoteObject extends UnicastRemoteObject implements
➥RemoteInterface{
  String name;
  public RemoteObject(String name) throws RemoteException{
    super(0, new SocketType("custom", null, null));
    this.name = name;
  }

  public String message(String message) throws RemoteException{
    String returnString = "My Name is:"+name+
➥",thanks for your message:"+message;
    System.out.println("Returning:"+returnString);
    return "My Name is:"+name+",thanks for your message:"+message;
  }

  public static void main (String args[]){
    try{
      RMISocketFactory.setSocketFactory(new CustomRMISocketFactory());
      System.setSecurityManager (new RMISecurityManager());
      //RMISocketFactory.setSocketFactory(new XorSocketFactory());
      //CustomRMISocketFactory());
      String myName = "ServerTest";
      RemoteObject theServer = new RemoteObject (myName);
      Naming.rebind("/"+myName,theServer);
      System.out.println("Ready to continue");
    } catch (Exception e){
      System.out.println("An Exception occurred while creating server");
      e.printStackTrace(System.out);
    }
  }
}
```

Listing 23.11 ***RemoteClient.java*****—Now Uses the New *CustomSocket***

```
import java.rmi.RMISecurityManager;
import java.rmi.server.RMISocketFactory;
import java.rmi.Naming;
public class RemoteClient {
  public static void main(String args[]){
    try{
      System.setSecurityManager(new RMISecurityManager());
      RMISocketFactory.setSocketFactory(new CustomRMISocketFactory());

      RemoteInterface server = (RemoteInterface) Naming.lookup("ServerTest");
      String serverString = server.message("Hello There");
```

```
        System.out.println("The server says :\n"+serverString);
      } catch (Exception e){
        System.out.println("Error while performing RMI:"+e);
        e.printStackTrace(System.out);
      }
    }
  }
```

Using the Activation Model

Another new feature in the implementation of RMI is the capability to remotely activate an object. The problem that RMI had before the Activator is that you always had to start an object and register it into the Registry as I have done in this chapter. However, there are often reasons why this solution isn't good enough.

If the remote object dies for some reason (because of a fault of exception), or if it thinks it's done processing (for example, if a state machine didn't reset), the object will not be available when your remote application attempts to use it. It's also possible that something might cause a remote object to fail to start all together.

Activation helps to solve this problem by giving the Registry the capability to use an Activator. The Activator will check the status of the remote object and perform whatever initialization is necessary to get it running again.

Building an Activatable Object

The first step to building a set of remote objects which can be Activated is to have each of the remote objects extend from the `java.rmi.activation.Activatable`, instead of the `UnicastRemoteObject` that you've seen through out this chapter.

Since your object is now extending Activatable, though, it must also alter its constructor signature.

```
public MyRemoteInterfaceImpl(ActivationID id, MarshalledObject data)
throws RemoteException {
// Register the object with the activation system
// then export it on an anonymous port
super(id, 0);
}
```

The major changes, however, need to go into the new main method. The setup for the Activator needs to perform several additional operations.

The first task is to define the location where the `Activatable` object will be found. This URL will be used by the remote deamon to create the object when it is required.

```
java.net.URL location = new java.net.URL("file:/src/se4/");
```

Once you know the location where the stub and skeleton files are located you next need to define a `CodeSource` object. The `CodeSource` constructor requires two items. The first is the location URL you just defined, and the second is a public key. You don't need to define the public key necessarily, so in this case it can be set to `null`.

```
CodeSource source = new CodeSource(location, null);
```

The next step is to get the system properties, and create an `ActivationGroupID`. The `ActivationGroupID` will be used to create an `ActivationDesc`. Now the `ActivationDesc` must be used to actually register the new object with the activatable object.

```
    Properties props = (Properties)System.getProperties().clone();
    ActivationGroupID agid = ActivationGroup.getSystem().registerGroup(
            new ActivationGroupDesc(props));
    MarshalledObject data = null;
    ActivationDesc desc = new ActivationDesc
➥(agid, "RemoteActivatableObject", source, data);
    RemoteInterface remoteInterface = (RemoteInterface)
➥Activatable.register(desc);
```

Now that you have a remote interface object you can rebind it, just like you did in the previous sections. However, once you bound the object, instead of having the system continue to wait for a connection, you can now exit the system.

```
Naming.rebind("ServerTest", remoteInterface);
System.out.println("Exported interface, ready to go");

//Now exit the program, the rmid will take over from here
System.exit(0);
```

NOTE When running the examples in this section make sure you are using the `RemoteClient` from Listing 36.3, not from Listing 36.11.

Listing 36.12 *RemoteActivatableObject.java*—Exporting Activatable and Performing Several Modifications Will Make the Object Activatable

```
import java.rmi.Naming;
import java.rmi.server.UnicastRemoteObject;
import java.rmi.RemoteException;
import java.rmi.RMISecurityManager;
import java.rmi.server.RMISocketFactory;
import java.rmi.activation.*;
import java.rmi.server.SocketType;
import java.rmi.MarshalledObject;
import java.security.CodeSource;
import java.util.Properties;


public class RemoteActivatableObject extends Activatable
➥ implements RemoteInterface{
```

```
   public RemoteActivatableObject(ActivationID id, MarshalledObject data)
      throws RemoteException {
      super(id, 0);
   }


   public String message(String message) throws RemoteException{
     String returnString = "Thanks for your message:"+message;
     System.out.println("Returning:"+returnString);
     return "Thanks for your message:"+message;
   }




   public static void main(String[] args) throws Exception {
     System.setSecurityManager(new RMISecurityManager());

     java.net.URL location = new java.net.URL("file:/src/se4/");
     CodeSource source = new CodeSource(location, null);
     Properties props = (Properties)System.getProperties().clone();
     ActivationGroupID agid = ActivationGroup.getSystem().registerGroup(
             new ActivationGroupDesc(props));
     MarshalledObject data = null;
     ActivationDesc desc = new ActivationDesc (agid,
➥ "RemoteActivatableObject", source, data);
     RemoteInterface remoteInterface = (RemoteInterface)
➥Activatable.register(desc);
     Naming.rebind("ServerTest", remoteInterface);
     System.out.println("Exported interface, ready to go");

     //Now exit the program, the rmid will take over from here
     System.exit(0);
   }
}
```

Listing 36.12 shows the new `RemoteActivatableObject`. To build the new program you must first compile `RemoteActivatableObject.java`, and then run `rmic` on it.

Finally, you can start the program by first starting the `rmiregistry`, then you must start the `rmid` which will actually instantiate the remote objects when they are required. Finally, you can run the `RemoteActivatableObject` and the `Remote Client` as you did before. So, roughly speaking you can create them as follows:

```
javac RemoteActivatableObject.java
rmic RemoteActivatableObject
start rmiregistry
rmid
```

Now the `rmid` will actually run continuously just like your previous `RemoteObject`, so you will now need another terminal window (or DOS prompt). From there you can start the `Activatable` object and run the client:

```
java RemoteActivatableObject
java RemoteClient
```

The results should be as follows:

```
G:\src\se4>java -Djava.rmi.server.codebase=file:/src/se4/
➥RemoteActivatableObject
Exported interface, ready to go

G:\src\se4>java RemoteClient
The server says :
Thanks for your message:Hello There
```

CHAPTER 37

Management API

In this chapter

JMAPI Components

The Java Management API (JMAPI) is a comprehensive subsystem for creating Java objects that can be managed by a central management tool, and also for creating the management tools themselves.

Within the Java management framework, there are three main components:

The Managed Object Server

Any number of managed "appliances"

A JMAPI applet presenting a user interface for managing appliances (which can range from toasters to mainframes)

The Managed Object Server contains a Managed Object Factory, which creates managed objects. Although the JMAPI system is managing appliances, most of the management logic resides in these managed objects.

The managed objects communicate with agent objects, usually residing on the appliances. These agent objects implement the requests of the managed objects. Agent objects sometimes need native libraries to control appliances. JMAPI includes special support for native libraries, allowing the agents to download native libraries for whatever hardware platform they are running on (assuming that a native library exists for that platform). Sun uses the term "appliances" in describing the devices managed by JMAPI—although most of the devices you deal with today may be computers, in the future you may be able to manage everyday household appliances with JMAPI.

A JMAPI applet presents the management user interface. Network management applications are often very complex, requiring many ways of presenting data and receiving input. The Admin View Module (AVM) contains many of these components. A JMAPI applet communicates with managed objects via managed object interfaces, which use RMI to transmit information.

JMAPI Applets

A JMAPI applet represents the user interface of the Java Management API. A typical applet enables a user to view available managed appliances and change various settings on those appliances. Unlike normal Web applets, JMAPI applets require some special applet parameters in order to communicate with the managed object server. JMAPI provides three different startup Web pages that can launch other JMAPI applets:

- `JmapiHome.html`
- `MOContentManagerApplet.html`
- `MOPropertyBookApplet.html`

JmapiHome.html

The `JmapiHome.html` page contains a launcher that can start other management applets. The launcher can use an optional page `Registry` object to limit the available applets. By default, the launcher displays all available pages. `JmapiHome.html` has several configuration parameters that are specified using the `<PARAM>` tag. The name values for these parameters are as follows:

- `host` The host name where the managed object server is running (required)
- `port` The port number of the managed object server (required)
- `domainName` The name of the management domain that this applet is managing (optional)
- `contextName` The name of a persistent context that is used to initialize the local management context (optional)
- `pageRegistry` The name of a page `Registry` object containing the information to be displayed by the launcher

MOContentManagerApplet.html

The `MOContentManagerApplet.html` page displays a content manager for a class of managed objects. Each type of managed object can have a presentation object for managing objects of that type. To manage an object from the `MOContentManagerApplet`, the object's type must have a presentation object defined. In the `<PARAM>` tag for `MOContentManagerApplet.html`, specify the `ManagedObjectClassName` parameter telling what type of object you want to manage.

MOPropertyBookApplet.html

The `MOPropertyBookApplet` displays a property book for a single object. This applet also requires that a presentation object is defined for any type of object you want to manage.

Accessing Managed Objects

The `MOFactory` class provides access to the managed object factory running on the managed object server. Using this class, you can create, modify, and delete managed objects. You can also enumerate through a set of objects, and query for objects matching a specific set of criteria.

Before you can perform any management functions, you must use the `initialize` method in `MOFactory` to specify the host name and port number of the managed object server:

```
MOFactory.initialize("mgmt_server", 1234);
```

To create a new instance of a management object, call the `newObj` method with the full name of the class:

```
MyManagedObject obj = (MyManagedObject) MOFactory.newObj(
    "demopkg.mgmt.MyManagedObject");
```

The get and set methods for managed objects require a security context to perform operations. You can pass null as a security context; for a production system, however, you should have a proper security context:

```
SecurityContext context = null;

obj.setSomething(context, "somethingValue");
obj.setSomethingElse(context, "otherValue");
```

After you create the object, you need to add it to the management server with the addObject method:

```
obj.addObject(context)
```

The modifyObject and deleteObject register object changes and object deletions with the managed object server:

```
obj.modifyObject(context);

obj.deleteObject(context);
```

The listMOClass method returns a vector containing all managed objects of a particular class:

```
Vector v = MOFactory.listMOClass("demopkg.mgmt.MyManagedObject");
```

You can specify an optional query object to search for managed objects with certain attributes. The QueryExp class contains methods for creating query expressions. You can pass a query expression to the listMOClass method to limit the search. This could be an enormous time saver. If there are a large number of managed objects, you don't want the server to send each object to your client program when you only need a small subset. It is better to let the server weed out the objects you don't want and only send you the ones you do.

Creating a Managed Object

Most of the time when you use JMAPI, you will be working with existing managed objects. Sometimes, however, you will need to create a managed object that is then visible to JMAPI applets.

Defining Properties Within Managed Objects

To make a property that is visible to JMAPI applets, you just provide get and set methods just like you do in the JavaBeans API. One difference between the JMAPI get/set methods and the Beans get/set methods is that the JMAPI methods take an additional SecurityContext parameter. The class definition shown in Listing 37.1 creates a managed object with a single property called "address".

Listing 37.1 Source Code for Simple *AddressMOImpl.java*

```
public class SimpleAddressMOImpl extends LogicalElementMOImpl
    implements SimpleAddressMOImpl
{
```

```
    PrismVar String address;

    public String getName(SecurityContext context)
    {
        return (String) getAttribute("address");
    }

    public void setName(SecurityContext context, String hostName)
    {
        setKnownAttribute("address", hostName);
    }
}
```


NOTE Notice that instead of the normal `.java` ending, managed objects within JMAPI are defined in files ending with `.mo`.

The `PrismVar` keyword in a managed object file identifies attributes within the managed object. Also, the `setKnownAttribute` enables you to set attributes persistently. In other words, when you set a known attribute, it gets saved in the database, and the next time the object is instantiated, it will retain that attribute value.

Defining Methods Within Managed Objects

Managed objects are implemented as RMI servers, and any method defined in the object's `.mo` file will be defined within RMI and can be called from a management applet. You only need to provide the implementation of the method; the JMAPI framework takes care of the rest.

Compiling a Managed Object

Because managed objects are defined in `.mo` files, you need a way to convert one of these files into a set of Java classes. You do this with the `Moco` program (the Managed Object COmpiler). To compile a managed object, just type:

```
java moco.Moco YourManagedObject.mo
```

The managed object compiler creates three Java source files for each managed object: the interface definition, the implementation, and the database operations. For a file named `SimpleAddressMO.mo`, the Java source files generated would be as follows:

- `SimpleAddressMO.java`
- `SimpleAddressMOImpl.java`
- `DBSimpleAddressMO.java`

CAUTION

If your managed object references other managed objects, you must include the `.mo` files on the command line for `Moco`.

Importing Managed Objects

Before a managed object can be used in the JMAPI system, you must import into the JMAPI database. The `importclasses` command enables you to import one or more class files into the system. If your class references other managed objects that are not yet in the database, you must import them all at once. The following command imports `SimpleAddressMO` into the JMAPI database:

```
importclasses SimpleAddressMO
```

After the managed object has been loaded into the system, a JMAPI applet can access it.

The Admin View Module

Although you may occasionally need to create new managed objects, you are more likely to create JMAPI applets. After all, there are only so many new kinds of objects to manage, but there are always new ways to display and manipulate objects.

Because management applications tend to require complex user interfaces, JMAPI provides a set of useful components called the Admin View Module (AVM). Although these components were originally intended for JMAPI applications, they do not depend on any other parts of JMAPI. In other words, you can use the AVM in any application you want without being dependent on the rest of JMAPI.

Content Managers and Selectable Objects

In a typical management application, you have a set of items that you can select and perform operations on. The Java AWT doesn't provide these capabilities by itself. Instead, that is left up to you, or in this case, to the AVM.

The AVM defines a `ContentManager` class, which is an abstract class responsible for displaying a set of objects, enabling you to select some of them and execute commands on them. Creating a content manager is a fairly complex job, but because the AVM provides several useful ones, you may not have to create one at all.

The `ContentManager` class uses `Selectable` interface to notify objects that they have been selected or deselected, and to find out what commands each object supports. Each object can support its own set of commands, which will be available on a menu when the object is selected. The `Selectable` interface contains the following methods:

```
public void select()

public void deselect()

public boolean isSelected()

public void toggleSelection()

public Command[] getCommands(String commandType)

public Command[] setCommands(String commandType, Commands[] commands)
```

The select, deselect, toggleSelection, and isSelected methods are used by content managers and other objects to control whether an object is selected. If the object needs to change its appearance based on its selection, it can do so in the implementation of these methods.

The getCommands and setCommands methods control the array of Command objects that the object supports. When an object is selected, its commands are presented on a menu. When a command is selected from the menu, the execute method in that command is executed to carry out the request.

In addition to the selection and command methods, the Selectable interface defines three string constants: SELECTED_COMMANDS, CREATE_COMMANDS, and VIEW_COMMANDS. When you get or set commands in a selectable, you must specify whether you want the commands for the create, view, or selected menu. These command types are used by content managers, which maintain these three menus.

The Command interface is very simple, containing only three methods:

```
public void execute(Object executor)

public String getLabel()

public String getName()
```

The execute method is called as a result of a menu selection and should carry out the requested operation. The getLabel method returns the string that is displayed on the menu. The getName method returns the name you have assigned to the command. This enables you to keep an internal version of a name while varying the label (the visual part), depending on the environment.

Listing 37.2 shows an applet that uses the SimpleContentManager class to demonstrate how to set up a command.

Listing 37.2 Source Code for *SimpleCMApplet.java*

```
import sunw.admin.avm.base.*;
import java.applet.*;
import java.awt.*;
import java.util.Vector;
import java.net.URL;

public class SimpleCMApplet extends Applet
{
    Frame currFrame;

    static String[] playmateInfo = {
        "Katy", "Sammy", "Bunnie"
    };

// For the play command, just print a dialog

    class PlayCommand implements Command {
        public String getLabel() { return "Play"; };
```

continues

Listing 37.2 Continued

```
        public String getName() { return "playCommand"; };

        public void execute(Object executor) {
            play(executor);
        }
    };

    public void init()
    {

// Load an image to display for the icon part of the simple content manager

        URL imgURL = null;
        try {
            imgURL = new URL(getDocumentBase(), "katyface.GIF");
        } catch (Exception ignore) {
        }

        Image img = getImage(imgURL);

        MediaTracker tracker = new MediaTracker(this);
        try {
            tracker.addImage(img, 0);
            tracker.waitForAll();
        } catch (Exception e) {
            e.printStackTrace();
        }

// Create a simple content manager

        SimpleContentManager cm = new SimpleContentManager(
            "Play Manager", img);

// Create the data for the content manager's table

        TableData data = new TableData(playmateInfo, "¦");

        cm.setTableData(data);

// Create an array of column names
        String[] cols = new String[1];
        cols[0] = "Name";

// Set up a filter to display the column names
        cm.setFilterPipe(new TableFilterPipe(data, cols));

// Create an empty query space
        cm.setQuerySpace(new QuerySpace());

// Set up the default sort pipe
        cm.setSortPipe(new TableSortPipe(cm.getFilterPipe(), cols));

// Cerate an array of column widths
        int[] widths = new int[1];
```

```
        widths[0] = 20;

// Set up the view properties pipe, which sets the column widths
        cm.setViewPipe(new TableViewPropertiesPipe(cm.getSortPipe(),
            cols, widths));

// Make the Content Manager look at the view pipe to get the column data
        cm.getViewPipe().addObserver(cm);

// Create an array of commands
        Command commands[] = new Command[1];
        commands[0] = new PlayCommand();

// Assign the commands to the content manager
        cm.setCommands(Selectable.SELECTED_COMMANDS,
            commands);

// Make the content manager process the data
        data.changed();

        setLayout(new GridLayout(1, 0));

// Create a top-level content manager to contain the simple manager
        TopLevelContentManager topCM = new TopLevelContentManager();

        add(topCM);

// Add the simple manager to the top manager
        topCM.add("Center", cm);

// Make the top-level manager receive events from the simple manager
        cm.addItemListener(topCM);

// Activate the simple manager (make it the current panel)
        topCM.select(cm);

// The command classes need a reference to this applet's frame
        currFrame = Util.findFrame(this);
    }

    protected void play(Object executor)
    {
        if (!(executor instanceof SimpleContentManager)) return;

// Get a reference to the current content manager
        SimpleContentManager cm = (SimpleContentManager) executor;

// Get the data table
        Table table = cm.getTable();

// Find the selected row
        int index = table.getSelectedIndex();

// Get the first column in the row
        String whichSelection = (String) table.getItem(index, 0);
```

continues

Listing 37.2 Continued

```
// Just put up a dialog showing who the playmate is
        InformationDialog info = new InformationDialog(
            currFrame, "Playing with "+ whichSelection);
        info.setVisible(true);
    }
}
```

In a typical management application, the command objects would invoke methods on managed objects. Because the content managers are not tied to the rest of the JMAPI framework, however, your command objects can perform any function you like. If you work at an airline, for example, you might create a content manager that displays a table of flights with commands such as `"create flight plan"`, `"cancel"`, or `"divert"`.

Icons

When creating a complex user interface, you often need to represent items graphically using an icon. Although you could create a subclass of the AWT's `Canvas` class, you would soon find yourself writing far more code than you like. The `Icon` class in the AVM implements the `Selectable` interface, allowing it to be managed by content managers. The `IconCanvas` class manages the display and possible selection of multiple icons.

To create an `Icon` object, just supply a name and an image or an AWT component. The following line creates an `Icon`:

```
Icon myIcon = new Icon(myImage, "My Image");
```

An `IconCanvas` object is actually a subclass of `Panel`, not `Canvas`. To put icons on the canvas, you just call the `add` method like you would for any other panel. You can also set up a layout manager for an `IconCanvas` to determine where to place the icons. You cannot add any objects other than icons to the canvas, however.

Listing 37.3 shows a sample applet that creates three icons and displays them.

Listing 37.3 Sample Applet

```
import sunw.admin.avm.base.*;
import java.applet.*;
import java.awt.*;
import java.net.URL;

public class IconApplet extends Applet
{

    public void init()
    {

// Load images to display in applet

        URL imgURL = null;
```

```
        try {
            imgURL = new URL(getDocumentBase(), "moeicon.gif");
        } catch (Exception ignore) {
        }

        Image moeImg = getImage(imgURL);

        try {
            imgURL = new URL(getDocumentBase(), "larryicon.gif");
        } catch (Exception ignore) {
        }

        Image larryImg = getImage(imgURL);

        try {
            imgURL = new URL(getDocumentBase(), "curlyicon.gif");
        } catch (Exception ignore) {
        }

        Image curlyImg = getImage(imgURL);

        MediaTracker tracker = new MediaTracker(this);
        try {
            tracker.addImage(moeImg, 0);
            tracker.addImage(larryImg, 0);
            tracker.addImage(curlyImg, 0);
            tracker.waitForAll();
        } catch (Exception e) {
            e.printStackTrace();
        }

// Create a canvas for the icons

        IconCanvas canvas = new IconCanvas();
        canvas.setLayout(new FlowLayout());

// Create the icons
        Icon moeIcon = new Icon(moeImg, "Moe");
        Icon larryIcon = new Icon(larryImg, "Larry");
        Icon curlyIcon = new Icon(curlyImg, "Curly");

// Add the icons to the canvas
        canvas.add(moeIcon);
        canvas.add(larryIcon);
        canvas.add(curlyIcon);

// Add the canvas to the applet
        setLayout(new GridLayout(1, 0));
        add(canvas);
    }
}
```

Figure 37.1 shows `IconApplet` in action. Notice that the `Icon` class displays both the image and the label.

FIG. 37.1
The `Icon` class makes it easy to display labeled, selectable images.

The Property Book

A property book is a way to separate information into logically separated "pages." Usually, a property book is associated with a particular object and contains the configuration information for that object. There is no requirement that a property book be associated with a specific item, however. A property book is similar to a tabbed panel, which you may have seen already in the Java Foundation Classes.

The property book has a column on the left side listing the various pages available. This listing is referred to as the index, and it is implemented by the `PropertyBookIndexPanel` class.

The bottom part of the property book can contain buttons that apply to each page in the book. Typically, you will have buttons such as Apply, Cancel, and Default. The `PropertyBookButtonsPanel` controls these buttons, and it cannot contain anything except buttons. This forces a fairly standard user interface for property books.

The top part of the book contains a menu bar but also has space for an "identity panel," which can contain information about the property book.

The main part of the property book displays one of many property book sections. Each section is an instance of the `PropertyBookSection` class, which is essentially a `Panel` but also contains two methods specific to properties: `apply` and `reset`. It is up to you how you implement these two methods.

In the simple case, you just need to create subclasses of `PropertyBookSection` for each different section you want, and then add the sections to the property book. Listing 37.4 shows a very simple and completely useless property book applet.

Listing 37.4 Source Code for *PropertyApplet.java*

```
import sunw.admin.avm.base.*;
import java.applet.*;
import java.awt.*;

public class PropertyApplet extends Applet
{
    public class InfoSection extends PropertySection
    {
        String who;

        public InfoSection(String who)
        {
            this.who = who;
```

```
            setLayout(new BorderLayout());

            add("Center",
                new Label("Here is the information about "+who));
        }
    }

    public void init()
    {
        PropertyBook book = new PropertyBook();

        PropertySection moeSection = new InfoSection("Moe");
        book.addSection("Moe", moeSection);

        PropertySection larrySection = new InfoSection("Larry");
        book.addSection("Larry", larrySection);

        PropertySection curlySection = new InfoSection("Curly");
        book.addSection("Curly", curlySection);

        PropertySection shempSection = new InfoSection("Shemp");
        book.addSection("Shemp", shempSection);

        PropertySection curlyJoeSection = new InfoSection("Curly Joe");
        book.addSection("Curly Joe", curlyJoeSection);

        setLayout(new GridLayout(1, 0));
        add(book);
    }
}
```


Task Pages

Task pages are a little bit like property books. They consist of multiple panels with different information. The big difference is that the task pages represent a sequence of steps. You most often encounter this kind of interface when installing new software. You usually have to enter your name and your product serial number, set the installation directory, and so on. A `TaskPage` object presents this same kind of interface, showing you one `TaskSection` at a time, enabling you to go forward and backward, and allowing you to cancel at any time. On the last step, you can also click on Finish to complete your task.

The `TaskSection` class is just a container class for two panels, including a graphics panel, which shows an image or a description of the current task. If this were the step where you enter your address, for example, you might put an image of an addressed envelope into the graphics panel. The directions panel contains all the fields involved in this particular step.

You create `TaskSection` by passing the graphics and directions panels to the `Constructor`:

```
public TaskSection(Panel graphics, Panel directions)
```

The `TaskSection` class is abstract, so you must create your own subclass.

The `TaskPage` class is a container for `TaskSection` objects. You just create it and call the `addSection` method with each new task section and a name for the section:

```
public void addSection(String sectionName, TaskSection section)
```

The `buttonPress` method is called whenever the user presses one of the buttons at the bottom of the task page:

```
public void buttonPress(int whichButton)
```

The possible values for the `whichButton` parameter are `BACK`, `CANCEL`, `FINISH`, `HELP`, and `NEXT`.

Like the `TaskSection` class, the `TaskPage` class is abstract, so you must create your own subclass of it. Listing 37.5 shows an applet that outlines thé steps for doing the hokey pokey and prints a dialog when you press Finish.

Listing 37.5 Source Code for *TaskApplet.java*

```
import sunw.admin.avm.base.*;
import java.applet.*;
import java.awt.*;

public class TaskApplet extends Applet
{
    class DirectionsTaskSection extends TaskSection
    {
        DirectionsTaskSection(Panel titlePanel, Panel directionsPanel)
        {
            super(titlePanel, directionsPanel);
        }
    }

    class HokeyPokeyTask extends TaskPage
    {
        public void buttonPress(int whichButton)
        {

// See if the Finish button was the one pressed

            if (whichButton == TaskPage.FINISH) {
                InformationDialog dialog = new InformationDialog(
                    Util.findFrame(this),
                    "That's what it's all about!");
                dialog.setVisible(true);
            }
        }
    }

    protected TaskSection createDirections(String title, String directions)
    {

// Create the title panel
        Panel titlePanel = new Panel();
        titlePanel.setLayout(new FlowLayout());
```

```
        titlePanel.add(new Label(title));

// Create the directions panel
        Panel directionsPanel = new Panel();
        directionsPanel.setLayout(new GridLayout(1, 0));

        TextArea area = new TextArea(directions, 10, 40);
        area.setEditable(false);

        directionsPanel.add(area);

        return new DirectionsTaskSection(titlePanel, directionsPanel);
    }

    public void init()
    {
        TaskPage page = new HokeyPokeyTask();

        TaskSection section = createDirections(
            "Step 1", "Put your left foot in");
        page.addSection("Step 1", section);

        section = createDirections("Step 2", "Take your left foot out");
        page.addSection("Step 2", section);

        section = createDirections("Step 3", "Put your left foot in");
        page.addSection("Step 3", section);

        section = createDirections("Step 4", "Shake it all about");
        page.addSection("Step 4", section);

        section = createDirections("Step 5", "Do the hokey pokey");
        page.addSection("Step 5", section);

        section = createDirections("Step 6", "Turn yourself around");
        page.addSection("Step 6", section);

        setLayout(new GridLayout(1, 0));
        add(page);
    }
}
```


Dialogs

Dialogs are a mainstay of form-based user interface. The AVM provides a number of commonly used dialogs, saving you the trouble of coding your own. One of the frustrating things encountered by developers when writing applets is that AWT dialogs require a `Frame` object. The `Util` class provides a handy way to get the `Frame` from an applet or any other AWT component. Just call `findFrame` and pass it a component (like the applet) in the `Frame` you are looking for:

```
Frame currentFrame = Util.findFrame(this);
```

InformationDialog The `InformationDialog` class presents a text message and an OK button. It also displays an icon indicating that it is an information message as opposed to an error. There are three different ways to create an information dialog:

```
public InformationDialog(Frame f)
```

```
public InformationDialog(Frame f, String message)
```

```
public InformationDialog(Frame f, String message, String title,
    boolean modal)
```

The following code fragment creates an information dialog with the infamous `Hello World!` message:

```
InformationDialog dialog = new InformationDialog(
    Util.findFrame(this), "Hello World!");
```

The modal flag in this example is true, indicating that no activity in the parent Frame may take place while the dialog is displayed. In other words, you must click OK before proceeding. Figure 37.2 shows the Hello World! dialog.

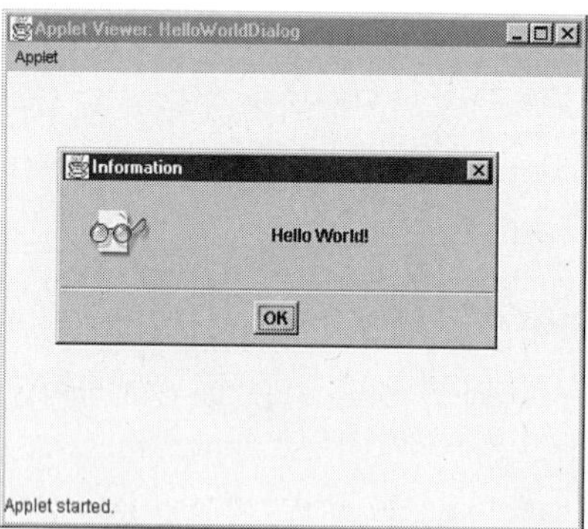

FIG. 37.2
An information dialog presents a message and an OK button.

ErrorDialog* and *WarningDialog The `ErrorDialog` class displays a dialog almost identical to the `InformationDialog` class, except that the icon next to the message and the title of the dialog indicate that it represents an error. The `Constructors` for the `ErrorDialog` are the same as for the `InformationDialog`:

```
public ErrorDialog(Frame f)
```

```
public ErrorDialog(Frame f, String message)
```

```
public ErrorDialog(Frame f, String message, String title,
    boolean modal)
```

Figure 37.3 shows an error dialog.

The `WarningDialog` class is identical to the `ErrorDialog` class, except that the icon and default title indicate a warning instead of an error. The `Constructors` for `WarningDialog` take the same form as the `ErrorDialog`.

FIG. 37.3
An error dialog is similar to an information dialog.

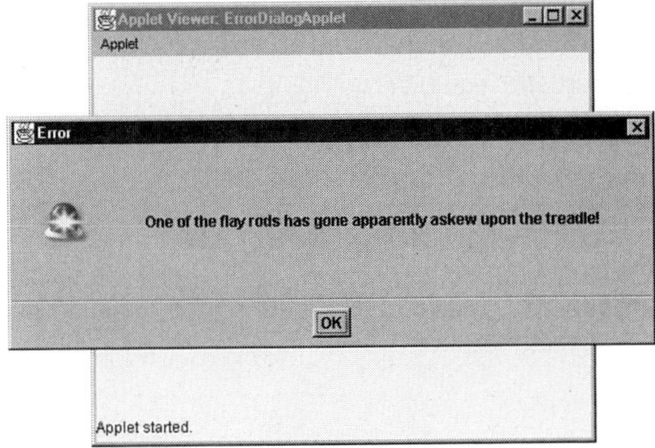

QuestionDialog Sometimes you need a dialog to do more than just present information. After all, the term *dialog* indicates two-way communication. The `QuestionDialog` class presents three buttons, Yes, No, and Cancel. Use the JavaBeans `ActionListener` class to retrieve the results from the dialog. Listing 37.6 shows an application that asks a question and then displays the result in an information dialog.

Listing 37.6 Source Code for *QuestionApplet.java*

```
import sunw.admin.avm.base.*;
import java.applet.*;
import java.awt.*;
import java.awt.event.*;

public class QuestionApplet extends Applet implements ActionListener
{
    public void start()
    {
        QuestionDialog dialog = new QuestionDialog(
            Util.findFrame(this), "Do you want to go on the cart?",
            "I'm not dead", true);

        dialog.addActionListener(this);

        dialog.setVisible(true);
    }

    public void actionPerformed(ActionEvent evt)
    {
        Object ob = evt.getSource();

        if (!(ob instanceof QuestionDialog)) return;

        String command = evt.getActionCommand();
        String response = null;

        if (command.equals("yes")) {
            response = "Why yes, I'll go on the cart.";
```

continues

Listing37.6 Continued

```
            } else if (command.equals("no")) {
                response = "I don't want to go on the cart.";
            } else if (command.equals("cancel")) {
                response = "I'm not dead.";
            }

            InformationDialog info = new InformationDialog(
                Util.findFrame(this), response, "Cart result", true);
            info.setVisible(true);
        }
    }
```

Figure 37.4 shows the `Question` applet in action.

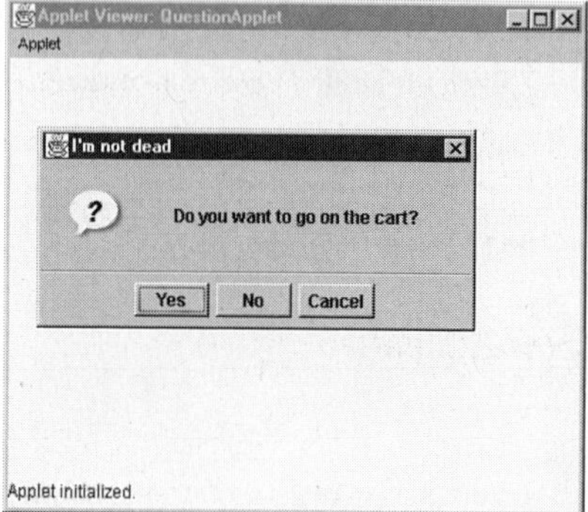

FIG. 37.4
A Question dialog waits for Yes, No, or Cancel.

ButtonDialog The `QuestionDialog` class is really just a special case of the more generic `ButtonDialog` class. A button dialog is laid out with a border layout, and any message you want to display should be added to the center section. The buttons appear along the south section of the dialog and can be any of the following standard buttons: Apply, Cancel, OK, and Reset. By default, only the OK and Cancel buttons are displayed. You can activate and deactivate the various buttons by calling `setVisible` on each button.

If you create a subclass of the a `ButtonDialog`, you can access the various buttons using the following local variables:

```
protected Button applyButton;

protected Button cancelButton;

protected Button helpButton;

protected Button okButton;

protected Button resetButton;
```

If you want to enable the Help button in a subclass of `ButtonDialog`, for example, just call `setVisible` like this:

```
helpButton.setVisible(true);
```

Because you sometimes want to use the dialog without creating a subclass (and if you've been using Java AWT since version 1.0, you're probably tired of creating subclasses), you can use the following methods to locate the buttons you may need:

```
public Button getApplyButton()

public Button getCancelButton()

public Button getHelpButton()

public Button getOKButton()

public Button getResetButton()
```


As with the `QuestionDialog`, you can get the results of a `ButtonDialog` by adding an action listener and examining the action command. The command values will be `apply`, `cancel`, `help`, `ok`, and `reset`—as you might expect.

ProgressDialog When an operation may take a long time, or you just want to keep the user informed as to what is going on, you can use a `ProgressDialog` object, which displays a progress bar on the screen. Typically, you call `setValues` to set the start, end, and current values of the dialog, and then call `setValue` to update the current value. Also, if you call `setIntervals`, you can make the progress bar appear as a series of blocks rather than a solid line. Listing 37.9 shows a progress dialog applet that uses a thread to update the dialog.

Listing 37.9 Source Code for *GaugeApplet.java*

```
import sunw.admin.avm.base.*;
import java.applet.*;
import java.awt.*;
import java.awt.event.*;

public class GaugeApplet extends Applet implements ActionListener
{
    ProgressDialog progress;
    Thread progressThread;
    boolean done;

    class ProgressThread implements Runnable
    {
        public void run()
        {
            int direction = 1;
            int value = 0;
            done = false;

            while (!done) {
                value = value + direction;
                if (value < 0) {
                    value = 0;
                    direction = 1;
                } else if (value > 100) {
                    value = 100;
                    direction = -1;
```

continues

Listing 37.9 Continued

```
                }
                progress.setValue(value);

                try {
                    Thread.sleep(250);
                } catch (Exception ignore) {
                }
            }
        }
    }

    public void init()
    {
        progress = new ProgressDialog(Util.findFrame(this),
            "Making progress");

        progress.setValues(0, 0, 100);
        progress.setIntervals(10);
        progress.addActionListener(this);

    }

    public void start()
    {
        progressThread = new Thread(new ProgressThread());
        progressThread.start();

        progress.setVisible(true);
    }

    public void stop()
    {
        if (progressThread != null) {

            done = true;
            progressThread = null;
            progress.setVisible(false);
        }
    }

    public void actionPerformed(ActionEvent evt)
    {
        Object ob = evt.getSource();

        if (!(ob instanceof ProgressDialog)) return;

        if (progressThread != null) {

            done = true;
            progressThread = null;
            progress.setVisible(false);
        }
    }
}
```

Figure 37.5 shows the GaugeApplet program in action.

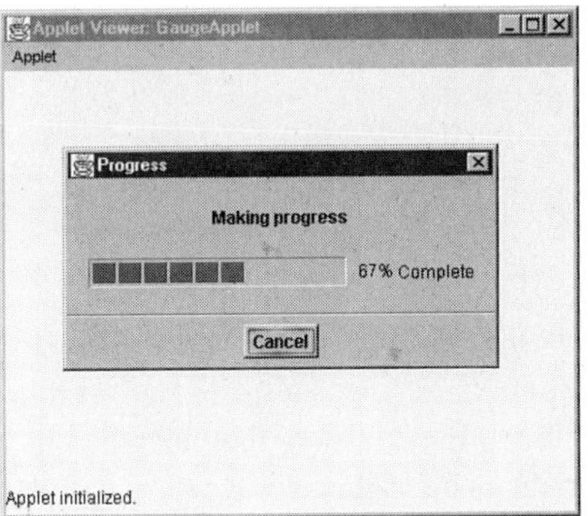

FIG. 37.5
A Progress dialog displays a progress bar and a message.

Self-Validating Fields

The AWT TextField class is certainly useful for getting information from the user; when you want something other than text strings, however, you must write code to make sure that the data in the field is in the correct format. Because you frequently need to read integers, doubles, and dates, the AVM provides the DateField, IntegerField, and DoubleField classes to automatically make sure that the text in the field is in the proper format.

IntegerField An integer field accepts only the digits 0–9 and returns the current value through the getValue method:

```
public int getValue();
```

Likewise, the setValue method enables you to change the value of the field:

```
public void setValue(int newValue);
```

There are a number of ways to create an integer field. You can create an empty field, initialize from an integer or a string, and also set the maximum number of columns in the field. The Constructors for IntegerField are as follows:

```
public IntegerField()

public IntegerField(int value)

public IntegerField(String text)

public IntegerField(int value, int cols)

public IntegerField(String text, int cols)
```

DoubleField The DoubleField class is almost identical to the IntegerField class except that it accepts floating-point numbers. The getValue method returns the current value and setValue changes it, just as with the IntegerField class:

```
public double getValue();

public void setValue(double newValue);
```

The `Constructors` for `DoubleField` are in the same form as `IntegerField`, except that the initial values are specified as doubles rather than integers:

```
public DoubleField()

public DoubleField (int value)

public DoubleField (String text)

public DoubleField (int value, int cols)

public DoubleField (String text, int cols)
```

DateField The `DateField` class provides validation for dates in a text field. Because dates are a little more complex than simple numbers, the `DateField` class is more complex than `IntegerField` or `DoubleField`. Although it has more methods than its numeric counterparts, `DateField` actually has fewer variations on its `Constructor`:

```
public DateField()

public DateField(Date date)

public DateField(String date)
```

You can retrieve the current date value as a `Date` object with `getDate`, or as a string with `getDateString`:

```
public Date getDate();

public String getDateString();
```

You can also set the date with either a `Date` object or a string:

```
public void setDate(Date newValue)

public void setDate(String newValue)
```

You can also manipulate the individual components of the date separately:

```
public int getDay()
public int getMonth()
public int getYear()

public boolean setDay(int day)
public boolean setDay(String day)
public boolean setMonth(int month)
public boolean setMonth(String month)
public boolean setYear(int year)
public boolean setYear(String year)
```

New Layout Managers

Along with all the new panels, the AVM has a few really useful new layout managers: `BulletinLayout`, `RowLayout`, `ColumnLayout`, and `FieldLayout`. Several of these layout managers are geared toward the kinds of interfaces usually found in network management applications.

BulletinLayout One of the lesser-known ways to lay out components in a panel is through the `null` layout manager. If you set the layout manager in a panel to `null`, you can move the components around manually using setLocation, setSize, and setBounds. Apparently, someone working on the AVM design decided that the null layout manager needed to come out of the closet, and now you have the BulletinLayout (think of it as the *Null*etin layout). After you set the layout manager of your panel to be a BulletinLayout, just add components and set their positions, like this:

```
setLayout(new BulletinLayout());

button b1 = new Button("Push Me");
add(b1);
b1.setSize(100,75);
b1.setLocation(200, 200);

button b2 = new Button("No, Push Me!");
add(b2);
b2.setBounds(30, 250, 100, 50);
```

If you have been fretting about whether the null layout manager will be removed in future versions of Java, use the BulletinLayout—it stands a better chance of being supported.

RowLayout* and *ColumnLayout Many times you just want to lay out all your columns in a row or a column. You could use a grid layout, but what if you don't know how many items you will have? The grid layout will start a new row or column if you add too many. The RowLayout and ColumnLayout classes enable you to create one long row or column of items. The height of the row is determined by the tallest component, just as the width of the column is determined by the widest component.

When you create a row or column layout, you can specify a layout alignment that specifies how each component will be aligned. These values tell whether the components should be left-aligned, right-aligned, centered, and so forth. The LAYOUT_ALIGNMENT class defines the possible layout values, which are CENTER, LEFT, RIGHT, TOP, BOTTOM, FIT, and EXPAND.

The Constructors for RowLayout are as follows:

```
public RowLayout();
public RowLayout(LAYOUT_ALIGNMENT alignment)
public RowLayout(LAYOUT_ALIGNMENT alignment, int hgap, int vgap)
```

Likewise, these are the Constructors for ColumnLayout:

```
public ColumnLayout();
public ColumnLayout(LAYOUT_ALIGNMENT alignment)
public ColumnLayout(LAYOUT_ALIGNMENT alignment, int hgap, int vgap)
```

After you set up these layout managers, you can add components by using the normal add method, without any special parameters.

ButtonLayout The ButtonLayout class is usually used for setting up rows of buttons, but it can handle any kind of component. It arranges the components from left to right in lines, centering each line. When no more components fit on a line, it moves down to the next line. Like the RowLayout and ColumnLayout classes, the Constructors for ButtonLayout come in three flavors:

```
public ButtonLayout();
public ButtonLayout(LAYOUT_ALIGNMENT alignment)
public ButtonLayout(LAYOUT_ALIGNMENT alignment, int hgap, int vgap)
```

FieldLayout The `FieldLayout` class provides an incredibly simple, yet incredibly useful function. When you create data-entry forms, you typically create a label and an input field. The `FieldLayout` class assumes that you want to do exactly that, and expects you to add a label followed by a field, over and over. The following code fragment adds a series of fields and their labels:

```
setLayout(new FieldLayout());
add(new Label("First Name: ");
textField firstNameField = new TextField(20);
add(firstNameField);
add(new Label("Last Name: ");
textField lastNameField = new TextField(20);
add(lastNameField);
```

A `FieldLayout` object has no alignment options, but you can still specify the `hgap` and `vgap` values in the `Constructor` if you like:

```
public FieldLayout();

public FieldLayout(int hgap, int vgap);
```

Parts of the Admin View Module have evolved into the Java Foundation Classes since it was originally designed. The remaining parts may also find themselves within JFC one day, although that remains to be seen. For now, the AVM provides a useful framework for displaying and manipulating managed objects within the JMAPI framework. ●

PART V

Databases

CHAPTER 38

Databases Introduced

In this chapter

ODBC and JDBC

This chapter is the introduction to a trilogy of chapters dealing with database access from a Java program. Standard relational data access is very important for Java programs because the Java applets by nature are not monolithic, all-consuming applications. Because applets by nature are modular, they need to read persistent data from data stores, process the data, and write the data back to data stores for other applets to process. Monolithic programs can afford to have their own proprietary schemes of data handling, but because Java applets cross operating system and network boundaries, you need published open data access schemes.

Java database connectivity (JDBC) is a part of the Java Enterprise APIs and provides cross-platform, cross-database access to databases from Java programs. The Enterprise APIs also consist of Remote Method Invocation (RMI) and serialization APIs (for Java programs to marshal objects across namespaces and invoke methods in remote objects), Java IDL (Interface Definition Language) for communicating with CORBA and other object-oriented systems, and Java JNDI (Java Naming and Directory Interface) for access to naming and directory services across the enterprise.

This chapter introduces relational concepts, as well as Microsoft's open database connectivity (ODBC). This chapter describes ODBC because of two major reasons:

- JDBC and ODBC are both based on SAG CLI (SQL Access Group Call Level Interface) specifications.
- JDBC design uses major abstractions and methods from ODBC.

The idea of basing JDBC design on ODBC is that because ODBC is so popular with ISVs (independent software vendors) as well as users, implementing and using JDBC will be easier for database practitioners who have earlier experience with ODBC. Also, Sun and Intersolv have developed a JDBC-ODBC bridge layer to take advantage of the ODBC drivers available in the market. So with the JDBC APIs and the JDBC-ODBC bridge, you can access and interact effectively with almost all databases from Java applets and applications.

Relational Database Concepts

Databases, as you know, contain data that's specifically organized. A database can be as simple as a flat file (a single computer file with data usually in a tabular form) containing names and telephone numbers of your friends or as elaborate as the worldwide reservation system of a major airline. Many of the principles discussed in this chapter are applicable to a wide variety of database systems.

Structurally, there are three major types of databases:

- Hierarchical
- Relational
- Network

During the 1970s and 1980s, the hierarchical scheme was very popular. This scheme treats data as a tree-structured system with data records forming the leaves. Examples of the hierarchical implementations are schemes like b-tree and multitree data access. In the hierarchical scheme, to get to data, users need to traverse down and up the tree structure. The most common relationship in a hierarchical structure is a one-to-many relationship between the data records, and it is difficult to implement a many-to-many relationship without data redundancy.

Relationships of the Database Kind

Establishing and keeping track of relationships between data records in database tables can be more difficult than maintaining human relationships!

There are three types of data record relationships between records:

- *One-to-one*—One record in a table is related to at least one record in another table. The book/ISBN relationship (where a book has only one ISBN and an ISBN is associated with only one book) is a good example of a one-to-one relationship.
- *One-to-many*—One record in a table can be associated with many records in another table. The purchase order/line items relationship (where a purchase order can have many line items but one line item can be associated with only a single purchase order) is an example of a one-to-many relationship.
- *Many-to-many*—This is similar to the student/class relationship (where a student is taking many courses with different teachers in a semester and a course has many students).

You might wonder how a database can remember these data relationships. This is usually accomplished either by keeping a common element like the student ID/class ID in both tables or by keeping a record ID table (called the *index*) of both records. Modern databases have many other sophisticated ways of keeping data record relationships intact to weather updates, deletes, and so on.

The network data model solved this problem by assuming a multirelationship between data elements. In contrast to the hierarchical scheme in which there is a parent-child relationship, in the network scheme, there is a peer-to-peer relationship. Most of the programs developed during those days used a combination of the hierarchical and network data storage and access models.

During the 1990s, the relational data access scheme came to the forefront. The relational scheme views data as rows of information; each row contains columns of data, called *fields*. The main concept in the relational scheme is that the data is uniform. Each row contains the same number of columns. One such collection of rows and columns is called a *table*. Many such tables (which can be structurally different) form a relational database.

Figure 38.1 shows a sample relational database schema (or table layout) for an enrollment database. In this example, the database consists of three tables: the Students table, which contains student information; the Courses table, which contains course information; and the StudentsCourses table, which has the student-course relationship. The Students table contains information such as student ID, name, address, and so on; the Courses table contains the course ID, subject name or course title, term offered, location, and so on.

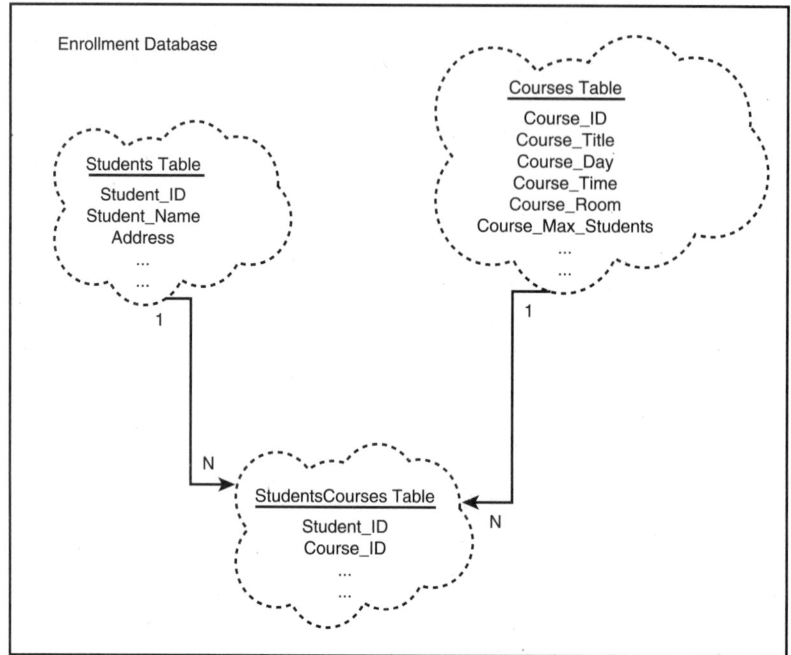

FIG. 38.1
A sample relational database schema for an enrollment database.

Now that you have the Students and Courses tables of data, how do you relate the tables? This is where the relational part of the relational database comes into the picture. To relate two tables, either the two tables will have a common column, or you will need to create a third table with two columns—one from the first table and the second from the second table.

Let's look at how this is done. In this example, to relate the Students table with the Courses table, you need to make a new table, StudentsCourses, which has two columns: Student_ID and Course_ID. Whenever a student takes a course, create a row in the StudentsCourses table with that Student_ID and the Course_ID. Thus the table has the student and course relationship. If you want to find a list of students and the subjects they take, go to the StudentsCourses table, read each row, find the student name corresponding to the Student_ID, from the Courses table find the course title corresponding to the Course_ID, and select the Student_Name and the Course_Title columns.

SQL

When relational databases started becoming popular, database experts wanted a universal database language to perform actions on data. The answer was Structured Query Language (SQL). SQL has grown into a mainstream database language that has constructs for data manipulation such as creating, updating, and deleting; data definition such as creating tables and columns; security for restricting access to data elements, creating users and groups; data management including backup, bulk copy, and bulk update; and most importantly, transaction processing. SQL is used along with programming languages such as Java, C++, and others and is used for data handling and interaction with the back-end database management system.

NOTE Each database vendor has its own implementation of SQL. For Microsoft SQL Server, which is one of the client/server relational DBMSs, SQL is called *Transact-SQL*, whereas Oracle SQL is called *PL/SQL*.

SQL became an ANSI (American National Standards Institute) standard in 1986 and later was revised to become SQL-92. JDBC is SQL-92-compliant.

Joins

Just because a database consists of tables with rows of data does not mean that you are limited to view the data in the fixed tables in the database. A *join* is a process in which two or more tables are combined to form a single table. A join can be *dynamic*, where two tables are merged to form a virtual table, or *static*, where two tables are joined and saved for future reference. A static join is usually a stored procedure that can be invoked to refresh the saved table, and then the saved table is queried. Joins are performed on tables that have a column of common information. Conceptually, there are many types of joins, which are discussed later in this section.

Before you dive deeper into joins, look at the following example, in which you fill the tables of the database schema in Figure 38.1 with a few records as shown in Tables 38.1, 38.2, and 38.3. These tables show only the relevant fields or columns.

Table 38.1 Students Table

Student_ID	Student_Name
1	John
2	Mary
3	Jan
4	Jack

Table 38.2 Courses Table

Course_ID	Course_Title
S1	Math
S2	English
S3	Computer
S4	Logic

Table 38.3 StudentsCourses Table

Student_ID	Course_ID
2	S2
3	S1
4	S3

The Inner Join A simple join, called an inner join, with the Students and StudentsCourses tables gives you a table like the one shown in Table 38.4. You get a new table that combines the Students and StudentsCourses tables by adding the Student_Name column to the StudentsCourses table.

Table 38.4 Inner Join Table

Student_ID	Student_Name	Course_ID
2	Mary	S2
3	Jan	S1
4	Jack	S3

Just because you are using the Student_ID to link the two tables doesn't mean you should fetch that column. You can exclude the key field from the result table of an inner join. The SQL statement for this inner join is as follows:

```
SELECT Students.Student_Name, StudentsCourses.Course_ID
FROM Students, StudentsCourses
WHERE Students.Student_ID = StudentsCourses.Student_ID
```

The Outer Join An outer join between two tables (such as Table1 and Table2) occurs when the result table has all the rows of the first table and the common records of the second table. (The first and second table are determined by the order in the SQL statement.) If you assume a SQL statement with the `FROM Table1,Table2` clause, in a left outer join, all rows of the first table (Table1) and common rows of the second table (Table2) are selected. In a right outer join, all records of the second table (Table2) and common rows of the first table (Table1) are selected. A left outer join with the Students table and the StudentsCourses table creates Table 38.5.

Table 38.5 Outer Join Table

Student_ID	Student_Name	Course_ID
1	John	<null>
2	Mary	S2

3	Jan	S1
4	Jack	S3

This join is useful if you want the names of all students regardless of whether they are taking any subjects this term and the subjects taken by the students who have enrolled in this term. Some people call it an if-any join, as in, "Give me a list of all students and the subjects they are taking, if any."

The SQL statement for this outer join is as follows:

```
SELECT Students.Student_ID,Students.Student_Name,StudentsCourses.Course_ID
FROM {
oj c:\enrol.mdb Students
LEFT OUTER JOIN c:\enrol.mdb
StudentsCourses ON Students.Student_ID = StudentsCourses .Student_ID
}
```


The full outer join, as you might have guessed, returns all the records from both the tables merging the common rows, as shown in Table 38.6.

Table 38.6 Full Outer Join Table

Student_ID	Student_Name	Course_ID
1	John	<null>
2	Mary	S2
3	Jan	S1
4	Jack	S3
<null>	<null>	S4

The Subtract Join What if you want only the students who haven't enrolled in this term or the subjects who have no students (the tough subjects or professors)? Then you resort to the subtract join. In this case, the join returns the rows that are not in the second table. Remember, a subtract join has only the fields from the first table. By definition, there are no records in the second table. The SQL statement looks like the following:

```
SELECT Students.Student_Name
FROM {
oj c:\enrol.mdb Students
LEFT OUTER JOIN c:\enrol.mdb
StudentsCourses ON Students.Student_ID = StudentsCourses.Student_ID
}
WHERE (StudentsCourses.Course_ID Is Null)
```

Joins and SQL Statements There are many other types of joins, such as the *self join*, which is a left outer join of two tables with the same structure. An example is the assembly/parts explosion in a bill of materials application for manufacturing. But usually, the join types you have learned about already are enough for normal applications. As you gain more expertise in SQL statements, you will start developing exotic joins.

In all these joins, you compared columns that have the same values; these joins are called *equi-joins*. Joins are not restricted to comparing columns of equal values. You can join two tables based on column value conditions (such as the column of one table greater than the other).

For equi-joins, because the column values are equal, you retrieve only one copy of the common column; then the joins are called *natural joins*. When you have a non–equi-join, you might need to retrieve the common columns from both tables.

When a SQL statement reaches a database management system, the DBMS parses the SQL statement and translates it to an internal scheme called a *query plan* to retrieve data from the database tables. This internal scheme generator, in all the client/server databases, includes an optimizer module. This module, which is specific to a database, knows the limitations and advantages of the database implementation.

In many databases—for example, Microsoft SQL Server—the optimizer is a cost-based query optimizer. When given a query, this optimizer generates multiple query plans, computes the cost estimates for each (knowing the data storage schemes, page I/O, and so on), and then determines the most efficient access method for retrieving the data, including table join order and index usage. This optimized query is converted into a binary form called the *execution plan*, which is executed against the data to get the result. There are known cases in which straight queries that take hours to perform are run through an optimizer and result in an optimized query that is performed in minutes. All the major client/server databases have a built-in query optimizer module that processes all the queries. A database system administrator can assign values to parameters such as cost, storage scheme, and so on and can fine-tune the optimizer.

An ODBC Technical Overview

ODBC is one of the most popular database interfaces in the PC world and is slowly moving into all other platforms. ODBC is Microsoft's implementation of the X/Open and SQL Access Group Call Level Interface specification. ODBC provides functions to interact with databases from a programming language, including adding, modifying, and deleting data and obtaining details about the databases, tables, views, and indexes.

This discussion on ODBC is relevant from the Java and JDBC point of view. It is instructive to note the similarities and differences between the JDBC and ODBC architectures. Also, the study of ODBC might give you some clues as to where JDBC is heading in the future.

Figure 38.2 shows a schematic view of the ODBC architecture. An ODBC application has five logical layers: application, ODBC interface, driver manager, driver, and the data source.

The application layer provides the GUI and the business logic and is written in languages such as Java, Visual Basic, and C++. The application uses the ODBC functions in the ODBC interface to interact with the databases.

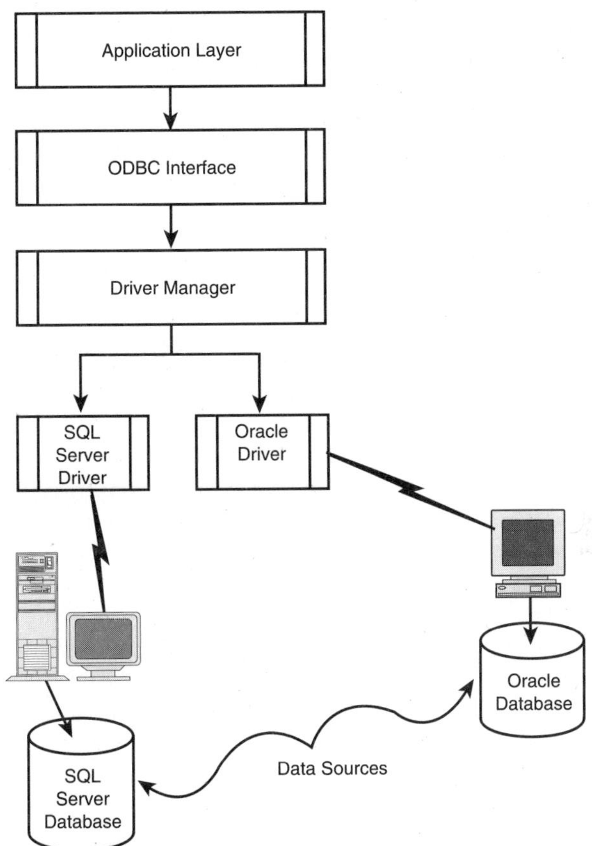

FIG. 38.2
An architecture schematic showing the five ODBC layers.

The driver manager layer is part of the Microsoft ODBC. As the name implies, it manages various drivers present in the system including loading, directing calls to the right driver, and providing driver information to the application when needed. Because an application can be connected to more than one database (such as legacy systems and departmental databases), the driver manager makes sure that the right DBMS gets all the program calls directed to it and that the data from the data source is routed to the application.

The driver is the actual component that knows about specific databases. Usually the driver is assigned to a specific database such as the Access driver, SQL Server driver, or Oracle driver. The ODBC interface has a set of calls such as SQL statements, connection management, information about the database, and so on. It is the driver's duty to implement all these functionalities. That means for some databases, the driver has to emulate the ODBC interface functions not supported by the underlying DBMS. The driver does the work of sending queries to the database, getting the data back, and routing the data to the application. For databases that are in local networked systems or on the Internet, the driver also handles the network communication.

In the context of ODBC, the data source can be a database management system or just the data store, which usually is a set of files in the hard disk. The data source can be as simple as a Microsoft Access database for the expense data of a small company or as exotic as a multiserver, multigigabyte data store of all the customer billing details of a telephone company. The data source might be handling a data warehouse or a simple customer list.

ODBC Conformance Levels

The major piece of an ODBC system is the driver, which knows about the DBMS and communicates with the database. ODBC doesn't require the drivers to support all the functions in the ODBC interface. Instead, ODBC defines API and SQL grammar conformance levels for drivers. The only requirement is that when a driver conforms to a certain level, it should support all the ODBC-defined functions on that level, regardless of whether the underlying database supports them.

NOTE The ODBC driver specification sets no upper limits of supported functionalities. This means a driver that conforms to Level 1 can and might support a few of the Level 2 functionalities. The driver is still considered Level 1 conformance because it doesn't support all Level 2 functions. An application, however, can use the partial Level 2 support provided by that driver.

As mentioned in the ODBC technical overview, it is the driver's duty to emulate the ODBC functions not supported by the underlying DBMS so that the ODBC interface is shielded from the DBMS implementation. As far as the ODBC interface and the application are concerned, a conformance to an ODBC level means all the functionalities are available regardless of the underlying DBMS.

NOTE Applications use API calls such as `SQLGetFunctions` and `SQLGetInfo` to get the functions supported by a driver.

Table 38.7 summarizes the levels of conformance for API and SQL.

Table 38.7 API and SQL Conformance Levels for ODBC

Type	Conformance Level	Description
API Conformance Levels	Core	All functions in SAG CLI specification. Allocates and frees connection, statement, and environment handles. Prepares and executes SQL statements. Retrieves the result set and information about the result set. Retrieves error information. Capability to commit and roll back transactions.

Type	Conformance Level	Description
	Level 1	Extended Set 1 is Core API plus capabilities to send and retrieve partial data set, retrieve catalog information, get driver and database capabilities, and more.
	Level 2	Extended Set 2 is Level 1 plus capabilities to handle arrays as parameters, scrollable cursor, call transaction DLL, and more.
SQL Grammar Conformance Levels	Minimum Grammar	CREATE TABLE and DROP TABLE functions in the Data Definition Language. SELECT, INSERT, UPDATE, and DELETE functions (simple) in the Data Manipulation Language. Simple expressions.
	Core Grammar	Conformance to SAG CAE 1992 specification. Minimum grammar plus ALTER TABLE, CREATE and DROP INDEX, and CREATE and DROP VIEW for the DDL. Full SELECT statement capability for the DML. Functions such as SUM and MAX in the expressions.
	Extended Grammar	Adds capabilities such as outer joins, positioned UPDATE, DELETE, more expressions, more data types, procedure calls, and so on to the Core grammar.

ODBC Functions and Command Set

The ODBC has a rich set of functions. They range from simple connect statements to handling multi–result set stored procedures. All the ODBC functions have the SQL prefix and can have one or more parameters, which can be of type input (to the driver) or output (from the driver). Let's look at the general steps required to connect to an ODBC source and then the actual ODBC command sequence.

Typical ODBC Steps In a typical ODBC program, the first steps are to allocate environment and connection handles using the functions SQLAllocEnv(<envHandle>) and SQLAllocConnect(<envHandle>,<databaseHandle>). After you get a valid database handle, you can set various options using SQLSetConnectOption(<databaseHandle>, <optionName>,<optionValue>). Then you can connect to the database using SQLConnect(<dataSourceName>,<UID>,<PW>, .. etc.).

The ODBC Command Sequence Now you are ready to work with statements. Figure 38.3 shows the ODBC command sequence to connect to a database, execute a SQL statement, process the result data, and close the connection.

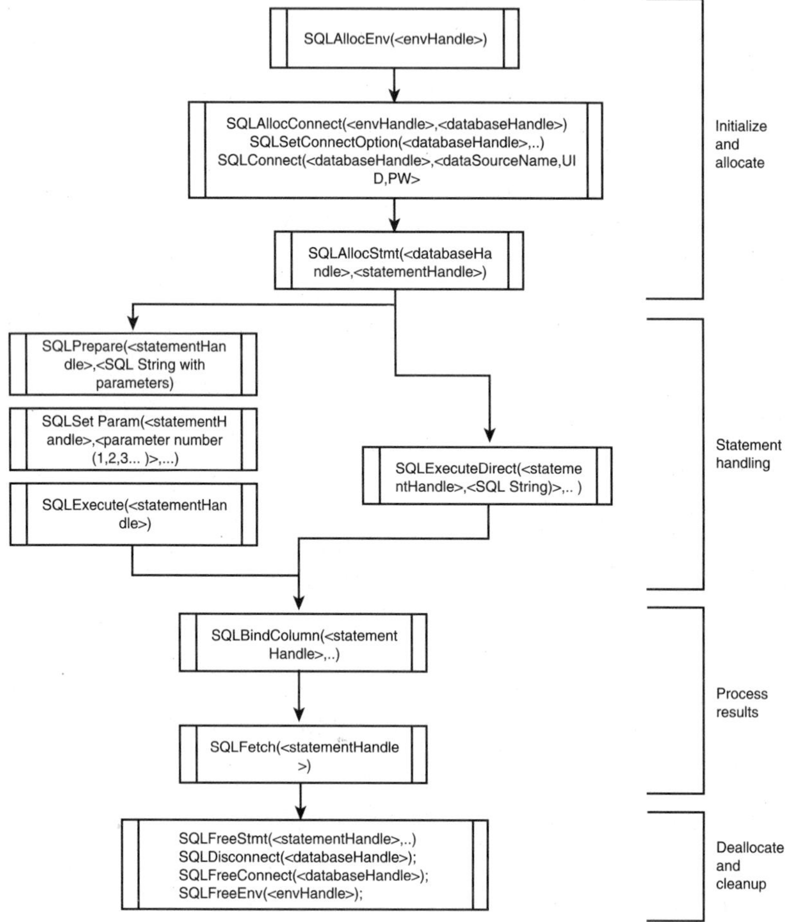

FIG. 38.3
The ODBC program flow schematic for a typical program.

First, allocate the statement handle using `SQLAllocStmt(<databaseHandle>, <statementHandle>)`. After the statement handle is allocated, you can execute SQL statements directly using the `SQLExecDirect` function, or you can prepare a statement using `SQLPrepare` and then execute with the `SQLExec` function. You first bind the columns to program variables and then read these variables after a `SQLFetch` statement for a row of data. `SQLFetch` returns `SQL_NO_DATA_FOUND` when there is no more data.

NOTE JDBC also follows similar strategy for handling statements and data. But JDBC differs in the data binding to variables.

Now that you have processed the data, it is time to deallocate the handles and close the database by using the following statement sequence:

```
SQLFreeStmt(<statementHandle>, ..)
SQLDisconnect(<databaseHandle>);
SQLFreeConnect(<databaseHandle>);
SQLFreeEnv(<envHandle>);
```

NOTE In JDBC, the allocate statements and handles are not required.

Because Java is an object-oriented language, you get the connection object, which then gives you the statement object.

As Java has automatic garbage collection, you don't need to free handles, delete objects, and so on. When an object loses scope, the JVM will reclaim the memory used by that object as a part of the automatic garbage collection. ■

Advanced Client/Server Concepts

A typical client/server system is at least a departmentwide system, and most likely an organizational system spanning many departments in an organization. Mission-critical and line-of-business systems such as brokerage, banking, manufacturing, and reservation systems fall into this category. Most systems are internal to an organization and also span the customers and suppliers. Almost all such systems are on a local area network (LAN), and they have wide area network (WAN) connections and dial-in capabilities. With the advent of the Internet/intranet and Java, these systems are getting more and more sophisticated and are capable of doing business in many new ways.

Take the case of Federal Express. Its Web site can now schedule package pickups, track a package from pickup to delivery, and get delivery information and time. You are now in the threshold of an era in which online commerce will be as common as shopping malls. Let's look at some of the concepts that drive these kinds of systems.

Client/Server System Tiers

Most of the application systems will involve modules with functions for a front-end GUI, business rules processing, and data access through a DBMS. In fact, major systems such as online reservation, banking and brokerage, and utility billing involve thousands of business rules, heterogeneous databases spanning the globe, and hundreds of GUI systems. The development, administration, maintenance, and enhancement of these systems involve handling millions of lines of code, multiple departments, and coordinating the work of hundreds if not thousands of personnel across the globe. The multitier system design and development concepts are applied to a range of systems from departmental systems to such global information systems.

NOTE In the two- and three-tier systems, an application is logically divided into three parts:

- *GUI (graphical user interface)*—Consists of the screens, windows, buttons, list boxes, and more.
- *Business logic*—The part of the program that deals with the various data element interactions. All processing is done based on values of data elements, such as the logic for determining the credit limit depending on annual income, the calculation of income tax based on tax tables, or a reorder point calculation logic based on the material usage belonging to this category.
- *DBMS*—Deals with the actual storage and retrieval of data.

Two-Tier Systems On the basic level, a two-tier system involves the GUI and business logic directly accessing the database. The GUI can be on a client system, and the database can be on the client system or on a server. Usually, the GUI is written in languages such as C++, Visual Basic, PowerBuilder, Access Basic, and LotusScript. The database systems typically are Microsoft Access, Lotus Approach, Sybase SQL Anywhere, or Watcom DB Engine and Personal Oracle.

Three-Tier Systems Most of the organizational and many of the departmental client/server applications today follow the three-tier strategy in which the GUI, business logic, and DBMS are logically in three layers. Here the GUI development tools are Visual Basic, C++, and PowerBuilder. The middle-tier development tools also tend to be C++ or Visual Basic, and the back-end databases are Oracle, Microsoft SQL Server, or Sybase SQL Server. The three-tier concept gave rise to an era of database servers, application servers, and GUI client machines. Operating systems such as UNIX, Windows NT, and Solaris rule the application server and database server world. Client operating systems such as Windows are popular for the GUI front end.

Multitier Systems Now with Internet and Java, the era of "network is the computer" and "thin client" paradigm shifts has begun. The Java applets with their own objects and methods created the idea of a multitiered client/server system. Theoretically, a Java applet can be a business rule, GUI, or DBMS interface. Each applet can be considered a layer. In fact, the Internet and Java were not the first to introduce the object-oriented, multitiered system concept. OMG's CORBA architecture and Microsoft's OLE (now ActiveX) architecture are all proponents of modular object-oriented, multiplatform systems. With Java and the Internet, these concepts became much easier to implement.

In short, the systems design and implementation progressed from the two-tiered architecture to the three-tiered architecture to the current internetworked, Java applet–driven, multitier architecture.

Transactions

The concept of transactions is an integral part of any client/server database. A transaction is a group of SQL statements that update, add, and delete rows and fields in a database. Transactions have an all or nothing property—either they are committed if all statements are successful, or the whole transaction is rolled back if any of the statements cannot be executed successfully. Transaction processing ensures the data integrity and data consistency in a database.

NOTE JDBC supports transaction processing with the `commit()` and `rollback()` methods. Also, JDBC has `autocommit()`, which when on, automatically commits all changes and when off, the Java program has to use the `commit()` or `rollback()` method to effect the changes to the data.

Transaction ACID Properties The characteristics of a transaction are described in terms of the Atomicity, Consistency, Isolation, and Durability (ACID) properties.

A transaction is *atomic* in the sense that it is an entity. All the components of a transaction occur or do not occur; there is no partial transaction. If only a partial transaction can happen, the transaction is aborted. The atomicity is achieved by the `commit()` or `rollback()` method.

A transaction is *consistent* because it doesn't perform any actions that violate the business logic or relationships between data elements. The consistent property of a transaction is very important when you develop a client/server system because there will be many transactions to a data store from different systems and objects. If a transaction leaves the data store inconsistent, all other transactions also will potentially be wrong, resulting in a systemwide crash or data corruption.

A transaction is *isolated* because the results of a transaction are self-contained. They don't depend on any preceding or succeeding transaction. This is related to a property called *serializability*, which means the sequence of transactions are independent; in other words, a transaction doesn't assume any external sequence.

Finally, a transaction is *durable*, meaning the effects of a transaction are permanent even in the face of a system failure. This means that some form of permanent storage should be a part of a transaction.

The Distributed Transaction Coordinator A related topic in transactions is the coordination of transactions across heterogeneous data sources, systems, and objects. When the transactions are carried out in one relational database, you can use the `commit()`, `rollback()`, `beginTransaction()`, and `endTransaction()` statements to coordinate the process. But what if you have diversified systems participating in a transaction? How do you handle such a system? As an example, let's look at the Distributed Transaction Coordinator (DTC) available as a part of the Microsoft SQL Server 6.5 database system.

In the Microsoft DTC, a transaction manager facilitates the coordination. Resource managers are clients that implement resources to be protected by transactions—for example, relational databases and ODBC data sources.

An application begins a transaction with the transaction manager and then starts transactions with the resource managers, registering the steps (enlisting) with the transaction manager.

The transaction manager keeps track of all enlisted transactions. The application, at the end of the multi–data source transaction steps, calls the transaction manager to either commit or abort the transaction.

When an application issues a commit command to the transaction manager, the DTC performs a two-phase commit protocol:

1. It queries each resource manager if it is prepared to commit.
2. If all resources are prepared to commit, the DTC broadcasts a commit message to all of them.

The Microsoft DTC is an example of a very powerful, next-generation transaction coordinator from the database vendors. As more and more multiplatform, object-oriented Java systems are being developed, this type of transaction coordinator will gain importance. Already many middleware vendors are developing Java-oriented transaction systems.

Cursors

A relational database query normally returns many rows of data. But an application program usually deals with one row at a time. Even when an application can handle more than one row—for example, by displaying the data in a table or spreadsheet format—it can still handle only a limited number of rows. Also, updating, modifying, deleting, or adding data is done on a row-by-row basis.

This is where the concept of cursors come into the picture. In this context, a *cursor* is a pointer to a row. It is like the cursor on the CRT—a location indicator.

Data Concurrency and Cursor Schemes

Different types of multiuser applications need different types of data sets in terms of data concurrency. Some applications need to know as soon as the data in the underlying database is changed. For example, in reservation systems, the dynamic nature of the seat allocation information is extremely important. Other applications such as statistical reporting systems need stable data; if data is constantly changing, these programs cannot effectively display any results. The different cursor designs support the need for the various types of applications.

A cursor can be viewed as the underlying data buffer. A fully scrollable cursor is one where the program can move forward and backward on the rows in the data buffer. If the program can update the data in the cursor, it is called a scrollable, updatable cursor.

CAUTION

An important point to remember when you think about cursors is transaction isolation. When a user is updating a row, another user might be viewing the row in a cursor of his own. Data consistency is important here. Worse, the second user also might be updating the same row!

NOTE The `ResultSet` in JDBC API is a cursor. But it is only a forward scrollable cursor–this means you can only move forward using the `getNext()` method.

ODBC Cursor Types ODBC cursors are very powerful in terms of updatability, concurrency, data integrity, and functionality. The ODBC cursor scheme allows positioned delete and update and multiple row fetch (called a *rowset*) with protection against lost updates.

ODBC supports static, keyset-driven, and dynamic cursors.

In the static cursor scheme, the data is read from the database once, and the data is in the snapshot recordset form. Because the data is a snapshot (a static view of the data at a point of time), the changes made to the data in the data source by other users are not visible. The dynamic cursor solves this problem by keeping live data, but this takes a toll on network traffic and application performance.

The keyset-driven cursor is the middle ground in which the rows are identified at the time of fetch, and thus changes to the data can be tracked. Keyset-driven cursors are useful when you implement a backward scrollable cursor. In a keyset-driven cursor, additions and deletions of entire rows are not visible until a refresh. When you do a backward scroll, the driver fetches the newer row if any changes are made.

NOTE ODBC also supports a modified scheme, in which only a small window of the keyset is fetched, called the *mixed cursor*, which exhibits the keyset-driven cursor for the data window and a dynamic cursor for the rest of the data. In other words, the data in the data window (called a `RowSet`) is keyset-driven, and when you access data outside the window, the dynamic scheme is used to fetch another keyset-driven buffer.

Cursor Applications You might be wondering where these cursor schemes are applied and why you need such elaborate schemes. In a short sentence, all the cursor schemes have their place in information systems.

Static cursors provide a stable view of the data because the data doesn't change. They are good for data mining and data warehousing types of systems. For these applications, you want the data to be stable for reporting executive information systems or for statistical or analysis purposes. Also, the static cursor outperforms other schemes for large amounts of data retrieval.

On the other hand, for online ordering systems or reservation systems, you need a dynamic view of the system with row locks and views of data as changes are made by other users. In such cases, you will use the dynamic cursor. In many of these applications, the data transfer is small, and the data access is performed on a row-by-row basis. For these online applications, aggregate data access is very rare.

Bookmarks The *bookmark* is a concept related to the cursor model, but is independent of the cursor scheme used. A bookmark is a placeholder for a data row in a table. The application program requests that the underlying database management system be a bookmark for a row. The DBMS usually returns a 32-bit marker that can later be used by the application program to get to that row of data. In ODBC, you use the `SQLExtendedFetch` function with the `SQL_FETCH_BOOKMARK` option to get a bookmark. The bookmark is useful for increasing performance of GUI applications, especially the ones in which the data is viewed through a spreadsheet-like interface.

Positioned *UPDATE/DELETE* This is another cursor-related concept. If a cursor model supports positioned UPDATE/DELETE, you can update/delete the current row in a ResultSet without any more processing, such as a lock, read, and fetch.

In SQL, a positioned UPDATE or DELETE statement is of the form

```
UPDATE/DELETE <Field or Column values etc.> WHERE CURRENT OF <cursor name>
```

The positioned UPDATE statement to update the fields in the current row is

```
UPDATE <table> SET <field> = <value> WHERE CURRENT OF <cursor name>
```

The positioned DELETE statement to delete the current row takes the form

```
DELETE <table> WHERE CURRENT OF <cursor name>
```

Generally, for this type of SQL statement to work, the underlying driver or the DBMS has to support updatability, concurrency, and dynamic scrollable cursors. But there are many other ways of providing the positioned UPDATE/DELETE capability at the application program level. Presently, JDBC doesn't support any of the advanced cursor functionalities. However, as the JDBC driver development progresses, I am sure there will be very sophisticated cursor management methods available in the JDBC API.

Replication

Data replication is the distribution of corporate data to many locations across the organization, and it provides reliability, fault-tolerance, data access performance due to reduced communication, and in many cases, manageability because the data can be managed as subsets.

As you have seen, the client/server systems span an organization, possibly its clients and suppliers—most probably in a wide geographic location. Systems spanning the entire globe aren't uncommon when you're talking about mission-critical applications, especially in today's global business market. If all the data were concentrated in a central location, it would be almost impossible for the systems to effectively access data and offer high performance. Also, if data were centrally located, in the case of mission-critical systems, a single failure would bring the whole business down. So, replicating data across an organization at various geographic locations is a sound strategy.

Different vendors handle replication differently. For example, the Lotus Notes groupware product uses a replication scheme in which the databases are considered peers and additions/updates/deletions are passed between the databases. Lotus Notes has replication formulas that can select subsets of data to be replicated based on various criteria.

Microsoft SQL Server, on the other hand, employs a publisher/subscriber scheme in which a database or part of a database can be published to many subscribers. A database can be a publisher and a subscriber. For example, the western region can publish its slice of sales data while receiving (subscribing to) sales data from other regions.

There are many other replication schemes from various vendors to manage and decentralize data. Replication is a young technology that is slowly finding its way into many other products. ●

CHAPTER 39

JDBC: The Java Database Connectivity

In this chapter

JDBC Overview

JDBC is a Java Database Connectivity API that is a part of the Java Enterprise APIs from Sun Microsystems, Inc. From a developer's point of view, JDBC is the first standardized effort to integrate relational databases with Java programs. JDBC has opened all the relational power that can be mustered to Java applets and applications. In this chapter and the next, you take an in-depth look at the JDBC classes and methods.

Java Database Connectivity is a set of relational database objects and methods for interacting with SQL data sources. The JDBC APIs are part of the Enterprise APIs of Java 1.1 and, thus, are a part of all Java Virtual Machine (JVM) implementations.

Even though the objects and methods are based on the relational database model, JDBC makes no assumption about the underlying data source or the data storage scheme. You can access and retrieve audio or video data from many sources and load into Java objects using the JDBC APIs. The only requirement is that there should be a JDBC implementation for that source.

Sun introduced the JDBC API specification in March 1996 as a draft Version 0.50 and open for public review. The specification went from Version 0.50 through 1.0 to 1.10 and now to 1.22. The JDK 1.1 includes JDBC. Therefore, you need not download JDBC separately. The JDBC Version 1.22 specification available at `http://java.sun.com/products/jdbc/` includes all the improvements from the review by vendors, developers, and the general public.

NOTE The JDBC Web site has four important documents related to the JDBC specification. They are JDBC Specification (`jdbc.spec-0122.pdf`), JDBC API documentation Part I—JDBC interfaces (`jdbc.api.1-0122.pdf`), and JDBC API documentation Part II—Classes and Exceptions (`jdbc.api.2-0122.pdf`). Also available with the JDK 1.1 documentation (`jdbc.pdf`) is the JDBC Guide: Getting Started.

Now look at the origin and design philosophies. The JDBC designers based the API on X/Open SQL Call Level Interface (CLI). It is not coincidental that ODBC is also based on the X/Open CLI. The Sun engineers wanted to gain leverage from the existing ODBC implementation and development expertise, and thus make it easier for independent software vendors (ISVs) and system developers to adopt JDBC. But ODBC is a C interface to Database Management Systems (DBMS), and thus is not readily convertible to Java. Therefore, JDBC design followed ODBC in spirit as well as in its major abstractions and implemented the SQL CLI with "a Java interface that is consistent with the rest of the Java system," as the JDBC specification describes it in section 2.4. Instead of the ODBC `SQLBindColumn` and `SQLFetch` to get column values from the result, for example, JDBC used a simpler approach (which you learn about later in this chapter).

How Does JDBC Work?

As previously discussed, JDBC is designed on the CLI model. JDBC defines a set of API objects and methods to interact with the underlying database. A Java program first opens a connection to a database, makes a Statement object, passes SQL statements to the underlying DBMS through the `Statement` object, and retrieves the results as well as information about the result sets. Typically, the JDBC class files and the Java applet reside in the client. They can be downloaded from the network also. To minimize the latency during execution, it is better to have the JDBC classes in the client. The DBMS and the data source are typically located in a remote server.

Figure 39.1 shows the JDBC communication layer alternatives. The applet and the JDBC layers communicate in the client system, and the driver takes care of interacting with the database over the network.

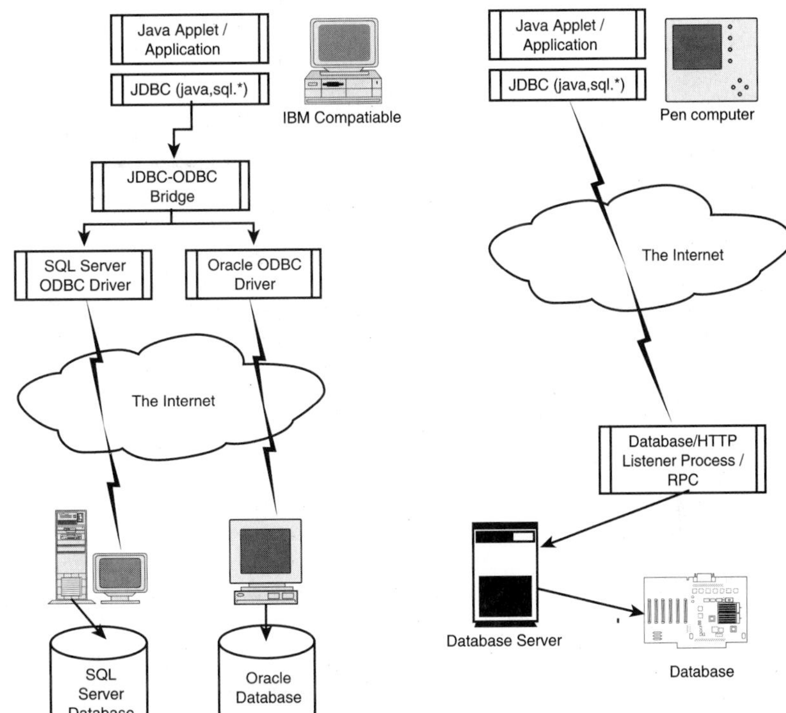

FIG. 39.1 JDBC communication layer alternatives: The JDBC driver can be a native library, like the JDBC-ODBC bridge, or a Java class talking across the network to an RPC or HTTP listener process in the database server.

The JDBC classes are in the `java.sql` package, and all Java programs use the objects and methods in the `java.sql` package to read from and write to data sources. A program using the JDBC will need a driver for the data source with which it wants to interface. This driver can be a native module (like the `JDBCODBC.DLL` for the Windows JDBC-ODBC bridge developed by Sun/Intersolv), or it can be a Java program that talks to a server in the network by using some RPC or an HTTP talker-listener protocol. Both schemes are shown in Figure 39.1.

It is conceivable that an application will deal with more than one data source—possibly heterogeneous data sources. (A database gateway program is a good example of an application that accesses multiple heterogeneous data sources.) For this reason, JDBC has a `DriverManager` whose function is to manage the drivers and provide a list of currently loaded drivers to the application programs.

Data Source, Database, or DBMS?

Although the word *database* is in the name JDBC, the form, content, and location of the data is immaterial to the Java program using JDBC so long as there is a driver for that data. Hence the notation data source to describe the data is more accurate than *database, DBMS, DB*, or just *file*. In the future, Java devices such as televisions, answering machines, or network computers will access, retrieve, and manipulate different types of data (audio, video, graphics, time series, and so on) from various sources that are not relational databases at all. Much of the data might not even come from mass storage. The data could be video stream from a satellite, for example, or audio stream from a telephone.

ODBC also refers to data sources rather than databases when describing in general terms.

Security Model

Security is always an important issue, especially when databases are involved. As of the writing of this book, JDBC follows the standard security model in which applets can connect only to the server from where they are loaded; remote applets cannot connect to local databases. Applications have no connection restrictions. For pure Java drivers, the security check is automatic. For drivers developed in native methods, however, the drivers must have some security checks.

NOTE With Java 1.1 and the Java Security API, you have the ability to establish "trust relationships," which enable you to verify trusted sites. You can then give applets downloaded from trusted sources more functionality by giving them access to local resources. For more information on Java security, refer to Chapter 34, "Java Security in Depth."

JDBC-ODBC Bridge

As a part of JDBC, Sun also delivers a driver to access ODBC data sources from JDBC. This driver is jointly developed with Intersolv and is called the JDBC-ODBC bridge. The JDBC-ODBC bridge is implemented as the `JdbcOdbc.class` and a native library to access the ODBC driver. For the Windows platform, the native library is a DLL (`JDBCODBC.DLL`).

Because JDBC is close to ODBC in design, the ODBC bridge is a thin layer over JDBC. Internally, this driver maps JDBC methods to ODBC calls and, thus, interacts with any available ODBC driver. The advantage of this bridge is that now JDBC has the capability to access almost all databases, as ODBC drivers are widely available. You can use this bridge (Version 1.2001) to run the sample programs in this and the next chapter.

JDBC Implementation

JDBC is implemented as the `java.sql` package. This package contains all the JDBC classes and methods, as shown in Table 39.1.

Table 39.1 JDBC Classes

Type	Class

Driver	`java.sql.Driver`
	`java.sql.DriverManager`
	`java.sql.DriverPropertyInfo`

Connection	`java.sql.Connection`

Statements	`java.sql.Statement`
	`java.sql.PreparedStatement`
	`java.sql.CallableStatement`

ResultSet	`java.sql.ResultSet`
Errors/Warning	`java.sql.SQLException` `java.sql.SQLWarning`
Metadata	`java.sql.DatabaseMetaData` `java.sql.ResultSetMetaData`

Date/Time	`java.sql.Date`
	`java.sql.Time`
	`java.sql.Timestamp`

Miscellaneous	`java.sql.Types` `java.sql.DataTruncation`

Now look at these classes and see how you can develop a simple JDBC application.

JDBC Classes—Overview

When you look at the class hierarchy and methods associated with it, the topmost class in the hierarchy is the `DriverManager`. The `DriverManager` keeps the driver information, state information, and more. When each driver is loaded, it registers with the `DriverManager`. The `DriverManager`, when required to open a connection, selects the driver depending on the JDBC URL.

JDBC URL

True to the nature of the Internet, JDBC identifies a database with an URL. The URL's form is as follows:

```
jdbc:<subprotocol>:<subname related to the DBMS/Protocol>
```

For databases on the Internet or intranet, the subname can contain the Net URL `//hostname:port/`. The `<subprotocol>` can be any name that a database understands. The `odbc` subprotocol name is reserved for ODBC-style data sources. A normal ODBC database JDBC URL looks like the following:

```
jdbc:odbc:<ODBC DSN>;User=<username>;PW=<password>
```

If you are developing a JDBC driver with a new subprotocol, it is better to reserve the subprotocol name with Sun, which maintains an informal subprotocol registry.

The `java.sql.Driver` class is usually referred to for information such as `PropertyInfo`, version number, and so on. This class could be loaded many times during the execution of a Java program using the JDBC API.

Looking at the `java.sql.Driver` and `java.sql.DriverManager` classes and methods as listed in Table 39.2, you see that the `DriverManager` returns a `Connection` object when you use the `getConnection()` method.

Table 39.2 *Driver, DriverManager,* and Related Methods

Return Type	Method Name	Parameter
`java.sql.Driver`		
`Connection`	`connect`	`(String url, java.util.Properties info)`
`boolean`	`acceptsURL`	`(String url)`
`DriverPropertyInfo[]`	`getPropertyInfo`	`(String url, java.util.Properties info)`
`int`	`getMajorVersion`	`()`
`int`	`getMinorVersion`	`()`
`boolean`	`jdbcCompliant`	`()`
`java.sql.DriverManager`		
`Connection`	`getConnection`	`(String url, java.util.Properties info)`
`Connection`	`getConnection`	`(String url, String user, String password)`
`Connection`	`getConnection`	`(String url)`
`Driver`	`getDriver`	`(String url)`

java.sql.DriverManager		
void	registerDriver	(java.sql. Driver driver)
void	deregisterDriver	(Driver driver)
java.util.Enumeration	getDrivers	()
void	setLoginTimeout	(int seconds)
int	getLoginTimeout	()
void	setLogStream	(java.io. PrintStream out)
java.io.PrintStream	getLogStream	()
void	println	(String message)
Class Initialization Routine		
void	initialize	()

Other useful methods include the `registerDriver()`, `deRegister()`, and `getDrivers()` methods. By using the `getDrivers()` method, you can get a list of registered drivers. Figure 39.2 shows the `JDBC` class hierarchy, as well as the flow of a typical Java program using the JDBC APIs.

In the following section, you will follow the steps required to access a simple database by using JDBC and the JDBC-ODBC driver.

Anatomy of a JDBC Application

To handle data from a database, a Java program follows these general steps. (Figure 39.2 shows the general JDBC objects, the methods, and the sequence.) First, the program calls the `getConnection()` method to get the `Connection` object. Then it creates the `Statement` object and prepares a `SQL` statement.

A `SQL` statement can be executed immediately (`Statement` object), can be a `compiled` statement (`PreparedStatement` object), or can be a call to a stored procedure (`CallableStatement` object). When the method `executeQuery()` is executed, a `ResultSet` object is returned. SQL statements such as `update` or `delete` will not return a `ResultSet`. For such statements, the `executeUpdate()` method is used. The `executeUpdate()` method returns an integer that denotes the number of rows affected by the SQL statement.

The `ResultSet` contains rows of data that are parsed using the `next()` method. In case of a transaction processing application, methods such as `rollback()` and `commit()` can be used either to undo the changes made by the SQL statements or permanently affect the changes made by the SQL statements.

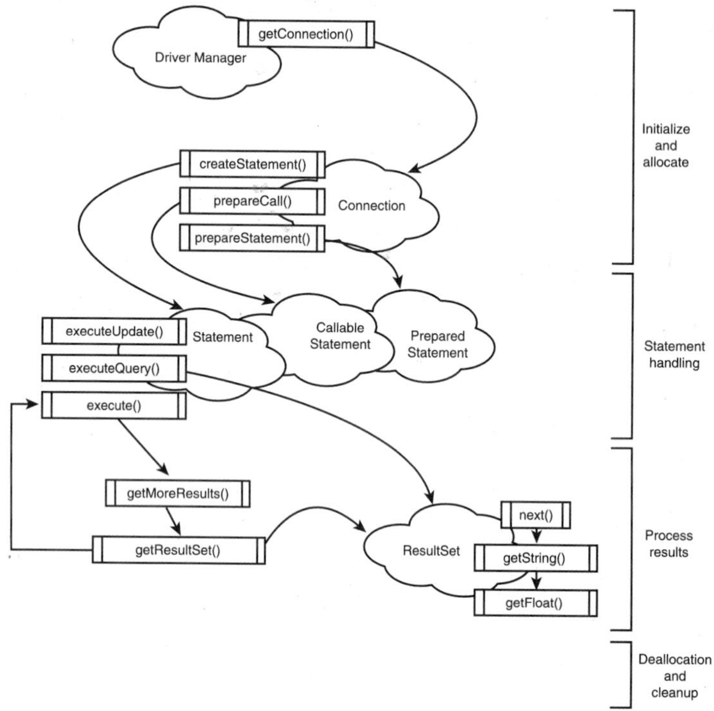

FIG. 39.2
JDBC class hierarchy and a JDBC API flow.

JDBC Examples

These examples access the Student database, the schema of which is shown in Figure 39.3. The tables in the examples that you are interested in are the Students table, Classes table, Instructors table, and Students_Classes table. This database is a Microsoft Access database. The full database and sample data are generated by the Access Database Wizard. You access the database by using JDBC and the JDBC-ODBC bridge.

Before you jump into writing a Java JDBC program, you need to configure an ODBC data source. As you saw earlier, the `getConnection()` method requires a data source name (DSN), user ID, and password for the ODBC data source. The database driver type or subprotocol name is `odbc`. So the driver manager finds out from the ODBC driver the rest of the details.

But wait, where do you put the rest of the details? This is where the ODBC setup comes into the picture. The ODBC Setup program runs outside the Java application from the Microsoft ODBC program group. The ODBC Setup program enables you to set up the data source so that this information is available to the ODBC Driver Manager, which in turn loads the Microsoft Access ODBC driver. If the database is in another DBMS form—say, Oracle—you configure this source as Oracle ODBC driver. In Windows 3.x, the Setup program puts this information in the `ODBC.INI` file. With Windows 95 and Windows NT 4.0, this information is in the Registry. Figure 39.4 shows the ODBC Setup screen.

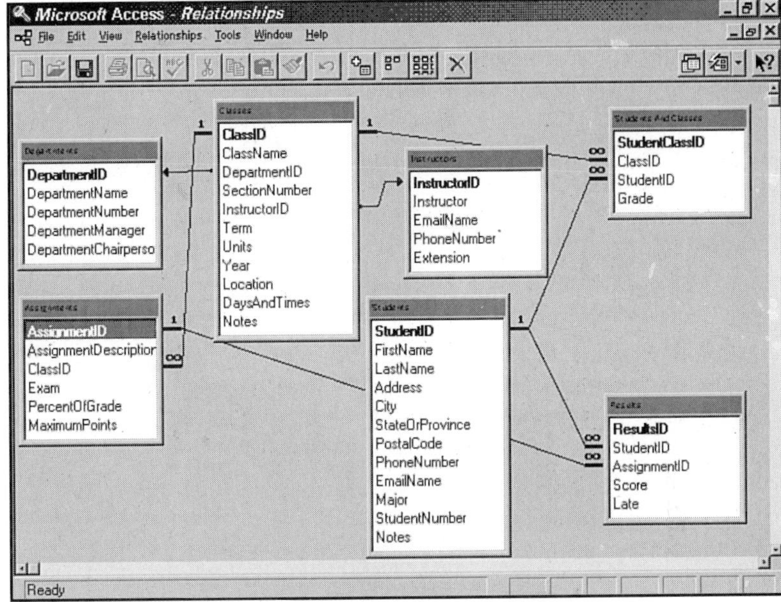

FIG. 39.3 JDBC example database schema.

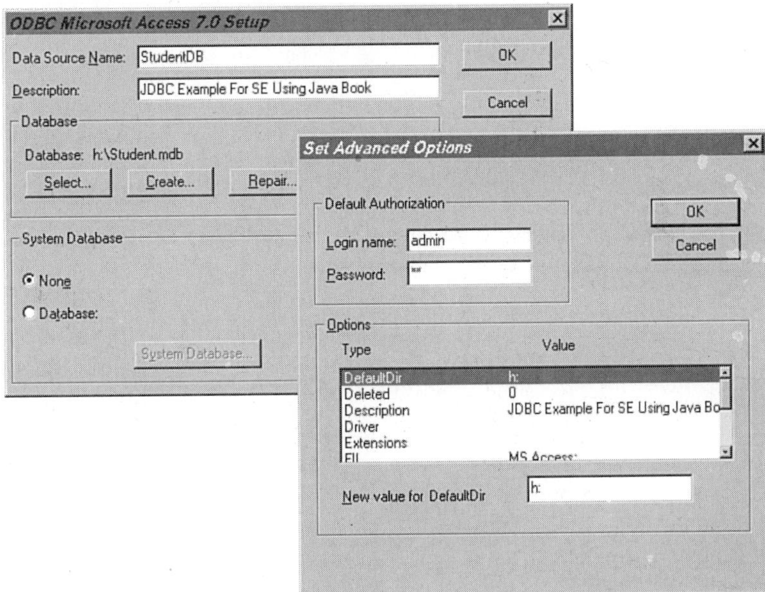

FIG. 39.4 ODBC Setup for the example database. After this setup, the example database URL is `jdbc:odbc:Student DB;uid="admin";pw="sa"`.

JDBC Query Example In this example, you list all the students in the database with a SQL `SELECT` statement. The steps required to accomplish this task using the JDBC API are listed here. For each step, the Java program code with the JDBC API calls follows the description of the steps.

```
//Declare a method and some variables.
public void ListStudents() throws SQLException {
   int i, NoOfColumns;
   String StNo,StFName,StLName;
   //Initialize and load the JDBC-ODBC driver.
   Class.forName ("jdbc.odbc.JdbcOdbcDriver");
   //Make the connection object.
   Connection Ex1Con = DriverManager.getConnection
➥( "jdbc:odbc:StudentDB;uid="admin";pw="sa");
   //Create a simple Statement object.
   Statement Ex1Stmt = Ex1Con.createStatement();
   //Make a SQL string, pass it to the DBMS, and execute the SQL statement.
   ResultSet Ex1rs = Ex1Stmt.executeQuery(
     "SELECT StudentNumber, FirstName, LastName FROM Students");
   //Process each row until there are no more rows.
   // Displays the results on the console.
   System.out.println("Student Number        First Name      Last Name");
   while (Ex1rs.next()) {
      // Get the column values into Java variables
      StNo = Ex1rs.getString(1);
      StFName = Ex1rs.getString(2);
      StLName = Ex1rs.getString(3);
      System.out.println(StNo,StFName,StLName);
      }
   }
```

As you can see, it is a simple Java program using the JDBC API. The program illustrates the basic steps needed to access a table and lists some of the fields in the records.

JDBC Update Example In this example, you update the `FirstName` field in the Students table by knowing the student's `StudentNumber`. As in the preceding example, the code follows the description of the step.

```
//Declare a method and some variables and parameters.
public void UpdateStudentName(String StFName, String StLName,
   String StNo) throws SQLException {
   int RetValue;
   // Initialize and load the JDBC-ODBC driver.
   Class.forName ("jdbc.odbc.JdbcOdbcDriver");
   // Make the connection object.
   Connection Ex1Con = DriverManager.getConnection
➥( "jdbc:odbc:StudentDB;uid="admin";pw="sa");
   // Create a simple Statement object.
   Statement Ex1Stmt = Ex1Con.createStatement();
   //Make a SQL string, pass it to the DBMS, and execute the SQL statement
   String SQLBuffer = "UPDATE Students SET FirstName = "+
   StFName+", LastName = "+StLName+
     " WHERE StudentNumber = "+StNo
   RetValue = Ex1Stmt.executeUpdate( SQLBuffer);
   System.out.println("Updated " + RetValue + " rows in the Database.");
   }
```

In this example, you execute the `SQL` statement and get the number of rows affected by the `SQL` statement back from the DBMS.

The previous two examples show how you can do simple yet powerful SQL manipulation of the underlying data by using the JDBC API in a Java program. In the following sections, you examine each JDBC class in detail.

The *Connection* Class

The `Connection` class is one of the major classes in JDBC. It packs a lot of functionality, ranging from transaction processing to creating statements, in one class as seen in Table 39.3.

Table 39.3 *java.sql.* Connection Methods and Constants

Return Type	Method Name	Parameter
Statement-Related Methods		
`Statement`	`createStatement`	`()`
`PreparedStatement`	`prepareStatement`	`(String sql)`
`CallableStatement`	`prepareCall`	`(String sql)`
`String`	`nativeSQL`	`(String sql)`
`void`	`close`	`()`
`boolean`	`isClosed`	`()`
Metadata-Related Methods		
`DatabaseMetaData`	`getMetaData`	`()`
`void`	`setReadOnly`	`(boolean readOnly)`
`boolean`	`isReadOnly`	`()`
`void`	`setCatalog`	`(String catalog)`
`String`	`getCatalog`	`()`
`SQLWarning`	`getWarnings`	`()`
`void`	`clearWarnings`	`()`
Transaction-Related Methods		
`void`	`setAutoCommit`	`(boolean autoCommit)`
`boolean`	`getAutoCommit`	`()`
`void`	`commit`	`()`
`void`	`rollback`	`()`
`void`	`setTransaction Isolation`	`(int level)`
`int`	`getTransaction Isolation`	`()`

The `TransactionIsolation` constants are defined in the `java.sql.Connection` as integers with the following values:

TransactionIsolation Constant Name	Value
TRANSACTION_NONE	0
TRANSACTION_READ_UNCOMMITTED	1
TRANSACTION_READ_COMMITTED	2
TRANSACTION_REPEATABLE_READ	4
TRANSACTION_SERIALIZABLE	8

As you saw earlier, the connection is for a specific database that can be interacted with in a specific subprotocol. The `Connection` object internally manages all aspects about a connection, and the details are transparent to the program. Actually, the `Connection` object is a pipeline into the underlying DBMS driver. The information to be managed includes the data source identifier, the subprotocol, the state information, the DBMS SQL execution plan ID or handle, and any other contextual information needed to interact successfully with the underlying DBMS.

NOTE The data source identifier could be a port in the Internet database server that is identified by the `//<server name>:port/` URL or just a data source name used by the ODBC driver or a full pathname to a database file in the local computer. For all you know, it could be a pointer to data feed of the stock market prices from Wall Street.

Another important function performed by the `Connection` object is the transaction management. The handling of the transactions depends on the state of an internal autocommit flag that is set using the `setAutoCommit()` method, and the state of this flag can be read using the `getAutoCommit()` method. When the flag is `true`, the transactions are automatically committed as soon as they are completed. There is no need for any intervention or commands from the Java application program. When the flag is `false`, the system is in the Manual mode. The Java program has the option to commit the set of transactions that happened after the last commit or roll back the transactions using the `commit()` and `rollback()` methods.

NOTE JDBC also provides methods for setting the transaction isolation modularity. When you are developing multi-tiered applications, multiple users will be performing concurrently interleaved transactions that are on the same database tables. A database driver has to employ sophisticated locking and data buffering algorithms and mechanisms to implement the transaction isolation required for a large-scale JDBC application. This is more complex when there are multiple Java objects working on many databases that could be scattered across the globe. Only time will tell what special needs for transaction isolation there will be in the new Internet/intranet paradigm.

After you have a successful `Connection` object to a data source, you can interact with the data source in many ways. The most common approach, from an application developer standpoint, is using the objects that handle the `SQL` statements. In JDBC, there are three main types of statements:

- Statement
- PreparedStatement
- CallableStatement

The Connection object has the createStatement(), prepareStatement(), and prepareCall() methods to create these statement objects. Chapter 40, "JDBC Explored," deals with the statement-type objects in detail.

Another notable method in the Connection object is the getMetadata() method that returns an object of the DatabaseMetaData type, which is the topic for the following section.

Metadata Functions

Speaking theoretically, metadata is information about data. The MetaData methods are mainly aimed at the database tools and wizards that need information about the capabilities and structure of the underlying DBMS. Many times these tools need dynamic information about the resultset, which a SQL statement returns. JDBC has two classes of metadata: ResultSetMetaData and DatabaseMetadata. As you can see from the method tables, a huge number of methods are available in this class of objects.

DatabaseMetaData

DatabaseMetaDatas are similar to the catalog functions in ODBC, where an application queries the underlying DBMS's system tables and gets information. ODBC returns the information as a resultset. JDBC returns the results as a ResultSet object with well-defined columns.

The DatabaseMetaData object and its methods give a lot of information about the underlying database. This information is more useful for database tools, automatic data conversion, and gateway programs. Table 39.4 gives all the methods for the DatabaseMetaData object. As you can see, it is a very long table with more than 100 methods. Unless they are very exhaustive GUI tools, most of the programs will not use all the methods. But, as a developer, there will be times when one needs to know some characteristic about the database or to see whether a feature is supported. It is those times when the following table comes in handy.

Table 39.4 *DatabaseMetaData* Methods

Return Type	Method Name	Parameter
boolean	allProceduresAreCallable	()
boolean	allTablesAreSelectable	()
String	getURL	()
String	getUserName	()
boolean	isReadOnly	()

continues

Table 39.4 Continued

Return Type	Method Name	Parameter
boolean	nullsAreSortedHigh	()
boolean	nullsAreSortedLow	()
boolean	nullsAreSortedAtStart	()
boolean	nullsAreSortedAtEnd	()
String	getDatabaseProductName	()
String	getDatabaseProductVersion	()
String	getDriverName	()
String	getDriverVersion	()
int	getDriverMajorVersion	()
int	getDriverMinorVersion	()
boolean	usesLocalFiles	()
boolean	usesLocalFilePerTable	()
boolean	supportsMixedCaseIdentifiers	()
boolean	storesUpperCaseIdentifiers	()
boolean	storesLowerCaseIdentifiers	()
boolean	storesMixedCaseIdentifiers	()
boolean	supportsMixedCaseQuotedIdentifiers	()
boolean	storesUpperCaseQuotedIdentifiers	()
boolean	storesLowerCaseQuotedIdentifiers	()
boolean	storesMixedCaseQuotedIdentifiers	()
String	getIdentifierQuoteString	()
String	getSQLKeywords	()
String	getNumericFunctions	()
String	getStringFunctions	()
String	getSystemFunctions	()
String	getTimeDateFunctions	()
String	getSearchStringEscape	()
String	getExtraNameCharacters	()
boolean	supportsAlterTableWithAddColumn	()

Return Type	Method Name	Parameter
boolean	supportsAlterTableWithDropColumn	()
boolean	supportsColumnAliasing	()
boolean	nullPlusNonNullIsNull	()
boolean	supportsConvert	()
boolean	supportsConvert	(int fromType, int toType)
boolean	supportsTableCorrelationNames	()
boolean	supportsDifferentTableCorrelation Names	()
boolean	supportsExpressionsInOrderBy	()
boolean	supportsOrderByUnrelated	()
boolean	supportsGroupBy	()
boolean	supportsGroupByUnrelated	()
boolean	supportsGroupByBeyondSelect	()
boolean	supportsLikeEscapeClause	()
boolean	supportsMultipleResultSets	()
boolean	supportsMultipleTransactions	()
boolean	supportsNonNullableColumns	()
boolean	supportsMinimumSQLGrammar	()
boolean	supportsCoreSQLGrammar	()
boolean	supportsExtendedSQLGrammar	()
boolean	supportsANSI92EntryLevelSQL	()
boolean	supportsANSI92IntermediateSQL	()
boolean	supportsANSI92FullSQL	()
boolean	supportsIntegrityEnhancement Facility	()
boolean	supportsOuterJoins	()
boolean	supportsFullOuterJoins	()
boolean	supportsLimitedOuterJoins	()
String	getSchemaTerm	()
String	getProcedureTerm	()

continues

Table 39.4 Continued

Return Type	Method Name	Parameter
String	getCatalogTerm	()
boolean	isCatalogAtStart	()
String	getCatalogSeparator	()
boolean	supportsSchemasInDataManipulation	()
boolean	supportsSchemasInProcedureCalls	()
boolean	supportsSchemasInTableDefinitions	()
boolean	supportsSchemasInIndexDefinitions	()
boolean	supportsSchemasInPrivilege Definitions	()
boolean	supportsCatalogsInDataManipulation	()
boolean	supportsCatalogsInProcedureCalls	()
boolean	supportsCatalogsInTableDefinitions	()
boolean	supportsCatalogsInIndexDefinitions	()
boolean	supportsCatalogsInPrivilege Definitions	()
boolean	supportsPositionedDelete	()
boolean	supportsPositionedUpdate	()
boolean	supportsSelectForUpdate	()
boolean	supportsStoredProcedures	()
boolean	supportsSubqueriesInComparisons	()
boolean	supportsSubqueriesInExists	()
boolean	supportsSubqueriesInIns	()
boolean	supportsSubqueriesInQuantifieds	()
boolean	supportsCorrelatedSubqueries	()
boolean	supportsUnion	()
boolean	supportsUnionAll	()
boolean	supportsOpenCursorsAcrossCommit	()
boolean	supportsOpenCursorsAcrossRollback	()
boolean	supportsOpenStatementsAcrossCommit	()
boolean	supportsOpenStatementsAcross Rollback	()

Return Type	Method Name	Parameter
int	getMaxBinaryLiteralLength	()
int	getMaxCharLiteralLength	()
int	getMaxColumnNameLength	()
int	getMaxColumnsInGroupBy	()
int	getMaxColumnsInIndex	()
int	getMaxColumnsInOrderBy	()
int	getMaxColumnsInSelect	()
int	getMaxColumnsInTable	()
int	getMaxConnections	()
int	getMaxCursorNameLength	()
int	getMaxIndexLength	()
int	getMaxSchemaNameLength	()
int	getMaxProcedureNameLength	()
int	getMaxCatalogNameLength	()
int	getMaxRowSize	()
boolean	doesMaxRowSizeIncludeBlobs	()
int	getMaxStatementLength	()
int	getMaxStatements	()
int	getMaxTableNameLength	()
int	getMaxTablesInSelect	()
int	getMaxUserNameLength	()
int	getDefaultTransactionIsolation	()
boolean	supportsTransactions	()
boolean	supportsTransactionIsolationLevel	(int level)
boolean	supportsDataDefinitionAndData ManipulationTransactions	()
boolean	supportsDataManipulation TransactionsOnly	()
boolean	dataDefinitionCausesTransaction Commit	()
boolean	dataDefinitionIgnoredIn Transactions	()

continues

Table 39.4 Continued

Return Type	Method Name	Parameter
ResultSet	getProcedures	(String catalog, String schemaPattern, String procedureNamePattern)
ResultSet	getProcedureColumns	(String catalog, String schemaPattern, String procedureNamePattern, String columnNamePattern)
ResultSet	getTables	(String catalog, String schemaPattern, String tableNamePattern, String types[])
ResultSet	getSchemas	()
ResultSet	getCatalogs	()
ResultSet	getTableTypes	()
ResultSet	getColumns	(String catalog, String schemaPattern, String tableNamePattern, String columnNamePattern)
ResultSet	getColumnPrivileges	(String catalog, String schema, String table, String columnNamePattern)
ResultSet	getTablePrivileges	(String catalog, String schemaPattern, String tableNamePattern)
ResultSet	getBestRowIdentifier	(String catalog, String schema, String table, int scope, boolean nullable)
ResultSet	getVersionColumns	(String catalog, String schema, String table)
ResultSet	getPrimaryKeys	(String catalog, String schema, String table)
ResultSet	getImportedKeys	(String catalog, String schema, String table)

Return Type	Method Name	Parameter
ResultSet	getExportedKeys	(String catalog, String schema, String table)
ResultSet	getCrossReference	(String primaryCatalog, String primarySchema, String primaryTable, String foreignCatalog, String foreignSchema, String foreignTable)
ResultSet	getTypeInfo	()
ResultSet	getIndexInfo	(String catalog, String schema, String table, boolean unique, boolean approximate)

As you can see in the table, the `DatabaseMetaData` object gives information about the functionality and limitation of the underlying DBMS. An important set of information that is very useful for an application programmer includes the methods describing schema details of the tables in the database, as well as table names, stored procedure names, and so on.

An example of using the `DatabaseMetaData` objects from a Java application is the development of multi-tier, scalable applications. A Java application can query if the underlying database engine supports a particular feature. If it does not, Java can call alternative methods to perform the task. This way, the application will not fail if a feature is not available in the DBMS.

At the same time, the application will exploit advanced functionality whenever it is available. This is what some experts call "interoperable and yet scalable." Interoperability is needed for application tools also—especially for general-purpose design and query tools based on Java that must interact with different data sources. These tools have to query the data source system to find out the supported features and proceed accordingly. The tools might be able to process information faster with data sources that support advanced features, or they may be able to provide the user with more options for a feature-rich data source.

ResultSetMetaData

Compared to the `DatabaseMetaData`, the `ResultSetMetaData` object is simpler and has fewer methods. But these will be more popular with application developers. The `ResultSetMetaData`, as the name implies, describes a `ResultSet` object. Table 39.5 lists all the methods available for the `ResultSetMetaData` object.

Table 39.5 *ResultSetMetaData* Methods

Return Type	Method Name	Parameter
`Int`	`getColumnCount`	`()`
`boolean`	`isAutoIncrement`	`(int column)`
`boolean`	`isCaseSensitive`	`(int column)`
`boolean`	`isSearchable`	`(int column)`
`boolean`	`isCurrency`	`(int column)`
`int`	`isNullable`	`(int column)`
`boolean`	`isSigned`	`(int column)`
`int`	`getColumnDisplaySize`	`(int column)`
`String`	`getColumnLabel`	`(int column)`
`String`	`getColumnName`	`(int column)`
`String`	`getSchemaName`	`(int column)`
`int`	`getPrecision`	`(int column)`
`int`	`getScale`	`(int column)`
`String`	`getTableName`	`(int column)`
`String`	`getCatalogName`	`(int column)`
`int`	`getColumnType`	`(int column)`
`String`	`getColumnTypeName`	`(int column)`
`boolean`	`isReadOnly`	`(int column)`
`boolean`	`isWritable`	`(int column)`
`boolean`	`isDefinitelyWritable`	`(int column)`
Return Values		
`int columnNo` `Nulls = 0`		
`int column` `Nullable = 1`		

`int Column`
`Nullable`
`Unknown = 2`		

As you can see from the preceding table, the `ResultSetMetaData` object can be used to find out about the types and properties of the columns in a resultset. You need to use methods such as `getColumnLabel()` and `getColumnDisplaySize()` even in normal application programs. Using these methods will result in programs that handle result sets generically, thus assuring uniformity across various applications in an organization as the names and sizes are taken from the database itself.

Before you leave this chapter, also look at the exception handling facilities offered by JDBC.

The *SQLException* Class

The `SQLException` class in JDBC provides a variety of information regarding errors that occurred during a database access. The `SQLException` objects are chained, so a program can read them in order. This is a good mechanism, as an error condition can generate multiple errors and the final error might not have anything to do with the actual error condition. By chaining the errors, you can actually pinpoint the first error. Each `SQLException` has an error message and vendor-specific error code. Also associated with a `SQLException` is a `SQLState` string that follows the `XOPEN SQLState` values defined in the SQL specification. Table 39.6 lists the methods for the `SQLException` class.

Table 39.6 *SQLException* Methods

Return Type	Method Name	Parameter
`SQLException`	`SQLException`	`(String reason, String SQLState, int vendorCode)`
`SQLException`	`SQLException`	`(String reason, String SQLState)`
`SQLException`	`SQLException`	`(String reason)`
`SQLException`	`SQLException`	`()`
`String`	`getSQLState`	`()`
`int`	`getErrorCode`	`()`
`SQLException`	`getNextException`	`()`
`void`	`setNextException`	`(SQLException ex)`

The *SQLWarnings* Class

Unlike the `SQLException` class, the `SQLWarnings` class does not cause any commotion in a Java program. The `SQLWarnings` are tagged to the object whose method caused the warning. So you should check for warnings using the `getWarnings()` method that is available for all objects. Table 39.7 lists the methods associated with the `SQLWarnings` class.

Table 39.7 *SQLWarnings* Methods

Return Type	Function Name	Parameter
SQLWarning	SQLWarning	(String reason, String SQLState, int vendorCode)
SQLWarning	SQLWarning	(String reason, String SQLState)
SQLWarning	SQLWarning	(String reason)
SQLWarning	SQLWarning	()
SQLWarning	getNextWarning	()
void	setNextWarning	(SQLWarning w)

CHAPTER 40

JDBC Explored

In this chapter

Statements

The `Statement` object does all of the work to interact with the Database Management System in terms of SQL statements. You can create many `Statement` objects from one `Connection` object. Internally, the `Statement` object would be storing the various data needed to interact with a database, including state information, buffer handles, and so on; but these are transparent to the JDBC application program.

NOTE When a program attempts an operation that is not in sync with the internal state of the system (for example, a `next()` method to get a row when no SQL statements have been executed), this discrepancy is caught and an exception is raised. This exception, normally, is probed by the application program using the methods in the `SQLException` object.

JDBC supports three types of statements:

- `Statement`
- `PreparedStatement`
- `CallableStatement`

Before you explore these different statements, see the steps that an SQL statement goes through.

A Java application program first builds the SQL statement in a string buffer and passes this buffer to the underlying DBMS through some API calls. An SQL statement needs to be verified syntactically, optimized, and converted to an executable form before execution. In the Call Level Interface (CLI) Application Program Interface (API) model, the application program through the driver passes the SQL statement to the underlying DBMS, which prepares and executes the SQL statement.

After the DBMS receives the SQL string buffer, it parses the statement and does a syntax check run. If the statement is not syntactically correct, the system returns an error condition to the driver, which generates an `SQLException`. If the statement is syntactically correct, depending on the DBMS, many query plans are usually generated that are run through an optimizer (often a cost-based optimizer). Then the optimum plan is translated into a binary execution plan. After the execution plan is prepared, the DBMS usually returns a handle or identifier to this optimized binary version of the SQL statement to the application program.

The three JDBC statement types (`Statement`, `PreparedStatement`, and `CallableStatement`) differ in the timing of the SQL statement preparation and the statement execution. In the case of the simple `Statement` object, the SQL is prepared and executed in one step—at least from the application program point of view. (Internally, the driver might get the identifier, command the DBMS to execute the query, and then discard the handle). In the case of a `PreparedStatement` object, the driver stores the execution plan handle for later use. In the case of the `CallableStatement` object, the SQL statement is actually making a call to a stored procedure that is usually already optimized.

NOTE As you know, stored procedures are encapsulated business rules or procedures that reside in the database server. They also enforce uniformity across applications, as well as provide security to the database access. Stored procedures last beyond the execution of the program, so the application program does not spend any time waiting for the DBMS to create the execution plan.

Now look at each type of statement more closely and see what each has to offer a Java program.

Statement

A `Statement` object is created using the `createStatement()` method in the `Connection` object. Table 40.1 shows all methods available for the `Statement` object.

Table 40.1 *Statement* Object Methods

Return Type	Method Name	Parameter
`ResultSet`	`executeQuery`	`(String sql)`
`int`	`executeUpdate`	`(String sql)`
`boolean`	`execute`	`(String sql)`
`boolean`	`getMoreResults`	`()`
`void`	`close`	`()`
`int`	`getMaxFieldSize`	`()`
`void`	`setMaxFieldSize`	`(int max)`
`int`	`getMaxRows`	`()`
`void`	`setMaxRows`	`(int max)`
`void`	`setEscapeProcessing`	`(boolean enable)`
`int`	`getQueryTimeout`	`()`
`void`	`setQueryTimeout`	`(int seconds)`
`void`	`cancel`	`()`
`java.sql.SQLWarning`	`getWarnings`	`()`
`void`	`clearWarnings`	`()`
`void`	`setCursorName`	`(String name)`
`ResultSet`	`getResultSet`	`()`
`int`	`getUpdateCount`	`()`

The most important methods are `executeQuery()`, `executeUpdate()`, and `execute()`. As you create a `Statement` object with a SQL statement, the `executeQuery()` method takes an SQL string. It passes the SQL string to the underlying data source through the driver manager and gets the `ResultSet` back to the application program. The `executeQuery()` method returns only one `ResultSet`. For those cases that return more than one `ResultSet`, the `execute()` method should be used.

CAUTION

Only one `ResultSet` can be opened per `Statement` object at one time.

For SQL statements that do not return a `ResultSet` like the `UPDATE`, `DELETE`, and `DDL` statements, the `Statement` object has the `executeUpdate()` method that takes a SQL string and returns an integer. This integer indicates the number of rows that are affected by the SQL statement.

NOTE The JDBC processing is synchronous; that is, the application program must wait for the SQL statements to complete. But because Java is a multithreaded platform, the JDBC designers suggest using threads to simulate asynchronous processing.

The `Statement` object is best suited for ad hoc SQL statements or SQL statements that are executed once. The DBMS goes through the syntax run, query plan optimization, and the execution plan generation stages as soon as this SQL statement is received. The DBMS executes the query and then discards the optimized execution plan; so, if the `executeQuery()` method is called again, the DBMS goes through all of the steps again.

The following example program shows how to use the `Statement` class to access a database.

▶ **See** "Anatomy of a JDBC Application," **p. 879**

In the example shown in Listing 40.1, you list all of the subjects (classes) available in the enrollment database and their locations, days, and times. The SQL statement for this is:

```
SELECT ClassName, Location, DaysAndTimes FROM Classes
```

You create a `Statement` object and pass the SQL string during the `executeQuery()` method call to get this data.

Listing 40.1 A Simple JDBC Example Listing Class Schedules

```
//Declare a method and some variables.
public void ListClasses() throws SQLException {
    int i, NoOfColumns;
    String ClassName,ClassLocation, ClassSchedule;
    //Initialize and load the JDBC-ODBC driver.
    Class.forName ("jdbc.odbc.JdbcOdbcDriver");
    //Make the connection object.
    Connection Ex1Con = DriverManager.getConnection( "jdbc:odbc:
StudentDB;uid="admin";pw="sa");
    //Create a simple Statement object.
    Statement Ex1Stmt = Ex1Con.createStatement();
```

```
        //Make a SQL string, pass it to the DBMS, and execute the SQL statement.
        ResultSet Ex1rs = Ex1Stmt.executeQuery( "SELECT ClassName, Location,
DaysAndTimes FROM Classes");
        //Process each row until there are no more rows.
        // And display the results on the console.
        System.out.println("Class          Location      Schedule");
        while (Ex1rs.next()) {
            // Get the column values into Java variables
            ClassName = Ex1rs.getString(1);
            ClassLocation = Ex1rs.getString(2);
            ClassSchedule = Ex1rs.getString(3);
            System.out.println(ClassName,ClassLocation,ClassSchedule);
        }
    }
```

As you can see, the program is very straightforward. You do the initial connection and create a `Statement` object. You pass the SQL along with the method `executeQuery()` call. The driver passes the SQL string to the DBMS, which performs the query and returns the results. After the statement is finished, the optimized execution plan is lost.

PreparedStatement

In the case of a `PreparedStatement` object, as the name implies, the application program prepares a SQL statement using the `java.sql.Connection.prepareStatement()` method. The `PreparedStatement()` method takes an SQL string, which is passed to the underlying DBMS. The DBMS goes through the syntax run, query plan optimization, and the execution plan generation stages, but does not execute the SQL statement. Possibly, it returns a handle to the optimized execution plan that the JDBC driver stores internally in the `PreparedStatement` object.

The methods of the `PreparedStatement` object are shown in Table 40.2. Notice that the `executeQuery()`, `executeUpdate()`, and `execute()` methods do not take any parameters. They are just calls to the underlying DBMS to perform the already-optimized SQL statement.

Table 40.2 *PreparedStatement* Object Methods

Return Type	Method Name	Parameter
`ResultSet`	`executeQuery`	`()`
`int`	`executeUpdate`	`()`
`boolean`	`execute`	`()`

One of the major features of a `PreparedStatement` is that it can handle `IN` types of parameters. The parameters are indicated in an SQL statement by placing the `?` as the parameter marker instead of the actual values. In the Java program, the association is made to the parameters with the `setXXXX()` methods, as shown in Table 40.3. All of the `setXXXX()` methods take the parameter index, which is 1 for the first `?`, 2 for the second `?`, and so on.

Table 40.3 *java.sql.PreparedStatement*—Parameter-Related Methods

Return Type	Method Name	Parameter
void	clearParameters	()
void	setAsciiStream	(int parameterIndex, java.io.InputStream x, int length)
void	setBinaryStream	(int parameterIndex, java.io.InputStream x, int length)
void	setBoolean	(int parameterIndex, boolean x)
void	setByte	(int parameterIndex, byte x)
void	1setBytes	(int parameterIndex, byte x[])
void	setDate	(int parameterIndex, java.sql.Date x)
void	setDouble	(int parameterIndex, double x)
void	setFloat	(int parameterIndex, float x)
void	setInt	(int parameterIndex, int x)
void	setLong	(int parameterIndex, long x)
void	setNull	(int parameterIndex, int sqlType)
void	setBignum	(int parameterIndex, Bignum x)
void	setShort	(int parameterIndex, short x)
void	setString	(int parameterIndex, String x)
void	setTime	(int parameterIndex, java.sql.Time x)
void	setTimestamp	(int parameterIndex, java.sql.Timestamp x)
void	setUnicodeStream	(int parameterIndex, java.io.InputStream x, int length)
Advanced Features—Object Manipulation		
void	setObject	(int parameterIndex, Object x, int targetSqlType, int scale)
void	setObject	(int parameterIndex, Object x, int targetSqlType)
void	setObject	(int parameterIndex, Object x)

In the case of the `PreparedStatement`, the driver actually sends only the execution plan ID and the parameters to the DBMS. This results in less network traffic and is well-suited for Java applications on the Internet. The `PreparedStatement` should be used when you need to execute the SQL statement many times in a Java application. But remember, even though the optimized execution plan is available during the execution of a Java program, the DBMS discards the execution plan at the end of the program. So, the DBMS must go through all of the steps of creating an execution plan every time the program runs. The `PreparedStatement` object achieves faster SQL execution performance than the simple `Statement` object, as the DBMS does not have to run through the steps of creating the execution plan.

The following example program shows how to use the `PreparedStatement` class to access a database. The database schema is shown in Chapter 39, "JDBC: The Java Database Connectivity." In this example, you optimize the example you developed in the `Statement` example.

See "Anatomy of a JDBC Application," **p. 879**

The simple `Statement` example in Listing 40.1 can be improved in a few major ways. First, the DBMS goes through building the execution plan every time, so you make it a `PreparedStatement`. Secondly, the query lists all courses that could scroll away. You improve this situation by building a parameterized query as shown in Listing 40.2.

Listing 40.2 Improving the Example with a *PreparedStatement*

```
 //Declare class variables
Connection Con;
PreparedStatement PrepStmt;
boolean Initialized = false;
private void InitConnection() throws SQLException {
    //Initialize and load the JDBC-ODBC driver.
    Class.forName ("jdbc.odbc.JdbcOdbcDriver");
    //Make the connection object.
    Con = DriverManager.getConnection(
➥"jdbc:odbc:StudentDB;uid="admin";pw="sa");
    //Create a prepared Statement object.
    PrepStmt = Ex1Con.prepareStatement( "SELECT ClassName,
➥Location, DaysAndTimes FROM Classes WHERE ClassName = ?");
    Initialized = True;
}

public void ListOneClass(String ListClassName) throws SQLException {
    int i, NoOfColumns;
    String ClassName,ClassLocation, ClassSchedule;
    if (! Initialized) {
        InitConnection();
    }
    // Set the SQL parameter to the one passed into this method
    PrepStmt.setString(1,ListClassName);
    ResultSet Ex1rs = PrepStmt.executeQuery()
    //Process each row until there are no more rows and
    // display the results on the console.
    System.out.println("Class Location Schedule");
    while (Ex1rs.next()) {
        // Get the column values into Java variables
        ClassName = Ex1rs.getString(1);
        ClassLocation = Ex1rs.getString(2);
        ClassSchedule = Ex1rs.getString(3);
        System.out.println(ClassName,ClassLocation,ClassSchedule);
    }
}
```

Now, if a student wants to check the details of one subject interactively, this sample program can be used. You can save execution time and network traffic from the second invocation onwards because you are using the `PreparedStatement` object.

CallableStatement

For a secure, consistent, and manageable multi-tier client/server system, the data access should allow the use of stored procedures. Stored procedures centralize the business logic in terms of manageability and also in terms of running the query. Java applets running on clients with limited resources cannot be expected to run huge queries. But the results are important to those clients. JDBC allows the use of stored procedures by the `CallableStatement` class and with the escape clause string.

A `CallableStatement` object is created by the `prepareCall()` method in the `Connection` object. The `prepareCall()` method takes a string as the parameter. This string, called an escape clause, is of the form

```
{[? =] call <stored procedure name> [<parameter>,<parameter> ...]}
```

The `CallableStatement` class supports parameters. These parameters are of the `OUT` kind from a stored procedure or the `IN` kind to pass values into a stored procedure. The parameter marker (question mark) must be used for the return value (if any) and any output arguments because the parameter marker is bound to a program variable in the stored procedure. Input arguments can be either literals or parameters. For a dynamic parameterized statement, the escape clause string takes the form

```
{[? =] call <stored procedure name> [<?>,<?> ...]}
```

The `OUT` parameters should be registered using the `registerOutparameter()` method (see Table 40.4) before the call to the `executeQuery()`, `executeUpdate()`, or `execute()` methods.

Table 40.4 *CallableStatement—OUT* Parameter Register Methods

Return Type	Method Name	Parameter
`void`	`registerOutParameter`	`(int parameterIndex, int sqlType)`
`void`	`registerOutParameter`	`(int parameterIndex, int sqlType, int scale)`

After the stored procedure is executed, the DBMS returns the result value to the JDBC driver. This return value is accessed by the Java program using the methods in Table 40.5.

Table 40.5 *CallableStatement* Parameter Access Methods

Return Type	Method Name	Parameter
boolean	getBoolean	(int parameterIndex)
byte	getByte	(int parameterIndex)
byte[]	getBytes	(int parameterIndex)
java.sql.Date	getDate	(int parameterIndex)
double	getDouble	(int parameterIndex)
float	getFloat	(int parameterIndex)
int	getInt	(int parameterIndex)
long	getLong	(int parameterIndex)
java.lang.Bignum	getBignum	(int parameterIndex, int scale)
Object	getObject	(int parameterIndex)
short	getShort	(int parameterIndex)
String	getString	(int parameterIndex)
java.sql.Time	getTime	(int parameterIndex)
java.sql.Timestamp	getTimestamp	(int parameterIndex)
Miscellaneous Functions		
boolean	wasNull	()

If a student wants to find out the grades for a subject, in the database schema shown in Chapter 39, you need to do many operations on various tables, such as find all assignments for the student, match them with class name, calculate grade points, and so on. This is a business logic well-suited for a stored procedure. In this example, you give the stored procedure a student ID and class ID, and it returns the grade. Your client program becomes simple, and all the processing is done at the server. This is where you will use a `CallableStatement`.

The stored procedure call is of the form

```
studentGrade = getStudentGrade(StudentID,ClassID)
```

In the JDBC call, you create a `CallableStatement` object with the `?` symbol as a placeholder for parameters, and then connect Java variables to the parameters as shown in Listing 40.3.

Listing 40.3 Displaying the Grade with a *CallableStatement*

```
public void DisplayGrade(String StudentID, String ClassID) throws SQLException {
    int Grade;
    //Initialize and load the JDBC-ODBC driver.
    Class.forName ("jdbc.odbc.JdbcOdbcDriver");
```

continues

Listing 40.3 Continued

```
    //Make the connection object.
    Connection Con = DriverManager.getConnection(
➥"jdbc:odbc:StudentDB;uid="admin";pw="sa");

    //Create a Callable Statement object.
    CallableStatement CStmt = Con.prepareCall({?=call getStudentGrade[?,?]});

    // Now tie the placeholders with actual parameters.
    // Register the return value from the stored procedure
    // as an integer type so that the driver knows how to handle it.
    // Note the type is defined in the java.sql.Types.
    CStmt.registerOutParameter(1,java.sql.Types.INTEGER);

    // Set the In parameters (which are inherited from the
    // PreparedStatement class)
    CStmt.setString(1,StudentID);
    CStmt.setString(2,ClassID);

    // Now we are ready to call the stored procedure
    int RetVal = CStmt.executeUpdate();

    // Get the OUT parameter from the registered parameter
    // Note that we get the result from the CallableStatement object
    Grade = CStmt.getInt(1);

    // And display the results on the console.
    System.out.println(" The Grade is : ");
    System.out.println(Grade);
}
```

As you can see, JDBC has minimized the complexities of getting results from a stored procedure. It still is a little involved, but is simpler. Maybe in the future these steps will become even more simple.

Now that you have seen how to communicate with the underlying DBMS with SQL, let's see what you need to do to process the results sent back from the database as a result of the SQL statements.

ResultSet Processing Retrieving Results

The `ResultSet` object is actually a tubular data set; that is, it consists of rows of data organized in uniform columns. In JDBC, the Java program can see only one row of data at one time. The program uses the `next()` method to go to the next row. JDBC does not provide any methods to move backwards along the `ResultSet` or to remember the row positions (called bookmarks in ODBC). After the program has a row, it can use the positional index (1 for the first column, 2 for the second column, and so on) or the column name to get the field value by using the `getXXXX()` methods. Table 40.6 shows the methods associated with the `ResultSet` object.

Table 40.6 *java.sql.ResultSet* Methods

Return Type	Method Name	Parameter
boolean	next	()
void	close	()
boolean	wasNull	()
Get Data By Column Position		
java.io.InputStream	getAsciiStream	(int columnIndex)
java.io.InputStream	getBinaryStream	(int columnIndex)
boolean	getBoolean	(int columnIndex)
byte	getByte	(int columnIndex)
byte[]	getBytes	(int columnIndex)
java.sql.Date	getDate	(int columnIndex)
double	getDouble	(int columnIndex)
float	getFloat	(int columnIndex)
int	getInt	(int columnIndex)
long	getLong	(int columnIndex)
java.lang.Bignum	getBignum	(int columnIndex, int scale)
Object	getObject	(int columnIndex)
short	getShort	(int columnIndex)
String	getString	(int columnIndex)
java.sql.Time	getTime	(int columnIndex)
java.sql.Timestamp	getTimestamp	(int columnIndex)
java.io.InputStream	getUnicodeStream	(int columnIndex)
Get Data By Column Name		
java.io.InputStream	getAsciiStream	(String columnName)
java.io.InputStream	getBinaryStream	(String columnName)
boolean	getBoolean	(String columnName)
byte	getByte	(String columnName)
byte[]	getBytes	(String columnName)
java.sql.Date	getDate	(String columnName)
double	getDouble	(String columnName)

continues

Table 40.6 Continued

Return Type	Method Name	Parameter
Get Data By Column Name (continued)		
float	getFloat	(String columnName)
int	getInt	(String columnName)
long	getLong	(String columnName)
java.lang.Bignum	getBignum	(String columnName, int scale)
Object	getObject	(String columnName)
short	getShort	(String columnName)
String	getString	(String columnName)
java.sql.Time	getTime	(String columnName)
java.sql.Timestamp	getTimestamp	(String columnName)
java.io.InputStream	getUnicodeStream	(String columnName)
int	findColumn	(String columnName)
SQLWarning	getWarnings	()
void	clearWarnings	()
String	getCursorName	()
ResultSetMetaData	getMetaData	()

As you can see, the `ResultSet` methods—even though there are many—are very simple. The major ones are the `getXXX()` methods. The `getMetaData()` method returns the metadata information about a `ResultSet`. The `DatabaseMetaData` also returns the results in the `ResultSet` form. The `ResultSet` also has methods for the silent `SQLWarnings`. It is a good practice to check any warnings using the `getWarning()` method that returns a `null` if there are no warnings.

Other JDBC Classes

Now that you have seen all of the main database-related classes, look at some of the supporting classes that are available in JDBC. These classes include the `Date`, `Time`, `TimeStamp`, and so on. Most of these classes extend the basic Java classes to add capability to handle and translate data types that are specific to SQL.

java.sql.Date

This package (see Table 40.7) gives a Java program the capability to handle SQL `DATE` information with only year, month, and day values.

Table 40.7 *java.sql.Date* Methods

Return Type	Method Name	Parameter
Date	Date	(int year, int month, int day)
Date	Date	(long date)
Date	valueOf	(String s)
String	toString	()
int	getHours	()
int	getMinutes	()
int	getSeconds	()
void	setHours	(int Hr)
void	setMinutes	(int Min)
void	setSeconds	(int Sec)
void	setTime	(long date)

java.sql.Time

As seen in Table 40.8, the `java.sql.Time` adds the `Time` object to the `java.util.Date` package to handle only hours, minutes, and seconds. `java.sql.Time` is also used to represent SQL `Time` information.

Table 40.8 *java.sql.Time* Methods

Return Type	Method Name	Parameter
Time	Time	(int hour, int minute, int second)
Time	Time	(long time)
Time	Time	valueOf(String s)
String	toString	()
int	getDate	()
int	getDay	()
int	getMonth	()
int	getYear	()
void	setDate	(int date)
void	setMonth	(int month)
void	setTime	(int time)
void	setYear	(int year)

java.sql.Timestamp

The `java.sql.Timestamp` package adds the `TimeStamp` class to the `java.util.Date` package (see Table 40.9). It adds the capability of handling nanoseconds. But the granularity of the subsecond timestamp depends on the database field as well as the operating system.

Table 40.9 *java.sql.Timestamp* Methods

Return Type	Method Name	Parameter
`TimeStamp`	`TimeStamp`	`(int year, int month, int date, int hour, int minute, int second, int nano)`
`TimeStamp`	`TimeStamp`	`(long time)`
`TimeStamp`	`valueOf`	`(String s)`
`String`	`toString`	`()`
`int`	`getNanos`	`()`
`void`	`setNanos`	`(int n)`
`boolean`	`after`	`(TimeStamp ts)`
`boolean`	`before`	`(TimeStamp ts)`
`boolean`	`equals`	`(TimeStamp ts)`

java.sql.Types

This class defines a set of `XOPEN` equivalent integer constants that identify SQL types. The constants are final types. Therefore, they cannot be redefined in applications or applets. Table 40.10 lists the constant names and their values.

Table 40.10 *java.sql.Types* Constants

Constant Name	Value
`BIGINT`	-5
`BINARY`	-2
`BIT`	-7
`CHAR`	1
`DATE`	91
`DECIMAL`	3
`DOUBLE`	8
`FLOAT`	6

Constant Name	Value
INTEGER	4
LONGVARBINARY	-4
LONGVARCHAR	-1
NULL	0
NUMERIC	2
OTHER	1111
REAL	7
SMALLINT	5
TIME	92
TIMESTAMP	93
TINYINT	-6
VARBINARY	-3
VARCHAR	12

java.sql.DataTruncation

This class provides methods for getting details when a `DataTruncation` warning or exception is thrown by an SQL statement. The data truncation could happen to a column value or parameter.

The main elements of a `DataTruncation` object are

- Index gives the column or parameter number.
- `parameter` flag `true` if the truncation is on a parameter and `false` if the truncation is on a column.
- `read` flag `true` if the truncation is during a read and `false` if the truncation is on a write.

The `DataTruncation` object also consists of a datasize element that has the actual size (in bytes) of the truncated value and the transfer size, which is the number of bytes actually transferred.

The various methods, as listed in Table 40.11, let the Java program retrieve the values of these elements. For example, the `getRead()` method returns `true` if data truncation occurred during a read and a `false` if the truncation occurred during a write.

Table 40.11 *java.sql.DataTruncation* Methods

Return Type	Method Name	Parameter
`int`	`getDataSize`	`()`
`int`	`getIndex`	`()`
`boolean`	`getParameter`	`()`
`boolean`	`getRead`	`()`
`int`	`getTransferSize`	`()`

JDBC in Perspective

JDBC is an important step in the right direction to elevate the Java language to the Java platform. The Java APIs—including the Enterprise APIs (JDBC, RMI, Serialization, and IDL), Security APIs, and the Server APIs—are the essential ingredients for developing enterprise-level, distributed, multi-tier client/server applications.

The JDBC specification life cycle happened in the speed of the Net—one Net year is widely clocked as equaling seven normal years. The JDBC specification is fixed, so the developers and driver vendors are not chasing a moving target.

JDBC Compliant

Sun has instituted the JDBC Compliant certification for drivers. A particular driver will be called JDBC Compliant if it passes JDBC compliance tests developed by Sun and Intersolv. At present, a driver should support at least ANSI SQL92 Entry Level to pass the compliance tests.

The JDBC Compliant certification is very useful for developers because they can confidently develop applications using JDBC and can be assured database access (in client machines) with JDBC Compliant drivers.

Another factor in favor of JDBC is its similarity to ODBC. Sun made the right decision to follow ODBC philosophy and abstractions, thus making it easy for ISVs and users to leverage their ODBC experience and existing ODBC drivers. In the JDBC specification, this goal is described as "JDBC must be implementable on top of common database interfaces."

By making JDBC a part of the Java language, you received all of the advantages of the Java language concepts for database access. Also, because all implementers have to support the Java APIs, JDBC has become a universal standard. This philosophy, stated in the JDBC specification as "provide a Java interface that is consistent with the rest of the Java system," makes JDBC an ideal candidate for use in Java-based database development.

Another good design philosophy is the driver independence of the JDBC. The underlying database drivers can either be native libraries—such as a DLL for the Windows system or Java routines connecting to listeners. The full Java implementation of JDBC is suitable for a variety of network and other Java OS computers, thus making JDBC a versatile set of APIs.

NOTE In my humble opinion, the most important advantage of JDBC is its simplicity and versatility. The goal of the designers was to keep the API and common cases simple and "support the weird stuff in separate interfaces." Also, they wanted to use multiple methods for multiple functionality. They have achieved their goals even in this first version.

For example, the `Statement` object has the `executeQuery()` method for SQL statements returning rows of data, and the `executeUpdate()` method for statements without data to return. Also, uncommon cases, such as statements returning multiple `ResultSets`, have a separate method: `execute()`.

As more applications are developed with JDBC, and as the Java platform matures, more and more features will be added to JDBC. One of the required features, especially for client/server processing, is a more versatile cursor. The current design leaves the cursor management details to the driver. I would prefer more application-level control for scrollable cursors, positioned update/delete capability, and so on. Another related feature is the bookmark feature, which is especially useful in a distributed processing environment such as the Internet.

PART VI

Component-Based Development

CHAPTER 41

JavaBeans

In this chapter

Self-Contained Components

JavaBeans adds to the Java platform the capability to create a complete application by simply linking together a set of self-contained components. Microsoft's Visual Basic and Borland's Delphi are both examples of applications that allow users to build full-blown applications by combining independent components. The success and popularity of these two applications alone speak volumes to the success of this style of application building.

Just as with other models, there is no restriction on the size or complexity of a JavaBeans component. In principle, JavaBeans components (or just Beans) can range from widgets and controls to containers and applications. The philosophy behind JavaBeans is to provide easy-to-implement functionality for the former, while allowing enough flexibility for the latter. In the spirit of this philosophy, you'll see how to create and use fairly simple Beans. However, after you finish reading this chapter, you'll have learned enough to create larger and more complex Beans, if you choose to do so. If you want to dive deeper into all the intricacies of JavaBeans, you might want to purchase a copy of Que's *Special Edition Using JavaBeans*, which goes into more detail on all the topics discussed in this chapter.

Important Concepts in Component Models

JavaBeans provides a platform-neutral component architecture. Examples of non-platform–neutral component architectures include COM/OLE for the Windows platform and OpenDoc for the Macintosh platform. A component written to be placed into an OpenDoc container, like ClarisWorks for example, can't be used inside a COM/OLE container like Microsoft Word. Because JavaBeans is architecture-neutral, Beans can be placed into any container for which a bridge exists between JavaBeans and the container's component architecture. Thus, a JavaBeans component could be used in both Microsoft Word and ClarisWorks. To accomplish this seemingly impossible feat, the JavaBeans specification adopts features common with the other popular component models. In particular, these features include the following:

- Component fields or properties
- Component methods or functions
- Events and intercommunication
- State persistence and storage

NOTE If you are familiar with component models already, you don't necessarily need to read this section. You can jump right into the next section, "The Basics of Designing a Java Bean."

Component Fields or Properties

For a component to be useful, it has to have a set of properties that define its state. For example, if you were to design a component that displayed some text, one of the properties of that component might be the foreground color of the font. Another property might be the type and size of the font. Taken as a whole, the set of properties that make up a component also define its state. For example, if the properties of one component completely match that of another, they are in the same state.

Properties are often used to define not only the appearance but also the behavior of components. This is because a component need not have any appearance at all. For example, a component in a spreadsheet might calculate the interest earned on some earnings column. If that component is not capable of displaying the data, then it probably shouldn't have any properties associated with appearance. It is likely, however, that it will have a property that defines the current interest rate.

Properties can range from Boolean values, to strings, to arrays, to other components. They can also be interdependent. Following the same example above, a component that displays the earnings column might want to be notified if the interest rate property of the other component changes.

Component Methods or Functions

The API, so to speak, of a component is the collection of methods or functions that it contains that other components and containers can call. There has to be some way for a container to modify a component's properties, notify it of an event (see below), or execute some functionality.

Different component models differ in how they make the properties and methods of their components available to other components. Because entire books have been written on how this is implemented for different models, suffice it to say that this is a common feature of component models. This topic will be discussed as it relates to JavaBeans in the section on Introspection later in the chapter.

Events and Intercommunication

A component by itself is a lonely component. Even though some components might have extensive functionality and many properties, in the true spirit of a component, it should only be useful when used in conjunction with other components. So if two components are sitting together in a container, how do they talk? How does one let the other know when it has done something the other really ought to know about?

The method by which most components communicate is through *event transmission*. One component (or the container) undergoes some action causing it to generate an event. For example, an event is generated when you click a button. Depending on the model, the component will notify the container, the interested components, or both, of the events. At the same time, the objects in the environment also act on events delivered to them. For example, the File dialog box displays itself when it hears that you just clicked a Browse button.

State Persistence and Storage

It is important for components to remember their state. This is so common that you may not even recognize it. When you open an application and it remembers the size and position of its window when it was last closed, it is maintaining (to some degree) a persistent state.

Also important is the capability to store and retrieve components. Sun Microsystems, Inc. likes to call this *packaging*. This is especially important in a distributed environment where the components are likely to be served up over a network.

The Basics of Designing a JavaBean

All good programmers recognize the importance of the design phase in programming. Thus, you'll start out by addressing how to design a Bean. As you will learn later, the way in which you design your Bean directly affects the way it behaves in containers. For example, the names you choose for the methods should follow specific design specifications. If you start from the beginning with these rules in mind, allowing your Bean to participate in Introspection does not require any additional programming on your part. Don't worry so much right now about what Introspection is; you'll get into that later.

Designing a Bean consists of the following steps:

1. Specifying the Bean's properties
2. Specifying the events the Bean generates or responds to
3. Defining which properties, methods, and events the Bean exposes to other Beans or to its container
4. Deciding miscellaneous issues, such as whether the Bean has its own Customization dialog box or whether it requires some prototypical state information

You'll start by designing some Beans. For the sake of a simple example, assume that you are developing two Beans; one Bean allows text to be entered into it, and the other displays some text. You can imagine how these Beans might be useful. By placing these two Beans into a container, you can use one to enter text that the other will then display. What types of properties do you think these Beans need to have? What events are these Beans interested in hearing about? What events do these Beans generate? Do these Beans expose all of their properties and events, or just some? At this point, you may not know the answers to these questions. The process is the important concept here; the details will become clearer as you progress through the chapter. Regardless, the first thing any Bean needs is a name. In this chapter, the sample Beans will be called `TextDisplayer` and `TextReader`.

Specifying the Bean's Properties

The `TextDisplayer` and `TextReader` Beans definitely need to have a property defining the text they hold. For example, say that the `TextDisplayer` Bean also contains properties defining the background color, the font, and the font color. The `TextReader` Bean also contains a property that defines how many columns of characters it can display. Table 41.1 lists the `TextDisplayer` Bean's properties and the Java types that will be used to implement them. Table 41.2 lists the `TextReader` Bean's properties and the Java types that will be used for them.

Table 41.1 The *TextDisplayer* Bean's Properties and Java Types

Property Name	Java Type
`OutputText`	`java.lang.String`
`BGColor`	`java.awt.Color`
`TextFont`	`java.awt.Font`
`FontColor`	`java.awt.Color`

Table 41.2 The *TextReader* Bean's Properties and Java Types

Property Name	Java Type
`InputText`	`java.lang.String`
`Width`	`int`

Specifying the Events the Bean Generates or Responds To

Our `TextDisplayer` Bean must respond to an event specifying that its text should change. Specifically, it must update its `OutputText` property and redraw itself. The `TextReader` Bean doesn't need to respond to any events, but it must generate (or fire) an event when the user changes its `InputText` property. This type of event is called a `PropertyChangeEvent`, for obvious reasons.

Properties, Methods, and Event Exposure

Because these Beans are particularly simple, you don't need to hide anything from the Beans' container or the other Beans interested in them. JavaBeans provides a mechanism for you that will use the names of your methods to extract the names and types of your properties and events. Rest assured that you will learn how this works as you go along. Later in the chapter, you'll learn how to explicitly define what information in a Bean is exposed to its environment.

Initial Property Values and Bean Customizers

You want to keep this example simple, so assume that your Beans do not need any prototypical information (you'll define default values for all their properties) and that they do not have their own Customization dialog box. This means that your Beans have a predefined state when they're instantiated and that they use the standard `PropertyEditors` for their properties. If you were designing a Bean that displays an HTML page, for example, specifying default values might not be possible. You would need to know what file to display when the Bean is instantiated. Table 41.3 shows your `TextDisplayer` Bean's properties and the default values it will hold. Likewise, Table 41.4 is for the `TextReader` Bean.

Table 41.3 Default Property Values for the *TextDisplayer* Bean

Property Name	Default Value
`TextOutput`	`"TextDisplayer"`
`BGColor`	`java.awt.Color.white`
`TextFont`	`Courier, normal, 12`
`FontColor`	`java.awt.Color.black`

Table 41.4 Default Property Values for the *TextReader* Bean

Property Name	Default Value
`TextInput`	`""` (an empty string)
`Width`	`40`

At this point, you've designed your Beans enough to begin coding. This will be an additive process because you haven't learned how to make the Beans do anything yet. All the code required to actually display the Beans isn't included in Listings 41.1 and 41.2 because it's mainly AWT-related and isn't relevant to this chapter. If you want to see the entire listings, please refer to the CD-ROM. In Figure 41.1 you can see your Beans hard at work inside the BeanBox. The BeanBox is a JavaBeans container that you can download from Sun's Web site; it's included in the BDK, or Beans Development Kit. Right now, the Beans are completely isolated. Because you haven't given the Beans any functionality yet, this is about as good as it gets. The preliminary code needed to instantiate our `TextDisplayer` Bean is shown in Listing 41.1.

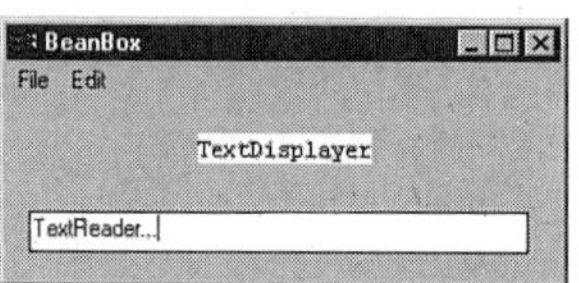

FIG. 41.1 Sun's BeanBox showing the `TextDisplayer` and `TextReader` Beans.

Listing 41.1 *TextDisplayer.java*—Preliminary Code for the *TextDisplayer* Bean

```
public class TextDisplayer extends Canvas implements PropertyChangeListener {
   // default constructor for this Bean.  This is the constructor that an
   // application builder (like Visual Basic) would use.
   public TextDisplayer() {
      this( "TextDisplayer", Color.white, new Font( "Courier", Font.PLAIN, 12 ),
            Color.black );
   }
```

```
   // custom constructor for this Bean.  This is the constructor you would
   // likely use if you were going to do all your coding from scratch.
   public TextDisplayer( String OutputText, Color BGColor, Font TextFont,
                         Color FontColor ) {
      super(); // call the Canvas's constructor.
      this.OutputText = OutputText;
      this.BGColor = BGColor;
      this.TextFont = TextFont;
      this.FontColor = FontColor;

      setFont( TextFont );          // set the Canvas's font.
      setBackground( BGColor );     // set the Canvas's background color.
      setForeground( FontColor ); // set the Canvas's foreground color.
   }

   // this Bean's properties.
   protected String OutputText;
   protected Color BGColor, FontColor;
   protected Font TextFont;
}
```

You might have noticed you have specified that your Bean implement an interface called `PropertyChangeListener`. This is so that the `TextDisplayer` Bean can update its `OutputText` property by receiving an event. How that works will be discussed in more detail later in the chapter. The preliminary code needed to instantiate your `TextReader` Bean is shown in Listing 41.2.

Listing 41.2 ***TextReader.java*—Preliminary Code for the *TextReader* Bean**

```
public class TextReader extends TextField {
   // default constructor for this Bean.  This is the constructor that an
   // application builder (like Visual Basic) would use.
   public TextReader() {
      this( "", 40 );
   }

   // custom constructor for this Bean.  This is the constructor that you would
   // likely use if you were doing your coding from scratch.
   public TextReader( String InputText, int Width ) {
      super( InputText, Width );
      this.InputText = InputText;
      this.Width = Width;
      setEditable( true );
   }

   // this Bean's properties.
   protected String InputText;
   protected int Width;
}
```

Creating and Using Properties

In Figure 41.1, you will notice that the `TextDisplayer` Bean displayed itself with a white background and black text. It did so because that's how you set its properties. If you had set the `FontColor` property to `red`, it would have displayed the text in red. If the properties of a component cannot be changed by other Beans, the usefulness of the Bean is reduced, as well as the reusability. For example, if you used the `TextDisplayer` Bean in an accounting package, you would need to change the Bean's `FontColor` property to `red` to indicate a negative value. So how do you let other Beans know that they can set (or read) this property? If you're coding from scratch, you can look at the documentation for the Bean. But what if you're in an application builder? Luckily, there's a way to do this without incurring any extra coding on your part. You'll see how that works a little later.

Two types of properties are supported by JavaBeans: single-value and indexed. In addition, properties can also be bound or constrained. A single-value property is a property for which there is only one value. As the name suggests, an indexed property has several values, each of which has a unique index. If a property is bound, it means that some other Bean is dependent on that property. In the continuing example, the `TextReader` Bean's `InputText` property is bound to our `TextDisplayer` Bean; the `TextReader` must notify the `TextReader` after its `InputText` field changes. A property is constrained if it must check with other components before it can change. Note that constrained properties cannot change arbitrarily—one or more components may not allow the updated value.

Single-Value Properties

All properties are accessed by calling methods on the owning Bean's object. Readable properties have a `getter` method used to read the value of the property. Writable properties have a `setter` method used to change the value of a property. These methods are not constrained to simply returning the value of the property; they can also perform calculations and return some other value. All the properties our Beans have are single-value.

At this point, you're ready to start talking about Introspection. The method by which other components learn of your Bean's properties depends on a few things. In general, though, this process is called Introspection. In fact, the class `java.beans.Introspector` is the class that provides this information for other components. The `Introspector` class traverses the class hierarchy of a particular Bean. If it finds explicit information provided by the Bean, it uses that. However, it uses design patterns to implicitly extract information from those Beans that do not provide information. Note that this is what happens for your Beans. Specific design rules should be applied when defining accessor methods so that the `Introspector` class can do its job. If you choose to use other names, you can still expose a Bean's properties, but it requires you to supply a `BeanInfo` class. For more about what a `BeanInfo` class is, see the section on Introspection. Here are the design patterns you should use:

```
public void set<PropertyName>( <PropertyType> value );
public <PropertyType> get<PropertyName>();
public boolean is<PropertyName>();
```

Note that the last pattern is an alternative `getter` method for Boolean properties only. `setter` methods are allowed to throw exceptions if they so choose. The accessor methods for the `TextDisplayer` Bean are shown in Listing 41.3. Notice that all the accessor methods have been declared as synchronized. Even though nothing serious could happen in this Bean, you should always assume that your Beans are running in multithreaded environments. Using synchronized accessor methods helps prevent race conditions from forming. You can check the `TextReader.java` file on your CD-ROM to see the accessor methods for the `TextReader` Bean.

Listing 41.3 *TEXTDISPLAYER.JAVA*—The Accessor Methods for the Properties in the *TextDisplayer* Bean

```
public synchronized String getOutputText() {
   return( OutputText );
}

public synchronized void setOutputText( String text ) {
   OutputText = text;
   resizeCanvas();
}

public synchronized Color getBGColor() {
   return( BGColor );
}

public synchronized void setBGColor( Color color ) {
   BGColor = color;
   setBackground( BGColor );   // set the Canvas's background color.
   repaint();
}

public synchronized Font getTextFont() {
   return( TextFont );
}

public synchronized void setTextFont( Font font ) {
   TextFont = font;
   setFont( TextFont );        // set the Canvas's font.
   resizeCanvas();
}

public synchronized Color getFontColor() {
   return( FontColor );
}

public synchronized void setFontColor( Color color ) {
   FontColor = color;
   setForeground( FontColor ); // set the Canvas's foreground color.
   repaint();
}
```

Figure 41.2 shows you what the property sheet of Sun's BeanBox shows for your `TextDisplayer` Bean. Notice that you can see the properties of the parent class, too. Your Bean inherits from `java.awt.Canvas`, which inherits from `java.awt.Component`, which inherits from `java.lang.Object`. The additional properties that you see are from the `java.awt.Component` class. This illustrates the principal drawback of using the automatic JavaBeans Introspection methods. In your own Beans, this might be the motivation for providing a `BeanInfo` class. Again, more on that is in the section on Introspection.

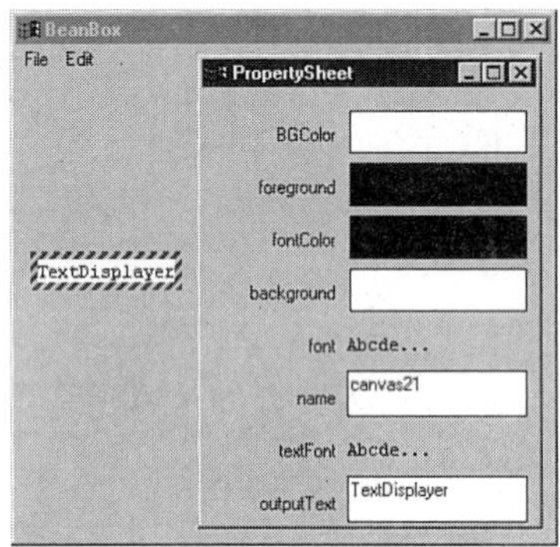

FIG. 41.2 The `PropertySheet` of Sun's BeanBox showing the Bean's exposed properties. Notice the properties of the parent class.

Indexed Properties

All indexed properties must be Java integers. Indexed properties can be read individually or as an entire array. The design patterns for indexed properties are as follows:

```
public <PropertyType> get<PropertyName>( int index );
public void set<PropertyName>( int index, <PropertyType> value );
public <PropertyType>[] get<PropertyName>();
public void set<PropertyName>( <PropertyType>[] value );
```

To illustrate, assume there is a `Meal` property that consists of an array of `Courses`:

```
public Course getMeal( int course);
public void setMeal( int course, Course dish );
public Course[] getMeal();
public void setMeal( Course[] dishes );
```

Bound Properties

As the programmer, you can decide which of your Bean's properties other components can bind to. To provide bound properties in your Beans, you must define the following methods:

```
public void addPropertyChangeListener( PropertyChangeListener l );
public void removePropertyChangeListener( PropertyChangeListener l );
```

To provide this functionality on a per-property basis, the following design pattern should be used:

```
public void add<PropertyName>Listener( PropertyChangeListener l );
public void remove<PropertyName>Listener( PropertyChangeListener l );
```

Beans wanting to bind to other components' properties should implement the `PropertyChangeListener` interface, which consists of the following method:

```
public void propertyChange( PropertyChangeEvent evt );
```

Whenever a bound property in a Bean is updated, it must call the `propertyChange()` method in all the components that have registered with it. The class `java.beans.PropertyChangeSupport` is provided to help you with this process. The code in Listing 41.4 shows you what is required in the `TextReader` Bean to allow its `InputText` property to be bound.

Listing 41.4. *TEXTREADER.JAVA*—Code Required to Make the *InputText* Property of the *TextReader* Bean a Bound Property

```
   // setter method for the InputText property.
   public synchronized void setInputText( String newText ) {
      String oldText = InputText;
      InputText = newText;
      setText( InputText );
      changeAgent.firePropertyChange( "inputText", new String( oldText ),
                                      new String( newText ) );
   }

   // these two methods allow this Bean to have bound properties.
   public void addPropertyChangeListener( PropertyChangeListener l ) {
      changeAgent.addPropertyChangeListener( l );
   }

   public void removePropertyChangeListener( PropertyChangeListener l ) {
      changeAgent.removePropertyChangeListener( l );
   }

   protected PropertyChangeSupport changeAgent = new PropertyChangeSupport( this
);
```

Constrained Properties

The process for providing constrained properties in your code is also fairly straightforward. You must define the following methods in your Bean:

```
public void addVetoableChangeListener( VetoableChangeListener l );
public void removeVetoableChangeListener( VetoableChangeListener l );
```

Just as with bound properties, you can make individual properties constrained using the following design pattern:

```
public void add<PropertyName>Listener( VetoableChangeListener l );
public void remove<PropertyName>Listener( VetoableChangeListener l );
```

Beans intended to constrain other components' properties should implement the `VetoableChangeListener` interface, which consists of the following method:

```
public void vetoableChange( PropertyChangeEvent evt );
```

Whenever a constrained property in a Bean is updated, it must call the `vetoableChange()` method in all the components that have registered with it. There is also a support class to help make this process easier. Use the class `java.beans.VetoableChangeSupport` to help manage your `vetoable` properties. The code in Listing 41.5 shows you what is required in the `TextReader` Bean to allow its `Width` property to be constrained.

Listing 41.5 *TEXTREADER.JAVA*—Code Required to Make the *Columns* Property of the *TextReader* Bean a Constrained Property

```
// setter method for the Columns property.
   public synchronized void setWidth( int newWidth )
   throws PropertyVetoException {
      int oldWidth = Width;
      vetoAgent.fireVetoableChange( "width", new Integer( oldWidth ),
                                    new Integer( newWidth ) );
      // no one vetoed, so change the property.
      Width = newWidth;
      setColumns( Width );
      Component p = getParent();
      if ( p != null ) {
         p.invalidate();
         p.layout();
      }
      changeAgent.firePropertyChange( "width", new Integer( oldWidth ),
                                      new Integer( newWidth ) );
   }

   // these two methods allow this Bean to have constrained properties.
   public void addVetoableChangeListener( VetoableChangeListener l ) {
      vetoAgent.addVetoableChangeListener( l );
   }

   public void removeVetoableChangeListener( VetoableChangeListener l ) {
      vetoAgent.removeVetoableChangeListener( l );
   }

   protected VetoableChangeSupport vetoAgent = new VetoableChangeSupport( this
);
```

In this particular example, we chose to make the `Width` property bound and constrained. A property does not have to be bound to be constrained. For example, to make the `Width` property constrained but not bound, we would remove the following line from Listing 41.5:

```
changeAgent.firePropertyChange( "width", new Integer( oldWidth ),
                                new Integer( newWidth ) );
```

Using Events to Communicate with Other Components

The whole idea behind the JavaBeans component model is to provide a way to create reusable components. To do this, Beans must be able to communicate with the other Beans in their environment and with their container. This is accomplished by means of `Listener` interfaces. You've already seen some of this with the `PropertyChangedEvent` from the last section. More detail about how this works follows.

Beans use the same event-handling scheme as AWT. This means that if your Bean needs to hear about events coming from another Bean, it must register itself with that Bean. To do this, it must implement the `Listener` interface for the event of interest. At the same time, if your Bean is no longer interested in hearing about some other Bean's event, it must unregister itself with that Bean. Any event that a Bean wants to fire must inherit from the `java.util.EventObject` class. For simple events, the `java.util.EventObject` class itself could be used; however, as with `java.lang.Exception`, using child classes provides clarity and is preferred. All `Listener` interfaces must inherit from the `java.util.EventListener` interface, and the same subclassing convention applies. The event handling method of a `Listener` interface should follow the design pattern for Introspection as shown here:

```
void <EventOccuranceName>( <EventObjectType evt );
```

Note that `<EventObjectType>` must inherit from `java.util.EventObject`. Here is an example of an event handler for a `DinnerServedListener` interface:

```
void dinnerServed( DinnerServedEvent evt ); // DinnerServedEvent inherits from
                                            // java.util.EventObject.
```

There is no restriction preventing an event handler method from throwing an exception. In addition, any one `Listener` interface can have any number of related event handlers.

There are two types of events that components can listen for: multicast events and unicast events.

Multicast Events

Multicast events are the most common types of events. The `PropertyChangeEvent`, which you have already been exposed to, is a multicast event because there can be any number of listeners. In that example, you had `addPropertyChangeListener()` and `removePropertyChangeListener()` methods, which allowed other components to register with the Bean as being interested in hearing when a bound property changed. The process is the same for any other type of multicast event, and the registration methods should follow the design pattern for Introspection as shown here:

```
public synchronized void add<ListenerType>( <ListenerType> listener );
public synchronized void remove<ListenerType>( <ListenerType> listener );
```

The keyword `synchronized` is not actually part of the design pattern. It is included as a reminder that race conditions can occur, especially with the event model, and precautions must be taken.

Unicast Events

Unicast events don't occur nearly as often as their counterpart, but they're just as useful. Unicast events can have only one listener. If additional components attempt to listen to the unicast event, a `java.util.TooManyListenersException` will be thrown. The following design pattern should be used when declaring unicast events:

```
public synchronized void add<ListenerType>( <ListenerType> listener ) throws
                                java.util.TooManyListenersException;
public synchronized void remove<ListenerType>( <ListenerType> listener );
```

Event Adapters

In some cases, it may be necessary to build an event adapter class that can transfer an event to a component. This comes into play especially for an application builder because the application doesn't know until runtime how the components will be linked together or how they will interact with each other's events.

An event adapter intervenes in the normal event-handling scheme by intercepting the events normally meant for another component. For example, assume that a user places a button and a text box in an application builder. If the user wants the text box to fill with the word "Pressed" when the button is pressed, the application builder can use an event adapter to call a method containing the user-generated code needed to do it. Here's how it will eventually work:

1. The event adapter registers with the event source. In other words, it calls an `addSomeEventListener()` method on the event source component.
2. The event source component fires an event by calling the event adapter's event-handler method, `someEvent()`. Keep in mind that the event source component doesn't care whether it's calling an event adapter. At this point, with the event fired, it can continue on with its business.
3. The event adapter calls the specific user-designed method on the final target component.
4. The code in the user-designed method fills in the text box component with the "Pressed" text.

Sometimes it helps to see some code. Listing 41.6 contains some pseudocode you can examine to see how an event adapter is written. The code in the example builds off the procedure listed previously. You won't be able to compile this code (notice the class keywords have been changed to pseudoclass), but it serves as an example you can build off of in your own Beans.

Listing 41.6. *ADAPTOREXAMPLE.JAVA*—Pseudocode Showing How to Implement an Adapter Class; This Code Might Be Generated by an Application Builder

```
// this pseudoclass example uses a unicast mechanism to keep things simple.

public interface SomeEventListener extends java.util.EventListener {
   public someEvent( java.util.EventObject e );
}

public pseudoclass button extends java.awt.Button {
   public void synchronized addSomeEventListener( SomeEventListener l )
                                throws java.util.TooManyListenersException {
      if ( listener != null ) {
         listener = l;
      } else throw new java.util.TooManyListenersException;
   }

   private void fireSomeEvent() {
      listener.someEvent( new java.util.EventObject( this ) );
   }

   private SomeEventListener listener = null;
}

public pseudoclass eventAdaptor implements SomeEventListener {
   public eventAdaptor( TargetObject target ) {
      this.target = target;
   }

   someEvent( java.util.EventObject e ) {
      // transfer the event to the user generated method.
      target.userDefinedMethod();
   }

   private TargetObject target;
}

public pseudoclass TargetObject {
   public TargetObject() {
      adaptor = new eventAdaptor( this );
   }

   public userDefinedMethod() {
     // user generated code goes here.
   }

   private eventAdaptor adaptor;
}
```

Introspection: Creating and Using *BeanInfo* Classes

You've already seen in the preceding sections and in the two Beans you designed how to use design patterns to facilitate automatic Introspection. You also saw that the automatic Introspection mechanism isn't perfect. If you look back at Figure 41.2, you'll see an example of this. Introspection is probably the most important aspect of JavaBeans because without it a container can't do anything with a Bean other than display it. As you become proficient at designing your own Beans, you'll find that you sometimes need to provide additional Introspection information for the users of your Beans. In the case of your Beans, this is to hide the parent class's properties to clear up ambiguities.

The `java.beans.Introspector` class, as discussed earlier in the chapter, does all the pattern analysis to expose the properties, methods, and events that a component has. As a first step, though, this class looks to see whether a `BeanInfo` class is defined for the Bean it's inspecting. If it finds one, it doesn't do any pattern analysis on the areas of the Bean for which the `BeanInfo` class supplies information. This means that you can selectively choose which information you want to provide and which information you want to be derived from analysis. To show how this is done, you'll design a `BeanInfo` class for our `TextDisplayer` Bean.

The first thing you need to do is define what information you'll provide and what you'll leave up to the `Introspector` class to analyze. For the sake of example, say that you'll choose to provide the properties of your Bean, and you'll let the `Introspector` class use analysis to expose the events and methods. Table 41.5 shows the names of the `TextDisplayer` Bean's properties and the user-friendly names you want to display. With that information defined, you can start working on your `BeanInfo` class, `TextDisplayerBeanInfo.class`. Notice how you simply appended "BeanInfo" to the class name. That's an Introspection design pattern; the `Introspector` class looks for `BeanInfo` information by appending "BeanInfo" to the class name of the Bean it's currently analyzing.

Table 41.5 The *TextDisplayer* Bean's Properties and User-Friendly Names

Property Name	User-Friendly Name
`OutputText`	`"Text String"`
`BGColor`	`"Background Color"`
`TextFont`	`"Text Font"`
`FontColor`	`"Text Color"`

All `BeanInfo` classes must implement the `java.beans.BeanInfo` interface. At first glance, that seems difficult; there are eight methods in the `java.beans.BeanInfo` interface! But remember the `Introspector` class has a set procedure for the way it looks for information. For the sake of clarity, that procedure is shown in the following list:

1. The `Introspector` class looks for a `BeanInfo` class for the Bean it's analyzing.
2. If a `BeanInfo` class is present, each method in the `BeanInfo` class is called to find out whether it can provide any information. The `Introspector` class will use implicit analysis to expose information for which the `BeanInfo` class denies any knowledge (returns a `null` value). If no `BeanInfo` class is found, the `Introspector` class will use implicit analysis for all the methods in the `java.beans.BeanInfo interface`.
3. The `Introspector` class then checks to see whether it has obtained explicit information for each of the methods in the `BeanInfo` interface. If it has not, it steps into the parent class (if one exists) and starts the process over for only those methods that it had to use analysis on.
4. When the `Introspector` class has gotten information from a `BeanInfo` class for all the methods in the `java.beans.BeanInfo` interface, or when there are no more parent classes to explore, the `Introspector` class returns its results.

To make your life easier as a programmer, Sun has provided a prebuilt class, `java.beans.SimpleBeanInfo`, that returns a `null` value for all the `BeanInfo` methods. That way, you can inherit from that class and override only the methods you choose. Listing 41.7 shows the `BeanInfo` class for the `TextDisplayer` Bean. Notice how you only override the `getPropertyDescriptors()` method. The parent class returns `null` for all the other methods in the `java.beans.BeanInfo` interface.

Listing 41.7 *TEXTDISPLAYERBEANINFO.JAVA*—The Entire *BeanInfo* Class for the *TextDisplayer* Bean Showing How to Provide Property Information

```
import java.beans.*;

public class TextDisplayerBeanInfo extends SimpleBeanInfo {
   // override the getPropertyDescriptors method to provide that info.
   public PropertyDescriptor[] getPropertyDescriptors() {
      PropertyDescriptor[] properties = new PropertyDescriptor[4];

      try {
         properties[0] = new PropertyDescriptor(
                      "Text String", BeanClass, "getOutputText",
➥"setOutputText" );
         properties[1] = new PropertyDescriptor(
                         "Text Color", BeanClass,
➥"getFontColor", "setFontColor" );
         properties[2] = new PropertyDescriptor(
                            "Text Font", BeanClass,
➥"getTextFont", "setTextFont" );
         properties[3] = new PropertyDescriptor(
                        "Background Color", BeanClass,
➥"getBGColor", "setBGColor" );
      } catch( IntrospectionException e ) {
         return( null ); // exit gracefully if we get an exception.
      }
```

continues

Listing 41.7 Continued

```
        return( properties );
    }

    private Class BeanClass = TextDisplayer.class;
}
```

Take a second to look at the try¦catch clause in Listing 41.7. Notice how you return a `null` value if you catch a `java.beans.IntrospectionException`. If you catch this exception, it usually means that you've provided an incorrect `getter` or `setter` method name. You should always return a `null` value if you catch this exception so that the `Introspector` class can still analyze your Bean. You should be able to extend this example to override the other methods in the `java.beans.BeanInfo` interface. Figure 41.3 shows the `PropertySheet` window of Sun's BeanBox for our `TextDisplayer` Bean. Notice how the user-friendly names for the properties have been used, and the parent class's properties are gone. Sweet success!

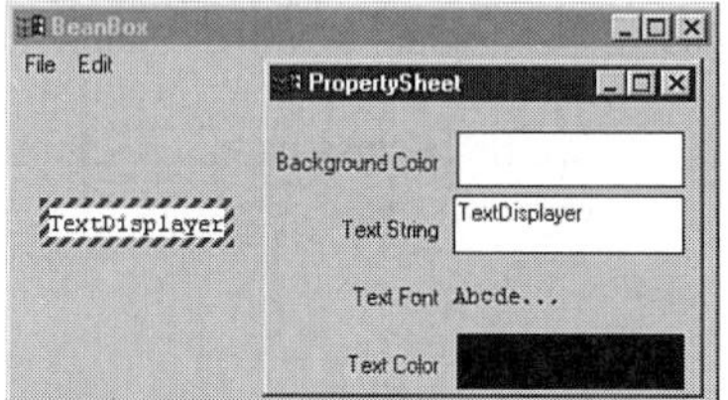

FIG. 41.3 The `PropertySheet` window of Sun's BeanBox showing the user-friendly names for the properties in the `TextDisplayer` Bean.

Customization: Providing Custom *PropertyEditors* and GUI Interfaces

So far you have seen how to create a Bean; how to expose its properties, methods, and events; and how to tweak the Introspection process. You might have noticed from the figures that the properties of a Bean have a `PropertyEditor`. For example, look at Figure 41.3. In the `PropertySheet` window, next to the `"Text String"` label, there's a `TextField` AWT component already filled with the value of the `OutputText` property. You didn't supply any code for this component, so how did Sun's BeanBox know to provide it? The answer is that the BeanBox application asked the `java.beans.PropertyEditorManager` what the default `PropertyEditor` was for an object of type `java.lang.String`, and displayed it.

Just because `PropertyEditors` and `Customizers` require a GUI environment doesn't mean a Bean can't function without one. For example, a Bean designed to run on a server might not use (or need) a GUI environment at all. The `java.beans.Beans` class and the `java.beans.Visibility` interface allow Beans to have different behavior in GUI and non-GUI environments.

PropertyEditors and the *PropertyEditorManager*

The class `java.beans.PropertyEditorManager` provides default `PropertyEditors` for the majority of the Java class types. So, if you use only native Java data types and objects, you're all set. But what if you design a Bean that has a property for which there's no default `PropertyEditor`? You'll run into this problem any time you design a custom property type. For those cases where there is no default `PropertyEditor`, you have to provide your own. Actually, you could redesign all the default `PropertyEditors`, too, if you choose, but you would only do this in rare cases, so this won't be discussed here. This means that you have to provide an additional class, by appending `Editor` to the class name, that the `PropertyEditorManager` can use. In most cases, you provide a subclass of `java.awt.Component`. The property sheet for your component will then pop up your custom `PropertyEditor` to allow your custom property to be edited. You won't actually design a custom `PropertyEditor` here because the majority of Beans won't require it, but an explanation of how to do it will be included. The requirements of a `PropertyEditor` are as follows:

1. Custom `PropertyEditors` must inherit from `java.awt.Component` so that they can be displayed in a property sheet. Note that this could simply mean inheriting from an AWT component like `java.awt.TextField`.
2. Custom `PropertyEditors` must derive their class name by postfixing `Editor` to the property class name unless they register themselves with the `PropertyEditorManager` for their container (see step 3). For example, the `PropertyEditor` for a custom property type `CustomProperty.class` must be named `CustomPropertyEditor.class`.
3. For custom `PropertyEditors` that do not follow the standard naming convention in step 2, the custom property type must register itself with the container's `PropertyEditorManager` by calling the `registerEditor()` method.
4. Custom `PropertyEditors` must always fire a `PropertyChange` event to update the custom property. This is a must! Otherwise, the container has no way of knowing to update the component.

You might be asking yourself, "Can I provide my own property sheet?" The answer is yes, and for complex Beans, this is absolutely imperative. Property sheets by nature are simple and relatively unuser-friendly. The following section discusses how to override the property sheet mechanism to provide your own customization dialog boxes.

Customization Editor

All application builders have to implement some method of customizing the Beans placed into their containers. Thus, the `PropertyEditor` mechanism and the idea of a property sheet were born. But what about the special cases where a Bean can be customized several different ways, or there are dozens of properties? The solution to this problem is called *customizers*. Bean developers can optionally supply customizer classes with their Beans to be used in place of standard property sheets. Even though the property sheet mechanism works just fine for the `TextReader` Bean, you'll create a customizer class anyway, to learn how it's done.

To implement a customizer class, a Bean must also provide a `BeanInfo` class. The class name of a Bean's customizer class is determined from a call to the `getBeanDescriptor()` method of the `java.beans.BeanInfo` interface. This is a little bit different from what you've encountered so far. There is no default Introspection design pattern for customizers; you must provide a `BeanInfo` class, even if the only information it provides is a `BeanDescriptor`. In fact, this is what you do for the `TextReaderBeanInfo.class` shown in Listing 41.8. Notice how the class inherits from `java.beans.SimpleBeanInfo`; the parent class implements the `java.beans.BeanInfo` class, and you simply override the `getBeanDescriptor()` method so that it returns something meaningful.

Listing 41.8 *TEXTREADERBEANINFO.JAVA*—The *BeanInfo* Class for the *TextReader* Bean Showing How to Provide Customizer Class Information

```
import java.beans.*;

public class TextReaderBeanInfo extends SimpleBeanInfo {
   // override the getBeanDescriptor method to provide a customizer.
   public BeanDescriptor getBeanDescriptor() {
      return( new BeanDescriptor( BeanClass, CustomizerClass ) );
   }

   private Class BeanClass = TextReader.class;
   private Class CustomizerClass = TextReaderCustomizer.class;
}
```

Although there isn't a design pattern for it, it's customary to name a customizer class by postfixing `Customizer` to the class name. Notice that you named the `TextReader` customizer `TextReaderCustomizer.class`. This is a good habit to get into.

The programmer has a tremendous amount of freedom when designing customizer classes. There are only two restrictions: The class must inherit from `java.awt.Component`, so that it can be placed in a `Panel` or `Dialog`, and it must implement the `java.beans.Customizer` interface. The customizer class is given a reference to the target component through a call to the `setObject()` method. After this point, what the customizer class does is its business, for the most part. Remember, though, that you'll be required (by the compiler) to acknowledge constrained properties because their accessor methods might throw `propertyVetoExceptions`. Finally, the `java.beans.Customizer` interface includes functionality for `PropertyChangeListeners`. Because the Bean's container may register itself as a listener with the customizer class, any property updates should be followed by a call to `firePropertyChange()`. The easiest way to do this is by using a `java.beans.PropertyChangeSupport` class as was done when discussing bound properties earlier.

Listing 41.9 shows most of the code for the `TextReaderCustomizer` class. Some of the AWT-specific code was removed for clarity. The full listing is available on the CD-ROM. Take a look at the `handleEvent()` method. This method is called by AWT when the user enters data. Notice how you were forced to catch `ProperyVetoExceptions` for the `setWidth()` accessor? You can also see how the `PropertyChangeListener` methods are used appropriately. Figure 41.4 shows what the customizer looks like when called up from within Sun's BeanBox.

Listing 41.9 *TEXTREADERCUSTOMIZER.JAVA*—The Code from *TextReaderCustomizer.java* Showing How to Implement a Customizer Class

```
public class TextReaderCustomizer extends Panel implements Customizer {
   public TextReaderCustomizer() {
      setLayout( new BorderLayout() );
   }

   public void setObject( Object target ) {
      component = (TextReader)target;
      // generate the User Interface (code removed for clarity)
   }

   public boolean handleEvent( Event event ) {
      if ( event.id == Event.KEY_RELEASE && event.target == InputText ) {
         String old_text = component.getInputText();
         String text = InputText.getText();
         component.setInputText( text );
         changeAgent.firePropertyChange( "inputText", old_text, text );
      } else if ( event.id == Event.KEY_RELEASE && event.target == Width ) {
         int old_width, width;
         old_width = component.getWidth();
         try {
            width = Integer.parseInt( Width.getText() );
            try {
               component.setWidth( width );
               changeAgent.firePropertyChange( "width",
➥new Integer( old_width ), new Integer( width ) );
            } catch( PropertyVetoException e ) {
               // do nothing... wait for acceptable data.
            }
         } catch( NumberFormatException e ) {
            // do nothing... wait for better data.
         }
      }
      return ( super.handleEvent( event ) );
   }

   public void addPropertyChangeListener( PropertyChangeListener l ) {
      changeAgent.addPropertyChangeListener( l );
   }

   public void removePropertyChangeListener(PropertyChangeListener l) {
      changeAgent.removePropertyChangeListener( l );
   }

   private TextReader component;
   private TextField InputText, Width;
   private PropertyChangeSupport changeAgent =
➥new PropertyChangeSupport( this );
}
```

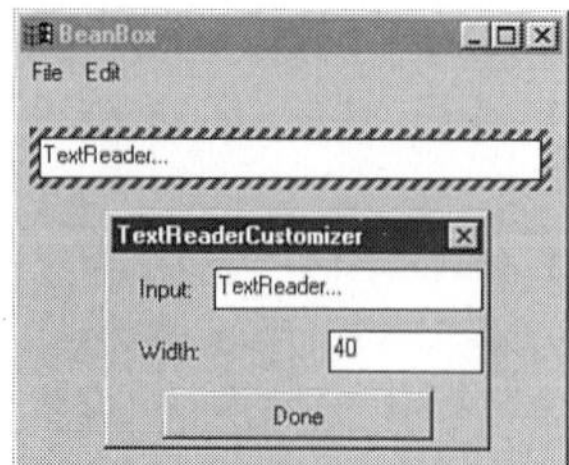

FIG. 41.4 Sun's BeanBox showing the `TextReader` Bean and its customizer dialog box.

Providing Alternative Behavior in Non-GUI Environments

Unfortunately, a GUI interface is not always available to a Bean. The most likely reason for this is that the Bean is being run in the background or on a server. Whatever the case, Beans that need to provide alternative or additional behavior in non-GUI environments can do so by using the `java.beans.Beans` class and the `java.beans.Visibility` interface.

The static methods `isDesignTime()` and `isGuiAvailable()` in the `java.beans.Beans` class can be used to check whether the Bean is being used in an application builder and a GUI environment is available. The method `isDesignTime()` returns `true` if the Bean is in an application builder and `false` if not. The method `isGuiAvailable()` returns `true` if a GUI environment is available to the Bean, and `false` if not.

Just because a GUI environment is available doesn't necessarily mean a container wants a Bean to use it. Similarly, a container might want to know whether a Bean isn't using the GUI environment, or even whether it needs one. A Bean and its container can communicate these things by implementing the `java.beans.Visibility` interface. The vast majority of Beans have no need for this interface, and it isn't necessary to implement it unless a Bean plans to use it. There are four methods in the interface:

```
public abstract boolean avoidingGui()
```

This method is called by a container to ask whether a Bean is currently avoiding the GUI environment. A Bean should return `true` for this method if it is actively avoiding the GUI environment. Notice that this is not the same as indicating that it doesn't need the GUI environment. For example, a container might use this information to free up resources being used by the GUI environment if a call to this method returns `true`.

```
public abstract void dontUseGui()
```

This method is called by the container to tell the Bean that even though a GUI environment may be available, the Bean shouldn't use it. For example, a container using a Bean on a server would call this method to tell the Bean there's no point in using the GUI environment. If a Bean chooses to comply with this method (and it should), then the Bean should return `true` for subsequent calls to `avoidingGui()`.

```
public abstract boolean needsGui()
```

This method is called by the container to ask whether a Bean absolutely has to have a GUI environment. If a Bean can function in a non-GUI environment, it should return `false`. Note that it's safe to return `true` and then never use the GUI environment, but it's not safe to return `false` and use it anyway.

```
public abstract void okToUseGui()
```

This method is called by a container to tell a Bean that a GUI environment is available and the Bean can use it. This method might also be called after `dontUseGui()` to indicate that a previously unavailable GUI environment is available again. Note that a call to this method in no way implies that a Bean should use the GUI environment, for example, if it wasn't planning to.

Enterprise JavaBeans

A new development on the horizon that utilizes the JavaBeans framework is known as Enterprise JavaBeans. *Enterprise JavaBeans* is a component model for building and deploying Java in a distributed multitier environment. Enterprise JavaBeans extends the JavaBeans component model to support server components.

Server Components

Unlike standard JavaBeans, Enterprise JavaBeans are designed to be server components. The advantage of running components on the server is that it enables a multitier construction. In a multitier architecture, much of the logic is placed on the server rather than the client.

Creating your application using a multitier design makes it much easier to increase its scalability, performance, and reliability. Using components from the Enterprise Beans allows you to develop extremely flexible multitier apps. These beans can be easily modified as your business rules or economic conditions evolve. In addition, like RMI components, Enterprise JavaBeans can be located anywhere, and the processing is independent of their location.

Adding Component "Run Anywhere"

Sun has long been touting the "write once, run anywhere" advantages of Java. Using Enterprise JavaBeans, this concept has been extended. Now not only can Java run on any platform, but Java components can be developed to run on any component execution system. The environment automatically maps the component to the specific system your server is using. So, if you have a server using DCOM, the enterprise system will map to DCOM. If your server is using CORBA, it maps to CORBA, and so on.

Partitioning Your Applications

Modern object-oriented designs typically split application design into three pieces. These pieces are the user interface, the business logic, and the data. Typically, the server is a relational database management system (DBMS), which the application communicates with but isn't actually part of the application itself. However, in a multitier architecture, the client application contains only user interface programming. The business logic and data are partitioned and moved into components deployed on one or more servers.

The result of moving the business and data logic to a server is that your application can take advantage of the power of multithreaded and multiprocessing systems. In addition, the server components can pool and share scarce resources, throughout all the user's applications. As system demands increase, Enterprise Beans that are heavily used can be replicated and distributed across multiple systems. This means that there is almost no limit to the scalablity of a multitier system. As system resources expire, you can always replicate another system to handle more of the load.

In addition to providing enhanced performance, the replication can be used to create many levels of redundancy. This redundancy helps to eliminate any single points of failure.

Reusability and Integration

Enterprise JavaBeans are accessed through a well-defined interface. The interface allows Enterprise Beans to be used to create reusable software building blocks, just like regular JavaBeans. A function can be created once and then used repeatedly in whatever application needs that functionality.

Nonvisual Components

Enterprise JavaBeans is a server component model for JavaBeans. Enterprise JavaBeans are specialized, nonvisual JavaBeans that run on a server. Just as with regular JavaBeans, an Enterprise Bean can be assembled with other Beans to create a new application.

Naming

Enterprise JavaBeans uses another of the new features of Java—JNDI (Java Naming and Directory Interface). JNDI defines a mechanism for mapping arbitrary system names to their actual computer location, much like the Internet's domain name system that allows you to map names like **www.yahoo.com** to the actual computer system the name represents. ●

CHAPTER 42

JavaIDL: A Java Interface to CORBA

In this chapter

What Is CORBA?

The Common Object Request Broker Architecture (CORBA) is a tremendous vision of distributed objects interacting without regard to their location or operating environment. CORBA is still in its infancy, with some standards still in the definition stage, but the bulk of the CORBA infrastructure is defined. Many software vendors are still working on some of the features that have been defined.

CORBA consists of several layers. The lowest layer is the Object Request Broker, or ORB. The ORB is essentially a remote method invocation facility. The ORB is language-neutral, meaning you can create objects in any language and use the ORB to invoke methods in those objects. You can also use any language to create clients that invoke remote methods through the ORB. There is a catch to the "any language" idea. You need a language mapping defined between the implementation language and CORBA's Interface Definition Language (IDL).

IDL is a descriptive language—you cannot use it to write working programs. You can only describe remote methods and remote attributes in IDL. This restriction is similar to the restriction in Java that a Java interface contains only method declarations and constants.

When you go from IDL to your implementation language, you generate a stub and a skeleton in the implementation language. The stub is the interface between the client and the ORB, while the skeleton is the interface between the ORB and the object (or server). Figure 42.1 shows the relationship between the ORB, an object, and a client wishing to invoke a method on the object.

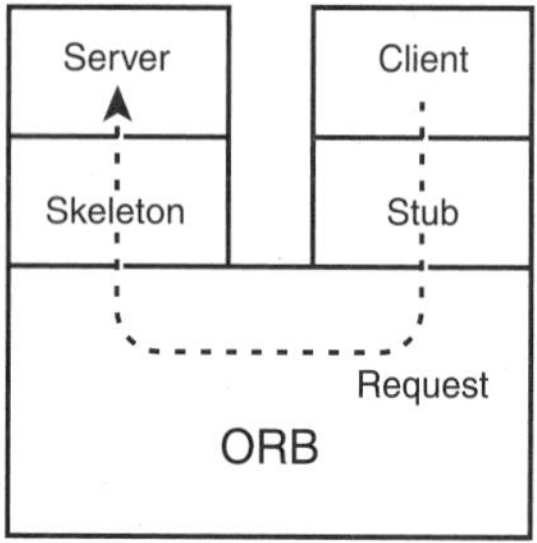

FIG. 42.1
CORBA clients use the ORB to invoke methods on a CORBA server.

While the ORB is drawn conceptually as a separate part of the architecture, it is often just part of the application. A basic ORB implementation might include the Naming service (discussed shortly) and a set of libraries to facilitate communication between clients and servers. Once a client locates a server, it communicates directly with that server, not going through any intermediate program. This permits efficient CORBA implementations.

The ORB is both the most visible portion of CORBA and the least exciting. CORBA's big benefit comes in all the services that it defines. Among the services defined in CORBA are

- Lifecycle
- Naming

- Persistence
- Events
- Transactions
- Querying
- Properties

These services are a subset of the full range of services defined by CORBA. The Lifecycle and the Naming services crystallize Sun's visionary phrase "the network is the computer." These services allow you to instantiate new objects without knowing where the objects reside. You might be creating an object in your own program space, or you might be creating an object halfway around the world, and your program will never know it.

The Lifecycle service allows you to create, delete, copy, and move objects on a specific system. As an application programmer you would prefer not to know where an object resides. As a systems programmer you need the Lifecycle service to implement this location transparency for the application programmer. One of the hassles you frequently run into in remote procedure call systems is that the server you are calling must already be up and running before you can make the call. The Lifecycle service removes that hassle by allowing you to create an object, if you need to, before invoking a method on it.

The Naming service allows you to locate an object on the network by name. You want the total flexibility of being able to move objects around the network without having to change any code. The Naming service gives you that ability by associating an object with a name instead of a network address.

The Persistence service allows you to save objects somewhere and retrieve them later. This might be in a file, or it might be on an object database. The CORBA standard doesn't specify which. That is left up to the individual software vendors.

The Event service is a messaging system that allows more complex interaction than a simple message call. You could use the Event service to implement a network-based observer-observable model, for example. There are event suppliers that send events, and event consumers that receive events. A server or a client is either push or pull. A push server sends events out when it wants to (it pushes them out), while a push client has a push method and automatically receives events through this method. A pull server doesn't send out events until it is asked—you have to pull them out of the server. A pull client does not receive events until it asks for them. It might help to use the term "poll" in place of "pull." A pull server doesn't deliver events on its own, it gives them out when it is polled. A pull client goes out and polls for events.

The Transaction service is one of the most complex services in the CORBA architecture. It allows you to define operations across multiple objects as a single transaction. This kind of transaction is similar to a database transaction. It handles concurrency, locking, and even rollbacks in case of a failure. A transaction must comply with a core set of requirements that are abbreviated ACID:

- Atomicity. A transaction is a single event. Everything in the transaction is either done as a whole or undone. You don't perform a transaction partially.

- Consistency. When you perform a transaction, you do not leave the system in an inconsistent state. For example, if you have an airline flight with one seat left, you don't end up assigning that seat to two different people if their transactions occur at the same time.
- Isolation. No other objects see the results of a transaction until that transaction is committed. Even if transactions are executing simultaneously, they have a sequential order with respect to the data.
- Durability. If you commit a transaction, you can be sure that the change has been made and stored somewhere. It doesn't get lost.

The Transaction service usually relies on an external transaction processing (TP) system.

The Object Querying service allows you to locate objects based on something other than name. For instance, you could locate all ships registered in Liberia or all Krispy Kreme donut locations in Georgia. This service would usually be used when your objects are stored in an object database.

The Properties service allows objects to store information on other objects. A property is like a sticky-note. An object would write some information down on a sticky-note and slap it on another object. This has tremendous potential because it allows information to be associated with an object without the object having to know about it.

The beauty of the whole CORBA system is that all of these services are available through the ORB interface, so once your program can talk to the ORB, you have these services available. Of course, your ORB vendor may not implement all of these services yet.

Sun's IDL to Java Mapping

In order to use Java in a CORBA system, you need a standard way to convert attributes and methods defined in IDL into Java attributes and methods. Sun has proposed a mapping and released a program to generate Java stubs and skeletons from an IDL definition.

Defining interfaces in IDL is similar to defining interfaces in Java since you are defining only the signatures (parameters and return values) of the methods and not the implementation of the methods.

IDL Modules

A module is the IDL equivalent of the Java package. It groups sets of interfaces together in their own namespace. Like Java packages, IDL modules can be nested. The following is an example IDL module definition (shown without any definitions, which will be discussed soon):

```
module MyModule {
     // insert your IDL definitions here, you must have at least
     // one definition for a valid IDL module
};
```

This module would be generated in Java as a package called `MyModule`:

```
package MyModule;
```

When you nest modules, the Java packages you generate are also nested. For example, consider the following nested module definition:

```
module foo {
     module bar {
          module baz {
// insert definitions here
          };
     };
};
```

Don't forget to put a semicolon after the closing brace of a module definition. Unlike Java, C, and C++, you are required to put a semicolon after the brace in IDL.

The Java package definition for interfaces within the `baz` module would be

```
package foo.bar.baz;
```

IDL Constants

As in Java, you can define constant values in IDL. The format of an IDL constant definition is

```
const type variable = value;
```

The type of a constant is limited to `boolean`, `char`, `short`, `unsigned short`, `long`, `unsigned long`, `float`, `double`, and `string`.

Constants are mapped into Java in an unusual way. Each constant is defined as a class with a single static final public variable, called `value`, that holds the value of the constant. This is done because IDL allows you to define constants within a module, but Java requires that constants belong to a class.

Here is an example of an IDL constant definition:

```
module ConstExample {
     const long myConstant = 123;
};
```

This IDL definition would produce the following Java definition:

```
package ConstExample;
public final class myConstant {
     public static final int value = (int) (123L);
}
```


IDL Data Types

IDL has roughly the same set of primitive data types as Java except for a few exceptions:

- The IDL equivalent of the Java `byte` data type is the `octet`.
- IDL supports the `String` type, but it is called `string`.

- Characters in IDL can have values only between 0 and 255. The JavaIDL system will check your characters to make sure they fall within this range, including characters stored in strings.
- IDL supports 16-, 32-, and 64-bit integers, but the names for the 32- and 64-bit types are slightly different. In IDL, the 32-bit value is called a `long`, while in Java it is called an `int`. The IDL equivalent of the Java `long` is the `long long`.
- IDL supports unsigned `short`, `int`, and `long` values. In Java, these values are stored in signed variables. You must be very careful when dealing with large unsigned values, since they may end up negative when represented in Java.

Enumerated Types

Unlike Java, IDL allows you to create enumerated types that represent integer values. The JavaIDL system turns the enumerated type into a class with public static final values.

Here is an example of an IDL enumerated type:

```
module EnumModule {
     enum Medals { gold, silver, bronze };
};
```

This definition would produce the following Java class:

```
package EnumModule;
public class Medals {
    public static final int gold = 0,
                   silver = 1,
                   bronze = 2;
    public static final int narrow(int i)throws
➥sunw.corba.EnumerationRangeException {
     if (gold <= i && i <= bronze) {
         return i;
     }
     throw new sunw.corba.EnumerationRangeException();
    }
}
```

Since you are also allowed to declare variables of an enumerated type, JavaIDL creates a holder class that is used in place of the data type. The holder class contains a single instance variable called `value` that holds the enumerated value. The holder for the `Medals` enumeration would look like:

```
package EnumModule;
public class MedalsHolder
{
    //     instance variable
    public int value;
    //     constructors
    public MedalsHolder() {
     this(0);
    }
    public MedalsHolder(int __arg) {
     value = EnumModule.Medals.narrow(__arg);
```

```
    }
}
```

You can create a MedalsHolder by passing an enumerated value to the constructor:

```
MedalsHolder medal = new MedalsHolder(Medals.silver);
```

The narrow method performs range checking on values and throws an exception if the argument is outside the bounds of the enumeration. It returns the value passed to it, so you can use it to perform passive bounds checking. For example,

```
int x = Medals.narrow(y);
```

will assign y to x only if y is in the range of enumerated values for Medals; otherwise, it will throw an exception.

Structures

An IDL struct is like a Java class without methods. In fact, JavaIDL converts an IDL struct into a Java class whose only methods are a null constructor and a constructor that takes all the structure's attributes.

Here is an example IDL struct definition:

```
module StructModule {
     struct Person {
          string name;
          long age;
     };
};
```

This definition would produce the following Java class declaration (with some JavaIDL-specific methods omitted):

```
package StructModule;
public final class Person {
    //     instance variables
    public String name;
    public int age;
    //     constructors
    public Person() { }
    public Person(String __name, int __age) {
     name = __name;
     age = __age;
    }
}
```

Like the enumerated type, a struct also produces a holder class that represents the structure. The holder class contains a single instance variable called value. Here is the holder for the Person structure:

```
package StructModule;
public final class PersonHolder
{
    //     instance variable
    public StructModule.Person value;
```

```
    //     constructors
    public PersonHolder() {
     this(null);
    }
    public PersonHolder(StructModule.Person __arg) {
     value = __arg;
    }
}
```

Unions

The union is another C construct that didn't survive the transition to Java. The IDL union actually works more like the variant record in Pascal, since it requires a "discriminator" value. An IDL union is essentially a group of attributes, only one of which can be active at a time. The discriminator indicates which attribute is in use at the current time. A short example should make this a little clearer. Here is an IDL union declaration:

```
module UnionModule {
     union MyUnion switch (char) {
          case 'a':      string aValue;
          case 'b':     long bValue;
          case 'c':      boolean cValue;
          default:     string defValue;
     };
};
```

The character value in the switch, known as the discriminator, indicates which of the three variables in the union is active. If the discriminator is 'a', the aValue variable is active. Since Java doesn't have unions, a union is turned into a class with accessor methods for the different variables and a variable for the discriminator. The class is fairly complex. Here is a subset of the definition for the MyUnion union:

```
package UnionModule;
public class MyUnion {
//     constructor
    public MyUnion() {
//     only has a null constructor
    }
    //     discriminator accessor
    public char discriminator() throws sunw.corba.UnionDiscriminantException {
//     returns the value of the discriminator
    }
    //     branch constructors and get and set accessors
    public static MyUnion createaValue(String value) {
//     creates a MyUnion with a discriminator of 'a'
    }
    public String getaValue() throws sunw.corba.UnionDiscriminantException {
//     returns the value of aValue (only if the discriminator is 'a' right now)
    }
    public void setaValue(String value) {
//     sets the value of aValue and set the discriminator to 'a'
    }
    public void setdefValue(char discriminator, String value)
throws sunw.corba.UnionDiscriminantException {
```

```
//      Sets the value of defValue and sets the discriminator. Although every
//      variable has a method in this form, it is only useful when you have
//      a default value in the union.
    }
}
```

The holder structure should be a familiar theme to you by now. JavaIDL generates a holder structure for a union. The holder structure for `MyUnion` would be called `MyUnionHolder` and would contain a single instance variable called `value`.

Sequences and Arrays

IDL sequences and arrays both map very neatly to Java arrays. Sequences in IDL may be either unbounded (no maximum size) or bounded (a specific maximum size). IDL arrays are always of a fixed size. Since Java arrays have a fixed size but the size isn't known at compile-time, the JavaIDL system performs runtime checks on arrays to make sure they fit within the restrictions defined in the IDL module.

Here is a sample IDL definition containing an array, a bounded sequence, and an unbounded sequence:

```
module ArrayModule {
     struct SomeStructure {
          long longArray[15];
          sequence <boolean> unboundedBools;
          sequence <char, 15> boundedChars;
     };
};
```

The arrays would be defined in Java as

```
public int[] longArray;
public boolean[] unboundedBools;
public char[] boundedChars;
```

Exceptions

CORBA has the notion of exceptions. Unlike Java, however, exceptions are not just a type of object, they are separate entities. IDL exceptions cannot inherit from other exceptions. Other than that, they work like Java exceptions and may contain instance variables.

Here is an example of an IDL exception definition:

```
module ExceptionModule {
     exception YikesError {
          string info;
     };

};
```

This definition would create the following Java file (with some JavaIDL-specific methods removed):

```
package ExceptionModule;
public class YikesError
```

```
        extends sunw.corba.UserException {
       //     instance variables
       public String info;
       //     constructors
       public YikesError() {
        super("IDL:ExceptionModule/YikesError:1.0");
       }
       public YikesError(String __info) {
        super("IDL:ExceptionModule/YikesError:1.0");
        info = __info;
       }
}
```

Interfaces

Interfaces are the most important part of IDL. An IDL interface contains a set of method definitions, just like a Java interface. Like Java interfaces, an IDL interface may inherit from other interfaces. Here is a sample IDL interface definition:

```
module InterfaceModule {
     interface MyInterface {
          void myMethod(in long param1);
     };
};
```

IDL classifies method parameters as being either `in`, `out`, or `inout`. An `in` parameter is identical to a Java parameter—it is a parameter passed by value. Even though the method may change the value of the variable, the changes are discarded when the method returns.

An `out` variable is an output-only variable. The method is expected to set the value of this variable, which is preserved when the method returns, but no value is passed in for the variable (it is uninitialized).

An `inout` variable is a combination of the two—you pass in a value to the method; if the method changes the value, the change is preserved when the method returns.

The fact that Java parameters are `in`-only poses a small challenge when mapping IDL to Java. Sun has come up with a reasonable approach, however. For any `out` or `inout` parameters, you pass in a holder class for that variable. The CORBA method can then set the `value` instance variable with the value that is supposed to be returned.

Attributes

IDL allows you to define variables within an interface. These translate into `get` and `set` methods for the attribute. An attribute may be specified as `readonly`, which prevents the generation of a `set` method for the attribute. For example, if you defined an IDL attribute as

```
attribute long myAttribute;
```

your Java interface would then contain the following methods:

```
int getmyAttribute() throws omg.corba.SystemException;
void setmyAttribute() throws omg.corba.SystemException;
```

Methods

You define methods in IDL like you declare methods in Java, with only a few variations. One of the most noticeable differences is that CORBA supports the notion of changeable parameters. In other words, you can pass an integer variable `x` to a CORBA method, and that method can change the value of `x`. When the method returns, `x` has the changed value. In a normal Java method, `x` would retain its original value.

In IDL, method parameters must be flagged as being `in`, `out`, or `inout`. An `in` parameter cannot be changed by the method, which is the way all Java methods work. An `out` parameter indicates a value that the method will set, but it ignores the value passed in. In other words, if parameter `x` is an `out` parameter, the CORBA method cannot read the value of `x`, it can only change it. An `inout` parameter can be read by the CORBA method and can also be changed by it.

Here is a sample method declaration using an `in`, an `out`, and an `inout` parameter:

```
long performCalculation(in float originalValue,
     inout float errorAmount, out float newValue);
```

Since Java doesn't support the notion of parameters being changed, the Java-IDL mapping uses special holder classes for `out` and `inout` parameters. The IDL compiler already generates holder classes for structures and unions. For base types like `long` or `float`, JavaIDL has built-in holders of the form `TypenameHolder`. For example, the holder class for the `long` type is called `LongHolder`. Each of these holder classes contains a public instance variable called `value` that contains the value of the parameter.

The other major difference between IDL and Java method declarations is in the way exceptions are declared. IDL uses the `raises` keyword instead of `throws`. In addition, the list of exceptions are enclosed by parentheses. Here is a sample method declaration that throws several exceptions:

```
void execute() raises (ExecutionError, ProgramFailure);
```

Creating a Basic CORBA Server

The interface between the ORB and the implementation of a server is called a skeleton. A skeleton for an IDL interface receives information from the ORB, invokes the appropriate server method, and sends the results back to the ORB. You normally don't have to write the skeleton itself; you just supply the implementation of the remote methods.

Listing 42.1 shows an IDL definition of a simple banking interface. You will see how to create both a client and a server for this interface in JavaIDL.

Listing 42.1 Source Code for *Banking.idl*

```
module banking {

     enum AccountType {
          CHECKING,
          SAVINGS
     };

     struct AccountInfo {
          string id;
          string password;
          AccountType which;
     };

     exception InvalidAccountException {
          AccountInfo account;
     };

     exception InsufficientFundsException {
     };

     interface Banking {

          long getBalance(in AccountInfo account)
               raises (InvalidAccountException);

          void withdraw(in AccountInfo account, in long amount)
               raises (InvalidAccountException,
                    InsufficientFundsException);

          void deposit(in AccountInfo account, in long amount)
               raises (InvalidAccountException);

          void transfer(in AccountInfo fromAccount,
               in AccountInfo toAccount, in long amount)
               raises (InvalidAccountException,
                    InsufficientFundsException);
     };
};
```

Compiling the IDL Definitions

Before you create any Java code for your CORBA program, you must first compile the IDL definitions into a set of Java classes. The `idlgen` program reads an IDL file and creates classes for creating a client and server for the various interfaces defined in the IDL file, as well as any exceptions, structures, unions, and other support classes.

To compile `Banking.idl`, the `idlgen` command would be

```
idlgen -fserver -fclient Banking.idl
```

idlgen allows you to use the C preprocessor to include other files, perform conditional compilation, and define symbols. If you do not have a C preprocessor, use the -fno-cpp option like this:

```
idlgen -fserver -fclient -fno-cpp Banking.idl
```

The -fserver and -fclient flags tell idlgen to create classes for creating a server and a client, respectively. You may not always need to create both, however. If you are creating a Java client that will use CORBA to invoke methods on an existing C++ CORBA server, you only need to generate the client portion. If you are creating a CORBA server in Java but the clients will be in another language, you only need to generate the server portion.

Using Classes Defined by IDL *structs*

When an IDL struct is turned into a Java class, it does not have custom hashCode and equals methods. This means that two instances of this class containing identical data will not be equal. If you want to add custom methods to these structs, you will have to create a separate class and define methods to convert from one class to the other.

One way to remedy this is to create a class that contains the same information as the IDL structure but also contains correct hashCode and equals methods, as well as a way to convert to and from the IDL-defined structure.

Listing 42.2 shows an Account class that contains the same information as the AccountInfo structure defined in Banking.idl.

Listing 42.2 Source Code for *Account.java*

```
package banking;

// This class contains the information that defines
// a banking account.

public class Account extends Object
{
// Flags to indicate whether the account is savings or checking
     public String id;     // Account id, or account number
     public String password;     // password for ATM transactions
     public int which;     // is this checking or savings

     public Account()
     {
     }

     public Account(String id, String password, int which)
     {
          this.id = id;
          this.password = password;
          this.which = which;
     }
```

Part VI Ch 42

continues

Listing 42.2 Continued

```
// Allow this object to be created from an AccountInfo instance

     public Account(AccountInfo acct)
     {
          this.id = acct.id;
          this.password = acct.password;
          this.which = acct.which;
     }

// Convert this object to an AccountInfo instance

     public AccountInfo toAccountInfo()
     {
          return new AccountInfo(id, password, which);
     }

     public String toString()
     {
          return "Account { "+id+","+password+","+which+" }";
     }

// Tests equality between accounts.
     public boolean equals(Object ob)
     {
          if (!(ob instanceof Account)) return false;
          Account other = (Account) ob;

          return id.equals(other.id) &&
               password.equals(other.password) &&
               (which == other.which);
     }

// Returns a hash code for this object

     public int hashCode()
     {
          return id.hashCode()+password.hashCode()+which;
     }
}
```

JavaIDL Skeletons

When you create a CORBA server, the IDL compiler generates a server skeleton. This skeleton receives the incoming requests and figures out which method to invoke. You only need to write the actual methods that the skeleton will call.

JavaIDL creates an `Operations` interface that contains Java versions of the methods defined in an IDL interface. It also creates a `Servant` interface, which extends the `Operations` interface. The skeleton class then invokes methods on the `Servant` interface. In other words, when you create the object that implements the remote methods, it must implement the `Servant` interface for your IDL definition.

NOTE This technique of defining the remote methods in an interface that can be implemented by a separate object is known as a TIE interface. In the C++ world, and even on some early Java ORBS, the IDL compiler would generate a skeleton class that implemented the remote methods. To change the implementation of the methods, you would create a subclass of the skeleton class. The subclass technique is often called a Basic Object Adapter, or BOA. The advantage of the TIE interface under Java is that a single object can implement multiple remote interfaces. You can't do this with a BOA object, because Java doesn't support multiple inheritance.

For example, your implementation for the `Banking` interface might be declared as

```
public class BankingImpl implements BankingServant
```

Listing 42.3 shows the full `BankingImpl` object that implements the `BankingServant` interface. Notice that each remote method must be declared as throwing `sunw.corba.Exception`.

Listing 42.3 Source Code for *BankingImpl.java*

```
package banking;

import java.util.*;

// This class implements a remote banking object. It sets up
// a set of dummy accounts and allows you to manipulate them
// through the Banking interface.
//
// Accounts are identified by the combination of the account id,
// the password and the account type. This is a quick and dirty
// way to work, and not the way a bank would normally do it, since
// the password is not part of the unique identifier of the account.

public class BankingImpl implements BankingServant
{
     public Hashtable accountTable;

// The constructor creates a table of dummy accounts.

     public BankingImpl()
     {
          accountTable = new Hashtable();

          accountTable.put(
               new Account("AA1234", "1017", AccountType.CHECKING),
               new Integer(50000));     // $500.00 balance

          accountTable.put(
               new Account("AA1234", "1017", AccountType.SAVINGS),
               new Integer(148756));     // $1487.56 balance

          accountTable.put(
               new Account("AB5678", "4456", AccountType.CHECKING),
               new Integer(7742));     // $77.32 balance
```

continues

Listing 42.3 Continued

```
        accountTable.put(
             new Account("AB5678", "4456", AccountType.SAVINGS),
             new Integer(32201));     // $322.01 balance
    }

// getBalance returns the amount of money in the account (in cents).
// If the account is invalid, it throws an InvalidAccountException

    public int getBalance(AccountInfo accountInfo)
    throws sunw.corba.SystemException, InvalidAccountException
    {

// Fetch the account from the table
        Integer balance = (Integer) accountTable.get(
             new Account(accountInfo));

// If the account wasn't there, throw an exception
        if (balance == null) {
             throw new InvalidAccountException(accountInfo);
        }

// Return the account's balance
        return balance.intValue();
    }

// withdraw subtracts an amount from the account's balance. If
// the account is invalid, it throws InvalidAccountException.
// If the withdrawal amount exceeds the account balance, it
// throws InsufficientFundsException.

    public synchronized void withdraw(AccountInfo accountInfo, int amount)
    throws sunw.corba.SystemException, InvalidAccountException,
        InsufficientFundsException
    {

        Account account = new Account(accountInfo);

// Fetch the account
        Integer balance = (Integer) accountTable.get(account);

// If the account wasn't there, throw an exception
        if (balance == null) {
             throw new InvalidAccountException(accountInfo);
        }

// If we are trying to withdraw more than is in the account,
// throw an exception

        if (balance.intValue() < amount) {
             throw new InsufficientFundsException();
        }
```

```
// Put the new balance in the account

            accountTable.put(account, new Integer(balance.intValue() -
                amount));
        }

// Deposit adds an amount to an account. If the account is invalid
// it throws an InvalidAccountException

        public synchronized void deposit(AccountInfo accountInfo, int amount)
        throws sunw.corba.SystemException, InvalidAccountException
        {

            Account account = new Account(accountInfo);

// Fetch the account
            Integer balance = (Integer) accountTable.get(account);

// If the account wasn't there, throw an exception
            if (balance == null) {
                throw new InvalidAccountException(accountInfo);
            }

// Update the account with the new balance
            accountTable.put(account, new Integer(balance.intValue() +
                amount));
        }

// Transfer subtracts an amount from fromAccount and adds it to toAccount.
// If either account is invalid it throws InvalidAccountException.
// If there isn't enough money in fromAccount it throws
// InsufficientFundsException.

        public synchronized void transfer(AccountInfo fromAccountInfo,
            AccountInfo toAccountInfo, int amount)
        throws sunw.corba.SystemException, InvalidAccountException,
            InsufficientFundsException
        {
            Account fromAccount = new Account(fromAccountInfo);
            Account toAccount = new Account(toAccountInfo);

// Fetch the from account
            Integer fromBalance = (Integer) accountTable.get(fromAccount);

// If the from account doesn't exist, throw an exception
            if (fromBalance == null) {
                throw new InvalidAccountException(fromAccountInfo);
            }

// Fetch the to account
            Integer toBalance = (Integer) accountTable.get(toAccount);
```

continues

Listing 42.3 Continued

```
// If the to account doesn't exist, throw an exception
          if (toBalance == null) {
               throw new InvalidAccountException(toAccountInfo);
          }

// Make sure the from account contains enough money, otherwise throw
// an InsufficientFundsException.

          if (fromBalance.intValue() < amount) {
               throw new InsufficientFundsException();
          }


// Subtract the amount from the fromAccount
          accountTable.put(fromAccount,
               new Integer(fromBalance.intValue() - amount));

// Add the amount to the toAccount
          accountTable.put(toAccount,
               new Integer(toBalance.intValue() + amount));
     }
}
```

Server Initialization

While JavaIDL is intended to be Sun's recommendation for mapping IDL into Java, it was released with a lightweight ORB called the Door ORB. This ORB provides just enough functionality to get clients and servers talking to each other but not much more.

Depending on the ORB, the initialization will vary, as will the activation of the objects. For the Door ORB distributed with JavaIDL, you initialize the ORB with the following line:

```
sunw.door.Orb.initialize(servicePort);
```

The `servicePort` parameter you pass to the ORB is the port number it should use when listening for incoming clients. It must be an integer value. Your clients must use this port number when connecting to your server.

After you initialize the ORB, you can instantiate your implementation object. For example,

```
BankingImpl impl = new BankingImpl();
```

Next, you create the skeleton, passing it the implementation object:

```
BankingRef server = BankingSkeleton.createRef(impl);
```

Finally, you activate the server by publishing the name of the object:

```
sunw.door.Orb.publish("Bank", server);
```

Listing 42.4 shows the complete JavaIDL startup program for the banking server.

Listing 42.4 Source Code for *BankingServer.java*

```
package banking;

public class BankingServer
{

// Define the port that clients will use to connect to this server
     public static final int servicePort = 5150;

     public static void main(String[] args)
     {

// Initialize the orb
          sunw.door.Orb.initialize(servicePort);

          try {

               BankingImpl impl = new BankingImpl();
// Create the server
               BankingRef server =
                    BankingSkeleton.createRef(impl);

// Register the object with the naming service as "Bank"
               sunw.door.Orb.publish("Bank", server);

          } catch (Exception e) {
               System.out.println("Got exception: "+e);
               e.printStackTrace();
          }
     }
}
```

Creating CORBA Clients with JavaIDL

Since the IDL compiler creates a skeleton class on the server side that receives remote method invocation requests, you might expect that it creates some sort of skeleton on the client side that sends these requests. It does, but the client side class is referred to as a stub.

The stub class implements the `Operations` interface (the same `Operations` interface implemented by the `Servant` class). Whenever you invoke one of the stub's methods, the stub creates a request and sends it to the server.

There is an extra layer on top of the stub called a reference. This reference object, which is the name of the IDL interface followed by `Ref`, is the object you use to make calls to the server.

There are two simple steps in creating a CORBA client in JavaIDL:

1. Create a reference to a stub using the `createRef` method in the particular stub.
2. Use the `sunw.corba.Orb.resolve` method to create a connection between the stub and a CORBA server.

You would create a reference to a stub for the banking interface with the following line:

```
BankingRef bank = BankingStub.createRef();
```

Next, you must create a connection between the stub and a CORBA server by "resolving" it. Since JavaIDL is meant to be the standard Java interface for all ORBs, it requires an ORB-independent naming scheme. Sun decided on an URL-type naming scheme of the format:

```
idl:orb_name://orb_parameters
```

The early versions of JavaIDL shipped with an ORB called the Door ORB, which is a very lightweight ORB containing little more than a naming scheme. To access a CORBA object using the Door ORB, you must specify the host name and port number used by the CORBA server you are connecting to and the name of the object you are accessing. The format of this information is

```
hostname:port/object_name
```

If you wanted to access an object named `Bank` with the Door ORB, running on a server at port 5150 on the local host, you would resolve your stub this way:

```
sunw.corba.Orb.resolve(
"idl:sunw.door://localhost:5150/Bank",
bank);
```

Remember that the `bank` parameter is the `BankingRef` returned by the `BankingStub.createRef` method. Once the stub is resolved, you can invoke remote methods in the server using the stub. Listing 42.5 shows the full JavaIDL client for the banking interface. As you can see, once you have connected the stub to the server, you can invoke methods on the stub just like it was a local object.

Listing 42.5 Source Code for *BankingClient.java*

```
import banking.*;

// This program tries out some of the methods in the BankingImpl
// remote object.

public class BankingClient
{

     public static void main(String args[])
     {

// Create an Account object for the account we are going to access.

          Account myAccount = new Account(
               "AA1234", "1017", AccountType.CHECKING);

          AccountInfo myAccountInfo = myAccount.toAccountInfo();
          try {
```

```
// Get a stub for the BankingImpl object

               BankingRef bank = BankingStub.createRef();
               sunw.corba.Orb.resolve(
                    "idl:sunw.door://localhost:5150/Bank",
                    bank);

// Check the initial balance
               System.out.println("My balance is: "+
                    bank.getBalance(myAccountInfo));

// Deposit some money
               bank.deposit(myAccountInfo, 50000);

// Check the balance again
               System.out.println("Deposited $500.00, balance is: "+
                    bank.getBalance(myAccountInfo));

// Withdraw some money
               bank.withdraw(myAccountInfo, 25000);

// Check the balance again
               System.out.println("Withdrew $250.00, balance is: "+
                    bank.getBalance(myAccountInfo));

               System.out.flush();
               System.exit(0);

          } catch (Exception e) {
               System.out.println("Got exception: "+e);
               e.printStackTrace();
          }
     }
}
```

Creating Callbacks in CORBA

Callbacks are a handy mechanism in distributed computing. You use them whenever your client wants to be notified of some event, but doesn't want to sit and poll the server to see if the event has occurred yet. In a regular Java program, you'd just create a callback interface and pass the server an object that implements the callback interface. When the event occurred, the server would invoke a method in the callback object.

As it turns out, callbacks are just that easy in CORBA. You define a callback interface in your IDL file and then create a method in the server's interface that takes the callback interface as a parameter. The following IDL file defines a server interface and a callback interface:


```
module callbackDemo
{
     interface callbackInterface {
          void doNotify(in string whatHappened);
     };
```

```
    interface serverInterface {
        void setCallback(in callbackInterface callMe);
    };
};
```

Under JavaIDL, the `setCallback` method would be defined as

```
void setCallback(callbackDemo.callbackInterfaceRef callMe)
    throws sunw.corba.SystemException;
```

Once you have the `callbackDemo.callbackInterfaceRef` object, you can invoke its `whatHappened` method at any time. At this point, the client and server are on a peer-to-peer level. They are each other's client and server.

Wrapping CORBA Around an Existing Object

When you create CORBA implementation objects you are tying that object to a CORBA implementation. While the `Servant` interface generated by the JavaIDL system goes a long way in separating your implementation from the specifics of the ORB, your implementation methods can throw the CORBA `SystemException` exception, tying your implementation to CORBA. This is not the ideal situation.

You can solve this problem, but it takes a little extra work up front. First, concentrate on implementing the object you want, without using CORBA, RMI, or any other remote interface mechanism. This will be the one copy you use across all your implementations. This object, or set of objects, can define its own types, exceptions, and interfaces.

Next, to make this object available remotely, define an IDL interface that is as close to the object's interface as you can get. There may be cases where they won't match exactly, but you can take care of that.

Once you generate the Java classes from the IDL definition, create an implementation that simply invokes methods on the real implementation object. This is essentially the same thing as a TIE interface, with one major exception—the implementation class has no knowledge of CORBA. You can even use this technique to provide multiple ways to access a remote object. Figure 42.2 shows a diagram of the various ways you might provide access to your implementation object.

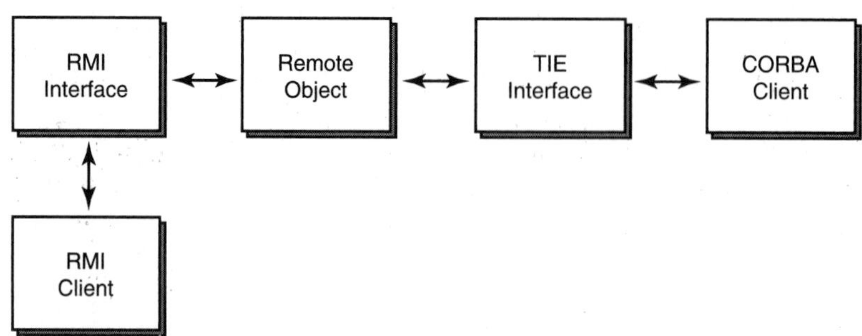

FIG. 42.2
A single object can be accessed by many types of remote object systems.

While this may sound simple, it has some additional complexities you must address. If your implementation object defines its own exceptions, you must map those exceptions to CORBA exceptions. You must also map between Java objects and CORBA-defined objects. Once again, the banking interface provides a good starting point for illustrating the problems and solutions in separating the application from CORBA.

The original banking interface was defined with a hierarchy of exceptions, a generic `BankingException`, with `InsufficientFundsException` and `InvalidAccountException` as subclasses. This poses a problem in CORBA, since exceptions aren't inherited. You must define a `BankingException` exception in your IDL file, such as the following:

```
exception BankingException {};
```

In addition, since you probably want the banking application itself to be in the banking package, change the IDL module name to `remotebanking`.

The implementation for the `Banking` interface in the `remotebanking` module must perform two kinds of mapping. First, it must convert instances of the `Account` object to instances of the `AccountInfo` object. This may seem like a pain and, frankly, it is. But it's a necessary pain. If you start to intermingle the classes defined by CORBA with the real implementation of the application, you will end up having to carry the CORBA portions along with the application, even if you don't use CORBA.

Mapping to and from CORBA-Defined Types

You can define static methods to handle the conversion from the application data types to the CORBA-defined data types. For example, the banking application defines an `Account` object. The `remotebanking` module defines this object as `AccountInfo`. You can convert between the two with the following methods:

```
// Create a banking.Account from an AccountInfo object

public static banking.Account makeAccount(AccountInfo info)
{
        return new banking.Account(info.id, info.password,
                info.which);
}

// Create an AccountInfo object from a banking.Account object

public static AccountInfo makeAccountInfo(banking.Account account)
{
        return new AccountInfo(account.id, account.password,
                account.which);
}
```

Your remote implementation of the banking interface needs access to the real implementation, so the constructor for the `RemoteBankingImpl` object needs a reference to the `banking.BankingImpl` object:

```
protected banking.BankingImpl impl;
```

```
public RemoteBankingImpl(banking.BankingImpl impl)
{
        this.impl = impl;
}
```

Creating Remote Method Wrappers

Now, all your remote methods have to do is convert any incoming `AccountInfo` objects to `banking.Account` objects, catch any exceptions, and throw the proper remote exceptions. Here is the implementation of the remote `withdraw` method:

```
// call the withdraw function in the real implementation, catching
// any exceptions and throwing the equivalent CORBA exception

public synchronized void withdraw(AccountInfo accountInfo, int amount)
throws sunw.corba.SystemException, InvalidAccountException,
        InsufficientFundsException, BankingException
{

        try {

// Call the real withdraw method, converting the accountInfo object
// to a banking.Account object first

                impl.withdraw( makeAccount(accountInfo), amount);

        } catch (banking.InvalidAccountException excep) {

// The banking.InvalidAccountException contains an Account object.
// Convert it to an AccountInfo object when throwing the CORBA exception

                throw new InvalidAccountException(
                        makeAccountInfo(excep.account));

        } catch (banking.InsufficientFundsException nsf) {
                throw new InsufficientFundsException();
        } catch (banking.BankingException e) {
                throw new BankingException();
        }
}
```

While it would be nice if you could get the IDL-to-Java converter to generate this automatically, it has no way of knowing exactly how the real implementation looks.

Using CORBA in Applets

Although the full CORBA suite represents a huge amount of code, the requirements for a CORBA client are fairly small. All you really need for a client is the ORB itself. You can access the CORBA services from another location on the network. This allows you to have very lightweight CORBA clients. In other words, you can create applets that are CORBA clients.

The only real restriction on applets using CORBA is that an applet can make network connections back only to the server it was loaded from. This means that all the CORBA services must be available on the Web server (or there must be some kind of proxy set up).

Since an applet cannot listen for incoming network connections, an applet cannot be a CORBA server in most cases. You might find an ORB that eludes this restriction by using connections made by the applet. Most Java ORBs available today have the ability to run CORBA servers on an applet for a callback object. For a callback, an applet might create a server object locally and then pass a reference for its server object to a CORBA server running on another machine. That CORBA server could then use the reference to invoke methods in the applet as a client.

Figure 42.3 illustrates how an applet might act as a CORBA server.

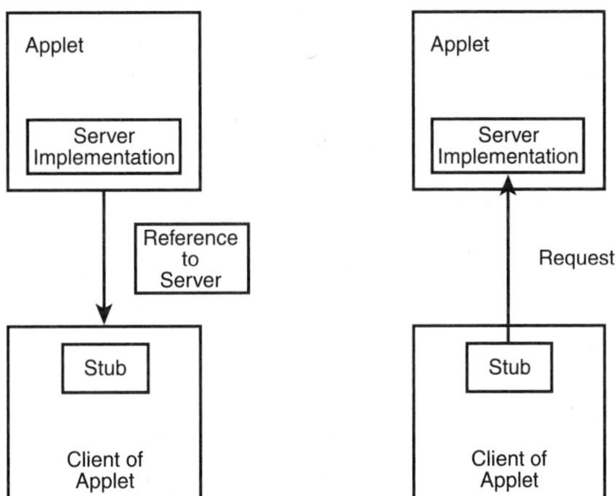

FIG. 42.3
An applet may act as a server by passing a reference to a local CORBA server.

Choosing Between CORBA and RMI

CORBA and RMI each have their advantages and disadvantages. RMI will be a standard part of Java on both the client and server sides, making it a good, cheap tool. Since it is a Java-only system, it integrates cleanly with the rest of Java. RMI is only a nice remote procedure call system, however.

CORBA defines a robust, distributed environment, providing almost all the necessary features for distributed applications. Not all of these features have been implemented by most vendors. Most CORBA clients are offered free, but you must pay for the server software. This is the typical pricing model for most Internet software nowadays. If you don't need all the neat features of CORBA and don't want to spend a lot of money, RMI might be the right thing for you.

Your company might feel that Java is not yet ready for "prime time." If this is the case but you believe that Java is the environment of the future, you should start working CORBA into your current development plans, if possible.

CORBA is a language-independent system. You can implement your applications in C++ today using many of the Java design concepts. Specifically, keep the application and the user interface separated and make the software as modular as possible. If you use CORBA between the components of your system, you can migrate to Java by slowly replacing the various components with CORBA-based Java software.

If you are a programmer trying to convince your skeptical management about the benefits of Java, use CORBA to make a distributed interface into one of your applications (hopefully you have a CORBA product for the language your application is written in). Next, write a Java applet that implements the user interface for your application using CORBA to talk to the real application. You have instantly ported part of your application to every platform that can run a Java-enabled browser. Hopefully, your applet will perform as well as the old native interface to the application.

This same technique will open your existing CORBA applications to non-traditional devices like cellular phones and PDAs. If you aren't ready to support those devices yet, at least you now have a pathway. ●

CHAPTER 43

Java—COM Integration

In this chapter

A Significant Extension

Microsoft's Java Virtual Machine, found in Java-enabled versions of Internet Explorer, contains several Windows-specific extensions that are not a part of standard Java. One of the most significant extensions is the integration with the Component Object Model, or COM.

CAUTION

The Java-COM integration in the Microsoft Java Virtual Machine is very platform-specific. You cannot use it to build platform-independent code. Any code that uses the Java-COM integration will certainly not pass the 100% pure Java test. Still, if you work with Microsoft products and you can use Java, you might as well use all the resources at your disposal.

A Brief Overview of COM

Many people have trouble distinguishing between OLE and ActiveX. In fact, many people say that ActiveX is just a fancy name for OLE. The reason for the confusion is that ActiveX and OLE are both based on COM.

COM provides a way for objects to communicate, whether they are in the same program, different programs on the same machine, or different programs on different machines. The network version of COM, called DCOM (Distributed COM), has only come into production with the introduction of NT 4.0. A version of DCOM for Windows 95 is also available from Microsoft's Web site at `http://www.microsoft.com/oledev`. DCOM should be embedded in future versions of Windows.

The goal of COM is not just to allow objects to communicate, but to encourage developers to create reusable software components. Yes, that is one of the stated goals of object-oriented development, but COM goes beyond a typical object-oriented programming language like Java. In Java or C++, you reuse a component by including it in your program. COM allows you to use components that are present on your machine, but are not specifically a part of your program. In fact, a successful COM object is used by many programs. The key here is that there is one copy of the COM object's code, no matter how many different programs use the object. Although you can arrange your Java classes so that there is no more than one copy of a particular class, you have to do it manually. With COM, this reuse is automatic.

Microsoft has embraced the notion of component-based software and has taken great strides to implement applications as a collection of reusable components. Internet Explorer, for instance, is implemented as a collection of components, with just a small startup program. The Java Virtual Machine in Internet Explorer, for instance, is a separate component that can be used by other applications.

Interfaces are the fundamental foundation of COM. If you understand Java interfaces, you understand COM interfaces. In Java, you can define a set of methods for a class and then also add other definitions by saying that an object implements a certain interface. In other words, in Java, the set of methods implemented by a class is determined by both the class definition and the interfaces it implements. COM doesn't support the notion of classes, only interfaces. The set of methods implemented by a COM object is determined only by the interfaces it implements.

Each interface has a unique identifier, called its GUID (Globally Unique Identifier), which is a 40-digit number (160 bits) that is generated such that there should never be two identical GUIDs. One of the important aspects of COM is that after you distribute software that presents a particular interface (with its unique GUID), you should never change that interface. You can't add to it, you can't remove things from it, you can't change the method signatures. If someone else is using one of your components and you change the interface in the next release, you'll break his software. If you need to change an interface, just create a new one instead.

NOTE GUIDs come from the DCE RPC standard where they are known as Universally Unique IDentifiers (UUID).

COM interfaces are defined by the COM Interface Definition Language (IDL), which is a superset of the DCE RPC IDL (an existing standard for remote procedure calls). Don't confuse COM IDL with CORBA IDL. Although they perform the same function, their syntax is very different. You can also use OLE's Object Definition Language (ODL) to define COM interfaces. Microsoft offers two different compilers for compiling interfaces. To compile IDL files, use MIDL, which comes with the Win32 SDK, or the Platform SDK. To compile ODL files, use MKTYPLIB, which comes with Visual J++, or the ActiveX SDK.

A COM object is accessed one of three basic ways: as an in-proc server, a local server, or a remote server. When you use an in-proc server object, it runs in the same address space as your program. A local server object runs as a separate program on the same machine, while a remote server object runs on a different machine.

Not only do COM interfaces have a unique identifier, so do COM objects. The unique identifier for an object is called its Class ID (CLSID). A CLSID is really a GUID, but it serves a specific purpose so it is given a separate name. These CLSID values are stored in the Windows Registry file and are used to find the particular DLL or EXE file that implements an object. Figure 43.1 shows a Registry entry for a CLSID that happens to be for a PowerPoint application. The various subkeys, such as LocalServer and InprocHandler, indicate which DLL or EXE file to use when the PowerPoint object is used as a local server or an in-proc server.

Other than the actual functions they perform, the only difference between OLE and ActiveX is that they use different interfaces. All OLE and ActiveX interfaces are defined and implemented using COM.

Defining COM Interfaces

To create a COM object, you must first create an interface using either IDL or ODL. Because the MKTYPLIB utility (the ODL compiler) comes with Visual J++, the examples in this chapter use ODL instead of IDL.

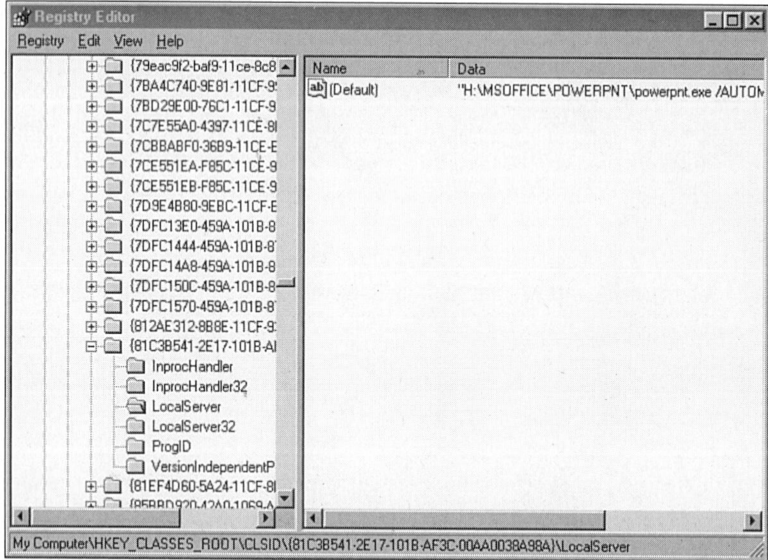

FIG. 43.1
The Registry entry for the LocalServer of a CLSID indicates the .EXE file that provides a specific COM interface.

Listing 43.1 shows a sample ODL file. There are a number things in this file that may seem foreign. By taking them one at a time, you see that things are not as complicated as they seem.

Listing 43.1 Source Code for *JavaObject.odl*

```
// JavaObject.odl

// First define the uuid for this type library
[
  uuid(D65E5380-6D58-11d0-8F0B-444553540000)
]

// Declare the type library

library LJavaObject
{

// Include the standard set of OLE types
    importlib("stdole32.tlb");

// Define the uuid for an odl interface that is a dual interface
// A dual interface is the most flexible because it supports the
// normal interface calling mechanism and also dynamic calling.
//
    [ odl, dual, uuid(D65E5381-6D58-11d0-8F0B-444553540000) ]

// Declare the IJavaObject interface (dual interfaces must inherit
// from the IDispatch interface)

    interface IJavaObject : IDispatch
    {
```

```
// Declare the reverseString method that takes a string as input
// and returns a string
        HRESULT reverseString( [in] BSTR reverseMe,
            [out, retval] BSTR *reversed );

// Declare the square method that takes an integer and returns
// an integer
        HRESULT square( [in] int squareMe,
            [out, retval] int *squared );
    }

// Declare a class that implements the IJavaObject interface
    [ uuid(10C24E60-6D5D-11d0-8F0B-444553540000) ]
    coclass JavaObject
    {
        interface IJavaObject;
    }
};
```


First of all, when you create a set of interfaces with ODL, you compile them into a type library. A type library is to an ODL file what a .CLASS file is to the Java source. A type library must have its own GUID, so the following statement declares the library and its GUID (remember that a GUID is another name for UUID):

```
[
uuid(D65E5380-6D58-11d0-8F0B-444553540000)
]

library LJavaObject
```

NOTE It may seem a little awkward, but you define an object's GUID just ahead of the object itself. In other languages, you usually start off with the object itself.

The `importlib` statement is similar to the `import` keyword in Java. In the previous example, it is importing a set of standard OLE definitions. After the `importlib` comes the definition of the `IJavaObject` interface:

```
[ odl, dual, uuid(D65E5381-6D58-11d0-8F0B-444553540000) ]

interface IJavaObject : Idispatch
{
```

Notice that the `uuid` keyword is accompanied by the `odl` and `dual` keywords. The bracketed area where you normally define the `uuid` is used for any kind of attribute. You almost always find `uuid` there, because every interface and class must have its own unique identifier.

Whenever you define an interface in ODL, you use the `odl` keyword. The `dual` keyword specifies that the interface is a dual interface.

COM has two different ways of invoking methods—through a lookup table or through a dispatch interface. The lookup table is better known as a `vtable`—a virtual method lookup table, similar to the `vtable` in C++. The dispatch interface allows you to perform dynamic method invocation. When you use a dispatch interface, there is an extra level of lookup that takes place before the method is invoked. This tends to be slower than a `vtable` method invocation, but is useful to interpreted languages like Visual Basic. To allow the maximum flexibility, you can implement your classes with both `vtable` and dispatch interfaces by declaring them as dual interfaces.

The method definitions also look rather strange:

```
HRESULT reverseString( [in] BSTR reverseMe,
[out, retval] BSTR *reversed );
```

Believe it or not, the `reverseString` method really returns a string, and not the `HRESULT` value you see declared. The `HRESULT` return value is necessary when creating this dual interface. The actual return value is specified by the `[out, retval]` attribute for one of the parameters. A parameter with an attribute of `[in]` is an input parameter, while those with an `[out]` attribute are output parameters.

The BSTR data type is a basic string and is the common way to represent strings in COM. There are other ways, but BSTR is compatible with OLE and also Visual Basic. You may be pleasantly surprised to know that the Java-COM compiler translates the definition of `reverseString` into this rather simple method declaration:

```
public String reverseString(String reverseMe)
throws com.ms.com.ComException
```

The definition of the `JavaObject` class at the bottom of the ODL file tells what interfaces a `JavaObject` class implements. In this case, there is a single interface: `IJavaObject`. If you look at different classes available on your system, especially OLE servers, you will find that most classes implement several different interfaces.

Compiling an ODL File

The MKTYPLIB program that comes with Visual J++, and also the ActiveX SDK, compiles an ODL file into a type library file, which has an extension of .TLB. The `MKTYPLIB` command to compile `JavaObject.odl` is:

```
mktyplib JavaObject.odl
```

By default, MKTYPLIB uses the C preprocessor, which allows you to use `#include` and other preprocessor directives. Unfortunately, this only works if you have a C preprocessor. If you don't, you must use the `/nocpp` option, like this:

```
mktyplib /nocpp JavaObject.odl
```

Generating a GUID

The JavaObject ODL file contains three different GUIDs. You don't have to make these values up (in fact, you shouldn't). Instead, Visual C++ and the ActiveX SDK (and probably other packages, too) come with a tool called GUIDGEN which randomly generates these values. It can format them in a number of ways and can even copy them to the Clipboard automatically so you can paste them into your source code. Figure 43.2 shows a sample GUIDGEN session.

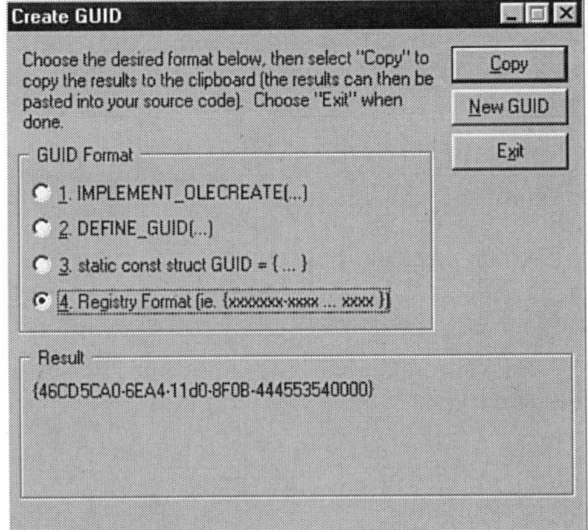

FIG. 43.2
The GUIDGEN tool automatically generates GUID values for you.

Creating COM Objects in Java

To create a Java object that implements one or more COM interfaces, you need to create special wrapper classes using the `JAVATLB` command. For example, to create the Wrapper classes for the information in `JavaObject.tlb` (which was compiled from `JavaObject.odl`), the `JAVATLB` command would be:

```
javatlb JavaObject.tlb
```

For the `JavaObject.tlb` file, `JAVATLB` creates an interface called `IJavaObject` and a Java class called `JavaObject`. These classes belong to the package `javaobject` (all lowercase) and are placed in the `\WINDOWS\JAVA\TRUSTLIB` directory. Remember that packages require their own subdirectory, so if you look in `\WINDOWS\JAVA\TRUSTLIB`, you will find a directory called javaobject that contains `IJavaObject.class` and `JavaObject.class`.

After the wrappers have been created, you only need to fill in the appropriate methods. Listing 43.2 shows the `JavaObjectImpl` class that implements the methods in the `IJavaObject` interface.

Listing 43.2 Source Code for *JavaObjectImpl.java*

```
import com.ms.com.*;
import javaobject.*;

public class JavaObjectImpl implements IJavaObject
{
```

continues

Listing 43.2 Continued

```
    public String reverseString(String in)
    throws ComException
    {
        StringBuffer buff = new StringBuffer();

// Start at the end of the input string and add characters
// to the string buffer. This puts the reverse of the string
// into the buffer.

        for (int i=in.length()-1; i >= 0; i—) {
            buff.append(in.charAt(i));
        }

// Return the contents of the buffer as a new string
        return buff.toString();
    }

    public int square(int val)
    throws ComException
    {
// Return the square of val
        return val * val;
    }
}
```

After you have compiled `JavaObjectImpl` (which you must compile with the Microsoft Java compiler, JVC), use the `JAVAREG` tool to put information about `JavaObjectImpl` into the system Registry. COM uses the Registry to locate COM objects and to find out how to run the server for a particular object. The following command registers `JavaObjectImpl` and gives it a `ProgID` of `JavaObject`:

```
JAVAREG /register /class:JavaObjectImpl /progid:JavaObject
```

CAUTION

Make sure that you do *not* put `.class` after `JavaObjectImpl` in the `JAVAREG` command. You want to give `JAVAREG` the name of the class, not the name of the file containing the class.

The `ProgID` value is a simple name that other programs like Visual Basic can use to locate the `JavaObject` class. `JAVAREG` creates an entry in the `HKEY_CLASSES_ROOT` section of the Registry called `JavaObject`, which contains a subkey called `CLSID` containing the class ID (GUID) for `JavaObjectImpl`. Figure 43.3 shows this Registry entry, as shown by the REGEDIT command.

`JAVAREG` also creates an entry under CLSID in `HKEY_CLASSES_ROOT`. The entry's key is the CLSID for `JavaObjectImpl` (the same CLSID contained in the `ProgID` entry for `JavaObject`). Figure 43.4 shows the entries made under the CLSID as shown by REGEDIT.

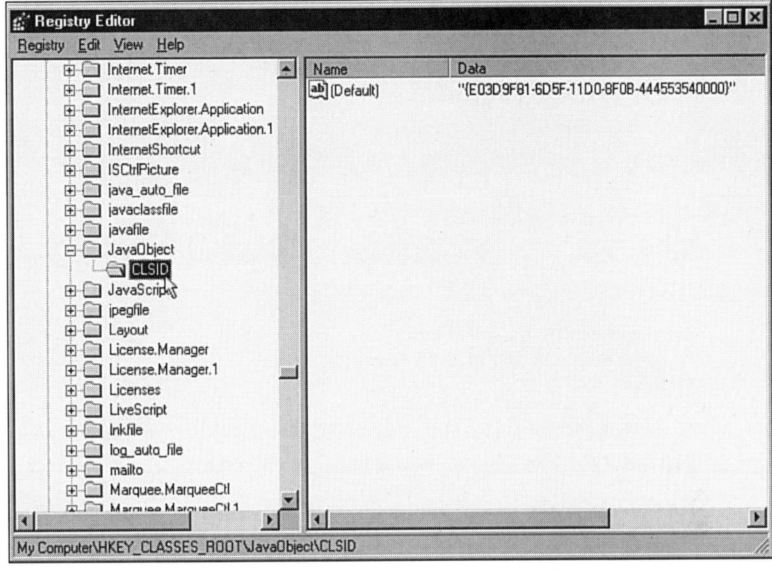

FIG. 43.3
A ProgID maps a simple text name to a 160-bit *CLSID* value.

The final step in making your class available to the rest of the world is to copy the JavaObjectImpl.class file into `\WINDOWS\JAVA\TRUSTLIB`.

NOTE If you have installed Windows 95 or Windows NT in a directory other than `\WINDOWS`, use that directory name followed by `\JAVA\TRUSTLIB`. For example, if you are running under Windows NT and it is installed in `\WINNT`, copy your file to `\WINNT\JAVA\TRUSTLIB`.

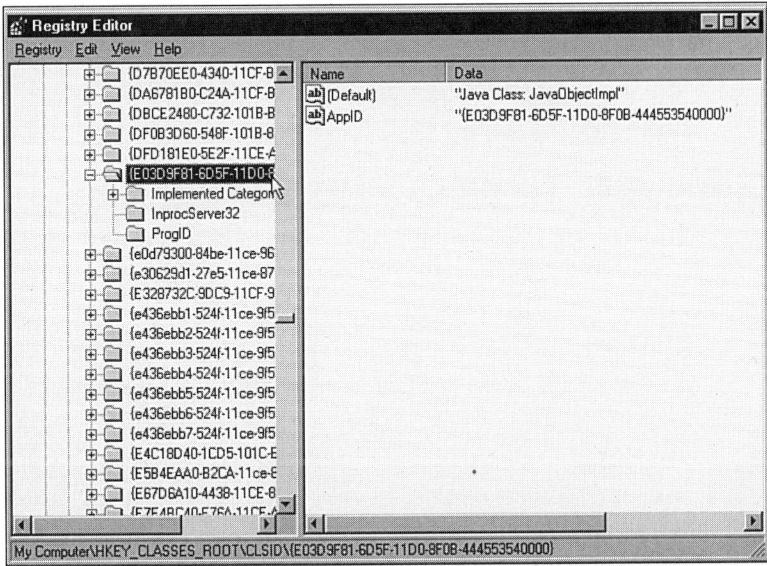

FIG. 43.4
JAVAREG makes a number of entries under the CLSID key.

Calling Java COM Objects from Visual Basic

If you have run JAVAREG to register your class, and you have copied the class to the TRUSTLIB directory, you should now be able to access your class from other programs. You can create a simple Visual Basic application to access this class. In the declaration section for the VB application, insert the following statement:

```
Dim javaob as Object
```

Next, the Form_Load subroutine, which is called when the VB application starts up, should look like this:

```
Private Sub Form_Load()
Set javaob = CreateObject("JavaObject")
End Sub
```

The JavaObject string is the ProgID for the object. If you used something else as the ProgID when you ran JAVAREG, you would use that name here.

Now you can make use of the methods in the JavaObject class. In this example VB application, there are two text fields: Text1 and Text2. The following subroutine takes the text from Text1, runs it through the reverseString method in JavaObject, and puts the resulting text in Text2:

```
Private Sub Text1_Change()
Text2.Text = javaob.reverseString(Text1.Text)
End Sub
```

Figure 43.5 shows this Visual Basic application in action.

FIG. 43.5
A Visual Basic application can use Java objects.

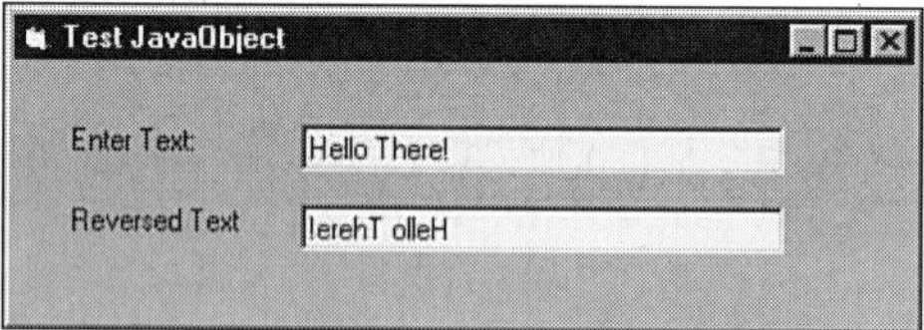

Calling Java Objects from Excel

Microsoft Excel and other Microsoft Office products have their own version of Visual Basic built-in. This means, of course, that you can also access Java objects from Excel!

> **CAUTION**
>
> You must use a 32-bit version of Excel for this to work. The 16-bit versions do not use 32-bit COM access, and cannot access Java objects. This example is shown with Excel 7.0a from the Office for Windows 95 suite.

To create an Excel function, start Excel and choose Insert, Macro, Module from the main menu, as shown in Figure 43.6.

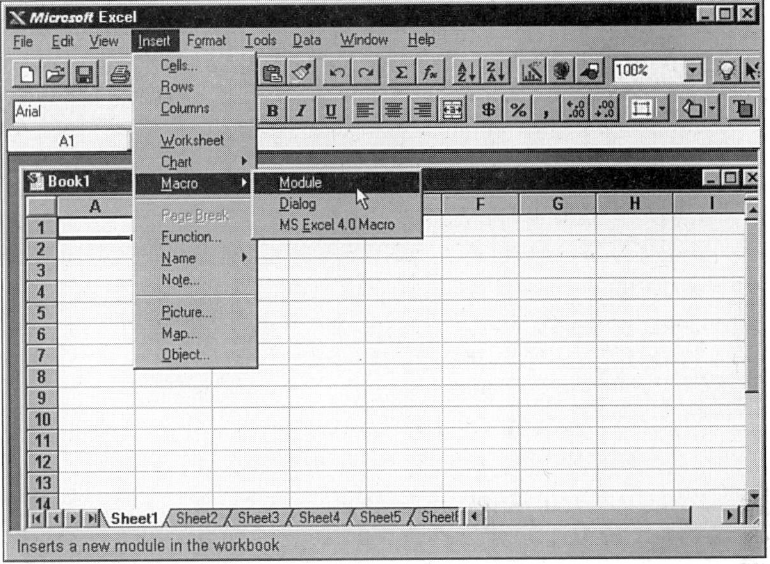

FIG. 43.6 To create an Excel function, you need to insert a code module.

The function must access the `JavaObject` class and then call `reverseString`. Listing 43.3 shows the `Reverser$` function.

Listing 43.3 *Reverser$* Function from ExcelDemo.xls

```
Function Reverser$(reverseMe$)
    Dim javaob As Object
    Set javaob = CreateObject("JavaObject")
    Reverser$ = javaob.reverseString(reverseMe$)
End Function
```

NOTE Make sure that you have a recent version of the Microsoft Java SDK. The earliest versions had problems with the COM integration.

After you have defined this function, you can use it in your spreadsheet. For example, assume that you want to take the information in cell A1 in the spreadsheet, reverse it, and place the results in cell A2. Just go to cell A2 and type the following formula:

```
=Reverser(A1)
```

Notice that there is no `$` at the end of `Reverser` in this case. Now, any text you type in A1 will automatically appear reversed in A2. Figure 43.7 shows a sample spreadsheet.

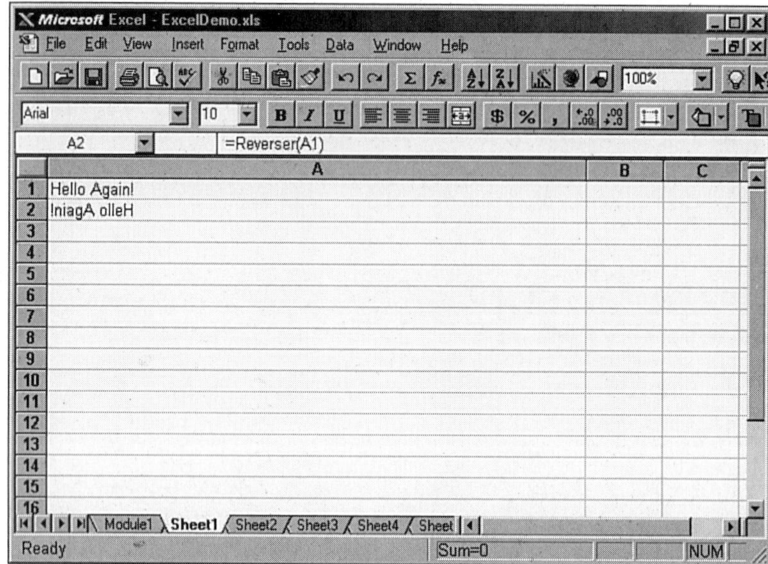

FIG. 43.7 Excel can use Java objects to perform interesting functions.

Calling COM Objects from Java

Just as you can access Java objects via COM, Java objects can access other COM-aware objects. This really opens up possibilities for you on the Windows platform. If you want to create a graph, you can use Excel's graphing capabilities. If you want to create a neatly formatted printout, you can create a document in Word and print it. The best part is you don't have to go through the pain of creating an ODL file, as long as you can get the type library for the application you want to use.

In the case of Microsoft Word, version 7, you can get the type library for free from Microsoft at **http://www.microsoft.com/WordDev/Articles/wb70endl.htm.**

After you have a type library, run `JAVATLB` on the library to create the Java wrappers. For example, the `JAVATLB` command for the Word 7 type library would be:

```
javatlb wb70en32.tlb
```

This command creates a `WordBasic` interface class that you can use. Because Word runs as a local server object, you have to do a little more work to access it.

The `LicenseMgr` object can access a local server object given the `CLSID` of the object. You don't want to look up the Word.Basic `CLSID` yourself and put it in the source code. Instead, you can access the system Registry from your program and discover the `CLSID` at runtime.

The `RegKey` class gives you access to the registry. Given a `RegKey` object, you retrieve subkeys by calling the `RegKey` constructor with the parent key. For instance, you want the key CLASSES_ROOT\Word.Basic\CLSID. You first need the `RegKey` for "CLASSES_ROOT." From that, you create a `RegKey` for Word.Basic, which is then used to create the `RegKey` for CLSID.

After you have the `RegKey` you want, you access the default value by calling the `enumValue` method. Listing 43.4 shows a demo program that runs Word 7.0, creates a simple "Hello World" document, and prints it.

Listing 43.4 Source Code for WordDemo.java

```
import wb70en32.*;
import com.ms.com.*;
import com.ms.lang.*;

public class WordDemo extends Object
{
    public static void main(String[] args)
    {
        try {

// Get the Registry Key for CLASSES_ROOT
            RegKey root = RegKey.getRootKey(RegKey.CLASSES_ROOT);

// From CLASSES_ROOT, get the key for Word.Basic
            RegKey wbkey = new RegKey(root,
                "Word.Basic", RegKey.KEYOPEN_READ);

// From Word.Basic, get the CLSID
            RegKey clsid = new RegKey(wbkey, "CLSID",
                RegKey.KEYOPEN_READ);

// Retrieve the CLSID from the CLSID key (it's the default value)
            String classID = ((RegKeyEnumValueString)clsid.
                enumValue(0)).value;

// Create a License Manager for accessing local server objects
            ILicenseMgr lm = (ILicenseMgr) new LicenseMgr();

// Get a reference to WordBasic
            WordBasic wb = (WordBasic)
                lm.createInstance(classID,
                    null, ComContext.LOCAL_SERVER);

// Create a new file
            wb.FileNewDefault();

// Insert some text
            wb.Insert("Hello World!");

            wb.InsertPara();

            wb.Insert("Hi there!");

// Print the text
            wb.FilePrintDefault();
```

continues

Listing 43.4 Continued

```
            } catch (Error e) {
                e.printStackTrace();
            }
        }
    }
```

Remember to use the `jview` command to run programs in the MS Java environment, rather than `java`.

If you want to see the methods available from the WordBasic object, use the OLE object viewer that comes with Visual J++ (OLE2VIEW) or the ActiveX SDK (OLEVIEW). Figure 43.8 shows the OLE2VIEW display of one of the methods in the `WordBasic` object.

One of the things you are bound to encounter with the WordBasic object, and others, is that some methods have parameters of the variant type. The Java-COM package comes with a `Variant` object that allows you to pass variant parameters. For example, if you want to call a method that takes two variant parameters, you create two instances of a `Variant` object. Variant parameters are used when parameters are optional. For this example, assume that the second parameter is optional and the first one is an integer. The sequence of events would go like this:

```
Variant p1 = new Variant(); // Create parameter 1
p1.putInt(5);     // Make the parameter value = 5

Variant p2 = new Variant(); // Create parameter 2
p2.noParam();     // Don't pass a value for this parameter

someObject.funMethod(v1, v2);     // Call the method
```

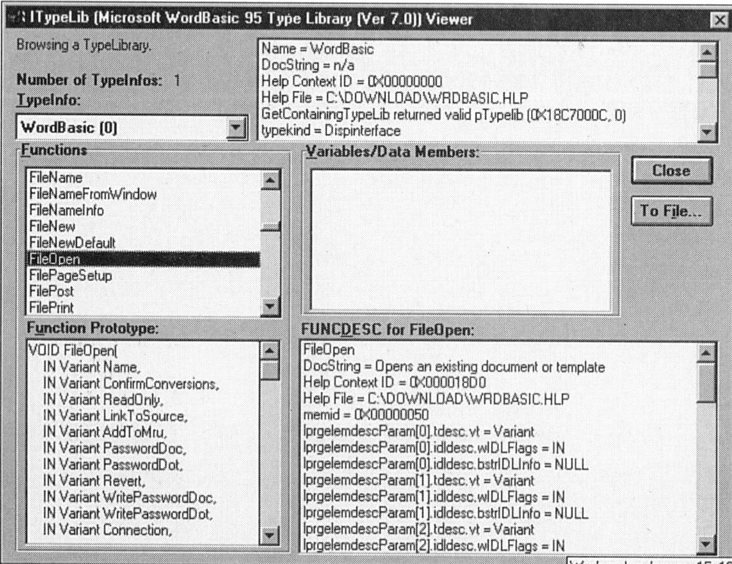

FIG. 43.8
OLEview and OLE2view allow you to examine the methods of COM objects.

Generally, there are `put` methods for the basic Java types like `int`, `short`, `double`, and so on. Also, for parameters that are passed by reference (ones that can also return a value), you use `putXXXRef`, like `putIntRef` or `putDoubleRef`. You can also use the `getXXX` and `getXXXRef` methods to retrieve the values stored in a `Variant` object. ●

PART VII

Advanced Java

CHAPTER 44

Java Media Framework

In this chapter

What Is the Java Media Framework?

In the first two incantations of Java, programmers were hard-pressed to use Java when they wanted to display complex media types like sound and video. Sure, Java had support for one audio type (au), but playing complex types like MIDI and WAV was not possible. In addition, video and animation could be done by creating slidelike presentations; but displaying AVI or MOV files again wasn't possible without a lot of work, and even then it wasn't practical. With the Java Media Framework, Java has come of multimedia age. The Java Media Framework provides the means to present all kinds of interesting media types. The Java Media Framework is an API for integrating advanced media formats into Java, such as video and sound. The media framework has several components, including media players, media capture, and conferencing. A key to any of these topics is in providing a timing mechanism, which determines when the next part of the media should be played. In other words, it's important to have a mechanism to keep a video stream playing at the same speed as an accompanying sound stream. Otherwise, you will end up with lips moving and somebody else's words coming out.

Creating a Media Player

To understand the Java Media Framework, it is best to jump straight in, by creating an applet that uses a media player. Putting a media player into an applet involves a few basic steps:

1. Create the URL for the media file.
2. Create the player for the media.
3. Tell the player to prefetch.
4. Add the player to the applet.
5. Start the player.

The first step is something you've done a dozen times already in this book. The next steps are what you need to do to create the player itself. To do this, you utilize the `Manager` class. The `Manager` class is actually the hub for getting both the timebase and the players. You need to give the manager the URL where the media file is located.

The first task is to create an URL for the media file and then to create the player. In the `BasicPlayer` class, this happens in the `init()` method, as shown in Listing 44.1.

Listing 44.1 Creating a Player and Its Associated URL

```
try {
      mediaURL = new URL(getDocumentBase(), mediaFile);
      player = Manager.createPlayer(mediaURL);
    }
    catch (IOException e) {
      System.err.println("URL for "+mediaFile+" is invalid");
    }
```

```
catch(NoPlayerException e) {
  System.err.println("Could not find a player for " + mediaURL);
        }
  }
```

By now you should be familiar with how the URL code is created in the second line of Listing 44.1. But just for review, the `getDocumentBase()` method returns the URL where the applet was originally loaded from, and with `mediaFile` representing the relative URL where the media file is located, the `mediaURL` ends up pointing to the fully qualified URL of the media file.

The next line is really the one you're interested in. The manager is asked to return the player that knows how to deal with the URL you've provided.

Note that there are two kinds of exceptions you need to catch in this situation. First, the URL constructor will throw an `IOException` if the URL isn't valid. Because we are using the `documentBase` of the applet, it's highly unlikely that this exception will ever occur for this particular example, but you need to catch this exception.

The second kind of exception is the `NoPlayerException`. This is a new one from the media package. This particular exception is thrown when the manager knows of no player that is designed for the media type the URL points to. For instance, if you had pointed to a `.wav` file and there was no player for the `.wav` file, the `NoPlayerException` would get thrown.

Prefetching the Media

The next step in the process is to prefetch the media. Prefetching causes two things to happen. First, the player goes through a process called realization. It then starts to download the media file so that some of it can be cached. This reduces the latency time before the player can start actually playing the media. Later in this chapter, we will go more into the states the player can go through, such as prefetch and realize. For now, it's sufficient to recognize that you need to ask the player to prefetch. As Listing 44.2 shows, in your most basic player you will do this in the `start()` method.

Listing 44.2 In the *start* Method, We Prefetch the Media We Are Going to Play

```
public void start() {
  if (player != null)
    //prefetch starts the player.
    //Prefetch returns immediately, just like getImage
    player.prefetch();
}
```

As you can see, all you need to do to prefetch the media is call the `prefetch` method on the player.

Adding the Player to Your Application

Adding the player to the application is actually kind of tricky. The player itself is not an AWT component. So you don't add the player itself, but its visual representation. To get the visual component, player has a method called `getVisualComponent()`. However, there is a catch—before you can get the visual component, the player must first be realized. Again, we will talk more about this later, but for now, it's important to understand that just as an image isn't valid right after you call `getImage()`, the player is not valid until it has been realized.

How then do you know whether the component has been realized? Well, player has a method called `getState()` that returns the state of the current player. If you wanted to, you could constantly check the state, and when the state of the player was finally realized, you could ask for the visual component.

Fortunately, there is a more efficient way. As you might recall, `Image` has an interface called `ImageObserver`. The media API has a similar method, called `ControllerListener`. `ControllerListener` has one method—`controllerUpdate(ControllerEvent)`. We can use the `controllerUpdate` method to know when the media has been fetched, as shown in Listing 44.3.

Listing 44.3 The *controllerUpdate* Method Is Called Each Time the Controller Changes State

```
public synchronized void controllerUpdate(ControllerEvent event)
{
    if (event instanceof RealizeCompleteEvent)
    {
        // Once the player has been realized add the
        //visual component to the screen
        if ((visualComponent = player.getVisualComponent()) != null)
            add("Center", visualComponent);

        // draw the component
        validate();
    }
}
```

The `controllerUpdate()` method is called each time the state of the controller changes. As we will see later in this chapter, the player is itself a controller, and it can go through many different state changes.

To differentiate between these changes, there are many events that can be generated. In this case, what we are looking for is the `RealizeCompleteEvent`. To determine which event has been received, we use the `instanceof` operator to evaluate whether the current event is of the class `RealizeCompleteEvent`. If it is, we know that the player has been realized, and we can now request the visual component from the player and add it to the application.

It is possible that the `getVisualComponent()` method will return a null. This happens when there is no visual representation of the media. For instance, a player for an audio file might not need to have a visual component. Obviously, that means you need to test for the null condition before adding it to the applet.

In addition, to make sure that the component is actually represented in the applet, you do need to make sure that the applet is validated. The `validate()` method forces any container, including an applet, to make sure that all the components that have been added are actually present on the screen.

Registering the Applet as a Listener

Before we can actually utilize the new `controllerUpdate()` method, we need to back up a step. You're probably already wondering how the player knows to inform the application about the changes. The answer is that it doesn't know right away. To have the player call `controllerUpdate()`, you must first register your application with the player. In traditional event listener fashion, this is done using player's `addControllerListener()` method.

Just like all `java.awt.event` listeners, after a component has been registered as a listener, its listener method will be called (in this case, `controllerUpdate()`) any time an event occurs. For the current purposes, you will add the `addControllerListener` code to the `init()` method of the applet, so the whole `init()` method now looks as shown in Listing 44.4.

Listing 44.4 In the *init()* Method, We Add *this* as a Listener to the Player

```
public void init() {
    String mediaFile = null;
    URL mediaURL = null;

    setLayout(new BorderLayout());

    if ((mediaFile = getParameter("file")) == null) {
      System.err.print ("Media File not present.");
      System.err.println("  Required parameter is 'file'");
    }
    else {
      try {
        mediaURL = new URL(getDocumentBase(), mediaFile);

        player = Manager.createPlayer(mediaURL);

        if(player != null) {
          //tell the player to add this applet as a listener
          player.addControllerListener(this);
        }
        else
          System.err.println("failed to creat player for " + mediaURL);
      }
      catch (IOException e) {
        System.err.println("URL for "+mediaFile+" is invalid");
      }
      catch(NoPlayerException e) {
        System.err.println("Could not find a player for " + mediaURL);
      }
    }
  }
```

Starting the Player

The next step in the process is to tell the player to start. However, just as with requesting the visual component, the player cannot be started until it has reached a certain state—namely, the player must have managed to complete the prefetching that we talked about earlier.

Technically speaking, as soon as the player has been realized, you can start it; however, it's unwise to do so because it's likely that the media will play choppily. The prefetching of the media allows the player to streamline some of the media so that it can smoothly play the whole thing.

To determine when the prefetch has been completed, we can look for a `PrefetchCompletedEvent`. After this event has been generated, the prefetching is complete. To utilize this knowledge, we will add the code shown in Listing 44.5 to the `controllerUpdate` method.

Listing 44.5 Start the Player After the Prefetch Is Complete

```
if (event instanceof PrefetchCompleteEvent) {
  // start the player once it's been prefetched
  player.start();
}
```

Cleaning Up and Stopping the Player

Being good public programmers, we must use the `stop()` method of the applet to clean up after ourselves. As you will recall, the `stop()` method is called when the browser leaves the current Web page. After the browser leaves the page, we should stop playing the media.

Stopping the player is easy to do; we just use the `stop()` method on the player. However, there is one additional step we should take—removing the media from memory. As you can well imagine, keeping a 2 or 3MB video that is no longer needed in memory is very wasteful and will eventually bring the whole system to its knees. Fortunately, player has a method for just this purpose: `deallocate()`. As soon as you know that you no longer need a media, you should tell the player to deallocate it so that it can be garbage-collected.

Using both the player's `stop()` and the `deallocate()` methods, you can create the applet's `stop()` method. Listing 44.6 shows what the complete `stop()` method should look like.

Listing 44.6 Stop the Player and Deallocate the Media in the *stop()* Method

```
public void stop()
{
    if (player != null)
    {
        // Stop media playback
        player.stop();
        //release resources for the media
        player.deallocate();
```

```
        }
    }
```

Putting It All Together

Now, you can put everything you have just learned together into a complete player. Listing 44.7 shows what the complete player looks like.

Listing 44.7 *BasicPlayer.java*—A Complete Media Player Using the Java Media Framework Classes

```
import java.applet.*;
import java.awt.*;
import java.net.*;
import java.io.*;
import javax.media.*;

/**
 * A basic media player Applet
 */
public class BasicPlayer extends Applet implements ControllerListener {
  // the media player
  Player player = null;

  // Component where video will appear
  Component visualComponent = null;
  /**
   * Read the applet file parameter and create the media player.
   */
  public void init() {
    String mediaFile = null;
    URL mediaURL = null;

    setLayout(new BorderLayout());

    if ((mediaFile = getParameter("file")) == null) {
      System.err.print("Media File not present.");
      System.err.println("  Required parameter is 'file'");
    }
    else {
      try {
        mediaURL = new URL(getDocumentBase(), mediaFile);

        player = Manager.createPlayer(mediaURL);

        if(player != null) {
          //tell the player to add this applet as a listener
          player.addControllerListener(this);
        }
        else
          System.err.println("failed to creat player for " + mediaURL);
      }
```

continues

Listing 44.7 Continued

```
      catch (IOException e) {
        System.err.println("URL for "+mediaFile+" is invalid");
      }
      catch(NoPlayerException e) {
        System.err.println("Could not find a player for " + mediaURL);
      }
    }
  }

  public void start() {
    if (player != null)
      //prefetch starts the player.
      //Prefetch returns immediately, just like getImage
      player.prefetch();
  }


  public void stop() {
    if (player != null) {
      // Stop media playback
      player.stop();
      //release resources for the media
      player.deallocate();
    }
  }


  //------  Controller interface method ----------

  /**
   * Whenever there is a media event,
   * the controllerUpdate method is called
   * for all the Player's listeners
   */
  public synchronized void controllerUpdate(ControllerEvent event) {
    if (event instanceof RealizeCompleteEvent) {
      // Once the player has been realized add
      // the visual component to the screen
      if ((visualComponent = player.getVisualComponent()) != null)
        add("Center", visualComponent);

      // draw the component
      validate();
    }

    else if (event instanceof PrefetchCompleteEvent) {
      // start the player once it's been prefetched
      player.start();
    }
  }
}
```

Compiling the BasicPlayer

To compile the BasicPlayer under JDK 1.2, simply use the javac compiler. However, under JDK1.1 it is also possible to compile the BasicPlayer. To do so, you need to first obtain a copy of the JMF classes from the vendor for your particular machine. For Windows 95/98, Windows NT, and Solaris users, you can obtain a set of classes from Sun Microsystems, Inc. at

`http://java.sun.com/products/java-media/jmf/1.0/`

After you have downloaded the files from these sites and installed them, you need to track down the media classes. In the case of the Sun installation, the file you want is called `jmf.jar` and is installed in the plug-ins directory (if you're using Netscape Navigator).

To compile the program, you need to include the `jmf.jar` file in your classpath and then run the javac program.

Running BasicPlayer

Before you can run the BasicPlayer, you must first create an HTML file with the appropriate file. In this case, we will use the sample MPEG file included with the JMF classes. Your HTML file should look similar to Listing 44.8.

Listing 44.8 ***BasicPlayer.html*****—A Basic HTML File That Includes Your Applet**

```
<html>
<body>
<applet code="BasicPlayer" width="320" height="300">
<param name="FILE" value="sample2.mpg">
Sorry, your browser does not support Java(TM) Applets.
</applet>
</body>
</html>
```

You now have two options for running BasicPlayer. First, you can use Netscape 4.03 with the final JDK 1.1 patch, or Internet Explorer 4, and if you have properly installed the media files from your vendor, you can now open the `BasicPlayer.html` file.

The second option is to use the Appletviewer program included with the JDK. To use Appletviewer, first make sure that you still have the `media.zip` file included in your classpath, and then simply run it the way you are used to:

```
Appletviewer BasicPlayer.html
```

If everything has gone as planned, you should see and hear the promotional Intel video start to play eventually.

The States of the Player

Now that you have made it through the most basic player, it's time to go back and take a look at the stages or states that the player goes through as it progresses. Figure 44.1 shows the states that a player goes through during normal operation.

FIG. 44.1
A player travels through many states before it is started.

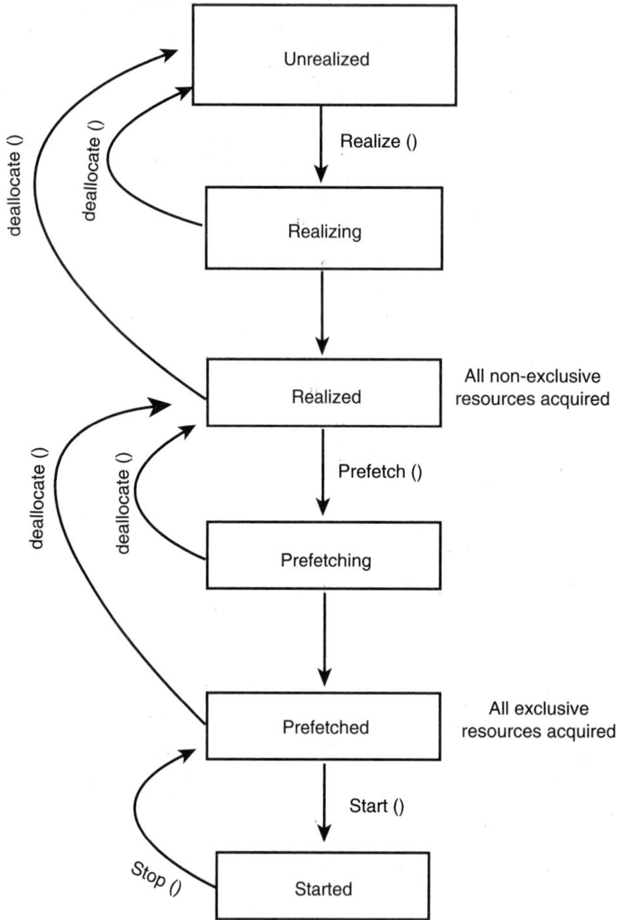

From Figure 44.1, you can see why we needed to track the state of the player before each method is called. The states of the player are as listed here:

Unrealized: When you first create a player, it is in the unrealized state. At this point, the player does not know anything about the media except what the URL to the media is. To move the player to the next stage, you can use the `realize()` method.

NOTE The `prefetch()` method will cause the `realize()` method to be run if the player is not yet realized. Therefore, you can skip over the `realize()` method as we did in the BasicPlayer and jump straight to the `prefetch()` method if you want.

Realizing: In the realizing state, the player determines the resource requirements for the particular media. For instance, it might require a rendering engine to play a FLIC file. In the realizing state, the player acquires all of these resources that are non-exclusive. A non-exclusive resource is a resource that can be shared with multiple players. The exclusive resources are acquired later in the prefetching state.

Realized: When a player enters the realized state, the `RealizeCompleteEvent` is issued. In the realized state, the player knows all the resources it will need in order to render the media. In addition, it knows enough about the media itself to be able to present the visual component of the media. The realized player has a "connection" to all the resources it will need, but it does not actually own any of the resources that would prevent another player from starting. These resources are known as scarce resources because they can not be shared among different programs within the computer.

Prefetching: To get the player to move into the prefetching state, you can use the `prefetch()` method. In the prefetching state, the player is preloading some of the media it is preparing to present. It also obtains those scarce resources it couldn't obtain back in the realizing state.

NOTE The `start()` method will cause the `prefetch()` method to be called on a player if the media has not been fetched yet. However, unlike `prefetch()`, `start` cannot be called on an unrealized player.

Also note that the prefetching state might have to be reentered if the media is repositioned, or if the timebase for the media is changed and requires additional amounts of the media to be downloaded and buffered.

Prefetched: Upon entering the prefetched state, a player issues the `PrefetchCompleteEvent`. When it is in the prefetched state, a player is ready to go. It has obtained all its resources and has enough of the media to begin playing. In short, it is ready to be started.

Started: As you saw in the BasicPlayer, to get a player to start you need to call the `start()` method. When a player is started, it enters the started state. After a player has been started, its clock is running and its media time has been set. If the player is not waiting for a particular time to start playing, it will begin immediately; otherwise, it will await the appropriate time and begin.

Adding Controls to the Player

Now that you have the player in your applet, what will you do if you want to let the user control the motion of the player? The Media API has thought ahead for you. Because obviously you don't want to be responsible for trying to figure out what controls are necessary for each type of player, the player has the capability to give you a set of controls using the `getControlPanelComponent()` method.

Like the `getVisualComponent()` method, the `getControlPanelComponent()` cannot be used until after the player has been realized. If you look back in the preceding section, you will see why. Until a player has been realized, it really doesn't know what type of media it will be playing.

Listing 44.9 shows a BasicPlayer with the control panel added. Figure 44.2 shows what it will look like when you run BasicPlayer.

Listing 44.9 Adding the Control Panel Is Simple and Easy in the *controllerUpdate* Method

```
import java.applet.*;
import java.awt.*;
import java.net.*;
import java.io.*;
import javax.media.*;

/**
 * A basic media player Applet
 */
public class BasicPlayer extends Applet implements ControllerListener {
  Player player = null;                  // the media player
  Component visualComponent = null;     // Component where video will appear
  Component controlComponent = null;
  /**
   * Read the applet file parameter and create the media player.
   */
  public void init() {
    String mediaFile = null;
    URL mediaURL = null;

    setLayout(new BorderLayout());

    if ((mediaFile = getParameter("file")) == null) {
      System.err.println("Media File not present.  Required parameter is
➥'file'");
    }
    else {
      try {
        mediaURL = new URL(getDocumentBase(), mediaFile);

        player = Manager.createPlayer(mediaURL);

        if(player != null) {
          //tell the player to add this applet as a listener
          player.addControllerListener(this);
        }
        else
          System.err.println("failed to creat player for " + mediaURL);
      }
      catch (IOException e) {
        System.err.println("URL for "+mediaFile+" is invalid");
      }
```

```
      catch(NoPlayerException e) {
        System.err.println("Could not find a player for " + mediaURL);
      }
    }
  }

  public void start() {
    if (player != null)
      //prefetch starts the player.
      //Prefetch returns immediately, just like getImage
      player.prefetch();
  }


  public void stop() {
    if (player != null) {
      // Stop media playback
      player.stop();
      //release resources for the media
      player.deallocate();
    }
  }


  //------  Controller interface method ----------

  /**
   * Whenever there is a media event, the
   * controllerUpdate method is called
   * for all the Player's listeners
   */
  public synchronized void controllerUpdate(ControllerEvent event) {
    if (event instanceof RealizeCompleteEvent) {
      // Once the player has been realized add
      // the visual component to the screen
      if ((visualComponent = player.getVisualComponent()) != null)
        add("Center", visualComponent);
      if ((controlComponent = player.getControlPanelComponent()) != null)
        if(visualComponent != null)
          add("South",controlComponent);
        else
          add("Center",controlComponent);


      // draw the components
      validate();
    }

    else if (event instanceof PrefetchCompleteEvent) {
      // start the player once it's been prefetched
      player.start();
    }
  }
}
```

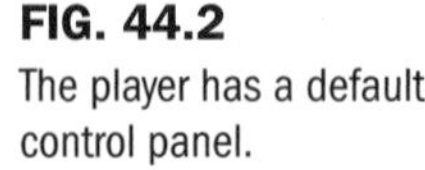
FIG. 44.2
The player has a default control panel.

Controlling the Player Programmatically

In addition to using the control panel, you can control the motion of the programmer using methods in player. You might want to do this for several reasons. One reason might be that you want to put up buttons to allow the player to control the player, but you don't want to use the default control panel. Another reason is that you might want to change the way the player is playing because of some other condition in your program.

Starting the Player

As you have already seen in the BasicPlayer example, player has a basic method—`start()`, which tells the player to start. However, there is a more fundamental method that allows you to start a player and specify when it will actually start displaying its media. The `syncStart()` method is the method that actually causes the player to start.

First, here's a brief review of what the `start()` method does. Based on the state of the player, the `start()` method will sequentially call first `prefetch()` for all the players under its control (later in this chapter, controlling multiple players is discussed) and bring them into the prefetched state, and then will call `syncStart()`.

Setting the Media Time

Often you would like to take one video and jump around it. It's not unlike playing tracks two and five on your CD player without playing through the whole CD. Fortunately, the media framework accommodates just such a need with the `setMediaTime()` method.

The `setMediaTime()` method takes a long number as a parameter, and that number represents the time in nanoseconds. Unlike with most time increments you might be familiar with (such as when sleeping a thread), you are not dealing in milliseconds here, but the finer nanosecond increment.

Changing the Rate of Play

Have you ever wanted to speed up or slow down video? How about play it backward? The player has a method for just such an activity. The method is `setRate()`, and it allows you to change the rate at which the media is played. However, you can use `setRate()` only before the player is actually started. Calling `setRate` on a started player causes an exception to be thrown.

The `setRate()` method might not be able to actually set the rate of the media play. You see, the only thing that's guaranteed is that a player will be able to play the media at a rate of 1.0. The `setRate()` method returns to you the actual rate that has been applied.

Fortunately, the AVI player supports playing the file at many different rates, so you can add a rate change to the BasicPlayer. Change the `controllerUpdate` method in BasicPlayer as shown in Listing 44.10.

Listing 44.10 Change the *controllerUpdate* Method to Adjust the Rate of Play

```
public synchronized void controllerUpdate(ControllerEvent event)
{
if (event instanceof RealizeCompleteEvent)
{
    // Once the player has been realized add the visual component to the screen
    if ((visualComponent = player.getVisualComponent()) != null)
        add("Center", visualComponent);
    if ((controlComponent = player.getControlPanelComponent()) != null)
        if(visualComponent != null)
            add("South",controlComponent);
        else
            add("Center",controlComponent);


    // draw the components
        validate();
}

else if (event instanceof PrefetchCompleteEvent)
{
    System.out.println("prefetching:"+(new Date()));
    player.setRate((float)2.0);
    // start the player once it's been prefetched
    player.start();
}
}
```

Changing the Sound Volume

The capability to change the volume of the sound for the player is very important. To change the volume, the JMF has dedicated a whole class: `GainControl`. The first step in changing the volume is to get the `GainControl` from the player. To do so, you can invoke the `getGainControl()` method.

Some players do not have an audio component to them. Those players return null from the `getGainControl` method, but for all others, after you have the `GainControl`, you can change the volume in many ways.

Perhaps the most obvious thing to do with the audio is to turn it off all together, or mute it. Lo and behold, the `GainControl` class just happens to have a `mute()` method for this purpose.

Aside from muting the volume altogether, there are two distinctly different ways to control the volume of the player. The first way is to adjust the volume based on a level. A level is an arbitrary number between 0 and 1.0. When set to 1.0, the volume is basically on full. Set to 0, it's almost indistinguishable from the muted setting.

To change the `GainControl`'s volume level, you can use the `setLevel()` method. There is also an accompanying `getLevel()` method to retrieve the level of the `GainControl`. Remember that the only valid numbers are between 0 and 1.0.

The problem with the level mechanism, however, is that it doesn't allow you as a programmer to know how loud the media will actually play. Typically, sound engineers deal with sound in terms of decibels. The level only tells you that if you set the level to 0.5, it's half as loud as at 1.0. Fortunately, the media API provides a means to set the decibel level of the volume. However, this technique is really only a guess on the media player's standpoint. It cannot account for things like the volume of your external speakers, but it instead makes a reasonable guess based on your system.

Resizing a Media Player

The media framework has the capability to allow you to resize a media component. Obviously, you want to be able to add a media player's visual component to a panel just like any other component. To let the LayoutManager do its work, it's necessary for the media player to allow you to resize the component.

To see this at work, we need do no more than change the `WIDTH` and `HEIGHT` parameters in the HTML file for the BasicPlayer. Because the border layout will automatically resize the visual component to fit, if you shrink the size of the applet, you will witness the automatic rescaling of the media component. Try using the HTML file as shown in Listing 44.11. Figure 44.3 demonstrates just what BasicPlayer will look like now.

Listing 44.11 *BasicPlayer2.html*—Reducing the *width* and *height* Parameters Helps Show Rescaling

```
<html>
<body>
        <applet code="BasicPlayer" WIDTH="160" HEIGHT="150">
        <param name="FILE" value="ExampleVideo.avi">
        Sorry, your browser does not support Java(TM) Applets.
        </applet>
</body>
</html>
```

FIG. 44.3
The media framework automatically rescales to the applet's size.

Adding a Progress Bar

As you know, downloading a multimegabyte file over the Internet can take a long time. In fact, it might seem an eternity during the time it takes to download a file. If the download takes too long, users are even likely to think that the whole system has hung.

However, if there is some activity from your applet, a user will realize that the system itself has not hung. The file won't take any less time to download, but the users might be a bit more tolerant. One perfect way to establish some activity is with a progress bar.

As you will recall, `ImageObservers` are notified each time more of the image is downloaded off of the Internet. Likewise, a media player generates an event, `CachingControlEvent`; underlying this is the `CachingControl`. Most players have a controller whose sole responsibility is to know the status of the download of the media. In addition, fortunately for you, the `CachingControl` has a progress-bar component. Much like the visual component and the control-component elements that the player has, the progress-bar component can be added to any container.

We can use the progress bar to add a great deal to the user's experience. Listing 44.12 shows the BasicPlayer with the progress bar added to it.

Listing 44.12 ***ProgressPlayer.java*—The BasicPlayer with a Progress Bar Added**

```
import java.applet.*;
import java.awt.*;
import java.net.*;
import javax.media.*;
import java.util.Date;

/**
 * A basic media player Applet
 */
public class ProgressPlayer extends Applet implements ControllerListener
{
    Player player = null;                    // the media player
    Component visualComponent = null;    // Component where video will appear
    Component controlComponent = null;
    Component progressBar = null;
    /**
```

continues

Listing 44.12 Continued

```
     * Read the applet file parameter and create the media player.
     */
    public void init()
    {
        System.out.println("init:"+(new Date()));
        String mediaFile = null;
        URL mediaURL = null;

        setLayout(new BorderLayout());

        if ((mediaFile = getParameter("file")) == null)
        {
            System.err.println("Media File not present.
➥   Required parameter is 'file'");
        }
        else
        {
            try
            {
                mediaURL = new URL(getDocumentBase(), mediaFile);
                player = Manager.createPlayer(mediaURL);

                if(player != null)
                {
                    //tell the player to add this applet as a listener
                    player.addControllerListener(this);
                }
                else
                  System.err.println("failed to creat player for " + mediaURL);
            }
            catch (MalformedURLException e)
            {
                System.err.println("URL for "+mediaFile+" is invalid");
            }
            catch(NoPlayerException e)
            {
                System.err.println("Could not find a player for " + mediaURL);
            }
        }
    }

    public void start()
    {
        if (player != null)
            //prefetch starts the player.
            //Prefetch returns immediately, just like getImage
            player.prefetch();
    }


    public void stop()
    {
        if (player != null)
```

```
        {
            // Stop media playback
            player.stop();
            //release resources for the media
            player.deallocate();
        }
    }


    //------  Controller interface method ----------

    /**
      * Whenever there is a media event, the controllerUpdate method is called
     * for all the Player's listeners
     */
    public synchronized void controllerUpdate(ControllerEvent event)
    {
        if (event instanceof RealizeCompleteEvent)
        {
            // Once the player has been realized add the
➥visual component to the screen
            if ((visualComponent = player.getVisualComponent()) != null)
                add("Center", visualComponent);
            if ((controlComponent = player.getControlPanelComponent()) != null)
                if(visualComponent != null)
                    add("South",controlComponent);
                else
                    add("Center",controlComponent);


            // draw the components
                validate();
        }

        else if (event instanceof PrefetchCompleteEvent)
        {
            System.out.println("prefetching:"+(new Date()));
            // start the player once it's been prefetched
            player.start();
        }
        else if (event instanceof CachingControlEvent) {

            // Put a progress bar up when downloading starts,
            // take it down when downloading ends.
            CachingControlEvent  cce = (CachingControlEvent) event;
            CachingControl      cc = cce.getCachingControl();
            long cc_progress       = cce.getContentProgress();
            long cc_length         = cc.getContentLength();

            if (progressBar == null)  // Add the bar if not already there ...
                if ((progressBar = cc.getProgressBarComponent()) != null) {
                    add("North", progressBar);
                    validate();
                }
```

continues

Part VII Ch 44

Listing 44.12 Continued

```
                    if (progressBar != null)  // Remove bar when finished downloading
                              if (cc_progress == cc_length) {
                                  remove (progressBar);
                                  progressBar = null;
                                  validate();
                              }
                 }
         }
}
```

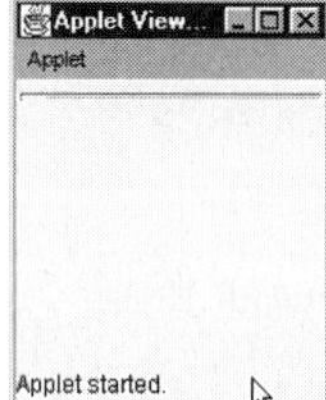

FIG. 44.4 While the player downloads the media, the progress bar shows the status.

Linking Multiple Players

When you have more than one player working on a panel, it's very likely that you would like to start and stop them with a single controller. To do this, you need to be able to link the controllers.

The player has a method for just this purpose: `addController()`. The purpose of the `addController` method is to tell the player to also control the other player. To review this means that with the line

```
masterPlayer.addController(slavePlayer);
```

`slavePlayer` is controlled by `masterPlayer`. However, before you can control another player, the slave player needs to be realized. The reason for this goes back to how much the player knows about itself when it's first created. As you will recall, before a player is actually realized, it doesn't even know what kind of media it will be playing. At that point, it doesn't know what kind of controller it will have, so it can't give control to another player.

To gain control of another player, the timebases for both players must be compatible. To make sure that this is the case, the master player will try to give the slave player its timebase. If this attempt fails, however, the `addController` method will throw an `IncompatibleTimeBaseException`.

Listing 44.13 is an example of the BasicPlayer with two side-to-side players, which are controlled with a single control. After the player starts, you will see a single control panel. Press the play button and they will both start.

Listing 44.13 The *Primary Player*

```
import java.applet.*;
import java.awt.*;
import java.net.*;
import javax.media.*;
import java.util.Date;

/**
 * A basic media player Applet
 */
public class PrimaryPlayer extends Applet implements ControllerListener
{
    Player player = null;                // the media player
    Player slavePlayer = null;
    Component visualComponent = null;    // Component where video will appear
    Component slaveVisualComponent = null;
    Component controlComponent = null;
    Component progressBar = null;
    /**
     * Read the applet file parameter and create the media player.
     */
    public void init()
    {
    String mediaFile = null;
        URL mediaURL = null;

        setLayout(new BorderLayout());

        if ((mediaFile = getParameter("file")) == null)
        {
            System.err.println("Media File not present.
➥  Required parameter is 'file'");
        }
        else
        {
            try
            {
                mediaURL = new URL(getDocumentBase(), mediaFile);
                player = Manager.createPlayer(mediaURL);
                slavePlayer = Manager.createPlayer(mediaURL);

                if(player != null)
                {
                    //tell the player to add this applet as a listener
                    player.addControllerListener(this);
                }
                else{
                  System.err.println("failed to creat player for " + mediaURL);
                }

                if(slavePlayer != null)
                {
```

continues

Listing 44.13 Continued

```
                    //tell the player to add this applet as a listener
                    slavePlayer.addControllerListener(this);
                }
                else{
                  System.err.println("failed to creat player for " + mediaURL);
                }

            }
            catch (MalformedURLException e)
            {
                System.err.println("URL for "+mediaFile+" is invalid");
            }
            catch(NoPlayerException e)
            {
                System.err.println("Could not find a player for " + mediaURL);
            }

        }
    }

    public void start()
    {
        if (player != null)
            //prefetch starts the player.
            //Prefetch returns immediately, just like getImage
            player.prefetch();
        if (slavePlayer !=null)
            slavePlayer.prefetch();
    }


    public void stop()
    {
        if (player != null)
        {
            // Stop media playback
            player.stop();
            //release resources for the media
            player.deallocate();
        }
    }


    //------  Controller interface method ----------

    /**
      * Whenever there is a media event, the controllerUpdate method is called
     * for all the Player's listeners
     */
    public synchronized void controllerUpdate(ControllerEvent event)
    {
        if (event instanceof RealizeCompleteEvent)
        {
```

```
            System.out.println("realized");
            // Once the player has been realized add the visual
➥ component to the screen
            if (event.getSource() == slavePlayer){
                System.out.println("slave");
                if ((slaveVisualComponent = slavePlayer.
➥getVisualComponent()) != null)
                    add("West", slaveVisualComponent);
                try{
                    player.addController (slavePlayer);
                }
                catch (IncompatibleTimeBaseException e)
                {
                    System.err.println("Could not attach player "+e);
                }
                validate();

            }
            else{
            if ((visualComponent = player.getVisualComponent()) != null)
                    add("East", visualComponent);
            if ((controlComponent = player.getControlPanelComponent()) != null)
                    if(visualComponent != null)
                        add("South",controlComponent);
                    else
                        add("Center",controlComponent);

            // draw the components
                validate();
            }

        }

        if (event instanceof PrefetchCompleteEvent){
        //player.setRate((float)2.0);
            // start the player once it's been prefetched
         //player.setMediaTime(20000);
            player.start();
        }
        else if (event instanceof CachingControlEvent) {

            // Put a progress bar up when downloading starts,
            // take it down when downloading ends.

            CachingControlEvent  e = (CachingControlEvent) event;
            CachingControl      cc = e.getCachingControl();
            long cc_progress       = e.getContentProgress();
            long cc_length         = cc.getContentLength();

            if (progressBar == null)  // Add the bar if not already there ...
                if ((progressBar = cc.getProgressBarComponent()) != null) {
                    add("North", progressBar);
                    validate();
                }
```

continues

Listing 44.13 Continued

```
                if (progressBar != null)  // Remove bar when finished downloading
                    if (cc_progress == cc_length) {
                        remove (progressBar);
                        progressBar = null;
                        validate();
                    }
            }
        }
    }
```

Creating Your Own Media Stream

Pull Media Streams

As you are aware, there are several ways to get data into a client. And more important, there are two basic subsets for retrieving data. One basic type is pull media streams, in which the client requests that the server send it something. This is how your Web browser works. You go out to a Web site and click on a URL. Your browser asks the server to send it that Web page, and off things go. The other type of datastream, which we will talk about later, is called push media. Push media results when the server automatically sends something to the client, or as some have put it, broadcasts information to your client.

Pull media is typical of many of the Internet protocols. For instance, the two most popular protocols on the Internet, HTTP and FTP, are both examples of pull streams. You have already seen how the HTTP protocol can be utilized in the BasicPlayer.

Next, you'll explore how to build your own pull stream.

Push Media Streams

Push streams have recently been popularized by Pointcast and Marimba. One basic advantage of pull streams is that you can guarantee that the client will receive 100 percent of all the data sent from the server. Because of this, your player does not need to know how to accommodate the gaps in data that push streams are likely to have. The push player needs to know how to handle gaps in data when they accrue, and it needs to be able to account for them.

A Larger Application

Now that you have read about all the controls for the player, you can put everything together and create your own custom control panel. You'll use all the methods you've learned to use up until now. See Listing 44.14.

Listing 44.14 *CustomPlayer.java*

```
import java.applet.*;
import java.awt.*;
import java.net.*;
import java.media.*;

/**
 * This is a Java Applet that demonstrates how to add your own
 * custom controls to the basic media player.
 */
public class ExtendedPlayer3 extends Applet implements ControllerListener
{
    Player player = null;                  // media player
    Component visualComponent = null;
➥// component in which the video is playing
    boolean running = false;               // indicates if the applet
➥ is currently running, because the user is on the page

    /**
     * The component of the media player that holds the gainControl reference.
     */
    GainControl gainControl = null;

    /**
     * Panel used to hold the custom controls in the Applets Layout Manager.
     */
    Panel controlPanel = null;

    /**
     * Runnable class used to monitor media progress and update the UI.
     */
    MediaProgressMonitor progressMonitor = null;

    /**
     * Buttons within the custom controls used to adjust Starting, Stopping,
     * Gain increase and Gain decrease.
     */
    Button startButton = null;
    Button stopButton = null;
    Button gainUpButton = null;
    Button gainDownButton = null;

    /**
   * Labels within the custom controls used to indicate adjustable media player
     * features.
     */
    Label controlLabel = null;
    Label gainLabel = null;
    Label muteLabel = null;
    Label mediaTimesLabel = null;

    /**
     * Checkbox within the custom controls used control the Mute feature of the
     * media player.
```

continues

Listing 44.14 Continued

```
     */
    Checkbox muteCheckbox = null;

    /**
Textfield within the custom controls used to indicate
➥ the current media player
     * position and total media file duration.
     */
    TextField timeText = null;

    /**
     * Read the applet file parameter and create the media player.
     */
    public void init()
    {
        String mediaFile = null;     // input filename from Applet parameter
        URL mediaURL = null;         // base URL for the
➥document containing the applet

        setLayout(new BorderLayout());

        /**
         * Get the media filename info.
         * The applet tag should contain the path to the
         * source media file, relative to the applet.
         */
        if ((mediaFile = getParameter("MediaFile")) == null)
        {
            System.err.println("Invalid media file parameter");
        }
        else
        {
            try
            {
                // Create an url from the file name and the url to the
                // document containing this applet.
                mediaURL = new URL(getDocumentBase(), mediaFile);

                // Create an instance of an appropriate
➥media player for this media type.
                player = Manager.createPlayer(mediaURL);

                if(player != null)
                {
                   // Add this applet as a listener for the media player events
                   player.addControllerListener(this);

                    // Create the duration monitor object:
                    progressMonitor = new MediaProgressMonitor(this);
                }
                else
                 System.err.println("Could not create player for " + mediaURL);
            }
```

```
            catch (MalformedURLException e)
            {
                System.err.println("Invalid media file URL!");
            }
            catch(NoPlayerException e)
            {
                System.err.println("Could not find a player to
➥ create for" + mediaURL);
            }
        }
    }

    /**
     * Start media file playback.  This method is called the first time
     * that the Applet runs and every time the user re-enters the page.
     *
     * Call prefetch() to prepare to start the player.  Prefetch returns
     * immediately, so this method does not call player.start().  The
     * controllerUpdate() method will call player.start() once the
     * player is Prefetched.
     */
    public synchronized void start()
    {
        if (player != null)
        {
            player.prefetch();
            running = true;
        }
    }

    /**
     * Stop media file playback and release resources before leaving
     * the page.
     */
    public synchronized void stop()
    {
        if (player != null)
        {
            progressMonitor.stop();
            player.stop();
            player.deallocate();
            running = false;
        }
    }

    /**
      * This controllerUpdate method must be defined in order to implement
     * a ControllerListener interface.  This method will be called whenever
     * there is a media event.
     */
    public synchronized void controllerUpdate(ControllerEvent event)
    {
        // do nothing if player is set to null
        if (player == null)
            return;
```

continues

Listing 44.14 Continued

```
        // When the player is Realized, get the visual component
        // and control component and add them to the Applet
        if (event instanceof RealizeCompleteEvent)
        {
            if ((visualComponent = player.getVisualComponent()) != null)
                add("Center", visualComponent);

            // Get pointer to the Gain Control of the media player.
            gainControl = player.getGainControl();

            // Create the custom control components.
            createCustomControls();
            if (visualComponent != null)
                add("South",controlPanel);
            else
                add("Center",controlPanel);

            // force the applet to draw the components
            validate();
        }

        // Once the player has Prefetched, start it
        else if (event instanceof PrefetchCompleteEvent)
        {
            if(running)
            {
                player.start();
                progressMonitor.start();
            }
        }

        // If we've reached the end of the media "rewind" it to the beginning.
        else if (event instanceof EndOfMediaEvent)
        {
            player.setMediaTime(0);
            if (running)
                player.start();
        }

        // A fatal player error has occurred
        else if (event instanceof ControllerErrorEvent)
        {
            progressMonitor.stop();
            player = null;
            System.err.println("FATAL ERROR: " +
➥((ControllerErrorEvent)event).getMessage());
        }
    }

    /**
     * This method handles the AWT details required to display
     * player controls.
     */
```

```
    public void createCustomControls()
    {
        controlPanel = new Panel();

        GridBagLayout gridBag = new GridBagLayout();
        GridBagConstraints gridBagCon = new GridBagConstraints();

        controlPanel.setFont(new Font("Arial", Font.PLAIN, 14));
        controlPanel.setLayout(gridBag);

        // Create the first row of AWT control components:
➥Label, Start Button, Stop Button.
        gridBagCon.fill = GridBagConstraints.BOTH;
        gridBagCon.weightx = 1.0;
        controlLabel = new Label("Controls:", Label.LEFT);
        makeControl(controlPanel, controlLabel, gridBag, gridBagCon);

        startButton = new Button("Start");
        makeControl(controlPanel, startButton, gridBag, gridBagCon);

        gridBagCon.gridwidth = GridBagConstraints.REMAINDER;
        stopButton = new Button("Stop");
        makeControl(controlPanel, stopButton, gridBag, gridBagCon);

        // Create the second row of AWT control components:
➥Label, GainUp Button, GainDown Button.
        gridBagCon.weightx = 1.0;
        gridBagCon.gridwidth = 1;
        gainLabel = new Label("Gain:", Label.LEFT);
        makeControl(controlPanel, gainLabel, gridBag, gridBagCon);

        gainUpButton = new Button("Loud");
        makeControl(controlPanel, gainUpButton, gridBag, gridBagCon);

        gridBagCon.gridwidth = GridBagConstraints.REMAINDER;
        gainDownButton = new Button("Soft");
        makeControl(controlPanel, gainDownButton, gridBag, gridBagCon);

       // Create the third row of AWT control components: Label, Mute checkbox.
        gridBagCon.gridwidth = GridBagConstraints.RELATIVE;
        gridBagCon.weightx = 1.0;
        muteLabel = new Label("Mute:", Label.LEFT);
        makeControl(controlPanel, muteLabel, gridBag, gridBagCon);

        gridBagCon.gridwidth = GridBagConstraints.REMAINDER;
        muteCheckbox = new Checkbox("");
        makeControl(controlPanel, muteCheckbox, gridBag, gridBagCon);

        // Create the third row of AWT control components:
➥Label, media time textbox.
        gridBagCon.gridwidth = 1;
        gridBagCon.weightx = 1.0;
        mediaTimesLabel = new Label("Current Time/Total Time:", Label.LEFT);
        makeControl(controlPanel, mediaTimesLabel, gridBag, gridBagCon);
```


continues

Listing 44.14 Continued

```
        gridBagCon.gridwidth = GridBagConstraints.REMAINDER;
        timeText = new TextField("0.0//0.0", 12);
        timeText.setEditable(false);
        makeControl(controlPanel, timeText, gridBag, gridBagCon);
    }

    /**
     * This method adds a control to the custom control layout manager.
     */
    protected void makeControl(Container parentComp, Component
➥ newComponent, GridBagLayout gridbag,    GridBagConstraints constraint)
    {
        gridbag.setConstraints(newComponent, constraint);
        parentComp.add(newComponent);
    }

    /**
     * This method captures all the events from the custom controls.  This
     * is where each control calls the media player control methods.
     */
    public boolean action(Event evt, Object arg)
    {
        if (evt.target instanceof Button)
        {
            // Process the button event:
            if ("Start".equals(arg))
            {
                player.start();
            }
            else if ("Stop".equals(arg))
            {
                player.stop();
            }
            else if ("Loud".equals(arg))
            {
                gainControl.setDB(2.0f);
            }
            else if ("Soft".equals(arg))
            {
                gainControl.setDB(-2.0f);
            }
            return(true);
        }
        else if (evt.target instanceof Checkbox)
        {
            // Set the player's Mute control based upon the checkbox state.
            if (muteCheckbox.getState() == true)
                gainControl.setMute(true);
            else
                gainControl.setMute(false);
            return(true);
        }
        else
            return(false);
```

```
    }
}

/**
 *    This class is used to continually monitor the progress
 *    of the playing media file.  The thread wakes up every 50 millisec
 *    and passes the progress info to the player controls in the applet.
 */
class MediaProgressMonitor implements Runnable
{
    ExtendedPlayer3 m_Applet = null;
    Thread thread = null;
    boolean running;

    public MediaProgressMonitor(ExtendedPlayer3 applet)
    {
        m_Applet = applet;
    }

    /**
     * This method is called when the user starts the Applet or returns
     * from another page.
     */
    public synchronized void start()
    {
        thread = new Thread(this);
        thread.start();
        running = true;
    }

    /**
     * This method is called when the user stops the Applet or
     * leaves the page.
     */
    public synchronized void stop()
    {
        running = false;
    }

    /**
     * This method is called after the start method has executed.
     * Every 50 milliseconds, check the media player's progress
     * and forward the results to the player's control component.
     */
    public void run()
    {
        String mediaDuration = null;
        String mediaTime = null;
        char tmpChar;

        // Get the total time of the media file and store for use later.
        long duration = m_Applet.player.getDuration();
        mediaDuration = new String(String.valueOf(duration / (long) 1e08));
        tmpChar = mediaDuration.charAt(mediaDuration.length() - 1);
        mediaDuration = String.valueOf(duration / (long) 1e09) + "." + tmpChar;
```

continues

Listing 44.14 Continued

```
            while (running)
            {
                // Update the media time text field.
                long currtime = m_Applet.player.getMediaTime();
                mediaTime = new String(String.valueOf(currtime / (long) 1e08));
                tmpChar = mediaTime.charAt(mediaTime.length() - 1);
                mediaTime = String.valueOf(currtime / (long) 1e09) + "." + tmpChar;
                m_Applet.timeText.setText(mediaTime + "/" + mediaDuration);

                try
                {
                    thread.sleep(50);
                }
                catch (InterruptedException e)
                {
                    System.err.println(e);
                }
            }
        }
    }
```

CHAPTER 45

Commerce and Java Wallet

In this chapter

Security Support with the JCC

As the number of users on the Internet grow, more and more companies want to sell products and services online. One of the biggest hurdles for online sales is security. Although the Java Security API provides the strong encryption needed to safely pass credit card and banking information back and forth over the Internet, there is still a need for a common set of APIs for performing electronic transactions. The Java Commerce Client (JCC) was designed to support all the features needed for online transactions.

The JCC includes a standard set of user interfaces, a framework for passing messages between clients and servers, and set of APIs for handling various aspects of online transactions.

One of the core features of the JCC is the *cassette*, which is a collection of classes performing a particular operation. You can think of a cassette as a larger version of an object—it consists of multiple objects and some extra information, but it "plugs in" to the commerce framework to perform some desired function.

NOTE The Java Commerce Client was originally called the Java Electronic Commerce Framework (JECF). You will probably still see it called JECF in many places, including Sun's documentation.

Commerce Messages

In a client/server environment, it is important to nail down a protocol early so that development can proceed on both the client and server sides. JCC defines a message format called Java Commerce Messages (JCM) to make it easy to define interactions between clients and servers.

JCM messages are human-readable text messages containing multiple `name=value` pairs like this:

```
buyer.billto.name = Mark Wutka
```

The contents of the message will vary from server to server. Typically, the message will contain information about the buyer, the order, the protocol, and any additional requirements.

JECF also defines a MIME type for JCMs so that e-mail programs, web servers, browsers, and other MIME-aware applications can deal with them. The MIME type is `application/x-java-commerce`, and a JCM has a file extension of `.jcm`.

Typically, the server will determine what kind of data needs to be sent to perform a transaction. Chances are, there will be a core set of `name=value` pairs that every server expects, and additional server-specific extensions that vary according to the type of server.

Creating Cassettes

Cassettes are the core of JCC. They perform all the operations needed to get information from the user, validate the transaction, and send it to a server. Cassettes are grouped into distinct areas indicating what type of operation they perform. The types of cassettes are instruments, protocols, operations, services, and user interfaces (UI).

An instrument cassette represents data used in a transaction. A typical instrument might represent a credit card, containing the credit card type, number, and expiration date. Another instrument might represent a bank account, containing the bank location, the account number, and the type of account.

A protocol is a communications mechanism between JCC and a commerce server. You have probably encountered the term "protocol" in reference to networking, where you find the File Transfer Protocol (FTP) and the Hypertext Transfer Protocol (HTTP). In the world of electronic commerce, you find protocols such as SET, which is a standard for secure electronic transactions. Although SET defines the interactions between a client and a server, the protocol cassette actually maps various protocols required by operation cassettes onto communication protocols. JCC has a protocol defined for making a purchase, for example. A protocol cassette for the SET protocol would implement the interface for the purchase protocol and perform purchases using the SET protocol.

An operation cassette represents a task that a user may want to perform. A very common operation cassette is one that implements a purchase operation, enabling the user to make a purchase. You might also need a sell operation enabling the user to sell something electronically. Most of the time, selling is performed on a server; cases may arise, however, where the user is doing the selling—as in a stock trade.

A UI cassette presents the user interface for performing various operations. An ATM UI might present all the operations found at an automatic teller machine, for example, although dispensing cash might be a little tricky because paper doesn't travel well over a modem and stores are hesitant to accept money that has been faxed. Still, you should be able to transfer money between accounts and possibly recharge a debit card.

A service cassette is a "helper" cassette that doesn't necessarily perform a transaction itself. A common service cassette might be a Rolodex of credit cards or a visual stock portfolio. A service cassette can also provide services to other cassettes. An operation cassette, for example, may use a service cassette to present a user interface when the operation is being performed.

The *CassetteControl* Class

Each cassette contains a class named `CassetteControl`, which contains information about the contents of a cassette, the kind of function it performs, the current version, and any cassettes it may depend on. The `CassetteControl` class is used when the cassette is first installed into the JCC environment, and also at runtime when the version is checked.

When you create your `CassetteControl` class, you must declare it as a subclass of `Cassette`. There is no `CassetteControl` base class. The `Cassette` class loader specifically looks for a class named `CassetteControl` and expects it to be a subclass of `Cassette`.

One of the helper classes that you will need when you create a `CassetteControl` object is the `CassetteIdentifier`, which contains the name and version information of a cassette. You can create a `CassetteIdentifier` one of three ways:

```
CassetteIdentifier()

CassetteIdentifier(String name)

CassetteIdentifier(String name, int majorVersion,
    int minorVersion)
```

If you create an empty cassette identifier using the `null` (empty) `Constructor`, you must set the name and version numbers with the `setName`, `setMajorVersion`, and `setMinorVersion` methods:

```
public void setName(String name)

public void setMajorVersion(int majorVersion)

public void setMinorVersion(int minorVersion)
```

If you set the cassette identifier using only the name, you must embed the version information in the name by using this form:

```
name_majorVersion.minorVersion
```

The `Constructors` of the following two cassette identifiers create identical identifiers, for example:

```
CassetteIdentifier("StockTrader", 3, 1)

CassetteIdentifier("StockTrader_3.1")
```

You use a cassette identifier in a `ControlCassette` object to provide the current version number of the cassette, as well as the identifiers for any other cassettes you may depend on.

Each `ControlCassette` object must return its current version in the `getCurrentVersionIdentifier` method. The following code fragment creates a version identifier on-the-fly:

```
public CassetteIdentifier getCurrentVersionIdentifier()
{
    return new CassetteIdentifier("StockTrader", 3, 1);
}
```

It is more efficient, of course, to create a `CassetteIdentifier` ahead of time and just return it every time `getCurrentVersionIdentifier` is called.

You also use a cassette identifier when returning the cassettes that your cassette depends on. The `getDependencyIdentifiers` method should return an array of cassette identifiers or `null` if there are no dependencies. Suppose, for example, that your cassette depends on cassettes named `TradeOMatic` and `LeatherPortfolio`. Your `getDependencyIdentifiers` method might look like this:

```
public CassetteIdentifier[] getDependencyIdentifiers()
{
    CassetteIdentifier dependencies[] =
        new CassetteIdentifier[2];

    dependencies[0] = new CassetteIdentifier(
        "TradeOMatic", 2, 1);
    dependencies[1] = new CassetteIdentifier(
        "LeatherPortfolio_2.4");

    return dependencies;
}
```

The `getJCMForLatestVersion` method should return an array of URLs telling JCC where to find newer versions of the cassette:

```
public URL[] getJCMForLatestVersion()
```

If another cassette needs a newer version of your cassette, the JCC will automatically check these URLs and download the needed version.

The `install` method in `CassetteControl` should register itself with JCC using one of the following methods:

```
public final void registerInstrumentType(
    String instrumentType, String className)

public final void registerProtocol(
    String protocolName, String className)

public final void registerOperation(
    String operationName, String className)

public final void registerService(
    String serviceName, String className)

public final void registerWalletUI(
    String walletUIName, String description,
    String className)
```

An `install` method for a `StockTrader` operation might look like this:

```
public void install()
    throws CassetteInstallationException
{
    registerOperation("StockTrader",
        "stocks.trader.cassettes.StockTrader");
}
```

When a cassette is removed from the system, JCC calls the `uninstall` method. If your cassette doesn't need to do anything to uninstall, just create an empty method like this:

```
public void uninstall()
{
}
```

When a cassette is started, its `init` method is called. When the cassette is stopped, its `shutdown` method is called:

```
public void init()
```

```
public void shutdown()
```

For the `CassetteControl` class, however, you don't need the `init` and `shutdown` methods, so just make them empty.

The `getExpirationDate` method returns the date when the cassette expires:

```
public Date getExpirationDate()
```

When the system needs to update a cassette, it first asks the cassette whether it is okay to update it. The `doUpdate` method is passed the date of the last update and should return `true` if it is okay to update, or `false` if it should not be updated:

```
public boolean doUpdate(Date lastUpdate)
```

The Instrument Cassette Class

An instrument, in the JCC world, represents a source of data. Usually, an instrument represents something such as a credit card, a bank account, or even a stock. In a typical scenario, a user visiting an online store would decide to make a purchase. The JCC applet would present a collection of instruments, perhaps even looking like a wallet, and the user would select an "instrument" for payment, such as a credit card. The applet would use the instrument along with an operation cassette and a protocol cassette to transmit the order to the online store. The operation cassette and protocol cassette would communicate with the credit instrument to get all the information needed to complete the sale—the account number, the expiration date, and so forth.

An instrument implements the `Instrument` interface, which is a high-level description of the interfaces that every instrument should support. The description is high level because the functions of different interfaces can vary so greatly that there would be no way to predict all the necessary methods to put into the interface. Besides, you don't want a stock instrument containing methods to get the credit card number and expiration date. Instead, the various types of instruments have their separate interfaces that implement the `Instrument` interface.

The JCC comes with a `GenericCreditCard` interface, for example, which implements the `Instrument` interface. As you might expect, the `GenericCreditCard` interface has methods to query the account number, expiration date, billing address, and cardholder's name.

The `Instrument` interface contains methods that indicate the type and general function of the instrument. The `getDescription` method returns a simple text description of the instrument, for example:

```
public String getDescription()
```

The `getType` method returns the type of instrument, which might be `"Visa"`, `"MasterCard"`, `"Amex"`, or `"Discover"`:

```
public String getType()
```

The `getName` method, on the other hand, returns the name of the instrument, such as `Sir ChargeAlot`:

```
public String getName()
```

The `getContext` method returns a string indicating how the instrument is used:

```
public String getContext()
```

The current JCC documentation gives `"pay"` and `"accumulate"` as examples of contexts. These will hopefully be standardized some time in the future to avoid possible conflicts of terminology.

The `getVisualRepresentation` method returns an AWT component that represents the instrument:

```
public Component getVisualRepresentation(
    CommerceContext context, Dimension dim)
```


The visual representation of an instrument allows for the kind of flashy representation that marketing folks love. The visual representation can display animations and even play audio clips. (For a credit card, I recommend the Eagles' "Take It to the Limit.")

The `getSimpleGraphic` method returns an image to use in various selection screens:

```
public Image getSimpleGraphics(
    CommerceContext context, Dimension dim)
```

The simple graphic is intended for container displays where the user selects from a group of instruments. A commerce applet might display a graphic of a wallet containing your credit cards. After you select a credit card, the applet would use the visual representation object for the rest of the transaction.

The `InstrumentAdministration` interface contains methods involved with creating and maintaining specific instruments. Several of these methods are used just to get the graphics components used for editing the instrument. The `getNewInstrumentUI` method, for example, returns an AWT container used for creating a new instrument:

```
public Container getNewInstrumentUI(DataStore instStore,
    CommerceContext context, Dimension dim)
```

The `getInstrumentEditUI`, on the other hand, returns a container used to edit existing instruments:

```
public Container getInstrumentEditUI(DataStore instStore,
    CommerceContext context, Dimension dim)
```

The `getInstrument` method returns an instrument from the database:

```
public Instrument getInstrument(DataStore instStore)
```

The `DataStore` object used in the `getInstrument`, and `new/edit` user interfaces provide a mechanism for storing and retrieving instruments from a database. A `DataStore` actually represents a database blob (Binary Large Object) in which instruments are stored using the Java serialization API. The `DataStore` object has only three methods:

```
public boolean commit() throws IOException
```

```
public void setObject(Serializable obj) throws IOException
```

```
public Serializable getObject() throws IOException
```

The `setObject` method stores an object in a data store; the `getObject` method retrieves an object from a data store. The `commit` method saves any data store changes and returns `true` if successful.

Because credit cards are one of the most prevalent forms of payment currently in use, the JCC includes a generic credit card interface that provides the kind of information commonly found on credit cards. This gives implementers of protocol and operation cassettes a base to work with so that they don't have to wait to see how other developers implement credit card instruments. If you create a credit card instrument, it should implement the `GenericCreditCard` interface.

The `GenericCreditCard` interface contains `get` and `set` methods for the items found in almost all credit cards. The `get/set` methods are as follows:

```
public String getPAN();     // PAN = Primary Account Number
public void setPAN(String primaryAccountNumber);

public String getExpireDate();
public void setExpireDate(String expireDate);

public String getCardholderName();
public void setCardholderName(String name);

public AddressRecord getBillingAddress();
public void setBillingAddress(AddressRecord address);
```

In addition, the `accept` method should return `true` if the current transaction is permitted:

```
public boolean accept();
```

Listing 45.1 shows an example instrument from the JCC package from Sun.

Listing 45.1 Source Code to *CCInstrument.java*

```
/* @(#)CCInstrument.java 1.21 11/07/97
 *
 * Copyright (c) 1996 Sun Microsystems, Inc. All Rights Reserved.
 *
 * Permission to use, copy, modify, and distribute this software
 * and its documentation for NON-COMMERCIAL or COMMERCIAL purposes and
 * without fee is hereby granted.
 * Please refer to the file http://java.sun.com/copy_trademarks.html
 * for further important copyright and trademark information and to
 * http://java.sun.com/licensing.html for further important licensing
 * information for the Java (tm) Technology.
 *
 * SUN MAKES NO REPRESENTATIONS OR WARRANTIES ABOUT THE SUITABILITY OF
 * THE SOFTWARE, EITHER EXPRESS OR IMPLIED, INCLUDING BUT NOT LIMITED
 * TO THE IMPLIED WARRANTIES OF MERCHANTABILITY, FITNESS FOR A
 * PARTICULAR PURPOSE, OR NON-INFRINGEMENT. SUN SHALL NOT BE LIABLE FOR
```

```
 * ANY DAMAGES SUFFERED BY LICENSEE AS A RESULT OF USING, MODIFYING OR
 * DISTRIBUTING THIS SOFTWARE OR ITS DERIVATIVES.
 *
 * THIS SOFTWARE IS NOT DESIGNED OR INTENDED FOR USE OR RESALE AS ON-LINE
 * CONTROL EQUIPMENT IN HAZARDOUS ENVIRONMENTS REQUIRING FAIL-SAFE
 * PERFORMANCE, SUCH AS IN THE OPERATION OF NUCLEAR FACILITIES, AIRCRAFT
 * NAVIGATION OR COMMUNICATION SYSTEMS, AIR TRAFFIC CONTROL, DIRECT LIFE
 * SUPPORT MACHINES, OR WEAPONS SYSTEMS, IN WHICH THE FAILURE OF THE
 * SOFTWARE COULD LEAD DIRECTLY TO DEATH, PERSONAL INJURY, OR SEVERE
 * PHYSICAL OR ENVIRONMENTAL DAMAGE ("HIGH RISK ACTIVITIES").  SUN
 * SPECIFICALLY DISCLAIMS ANY EXPRESS OR IMPLIED WARRANTY OF FITNESS FOR
 * HIGH RISK ACTIVITIES.
 */

package com.sun.commerce.gencc;
import javax.commerce.util.AddressRecord;
import java.awt.*;
import java.net.URL;
import javax.commerce.util.Money;
import java.io.*;
import javax.commerce.base.*;
import javax.commerce.gui.*;
import javax.commerce.gui.image.*;
/**
 * A generic credit card object in the user's wallet.
 *
 * @author Daniel J. Guinan
 * @author Java Commerce Team
 * @version @(#)CCInstrument.java 1.21 11/07/97
 */
public class CCInstrument implements GenericCreditCard
{
  // The data that is to be stored for this instrument
  /** The Primary Account Number of this credit-card */
  protected String PAN = null;

  /** The expiration date of this credit-card */
  protected String expireDate = null;
  /** The description of this credit-card */
  protected String description = null;
  /** The name of the cardholder of this credit-card */
  protected String cardholderName = null;
  /** The billing address for this credit-card */
  protected AddressRecord billingAddress = null;
  /** The local alias (the name in the wallet) of this credit-card */
  protected String localAlias = null;
  /** The name of the image (taken from the /graphics directory in
   * the cassette */
  protected String imageName = null;
  // Declare any variables that are NOT to be stored with the
  // instrument as transient
  /** We keep the image around so that we don't have to re-create it */
  private transient Image theImage=null;
  /** This dummy frame is present to do image processing.  AWT 1.1 requirement
*/
```

Part VII

Ch 45

continues

Listing 45.1 Continued

```
private static transient Frame dummy=null;
/** Constructor
 * @param desc The description of the card to find in the wallet
 * @param cardno The primary account number (the credit-card number)
 * @param expire The expiration date of the credit-card
 * @param holder The cardholder name
 * @param addr The card's billing address
 * @param gra The card's local alias
 */
public CCInstrument (String desc,
       String cardno,
       String expire,
       String holder,
       AddressRecord addr,
       String gra,
       String imagenm)
{
description = desc;
PAN = cardno;
expireDate = expire;
cardholderName = holder;
billingAddress = addr;
localAlias = gra;
imageName = imagenm;
}

/*******************************************************************
 * Instrument interface specific methods
 *******************************************************************/
/** Returns the description of the instrument
 * @return description
 */
public String getDescription ()
{ return description; }
/** Sets the description of the instrument.
 * @param x The description of the credit-card.
 */
public void setDescription (String x)
{ description = x; }
/** Returns the context that this credit-card is generally used within.
 * @return always returns "pay" for generic credit cards
 */
public String getContext() { return "pay"; }
/** Sets the instrument type
 * @return In the case of Generic Credit Card, it always returns the
* constant <tt>CCAdmin.Type_Name</tt>
 */
public String  getType ()
{ return CCAdmin.TYPE_NAME; }
/**
* Returns the name the user associated with the specific instance
* of the credit card
 * @return The local (wallet name) name of the credit-card.
 */
```

```
public String getName()
{ return localAlias;}
/**
* Set the user-defined name of this instance of the credit card.
 * @param x The local alias (wallet name) name of the credit-card.
 */
public void setName(String x)
{ localAlias = x; }
/**
 * This method retrieves the visual representation of this instrument.
 * Since this method returns a Component, it can be active imagery
 * (e.g. an animation), or other such thing.
 *
 * @param media The CommerceContext used to fetch imagery from
 *   the jecf, a file, a URL, or the cassette.
 *
 * @param dim A hint as to the size of the image required.  Since
 *   proportions are important, we will not be returning
 *   an image exactly this size.  Rather, we will ensure
 *            that our returned image is proportionally correct,
 *            yet fits within these dimensions.
 *
 * @return Component A component with branding imagery associated with
 *                   this instrument.
 */
public Component getVisualRepresentation(CommerceContext media, Dimension dim)

{
  try  // We will do the simplest thing — wrap the simple imagery
  {    // into a canvas and return it.
    Image img = getSimpleGraphic(media, dim);
    CWImage cimg = new CWImage(img,dim);
    //cimg.waitForDimensions();
    return cimg;

  } catch(Exception e) { return new Label("No Imagery"); }
}
/**
 * This method retrieves the image that is associated with this
 * instrument.
 *
 * @param media The CommerceContext used to fetch imagery from
 *              the jecf, a file, a URL, or the cassette.
 *
 * @param dim A hint as to the size of the image required.  Since
 *            proportions are important, we will not be returning
 *            an image exactly this size.  Rather, we will ensure
 *            that our returned image is proportionally correct,
 *            yet fits within these dimensions.
 *
 * @return Image The image representing this instrument.
 */
public Image getSimpleGraphic(CommerceContext media, Dimension dim)
{
  try
```

continues

Listing 45.1 Continued

```
    {
      Image img,timg;
      if(dummy==null)         // We need a dummy frame to do image processing
      {                       // create it if we haven't already
        dummy = new Frame();
        dummy.addNotify();    // We need the Frame's peer to exist for
      }                       // this to work.. This forces that to happen.
      // We need a MediaTracker to ensure our processing results in
      // images that are ready for display
      //MediaTracker mt = new MediaTracker(dummy);
      if(theImage==null)  // If we haven't created the image, create it
      {
        timg = media.getImage(this,"graphics/"+imageName);
        //mt.addImage(timg,1);
        //mt.waitForID(1);

        // We will use the dummy frame to create a duplicate of the
        // image that we can do image processing on.
 img =dummy.createImage(160,100);
 Graphics g = img.getGraphics();
 Color chromaKey = new Color(255,0,255);
 g.setColor( chromaKey );
 g.fillRect(0,0,160,100);
 stampGraphic(g,160,100);
 g.dispose();
 theImage = ImageTools.mergeImages(timg,img,chromaKey);
      }

      return theImage;
    }
    catch(Exception e)
      { System.out.println(e); e.printStackTrace(System.out); return null; }
  }
  /**
   * This method writes out specific card related data on top of the
   * branding image, so the user can see the difference between two
  * instances of the same type of Credit Card.
   *
   * @param img The image to stamp with specific information
   */
  void stampGraphic(Graphics g, int w, int h)
  {
    try
    {
      Font f = new Font("Helvetica",Font.BOLD,11);
      g.setColor(Color.black);
      g.setFont(f);
      FontMetrics fm = g.getFontMetrics();
      Rectangle bounds = new Rectangle(0,0,w-1,h-1);
      //String drawStr = localAlias+"\n\n\n"+PAN+"\n"+expireDate+
      // "\n"+cardholderName;
      String drawStr = "\n\n"+PAN+"\n"+expireDate+"\n"+cardholderName;
      TextDraw.drawCentered(g,fm,drawStr,bounds,2,0,TextDraw.CENTERED);
      bounds = new Rectangle(1,1,w-1,h-1);
```

```
    g.setColor( new Color(254,254,254) );
    TextDraw.drawCentered(g,fm,drawStr,bounds,2,0,TextDraw.CENTERED);
  }
  catch(Exception e)
    { System.out.println(e); e.printStackTrace(System.out); }
}
/*****************************************************************
 * GenericCreditCard interface specific methods
 *****************************************************************/
/* Check if this instrument allows this purchase
 * Has the option of returning false and keeping all data un-available
 * In this type of sceneraio, the data would be unavailable by default,
 * and would only become available if a valid accept() occurs...
 * (e.g. — having a boolean OKAYTOGIVEOUTINFO; variable that is checked
 * by each getter()..  set OKAYTOGIVEOUTINFO=true; only if accept
 * succeeds).
 *
 * @return true=is acceptable, false=is not acceptable
 */
public boolean accept()
{
  // Has the option of returning false and keeping all data unavailable
  // In this type of scenario, the data would be unavailable by default,
  // and would only become available if a valid accept() occurs...
  // (e.g. -- having a boolean OKAYTOGIVEOUTINFO; variable that is checked
  // by each getter()..  set OKAYTOGIVEOUTINFO=true; only if accept
  // succeeds).
  return true;
}
/**
* Returns the credit-card number
 * @return the Instrument's card number
 */
public String getPAN()
{ return PAN; }
/**
* Returns the card's expiration date
 * @return the Instrument's expire date
 */
public String getExpireDate()
{ return expireDate; }
/**
* Returns the cardholder's name as known by the issuing institution
 * @return the Instrument's cardholder name
 */
public String getCardholderName()
{ return cardholderName; }
/**
* Return's the cardholder's billing address
 * @return the Instrument's cardholder address
 */
public AddressRecord getBillingAddress()
{ return billingAddress; }

/**
```

Part VII Ch 45

continues

Listing 45.1 Continued

```
    * Sets the credit-card number for this instance
    * @param the card number in string format
     */
    public void setPAN(String x)
    { PAN = x; }
    /**
    * sets the card's expiration date
     *@param the expiration date as a string
     */
    public void setExpireDate(String x)
    { expireDate = x; }
    /** Sets the cardholder's name as known by the issuing institution
    * the cardholder's name
     */
    public void setCardholderName (String x)
    { cardholderName = x; }
    /**
    *  Sets the billing address as an AddressRecord
    * @param The billing address as an AddressRecord
     */
    public void setBillingAddress (AddressRecord x)
    { billingAddress = x; }
  } // end of CCInstrument
```

The Protocol Cassette

A protocol cassette handles the communications between a client and a server. An example of a protocol cassette is one that handles the SET (Secure Electronic Transaction) protocol. Because protocols vary so much, there is very little in common between different protocol cassettes. The `Protocol` interface defines the few methods that all protocol cassettes must share.

The `canUseInstrument` method returns `true` if the protocol supports a particular instrument:

```
public boolean canUseInstrument(Instrument instrument)
```

Sun recommends the following code structure when determining whether an instrument is supported:

```
if ( !(instrument instanceof NeededInterface_1) )
    return false;

if ( !(instrument instanceof NeededInterface_2) )
    return false;

if ( !(instrument instanceof NeededInterface_3) )
    return false;

return true;
```

The `getName` method returns the name of the protocol as it was registered by the control cassette:

```
public String getName()
```

The `setProtocolJCM` tells the protocol cassette to read a JCM and extract information:

```
public void setProtocolJCM(JCM protocolJCM)
```

The `setWalletGate` method gives the protocol a `WalletGate` object, which is used to get permission to perform particular operations:

```
public void setWalletGate(WalletGate gate)
```

According to Sun, the wallet gate and the protocol portion of the JCM may soon be merged into the `CommerceContext` object, so the `setProtocolJCM` and `setWalletGate` methods may disappear in future releases of the JCC API.

The `setCommerceContext` method assigns a commerce context to the current protocol:

```
public void setCommerceContext(CommerceContext context)
```

A commerce context contains information specific to the current operation. Sun predicts that future versions of JCC will assign the commerce context when the protocol is created, eliminating the need for the `setCommerceContext` method.

The `PurchaseProtocol` interface defines a typical protocol for making purchases. As complex as the purchase process is in an electronic environment, the `PurchaseProtocol` interface contains only one method:

```
public boolean actUpon(Instrument instrument,
    PurchaseParams purchase) throws TransactionException
```

Listing 45.2 shows an example protocol from Sun that is provided in the JCC package.

Listing 45.2 Source Code for *DemoProtocol.java*

```
/*
 * @(#) @(#)DemoProtocol.java 1.7 11/07/97
 *
 * Copyright (c) 1996 Sun Microsystems, Inc. All Rights Reserved.
 *
 * Permission to use, copy, modify, and distribute this software
 * and its documentation for NON-COMMERCIAL or COMMERCIAL purposes and
 * without fee is hereby granted.
 * Please refer to the file http://java.sun.com/copy_trademarks.html
 * for further important copyright and trademark information and to
 * http://java.sun.com/licensing.html for further important licensing
 * information for the Java (tm) Technology.
 *
 * SUN MAKES NO REPRESENTATIONS OR WARRANTIES ABOUT THE SUITABILITY OF
 * THE SOFTWARE, EITHER EXPRESS OR IMPLIED, INCLUDING BUT NOT LIMITED
 * TO THE IMPLIED WARRANTIES OF MERCHANTABILITY, FITNESS FOR A
 * PARTICULAR PURPOSE, OR NON-INFRINGEMENT. SUN SHALL NOT BE LIABLE FOR
 * ANY DAMAGES SUFFERED BY LICENSEE AS A RESULT OF USING, MODIFYING OR
 * DISTRIBUTING THIS SOFTWARE OR ITS DERIVATIVES.
 *
 * THIS SOFTWARE IS NOT DESIGNED OR INTENDED FOR USE OR RESALE AS ON-LINE
```

continues

Listing 45.2 Continued

```
 * CONTROL EQUIPMENT IN HAZARDOUS ENVIRONMENTS REQUIRING FAIL-SAFE
 * PERFORMANCE, SUCH AS IN THE OPERATION OF NUCLEAR FACILITIES, AIRCRAFT
 * NAVIGATION OR COMMUNICATION SYSTEMS, AIR TRAFFIC CONTROL, DIRECT LIFE
 * SUPPORT MACHINES, OR WEAPONS SYSTEMS, IN WHICH THE FAILURE OF THE
 * SOFTWARE COULD LEAD DIRECTLY TO DEATH, PERSONAL INJURY, OR SEVERE
 * PHYSICAL OR ENVIRONMENTAL DAMAGE ("HIGH RISK ACTIVITIES").  SUN
 * SPECIFICALLY DISCLAIMS ANY EXPRESS OR IMPLIED WARRANTY OF FITNESS FOR
 * HIGH RISK ACTIVITIES.
 */
// Things to be done to this code are marked with ?? or UNDONE:
package com.sun.commerce.example.demoprot;

import java.awt.*;
import java.awt.Event;
import java.io.*;
import java.net.*;
import java.security.*;
import java.util.*;

import javax.commerce.base.*;
import javax.commerce.base.WalletUserPermit;
import javax.commerce.cassette.*;
import javax.commerce.database.*;
import com.sun.commerce.gencc.GenericCreditCard;
import javax.commerce.gui.ProgressBar;
import javax.commerce.util.Money;

/**
 * The DemoProtocol is a protocol that is intended to be used for
 * Demo purposes.  It does not actually perform a transaction or
 * open any network connections.  It mostly puts up a progress
 * bar and pretends that it performed a transaction.  This protocol
 * will accept any instrument.
 *
 * @see PurchaseProtocol
 * @see ActionBase
 * @see ActionParameter
 */
public class DemoProtocol implements PurchaseProtocol, Runnable
{
 /** The registration name of the protocol */
 public static final String PROTOCOL_NAME="Demo";

 /** The instrument being used in the demo protocol */
 Instrument instrument;

 private PurchaseParams pp;

 private ProgressBar pbar;

 private JCM jcm=null;

 private String failure=null;
```

```
private boolean protocolDone = false;

private CommerceContext media;

/** Constructor
 */
public DemoProtocol() {}

/**
 * Returns the registration name of the Demo Protocol.
 *
 * @return String The registration name of the Demo Protocol.
 */
public String getName() { return PROTOCOL_NAME; }

/**
 * Called by the Operation to set the protocol's JCM.
 *
 * @param prjcm The part of the JCM that applies to the protocol.
 */
public void setProtocolJCM(JCM prjcm) { jcm=prjcm; }

public void setWalletGate(WalletGate wg)
 {}

  public void setCommerceContext(CommerceContext ccntxt)
  {
    media=ccntxt;
  }
  /**
   * Pretends to perform the transaction.  Uses the passed instrument and
   * parameters present a convincing progress bar.
   *
   * @param inst The CreditCard instrument used for the transaction
   *
   * @param ap The parameters used for the payment
   *
   * @return boolean true= success
   */
 synchronized public boolean actUpon(Instrument inst, PurchaseParams pp)
  throws TransactionException
 {
  // record parameters and double-check the instrument is of
  // the correct type.

  this.pp=pp;

  pbar = new ProgressBar (media,"Paying "+
     ((javax.commerce.util.Invoice)pp.getInvoice()).getTotal().toString ()+
     " using "+pp.getInstrument().instrument.getDescription ());
  pbar.setTitle (pp.getMerchant().getGeneralURL().toString ());

  instrument=inst;
```

continues

Listing 45.2 Continued

```
  if (true) {
   System.out.println("Running Protocol in the same thread.");
   commit();
  } else {
   System.out.println("Running Protocol as a sepparate thread.");
   // Start the thread that will monitor the transaction
   Thread t = JECF.makeThread(this);
   t.start();
   while (!protocolDone) {
    try { wait();
    } catch (InterruptedException ignored) {}
   }
  }

  if (failure != null){
    System.out.println("Failure: " + failure);
    throw new TransactionException(failure);
  }

   // Return DONE -> An exception will be raised for an error condition
  return true;
 }

  /**
   * Check to see if this Protocol can use a specific instrument
   *
   * @param instrument The instrument to check
   *
   * @return boolean true=can use, false=cannot use
   */
 public boolean canUseInstrument(Instrument instrument)
 {
  return true;
 }

 private void pause(int milliseconds) {
  Thread thisThread = Thread.currentThread();
  try { thisThread.sleep(500);
  } catch (InterruptedException ignored) {}
 }

 private void setFailure(String newFailure) {
  failure=newFailure;
  if (newFailure != null) {
   System.out.println("setFailure(" + failure + ")");
   throw new RuntimeException(failure);
  }
 }

 private void checkCancelled (boolean cancelled) {
  if (cancelled) {
   setFailure("User Cancelled Transaction");
  }
 }
```

```
private void getJcmInfo() {
 if (jcm!=null)
  try { setFailure(jcm.getString("failure"));
  } catch (JCMException ignored) { }
 if (jcm!=null) {
  System.out.println("Displaying JCM:");
  Enumeration leaves = jcm.elements() ;
  while (leaves.hasMoreElements()) {
   String[] leaf = (String[]) leaves.nextElement();
   if (leaf != null) {
    System.out.print("    " + leaf[0] + "=");
    for (int i=1; i<leaf.length; i++) {
     System.out.print(leaf[i] + " ");
    }
    System.out.println("");
   }
  }
 } else {
  System.out.println("No JCM was set!");
 }
}

private Random rand = new Random();
int rand(int minValue, int maxValue) {
 return minValue + Math.abs(rand.nextInt()%(maxValue-minValue));
}

synchronized protected boolean commit()
{
 try {
  getJcmInfo();
  // Start the progress bar
  pause(500);
  checkCancelled(pbar.showProgress (0, "Initiating Communications"));
  for (int i=rand(5,15); i<100; i+=rand(5,15)) {
   pause(rand(10,500));
   checkCancelled(pbar.showProgress (i, "Transaction is " + i + "% done."));
  }
  pause(500);
  pbar.showProgress (100, "Transaction is complete.");

  return true;
 } catch (RuntimeException ignored) {
  return false;
 } finally {
  protocolDone=true;
  notify();
  pbar.done ();
 }
}

public void run(){
 commit();
}
}
```

The Operation Cassette

The operation cassette is really the hub of JCC. When an operation is selected, the operation's user interface collects the information needed to complete the transaction, gets the necessary instruments, and activates a protocol to complete the deal.

NOTE As with the rest of the Java Commerce Client, the information in this section is subject to change. Sun suggests that some of the information in the `Operation` interface will be merged into the `CommerceContext` object in a future release.

The `Operation` interface and its partners represent a pretty complex system that takes some time to adjust to. Most of the methods in the `Operation` interface itself are used to set up the initial context for the operation. The `setJCM` gives the `Operation` object a JCM to parse and retrieve information related to the operation:

```
public void setJCM(JCM message) throws Exception
```

The `getJCMDescription` method returns a description of the required and optional parameters for this operation:

```
public String[] getJCMDescription()
```

The description strings are returned in the form `"name=description"`.

The `setWalletGate` method gives the operation a `WalletGate`, which it uses to get various security permissions:

```
public void setWalletGate(WalletGate gate)
```

The `setID` method gives the operation its row ID from the database:

```
public void setID(RowID id)
```

The `setCommerceContext` method sets the current context for the operation:

```
public void setCommerceContext(CommerceContext context)
```

In the future, some of the other parameters may be merged into the commerce context, and the context itself may be part of the `Constructor` for the operation.

The `execute` method starts the operation, which then brings up a `UI` object to collect the information for the operation:

```
public String execute() throws Exception
```

The Service Cassette

A service cassette is a utility cassette used by other cassettes within JCC. There is no service interface, but there is a `ServiceUI` because most service cassettes perform user interface functions. In addition, the `ServiceUI` interface is used by the `Operation` interface for a user interface.

The `getClientContainer` method in the `ServiceUI` interface returns the container that represents the user interface:

```
public Container getClientContainer(
    CommerceContext context, Dimension dim)
```

The `getSelectedImage` and `getUnselectedImage` methods return the images used to represent the service if it is shown inside another container as something to be selected:

```
public Image getSelectedImage(
    CommerceContext context, Dimension dim)

public Image getUnselectedImage(
    CommerceContext context, Dimension dim)
```

The `getSelectorText` returns the text that serves as a label for the image when shown as an image:

```
public String getSelectorText()
```

Finally, the `setWalletGate` method gives the `ServiceUI` a `WalletGate` object for security operations:

```
public void setWalletGate(WalletGate gate)
```

Listing 45.3 shows an example Rolodex service from Sun's examples in the JCC package.

Listing 45.3 Source Code for *Rolodex.java*

```
/*
 * @(#)Rolodex.java     1.1 97/10/29
 *
 * Copyright (c) 1996 Sun Microsystems, Inc. All Rights Reserved.
 *
 * Permission to use, copy, modify, and distribute this software
 * and its documentation for NON-COMMERCIAL or COMMERCIAL purposes and
 * without fee is hereby granted.
 * Please refer to the file http://java.sun.com/copy_trademarks.html
 * for further important copyright and trademark information and to
 * http://java.sun.com/licensing.html for further important licensing
 * information for the Java (tm) Technology.
 *
 * SUN MAKES NO REPRESENTATIONS OR WARRANTIES ABOUT THE SUITABILITY OF
 * THE SOFTWARE, EITHER EXPRESS OR IMPLIED, INCLUDING BUT NOT LIMITED
 * TO THE IMPLIED WARRANTIES OF MERCHANTABILITY, FITNESS FOR A
 * PARTICULAR PURPOSE, OR NON-INFRINGEMENT. SUN SHALL NOT BE LIABLE FOR
 * ANY DAMAGES SUFFERED BY LICENSEE AS A RESULT OF USING, MODIFYING OR
 * DISTRIBUTING THIS SOFTWARE OR ITS DERIVATIVES.
 *
 * THIS SOFTWARE IS NOT DESIGNED OR INTENDED FOR USE OR RESALE AS ON-LINE
 * CONTROL EQUIPMENT IN HAZARDOUS ENVIRONMENTS REQUIRING FAIL-SAFE
 * PERFORMANCE, SUCH AS IN THE OPERATION OF NUCLEAR FACILITIES, AIRCRAFT
 * NAVIGATION OR COMMUNICATION SYSTEMS, AIR TRAFFIC CONTROL, DIRECT LIFE
 * SUPPORT MACHINES, OR WEAPONS SYSTEMS, IN WHICH THE FAILURE OF THE
 * SOFTWARE COULD LEAD DIRECTLY TO DEATH, PERSONAL INJURY, OR SEVERE
 * PHYSICAL OR ENVIRONMENTAL DAMAGE ("HIGH RISK ACTIVITIES").  SUN
 * SPECIFICALLY DISCLAIMS ANY EXPRESS OR IMPLIED WARRANTY OF FITNESS FOR
 * HIGH RISK ACTIVITIES.
```

continues

Listing 45.3 Continued

```
 */
package com.sun.commerce.example.rolodex ;
import java.awt.*;
import javax.commerce.database.* ;
import javax.commerce.cassette.* ;
import javax.commerce.util.*;
import javax.commerce.base.*;
import java.util.* ;
import java.io.* ;
import java.security.* ;
import javax.commerce.base.Constants;
import javax.commerce.gui.InfoDialog;

/**
 * @author Surya Koneru
 * @(#)Rolodex.java     1.1 97/10/29
 */
public class Rolodex implements ServiceUI
{
  public static final String SERVICE_NAME = new String("Rolodex");


  public WalletGate wgate;
  private WalletAdminPermit wap;
  private DatabaseOwnerPermit dop;

  /**
   * This method will always be called before any other ServiceUI methods
   *
   * @param gate A WalletGate to allow the service to utilize wallet-level
   *             functionality.
   */
  public void setWalletGate(WalletGate gate)
  {
    wgate=gate;
    wap = gate.getWalletAdminPermit( new Ticket( "W_OWNER"));
    dop = wap.getDatabaseOwnerPermit();
  }

  /**
   * This method fetches a service's client container for display within
   * the encompassing WalletUI.  The ServiceUI author is urged to use
   * commerce widgets, but it is not neccessary.<br><br>
   *
   * This method, in general, returns an a light-weight container that
   * has transparent characteristics.  It may,
   * however, return any Container.
   *
   * @param ccontext A CommerceContext that may be used to fetch imagery
   *                 and for use in constructing the ServiceUI. The
   *                 UIFactory of this CommerceContext models the
   *                 current WalletUI.
```

```
     *
     * @param hint The initial dimensions of the Service UI.  The returned
     *            container is likely to be resized many times, however.
     *
     * @return Container The AWT Container that represents the Service's UI.
     *                   This Container should have dimensions that match
     *                   the passed in hint.
     */
    public Container getClientContainer(CommerceContext ccontext,
                                        Dimension hint)
    {
      return new RolodexPanel(ccontext,dop);
    }

    /**
     * Used to fetch the image displayed on the WalletUI selector when the
     * selector for this service is not selected.
     *
     * @param factory A CommerceContext that may be used to fetch imagery.
     * @param size The size of the requested image (Generally 16x16 pixels)
     *
     * @return Image The image to display when this serivce is not selected.
     */
    public Image getUnselectedImage(CommerceContext factory, Dimension size)
    { return null; }

    /**
     * Used to fetch the image displayed on the WalletUI selector when the
     * selector for this service is selected.
     *
     * @param factory A CommerceContext that may be used to fetch imagery.
     * @param size The size of the requested image (Generally 16x16 pixels)
     *
     * @return Image — The image to display when this service is selected.
     */
    public Image getSelectedImage(CommerceContext factory, Dimension size)
    { return null; }

    /**
     * Used to fetch the text that will be displayed on the WalletUI selector.
     *
     * @return String -- The text to display on the WalletUI selector for this
     *                   service.
     */
    public String getSelectorText() { return SERVICE_NAME; }
  }
```


The User Interface Cassette

A user interface cassette contains a `WalletUI` object, a `TransactionListener`, an `ActionListener`, and a `UIFactory`.

The `WalletUI` interface defines a set of methods that indicate which operations and services are available in the UI, and also information about the current security context. The `addOperation` method adds an operation to the operations available from this user interface and returns a unique index number:

```
public int addOperation(Operation op)
```

The `canUseOperation` method returns `true` if the user interface cassette is compatible with a particular operation:

```
public boolean canUseOperation(Operation op)
```

The `addSelector` method adds a service to the available services and returns a unique index number:

```
public int addSelector(ServiceUI service)
```

The `removeSelector` method removes a service from the user interface:

```
public void removeSelector(int index)
```

The `addSelector` and `removeSelector` methods deal with objects visible from the user interface. If an operation is added that has a user interface component, the `addOperation` method will likely call the `addSelector` method to add it to the visible items. Thus if an operation has a visible component, you can use `removeSelector` to remove it because there is no `removeOperation` method.

The `setCommerceContext` method sets the current context for the user interface and should be called immediately after the user interface is instantiated:

```
public void setCommerceContect(CommerceContext context)
```

The `init` method must be called after the commerce context has been set, but before any other operations are performed:

```
public void init()
```

The `getName` method returns the name of the user interface cassette as it was registered by the `CassetteControl` class:

```
public String getName()
```

The `select` method selects a different object within the user interface:

```
public void select(int selectorIndex)
```

The selection value should be the unique index of one of the available selectors.

The `populate` method tells the user interface to draw itself in an AWT container:

```
public void populate(Container cont)
```

Bear in mind that the `populate` method might be operating on a visible container. Therefore, if you do ugly things such as adding a bunch of objects and then removing them, your user interface is liable to appear a little wacky.

Listing 45.4 shows a demo user interface cassette from Sun's JCC examples.

Listing 45.4 Source Code for *DemoUI.java*

```
/*
 * @(#)DemoUI.java 1.23 11/07/97
 *
 * Copyright (c) 1997 Sun Microsystems, Inc. All Rights Reserved.
 *
 * Permission to use, copy, modify, and distribute this software
 * and its documentation for NON-COMMERCIAL or COMMERCIAL purposes and
 * without fee is hereby granted.
 * Please refer to the file http://java.sun.com/copy_trademarks.html
 * for further important copyright and trademark information and to
 * http://java.sun.com/licensing.html for further important licensing
 * information for the Java (tm) Technology.
 *
 * SUN MAKES NO REPRESENTATIONS OR WARRANTIES ABOUT THE SUITABILITY OF
 * THE SOFTWARE, EITHER EXPRESS OR IMPLIED, INCLUDING BUT NOT LIMITED
 * TO THE IMPLIED WARRANTIES OF MERCHANTABILITY, FITNESS FOR A
 * PARTICULAR PURPOSE, OR NON-INFRINGEMENT. SUN SHALL NOT BE LIABLE FOR
 * ANY DAMAGES SUFFERED BY LICENSEE AS A RESULT OF USING, MODIFYING OR
 * DISTRIBUTING THIS SOFTWARE OR ITS DERIVATIVES.
 *
 * THIS SOFTWARE IS NOT DESIGNED OR INTENDED FOR USE OR RESALE AS ON-LINE
 * CONTROL EQUIPMENT IN HAZARDOUS ENVIRONMENTS REQUIRING FAIL-SAFE
 * PERFORMANCE, SUCH AS IN THE OPERATION OF NUCLEAR FACILITIES, AIRCRAFT
 * NAVIGATION OR COMMUNICATION SYSTEMS, AIR TRAFFIC CONTROL, DIRECT LIFE
 * SUPPORT MACHINES, OR WEAPONS SYSTEMS, IN WHICH THE FAILURE OF THE
 * SOFTWARE COULD LEAD DIRECTLY TO DEATH, PERSONAL INJURY, OR SEVERE
 * PHYSICAL OR ENVIRONMENTAL DAMAGE ("HIGH RISK ACTIVITIES").  SUN
 * SPECIFICALLY DISCLAIMS ANY EXPRESS OR IMPLIED WARRANTY OF FITNESS FOR
 * HIGH RISK ACTIVITIES.
 */
package com.sun.commerce.example.demoui ;
import javax.commerce.database.* ;
import javax.commerce.cassette.* ;
import javax.commerce.util.*;
import java.util.* ;
import java.io.* ;
import java.security.* ;
import javax.commerce.base.*;
import javax.commerce.gui.*;
import java.awt.*;
import java.awt.event.*;

/**
 * @author Daniel J. Guinan
 * @version @(#)DemoUI.java 1.23 11/07/97
 *
 */
public class DemoUI implements WalletUI, ActionListener, TransactionListener
{
  class ServiceNode
  {
```

continues

Listing 45.4 Continued

```
    public ServiceUI service;
    public Container container;
    public CWSelector button;
    public int selectorIndex;

    public ServiceNode(ServiceUI sui, CommerceContext media,
         String buttontext, int index)
    {
      service=sui;
      container=null;
      selectorIndex=index;
      Dimension d = new Dimension(20,20);
      button=new CWSelector(media,buttontext,
       sui.getUnselectedImage(media,d),
       sui.getSelectedImage(media,d));
    }
  }

  public static final String WALLETUI_NAME = "DemoUI";
  public static final String WALLETUI_DESCRIPT = "Demonstration
➥Wallet User Interface";

  public static final Color INACTIVE_COLOR = Color.lightGray;
  public static final Color ACTIVE_COLOR = new Color(150,175,255);

  private CommerceContext context;
  private UIFactory widgets;

  private CWPanel loadingPanel;
  private CWPanel selectionPanel;
  private Container currentClient = null;
  private CWPanel masterContainer = null;
  //  private CWSelector selectedButton = null;
  private ServiceNode currentlySelected = null;

  private Hashtable serviceTable = new Hashtable();  // (name, ServiceNode)
  private Hashtable idxMapping = new Hashtable();    // (Integer, name)
  private Hashtable pendingTable = new Hashtable();  // (Operation, name)

  private int currentIdx = 0;

  ///////////////////////////////////////////////////////////////
  ///////////////// WalletUI Interface Methods //////////////////
  ///////////////////////////////////////////////////////////////

 /**
   * Init() is called after the current CommerceContext and
   * CommerceUIFactory objects are set, but before any other
   * calls are made into the WalletUI.  It is here that initialization
   * code should be executed.<br><br>
   *
   * PLEASE NOTE:  This is not where the UI is shown.  That occurs
   * in the populate() method.
   */
```

```
public void init()
{

}

/**
 * Retrieves the current CommerceContext.
 *
 * @return CommerceContext -- The current CommerceContext
 */
public CommerceContext getCommerceContext()
{ return context; }

/**
 * Sets the current CommerceContext (THIS METHOD IS ALWAYS
 * CALLED DIRECTLY AFTER OBJECT INSTANTIATION)
 *
 * @param ccontext The CommerceContext to use as current.
 */
public void setCommerceContext(CommerceContext ccontext)
{
  context=ccontext;
  new CommonGraphics(ccontext);  // Load static common graphics...
  widgets=new DemoUIFactory();
  context.setUIFactory( widgets );

  loadingPanel = new CWPanel(ccontext);
  loadingPanel.setLayout(new BorderLayout());
  currentClient=loadingPanel;
  CWLabel loading = new CWLabel(ccontext,"Loading...",CWLabel.CENTER);
  loading.setFont(new Font("GilSans",Font.BOLD,20));
  loading.setForeground(Color.white);
  loadingPanel.add(loading,BorderLayout.CENTER);
}

/**
 * This method is called to add a Service selector.
 *
 * @param service The ServiceUI being added.
 * @return int -- The unique index of the selector created.
 */
public int addSelector(ServiceUI service)
{
System.out.println("DEMOUI: Adding service = "+service.getSelectorText());

  int ret=currentIdx++;
  String selectorText = service.getSelectorText();

  //UNDONE: Freak out if the selectorText is already there..
  if( serviceTable.get(selectorText)!=null )
    {
boolean unique=false;
int index=1;
String name=null;
while(!unique)
```

continues

Listing 45.4 Continued

```
    {
      name = selectorText+" "+(++index);
      if(serviceTable.get(name)==null) unique=true;
    }
  selectorText=name;
      }
    //return -1;

    idxMapping.put( new Integer(ret), selectorText );

    ServiceNode sn = new ServiceNode(service,context,selectorText,ret);
    serviceTable.put(selectorText, sn);
    selectionPanel.add(sn.button);
    sn.button.addActionListener(this);
    // Do we really want to do this??
    selectionPanel.validateAll();

    return ret;
  }

  /**
   *
   * @param op The Operation that should have a selector added for it.
   * @return int — The unique index of the selector created.
   */
  public int addOperation(Operation op)
  {
    int idx = -1;
    if(op instanceof ServiceUI)
      {
  idx= addSelector((ServiceUI)op);
  select(idx);
  String name = (String)idxMapping.get( new Integer(idx) );
  ServiceNode sn = (ServiceNode)serviceTable.get(name);
  sn.button.setPending(true);
  pendingTable.put(op,name);
  op.addTransactionListener(this);
      }

    //UNDONE: Exception??
    return idx;
  }

  public void transactionPerformed(TransactionEvent evt)
  {
    Operation source = (Operation)evt.getSource();
    String name = (String)pendingTable.get(source);
    if(name==null) return;
    pendingTable.remove(source);
    ServiceNode sn = (ServiceNode)serviceTable.get(name);
    sn.button.setPending(false);
  }
```

```
/**
 * This method is called to remove a Service selector.
 *
 * @param int The unique index of the Service selector to remove.  This
 *            is the same index returned by addSelector().
 */
public void removeSelector(int idx)
{
  Integer i = new Integer(idx);
  String stext = (String)idxMapping.get(i);
  if(stext==null)
    {
System.out.println("Cannot remove selector: Index "+idx+
    " is not valid!");
return; //Not there??
    }

  ServiceNode sn = (ServiceNode)serviceTable.get(stext);
System.out.println(">> Removing Service "+stext);
//    selectionPanel.setCanInvalidate(false);
  selectionPanel.remove(sn.button);
  sn.button.removeActionListener(this);

  idxMapping.remove(i);
  serviceTable.remove(stext);
  selectionPanel.validateAll(); // we removed a button...
  if(sn.selectorIndex==idx)
  {
    //If this guy is currently selected, change...
    Enumeration e = serviceTable.elements();
    sn = (ServiceNode)e.nextElement();
    if(sn!=null) select(sn.selectorIndex);
    else showClient(null);
  }
}


/**
 * This method is called to force the WalletUI to change it's focus to
 * a particular service.
 *
 * @param idx The uniqe index of the Service selector to select.  This
 *            is the same index returned by addSelector().
 */
public void select(int idx)
{
  Integer i = new Integer(idx);
  String stext = (String)idxMapping.get(i);
  if(stext==null) return; // Not there??

  showClient(stext);
}
```


continues

Listing 45.4 Continued

```
/**
 * This method is used to determine compatibility with Operations.  When
 * Operations or WalletUIs are installed, this method is called on all
 * WalletUIs against all Operations to generate a compatibility list.
 * <br><br>
 *
 * It is this compatibility list that appears in the user's preferences,
 * allowing a user to change their "preferred" UI for various operations.
 * <br><br>
 *
 * In general, this method will check interfaces of the Operation and return
 * true if it feels that it can accomidate the Operation's UI requirements.
 * <br><br>
 *
 * @param op The operation to check for UI compatibility.
 * @return boolean — true=compatible with operation, false=not compatible
 *
 * @see WalletUI.addOperation
 */
public boolean canUseOperation(Operation op)
{
  //The demonstration UI works with any operation that implements ServiceUI...
  if(op instanceof ServiceUI) return true;
  else return false;
}



/**
 * Retrieves the registration name of this WalletUI.  This name must match
 * the registration name used in the CassetteControl.install() method when
 * registering this UI.
 *
 * @return String -- The registration name of this WalletUI.
 */
public String getName()
{
  return WALLETUI_NAME;
}


/**
 * This method is called to present the WalletUI.  In general, this happens
 * right before the JECF performs a show() on the frame that contains the
 * various widgets that represent the WalletUI.  The whole of the WalletUI
 * will be shown within the container passed in this method.  The following
 * considerations should be carefully taken into account by WalletUI cassette
 * writers:<br><br>
 *
 * <li> The container passed to this method is probably, but not
 *      necessarily a Frame or an Object that inherets Frame.
 *      (NOTE: Never cast this Container to Frame)
 *
```

```
 * <li> The container may change dimensions.  It is expected that the
 *      User will resize the Window, causing this container to resize
 *      as a result.  The UI must be written to accommodate this (i.e.
 *      stretch).
 *
 * <li> Do not rely on any characteristics of any AWT components that
 *      may exist above this Container.  Those characteristics are
 *      subject to change at any time, forcing any cassettes that rely
 *      upon them to become obsolete.
 *
 * <li> The populate method may be populating a live AWT component
 *      (i.e. already shown).
 * </ul>
 *
 * @param c The container that the WalletUI should be drawn within.
 */
public void populate(Container c)
{
  masterContainer = new CWPanel(context);
  c.setLayout(new BorderLayout(0,0));
  c.add(masterContainer,BorderLayout.CENTER);
  masterContainer.setLayout(new BorderLayout(0,0));

  currentClient=loadingPanel;
  masterContainer.add(currentClient,BorderLayout.CENTER);
  loadingPanel.validateAll();

  selectionPanel = new SelectionPanel(context);
  selectionPanel.setLayout( new VFlowLayout(VFlowLayout.
➥TOP¦VFlowLayout.HORZ_LEFT) );

  masterContainer.add(selectionPanel,BorderLayout.EAST);
}

/////////////////////////////////////////////////////////////////
//////////////////////// Private Methods ////////////////////////
/////////////////////////////////////////////////////////////////

public void actionPerformed(ActionEvent evt)
{
  Object source = evt.getSource();
  if(source instanceof CWSelector)
  {
    CWSelector bt = (CWSelector)source;

    String item = bt.getLabel();
    showClient(item);
    //cardLayout.show(switchPanel,item);
  }
}

private void showClient(String stext)
{
  Container newClient;
```

Part VII Ch 45

continues

Listing 45.4 Continued

```
    // Tell the selector it is not current anymore.
    if(currentlySelected!=null) currentlySelected.button.setCurrent(false);

    if(stext==null) // What is this??
    {
      newClient = loadingPanel;
      currentlySelected=null;
    }
    else // Get the new client
    {
      ServiceNode sn = (ServiceNode)serviceTable.get(stext);
      newClient = sn.container;
      currentlySelected = sn;
      // Tell the new selector it is not current anymore.
      sn.button.setCurrent(true);
    }

    // If this is the first time, do something special.
    if(newClient == null) firstTimeShowClient(stext);
    else // Just change the page
    {
      //if(currentClient!=null)
      masterContainer.swapComponentValid(currentClient,newClient,
      BorderLayout.CENTER);
      currentClient=newClient;
    }

    //reLayoutPaintMaster();
  }

  /*  void reLayoutPaintMaster()
  {
    // Relayout and repaint everything...
    if(masterContainer instanceof CWBasePanel)
      ((CWBasePanel)masterContainer).validateAll();
    else if(masterContainer instanceof CWidget)
      ((CWidget)masterContainer).validateAll();
    else { masterContainer.validate(); masterContainer.repaint(); }
  }*/

  private void firstTimeShowClient(String stext)
  {
    // Show the loading loadingPanel
    if(currentClient!=loadingPanel)
    {
      masterContainer.swapComponentValid(currentClient,loadingPanel,
      BorderLayout.CENTER);
      currentClient=loadingPanel;
      context.showStatus("Loading...");
    }

    // Do the normal stuff...
    ServiceNode sn = (ServiceNode)serviceTable.get(stext);
```

```
    Container clientArea =
      sn.service.getClientContainer(context,
        loadingPanel.getSize() );
    clientArea.setSize(loadingPanel.getSize());
    clientArea.setLocation(loadingPanel.getLocation());
    sn.container=clientArea;

    // swap
    masterContainer.swapComponentValid(currentClient,clientArea,
           BorderLayout.CENTER);
    currentClient=clientArea;
    context.showStatus("");
  }

}
```


The Java Commerce Client is a very new API and will likely go through several changes before it really makes an impact on the Internet. Although this chapter has covered the construction of commerce client objects, you will probably not have to write your own commerce objects. Instead, you should be able to get cassettes from various vendors and online stores. If you are creating your own `Shopping Cart` applet, however, you will probably want to write your own UI cassette and still leave the lower-level cassettes to other developers. ●

CHAPTER 46

Data Structures and Java Utilities

In this chapter

What Are Data Structures?

The `java.util` package provides several useful classes that give important functionality to the Java runtime environment. These classes provide much of the code that you frequently end up writing yourself when you write in C++. The creators of Java realized that one of the things people really like about Smalltalk is the abundance of useful utility classes.

The `java.util` package focuses mostly on container objects—that is, objects that contain or hold other objects. In addition to the containers, the package also adds a handy utility class for breaking up a string into words (tokens), expanded support for random numbers and dates, and a carryover from Smalltalk called *observables*.

Data structure is a general computer science term for an object that holds a collection of other objects. For instance, an array is the simplest data structure. Data structures can vary in complexity, but ultimately their goal is to hold and manipulate objects.

Some data structures, like arrays, keep data in one long list. Others, like trees, keep the data sorted in non-linear storage compartments. Each type of data structure has its advantages and disadvantages. For instance, trees are extremely efficient at finding and inserting sorted data, while hashtables are even more efficient at finding data, but at the cost of more memory usage.

Collections

One significant design change in the Java 1.2 API is the creation of a group of classes called the Collection API. The Collection API provides a common set of interfaces for all data structures in the `java.util` package.

Before collections, converting between one data structure and another required some non-trivial amount of work. However, the Collection API provides a uniform mechanism for doing this. In addition, the Collection API is designed to allow characteristics, such as the ordering of an object, to be used in many types of structures.

Now you can choose the proper data structure based on its performance characteristics, without having to worry about the implementation mechanics.

Collection Interface

At the root of the Collection API is the `Collection` interface. The goal of the `Collection` interface is to provide all the common methods all collection classes will have. Now, not 100 percent of all collections will actually provide an implementation for all of the methods. If a method isn't implemented in a `Collection` and you try to call that method anyway, the method will probably throw an `UnsupportedOperationException`.

As you might expect, the `Collection` interface provides mechanisms for inserting new objects into the collection. The first method allows you to insert a single element. The second allows you to add all of the elements in another collection.

```
boolean add(Object o)
boolean addAll(Collection c)
```

To get objects out of the collection, you can choose from three methods. The first two return the contents of the container in an array. The interesting thing about the second of these methods is that you pass into it an array of the object type you wish to return. The last of these methods returns a new class called `Iterator`. You'll see how `Iterator` works later in this chapter.

```
Object[] toArray()
Object[] toArray(Object[] a)
Iterator iterator()
```

You can also remove objects from the collection, either by emptying the array (`clear()`) or by removing a specific object (`remove()`). In addition, you can remove a set of objects by removing all the objects in the collection that also exist in the collection passed as a parameter; or you can retain the objects in the collection that's passed in and remove all the rest of the elements.

```
void clear()
boolean remove(Object o)
boolean removeAll(Collection c)
boolean retainAll(Collection c)
```


The final set of methods allows you to check the status of the collection. The first two allow you to determine if an object or a set of objects is included in a collection. The third method determines if the collection is empty, and the fourth returns the number of elements in the collection.

```
boolean contains(Object o)
boolean containsAll(Collection c)
boolean isEmpty()
int size()
```

The `Collection` interface is implemented by several classes throughout this chapter, so you'll find examples of how to use each of these methods later.

List Interface

The `Collection` interface is extended and specialized with two sub-interfaces, `List` and `Map`. The `List` interface builds on `Collection` and adds some methods for a collection that store the objects in order.

NOTE The creation of the `java.util.List` interface in the 1.2 API has created a name conflict with `java.awt.List`. If you import both `java.awt.*` and `java.util.*`, you will have to do some extra work to use the `List`. You can do this two ways: by importing `java.util.List` specifically, or by using the fully qualified name of the `List` (`java.util.List`) instead of just `List`.

The primary enhancement that an ordered list adds is the concept of an index. The index is the location where the object is actually stored. So, the `List` adds several methods that deal with this concept.

The two new `add()` methods allow you to insert elements at a particular index and shift the elements after that index down so that the remaining objects are shifted in the collection to come after the new object(s). In addition, you can now substitute an object at a particular index with the new one, using the `set()` method.

```
void add(int index, Object element)
boolean addAll(int index, Collection c)
Object set(int index, Object element)
```

You can also get the objects out of the container in three new ways. The first two return a new iterator called a `ListIterator`, which provides bidirectional access. The first of these two methods returns a `ListIterator` of the entire collection, the second returns just an iterator of the collection starting at the specified index. The third method allows you to retrieve just the object at the specified index.

```
ListIterator listIterator()
ListIterator listIterator(int index)
Object get(int index)
```

Obviously you will also want to be able to remove objects from the collection in some new ways too. The first of the new methods removes the element at the specified index, while the second removes all of the objects from the `fromIndex` up to (but not including) the `toIndex`.

```
Object remove(int index)
void removeRange(int fromIndex, int toIndex)
```

Finally, it is often useful to know the index where an element is positioned in the collection. The three methods for getting the element will return either the index where the element is stored, or, if the element is not found, they will return `-1`. The first of these methods returns the first index where a matching object is found and starts to look at the `startingIndex`. The second simply returns the last index where the object can be found, and the last method returns the last index, so long as it is not less than the `minIndex`.

```
int indexOf(Object o, int startingIndex)
int lastIndexOf(Object o)
int lastIndexOf(Object o, int minIndex)
```

Map Interface

The second interface which extends from `Collection` is the `Map` interface. Unlike a `List`, a `Map` ensures that there will be at most one instance of an object and at most one null in the collection. `Map` contains an element and a key value; the key determines where in the `Map` the element should be placed, and the keys can not be duplicated in the `Map`.

To insert elements into `Map` you must provide both the key and the value. So, obviously a new method is required to do just that (`put()`). In addition, because `Map` needs to know the key, it's not possible to just copy any collection and insert it into the collection. Instead, the `putAll()` method copies the elements and uses their associated keys.

```
Object put(Object key, Object value)
void putAll(Map t)
```

To get objects out of a `Map`, you generally don't need to know the object itself, but rather its key. The `get()` method returns the element with the matching key. In addition, `Map` can return a new interface called a `Set`. The two methods return either the `Set` for the entries or the keys. The last new method for getting the elements in the collection returns a regular collection of the elements in `Map`.

```
Object get(Object key)
Set entrySet()
Set keySet()
Collection values()
```

Like inserting new elements into `Map`, removing elements is done via the key value, not the element itself via the `remove()` method.

```
Object remove(Object key)
```

The last of the new `Map` methods determines if a specified key or element is found. The `containsKey()` method returns `true` if the key exists in `Map`, while `containsValue()` returns `true` if the indicated object is mapped in `Map` via one or more keys.

```
boolean containsKey(Object key)
boolean containsValue(Object value)
```


Iterator Interface

As you've seen, a `Collection` allows you to view its contents via a new interface called the `Iterator` interface. If you are familiar with the `Enumeration` interface, which has existed in the Java API since the 1.0 version, the `Iterator` will be very familiar. However, the `Iterator` also allows you to remove an element from the underlying collection.

The three methods first allow you to know if there are any additional elements in `Iterator`.

```
boolean hasNext()
```

Second, `Iterator` will return the next element in `Iterator`.

```
Object next()
```

Finally, you can remove the last element read from `Iterator` from the underlying collection.

```
void remove()
```

ListIterator Interface

A `List` has the ability to provide a more specific form of the `Iterator`. The `ListIterator` takes advantage of the indexing in the `List` and allows you to perform several additional operations.

The first new capability is the ability to insert a new object, or to change the value of the one you just read. So `add()` will insert a new object, while `set()` replaces the object that was just read out of the `Iterator` with the one specified.

```
void add(Object o)
void set(Object o)
```

In addition to being able to read the next element in `Iterator`, a `ListIterator` also allows you to read the previous element. So `ListIterator` adds `hasPrevious()` in addition to the `hasNext()` method.

```
boolean hasPrevious()
```

Obviously you will also want to retrieve the previous object as well, so, in addition to the `next()` method, a `ListIterator` also has a `previous()` method.

```
Object previous()
```

Finally, since you're looking at a list, you can also get the index values of the next or previous elements.

```
int nextIndex()
int previousIndex()
```

The *Vector* Class

Java arrays are powerful, but they don't always fit your needs. Sometimes you want to put items in an array, but you don't know how many items you will be getting. One way to solve this is to create an array larger than you think you'll need. This was the typical approach in the days of C programming. The `Vector` class gives you an alternative to this. A *vector* is similar to an array in that it holds multiple objects, and you retrieve the objects using an index value. The big difference between arrays and vectors is that vectors automatically grow when they run out of room. They also provide extra methods for adding and removing elements that you would normally have to do manually in an array, such as inserting an element between two others. Effectively, a vector is an extensible array.

Before the 1.2 API, `Vector` extended just `Object`. Now with the 1.2 API, it extends from `AbstractList`, which implements `List`.

Creating a Vector

When you create a vector, you can specify how big it should be initially and how fast it should grow. You can also just set the vector's initial size and let it figure out how fast to grow, or you can let the vector decide everything for itself. To accomplish these various forms of initialization, the `Vector` class has three constructors.

```
public Vector()
```

creates an empty vector.

```
public Vector(int initialCapacity)
```

creates a vector with space for `initialCapacity` elements.

```
public Vector(int initialCapacity, int capacityIncrement)
```

creates a vector with space for `initialCapacity` elements. Whenever the vector needs to grow, it grows by `capacityIncrement` elements.

JDK 1.2 adds one more constructor to support the Collection API, discussed at the end of this chapter. The new constructor creates a vector that initially has all the elements in the `Collection`, in the order they appear from the `Collection`'s `Iterator`.

```
public Vector(Collection c)
```

If you have some idea of the typical number of elements you will be adding, go ahead and set up the vector with space for that many elements. If you don't use all the space, that's okay; you just don't want the vector to have to allocate more space over and over.

CAUTION

If you do not specify a capacity increment, the vector doubles its capacity when it grows. If you have a large vector, this may not be the desired behavior. When you are adding many elements to a vector, you should set a specific capacity increment. Even if you're not adding a large number of elements because growing the array can be a costly operation, if you're lucky enough to have a good idea how many objects will likely be in the vector you should create the vector with that initial capacity.

Adding Objects to a Vector

In addition to the standard `List` methods, there are two ways to add new objects to a vector. You can add an object as the last element in the vector, or you can insert an object between two existing objects. The `addElement` method adds an object as the last element:

```
public final synchronized void addElement(Object newElement)
```

The `insertElementAt()` method adds a new object at a specific position. The `index` parameter indicates where in the vector the new object should be placed:

```
public final synchronized void insertElementAt(Object newElement, int index)
     throws ArrayIndexOutOfBoundsException
```

If you try to insert the new element at a position that does not exist yet—for example, if you try to insert at position 9 and there are only five elements in the vector—you get an `ArrayIndexOutOfBoundsException`.

You can change the object at a specific position in the vector with the `setElementAt` method:

```
public final synchronized void setElementAt(Object ob, int index)
     throws ArrayOutOfBoundsException
```

This method works almost exactly like the `insertElementAt` method, except that the other elements in the vector are not shifted over to make room for a new object. In other words, the new object replaces the old one in the vector.

Accessing Objects in a Vector

Unfortunately, accessing objects in a vector is not as simple as accessing array elements. Instead of giving an index surrounded by brackets (`[]`), you use the `elementAt` method to access vector elements. The vector equivalent of `someArray[4]` is `someVector.elementAt(4)`. The format of the `elementAt` method is:

```
public final synchronized Object elementAt(int index)
     throws ArrayIndexOutOfBoundsException
```

You can also access the first and last elements in a vector with the `firstElement` and `lastElement` methods:

```
public final synchronized Object firstElement()
    throws NoSuchElementException
public final synchronized Object lastElement()
    throws NoSuchElementException
```

If no objects are stored in the vector, these methods both throw a `NoSuchElementException`.

You can test to see whether a vector has no elements using the `isEmpty` method:

```
public final boolean isEmpty()
```

Many times you want to use a vector to build up a container of objects but then convert the vector over to a Java array for speed purposes. You usually only do this after you have all the objects you need. For instance, if you are reading objects from a file that can contain any number of objects, you store the objects in a vector. When you have finished reading the file, you create an array of objects and copy them out of the vector. The `size` method tells you how many objects are stored in the vector:

```
public final int size()
```

After you know the size of the vector, you can create an array of objects using this size. The `Vector` class provides a handy method for copying all the objects in a vector into an array of objects:

```
public final synchronized void copyInto(Object[] obArray)
```

If you try to copy more objects into the array than it can hold, you get an `ArrayIndexOutOfBounds` exception. The following code fragment creates an object array and copies the contents of a vector called `myVector` into it:

```
Object obArray[] = new Object[myVector.size()]; // Create object array
myVector.copyInto(obArray);  // Copy the vector into the array
```

The *Enumeration* Interface

If you want to cycle through all the elements in a vector, you can use the elements method to get an `Enumeration` object for the vector. An `Enumeration` is responsible for accessing elements in a data structure sequentially. It contains two methods.

```
public abstract boolean hasMoreElements()
```

returns `true` while there are still more elements to access. When there are no more elements left, this method returns `false`.

```
public abstract Object nextElement()
    throws NoSuchElementException
```

returns a reference to the next element in the data structure. If there are no more elements to access and you call this method again, you get a `NoSuchElementException`.

In the case of the `Vector` class, the `elements()` method returns an `Enumeration` interface for the vector:

```
public final synchronized Enumeration elements()
```

The following code fragment uses an `Enumeration` interface to examine every object in a vector:

```
Enumeration vectEnum = myVector.elements();     // get the vector's
enumeration

while (vectEnum.hasMoreElements())     // while there's something to get...
{
     Object nextOb = vectEnum.nextElement();     // get the next object
     // do whatever you want with the next object
}
```

This loop works the same for every data structure that can return an `Enumeration` object. A data structure typically has an `elements()` method, or something similar, that returns the `enumeration`. After that, the kind of data structure doesn't matter—they all look the same through the `Enumeration` interface.

Searching for Objects in a Vector

You can always search for objects in a vector manually, by using an `enumeration` and doing an element-by-element comparison, but you will save a lot of time by using the built-in search functions.

If you just need to know whether an object is present in a vector, use the `contains()` method. For example:

```
public final boolean contains(Object ob)
```

returns `true` if `ob` occurs at least once in the vector, or `false` if not.

You can also find out an object's position in a vector with the `indexOf()` and `lastIndexOf()` methods. For example:

```
public final int indexOf(Object ob)
```

returns the position in the vector where the first occurrence of `ob` is found, or `-1` if `ob` is not present in the vector.

```
public final synchronized int indexOf(Object ob, int startIndex)
     throws ArrayIndexOutOfBoundsException
```

returns the position in the vector where the first occurrence of `ob` is found, starting at position `startIndex`. If `ob` is not in the vector, it returns `-1`. If `startIndex` is less than 0, or greater than or equal to the vector's length, you get an `ArrayOutOfBoundsException`.

```
public final int lastIndexOf(Object ob)
```

returns the position in the vector where the last occurrence of `ob` is found, or `-1` if `ob` is not present in the vector.

```
public final synchronized int lastIndexOf(Object ob, int startIndex)
     throws ArrayOutOfBoundsException
```

returns the position in the vector where the last occurrence of `ob` is found, starting at position `startIndex`. If `ob` is not in the vector, it returns `-1`. If `startIndex` is less than 0 or greater than or equal to the vector's length, you get an `ArrayOutOfBoundsException`.

Removing Objects from a Vector

You have three options when it comes to removing objects from a vector. You can remove all the objects, remove a specific object, or remove the object at a specific position. The `removeAllElements` method removes all the objects from a vector:

```
public final synchronized void removeAllElements()
```

The `removeElement` method removes a specific object from a vector:

```
public final synchronized boolean removeElement(Object ob)
```

If the object occurs more than once, only the first occurrence is removed. The method returns `true` if an object was actually removed, or `false` if the object was not found in the vector.

The `removeElementAt` method removes the object at a specific position and moves the other objects over to fill in the gap created by the removed object:

```
public final synchronized void removeElementAt(int index)
     throws ArrayIndexOutOfBoundsException
```

If you try to remove an object from a position that does not exist, you get an `ArrayIndexOutOfBoundsException`.

Changing the Size of a Vector

A vector has two notions of size—the number of elements currently stored in the vector and the maximum capacity of the vector. The `capacity` method tells you how many objects the vector can hold before having to grow:

```
public final int capacity()
```

You can increase the capacity of a vector using the `ensureCapacity` method. For example:

```
public final synchronized void ensureCapacity(int minimumCapacity)
```

tells the vector that it should be able to store at least `minimumCapacity` elements. If the vector's current capacity is less than `minimumCapacity`, it allocates more space. The vector does not shrink the current capacity if the capacity is already higher than `minimumCapacity`.

If you want to reduce a vector's capacity, use the `trimToSize` method:

```
public final synchronized void trimToSize()
```

This method reduces the capacity of a vector down to the number of elements it is currently storing.

The `size` method tells you how many elements are stored in a vector:

```
public final int size()
```

You can use the `setSize` method to change the current number of elements:

```
public synchronized final void setSize(int newSize)
```

If the new size is less than the old size, the elements at the end of the vector are lost. If the new size is higher than the old size, the new elements are set to `null`. Calling `setSize(0)` is the same as calling `removeAllElements()`.

The *Hashtable* Class

The `Hashtable` class is the most common implementation of the `Map` collection and provides methods for associating one object with another. Hashtables are often used to associate a name with an object and retrieve the object based on that name. In a dictionary, the name object is called a *key*, and it can be any kind of object. The object associated with the key is called the *value*. A key can be associated with only one value, but a value can have more than one key.

Effectively you can think of the `Hashtable` class as a class that uses the hash codes of the key objects to perform the lookup. It groups keys into *buckets* based on their hash code. When it goes to find a key, it queries the key's hash code, uses the hash code to get the correct bucket, and then searches the bucket for the correct key. Usually, the number of keys in the bucket is small compared to the total number of keys in the hashtable, so the hashtable performs only a fraction of the comparisons performed in most collections like a vector.

The hashtable has a capacity, which tells how many buckets it uses, and a load factor, which is the ratio of the number of elements in the table to the number of buckets. When you create a hashtable, you can specify a load factor threshold value. When the current load factor exceeds this threshold, the table grows—that is, it doubles the number of buckets and then reorganizes the table. The default load factor threshold is 0.75, which means that when the number of elements stored in the table is 75 percent of the number of buckets, the number of buckets is doubled. You can specify any load factor threshold greater than 0 and less than or equal to 1. A smaller threshold means a faster lookup because there will be few keys per bucket (maybe no more than one), but the table will have far more buckets than elements, so there is some wasted space. A larger threshold means the possibility of slower lookups, but the number of buckets is closer to the number of elements.

The `Hashtable` class has three constructors.

```
public Hashtable()
```

creates a new hashtable with a default capacity of 101 and a default load factor threshold of 0.75.

```
public Hashtable(int initialCapacity)
```

creates a new hashtable with the specified initial capacity and a default load factor threshold of 0.75.

```
public Hashtable(int initialCapacity, float loadFactorThreshold)
     throws IllegalArgumentException
```

creates a new hashtable with the specified initial capacity and threshold. If the initial capacity is 0 or less, or if the threshold is 0 or less, or greater than 1, you get an `IllegalArgumentException`.

Storing Objects in a Hashtable

To store an object in a dictionary with a specific key, use the `put()` method:

```
public abstract Object put(Object key, Object value)
     throws NullPointerException
```

The object returned by the `put` method is the object previously associated with the key. If there was no previous association, the method returns `null`. You cannot have a `null` key or a `null` value. If you pass `null` for either of these parameters, you get a `NullPointerException`.

Retrieving Objects from a Hashtable

The `get()` method finds the object in the hashtable associated with a particular key:

```
public abstract Object get(Object key)
```

The `get()` method returns `null` if there is no value associated with that key.

Removing Objects from a Hashtable

To remove a key-value pair from a dictionary, call the `remove()` method with the key. For example:

```
public abstract Object remove(Object key)
```

returns the object associated with the key, or `null` if no value is associated with that key.

The `Dictionary` class also provides some utility methods that give you information about the dictionary. The `isEmpty()` method returns `true` if no objects are stored in the dictionary:

```
public abstract boolean isEmpty()
```

The `size` method tells you how many key-value pairs are currently stored in the dictionary:

```
public abstract int size()
```

The `keys` method returns an `Enumeration` object that allows you to examine all the keys in the dictionary, whereas the `elements()` method returns an `Enumeration` for all the values in the dictionary:

```
public abstract Enumeration keys()

public abstract Enumeration elements()
```

In addition to these methods, the `Hashtable` has a few more methods for the `Map` interface.

```
public synchronized void clear()
```

removes all the elements from the hashtable. This is similar to the `removeAllElements` method in the `Vector` class.

```
public synchronized boolean contains(Object value)
     throws NullPointerException
```

returns `true` if `value` is stored as a value in the hashtable. If `value` is `null`, it throws a `NullPointerException`.

```
public synchronized boolean containsKey(Object key)
```

returns `true` if `key` is stored as a key in the hashtable.

When a hashtable grows in size, it has to rearrange all the objects in the table over the new set of buckets. In other words, if there were 512 buckets and the table grew to 1,024 buckets, you need to redistribute the objects over the full 1,024 buckets. An object's bucket is determined by a combination of both the hash code and the number of buckets. If you were to change the number of buckets but not rearrange the objects, the hashtable might not be able to locate an existing object because its bucket was determined based on a smaller size. The `rehash()` method, (which is automatically called when the table grows) recomputes the location of each object in the table.

The *Properties* Class

The `Properties` class is a special kind of dictionary that uses strings for both keys and values. It is used by the `System` class to store system properties, but you can use it to create your own set of properties. The `Properties` class is actually just a hashtable that specializes in storing strings.

You can create a new `Properties` object with the empty constructor:

```
public Properties()
```

You can also create a `Properties` object with a set of default properties. When the `Properties` object cannot find a property in its own table, it searches the default properties table. If you change a property in your own `Properties` object, it does not change the property in the default `Properties` object. This means that multiple `Properties` objects can safely share the same default `Properties` object. To create a `Properties` object with a default set of properties, just pass the default `Properties` object to the constructor:

```
public Properties(Properties defaultProps)
```

Setting Properties

You set properties using the same `put()` method that all dictionaries use:

```
public Object put(Object key, Object value)
     throws NullPointerException
```

Querying Properties

The `getProperty()` method returns the string corresponding to a property name, or `null` if the property is not set:

```
public String getProperty(String key)
```

If you specify a default `Properties` object, that object is also checked before `null` is returned. You can also call `getProperty` and specify a default value to be returned if the property is not set:

```
public String getProperty(String key, String defaultValue)
```

In this version of the `getProperty` method, the default `Properties` object is completely ignored. The value returned is either the property corresponding to the key, or, if the property is not set, `defaultValue`.

CAUTION

Because the `Properties` class uses the `put()` method from the `Dictionary` class, you can store objects other than strings in a `Properties` object. However, if you store a property that is not a `String` or a subclass of `String`, you get a `ClassCastException` when you try to retrieve it with the `getProperty()` method. It is a good practice to use the `toString()` method in an object to ensure that you are storing a string representation and not a non-string object.

You can get an `Enumeration` object for all the property names in a `Properties` object, including the default properties, with the `propertyNames()` method:

```
public Enumeration propertyNames()
```

Saving and Retrieving Properties

Because the `Properties` class is so useful for storing things like a user's preferences, you need a way to save the properties to a file and read them back the next time your program starts. You can use the `load()` and `save()` methods for this.

```
public synchronized void save(OutputStream out, String header)
```

saves the properties on the output stream `out`. The header string is written to the stream before the contents of the `Properties` object.

```
public synchronized void load(InputStream in)
     throws IOException
```

reads properties from the input stream. It treats the `#` and `!` characters as comment characters and ignores anything after them up to the end of the line, similar to the `//` comment characters in Java.

Listing 46.1 shows a sample file written by the `save()` method.

Listing 46.1 File Written by the *save()* Method

```
#Example Properties
#Mon Jun 17 19:57:39  1996
foo=bar
favoriteStooge=curly
helloMessage=hello world!
```

The `list()` method is similar to the `save()` method, but it presents the properties in a more readable form. It displays the contents of a properties table on a print stream in a nice, friendly format, which is handy for debugging. The format of the `list()` method is as follows:

```
public void list(PrintStream out)
```

The *Stack* Class

A stack is a handy data structure that adds items in a last-in, first-out manner. In other words, when you ask a stack to give you the next item, it hands back the most recently added item. Think of the stack as a stack of cafeteria trays. The tray on the top of the stack is the last tray you put on the stack. Every time you add another tray it becomes the new top of the stack.

The `Stack` class is implemented as a subclass of `Vector`, which means that all the vector methods are available to you in addition to the stack-specific ones. You create a stack with the empty constructor:

```
public Stack()
```

To add an item to the top of the stack, you push it onto the stack:

```
public Object push(Object newItem)
```

The object returned by the `push()` method is the same as the `newItem` object. The `pop()`method removes the top item from the stack:

```
public Object pop() throws EmptyStackException
```

If you try to pop an item off an empty stack you get an `EmptyStackException`. You can find out which item is on top of the stack without removing it by using the `peek()` method:

```
public Object peek() throws EmptyStackException
```

The `empty()` method returns `true` if there are no items on the stack:

```
public boolean empty()
```

Sometimes you may want to find out where an object is in relation to the top of the stack. Because you don't know exactly how the stack stores items, the `indexOf()` and `lastIndexOf()` methods from the `Vector` class might not do you any good. The `search()` method, however, tells you how far an object is from the top of the stack:

```
public int search(Object ob)
```

If the object is not on the stack at all, `search()` returns `-1`.

The fragment of code in Listing 46.2 creates an array of strings and then uses a stack to reverse the order of the words by pushing them all on the stack and popping them back off.

Listing 46.2 Example Usage of a Stack

```
String myArray[] = { "Please", "Reverse", "These", "Words" };

Stack myStack = new Stack();

// Push all the elements in the array onto the stack

for (int i=0; i < myArray.length; i++) {
    myStack.push(myArray[i]);
}
// Pop the elements off the stack and put them in the
// array starting at the beginning

for (int i=0; i < myArray.length; i++) {
    myArray[i] = (String) myStack.pop();
}

// At this point, the words in myArray will be in
// the order: Words, These, Reverse, Please
```

The *Date* Class

The `Date` class represents a specific date and time. It is centered around the Epoch, which is midnight GMT on January 1, 1970. Although there is some support in the `Date` class for referencing dates as early as 1900, none of the date methods function properly on dates occurring before the Epoch.

The empty constructor for the `Date` class creates a `Date` object from the current time:

```
public Date()
```

You can also create a `Date` object using the number of milliseconds from the Epoch, the same kind of value returned by `System.currentTimeMillis()`:

```
public Date(long millis)
```

You can also get the milliseconds since the Epoch by using the static `UTC` method in the `Date` class (UTC stands for Universal Time Coordinates):

```
public static long UTC(int year, int month, int date,
int hours, int minutes, int seconds)
```

The following `Date` constructors allow you to create a `Date` object by giving a specific year, month, day, and so on:

```
public Date(int year, int month, int date)
public Date(int year, int month, int date, int hours, int minutes)
public Date(int year, int month, int date, int hours, int minutes, int seconds)
```

There are several important things to note when creating dates this way:

- The `year` value is the number of years since 1900. For instance, the year value for 1984 would be 84.
- Months are numbered starting at 0, not 1. January is month 0.
- Dates (the day of the month) are numbered starting at 1, just to add some confusion, so the 11th day of the month would have a date value of 11.
- Hours, minutes, and seconds are all numbered starting at 0, which, unlike the months, is correct. An hour value of 1 means 1 a.m.

The `Date` class also has the capability to create a new `Date` object from a string representation of a date:

```
public Date(String s)
```

The following statements all create `Date` objects for January 12, 1992 (the birthday of the HAL 9000 computer):

```
Date d = new Date("January 12, 1992");
Date d = new Date(92, 0, 12);
Date d = new Date(695174400000l);      // milliseconds since the epoch
Date d = new Date(Date.UTC(92, 0, 12, 0, 0, 0));
```


NOTE Whenever you create a date using specific year, month, day, hour, minute, and second values, or when you print out the value of a `Date` object, it uses the local time zone. The `UTC` method and the number of milliseconds since the Epoch are always in GMT (Greenwich Mean Time).

Comparing Dates

As is true with all subclasses of `Object`, you can compare two dates with the `equals()` method. The `Date` class also provides methods for determining whether one date comes before or after another. The `after()` method in a `Date` object returns `true` if the date comes after the date passed to the method:

```
public boolean after(Date when)
```

The `before()` method tells whether a `Date` object occurs before a specific date:

```
public boolean before(Date when)
```

Suppose you defined `date1` and `date2` as:

```
Date date1 = new Date(76, 6, 4);      // July 4, 1976
Date date2 = new Date(92, 0, 12);      // January 12, 1992
```

For these two dates, `date1.before(date2)` is `true`, and `date1.after(date2)` is `false`.

Converting Dates to Strings

You can always use the `toString()` method to convert a date to a string. It converts the date to a string representation using your local time zone. The `toLocaleString()` method also converts a date to a string representation using the local time zone, but the format of the string is slightly different:

```
public String toLocaleString()
```

The `toGMTString()` method converts a date to a string using GMT as the time zone:

```
public String toGMTString()
```

The following example shows the formats of the different string conversions. The original time was defined as midnight GMT, January 12, 1992. The local time zone is Eastern Standard, or five hours behind GMT.

```
Sat Jan 11 19:00:00  1992          // toString
01/11/92 19:00:00                // toLocaleString
12 Jan 1992 00:00:00 GMT           // toGMTString
```

Changing Date Attributes

You can query and change almost all the parts of a date. The only two things that you can query but not change are the time zone offset and the day of the week a date occurs on. The time zone offset is the number of minutes between the local time zone and GMT. The number is positive if your time zone is behind GMT—that is, if midnight GMT occurs before midnight in your time zone. The format of `getTimezoneOffset()` is:

```
public int getTimezoneOffset()
```

The `getDay()` method returns a number between 0 and 6, where 0 is Sunday:

```
public int getDay()
```

Remember that the day is computed using local time.

If you prefer to deal with dates in terms of the raw number of milliseconds since the Epoch, you can use the `getTime()` and `setTime()` methods to modify the date:

```
public long getTime()
public void setTime(long time)
```

You can also manipulate the individual components of the dates using these methods:

```
public int getYear()
public int getMonth()
public int getDate()
public int getHours()
public int getMinutes()
public int getSeconds()

public void setYear(int year)
public void setMonth(int month)
public void setDate(int date)
```

```
public void setHours(int hours)
public void setMinutes(int minutes)
public void setSeconds(int seconds)
```

The *BitSet* Class

The `BitSet` class provides a convenient way to perform bitwise operations on a large number of bits, and to manipulate individual bits. The `BitSet` automatically grows to handle more bits. You can create an empty bit set with the empty constructor:

```
public BitSet()
```

If you have some idea how many bits you will need, you should create the `BitSet` with a specific size:

```
public BitSet(int numberOfBits)
```

Bits are like light switches, they can be either on or off. If a bit is set, it is considered on, whereas it is considered off if it is cleared. Bits are frequently associated with Boolean values because each has only two possible values. A bit that is set is considered to be `true`, whereas a bit that is cleared is considered to be `false`.

You use the `set()` and `clear()` methods to set and clear individual bits in a bit set:

```
public void set(int whichBit)
public void clear(int whichBit)
```

If you create a bit set of 200 bits and you try to set bit number 438, the bit set automatically grows to contain at least 438 bits. The new bits will all be cleared initially. The `size()` method tells you how many bits are in the current bit set:

```
public int size()
```

You can test to see whether a bit is set or cleared using the `get()` method:

```
public boolean get(int whichBit)
```

The `get()` method returns `true` if the specified bit is set, or `false` if it is cleared.

There are three operations you can perform between two bit sets. These operations manipulate the current bit set using bits from a second bit set. Corresponding bits are matched to perform the operation. In other words, bit 0 in the current bit set is compared to bit 0 in the second bit set. The bitwise operations are:

- The `or` operation sets the bit in the current bit set if either the current bit or the second bit is set. If neither bit is set, the current bit remains cleared.
- The `and` operation sets the bit in the current bit set only if the current bit and the second bit are set. Otherwise, the current bit is cleared.
- The `xor` operation sets the bit in the current bit set if only one of the two bits is set. If both are set, the current bit is cleared.

The format of these bitwise operations is:

```
public void or(Bitset bits)
public void and(Bitset bits)
public void xor(Bitset bits)
```

The *StringTokenizer* Class

The `StringTokenizer` class helps you parse a string by breaking it up into tokens. It recognizes tokens based on a set of delimiters. A token is considered to be a string of characters that are not delimiters. For example, the phrase "I am a sentence" contains a number of tokens with spaces as delimiters. The tokens are I, am, a, and sentence. If you were using the colon character as a delimiter, the sentence would be one long token called "I am a sentence" because there are no colons to separate the words. The `StringTokenizer` is not bound by the convention that words are separated by spaces. If you tell it that words are only separated by colons, it considers spaces to be part of a word.

You can even use a set of delimiters, meaning that many different characters can delimit tokens. For example, if you had the string "Hello. How are you? I am fine, I think," you would want to use a space, period, comma, and question mark as delimiters to break the sentence into tokens that are only words.

The string tokenizer doesn't have a concept of words itself; it only understands delimiters. When you are parsing text, you usually use whitespace as a delimiter. Whitespace consists of spaces, tabs, newlines, and returns. If you do not specify a string of delimiters when you create a string tokenizer, it uses whitespace.

You create a string tokenizer by passing the string to be tokenized to the constructor:

```
public StringTokenizer(String str)
```

If you want something other than whitespace as a delimiter, you can also pass a string containing the delimiters you want to use:

```
public StringTokenizer(String str, String delimiters)
```

Sometimes you want to know what delimiter is used to separate two tokens. You can ask the string tokenizer to pass delimiters back as tokens by passing `true` for the `returnTokens` parameter in this constructor:

```
public StringTokenizer(String str, String delimiters, boolean returnTokens)
```

The `nextToken()` method returns the next token in the string:

```
public String nextToken()
     throws NoSuchElementException
```

If there are no more tokens, it throws a `NoSuchElementException`. You can use the `hasMoreTokens()` method to determine whether there are more tokens before you use `nextToken()`:

```
public boolean hasMoreTokens()
```

You can also change the set of delimiters on-the-fly by passing a new set of delimiters to the `nextToken()` method:

```
public String nextToken(String newDelimiters)
```

The new delimiters take effect before the next token is parsed and stay in effect until they are changed again.

The `countTokens()` method tells you how many tokens are in the string, assuming that the delimiter set doesn't change:

```
public int countTokens()
```

You may have noticed that the `nextToken()` and `hasMoreTokens()` methods look similar to the `nextElement()` and `hasMoreElements()` methods in the `Enumeration` interface. They are so similar, in fact, that the `StringTokenizer` also implements an `Enumeration` interface that is implemented as:

```
public boolean hasMoreElements() {
    return hasMoreTokens();
}

public Object nextElement() {
    return nextToken();
}
```

The following code fragment prints out the words in a sentence using a string tokenizer:

```
String sentence = "This is a sentence";
StringTokenizer tokenizer = new StringTokenizer(sentence);

while (tokenizer.hasMoreTokens())
{
     System.out.println(tokenizer.nextToken());
}
```


The *Random* Class

The `Random` class provides a random number generator that is more flexible than the random number generator in the `Math` class. Actually, the random number generator in the `Math` class just uses one of the methods in the `Random` class. Because the methods in the `Random` class are not static, you must create an instance of `Random` before you generate numbers. The easiest way to do this is with the empty constructor:

```
public Random()
```

One handy feature of the `Random` class is that it lets you set the random number seed that determines the pattern of random numbers. Although you cannot easily predict what numbers will be generated with a particular seed, you can duplicate a series of random numbers by using the same seed. In other words, if you create an instance of `Random` with the same seed value every time, you will get the same sequence of random numbers every time. This might not be good for writing games and would be financially devastating for lotteries, but it is useful when writing simulations where you want to replay the same sequences over and over. The empty constructor uses `System.currentTimeMillis` to seed the random number generator. To create an instance of `Random` with a particular seed, just pass the seed value to the constructor:

```
public Random(long seed)
```

You can change the seed of the random number generator at any time using the `setSeed()` method:

```
public synchronized void setSeed(long newSeed)
```

The `Random` class can generate random numbers in four different data types.

```
public int nextInt()
```

generates a 32-bit random number that can be any legal `int` value.

```
public long nextLong()
```

generates a 64-bit random number that can be any legal `long` value.

```
public float nextFloat()
```

generates a random `float` value between 0.0 and 1.0, though always less than 1.0.

```
public double nextDouble()
```

generates a random `double` value between 0.0 and 1.0, always less than 1.0. This is the method used by the `Math.random()` method.

There is also a special variation of random number that has some interesting mathematical properties. This variation is called `nextGaussian`.

```
public synchronized double nextGaussian()
```

returns a special random `double` value that can be any legal `double` value. The mean (average) of the values generated by this method is 0.0, and the standard deviation is 1.0. This means that the numbers generated by this method are usually close to zero and that very large numbers are fairly rare.

The *Observable* Class

The `Observable` class allows an object to notify other objects when it changes. The concept of observables is borrowed from Smalltalk. In Smalltalk, an object may express interest in another object, meaning that it would like to know when the other object changes.

When building user interfaces, you might have multiple ways to change a piece of data, and changing that data might cause several different parts of the display to update. For instance, suppose that you want to create a scrollbar that changes an integer value and, in turn, that integer value is displayed on some sort of graphical meter. You want the meter to update as the value is changed, but you don't want the meter to know anything about the scrollbar. If you are wondering why the meter shouldn't know about the scrollbar, what happens if you decide you don't want a scrollbar but want the number entered from a text field instead? You shouldn't have to change the meter every time you change the input source.

You would be better off creating an integer variable that is observable. It allows other objects to express interest in it. When this integer variable changes, it notifies those interested parties (called observers) that it has changed. In the case of the graphical meter, it would be informed that the value changed and would query the integer variable for the new value and then redraw itself. This allows the meter to display the value correctly no matter what you are using to change the value.

This concept is known as Model-View-Controller. A model is the nonvisual part of an application. In the preceding example, the model is a single integer variable. The view is anything that visually displays some part of the model. The graphical meter is an example of a view. The scrollbar could also be an example of a view because it updates its position whenever the integer value changes. A controller is any input source that modifies the view. The scrollbar, in this case, is also a controller (it can be both a view and a controller).

In Smalltalk, the mechanism for expressing interest in an object is built right in to the `Object` class. Unfortunately, for whatever reason, Sun separated out the observing mechanism into a separate class. This means extra work for you because you cannot just register interest in an `Integer` class; you must create your own subclass of `Observable`.

The most important methods to you in creating a subclass of `Observable` are `setChanged()` and `notifyObservers()`. The `setChanged()` method marks the observable as having been changed, so that when you call `notifyObservers()` the observers are notified:


```
protected synchronized void setChanged()
```

The `setChanged()` method sets an internal `changed` flag that is used by the `notifyObservers()` method. It is automatically cleared when `notifyObservers()` is called, but you can clear it manually with the `clearChanged()` method:

```
protected synchronized void clearChanged()
```

The `notifyObservers()` method checks to see whether the `changed` flag has been set, and if not, it does not send any notification:

```
public void notifyObservers()
```

The following code fragment sets the `changed` flag and notifies the observers of the change:

```
setChanged();            // Flag this observable as changed
notifyObservers();       // Tell observers about the change
```

The `notifyObservers()` method can also be called with an argument:

```
public void notifyObservers(Object arg)
```

This argument can be used to pass additional information about the change—for instance, the new value. Calling `notifyObservers()` with no argument is equivalent to calling it with an argument of `null`.

You can determine whether an observable has changed by calling the `hasChanged()` method:

```
public synchronized boolean hasChanged()
```

Observers can register interest in an observable by calling the `addObserver()` method:

```
public synchronized void addObserver(Observer obs)
```

Observers can deregister interest in an observable by calling `deleteObserver()`:

```
public synchronized void deleteObserver(Observer obs)
```

An observable can clear out its list of observers by calling the `deleteObservers()` method:

```
public synchronized void deleteObservers()
```

The `countObservers()` method returns the number of observers registered for an observable:

```
public synchronized int countObservers()
```

Listing 46.3 shows an example implementation of an `ObservableInt` class.

Listing 46.3 Source Code for *ObservableInt.java*

```
import java.util.*;

// ObservableInt - an integer Observable
//
// This class implements the Observable mechanism for
// a simple int variable.
// You can set the value with setValue(int)
// and int getValue() returns the current value.

public class ObservableInt extends Observable
{
     int value;     // The value everyone wants to observe

     public ObservableInt()
     {
          value = 0;     // By default, let value be 0
     }

     public ObservableInt(int newValue)
     {
          value = newValue;     // Allow value to be set when created
     }

     public synchronized void setValue(int newValue)
     {
//
// Check to see that this call is REALLY changing the value
//
          if (newValue != value)
          {
               value = newValue;
               setChanged();     // Mark this class as "changed"
               notifyObservers();     // Tell the observers about it
          }
     }
```

```
    public synchronized int getValue()
    {
        return value;
    }
}
```

The `Observable` class has a companion interface called `Observer`. Any class that wants to receive updates about a change in an observable needs to implement the `Observer` interface. The `Observer` interface consists of a single method called `update()` that is called when an object changes. The format of `update()` is:

```
public abstract void update(Observable obs, Object arg);
```

where `obs` is the observable that has just changed, and `arg` is a value passed by the observable when it called `notifyObservers()`. If `notifyObservers()` is called with no arguments, `arg` is `null`.

Listing 46.4 shows an example of a `Label` class that implements the `Observer` interface so that it can be informed of changes in an integer variable and update itself with the new value.

Listing 46.4 Source Code for *IntLabel.java*

```
import java.awt.*;
import java.util.*;

//
// IntLabel - a Label that displays the value of
// an ObservableInt.

public class IntLabel extends Label implements Observer
{
    private ObservableInt intValue;    // The value we're observing

    public IntLabel(ObservableInt theInt)
    {
        intValue = theInt;

// Tell intValue we're interested in it

        intValue.addObserver(this);

// Initialize the label to the current value of intValue

        setText(""+intValue.getValue());
    }

// Update will be called whenever intValue is changed, so just update
// the label text.

    public void update(Observable obs, Object arg)
    {
```

continued

Listing 46.4 Continued

```
          setText(""+intValue.getValue());
     }
}
```

Now that you have a model object defined in the form of the `ObservableInt` and a view in the form of the `IntLabel`, you can create a controller—the `IntScrollbar`. Listing 46.5 shows the implementation of `IntScrollbar`.

Listing 46.5 Source Code for *IntScrollbar.java*

```
import java.awt.*;
import java.util.*;

//
// IntScrollbar - a Scrollbar that modifies an
// ObservableInt.  This class functions as both a
// "view" of the observable, since the position of
// the scrollbar is changed as the observable's value
// is changed, and it is a "controller," since it also
// sets the value of the observable.
//
// IntScrollbar has the same constructors as Scrollbar,
// except that in each case, there is an additional
// parameter that is the ObservableInt.
// Note:  On the constructor where you pass in the initial
// scrollbar position, the position is ignored.

public class IntScrollbar extends Scrollbar implements Observer
{
     private ObservableInt intValue;

// The bulk of this class is implementing the various
// constructors that are available in the Scrollbar class.

     public IntScrollbar(ObservableInt newValue)
     {
          super();     // Call the Scrollbar constructor
          intValue = newValue;
          intValue.addObserver(this);        // Register interest
          setValue(intValue.getValue());     // Change scrollbar position
     }

     public IntScrollbar(ObservableInt newValue, int orientation)
     {
          super(orientation);          // Call the Scrollbar constructor
          intValue = newValue;
          intValue.addObserver(this);        // Register interest
          setValue(intValue.getValue());     // Change scrollbar position
     }
```

```
    public IntScrollbar(ObservableInt newValue, int orientation,
         int value, int pageSize, int lowValue, int highValue)
    {
         super(orientation, value, pageSize, lowValue, highValue);
         intValue = newValue;
         intValue.addObserver(this);        // Register interest
         setValue(intValue.getValue());     // Change scrollbar position
    }

// The handleEvent method checks with the parent class (Scrollbar) to see
// if it wants the event, if not, just assumes the scrollbar value has
// changed and updates the observable int with the new position.

    public boolean handleEvent(Event evt)
    {
         if (super.handleEvent(evt))
         {
              return true;      // The Scrollbar class handled it
         }
         intValue.setValue(getValue());     // Update the observable int
         return true;
    }

// update is called whenever the observable int changes its value

    public void update(Observable obs, Object arg)
    {
         setValue(intValue.getValue());
    }
}
```


This may look like a lot of work, but watch how easy it is to create an applet with an `IntScrollbar` that modifies an `ObservableInt` and an `IntLabel` that displays one. Listing 46.6 shows an implementation of an applet that uses the `IntScrollbar`, the `ObservableInt`, and the `IntLabel`.

Listing 46.6 Source Code for *ObservableApplet1.java*

```
import java.applet.*;
import java.awt.*;


public class ObservableApplet1 extends Applet
{
     ObservableInt myIntValue;

     public void init()
     {

// Create the Observable int to play with

          myIntValue = new ObservableInt(5);
```

continued

Listing 46.6 Continued

```
          setLayout(new GridLayout(2, 0));

// Create an IntScrollbar that modifies the observable int

          add(new IntScrollbar(myIntValue,
               Scrollbar.HORIZONTAL,
               0, 10, 0, 100));

// Create an IntLabel that displays the observable int

          add(new IntLabel(myIntValue));
     }
}
```

You might notice when you run this applet that the label value changes whenever you update the scrollbar; yet the label has no knowledge of the scrollbar, and the scrollbar has no knowledge of the label.

Now, suppose that you also want to allow the value to be updated from a `TextField`. All you need to do is create a subclass of `TextField` that modifies the `ObservableInt`. Listing 46.7 shows an implementation of an `IntTextField`.

Listing 46.7 Source Code for *IntTextField.java*

```
import java.awt.*;
import java.util.*;

//
// IntTextField - a TextField that reads in integer values and
// updates an Observable int with the new value.  This class
// is both a "view" of the Observable int, since it displays
// its current value, and a "controller" since it updates the
// value.

public class IntTextField extends TextField implements Observer
{
     private ObservableInt intValue;

     public IntTextField(ObservableInt theInt)
     {
// Initialize the field to the current value, allow 3 input columns

          super(""+theInt.getValue(), 3);
          intValue = theInt;
          intValue.addObserver(this);     // Express interest in value
     }

// The action for the text field is called whenever someone presses "return"
// We'll try to convert the string in the field to an integer, and if
// successful, update the observable int.
```

```
     public boolean action(Event evt, Object whatAction)
     {
          Integer intStr;          // to be converted from a string

          try {     // The conversion can throw an exception
               intStr = new Integer(getText());

// If we get here, there was no exception, update the observable

               intValue.setValue(intStr.intValue());
          } catch (Exception oops) {
// We just ignore the exception
          }
          return true;
     }

// The update action is called whenever the observable int's value changes.
// We just update the text in the field with the new int value

     public void update(Observable obs, Object arg)
     {
          setText(""+intValue.getValue());
     }
}
```


After you have created this class, how much code do you think you have to add to the applet? You add one line (and change `GridLayout` to have three rows). Listing 46.8 shows an implementation of an applet that uses an `ObservableInt`, an `IntScrollbar`, an `IntLabel`, and an `IntTextField`.

Listing 46.8 Source Code for *ObservableApplet2.java*

```
import java.applet.*;
import java.awt.*;

public class ObservableApplet2 extends Applet
{
     ObservableInt myIntValue;

     public void init()
     {

// Create the Observable int to play with

          myIntValue = new ObservableInt(5);

          setLayout(new GridLayout(3, 0));

// Create an IntScrollbar that modifies the observable int

          add(new IntScrollbar(myIntValue,
               Scrollbar.HORIZONTAL,
```

continued

Listing 46.8 Continued

```
                    0, 10, 0, 100));

// Create an IntLabel that displays the observable int

        add(new IntLabel(myIntValue));

// Create an IntTextField that displays and updates the observable int

        add(new IntTextField(myIntValue));
    }
}
```

Again, the components that modify and display the integer value have no knowledge of each other; yet whenever the value is changed, they are all updated with the new value. ●

CHAPTER 47

java.lang

The *java.lang* Packages

Of all the Java API packages, `java.lang` is the most important. It contains classes that provide a solid foundation for the other Java packages. It is safe to say that the `java.lang` package is the one Java package that does not require any other packages to exist.

The `java.lang` package includes the following classes:

- `Object` is the root class from which all other classes derive. If you don't explicitly state which class your new subclass extends, it extends `Object`.
- `Class` represents a Java class. For every class defined in Java, there is an instance of `Class` that describes it.
- `ClassLoader` provides a way to add new classes to the Java runtime environment.
- `Compiler` provides access to the Just-In-Time compiler, if available.
- `Math` provides a number of well-known math functions.
- `Number` is the base class for the Java numeric classes, which are `Double`, `Float`, `Integer`, and `Long`. These classes are called object wrappers because they present an object interface for the built-in primitive types.
- `Package` defines information about a package such as the version number, specification title, and vendor. Using the `Package` class, JDK 1.2 apps can be sure they are using the correct version of a package.
- `Process` represents an external program started by a `Runtime` object.
- `Runtime` provides many of the same functions as `System`, but also handles the running of external programs.
- `RuntimePermission` defines the level of runtime access. For more information see Chapter 34, "Java Security in Depth."
- `String` provides methods for manipulating Java strings.
- `StringBuffer` is used for creating Java strings, especially ones that change length frequently.
- `System` provides special system-level utilities.
- `Thread` represents a thread of execution in a Java program. Each executing program can have multiple threads running.
- `ThreadGroup` allows threads to be associated with each other. Some thread operations can only be performed by threads in the same `ThreadGroup`.
- `Throwable` is the base class for Java exceptions. Any object that is caught with the `catch` statement, or thrown with the `throw` statement, must be a subclass of `Throwable`.
- `SecurityManager` defines the security restrictions in the current runtime environment. Many of the Java classes use the `SecurityManager` to verify that an operation is allowed.
- `Boolean`, `Byte`, `Character`, `Double`, `Float`, `Integer`, `Long`, and `Short` are object wrappers for their native data types. For instance, `Character` wraps a `char` data type.

In addition to these classes, the `java.lang` package defines four interfaces:

- `Cloneable` must be implemented by any object that can be cloned or copied.
- `Comparable` is used to define the ordering of objects. This is very useful for classes like `java.util.List`.
- `Runnable` is used in conjunction with the `Thread` class.
- `Runtime.MemoryAdvice` is used in conjunction with the `Runtime` class to define the level of urgency for `Runtime`'s garbage collection.

The *Object* Class

The `Object` class is the base class of every class in Java. It defines the methods that every class in Java supports.

Testing Object Equality

You should already be aware that the == operator only tells whether two objects are really the same object. This is not the same as testing whether the objects contain the same information. The `equals()` method in the `Object` class enables you to define a way to tell whether two objects contain the same information. For instance, you and I might both own the same model of car, but `myCar == yourCar` is not true—they are two different objects. However, if you test this with `myCar.equals(yourCar)`, they would contain the same information. The format of the `equals()` method is

```
public boolean equals(Object ob)
```

Listing 47.1 shows a sample class with an `equals()` method that does an attribute-by-attribute comparison of two objects.

Listing 47.1 Source Code for *EqualityTest.java*

```
public class EqualityTest
{
     protected String someName;
     protected int someNumber;
     protected Object someObject;

     public boolean equals(Object otherOb)
     {
          EqualityTest other;

// First, test to see if these are the same object
          if (otherOb == this) return true;

// Next, make sure the other object is the same class
          if (!(otherOb instanceof EqualityTest)) return false;
```

continues

Listing 47.1 Continued

```
// Cast otherOb to this kind of object (EqualityTest) for accessing
// the attributes.
          other = (EqualityTest) otherOb;

// Now, compare each attribute of the objects to see if they are equal.
// Notice that on primitive data types like int you should use ==
          if (someName.equals(other.someName) &&
               (someNumber == other.someNumber) &&
               (someObject.equals(other.someObject))) return true;

// Looks like they are not the same object, so the compare result is false
          return false;
     }
}
```

String Representations of Objects

Many times, especially during debugging, you need to print out an object to an output stream. The `toString()` method in `Object` was created just for this purpose. The format of `toString()` is

```
public String toString()
```

The default implementation of `toString()` prints out the object's class name and its hash code. You might want to provide additional information in your own objects. For instance, if you defined an `Employee` object, you might want the `toString()` method to print out the employee's ID number:

```
public String toString()
{
     return "Employee #"+this.employeeID;
}
```

The `toString()` method is a convenience for creating a string representation of objects. It is not intended to be a mechanism for saving all the information for an object, thus there is no corresponding `fromString()` method.

Cloning Objects

The `clone()` method creates a duplicate copy of an object. For an object to be cloned, it must support the `Cloneable` interface. The `Cloneable` interface does not have any methods itself—it serves only as an indicator to show that an object can be cloned. An object can choose to implement `Cloneable` but still not support the cloning operation, by throwing a `CloneNotSupportedException` in the `clone()` method. The format for the `clone()` method is

```
protected Object clone()
     throws CloneNotSupportedException, OutOfMemoryError
```

Because the `clone()` method copies only primitive data types and references to objects, there are times when you will need to create your own `clone()` method. For example, take the following class:

```
public class StoogesFilm extends Object implements Cloneable
{
     public String[] stooges;

     public StoogesFilm()
     {
          stooges = new String[3];
          stooges[0] = "Moe";
          stooges[1] = "Larry";
          stooges[2] = "Curly";
     }
}
```

The default `clone()` method for `StoogesFilm` copies only the reference to the `stooges` array. Unfortunately, if the newly cloned object decides that Shemp will be the third stooge rather than Curly, and thus changes the `stooges` array, it will change for both copies:

```
StoogesFilm film1 = new StoogesFilm();      // Create a StoogesFilm
System.out.println("The third stooge in film 1 is "+film1.stooges[2]);

StoogesFilm film2 = (StoogesFilm) film1.clone();
// Create a copy of the first film
film2.stooges[2] = "Shemp";      // Substitute Shemp for Curly

System.out.println("The third stooge in film 1 is now "+film1.stooges[2]);
System.out.println("The third stooge in film 2 is "+film2.stooges[2]);
```

The output from this code segment would be

```
The third stooge in film 1 is Curly
The third stooge in film 1 is now Shemp
The third stooge in film 2 is now Shemp
```


You can solve this problem by creating a `clone()` method that clones the `stooges` array:

```
public Object clone() throws CloneNotSupportedException
{
// Create an initial clone of the object using the default clone method
     StoogesFilm returnValue = (StoogesFilm)super.clone();

// Now create a separate copy of the stooges array
     returnValue.stooges = (String[])stooges.clone();
     return returnValue;
}
```

After you add this method, the output from the previous code segment becomes

```
The third stooge in film 1 is Curly
The third stooge in film 1 is now Curly
The third stooge in film 2 is now Shemp
```

Finalization

The `finalize()` method is called on an object when it is about to be removed from memory by the garbage collector. Normally, your objects will not need to override the `finalize()` method, but if you have allocated resources outside the Java Virtual Machine (usually via native methods), you may need to implement a `finalize()` method to free up those resources. The format of the `finalize()` method is

```
protected void finalize() throws Throwable
```

CAUTION

Make sure that your `finalize()` method calls `super.finalize` at some point; otherwise, the resources allocated by the superclass will not be freed correctly.

A typical `finalize()` method would look like

```
protected void finalize() throws Throwable
{
     super.finalize();      // ALWAYS do this in a finalize method
// (other code to free up external resources)
}
```

Serializing Objects

The notion of serializing objects appeared in version 1.1 of the Java API. Object serialization refers to the storage and retrieval of the data stored in the object. You would use object serialization to save the contents of an object in a file or to send an object over a network. You can protect attributes from being serialized. For instance, you might have a handle to an open file, which might not make sense when the object is retrieved on some other system. You can mark attributes as being `transient`, which will prevent the system from serializing them. For example, suppose that you have an `InputStream` that you do not want to be serialized. You can declare it as `transient`:

```
public transient InputStream myStream;
     // Don't serialize this attribute
```

For an object to be serialized, it must implement the `java.io.Serializable` interface. Like the `Cloneable` interface, the `java.io.Serializable` interface does not contain any methods. It serves only as a flag to indicate that an object can be serialized. Oddly enough, although the `java.io.Serializable` interface does not contain any methods, there are two methods you must implement if your object requires custom serialization:

```
private void writeObject(java.io.ObjectOutputStream out)
     throws IOException
private void readObject(java.io.ObjectInputStream in)
     throws IOException, ClassNotFoundException
```

Your `readObject()` and `writeObject()` methods must be declared exactly as they are in the preceding code. The serialization code contains special checks for these methods. You probably won't have to implement your own `readObject()` and `writeObject()` methods, but it is nice to know that you can if you need to. There are cases where you can take shortcuts in serializing an object, or you might want to prevent certain attributes contained in the object from being serialized, but you don't want to mark those attributes as `transient` (for instance, you might want the serialization of those attributes to be dependent on the current state of the object).

Hash Codes

The `hashCode()` method in an object returns an integer that should be unique for each object. The `hashCode()` value is used by the `Hashtable` class when storing and retrieving objects. You can usually just rely on the default implementation, but just in case you decide you have a much better way to compute a hash code for your object, the format for the `hashCode()` method is

```
public int hashCode()
```

A hash table is an associative array that uses non-numeric "keys" as indices. In other words, it's similar to an array whose index values can be something other than numbers. It uses hash codes to group objects into *buckets*. When it searches for an object, it only searches through the bucket for that object's hash code.

CAUTION

If you create your own `hashCode()` method, make sure that it returns the same hash value for two objects that are equivalent. The `Hashtable` class uses the `hashCode()` to help locate equivalent objects, and if the hash values for two objects are different, the `Hashtable` class assumes that they are different and never even checks the `equals()` method.

wait() and *notify()*

The `wait()` and `notify()` methods provide a way for objects running in separate threads to signal each other when something interesting occurs. For example, one object might be writing information into an array that another object is reading. The reader calls `wait()` to wait until the writer is finished. When the writer is finished, it calls `notify()` to signal to the reader that it is done. Effectively, the reader thread will sleep until it receives the notify signal from the writer thread. The idea might sound simple, but there are several important items to consider:

- If `notify()`is called before an object starts waiting, the notification is ignored. This could cause an object to wait for a signal that never comes. Consider the following scenario. An object called `Bob` is going to wait until the sky turns blue. Object `Sun` notifies `Bob` that the sky is blue (like it always is). This works fine, except when the following happens.

  Your program starts up. `Sun` automatically notifies `Bob` that the sky is blue. However, `Bob` hasn't started waiting yet, so the notification is ignored. Moments later `Bob` gets to the point that he is going to wait. Unfortunately, `Sun` has already done its notification, so `Bob` is going to wait forever for the notification. To fix this situation, you should set up a flag to indicate whether the object should wait. If when `Sun` has notified `Bob` the first time a skyIsBlue variable had been set to true, and Bob checked this variable before he issued the wait(), he never would have started to wait, and the problem would have been solved.

- notify() and wait() must both be called from within synchronized methods or blocks. In addition, the method cannot be called from a thread other than the one that is running. Consider the Sun and Bob example above. Sun can not issue a Bob.wait() command. If it does, an IllegalMonitorStateException will be thrown.
- Because it is possible for wait() to be interrupted with an exception, you should put it inside a while loop that checks the wait flag and then calls wait().

The wait() method comes in three forms:

```
public final void wait()
throws InterruptedException, IllegalMonitorStateException
```

waits forever until a notify() is sent.

```
public final void wait(long timeout)
throws InterruptedException, IllegalMonitorStateException
```

waits timeout seconds for a notify() and then returns.

```
public final void wait(long timeout, int nano)
throws InterruptedException, IllegalMonitorStateException
```

waits timeout seconds and nano nanoseconds for a notify() and then returns.

The notify() method comes in two forms:

```
public final void notify() throws IllegalMonitorStateException
```

sends a notification to a thread that is waiting on this object. If multiple threads are waiting, it sends the notification to the thread that has waited the longest.

```
public final void notifyAll() throws IllegalMonitorStateException
```

sends a notification to every thread waiting on this object.

CAUTION

The notify(), notifyAll(), and wait() methods must be called from synchronized methods or synchronized blocks. In addition, notify() must be called from a method or block that is synchronized on the same object as the corresponding wait(). In other words, if some object, myObject, calls wait() and another object calls myObject.notify(), the calling block or method must be synchronized on myObject. This is shown in the following pseudo code.

```
public class MyObject{
    public synchronized wait(){
        wait()
    }
}

public class AnotherObject{
    public void notifyIt(MyObject myObject){
```

```
        synchronized(myObject){
            myObject.notify();
        }
    }
}
```

Listing 47.2 shows an example use of `wait()` and `notify()` for implementing a signaling system.

Listing 47.2 Source Code for *Signaler.java*

```
/**
 * This class provides a signaling mechanism for objects.
 * An object wishing to send a signal calls the signal method.
 * An object receiving the signal would wait for a signal with
 * waitForSignal.  If there is no signal pending, waitForSignal
 * will wait for one.  If there are multiple signals sent, the
 * class will keep track of how many were sent and will not call
 * wait until there are no more pending signals.
 * There should only be one object waiting for a signal at any given
 * time.

 */

public class Signaler extends Object
{
     protected int signalCount;     // the number of pending signals
     protected boolean isWaiting;     // is an object waiting right now?
     protected boolean sentNotify;     // Did someone send a notify?

/**
 * Creates an instance of a signaler
 */
     public Signaler()
     {
          signalCount = 0;     // no pending signals
          isWaiting = false;     // no one waiting
     }

/**
 * Sends a signal to the object waiting for a signal.
 * @exception Exception if there is an error sending a notification
 */
     public synchronized void signal()
     throws Exception
     {
          signalCount++;     // Increment the number of pending signals
          if (isWaiting)     // If an object is waiting, notify it
          {
               try {
                    sentNotify = true;
                    notify();
```

continues

Listing 47.2 Continued

```
                } catch (Exception IllegalMonitorStateException) {
                    throw new Exception("Error sending notification");
                }
            }
        }

    /**
     * Waits for a signal.  If there are signals pending, this method will
     * return immediately.
     */
        public synchronized void waitForSignal()
        {
            while (signalCount == 0)     // If there are no signals
                                    // pending, wait for a signal
            {
                sentNotify = false;
                isWaiting = true;      // Yes, someone is waiting

    // Want to keep looping until a notify is actually sent, it is possible
    // for wait to return without a notify, so use sentNotify to see if we
    // should go back to waiting again.

                while (!sentNotify)
                {
                    try {
                        wait();
                    } catch (Exception waitError) {
                        // Shouldn't really ignore this, but...
                    }
                }
                isWaiting = false;      // I'm not waiting any more
            }
            signalCoun--;      // one fewer signal pending
        }
    }
```

If you are familiar with Java's `synchronized` method specifier, you might be wondering how `notify()` can ever be called in the `Signaler` class. If you aren't wondering that, either you know the answer or you don't see the problem. The problem is that `waitForSignal()` and `signal` are both synchronized. If some thread is blocked on the `wait()` call in the middle of the `waitForSignal()` method, the `signal()` method can't be called because of the synchronization lock. The reason that the `Signaler` class works is because the `wait()` method releases the synchronization lock when it is called and acquires it again when it returns.

Getting an Object's Class

You can retrieve the instance of the `Class` object that corresponds to an object's class using the `getClass()` method:

```
public final Class getClass()
```

The *Class* Class

The `Class` class contains information that describes a Java class. Every class in Java has a corresponding instance of `Class`. There is even an instance of `Class` that describes `Class` itself. In case you are wondering what would happen if you tried the line:

```
Class newClass = new Class();
```

you can't. There is no public constructor for the `Class` object. You can, however, get hold of an instance of `Class` in one of three ways:

- Use the `getClass()` method in an object to get that object's `Class` instance.
- Use the static method `forName()` in `Class` to get an instance of `Class` using the name of the class.
- Load a new class using a custom `ClassLoader` object.

Dynamic Loading

The `Class` class is a powerful construct that allows you to do things that you can't do in C++. You typically instantiate a class with a statement like this:

```
Object vehicle = new Car();
```

Suppose, however, that you would like to create a `vehicle` using the name of the class you want to instantiate. You could do something like this:

```
String vehicleClass = (some string representing a class name)
     Object vehicle;
     if (vehicleClass.equals("Car")
     {
          vehicle = new Car();
     }
     else if (vehicleClass.equals("Airplane")
     {
          vehicle = new Airplane();     }
```


This is better, but it is still not flexible enough. Suppose that you add a new class called `Train`. You do not want to have to add an `else if` to check for `Train`. This is where `Class` comes in. You can perform the equivalent of the code using `Class.forName()` and `Class.newInstance()`:

```
     Object vehicle;
// First get the class named by vehicleClass
     Class whichClass = Class.forname(vehicleClass);
// Now ask the class to create a new instance
vehicle = whichClass.newInstance();
```

The `forName()` method in `Class` is defined as:

```
public static Class forName(String className)
     throws ClassNotFoundException
```

and returns the instance of `Class` that corresponds to `className`, or it throws a `ClassNotFoundException`. The `newInstance()` method is defined as:

```
public Object newInstance()
     throws InstantiationException, IllegalAccessException
```

and returns a new instance of the class, or throws an exception if there was an error instantiating the class.

CAUTION

You can only use `newInstance()` to instantiate objects that provide an empty constructor (a constructor that takes no parameters). If you try to use `newInstance()` to instantiate an object that does not have an empty constructor, you get a `NoSuchMethodError` error. You should be ready to catch the `NoSuchMethodError`. Remember that it is an error and not an exception, so just catching `Exception` will not grab it.

Getting Information About a Class

You can also use `Class` to get interesting information about a class:

```
public String getName()
```

returns the name of the class.

```
public boolean isInterface()
```

returns `true` if the class is actually an interface.

```
public Class getSuperclass()
```

returns the superclass of the class.

```
public Class[] getInterfaces()
```

returns an array containing `Class` instances for every interface the class supports.

```
public ClassLoader getClassLoader()
```

returns the instance of `ClassLoader` responsible for loading this class into the runtime environment.

The Reflection API introduced in Java 1.1 added a number of methods to the `Class` class for examining the attributes and methods of a class. These methods were:

```
public Class[] getInterfaces()
public Class getComponentType()
public int getModifiers()
public Class getDeclaringClass()
public Class[] getClasses()
public Field[] getFields() throws SecurityException
public Method[] getMethods() throws SecurityException
public Constructor[] getConstructors() throws SecurityException
public Field getField(String name)
     throws NoSuchFieldException, SecurityException
```

```
public Method getMethod(String name, Class parameterTypes[])
     throws NoSuchMethodException, SecurityException
public Constructor getConstructor(Class parameterTypes[])
     throws NoSuchMethodException, SecurityException
public Class[] getDeclaredClasses() throws SecurityException
public Field[] getDeclaredFields() throws SecurityException
public Method[] getDeclaredMethods() throws SecurityException
public Constructor[] getDeclaredConstructors() throws SecurityException
public Field getDeclaredField(String name)
     throws IllegalArgumentException, SecurityException
public Method getDeclaredMethod(String name, Class parameterTypes[])
     throws NoSuchMethodException, SecurityException
public Constructor getDeclaredConstructor(Class parameterTypes[])
     throws NoSuchMethodException, SecurityException
```

These Reflection API methods are discussed in depth in Chapter 48, "Reflection."

The *Package* Class

New in the 1.2 API is a class called `Package`. The `Package` class is used primarily to help you determine the version of each of the packages loaded in the system. Normally the version information will actually be stored in the Manifest file for that particular package.

To obtain a `Package` there are two static methods. The `getPackage()` method will get just one specific package, while `getAllPackages()` will return an array of all the packages currently know by the classloader:

```
static Package getPackage(String packageName)
```

```
static Package[] getAllPackages()
```


Once you have the `Package` object you can obtain information about it, such as its title, the name of the vendor that produced the package, the name of the package (which you would know if you used the `getPackage()` method, but not if you used `getAllPackages()`), the URL where a sealed package came from, the name of the specification the package implements, the hash code of the `Package` (from its name), and the version of the package.

```
String getImplementationTitle()
String getImplementationVendor()
String getImplementationVersion()
String getName()
URL getSealBase()
String getSpecificationTitle()
int
boolean isCompatibleWith(String Desired)
boolean isSealed()
String toString()
```

The *String* Class

The `String` class is one of the most useful classes in the Java API. It enables you to create and manipulate strings of characters. Keep in mind that Java strings are immutable; in other words, you cannot change the contents of a string. On the surface, this makes the `String` class look useless. After all, what good is it to create strings that you can't change? The way you manipulate strings in Java is to create new strings based on other strings. In other words, instead of changing the string "father" to "grandfather," you create a new string that is "grand" + "father". The `StringBuffer` class provides ways to directly manipulate string data.

Creating Strings

Java provides many string constructors:

```
public String()
```

creates an empty string.

```
public String(String value)
```

creates a new string that is a copy of `value`.

```
public String(char[] value)
```

creates a new string from the characters in `value`.

```
public String(char[] value, int from, int count)
throws StringIndexOutOfBoundsException
```

creates a new string from the characters in `value`, starting at offset `from` that is `count` characters long.

```
public String(byte[] value, int hibyte)
```

creates a new string from the characters in `value`, using `hibyte` as the upper 8 bits in each character. (Remember that Java characters are 16 bits, not 8 as in C.)

```
public String(byte[] value, int hibyte, int from, int count)
     throws StringIndexOutOfBoundsException
```

creates a new string from the characters in `value`, starting at offset `from`, `count` characters long, and using `hibyte` as the upper 8 bits in each character.

```
public String(StringBuffer buffer)
```

creates a new string from the contents of a `StringBuffer`.

Here is an example of different ways to create the string `"Foo"`:

```
String foo1 = new String("Foo");

char foochars[] = { 'F', 'o', 'o' };
String foo2 = new String(foochars);

char foo2chars[] = { 'B', 'a', 'r', 'e', 'F', 'o', 'o', 't' };
String foo3 = new String(foo2chars, 4, 3);     // from offset 4, length of 3

byte foobytes[] = { 70, 111, 111 };      // ascii bytes for Foo
String foo4 = new String(fooBytes, 0);      // use 0 as upper 8 bits

byte foo2bytes[] = { 66, 97, 114, 101, 70, 111, 111, 116 }; // ascii BareFoot
String foo5 = new String(foo2Bytes, 0, 4, 3); // 0 as upper 8 bytes, offset 4,
➥length 3
```

```
StringBuffer fooBuffer = new StringBuffer();
fooBuffer.append('F');
fooBuffer.append("oo");
String foo6 = new String(fooBuffer);
```

The `String` class also provides a number of static methods for creating strings from other objects. The following `valueOf()` methods create a string representation from a primitive data type:

```
public static String valueOf(boolean b);
public static String valueOf(char c);
public static String valueOf(int i);
public static String valueOf(long l);
public static String valueOf(float f);
public static String valueOf(double d);
```

Some `valueOf()` methods are equivalent to other methods in `String` and `Object`. For instance

```
public static String valueOf(Object ob)
```

is the same as the `toString()` method in `Object`. The methods

```
public static String valueOf(char[] data);
public static String copyValueOf(char[] data);
```

are the same as the `String` constructor:

```
public String(char[] data)
```

Likewise, the methods

```
public static String valueOf(char[] data, int from, int count)
public static String copyValueOf(char[] data, int from, int count)
```

are equivalent to the `String` constructor

```
public String(char[] data, int from, int count)
```


String Length

The `length()` method returns the length of a string:

```
public int length()
```

Notice that unlike the `length` attribute for arrays, `length()` in the `String` class is a method. The only time you access `length` as an attribute is on an array. Any time you are using a standard Java class, `length()` will be a method call.

Comparing Strings

Because strings are Java objects, you can use == and the `equals()` method to compare strings. You should be extremely careful about using == to compare two strings. For instance, in the following code segment:

```
String a = new String("Foo");
String b = new String("Foo");
```

the comparison `a == b` would be `false` because `a` and `b` are two different objects, even though they have the same value. The comparison `a.equals(b)` would be `true`, however, because they both have a value of `"Foo"`.

The `String` class also provides a handy, case-free comparison:

```
public boolean equalsIgnoreCase(String anotherString)
```

This method compares two strings but ignores the case of the letters, so where `"Foo".equals("FOO")` is `false`, `"Foo".equalsIgnoreCase("FOO")` is `true`.

If you want to find out whether one string comes before another alphabetically, you can use the `compareTo()` method:

```
public int compareTo(String anotherString)
```

This method returns `0` if the two strings are equal, a number less than 0 if the string comes before `anotherString`, or a number greater than 0 if the string comes after `anotherString`. For example, `"foo".compareTo("bar")` would return a positive number because `"foo"` comes after `"bar"`.

You can also compare portions of strings. The `startsWith()` method returns `true` if the beginning of the string starts with another string:

```
public boolean startsWith(String anotherString)
```

A variation on `startsWith()` returns `true` if the string matches another string starting at a certain position:

```
public boolean startsWith(String anotherString, int offset)
```

For instance, `"barefoot".startsWith("foo", 4)` would be `true`, because `"foo"` appears in `"barefoot"` starting at location 4 (remember that string offsets start at 0).

You can also use `endsWith()` to see whether a string ends with another string:

```
public boolean endsWith(String anotherString)
```

Sometimes you want to compare part of a string with part of another string. You can use `regionMatches()` to do this:

```
public boolean regionMatches(int from, String anotherString, int otherFrom, int
➥len)
```

This method compares the characters in the string starting at offset `from` with the characters in `anotherString` starting at offset `otherFrom`. It compares `len` characters.

You can also do case-free comparisons with an alternate version of `regionMatches()`:

```
public boolean regionMatches(boolean ignoreCase, int from, String anotherString,
    int otherFrom, int len)
```

The only difference between this version of `regionMatches()` and the previous one is the `ignoreCase` parameter, which, when set to `true`, causes the comparison to ignore the case of letters and considers a and A to be equivalent.

Searching Strings

Many times you need to find out whether a certain string or character is present within a string and, if so, where. The `indexOf()` method searches through a string for a character or string and returns the offset of the first occurrence:

```
public int indexOf(int ch)
public int indexOf(String anotherString)
```

These methods return the location in the string where the first match occurred or `-1` if the character or string was not found. Because you probably want to search for more than just the first occurrence, you can call `indexOf()` with the starting location for the search:

```
public int indexOf(int ch, int startingOffset)
public int indexOf(String anotherString, int startingOffset)
```

The `lastIndexOf()` methods perform a similar search, only starting from the end of the string and working backwards:

```
public int lastIndexOf(int ch)
public int lastIndexOf(String anotherString)
```

You can also give the starting offset of the search. `lastIndexOf()` searches backwards from the offset:

```
public int lastIndexOf(int ch, int startingOffset)
public int lastIndexOf(String anotherString, int startingOffset)
```

Extracting Portions of a String

The `String` class provides several methods for extracting sections from a string. The `charAt` function allows you to get the character at offset `index` from the string:

```
public char charAt(int index) throws StringIndexOutOfBoundsException
```

For example, `"bar".charAt(1)` would return the character `'a'`. You can get the entire string as an array of characters using `toCharArray()`:

```
public char[] toCharArray()
```

Remember that the array returned by `toCharArray()` is a copy of the characters in the string. You cannot change the contents of the string by changing the array. The `substring()` method returns the portion of a string starting from offset `index`:

```
public String substring(int index)
```

You can also call `substring()` with an ending index. This version of `substring()` returns the portion of the string starting at `startIndex` and going up to, but not including, `endIndex`:

```
public String substring(int startIndex, int endIndex)
    throws StringIndexOutOfBoundsException
```

Changing Strings

Although it's true that you don't actually change strings in Java, there are several methods that create new strings based on the old string. The `concat()` method, for instance, appends a string to the current string and returns the new combined string:

```
public String concat(String otherString)
```

The method call `"foo".concat("bar")` would return the string `"foobar"`.

`toLowerCase()` and `toUpperCase()` return copies of a string with all the letters converted to lower- and uppercase, respectively:

```
public String toLowerCase()
public String toUpperCase()
```

`"FooBar".toLowerCase()` would return `"foobar"`, whereas `"FooBar".toUpperCase()` would return `"FOOBAR"`.

The `trim()` method removes the leading and trailing whitespace from a string. Whitespace is made up of spaces, tabs, form feeds, new lines, and carriage returns. In other words, `' '`, `'\t'`, `'\f'`, `'\n'`, and `'\r'`:

```
public String trim()
```

For example, `" Hi Ceal! ".trim()` would return `"Hi Ceal!"`.

Finally, you can replace all occurrences of one character with another using `replace`:

```
public String replace(char oldChar, char newChar)
"fooble".replace('o', 'e') would return "feeble".
```

The *StringBuffer* Class

The `StringBuffer` class is a workbench for building strings. It contains methods to add new characters to the buffer and then convert the final result to a string. Unlike the `String` class, when you add characters to a `StringBuffer`, you do not create a new copy of the `StringBuffer`. This makes it more efficient for building strings.

Creating a *StringBuffer*

The easiest way to create a `StringBuffer` is using the empty constructor:

```
public StringBuffer()
```

You can also create a `StringBuffer` with an initial length:

```
public StringBuffer(int length)
```

Finally, you can create a `StringBuffer` from a string, where the contents of the string are copied to the `StringBuffer`:

```
public StringBuffer(String str)
```

Adding Characters to a *StringBuffer*

The `insert()` methods allow you to insert characters, strings, and numbers into a `StringBuffer`. You can insert a character representation of one of the primitive data types with one of these `insert()` methods:

```
public StringBuffer insert(int offset, boolean b) throws
➥StringOutOfBoundsException
public StringBuffer insert(int offset, char c) throws StringOutOfBoundsException
public StringBuffer insert(int offset, int i) throws StringOutOfBoundsException
public StringBuffer insert(int offset, long l) throws StringOutOfBoundsException
public StringBuffer insert(int offset, float f) throws
➥StringOutOfBoundsException
public StringBuffer insert(int offset, double d) throws
➥StringOutOfBoundsException
```

In each of these methods, the offset parameter indicates the position in the `StringBuffer` where the characters should be inserted. The instance of `StringBuffer` returned by each of these is not a copy of the old `StringBuffer` but another reference to it. You can safely ignore the return value.

You can insert a string into a `StringBuffer` with:

```
public StringBuffer insert(int offset, String str)
     throws StringOutOfBoundsException
```

You may also insert a string representation of an object with:

```
public StringBuffer insert(int offset, Object ob)
     throws StringOutOfBoundsException
```

This method uses the `toString()` method in the `Object` to create a string representation of the object. Finally, you can insert an array of characters into a `StringBuffer` with


```
public StringBuffer insert(int offset, char[] data)
     throws StringOutOfBoundsException
```

For each `insert()` method, there is a corresponding `append()` method that adds characters to the end of a `StringBuffer`:

```
public StringBuffer append(boolean b)
public StringBuffer append(char c)
public StringBuffer append(int i)
public StringBuffer append(long l)
public StringBuffer append(float f)
public StringBuffer append(double d)
public StringBuffer append(String str)
public StringBuffer append(Object ob)
public StringBuffer append(char[] data)
```

StringBuffer Length

A `StringBuffer` has two notions of length:

- The number of characters currently in the buffer
- The maximum capacity of the buffer

The `length()` method returns the total number of characters currently in the buffer:

```
public int length()
```

The `capacity()` method returns the maximum capacity of the buffer:

```
public int capacity()
```

The `StringBuffer` automatically grows when you add characters, so why should you be concerned with the capacity? Whenever the buffer grows, it must allocate more memory. If you specify the capacity up front to be at least as large as you expect the string to be, you will avoid the overhead of allocating additional space. The `ensureCapacity()` method tells the `StringBuffer` the minimum number of characters it needs to be able to store:

```
public void ensureCapacity(int minimumAmount)
```

You can use the `setLength()` method to change the length of a `StringBuffer`:

```
public void setLength(int newLength)
     throws StringOutOfBoundsException
```

If the new length is shorter than the previous length, any characters beyond the new length are lost.

Getting and Setting Characters in a *StringBuffer*

You can manipulate individual characters in a `StringBuffer` using the `charAt()` and `setCharAt()` methods. The `charAt()` method returns the character at a particular offset in the `StringBuffer`:

```
public char charAt(int offset)
     throws StringIndexOutOfBoundsException
```

The `setCharAt()` method changes the character at a particular offset in the buffer:

```
public void setCharAt(int offset, char newChar)
     throws StringIndexOutOfBoundsException
```

The `getChars()` method allows you to copy a range of characters from a `StringBuffer` into an array of characters. You must specify the beginning and ending offsets in the `StringBuffer`, the destination array of characters, and the offset in the array to copy to

```
public void getChars(int beginOffset, int endOffset, char[] dest, int destOffset)
      throws StringIndexOutOfBoundsException
```

Creating a String from a *StringBuffer*

After you have built up a string in a `StringBuffer`, you can turn it into a `String` with the `toString()` method, which overrides the `toString()` method in the `Object` class:

```
public String toString()
```

NOTE When you use the `toString()` method in `StringBuffer` to create a `String`, the `String` and the `StringBuffer` share the same buffer to avoid excess copying. If the `StringBuffer` is subsequently changed, it first makes a copy of the buffer before making the change.

The *Thread* Class

A thread represents a single thread of execution in a Java program. A thread has an associated `Runnable` interface, which can be the thread itself. The `Runnable` interface implements a `run()` method, which contains the code executed by the thread. Think of the thread as a motor that drives a `Runnable` interface. Threads also have a notion of thread groups, which implement a security policy for threads. You do not want a "rogue" thread to go around putting other threads to sleep or changing their priorities. A thread may only manipulate threads in its own thread group or in a subgroup of its own thread group.

Creating a Thread

You can create a thread using the empty constructor:

```
public Thread()
```

When you create a thread without specifying a `Runnable` interface, the thread uses itself as the `Runnable` interface. The default implementation of the `run()` method in the `Thread` class just returns without doing anything. To specify an alternate `Runnable` interface, use this variation of the `Thread` constructor:

```
public Thread(Runnable target)
```

When the thread is started, it invokes the `run()` method in `target`. When you create a thread, it gets added to the `thread` group of the current thread. If you want the thread to belong to a different group, you must do it when you create the thread:

```
public Thread(ThreadGroup group, String name)
```

The `name` parameter is an optional thread name you might want to use to be able to tell threads apart. You can pass `null` as the thread name if you don't feel like naming it. The other thread constructors are combinations of the previous constructors:

```
public Thread(String name)
public Thread(Runnable target, String name)
public Thread(ThreadGroup group, Runnable target)
public Thread(ThreadGroup group, Runnable target, String name)
```


Starting and Stopping Threads

The `start()` and `stop()` methods control the initial startup and final ending of a thread:

```
public synchronized void start()
     throws IllegalThreadStateException
public final void stop()
public final void stop(Throwable stopThrowable)
```

The `start()` method throws an `IllegalThreadStateException` if the thread is already running. Prior to JDK 1.2, typically you would stop a thread by calling the `stop()` method with no arguments, which throws a `ThreadDeath` error to the thread. You can throw something other than `ThreadDeath` by using the second variation of the `stop()` method. A thread may also throw a `ThreadDeath` error instead of calling its own `stop()` method. As of Java 1.2, however, you should no longer call the `stop()` method. The problem is that `stop()` is inherently unsafe because it can cause a lockup if the thread has some object synchronized or has a lock on some scarce resource. Instead, make sure that your `run()` method will end.

CAUTION

Java allows you to catch the `ThreadDeath` error, which you should only do in the rare circumstance that a `finalize()` method will not suffice. If you catch `ThreadDeath`, you must make sure that you throw it again; otherwise, your thread will not die.

Waiting for Thread Completion

Suppose that you have an application that does some heavy computation and then does some other work before using the computation. You could split the heavy computation off into its own thread, but then how do you know when it is finished? You use the `join()` method:

```
public final void join() throws InterruptedException
```

The following code segment illustrates a possible use of the `join()` method:

```
Double finalResult;      // place for computation thread to store result
Thread computeThread = new HeavyComputationThread(finalResult);
computeThread.start();
// do some other stuff
computeThread.join();      // Wait for the heavy computations to finish
```

Because you may not want to wait forever, `join()` also supports a timeout value:

```
public final synchronized void join(long millis)
     throws InterruptedException
public final synchronized void join(long millis, int nanos)
     throws InterruptedException
```

These `join()` methods only wait for `millis` milliseconds, or `millis` milliseconds + `nanos` nanoseconds.

Sleeping and Yielding

Perhaps the most common thing you will want to do with threads is to stop and just wait a few moments. If you want your thread to wait for a period of time before proceeding, use the `sleep()` method:

```
public static void sleep(long millis)
     throws InterruptedException
public static void sleep(long millis, int nanos)
     throws InterruptedException
```

These methods suspend execution of the thread for the `millis` milliseconds, or `millis` milliseconds + `nanos` nanoseconds. The `sleep()` method is often used for animation loops:

```
public void run()
{
```

```
        while (true) {            // do animation forever
            changeCurrentFrame();     // do the next animation frame
            repaint();     // redraw the screen
            try {
                sleep(100);      // Wait 100 ms (1/10th of a second)
            } catch (InterruptedException insomnia) {
                // got interrupted while sleeping
            }
        }
}
```

If you have a thread that "hogs" the CPU by performing many computations, you might want to have it yield the CPU for other threads to get in some execution time. You can do this with the `yield()` method:

```
public static void yield()
```

For example, suppose that you have a loop like this:

```
int sum = 0;
for (int i=0; i < 10000; i++) {
     for (int j=0; j < 10000; j++) {
          sum = sum + (i * j);
     }
}
```

This loop is going to run for a long time, and if it is running as one thread in a larger program, it could hog the CPU for extended periods. If you place a call to `Thread.yield()` after the inner loop, the thread politely relinquishes the CPU occasionally for other threads:

```
int sum = 0;
for (int i=0; i < 10000; i++) {
     for (int j=0; j < 10000; j++) {
          sum = sum + (i * j);
     }
     Thread.yield();     // give other threads a chance to run
}
```


NOTE You are not required to call `yield()` to give other threads a chance to run. Most Java implementations support preemptive scheduling, which allows other threads to run occasionally, even when one executes a loop like the previous one. Not all implementations support preemptive scheduling, so a strategically placed `yield()` statement will help those implementations run smoothly.

Daemon Threads

A Java program usually runs until all its threads die. Sometimes, however, you have threads that run in the background and perform cleanup or maintenance tasks that never terminate. You can flag a thread as a *daemon thread*, which tells the Java Virtual Machine to ignore the thread when checking to see whether all the threads have terminated. In other words, a Java program runs until all its non-daemon threads die. Non-daemon threads are referred to as *user threads*.

NOTE The word *daemon* is pronounced either "day-mon" or "dee-mon." It originated back in the pre-UNIX days and supposedly stood for "Disk And Execution Monitor." Under UNIX, a daemon is a program that runs in the background and performs a useful service, which is similar to the concept of a Java daemon thread.

To flag a thread as a daemon thread, use the `setDaemon()` method:

```
public final void setDaemon(boolean on)
     throws IllegalThreadStateException
```

The `on` parameter should be `true` to make the flag a daemon thread or `false` to make it a user thread. You may change this setting at any time during the thread's execution. The `isDaemon()` method returns `true` if a thread is a daemon thread or `false` if it is a user thread:

```
public final boolean isDaemon()
```

Thread Priority

Java's thread scheduling is simple. Whenever a thread blocks—that is, when a thread either suspends, goes to sleep, or has to wait for something to happen—Java picks a new thread from the set of threads that are ready to run. It picks the thread with the highest priority. If more than one thread has the highest priority, it picks one of them. You can set the priority of a thread with the `setPriority()` method:

```
public final void setPriority(int newPriority)
     throws IllegalArgumentException
```

A thread's priority must be a number between `Thread.MIN_PRIORITY` and `Thread.MAX_PRIORITY`. Anything outside that range triggers an `IllegalArgumentException`. Threads are assigned a priority value of `Thread.NORM_PRIORITY` by default. You can query a thread's priority with `getPriority()`:

```
public final int getPriority()
```

Getting Thread Information

The `Thread` class provides a number of static methods to help you examine the current thread and the other threads running in a thread's group. The `currentThread()` method returns a `Thread` object for the currently executing thread:

```
public static Thread currentThread()
```

The `dumpStack()` method prints a stack trace for the current thread:

```
public static void dumpStack()
```

You can use the `countStackFrames()` method to find out how many stack frames a thread has. This is the number of frames that would be dumped by the `dumpStack()` method:

```
public int countStackFrames()
```

Because the `countStackFrames()` method is an `instance()` method, whereas the `dumpStack()` method is a static method that dumps the current thread's stack frame, the following call always returns the number of stack frames that would be dumped by an immediate call to `dumpStack()`:

```
int numFrames = Thread.currentThread().countStackFrames();
```

The `enumerate()` method fills an array with all the `Thread` objects in the current thread group:

```
public static int enumerate(Thread[] threadArray)
```

You need to know how many threads will be returned because you have to allocate the `threadArray` yourself. The `activeCount()` method tells you how many threads are active in the current thread group:

```
public static int activeCount()
```

The program in Listing 47.3 displays the threads in the current thread group.

Listing 47.3 Source Code for *DumpThreads.java*

```
public class DumpThreads
{
     public static void main(String[] args)
     {
// Find out how many threads there are right now
          int numThreads = Thread.activeCount();

// Allocate an array to hold the active threads
          Thread threadArray[] = new Thread[numThreads];

// Get references to all the active threads in this thread group
          numThreads = Thread.enumerate(threadArray);

// Print out the threads
          for (int i=0; i < numThreads; i++) {
               System.out.println("Found thread: "+threadArray[i]);
          }
     }
}
```


The *ThreadGroup* Class

The `ThreadGroup` class implements a security policy that only allows threads in the same group to modify one another. For instance, a thread can change the priority of a thread in its group or put that thread to sleep. Without thread groups, a thread could wreak havoc with other threads in the Java runtime environment by putting them all to sleep or, worse, terminating them. Thread groups are arranged in a hierarchy where every thread group has a parent group. Threads may modify any thread in their own group or in any of the groups that are children of their group. You can create a thread group simply by giving it a name:

```
public ThreadGroup(string groupName)
```

You can also create a `ThreadGroup` as a child of an existing `ThreadGroup`:

```
public ThreadGroup(ThreadGroup existingGroup, String groupName)
     throws NullPointerException
```

Several of the `ThreadGroup` operations are identical to `Thread` operations, except that they operate on all the threads in the group:

```
public final synchronized void suspend()
public final synchronized void resume()
public final synchronized void stop()
public final void setDaemon(boolean daemonFlag)
public final boolean isDaemon()
```

You can limit the maximum priority any thread in a group can have by calling `setMaxPriority()`:

```
public final synchronized void setMaxPriority(int priority)
```

You can query the maximum priority for a thread group with `getMaxPriority()`:

```
public final int getMaxPriority()
```

You can find out the parent of a thread group with `getParent()`:

```
public final ThreadGroup getParent()
```

The different `enumerate()` methods let you find out what threads and thread groups belong to a particular thread group:

```
public int enumerate(Thread[] threadList)
public int enumerate(Thread[] threadList, boolean recurse)
public int enumerate(ThreadGroup[] groupList)
public int enumerate(ThreadGroup[] groupList, boolean recurse)
```

The `recurse` parameter in the `enumerate()` methods causes `enumerate()` to trace down through all the child groups to get a complete list of its descendants. You can get an estimate of how many threads and thread groups are active in this group by using `activeCount()` and `activeGroupCount()`:

```
public synchronized int activeCount()
public synchronized int activeGroupCount()
```

The *Throwable* Class

The `Throwable` class is not very big, but the part it plays in Java is huge. Every error and exception in Java is a subclass of `Throwable`. Although you will usually create a subclass of `Throwable`, you can instantiate one using one of these two constructors:

```
public Throwable()
public Throwable(String message)
```

The `message` parameter is an optional error message that is associated with the throwable. You can fetch a throwable's message with the `getMessage()` method:

```
public String getMessage()
```

One of the handy features of the `Throwable` class, especially during debugging, is the `printStackTrace()` method:

```
public void printStackTrace()
public void printStackTrace(PrintStream stream)
```

These methods print a traceback of the method calls that led to the exception. The default output stream for the stack trace is `System.out`. You can use the second version of the method to print to any stream you want, such as `System.err`. You might have a case where you catch an exception, perform some cleanup work, and then throw the exception for another object to catch. If you throw the exception that you caught, the stack trace shows where the exception originally occurred. If you would prefer the stack trace to show only where the exception was first caught—if you want to hide the lower-level details, for instance—use the `fillInStackTrace()` method:

```
public Throwable fillInStackTrace()
```

The following code segment shows how you can use `fillInStackTrace()` to hide where an exception was originally thrown:

```
try {
     // do something interesting
} catch (Throwable somethingBadHappened) {
     // do some cleanup work
     throw somethingBadHappened.fillInStackTrace();
}
```

In this example, a stack trace would show the exception originally being thrown at the point of the `fillInStackTrace()` and not within the `try` statement or one of the methods it calls.

The *System* Class

The `System` class is a grab bag of useful utility methods that generally deal with the runtime environment. Some of the methods in the `System` class are also found in the `Runtime` class.

System Input and Output Streams

The `System` class contains three public data streams that are used quite frequently:

```
public static InputStream in
public static PrintStream out
public static PrintStream err
```

C programmers should recognize these as the Java equivalents of `stdin`, `stdout`, and `stderr`. When you are running a Java application, these streams usually read from and write to the window where you started the application. You are probably safest not trying to use the `System.in` stream within an applet because different browsers treat the stream differently. As for the `System.out` and `System.err` streams, Netscape sends them to the Java console window, whereas Appletviewer sends them to the window where Appletviewer was started. `System.err` is typically used for printing error messages, whereas `System.out` is used for other information. This is only a convention used by developers. You may, if you want, print error messages to `System.out` and print other information to `System.err`.

The `arraycopy()` method is another frequently used member of the `System` class:

```
public static void arraycopy(Object source, int sourcePosition,
     Object dest, int destPosition, int length)
     throws ArrayIndexOutOfBoundsException, ArrayStoreException
```

This method provides a quick way to copy information from one array to another. It copies `length` elements from the array `source`, starting at offset `sourcePosition`, into the array `dest`, starting at offset `destPosition`. This method saves time over copying elements individually within a loop. For example, consider the following loop:

```
int fromArray[] = { 1, 2, 3, 4, 5 };
int toArray[] = new int[5];
for (int i=0; i < fromArray.length; i++) {
     toArray[i] = fromArray[i];
}
```

This can be implemented more efficiently using `arraycopy`:

```
int fromArray[] = { 1, 2, 3, 4, 5 };
int toArray[] = new int[5];
System.arraycopy(fromArray, 0, toArray, 0, fromArray.length);
```

Getting the Current Time

If you have ever wondered exactly how many milliseconds have elapsed since midnight GMT on January 1, 1970, the `currentTimeMillis()` method would be more than happy to tell you:

```
public static long currentTimeMillis()
```

Other than being the dawning of the Age of Aquarius, there is nothing significant about that particular time; it was just chosen as a reference point by the original UNIX wizards. The most common use of the `currentTimeMillis()` function is in determining elapsed time. For example, if you want to figure out how many milliseconds a loop took to execute, get the time before executing the loop, then get the time after executing the loop, and subtract the time values:

```
long startTime = System.currentTimeMillis(); // record starting time
int sum = 0;
for (int i=0; i < 100000; i++) {
     sum += i;
}
long endTime = System.currentTimeMillis(); // record end time
System.out.println("The loop took "+
    ➥(endTime - startTime) + " milliseconds.");
```

NOTE Although it is possible to compute the current date and time using `currentTimeMillis()`, you are much better off using the `Date` class in `java.util` to get the current date and time.

Exiting the Virtual Machine

A Java program normally exits when all its user threads finish running. If you have spawned a large number of threads and decide that you want the program to quit, you don't have to kill off all the threads—you can just make the VM terminate by calling `System.exit`:

```
public static void exit(int exitCode)
```

The `exitCode` parameter is the exit code used by the VM when it terminates. You should only use this method from Java applications: applets are typically forbidden from calling this method and get a `SecurityException` thrown back in their face if they try it.

Getting System Properties

System properties are roughly the Java equivalents of environment variables. When you start a Java program, you can define properties that a Java application can read. The `getProperty()` method returns a string that corresponds to a property or `null` if the property doesn't exist:

```
public static String getProperty(String propertyName)
```

To save you the trouble of having to check for `null` each time, you can call `getProperty()` with a default value that is returned instead of `null` if the property isn't set:

```
public static String getProperty(String propertyName,
     String defaultValue)
```

The program in Listing 47.4 illustrates how to use `getProperty()`.

Listing 47.4 Source Code for *PrintProperty.java*

```
public class PrintProperty extends Object
{
     public static void main(String[] args)
     {
          String prop = System.getProperty("MyProperty",
              ➥"My Default Value");
          System.out.println("MyProperty is set to: "+prop);
     }
}
```

When you run the program with the `java` command, use the `-D` option to set properties. For example:

```
java -DMyProperty="Hi There" PrintProperty
```

This command causes the application to print out

```
MyProperty is set to: Hi There
```

If you run the program without setting `MyProperty`, it prints:

```
MyProperty is set to: My Default Value
```

`getProperties()` and `setProperties()` let you query and set the system properties using a `Properties` class:

```
public static Properties getProperties()
public static void setProperties(Properties prop)
```

▶ **See** "The Properties Class," **p. 1061**

Forcing Garbage Collection

The garbage collector normally just runs in the background, occasionally collecting unused memory. You can force the garbage collector to run using the `gc` method:

```
public static void gc
```

Similarly, you can force the `finalize()` methods to be executed in objects that are ready to be collected using the `runFinalization()` method:

```
public static void runFinalization()
```

Loading Dynamic Libraries

When you have a class that calls native methods, you need to load the libraries containing the methods. The `loadLibrary()` method searches through your path for a library matching `libname`:

```
public static void loadLibrary(String libname) throws UnsatisfiedLinkError
```

If you already know the full pathname of the library, you can save a little time by calling the `load()` method rather than `loadLibrary`:

```
public static void load(String filename) throws UnsatisfiedLinkError
```

The *Runtime* and *Process* Classes

The `Runtime` class provides many of the same functions as the `System` class but adds the capability to query the amount of memory available and to run external programs. The `Runtime` methods that are the same as the methods in `System` are

```
public void exit(int exitCode)
public void gc()
public void runFinalization()
public synchronized void load(String filename)
     throws UnsatisfiedLinkError
public synchronized void loadLibrary(String libname)
     throws UnsatisfiedLinkError
```

NOTE Unlike the `System` class methods, the `Runtime` class methods are not static, which means that you must have an instance of `Runtime` to call them. Instead of using `new` to create an instance, use the `Runtime.getRuntime()` method.

Querying Available Memory

The `freeMemory()` and `totalMemory()` methods tell you how much memory is free for you to use and how much memory is available to the Java VM:

```
public long freeMemory()
public long totalMemory()
```

The following code segment prints the percentage of memory that is free:

```
Runtime r = Runtime.getRuntime();
int freePercent = 100 * r.freeMemory() / r.totalMemory();
System.out.println(freePercent + "% of the VM's memory is free.");
```

Running External Programs

Even though Java is a wonderful and powerful programming environment, you might occasionally have to run external programs from your application. The `exec()` methods allow you to do just that:

```
public Process exec(String command) throws IOException
public Process exec(String command, String[] envp) throws IOException
public Process exec(String[] cmdArray) throws IOException
public Process exec(String[] cmdArray, String[] envp) throws IOException
```

The `envp` parameter in the `exec()` methods contains environment-variable settings for the program to be run. The strings in `envp` should be in the form `name=value`. The instance of the `Process` class returned by `exec` allows you to communicate with the external program, wait for it to complete, and get its exit code. The following methods in the `Process` class return input and output streams for you to send data to, and receive data from, the external program:


```
public abstract InputStream getInputStream()
public abstract InputStream getErrorStream()
public abstract OutputStream getOutputStream()
```

The `getInputStream()` method returns a stream that is hooked to the output of the external program. If the external program was a Java program, the input stream would receive everything written to the external program's `System.out` stream. Similarly, the `getErrorStream` returns a stream that is hooked to the error output of the external program, or what would be the `System.err` for a Java program. The `getOutputStream()` returns a stream that supplies input to the external program. Everything written to this stream goes to the external program's input stream, similar to the `System.in` stream.

If you want to kill off the external program before it completes, you can call the `destroy()` method:

```
public abstract void destroy()
```

If you would rather be polite and let the program complete on its own, use the `waitFor()` method to wait for it to complete:

```
public abstract int waitFor() throws InterruptedException
```

The value returned by `waitFor()` is the exit code from the external program. You can also check the exit code with the `exitValue()` method:

```
public abstract int exitValue() throws IllegalThreadStateException
```

If the external program is still running, the `exitValue()` method will throw an `IllegalThreadStateException`.

The *Math* Class

If the term *math class* makes you squeamish, you better sit down for this section. The `Math` class is a collection of useful numeric constants and functions, from simple minimum and maximum functions to logarithms and trig functions.

min and *max*

The `min` and `max` functions, which return the lesser and greater of two numbers, come in four flavors—`int`, `long`, `float`, and `double`:

```
public static int min(int a, int b)
public static long min(long a, long b)
public static float min(float a, float b)
public static double min(double a, double b)

public static int max(int a, int b)
public static long max(long a, long b)
public static long max(float a, float b)
public static double max(double a, double b)
```

Absolute Value

`abs`, the absolute value function, which converts negative numbers into positive numbers while leaving positive numbers alone, also comes in four flavors:

```
public static int abs(int a)
public static long abs(long a)
public static float abs(float a)
public static double abs(double a)
```

Random Numbers

It is difficult to write a good game without a random number generator, so the `Math` class kindly supplies the `random()` method:

```
public static synchronized double random()
```

The `random()` method returns a number between 0.0 and 1.0. Some of the other variations you might want are as follows:

```
int num = (int)(10.0 * Math.random());      // random number from 0 to 9
int num = (int)(10.0 * Math.random()) + 1;     // random number between 1 and 10
```

▶ **See** "The Random Class," **p. 1069**

Rounding

Rounding sounds like a simple process, but there are quite a few options available for rounding numbers. First of all, you can round off a `float` and turn it into an `int` with:

```
public static int round(float a)
```

This code rounds to the closest whole number, which means that 5.4 gets rounded to 5, but 5.5 gets rounded to 6. You can also round off a `double` and turn it into a `long` with:

```
public static long round(double a)
```

The other rounding functions work exclusively with the `double` type. The `floor()` method always rounds down, such that `Math.floor(4.99)` is `4.0`:

```
public static double floor(double a)
```

Conversely, `ceil` always rounds numbers up, such that `Math.ceil(4.01)` is `5.0`:

```
public static double ceil(double a)
```

Finally, the `rint()` method rounds to the closest whole number:

```
public static double rint(double a)
```

Powers and Logarithms

One of the most familiar power-related functions is the square root, which is returned by the `sqrt` method:

```
public static double sqrt(double a) throws ArithmeticException
```

You, of course, get an `ArithmeticException` if you try to take the square root of a negative number. This is a mathematical no-no.

The `pow()`method raises `x` to the `y` power:

```
public static double pow(double x, double y) throws ArithmeticException
```

The `pow()` function requires a bit of care. If `x == 0.0`, `y` must be greater than 0. If `x` < 0.0, `y` must be a whole number. If either of these two conditions is violated, you receive a friendly `ArithmeticException` as a reminder not to do it again.

You can use the `pow()` method to take the Nth root of a number. Just use `pow(x, 1.0/N)`, where *N* is the root you want to take. For example, to take the square root, use N=2, so `pow(x, 1.0/2.0)` returns the square root of `x`. For a cube root, use N=3, or `pow(x, 1.0/3.0)`. But remember that if you use this technique, `x` must be a positive number.

The `log()` method returns the natural log of a number:

```
public static double log(double a) throws ArithmeticException
```

To refresh your memory, if the natural log of `x` is equal to `y`, then the constant `e` (about 2.718) raised to the `y` power equals `x`. For example, the natural log of `e` is 1.0 because `e` to the first power equals `e`. The natural log of 1.0 is 0.0 because `e` to the zero power is 1 (as it is for any number raised to the zero power). You cannot take the log of 0 or any number less than 0. After all, there is no power you can raise e to and come up with 0. The same is true for negative numbers. Even though you can use the `pow()` method to raise any number to any power, the `Math` class provides the `exp()` method as a shortcut for raising e to a power:

```
public static double exp(double a)
```

The `log()` and `exp()` functions are inverses of each other; they cancel each other out. In other words, `log(exp(x)) == x`, for any x. Also, `exp(log(x)) == x`, for any x > 0 (remember, you cannot take a `log()` of a number <= 0).

A base-10 logarithm is another common type of logarithm. Where the `log()` of a number is the power you would raise e to, a base-10 logarithm is the power you raise 10 to. The `Math` class does not provide a log base-10 function, but you can use a simple mathematical property to compute the log base-10. The property is this: "The log base-N of a number is the natural log of the number divided by the natural log of N." So, the log base-10 of x is `log(x) / log(10)`. If you need to compute the log base-2 of x, another common log, it is `log(x) / log(2)`.

Trig Functions

The old favorite trig functions of sine, cosine, and tangent are available in the `Math` class:

```
public static double sin(double angle)
public static double cos(double angle)
public static double tan(double angle)
```

These functions take their angle value in radians, which is a number between 0 and 6.2831 (2 * pi). You can convert a degree value to radians by multiplying it by pi/180.0, or 0.017453. Trig angles have a "period" of 6.2831, which means that some angle x is the same as x + 6.2831, and also the same as x - 6.2831, and generally, x + 6.2831 * any whole number.

The inverse functions of sine, cosine, and tangent are arcsin, arccosine, and arctangent. They are available in the following methods:

```
public static double asin(double x)
public static double acos(double x)
public static double atan(double x)
public static double atan2(double y, doubly x)
```

The `asin()` and `acos()` functions return a radian value between -3.1415 and 3.1415. If you prefer to have your radians go from 0 to 6.2831, you can always add 6.2831 to any negative radian value. It doesn't matter to the trig functions. The `atan()` is a little less accurate. It only returns values between -1.5708 and 1.5708 (-pi/2 to pi/2). The `atan2()` function, however, returns values from -3.1415 to 3.1415. Where the `atan()` function usually takes a ratio of y/x and turns it into an angle, `atan2()` takes y and x separately. This allows it to make the extra calculations to return an angle in the full -pi to pi range.

Mathematical Constants

The `Math` class defines the constants `PI` and `E` for you because they are used so frequently:

```
public static final double E;
public static final double PI;
```

The Object Wrapper Classes

Many Java classes prefer to work with objects and not the primitive data types. The wrapper classes provide object versions of the primitive data types. In addition to making the primitive types look like objects, these wrapper classes also provide methods for converting strings to the various data types and also type-specific methods. Each of the wrapper classes contains a static attribute named `TYPE` that contains the wrapper's `Class` object. The definition for the `TYPE` attribute in each wrapper class is identical:

```
public final static Class TYPE;
```

The *Character* Class

The `Character` class provides a wrapper for the `char` data type. In addition, it contains methods for converting characters to numeric digits and vice versa. This class also contains methods for testing whether a character is a letter, digit, and so on. The only constructor available for the `Character` class takes the value of the character it represents as its only parameter:

```
public Character(char value)
```

You can use the `charValue` method to get the `char` value stored in a `Character` object:

```
public char charValue()
```

The `Character` class contains many static methods to classify characters:

Method	Description
`isDigit()`	A numeric digit between 0–9
`isLetter()`	An alphabetic character
`isLetterOrDigit()`	An alphabetic character or numeric digit
`isLowerCase()`	A lowercase alphabetic character
`isUpperCase()`	An uppercase alphabetic character
`isJavaLetter()`	A letter, '$', or '_'
`isJavaLetterOrDigit()`	A letter, digit, '$', or '_'
`isSpace()`	A space, new line, return, tab, or form feed
`isTitleCase()`	Special two-letter upper- and lowercase letters

Each of these classification methods returns a `boolean` value that is `true` if the letter belongs to that classification. For example, `isLetter('a')` returns `true`, but `isDigit('a')` returns `false`. The `toUpperCase()` and `toLowerCase()` methods return an uppercase or lowercase version of a character:

```
public static char toUpperCase(char ch)
public static char toLowerCase(char ch)
```

The `Character` class also supplies some digit conversion methods to help convert numbers into strings and strings into numbers:

```
public static int digit(char ch, int radix)
public static char forDigit(int digit, int radix)
```

The `digit()` method returns the numeric value that a character represents in the specified radix (the radix is the number base, like 10 for decimal or 8 for octal). For example, `Character.digit('f', 16)` would return 15. You can use any radix between `Character.MIN_RADIX` and `Character.MAX_RADIX`, which are 2 and 36, respectively. If the character does not represent a value in that radix, `digit` returns `-1`.

The `forDigit()` method converts a numeric value to the character that would represent it in a particular radix. For example, `Character.forDigit(6, 8)` would return `'6'`, whereas `Character.forDigit(12, 16)` would return `'c'`.

The *Boolean* Class

The `Boolean` class is the object wrapper for the `boolean` data type. It has two constructors—one that takes a `boolean` value, and one that takes a string representation of a `boolean`:

```
public Boolean(boolean value)
public Boolean(String str)
```

In the second version of the constructor, the value of the `Boolean` class created is `false` unless the string is equal to `true`. The string is converted to lowercase before the comparison, so a value of `true` would set the Boolean object to `true`. You can retrieve the `boolean` value stored in a `Boolean` object with the `booleanValue()` method:

```
public boolean booleanValue()
```

The `Boolean` class even has object wrapper versions of `true` and `false`:

```
public final static Boolean TRUE
public final static Boolean FALSE
```

The `valueOf()` method is an alternate way of creating a `Boolean` object from a string:

```
public static Boolean valueOf(String str)
```

This method is equivalent to the `Boolean` constructor that takes a string as an argument. You can also fetch `boolean` system parameters using the `getBoolean()` method:

```
public static boolean getBoolean(String propName)
```

This method looks for the property named by `propName` in the system properties, and if it finds a property with that name, it tries to convert it to a `boolean` using the `valueOf` method. If the value of the property is true, the method returns `true`. If the value of the property is not true, or if there was no such property, this method returns `false`.

The *Number* Class

The object wrappers for the `int`, `long`, `float`, and `double` types are all subclasses of the abstract `Number` class. This means that any class that expects an instance of a `Number` may be passed an `Integer`, `Long`, `Float`, or `Double` class. The four public methods in the `Number` class are responsible for converting a number to a particular primitive type:

```
public byte byteValue()
public short shortValue()
public abstract int intValue()
public abstract long longValue()
public abstract float floatValue()
public abstract double doubleValue()
```

The *Integer* Class

The `Integer` class implements an object wrapper for the `int` data type, provides methods for converting integers to strings, and vice versa. You can create an `Integer` object from either an `int` or a string:

```
public Integer(int value)
public Integer(String s) throws NumberFormatException
```


When creating an integer from a string, the `Integer` class assumes that the radix (number base) is 10, and if the string contains non-numeric characters, you receive a `NumberFormatException`. Like the `getBoolean()` method in the `Boolean` class, the `getInteger()` method converts a string from the system properties. If the property is not set, it returns `0` or a default value that you can pass as the second parameter. The default value can be passed either as an `int` or as an `Integer`:

```
public static Integer getInteger(String paramName)
public static Integer getInteger(String paramName, int defaultValue)
public static Integer getInteger(String paramName, Integer defaultValue)
```

The `Integer` class also provides methods for converting strings into integers, either as an `int` or an `Integer`. You may also specify an alternate radix (number base):

```
public static int parseInt(String s) throws NumberFormatException
public static int parseInt(String s, int radix) throws NumberFormatException
public static Integer valueOf(String s) throws NumberFormatException
public static Integer valueOf(String s, int radix) throws NumberFormatException
```

The only difference between `parseInt()` and `valueOf()` is that `parseInt()` returns an `int`, whereas `valueOf()` returns an `Integer`.

Many times you will need to convert a string into a number without knowing the number base ahead of time. The `decode()` method understands decimal, hexadecimal, and octal numbers:

```
public static Integer decode(String str) throws NumberFormatException
```

The `decode()` method figures out the base by looking at the beginning of the number. If it starts with 0x or 0X, it is assumed to be a hex number. If it starts with 0, the number is assumed to be octal; otherwise, the number is assumed to be decimal.

You can use the `toString()` method to convert an integer to a string. There are two static versions of the `toString()` method that should not be confused with the instance method `toString()` that is defined for all subclasses of `Object`. The static methods take an `int` as a parameter and convert it to a string, allowing you to specify an alternate radix. The instance method `toString()` converts the value of the `Integer` instance into a base-10 string representation:

```
public static String toString(int i)
public static String toString(int i, int radix)
```

Finally, the `Integer.MIN_VALUE` and `Integer.MAX_VALUE` constants contain the minimum and maximum values for integers in Java:

```
public final static int MIN_VALUE
public final static int MAX_VALUE
```

The *Long* Class

The `Long` class is identical to the `Integer` class, except that it works a wrapper for `long` values rather than `int` values. The constructors for `Long` are

```
public Long(long value)
public Long(String s) throws NumberFormatException
```

You can fetch `Long` values from the system properties using `getLong()`:

```
public static Long getLong(String paramName)
public static Long getLong(String paramName, long defaultValue)
public static Long getLong(String paramName, Long defaultValue)
```

The `parseLong()` and `valueOf()` methods convert strings into `long` data types and `Long` objects, respectively:

```
public static long parseLong(String s) throws NumberFormatException
public static long parseLong(String s, int radix) throws NumberFormatException
public static Long valueOf(String s) throws NumberFormatException
public static Long valueOf(String s, int radix) throws NumberFormatException
```

The `toString()` static methods convert `long` data types into strings:

```
public static String toString(long l)
public static String toString(long l, int radix)
```

Finally, the `Long.MIN_VALUE` and `Long.MAX_VALUE` constants define the minimum and maximum values for long numbers:

```
public final static long MIN_VALUE
public final static long MAX_VALUE
```

The *Byte* Class

The `Byte` class also bears a striking similarity to the `Integer` class. The `Byte` class has two constructors:

```
public Byte(byte value)
public Byte(String s) throws NumberFormatException
```

Unlike the `Integer` and `Long` classes, the `Byte` class does not contain any methods to fetch information from the system properties. You can, however, parse strings into bytes. The `parseByte()` and `valueOf()` methods convert strings into `byte` data types and `Byte` objects, respectively:

```
public static byte parseByte(String s) throws NumberFormatException
public static byte parseByte(String s, int radix) throws NumberFormatException
public static Byte valueOf(String s) throws NumberFormatException
public static Byte valueOf(String s, int radix) throws NumberFormatException
```

Once again, you can use `decode` to convert a decimal/hex/octal string into a `Byte`:

```
public static Byte decode(String s) throws NumberFormatException
```

The `toString()` static methods convert `byte` data types into strings:

```
public String toString()
public static String toString(byte l)
```

Finally, the `Byte.MIN_VALUE` and `Byte.MAX_VALUE` constants define the minimum and maximum values for long numbers:

```
public final static byte MIN_VALUE
public final static byte MAX_VALUE
```


The *Short* Class

By this time, you have probably noticed a pattern for the `Integer`, `Long`, and `Byte` classes. The `Short` class follows this same pattern. In other words, the `Short` class supports the following methods:

```
public Short(short value)
public Short(String s) throws NumberFormatException
public static short parseShort(String s) throws NumberFormatException
public static short parseShort(String s, int radix) throws NumberFormatException
public static Short valueOf(String s) throws NumberFormatException
public static Short valueOf(String s, int radix) throws NumberFormatException
public static Short decode(String s) throws NumberFormatException
public String toString()
public static String toString(short l)
public final static short MIN_VALUE
public final static short MAX_VALUE
```

The *Float* Class

The `Float` class provides an object wrapper for the `float` data type. In addition to string conversions, it provides a way to directly manipulate the bits in a `float`. You can create a `Float` by giving either a `float`, `double`, or string representation of the number:

```
public Float(float value)
public Float(double value)
public Float(String s) throws NumberFormatException
```

The `Float` class lacks the methods for fetching system properties that are present in the `Integer` and `Long` classes, but it does provide methods for converting `to` and `from` strings. JDK 1.2 has added a `float` equivalent of the `parseInt()` and `parseLong()` methods, and `float` has several other related methods:

```
public static Float valueOf(String s) throws NumberFormatException
public static String toString(float f)
public static float parseFloat(String floatString)
```

Floating-point numbers have a special notation for infinity, as well as for "Not a Number." You can test for these values with `isInfinite()` and `isNaN()`, which come in both static and instance varieties:

```
public static boolean isInfinite(float f)
public static boolean isNaN(float f)
public boolean isInfinite()
public boolean isNan()
```

If you want to manipulate the individual bits of a floating-point number, you can convert it to an `int` using the `floatToIntBits()` method:

```
public static int floatToIntBits(float f)
```

Both `float` and `double` values are stored in IEEE 754 format. This method is probably not useful to you unless you are familiar with the format, but there are applications that depend on getting a hold of this information. After you have manipulated the bits in the `int` version of the number, you can convert it back to a `float` with:

```
public static float intBitsToFloat(int bits)
```

You should keep in mind that this bitwise representation is not the same as converting a `float` to an `int`. For example, `Float.floatToIntBits((float)42)` returns an integer value of 1109917696, which is a few orders of magnitude different from the original value.

In addition to the typical `MIN_VALUE` and `MAX_VALUE` constants, the `Float` class also provides constants for `NEGATIVE_INFINITY`, `POSITIVE_INFINITY`, and "Not a Number," or `NaN`:

```
public final static float MIN_VALUE
public final static float MAX_VALUE
public final static float NEGATIVE_INFINITY
public final static float POSITIVE_INFINITY
public final static float NaN
```

The *Double* Class

The `Double` class provides the same functionality as the `Float` class, except that it deals with the `double` data type rather than `float`. You can create a `Double` using either a `double` or a string:

```
public Double(double value)
public Double(String s) throws NumberFormatException
```

You can convert a `double` to a string and vice versa with `toString()` and `valueOf()`:

```
public static String toString(double d)
public static double parseDouble(String doubleString)
public static Double valueOf(String s) throws NumberFormatException
```

`Double` also provides methods to check for infinity and "Not a Number" with static and instance versions of `isInfinite()` and `isNaN()`:

```
public static boolean isInfinite(double d)
public static boolean isNaN(double d)
public boolean isInfinite()
public boolean isNaN()
```

You can manipulate the bits of a double, which are also stored in IEEE 754 format, using the `doubleToLongBits()` and `longBitsToDouble()` methods:

```
public static long doubleToLongBits(double d)
public static double longBitsToDouble(long bits)
```

Finally, the `Double` class also defines its own `MIN_VALUE`, `MAX_VALUE`, `POSITIVE_INFINITY`, `NEGATIVE_INFINITY`, and `NaN` constants:

```
public final static double MIN_VALUE
public final static double MAX_VALUE
public final static double NEGATIVE_INFINITY
public final static double POSITIVE_INFINITY
public final static double NaN
```


The *Void* Class

To round out the set of wrappers for primitive types, Sun created a `Void` class. Because a void type contains no information, you might expect that the `Void` class would have no constructors or methods. Things are exactly as you would expect. The only thing contained in the `Void` class is the `TYPE` attribute that is common to all wrapper classes.

The *java.math.BigInteger* Class

Although it is a subclass of `Number`, the `BigInteger` class is not a wrapper class for an existing data type. Instead, it implements a large set of arithmetic operations for very large integer numbers. These operations are often used for cryptography applications where you work with numbers containing hundreds or even thousands of bits. `BigInteger` is not actually a part of the `java.lang` package, but is instead in `java.math`, along with the `BigDecimal` class, which implements very large fixed-point numbers.

Creating a *BigInteger*

A `BigInteger` value is essentially as large as it needs to be. If you need 927 digits, you got it! You can create a `BigInteger` object in a variety of ways. In the simple case, you can create a `BigInteger` from an existing `long` value:

```
public BigInteger valueOf(long l)
```

NOTE The `valueOf()` method performs the same function as a constructor in that it creates a new instance of a `BigInteger`. It isn't implemented as a constructor because it is able to use existing constant `BigInteger` objects for numbers like 0 and 1.

You can also use a string to represent a number. This is useful when the number you are creating is too large to store in a `long` data type.

```
public BigInteger(String str)
```

You can create a `BigInteger` from an array of bytes:

In this case, the array of bytes is really like an array of bits. The leftmost bit in the first byte is the most significant bit in the number. Remember that these bytes are not ASCII representations of digits; they contain the actual number. You can fetch a byte array containing the representation of a `BigInteger` with

```
public byte[] toByteArray()
```

When performing cryptography, you often need to create a large random number. The `BigInteger` class has the capability to create such a number:

When you create the random number, the `bits` parameter indicates the size in bits of the number you are creating. The `randomSource` object is used to generate the random bits. The resulting number is always positive.

An important aspect of random number generation, especially in the area of cryptography, is the probability that a number is prime. You can generate a random number that has a certain probability of being prime:

```
public BigInteger(int bits, int certainty, Random randomSource)
```

This additional `certainty` parameter indicates how certain the constructor should be that a number is prime. The probability is given as `1 - ( 1 / (2 ^ certainty))`. A certainty value of 0 would generate a 0 probability (`2 ^ 0 = 1`, so the formula is `1 - 1/1`), meaning that the number is probably not prime. A certainty of 1 generates a probability of 0.5, and a certainty of 10 gives a probability of 0.999 (1 - 1/1024). For this constructor, the `bits` parameter must be at least 2.

Because there is no built-in support for big numbers in Java, the `BigInteger` class must provide methods for common numerical operations. Here are the available methods:

```
public BigInteger add(BigInteger otherValue)
public BigInteger subtract(BigInteger otherValue)
public BigInteger multiply(BigInteger otherValue)
public BigInteger divide(BigInteger otherValue)
```

```
public BigInteger remainder(BigInteger otherValue)
public BigInteger[] divideAndRemainder(BigInteger otherValue)
public BigInteger pow(int exponent)
public BigInteger gcd(BigInteger otherValue)
public BigInteger abs()
public BigInteger negative()
public BigInteger signum()
public BigInteger mod(BigInteger modValue)
public BigInteger modPow(BigInteger exponent, BigInteger modValue)
public BigInteger modInverse(BigInteger modValue)
public BigInteger shiftLeft(numBits)
public BigInteger shiftRight(numBits)
public BigInteger and(BigInteger otherValue)
public BigInteger or(BigInteger otherValue)
public BigInteger xor(BigInteger otherValue)
public BigInteger not()
public BigInteger andNot(BigInteger otherValue)
public boolean testBit(int bitNumber)
public BigInteger setBit(int bitNumber)
public BigInteger clearBit(int bitNumber)
public BigInteger flipBit(int bitNumber)
public int getLowestSetBit()
public int bitLength()
public int bitCount()
public boolean isProbablePrime(int certainty)
public int compareTo(BigInteger otherValue)
public boolean equals(Object x)
public BigInteger min(BigInteger otherValue)
public BigInteger max(BigInteger otherValue)
```

Finally, you can convert a `BigInteger` value into a numeric data type, but you may lose precision if the number is too large to fit in the data type:

```
public int intValue()
public long longValue()
public float floatValue()
public double doubleValue()
```


The *java.math.BigDecimal* Class

The `BigDecimal` class represents a large, fixed-point number. Like `BigInteger`, it is also a subclass of `Number` but is not a wrapper for a native Java type. A `BigDecimal` number is similar to a `BigInteger` number, except that it has an extra scale parameter that indicates how many digits are to the right of the decimal point.

Creating a *BigDecimal*

You can create a `BigDecimal` number from a double, or from a string of digits:

```
public BigDecimal(double doubleValue)
public BigDecimal(String digits)
```

You can also create a `BigDecimal` from a `BigInteger`. You can supply an optional `scale` parameter that indicates the number of digits to the right of the decimal point. For example, a number 123456789 with a scale of 4 would be the number 12345.6789:

```
public BigDecimal(BigInteger bigVal)
public BigDecimal(BigInteger bigVal, int scale)
```

You can also create a `BigDecimal` from a `long` value with the `valueOf()` method:

```
public BigDecimal valueOf(long longValue)
public BigDecimal valueOf(long longValue, int scale)
```

One of the issues you must deal with when performing fixed-point calculations is rounding. The `BigDecimal` class has several different rounding options:

ROUND_DOWN	Always round down
ROUND_HALF_UP	Round up when last digit >= 5
ROUND_HALF_DOWN	Round up when last digit > 5
ROUND_UP	Always round up
ROUND_CEILING	Round positive numbers up, negative numbers down
ROUND_FLOOR	Round positive numbers down, negative numbers up
ROUND_HALF_EVEN	If the number immediately left of the decimal point is odd, works like ROUND_HALF_UP. If the number to the left of the decimal is even, works like ROUND_HALF_DOWN.
ROUND_UNNECESSARY	Don't round at all

These rounding values are used only in division operations and when changing the scale of a number.

Like the `BigInteger` class, the `BigDecimal` class must provide methods for common numerical operations. Here are the available methods:

```
public BigDecimal add(BigDecimal otherValue)
public BigDecimal subtract(BigDecimal otherValue)
public BigDecimal multiply(BigDecimal otherValue)
public BigDecimal divide(BigDecimal otherValue, int roundingMode)
public BigDecimal divide(BigDecimal otherValue,
    int scale, int roundingMode)
public BigDecimal abs()
public BigDecimal negate()
public int signum()
public BigDecimal setScale(int scale)
public BigDecimal setScale(int scale, int roundingMode)
public BigDecimal movePointLeft(int numPositions)
public BigDecimal movePointRight(int numPositions)
public int compareTo(BigDecimal otherValue)
public boolean equals(Object x)
public BigDecimal min(BigDecimal otherValue)
public BigDecimal max(BigDecimal otherValue)
```

You can convert a `BigDecimal` value into a numeric data type, but you may lose precision if the number is too large to fit in the data type:

```
public int intValue()
public long longValue()
public float floatValue()
public double doubleValue()
public BigInteger toBigInteger()
```

The *ClassLoader* Class

The `ClassLoader` class contains methods for loading new classes into the Java runtime environment. One of Java's most powerful features is its capability to load new classes on-the-fly. This class, along with the `Class` class makes dynamic class loading possible. All the methods in `ClassLoader` are protected, which means that they are only accessible to subclasses of `ClassLoader`. In fact, all but one of the methods in `ClassLoader` are final, leaving a single abstract method to be implemented by the individual class loaders. This abstract method is `loadClass()`:

```
protected abstract Class loadClass(String className, boolean resolve)
     throws ClassNotFoundException
```

The `loadClass()` method is responsible for finding the class information, whether in a local file or across the network, and creating a class from it. The `loadClass()` method obtains an array of bytes that represent the entire contents of the `.class` file for the class to be loaded and then calls `defineClass` to create an instance of `Class` for the new class:

```
protected final Class defineClass(byte data[], int offset, int length)
```

The `length` parameter is the number of bytes that define the class, and `offset` is the location of the first byte of the data for the class in the `data` array.

If the `resolve` parameter in `loadClass()` is `true`, the `loadClass()` method is responsible for calling the `resolveClass()` method before returning:

```
protected final void resolveClass(Class c)
```

The `resolveClass()` method makes sure that all classes referenced by class `c` have been loaded and resolved. A class cannot be used until it has been resolved. When a class is resolved, its class loader is responsible for locating any other classes it references. This is not convenient when a class references `java.lang.Object`, for instance. Rather than forcing you to write class loaders that know how to load all the system classes, the `ClassLoader` class gives you a hook into the system class loader, so if you are unable to locate a class, you can try the system class loader before giving up:

```
protected final Class findSystemClass(String name)
     throws ClassNotFoundException
```

Listing 47.5 shows a sample class loader that loads classes from an alternate directory.

Listing 47.5 Source Code for *MyClassLoader.java*

```
import java.io.*;
import java.util.*;

// This class loader uses an alternate directory for loading classes.
// When a class is resolved, its class loader is expected to be able
// to load any additional classes, but this loader doesn't want to have
// to figure out where to find java.lang.Object, for instance, so it
// uses Class.forName to locate classes that the system already knows
// about.

public class MyClassLoader extends ClassLoader
{
     String classDir;     // root dir to load classes from
     Hashtable loadedClasses;     // Classes that have been loaded

     public MyClassLoader(String classDir)
     {
          this.classDir = classDir;
          loadedClasses = new Hashtable();
     }

     public synchronized Class loadClass(String className,
          boolean resolve) throws ClassNotFoundException
     {
          Class newClass = (Class) loadedClasses.get(className);

// If the class was in the loadedClasses table, you don't
// have to load it again, but you better resolve it, just
// in case.
          if (newClass != null)
          {
               if (resolve) // Should we resolve?
               {
                    resolveClass(newClass);
               }
               return newClass;
          }

          try {
// Read in the class file
               byte[] classData = getClassData(className);
// Define the new class
               newClass = defineClass(classData, 0,
                    classData.length);
          } catch (IOException readError) {

// Before you throw an exception, see if the system already knows
// about this class
               try {
                    newClass = findSystemClass(className);
                    return newClass;
               } catch (Exception any) {
                    throw new ClassNotFoundException(className);
```

```
            }
        }

// Store the class in the table of loaded classes
        loadedClasses.put(className, newClass);

// If you are supposed to resolve this class, do it
        if (resolve)
        {
            resolveClass(newClass);
        }

        return newClass;
    }

// This version of loadClass uses classDir as the root directory
// for where to look for classes, it then opens up a read stream
// and reads in the class file as-is.

    protected byte[] getClassData(String className)
    throws IOException
    {
// Rather than opening up a FileInputStream directly, you create
// a File instance first so you can use the length method to
// determine how big a buffer to allocate for the class

        File classFile = new File(classDir, className+".class");

        byte[] classData = new byte[(int)classFile.length()];

// Now open up the input stream
        FileInputStream inFile = new FileInputStream(classFile);

// Read in the class
        int length = inFile.read(classData);

        inFile.close();

        return classData;
    }
}
```


Listing 47.6 shows a simple class for testing the loader.

Listing 47.6 Source Code for *LoadMe.java*

```
public class LoadMe extends Object
{
    public LoadMe()
    {
    }
```

continues

Listing 47.6 Continued

```
     public String toString()
     {
          return "Hello!  This is the LoadMe object!";
     }
}
```

The `TestLoader` program, shown in Listing 47.7, uses `MyClassLoader` to load the `LoadMe` class and print it out. It expects the `LoadMe.class` file to be in a subdirectory called `TESTDIR`.

Listing 47.7 Source Code to *TestLoader.java*

```
//
// This program uses MyTestLoader to load the LoadMe class.
//

public class TestLoader extends Object
{
     public static void main(String[] args)
     {
// Create the class loader.  Note: myLoader must be declared as MyClassLoader
// and not ClassLoader because the loadClass method in ClassLoader is
// protected, not public.

          MyClassLoader myLoader = new MyClassLoader("testdir");

          try {
// Try to load the class
               Class loadMeClass = myLoader.loadClass("LoadMe", true);
// Create a new instance of the class
               Object loadMe = loadMeClass.newInstance();
// Print out the string representation of the instance
               System.out.println(loadMe);
          } catch (Exception oops) {
// If there was an error, just print a whole stack trace
               oops.printStackTrace();
          }
     }
}
```

The *SecurityManager* Class

The `SecurityManager` class is one of the keys to Java's security. It contains an assortment of methods to check to see whether a particular operation is permitted. The various Java system classes, such as the `Applet` class, the network classes, and the file classes, all check with the security manager before performing potentially hazardous operations. If the security manager decides that something is not permitted, it will throw a `SecurityException`. The `System` class provides methods for accessing the current security manager and for setting the security manager if one isn't already defined. You may not change security managers after one has been set. These methods are in the `System` class, not the `SecurityManager` class:

```
public static SecurityManager getSecurityManager()
public static void setSecurityManager(SecurityManager)
     throws SecurityException
```

The *Compiler* Class

If Java were to remain an interpreted-only language, it would not survive in the business world against compiled languages like C++. Just-In-Time (JIT) compilers give Java that extra speed boost it needs. A JIT compiles methods to native machine instructions before executing them. The compilation only occurs once per method. Some JITs may compile entire classes, rather than one method at a time. The `Compiler` class lets you exercise a little control over the JIT.

You can ask the JIT to compile a specific class by passing a `Class` instance to the `compileClass()` method:

```
public static boolean compileClass(Class clazz)
```

The `compileClass()` method returns `true` if the compilation succeeded, or `false` if either the compilation failed or no JIT is available. This is useful if you need to invoke a method and you don't want to take the one-time compilation hit when you invoke the method. You ask the JIT to precompile the entire class before you start invoking methods.

The `compileClasses()` method is similar to the `compileClass()` method, except that it compiles a set of classes:

```
public static boolean compileClasses(String classes)
```

The `classes` parameter contains the name of the classes you want to compile. This might be something like `java.lang.*`. You should consult the documentation for your JIT (if it is available) to find out more on this method.

You can selectively disable and enable the JIT compiler with the disable and enable methods:

```
public static void disable()
public static void enable()
```

Finally, the `command()` method allows you to pass arbitrary commands to the compiler. This method is JIT-specific, so you should consult the documentation for a particular JIT to find out what commands it supports. The format for the `command()` method is

```
public static Object command(Object any)
```

- How to catch exceptions

  There are several types of exceptions that Java insists that you handle in your program. To do this, you must catch the exception and then perform some action.

- Creating and throwing your own exceptions

  Java's `Exception` class enables you to create custom exception objects. You can create and throw these custom exception objects in your programs.

- About Java's `Event` class

  When you understand how the `Event` class works, you're better prepared to deal with events in your Java programs.

- Handling all events, including the all-important mouse and keyboard events

  The only way your program can interact with the user is through events. Obviously, handling events is a Java programming must.

- How to create and send your own event objects

  Sometimes you want to create and deliver your own event objects in response to other Java events.

CHAPTER 48

Reflection

In this chapter

What Is Reflection?

According to Sun, Reflection is a "small, type-safe and secure API which supports introspection about the classes and objects in the current JVM." This may need a bit of translation to some of you, if not most. Essentially, the key word in the definition is *introspection*. Using Reflection, you can take an object, such as a `Vector`, look at it under a microscope, and find out what classes it extends and what methods and variables it has; and you can do this without knowing that the object is a vector.

To accomplish the task of inspection, Sun had to add a couple of classes in the `java.lang` package, including `Field`, `Method`, and `Constructor`. Each of these classes is used to obtain information about their respective characteristics from an object. In addition, to handle the rest of the class, Sun has added the `Array` and `Modifier` classes.

Surrounding the whole use of Reflection is the enhanced Java Security Model. The security model prevents classes that don't have access to methods, fields, constructors, and so on from being able to see them. How the security model works with Reflection is through a fairly tight coupling of some new class methods with the security manager. To do this, the `SecurityManager` itself has been granted an additional method—`checkMemberAccess()`. When a class is asked to produce its `Method` class (note: only a class is allowed to create a `Method`, `Field` or `Constructor` class) it first queries the `SecurityManager` to determine if it's okay to give the requesting class a copy of its `Method` class. If it is, fine; if not, the request is denied. If this sounds like someone trying far too hard to use the word class, look at it this way: Let's say you have a scenario where the object `Requestor` wants to know the methods of object `Provider`. In `Requestor`, you want to know what constructors are available in `Provider`. To do this, you might create two classes as seen in Listing 48.1.

NOTE As of JDK 1.2, you can also define the accessibility of a class by extending the `AccessibleObject` or using the `ReflectPermission` class.

Listing 48.1 *Requestor* Class Requests Information from the *Provider* Class

```
/*
 *
 * Requestor
 *
 */
import java.lang.reflect.*;
public class Requestor{
     public void requestConstuctors(){
          try{
               Constructor con[]= Class.forName("Provider").
➥getDeclaredConstructors();
               for (int x=0;x<con.length;x++)
                    System.out.println("Constructor "+x+" = "+con[x]);
          } catch (ClassNotFoundException se){
               System.out.println("Not allowed to get class info");
          }
```

```
    }

    public static void main(String args[]){
        Requestor req = new Requestor();
        req.requestConstuctors();
    }
}

/*
 *  Provider
 *
 */
class Provider{
    public Provider(){
    }

    public Provider(String s){
    }
}
```

After you compile this class, which should be called `Requestor.java` (note that you must compile it using the JDK 1.1 or 1.2; this won't work under 1.0), you can then run the `Requestor` program (also using 1.1 or 1.2). The output you get looks like this:

```
Constructor 0 = public Provider()
Constructor 1 = public Provider(String)
```

That's a pretty neat trick, and one that you quite simply couldn't accomplish without Reflection. Under other languages, such as C/C++, access to methods can be accomplished using method pointers. Because Java has no pointers, it's necessary to have this Reflection model to gain access to runtime methods.

Creating a Class Knowing Only the List of Constructors

Let's try something else. Instantiate the `Provider` class using the `Provider (String)` method. Under JDK 1.0, this was simply impossible (without using the direct approach, of course). Listing 48.2 shows just how to do this. Notice that I've cheated a bit by using the null parameter version of `newInstance()` method for the parameters (which can only be done because I know that the parameter (`String`) has a null constructor).

Part VII Ch 48

Listing 48.2 Requestor Creates a Provider Without Knowing the Constructor Name

```
/*
 *
 * Requestor
```

continues

Listing 48.2 Continued

```
 *
 */
import java.lang.reflect.*;
public class Requestor{
    public void requestConstuctors(){
        Class cl;
        Constructor con[];
        try{
            cl = Class.forName("Provider");
            con = cl.getDeclaredConstructors();
            for (int x=0;x<con.length;x++)
                System.out.println("Constructor "+x+" = "+con[x]);
            Class param[] = con[1].getParameterTypes();
            Object paramValues[] = new Object[param.length];
            for (int x=0;x<param.length;x++){
                if (!param[x].isPrimitive()){
                    System.out.println("param:"+param[x]);
                    paramValues[x]=param[x].newInstance();
                }
            }
            Object prov = con[1].newInstance(paramValues
        } catch (InvocationTargetException e){
        System.out.println("There was an InvocationEception and
➥ we were not allowed to get class info: "+e.getTargetException());
        } catch (Exception e){
        System.out.println("Exception during construction:"+e);
        }
    }

    public static void main(String args[]){
        Requestor req = new Requestor();
        req.requestConstuctors();
    }
}

class Provider{
    String me;
    public Provider(){
        me = new String();
    }

    public Provider(String x){
        this.me=me;
    }
}
```

Of course this whole system works, but probably isn't very practical. After all, it's not very often that all you want to do is construct a defaulted object, and at the same time that object doesn't have a null constructor of its own. The more likely time when this comes in handy is when you want to instantiate an object which has a constructor that you expect. For example, if you were to build up an API and the basis of one class is a constructor that takes several parameters, each class that extends your base class has to overload this constructor. That seems simple enough, right? For instance, take the ever popular car model. There will be two classes: `Car` and `Tires` (see Listing 48.3).

Listing 48.3 A *Car* with *Tires*

```
public class Tires {
     int number;
     float diameter;
}

public class Car{
     Tires tires;
     public Car (Tires tires){
          this.tires = tires;
     }
}
```

There's no need to fill out the rest of this class because it's irrelevant for the current discussion. The point is that the class `Car` obviously needs to receive a `Tires` object from an outside source. When you go to create a subclass, let's say Saturn and BMW, you still need to get the `Tires` model from an outside source as seen in Listing 48.4.

Listing 48.4 Saturn and BWM *Cars* with *Tires*

```
public class Saturn extends Car{
     public Saturn(Tires tires){
          super(tires);
     }
}

public class BMW extends Car{
     public BMW(Tires tires){
          super(tires);
     }
}
```


The only problem now is that, under JDK 1.0, you had no truly object-oriented way to handle each new type of car without coding at least its constructor into the program. You might think that this sounds like an interface solution, but unfortunately interfaces aren't broad enough to handle this situation. Interfaces allow you to create templates for methods, but not constructors. This means that every time a new car line is introduced, you need to go back, find every instance where the new car needed to be added, and add it in manually. Now, using Reflection this becomes very easy to do, as seen in Listing 48.5.

Listing 48.5 The Complete *CarShop* Creates *Cars* Using Reflection

```
/*
 *
 * CarShop
 *
 */
import java.lang.reflect.*;

public class CarShop {
     Car carList[];

     public CarShop (){
          carList = new Car[2];
          createCar("Saturn",0);
          createCar("BMW",1);
     }

     public void createCar(String carName,int carNum){
          try{
               //create the Tires array, which you'll use as a
               //the parameter to the constructor
               Object constructorParam[] = new Tires[1];
               constructorParam[0]= new Tires();

               //get the class name for the car that you want
               Class cl = Class.forName(carName);

               //create an array of Classes, and use this to
               //array to find the constructor that you want
               Class parameters[] = new Class[1];
               parameters[0]= Class.forName("Tires");
               Constructor  con = cl.getDeclaredConstructor(parameters);

               //create a car instance for the carList
               carList[carNum] = (Car)con.newInstance(constructorParam);
          } catch (Exception e){
               System.out.println("Error creating "+carName +":"+e);
          }
     }

     public static void main(String args[]){
          new CarShop();
     }
}
```

In this example, the most important thing is obviously the `createCar()` method. Here, it's broken down step-by-step:

```
Object constructorParam[] = new Tires[1];
               constructorParam[carNum]= new Tires();
```

As you saw earlier using Reflection, the method `newInstance`, which allows you to create a new instance of a class, takes as its parameter an array of objects (`Object []`). As a result, take a look at the constructor you hope to use:

```
Car (Tires tire)
```

This constructor has one parameter and is of type `Tires`, so you need to create an array (of one) with a `Tire` object as the first (and only) element:

```
Class cl = Class.forName(carName);
```

Next, you need to get the class that you're looking for. Notice that you're doing this just by knowing the name of the class. This means that you can even create a `<PARAM>` value that would contain a list of all the currently known cars:

```
Class parameters[] = new Class[1];
 parameters[0]= Class.forName("Tires");
 Constructor  con = cl.getDeclaredConstructor(parameters);
```

The next step is to find the constructor that matches the one you're looking for. To do this, you must create an array of classes. Each of the elements of this array is a class that matches the order of the parameters for the constructor you're looking for:

```
carList[carNum] = (Car)con.newInstance(constructorParam);
```

Now that you have obtained the correct constructor and put the parameter array together, you can finally create a new instance of the car. You're probably saying to yourself, "All this for what I could have written as: `carList[carNum] = new Saturn(new Tire());`?"

Yes, that's true, but to really account for this situation you would have needed to have an `if` loop that looked like the following:

```
if (carName.equals("Saturn"))
     carList[carNum] = new Saturn(new Tire());
   else if (carName.equals("BMW"))
     carList[carNum] = new BMW(new Tire());
```

Each time you added a new car, you'd have to go back in and add another `if` loop. With Reflection, this isn't necessary.

Inspecting a Class for Its Methods

In addition to discovering class methods, Reflection can also be used to help you discover which methods a class has. To do this, a very similar method to `getDeclaredConstructors()` has been created, called `getDeclaredMethods()`.

Obtaining a List of Methods

Going back to the `Requestor/Provider` example used in Listing 48.1, in addition to listing the constructors, you'll add a couple of methods to the `Provider` class and see what happens when you request them in the `Requestor` class, as shown in Listing 48.6.

Listing 48.6 Reflection Reveals Methods as Well as Constructors

```
/*
 *
 * Requestor
 *
 */
import java.lang.reflect.*;

public class Requestor{
     public void requestConstuctors(){
          Class cl;
          Constructor con[];
          Method meth[];
          try{
               cl = Class.forName("Provider");
               con = cl.getDeclaredConstructors();
               for (int x=0;x<con.length;x++)
                    System.out.println("Constructor "+x+" = "+con[x]);

               meth = cl.getDeclaredMethods();
               for (int x=0;x<meth.length;x++)
                    System.out.println("Method "+x+" = "+meth[x]);

          } catch (NoSuchMethodException e){
               System.out.println(
         ➥"There was an exception and we were not allowed to get
➥class info: "+e);

}
     }

     public static void main(String args[]){
          Requestor req = new Requestor();
          req.requestConstuctors();
     }
}

class Provider{
     int x;
     public Provider(){
          this.x=0;
     }

     public Provider(int x){
          this.x=x;
     }

     public boolean testMe(boolean test){
          return !test;
     }

     public int addThree(int num){
          return num+3;
     }
```

```
     public char letterD(){
          return 'D';
     }

}
```

Now, when you compile `Requestor.java` and run it, the output you see should look like this:

```
Constructor 0 = public Provider()
Constructor 1 = public Provider(int)
Method 0 = public boolean Provider.testMe(boolean)
Method 1 = public int Provider.addThree(int)
Method 2 = public char Provider.letterD()
```

As you can see, the method contains not only the same modifiers and parameters as the constructor did, but also return type. This should not be surprising to you because this is a critical component of any method. However, make a change to the `Provider` class as shown in Listing 48.7.

Listing 48.7 The *Provider* Class Extending *java.applet.Applet*

```
/*
 *
 * Provider
 *
 */

class Provider extends java.applet.Applet{
     int x;
     public Provider(){
          this.x=0;
     }

     public Provider(int x){
          this.x=x;
     }

     public boolean testMe(boolean test){
          return !test;
     }

     public int addThree(int num){
          return num+3;
     }

     public char letterD(){
          return 'D';
     }

}
```

Now if you run Requestor again, the output should look like this:

```
Constructor 0 = public Provider()
Constructor 1 = public Provider(int)
Method 0 = public boolean Provider.testMe(boolean)
Method 1 = public int Provider.addThree(int)
Method 2 = public char Provider.letterD()
```

Can you tell the difference? No, because there is no difference. Despite the fact that you just made Provider extend java.applet.Applet, which itself has a number of methods, these methods do not show up in the listing from getDeclaredMethods(). This is because getDeclaredMethods()returns all the methods that are declared by the current class (or interface) but does not return those methods the class obtains by inheritance.

You might be asking yourself, "Does this mean if I override or overload a method I won't be able to detect it because it was obtained through inheritance?" The answer is no on both counts—you will see these methods. Overloaded methods are actually new, so they are not obtained through inheritance; and overridden methods are included in the methods list to avoid this confusion.

Using *getDeclaredMethod()* to Invoke a Method

As you may have guessed, just like with the constructor example, invoking a method for the sake of invoking it really isn't useful except in rare instances, like writing a debugger.

Just like its constructor counterpart, getDeclaredConstructors(), getDeclaredMethods() has a sibling method, getDeclaredMethod(), that will obtain just the specific method you are looking for:

```
public Method getDeclaredMethod(String name, Class parameterTypes[])
```

Right away you might notice that getDeclaredMethod takes an additional parameter. This is because, as with a constructor, it's necessary to find a method based on its parameter list. But when you were looking for a constructor, it wasn't necessary to know the *name* of the constructor, because every constructor's name is the same as the class. To find a method, however, you need to specify the method name as well.

Just like its constructor counterpart, getDeclaredMethod does throw a NoSuchMethodException if no method matches the signature you are looking for. This, of course, means that you need to enclose any getDeclaredMethod() in a try-catch block.

Now go back to the car example and make a few changes as shown in Listing 48.8.

Listing 48.8 The *Car* Example with Several Changes

```
class Car{
     Tires tires;
     boolean running = false;

     public Car (Tires tires){
```

```
            this.tires = tires;
        }
}


class Saturn extends Car{
        public Saturn(Tires tires){
            super(tires);
        }

        public boolean start(){
            running = true;
            System.out.println("The Saturn is now running");
            return true;
        }
}

class BMW extends Car{
        public BMW(Tires tires){
            super(tires);
        }

        public boolean start(){
            running = true;
            System.out.println("The BMW is now running");
            return true;
        }

}
```

First, modify the `Car` classes and add a `start()` method to the Saturn and BMW cars. Don't add the `start()` method to `Car`; that would make life too easy. Next you need to add a method to the `CarShop` class to allow it to start the cars. In this case, call the method `startCar()` and call it right after you've added the Saturn and BMW to your motor pool, as shown in Listing 48.9.

Listing 49.9 The Complete *CarShop* for Use with the New *Cars*

```
/*
 *
 * CarShop
 *
 */
import java.lang.reflect.*;

public class CarShop {
        Car carList[];

        public CarShop (){
            carList = new Car[2];
```

continues

Listing 49.9 Continued

```
        createCar("Saturn",0);
        createCar("BMW",1);
        startCar(1);
    }

    public void createCar(String carName,int carNum){
        try{
            //create the Tires array, that you'll use as a
            //the parameter to the constructor
            Object constructorParam[] = new Tires[1];
            constructorParam[0]= new Tires();

            //get the class name for the car that you want
            Class cl = Class.forName(carName);

            //create an array of Classes, and use this to
            //array to find the constructor that you want
            Class parameters[] = new Class[1];
            parameters[0]= Class.forName("Tires");
            Constructor  con = cl.getDeclaredConstructor(parameters);

            //create a car instance for the carList
            carList[carNum] = (Car)con.newInstance(constructorParam);
        } catch (Exception e){
            System.out.println("Error creating "+carName +":"+e);
        }
    }

    public void startCar(int num){
        try{


            //create an array of Classes, and use this to
            //array to find the method you want
            //since you are actually looking for a null parameter
            //this is an array of 0
            Class parameters[] = new Class[0];
            Class carType = carList[num].getClass();
            Method meth = carType.getDeclaredMethod("start",parameters);

            //create a car instance for the carList
            meth.invoke(carList[num],parameters);
        } catch (Exception e){
            System.out.println("Error starting car "+num +":"+e);
        }
    }


    public static void main(String args[]){
        new CarShop();
    }
}
```

Now when you run this application, it should notify you that the BMW is now running. It's important to point out something about the `invoke()` method. `invoke()` requires two parameters. The second parameter is the array of parameters required to invoke the method just as the parameter array was used in the `newInstance()` method of constructor. However, `invoke()` also needs to know which object the method is being called upon, so the first parameter of `invoke()` is the correct object. What happens if the object doesn't have a `start()` method? Well, it actually goes a bit further than that. If the object is not an instance of the class that declared the method, then an exception is thrown.

Going back to Listing 48.9 again, notice that, to obtain the method `start()`, you need to be operating on the class `BMW` or `Saturn` and not on the object instances of these classes. `java.lang.Object` has been blessed with a new method called `getClass()`, which helps you solve this problem easily.

At this point, a good object-oriented programmer might ask, "Why would I ever want to use this method to invoke a method?" After all, a much better design would have you using either an interface or the `start()` method, which would be in the `car()` class. Under either of these two scenarios it would be unnecessary to find the method before invoking it. This is true, except that the world is not always perfect. Without the capability to invoke methods like this with Reflection, you have put a fairly substantial limitation on programming architecture. Much more importantly, the `getDeclaredMethod()`can frequently be used to provide another method with a method pointer. This means the portion of the method signature that becomes important is the parameter list and not necessarily the method name. This level of extension allows you to create multiple methods, which require similar processing, without the need to create multiple process layers.

Invoking Methods That Use Native Types as Parameters

One limitation of the system you've seen so far is that you have not seen how to invoke any methods or constructors that have native types as parameters. For instance, consider the `NewCar` in listing 49.10 below.

Listing 49.10 The *NewCar* Has a Constructor that Requires an *int*

```
public class NewCar{
  int numTires;
  public NewCar(int numTires){
     this.numTires = numTires;
  }

  public int getTireCount(){
    return numTires;
  }

}
```

To invoke the constructor for `NewCar` you must provide an `int`. The `getDeclaredContructor()` method, however, requires an array of class objects. How do you get the class for an `int`? Well, to handle this very situation the language allows you to add a `.class` to any native type and obtain a class object representing the type.

The next challenge is providing an object that represents the native type. You have probably already guessed that you need to use the wrapper classes in `java.lang`, in this case `java.lang.Integer`. Listing 49.11 below shows a brief example that instantiates the `NewCar`.

Listing 49.11 The *TestNewCar* Creates a New Instance of the *NewCar* Class.

```
import java.lang.reflect.Constructor;

public class TestNewCar{
   public static void main(String args[]){
      try{
        Class car = Class.forName("NewCar");

        Class param[] = {int.class};

        Constructor con = car.getDeclaredConstructor(param);

        Object values[] = {new Integer(4)};

        Object carObj = con.newInstance(values);

        System.out.println("The car has "+((NewCar)carObj).getTireCount()
➥ +" tires");
      }catch (Exception e){
        System.out.println("Something went wrong while invoking NewCar");
        e.printStackTrace(System.err);
      }
   }
}
```

Getting the Declared Fields of a Class

The final aspect of Reflection covered in this chapter is obtaining a list of the fields that a class has. As you might have guessed, the two methods most useful in this endeavor are `getDeclaredFields()` and `getDeclaredField()`. In the previous `Provider` class (Listing 48.7), you already had a variable (x), so all you need to do now is take the `Requestor` class one step further, as shown in Listing 48.12.

Listing 48.12 *Requestor* Application That Gets Fields

```
/*
 *
 * Requestor
```

```
 *
 */
import java.lang.reflect.*;

public class Requestor{
     public void requestConstuctors(){
          Class cl;
          Constructor con[];
          Method meth[];
          Field  field[];
          try{
               cl = Class.forName("Provider");
               con = cl.getDeclaredConstructors();
               for (int x=0;x<con.length;x++)
                    System.out.println("Constructor "+x+" = "+con[x]);

               meth = cl.getDeclaredMethods();
               for (int x=0;x<meth.length;x++)
                    System.out.println("Method "+x+" = "+meth[x]);

               field = cl.getDeclaredFields();
               for (int x=0;x<field.length;x++)
                    System.out.println("Field "+x+" = "+field[x]);


          } catch (Exception e){
               System.out.println("There was an exception and you were
➥not allowed to get class info: "+e);
          }
     }

     public static void main(String args[]){
          Requestor req = new Requestor();
          req.requestConstuctors();
     }
}
```

If you've been following the previous two examples, you have probably already guessed that the resulting output from your new `Requestor` looks like this:

```
Constructor 0 = public Provider()
Constructor 1 = public Provider(int)
Method 0 = public boolean Provider.testMe(boolean)
Method 1 = public int Provider.addThree(int)
Method 2 = public char Provider.letterD()
Method 3 = public boolean Provider.mouseDown(java.awt.Event,int,int)
Field 0 = int Provider.x
```

`Field()` itself can be used to provide a number of widening and narrowing conversions on `Field` types, but that area is left to you for further investigation. ●

CHAPTER 49

Extending Java with Other Languages

In this chapter

Native Methods, a Final Frontier for Java

The topic of native methods has been called one of the "final frontiers" of Java, and rightfully so! That's only because this potent feature empowers the Java developer to potentially do just about anything that can be programmatically done on a computer—assuming that a Java implementation exists for it, of course. Native methods enable programmers to extend the reach of Java, by selectively implementing methods in other programming languages such as C or C++ when the problem cannot be solved using Java alone.

> Prior to the evolution of JDK 1.1, native methods was one of those foreboding, "rocket-science" Java topics that was seldom discussed and even less understood. And not without ample reason, either! Then, the very implementation of the native method interface within JVMs had differed quite drastically, depending on the vendor implementing it. Due to myriad shortcomings, Sun's native method specification under JDK 1.02 was superseded by proprietary interfaces such as Netscape's Java Runtime Interface (JRI), Microsoft's Raw Native Interface (RNI), and the Java/COM interface. The lack of a unified interface meant that the developer had to implement a separate native method binary for each JVM used, even though they may all have targeted the same platform!

Given the prevailing situation, it was none too surprising that the native method specification was thoroughly overhauled under the JDK 1.1. The new and improved version, called the Java Native Interface (JNI), simplifies matters by presenting a unified interface for incorporating native methods, irrespective of the JVM used, assuming that the vendor conforms to the JNI specification for supporting native methods. JNI was developed following extensive consultations between Sun Microsystems, Inc. and other Java licensees, and bears very close resemblance to Netscape's JRI specification.

NOTE Some confusion still exists as to whether Microsoft will be adopting the JNI standard within its JVM implementation. So far, Microsoft has insisted that it will not be adopting JNI, but rather will support only the RNI and Java/COM interfaces. This is actually one of the parts of the lawsuit between Sun and Microsoft that you may have heard of. Hopefully by year-end 1998 we will have a better idea of what to expect in the future.

The Case for "Going Native"

Java purists may consider incorporating C or C++ code within Java programs as an act of heresy! Why in the world would someone want to program in anything but Java, given the power and flexibility of the platform-independent JDK? The reasons are many:

- Java programmers may need access to specialized operating system facilities that are not available directly through the JDK.
- You may need direct access to a peripheral device such as a video card, sound card, or modem to make optimal usage of available functionality.

- The Java program may need to interface with third-party middleware and messaging systems (such as IBM's MQ Series, Sybase's Open Server, Momemtum's XIPC, Lotus Notes, and so on) or proprietary enterprise software systems such as SAP R/3, PeopleSoft, Baan, and so on. Because these software solutions come with their own (usually C-based) proprietary interface APIs, native methods is the only alternative for their integration with Java.
- A ton of legacy code already exists at the back end that would continue to work seamlessly, irrespective of the user interface. The continual movement of legacy systems to a Java-based intranet/Internet computing environment without extensive code rewrite is a compelling reason for their rapid integration via native methods.
- Certain highly time-critical operations within real-time Java systems may need functionality to be implemented as assembly code. In a situation like this, using native methods is usually the only answer.

Incorporating native methods may bring certain benefits, but there is certainly a price to be paid:

- Your Java code loses one of its chief strengths: portability. Because native method implementation is platform-specific, your native library will have to be re-implemented and recompiled for each and every platform your Java system will have to run on.
- Browser security manager policies may prevent you from loading applets that link to dynamically loadable libraries implementing the native methods. Consequently, native methods can be used hassle-free only from within Java applications and not applets.

NOTE Future versions of browsers may well have a fully customizable security manager, where the user can load applets implementing native methods on a selective basis. Sun's HotJava browser currently provides a customizable security manager.

- Native methods usage involves the management of additional header and C interface files. The creation of complex native methods itself requires not only a great deal of Java programming expertise, but also expertise of the implementation language and platform.

JNI Highlights

As mentioned before, JVM's full compliance with the JDK 1.1 specification presents the same standard native method interface—the JNI—irrespective of the platform. The highlights of the JNI are as follows:

- Native methods can create, update, and inspect Java objects.
- Java can pass any primitive data types or objects as parameters to native methods.
- Native methods can return either primitive data types or objects back to the Java environment.
- Java instance or class methods can be called from within native methods.
- Native methods can catch and throw Java exceptions.

- Runtime type checking can be performed within native methods.
- Native methods can implement synchronization to support multithreaded access.

Writing Native Methods

If you still think native methods are the way to go, it is time to dive into the mysterious waters of the sea of JNI.

NOTE All the JNI examples given here are written with the Solaris operating environment in mind, and the native methods are implemented using C. The examples should work fine on other platforms, as long as the shared library is created properly for that platform.

All native methods are implemented in JNI by closely following a basic six-step program.

Step One—Write the Java Code

Looking at Listing 49.1, you see that the keyword `native`, within the declaration of the method `greet`, indicates that it is implemented outside Java and in a different programming language. Additionally, the static block tells Java to load the shared library (`libsayhello1.so`, in the case of Solaris), within which you can find the actual implementation of the method at runtime.

Listing 49.1 ***SayHello1.java*—Native Methods Demo Program**

```
public class SayHello1 {
     public native void greet();

     static {
     System.loadLibrary("sayhello1");
     }
          public static void main(String[] args) {
          new SayHello1().greet();
     }
}
```

The `main` method just invokes a new instance of the class `SayHello1` and invokes the native method `greet`. Notice that the native method is invoked just like any ordinary instance method.

Step Two—Compile the Java Code to a Class File

No surprises here. Just compile the Java source file using the `javac` compiler as usual:

```
javac SayHello1.java
```

Step Three—Generate the JNI-Style Header File

Apply javah—the C header and stub file generator given to you as part of the JDK—on the compiled class file to generate the JNI header file for the class. JNI, unlike the native method interface specification under JDK 1.02, does not make use of stub files.

```
javah -jni SayHello1
```

This generates the corresponding header file, SayHello1.h, to the local directory (see Listing 49.2).

NOTE The generated header file always has the naming convention SomeClassFile.h, where the class SomeClassFile contains the native method declaration, within your Java source.

Listing 49.2 *SayHello1.h*—Generated Header File

```
/* DO NOT EDIT THIS FILE - it is machine generated */
#include <jni.h>
/* Header for class SayHello1*/

#ifndef _Included_SayHello1
#define _Included_SayHello1
#ifdef __cplusplus
extern "C" {
#endif
/*
 * Class:     SayHello1
 * Method:    greet
 * Signature: ()V
 */
JNIEXPORT void JNICALL Java_SayHello1_greet
  (JNIEnv *, jobject);

#ifdef __cplusplus
}
#endif
#endif
```

Step Four—Implement the Native Method

The native method can now be developed, after making sure to include the generated header file within the native method implementation file. The native method prototypes can be taken from the header file, to simplify matters (see Listing 49.3).

There are no restrictions for naming the native method implementation file. However, it is better to choose a filename for the method that has some relationship to the actual Java file within which the native method is declared.

Listing 49.3 ***MyHello1.c*—Native Method Implementation Program**

```
#include "SayHello1.h"
#include <stdio.h>
JNIEXPORT# void JNICALL# Java_SayHello1_greet ( JNIEnv *env, jobject this) {
     printf("Hi folks! Welcome to the netherworld of native methods!\n");
}
```

Step Five—Create the Shared Library

This step varies quite a bit, depending on the target platform, and requires the availability of a compiler that enables you to create a shared library. For Solaris, a shared object is created quite easily by using the appropriate compiler option. It is important that the path of the standard JDK 1.2 includes files that are properly denoted during the compilation process.

The following command has the effect of creating the shared object `libsayhello1.so` on Solaris platforms, for example.

```
cc -G MyHello1.c -I $JAVAHOME/include -I $JAVAHOME/include/solaris -o
➥libsayhello1.so
```

For Windows 95 and Windows NT, you can create a DLL for the native implementation as follows:

```
cl MyHello1.c -I$JAVAHOME\include -I$JAVAHOME\include\win32 -Fesayhello1.dll -MD
➥-LD -nologo
$JAVAHOME\lib\javai.lib
```

NOTE For Windows 95 and Windows NT, you can use any C or C++ compiler that enables you to create DLLs. You have to make sure that you include the path of the relevant JDK, including files, when you create the DLL.

Step Six—Run the Java Program

Running the application as

```
java SayHello1
```

produces the following output:

```
Hi folks! Welcome to the netherworld of native methods!
```

On Solaris platforms, please note that the environment variable `LD_LIBRARY_PATH` should contain the path of the newly created shared object.

Accessing Object Fields from Native Methods

JNI methods can easily access and even alter the member fields of the invoking object. This is done by using the various JNI accessor functions made available to programmers via the interface pointer that is passed by default as the first argument to every JNI method. The JNI interface pointer is of type `JNIEnv`. The second argument differs on the nature of the native method. For a non-static native method, the argument is a reference to the object; whereas for a static method, it is a reference to its Java class.

Accessing Java object members through the accessor functions is what ensures the portability of the native method implementation. Assuming the vendor of a VM implements the JNI, your native methods should work irrespective of how the Java objects are maintained internally.

Take a look at the function prototype back in Listing 49.3.

```
JNIEXPORT# void JNICALL# Java_SayHello1_greet ( JNIEnv *env, jobject this)
```

You see that the first two arguments for this method are passed by default by the Java environment. The interface pointer `env` gives you access to the accessor functions, and the object reference `this` refers to the instance that invoked the native method.

Listing 49.4 is a modification of Listing 49.1. Here, you have added a couple of `public` fields to `class`, and you see how they can be accessed and changed in Listing 49.5.

Listing 49.4 *SayHello2.java*—Java Program to Demonstrate Object Access from Native Methods

```
public class SayHello2 {

          public String aPal = "Java Joe";
          public int age=0;
          public native void greet();


          static {
               System.loadLibrary("sayhello2");
          }

          public void howOld() {
               System.out.println(aPal + " is " + age + "years old today!");
          }
          public static void main(String[] args) {
               SayHello2 mySayHello2 = new SayHello2();
               mySayHello2.greet();
               mySayHello2.howOld();
          }
}
```

Listing 49.5 *MyHello2.c*—Native Method Implementation Program to Demonstrate Object Access

```
#include "SayHello2.h"
#include <studio.h>
JNIEXPORT# void JNICALL# Java_SayHello2_greet ( JNIEnv *env, jobject this) {
    jfieldID jf;
```

continues

Listing 49.5 Continued

```
    jclass jc;
    jobject jobj;
    const jbyte *pal;
       jint new_age=2;
       jc = (*env)->GetObjectClass(env, this);
       jf = (*env)->GetFieldID(env,jc,"aPal","Ljava/lang/String;");
       jobj = (*env)->GetObjectField(env,this,jf);
       pal = (*env)->GetStringUTFChars(env,jobj,0);
       printf("Hi %s! Welcome to the netherworld of native methods!\n", pal);
       jf = (*env)->GetFieldID(env,jc,"age","I");
       (*env)->SetIntField(env,this,jf,new_age);
}
```

In Listing 49.5, you see how you can not only access the value of a Java field, but can also reset Java field values from within the native method itself.

The Java class file and shared library are created as before, and on execution, you get the following output:

```
Hi Java Joe! Welcome to the netherworld of native methods!
Java Joe is 2 years old today!
```

TROUBLESHOOTING

Why am I getting all the exception errors?

If you get a ton of Java exception errors, the most likely cause could be an incorrect type signature for your `GetMethodID()` function call. Verify that the signature is correct and recompile your shared library.

Object fields are accessed and used within native methods by following these four steps:

1. Get the class type of the invoking object.
2. Get the field ID.
3. Use the appropriate `GetField()/SetField()` accessor functions to `retrieve/set` the object field.
4. Convert the retrieved object field as needed to use within the native method.

The `GetObjectClass` is used to determine the class of the object invoking the native method. You see that before the value of an object member field is accessed, you first need to obtain a `fieldID` for it. The `GetFieldID` accessor function needs to know the exact field name, as well as its type signature. Table 49.1 denotes the possible JVM type signatures.

Table 49.1 JVM Type Signatures

Type Signature	Java Type
`Z`	`boolean`
`B`	`byte`
`C`	`char`
`S`	`short`
`I`	`int`
`J`	`long`
`F`	`float`
`D`	`double`
`Lfully-qualified-class;`	`fully-qualified-class`
`[type`	`type[]`
`(arg-types)ret-type`	`method type`

Because the accessed field is of type `String`, its type signature is `Ljava/lang/String`.

The JNI interface pointer provides many functions to access the actual member field, depending on its type.

Table 49.2 shows the various `GetField()` functions that are available.

Table 49.2 Accessor Functions for Java Field Access

GetField **Routine Name**	**Native Type**	**Java Type**
`GetObjectField()`	`jobject`	`Object`
`GetBooleanField()`	`jboolean`	`boolean`
`GetByteField()`	`jbyte`	`byte`
`GetCharField()`	`jchar`	`char`
`GetShortField()`	`jshort`	`short`
`GetIntField()`	`jint`	`int`
`GetLongField()`	`jlong`	`long`
`GetFloatField()`	`jfloat`	`float`
`GetDoubleField()`	`jdouble`	`double`

You make use of the `GetObjectField` function because the target field accessed is a Java object. Also, you have to declare an equivalent native type to store the accessed Java field within the native method.

Lastly, you see that object fields can have their values altered by making use of the appropriate `SetField()` function. You make use of the `SetIntField()` function because the target field set is of type `int`. As before, it is important to declare the correct native type to store the value of the native field that is passed to the Java environment.

Table 49.3 shows the various `SetField()` functions that are available.

Table 49.3 Accessor Functions for Setting Java Field Values

SetField **Routine Name**	**Native Type**	**Java Type**
`SetObjectField()`	`jobject`	`Object`
`SetBooleanField()`	`jboolean`	`boolean`
`SetByteField()`	`jbyte`	`byte`
`SetCharField()`	`jchar`	`char`
`SetShortField()`	`jshort`	`short`
`SetIntField()`	`jint`	`int`
`SetLongField()`	`jlong`	`long`
`SetFloatField()`	`jfloat`	`float`
`SetDoubleField()`	`jdouble`	`double`

Table 49.4 denotes the primitive types that can be used within native functions.

Table 49.4 Primitive Types

Java Type	**Native Type**	**Description**
`boolean`	`jboolean`	unsigned 8 bits
`byte`	`jbyte`	signed 8 bits
`char`	`jchar`	unsigned 16 bits
`short`	`jshort`	signed 16 bits
`int`	`jint`	signed 32 bits
`long`	`jlong`	signed 64 bits
`float`	`jfloat`	32 bits
`double`	`jdouble`	64 bits
`void`	`void`	N/A

Accessing Java Methods from Native Methods

The process of invoking a Java method from within a native method is a little complicated. By using the techniques demonstrated in Listings 49.6 and 49.7, however, you will also be able to call other native methods from within a native method. In fact, a native method can even call itself recursively, if need be. Listing 49.6 is a good example of how a Java method can be invoked from a native method, with arguments passed to it. Listing 49.7 shows the C implementation and demonstrates the actual JNI syntax for accessing Java methods from native methods.

Listing 49.6 ***SayHello3.java*****—Java Program to Demonstrate Java Method Access from Native Methods**

```
public class SayHello3 {

        public  String rectArea(int l, int b ) {
            return "The area of the rectangle is " + l*b + " units" ;
        }
        public native void calc();

        static {
            System.loadLibrary("sayhello3");
        }

        public static void main(String[] args) {
            new SayHello3().calc();
        }
}
```

Listing 49.7 ***MyHello3.c*****—Native Method Implementation to Demonstrate Java Method Access**

```
    #include "SayHello3.h"
    #include <studio.h>
    JNIEXPORT# void JNICALL# Java_SayHello3_greet ( JNIEnv *env, jobject this)
{
        jmethodID jm;
        jclass jc;
        jobject jo;
        const jbyte *area;
        jint x,y ;
        x =20;
        y =20;
        jc = (*env)->GetObjectClass(env, this);
        jm = (*env)->GetMethodID(env,jc,"rectArea","(II)Ljava/lang/
➥      String;",x,y);
        jo= (*env)->CallObjectMethod(env,this,jm,x,y);
        area = (*env)->GetStringUTFChars(env,jo,0);
        printf("%s\n",area);

}
```

The Java class file and shared library is created as before, and on execution, you get this output:

```
The Area of the Rectangle is 400 units
```

Object methods can be called from within native methods by following these five steps:

1. Get the class type of the invoking object.
2. Get the method ID.
3. Initialize the variables that need to be passed as parameters to the Java method.
4. Use the appropriate `CallMethod()` accessor function to invoke the method.
5. Convert the returned object field as needed for use within the native method.

Looking at the type signatures in Table 49.1, you can deduce that the type signature for the Java method `rectArea()` in Listing 49.6 is `(II)Ljava/lang/String;`. This is because the method takes in two `int`s and returns back a `String` object.

Table 49.5 shows the various `CallMethod()` accessor functions that are available.

Table 49.5 Accessor Functions to Invoke Java Methods from Native Methods

CallMethod **Routine Name**	**Native Type**	**Java Type**
`CallVoidMethod()`	`void`	`void`
`CallObjectMethod()`	`jobject`	`Object`
`CallBooleanMethod()`	`jboolean`	`boolean`
`CallByteMethod()`	`jbyte`	`byte`
`CallCharMethod()`	`jchar`	`char`
`CallShortMethod()`	`jshort`	`short`
`CallIntMethod()`	`jint`	`int`
`CallLongMethod()`	`jlong`	`long`
`CallFloatMethod()`	`jfloat`	`float`
`CallDoubleMethod()`	`jdouble`	`double`

Accessing Static Fields

Thus far you have seen how to work with functions that work on instance fields and methods. You can access static fields and methods of Java objects in much the same way by using some of the special functions shown here.

`GetStaticFieldID()` The signature of the field accessed can be obtained from Table 49.1. After the signature has been obtained, the `GetStaticFieldID()` is used exactly as the `GetFieldID()` function.

`GetStaticField()` Table 49.6 shows the various `GetStaticField()` functions that can be used to access static fields. The selected function will depend on the data type of the Java field accessed.

Table 49.6 Accessor Functions for Accessing Static Java Fields

GetStaticField **Routine Name**	**Native Type**	**Java Type**
`GetStaticObjectField()`	`jobject`	`Object`
`GetStaticBooleanField()`	`jboolean`	`boolean`
`GetStaticByteField()`	`jbyte`	`byte`
`GetStaticCharField()`	`jchar`	`char`
`GetStaticShortField()`	`jshort`	`short`
`GetStaticIntField()`	`jint`	`int`
`GetStaticLongField()`	`jlong`	`long`
`GetStaticFloatField()`	`jfloat`	`float`
`GetStaticDoubleField()`	`jdouble`	`double`

`SetStaticField()` Table 49.7 shows the available accessor functions that can be used to modify the value of static Java fields. The chosen function will depend on the type of the target static field.

Table 49.7 Accessor Functions for Setting Static Field Values

SetStaticField **Routine Name**	**Native Type**	**Java Type**
`SetStaticObjectField()`	`jobject`	`Object`
`SetStaticBooleanField()`	`jboolean`	`boolean`
`SetStaticByteField()`	`jbyte`	`byte`
`SetStaticCharField()`	`jchar`	`char`
`SetStaticShortField()`	`jshort`	`short`
`SetStaticIntField()`	`jint`	`int`
`SetStaticLongField()`	`jlong`	`long`
`SetStaticFloatField()`	`jfloat`	`float`
`SetStaticDoubleField()`	`jdouble`	`double`

Accessing Static Methods

Static Java methods can be invoked just like instance methods, but by making use of the functions `GetStaticMethodID()` and `CallStaticMethod()`.

`GetStaticMethodID()` The usage of this function is identical to that of `GetMethodID()`. The developer will have to determine the method signature using Table 49.1, before invoking the function.

`CallStaticMethod` Table 49.8 shows a listing of the available `CallStaticMethod()` accessor functions. The developer will have to choose the appropriate one based on the Java type of the data returned from the function call.

Table 49.8 Accessor Functions for Invoking Static Java Methods

***CallStaticMethod* Routine Name**	**Native Type**	**Java Type**
`CallStaticVoidMethod()`	`void`	`void`
`CallStaticObjectMethod()`	`jobject`	`Object`
`CallStaticBooleanMethod()`	`jboolean`	`boolean`
`CallStaticByteMethod()`	`jbyte`	`byte`
`CallStaticCharMethod()`	`jchar`	`char`
`CallStaticShortMethod()`	`jshort`	`short`
`CalStaticIntMethod()`	`jint`	`int`
`CallStaticLongMethod()`	`jlong`	`long`
`CallStaticFloatMethod()`	`jfloat`	`float`

Exception Handling Within Native Methods

JNI methods can throw exceptions that can then be handled within the invoking Java object. Following are some of the important functions available within the JNI interface pointer for exception handling:

`Throw`

```
jint Throw(JNIEnv *env, jthrowable obj);
```

causes a `java.lang.Throwable` object to be thrown.

Parameters:

`env` The JNI interface pointer

`obj` A `java.lang.Throwable` object

Returns:

0 On success

Negative number On failure

`ThrowNew`

```
jint ThrowNew(JNIEnv *env,  jclass classz, const char *msg);
```

initializes and constructs a new exception object instance of type `classz` with the diagnostic `msg` and throws it.

Where:

`env` The JNI interface pointer

`classz` A subclass of `java.lang.Throwable`

`msg` A diagnostic message for the class constructor

Returns:

0 On success

Negative number On failure

`FatalError`

```
void FatalError(JNIEnv *env, char *msg);
```

raises an unrecoverable fatal error

Where:

`env` The JNI interface pointer

`msg` An error message

CHAPTER 50

Java Versus C(++)

In this chapter

Common Ancestry

The Java and C++ programming languages both share the C language as a common ancestor, and thus the three languages share many features and syntactic constructs. But it will be clear to any C or C++ programmers reading this book that there are also many differences. The languages are similar, but certainly not identical. C programmers will find that Java is mostly additive, that it forms a superset of C. Although it is true that some loved (and hated) features of C are missing in Java—most notably the pre-processor and support for pointers—there are far more areas where Java introduces new constructs and new features. Most obvious in the latter category is Java's support for the object-oriented programming paradigm.

C++ programmers will find the differences between C++ and Java more subtle. Some are fairly minor, like the scope of a variable declared within a `for` loop control statement. Others, unfortunately, are quite profound, like the Java object reference model and its support for polymorphic behavior.

This chapter contains a concise comparison of C, C++, and Java. If you have prior experience with C or C++, you can use this chapter to accelerate your progress with Java. If you don't have prior experience, you can use this chapter to gain some insights into how Java evolved. And no matter what your background, you can use this chapter as a quick reference.

Basic Java Syntax

There are many small differences between C/C++ and Java. None of these are particularly difficult to understand, but there are quite a few of them, and they can be difficult to remember. This first section covers the most basic differences.

Lexical Structure

The lexical structures of Java, C, and C++ are nearly the same. The source code for the program is broken down into tokens that combine to form expressions and statements. All three languages are freeform languages, which means that there are no special rules for the positioning of tokens in the source stream. Whitespace, consisting of blanks, tabs, and newlines, can be used in any combination to separate tokens. As in C and C++, semicolons are used to delimit statements. Anywhere a single statement is required, multiple statements can be combined within braces to form a single compound statement.

CAUTION

Although whitespace can be used to separate tokens, it cannot be used to separate the components of a token. For example, whitespace cannot be placed between the two characters of an operator such as ++ or *=.

Comments

There are three forms of comments in Java:

- The traditional C comment, introduced with `/*`, and encompassing all text up to the first `*/`.
- The BCPL comment, which is introduced with `//` and continues until the end of the current line. Everything to the right of the `//` on the current line is a comment.
- The Javadoc comment, introduced with `/**`, and encompassing all text up to the first `*/`. Although Javadoc comments look like traditional C comments, they have special meaning.

▶ **See** "JDK Tools: Javac, AppletViewer, Javadoc," (ed says maybe CH04), **p. 56**

The following code fragment illustrates the three styles:

```
/* This is the first line of a multi-line comment
this is the second line of the comment */
int tableSize;  // This is a single line comment
/** This is a Javadoc comment */
```

NOTE As in C and C++, Java comments do not nest. Take a look at the following example:

```
/* This is a line of a comment
/* Someone might think this is a nested comment */
But this line is no longer part of a comment
*/ n
```

> **CAUTION**
>
> Many C and C++ programmers are used to being able to nest comments, despite the preceding note. This is because some C and C++ compiler vendors have added support for nested comments to their products. Don't be fooled into thinking that these extensions are actually part of the C or C++ language—they aren't!

What's Missing

A number of constructs from C and C++ are not present and not supported in Java. Some of these, like the lack of pre-processor, get special attention later in this chapter. Others are more minor and are collected here. In most situations, you can achieve similar results using alternate Java syntax.

No Pointers Pointers are not supported in Java in any way, although the Java reference model is very similar to the use of pointers in C++. There are no pointer operators, and there is no way of directly manipulating memory locations by address. Furthermore, memory cannot be allocated and de-allocated at programmer convenience as is the case in both C and C++.

No C++ Reference In C++, reference variables can be defined to refer to any native or abstract data type. In Java, all objects of class type are manipulated via references, so no special syntax is necessary. However, there is no way in Java to declare a reference to a native type.

Instead, one of the Java wrapper classes defined in `java.lang` can be used (for example, `Integer`, `Float`, and so on).

▶ **See** "Primitive Types and `java.lang` Wrapper Classes," **p. 1171**

No Structs, Unions, or Enums The C and C++ strict construct no longer exists. A C struct can be mimicked in Java by defining a class with all data elements public and with no methods. The enum construct isn't supported either, but can be mimicked by defining a class with no methods, and with all data elements public, static, and final. C and C++ unions are not supported and there is no trivial way to provide similar functionality.

No *consts* The `const` keyword, although reserved in Java also, isn't currently used for anything. In C++, use of the `const` modifier was encouraged to eliminate the need for `#define` constants. In Java, the `final` modifier can be used to achieve a similar effect: Data elements in a class that are declared to be final must be initialized when they are declared, and thereafter cannot be modified.

The Runtime Library

C programmers are accustomed to using the C runtime library in every program they write. The very first C program a programmer creates is traditionally the "Hello world" program, in which the following line appears:

```
printf ("Hello, world!\n");
```

The `printf` function is defined in the C runtime library and is available to be used in any C program.

In C++, the equivalent functionality is usually provided by classes and methods in the `iostream` class library. The traditional first program for a C++ programmer might contain a line like the following:

```
cout << "Hello again, world!\n";
```

The functionality provided by the `iostream` class library is again available to any C++ program.

In Java, the functionality you have come to expect in the C runtime library, or in the standard C++ class libraries, is provided in the Java API. The API defines a large number of classes, each with many different methods. The traditional first program might now contain the line

```
System.out.println ("Hello from Java!");
```

The `println` method is defined in the `PrintStream` class. `System.out` is an instance of the `PrintStream` class. The important thing is that the functionality provided by the Java API, which includes everything that the old C runtime library does and much more, is available to every Java program you write.

The Structure of Java Programs

When you first start reading Java code, two things strike you right away. First is the minor syntax differences like the ones listed in the previous section. Second is the overall structure of the Java program.

The Big Picture

In C, the big picture of a program is that it is a collection of procedures or functions that interact with one another. Processing begins with the function called `main`, and from there all the functions call one another. In Java, the big picture is of a collection of class definitions, the instances of which are interrelated and interact. In some respects, this is the essence of object-oriented programming.

Java programs themselves are classes and come in two main flavors. Applications are classes that have a `main` method, and applets are classes that extend the `Applet` class.

NOTE The definitions of application and applet are not mutually exclusive. By creating a class that both extends the `Applet` class and has a `main` method, it is possible to write one program that can be used as either application or applet at the user's choice.

In this context, as in many others, C++ is halfway between C and Java. C programs are collections of functions, Java programs are collections of classes, and C++ programs are collections of both functions and classes.

Methods Yes, Functions No

As pointed out, C programs are just collections of functions. In C++, most programs are collections of classes, similar to programs in Java. However, a C++ program begins execution with the function called `main`, just as C programs do. Moreover, C++ provides explicit support for functions that behave like C functions, in addition to methods that are part of class definitions. Java is much more pure in its object orientation than C++, however, and, as such, provides no support for functions except as methods defined within a class.

If you must create functionality similar to that provided by C and C++ functions (a math library, for instance), you can do so by creating a utility class that consists only of static methods and static data items.

No Pre-Processor

When many C and C++ programmers learn that the pre-processor no longer exists in Java, they are quite skeptical. The truth is that the pre-processor isn't supported in Java because the language no longer has need of it.

Constant Values There are no `#define` constants in Java. As previously seen, data elements in a class definition can be declared to be final, however, in which case their initial values can never be changed. To get as close as possible to the functionality of a `#define`, you would create those data elements to be public, static, and final.

NOTE The Java equivalent to the C `#define` is far superior. Its name is protected by the compiler, it has a true data type, and its use can be verified for correctness by the compiler.

Macros C macros, also implemented with the `#define` construct of the pre-processor, were designed to provide a function-like construct that could be implemented at compile time, thus avoiding the runtime overhead associated with a function invocation. Java does not provide an equivalent to the C macro. Remember, however, that C macros are extremely error-prone and are a fairly consistent source of program bugs. C++ programmers are encouraged to forego the `#define` macro in favor of the C++ inline function. Java does not explicitly support the `inline` keyword, but Java compilers are free to inline any function they choose to as part of their general optimization process.

Source File Inclusion Java does not provide anything equivalent to the C `#include` directive for source file inclusion. In practice, however, there is little need for this in Java code. The two most common uses of the `#include` in C are for the creation of `#define` constants and for the declaration of function prototypes. As just seen, Java supports constant values through quite a different syntax, which doesn't require source file inclusion. And because Java doesn't support a method declaration separate from its definition, there is no need for prototypes.

NOTE C compilers only support very limited forms of forward reference, meaning that symbols—function names in this case—must be declared before they are used. In practice, this means that C programmers must either provide a function prototype—a declaration—or must ensure that the function definition comes before the first time the function is used. Java, on the other hand, supports very liberal forward references, thus eliminating the need for separate function declarations.

The following code fragments illustrate the different pre-processor issues just discussed. The first fragment is C++:

```
#include <iosteam.h>
#define PLAYERS 2

class Game
{
public:
Game()
{ cout << "Constructing the Game\n"; }
};
Now look at the Java equivalent:
import java.lang.*;
class Game{
public Game()
{ System.out.println ("Constructing the Game"); }
public static final int PLAYERS=23;
}
```

Notice how the `import` statement appears to take the place of the `#include`. The two statements are superficially similar, but in fact accomplish quite different objectives. The `#include` does a straight source file inclusion on the part of the C pre-processor. Because the pre-processor doesn't understand C syntax (it's basically a batch-mode text editor), the source file being included could contain anything. The `import` statement doesn't actually include anything, but rather tells the compiler where to look for classes that you want to make use of.

The preceding example imports the `java.lang` package. In fact, that is the one package that the Java compiler will import automatically, with or without an import statement. You can make use of classes in `java.lang` without explicitly importing them yourself.

Source Filenames

At the moment, most development kits for Java, including the Sun JDK, require that the definition of a public class be contained in a source file of the same name. Thus, the definition of the `InventoryItem` class would have to be contained in a source file named `InventoryItem.java`.

Although the current naming restrictions apply only to the definition of public classes, it is common practice in the Java community to define one class per source file, regardless of whether the class is public or not. This practice will be a little unfamiliar to many C and C++ programmers, who might be amazed at the number of source files used in the creation of a single Java program. However, it does make Java source code much easier to find—both for you and for the compiler—and lends some consistency to file naming.

Java Data Types

Java support for data types is stronger and more specific than that in C or C++. In this section, you look at integral data types, Unicode characters, Booleans, floating-point types, and aggregate types. You also take a look at converting from one Java data type to another.

Integral Data Types

It is in the integral data types that you see most of the differences between Java and C/C++. Much of what was platform-dependent in C or C++ is now clearly defined in Java. Table 50.1 summarizes the differences.

Table 50.1 Comparison of Java and C/C++ Data Types

Data Type	C/C++	Java
`byte`	Didn't exist; `char` instead	8 bits usually used
`char`	8 bits; one ASCII or EBCDIC character	16 bits one Unicode character
`short`	At least 16 bits	16 bits
`int`	Usually 16 or 32 bits	32 bits
`long`	At least 32 bits	64 bits

NOTE There are no unsigned integral data types in Java.

Unicode Characters

In Java, the `char` and `String` data types are not single-byte ASCII or EBCDIC values, but are instead 16-bit values taken from the Unicode character set. The larger data type means that a larger number of possible values are supported, giving greater flexibility to programmers in non-English or multilingual environments. In the Unicode set, the first 256 characters are identical to the ASCII characters 0x00-0xFF (which is also ISO standard ISO8859-1).

Specific values from the Unicode character set can be represented in Java using the syntax `\uhhhh`, where `h` is a hexadecimal character representing four of the 16 bits in the Unicode character. In fact, you don't need to specify all four hex digits; if fewer than four digits are specified, then the high-order bits are set to zero.

NOTE Java also supports C and C++ escape sequences such as `\n`, `\r`, and `\t` to represent non-printing control characters.

The *boolean* Data Type

Neither C nor C++ provides a native `boolean` data type. In both those languages, most programmers use `int` variables to hold Boolean values, with the convention that a value of 0 represents `false` and a value of 1 represents `true`. Furthermore, the logical and relational operators in C and C++ all produce integer values, and the control statements on loops or an `if` statement both take integer values as control expressions.

In Java, the native `boolean` data type is used in all these situations. The `boolean` data type supports only two possible values: `true` and `false`. The relational and logical operators all produce values of `boolean` type, and the logical operators will only accept operands that are of `boolean` type. The control expression in Java loops and the Java `if` statement may only have `boolean` type.

CAUTION

The words `true` and `false` are values of the `boolean` type, just as 1, 2, or 3 are values of an integer type. Even though they are not defined as keywords in the Java language grammar, they are nonetheless reserved, so you can't use them as variable or class names.

Floating-Point Types

Java supports float and double data types, just as C and C++ do. However, in those languages, the behavior of those data types is platform-dependent. In Java, all floating-point behavior—including the limits that float and double variables can take—is defined by the IEEE 754 standard for floating-point arithmetic.

NOTE Most modern C and C++ compilers also provide support that is consistent with IEEE 754. For most programmers, therefore, Java formalizes behavior that they are already familiar with.

Aggregate Data Types

Aggregate data types, including strings and arrays, are implemented somewhat differently in Java. Most notably, `String` is a native data type in Java, and the + operator can be used to concatenate strings. Also, arrays and strings both have known lengths that can be reliably depended on at runtime. As in C and C++, arrays must be statically sized. Dynamically sized aggregates in Java are supported by way of the `Vector` class. (See the section "Aggregates: Strings, Arrays, and Vectors" later in this chapter for more information.)

Type Conversion and Casting

C and C++ both support ad hoc type conversions all over the place—in expression evaluation, assignments, and function invocations, to name a few places. Java also supports ad hoc conversions, but only under very controlled circumstances. In particular, if a conversion is a narrowing conversion (one that could result in a loss of precision), then the conversion will only be allowed with an explicit cast. Consider the following example:

```
byte b=126;
int i=17;
float f=(float)3.50;
b = (byte) (b+i);   // cast to byte required
i = (int) f;          // cast to int required
f = i;               // no cast required...
// this is not a narrowing conversion
```

Objects and Classes

Java and C++ both support the object-oriented programming paradigm, and hence they both have support for objects and classes, which C does not. When you are comparing Java and C, all the syntax that supports object orientation—including support for objects and classes—for inheritance and for interfaces, will be new. If you are a C programmer unfamiliar with object-orientation, then it would be best for you to refer back to the material in Chapter 5, "Object-Oriented Programming," and Chapter 11, "Classes."

Even though both C++ and Java support object-orientation, and both include support for objects and classes, there are a number of subtle and important differences between the two languages in these areas. This section is a collection of the major differences.

Declaring Reference Types

In addition to the primitive data types (`char`, `int`, and so on) are objects, arrays, vectors, and strings. All these are manipulated by reference rather than by value and are referred to as reference types. Consider the following declaration:

```
GameTable chessBoard;
```

If GameTable is a class you have previously defined somewhere, then the preceding declaration would be syntactically correct in both C++ and Java. However, in C++, this would have created a new instance of the GameTable class. In Java, the preceding declaration is only a declaration of the variable chessBoard to be of reference type; it is a reference to a GameTable, but it doesn't yet refer to any particular instance of that class. In Java, you must also instantiate the object, using the new operator:

```
GameTable chessBoard;
chessBoard = new GameTable ();
```

NOTE In Java, as in C and C++, the declaration of a variable and its initialization can be combined into one statement:

```
GameTable chessBoard = new GameTable ();
```

The above line declares the variable chessBoard to be a reference to a GameTable, and also instantiates a new GameTable that chessBoard now refers to.

Manipulating References

When manipulating objects in Java, it is again important to remember that you are manipulating references, not instances. In the following code fragment, variables b1 and b2 are distinct variables, and therefore can hold distinct references; but following the assignment, they both refer to the same instance:

```
Box b1, b2;         // 2 references to type Box
b1=new Box(2,2);    // instantiate b1
b2=b1;              // b1 and b2 now both refer to the
                    // same instance
```

The object/reference relationship in Java is also significant when you are comparing references. Take a look at the following code fragment:

```
Box b1, b2;         // 2 references to type Box
b1=new Box(2,2);    // instantiate b1
b2=new Box(2,2);    // instantiate b2 with same values
if (b1==b2)         // This expression compares false
```

In the final line of the example, the references b1 and b2 are being compared. By default, this only compares true if the two references are actually referring to the same instance. Because b1 and b2 are referring to two different instances (albeit with the same values), the comparison has to yield false.

TIP All classes in Java inherit from the Object base class, which defines an isEquals method with the previously mentioned behavior. If you want comparisons such as the one you've just seen to behave differently, just override isEquals in your own class to produce true or false according to your own criteria.

Method Invocation Call-by-Value and Call-by-Reference

Like C and C++, the default behavior of method invocations in Java is call-by-value. Remember, though, that objects are always manipulated by reference. This means that when you call a method and attempt to pass an object as an argument, you are really passing a reference to that object; the "value" being passed is a reference to an object. In effect, by passing native types as arguments to a Java method, it is call-by-value; when passing reference types, it is call-by-reference.

If you need to call a method and pass a reference by value, you can achieve the same effect by taking a local copy of the object first, as in the following code:

```
Box b1 = new Box (2,2);
valueMethod ( new Box (b1) );
```

In this case, the reference being passed to `valueMethod` is a new instance that is being initialized with `b1`. Any changes made to the reference within the method will not affect `b1`.

Primitive Types and *java.lang* Wrapper Classes

In the `java.lang` package, several classes are defined that "wrap" a primitive data type in a reference object. For example, an `int` value can be wrapped in an `Integer` object. One of these wrapper classes exists for each of the primitive data types. There are a number of interesting ways in which these wrapper classes can be used to make your life easier.

Passing Primitive Types by Reference There is no explicit reference syntax in Java analogous to the `&` reference syntax in C++. For example, in C++, a method can be defined to take a reference to an argument being passed, rather than taking the argument's value. In Java, to pass a primitive data type by reference, you must first wrap the value in an object as follows:

```
int j = 17;
Integer arg = new Integer (j);
methodCalledByReference ( arg );
```

CAUTION

Note that the wrapper classes supplied in `java.lang` do not provide methods for setting or updating the values of primitive type that they contain, which limits their usefulness in situations such as that outlined in the preceding. If you find yourself trying this too often, you might be thinking C++ instead of thinking Java.

Adding Primitive Types to a Vector The Java `Vector` class allows you to create a dynamically sized aggregate of reference types. However, because the elements in the vector must be references, you can't add values of the primitive types to a vector. Instead, wrap the primitive value in a wrapper object and add that new object to the vector. Here's an example:

```
Vector sizes = new Vector ();
Integer small= new Integer (5);
sizes.addElement (small);
```

The `int` value `5` has been wrapped in the `small` object, which has then been added to the `sizes` vector.

NOTE Because Java hashtables also are designed to store object references, the preceding comments apply to hashtables as well as to vectors.

Converting Primitive Types to Strings The `java.lang` wrapper classes each define a method called `toString` that converts the primitive value to a Java `String`. This can be very useful when you need a `String` but only have a value of a primitive data type. In the following example, you need a `String` version of a floating-point value, so that you can pass it as an argument to the `drawString` method from within an Applet's `paint` method:

```
Float temp = new Float (this.interestRate);
g.drawString ( temp.toString(), 10, 10 );
```

As you can see, you first wrap the `interestRate` value in a `Float` object. Then you invoke the `Float` object's `toString` method to create a valid Java `String`, which you then pass to `drawString`.

The Object Life Cycle

Like any other data element or data structure, Java objects have a definite life cycle: They are created, they have a useful life, and then they are destroyed. This is also true of objects created as part of a C++ program. There are differences, however, in how the two languages manage the life cycle of an object.

When Objects Are Created In C++, an object is created in one of two ways. If an object is being stored in a variable, then the object is instantiated— created—when the variable comes into scope. It is destroyed when the object goes out of scope. If a C++ object is being manipulated via a pointer, however, it is only instantiated when the `new` operator is used.

Life in Java is a little simpler than this. There is only one way to create and use Java objects, and that is by reference. Hence, an object doesn't exist until it is created with the `new` operator:

```
Table r;            // Table object doesn't yet exist
r = new Table ();   // Only now does the Table object exist
```

This is very similar to the C++ syntax that would be used if the object were to be manipulated via a pointer:

```
Table *r;           // C++ code to create pointer
r = new Table ();   // C++ code to instantiate Table object
```

As in C++, it is only when the object is actually instantiated that a constructor method is invoked.

NOTE Both Java and C++ constructor methods can be overloaded. That is, there can be more than one of them as long as their signatures (the number and types of the arguments) are different.

When Objects Are Destroyed How a C++ object is destroyed depends on how it was created. If an object is being stored in a variable, then the object is destroyed when the variable goes out of scope. If a C++ object was created using the `new` operator, then it is only destroyed when the programmer explicitly requests it with the `delete` operator.

Once again, things in Java are a little different. An object is created when it is instantiated with the `new` operator. An object is destroyed, at least in principle, when there are no longer any references to it. Consider the following little code fragment:

```
Square s1 = new Square (5);
Square s2 = new Square (10);
s2=s1;
```

As soon as you perform the final assignment, both `s1` and `s2` refer to the same object. There are no longer any references to the `Square` object that was created as `Square(10)`. It is at that point that the object created as `Square(10)` is, in principle, destroyed.

Why do I keep saying "in principle?" Because Java uses a form of dynamic memory management known as garbage collection. This means that memory deallocation is done automatically by the Java garbage collector, rather than under the control of the programmer. Because the garbage collector usually runs in a separate thread, it would be more accurate to say that an object "is eligible for garbage collection" rather than to say that it is "destroyed." The distinction is really only academic, however; whether it is destroyed or just made ready for garbage collection, the reality is that the object can no longer be used in the program. For all practical purposes, that object has ceased to exist.

NOTE Although Java supports constructors, it doesn't support explicit destructors, as in C++. There is a `finalize` method, however, that you can override in your class definition, and that is invoked when the object is garbage collected. Because the timing of garbage collection is not predictable, however, the `finalize` method is not as commonly used as a destructor is in C++.

Java References Versus C++ Pointers

It has probably become clear to you in this section that much of the Java syntax for manipulating objects is very similar to that used in C++—right down to the use of the `new` operator to instantiate an object. But when using the `new` operator in C++, you are given an address of an object, which you can then assign to a pointer variable. In Java, the `new` operator returns an object reference to you that you can then assign to a reference variable.

Some people, especially those new to Java, feel that the use of references in Java is really the same as the use of pointers in C++—that it is the same construct with a different name. There is some truth to this, and if you are familiar with C++ syntax you will likely find the Java syntax quite easy to pick up. But there is an important difference. In Java, all the memory management is done for you automatically, and you can never manipulate a memory address directly. Whether the Java interpreter uses pointers underneath it all to implement references isn't really important. What's important is that Java programs will, in this regard, be more stable and reliable than their C and C++ counterparts.

NOTE C++ programmers are familiar with `this`, which is a pointer variable containing the address of the object for which a method was invoked. In Java, you have `this` as well, only now it is a reference instead of a pointer. Other than that, its meaning is the same.

Aggregates: Strings, Arrays, and Vectors

Like C and C++, Java provides a number of mechanisms for creating aggregates of values, whether those values be of primitive type or of a reference type. In this section, you look at the three most common aggregates in Java: strings, arrays, and vectors.

Strings

In Java, strings are handled much as they are in C++. The most significant exception is that after a `String` is declared, its contents cannot be changed. To actually modify a `String`, you must create a `StringBuffer` object that can be initialized with a `String` and then modified. You can then create a new `String` with the contents of the `StringBuffer`. The following code fragment illustrates such a process:

```
//create the initial String object
String badString = new String("This is a String");
// create the StringBuffer that we can modify
StringBuffer correction = new StringBuffer(badString);
// make the modification to the StringBuffer object
correction.insert(12,=i=);
// create a new String object with the corrected contents
String goodString = new String(correction);
```

NOTE Java `String`s, like many other Java objects, have known and dependable sizes. For a `String` object, the `length` method returns the length of the `String` as an `int`. It is not possible for `String`s to "overflow" as it is in C and C++.

Arrays

Java arrays are very similar to C and C++ arrays. They are homogenous aggregates (that is, each element is of the same data type), and they have a fixed size. However, there are also some subtle differences.

Arrays of Primitive Types In Java, arrays are instances of a hidden array class—hidden in the sense that there is no `Array` keyword to denote the class name. Nonetheless, arrays must be instantiated just as other objects must. The following example declares `myArray` to be an array of `int`s:

```
int[] myArray;
```

NOTE In Java, the empty square brackets that indicate `myArray` are an array reference that can be placed just after the data type (as in the preceding), or can be placed after the variable name:

```
int myArray[];
```

Placing them immediately after the type name is the preferred Java style.

At this point, however, `myArray` is a reference variable that doesn't refer to anything. You must still instantiate the array object:

```
myArray = new int[10];
```

The size of a Java array is fixed at compile time, just as it is in C and C++. If you need to create a dynamically sized array, use a vector instead.

As in C++, the two steps outlined above can be combined onto one statement, as follows:

```
int[] myArray = new int[10];
```

C and C++ programmers are used to being able to initialize arrays at the time they are declared, using syntax similar to the following:

```
// declaring and initializing a C array
int powers[3] = {3,9,27};
```

In such situations, the size of the array can be omitted; the compiler determines the size of the array based on the number of initial values supplied.

The same syntax can be used in Java. The following example accomplishes three distinct tasks: it declares `powers` to be an array of `int`s, instantiates the array, and initializes each element in the array. The size of the array is taken from the number of initializers:

```
int[] powers = {3,9,27};
```

The empty square brackets are also used to denote an array when the array is being passed to a method as an argument. The following example shows an array of `int`s and an array of `char`s being accepted as arguments in a method definition:

```
public syntaxExample(int[]  thisInt,
char[] thisChar)
{
// method body goes here
}
```

Arrays of References As in C and C++, it is also possible to have Java arrays of non-primitive types. In Java, such arrays are of reference types; that is, such an array will be an array of references. The basic syntax still holds. The following example creates an array of 31 `Month` references:

```
Month[] year = new Month[12];
```

After the preceding line has been executed, an array of 12 `Month` references will have been instantiated, and `year` will be a reference variable that refers to that array. But none of the 12 elements in the array yet refer to anything. You have instantiated the array, but you have not yet instantiated any of the 12 `Months`. If the `Month` class has a constructor that takes a `String` as an argument, you might go ahead and instantiate the elements of the array as follows:

```
year[0] = new Month ("January");
year[1] = new Month ("February");
year[2] = new Month ("March");
// ... and so on
```

NOTE Java arrays, like their C and C++ counterparts, use only zero-origin subscripting. Thus, an array of 12 elements has valid subscripts from 0 to 11 inclusive.

Java arrays, like Java `Strings`, have fixed and dependable sizes. Each array object has a `length` variable associated with it that contains the correct length of the array. In the preceding example, `year.length` would be 12.

Vectors

In C and C++, dynamic memory allocation under the control of the programmer is a time-honored tradition—unfortunately a tradition that has produced some pretty unstable code over the years. In Java, such dynamic memory allocation is not directly possible. However, there are many situations in which a data structure of dynamic size is critical to the solution of the problem. In such situations, Java programmers can turn to the `Vector` class.

Java `Vectors` are like dynamically sized arrays. They consist of a dynamic number of references to objects. References can be added to and removed from the `Vector` at will, using methods such as `addElement` and `removeElement`. Because all Java classes inherit from the `Object` class, it follows that the elements in a Java `Vector` can be references to any `Java` class.

NOTE When a reference is retrieved from a `Vector`, it is of type `Object`. It must therefore be cast to be of the appropriate reference type before it can be used reliably.

Each element in a `Vector` is numbered, with element numbers beginning at 0. This is consistent with the subscripting of Java arrays and with the use of arrays in C and C++. Java `Vectors`, like Java arrays and strings, have dependable sizes. The `size` method in the `Vector` class returns the number of elements currently stored in the `Vector`.

The following code fragment shows a `Vector` of `Months`, very similar to the array of `Months` we had a few pages ago:

```
MonthVector = new Vector();
MonthVector.addElement (new Month ("January");
MonthVector.addElement (new Month ("February");
MonthVector.addElement (new Month ("March");
// and so on...
```

For more information on `Vectors`, take a look at Chapter 33, which covers the `java.util` package.

▶ **See** "`java.util`," **p. 35**

Class Hierarchies and Inheritance

Most Java programs, like most C++ programs, make extensive use of inheritance, in which one class is defined in terms of another. The new class, also called the derived class or the subclass, is said to inherit all the characteristics of the original class—also called the base class or the superclass. When a base class itself inherits characteristics from another class, the result is said to be a class hierarchy. (For more on inheritance, see Chapter 5 on object-oriented programming.)

NOTE In a class hierarchy, one class may be both a subclass of some class and a superclass of another. This should not strike you as being strange. In real life, someone's parent is also someone else's child.

In Java, all classes are subclasses of the `Object` base class and inherit all its characteristics.

The Syntax of Inheritance

The syntax for creating derived classes in Java is different from C++. When deriving a subclass from a superclass, Java uses the `extends` keyword in the new class's definition. The following example contrasts the syntax for both C++ and Java. In both cases, you are creating a class called `CaptionedRectangle`, which inherits from the `Rectangle` base class.

First, the C++ version:

```
class CaptionedRectangle : public Rectangle
{
// definition of class here
}
```

Now here's the Java equivalent:

```
class CaptionedRectangle extends Rectangle
{
// definition of class here
}
```

The *instanceof* Operator

The `instanceof` operator is a real bit of convenience. This operator takes two operands: a reference on the left and the name of a class on the right. The operator returns `true` if the object referred to by the reference is an instance of the class on the right or of any of its subclasses. In the following example, you only want to invoke the `checkInsurance` method if `obj` refers to an object of the `Vehicle` class:

```
void quarterlyUpdates (Object obj)
{
if ( obj instanceof Vehicle )
{
obj.checkInsurance ();
}
}
```

NOTE Because all classes are derived from `Object`, the expression `(obj instanceof Object)` will always return `true`.

Inheritance and Polymorphism

In Java, a variable declared to be of some class type can actually be used to refer to any object of that class or of any of its subclasses. Given the earlier classes `Rectangle` and `CaptionedRectangle`, you could have the following:

```
void updateScreen ( Rectangle r )
{
r.display ();
}
```

If `r` happens to refer to a `Rectangle` object, then the `display` method from the `Rectangle` class is invoked (if there is one). If `r` refers to a `CaptionedRectangle`, then the `display` method of the `CaptionedRectangle` class is invoked. This is the essence of polymorphism, a concept in object-oriented programming in which a single interface (in this case, the `display` method) can actually have multiple implementations.

NOTE C++ programmers are familiar with this behavior. However, for a C++ class hierarchy to exhibit this behavior, the `display` method in the base class must be declared to be `virtual`. Java methods are all "virtual" in the C++ sense.

Interfaces Versus Multiple Inheritance

In C++, one class may inherit the characteristics of multiple base classes—a concept known as multiple inheritance. A Java class, by contrast, may only inherit the characteristics of one base class. A Java class, however, may be said to `implement` a Java interface. For example, you might have the following:

```
class CaptionedRectangle
extends Rectangle
implements Displayable
{
// class definition goes here
}
```

A Java interface is similar to a class, but its data items are all static and final, and its methods are all abstract. Within the definition of the new class, each of the methods in the interface must be given actual definitions. The interface is really a form of guarantee: If a class is defined to implement an interface, it is a guarantee to the user of the class that each of the methods in the interface will be fully defined in the class. Interfaces are covered in depth in Chapter 12, "Interfaces."

NOTE The multiple inheritance mechanism in C++ has a number of subtle problem areas. As a result, the most reliable and common use of multiple inheritance in C++ programs is when there is one primary chain of inheritance, and any other classes used as base classes are collections of utility methods and constant values. This behavior is formalized in the Java interface construct.

The *super* Reference

Just as you have a `this` reference, which refers to the object for which a method has been invoked, you also have a `super` reference, which refers to the `this` object's parent class. It can be used in situations when a method in the derived class needs to explicitly invoke a method from the superclass. Consider the following example of a `display` method defined within the `captionedRectangle` class:

```
void display ()
{
System.out.println (this.caption);
super.display ();
}
```

The `super` reference can also be used on the first line of a base class constructor method to explicitly invoke a superclass constructor. Once again, it is instructive to compare the C++ and Java equivalents here. The following is one possibility in C++ of a `CaptionedRectangle` constructor that takes five arguments: four that define the `Rectangle`, and one that defines the caption of the `CaptionedRectangle`:

```
// C++ constructor
CaptionedRectangle::CaptionedRectangle
 ( int x, int y, int width, int height, String caption ):
Rectangle ( x,y,width,height )
{
// body of CaptionedRectangle constructor here
}
```

The Java equivalent might be the following:

```
// Java constructor
CaptionedRectangle
 ( int x, int y, int width, int height, String caption )
{
super ( x,y,width,height );
// balance of CaptionedRectangle constructor here
}
```

No Scope Resolution Operator

Many C++ programmers are alarmed to find that there is no scope resolution operator (the double colon ::) in Java. In fact, there is no way in Java to elect to invoke a method from a specific class in a hierarchy.

TIP If the method you want to invoke is in the superclass, then the method can be invoked using the `super` reference.

NOTE Many new Java programmers attempt to invoke a method from elsewhere in the hierarchy using multiple `super`s, something like `super.super.display()`. This is an interesting idea, but it's not Java!

Statements

By and large, Java supports the same control statements as C++, which in turn are pretty much the same as in the original C language. The areas of difference are highlighted in this section.

See "Control Flow," **p. 143**

Loops

The loop statements in Java are virtually identical to their counterparts in C++. However, in Java, it is possible to add a label to a loop. The label can then be used as an argument on a `break` or `continue` statement. Here is an example:

```
start:
for(int j=0;j<20;j++)
for(int k=0;k<20;k++)
for(int l=0;l<20;l++)
if ((j+k+l)==20) break start;
```

When the `break` statement is encountered in the `if` statement, the outermost loop is broken. This is one effect that was very difficult to achieve in C or C++ without the use of `goto`.

NOTE Because this was the only use of a `goto` that was generally accepted in practice, and because the `goto` is no longer required to achieve this effect, the `goto` statement has been eliminated from the Java syntax.

You might notice in the preceding example that the control variables (j, k, and l) are defined in the `for` loop control statement. This is very convenient in those common situations where the control variable is only relevant within the loop and has no real meaning outside of the loop. This syntax is also legal in C++, but there is a subtle difference. In C++, the scope of the control variable begins with the `for` loop control statement but then continues to the end of the block. In Java, the scope of the control variable is only the body of the loop. The variable is undefined elsewhere in the block.

Conditionals

The explicit condition in the Java `if` statement and the implicit conditions in the various Java loops all require an expression that produces a Boolean value. This is not true in C or C++, where the expression can produce any value at all; a non-zero value is taken to be true, and a zero value is taken to be false. Thus, a whole category of C and C++ errors is eliminated:

```
// The world's most common C error
// luckily enough, this will no longer compile in Java!
if ( x = 5 )
{
}
```

Synchronized Statements

With the addition of support for multithreading to the list of Java features comes a few problem areas. Specifically, you may have sections of code in which multiple threads might modify objects simultaneously, possibly corrupting the object. The `synchronized` statement deals with these critical sections by blocking the execution of code until exclusive access to the object can be acquired.

The syntax for the `synchronized` statement is

```
synchronized (expression) statement
```

where the `expression` yields a reference to the object to be protected, and `statement` is a block of code to be executed after primary control of the object is acquired.

```
public swapFirstValues(int[] k)
{
synchronized(k)
{
int temp;
temp=k[0];
k[0]=k[1];
k[1]=temp;
}
}
```

CAUTION

Do not use the `synchronized` statement if the object is never accessed by more than one thread, as it introduces needless processing overhead at runtime.

For more information on threads, refer back to the material in Chapter 13, "Threads."

Operators and Expressions

The list of operators Java supports is almost identical to that of C++, as is the order of precedence and associativity of those operators (see Chapter 9). Here are the major differences:

- The `instanceof` operator has been added, as you've already seen.

▶ **See** "The `instanceof` Operator," earlier in this chapter, **p. 1177**

- The + operator can now be used with two `String` objects to concatenate them.

- The right shift operator (>>) now explicitly sign-extends the value, while the new logical right shift operator (>>>) populates vacant spaces with zero-bits.
- As you've seen, the relational and logical operators all produce Boolean results, and the logical operators only take Boolean operands.

▶ **See** "The `boolean` Data Type," **p. 1168**

- The scope resolution operator has been removed.

▶ **See** "No Scope Resolution Operator," **p. 1179**

- The comma operator has been removed.

NOTE Although the comma has been removed, it can still be used within a `for` loop control statement to separate multiple control expressions, as in the following:

```
for (i=5,j=0; i>j; i--,j++) n
```

Unlike in C++, Java operators cannot be overloaded. This means that the meaning of an operator is fixed by the grammar of the language. Any special behavior that you want to implement must be done by using an explicit method invocation.

Java expressions are evaluated in a much more predictable fashion than in C or C++. In any expression that involves one operator and two operands, the left operand is always evaluated first and the right operand is evaluated second. In method invocations, the argument list is evaluated strictly left-to-right.

Name Spaces

Name spaces essentially define the scope of a name or symbol—that portion of a program or collection of classes in which the name or symbol has meaning. More importantly, distinct name spaces protect variable and method names from conflicts—so-called name collisions.

The first and simplest difference between Java and C or C++ is that, in Java programs there are no global variables or functions of any kind. This helps to keep name-space violations and conflicts to a minimum.

Java also incorporates the concept of packages to help you manage your name spaces. A package is a collection of classes. Each package has its own name space. In practice, this means that the name of a class is combined with its associated package to create a globally unique class name. Because method and variable names are managed locally within a class, the possibility of name collisions is essentially eliminated.

▶ **See** "Packages," **p. 185**

NOTE Because the classes and methods of the Java API all belong to predefined packages, it is not possible for someone to create classes or methods that either deliberately or inadvertently conflict with system-supplied classes or methods. This is for system security and for protecting the user from programmer error.

Java was designed from the ground up to be Internet-enabled. Packages, and the name space protection they provide, were necessary to provide robustness in the distributed Internet environment. But although packages may have been necessary because of the Internet, they have the added benefit of eliminating the name collisions that are possible with C and C++. ●

PART VIII

Debugging Java

CHAPTER 51

Debugging Java Code

In this chapter

The Architecture of the *sun.tools.debug* Package

One of the hurdles for anyone developing in a new language and execution environment such as Java is learning the appropriate techniques and tools that are available for finding problems in the applications being written (such as bugs). Besides providing the standard constructs for creating well-designed, object-oriented applications (inheritance, encapsulation, and polymorphism), Java includes new features such as exceptions and multithreading. These features add a new level of complexity to the debugging process.

To get Java to market as quickly as possible, Sun initially chose not to create a development environment to support the creation of Java applications and applets. Instead, Sun provided features and facilities for developers like us to use to create these advanced tools. One of these facilities is the `sun.tools.debug` package, called the Java Debugger (JDB) API. The API consists of a set of classes that allow the creation of custom debugging aids that may interact directly with an application/applet running within a local or remote instance of the JVM.

The package contains one public interface and 20 public classes that work together to allow you to implement a debugger. The debugging interface is modeled after the client/server architecture. The JVM is on the server that hosts the target application, and your debugger is a client that acts as the interface to control the target application. To understand the model, each class of the JDB API is discussed within the following five categories:

- Client/server debugger management
- Stack management
- Special types
- Thread management
- Native types

The way that your debugger interacts with the running application is through a series of remote classes that act as proxies to the objects in your application. A proxy acts as an intermediary between your debugger and the host JVM. You might think of a proxy as a celebrity with an agent who acts as the public point of contact. You never communicate directly with the celebrity, just with the agent. The agent's sole responsibility is to send messages to the celebrity and relay responses back to the interested party. This is exactly what classes implemented in the `sun.tools.debug` package do. The proxy model keeps the classes small and gives a clean interface for interacting with the host JVM.

NOTE Many methods in the JDB API throw the generic `Exception` exception. This should not be confused with the exceptions that you may or may not want to catch. The exceptions thrown by the API typically represent hard-error situations that occur within the JVM as it is servicing a debugger client request.

Before I get into detail on the classes in the `sun.tools.debug` package, it might be helpful to see how these classes fit together hierarchically. Figure 51.1 shows the hierarchy (in loose OMT format) for the JDB API classes.

Client/Server Debugger Management

One of the most interesting aspects of the debugging facilities that are built into the JVM is their client/server nature. By using the `RemoteDebugger` class in conjunction with your implementation of the `DebuggerCallback` interface, you can literally control all aspects of the JVM as it runs an application/applet on your behalf. The debugger client communicates with the JVM via a private TCP/IP connection using a proprietary and undocumented protocol (for security reasons). This private connection is why the source code for the Debugger API is not available in the JDK.

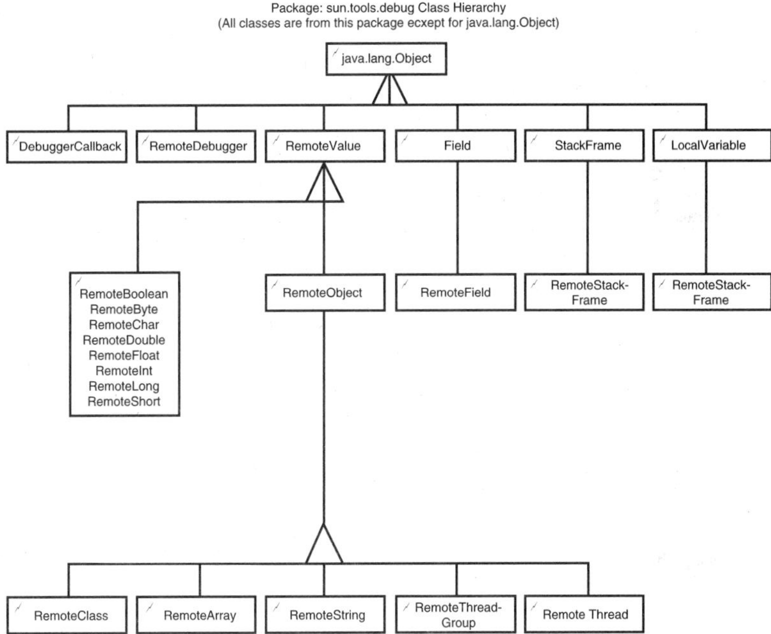

FIG. 51.1
Class hierarchy for the JDB API.

NOTE Two more classes can be placed in this category: `RemoteClass` and `RemoteThread`. `RemoteClass` supports breakpoint and exception management, as well as descriptive information on the class structure. `RemoteThread` supports the control of running threads by manipulating the execution state. As they are subclasses of `RemoteObject`, you will find them described in detail in the section "Special Types" later in this chapter.

***DebuggerCallback* Interface** The `DebuggerCallback` interface is used to provide a mechanism for the JVM's debugger agent to notify your debugger client when something of note has happened within the target application. These "events" are handled via `callback` methods that support breakpoints, exceptions, termination, thread death, and console output. The public API for the `DebuggerCallback` interface is shown in Listing 51.1.

Listing 51.1 Public API for the *DebuggerCallback* Interface

```
public interface DebuggerCallback {
    public abstract void printToConsole( String text ) throws Exception;
    public abstract void breakpointEvent( RemoteThread t ) throws Exception;
    public abstract void exceptionEvent( RemoteThread t,
 String errorText) throws Exception;
    public abstract void threadDeathEvent( RemoteThread t ) throws Exception;
   public abstract void quitEvent() throws Exception;
}
```

Table 51.1 lists each of the public member methods and what they do.

Table 51.1 The *DebuggerCallback* Interface Public Member Methods

Name	Description
`printToConsole`	Called whenever your target applet sends output to `System.out` or `System.err` and when the debugger agent in the host VM has messages (especially if you create your `RemoteDebugger` with the `verbose` flag set to true).
`breakpointEvent`	Called when a breakpoint has been reached in the target application. `t` is the thread that was running when the breakpoint was reached.
`exceptionEvent`	Happens when an exception is thrown in the target application. `t` is the thread that was running when the exception occurred, and `errorText` contains the message sent with the exception.
`threadDeathEvent`	Signals that thread `t` has stopped in the target application.
`quitEvent`	Informs you that the target application has ended. This can be a result of calling `System.exit()` or returning from the main thread of the application.

RemoteDebugger If the `DebuggerCallback` interface is the eyes and ears of your debugger, then the `RemoteDebugger` class is the mouth and hands. The `RemoteDebugger` class is your "proxy" to the control of the JVM instance that is hosting the target application/applet being debugged.

To use the `RemoteDebugger` class, you must first create a class that implements the `DebuggerCallback` interface. This class becomes an argument to the constructor of a `RemoteDebugger` instance. (Typically, your debugger's main class would fulfill this requirement.) There are two ways to create a `RemoteDebugger` instance:

- Connect to a remote instance of the JVM
- Have an instance of the `java` command started for you

Both run as separate processes and use TCP/IP internally to "talk" to your debugger. After you have created an instance of `RemoteDebugger`, you will be in direct control of the target application that you will be debugging. You can then begin to make calls against your `RemoteDebugger` instance to manipulate your debugging session.

Figure 51.2 shows that the JVM, `RemoteDebugger`, and `DebuggerCallback` are related at execution time.

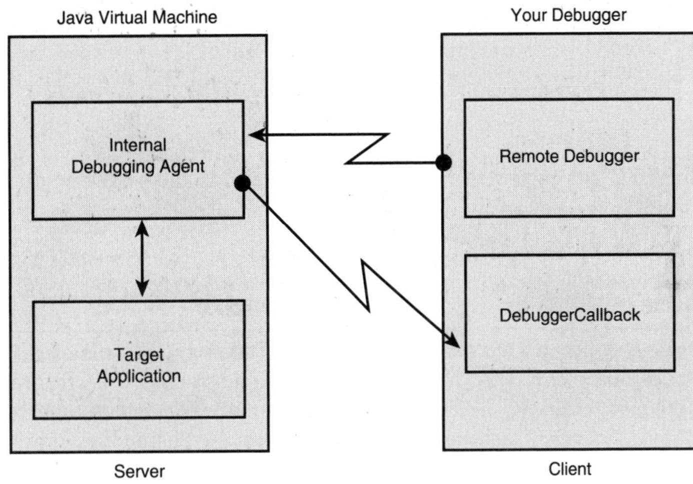

FIG. 51.2 Relationship between the JVM, `RemoteDebugger`, and `DebuggerCallback`.

The public API for the `RemoteDebugger` class is shown in Listing 51.2.

Listing 51.2 Public API for the *RemoteDebugger* Class

```
public class RemoteDebugger {
    public RemoteDebugger( String host,
        String password,
        DebuggerCallback client,
        boolean verbose ) throws Exception;

   public RemoteDebugger( String javaArgs,
        DebuggerCallback client,
        boolean verbose ) throws Exception;

    public void addSystemThread()
    public void addSystemThread(thread t);
    public void close();
    public RemoteObject get( Integer id );
    public RemoteClass[] listClasses() throws Exception;
    public RemoteClass findClass( String name ) throws Exception;
    public RemoteThreadGroup[] listThreadGroups( RemoteThreadGroup tg )   throws
➥Exception;
    public void gc( RemoteObject save_list[] ) throws Exception;
    public void trace( boolean traceOn ) throws Exception;
```

continues

Listing 51.2 Continued

```
    public void itrace( boolean traceOn ) throws Exception;
    public int totalMemory() throws Exception;
    public int freeMemory() throws Exception;
    public RemoteThreadGroup run( int argc,
        String argv[]) throws Exception;

    public String[] listBreakpoints() throws Exception;
    public String[] getExceptionCatchList() throws Exception;
    public String getSourcePath() throws Exception;
    public void setSourcePath( String pathList ) throws Exception;

}
```

Table 51.2 lists each of the public member methods and what they do.

Table 51.2 The *RemoteDebugger* Class Public Member Methods

Name	Description
`RemoteDebugger (String host, String password, DebuggerCallback, client boolean verbose)`	The first constructor is used to connect to an existing remote JVM. The `host` argument is the DNS name of the target machine running the JVM. `password` is part of the security mechanism used to debug remote applications securely. `client` is your object that implements the `DebuggerCallback` interface described previously. And, when set to true, `verbose` causes informational messages to be sent to `client.printToConsole()` from the host's JVM.
`RemoteDebugger (String javaArgs, Debugger Callback client, boolean verbose)`	The second constructor is very similar to the first, except that it is used to debug Java applications locally. This is probably fine for most GUI applications, but a console application is difficult to debug in this way because the target's output becomes interspersed with the debugger's own informational output. The `javaArgs` argument should contain valid optional arguments to the `java` command (excluding the target class). The `client` and `verbose` arguments work as mentioned previously.
`addSystemThread()`	Add the calling thread to the list of threads that are not suspended by the debugger. These threads are usually Threads used by the debugger itself.

Name	Description
`addSystemThread (Thread t)`	Add the specific thread `t` to the list of threads that the debugger will not suspend.
`close()`	Closes down the remote target application/applet and the host JVM.
`get(Integer id)`	Returns a proxy for the object identified by `id`. The returned `RemoteObject` instance may be cast to its appropriate type. Use `ClassName` or `instanceof` to test its type.
`ListClasses()`	Returns an array of `RemoteClass` instances that are resident in the host JVM.
`FindClasses(String name)`	Searches the host JVM for a class called `name`. If the class is not in the VM's class cache, then it is searched for on the target machine. If it is not found, a `null` is returned. Partial names may be passed in, but there may be ambiguities between user and system classes with the same name.
`ListThreadGroups (RemoteThreadGroup tg)`	Returns an array of `RemoteThreadGroup` instances for the thread groups that are contained in `tg`. If `tg` is null, then all thread groups are returned.
`gc(RemoteObject save_list[])`	Causes the garbage collector to be run on the host's JVM in order to free all objects that were requested by this debugger instance. Any objects that were sent to the `RemoteDebugger` are not garbage collected until this call is made, or the debugger exits. `save_list` is used to prevent any specific objects that are still being examined by this debugger instance from being collected.
`trace(boolean traceOn)`	Toggles the state of the method `trace` flag in the remote JVM. This command is only valid if you created your `RemoteDebugger` instance using the constructor that takes `javaArgs` as the first argument, or if the remote debugging host is one of the _g variants.
`itrace(boolean traceOn)`	Toggles the state of the instruction `trace` flag in the remote JVM. This command is only valid if you created your `RemoteDebugger` instance using the constructor that takes `javaArgs` as the first argument, or if the remote debugging host is one of the _g variants.

continues

Table 51.2 Continued

Name	Description
`TotalMemory()`	Returns the total amount of memory available for use by the host JVM.
`FreeMemory()`	Returns the amount of memory currently available for use by the host JVM.
`run(int argc,String argv[])`	Causes the host JVM to load in and run a Java class. `argv` is an array of Strings that represents the command line to execute. The class name must be the first array element. `argc` is the number of elements that are valid. The `RemoteThreadGroup` instance that the class is running in is returned on success, otherwise `null` is returned.
`ListBreakpoints()`	Returns the list of breakpoints that are currently active in the host JVM. The format of the breakpoint list is either `class.method_name` or `class:line_number`.
`GetExceptionCatchList()`	Returns an array of names of the exceptions that the host JVM will send to the debugger as if they were breakpoints.
`GetSourcePath()`	Returns the path string that the host JVM uses when searching for the source files associated with a given class. The format is system-dependent.
`setSourcePath(String pathList)`	Sets the path string that the host JVM uses when searching for the source files associated with a given class.

NOTE When you start up `java` or `appletviewer` with the `-debug` flag, a special password is displayed. This value must be used for the `password` argument.

NOTE Remember, the output of the method `trace` and the instruction `trace` is displayed on the console of the host VM.

Special Types

The classes in this category represent proxies that give you access to runtime instance data within the host JVM containing your target. These classes are considered special because they are used to represent information on data and control elements other than native types. These proxies allow you to inspect and interact with objects and classes that are loaded in the host JVM. For example, `RemoteObject` and its subclasses represent objects that your target applet has instantiated.

RemoteValue `RemoteValue` is an abstract class that sits at the root of the tree of classes and acts as a proxy to the remote JVM. This class essentially contains an interface implemented by the classes that follow the interface down the tree. Because the class contains abstract methods, you never explicitly instantiate it; rather, you can assume that any of the subclasses consistently and safely implement the methods of `RemoteValue`.

The public API for the `RemoteValue` class is shown in Listing 51.3.

Listing 51.3 Public API for the *RemoteValue* Class

```
public class RemoteValue
      implements sun.tools.java.AgentConstants {  // An undocumented
                                                 // interface containing static
                                                 // constants used internally
                                                 // by RemoteValue
      public String description();
      public static int fromHex( String hexStr );
      public final int getType();
      public final boolean isObject();
      public final boolean isString();
      public static String toHex( int n );
      public abstract String typeName() throws Exception;
}
```

Table 51.3 lists each of the public member methods and what they do.

Table 51.3 The *RemoteValue* Class Public Member Methods

Name	Description
`description()`	Returns a literal description for this instance of the `RemoteValue`.
`fromHex(String hexStr)`	Converts the number in `hexStr` from its hexadecimal representation to an integer value.
`getType()`	Returns the internal numeric identifier for this `RemoteValue`'s type. This value is primarily used internally by the proxy.
`isString()`	Returns `true` if the `RemoteValue` is a string.
`isObject()`	Returns `true` if the `RemoteValue` instance is an object type versus a native language type (for example, `boolean`).
`toHex(int n)`	Converts the integer value to its hexadecimal representation in String form.
`typeName()`	Returns the literal type name associated with this instance of `RemoteValue`.

NOTE See ShowTypeCodes.java on the CD-ROM for a very simple utility that displays these values.

RemoteField The RemoteField proxy class is similar to the RemoteValue class, except that it pertains to fields of a RemoteClass or RemoteObject instance. This class provides detailed descriptive information about a field in an object instance or class definition. A field may be any of the following: an instance variable, a static (class) variable, an instance method, or a static (class) method. The public API for the RemoteField class is shown in Listing 51.4.

Listing 51.4 Public API for the *RemoteField* Class

```
public class RemoteField
       extends sun.tools.java.Field    // An undocumented class containing the
                                       // instance variables that hold the
                                       // representative values of the
                                       // RemoteField
implements sun.tools.java.AgentConstants {     // An undocumented interface
                                               // containing static
                                               // constants used internally by
                                               // RemoteField
       public String getModifiers();
       public String getName();
       public String getType();
       public boolean isStatic();
       public String toString();
       public String getTypedName()
}:
```

Table 51.4 lists each of the public member methods and what they do.

Table 51.4 The *RemoteField* Class Public Member Methods

Name	Description
getModifiers()	Returns the access modifiers for this RemoteField in literal form (for example, public or private).
getName()	The literal field name.
getType()	The type of this field as a String (such as int, boolean, or java.lang.String).
isStatic()	Returns true if the field is designated as static (see getModifiers(), discussed previously).
toString()	Returns the value of this field in String form, as opposed to its native type.
getTypedName()	Returns a string that describes the field and its type name.

RemoteObject `RemoteObject` is a proxy that allows you to interface with an instance of a class in the host JVM. It is used to access detailed information about the object instance in question, including its class, field information, and field values. The `RemoteObject` is what you use to enumerate through an object instance's data.

CAUTION

You should be aware that, as you request `RemoteObject` (or any subclass) instances from the host JVM, the host JVM will keep these instances in a nongarbage collected area of memory. Your debugger should either (periodically or on command) call the `RemoteDebugger.gc()` method to release any `RemoteObject` instances in which you are no longer interested.

The public API for the `RemoteObject` class is shown in Listing 51.5.

Listing 51.5 Public API for the *RemoteObject* Class

```
public class RemoteObject
    extends RemoteValue {

    public String description();
    public final RemoteClass getClazz();
    protected void finalize() throws Exception;
    public RemoteField getField( int slotNum ) throws Exception;
    public RemoteField getField( String name ) throws Exception;
    public RemoteValue getFieldValue( int slotNum ) throws Exception;
    public RemoteValue getFieldValue( String name ) throws Exception;
    public RemoteField[] getFields() throws Exception;
    public final int getId();
    public String toString();
    public String typeName() throws Exception;
}:
```

Table 51.5 lists each of the public member methods and what they do.

Table 51.5 The *RemoteObject* Class Public Member Methods

Name	Description
`description`	Overrides `RemoteValue.description()`.
`getClazz()`	Returns an instance of `RemoteClass` that corresponds to this object instance.
`getField()`	This overloaded method returns an instance of `RemoteField` that is based on either a slot number representing the physical position of this field within the object or the literal name of the field. If the field does not exist (`slotNum` or `name` is invalid), then `Exception` is thrown. If `name` is not found, the `RemoteField` instance is returned as a null.

continues

Table 51.5 Continued

Name	Description
`getFieldValue()`	This overloaded method returns the value of this field as an instance of `RemoteValue`. The search is based on either a slot number representing the physical position of this field within the object or the literal name of the field. If the field does not exist (`slotNum` or `name` is invalid), then `Exception` is thrown. If `name` is not found, the `RemoteValue` instance is returned as a null.
`getFields()`	Returns a list of `RemoteField` instances representing all of the non-static instance variables defined in this object's class. An exception is thrown if host JVM encounters any problems processing the request.
`getId()`	Returns the instance ID that is used uniquely to identify this object in the host JVM.
`toString()`	Returns a representation of the object in String form. This is completely dependent on the type of object instance being used.
`typeName()`	Overrides `RemoteValue.typeName()`.
`finalize`	Contains code that needs to be executed when this object is collected by the garbage collector.

RemoteClass `RemoteClass` represents one of the larger APIs in the `sun.tools.debug` package and provides details on every aspect of a class definition, including its superclass, fields (static and instance), the interfaces implemented, and methods. As it is a descendent of `RemoteObject`, remember to `gc()` the instance at some point when your debugger is finished with it. You can retrieve instances of `RemoteClass` from `RemoteDebugger`, `RemoteObject`, and `RemoteStackFrame` instances.

The public API for the `RemoteClass` class is shown in Listing 51.6.

Listing 51.6 Public API for the *RemoteClass* Class

```
public class RemoteClass extends RemoteObject {

    // Descriptive methods:
    public String description();
    public RemoteObject getClassLoader() throws Exception;
    public RemoteField getField( int slotNum ) throws Exception;
    public RemoteField getField( String name ) throws Exception;
    public RemoteValue getFieldValue( int slotNum ) throws Exception;
    public RemoteValue getFieldValue( String name ) throws Exception;
    public RemoteField[] getFields() throws Exception;
    public RemoteField getInstanceField( int slotNum ) throws Exception;
    public RemoteField[] getInstanceFields() throws Exception;
    public RemoteClass[] getInterfaces() throws Exception;
```

```
    public RemoteField getMethod( String name ) throws Exception;
    public String[] getMethodNames() throws Exception;
    public RemoteField[] getMethods() throws Exception;
    public String getName() throws Exception;
    public RemoteField[] getStaticFields() throws Exception;
    public RemoteClass getSuperclass() throws Exception;
    public String getSourceFileName();
    public boolean isInterface() throws Exception;
    public String toString();
    public String typeName() throws Exception;

    // Debugging management methods:
    public InputStream getSourceFile() throws Exception;
    public void catchExceptions() throws Exception;
    public void ignoreExceptions() throws Exception;
    public String setBreakpointLine( int lineNo ) throws Exception;
    public String setBreakpointMethod( RemoteField method ) throws Exception;
    public String clearBreakpoint( int pcLocation ) throws Exception;
    public String clearBreakpointLine( int lineNo ) throws Exception;
    public String clearBreakpointMethod( RemoteField method ) throws Exception;
    public int[] getLineNumbers() throws Exception
    public int getMethodLineNumber(int index) throws IIndexOutOfBoundsException,
 NoSuchLineNumberException, Exception
    public int getMethodLineNumber(String name) throws NoSuchMethodException,
 NoSuchLineNumberException, Exception
}
```

Tables 51.6 and 51.7 list each of the public member methods and what they do.

Table 51.6 The *RemoteClass* Class Descriptive Public Member Methods

Name	Description
`description`	Overrides `RemoteObject.description()`.
`getClassLoader()`	Returns a `RemoteObject` instance that represents the class loader for this class.
`getField()`	This overloaded method returns an instance of `RemoteField` for a static member based on either a slot number that represents the physical position of this field within the object, or based on the literal name of the field. If the field does not exist (`slotNum` or `name` is invalid), then `Exception` is thrown. If `name` is not found, the `RemoteField` instance is returned as a null.
`getFieldValue()`	This overloaded method returns the value of a static field as an instance of `RemoteValue`. The search is based on either a slot number that represents the physical position of this field within the object, or the literal name of the field. If the field does not exist (`slotNum` or `name` is invalid), then `Exception` is thrown. If `name` is not found, the `RemoteValue` instance is returned as a null.

continues

Table 51.6 Continued

Name	Description
`getFields()`	Overrides `RemoteObject.getFields()` but returns an array of `RemoteField` instances that represent all of the static fields available in this class.
`getInstanceField()`	Returns an `instance` field description as an instance of `RemoteField`. The search is based on a slot number representing the physical position of this field within the object. If the field does not exist (`slotNum` invalid), then `Exception` is thrown. Note that there is no instance data in the field when called in this context.
`getInstanceFields()`	Returns an array of `RemoteField` instances representing all of the instance fields available in this class. Note that there is no instance data in the field when called in this context.
`getInterfaces()`	Returns an array of `RemoteClass` instances representing each of the interfaces implemented by this class.
`getMethod()`	Uses `name` to look up and return, an instance of `RemoteField` that describes the signature for the specified method.
`getMethodNames()`	Returns a `String` array containing the names of all methods implemented in this class.
`getMethods()`	Returns an array of `RemoteField` instances representing all methods implemented in this class.
`getName()`	Returns a String containing the name of this class.
`getSourceFileName()`	Returns the filename that contained the Java source statements used to compile this class. This is just a base name and extension (format is OS dependent) without any path information (for example, `MyClass.java`).
`getStaticFields()`	Returns an array of `RemoteField` instances representing all of the static fields available in this class.
`getSuperclass()`	Returns a `RemoteClass` instance for the superclass of this class. If no superclass was specified (no `extends` clause was used in the class definition), then an instance of `java.lang.Object` is returned.
`isInterface()`	Returns true if this `RemoteClass` instance represents an interface versus a class definition.
`toString()`	Overrides `RemoteObject.toString()`.
`typeName()`	Overrides `RemoteObject.typeName()`.

Name	Description
`getLineNumbers`	Returns the source file line numbers from the class that have code associated with them, in the form of an array.
`getMethodLineNumber`	This method returns the first line of the method that is specified by either a string or the index number.

Table 51.7 The *RemoteClass* Debugging Management Public Member Methods

Name	Description
`getSourceFile()`	Returns an `InputStream` instance that you may use to display lines from the source file used to create this class (if it is available—a non-null return value). This method is for providing a `list` type of command in your debugger implementation or for providing interactive source-level debugging. The returned `InputStream` is typically cast to a `DataInputStream` prior to use.
`catchExceptions()`	Tells the host JVM to return control to your debugger when an instance of this class is thrown. A `ClassCastException` is thrown if this class is not a subclass of `Exception`. This makes the exception appear as a breakpoint to your debugger and causes `DebuggerCallback.exceptionEvent()` to be called.
`ignoreExceptions()`	Tells the host JVM not to signal your debugger in the case of this exception being thrown. The host JVM still throws the exception, just not to you. A `ClassCastException` is thrown if this class is not a subclass of `Exception`. In practice, it is assumed that `catchExceptions()` has already been called for this class.
`setBreakpointLine()`	Allows your debugger to set a breakpoint based on the source file line number in `lineNo`. If `lineNo` is out of range or some other error occurs, a message is returned. Otherwise, an empty string ("") is returned on success. If successful, when your breakpoint is hit, your `DebuggerCallback.breakpointEvent()` is called.
`setBreakpointMethod()`	Allows your debugger to set a breakpoint based on an instance of `RemoteField` that contains a reference to a method in this class. The breakpoint is placed on the first line of the method. If, for some reason, `method` is invalid, an empty string ("") is returned on success. If successful, your `DebuggerCallback.breakpointEvent()` is called when your breakpoint is hit.

continues

Table 51.7 Continued

Name	Description
`clearBreakpoint()`	Your debugger may remove breakpoints using a valid Program Counter (PC) value as specified in `pcLocation`. If, for some reason, `pcLocation` is invalid, an error message is returned. Otherwise, an empty string ("") is returned. This method has limited value as there is no documented method for specifying a breakpoint in this manner.
`clearBreakpointLine()`	Removes a breakpoint that was previously specified for `lineNo`. If, for some reason, `lineNo` is invalid, an error message is returned. Otherwise, an empty string ("") is returned.
`clearBreakpointMethod()`	Removes a breakpoint that was previously specified for `method`. If, for some reason, `method` is invalid, an error message is returned. Otherwise, an empty string ("") is returned.

RemoteArray In Java, arrays are objects, which applies to how your debugger views arrays. So, you have a special type that is called `RemoteArray`. This type allows you to interrogate the runtime instance of an array in the host JVM. One of the differences in the `RemoteArray` class is that there is no way to get directly to its `RemoteField` information. So, in your debugger, you would use `RemoteObject.getField()` to get this information. Then you would use `RemoteObject.getFieldValue()` and cast its return type to `RemoteArray` to access the actual elements of the array.

The public API for the `RemoteArray` class is shown in Listing 51.7.

Listing 51.7 Public API for the *RemoteArray* Class

```
public class RemoteArray extends RemoteObject {
     public String arrayTypeName( int type );
     public String description();
     public final RemoteValue getElement( int index ) throws Exception;
     public final int getElementType() throws Exception;
     public final RemoteValue[] getElements() throws Exception;
     public final RemoteValue[] getElements( int beginIndex, int endIndex
➥)throws Exception;
     public final int getSize();
     public String toString();
     public String typeName();
}
```

Table 51.8 lists each of the public member methods and what they do.

Table 51.8 The *RemoteArray* Class Public Member Methods

Name	Description
`arrayTypeName()`	Returns a string that contains the type of array elements as a String. The `type` argument is supplied by calling `getElementType()`, which is defined later. For any type that is a subclass of `java.lang.Object`, the string `Object` is returned. You need to use `RemoteValue.typeName()` on the `RemoteValue` instance returned by `getElement()` or `getElements()` in order to get the actual object class name.
`description`	Overrides `RemoteObject.description()`.
`getElement()`	Returns an instance of `RemoteValue` containing the value of the array at `index`. `getElement` throws an `ArrayIndexOutOfBoundsException` if `index` subscripts off the array's boundary.
`getElementType()`	Returns a numeric identifier (defined internally) that represents the data type of the elements contained in the array. Use `arrayTypeName()`, defined previously, to get the literal associated with this type of designator.
`getElements()`	This overloaded method is used to return an array of either all or a subset of `RemoteValue` instances. If you specify no arguments, then all values are returned. If you specify `beginIndex` (zero based) and `endIndex` (maximum of `getSize() - 1`), then that specific subset of `RemoteValue` instances is returned. If either index is invalid, then an `ArrayIndexOutOfBoundsException` is thrown.
`getSize()`	Returns the actual number of elements contained in this array instance.
`toString()`	Overrides `RemoteObject.toString()`.
`typeName()`	Overrides `RemoteObject.typeName()`.

RemoteString `RemoteString` is the last of the "special types." It is considered special because it is a subclass of `RemoteObject`, but it is close to being a native type because of the way the compiler treats it. This class is very simple—just about all you can do with a string is display its contents.

The public API for the `RemoteString` class is shown in Listing 51.8.

Listing 51.8 Public API for the *RemoteString* Class

```
public class RemoteString extends RemoteObject {
     public String description();
     public String toString();
     public String typeName();
}
```

Table 51.9 lists each of the public member methods and what they do.

Table 51.9 The *RemoteString* Class Public Member Methods

Name	Description
`description`	Overrides `RemoteObject.description()` and returns the value in the `String` object or literal `null`.
`toString`	Overrides `RemoteObject.toString()` and returns the value in the `String` object or literal `null`.
`typeName`	Overrides `RemoteObject.typeName()`.

Native Types

The native types classes are all proxies based on `RemoteValue` that are used to examine any type of field or stack variable based on a nonobject native type. Native types all share an identical interface to allow complete polymorphic use via the `RemoteValue` abstract type.

The native types supported by this API are described in Table 51.10.

Table 51.10 Native Types Supported by the *RemoteXXX* Classes

Native Type	RemoteXXX Class
`boolean`	`RemoteBoolean`
`byte`	`RemoteByte`
`char`	`RemoteChar`
`double`	`RemoteDouble`
`float`	`RemoteFloat`
`int`	`RemoteInt`
`long`	`RemoteLong`
`short`	`RemoteShort`

The public API shared by the native type classes is shown in Listing 51.9. The `XXX` portion of the `<RemoteXXX>` tag can be replaced with any of the native types using proper capitalization (for example, `RemoteBoolean` for Boolean), as described in Table 51.10.

Listing 51.9 Public API for the Set of *RemoteXXX* Classes

```
public class <RemoteXXX> extends RemoteValue {
    public <native type> get();
    public String toString();
    public String typeName();
}
```


Table 51.11 lists each of the public member methods and what they do.

Table 51.11 The *RemoteXXX* Class Public Member Methods

Name	Description
`get`	Returns the value contained in the `RemoteXXX` class as a native value. The `<native type>` designator as shown in Listing 51.9 may be replaced with any type from the Native Type column of Table 51.10 based on the actual `RemoteXXX` class that the current instance represents. For example, a `RemoteBoolean` class returns a real boolean value from its `get( )` method.
`toString`	Overrides `RemoteObject.toString()`.
`typeName`	Overrides `RemoteObject.typeName()`.

Stack Management

After you get to a point in your debugger where you can begin to stop execution to examine things, then the stack becomes very important. In the JVM, everything that describes the state of the current method being executed is held in a stack frame. The stack frame includes items such as the method arguments, local variables, program counter (PC), method name, and so on. The `RemoteStackFrame` represents all of the execution time characteristics of a running Java method and is the proxy to this unit of control from your debugger. The `RemoteStackFrame`, in turn, provides you with information on data that is physically resident in this stack frame via `RemoteStackVariable` instances. These instances are the proxies to the actual variables that are available for the method currently in context. Currently in context can be defined as the stack frame method that is active.

StackFrame The `StackFrame` class is very thin and basically used as a placeholder to represent a method in a suspended thread in the host JVM. It is used as the superclass for `RemoteStackFrame` and only includes a constructor that doesn't take arguments and a `toString()` method for retrieving this object's value in a String.

The public API for the `StackFrame` class is in Listing 51.10.

Listing 51.10 Public API for the *StackFrame* Class

```
public class StackFrame {
     public StackFrame();
     public String toString();
}
```

RemoteStackFrame The `RemoteStackFrame` class is the proxy that allows you to interact with the stack frame of a suspended thread in the host JVM. The `RemoteStackFrame` instance can basically describe the execution state of itself and enumerate through its variables. Your debugger uses this class in conjunction with the other debugger classes to display the state of the method that is in context.

The public API for the `RemoteStackFrame` class is shown in Listing 51.11.

Listing 51.11 Public API for the *RemoteStackFrame* Class

```
public class RemoteStackFrame extends StackFrame {
     public int getLineNumber();
     public RemoteStackVariable getLocalVariable( String name )
          throws Exception;
     public RemoteStackVariable[] getLocalVariables() throws Exception;
     public String getMethodName();
     public int getPC();
     public RemoteClass getRemoteClass();
}
```

Table 51.12 lists each of the public member methods and what they do.

Table 51.12 The *RemoteStackFrame* Class Public Member Methods

Name	Description
`getLineNumber()`	Returns the line number relative to the beginning of the source file that is associated with the current position of this stack frame in a suspended thread.
`getLocalVariable()`	Returns the `RemoteStackVariable` instance associated with `name` in this `RemoteStackFrame` instance.
`getLocalVariables()`	Returns an array of `RemoteStackVariable` instances that are available in this `RemoteStackFrame` instance.
`getMethodName()`	Returns a String containing the name of the method that is represented by this `RemoteStackFrame` instance.
`getPC()`	Returns the JVM's PC relative to the first bytecode of the method that this `RemoteStackFrame` instance represents. The PC is like a pointer into the Java bytecode stream and is moved as each bytecode is interpreted by the VM.

Name	Description
`getRemoteClass()`	Returns an instance of `RemoteClass` that defines the method represented by this `RemoteStackFrame` instance.

RemoteStackVariable The `RemoteStackVariable` class is the proxy that gives you access to the values contained in a `RemoteStackFrame` instance. The method arguments and the local variables are all returned as `RemoteStackVariable` instances that hold the state, the identification of the variable, and its current value.

The public API for the `RemoteStackVariable` class is shown in Listing 51.12.

Listing 51.12 Public API for the *RemoteStackVariable* Class

```
public class RemoteStackVariable extends LocalVariable {
      // This is a private class that contains the data
      // items that are exposed via Remote-
      // StackVariable methods
      public String getName();
      public RemoteValue getValue();
      public boolean inScope();
}
```

Table 51.13 lists each of the public member methods and what they do.

Table 51.13 The *RemoteStackVariable* Class Public Member Methods

Name	Description
`getName`	Returns a String that contains the literal name of this `RemoteStackVariable` instance.
`getValue`	Returns a `RemoteValue` instance that contains the data value for this variable at this moment. This object may be cast to an appropriate `RemoteValue` subclass.
`inScope`	Returns true if this `RemoteStackVariable` instance is currently in scope. A `RemoteStackVariable` is out of scope if the block that defines it is not in context—for example, a counter defined within a `for` loop construct or an exception variable defined within a `catch` statement.

Thread Management

One of the more challenging tasks when writing Java applications is how to debug threads. Fortunately for us Java developers, Sun has included special classes to help debug multithreaded applications. The thread manager in Java is based on two constructs: a thread group and the threads themselves. Java uses the thread group to help categorize and isolate related sets of independent execution paths, or threads.

The debugging aids for multithreaded applications allow us to examine and control the execution of both thread groups and individual threads. This control and execution is accomplished through the `RemoteThreadGroup` and `RemoteThread` classes.

One of the complexities of debugging multithreaded applications is how to manipulate the individual threads that are active. When you set a breakpoint in a given class's method, all threads that cross that execution path will break. What actually happens is that the current thread breaks, and the other threads along the same path suspend. In this situation, you may use the `RemoteThreadGroup` and `RemoteThread` class to resume the other related threads while you continue to debug (`step`, `examine`, and more) the single thread that you are interested in. Keeping that in mind, the techniques for debugging a multithreaded application are essentially identical to debugging a single-threaded application.

Debugging multithreaded applications can be difficult depending on the logic of how the threads share data. The Java language provides many built-in facilities to allow you to control the concurrency of access that threads have over shared data. The `synchronized` keyword, the `wait()` and `notify()` methods of the `Object` class, and the `sleep()` and `yield()` methods of the `Thread` class provide features that help you design your logic so that sharing data is accomplished safely in a threaded application. Debugging facilities can help you identify areas of logic that are missing these concurrency primitives.

The following two topics—`RemoteThreadGroup` and `RemoteThread`—describe the proxy classes that allow us to do this manipulation.

RemoteThreadGroup The `RemoteThreadGroup` class is a proxy to an instance of a real thread group running in the host JVM. As such, it represents a container that can hold instances of `RemoteThread` as well as embedded `RemoteThreadGroup` instances. The interface for `RemoteThreadGroup` is rather simple and provides the ability to retrieve a list of remote threads and stop the execution of all threads and thread groups that are contained within the current group.

The public API for the `RemoteThreadGroup` class is in Listing 51.13.

Listing 51.13 Public API for the *RemoteThreadGroup* Class

```
public class RemoteThreadGroupextends RemoteObject {
     public String getName() throws Exception;
     public RemoteThread[] listThreads( boolean recurse ) throws Exception;
     public void stop() throws Exception;
}
```

Table 51.14 lists each of the public member methods and what they do.

Table 51.14 The *RemoteThreadGroup* Class Public Member Methods

Name	Description
`getName`	Returns the name of the current `RemoteThreadGroup` instance.
`listThreads`	Returns an array of `RemoteThread` instances that exist in the current `RemoteThreadGroup` instance. If `recurse` is set to true, then all embedded `RemoteThreadGroups` are traversed and their member `RemoteThread` instances are returned as well.
`stop`	Stops the execution of all threads belonging to this thread group. This is very useful if you are debugging a multithreaded application with many thread instances running on the same execution path. Alternatively, you could use `listThreads()` and manually choose the threads to stop.

RemoteThread The `RemoteThread` class is at the heart of multithreaded debugging for Java applications. It provides the interface to control the execution of a thread after execution has been stopped. Execution may be stopped by a breakpoint being reached, an explicit call to `suspend()`, or a call to `stop()`. After the thread of execution has been suspended (somehow), you may examine the current state of the thread, single step through the thread, manipulate the stack frame, and examine any variables that are in scope. Implementing the use of `RemoteThread` in your debugger means that you now have everything you need to manage the execution of remote threads.

Because its API is so large, the `RemoteThread` class can be broken up into three categories:

- Basic thread control. Methods that control the overall execution state of the current thread instance.
- Execution path control. Methods that control program flow after a thread has been suspended (either manually, from a caught exception, or because a breakpoint was reached).
- Stack frame control. Methods that manipulate the stack frame and examine local variables and arguments in the current frame.

The public API for the `RemoteThread` class is in Listing 51.14.

Listing 51.14 Public API for the *RemoteThread* Class

```
public class RemoteThreadextends RemoteObject {

    // Basic Thread Control
    public String getName() throws Exception;
    public String getStatus() throws Exception;
    public boolean isSuspended();
    public void resume() throws Exception;
    public void stop() throws Exception;
    public void suspend() throws Exception;
```

continues

Listing 51.14 Continued

```
    // Execution path control
    public void cont() throws Exception;
    public void next() throws Exception;
    public void step( boolean skipLine ) throws Exception;

    // Stack frame control
    public void down( int nFrames ) throws Exception;
    public RemoteStackFrame[] dumpStack() throws Exception;
    public RemoteStackFrame getCurrentFrame() throws Exception;
    public int getCurrentFrameIndex();
    public RemoteStackVariable getStackVariable( String name )
         throws Exception;
    public RemoteStackVariable[] getStackVariables() throws Exception;
    public void resetCurrentFrameIndex();
    public void setCurrentFrameIndex( int iFrame );
    public void up( int nFrames ) throws Exception;
}
```

Table 51.15 lists each of the public member methods relating to basic thread control and what they do.

Table 51.15 The *RemoteThread* Class Public Member Methods for Basic Thread Control

Name	Description
`getName()`	Returns a String containing the name of this `RemoteThread` instance.
`getStatus()`	Returns a String containing the literal status of this `RemoteThread` instance.
`isSuspended()`	Returns true if this `RemoteThread` instance is suspended.
`resume()`	Resumes execution of this `RemoteThread` instance from the current program counter. It is assumed that the thread is currently suspended.
`stop()`	Terminates execution of this `RemoteThread` instance. You cannot resume execution after you stop the thread, but you can examine the current stack frame.
`suspend()`	Suspends execution of this `RemoteThread` instance at its current location. This is similar to the thread instance receiving a breakpoint. Once suspended, you may use execution path control methods to step through the thread and the stack frame control methods to examine the variables of the current frame. Execution of the thread may continue upon execution of the `resume()` method.

Table 51.16 lists each of the public member methods relating to execution path control and what they do.

Table 51.16 The *RemoteThread* Class Public Member Methods for Execution Path Control

Name	Description
`cont()`	Resumes the current `RemoteThread` instance from a breakpoint. If the thread is suspended, use `resume()` instead of `cont()`.
`next()`	Executes to the next line of source in the current `RemoteThread` instance and does not "step into" any method calls on the way. That is, it executes any intermediate method calls without giving you the opportunity to stop and examine variables and more. This method throws an `IllegalAccessError` exception if the thread is not suspended or processing a breakpoint. Also, if there is no line number information for this class, then `next` operates like the `step()` method below.
`step()`	Executes either the next instruction or goes to the next line if `skipLine` is true. Executing `step(false)` at this point puts the PC at the first instruction of `evaluateCounter()`, whereas calling `next()` executes the call to `evaluate-Counter()` and leaves the PC pointing to the first instruction of line 3.

NOTE Unlike `next()`, `step()` "steps into" any intermediate method calls that are encountered on the way. The following lines of source are an example (where PC is the current program counter):

```
1: myCounter += 1;
2: evaluateCounter( myCounter );
3: System.out.println( "myCounter: " + myCounter );
```

Table 51.17 lists each of the public member methods relating to stack frame control and what they do.

Table 51.17 The *RemoteThread* Class Public Member Methods for Stack Frame Control

Name	Description
`down()`	Moves the stack frame that is currently in context for this `RemoteThread` instance down `nFrames` levels. This is typically used after executing the `up()` method in order to "walk" back down the call stack frames. This command, when used in conjunction with `up()`, may be used to help implement an interactive call stack window. If this `Remote-Thread` instance is not suspended or at a

continues

Table 51.17 Continued

Name	Description
	breakpoint, then an `IllegalAccessError` exception is thrown. Also, if `nFrames` is too great (for example, you try to go past the bottom frame on the execution stack), an `ArrayOutOfBounds` exception is thrown.
`dumpStack()`	Returns an array of `RemoteStackFrame` instances representing the execution stack up to and including the current stack frame. To display the call stack, you can iterate through the array of `RemoteStackFrame` instances and call its `toString()` method.
`getCurrentFrame()`	Returns the `RemoteStackFrame` instance for the current frame.
`getCurrentFrameIndex()`	Returns the index to the current `RemoteStackFrame` in the execution stack.
`getStackVariable()`	Returns the `RemoteStackVariable` instance associated with `name` in the current stack frame. A `null` instance is returned if `name` is not found.
`getStackVariables()`	Returns the array of `RemoteStackVariable` instances that are contained in the current stack frame. These represent both arguments to the method and local variables (whether they are in scope at this point).
`resetCurrentFrameIndex()`	Restores the current stack frame to its state prior to making any calls to `up()`, `down()`, or `setCurrentFrameIndex()`.
`setCurrentFrameIndex()`	Establishes the stack frame at level `iFrame` to be the current stack frame in the host JVM.
`up()`	Moves the stack frame that is currently in context for this `RemoteThread` instance up `nFrames` levels. This is typically used after a breakpoint in order to "walk" up the call stack frames. When used in conjunction with `down()`, this command may be used to help implement an interactive call stack window. If this `RemoteThread` instance is not suspended or at a breakpoint, then an `IllegalAccessError` exception is thrown. Also, if `nFrames` is too great (for example, you try to go past the top frame on the execution stack), an `ArrayOutOfBounds` exception is thrown.

Putting It All Together

By now, you are probably asking yourself, "How can I take advantage of all of this great technology?" First, you can simply use the JDB described in the next section. Or, you might choose to think of JDB as a sample application and write your own debugger. In this case, the section provides you with some basic guidelines for using the classes in the `sun.tools.debug` package.

On the CD-ROM included with this book is a file called `DebuggerSkeleton.java`. This is a shell for a debugger that is based on the `sun.tools.debug` package. `DebuggerSkeleton.java` shows how to get started by implementing the `DebuggerCallback` interface and instantiating an instance of the `RemoteDebugger` class.

You can use the following steps as a guide in implementing a custom debugging aid with the JDB API:

1. Create a base class that implements the `DebuggerCallback` interface.
2. Create a set of state-oriented instance variables in your base class to hold items such as your instance of `RemoteDebugger`, the current thread group, and the current thread (this is the same model used by JDB).
3. Create an instance of `RemoteDebugger` using either of the two constructors available. The constructor you choose depends on whether you want to debug remotely, locally, or both.
4. If you are creating a command line-based debugger, start up a command loop to accept interactive debugging commands. If you are developing a GUI-based debugger, then your command's logic will typically be executed from button or menu events.
5. You may organize your command processing along the following lines, as shown in Table 51.18.

Table 51.18 Command Processing Organization

Category	Description
General	These commands handle the general flow of the debugger's control. You can take advantage of the `RemoteDebugger` class instance to handle these commands. Consider options such as context commands (set the current thread group and thread), memory commands, tracing, and more as potential commands for this category.
Informational	These commands display information on the current debugging target. You use instances of `RemoteObject`, `RemoteClass`, and `RemoteStackFrame` to display objects, classes, methods, variables, and source lines.
Breakpoints	These commands are used to set/reset breakpoints and exceptions. These may be implemented by the methods in `RemoteClass` and `RemoteThread`.
Execution	These are the commands that may be used once a breakpoint happens, a thread suspends, or an exception is thrown. You can use `RemoteClass` and `RemoteThread` again to process these requests.

The JDB in Depth

Now that you have a good understanding of the underlying debugging facilities in the JDK, JDB can be examined. JDB really serves two purposes:

- To be an interactive debugging aid for Java programmers
- To serve as a sample application for applying the classes in the JDB API

Our discussion of JDB covers all of the commands in detail and describes the major portions of the JDB API as they are used.

Basic Architecture

As an application, JDB is patterned after the DBX debugger found on many UNIX systems. This is a command line–oriented debugger that allows you to interact with a running application by entering English-like commands for examining and controlling its execution state. These commands allow you to examine variables, set breakpoints, control threads, and query the host JVM about the classes that it has loaded. You may also have the host JVM load classes for you in advance so that you can set breakpoints in methods prior to their execution.

To understand fully the architecture of JDB, it may be helpful to print out or have access to its source while you are reading this section. When you install the JDK, there is a relatively small ZIP file in the installed JDK root directory (typically, `\ JAVA` in the Windows versions) called `SRC.ZIP`. This file contains the Java source files for all of the publicly documented Java classes, including the class that is the foundation for JDB. The `SRC.ZIP` file must be unzipped with the Use Directory Names option to preserve the source tree. The source tree follows the package-naming convention used in the JDK.

For example, if you unzip the `SRC.ZIP` file into a directory under `\JAVA` called `SRC`, you would find two subdirectories under `\JAVA\SRC` called `\JAVA\SRC\JAVA` and `\JAVA\SRC\SUN`. These represent the Java source files in the `java.*` and `sun.*` collection of packages, respectively.

The source to JDB is based on a class called `TTY`, or `sun.tools.ttydebug.TTY`. The source file (assuming the directory structure in the preceding) would be in `\JAVA\SRC\SUN\TOOLS\TTYDEBUG\TTY.JAVA`.

As you look at `TTY.java`, the first thing you will probably notice is that TTY is a simple class that derives from `Object`, as all classes with no `extends` clause do. But, it does implement the `DebuggerCallback` interface, as mentioned previously in the section "Putting It All Together."

You should note that there are a few instance variables to help support application currency. Specifically, a reference to a `RemoteDebugger` instance (`debugger`), a `RemoteThreadGroup` (`currentThreadGroup`), and a `RemoteThread` (`currentThread`) are needed to maintain context within the currently executing application. This helps when implementing most of the commands that query for information from a suspended thread and method. After a few private methods, you will see the methods defined in `DebuggerCallback`, allowing `TTY` to complete its contract by implementing this interface.

It is now probably easier to jump to the bottom of the source and see its real structure. It starts with a `main` method that will be called first when `TTY.class` is loaded and run. This `main` essentially parses, collects, and verifies all of the command-line arguments and, if everything looks good, creates an instance of the `TTY` class. The rest of the processing takes off from `TTY`'s custom constructor.

The only constructor in `TTY` takes seven arguments; these arguments specify the following:

- Location and connection information for the remote JVM
- The class file to load (optional)
- Output files for the debugger and remote JVM
- A Boolean flag to denote whether you want lots of informational messages returned by the remote JVM as your debugging session is active

Once in the constructor, the remote debugger instance is created and, if specified, the initial class is loaded. Creating an instance of `RemoteDebugger` actually causes a JVM to be started for you in the remote system (even if no starting class is specified). After that, a check is made for an input command file. Finally, the command processing loop is started.

The command loop's real functionality lies in a method called `executeCommand` that expects a tokenized version of the input command line. `executeCommand` is simply a series of cascading `if-else-if` statements that check to see if the first token of the input argument matches one of the predefined sets of commands supported by JDB. If so, then the helper method associated with that command is executed. Otherwise, an appropriate error message is displayed (`"Huh? Try help..."`).

Now that you have a feel for the general structure of JDB and its source (the `TTY` class), look at the actual command-line arguments and commands supported by JDB.

The JDB Command Line

To start JDB in its simplest form, you can type **jdb <Enter>** at your command prompt. JDB then performs its initialization and presents you with a > prompt. In fact, three "formal" command lines start JDB in various modes, as follows:

1. Start JDB and create a `VM` instance on this machine with no class loaded:

   ```
   JDB [-dbgtrace] [<java-args>]
   ```

Option	Meaning
`-dbgtrace`	If specified, enables verbose messages to be returned from the JVM instance that is created in order to run the target Java application/applet. These messages are sent to the `printToConsole` callback method and have the format `[debugger: <some message>]`. That way, you can filter them in your `printToConsole` implementation and send them to a log file or window, for example.
`<java-args>`	This is an optional subset of the arguments that you can specify when running the `java` command to start an instance of the JVM. The

currently recognized options are the following: `-cs`, `-checksource`, `-noasyncgc`, `-prof`, `-v`, `-verbose`, `-verify`, `-noverify`, `-verifyremote`, `-verbosegc`, `-ms`, `-mx`, `-ss`, `-oss`, `-D`, and `-classpath`.

2. Start JDB and create a VM instance on this machine with `<classname>` loaded:

```
JDB [-dbgtrace] [<java-args>] <classname> [<args>]
```

Option	Meaning
`-dbgtrace`	Same as above.
`<java-args>`	Same as above.
`<classname>`	This mandatory argument is the .class file to load initially into the JVM and control by the debugger. Use the `run` command to begin execution.
`<args>`	This argument represents any arguments needed by `<classname>`. It must be specified here, as there is no way to set up arguments for `<classname>`'s `main` method after JDB starts up.

3. Start JDB and connect to a remote VM instance that is already running a class:

```
JDB [-dbgtrace] [-host <hostname>] -password <password>
```

Option	Meaning
`-dbgtrace`	Same as above.
`-host <hostname>`	This optional argument specifies a DNS name or IP address of a computer runningthe host JVM for the Java application/applet that you will be debugging. If this argument is not specified, then `localhost` is automatically assumed.
`-password <password>`	This mandatory argument is the password that was displayed on the console when the JVM hosting the application/applet to be debugged was loaded. It is generated by `java` or `appletviewer` when the flag is specified on the respective command lines.

After you enter one of the JDB command lines, the initialization process described previously takes over and, eventually, the interactive prompt (>) appears.

JDB Input Files

If you choose to run a debug session repeatedly with a specific set of commands, you can create a command input file for JDB to use automatically. The command file is a simple ASCII text file in which each line contains a valid JDB command followed by the line delimiter that is appropriate to the OS you are running JDB on (for example, `CR/LF` for Wintel). JDB looks in three places, in the order shown in Table 51.19, for a command input file.

Table 51.19 Locations for the JDB Command Input File

Directory (System Property)	Filename	Example
USER.HOME	JDB.INI	C:\JAVA\JDB.INI
USER.HOME	JDBRC	/JAVA/.JDBRC
USER.DIR	STARTUP.JDB	./STARTUP.JDB

If one of the aforementioned files is found, JDB reads each line and processes the command as if it were typed in at the console. If you want JDB to exit quietly when it has finished processing the file, place a quit or exit command as the last line in the command file. Otherwise, you are left at the JDB prompt with any output from the processed commands visible on the console window. Also, because the calls made to `printToConsole` are sent to `System.out`, you may redirect the results of these commands to an output file using command-line redirection.

The JDB Command Set

Now that you know how to start JDB, it is useful to know how to operate it as well. To show some of the features of the JDB command set, I use a small, threaded application where each thread increments a shared counter and displays the value. Listing 51.15 contains the application.

Listing 51.15 *MTTest.java*—Sample Buggy Application

```
public class MTTest extends Thread {
    static int count = 0;
    static Object sema = new Object();

    public MTTest( ThreadGroup theGroup, String threadName ) {
         super( theGroup, threadName );
     }

    public void run() {
          String  myName = getName();
          while (true) {
               synchronized (sema) {
                    if(count < 30) {
                       System.out.println( myName + ": " + count );
                       count += 1;
                   } else break;
               }
               yield();
         }
         System.out.println( "Exiting " + getName() );
     }

    public static void main( String[] args ) {
         ThreadGroup   theGroup;              // To contain the threads
```

continues

Listing 51.15 Continued

```
         MTTest[]      theThreads;            // Array of threads
         // Wait for the user to hit <Enter> to start
        System.out.print( "MTTest: Press the <Enter> key to begin." );
        System.out.flush();
        try { System.in.read(); }
        catch (java.io.IOException e) {}
        System.out.println("");
        // Create the thread group
        theGroup = new ThreadGroup( "MTThreads" );
        // Create the thread array
        theThreads = new MTTest[3];
        // Create and start the threads
        for (int i = 0; i < theThreads.length ; ++i) {
            theThreads[i] = new MTTest( theGroup, "T" + Integer.toString(i));
            if (theThreads[i] != null)
                 theThreads[i].start();
         }
    }
}
```

One of the first things to know about debugging anything with JDB that is multithreaded is that it is best to have the target application wait until you are ready and run it in a separate process space. Running in a separate process space prevents the target application's output from getting interspersed with the debugger output. Also, having the application wait for you means that it won't start running as soon as you start up the JVM that will run your application.

To follow along with the examples associated with each command, complete the following steps:

1. Use the following command line to compile `MTTest` with debug information (line numbers and local variable information):

   ```
   javac  -g  MTTest.java
   ```

2. Open up two command windows: one for the JVM to run `MTTest` and the other to run JDB within. From the first command window, start up the JVM as follows:

   ```
   java  -debug  MTTest
   ```

   The `-debug` option told the JVM that I was going to communicate with it via external proxies, and `MTTest` is the name of the class file to load. After `java` is started, it displays the following information on the system console:

   ```
   Agent password=xxxxxx
   ```

   where `xxxxxx` is the password to use when starting up JDB, which is the next step.

3. In the second command window, enter the following command to start JDB and connect to the running JVM:

   ```
   jdb  -host localhost  -password xxxxxx
   ```

4. To put the debugging session at an interesting point, enter the following in your JDB command window; you are setting a breakpoint at the start of the `run` method of `MTTest`:

```
>stop in MTTest.run
Breakpoint set in MTTest.run
```

   (Don't worry about what the commands mean—we get to them in a future section.)

5. In the console window that is actually running `MTTest` (see step 2), press Enter to let `MTTest` start to execute. You should almost immediately hit a breakpoint and see the following in the JDB console window:

```
Breakpoint hit: MTTest.run (MTTest:12)
T0[1]
```


Now that everything is ready to go, the specific commands that are implemented by JDB can be examined. For clarity, I have broken the commands into groupings based on their functionality. By using these categories, you can put each command into its respective slot (see Table 51.20).

Table 51.20 JDB Commands by Group

General	Context	Information	Breakpoint	Exception	Threads
help/?	load	classes	stop	catch	suspend
exit/quit	run	dump	clear	ignore	resume
memory	threadgroup	list	step	kill	down
gc	thread	locals	next	up	
itrace	use	methods	cont		
trace			print		
!!			threadgroups		
			threads		
			where		

NOTE `kill`, `next`, `itrace`, and `trace` are undocumented but implemented commands.

The rest of this section describes each command and its function.

General Commands

These are the commands that are used to control some of the features of the debugger or interrogate the state of the remote JVM.

help/? Syntax: `help` [or `?`]

This command displays a list of the "documented" commands that are supported by JDB.

exit/quit Syntax: `exit [ or quit ]`

Uses: `RemoteDebugger.close()`

This command terminates your debugging session and JDB. The connection between JDB and the remote JVM is broken. If debugging locally, the VM is shut down.

memory Syntax: `memory`

Uses: `RemoteDebugger.freeMemeory()` and `RemoteDebugger.totalMemory()`

This command displays the total amount of used and free memory in the remote JVM. For example, on my system, the `memory` command displays the following:

```
Free: 2674104, total: 3145720
```

gc Syntax: `gc`

Uses: `RemoteDebugger.gc()`

This command causes the garbage collection task to run on the remote JVM. The classes that are not in use by the debugger are freed. JDB automatically tells the JVM not to garbage collect the classes involved with the current `RemoteThreadGroup` and `RemoteThread` instances. If you are having a long debug session, then you should use the `gc` command to occasionally remove the `RemoteClass` instances that have been cached on your behalf by the remote JVM.

***itrace* (an Undocumented Command)** Syntax: `itrace on ¦ off`

Uses: `RemoteDebugger.itrace()`

This command enables (on) or disables (off) bytecode instruction tracing on the remote JVM that is hosting your application. The output is sent to `System.out` on the remote JVM and cannot be intercepted from within your debugging session.

The following is sample output from an itrace:

```
1393B58    6B4AD8        ifeq goto   6B4ADD (taken)
1393B58    6B4ADD        aload_0 => java.net.SocketInputStream@139EE80/1481298
1393B58    6B4ADE        aload_1 => byte[][2048]
1393B58    6B4ADF        iload_2 => 0
1393B58    6B4AE0        iload_3 => 2048
1393B58    6B4AE1        invokenonvirtual_quick
java/net/SocketInputStream.socketRead([BII)I (4)
```

***trace* (an Undocumented Command)** Syntax: `trace on ¦ off`

Uses: `RemoteDebugger.trace()`

This method enables (on) or disables (off) method call tracing on the remote JVM that is hosting your application. The output is sent to `System.out` on the remote JVM and cannot be intercepted from within your debugging session.

The following is sample output from a `trace`:

```
# Debugger agent [ 3] ¦ ¦ ¦ < java/lang/Runtime.traceMethodCalls(Z)V returning
# Debugger agent [ 2] ¦ ¦ < sun/tools/debug/Agent.handle(ILjava/io/
```

```
➥DataInputStream;
Ljava/io/DataOutputStream;)V returning
# Debugger agent [ 2] ¦ ¦ > java/io/DataOutputStream.flush()V (1) entered
# Debugger agent [ 3] ¦ ¦ ¦ > java/io/BufferedOutputStream.flush()V (1) entered
# Debugger agent [ 4] ¦ ¦ ¦ ¦ > java/net/SocketOutputStream.write([BII)V (4)
➥entered
# Debugger agent [ 5] ¦ ¦ ¦ ¦ ¦ > java/net/SocketOutputStream.socketWrite([BII)V
➥(4) entered
# Debugger agent [ 5] ¦ ¦ ¦ ¦ ¦ < java/net/SocketOutputStream.socketWrite([BII)V
➥returning
# Debugger agent [ 4] ¦ ¦ ¦ ¦ < java/net/SocketOutputStream.write([BII)V
➥returning
# Debugger agent [ 4] ¦ ¦ ¦ ¦ > java/io/OutputStream.flush()V (1) entered
# Debugger agent [ 4] ¦ ¦ ¦ ¦ < java/io/OutputStream.flush()V returning
# Debugger agent [ 3] ¦ ¦ ¦ < java/io/BufferedOutputStream.flush()V returning
# Debugger agent [ 2] ¦ ¦ < java/io/DataOutputStream.flush()V returning
# Debugger agent [ 2] ¦ ¦ > java/io/FilterInputStream.read()I (1) entered
# Debugger agent [ 3] ¦ ¦ ¦ > java/io/BufferedInputStream.read()I (1) entered
# Debugger agent [ 4] ¦ ¦ ¦ ¦ > java/io/BufferedInputStream.fill()V (1) entered
# Debugger agent [ 5] ¦ ¦ ¦ ¦ ¦ > java/net/SocketInputStream.read([BII)I (4)
➥entered
# Debugger agent [ 6] ¦ ¦ ¦ ¦ ¦ ¦ > java/net/SocketInputStream.socketRead([BII)I
➥(4) entered
```

The format of the call information uses the signature described in the section on the class file, which is described in a subsequent section on the .class file structure.

!! (Repeat Last Command) Syntax: `!!`

This command re-executes, or repeats, the last entered command. It is not something that is implemented by any remote class; rather, this command is just a feature that is enabled by the JDB command processor.

Context Commands

These commands are used to establish context for the debugging session. They set up the state of the remote JVM and the instance variables used operationally by `TTY`. To use just about any of the commands in JDB, the current thread group and current thread must be set. The initial context is set automatically when you use the `run` command; otherwise, you must manually set it using the `threadgroup` and `thread` commands.

load Syntax: `load <classname>`

Uses: `RemoteDebugger.findClass()`

`load` causes the remote JVM to search for and `load <classname>`. If you do not fully qualify the name of the class to `load`, the VM tries to look in well-known packages to complete the name. If the class is not found, an error message is returned. Also, an error message is displayed if no `<classname>` is provided. This command does not affect the current context.

run Syntax: `run [ <classname> [args] ]`

Uses: `RemoteClass.getQualifiedName` and `RemoteDebugger.run()`

This command loads and begins execution of `<classname>` or the last `<classname>` specified on the previous call to the `run` command. Error messages are returned if the class can't be found or if there is a general failure in attempting to start `<classname>`. This command also sets the context by establishing initial values for the `currentThreadGroup` and `currentThread`.

threadgroup Syntax: `threadgroup <thread group name>`

Uses: `RemoteDebugger.listThreadGroups` and `RemoteThreadGroup.getName`

This command establishes `<thread group name>` as the default thread group by putting a reference to its `RemoteThreadGroup` instance in the `currentThreadGroup` instance variable. This command is required for using any of the commands that are relating to breakpoints, exception, and thread management. For example, you could enter:

```
>threadgroup MTThreads
```

to specify the current default thread group.

thread Syntax: `thread t@<thread id> ¦ <thread id>`

`<thread id>` is an integer constant representing a thread's ID number. (See the `threads` command.)

Uses: `RemoteThreadGroup.listThreads`

This command sets `<thread id>` as the current thread in context relative to the current thread group by putting a reference to its `RemoteThread` instance in the `currentThread` instance variable. This command is required for using any of the commands relating to breakpoints, exception, and thread management. It is typically used in conjunction with the `threadgroup` command. For example, you could enter:

```
>thread 5
T0[1]
```

to specify the current default thread. `T0[1]` is now the new prompt showing you that your context is in thread `T0`, which is the first thread in the current thread group.

use Syntax: `use [source file path]`

Uses: `RemoteDebugger.getSourcePath` and `RemoteDebugger.setSourcePath`

This command is used to display or set the path that the remote JVM uses to find .class and .java files. If called without any arguments, then the current source file path is displayed. If called with a path (formatted like the classpath system property), then the source file path is updated accordingly. For example, to display the current class/source path and then change it, use this:

```
>use
.;c:\java\lib\classes.zip
>use .;c:\java\lib\classes.zip;c:\java\lib\classdmp.zip
>use
.;c:\java\lib\classes.zip;c:\java\lib\classdmp.zip
```

Information Commands

These commands are used to display information about the classes that are currently loaded and known to the remote JVM. They are list-oriented in nature and depend on the context being established as described previously.

classes Syntax: `classes`

Uses: `RemoteDebugger.listClasses` and `RemoteClass.description`

This command displays the class and interface names that are currently known to the remote JVM hosting the debugging target. If this list is unusually large, try running the `gc` command to free instances of `RemoteClass` that are being held on your behalf by the remote JVM and the `RemoteDebugger` agent.

The following is sample output from the `classes` command after starting up `MTTest`:

```
0x1393768:class(MTTest)
0x1393778:class(sun.tools.debug.Agent)
0x13937a0:class(java.lang.Runtime)
0x1393818:class(java.net.ServerSocket)
0x1393830:class(java.net.PlainSocketImpl)
0x1393840:class(java.net.SocketImpl)
0x1393890:class(java.net.InetAddress)
```

dump Syntax: `dump t@<thread id> ¦ $s<slot id> ¦ 0x<class id> ¦ <name>`

`t@<thread id>` represents a valid thread ID within the current thread group; `$s<slot id>` represents the slot/offset to a variable in a stack frame; `0x<class id>` represents the numeric identifier for a currently loaded class; or `<name>` represents the literal `this`, a valid class name, a field name (for example, `class.field`), an argument name, or a local variable name.

Uses: `RemoteThreadGroup.listThreads`, `RemoteThread.getStackVariables`, `RemoteStackVariable.getValue`, `RemoteDebugger.get`, and `RemoteDebugger.findClass`

This command dumps the detailed description of the specified thread, stack-based variable, class, field, named local variable, or named argument. If an argument, variable, or field is requested, its name and value are displayed. If a thread or class is specified, a detailed description of the thread or class is displayed, including instance variables and their current values.

The following is an example of dumping the `MTTest` class:

```
T0[1] dump MTTest       // Could also have entered: dump 0x1393768
 "MTTest" is not a valid field of (MTTest)0x13a0ca8
MTTest = 0x1393768:class(MTTest) {
superclass = 0x1393008:class(java.lang.Thread)
loader = null

private static Thread activeThreadQ = null
private static int threadInitNumber = 2
public static final int MIN_PRIORITY = 1
public static final int NORM_PRIORITY = 5
public static final int MAX_PRIORITY = 10
static int count = 0
```

```
}
T0[1]
```

Note that the second line is a result of the search algorithm used by the `dump` command.

list Syntax: `list [line number]`

Uses: `RemoteThread.getCurrentFrame`, `StackFrame.getRemoteClass`, `RemoteClass.getSourceFileName`, `RemoteClass.getGetSourceFile`

This command displays one or more source lines for the current thread's current method. There must be a thread in context that is running but in a suspended state. Also, the line number, if specified, must be relative to the top of the source file that defines the current method. Otherwise, if you don't specify a line number, then the current line is displayed. This listing includes the four lines of source immediately before and after the specified line.

The following is how a list with no arguments should look for `MTTest` at the current breakpoint:

```
T0[1] list
6               }
7
8               public void run() {
9
10      =>              String  myName = getName();
11
12                      while (true) {
13                              synchronized (sema) {
15                                      if (count < 30) {
T0[1]
```

The => in line 10 denotes the current line of source.

locals Syntax: `locals`

Uses: `RemoteThread.getStackVariables`

This command displays all arguments to the current method and local variables that are defined in this stack frame. You must have a thread in context, and you must have compiled your code with the `-g` option to get symbol table information for the local variables and arguments available for debugging.

For example, if you entered **locals**, you should see the following:

```
T0[1] locals
Method arguments:
this = Thread[T0,5,MTThreads]
Local variables:
myName is not in scope.
T0[1]
```

The `this` argument is present in all methods and is pushed on the stack implicitly by the JVM invocation logic. The `myName` variable is not in scope yet, as you are at a breakpoint at the beginning of the method.

methods Syntax: `methods <classname> ¦ 0x<class id>`

Uses: `RemoteDebugger.get`, or `RemoteDebugger.findClass` and `RemoteClass.getMethods` This command displays all of the methods in the specified class, including the signature of each. The methods list for `MTTest` should look like this:

```
T0[1] methods MTTest
void <init>(ThreadGroup, String)
void run()
void main(String[])
T0[1]
```

The `<init>` method is a special name and represents the constructor for this class.

print Syntax: `print t@<thread id> ¦ $s<slot id> ¦ 0x<class id> ¦ <name>`

`t@<thread id>` represents a valid thread ID within the current thread group; `$s<slot id>` represents the slot/offset to a variable in a stack frame; `0x<class id>` represents the numeric identifier for a currently loaded class; `<name>` represents the literal `this`, a valid class name, a field name (for example, `class.field`), an argument name, or a local variable name.

Uses: `RemoteThreadGroup.listThreads`, `RemoteThread.getStackVariables`, `RemoteStackVariable.getValue`, `RemoteDebugger.get`, and `RemoteDebugger.findClass`

This command displays a simple description of the specified thread, stack-based variable, class, field, named local variable, or named argument. If an argument, variable, or field is requested, then its name and value are displayed. If a thread or class is specified, then the name and ID of the thread or class are displayed.

The following is an example of printing the `MTTest` class:

```
T0[1] print MTTest
MTTest = 0x1393768:class(MTTest)
T0[1]
```

threadgroups Syntax: `threadgroups`

Uses: `RemoteDebugger.listThreadGroups`, `RemoteThreadGroup.getName`, and `RemoteThreadGroup.description`

This command displays the name and description of all active thread groups in the remote JVM.

The `threadgroups` command for `MTTest` looks like this:

```
T0[1] threadgroups
1. (java.lang.ThreadGroup)0x13930b8 system
2. (java.lang.ThreadGroup)0x139ec60 main
3. (java.lang.ThreadGroup)0x13a0b00 MTThreads
T0[1]
```

threads Syntax: `threads [thread group name]`

Uses: `RemoteDebugger.listThreadGroups`, `RemoteThreadGroup.getName`, `RemoteThreadGroup.listThreads`, `RemoteThread.getName`, `RemoteThread.description`, and `RemoteThread.getStatus`

This command displays the list of threads for the current or specified thread group. If the current or specified thread group has embedded thread groups, their threads are listed as well.

Issuing the `threads` command for `MTTest`'s named thread group `MTThreads` should give you something that is similar to the following:

```
T0[1] threads MTThreads
Group MTThreads:
1. (MTTest)0x13a0b30 T0 at breakpoint
2. (MTTest)0x13a0b90 T1 suspended
3. (MTTest)0x13a0bd0 T2 suspended
T0[1]
```

where Syntax: `where [ all ¦ <thread id> ]`

Uses: `RemoteThreadGroup.listThreads`, `RemoteThread.dumpStack`, and `RemoteStackFrame.toString`

This command displays the call stack (the list of methods that were called to get to this point) for the current thread (as set with the `thread` command), all threads (for the current thread group as set with the `threadgroup` command), or the specified thread (by its ID).

On my system, the command `where all` gives the following result:

```
T0[1] where all
Finalizer thread:
Thread is not running (no stack).
Debugger agent:
[1] sun.tools.debug.Agent.handle (Agent:590)
[2] sun.tools.debug.Agent.run (Agent:324)
[3] java.lang.Thread.run (Thread:294)
Breakpoint handler:
[1] java.lang.Object.wait (Object:152)
[2] sun.tools.debug.BreakpointQueue.nextEvent (BreakpointQueue:51)
[3] sun.tools.debug.BreakpointHandler.run (BreakpointHandler:184)
main:
[1] MTTest.main (MTTest:51)
T0:
 [1] MTTest.run (MTTest:12)
T1:
Thread is not running (no stack).
T2:
Thread is not running (no stack).
T0[1]
```

Breakpoint Commands

These commands allow you to set/remove and control execution flow from a breakpoint. Breakpoints are the fodder for most debugging sessions in that just about the only way to do anything while debugging is to stop the application. Or, in Java's case, a thread must be stopped unconditionally at some point. That's exactly what a breakpoint does. After you have established a breakpoint (you have already seen this briefly in step 4 while setting up the debugging session), you execute your program/thread until the execution path reaches that point. When it does, the execution of that thread stops, and you regain control of the remote JVM and your application.

Now you can set up and remove breakpoints, "walk" through your program using the `step` and `next` commands, or use `cont` to continue execution.

stop Syntax 1: `stop in <classname>.method ¦ 0x<class id>.method`

Uses: `RemoteDebugger.findClass` or `RemoteDebugger.get`, `RemoteClass.getMethod`, and `RemoteClass.setBreakpointMethod`

Syntax 2: `stop at <classname>:line number ¦ 0x<class id>:line number`

Uses: `RemoteDebugger.findClass` or `RemoteDebugger.get` and `RemoteClass.setBreakpointLine`

This command sets a breakpoint at the first bytecode instruction of the specified method (Syntax 1) or at the first bytecode instruction of the specified line. If Syntax 2 is used, line number is relative to the beginning of the source file that contains `<classname>/<class id>`. If `stop` is issued with no arguments, then the existing breakpoints are displayed. When a breakpoint is placed on a method that is part of a multithreaded application/applet, it applies to all active threads when they cross that method or line of code. The breakpoint remains active until it is removed with the `clear` command.

The following example lists the current breakpoints, sets one at line 14 of `MTTest`, and then displays the breakpoint list again:

```
T0[1] stop
Current breakpoints set:
MTTest:10
T0[1] stop at MTTest:12
Breakpoint set at MTTest:12
T0[1] stop
Current breakpoints set:
MTTest:12
MTTest:10
T0[1]
```

clear Syntax 1: `clear <classname>.method ¦ 0x<class id>.method`

Uses: `RemoteDebugger.findClass` or `RemoteDebugger.get`, `RemoteClass.getMethod`, and `RemoteClass.clearBreakpointMethod`

Syntax 2: `clear <classname>:line number ¦ 0x<class id>:line number`

Uses: `RemoteDebugger.findClass` or `RemoteDebugger.get`, and `RemoteClass.clearBreakpointLine`

This command clears an existing breakpoint at the first bytecode instruction of the specified method (Syntax 1) or at the first bytecode instruction of the specified line. If Syntax 2 is used, line number is relative to the beginning of the source file that contains `<classname>/<class id>`. If `clear` is issued with no arguments, then the existing breakpoints are displayed. When a breakpoint is cleared from a method that is part of a multithreaded application/applet, then it affects all active threads when they cross that method or line of code.

The following example lists the current breakpoints, clears one at the start of `MTTest.run`, and then displays the breakpoint list again:

```
T0[1] clear
Current breakpoints set:
MTTest:12
MTTest:10
T0[1] clear MTTest.run
Breakpoint cleared at MTTest.run
T0[1] clear
Current breakpoints set:
MTTest:12
T0[1]
```

step Syntax: `step`

Uses: `RemoteThread.step`

This command executes the next instruction of the currently stopped thread. If the next instruction is a method call, execution stops at the first instruction of the method being invoked. An error is generated if there is no current thread or the current thread is not suspended at a breakpoint.

***next* (An Undocumented Command)** Syntax: `next`

Uses: `RemoteThread.next`

Like `step`, the `next` command steps execution of the currently stopped thread to the next instruction. But, if the `next` instruction is a method invocation, then the method is called and control returns to the debugger upon return from the method being executed. At that point, the current instruction is the one immediately following the call. As with `step`, an error is generated if there is no current thread or the current thread is not suspended at a breakpoint.

cont Syntax: `cont`

Uses: `RemoteThreadGroup.listThreads`, `RemoteThread.cont`, and `RemoteThread.resetCurrentFrameIndex`

This command continues the execution of all suspended threads in the default thread group. The command is useful when you have been single-stepping through a thread and want to let the application simply run until the next breakpoint or exception occurs.

Exception Commands

These commands control which exception classes should be caught or ignored by JDB. One of the more interesting aspects of Java is the notion of exceptions. Exceptions are kind of like intelligent breakpoints that you can code logic for directly within your application. They are typically used to trap very specific exceptional situations that should not occur under normal use.

A feature of the JDB API is the ability to register your interest in a specific exception and have it behave like a breakpoint so that you can step through the logic coded in the `catch` block of the exception handling code. If you choose not to handle a breakpoint in this manner, then the debugging client is notified as if a nonrecoverable breakpoint were reached. That control is returned to the debugger, but you will not be able to step through the exception logic in the catch block.

catch Syntax: catch [<classname> 0x<class id>]

Uses: RemoteDebugger.getExceptionCatchList, RemoteDebugger.findClass, or RemoteDebugger.get and RemoteClass.catchException

This command causes the debugger to catch (via DebuggerCallback.exceptionEvent) occurrences of the exception class specified by <classname>/0x<class id> when thrown by the remote JVM. Throwing the exception class causes execution to stop, as if a breakpoint were placed at the first executable statement of the catch block that is currently active when trying the specified exception. In other words, all try-catch blocks in the application that "catch" the specific exception will become breakpoints. If no class is specified, then the existing caught exceptions are displayed. An error is generated if the specified class is not a subclass of Exception.

ignore Syntax: ignore [<classname> 0x<class id>]

Uses: RemoteDebugger.getExceptionCatchList, RemoteDebugger.findClass or RemoteDebugger.get, and RemoteClass.ignoreException

This command causes the debugger to stop catching occurrences of the exception class specified by <classname>/0x<class id> when thrown by the remote JVM. This does not stop the exception from being thrown, but it does stop the debugger from being able to catch the exception as if it were a breakpoint. If no class is specified, then the existing caught exceptions are displayed. An error is generated if the specified class is not a subclass of Exception.

Thread Commands

These commands are used to control the execution state and stack of currently active threads. The thread control commands are something like a manual breakpoint, in that you can stop a thread in its tracks without needing to code a breakpoint. This can be extremely useful in situations where you have inadvertently coded an endless loop and can't see where the flawed logic exists. You can also resume execution of a thread you have suspended as well as remove it entirely. After you have suspended a thread, you can then manipulate the current frame within the call stack that is active. This allows you to examine arguments and local variables in methods that called the currently suspended method.

suspend Syntax: suspend [thread-id [thread-id ...]]

Uses: RemoteThreadGroup.listThreads and RemoteThread.suspend

This command suspends (stops) the execution of the specified thread(s) or all nonsystem threads if no thread is specified. This causes a one-time breakpoint to occur at the currently executing instruction in the affected thread(s).

resume Syntax: resume [thread-id [thread-id ...]]

Uses: RemoteThreadGroup.listThreads and RemoteThread.resume

This command resumes (continues) execution of the specified thread(s) or all nonsystem threads if no thread is specified. This allows the affected thread to run as if no breakpoints ever existed at the previously suspended code location.

***kill* (An Undocumented Command)** Syntax: `kill <thread group name> <thread id>`

Uses: `RemoteThreadGroup.listThreads`, `RemoteThread.stop`, and `RemoteThreadGroup.stop`

This command terminates (permanently stops) the execution of either all threads in the specified thread group or just the specified thread (by ID). After a thread or thread group has been terminated, it may not be resumed, and no breakpoint commands (`step`, `next`, `cont`) may be applied. An error is generated if no arguments are specified or if the specified name or ID is bad.

up Syntax: `up [ n frames ]`

Uses: `RemoteThread.up`

This command moves the context of the current stack frame from its current position up one (the default), or n frames. A frame represents the execution state for a method that was being executed prior to calling into another method. The execution state includes the location of the line being executed when the method call was made, the line's arguments (and their current values), and the line's local variables (and their current values). At this point, the method's state is "pushed," and a new frame is created for the method being called. Each time a method is subsequently called from within the next method, the current frame is pushed and a new frame is put into context. By moving "up" the call stack, the prior method's arguments and variables may be examined.

down Syntax: `down [ n frames ]`

Uses: `RemoteThread.down`

This command is used after using the `up` command. `down` moves the context of the current stack frame from its current position down one (the default), or n frames. By moving "down" the call stack, you progress toward the current state of execution prior to the last suspended point in the current thread (whether from a breakpoint, caught exception, or explicit call to `suspend`).

JDB Wrap-Up

As you can see from the number of commands (33 distinct ones), JDB is actually a very powerful debugging facility.

It is an excellent example of how to implement a debugger using Sun's JDB API. Furthermore, it is a great sample application for Java system programming. In reality, it would not take much work to wrap some GUI functionality around the `TTY` class to make it a little more visually appealing (subclass it, add a multiline text field for the output, set up menu items for the command groups, create pop-up windows, and more). Even if you don't work with the GUI functionality in this manner, you can use JDB to debug your applications on any platform that is supported by the Sun JDK.

What about debugging strategies? The biggest point to keep in mind is that if you are running into problems in a multithreaded application, you are going to want to liberally use breakpoints and exceptions. The nice thing about throwing exceptions in your own code is that you can catch them like breakpoints without having to know specific source line numbers or method names and ignore them as well. (Remember, an exception does not have to mean that a catastrophic error has occurred. It is simply a signal from one piece of code to another.) You can create an exception to throw when a loop counter goes beyond a certain value, when a socket receives a particular message, and so on. The ways that exceptions can be used are truly limitless.

Another important feature to use is the `where` command. You will not realize you are in a recursive situation unless you see what the call stack looks like. Your logic may have intentional recursion, but it is not a technique that the average business application uses on a regular basis. After you have a feel for the look of the call stack, you can then use the `up` and `down` commands to move your context through the call stack and check out local variables/arguments that might be affecting your execution.

The last strategy is to have an in-depth understanding of how your compiled class files are formatted and how the JVM uses them. That's what is covered in the next two chapters. ●

CHAPTER 52

Understanding the *.class* File

In this chapter

A Fundamental Measurement

The `.class` file is the fundamental unit of measure for a Java application with respect to the Java Virtual Machine (JVM). It represents a contract of sorts between a compiler and an implementation of the JVM. I mention "a compiler" versus "a Java compiler" because, as you will see, any language compiler can potentially generate `.class` files and Java bytecodes.

Physically, the `.class` file is an ordered set of bytes representing extremely dynamic structures and arrays that describe the compiled version (or runtime image) of an executable unit, called a class. Most of the components that make up the `.class` file have a fixed structure followed by a set of variable-length structures. Some pieces are mandatory, and others are optional. The important thing to keep in mind is that a process that generates a `.class` file must do so in the exact format and style in this chapter. Otherwise, the JVM's class loader and verifier will not accept the submitted `.class` file.

Elements of the *.class* File

Keeping the `.class` file in the byte stream–oriented format is very critical for quickly loading and parsing the information it contains. Implementers of class loaders might take advantage of the stream I/O classes in Java—for example, to easily read in a `.class` file piece by piece, parsing as it is read, or to read it into a byte array and parse it manually.

The concept to keep in mind is that you must read in each section, in order, until its information is exhausted. Also, you can't really read in a section of the file without reading its descriptive information first. For example, a portion of the file is called the Constant Pool. The first item that you read in is the number of elements that will follow. Then, for each element that you read in, a descriptor tells you the format of the next element. Finally, you read in the actual element based on its specific format.

The file itself can be broken up into logical sections:

- At its highest level, the `.class` file represents a single compiled Java class. When you compile a Java source file (`.java` file) for every class defined within that one file, the compiler generates a `.class` file for each one.
- The next level is the basic class structure. This level includes information about the class's properties and subsections for describing the constant values collected for the class (the Constant Pool) when it was compiled, followed by the class's interfaces, fields, methods, and class-level attributes.
- Then, each subsection can be looked at independently: the Constant Pool and its elements, the table of interfaces, the field table including properties and attributes, and the method table including properties and attributes.

NOTE The information described in this chapter was gleaned from two sources:

- The online reference materials at the old JavaSoft Web site (`www.javasoft.com`) and Sun Web site (`www.sun.com`).

- Sessions at JavaOne, Sun's Worldwide Java Developer Conference held in San Francisco in May, 1996.

Definitions

In order to fully understand the contents of the `.class` file, you need to first define some common structures that are used by the various sections it includes. In this section, you examine the Constant Pool, the format of a signature or type definition, and attributes.

The Constant Pool

The idea of a Constant Pool might be a new concept to you, but Constant Pools have been used since the early days of compilers and runtime systems. A Constant Pool is used to contain each distinct literal value encountered while the source code for a class is being compiled. A literal value in this case might be an actual numeric value, a string literal, a class name, type description, or method signature.

Each time one of these literal values is encountered, the Constant Pool is searched for a matching value in order to avoid putting duplicate values into the pool. If the value is found, its existing location in the Constant Pool is inserted into the class definition or compiled bytecode stream. If the value isn't found in the Constant Pool, it is added. At load time, the Constant Pool is placed into an array-like structure in memory for quick access. Then, as the rest of the class is loaded, and at runtime whenever a literal is needed, its value is located in the Constant Pool by its index and retrieved.

The use of a Constant Pool keeps the size of the compiled class smaller; hence, it loads faster. At runtime, the Sun implementation of the JVM has a mechanism to make resolving a Constant Pool reference occur only the first time a distinct value is needed. After that, the resolved value can be directly referenced in a special array off the Constant Pool. The actual mechanism is supported by a special set of internal bytecodes called the *quick instructions*. Because they are strictly implementation-dependent, they are not part of the formal definition of the Java bytecodes.

The Constant Pool as it is recorded in the `.class` file is in a very compacted format. It begins with a 16-bit unsigned integer value that is the count of elements that follow plus one. (The extra count is for the zero'th element that is only used at runtime and not included in the elements contained in the `.class` file.) What follows the count value is a variable-length array with each element being a variable-length structure and no padding between elements.

Twelve different types of values and associated structures can be stored in the Constant Pool. Each structure begins with a single byte-sized integer value called a *tag* (see Table 52.1). The tag is used to determine the format of the bytes that follow which make up the remainder of this element's structure.

Table 52.1 Constant Pool Tags

Tag	Meaning	Note
1	`Utf8` string	
2	`Unicode` string	Not used at this point
3	`Integer` value	
4	`Float` value	
5	`Long` value	
6	`Double` value	
7	Class reference	Only refers to class name
8	String	
9	Field reference	Only used in bytecode stream
10	Method reference	Only used in bytecode stream
11	Interface method	Only used in bytecode stream
12	Name and type reference	

Now that you know the tag values, let's look at each Constant Pool element type. All tags are one byte long, and all lengths and indexes are 16-bit unsigned integer values, unless otherwise noted.

Tag 1: The *Utf8* String The `Utf8` constant is used to represent `Unicode` string values in as small a representation as possible (see Table 52.2). In a `Utf8` string, a character will use from 1–3 bytes depending on its value. It is very oriented towards ASCII values in that all nonnull ASCII characters will fit in a single byte. The `.class` file depends heavily on this Constant Pool entry type, in that all actual string values (including class, field, and method names, types, and method signatures) are stored in `Utf8` constants.

Table 52.2 The *Utf8* String Constant

Field	Number of Bytes	Value
`Tag`	1	1
`Size`	2	Length in bytes of the `Utf8` string.
`Data`	(Size)	The actual `Utf8` string.

Tag 2: The *Unicode* String The `Unicode` constant is intended to hold an actual `Unicode` string but is not used in the `.class` file itself (see Table 52.3). It can be used internally to hold a true `Unicode` string at runtime. Its format is similar to the `Utf8` constant, but each character is a true 16-bit `Unicode` character.

Table 52.3 The *Unicode* String Constant

Field	Number of Bytes	Value
`Tag`	1	2
`Size`	2	Number of characters in the `Unicode` string.
`Data`	(Size * 2)	The actual `Unicode` string.

Tags 3 and 4: *Integer* and *Float* Values The `Integer` and `Float` constants are used to hold integer and float constant values, respectively, that can be used as initializers to fields or variables, as well as hard-coded literal values within a Java statement (see Table 52.4).

Table 52.4 The *Integer* and *Float* Constants

Field	Number of Bytes	Value
`Tag`	1	3 for `Integer`; 4 for `Float`.
`Data`	4	Actual integer or float value in big-endian (MSB first) order.

Tags 5 and 6: *Long* and *Double* Values The `Long` and `Double` constants are used to hold long and double constant values, respectively, that can be used as initializers to fields or variables, as well as hard-coded literal values within a Java statement (see Table 52.5). For internal reasons, each `Long` and `Double` constant uses up two elements in the Constant Pool. So if a `Long` constant starts at Constant Pool location 4, the next constant will be placed in location 6.

Table 52.5 The *Long* and *Double* Constants

Field	Number of Bytes	Value
`Tag`	1	5 for `Long`; 6 for `Double`.
`Data`	8	Actual long or double value in big-endian (MSB first) order.

Tag 7: The *Class* Reference The `Class` reference constant is an indirection that is used to refer to the actual literal name of a class (see Table 52.6). All class names used within the `.class` file are referred to in this way, except when used in a field, variable, argument, or return type declaration (see the upcoming section "Type Information"). Also, because arrays are objects in Java, all array references are based on a `Class` reference constant.

Table 52.6 The *Class* Reference Constant

Field	Number of Bytes	Value
`Tag`	1	7
`Index`	2	Location of a `Utf8` string in the Constant Pool containing the fully qualified class name.

Tag 8: The *String* Reference The `String` reference is another indirection used whenever an actual string literal is encountered in the class definition or bytecode stream (see Table 52.7). This string can be used as an initializer to a `String` variable, directly in a Java expression, or as an argument to a method call.

Table 52.7 The *String* Reference Constant

Field	Number of Bytes	Value
`Tag`	1	8
`Index`	2	Location of a `Utf8` string in the Constant Pool containing the actual string value.

Tags 9, 10, and 11: The *Field*, *Method*, and *Interface Method* Reference The `Field`, `Method`, and `Interface Method` reference constants are used within the compiled Java bytecode stream in order to dynamically reference a field or method that resides in another class or interface (see Table 52.8). The `Class` reference is used to dynamically load in the referenced class, and the `Name` and `Type` reference is used to find the specified field to use or method to call.

Table 52.8 The *Field*, *Method*, and *Interface Method* Reference Constants

Field	Number of Bytes	Value
`Tag`	1	9 for `Field`; 10 for `Method`; 11 for `Interface Method`.
`Class Index`	2	Location of a `Class` reference in the Constant Pool containing the following `Field` or `Method` reference.
`Name/Type`	2	Location of a `Name` and `Type Index` reference in the Constant Pool describing a field or method.

Tag 12: The *Name* and *Type* Reference The `Name` and `Type` reference is used to hold the actual name of a field, variable, method, or argument and its associated type or signature (see Table 52.9). These constant types are used anywhere fields, variables, methods, or arguments are defined and used. See the following section, "Type Information," for the exact format of the contents of the `Description` field.

Table 52.9 The *Name* and *Type* Reference Constants

Field	Number of Bytes	Value
`Tag`	1	12
`Name Index`	2	Location of a `Utf8` string in the Constant Pool containing the name of a field, `var`, `arg`, or method.
`Description Index`	2	Location of a `Utf8` string in the Constant Pool containing the `Name`'s type or signature.

Type Information

In order to have a consistent way of describing the data types of fields, variables, arguments, and the signatures of methods, the `.class` file uses a very abbreviated notation. Essentially, each native type known by the JVM is represented by a single-character shortcut for its full name, with classes and arrays denoted by a special character for modification. Each type and signature shortcut is kept in a `Utf8` formatted string in the Constant Pool. For the type of a field or variable, it is just a single type description; for a method signature, it is a series of type descriptions put together with the arguments first (in order, surrounded by parentheses), followed by the shortcut for the method's result type.

Table 52.10 shows the abbreviated type name followed by its real data type.

Table 52.10 Data Type Abbreviations Used by the *.class* File

Abbreviation	Java Type	Notes
`B`	`byte`	
`C`	`char`	
`D`	`double`	
`F`	`float`	
`I`	`int`	
`J`	`long`	
`S`	`short`	
`Z`	`boolean`	
`V`	`void`	Only used for methods.
`L`<*classname*>`;`	`class`	The capital letter L followed by a fully qualified class name terminated by a semicolon. Note that forward slashes, not periods, are used to delimit the actual package name tokens for the class name.
`[`	Array dimension	An open bracket is used to denote each dimension of an array.

Part VIII

Ch 52

In order to see how these abbreviations are used, take a look at Listing 52.1. You define a simple Java class, and for each variable and method, you put its shorthand version in a comment.

Listing 52.1 Shorthand Types and Signatures

```
class foo {

//     TYPE             FIELD NAME                SHORT-HAND VERSION

       int              simpleInt;             // I
       boolean          simpleBool;            // Z
       float[]          floatArray;            // [F
       char[][]         twoDimCharArray;       // [[C
       String[][][]     threeDimStringArray;   // [[[Ljava/lang/String;
                                               // Note the use of slashes here

       void DoSomething( long arg1, double[][] arg2 ) { }
       //  (J[[D)V
       //  Two arguments, a long and a two dimension double array, returning
       //  nothing.

       java.net.Socket OpenSocket( String hostname, int port ) { }
       //  (Ljava/lang/String;I)Ljava/net/Socket;
       //  Two arguments, a String object and an integer, returning a Socket
       //  object.

       void NoArgsNoResult( ) { }
       //  ()V
       //  No arguments, returning nothing

}
```

Attributes

Attributes are the mechanism that the designers of the `.class` file structure created to allow additional descriptive information about the class to be included in the file without changing its semantics. Attributes are dynamically structured modifiers that contain both mandatory and optional properties affecting the class, its fields, and its methods. For example, information on local variables, arguments, and the compiled bytecode for a method are contained in a mandatory attribute called the `Code` attribute.

Also, with respect to using attributes to extend the information in a `.class` file, Microsoft's JVM implementation provides support for interoperability with COM objects by adding new attributes to the `.class` file. A class loader and JVM implementation only need to recognize the mandatory attributes and can ignore the rest. That way, a class compiled for one VM can still be read (and possibly executed) by another VM.

CAUTION

Obviously, if you created a .class file that depended on a VM that supported COM objects, for example, it would not run with the Sun JVM 1.0.2.

Table 52.11 gives a brief description of the attributes that are recognized by Sun's JVM Version 1.0.2.

Table 52.11 Sun 1.0.2 Java .class File Attributes

Attribute Name	Mandatory	Level	Purpose
`SourceFile`	No	Class	Names the file containing Java source for this `.class` file.
`ConstantValue`	Yes	Field	Holds value of an initializer for a native typed field.
`Exceptions`	Yes	Method	Defines the exceptions that are thrown by this method.
`Code`	Yes	Method	Defines the physical structure and bytecodes for a method.
`LineNumberTable`	No	Code	Contains a program counter to the line number table for use in debugging.
`LocalVariableTable`	No	Code	Contains local variable descriptive information for use in debugging.

When `.class` file elements use attributes, they are kept in a table and are preceded by an unsigned 16-bit integer count field holding the number of attributes that immediately follow. The attributes physically are named variable-length structures that are similar in some respects to the entries in the Constant Pool described earlier in this section. Each attribute begins with a fixed-length portion and is followed by a variable number of fields. Attributes can also be nested in order to allow for extensions to the information that they contain.

All attribute definitions have the same first two fields, as shown in Table 52.12.

Table 52.12 Attribute Definition: The Fixed Portion

Field	Number of Bytes	Value
`Name Index`	2	Location of a `Utf8` string in the Constant Pool containing the literal name of this attribute, as defined in Table 52.11.
`Length`	4	An unsigned integer containing the number of bytes of data that follow, excluding the six bytes that make up the fixed portion (`Name Index` and `Length`).
`Data`	(`Length`)	The actual variable length structure associated with this specific attribute definition.

NOTE I describe each attribute's meaning and structure in context with its actual position in the `.class` file. In those discussions, it is assumed that each attribute begins with the `Name Index` and `Length` fields described in Table 52.12.

The *.class* File Structure

Now that I have defined the dynamic elements that are used in the `.class` file, you can finally discover its real structure. Table 52.13 shows the first level of description for the fields in the `.class` file.

Table 52.13 First Level Fields in the *.class* File Structure

Field	Number of Bytes	Value
`Magic Number`	4	This value acts as a signature and is used to help ensure the validity of the actual `.class` file. As of this writing, it must be the 32-bit value `0xCAFEBABE`.
`Minor Version`	2	Minor version number used by the compiler that generated this `.class`. This integer value is currently `3` in the JDK 1.0.2 javac compiler.
`Major Version`	2	Major version number used by the compiler that generated this `.class`. This integer value is currently `45` in the JDK 1.0.2 javac compiler.
`Constant Pool Size`	2	Number of entries in the following Constant Pool plus one. That is, this value represents the actual number of entries in the runtime version of the Constant Pool, which includes the zero'th entry. That entry is not included in Table 52.14.
`Constant Pool`	Varies	The actual Constant Pool entries as described in the earlier section "The Constant Pool."
`Class Flags`	2	A series of bit flags (defined in the following section) that specify the access permissions for this class or interface definition.
`Class Name`	2	Index to a `Class` reference in the Constant Pool representing the fully qualified name of this class.
`Superclass Name`	2	Index to a `Class` reference in the Constant Pool representing the fully qualified name for

Field	Number of Bytes	Value
		the ancestor class to this one. If this value is zero, `Class Name` must refer to `java.lang.Object` (the only class without a direct ancestor).
`No. of Interfaces`	2	The count of interfaces implemented by this class.
`Interface List`	(Number * 2)	An array of Constant Pool indexes pointing to `Class` reference entries that name the interfaces that this class implements. This array must be in the same order as the `implements` clause encountered when this class was compiled.
`No. of Fields`	2	The count of fields (`static` and `instance`) that are defined in this class.
`Field Table`	Varies	An array of field information structures as defined in the following section.
`No. of Methods`	2	The count of methods (`static` and `instance`) that are defined in this class.
`Method Table`	Varies	An array of `Method Information` structures as defined in the following section.
`No. of Attributes`	2	The count of attributes that are defined for this class.
`Attribute Table`	Varies	The table of attributes included in this `.class` file. The only attribute recognized at this level by the Sun JVM 1.0.2 is the `SourceFile` attribute defined previously.

As you can now see, the `.class` file even at its highest level is very dynamic. There is no way to read in the top level and then go deeper and read the parts that you are interested in. It is totally sequential in nature and physical structure. Most of the individual fields are pretty clear from their description. The only exceptions are the flags and embedded arrays for the fields and methods.

The *Class Flags* Field

The `Class Flags` field is a 16-bit unsigned integer that is used to represent a set of Boolean values that define the structure and access permissions for this `.class` file (see Table 52.14). They are predominantly used by the verification pass of the JVM to denote whether this is a class or interface, and modifiers with respect to class visibility and extension.

Table 52.14 Class Flag Value Definitions

Bit Position (LSb = 1)	Logical Name	Applies to Class	Interface	Definition of Set
1	`PUBLIC`	Yes	Yes	The class is accessible from other classes outside of this package.
5	`FINAL`	Yes	No	This class cannot be subclassed.
6	`SUPER`	Yes	Yes	Calls to methods in the superclass are specially cased.
10	`INTERFACE`	No	Yes	This class represents an interface definition.
11	`ABSTRACT`	Yes	Yes	This class or interface is abstract and has methods that must be coded in a subclass or interface implementation.

The *Field Information* Structure

The `Field Information` structure is a second-level set of information used to describe the name, type, and access permissions associated with a field of this class (see Table 52.15). The fields can be `instance` or `static` (class variables) and can represent native types, specific object references, or arrays of either one. The JVM uses this information to allocate the appropriate amount of space for the class definition in memory and each instance's data space in memory.

Table 52.15 Fields in the *Field Information* Structure

Field	Number of Bytes	Value
`Field Flags`	2	A series of bit flags that define the access permissions for this field.
`Field Name`	2	Index to a `Utf8` string in the Constant Pool representing the name of this field.
`Type`	2	Index to a `Utf8` string in the Constant Pool representing the type definition in the format described in the "Type Information" section.
`No. of Attributes`	2	The count of attributes that are defined for this field.
`Attribute Table`	Varies	The table of attributes associated with this field. The only attribute recognized at this level by the Sun JVM 1.0.2 is the `ConstantValue` attribute defined previously.

Table 52.16 defines the meaning for the access flags associated with a field.

Table 52.16 Field Flag Value Definitions

Bit Position (LSb = 1)	Logical Name	Applies to Class	Interface	Definition of Set
1	`PUBLIC`	Yes	Yes	The field is accessible from other classes outside this package.
2	`PRIVATE`	Yes	No	The field is only accessible from this class. No subclasses or classes outside this package can access it.
3	`PROTECTED`	Yes	No	The field is only accessible from this class and its subclasses.
4	`STATIC`	Yes	Yes	The field is considered a class level field and only has one occurrence in memory that is shared by all instances of this class.
5	`FINAL`	Yes	Yes	This field is only present in this class definition and cannot be overridden or have a value assigned into it after it is initialized.
7	`VOLATILE`	Yes	No	Denotes that this field's value is not guaranteed to be consistent between accesses. So the compiler will not generate optimized code with respect to this field.
8	`TRANSIENT`	Yes	No	This field's value is only valid while an instance of the class is in memory at runtime. Its value, if written to, or read from persistent storage, is ignored.

The *ConstantValue* Attribute

`ConstantValue` is a mandatory attribute found in the field information structure of the `.class` file. It is used to hold the values that were used to initialize the native typed (non-object) fields in a class when they were defined (see Table 52.17).

Table 52.17 Fields Unique to the *ConstantValue* Attribute

Field	Number of Bytes	Value
`Value`	2	Location in the Constant Pool of either an `Integer` constant, a `Long` constant, a `Float` constant, or a `Double` constant.

The type of constant referred to by the `Value` field is determined by the following table:

Constant Pool Type	Holds Values For
`Integer` constant	`boolean`, `byte`, `char`, `integer`, and `short` initializers
`Long` constant	`long` initializers
`Float` constant	`float` initializers
`Double` constant	`double` initializers

The *Method Information* Structure

The `Method Information` structure is a second-level set of information that is used to describe the name, signature, and access permissions for a method in this class (see Table 52.18). Methods can be instance-oriented (only callable from an instance of this class), or they can be `static` methods (callable whether an instance of this class is present or not). The JVM uses the information in these structures, along with the attributes for this method, to create the internal method table for instances of this class or interface to use.

Table 52.18 Fields in the *Method Information* Structure

Field	Number of Bytes	Value
`Method Flags`	2	A series of bit flags that define the access permissions for this method.
`Method Name`	2	Index to a `Utf8` string in the Constant Pool representing the name of this method.
`Signature`	2	Index to a `Utf8` string in the Constant Pool representing this method's signature definition in the format described in the "Type Information" section.
`No. of Attributes`	2	The count of attributes that are defined for this method.
`Attribute Table`	Varies	The table of attributes associated with this method. The only attributes recognized at this level by the Sun JVM 1.0.2 are the `Exceptions` and `Code` attributes defined previously.

Table 52.19 defines the meaning for the access flags associated with a method.

Table 52.19 Field Flag Value Definitions

Bit Position (LSb = 1)	Logical Name	Applies to Class	Interface	Definition of Set
1	PUBLIC	Yes	Yes	The method is accessible from other classes outside this package.
2	PRIVATE	Yes	No	The method is only accessible from this class. No subclasses or classes outside this package can access it.
3	PROTECTED	Yes	No	The method is only accessible from this class and its subclasses.
4	STATIC	Yes	No	The method is considered a class level method and can be called whether an instance of this class exists or not.
5	FINAL	Yes	No	This method is only present in this class definition and cannot be overridden.
6	SYNCHRONIZED	Yes	No	This method is callable in a multi-threaded scenario and will have its access controlled and locked with a monitor.
9	NATIVE	Yes	No	This method's implementation is not in Java bytecodes but in some other external form. It must conform to the native call interface specification of the JVM.
11	ABSTRACT	Yes	Yes	This method's signature is only defined in this class and must be implemented in a subclass. It effectively turns this class into an abstract class.

The *Exceptions* Attribute `Exceptions` is a mandatory attribute found in the `Method Information` structure of the `.class` file for a given method (see Table 52.20). It defines the list of exceptions that are thrown by the method containing this attribute. They are in the same order as found in the `throws` clause that was present in the `.java` source file when this class was compiled. This information is used by the class loader and JVM to verify that a method is permitted to throw a given exception.

Table 52.20 Fields Unique to the *Exceptions* Attribute

Field	Number of Bytes	Value
`Count`	2	Number of elements in the following table of `Utf8` Constant Pool entries.
`Table`	(Count * 2)	An array of indexes to `Utf8` Constant Pool entries.

The *Code* Attribute `Code` is a mandatory attribute of the `Method Information` structure; it defines the actual compiled representation of its source statements (see Table 52.21). The first two fields are used by the JVM to know how much space to define for its stack frame. The bytecodes are executed at runtime, the `Exceptions` are monitored and handled at runtime, and the attributes (if present at all) are used while debugging. In Sun's javac compiler, the `LineNumberTable` and `LocalVariableTable` are inserted when using the `-g` option. These attributes are detailed following this description of the `Code` attribute.

Table 52.21 Fields Unique to the *Code* Attribute

Field	Number of Bytes	Value
`Stack Depth`	2	Maximum allowable depth of the JVM's expression stack.
`No. Locals`	2	Number of local variables (including arguments) defined in this method.
`Code Length`	4	Number of bytes used by the following stream of bytecodes.
`bytecodes`	(`Code Length`)	Stream of Java bytecodes representing the compiled version of this method's statements.
`Exception Count`	2	Number of exceptions that are caught inside this method as described by Table 52.22.
`Exceptions`	(Count * 8)	An ordered table of fixed-length structures (described in Table 52.22) that detail each `try-catch` clause coded in this method.
`Attribute Count`	2	Number of attributes defined in the following attribute table.

Field	Number of Bytes	Value
`Attribute Table`	Varies	Table of attributes provided for this method's `Code` attribute. Currently, only the `LineNumberTable` and `LocalVariableTable` subattributes are supported.

The embedded Exception table has the following format, shown in Table 52.22.

Table 52.22 Fields in the *Code* Attribute's Embedded Exception Table

Field	Number of Bytes	Value
`PC Start`	2	First bytecode of the `try` block that this exception is to handle.
`PC End`	2	Bytecode address where this exception handler is no longer active (the bytecode immediately after the `try` block).
`PC Exception Handler`	2	Bytecode location of the beginning of the actual exception handler.
`Exception Type`	2	Index into the Constant Pool of a `Class` reference constant representing the actual exception to be handled.

The definition of the embedded attributes of the `Code` attribute are discussed in the following sections.

The *LineNumberTable* Attribute `LineNumberTable` is an optional attribute of the `Code` attribute; it contains a table of program counter to line number translation entries (see Table 52.23). They are in order by PC location and can contain duplicate line number references. This anomaly is the result of the way that code is generated in general, and by optimizations performed on the generated Java bytecodes as they are created by Sun's javac compiler.

Table 52.23 Fields Unique to the *LineNumberTable* Attribute

Field	Number of Bytes	Value
`Count`	2	Number of elements in the following line number information table.
`Table`	(Count * 4)	A table containing line number information elements as described in Table 52.24.

The actual line number table elements have the following fixed-length structure, as shown in Table 52.24.

Table 52.24 Fields in the *LineNumberTable* Attribute's Line Number Table

Field	Number of Bytes	Value
`PC Start`	2	Program counter location of the start of some bytecodes associated with a given line number.
`Line Number`	2	The actual line number (relative to the start of the .java source file) where these generated bytecodes came from.

The *LocalVariableTable* Attribute `LocalVariableTable` is an optional attribute of the `Code` attribute; it contains a table of entries describing the local variables present in this method and their associated scope (see Table 52.25). They are not in order and include entries representing the arguments for this method. One point to note here is that every nonstatic method contains at least one argument (even if there are no arguments in the method's signature) representing the current object instance for this class.

Table 52.25 Fields Unique to the *LocalVariableTable* Attribute

Field	Number of Bytes	Value
`Count`	2	Number of elements in the following local variable information table.
`Table`	(Count * 10)	A table containing local variable information elements as described in Table 52.26.

The actual local variable table elements have the following fixed-length structure, as shown in Table 52.26.

Table 52.26 Fields in the *LocalVariableTable* Attribute's Local Variable Table

Field	Number of Bytes	Value
`PC Start`	2	Program counter location where this variable goes into scope.
`Scope Size`	2	The number of bytecodes beginning with `PC Start` where this variable remains in scope—for example, `Scope= ['PC Start' to ('PC Start' + 'Scope Size' - 1)].`
`Name`	2	Location of a `Utf8` string in the Constant Pool containing the literal variable name.
`Type`	2	Location of a `Utf8` string in the Constant Pool containing the type information for this variable (as defined in the "Type Information" section).
`Variable Slot`	2	The slot, or offset, in this method's stack frame where the variable's value is kept.

The *SourceFile* Attribute

`SourceFile` is an optional attribute that is used in the high-level `.class` file structure to hold the name of the source file that was used to compile this `.class` file (see Table 52.27). It is primarily useful for debugging systems to be able to search for the source file and display source lines as required.

Table 52.27 Fields Unique to the *SourceFile* Attribute

Field	Number of Bytes	Value
`File Name`	2	Location of a `Utf8` string in the Constant Pool containing the literal `.java` filename.

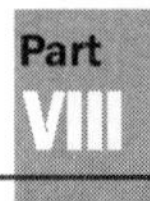

So Now What Can I Do?

Now that you have a fairly good understanding of the physical format of the class structure, you can do many things with this information, such as the following:

- It can help you in understanding how a Java language compiler represents the source information in binary format.
- In debugging, it can help you to effectively use JDB.
- When you attempt to implement a custom debugging aid with the Java Debugger API, this information can help you parse the `.class` file.
- It can help you create your own `.class` file reader.

Personally, I chose a derivative of the fourth alternative. In order to gain a full understanding of the nuances that a `.class` file reader needed to be able to deal with, I implemented a Java application to help me out. I created a package and utility for parsing a `.class` file and converting its information into a displayable string format. The driver utility is called `ClassFileDump`, and the package is called `com.Que.SEUsingJava.ClassFile`.

The utility itself is very simple and just reads some command-line arguments and passes them on to the main class in the package. The package is comprised of 32 classes that are contained in eight Java language source files. The starting class to the package is called `ClassHeader` and has a simple constructor taking no arguments and two primary methods. The first primary method is called `read` and takes a single argument of a `java.io.DataInputStream` instance. This instance should be associated with an open `.class` file. `read` is completely responsible for loading and parsing the `.class` file. It does this by passing the input stream to the 31 other support classes in the package.

Each class in the package knows about a specific structure or attribute of the `.class` file and understands how to read it and convert it to a `String`. After the `read` method returns, the utility calls the `toString` method on the `ClassHeader` instance. The `toString` method takes advantage of the other class instances in the package to convert their respective member data items to `String` values. The `toString` method then returns this large string to the driver utility, where it is sent to `System.out`.

NOTE The `ClassFileDump` utility can be found on the CD-ROM in two formats. The first one is the source to the utility and package and is called `CLASSDMP_SOURCE.ZIP`. The second format is the executable Java bytecode version and is in a file called `CLASSDMP_LIB.ZIP`. This file is in the proper format to add to your `CLASSPATH` environment variable. For example, if you put `CLASSDMP_LIB.ZIP` in your JDK's `\LIB` directory, you can modify your classpath to be the following:

```
;c:\java\lib\classes.zip;c:\java\lib\classdmp_lib.zip
```

After you have done that, you can execute the utility from anywhere that the `java` command is available.

The command line for `ClassFileDump` looks like the following:

```
java  ClassFileDump  <.class filename>
```

For example,

```
java  ClassFileDump  ClassFileDump.class
```

causes the contents of the `ClassFileDump` utility's `.class` file to be sent to `System.out`, the console. I chose to send output there because it can be easily redirected to a file.

CHAPTER 53

Inside the Java Virtual Machine

In this chapter

Elements of the JVM

The concept and implementation of virtual machines (VMs) have been around for quite some time. One of the earliest commercial environments with this architecture was the UCSD p-System. This system was created by Dr. Kenneth Bowles at the University of Southern California, San Diego, in the 1970s. Dr. Bowles was able to create a company, called SofTek Microsystems, to market the operating system. In fact, the p-System was the core operating system for the Apple. It was also the alternative operating system to PC-DOS for the IBM PC after the PC's introduction in 1980.

Like the Java environment, the UCSD p-System was based on a primary language (Pascal). The UCSD p-System had a set of primitive core libraries, a machine-independent object file format, a set of byte-oriented pseudocodes, and a VM definition to interpret them. The p-System and its version of Pascal even had advanced features such as a full-screen user interface, concurrency primitives, and a dynamic library mechanism called units. The p-System was ported to many architectures and had widespread success in the vertical software market.

So, if the p-System was so much like Java, why isn't it still around today? When I asked Sun's chief technology officer, Eric Schmidt, this question, he simply replied, "Have you ever known a university that knew how to market software?" The point of this is that Java is not so unique or new. The Java environment is a success because it has the sponsorship of a very successful company and a much more mature industry.

When you look at the Java environment, you see five major elements:

- Java language
- Bytecode definitions
- Java/Sun core class libraries
- JVM specification
- `.class` file structure

Of these items, the .class file structure, bytecode definitions, and JVM specifications are really what enabled Java technology to become as widespread (or ubiquitous) as quickly as it has. Thus, the designers of Java gained almost instant portability of any .class file to any computer/chip-set with an implementation of the JVM. This portability applied regardless of what kind of host computer/chip-set was used to compile the source. The concept of "write once, run anywhere" is being realized because of the widespread implementation of the JVM on a wide array of hardware platforms and architectures.

The remainder of this section describes some of the technical details involved with Sun's implementation of the JVM. Clearly, many vendors have created JVM implementations (Natural Intelligence, Netscape, Microsoft, and more). All of the vendors have contributed some unique features to their implementations. But, what is fundamentally important is that they all support Sun's initial specification for the `.class` file structure, bytecode definitions, and virtual machine.

The Architecture of a Virtual Machine

So, what really is a virtual machine? It is a software concept that is based on the notion of an imaginary computer with a logical set of instructions, or pseudocodes, that define the operations this computer can perform. A VM-oriented compiler will typically take some source language. Instead of generating machine code instructions targeted to a particular hardware architecture, it generates pseudocode streams that are based on the imaginary computer's instruction set.

The other side of the equation is how these instructions get executed. This is where an interpreter, or what the Java world has been referring to as the VM, takes its role. An interpreter is really just an application that understands the semantics of the pseudocodes for this imaginary computer and converts them to machine code instructions for the underlying hardware to which the interpreter has been targeted. The VM also creates a runtime system internally to support implementing the semantics of the instructions as they are executed. The runtime system is also responsible for loading object (or .class) files, memory management, and garbage collection.

Because of the inconsistency in the hardware platform facilities that are used to host a VM, they are typically based on the concept of a stack machine. A stack machine does not use any physical registers to pass information between instructions. Instead, it uses a stack to hold frames representing the state of a method, operands to the bytecodes, space for arguments to the methods, and space for local variables. There is one pseudoregister called the program counter—a pointer into the bytecode array of the currently executing instruction.

The actual logic for the interpreter phase of the VM is a very simple loop. Figure 53.1 represents a flowchart view of the logic that is typically used by a stack-based VM interpreter.

There are two important points to note about how the interpreter actually processes the bytecode instructions:

- The majority of all semantic routines that perform the action associated with a given bytecode get their operands from the stack and place their results back on the stack.
- The actual bytecodes will typically have arguments that are in line in the bytecode stream immediately following the bytecode itself.

For example, there are bytecodes that push values from the Constant Pool onto the stack. These bytecodes have, as an argument, the index of the value in the Constant Pool. When the semantic for that bytecode is complete, the value will be on the top of the stack, and the program counter will point to the bytecode immediately following the argument. Here is what the bytecode stream might look like for the Load Constant-2 Bytecode:

```
ldc2    index byte 1    index byte 2    <next bytecode>
```

Something else that may not be readily apparent is that method calls, exception handlers, and monitors (the locks used by the `synchronize` language keyword) are all handled by specific bytecodes. They are not the responsibility of the interpreter loop itself. The loop is very stupid in that all it knows how to do is get a bytecode and fire off its associated semantic routine.

FIG. 53.1
The JVM interpreter loop.

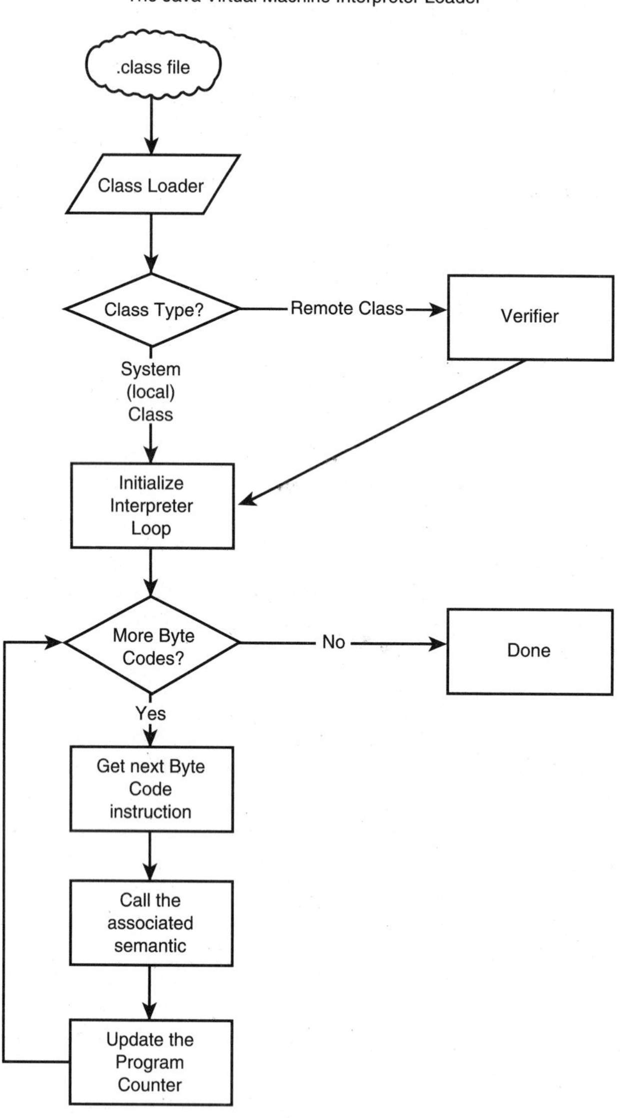

Finally, there are other techniques that an interpreter may use to process the stream of bytecodes representing the executable instructions for the VM. One common optimized interpreter technique is called a threaded interpreter (not to be confused with multithreading). A threaded interpreter does not use a loop-based approach to traverse the stream of bytecodes. Instead, the interpreter actually jumps from bytecode semantic to bytecode semantic in a similar way that a needle and thread are used to make stitches. The big advantage to this technique is that there is no overhead for the interpreter loop, the instructions are executed, and a simple jump is performed at the end. Because this is an implementation choice, it does not affect the .class file structure and, hence, is an option open to people developing their own VMs.

The other optimization that is becoming increasingly popular is the use of what is called a Just-in-Time (JIT) compiler. The Microsoft JVM, Microsoft Internet Explorer 4.0, and Netscape Navigator 4.0 all include JIT technology. The idea of the JIT compiler is that instead of interpreting each instruction of the bytecode stream, the set of bytecodes is directly translated into an equivalent set of machine code instructions for the target system at runtime. This new translated machine code version of the method is then stored and used whenever a call is made to that particular method. So, you get the portability based on the .class file and bytecodes. You also get close-to-native code performance after taking the one-time, up-front translation from bytecode to machine code.

Now that you have a better feel for the architecture of the VM, let's examine how it deals with memory management.

Memory Management and Garbage Collection

One of the major decisions that implementers of runtime systems face is how to handle dynamic memory requirements that are placed on the systems by the programs that are executing within them. The runtime system designer must choose between making the user of the system responsible for memory management or making the runtime system smart enough to handle this task.

If you have ever coded in any compiled 3GL such as C, C++, or Pascal, then you have experienced the "pleasure" of handling your own memory management. These languages have runtime systems that give you primitive methods for allocating and deallocating arbitrarily sized blocks of memory from a larger chunk of memory called a heap. Allocating your application's memory needs from the heap is not a problem if your application has relatively few dynamic memory requirements, but most object-oriented applications tend to create and destroy relatively small objects on a frequent basis.

To help deal with this problem, most runtime systems have a heap manager that actively maintains the heap in a state where memory is available as much as possible. One of the major problems that the heap manager tries to solve is called *fragmentation*, which is a result of allocating and deallocating lots of small, nonuniform pieces of memory from the heap. Typically, a heap is managed by tracking memory in two lists:

- Free block list
- Allocated block list

When a request is made to the heap manager for a chunk of memory, the free list is searched for a block that can fulfill this request. Most modern heap managers keep the free list in ascending order of the free blocks' sizes. This allows the allocation mechanism to use a "first-fit strategy," finding the first-available, smallest block of memory that can satisfy the request. This strategy helps keep fragmentation of the heap to a minimum.

Another technique that heap managers use to keep fragmentation of the heap to a minimum is called coalescing. As memory is returned to the heap, a new block is placed in the free list. As this process occurs, the free list is examined to see if the piece of memory being returned immediately precedes or follows another free block. If this is the case, then the two blocks are merged together, creating one larger free block.

Another issue in heap management is how to deal with a request for more memory than an individual block on the free list can provide. Such a request requires that the heap manager take some very proactive steps in order to create more memory. The solution is a technique called compaction. Compaction is the process of merging all free blocks together by moving the allocated memory (memory between the free blocks) to one end of the heap, thereby creating one large, coalesced free block. The real difficulty with this process is that the runtime system must know the location of every variable (stack-based or dynamic) that refers to any heap-based object in memory. The system must then update the variable with the new location of the object that it refers to. This process is very expensive in both time and memory overhead, but compaction is a reality in any heap-based allocation system.

The other major problem with being responsible for your own memory allocation and, specifically, deallocation is the concept of dangling references, or garbage. This refers to objects in memory that you allocated but have lost the reference (or pointer) to, so you cannot explicitly deallocate the memory. Dangling references are very easy to create. The following C++ code shows a typical way to create a dangling reference:

```
int *iArray;
// Create initial array
iArray = new int[3];
...
// Grow the array
if (iArrayCount == 3) {
    int *tempArray = new int[6];
    for (int i = 0;i < 3;++i) tempArray[I] = iArray[I];
    // MAKE A DANGLING REFERENCE:
    iArray = tempArray;
}
```

Once `iArray` is overwritten with `tempArray`, the memory chunk originally pointed to by `iArray` is orphaned and now garbage. The memory chunk cannot be reclaimed during compaction, because it is not on the free list. The only way to deal with this situation is via garbage collection.

Garbage collection is a technique in which all allocated memory objects that are no longer needed or referred to may be reclaimed back to the free list without an explicit deallocation. It is a process of the heap management system, and memory blocks must be structured in specific ways to take advantage of it. Two common garbage collection techniques can be used: reference counting, and mark and sweep.

Reference counting requires that each object instance in the heap maintain a field called the reference count. As a field or variable is assigned a reference to an object, that object's reference count is increased by one. When the field or variable that refers to the object goes out of scope or is destroyed, the reference count is decreased by one. When an object's reference count reaches zero, it is no longer in use and its space may be collected. This algorithm is fast during collection but has a performance penalty when any assignment is without objects or an object is passed as an argument. For each of these situations, the reference count must be maintained at runtime, causing general slow-downs of the runtime system.

The mark and sweep algorithm requires that each object contain a bit field called the mark bit, or it is required that an external array is created when the algorithm runs to hold the mark bit. The algorithm begins by traversing all allocated blocks of memory in the heap and resetting the marked bit for that block. Next, examine all fields and variables that refer to objects in the heap, setting the marked bit of the heap object to true. Finally, sweep through the allocated heap objects and look for any that are not marked. Then, either reclaim the space by putting the unused objects on the free list, or copy the "live" objects to the end of the heap. Then, reclaim the original area back to the free list and compact (a variant of mark and sweep known as stop and copy). This algorithm has low storage overhead and does not affect runtime performance overall but may cause longer-than-desired lags in time when the garbage collector runs.

Now that you can see how difficult a problem heap and memory management can be, especially for the non-Java developer, take a look at how the Java runtime system handles these problems.

First, the JVM uses two separate heaps for dynamic and static memory allocation. All class definitions, the Constant Pool, and method tables are kept in a nongarbage collected heap. Once a class definition has been read in, the structural information and methods stay in memory. This does add a little storage overhead, but improves performance for classes that come and go relatively frequently within an application.

The second heap is split into two areas that grow in opposite directions. One area is used to hold object instances, and the other contains "handles" to those instances. The runtime image of fields and variables in your Java application that reference object instances do not actually contain pointers to those objects. They contain pointers to a special, fixed-size, heap-based memory object called a handle. The handle is a structure that contains two pointers: one to the object's method table and the other to the actual object instance. The advantage to this layout is that the handles never move in memory, so there is never a need to keep track of which variables point to which objects when updating pointers after compacting. You simply update the pointer value of the handle structure.

The object space of the heap is managed in a traditional fashion in that there is a free list and an allocated object list. As objects are instantiated, the free list is searched for the "first-fit block." Also, if possible, coalescing happens during this phase (as opposed to when an instance is put back on the free list) in order to make the garbage collection process faster. In addition, the dangling reference problem is eliminated by Java, as you are not responsible for explicit object deallocations. The Java language has a `new` operator but no corresponding `delete`.

The garbage collection algorithm used by the JVM applies to all objects in the dynamic heap. The algorithm runs synchronously whenever the heap manager cannot find any memory in the free space list. Or, it may also run asynchronously in that a thread for the garbage collector is kicked off whenever the system is idle for a sufficient period of time. (This is of dubious value, because the asynchronous garbage collector will be interrupted and have to start again if a runnable class becomes ready.) And, you may manually initiate the garbage collection algorithm by calling the method `System.gc()`. For highly interactive applications where idle processing may be at a minimum, you might occasionally want to call the garbage collector manually.

The actual garbage collector used by the JVM is an implementation of the stop-and-copy algorithm. But, there is a difference. Normally, after the garbage collector finishes its compaction phase, all variables and fields that relate to an object would need to change. But, because all object reference variables are handle-based, we don't need to find and update all variables that point to active objects. You can simply update the handle in the heap to point to the just-moved object instance. The algorithm is pretty fast but not ready for real-time applications.

One last aspect to the JVM's garbage collector is the notion of a `Finalizer` method. A `Finalizer` is a special method called `finalize` that is declared in the base class `java.lang.Object`. It has the following prototype:

```
protected void finalize () throws Throwable;
```

The `finalize` method is used for cleaning up external resources (such as open files) that would not normally be performed in routine garbage collection. The garbage collector calls the `finalize` method just prior to garbage collecting an object instance. The problem is that garbage collection is not run immediately when you call the `System.gc()` method; it is simply scheduled to run. The garbage collector thread runs at a very low priority and may get interrupted frequently. In fact, the garbage collector may never get to dispose of your object before the application terminates. So, generally speaking, the usefulness of implementing the `finalize` method is questionable.

You can do one other trick in a `finalize` method—"resurrect" an object instance. It is possible for you to place the value of the `this` field into some other object reference and stop the object from being garbage collected. At that point, though, the garbage collector will not call the `finalize` method again, even when the object instance is really ready for garbage collection.

That's all there is to heap management in Java: One heap contains a fixed table of class information and methods, and another heap holds the handle table and object instances. You don't explicitly deallocate anything (although setting an unused object variable to null will act as a hint to the garbage collector and heap), and the garbage collector may be run manually by calling `System.gc()`.

Class File Verification

The last real algorithm that I cover for the JVM is verification. Verification is a process that is applied to certain class files as they are loaded. Because Java is oriented toward applications whose pieces (.class files) are potentially scattered anywhere around the globe, you need a mechanism that can prove these nonlocal classes can be properly executed by the JVM. By default, the `java` command will put all classes that were not loaded from the local hard drive through the verification process. Whether a class is put through the verification process is a function of the Class Loader and is controlled by arguments that you may specify on the `java` command line. In the case of browsers that support Java applets, all nonsystem classes are put through verification.

The verifier exists basically to subvert or thwart any attempts to create or pass off a hostile .class file. Because classes are loaded over the network from a typically unknown source, the verifier is applied to them to make sure they conform to the contract between a .class file and the JVM specification. Another benefit of the verification step is that it speeds execution of the Java bytecodes at runtime. The speed is increased because the form is good, and the bytecodes don't have to verify their own arguments at each execution. The verifier also checks the overall integrity of the .class file.

The verification process can be broken up into four phases. The first three are performed at class-load time, with the fourth performed by a subset of the actual Java bytecodes.

The first phase could be called the syntax check phase. It is responsible for ensuring the structural and syntactic integrity of the .class file being loaded. The following areas are examined during this phase:

- The magic number.
- The version number. Checked to be sure it is in sync with this VM implementation.
- Mandatory attributes. Checked to be sure they exist and are properly formed.
- The Constant Pool. Verifies that only valid item types are contained.

The second phase is used to check the "semantic" consistency of the .class file. It is responsible for checking the following areas:

- The access flags. Checks that they are not being violated for the class, its fields, and its methods.
- The lineage of the object. Verifies the superclass field, for example.
- The Constant Pool items. Checks that these items are well-formed (for example, the Strings are strings, and so on).

The third phase is the most intense and is called the bytecode verifier. This phase performs a data-flow analysis on the actual bytecode stream that is contained in each method definition in the class. The following list represents the major features of the bytecode verifier, which ensures the following:

- The stack is in a consistent state for each bytecode encountered. That is, it verifies there is no under- or overflow of the expression stack.
- The arguments to the operands are in the appropriate domain.
- The types of values being put in or referenced from fields, arguments, and variables are correct for their usage.
- The arguments passed to method calls are of the right form.
- No field or variable is accessed without being properly initialized.

The final phase is actually performed at runtime and involves checks that could not be performed in phase three, because not all referenced classes are necessarily loaded in that phase. For each instruction that dynamically refers to another class (either a field or method), the linkage is examined. Then, the access permissions are checked. Furthermore, if all is OK, the referenced class is instantiated. Also, if the current bytecode references anything in the Constant Pool, it is resolved, and a special _quick variant of the bytecode instruction is replaced at that point in the bytecode stream. The _quick variants assume that the value required is directly accessible with no intermediate Constant Pool resolution requirement.

The JVM Bytecodes

This final section is a reference for the actual JVM bytecode instructions. There is not enough space in this section to include all of the details that are actually required to implement a JVM, but you should be able to write a simple bytecode disassembler with this information. Table 53.1 contains the following columns:

Instruction	The literal mnemonic for this OpCode
OpCode	The actual unsigned bytecode value
#Args	The number of byte-sized operands in the bytecode stream that immediately follow the OpCode for this instruction
Description	The basic semantics of this instruction

When the JVM interpreter loop is running, there is actually one logical register that is used—the Program Counter, which represents the address in the bytecode stream of the currently executing instruction. Some of the instructions modify this Program Counter in order to alter the flow of execution. Otherwise, execution flows sequentially through the bytecode stream from instruction to instruction.

Table 53.1 Java Bytecode Instructions in OpCode Order

Instruction	Op Code	# Args	Description
nop	0	0	Does nothing, a No Operation.
aconst_null	1	0	Pushes the null object reference on the stack.
iconst_m1	2	0	Pushes the integer constant -1 on the stack.
iconst_0	3	0	Pushes the integer constant 0 on the stack.
iconst_1	4	0	Pushes the integer constant 1 on the stack.
iconst_2	5	0	Pushes the integer constant 2 on the stack.
iconst_3	6	0	Pushes the integer constant 3 on the stack.
iconst_4	7	0	Pushes the integer constant 4 on the stack.
iconst_5	8	0	Pushes the integer constant 5 on the stack.

Instruction	Op Code	# Args	Description
`lconst_0`	9	0	Pushes the long constant `0` on the stack.
`lconst_1`	10	0	Pushes the long constant `1` on the stack.
`fconst_0`	11	0	Pushes the float constant `0` on the stack.
`fconst_1`	12	0	Pushes the float constant `1` on the stack.
`fconst_2`	13	0	Pushes the float constant `2` on the stack.
`dconst_0`	14	0	Pushes the double constant `0` on the stack.
`dconst_1`	15	0	Pushes the double constant `1` on the stack.
`bipush`	16	1	Pushes a 1-byte signed value on the stack as an integer.
`sipush`	17	2	Pushes a 16-bit signed value on the stack as an integer.
`ldc1`	18	1	Uses arg as an 8-bit index into the Constant Pool and puts the associated item on the stack.
`ldc2`	19	2	Uses arg as a 16-bit index into the Constant Pool and puts the associated item on the stack.
`ldc2w`	20	2	Uses arg as a 16-bit index into the Constant Pool and pushes the long or double at that position on the stack.
`iload`	21	1	Pushes the value of the integer local variable at the index specified by the argument in the current method frame on the stack.
`lload`	22	1	Pushes the value of the long local variable at the index and index+1 specified by the argument in the current method frame on the stack.
`fload`	23	1	Pushes the value of the float local variable at the index specified by the argument in the current method frame on the stack.
`dload`	24	1	Pushes the value of the double local variable at the index and index+1 specified by the argument in the current method frame on the stack.
`aload`	25	1	Pushes the value of the object reference local variable at the index specified by the argument in the current method frame on the stack.

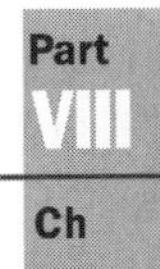

continues

Table 53.1 Continued

Instruction	Op Code	# Args	Description
`iload_0`	26	0	Pushes the value of the integer local variable at index 0 in the current method frame on the stack.
`iload_1`	27	0	Pushes the value of the integer local variable at index 1 in the current method frame on the stack.
`iload_2`	28	0	Pushes the value of the integer local variable at index 2 in the current method frame on the stack.
`iload_3`	29	0	Pushes the value of the integer local variable at index 3 in the current method frame on the stack.
`lload_0`	30	0	Pushes the value of the long local variable at index 0 and 1 in the current method frame on the stack.
`lload_1`	31	0	Pushes the value of the long local variable at index 1 and 2 in the current method frame on the stack.
`lload_2`	32	0	Pushes the value of the long local variable at index 2 and 3 in the current method frame on the stack.
`lload_3`	33	0	Pushes the value of the long local variable at index 3 and 4 in the current method frame on the stack.
`fload_0`	34	0	Pushes the value of the float local variable at index 0 in the current method frame on the stack.
`fload_1`	35	0	Pushes the value of the float local variable at index 1 in the current method frame on the stack.
`fload_2`	36	0	Pushes the value of the float local variable at index 2 in the current method frame on the stack.
`fload_3`	37	0	Pushes the value of the float local variable at index 3 in the current method frame on the stack.

Instruction	Op Code	# Args	Description
dload_0	38	0	Pushes the value of the double local variable at index 0 and 1 in the current method frame on the stack.
dload_1	39	0	Pushes the value of the double local variable at index 1 and 2 in the current method frame on the stack.
dload_2	40	0	Pushes the value of the double local variable at index 2 and 3 in the current method frame on the stack.
dload_3	41	0	Pushes the value of the double local variable at index 3 and 4 in the current method frame on the stack.
aload_0	42	0	Pushes the value of the object reference local variable at index 0 in the current method frame on the stack.
aload_1	43	0	Pushes the value of the object reference local variable at index 1 in the current method frame on the stack.
aload_2	44	0	Pushes the value of the object reference local variable at index 2 in the current method frame on the stack.
aload_3	45	0	Pushes the value of the object reference local variable at index 3 in the current method frame on the stack.
istore	45	1	Pops the integer value from the stack and stores it into the local variable at the index specified by the argument in the current method frame.
iaload	46	0	Pops an array index and an integer array object reference off the stack and pushes the element at `index` back onto the stack.
laload	47	0	Pops an array index and a long array object reference off the stack and pushes the element at `index` back onto the stack.
faload	48	0	Pops an array index and a float array object reference off the stack and pushes the element at `index` back onto the stack.

continues

Table 53.1 Continued

Instruction	Op Code	# Args	Description
`daload`	49	0	Pops an array index and a double array object reference off the stack and pushes the element at `index` back onto the stack.
`aaload`	50	0	Pops an array index and an array object reference off the stack and pushes the element at `index` back onto the stack.
`baload`	51	0	Pops an array index and a signed byte array object reference off the stack and pushes the element at `index` back onto the stack.
`caload`	52	0	Pops an array index and a char array object reference off the stack and pushes the element at `index` back onto the stack.
`saload`	53	0	Pops an array index and a short array object reference off the stack and pushes the element at `index` back onto the stack.
`lstore`	55	1	Pops the long value from the stack and stores it in the local variable at `index` and `index+1` specified by the argument in the current method frame.
`fstore`	56	1	Pops the `float` value from the stack and stores it in the local variable at the index specified by the argument in the current method frame.
`dstore`	57	1	Pops the double value from the stack and stores it in the local variable at `index` and `index+1` specified by the argument in the current method frame.
`astore`	58	1	Pops the object reference from the stack and stores it in the local variable at the index specified by the argument in the current method frame.
`istore_0`	59	0	Pops the integer value from the stack and stores it in the local variable at index 0 in the current method frame.
`istore_1`	60	0	Pops the integer value from the stack and stores it in the local variable at index 1 in the current method frame.

Instruction	Op Code	# Args	Description
`istore_2`	61	0	Pops the integer value from the stack and stores it in the local variable at index 2 in the current method frame.
`istore_3`	62	0	Pops the integer value from the stack and stores it in the local variable at index 3 in the current method frame.
`lstore_0`	63	0	Pops the long value from the stack and stores it in the local variable at index 0 and 1 in the current method frame.
`lstore_1`	64	0	Pops the long value from the stack and stores it in the local variable at index 1 and 2 in the current method frame.
`lstore_2`	65	0	Pops the long value from the stack and stores it in the local variable at index 2 and 3 in the current method frame.
`lstore_3`	66	0	Pops the long value from the stack and stores it in the local variable at index 3 and 4 in the current method frame.
`fstore_0`	67	0	Pops the float value from the stack and stores it in the local variable at index 0 in the current method frame.
`fstore_1`	68	0	Pops the float value from the stack and stores it in the local variable at index 1 in the current method frame.
`fstore_2`	69	0	Pops the float value from the stack and stores it in the local variable at index 2 in the current method frame.
`fstore_3`	70	0	Pops the float value from the stack and stores it in the local variable at index 3 in the current method frame.
`dstore_0`	71	0	Pops the double value from the stack and stores it in the local variable at index 0 and 1 in the current method frame.
`dstore_1`	72	0	Pops the double value from the stack and stores it in the local variable at index 1 and 2 in the current method frame.

continues

Table 53.1 Continued

Instruction	Op Code	# Args	Description
`dstore_2`	73	0	Pops the double value from the stack and stores it in the local variable at index 2 and 3 in the current method frame.
`dstore_3`	74	0	Pops the double value from the stack and stores it in the local variable at index 3 and 4 in the current method frame.
`astore_0`	75	0	Pops the object reference from the stack and stores it in the local variable at index 0 in the current method frame.
`astore_1`	76	0	Pops the object reference from the stack and stores it in the local variable at index 1 in the current method frame.
`astore_2`	77	0	Pops the object reference from the stack and stores it in the local variable at index 2 in the current method frame.
`astore_3`	78	0	Pops the object reference from the stack and stores it in the local variable at index 3 in the current method frame.
`iastore`	79	0	Pops an integer value, an array index, and an integer array object reference off the stack and stores the integer value in the array element at `index`.
`lastore`	80	0	Pops a long value, an array index, and a long array object reference off the stack and stores the long value in the array element at `index`.
`fastore`	81	0	Pops a float value, an array index, and a float array object reference off the stack and stores the float value in the array element at `index`.
`dastore`	82	0	Pops a double value, an array index, and a double array object reference off the stack and stores the double value in the array element at `index`.
`aastore`	83	0	Pops an object reference, an array index, and an object reference array object reference off the stack and stores the object reference in the array element at `index`.

Instruction	Op Code	# Args	Description
`bastore`	84	0	Pops a signed byte value, an array index, and a signed byte array object reference off the stack and stores the signed byte value in the array element at `index`.
`castore`	85	0	Pops a `char` value, an array index, and a `char` array object reference off the stack and stores the `char` value in the array element at `index`.
`sastore`	86	0	Pops a short value, an array index, and a short array object reference off the stack and stores the short value in the array element at `index`.
`pop`	87	0	Pops the word from the top of the stack.
`pop2`	88	0	Pops two words from the top of the stack.
`dup`	89	0	Duplicates the word at the top of the stack.
`dup_x1`	90	0	Duplicates the word at the top of the stack and puts the duplicate value two words down.
`dup_x2`	91	0	Duplicates the word at the top of the stack and puts the duplicate value three words down.
`dup2`	92	0	Duplicates the two words at the top of the stack.
`dup2_x1`	93	0	Duplicates the two words at the top of the stack and puts the duplicate values two words down.
`dup2_x2`	94	0	Duplicates the two words at the top of the stack and puts the duplicate value three words down.
`swap`	95	0	Swaps the two words at the top of the stack.
`iadd`	96	0	Pops the two integer values off the stack, adds them, and pushes the result on top of the stack.
`ladd`	97	0	Pops the two long values off the stack, adds them, and pushes the result on top of the stack.
`fadd`	98	0	Pops the two float values off the stack, adds them, and pushes the result on top of the stack.

continues

Table 53.1 Continued

Instruction	Op Code	# Args	Description
dadd	99	0	Pops the two double values off the stack, adds them, and pushes the result on top of the stack.
isub	100	0	Pops the two integer values off the stack, subtracts them, and pushes the result on top of the stack.
lsub	101	0	Pops the two long values off the stack, subtracts them, and pushes the result on top of the stack.
fsub	102	0	Pops the two float values off the stack, subtracts them, and pushes the result on top of the stack.
dsub	103	0	Pops the two double values off the stack, subtracts them, and pushes the result on top of the stack.
imul	104	0	Pops the two integer values off the stack, multiplies them, and pushes the result on top of the stack.
lmul	105	0	Pops the two long values off the stack, multiplies them, and pushes the result on top of the stack.
fmul	106	0	Pops the two float values off the stack, multiplies them, and pushes the result on top of the stack.
dmul	107	0	Pops the two double values off the stack, multiplies them, and pushes the result on top of the stack.
idiv	108	0	Pops the two integer values off the stack, divides them, and pushes the result on top of the stack.
ldiv	109	0	Pops the two long values off the stack, divides them, and pushes the result on top of the stack.
fdiv	110	0	Pops the two float values off the stack, divides them, and pushes the result on top of the stack.

Instruction	Op Code	# Args	Description
ddiv	111	0	Pops the two double values off the stack, divides them, and pushes the result on top of the stack.
irem	112	0	Pops the two integer values off the stack, divides them, and pushes the remainder on top of the stack.
lrem	113	0	Pops the two long values off the stack, divides them, and pushes the remainder on top of the stack.
frem	114	0	Pops the two float values off the stack, divides them, and pushes the remainder on top of the stack.
drem	115	0	Pops the two double values off the stack, divides them, and pushes the remainder on top of the stack.
ineg	116	0	Pops the integer value off the stack, calculates its arithmetic negation, and pushes the result on top of the stack.
lneg	117	0	Pops the long value off the stack, calculates its arithmetic negation, and pushes the result on top of the stack.
fneg	118	0	Pops the float value off the stack, calculates its arithmetic negation, and pushes the result on top of the stack.
dneg	119	0	Pops the double value off the stack, calculates its arithmetic negation, and pushes the result on top of the stack.
ishl	120	0	Pops the shift count and the integer value, shifts the value left by the low 5 bits of the shift count, and pushes the integer result on top of the stack.
lshl	121	0	Pops the shift count and the long value, shifts the value left by the low 6 bits of the shift count, and pushes the long result on top of the stack.

continues

Table 53.1 Continued

Instruction	Op Code	# Args	Description
ishr	122	0	Pops the shift count and the integer value, arithmetically shifts the value right (extending the sign) by the low 5 bits of the shift count, and pushes the integer result on top of the stack.
lshr	123	0	Pops the shift count and the long value, arithmetically shifts the value right (extending the sign) by the low 6 bits of the shift count, and pushes the long result on top of the stack.
iushr	124	0	Pops the shift count and the integer value, logically shifts the value right (not extending the sign) by the low 5 bits of the shift count, and pushes the integer result on top of the stack.
iushr	125	0	Pops the shift count and the long value, logically shifts the value right (not extending the sign) by the low 6 bits of the shift count, and pushes the long result on top of the stack.
iand	126	0	Pops two integer values off the stack, performs a bitwise, and then puts the result back on top of the stack.
land	127	0	Pops two long values off the stack, performs a bitwise, and then puts the result back on top of the stack.
ior	128	0	Pops two integer values off the stack, performs a bitwise or then puts the result back on top of the stack.
lor	129	0	Pops two long values off the stack, performs a bitwise or then puts the result back on top of the stack.
ixor	130	0	Pops two integer values off the stack, performs a bitwise x or puts the result back on top of the stack.
lxor	131	0	Pops two long values off the stack, performs a bitwise x or puts the result back on top of the stack.
iinc	132	2	Increments the integer local variable at index (arg1) in the current method frame by the signed 8-bit value in (arg2).

Instruction	Op Code	# Args	Description
`i2l`	133	0	Pops an integer value off the stack, converts it to a long, and pushes it on the stack.
`i2f`	134	0	Pops an integer value off the stack, converts it to a float, and pushes it on the stack.
`i2d`	135	0	Pops an integer value off the stack, converts it to a double, and pushes it on the stack.
`l2i`	136	0	Pops a long value off the stack, converts it to an integer, and pushes it on the stack.
`l2f`	137	0	Pops a long value off the stack, converts it to a float, and pushes it on the stack.
`l2d`	138	0	Pops a long value off the stack, converts it to a double, and pushes it on the stack.
`f2i`	139	0	Pops a float value off the stack, converts it to an integer, and pushes it on the stack.
`f2l`	140	0	Pops a float value off the stack, converts it to a long, and pushes it on the stack.
`f2d`	141	0	Pops a float value off the stack, converts it to a double, and pushes it on the stack.
`d2i`	142	0	Pops a double value off the stack, converts it to an integer, and pushes it on the stack.
`d2l`	143	0	Pops a double value off the stack, converts it to a long, and pushes it on the stack.
`d2f`	144	0	Pops a double value off the stack, converts it to a float, and pushes it on the stack.
`int2byte`	145	0	Pops an integer value off the stack, converts it to a signed byte, and pushes it on the stack.
`int2char`	146	0	Pops an integer value off the stack, converts it to a `char`, and pushes it on the stack.
`int2short`	147	0	Pops an integer value off the stack, converts it to a short, and pushes it on the stack.
`lcmp`	148	0	Pops long `value2` and long `value1` from the stack. If `value1` is greater than `value2`, push integer `1` on the stack. If `value1` equals `value2`, push integer `0` on the stack. If `value1` is less than `value2`, push integer `-1` on the stack.

continues

Table 53.1 Continued

Instruction	Op Code	# Args	Description
`fcmpl`	149	0	Pops float `value2` and float `value1` from the stack. If `value1` is greater than `value2`, then push integer `1` on the stack. If `value1` equals `value2`, then push integer `0` on the stack. If `value1` is less than `value2` or either value is `NaN`, then push integer `-1` on the stack.
`fcmpg`	150	0	Pops float `value2` and float `value1` from the stack. If `value1` is greater than `value2`, then push integer `1` on the stack. If `value1` equals `value2`, then push integer `0` on the stack. If `value1` is less than `value2` or either value is `NaN`, then push integer `1` on the stack.
`dcmpl`	151	0	Pops double `value2` and double `value1` from the stack. If `value1` is greater than `value2`, then push integer `1` on the stack. If `value1` equals `value2`, then push integer `0` on the stack. If `value1` is less than `value2` or either value is `NaN`, then push integer `-1` on the stack.
`dcmpg`	152	0	Pops double `value2` and double `value1` from the stack. If `value1` is greater than `value2`, then push integer `1` on the stack. If `value1` equals `value2`, then push integer `0` on the stack. If `value1` is less than `value2` or either value is `NaN`, then push integer `1` on the stack.
`ifeq`	153	2	Pops an integer value off the stack. If it is equal to 0, then the two args are added together and added to the current Program Counter; otherwise, the next instruction is executed.
`ifne`	154	2	Pops an integer value off the stack. If it is not equal to 0, then the two args are added together and added to the current Program Counter; otherwise, the next instruction is executed.
`iflt`	155	2	Pops an integer value off the stack. If it is less than 0, then the two args are added together and added to the current Program Counter; otherwise, the next instruction is executed.

Instruction	Op Code	# Args	Description
`ifge`	156	2	Pops an integer value off the stack. If it is greater than or equal to 0, then the two args are added together and added to the current Program Counter; otherwise, the next instruction is executed.
`ifgt`	157	2	Pops an integer value off the stack. If it is greater than 0, then the two args are added together and added to the current Program Counter; otherwise, the next instruction is executed.
`ifle`	158	2	Pops an integer value off the stack. If it is less than or equal to 0, then the two args are added together and added to the current Program Counter; otherwise, the next instruction is executed.
`if_icmpeq`	159	2	Pops integer `value2` and integer `value1` from the stack. If `value1` equals `value2`, then the two args are added together and added to the current Program Counter; otherwise, the next instruction is executed.
`if_icmpne`	160	2	Pops integer `value2` and integer `value1` from the stack. If `value1` is not equal to `value2`, then the two args are added together and added to the current Program Counter; otherwise, the next instruction is executed.
`if_icmplt`	161	2	Pops integer `value2` and integer `value1` from the stack. If `value1` is less than `value2` then the two args are added together and added to the current Program Counter; otherwise the next instruction is executed.
`if_icmpge`	162	2	Pops integer `value2` and integer `value1` from the stack. If `value1` is greater than or equal to `value2`, then the two args are added together and added to the current Program Counter; otherwise, the next instruction is executed.
`if_icmpgt`	163	2	Pops integer `value2` and integer `value1` from the stack. If `value1` is greater than `value2`, then the two args are added together and added to the current Program Counter; otherwise, the next instruction is executed.

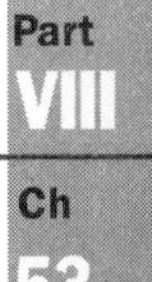

continues

Table 53.1 Continued

Instruction	Op Code	# Args	Description
`if_icmple`	164	2	Pops integer `value2` and integer `value1` from the stack. If `value1` is less than or equal to `value2`, then the two args are added together and added to the current Program Counter; otherwise, the next instruction is executed.
`if_acmpeq`	165	2	Pops object reference `value2` and object reference `value1` from the stack. If the values refer to the same object, then the two args are added together and added to the current Program Counter; otherwise, the next instruction is executed.
`if_acmpne`	166	2	Pops object reference `value2` and object reference `value1` from the stack. If the values do not refer to the same object, then the two args are added together and added to the current Program Counter; otherwise, the next instruction is executed.
`goto`	167	2	Adds the two args together, constructing a 16-bit value, and adds to the current Program Counter.
`jsr`	168	2	Adds the two args together, constructing a 16-bit integer value. Pushes the Program Counter location of the instruction immediately following this one onto the stack. Adds the 16-bit value to the Program Counter to move the flow of execution to the subroutine. At the entry to the subroutine, the return address is popped off the stack and saved in a local variable for later use in the `ret` and `ret_w` instructions. (This instruction is used when the JVM processes a `finally` block.)
`ret`	169	1	Uses the argument as an index into the method's frame to a local variable that contains the return address of the caller. The return address is then put into the Program Counter to move the flow of execution back to the caller of this subroutine. (This instruction is used when the JVM processes a `finally` block.)

Instruction	Op Code	# Args	Description
`tableswitch`	170	>12	Represents the compiled implementation of a switch statement where the location of the desired case is on the stack. After the OpCode, there may be 0 to 3 bytes of padding in order to bring the next arguments to a 4-byte boundary. The next three arguments help describe the size of the table. After the pad bytes is a 32-bit integer representing the offset into the table for the `default` block. Then follows two 32-bit values representing the lowest and highest allowable index values, respectively. Next is the actual table. The table is an array of 32-bit integers containing the offsets from the beginning of this instruction to the block of code for a `case` in the `switch` statement. There are (high-index – low-index + 1) 32-bit entries in the table, with the first entry considered to be at offset zero. The `index` to be used in the actual lookup is an integer that must be popped off the stack. If the index value is not in the range `[low-index, high-index]`, then the address for the `default` block is used. Otherwise, the value of `low-index` is subtracted from the `index` off the stack to determine the table slot containing the new offset where the execution point should be moved.
`lookupswitch`	171	>12	Represents the compiled implementation of a `switch` statement that is based on determining the `index` by matching up an integer key, which is located on the stack with a value in the table. After the OpCode, there may be 0 to 3 bytes of padding in order to bring the next arguments to a 4-byte boundary. The next two arguments help describe the size of the table. After the pad bytes is a 32-bit integer representing the offset into the table for the `default` block. Then follows a 32-bit value representing the number of `match/offset` pairs that make up the table elements. Next is the actual table. The table is an array of 32-bit integer pairs containing a value to compare the `key` with and

continues

Table 53.1 Continued

Instruction	Op Code	# Args	Description
			the offset from the beginning of this instruction to the block of code for a matching `case` in the `switch` statement. The `key` to be used in the actual match is an integer that must be popped off the stack. If the `key` does not match any of the entries in the table, then the address for the `default` block is used. Otherwise, the index value of the matching table entry is added to the Program Counter. Execution continues from that point.
`ireturn`	172	0	Pops an integer value from the current method's stack. This integer value is then pushed onto the stack of the caller's method frame. Control is then returned to the caller's method.
`lreturn`	173	0	Pops a long value from the current method's stack. This long value is then pushed onto the stack of the caller's method frame. Control is then returned to the caller's method.
`freturn`	174	0	Pops a float value from the current method's stack. This float value is then pushed onto the stack of the caller's method frame. Control is then returned to the caller's method.
`dreturn`	175	0	Pops a double value from the current method's stack. This double value is then pushed onto the stack of the caller's method frame. Control is then returned to the caller's method.
`areturn`	176	0	Pops an object reference value from the current method's stack. This object reference value is then pushed onto the stack of the caller's method frame. Control is then returned to the caller's method.
`return`	177	0	Control is returned to the caller's method without pushing any result value onto the caller's stack.
`getstatic`	178	2	Gets a value from a class's static field. The arguments are added together to create 16-bit offset into the Constant Pool to a Field Reference entry. The class and field are

Instruction	Op Code	# Args	Description
			resolved, and the size of the value and its offset into the class are determined. Based on the knowledge of its size, the value is retrieved from the class's static field area and pushed on top of the stack.
`putstatic`	179	2	Puts a value into a class's static field. The arguments are added together to create 16-bit offset into the Constant Pool to a Field Reference entry. The class and field are resolved, and the size of the value and its offset into the class are determined. Based on the knowledge of its size, the value is popped from the stack. The value is then placed into the class's static field area at the offset determined from the field information.
`putfield`	181	2	Puts a value into an object's nonstatic field. The arguments are added together to create 16-bit offset into the Constant Pool to a Field Reference entry. The class and field are resolved, and the size of the value and its offset into the object are determined. Based on the knowledge of its size, the value is first popped from the stack, followed by the actual object reference. The value is then placed into the object reference at the offset determined from the field information.
`getfield`	182	2	Gets a value from an object's nonstatic field. The arguments are added together to create 16-bit offset into the Constant Pool to a Field Reference entry. The class and field are resolved, and the size of the value and its offset into the object are determined. Next, the actual object reference is popped off the stack. The value is then retrieved from the object reference at the offset determined from the field information and pushed on top of the stack.
`invokevirtual`	182	2	Invokes an instance method of the object reference on the stack based on dynamic type lookup. The arguments are added together to create a 16-bit offset into the Constant Pool to a Method Reference entry. The class, method signature, and location of the method's

continues

Table 53.1 Continued

Instruction	Op Code	# Args	Description
			bytecodes are resolved dynamically to determine the number of arguments and the sizes that need to be popped off the stack. Next, the arguments are popped off the stack, followed by the object reference of the class containing the method to be called. The object reference and arguments (in that order) become the first local variables in the new frame that is created for the method to be called. Finally, control is passed to the method.
`invokenonvirtual`	183	2	Invokes an instance method of the object reference on the stack based on compile-time type lookup. Logic is identical to `invokevirtual`, except that the class information has already resolved.
`invokestatic`	184	2	Invokes a class's static method. Logic is similar to `invokenonvirtual`, except that there is no object reference behind the arguments on the stack (as static methods don't require an object of this type to be instantiated).
`invokeinterface`	185	4	Invokes an object's interface method. Logic is similar to `invokevirtual`, except that the number of arguments to the method is present as the third argument of the OpCode. The fourth argument is reserved and not used.
`new`	187	2	Creates a new object based on the class type defined by the arguments. The arguments are added together to create a 16-bit Constant Pool index to a Class Reference entry. The class information is resolved, and a new object reference is created for the class. The object reference is then pushed on the top of the stack.
`newarray`	188	1	Allocates a new array containing elements from one of the Java native data types. The number of elements to allocate is on the stack at entry to this OpCode. The argument to this OpCode may be one of the following type designators: `boolean, 4`; `char, 5`; `float, 6`; `double, 7`; `byte, 8`; `short, 9`; `int, 10`; `long, 11`.

Instruction	Op Code	# Args	Description
anewarray	189	2	Allocates a new array containing elements of object references. The number of elements to allocate is on the stack at entry to this OpCode. The arguments to this OpCode, when added together, make up a 16-bit Constant Pool index to the class type that will be referenced by the array elements.
athrow	191	0	Throws an exception. The top of the stack must contain an object reference that is subclassed from `Throwable`. The specified exception object is popped off the stack and thrown. The process of throwing an exception requires the current method's frame to be searched for an appropriate exception handler. If one is found, the Program Counter is set to the address of the first bytecode of the handler. Otherwise, this method frame is popped, and the exception is rethrown to the caller of this method.
checkcast	192	2	Verifies that a cast operation is valid given the type of object reference on the top of the stack. The arguments are added together to create a 16-bit Constant Pool index to a Class Reference entry. The class information is resolved. The type of object reference on the top of the stack is compared to the type of class specified by the Constant Pool entry. If the object on the stack is an instance of the class found in the Constant Pool or one of its superclasses, execution continues with the next instruction. Otherwise, a `ClassCastException` is thrown.
instanceof	193	2	Verifies that an object is of the specified type based on the arguments. The arguments are added together to create a 16-bit Constant Pool index to a Class Reference entry. The class information is resolved and the object reference is popped off the stack. The type of the object is compared to the type of class specified by the Constant Pool entry. If the object on the stack is an instance of the class found in the Constant Pool or one of its superclasses, then the integer value `1` is

continues

Table 53.1 Continued

Instruction	Op Code	# Args	Description
			pushed on the stack. Otherwise, the value `0` is pushed on the stack.
`monitorenter`	194	0	Enters a monitored section of the current bytecode stream and pops the object reference off the top of the stack. Try to allocate an exclusive lock on the object reference. If another monitor already has this object locked, wait for it to become unlocked. If the object is already locked, then just continue. Otherwise, allocate a new exclusive lock on the object.
`monitorexit`	195	0	Leaves a monitored section of the current bytecode stream and pops the object reference off the top of the stack. The exclusive lock on the object reference is removed. If no other threads have this object locked, then any other threads waiting for this object are notified that the object is now available.
`wide`	196	1	Provides for a 16-bit index in local variable load, store, and increment OpCodes. This is possible by adding the 8-bit quantity in (`arg1`) to the index in the argument of the succeeding OpCode in the bytecode stream that follows this one.
`multianewarray`	197	3	Allocates a new multidimensional array containing elements of object references. The number of elements to allocate per dimension are on the stack at the entry to this OpCode. The first two arguments to this OpCode, when added together, make up a 16-bit Constant Pool index to the class type that will be referenced by the array elements. The third argument is the number of dimensions that the array is to contain.
`ifnull`	198	2	Pops an object reference off the stack. If it is `null`, then the two args are added together and added to the current Program Counter. Otherwise, the next instruction is executed.
`ifnonnull`	199	2	Pops an object reference off the stack. If it is not `null`, then the two args are added together and added to the current Program Counter. Otherwise, the next instruction is executed.

Instruction	Op Code	# Args	Description
goto_2	200	4	Adds the four args together, constructing a 32-bit value, and adds to the current Program Counter.
jsr_w	201	4	Adds the four args together, constructing a 32-bit integer value. Push the Program Counter location of the instruction immediately following this one onto the stack. At entry to the subroutine, the return address is popped off the stack and saved in a local variable for later use in the `ret` and `ret_w` instructions. Add the 32-bit value to the Program Counter to move the flow of execution to the subroutine. (This instruction is used when the JVM processes a `finally` block.)
breakpoint	202	0	Stops execution and passes control to the JVM's breakpoint handler.
ret_w	209	2	Adds the two arguments together to create a 16-bit index into the method's frame to a local variable that contains the return address of the caller. The return address is then put into the Program Counter to move the flow of execution back to the caller of this subroutine. (This instruction is used when the JVM processes a `finally` block.)

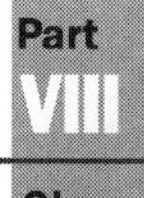

PART IX

JavaScript

CHAPTER 54

Java Versus JavaScript

In this chapter

Java and JavaScript

If you're reading this book from beginning to end, by now you should have a pretty good idea of what Java is and what it can do for you. Now that you are approaching the end of this book, it is time to introduce you to another language you will encounter if you plan to build Java applets on the Web. The next few chapters bring you to a greater understanding of the features of Netscape's new scripting language, JavaScript. You learn how it differs from Sun's Java and how you can use JavaScript to dramatically enhance your Web pages. You see that JavaScript and Java are distinct languages that can work together in a Web browser environment to create pages that are highly interactive.

Programmers often are confused by the similar names of Java and JavaScript. If you were to say to a friend, "I program in JavaScript," more often than not, that person will respond with something like, "Oh, perhaps then you can help me with this Java applet...."

It is a common misconception that Java and JavaScript are just part of the same language. This is far from true. Although they are similarly named, there are quite a few differences between them, the first of which is their origin. Around June of 1991, Java was developed at Sun Microsystems and was originally called Oak. It was officially announced (after much development and a name change) in May 1995 at SunWorld '95. JavaScript was developed at Netscape Communications Corporation and was originally called LiveScript. Sun renamed Oak to Java because of copyright issues with another language already called Oak, and Netscape changed LiveScript to JavaScript after an agreement with Sun to develop JavaScript as a language for non-programmers. JavaScript was first released with Netscape 2.0.

Before you delve into some of the differences between these two languages, let's get an overview of the major distinctive points and then discuss each in more depth. Table 54.1 lists some of the major distinctions between Java and JavaScript.

Table 54.1 JavaScript and Java Comparison

JavaScript	Java
Developed by Netscape.	Developed by Sun.
Code is interpreted by client (Web browser).	Code is compiled and placed on server before execution on client.
Object-based. Objects are built in but are not classes and cannot use inheritance.	Object-oriented. Everything is an extensible class that can use inheritance.
Data types need not be declared (loose typing).	Data types must be declared (strong typing).
Runtime check of object references (static binding).	Compile-time check of object references (dynamic binding).
Restricted disk access (must ask before writing a file).	Restricted disk access (levels of access set by user; cannot automatically write to disk).

JavaScript	Java
Scripts are limited to Web browser functionality.	Compiled code can run either as a Web applet or a standalone application.
Scripts work with HTML elements (tags).	Can handle many kinds of elements (such as audio and video).
The language is rapidly evolving and changing in functionality.	Most major changes are complete.
There are few libraries of standard code with which to build Web.	Java comes with many libraries bundled with the language.

JavaScript Is Not Java

The first thing you need to know is that JavaScript is not Java. It is almost becoming a mantra for JavaScript programmers who constantly face Java questions, even though the forum (such as the newsgroup) is clearly JavaScript.

You can write JavaScript scripts and never use a single Java applet. The reason JavaScript has adopted Java's name (in addition to the agreement with Sun Microsystems) is because the language has a similar syntax to Java. Netscape also recognized the momentum building behind Java and leveraged the name to strengthen JavaScript. If you have programmed in Java, then you will find that JavaScript is both intuitive and easy for you to pick up. There is not much new for you to learn. The nicest thing about JavaScript, though, is that you don't need to have any experience using Java to rapidly create useful scripts.

To give you an example of the similar nomenclature in Java and JavaScript, look at how each language would handle a specific function called from a specific object.

Suppose in Java you have a class called `MyClass` that contains a method called `MyMethod`. You could call `MyMethod` in this way:

```
foo = new MyClass();
result = foo.MyMethod(parameter1, parameter2);
```

In JavaScript, you can do the same thing. If you have a function called `MyObject` defined by:

```
function MyObject(parameter) {
this.firstone = parameter;
this.MyFunction = MyFunction;
}
```

assuming that `MyFunction()` has been previously defined, you can then call `MyFunction` by:

```
foo = new MyObject(parameter);
foo.MyFunction(someparameter);
```

In the first part, you have created two properties (basically slots for information inside the object) called `firstone` and `MyFunction`. In the second part, you see how you can create a specific instance of an object and use that new object's methods.

There are many similarities like this between the languages. See the next chapter for details of the JavaScript syntax.

▶ **See** Chapter 56, "Starting with JavaScript," for more information, **p. 1333**

Interpreted Versus Compiled

JavaScript code is almost always placed within the HTML document where it will be running. When you load a page that contains JavaScript code, the Web browser contains a built-in interpreter that takes the code as it is loaded and executes the instructions (sometimes on-the-fly, before you see anything on that window). This means that you can usually use View Source (choose View, Document Source in the Netscape menu) to see the code inside the HTML document.

JavaScript uses the `<script>...</script>` tag, similar to Java's `<applet>...</applet>` tag. Everything within the `<script>...</script>` is ignored by Netscape's HTML parser, but is passed on to the JavaScript interpreter. For Web browsers that do not support the `<script>...</script>` tag, it is customary to further enclose the JavaScript code in comments. Here is an example in Listing 54.1.

Listing 54.1 JavaScript Code in an HTML Document

```
<html>
<head>
<title>JavaScript Hello!</title>
<script language="JavaScript">
<!-- // to hide from old browsers
var textData = "Hello World!";
function showWorld(textInput) {
document.write(textInput);
}
//to ignore end comment -->
</script>
</head>
<body bgcolor=white>
<script language="JavaScript">
<!--
showWorld(textData);
// -->
</script>
</body>
</html>
```

The script in Listing 54.1 shows how JavaScript can appear in both the `<head>` and `<body>` elements of an HTML document. This script first loads the function within the `<head>` element. (All of the code is read from the top down—remember this when you refer to other pieces of code so you don't refer to code that hasn't been loaded yet.) When the browser encounters the `showWorld(textData)` line in the `<body>` element, the browser displays the text value of `textData`—in this case, `"Hello World!"`.

If you were to do something similar in Java, you would write the code in Java in an editor, compile the code to a .class file, and place that file on your server. You would then use the now familiar `<applet>...</applet>` to embed this applet in your HTML document. For example, the Java code would appear as:

```
public class HelloWorld extends java.applet.Applet {
public static void main (String args []) {
System.out.println("Hello World");
}
}
The HTML code would appear as:
<html>
<head>
<title>Java Example</title>
</head>
<body>
<applet code="HelloWorld.class" width=150 height=25>
</applet>
</body>
</html>
```

The benefits of having code interpreted by the browser instead of compiled by a compiler and run through the browser is primarily that you—as a JavaScript developer—can very quickly make modifications to your code and test the results via the browser. If you use Java, you must change the code, compile it, upload it again (if you are testing on your own Web server), and then view it in your browser. Interpreted code is typically not as fast as compiled code, but for the limited scope of JavaScript, you will probably see scripts run a little faster than their Java counterparts (with equivalent functions, such as a scrolling text ticker).

The drawback to having your JavaScript code on the HTML document is that any code you write will be exposed to anyone else who accesses your page—even those who want to use your code for their own projects. For small scripts, this is not much of a problem, nor is it a problem for large projects—if you don't mind having your efforts used on other pages or improved upon by others. If you have a large project in which you want to keep your code private, you might consider using Java instead. With the recent implementation of the SRC attribute, your scripts can now be pulled out of the HTML page and placed in their own file. This dramatically increases their usefulness if you have scripts that you want to reuse often. Overall, it is more convenient for JavaScript coders to be able to see the results of their changes on-the-fly in the browser than it is for the code/compile/upload/view of Java.

One feature of this interpreted nature of JavaScript is that you can test out statements on-the-fly (such as `eval(7*45/6)` or `document.write("hi1")`). If you are using Netscape Navigator 2.0 or later, try typing **javascript:** or **mocha:** in the URL window. You see that the browser window changes into interpreter mode with a large frame above a smaller frame. You can type in JavaScript commands in the smaller frame input box and see the results displayed in the larger frame (see Figure 54.1).

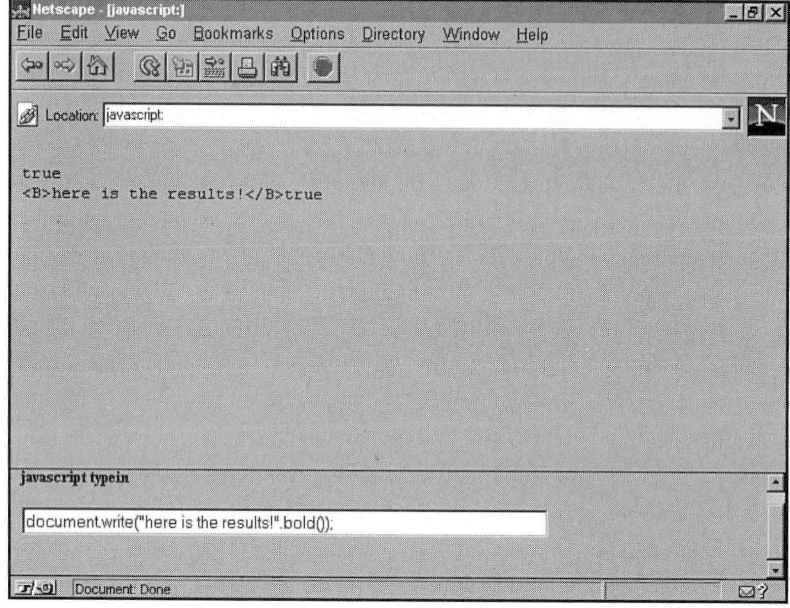

FIG. 54.1 The JavaScript Interpreter evaluates statements you type in the lower window and displays the results in the upper window. (Mac and Windows versions vary in their display.)

Object Based Versus Object Oriented

JavaScript takes liberally from Java in respect to its overall language structure, but lacks many of the features that make Java an object-oriented language. JavaScript has built-in objects (such as `Navigator`, `Window`, or `Date`) that access many browser elements such as windows, links, and images. Java typically cannot access any of these browser elements and is restricted to the area (or bounding box) that contains it and any Java windows it subsequently creates.

JavaScript allows you to create new objects that are really functions. Objects in JavaScript are not true objects because they do not implement inheritance and other features that Java does. For instance, you cannot create a new class `MyWindow` that inherits properties of the JavaScript object `window` (the top-level object in JavaScript).

Although this limitation may at first seem very constricting, you can still create many useful functions within JavaScript that can perform many of the same tasks that an equivalent Java applet can do.

Due to these built-in objects, JavaScript really shines when it comes to accessing or manipulating browser-based attributes, such as the current time, the value of a given form element, the third window in your browser, the link you visited five clicks ago, and so on.

Java code can be written to allow a programmer to do just about anything on a computer as a standalone application or a Java applet. But, JavaScript fills a major gap (at least in the context of Java applets and Web browsers) by acting as a glue by which Java and the browser can communicate. Via JavaScript, you could enter information into a form field in an HTML document, and a Java applet on that page could use that input to display new information. JavaScript allows

Java applets to gain access to properties of an HTML page and allows non-programmers access to various parts of a Java applet—such as public variables.

Although JavaScript does not allow inheritance, there is an interesting new feature called prototype. Prototype allows you to add new properties to any object that you created (with the `new` statement) and even add new properties to existing built-in objects. What this means is you can extend existing instances of objects even after they have been defined.

For example, you have an object `House` that has the properties of `Light`, `GarageDoor`, and `BurglarAlarm`. You might already have an instance of this called `myHouse`. But now you want to extend `House` by adding `ChimneySmoke`. Instead of re-defining all of your objects, you can use

```
House.prototype.ChimneySmoke = ChimneySmoke.
```

Now the instance called `myHouse` can access this new property `ChimneySmoke` by using

```
myHouse.ChimneySmoke.
```

Strong Typing Versus Loose Typing

When you are writing JavaScript code, variables don't need to have data types when they are declared. This loose typing means that it is much easier for JavaScript writers to work on creating and manipulating variables without worrying if the data was an `int`, `float`, and so on.

In Java, you must explicitly declare what data type a variable will be before you use it. This is called strong typing and contributes to the overall stability of Java code; but it can cause problems for new programmers. JavaScript allows you to ignore this and assumes that the type of value you first assign to a variable is the type you intended it to be. For instance, if you had a variable `HouseType` and you assigned it a value of "Victorian," JavaScript assumes you meant `HouseType` to be a string all along and does not complain if you did not specifically set `HouseType` to a string. However, if you had first assigned a value of 4 to `HouseType`, JavaScript now assumes it is of type `INT`. Overall, this makes for faster and easier script writing and eliminates needless debugging for variable declarations. However, you must be careful to assign the correct type of value to a variable.

This loose typing demonstrates one of the areas in which JavaScript seeks to simplify the process of writing code. Because JavaScript is directed toward non-programmers or minimal programmers, the developers sought to simplify the language in as many ways as possible while still keeping much of the flexibility. Other examples of loose-typed language include HyperTalk, dBASE, and AppleScript.

Dynamic Versus Static Binding

Because JavaScript is interpreted on the client's browser, object references are checked on-the-fly as opposed to Java's static binding at compile time. Binding simply means that a variable name is bound to a type—either statically through an explicit declaration of a type with a variable, or dynamically through an implicit association determined by the computer at compile or runtime. Because of JavaScript's dynamic nature, objects in JavaScript can be created on-the-fly as well, and might change the functionality of the script due to some outside factor (time, customer responses, and so on). The `Date` object is often used to get information about the Web browser's current date, time, day of the year, and more. This object is created at the time the JavaScript code is interpreted in order to get the correct information.

Java programs—with static binding—are typically more stable, because the entire process of compiling the code has already been completed via the Java compiler. Any bad or missing object references have been corrected. This is an advantage when you want the given application to load and run quickly on the user's machine.

Restricted Disk Access

Security is a hot issue in today's Internet and intranet Web industry for many good reasons. One of the greatest fears people have when they use the Web (or other Internet applications such as e-mail) is that a hostile program will enter their computer and damage or compromise their sensitive data. Java has a comprehensive way of dealing with security that allows it to do useful things on your computer while keeping it isolated from your sensitive documents. Java applets typically cannot write to your hard drive at all, or if they do, it is in some extremely limited way.

Because JavaScript can control so many aspects of your browser, for a while there was some concern that JavaScript was less safe than Java. This was primarily due to bugs in early versions of JavaScript that allowed it to send the contents of the file containing your bookmarks and e-mail address to another remote site through a hidden form, or acquire a list of all the files on your machine. These problems have been eliminated, and JavaScript is now—for the most part—as safe as any Java applet you might run via your browser.

Note that JavaScript can write to your hard drive—an essential feature your Web browser has to write to its cache or save files downloaded via the Web. However, it requires now that you specifically click Accept in a dialog box to download a file. In a sense, JavaScript is more versatile than Java in this respect, because it allows you to use your browser to create files to save and work with at a later time.

If you are concerned that some kind of hostile code might damage your machine, you should be aware that the possibility of virus infection has been around for a long time. Java, with its assertion of security, has only focused more attention to security issues. Soon, with JavaScript's tainting (a system of marking data so that it cannot be sent via a form or mailto: link via JavaScript) and Java's digital signatures (an electronic verification of the origin or identity of the code or information), you will be able to verify that any code—be it Java or JavaScript—comes from some trusted source. This is very good, because you will be able to allow Java to perform more sensitive tasks such as update your Oracle database or send and auto-install updated versions of software on your machine.

Also note that your Web browser (and JavaScript through the browser) can also write information to a file called a cookie. This is a file on your machine that allows Web sites to store information about you that could be retrieved when you visit that site again. Only the site that wrote the information to the cookie can retrieve it, and it is usually only used to maintain some kind of temporary information about you to carry across different pages (such as a user ID or the fact that you are from Florida).

Different Functionality (Scope Limitations) and Code Integration with HTML

JavaScript is limited in scope to your Web browser (either Netscape Navigator or Microsoft Internet Explorer). Java, on the other hand, can run as a standalone application (like Microsoft Word) or within the context of a browser as an applet. It is a testimony of the versatility of Java that it has adapted so quickly to the Web. It was originally intended to run as operating system and controls on set-top boxes or other small communication appliances. Given that Java will eventually outstrip C++ as the programming language of choice (at least for Internet programmers, if not for all programmers, as its speed increases), it has the functionality and versatility to run in many different operating systems.

JavaScript is a smaller language for a more limited audience of Web browser programmers. JavaScript gives to Web programmers the ability to access and modify all of the HTML tags, form elements, window elements, images, bookmarks, links, and anchors in a Web browser. It enables the programmer to create Web sites that respond and change based on many factors such as the time of day or some user profile (see Figure 54.2). JavaScript allows Java applets, scripts, and browser plug-ins to communicate with each other. This actually is a suite of technologies called LiveConnect from Netscape and requires some additional code in the Java applet or plug-in to be "aware" of JavaScript.

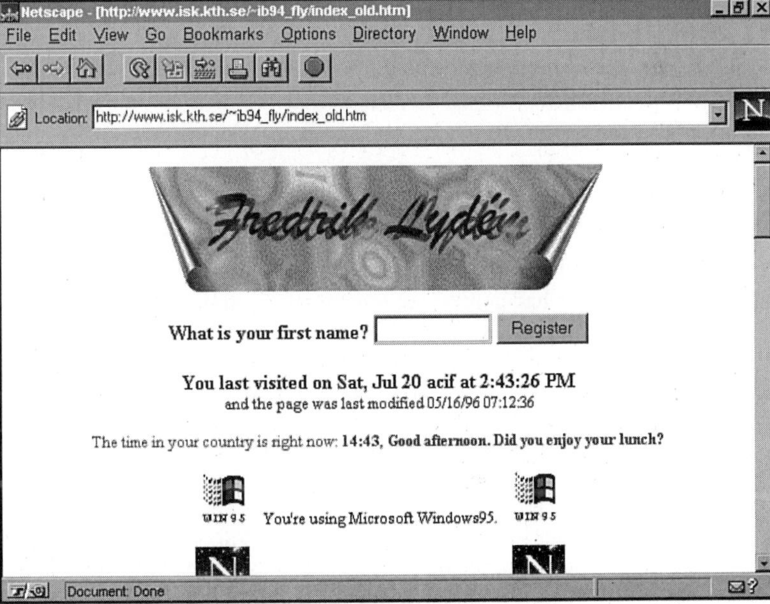

FIG. 54.2
This page displays information based on the time of day.

JavaScript can create HTML files on-the-fly, change attributes of a page instantly (such as the background color), and allows the client machine to perform many functions that were traditionally allowed only through CGIs, such as a TicTacToe game. JavaScript allows for form input validation, where incorrect responses are checked before they are sent back to the browser, which is much more difficult to do in Java than in JavaScript. Essentially, to get the functionality of JavaScript in Java, you would have to rebuild a mini-browser into your code—a fairly inefficient solution.

Also, JavaScript can be integrated directly into the HTML of your document. Event handlers, such as `onClick`, can modify the behavior of your browser beyond just accessing new documents. You can create simple calculators in JavaScript that take advantage of the GUI already present in the browser, as well as the layout capabilities already in place via the presence of HTML forms or `TABLE` elements. In other words, you can use your browser to do more than just access documents. You can use it as a front end to just about any kind of application. If you use Java, you have GUI capabilities, but you have to manually activate and resolve these capabilities, which might require significant programming on your part. In JavaScript, though, you let the browser handle most of the GUI problems and concentrate on your creative project.

Here are some examples of how you can integrate JavaScript statements into your HTML. You saw in Listing 54.1 how you can create scripts via the `<script>` tag. You can also embed JavaScript statements directly into your HTML:

```
<a href="" onMouseover="alert('you noticed me!');">pass
your mouse over here for a message!</a>
```

Instead of showing the URL in the status bar, passing the mouse over the text of the hyperlink brings up a new dialog box that displays the `you noticed me!` text. To do this in Java, you would have to create an applet that draws the link text to the screen, write the code that monitors the mouse location (probably as a separate thread), and write more code to create and destroy the resulting dialog box. Needless to say, the JavaScript solution is much easier to implement for the casual Web designer. Also, with LiveConnect, you can let a Java applet tell JavaScript to open the window and do other tasks without having to write additional code.

Look at the following JavaScript example:

```
<img width="&{imgwidth}";%" height=40>
```

Here, JavaScript allows you to set a value to an HTML attribute via a JavaScript expression. In this case, if you had defined `imgwidth` to be 50, the resulting image would have a scaled width of 50 percent of the window size. Again, if you had to do this in Java, you would have a significant amount of code to create—just to mimic the same ability. Even then, you could not easily share the value of `imgwidth` with other applets.

Overall, the ability to integrate JavaScript code directly in the HTML source allows Web programmers to quickly take advantage of the browser's built-in GUI. Casual scripters can both leverage their HTML experience as well as any familiarity with Java. Java allows you to create amazing new applications that can be executed on many operating systems that have had the Java interpreter ported to them.

The capacity for Java to create as diverse a range of applications as C++ is not disputed. However, if you are a Web page designer who doesn't have the time to learn how to program Java, you will find that JavaScript is very useful. On the other hand, if you dislike using proprietary code in your HTML that only functions with two browsers (even though together they hold almost 90 percent of the current browser market share), you may decide to tough it out by using just Java.

Rapid Evolution Versus Relative Stability

JavaScript is the newer of the two languages and, as such, is undergoing a more dramatic series of changes and improvements. As of this writing, Java Version 1.0.2 is relatively stable. Most of the statements, operators, syntax, and so on have been well-defined and most likely will not change significantly in subsequent versions. JavaScript has been rapidly evolving from the original goal of providing form verification on the client side (instead of a server-side CGI) to having the potential to simulate a simple game such as Pong or breakout. Some of the features of JavaScript include:

- Java-JavaScript communication
- JavaScript-Plug-in communication
- Determination of installed plug-ins
- Data Tainting (security enhancements)
- Image reflection (dynamic listing of all images)
- New event handlers (`onMouseOut` and more)
- New attributes to the `<script>` tag (SRC)
- New built-in objects (array, string, and so on)
- New operators (`typeof`)
- Object prototypes

As you can see, JavaScript is changing and growing. It provides a powerful way for non-programmers (or light programmers) to do the following:

- Access Java applet methods
- Enable plug-ins and applets to communicate with other elements (other plug-ins, scripts, and applets)
- Validate form information on the client side (before it is sent back to the Web server)
- Generate HTML on-the-fly or based on environment variables (time, date, location, and so on)
- Create simple interactive programs (such as a TicTacToe game) completely in JavaScript

The drawback to this is subtle. It may seem at first that adding new features with every new release of Netscape would be looked upon as a wonderful thing. For the most part this is true, except now when you sit down at your latest browser and begin programming with JavaScript. You have to ask yourself if the feature you are using is going to be available to a large audience (specifically, the target audience for your Web site). Not everyone updates their browser every few months, so every release tends to segment your audience. Another drawback is that, for every feature added to a language, it opens the possibility that a bug snuck in as well.

For now, it is a good strategy to take advantage of only those features of JavaScript that have persisted through Version 2.02 of Netscape. If you use 3.0-specific features, be sure to mention this on the page to inform your visitors. So, another difference between Java and JavaScript is that, although Java is more powerful and relatively stable as a language, JavaScript is growing with each version.

It is exciting to see how much a scripter can do now with JavaScript. With 3.0, I have seen simple paint programs, Pong games, and even LED clocks that change every second. Many of these scripts would be fairly indistinguishable from their Java counterparts.

NOTE If you discover a feature you would like to add to JavaScript, you have the unique opportunity to talk to the developer of JavaScript (Brendan Eich at Netscape). I expect that the expansion of features in JavaScript will continue, especially now that it is being compared to Microsoft's Visual Basic Script. If you find JavaScript too limited in some way, you may be able to change it in future versions. Brendan tries to respond to all email he gets, but with such a high volume, it may take a while for him to respond–if at all.

Libraries

Sun delivers Java with a standard set of libraries that act to dramatically enhance its usefulness. Instead of having to write all the code to handle images, sockets, and so on, the programmers at Sun have done this for you. You simply have to learn the standard APIs so you can quickly write terminal emulators, word processors, and more.

JavaScript—because of its relative youth—has not had time to build up any assemblage of standard code with which to build Web-based applications. One major problem that stalled this development was that you were forced to embed your code in the HTML document in which you wanted to use the script. With the addition of the SRC attribute to the `<script>` tag, you can now write your code in a separate file and merely reference the script in the page. It is similar to the `CODE` attribute in the `<applet>` tag (this page would load all of the JS files, display the correct title at the top of the window, and display a clock above the `Welcome to my home page` text):

```
<html>
<head>
<script language="JavaScript" src="header.js"></script>
</head>
<body>
<script language="JavaScript"
src="http://www.foo.com/scripts/timer.js"></script>
<script language="JavaScript" src="body.js"></script>
</body>
</html>
```

- HEADER.JS:

```
document.write("<title>Welcome!</title>");
alert("Welcome To My Homepage!");
```

- BODY.JS:

```
document.write("Welcome to my home page!");
```

The ability to refer to a JavaScript file via the `SRC` attribute allows you to reuse scripts much more readily than before. It is expected to be only a matter of time before standard libraries of code are developed and easily accessible. It is somewhat ironic that you can find more standard code for Java now than you can for JavaScript, given that Java is more complicated.

JavaScript and Java Integration

There are many other examples of differences between Java and JavaScript, such as memory requirements (and limitations), threads (Java has them, JavaScript doesn't), and more. But I think that the differences presented in this chapter will help you to perhaps change your perception of JavaScript.

You should begin to think of JavaScript not as simply an aspect of Java, but instead a complementary language that allows you to greatly control the behavior of your browser. You can now pass more of the computation and interactivity from your server down to the user's client browser—thus relieving some of the load and improving the performance of your server. JavaScript is not an all-purpose or a universal scripting language, but in the confines of HTML, plug-ins, browser events, and windows, JavaScript shines as an easy way to add interactivity to your Web pages. You will see this in the next chapter.

The decision to use Java or JavaScript will depend not only on your skills as a programmer, but also on the scope of the Web-related task at hand. Look carefully at the task and see if the scrolling text, spinning icon, or calculator might more easily be implemented in JavaScript. If you need to control most of the browser window with specialized text or perhaps have a highly sophisticated application, then Java is surely the way to go.

The next chapter introduces you to the syntax of JavaScript and gives you a good idea of its capabilities. You may find that programming in JavaScript is as much fun as creating Java applets. ●

CHAPTER 55

Starting with JavaScript

In this chapter

The Basics

By now you have read a lot about the newest version of Java, and in the previous chapter, I began to talk about one of Java's partners in Web development—JavaScript. You may be wondering (if you jumped straight to this chapter or are reading this in the bookstore) why there is a chapter on JavaScript in a book about Java. The reason is quite simple. JavaScript complements Java's capabilities in the Web browser environment. It allows people with little or no programming experience who are daunted by Java's complexity to create interactive and Web-based applications.

JavaScript is a scripting language that is loosely based on Java. By imbedding JavaScript code in an HTML document, you can have greater control of your user's experience as well as pass a larger amount of computation (originally only available via CGI scripts) down to the client-side browser. These scripts are read sequentially by the browser as it is loading a page and can execute commands immediately—which may affect the page even before it completes loading.

Because JavaScript lives inside your HTML document, it can either exist as a complete script that is embedded in the `<head>` or `<body>` elements, or it can consist of event handlers that are written directly into the HTML code.

In Listing 55.1, you can see how to build the skeleton of a JavaScript script in a document via the `<script>` tag.

Listing 55.1 The Script Tag

```
<SCRIPT LANGUAGE="JavaScript">
<!-- HTML comment tags to hide script from old browsers
[JavaScript statements...]
// End hiding the code from old browsers -->
</SCRIPT>
```

You can see from this example that the `<script>` tag is somewhat similar to the `<applet>` tag you use when you embed Java code. The `SCRIPT` tag has an attribute called `LANGUAGE` that allows you to specify in which language the browser needs to interpret the following code. This makes the `<script>` tag versatile, in that you may eventually use it to embed Visual Basic Script, TCL, Perl, and more scripts.

Another attribute to the `<script>` tag is `SRC`. Implemented in Netscape 3.0, the `SRC` attribute allows you to write all of your script in another file and reference that file—instead of having to paste all of the statements in the HTML. If you use the `SRC` tag, anything you place between the `<script>...</script>` is ignored. Thus, you can place alternative HTML for non-JavaScript-enabled browsers. Listing 55.2 uses the `SRC` attribute.

Listing 55.2 JavaScript with *SRC*

```
<SCRIPT LANGUAGE="JavaScript" SRC="footer.js">
You must not have a JavaScript Enabled Browser if
you see this (poor you!) Click <A HREF="foo.html">here</A>
to go to another page.
</SCRIPT>
```

In Listing 55.2, the browser loads the script contained within FOOTER.JS as if it had been typed in the HTML document.

Your First Script

When you start learning about JavaScript, you will find it very useful to begin with the basics. Immediately start up your Web browser (Netscape Communicator or Microsoft Internet Explorer) and test out what you learn.

Let's begin with a simple script and explain what will happen when you load this page. Listing 55.3 is an example of the typical "Hello World!" program that is very popular for testing out new languages. In this example, you are essentially telling the browser to display the string "Hello World!" as if you had directly typed that string in your HTML document. (Note that I usually capitalize my HTML or JavaScript tags. This is simply a programming convention, but it makes the code easier to read.)

Listing 55.3 "Hello World!" Implemented in JavaScript

```
<HTML>
<HEAD>
<SCRIPT LANGUAGE="JavaScript">
<!-- Hide me from old browsers
document.write("Hello World!");
// End Hiding -->
</SCRIPT>
</HEAD>
<BODY>
Are you ready for JavaScript?
</BODY>
</HTML>
```


Try this one out on your browser and see the results.

Basically, the browser reads this code into the JavaScript interpreter. The text string "Hello World!" is passed to the `write` function of the `document` object, which in turn instructs the browser to display the phrase `"Hello World!"` on a new page. Notice that the actual code is not displayed in the browser window. This is because the HTML parser never received this code, as it was passed to the JavaScript interpreter after the HTML parser encountered the `<SCRIPT>` tag.

Events

Most of the time, you will be building scripts that do such things as store information, display data in a certain format, perform some calculations, or respond to user actions (called events). JavaScript has all of the elements that make up a powerful scripting language and can handle all of these tasks. One of the primary tasks JavaScript is used for is intercepting and handling events. Just about any way you respond to your browser can be intercepted by JavaScript. Furthermore, your response can trigger other events, or functions.

Essentially, functions are stored chunks of code that are executed at some interval—either immediately, when the document is loaded, or in response to some triggered event. Think of functions as collections of instructions that allow you to pull out some behavior you might want to perform over and over again or possibly reuse.

When JavaScript encounters an event, it passes it to an event handler. Event handlers are tags that point to the specific functions to be executed. Table 55.1 lists the events and handlers in JavaScript.

Table 55.1 Events and Event Handlers in JavaScript

Event	Event Handler	To Trigger Event
blur	`onBlur`	In a form element, user clicks (tabs) away from element.
click	`onClick`	In a form element or link, user clicks element.
change	`onChange`	In a form text, text area, or select object, user changes value.
focus	`onFocus`	In a form element, user clicks (tabs) to element.
load	`onLoad`	Happens when page is loaded.
mouseover	`onMouseOver`	Happens when mouse is passed over links or anchors.
select	`onSelect`	In a form, user selects input field.
submit	`onSubmit`	In a form, user submits a form (clicks the Submit button).
unload	`onUnload`	User leaves the page.

Using Event Handlers

Although you can use event handlers anywhere in your JavaScript scripts, you usually place them either inside HTML form elements or alongside anchors or links. The reason for this is that JavaScript uses the HTML form as a way to send data to your JavaScript script or perform some "preprocessing" on the data, not just to send data back to the server.

For example, an enrollment form on your site asks the users a number of questions about themselves, and you want to make sure they at least fill out their names and ages. Before JavaScript, the form was submitted directly back to the Web server, which checked that the appropriate fields were filled out. Then, if they weren't, the form was sent back to the users, asking for the appropriate information. Now, JavaScript can check this field before it is sent and ask the users to fill out that information, without all the overhead of reconnecting to the remote server.

Let's look at an example of how you might add an event handler to your existing HTML code. Most of the time, you follow this general syntax:

```
<TAG eventHandler="JavaScript code">
```

Of course, `TAG` is some HTML tag, and `eventHandler` is any one of the event handlers you saw in Table 55.1. The `"JavaScript code"` can be any valid JavaScript code but is usually a call to a function that you loaded earlier in the document. Listing 55.4 demonstrates an embedded JavaScript event handler in a common hypertext link. When you click the link, a dialog box displays the text, followed by an OK button for you to click to return to the page.

Listing 55.4 An Event Handler in an *HREF*

```
<A HREF="#" onClick="alert('Wow! It Works!');">Click here for a message!</A>
```

There is a lot to notice in this example:

- No URL is found in the `HREF` attribute. Why? You probably don't want the browser to go to another page while the user is viewing the pop-up window. When the user clicks the link, not only is the `onClick` activated, but the browser attempts to go to the location specified in the `HREF`. In this case, you are using this link for its `onClick` event handler and not its hypertext reference. An alternative would be to type:

  ```
  <a href="javascript:alert('Wow It Works!')>Click here</a>
  ```

- `onClick` has mixed case. Although HTML is not case sensitive, JavaScript is. This is important to remember when you are creating functions and variables.
- `alert(...)` is the standard function for bringing up an alert dialog box on the screen. Notice how this function, and all JavaScript functions, behave similarly to Java in that they use parentheses to contain their arguments. In this case, the argument is the string `'Wow! It Works!'`. Notice also that the quotation marks of that string are single. When you need to use quotation marks within quotation marks, you nest them by alternating the single and double quotation marks. If you need more than two "levels" of quotations in a given element, you should probably think about an alternate way to eliminate that need.
- The JavaScript code in quotation marks—`"alert('Wow! It Works!');"`—ends in a semicolon. You use the semicolon to end a statement in JavaScript, which is similar to

Part IX Ch 55

Perl and other languages (including Java). Unlike Perl, the use of the semicolon is optional.

Now that you have seen the two main ways you can implement JavaScript in your HTML code (either in scripts contained by the <SCRIPT>...</SCRIPT> tags or directly embedded in HTML form elements and links), let's look at the building blocks of JavaScript code.

Variables

To create a variable in JavaScript, you simply declare it using the keyword `var`. You can initialize this variable with some value when you declare it, but it is not required. Listing 55.5 shows some examples of variables created in JavaScript.

Listing 55.5 Variable Declaration in JavaScript

```
var foo = 23
var a, b, c = "letter"
var aNumber = "99"
var isItTrue = false
var flag1 = false , bingo = null , star
```

JavaScript is relatively unique in that you cannot explicitly set a type to a variable, such as casting a string to an integer, like you would in Java. Types are found in JavaScript, but they are set implicitly. This means that the type a variable has is defined by the context in which it is either defined or used.

When you initialize a variable with a string value (as variables `a`, `b`, and `c` in Listing 55.5), it is a string type; if you initialize it with a number, it becomes an integer type value (as in variable `foo` in Listing 55.5). The following places a number of variables within a single statement:

```
bax + bay + baz
```

This code attempts to treat all of the variables as having the same type as the first variable. If `bax` was a string and `bay` and `baz` were originally integers, JavaScript would treat `bar` and `baz` as if they were strings. The implicit nature of JavaScript variables allows you to reuse variables easily without worrying about their type.

If you set some variable day to `"Tuesday"` and later in the script decide to assign `46` to day, the JavaScript interpreter (inside the browser) will not complain. Because of this, however, you should be careful when naming your variables so that they do not overlap in scope and cause strange errors in your scripts. You will find it extremely helpful to experiment with declaring and setting variables from the interpreter window I talked about earlier. (In Netscape, just type **javascript:** in the open URL window.)

Table 55.2 contains a list of the possible implicit data types in JavaScript, along with their possible values:

Table 55.2 Data Types in JavaScript

Data Type	Values
Number	100, -99.99, 0.000001
Boolean	true, false
Strings	"this is a string", "This is another", "5555"
Null	A special keyword with a null value

Variable Names

JavaScript follows the same naming rules for creating variable names as Java. Your variable must start with a letter or an underscore and can contain subsequent numbers, letters, or underscores. Listing 55.6 gives you a sampling of possible variable names in JavaScript. Remember to keep your names unique; also remember that, in JavaScript, names are case sensitive.

Listing 55.6 Variable Name Examples

```
Too_hot
cold999
_100JustRight
This_is_a_long_variable_name_but_it_is_valid000
```

Variable Scope

Earlier, I mentioned that you want to keep your variable names distinct from one another to prevent overwriting values; but what if you really want to use the same name? This is where variable scope comes into play. Global variables are accessible by your entire script and all of its functions. Local variables are accessible only to the function from which they were created. Those variables are destroyed when that function is complete. To define a variable as a global variable, simply assign a value to it (such as `"foo = 95"`).

To define a local variable inside a function, use the `var` keyword.

Literals

You can think of a literal as the value on the right side of an equality expression. It is the concrete way to express values in JavaScript and is very similar to Java's method. Here is a list of literals and their possible values:

- Integers:

  Decimal expression as a series of digits not starting with a zero:

  (77, 56565565)

Octal expression as a series of digits starting with a zero:

08988

Hexidecimal expression as 0X followed by any digits.

- Floating point:

  Expressed as a series of zero or more digits followed by a period (.) and one or more digits.

  Expressed in scientific notation as a series of digits followed by E or e and some digits for the exponent (such as -4.666E30).
- Boolean. True or false.
- String. Zero or more characters enclosed by single or double quotation marks.

Strings can contain special characters that affect how they are eventually displayed:

- `\b`—Backspace
- `\f`—Linefeed
- `\n`—New line character
- `\r`—Carriage return
- `\t`—Tab character
- `\"`—An escaped quotation mark—a way to display double quotation marks inside a string
- `\'`—Another escaped quotation mark for the single quote

Expressions and Operators

Having values is not enough for a language to be useful. You must have some way to manipulate these values meaningfully. JavaScript uses expressions to manipulate numbers, strings, and so on. An expression is a set of literals, operators, subexpressions, and variables that evaluate to value. You can use expressions to assign a value to a variable, as in:

```
today = "Friday"
```

Or an expression can simply evaluate to a value, as in :

```
45 - 66
```

JavaScript uses arithmetical expressions that evaluate to some number, string expressions that evaluate to another string, and logical expressions that evaluate to `true` or `false`. Operators behave very similarly to their cousins in Java. Table 55.3 summarizes the various operators that are available in JavaScript.

<table>
<tr><th colspan="2">Table 55.3 JavaScript Operators</th></tr>
<tr><th>Operator</th><th>Explanation</th></tr>
<tr><td colspan="2">Computational</td></tr>
<tr><td>+</td><td>Numerical addition and string concatenation</td></tr>
<tr><td>-</td><td>Numerical subtraction and unary negation</td></tr>
<tr><td>*</td><td>Multiplication</td></tr>
<tr><td>/</td><td>Division</td></tr>
<tr><td>%</td><td>Modulus (remainder)</td></tr>
<tr><td>++</td><td>Increment (pre and post)</td></tr>
<tr><td>--</td><td>Decrement (pre and post)</td></tr>
<tr><td colspan="2">Logical</td></tr>
<tr><td>==, !==</td><td>Equality and inequality (not assignment)</td></tr>
<tr><td><</td><td>Less than</td></tr>
<tr><td><=</td><td>Less than or equal to</td></tr>
<tr><td>></td><td>Greater than</td></tr>
<tr><td>=></td><td>Greater than or equal to</td></tr>
<tr><td>!</td><td>Logical negation (NOT)</td></tr>
<tr><td>&&</td><td>Logical AND</td></tr>
<tr><td>||</td><td>Logical OR</td></tr>
<tr><td>?</td><td>Trinary conditional selection</td></tr>
<tr><td>,</td><td>Logical concatenation</td></tr>
<tr><td colspan="2">Bitwise</td></tr>
<tr><td>&</td><td>Bitwise AND</td></tr>
<tr><td>|</td><td>Bitwise OR</td></tr>
<tr><td>^</td><td>Bitwise exclusive OR (XOR)</td></tr>
<tr><td>~</td><td>Bitwise NOT</td></tr>
<tr><td><<</td><td>Left shift</td></tr>
<tr><td>>></td><td>Right shift</td></tr>
<tr><td>>>></td><td>Unsigned right shift</td></tr>
</table>

Table 55.3 Continued

Operator	Explanation
Assignment	
=	Assignment
X=	Aggregate assignment (where X can be +, -, *,/,%, &, ^, <<, >>, |, >>>,~) Example: (A += B is equivalent to A = A + B)

The operator precedence is identical to Java's. JavaScript uses lazy evaluation going from left to right. If, while evaluating an expression, it encounters a situation where the expression must be `false`, it does not evaluate the rest of the expression and returns `false`. If you want to group expressions to be evaluated first, use the parentheses. For example:

```
(56 * 99) + (99 - (44 / 5))
```

A handy expression is the conditional expression. Very underused, this expression allows you to evaluate some condition quickly and return one of two values. Its syntax is:

```
(condition) ? value1 : value2
```

If the condition is `true`, then the first value is returned; otherwise, the second is returned. For example:

```
isReal = (Imagination <= Reality) true : false
```

Control Statements

Now that you have assignment and mathematical operators, you can assign values to variables, perform simple math expressions, and so on. But you still don't have the ability to write any kind of meaningful JavaScript code. You need to have some way of controlling the flow of statement evaluation, making decisions based on values, ignoring some statements, and looping through a series of statements until some condition is met.

This is where control statements come into play. JavaScript groups these statements into conditional (`if...else`), loop (`for`, `while`, `break`, `continue`), object manipulation (`for...in`, `new`, `this`, `with`), and comments (`//`, `/*...*/`). Examples of each of these statements are explored in this section. (I come back to the object manipulation statements later, after you learn about JavaScript's object model.)

JavaScript uses brackets to enclose a series of statements into a complete chunk of code. When JavaScript encounters these chunks, all of the statements within are evaluated (unless, of course, JavaScript encounters another branch beforehand, as you learn soon).

Conditional Statements

These are statements that allow your script to make decisions based on criteria you select.

if...else When you want to execute some block of code based on some other condition, you can use the `if` statement. Its syntax is:

```
if ( someExpressionIsTrue) {
zero or more statements...
}
```

If you want to either execute some block of code or another, you can use the `if...else` statement, which forces the execution of one block or the other. Its syntax is:

```
if ( someExpressionIsTrue) {
some statements...
}
else {
some other statements...
}
```

NOTE If you want to execute just one line of code, you can omit the brackets. This is not recommended, however, because your code will not be as easy to follow later.

Listing 55.7 shows how you might implement an `if...else` statement. It also shows you how you can chain together multiple `else` and `if` statements.

Listing 55.7 *if...else* Statement Chaining

```
if...else statement
if ( jobs < 100) && (money <= budget) {
poor = true;
free = (99 - x) / jobs ;
}
else if (jobs != overTime) {
workers = "Strike"
}
else {
poor = false;
workers = "Happy";
}
```

In a moment, I will talk about functions and how they are constructed in JavaScript (refer to the "Functions in JavaScript" section later in this chapter). For now, let's start with a working definition of a function as some set of instructions that performs an action or returns a value. Because a function can return a value, it can return a Boolean `true` or `false`. Furthermore, you can use a function call in an `if` statement as the test. Listing 55.8 shows how you might implement this.

Listing 55.8 Using a Function as a Conditional

```
if ( pageIsLoaded) {
alert ("All Done!");
done = true;
}
else {
done = false; }
```

Loop Statements

Sometimes you want to execute a series of statements over and over again until some condition is met. An example of this is to play a sound in the background of your page until the user clicks Stop! or to repeatedly divide some number by 6 until it is less than 50. This action is performed in JavaScript by the `for` and the `while` structures.

for A `for` loop repeats some series of statements until some condition is met. The `for` loop structure is virtually identical to the structure in Java. Its syntax is:

```
for ([some initial expression] ; [condition] ; [increment expression] ) {
some expressions...
}
```

You build a `for` loop by setting up three expressions that follow a more or less standard format. The initial expression can be of any degree of complexity, but it usually is simply an initial assignment of value to the counter variable. In the second expression, the condition is executed once for each pass through the expressions. If the expression evaluates to `true`, then the block of expressions is executed. If the expression evaluates to `false`, the `for` loop is completed and the interpreter jumps down the next expression after the loop. The increment expression is evaluated after each pass through the loop and is usually where the "counter" variable is incremented or decremented. Essentially, this means you initialize some counter, test some condition, execute the enclosed statements if `true`, increment the counter, test the condition again, and so on.

Although not required, you should use the increment expression to change some value that will eventually render the condition expression false. Otherwise, your `for` loop will run forever (or until you get tired of waiting and reboot your computer).

Listing 55.9 gives you a simple example of a `for` loop in JavaScript.

Listing 55.9 An Example of a *for* Loop

```
<script language="JavaScript">
var myMessage = "Here we go again! <br>";
var numberOfRepeats = 100;
for ( i=0; i < numberOfRepeats ; i++) {
document.write(myMessage);
}
</script>
```

while The `while` loop is a simpler version of the `for` loop in that it tests some expression each time around and escapes if that expression is `false`. You will probably use `while` loops when the variable you are testing for is also present inside the statement block that you are executing during each loop. Note that the condition is tested first before the statements are executed, and that the condition is tested only once for each loop. Here is the standard syntax for a `while` loop:

```
while (somecondition) {
some statements;
}
```

Listing 55.10 repeatedly displays a series of lines that state the current value of `tt` until `tt` is greater than or equal to `xx`, which, in this case, is 55.

Listing 55.10 An Example of a *while* Loop

```
<script language="JavaScript">
tt = 0
xx = 55
while ( tt <= 55) {
tt += 1;
document.write ("The value of tt is " + tt +". <br> ");
}
</script>
```

break and *continue*

Sometimes you might want to have a finer degree of control over your block of statements within a `for` or `while` loop. Occasionally, you might want to arbitrarily jump out of a loop and continue down to the `next` statement. Or, you might want to stop the execution of statements in the current loop and start a new loop. You can achieve both of these options by using `break` and `continue`. `break` causes the `for` or `while` loop to terminate prematurely and the execution to jump down to the next line after the loop. `continue` stops the current loop and begins a new one.

It is easy to get these statements confused, and their purpose may become unclear over time. An easy way to remember how these work is to think of `break` as breaking the loop, which renders the loop inoperable. Then, the program continues down. You can think of `continue` as a way of skipping whatever is below it and starting again. Listings 55.11 and 55.12 mirror Listings 55.9 and 55.10 and illustrate these control statements.

Listing 55.11 Breaking Out of a *for* Loop

```
<script language="JavaScript">
var myMessage = "Here we go again! <br>";
var numberOfRepeats = 100;
for ( i=0; i < numberOfRepeats ; i++) {
document.write(myMessage);
if ( i <0) {
document.write("Invalid Number!");
break
}
}
</script>
```

Listing 55.12 Continuing a *while* Loop

```
<script language="JavaScript">

var tt = 0;
xx = 55
while ( tt <= 55) {
tt += 1;
if (tt < 0) {
continue;
}
document.write ("The value of tt is " + tt +". <br> ");
}
</script>
```

Comments

Every language needs to have some way to document exactly what is going on, especially if you ever intend to reuse your code. It may seem obvious to you when you are deep in the zone of programming your cool new script. But a few days later, you may find yourself wondering, "What was I thinking?" It's always a good idea to comment your code. I talk about comments here, in control statements, essentially because they are a way of telling the JavaScript interpreter to skip over some piece of code or comments, no matter what.

Comments are similar to a `for` loop that is initially and always `false`. JavaScript supports two kinds of comments:

- Line-by-line version (`//`)
- Multiple-line version (`/* ... */`)

You can place anything you want in either of these comments, except for one thing. Do you remember when I talked about using HTML comments to keep the older browsers from erroneously displaying JavaScript code? In other words, you cannot use `-->` in your comments unless you are really intending the script to end.

Notice also that you must place the single-line comment in front of the HTML end comment notation. This is because the JavaScript interpreter does not recognize `-->` as anything meaningful and gives you an error if you forget to use `//` before it.

Why, then, doesn't the initial line (something such as "Hide me from old browsers") after the beginning HTML comment give you a JavaScript error? The reason is that the interpreter ignores everything else on the line containing `<--`. This is handy for you, because you can use this line to describe your script, and so forth.

Listing 55.13 shows both ways of displaying comments.

Listing 55.13 An Example of Displaying Comments

```
<html>
<script language = "JavaScript">
<!-- Hide this code from old browsers.
one = 1
two = 2
// three = 99 everything on this line is ignored....
four = 4 ;
five = 5 ; /* everything on this line, and all
subsequent lines will be ignored, until
we get to the closing comment */
six = 6;
// remember to comment out the last line if you are using the HTML comments also
-->
//You must not have JavaScript if you see this line...
</script>
</html>
```

Functions in JavaScript

You have now reached one of the most interesting parts of JavaScript. The heart of most scripts that you build will consist of functions. You can think of a function as a named series of statements that can accept other variables or statements as arguments. Remember how the `if` statement was constructed:

```
 if (someTest) {
zero or more statements
}
You build functions in a very similar way:
function someFunction (arguments) {
some statements
return someValue;
}
```

Let's discuss functions in greater detail. As I mentioned earlier in this chapter, functions are blocks of code that you can reuse over and over again just by calling the blocks by name and optionally passing some arguments to them. Functions form the heart of most of the scripts you will build and are almost as fundamental to JavaScript as classes are to Java.

You will see that JavaScript comes with many built-in functions for you to use and allows you to create your own as well. Suppose, for instance, that you want to use JavaScript to create a small HTML page. You can use functions to pull out each of the subtasks you want to do, which makes your code much easier to modify, read, and reuse. Let's look at Listing 55.14.

Listing 55.14 A Simple Example Using Functions

```
<html>
<head>
<script language="javaScript">
<!-- remember me?
var age = 0;
function myHeader (age) {
document.write("<TITLE>The " + age + "Year Old Page</TITLE>");
}
function myBody (date, color) {
document.write (" <body bgcolor=" + color + " >");
document.write ("<h3>Welcome to My Homepage!</h3>");
document.write ("The date is " + date + "<br>");
}
function manyLinks (index) {
if (index == 1) {
return "http://www.yahoo.com";
}
else if (index == 2){
return "http://home.netscape.com";
}
else return "http://www.idsoftware.com" ;
}
// return the title
myHeader(33);
// done for the moment! -->
</script>
</head>
<script language=JavaScript>
<!--
myBody("July 22, 1996", "#ffffff");
document.write("<a href=" + manyLinks(2) + ">Here's a link!</a>");
// -->
</script>
```

In this example, each function encapsulates some HTML code. You can see how you pass information into each function by means of the arguments. JavaScript passes values by reference, meaning that when you pass a value to a function, you are really just passing a value pointer to the function. (A value pointer is just an address, similar to how a house address on an envelope gives information about how to find the house.) If the function modifies that value, the value is changed for the entire script, not just the scope of the function. The result of the code is shown in Figure 55.1.

Also, notice the behavior of return. You can optionally return an explicit value back to the statement that called the function (as in return `http://...`). The value returned can be of any valid JavaScript type. If no value is explicitly returned, JavaScript returns `true` upon successful completion of the function.

Notice the difference between defining the function and calling the function. You define (or store into memory) the function by using the function keyword. None of the statements inside the function are executed until the function is called by using the function name elsewhere in the script.

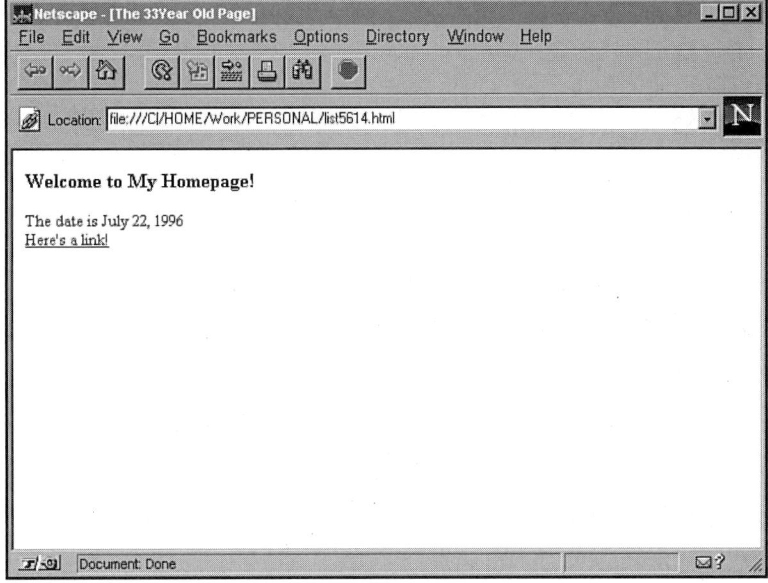

FIG. 55.1 Output from Listing 55.14.

> **CAUTION**
>
> You must be careful how you write your scripts when you use functions. Because JavaScript reads scripts from the top down and left to right, you cannot call functions that have not yet been read in by the interpreter.
>
> Suppose, for example, you have two functions: `myFirst()` and `mySecond()`. If `myFirst()` appears above `mySecond()`, then `myFirst()` cannot immediately use the `mySecond()` function. Because of this linear interpretation and loading of code, you should instead load all of your functions first (usually in the <HEAD> area) and then call the functions afterwards. It is good practice to place your functions in the <HEAD> element, because this ensures that all of the code will be loaded into memory before your script begins to execute commands.
>
> Remember that you don't necessarily need to pass any information to a function for it to be useful. You might create a function that writes to the page all of the many lines of HTML that make up the headers of your HTML pages. After you have written the function once, all you have to do is call it as often as you need—saving you many keystrokes of typing later.

Arrays

While I am on the subject of functions, it is convenient to introduce another extremely useful construct in JavaScript—the array. An array is simply an ordered set of values that can be accessed by a common name and an index (a number representing at what place in the series that value is located). Before Netscape 3.0, you were forced to create arrays yourself by using a function you will see quite often in scripts on the Internet. Listing 55.15 shows how to create a function that builds an array for you.

Listing 55.15 An Array Builder

```
function MakeArray(n) {
this.length = n;
for (var i = 1; i <= n; i++;) {
this[i] = " " }
return this
}
}
```

You may notice a new keyword here called `this`. `this` is a special keyword that refers to the current object. I talk about this and another keyword you haven't encountered, `new`, later in this section. To create a new array, you simply assign the results of `MakeArray` to some name, as shown here:

```
Letterman = new MakeArray(10);
```

The `new` keyword is a way of telling JavaScript that the function to the right of it is an object constructor, and JavaScript treats it accordingly. To access values in your new array or set any of the values, use this syntax:

```
Letterman[1] = "A list"
Letterman[3] = "Not so popular"
```

In Netscape 3.0, arrays are built in, so all you need to do is use `Array` instead of your `MakeArray` function. In the previous case, this would be:

```
Letterman = new Array();
```

You can either set the size of the array when you initialize it or assign some null value to the highest element in the array.

Built-In Functions

There are a few built-in functions in JavaScript. Table 55.4 lists them with a short description of the function of each.

Table 55.4 Built-In Functions

Function	Description
`escape(str)`	Converts strings to HTML special characters (such as " " to %20).
`unescape(str)`	Inverse of `escape()`. %20 to " ".
`eval (str)`	Evaluates a string `str` as a JavaScript expression.
`parseFloat (str, radix)`	Converts a string to a floating-point number (if possible).
`parseInt (str)`	Converts a string to an integer value (if possible).

Now that I have touched on functions that group together statements, let's look at the equivalent structure for data in general—the all-important object.

Objects

Because you surely have read some part of the rest of this book (unless you decided to skip to this part first!), you have come face to face with Java objects. Basically, objects are a way of organizing data and the manipulations you might associate with that data. In Java, you have classes and methods, but in JavaScript, you have objects and functions. As I mentioned before, JavaScript comes preloaded with many very useful objects and functions. This section familiarizes you with Netscape's object model and summarizes each of the many built-in objects.

Dot Notation

JavaScript borrows from Java the system of accessing properties and methods (JavaScript freely mixes the terms function and method) by the use of the dot notation.

Basically, you access information by first naming the top-level object that contains it, as well as all subsequent objects (or methods) that focus in on that information. Suppose you have an object called `car` that contains an object called `door`. Suppose `door` contains another object called `doorhandle` that uses a method called `openDoor()`. You could use this method at any time by using this syntax:

```
car.door.doorhandle.openDoor()
```

Let's say also that the `door` object has an attribute called `color`, and that `color` has a value of `"Red"`. You could assign that value to another variable by using a notation similar to this:

```
myColor = car.door.color.value ;
```

Methods and Properties

JavaScript objects contain data in the forms of properties and methods. Properties are basically named values that are associated with a given object. Properties are accessed through that object. In the previous example of the `car`, `door` would have the property of `color`.

Properties are handy and intuitive ways of storing information about an object. Methods (or functions) tend to be blocks of code that perform some operations on the object's properties. Or, methods perhaps store their results in one of the properties. The `openDoor()` function is a method of the object `doorhandle`. When I discuss the objects that are built in to Navigator, I cover their associated methods and properties as well.

The *Window* Object

The `Window` object is the top-level object in JavaScript. It contains all other objects except the navigator object, which is not tied to any particular window. Because most of your work is done inside a Navigator window, this is a useful object that you should become familiar with.

The `Window` object contains methods to open and close windows, bring up an alert dialog box (where you just click OK), bring up a confirm dialog box (you click Yes or No), and bring up a prompt dialog box (where you type in some information). The `Window` object also contains properties for all frames that `window` contains and all child windows `Window` creates. It also allows you to change the status line at the bottom of the window (where you see those ticker-tape messages on many pages).

Table 55.5 lists all of the properties and methods of the `Window` object.

Table 55.5 Properties and Methods of the *Window* Object

Properties	Description
`defaultStatus`	The default message in the status bar.
`document`	The current document contained in the window.
`frames`	An array that describes all of the frames (if any) in the window.
`frame`	A `frame` object.
`length`	Reflects the number of frames (if any) in the window.
`name`	The name of the window.
`parent`	Synonymous with the name of the window. Contains the `frameset` tags.
`self`	Synonymous with the name of the window and refers to the current window.
`status`	Value appears in the window's status bar. Usually only lasts a moment before overwritten by some other event.
`top`	Synonymous with the name of the window and represents the topmost window.
`window`	Synonymous with the name of the window and refers to the current window.
`location`	A string specifying the URL of the current document.
Methods	**Description**
`alert`	Brings up an alert dialog box.
`close`	Closes the window.
`confirm`	Brings up a dialog box with Yes or No buttons and a user-specified message.
`open`	Opens a new window.
`prompt`	Brings up a window with user-specified text and an input box that allows the user to type in information.
`setTimeout`	Sets a time in milliseconds for an event to occur.
`clearTimeout`	Resets value set by `setTimeout`.

The *Document* Object

The `Document` object is extremely useful because it contains so much information about the current document, and it can create HTML on-the-fly with its `write` and `writeln` methods. Table 55.6 lists the properties and methods of the document object, as well as short descriptions of their purpose.

Table 55.6 Properties and Methods of the *Document* Object

Properties	Description
`alinkColor`	Reflects the `ALINK` attribute (in the `<body>` tag).
`anchors`	An array listing all of the HTML anchors in the document (`<a name>`).
`anchor`	An anchor object.
`bgColor`	Reflects the value of the `BGCOLOR` attribute.
`cookie`	Reflects the value of a Netscape cookie.
`fgColor`	The value of the `TEXT` attribute (in the `<body>` tag).
`forms`	An array listing all the forms in the document.
`form`	A form object.
`history`	An object containing the current browser history (links visited, number of links visited, and link URLs).
`lastModified`	The date the document was last modified.
`linkColor`	Reflects the `LINK` attribute of the `<body>` tag.
`links`	An array of all HTML links in the document (`<a href>`).
`link`	A link object.
`location`	The URL of the document.
`referrer`	The URL of the document that called the current document.
`title`	Reflects the title of the document.
`vlinkColor`	Reflects the color listed in the `VLINK` attribute.
Methods	**Description**
`clear`	Clears the window of all content.
`close`	After an `open` causes the string buffer to be written to the screen.
`open`	Begins a string to be written to the screen. Needs a `close` to actually force the writing.
`write`	Writes some expression to the current window.
`writeln`	Same as `write` but adds a `newline` character at the end.

The *Form* Object

This object is created every time JavaScript encounters a `<form>...</form>` in your HTML documents. It contains all of the information stored in your form and can be used to submit information to a function or back to the server. Table 55.7 describes the properties and methods of the `Form` object.

Table 55.7 Properties and Methods of the *Form* Object

Properties	Description
`action`	Reflects the HTML `ACTION` attribute of the `<form>` tag.
`button`	A button object (`<input type=button>`).
`checkbox`	A checkbox object (`<input type= checkbox>`).
`elements`	An array listing all elements in a form.
`encoding`	The value of the `ENCTYPE` attribute (for HTML uploads in Netscape).
`hidden`	A hidden object (`<input type=hidden>`).
`length`	The number of elements in the form.
`method`	The `METHOD` attribute of `<form>`.
`password`	A password object (`<input type=password>`).
`radio`	A radio object (`<input type=radio>`).
`reset`	A reset button object.
`select`	A select object (`<select>...<select>`).
`submit`	A submit button object.
`target`	The `TARGET` attribute of `<form>`.
`text`	A text object (`<input type=text>`).
`textarea`	A textarea object (`<textarea>...</textarea>`).
Method	**Description**
`submit`	Submits the form to the location in the `ACTION` attribute.

The *Navigator* Object

The `Navigator` object is distinct from the `window` object in that it contains information about the browser that persists across any given window. In Netscape 3.0, JavaScript adds two new properties—an object called `mimeTypes`, which lists all of the `mimeTypes` the browser can handle, and `plug-ins`, which lists all of the registered plug-ins the browser can use. Table 55.8 summarizes the properties of the `Navigator` object (it has no associated methods).

Table 55.8 *Navigator* Object Properties

Properties	Description
`appCodeName`	The code name of the browser, such as "Mozilla."
`appName`	The name of the browser, such as "Netscape."
`appVersion`	Contains the version information of the browser, such as "2.0 (Win95, I)."
`userAgent`	Contains the user-agent header that the browser sends to the server to identify itself, such as "Mozilla/2.0 (Win95, I)."
`mimeTypes`	An array reflecting all possible MIME types the browser can either handle itself or pass on to a plug-in or helper application (Netscape 3.0).
`plug-ins`	An array of registered plug-ins that the browser currently has loaded.

The *String* Object

Other objects are built in to JavaScript that are not specific to either the browser or the window. The first of these is the `String` object. This object is very useful because you can use its methods to modify and add HTML modifications without changing the string itself. One thing to notice about this object is that you can string together any number of its methods to create multilayers of HTML encoding. For example:

```
"Hello!".bold().blink()
```

would return:

```
<blink><b>Hello!</b></blink>
```

Table 55.9 describes this object.

Table 55.9 Properties and Methods of the *String* Object

Property	Description
`length`	The number of characters in the string.
Methods	**Description**
`anchor`	Converts string to an HTML anchor.
`big`	Encloses string in `<big>...</big>`.
`blink`	Encloses string in `<blink>...</blink>`.
`bold`	Encloses string in `<b>...</b>`.
`charAt`	Returns the character at some index value. Index reads from left to right. If `char` not found, it returns a -1.

continues

Table 55.9 Continued

Methods	Description
`fixed`	Encloses string in `<tt>...</tt>`.
`fontcolor`	Encloses string in `<font color=somecolor>...</font>`.
`indexOf`	Looks for the first instance of some string and returns the index of the first character in the target string, or gives a -1 if not found.
`italics`	Encloses string in `<i>...</i>`.
`lastIndexOf`	Same as `indexOf`, only begins searching from the right to find the last instance of the search string, or -1 if not found.
`link`	Converts string into a hyperlink.
`small`	Encloses string in `<small>...</small>`.
`strike`	Encloses string in `<strike>...</strike>`.
`sub`	Encloses string in `<sub>...</sub>`.
`substring`	Given a start and end index, returns the string contained by those indices.
`sup`	Encloses string in `<sup>...</sup>`.
`toLowerCase`	All uppercase characters are converted to lowercase (`UpPeRcAsE` becomes `uppercase`).
`toUpperCase`	All lowercase characters are converted to uppercase.

The *Math* Object

The `Math` object is both a set of methods that allows you to perform higher-level mathematical operations on your numerical data and a set of properties that contain some common mathematical constants. You can use the `Math` object anywhere in your scripts, as long as you reference the methods like this:

```
Math.PI
```

Or you can use the `with` keyword to contain a series of `math` statements:

```
with (Math) {
foo = PI
bar = sin(foo)
baz = tan(bar/foo)
}
```

Table 55.10 gives you a list of the `Math` properties and methods.

Table 55.10 *Math* Properties and Methods

Properties	Methods
E	abs
LOG2E	acos
SQRT1_2	asin
LN2	atan
LOG10E	ceil
SQRT2	cos
LN10	exp
PI	floor
	log
	max
	min
	pow
	random
	round
	sin
	sqrt
	tan

The *Date* Object

The final object I examine here is the `Date` object. This object allows you to grab information about the client's current time, year, month, date, and more. In addition, you can quickly create new date objects that can simplify keeping track of dates or time intervals between events. You can even parse a text string for date information that can be used elsewhere as a `Date` object. This object is most commonly used to create dynamic clocks, change page attributes (such as the background color) based on the time of day, and so on. Table 55.11 gives you a view of the `Date` object's methods (it has no properties).

Table 55.11 Methods of the *Date* Object

Method	Description
`getDate`	Returns the current date.
`getDay`	Returns the day of the week from a date object.
`getHours`	Returns the current number of hours since midnight.
`getMinutes`	Returns the current number of minutes past the hour.
`getMonth`	Returns the number of months since January.
`getSeconds`	Returns the number of seconds past the minute.
`getTime`	Returns the current time from the specified date object.
`getTimeZoneOffset`	Returns the offset in minutes for the current location (either more or less than GMT, or Greenwich Mean Time).
`getYear`	Returns the year from the `Date` object.
`parse`	Returns the number of milliseconds since January 1, 1970 00:00:00 for the current locale from the `Date` object.
`setDate`	Argument used to set a `Date` object.
`setHours`	Argument sets the hours of the `Date`.
`setMinutes`	Argument sets the minutes of the `Date`.
`setMonth`	Argument sets the month value.
`setSeconds`	Argument sets the seconds value.
`setTime`	Argument sets the time value of the specified `Date` object.
`setYear`	Argument sets the year value for the specified `Date` object.
`toGMTString`	Converts a date to a string using the standard GMT conventions (for example, Wed, 24 Jul 12:49:08 GMT).
`toLocaleString`	Converts a date to a string but is aware of the locale's convention instead of GMT. (7/24/96 10:50:02).
`UTC`	Opposite of `toGMTString`. Converts a string into the number of milliseconds since the epoch.).

A Final Example

As a final example of what JavaScript can do, Listing 55.16 is the source code for a Web page that displays the current time every second. You can see all of the elements that have been discussed previously in this chapter somewhere within this example. Essentially, this program gets a `Date` object every second; parses that object for the current minutes, seconds, and hours; converts those values to a string; and then sets a form input field to that value. Using a form in this way is quite common in JavaScript. Instead of being a way to input data, the text input field becomes a "screen" to display the time.

Listing 55.16 A JavaScript Clock

```
<HTML>
<HEAD>
<TITLE>JavaScript Clock</TITLE>
<script Language="JavaScript">
<!-- Hide me from old browsers - hopefully
// Netscapes Clock - Start
// this code was taken from Netscapes JavaScript documentation at
// www.netscape.com on Jan.25.96
var timerID = null;
var timerRunning = false;
function stopclock (){
if(timerRunning)
clearTimeout(timerID);
timerRunning = false;
}
function startclock () {
// Make sure the clock is stopped
stopclock();
showtime();
}
function showtime () {
var now = new Date();
var hours = now.getHours();
var minutes = now.getMinutes();
var seconds = now.getSeconds()
var timeValue = "" + ((hours >12) ? hours -12 :hours)
timeValue += ((minutes < 10) ? ":0" : ":") + minutes
timeValue += ((seconds < 10) ? ":0" : ":") + seconds
timeValue += (hours >= 12) ? " P.M." : " A.M."
document.clock.face.value = timeValue;
// you could replace the above with this
// and have a clock on the status bar:
// window.status = timeValue;
timerID = setTimeout("showtime()",1000);
timerRunning = true;
}
// Netscapes Clock - Stop
// end -->
</script>
</HEAD>
<BODY bgcolor="#ffffff" text="#000000" link="#0000ff"
alink="#008000" vlink="800080" onLoad="startclock()">
<!-- main -->
<table >
<tr>
<td colspan=3>
<form name="clock" onSubmit="0">
```


continues

Listing 55.16 Continued

```
<div align=right>
<input type="text" name="face" size=12 value="">
</div>
<center><b><font size=-1 >Welcome to My HomePage!</font></b></center><p>
</table>
</BODY>
</HTML>
```

Let's go through this script and see how it works to create the changing clock you will see in your browser.

After the initial HTML code starting the page, the browser sees the `<SCRIPT>` tag and begins to pass the code into the JavaScript interpreter. The HTML comment `<--` hides the JavaScript code from old browsers.

The next three lines are comments that JavaScript ignores.

The next two lines initialize `timerID` to `null` (a special value that acts as a placeholder) and `timerRunning` to `false` (a Boolean value). The variable `timerID` is used in the `setTimeOut` and `clearTimeOut` function. It just acts as a name to keep track of that specific countdown.

The next five lines define a function called `stopclock` which tests if the `timerRunning` value is true. If so, it calls `clearTimeout` which frees up the countdown timer called `timerID`.

The next five lines (after a space) define a function called `startclock`. All `startclock` does is call `stopclock` and then the function `showtime`. It's important to stop the clock before calling `showtime`, because `showtime` resets the countdown timer `timerID`.

The next 16 lines define the heart of the script, called `showtime`. This function creates a new `Date` object called `now` and gets the hours, minutes, and seconds values from that object and assigns them to the variables `hour`, `minutes`, and `seconds`, respectively. By creating this new object every time `showtime` is called, the script is getting the most recent time possible, which is why the clock changes every second.

After the hours, minutes, and seconds are retrieved from the `Date` object, a new variable `timeValue` is created, which is a `String` object, and it assigns the corrected value of hours to this string. (The `(hours >12) ? hours -12 :hours` expression converts the hours from 24-hour time to 12-hour time.) The next `timeValue` assignments append the values of minutes and seconds to the `timeValue` string—correcting for tens of minutes.

The line

```
document.clock.face.value = timeValue
```

places the resulting string into the form text input field that is defined later. By assigning this value to that field, it causes that value to appear in that box on the page.

The next line in the function `showtime` (following the three comments) starts a countdown of one second and calls it `timerID`. After one second, the function `showtime` is called again—essentially, this is a way of calling a `this` function over and over again every second.

The last line in the `showtime` function sets the `timerRunning` value to the Boolean true which would affect the `stopclock` function (breaking the one-second loop which `timerID` had been causing). To test this, run this script and then in the URL input window (at the top of the browser window), type:

```
javascript:stopclock()
```

You see that the clock stops. Typing

```
javascript:startclock()
```

in the URL gets the clock running again.

After the function `showtime`, the rest of the lines close out the script and create via HTML a table that contains a form called `clock` with one input field called `face`.

Notice that, in the `<BODY>` tag the `onLoad="startclock()"` statement, after the entire page is loaded into the window, the `onLoad` event handler is triggered, and the `startclock` function is called, which begins the script. ●

PART X

Java Resources

CHAPTER 56

Java Resources

In this chapter

Web Sites

Keeping on top of resources for something that changes as rapidly as the Java world is a daunting task, to say the least. As a result, any listing of Java resources is going to be obsolete before it's completed.

Rather than providing a comprehensive listing of every site that mentions Java (Digital's AltaVista Web search engine returns more than hundreds of thousands of hits on the word "java"), this list is intended to provide information on a few of the ever-expanding number of Java Web sites as well as data on good places to look for more Web sites. So, these sites are by no means the totality of what's out there—this is a starting point for you to begin your Java reference bookmark lists. These sites are in no particular order and have no other qualification beyond the fact that I think that Java programmers of all levels will find them useful in some way.

Because one of Java's main strengths lies in its capability to embed applets into Web pages, it's natural that the Web is an excellent source of information for Java development. These Web sites provide a great deal of information, from API calls to the latest news in the world of Java—an invaluable resource for any level of Java programmer.

Earthweb's developer.com

`http://www.gamelan.com/`

Originally known as Gamelan (pronounced "gamma-lahn"), this is the granddaddy of all Java resource sites offering a huge listing of just about anything available on the Web for Java. From its extensive applet collection to its listing of other outside Java resources, Gamelan is a great place to start browsing to see what other Java programmers are up to.

Focus on Java

`http://java.miningco.com`

Focus on Java's Java Guide in which John Zukowski offers a vast collection of exceptional information on Java. John hand picks the best Java tidbits, identifies the best books and tools, and provides insight into the disparate directions Java is headed. His resource collection is a library of Java resources categorized by type.

Inside Java

`http://www.inside-java.com`

Inside Java is a very good source for Java programmers. Here, you can find listings for articles, what's new in the field of Java, recourses, a forum for Java discussions, plus chats on Java. They keep you up to date on what's going on with changes, updates, and new releases—a good URL to add to your bookmarks.

Java Applet Rating Service (JARS)

`http://www.jars.com/`

The main focus of JARS is to provide ratings for Java applets that are available on the World Wide Web. Each applet is reviewed by a panel of independent judges, including some of this book's authors, who base the rating on a set of criteria. If an applet achieves specified totals for its rating, distinction might be recognized by the following JARS awards:

- Top 1 percent Web Applet
- Top 5 percent Web Applet
- Top 25 percent Web Applet
- Top 10 Web Applet (of the month)
- Top 100 Web Applet (of the month)

In addition, applets with publicly available source code are further acknowledged, and a link to the source is provided when possible.

JARS is a great site for checking out other programmers' applets and seeing how yours stacks up against the rest of the world.

The Java Boutique

`http://javaboutique.internet.com/`

The Java Boutique has many URL listings, along with applets, reviews, forums, how-to's, and many other interesting features.

Java Developer's Journal

`http://www.javadevelopersjournal.com/java/`

Java Developer's Journal has free Java courses, a free three-month trial subscription to its *Java Developer's Journal* magazine, free software, and so on. This site includes a nice feature of product reviews that can help when you want to buy software.

Java Developers Connection

`http://java.sun.com/jdc`

A free resource from Sun providing up-to-date material and prerelease software—a must visit for any serious developer.

Java Lobby

`http://www.javalobby.org`

The Java Lobby is a group of Java developers dedicated to insuring the "Write Once Run Anywhere" promise of Java. They lobby to make sure that Java is always kept pure.

Java Resources from Netscape

`http://developer.netscape.com/library/documentation/javalist.html`

Java Resources from Netscape offers a comprehensive listing of Java technical information for use with its products. At this site, you can find multiple listings and third-party listings covering just about anything you might want to know about Java.

Java World

`http://www.javaworld.com/`

A monthly online magazine, *Java World* is IDG's magazine for the Java community. Here you find informative links to resources and how-to's. You can search for specific information and check out its "Nuts & Bolt's" section for great information on software usage.

JavaBeans Site

`http://java.sun.com/beans`

The root of all JavaBeans information is this wonderful site that includes information and links to a variety of information on JavaBeans and JavaBeans projects.

Sun's Home Page

`http://java.sun.com/`

This is probably the best place to start when looking for Java resources. It's the home of Sun. Here you can find extensive documentation on the Java API, the JDK, and the Java language itself. You can download the latest versions of the JDK and other Java-related tools. Anyone serious about programming in Java should explore this site fully and return frequently. You can also find timely information that you can't find anywhere else.

Javology—The Online Ezine of Java News and Opinion

`http://www.javology.com/javology`

Javology is a slick online magazine that covers the current events taking place in the Java world. With articles about breaking news, interviews with the movers and shakers in the Java community, and other up-to-date information about what's happening with Java, *Javology* helps people who are interested in Java stay on top of what's going on.

Microsoft's Java Home Page

`http://www.microsoft.com/java`

Microsoft's site on Java includes information on Microsoft's implementation of Java and offers links to Microsoft Java tools. Be aware that Microsoft has been altering its Java VM and the core APIs, but if that's okay with you, jump into this site.

Swing Connection

`http://java.sun.com/products/jfc/swingdoc-current/`

This site is the home of the Swing (JFC) project offering timely tips and techniques on using JFC, as well as information about upcoming features.

Team Java

`http://www.teamjava.com/`

Team Java is intended to assist Java consultants by providing information regarding available jobs, news, educational materials, and other useful Java resources. Team Java also has an applet-of-the-day service called Java the Hut. Overall, this site is very useful for people who use, or plan to use, Java in a professional environment. Even weekend Java warriors will find this site useful.

Newsgroups

UseNet newsgroups can be a great source of information. They can also be a major pain when people stop being helpful and start arguing about whatever they feel like arguing about. If you're familiar with UseNet, and feel comfortable using it, these newsgroups are a valuable asset. If you're not familiar with UseNet news, it's best to just observe for awhile, get a feel for the system, stay out of flame wars, and read the FAQ before starting to post.

With that said, the many UseNet newsgroups on Java worth mentioning are as follows:

- comp.lang.java Java language and programming
- comp.lang.java.advocacy Java proponents speak out
- comp.lang.java.announce Java products and other services announced (moderated)
- comp.lang.java.beans JavaBeans discussions and programming
- comp.lang.java.databases Java database programming
- comp.lang.java.gui Graphical interface tips and help
- comp.lang.java.help General help with the Java language and programming
- comp.lang.java.machine Java virtual machine discussions
- comp.lang.java.programmer Java programmer help
- comp.lang.java.security Java security discussions
- comp.lang.java.softwaretools Discussion of Java tools to help you be more productive
- alt.www.hotjava HotJava World Wide Web browser

NOTE Be aware that not all news servers make the alt. hierarchy of newsgroups available to its subscribers. If you have trouble locating it, contact your news administrator.

The Northeast Parallel Architecture Server at Syracuse University tracks comp.lang.java, among other newsgroups. This is a handy way to get all the comp.lang.java postings regarding, for example, garbage collection.

Mailing Lists

In addition to the mailing list administered by Java-SIG and run by various smaller groups, a few lists are run out of Sun.

Here's the address for the list:

```
java-interest@java.sun.com
```

NOTE This is an extremely high-traffic group, with more than 20,000 subscribers and dozens of posts every day. The list isn't moderated, so this isn't a place for you if you're easily overwhelmed.

You can subscribe to the list by sending the words **subscribe java-interest** in the body of your message to this address:

```
majordomo@java.sun.com
```

All the traffic on the Sun lists is gated to comp.lang.java; it's not necessary to read both the mailing list and the newsgroup. For more information about Sun's mailing lists, take a look at this address:

```
http://java.sun.com/mail.html
```

Support for Porting Issues

Java is a popular language, and a lot of people are working hard to see that it becomes a truly universal one by porting it to as many platforms as possible. The following listing tells where to connect with some of the porters.

Amiga Porting Issues

Mattias Johansson (`matj@o.lst.se`) in Sweden runs Porting Java to Amiga, or P'Jami.

There are three email lists:

```
amiga-hotjava-dev@mail.iMNet.de
```

This is a closed list. Participants must be approved by the list administrator.

```
amiga-hotjava@mail.iMNet.de
```

This is an open mailing list for the exchange of information. To subscribe, send the words **subscribe amiga-hotjava** in the body of your message to

```
mafordom@mail.iMNet.deamiga-hotjava-announce@mail.iMNet.de
```

This last list broadcasts announcements of Amiga ports. To subscribe, send the words **subscribe amiga-hotjava-announce** in the body of a message to majordomo@mail.iMNet.de.

DEC Alpha OSF/1 Port

This section covers patches and information about a DEC Alpha port. The Web page is maintained by Greg Stiehl.

Web site: http://www.NetJunkies.Com/Java/osf1-port.html

email: stiehl@NetJunkies.com

Linux Porting Issues

Linux is the free, IBM-compatible version of UNIX. Karl Asha (karl@blackdown.com) maintains several resources for people interested in porting and using Java and HotJava with Linux. .

The Web site is found at this address:

http://www.blackdown.org/java-linux.html

There are two mailing lists for Linux issues: java-linux and java-linux-announce. The first is a discussion list and the second is a broadcast list.

The address for the mailing list is java-linux@java.blackdown.org

To subscribe to this list, send the word **subscribe** in the subject line of a message to this address:

java-linux-request@java.blackdown.org

or

java-linux-announce-request@java.blackdown.org

An anonymous FTP distribution of the Linux Java port is available from this address:

ftp://substance.blackdown.org:/pub/Java

NEXTSTEP Porting Issues

Bill Bumgarner (bbum@friday.com) maintains an open mailing list for the discussion of porting and integration esoterica that are unique to the NeXT platform.

To subscribe, send the word subscribe in the body of a message to this address:

next-java-request@friday.com

Here's the address to mail to the list:

next-java-@friday.com

PART XI

Appendix

APPENDIX A

What's on the CD-ROM

In this appendix

This book's CD-ROM includes sample applets, as well as valuable programs, utilities, and other information. This appendix gives you a brief overview of the contents of the CD-ROM. For a more detailed look at any of these parts, load the CD-ROM and browse the contents.

Example Code from the Book

Complete examples of applets and applications from the book are included on the CD-ROM—organized by chapter for quick and easy location and use.

Third-Party Software

Included on this CD-ROM is software that will help you in programming Java, including:

- JBuilder™ Publisher Edition
- JBuilder™2 Tutorials
- Tek-Tools, Inc.'s Kawa

Bonus Software

Bundled on this CD-ROM are software packages that you might find useful, including:

- Adobe Systems, Inc.'s Acrobat Reader 3.01
- EarthLink Network's TotalAccess 2.0
- Microsoft's Internet Explorer 4.01
- Netscape Communicator 4.04

Index

Symbols

A

B

C

D

E

F

G

H

K

L

M

N

P

Q-R

S

T

U

X-Y-Z

Java 1.2 Unleashed

Jamie Jaworski

Extensive coverage of the latest Java 1.2 technologies. Ideal for the intermediate- to expert-level user, this guide explores the new Java extensions and APIs, JavaBeans, JavaOS, and other new Java-based technologies; guides the reader in using JDBC to gain database connectivity; teaches effective programming strategies and application development, and investigates Java security. Using expert tips, advice, and real-world examples, this comprehensive guide and reference is ideal for readers wanting to master professional-level programming with Java.

$49.99 U.S. — *Accomplished – Expert*

$71.95 CAN — *1,200 Pages*

1-57521-389-3 — *PUB 8/98*

JFC Unleashed

This programmer's tutorial helps the reader understand how to build client and server applications utilizing all the features of the new Java Foundation Classes.

Extensive use of code samples demonstrates how to put each feature to use.

Complete coverage of the Swing Toolkit, Pluggable Look and Feel, and Drag and Drop.

$39.99 U.S. — *Accomplished – Expert*

$57.95 CAN — *800 Pages*

0-7897-1466-3 — *PUB 9/98*

Java 1.2 Class Libraries Unleashed

Serves as a nuts-and-bolts, code-level book for programmers who want to use Java Class Libraries.

Examines specifications, major vendors' libraries, compilers, and SDKs.

Shows readers how to use and create class libraries to meet their personalized needs.

$49.99 U.S — *Accomplished – Expert*

$71.95 CAN — *1,200 Pages*

0-7897-1292-X — *PUB 8/98*

Using Visual J++ 6

Using Visual J++ 6 is a task-based reference that uses clear organization, step-by-step tasks, abundant code samples, and new cross-indexing techniques to teach Visual J++. This book covers all aspects of using Visual J++ to build a wide range of Java applets and applications, ActiveX objects, COM/DCOM objects, and more. The book also covers some of the more advanced features of the Java 1.2 language.

Using Visual J++ 6 accomplishes these goals by anticipating the needs of the user, providing strong navigation and accessibility to the content. This book provides a powerful price/content value proposition versus other books in the marketplace.

$29.99 U.S. — *Beginner – Intermediate*

$42.95 CAN — *800 Pages*

0-7897-1400-0 — *PUB 8/98*

Sams Teach Yourself Visual J++ 6 in 21 Days

This easy-to-use tutorial teaches you everything you need to know about Visual J++ 6.

Hands-on practical approach and well-documented code examples ensure that readers understand and learn Visual J++ programming techniques.

This book is an excellent companion to the #1 Java tutorial, *Sams Teach Yourself Java 1.2 in 21 Days.*

$29.99 U.S. — *Beginner – Intermediate*

$42.95 CAN — *600 Pages*

0-672-31351-0 — *PUB 9/98*

Mitchell Waite Signature Series: Data Structures and Algorithms in Java

Not filled with obtuse mathematics and difficult proofs, *MWSS: Data Structures and Algorithms in Java* removes the mystique from DS&A. It does this in two ways. First, the text is written in a straightforward style, making it accessible to anyone. Second, unique new Java demonstration programs, called "Workshop Applets," are provided with the book. These Workshop Applets provide interactive "moving pictures" that the user can control and modify by pressing buttons. The book's text describes specific operations the user can carry out with these Workshop Applets, and the applets then reveal the inner workings of an algorithm or data structure.

$49.99 U.S. — *Accomplished – Expert*

$71.95 CAN — *600 Pages*

1-57169-095-6 — *PUB 8/98*

NOTE: This CD-ROM uses long and mixed-case filenames requiring the use of a protected-mode CD-ROM driver.